The Great Book of French Cuisine

Henri Paul Pellaprat

The Great Book of French Cuisine

Over 2,000 recipes by the director of the École du Cordon Bleu, Paris

Edited by
RENÉ KRAMER *and* DAVID WHITE

Adapted for the American kitchen by
AVANELLE DAY

THE VENDOME PRESS

Distributed in the United States of America by
Rizzoli International Publications
through St. Martin's Press
175 Fifth Avenue
New York, NY 10010

Title of the original work: L'ART CULINAIRE MODERNE

Library of Congress Catalog Card Number: 65-25779
Printed and bound in Italy

TYPOGRAPHIC DESIGN BY JEANETTE YOUNG
ISBN: 0-86565-149-3

ACKNOWLEDGMENTS

Grateful acknowledgment is made to the following contributors for their valuable help in bringing Pellaprat's classic book up to date:

Mesdames Colette Guéden, Lucia Mazzucchetti; *Mesdemoiselles* Madeleine Decure, Helga Lund; *Messieurs* Alex Allegrier, François d'Athis, Walter Bickel, Pierre Boutines, Pino Braguti, Octave Brust, Franco Corpora, Claude Desarzens, Jean Doreau, Wilfred Fance, Marc Fatio, Dagobert Fehlmann, Werner Fischer, Giuseppe Fontana, Herbert Gömöri, Charles Goetz, César Gosi, Marco Guarnori, Roger Guillaume, Jean Guinot, Georges Guth, Paul Heinz, Arthur Hope, Hublet, René Lacroix, Fred Laubi, Leone Legnani, Jean Liban, Xavier Maier, Philippe Marnier-Lapostolle, Pierre Mengelatte, Flavien Monod, Luigi Morandi, Bruno Mosca, Franco Puricelli, Gilbert Rohrer, Natale Rusconi, Herbert Seidel, Charles Vaucher, Stefano Zaccone, Franco Zecca

In the preparation of the American edition, grateful acknowledgment is made to The Taylor Wine Company, Hammondsport, N.Y., and to the California Wine Institute, for information on the wine industry in the United States; to Dr. G. Robert DiMarco and Dr. Myron Solberg of the Department of Food Science, Rutgers University, for checking the chapter on meat; and to Alice Roberts for editorial supervision.

Thanks are also extended to the following individuals and business organizations for assistance in the preparation of the illustrations:

Photography—Messieurs Jean Froehlich, La Chaux-de-Fonds, Switzerland; Eric Muller-Grunitz, Aschaffenburg, Germany; Jacques Primois, Paris

Preparation of foods for presentation—Restaurant Lucas Carton, Paris; Hotel Carlton Senato, Milan; Grand Hotel des Bains, Venice; Hotel Gritti-Palace, Venice; Kranzler Konditorei, Frankfurt; Lacroix, Pâté Manufacturer, Frankfurt; Manuel & Cie, Candy Manufacturers, Lausanne; Restaurant Möwenpick, Zurich; Parkhotel, Frankfurt; Pizzeria "A Santa Lucia," Milan; La Caravelle, New York

ACKNOWLEDGMENTS

Displays of silverware—Béard S.A., Montreux; Christofle, Paris, London, and New York; Dominici, Venice; Mappin and Webb, Paris and London; Steiger, Lausanne and Berne

Displays of china, pottery, and glassware—Copeland; Richard Ginori, Venice, Paris, and New York; Meissen; Primavera, Atelier d'Art du Printemps, Paris; Baccarat, Saint-Louis, Val-Saint-Lambert, France; Venini, Venice

Displays of table linens—Jesurum, Lace Manufacturer, Venice

Use of interiors—Hotel Gritti-Palace, Venice; Primavera, Atelier d'Art du Printemps, Paris; Zéberli Gallery, Lausanne; Marc Leyvraz, Wine Producer and Dealer, Rivaz, Switzerland

CONTENTS

ILLUSTRATIONS IN COLOR

ILLUSTRATIONS IN COLOR

Illustrations in Color

ILLUSTRATIONS IN COLOR

INTRODUCTION

by Michael Field

Since it was first published in 1935, Henri-Paul Pellaprat's great work, *L'Art culinaire moderne,* has been translated into five languages and has sold 750,000 copies throughout the world. This, the first American edition, makes its propitious debut in the land which, in many ways, needs it the most. Here, in the United States, the encroaching tide of "convenience" foods, dehydrated foods, synthetic sauces, and frozen dinners threatens to engulf us all; not only are our palates being brutalized, slowly and insidiously, but we are in danger of forgetting what the aroma, taste, and even appearance of good, honest food can be. However, with this edition of Henri-Paul Pellaprat's book before us we can again take heart. Translated by Avanelle Day and David White into practical American terms, it reaffirms lucidly, persuasively, and precisely the dignity of man's relation to the food he eats. And because Pellaprat was French, and a culinary genius as well, his book was conceived in terms of the French cuisine, surely the only cuisine in the Western world which can lay claim to being called an art.

Through the years much has been written about French cooking, its genesis, its architechtonics, and its technical culmination in *la haute cuisine*—its higher mathematics, as it were. But few writers have so succinctly described the skeletal structure of French cooking as did Maurice-Edmund Saillant, who wrote under the *nom de plume* of Curnonsky, and who was known throughout France as the "Prince of Gastronomes"; his brilliant analysis has become by now the classic formulation.

In his glowing and affectionate preface to his friend Pellaprat's *L'Art culinaire moderne* it is fitting indeed that Curnonsky chose to state: "This volume . . . is a veritable encyclopedia of the table and textbook of good living; it sums up half a century of professional experience and teaching. It contains the essentials of all kinds of cookery, and above all of the four types of French cookery:

"*La haute cuisine*—the most elaborate and sophisticated cooking, one of the greatest achievements of France.

"*La cuisine bourgeoise*—middle-class family cooking, the triumph of both *cordons bleus* and housewives; Pellaprat is a fervent feminist who has rendered homage to the finesse, the grace, and the simplicity which these women have contributed to French cookery.

"*La cuisine regionale*—the provincial cookery of France, unique in the world because of the diversity, richness, and originality of its countless local dishes and specialties.

"*La cuisine impromptue*—the cooking which uses the materials at hand, and the simplest and quickest methods."

Curnonsky goes on to say that "Pellaprat has made the most judicious choice from among the innumerable recipes of these four types of cookery," which, indeed, he has.

In reality, Curnonsky's categories overlap more often than not, or blur, particularly when for sociological, economic, or fashionable reasons, certain dishes begin to lose their specific profiles. Pellaprat was, of course, aware of this. French cooking was for him a dynamic process, and his procedures and recipes kept constant pace with its movement; thus the recipes have a surprising quality of contemporaneity and are never needlessly complex or contrived, whether they depart from tradition or not. Even the numerous foreign dishes in the book reflect his profound culinary intelligence and penetrating eye. The Italian, Spanish, Indian, and other dishes that he tasted and recorded on his extensive travels are reproduced with remarkable fidelity. But whatever the recipe, it is clearly apparent throughout the book that Pellaprat never lost sight of Curnonsky's oft-stated dictum that in really fine cooking "ingredients should taste of what they are."

Born in Paris in 1869, Henri-Paul Pellaprat knew from the age of twelve (it was then that he began his apprenticeship as a pastry cook) that he was destined to become a chef. Year after year he worked with the feverish dedication of which only French cooks seem capable, and explored every branch of the French culinary art, including even what Curnonsky called that "exquisite ornament of French cuisine"—confectionery. Pellaprat also knew the rigors and joys of working in the restaurant kitchens of the most famous chefs of the time, Père Lépey of the Café de la Paix, Casimir Moisson at La Maison Dorée, and, on various occasions, with such illustrious men as Bignon, Maire, and Prillard. So lively and investigating a culinary mind as

Pellaprat's, coupled with a gift for articulation rare in chefs, led him inevitably to a pedagogic post at the Cordon Bleu Cooking School in Paris. His teaching activities were interrupted in 1914 by a year's stay in the army, from which he was discharged in order to support his seven children. After subsequent work as a chef in the Restaurant Lucas Carton, and the Terminus Demain, he returned to the Cordon Bleu School when it reopened after the war. There he remained, immersed in his teaching, culinary experimentation, and testing, all of which were to prove so meaningful and productive when he retired from the school in 1932.

Then at last it was possible for Pellaprat to distill his years of theoretical and empirical explorations in the kitchen and classrooms into a number of books on baking and cooking, culminating in the monumental *L'Art culinaire moderne*, his last published work.

Translating, at best, is an arduous and often thankless task, but translating a cookbook, and a great one at that, would be enough to give most translators pause. Recipe ingredients must be precisely remeasured, and differences between measuring by scales, as the French do, and measuring by volume, as we do, must be taken into account. And French flours and creams are different from ours; their flour is softer and their cream thicker. The manner in which these ingredients are reinterpreted for American use will, more often than not, determine the success or failure of a particular dish.

American cooks everywhere, be they practitioners of *la haute cuisine*, or day-to-day exponents of *la cuisine bourgeoise*, or only neophytes who have just begun to cook, must be grateful for the devotion, skill, and care that Avanelle Day and David White have brought to their task. Their adaptation of Pellaprat's recipes is faithful to the original without being rigid, and lucid and helpful without condescension. Whether we actually cook from this book or simply read it, an inexhaustible fund of knowledge and pleasure awaits us in this American adaptation—*Modern French Culinary Art.*

SUGGESTIONS FOR USING THIS BOOK

The recipes in the book have been planned to be as detailed and helpful as possible. They include cooking times and temperatures, and the various procedures are described in the order in which they are to be carried out. When a recipe or its presentation requires a preparation for which the recipe is given elsewhere, the title of the recipe referred to is capitalized (Béchamel Sauce, Tomato Fondue, Duchess Potatoes, etc.) in the list of ingredients and in the text and will be found in the index in alphabetical order and also under its category (Sauce, etc.). When there is an illustration for a recipe, a page reference for the illustration is given, and the page on which the recipe appears is given in the caption. Illustrations are indicated in the index. Most of the ingredients required are readily available to the American housewife; for those which are not—and a few are inevitable—alternatives are suggested.

The use of English, French, and occasionally other languages in the titles of recipes, with and without translations, is purposely inconsistent. Many French names for dishes cannot be translated at all, others in part only. When English serves the purpose it has been used and the original French title given in parentheses if it conveys additional information. If the French (or Italian, Russian, etc.) title is either familiar or untranslatable (or both), the original language is used, and an English descriptive title added in parentheses. Recipes with titles in two languages are listed under both titles in the index.

Before beginning to use the recipes, the reader will find it helpful to survey the table of contents, index, and list of illustrations to get an idea of the scope and organization of the book and to facilitate locating recipes and information. Chapter 3, The Principles and Basic Materials of Cookery, will repay a careful preliminary study, particularly the section on Various Methods of Cooking and Their Technology and the recipes for basic stocks, doughs, forcemeats, etc. Culinary Techniques in Pictures (pages 1047–94) contains step-by-step illustrations of various procedures; references to these appear in the related recipes. Cooking terms are defined in the Glossary.

The New Pellaprat

MODERN FRENCH CULINARY ART

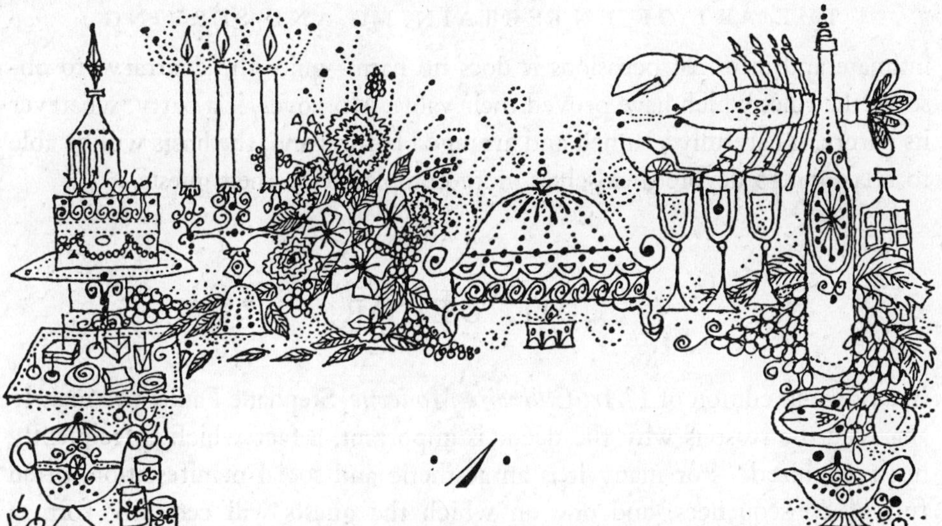

1

THE ART OF ENTERTAINING AND SERVING

The arts of entertaining and of serving are a little like the art of creating a theatrical production, in which the text, the actors, the decor, the music are the major elements which must be coordinated by the producer. He brings out their various qualities and above all sees that they are in harmony with one another. The host or hostess must play a similar part. The quality of the dishes, the harmonious sequence of the menu, the choice of wines require as much care, as much subtlety as the table decorations and the attention which surrounds each guest. Entertaining means giving. And the way in which we give, in our own sphere, is as important as what we give.

Entertaining means honoring one's guests; the same consideration must be shown to friends and to celebrities, to affection and to power. For family and friends, customs are modified, made more flexible and personal. But everyone who entertains should nevertheless be familiar with the fundamental rules which govern the preparation of a dinner, a luncheon, or a traditional tea. In spite of the exigencies of modern life, the universal tendency toward simplification, and the very difficult problem of service, there are still occasions on which the basic requirements—which are unchanged—must be observed, or at least approached as closely as possible. And even on the most intimate and informal occasions it does no harm—quite the contrary—to observe the rules which have proved their value. Moreover, if a party, whatever its nature, is carefully planned and arranged beforehand, the hosts will be able to relax and to devote themselves more completely to their guests.

THE DECOR

In a previous edition of *L'Art Culinaire Moderne*, Stephane Faniel pertinently analyzed the reasons why the decor is important, a fact which is frequently not recognized. "For many it is an aesthetic and social manifestation, often full of consequences, and one on which the guests will certainly form a judgment."

The atmosphere of a meal consists of a thousand imponderable elements, all aimed at the essential purpose of putting everyone at ease. Here the hostess's great gift comes into play—to put herself in the position of others, to think in advance of what they would enjoy, to remember their dislikes—in fact, to take charge, for however short a time, of their pleasure. Some will feel happier in rather formal surroundings, at a very sophisticated table, equipped with all that is best in china, linen, crystal, and silver. Others will attach more importance to the dazzling freshness of flowers, the smiling grace and informality of a more imaginative table. But all guests will appreciate the personal note, the attentions that discreetly remind them that everything has been done for *their* pleasure, *their* comfort, and *their* relaxation.

Unfortunately one cannot always know the precise tastes of all of one's guests, but at least one knows their age, their occupation or profession, their native region or nationality. Anything which will, in one form or another, evoke, recall, or underline the personality of the guests of honor is welcome.

In the best productions the audience does not see the wheels go around, just as true elegance consists in not drawing attention to oneself. Nevertheless, the fact that the wheels are invisible does not mean that they are missing; this is only a warning against an excessive show of the means being used or the belongings that one has.

The extreme case is a grand ceremonial dinner where the loveliest silver, the most dazzling crystal, the most delicate china, and the finest linen are laid out; but in order to use all these one must also have the necessary staff. This staff may quite well be engaged only for one evening. Equally, if one has a staff, the objects used must be up to the level of the service. If necessary, equipment can be hired from specialized firms. The constant aim, here as elsewhere, must be to achieve harmony—harmony between the hosts and the arrangement of the meal and of the table, between the staff and the equipment, between the general decoration of the room and that of the table. One does not engage two menservants in tailcoats and white gloves to place plates of peasant pottery, however charming, on table mats, any more than a hostess alone, or with the assistance of a single servant, can pull out all the stops of ceremonial service.

There must be harmony, too, between the size of the room and the number of guests, whether it is a large room and a numerous party or a small room and a family gathering. A formal dinner or a party can only succeed if the guests have enough space, for themselves, between one another, and for those around them. The most trying kind of embarrassment is to feel that one is embarrassing others. The staff must be able to move freely. The table must be big enough for the glasses, plates, covers, and various accessories not to be cramped. It is better to have two fewer guests than to "squash" either objects or people. Attention must also be paid to ventilation and temperature. How many delightful occasions are spoiled by a room so hot that people are made uncomfortable!

Tradition has it that the style of the silver should determine that of the plates and glasses and that all should, as far as possible, be of the same style and period. Obviously, one avoids all risks by setting a table in a single style, especially a good one. But the development of modern taste (or dare we say of taste as such?) makes it permissible to deviate from this golden rule. There need be nothing discordant in using beautiful old plates with contemporary cutlery, the quality of which may be superb. We must be quite clear about this: principles have an undeniable value and rules are useful; the matter is one of codifying the language of good breeding. But, quite apart from the fact that languages evolve, rules and a thorough knowledge of them must never be allowed to paralyze initiative. Such initiative should only be taken if one is sure of oneself, but then one should not hesitate. Is anyone nowadays horrified to find a Renoir hanging on the walls of a drawing room furnished with Louis XV furniture, or a Braque in an Empire-style study?

The important factors are taste, discernment, and an infinite amount of tact. The producer knows quite well that a harmony, more difficult but by no means less subtle, may be achieved by contrast as well as by the use of similar elements.

A discreet progression should be observed in the utilization of the various elements—silver, china, glass. It would be unfortunate if for lack of knowledge of how to graduate the choice of plates or glasses the meal were to finish less elegantly than it began. Even if there is no progression, there should be no regression. The same principles apply here as to the progression of wines.

In the past, centerpieces were large, ornate pieces of plate, complicated in design and often allegorical in theme. These may still be used for very traditional receptions, but nowadays flowers, possibly reflected in a discreet mirror base, are preferred; they are an inexhaustible source of decoration, from the simplest to the most sumptuous. The decorative theme may, according to individual taste, spread some way beyond the center of the table, but the flowers must not engulf the place settings; a table turned into a greenhouse or a florist's display window is distinctly out of place. Nor should the flowers be too strongly scented, otherwise they may overpower or form dubious alliances with the subtle odors of well-cooked food.

The lighting gives the finishing touch to the table, to the whole of the decor. Wherever possible, the gentle, warm, and living light of candles should be used in the evening. Candelabra and chandeliers give a table a sparkle, a shimmer, for which there is no substitute. But their use does not exclude a source of indirect or filtered electric light.

Obviously the decor will vary with the time of day and with the nature of the meal or party. In the following paragraphs we analyze possible preparations for various meals, from breakfast to a formal dinner (see illustrations on pages 16–18). Naturally the suggestions we make can always be changed to suit the house, the equipment, and the staff available. From the first ray of morning sunshine to the last glimmer of the last candle, it is the warmth of the welcome that counts.

Breakfast

The tea or coffee service may be placed in front of the hostess, who pours the tea or coffee and passes the cups around, with cream and sugar following on a small tray for the guests to serve themselves. Butter, marmalade or jam, and honey are served in separate dishes, each with its own serving piece, placed on the table within easy reach of the guests. There should also be salt and pepper cellars for dishes that require additional seasoning. Toast may be placed on a toast rack or, better, toasted in an electric toaster that is on a tea cart or side table. If rolls are served, arrange them attractively in a dish or basket and place it on the table.

Naturally the service can be less formal, without being any the less attentive. Especially in the country, it is permissible to be fanciful as long as taste and attentiveness prevail. Guests from other countries will be very grateful if they are allowed to follow their national customs in the matter of breakfast.

Luncheon

The luncheon table may be laid with either a cloth or table mats. An informal elegance is entirely suitable. Lacking more original ideas, one may use a bowl of fruit or flowers as a centerpiece; either makes a pleasant and gracious decoration.

The place settings are the same as for dinner but simplified in accordance with the menu and the wines served. (See the section on Dinner, pages 6–8.) Two glasses per guest are enough. The luncheon knife is always placed to the right of the plate with the cutting edge turned toward it. Next to it place the oyster or melon fork, if required. The luncheon fork goes at the left of the plate. The dessert fork and cheese knife may be placed behind the plate at the foot of the glasses or brought in on dessert plates, as the fruit knife is.

Tea

The hostess herself serves the guests, passing to them the filled cups, the sugar bowl, cream pitcher, and plates of toast or sandwiches and cakes.

There are two customary ways of serving. One is to use a large table around which the guests are invited to sit. At each place there is a tea plate, a fork (if one is needed), and a tea-size napkin. The tea service stands on a tray and cups and saucers are placed in stacks of two near the hostess's place. She, while seated, pours the beverage and passes it to the guests. Cream, lemon, and sugar are passed on a tray for the guests to serve themselves. Toast, sandwiches, and cakes are passed around the table on separate plates.

The alternate method is to place the tea service on a small table, along with the cups, saucers, and small plates. The hostess, assisted by a young girl, will hand each guest his cup and plate. This method is less formal and is preferable if the guests come and go at various times. It also gives the hostess more opportunity to mingle with her guests.

The cups should be emptied into a waste basin, a part of the tea service, before they are refilled.

Bridge Teas

At a bridge tea, the serving is done from a tea cart. The space on the trays is limited, and all the hostess's ingenuity is needed to find room for the necessary objects—cups, saucers, glasses, cake plates, etc. The assistance of a young girl, who will carry the teapot and sugar bowl, pour out, and remove cups to be refilled, will simplify the serving problem. If possible, use small side tables, to avoid putting food and drink on the card tables.

Canapés, sandwiches, pastries, and petits fours may be served, and, in addition to tea, the drinks may include fruit juice, port, whisky, etc. Passionate bridge players may remain indifferent to these delights, but most guests will do them justice.

Bridge is no longer the only game which can be made the occasion for such a tea; any game that is fashionable will do. The newer games, less traditional than bridge, are appropriate for quite informal parties.

Cocktails

In today's homes, a corner of a room, or a piece of furniture, is often reserved for the purpose of a "house bar" and for the preparation of cocktails. Either its purpose is announced by suitable decorations or the equipment is concealed. A popular custom is to adapt for this purpose a marquetry cabinet with doors which, when opened, reveal the contents, perhaps multiplied by a mirror lining. Many pieces of furniture, from bureaus to all kinds of cabinets, lend themselves to transformation into a drawing-room bar.

Remember that champagne and whisky are also popular at cocktail time. A bottle of good dry white wine needs no apology among close friends. Aperitifs may also be served to those who prefer them.

Cocktails are easily prepared in a beaker or shaker (see pages 33ff).

Be sure to have fruit juice on hand, and remember that canapés are always appreciated with cocktails. These should be small and require no plates or cutlery.

Dinner

Even if the number of guests is small, dinner always involves some formality. Our suggestions on table decorations and service may be helpful here. The general considerations involved in giving a well-regulated dinner have already been discussed. Here we present the details of the table setting.

The glasses are placed in a row behind the plate, starting on the left with the champagne glass, then the water glass, Burgundy glass, and Bordeaux glass. Sometimes a glass for white wine is added.

The napkins are folded simply, without any attempt at elaboration, and put on the plates, unless the soup is brought in before the guests come to the table; in that case, the napkins, like the bread, are put at the left of the plate. When there are many guests, place cards may be put behind the plate, next to the glasses. For a large dinner, it is customary for the hostess to provide handwritten menus, which are also put behind the plate.

The dessert plates and appropriate cutlery, together with the finger bowls, may be laid out on the butler's tray in advance, if there is room. The coffee service and cups, as well as the liqueurs, will be carried into the drawing room when the guests leave the table.

The place setting for a dinner is as follows:

A flat plate on which the napkin is laid. (The soup plate is handed, ready filled, when the guests are seated, unless it has been set in place beforehand.)

Table knife, cutting edge turned toward the plate.

Fish knife.

Soup spoon. In France, the convex side is laid uppermost. In Great Britain and the United States, the hollow side is turned up. The same applies to forks.

Oyster fork or melon fork, if required.

Table fork. This is changed with each course, together with the plate.

Fish fork.

Dessert knife and fork or spoon. In Great Britain these are sometimes placed behind the plate. In France, they are more frequently brought in on the dessert plate. In the United States, they may be brought in on the dessert plate at the time the dessert is served, or fork or spoon may be placed on the table at the time the cover is laid, having the fork on the left of the plate and the spoon on the right.

If finger bowls are to be used, fill them one-third full with warm water and place each, with a small doily under it, on a dessert plate, which is placed before the guest. Then the guests will move the finger bowls and doilies to a position just behind the dessert plate and a little to the left. If fruit is to be served after the dessert course, do not put finger bowls on the dessert plates.

Instead, place dessert silver at each place, unless it has been previously laid, and then serve the dessert. When the dessert is finished, replace each dessert plate with a fruit plate which has on it a finger bowl and doily in the center, the fruit knife to the left of the bowl, and the spoon to the right. The guest places the finger bowl and doily on the table at the top of the plate, and the silver on the table, the fork on the left of the bowl and the spoon on the right. The fruit bowl is passed.

Holiday Parties

Dinners or suppers on Christmas Eve or New Year's Eve, whether celebrated intimately in a small group or by a large number of friends, must have a domestic solemnity. Christmas Eve is traditionally more of a family affair, quieter; in France the party usually follows the celebration of midnight Mass. New Year's Eve, a purely secular occasion, is more animated, not to say exuberant. Decorations on these occasions are a matter of personal taste, a time for new and gay ideas. The charming bric-a-brac of angel's hair, glass balls, tinsel, etc., must be used with discernment. Holly, gilded leaves, and flowers are also useful, though the real art is to create a sparkle of life and gaiety which, in the nature of things, is dormant in winter. There is always room for a Christmas tree, small or large. Candles are more than ever indicated.

For these occasions, nothing is too beautiful. Once a year, one can indulge in an accumulation of crystal, silver, china, an abundance of light and reflections, without fear of criticism. But as always, good taste will keep the display within bounds.

As to the menu, it remains traditional: oysters or cold consommé, chicken in aspic (or turkey, at Christmas), foie gras, Christmas chocolate log. That is only the basis; regional specialties will evoke more or less distant provinces. One must experiment with innovations while carefully preserving the atmosphere of tradition. A successful Christmas Eve or New Year's Eve party can be an enchanted memory for a whole year.

SERVICE FOR A FORMAL DINNER

Undoubtedly the number of private houses where service on the grand scale is still practiced has decreased in recent years. Nevertheless, many still survive, more perhaps than is generally believed. In any case, the information and suggestions which we offer concerning service at receptions and formal dinners are valuable even for occasions on a reduced scale.

Present-day usage demands quick service. For this reason the dishes leave the kitchen ready carved, with joints, birds, and game re-formed in their original shape. In first-class and distinguished restaurants the dishes are first presented to the customer and then carved at a side table placed in front of or next to the customer's table. Carving methods and the traditional preparation in front of the customer are described and illustrated in Culinary Techniques in Pictures.

In houses of great tradition and at ceremonial meals, the butler, in white gloves, will present the dish on the guest's left, starting with the lady sitting on the host's right and finishing with the hostess. A second servant starts with the gentleman seated on the right of the hostess and finishes with the host. If the dish is accompanied by a sauce, it is best to have another servant offer the sauce immediately. Usually, however, the same servant who presents the dish holds the sauceboat in his right hand and the dish in his left, and turns slightly to present the sauceboat as soon as the guest has served herself or himself to the dish.

As soon as the guests have finished, the plates, knives, and forks are removed and replaced by warmed plates (except for cold dishes, of course) and new cutlery. After entrées and dishes in a sauce have been served, the roast usually follows, accompanied by salad. However, if the menu includes a cold dish, the salad will be served with the latter.

We recommend that both food and serving dishes be very hot. When hot dishes have been carved and prepared, they must be put back into the oven for a moment. The underside of a dish must be wiped when it is removed from the oven, to avoid soiling the staff's white gloves. If the dining room is rather far away from the kitchen the dishes should be covered to keep the food hot. The cover is removed outside the dining room door. If the serving dish does not have a cover, a warmed deep plate may be used instead.

After the roast and salad comes the cheese course. It is usual to offer two kinds of cheese, one soft and one hard, say Camembert and Gruyère, or Brie and Edam, for the guests to choose from. For the cheese course, each guest is handed a small plate with the cheese knife lying on it.

After the cheese course, the staff will remove the cutlery and salt cellars, brush off the crumbs, working from the right-hand side of each guest, and then set finger bowls filled with lukewarm, perfumed water.

Ices or desserts are usually served by the manservant, using an ice-cream ladle or a spoon for the dessert. On ceremonial occasions the plates of petits fours and dessert will be handled by the manservant, but on more informal ones they are placed on the table and the guests serve themselves when invited to do so by the hostess.

The dinner is now concluded and the host and hostess rise to indicate that the time has come to go into the drawing room. At large dinners the staff quickly draws back the chairs so that the guests can leave the dining room without noise or obstacle. When the dinner is a ceremonial one, each gentleman will offer his arm to his dinner partner to lead her out of the room. Coffee and liqueurs are served in the drawing room.

On formal or ceremonial occasions, the party will break up not later than 11 P.M. It is only on more intimate occasions that the evening is prolonged, and it is then the duty of the host and hostess to circulate refreshments—lemonade, orangeade, iced coffee, etc.

When the guests start to leave, the valet or chambermaid must be in the cloakroom in order to hand over the coats and help the guests into them. The chambermaid must stay until the last guest has gone, if only in case there is a button to sew on at the last moment.

As we suggested earlier, it is possible to hold very charming and very brilliant receptions without the help of a large staff. The whole art is to prepare everything in advance so that the host and hostess are not constantly forced to leave their guests. It is better to have a cold buffet, where everyone can serve himself and the host and hostess can really devote themselves to their guests, than one of those ghastly dinners at which every time the hostess gets up, everyone feels he must offer to help, only to let her do it alone in the end after all. (See the section on Cold Buffets, pages 23–33.)

In conclusion, no guest must ever be allowed to feel for a second that he is causing trouble. Let us repeat what we said at the beginning: the secret of successful entertainment is to put everyone at ease. Entertaining successfully also means making friends, and what in the world is of greater value?

MENUS

The great traditional menus of ten to twelve courses belong to the past. Even a menu of six to seven courses has become exceptional. Though these elaborate menus have vanished as the result of changing customs, social necessity, and even the demands of health and beauty, our present menus are worthy successors.

The composition of a grand traditional menu was roughly as follows:

1. Soup—clear or thickened.
2. Hot hors d'oeuvre.
3. Cold hors d'oeuvre.
4. Fish.
5. A remove of meat, poultry, or game—usually a piece of roasted or braised meat with a garnish. (A remove—French *relevé*—is a dish which follows another; it usually preceded the entrée.)
6. Entrée. Many dishes could be served as an entrée, but it was usually a dish in a sauce.
7. Roast—usually poultry or game. The roast was accompanied by a green salad, but this could also be served separately.
8. Sherbet or water ice (sorbet). It used to be compulsory to serve an ice after the roast, to cleanse the palate for the next courses.
9. Cold entrée. This could be a foie gras pâté or parfait, an artistic presentation of lobster or rock lobster, a cold chicken or other cold dish.
10. Side dishes (entremets). These included not only desserts and ices but also vegetables and cheeses.
11. Dessert and fruit.

A menu for what is described as a "simple dinner" at the beginning of the nineteenth century is given in Antonin Carême's book *Le Maître d'Hôtel Français*. It consisted of two soups, two hors d'oeuvre, two removes, two removes of soup, twenty entrées, four different roasts, two large, two medium-sized and sixteen smaller side dishes of eggs, vegetables, and desserts.

Toward the middle of the nineteenth century radical deletions began to be made, as this menu for a dinner at the court of Napoleon III shows.

Dinner at the Tuileries on February 1, 1858

Potage printanier
Rice in consommé

Turbot with lobster and Hollandaise sauce

Fillet of beef jardinière
Small chicken, fricasseed

Pheasant Perigord style
Chaud-froid of partridge
Rice casseroles Toulouse style
Strasbourg pâté de foie gras

Venison
Woodcock
Rouen duck

Asparagus
French beans

Puff-paste gâteau Pompadour
Orange and tangerine jelly
Timbale Chateaubriand
Basket of apricots with rice

At the beginning of the twentieth century, the number of dishes was again reduced. The menu, even at a banquet, was something like this: one soup, thick or clear; one fish dish; one remove or entrée; one roast, usually accompanied by a salad; one vegetable dish; one side dish, hot or cold, followed by an ice; dessert. At very elegant dinners, a cold hors d'oeuvre—caviar, melon, oysters, etc.—was served, contrary to general usage. The chief simplification consisted in serving only one dish for each course.

The remarkable simplification of menus in our second half of the twentieth century should be noted. Even on the occasion of the marriage of King Baudouin of the Belgians to Doña Fabiola de Mora y Aragon on December 13, 1960, only the following simple meal was served:

Clear soup Diane
Lobster with herbs
Saddle of boar Nesselrode with chestnut purée
Strasbourg foie gras in sherry jelly
Royal parfait

Some other recent menus for important occasions follow.

Luncheon of the Disciples of Antonin Carême, 1959

Foie gras parfait
Sole soufflé Abel Luquet
Saddle of lamb Antonin Carême
Cointreau sherbet
Cold sliced Nantes duck with orange
Selection of cheeses
Omelette Duc de Praslin

Luncheon at the Jean-Drouant Hotel School, Paris

Terrine Lucullus with toast, or
Russian-style pink salmon with mayonnaise

*

Royal chicken with morels, or
grilled entrecôte Maître d'Hôtel

*

Selection of spring vegetables
Salad
Selection of cheeses
Choice of desserts

Dinner given by the French Culinary Academy
in honor of Monsieur Eugène Lacroix
at Lucas Carton, Paris

Salmon trout, Hermitage sauce
Timbale of sweetbreads with peas
Roast beef, Macaire potatoes
Terrine Brillat-Savarin, lettuce hearts
Delices de France
Peaches Madeleine
Rock of vanilla ice
Petits fours

Pouilly-Fuissé 1956
Château Montrose 1937
Irroy Champagne 1950

All these menus show that while the number of dishes offered has decreased considerably and some changes have been made in the composition of the dishes, the basic construction of the menu has not changed.

However, there have been major changes of detail. Before going into these it is necessary to explain what an entrée was in a traditional menu. It never meant, as one might expect, the first dish on a menu. In a traditional menu, without any exception whatsoever, the entrée followed the dish known as a remove, which was served after the fish if fish appeared on the menu. In principle, an entrée should be a hot dish in a white or brown sauce, though at a formal dinner a cold dish may be served instead. Although this principle is inviolable for formal dinners, ordinary usage must be taken into account. Thus in certain restaurant menus there is a choice of several courses and the first is described as the "entrée" or "first course."

The most important changes that have taken place in menus are the result of the present-day way of life. Nobody wants to spend a long time at table. Nor does anyone wish to put on weight, so people tend to be active after meals. A large roast is no longer as popular as it used to be, especially for luncheon. Small, easily digested dishes are preferred—quickly sautéed

Decor is an aesthetic and social manifestation (Hotel Gritti Palace, Venice) ▶

▲ A continental breakfast table

A family luncheon table ▼

A dinner table for guests ▲

▼ Elegance and formality in a restaurant

meats, poultry, or grills. Ragouts have become much less popular. People want a light, appetizing meal, with plenty of vegetables, salad, and fruit—in fact, a meal which does not overload the digestion and after which work can be resumed without any difficulty. There are no absolute rules, but in practice a present-day luncheon may be something like this:

1. A cold hors d'oeuvre, an egg dish, or fish. (Some people like soup at lunch time.)
2. A hot entrée or a grilled meat, garnished. In summer cold meat may be served, accompanied by salad.
3. Cheese.
4. A small dessert: ice, stewed fruit, pastry, or fresh fruit.

The evening meal may be more substantial, since time is not so limited. Nevertheless, dinners also are far less rich than they used to be. A dinner consists of:

1. Clear or thick soup, or a small cold hors d'oeuvre.
2. Fish, a hot entrée, or a dish of garnished vegetables.
3. A roast garnished with vegetables. (If entrée is substantial, a small cold dish with salad may be served instead.)
4. A hot or cold dessert or an ice, if possible with fruit.

All this still makes for a rather plentiful evening meal, which will be reduced to three courses on everyday occasions. Banquets and formal dinners are, of course, arranged differently. Before we come to these, certain rules that are compulsory both for the daily menu and more important occasions must be explained.

A correct menu, gastronomically speaking, is much more difficult to select than one might think. In planning menus for a restaurant or a household, some fundamental principles must be borne in mind, of which these are the most important:

1. The same meat or poultry must never appear twice on one menu, even if prepared in different ways.
2. Colors must be alternated—that is, one must not serve two white or two brown sauces in succession. If there is fish in a white sauce it must not be followed by chicken in a white sauce.
3. Garnishes must be varied. If one serves mushrooms, tomatoes, or artichoke bottoms as garnish for a fish dish, these cannot be served with another course. It is, however, permissible to use truffles to garnish a cold dish even if they have already accompanied a previous dish.

◀ A hunt breakfast

4. Cooking methods must be varied. A boiled or poached fish cannot be followed by boiled chicken, for example. An exception may be made only if the menu is a very full one, and even then only if other dishes have been served between the two similar ones.
5. A thick and nourishing soup is served only in cold weather. The same applies to fat or filling dishes, which are only served in winter.
6. A canned vegetable should not be served during or immediately after the season of the fresh one. If, for instance, the asparagus season is just over, canned asparagus will not be served unless the customer in a restaurant expressly asks for it. However, the rule does not apply to the excellent deep-frozen vegetables now available.
7. Menus should be written in clear and comprehensible language. Technical hotel expressions are usually Greek to the layman. They should be correct, without a single error. A menu that is handwritten or typewritten (top copy) is always pleasanter than a mimeographed one.

These rules apply to daily meals and even more to formal occasions. It is not easy to compose menus of this kind. The chef must bear in mind not only the customer's wishes, the cost, the time of year, but a lot of other things as well. A wedding breakfast will be quite different from the closing banquet of a scientific congress. A hunting breakfast has quite a different character from a diplomatic dinner. But even on the most formal occasions, it is unusual to go beyond the courses which follow:

1. A small, first-class thick soup or clear soup served in cups. At a large official dinner a cold hors d'oeuvre—caviar, oysters, foie gras parfait, etc.—may be served before the soup.
2. Fish or shellfish.
3. An entrée or a roast garnished with vegetables.
4. A cold dish with a salad or a fine vegetable—or even a roast if a very light entrée is served.
5. Cheese.
6. A hot or cold dessert or an ice.
7. Fruit.

Salad, vegetables, and fruit must be included in all meals. The question of cheese at large dinners is a controversial one; many connoisseurs maintain that it is out of place at an elaborate dinner. In France, cheese is served before the dessert, but in some countries it is eaten at the end of the meal.

Here is a selection of menus, some simple, some more elaborate, for various seasons and special circumstances.

Spring

LUNCHEON

Avocados with seafood
Lamb noisettes Salvatore
Cheese
Fruit Salad

DINNER

Chicken broth
Cheese straws
Asparagus with three sauces
German-style saddle of venison
Endive salad
Charlotte Russe

Summer

LUNCHEON

Hors d'oeuvre platter
Venison steak Madame Lacroix
Hearts of lettuce
Cheese
Strawberries with Chantilly cream

DINNER

Cream soup Ilona
Crayfish tails au gratin
Chicken in Riesling wine
Noodles Alsatian style
Beatrice salad
Iced soufflé with strawberries

Autumn

LUNCHEON

Poached eggs Massena
Brisket of beef Flemish style
Cheese
Cream à la Vigneron

DINNER

Consommé Madrilène
Pike quenelles Lyonnaise
Pheasant Vallée d'Auge
Mercedes salad
Pears Cardinal

Winter

LUNCHEON

Artichokes à la Grecque
Sweetbread fillets Jèrome
Cheese
Profiteroles with chocolate sauce

DINNER

Lobster cocktail
Soup à la Reine
Saddle of hare à la bergère
Simone salad
Ice pudding Diane

Wedding Breakfast

Rich hors d'oeuvre
Cream Duquinha
Salmon trout Doria
Breasts of guinea fowl with lichee nuts
Hearts of palm Milanese
Soufflé with almonds; zabaglione with port

Diplomatic Dinner

Clear turtle soup with sherry
Fillets of sole Atelier
Saddle of lamb Richelieu
Lettuce hearts with celery
Sliced duck in aspic with oranges
Savarin Othello

Closing Dinner for a Congress or Convention

Melon cocktail
Consommé à la diable
Red mullet Niçoise
Spit-roasted chicken
Green peas French style
Cress and beet salad
Kirsch parfait
Friandises

Christmas Eve

Lobster medallions Windsor style
Consommé
Fillets of sole Nabuchu
Turkey breasts Tamburlaine
Apples Marie-Louise
Chicory and tomato salad
Biscuit glacé with small cakes

COLD BUFFETS

An invitation to a cold buffet not only indicates the eclectic taste of the hosts but is also most likely to promise a successful party. It provides the opportunity for a real spectacle of culinary art and color, ranging from the simplest to the most splendid, depending on the brilliance and importance you wish to give to the occasion, and on the standing and taste of your guests. Whether it is a simple buffet for friends or a ceremonial occasion, aesthetic beauty and culinary skill are bound to triumph.

According to their wishes and facilities, the hosts may have the buffet prepared by their own staff or by a catering firm which will send the food to their home. In some circumstances a reception at which a cold buffet is served is given at a hotel which specializes in this service.

For a cold buffet at home hosts with a limited number of rooms at their disposal will choose one, for instance the dining room, in which the cold buffet will be set out. If possible this should not be the same room as that in which they receive their guests. The buffet, laid out on a long and preferably narrow table covered with a cloth reaching to the floor, will be the center of attention. The table should be neither too high nor too large, in order to make service easier. A second smaller table will be set aside for drinks, which the staff will hand around to the guests. Lacking a serving staff, you may serve drinks on a chest, desk, or any other convenient place, in addition to the table. Do not forget to provide enough plates, cutlery, and napkins. The size of the plates must be suitable for the dishes provided. If the guests are to serve themselves, put these accessories in a place where they will not interfere with the guests' freedom of movement.

The table decorations are of the utmost importance. A lace tablecloth will bear witness to the host's taste. Alternatively, a white tablecloth, whether or not it is of damask, will give a note of sober elegance. If there is no serving staff, the floral decorations, tastefully arranged and harmonizing with the colors of the food, may be high and sumptuous; otherwise they should not be too bulky, in order not to hamper the staff. In the evening, candelabra, chandeliers, and candlesticks will give a festive air to your buffet table and the soft light of the candles will create an exquisite atmosphere.

Some suggestions for buffets for various occasions follow.

Cocktail Buffet

The more subtle and colorful your buffet, the more it will be appreciated by your guests. Platters or trays should not be so large that the staff cannot pass them easily without inconveniencing the guests.

We suggest the following selection:

Small chou-paste puffs filled with anchovy, cheese, caraway seeds, ham.

Smoked eel or fish canapés with pickled cucumber; canapés of dried beef with stuffed olives; raw ham canapés with gherkins; cheese cubes sprinkled with caraway seeds and garnished with grated white of hard-cooked egg.

Puff-paste boats filled with truffled chicken salad; canapés of white bread with Gervais cheese; canapés of rye bread with slices of tomato and Emmentaler cheese sprinkled with paprika; slices of apple cooked slowly in butter and wrapped in slices of lean grilled bacon.

Canapés of shrimp and fresh butter; cornets of dried beef filled with cream cheese; canapés of hard-cooked eggs and caviar.

Whole grapefruit into which small slices of salami, round slices of gherkins and pickled cucumbers, small cocktail onions pickled in vinegar, pieces of pimiento, and cheese cubes dusted with paprika are stuck with toothpicks. Surround with small pieces of puff paste cut in fancy shapes. Or grapefruit stuck with black olives, radishes, slices of pickled cucumber, cheese cubes dusted with paprika.

Whole head of red cabbage, stuck with crayfish tails, black olives, stuffed olives, small radishes, small celery hearts. Surround with small sausages and pieces of puff paste cut in fancy shapes.

Slices of fresh cucumber spread with salmon; small canapés of rye bread spread with cream cheese with a slice of tomato on top; canapés of Swedish bread spread with salmon mousse and cream cheese.

Puff-paste boats filled with truffled lobster salad. Gorgonzola and creamed Gruyère cheese mixed with diced rye bread and served in paper cups.

Canapés of wholewheat bread, buttered and spread with cheese and garnished with pimientos.

Thin slices of buttered white bread with a slice of tomato topped with a small artichoke bottom on each; slices of cheese garnished with sweet peppers.

Salted almonds.

DRINKS: All cocktails, aperitifs, white wine, champagne, fruit juice, tomato juice.

Danish Buffet

As the name indicates, this gastronomic novelty came to us from Denmark. It is very popular in Scandinavia and is becoming more and more so in other countries. It is the ideal formula for a summer party in the country. The food can be served on pottery dishes laid on countrified homespun tablecloths. The dishes may be selected among the following:

Sliced roast pork garnished with pickled cucumbers, lettuce hearts, and sliced tomatoes.

Sliced pickled tongue with lettuce hearts.

Cold sliced roast beef garnished with fresh cucumbers.

Sliced boiled ham garnished with fresh cucumbers.

Danish caviar, chopped onions, parsley, and radishes.

Hard-cooked eggs in mayonnaise, garnished with tomatoes, asparagus, and lettuce leaves.

Shrimp in cocktail sauce, surrounded with lettuce leaves.

Julienne of pickled tongue and beets mixed with mayonnaise, garnished with cucumbers, tomatoes, and sliced sweet peppers.

Salad of asparagus tips in Chantilly mayonnaise.

Seafood salad with Chantilly mayonnaise seasoned with catsup.

Quartered hard-cooked eggs and sliced tomatoes, garnished with parsley.

Asparagus tips.

Cornets of smoked salmon with asparagus tips and parsley.

Small Tartare steaks on lettuce leaves, egg yolks and salt served separately.

Sliced wholewheat, white, and rye bread arranged on a breadboard, with fresh butter.

Small pickled onions, black olives, radishes, gherkins, and pickles.

Small fillets of cold pork garnished with orange sections.

Danish pâté de foie gras in jelly, garnished with lettuce leaves and slices of grilled bacon.

Gripsholm-style herring salad (pickled herring, diced apple and cucumber, mayonnaise, sour cream, and horseradish).

Sardines marinated with catsup.

Canned smoked herring.

Salad of herring, cucumbers, and macédoine of vegetables, with sweet and sour dressing.

Matjes herring garnished with onion rings.

Smoked mussels with mayonnaise.

Pickled herring garnished with gherkins and cucumber.

DRINKS: For a reception in the country, first serve an aperitif and in summer Bellini cocktails; with the buffet serve white and rosé wine, local wine, Danish beer, fruit juice, carbonated beverages.

Formal Buffet

At home. Many recipes and suggestions for simple dishes will be found in Chapter 5, Cold Hors d'Oeuvre. Skill, taste, and culinary experience will enable you to prepare fine cold dishes ranging from fish to game, which will give great pleasure to your guests. Fruit salads, cold zabaglione in coupes, charlottes, savarins, parfaits, and iced coupes will be the favorite desserts, with plates of petits fours and cakes.

If you have more than ten guests, prepare two plates of each dish.

Choose the drinks to suit the dishes and the time of day; in the late morning and at lunch time serve vermouth, sherry, Bellini cocktails, white and rosé wine, champagne; in the evening, all aperitifs, cocktails, wines, fruit juice, and carbonated beverages.

In a hotel. A formal buffet in a first-class hotel is always an occasion of great brilliance (see illustration, pages 36–37).

To avoid confusion, the chef and some of his assistants, or the waiters, will stand behind the buffet tables to serve the guests. The number of servers will depend on the number of guests. The guests themselves will choose the dishes they want. To avoid gastronomic and culinary incompatibility, the serving staff will not place fish and poultry, shellfish and game, etc., on the same plate. Soup is optional; it will be hot or cold according to the time of year. If only one dessert is provided, for example, Oranges Riviera (see illustration, page 38), it will be served to the guests in portions.

The drinks will be served in the appropriate glasses, placed on silver trays handed around by waiters. If the guests sit down to eat, the waiters will go around pouring wine for each place setting, as requested by the guests. It is not usual to serve beer at a formal buffet unless a guest asks for it especially.

Dishes for formal and ceremonial buffets. A selection of dishes may be made from the list which follows. An asterisk indicates that the recipe is included in this section. Recipes for the other dishes listed will be found in the relevant chapters by consulting the index. When the ingredients of a recipe include elements to be prepared in advance, the title is capitalized (Chantilly Sauce, Truffles Surprise) and the recipe can be located from the index.

Hors d'oeuvre cocktails

Shellfish

All cold lobster and rock lobster dishes (see illustrations, pages 36, 515, 516)

Fish

Cold Cod Russian Style (see illustration, page 441)
Salmon in an artistic presentation (see illustrations, pages 463, 465)
Salmon Steaks Louis XVI*
Salmon Moscow Style (see illustration, page 463)
Cornets of Smoked Salmon Russian Style (see illustration, page 222)
Any other cold salmon dishes
Fillets of Sole Floralies (see illustration, page 442)
Trout: any cold trout dishes that are sufficiently showy

⚜ SALMON STEAKS LOUIS XVI

2 fillets of salmon (2¼ pounds without bones and skins)
50 jumbo shrimp tails
hot fish stock (court bouillon) to cover fish
mayonnaise
1¼ cups jellied clear stock
1 cup each cooked julienne carrots, green beans, and peas
1 cup raw julienne celery strips
24 small poached mushroom caps
8 ounces red caviar
12 ripe olives
3 tangerine sections
chives
4 hen's eggs, or 12 quail or gull eggs, hard-cooked
1¼ cups melted jellied stock
23 cherry tomatoes
salt
ground black pepper
7-ounce can pimiento
honeydew balls from large honeydew melon
Chantilly Sauce or Green Mayonnaise

Wrap salmon in buttered paper or cheesecloth and place in a deep baking dish. Add enough fish stock (court bouillon) to cover. Cook in a preheated moderate oven (350° F.) 15 minutes or until the fish is flaky but still holds its shape. Chill until ready to serve with a plate placed on top of it to give a small amount of pressure. Cook shrimp; peel, devein, and set aside. Combine 1 cup mayonnaise and ¾ cup of the jellied stock, having it about half set. Fold in the carrots, green beans, peas, and celery. Turn the mixture into a lightly oiled 1½-quart round shallow mold. Just before serving, unmold onto a very large plate or tray. Frost top and sides completely with mayonnaise. Decorate top as desired with 2 of the poached mushroom caps, a little of the red caviar, 2 of the ripe olives, the tangerine sections, chives, and 3 wedges of the hard-cooked eggs. Brush melted jellied stock over decorations, saving remaining melted stock for later use. Place shrimp around the mold. Cut the chilled salmon into 22 uniform slices and arrange them around the shrimp, with the rounded ends pointed inward. Stuff the remaining mushrooms with the rest of the caviar and place one on each pointed end of salmon slices. Brush both shrimp and salmon with melted jellied stock. Remove and discard centers of tomatoes, sprinkle the cavities with salt and black pepper, and drain well. Drain and discard oil from pimientoes. Put pimientoes through a sieve, and mix with remaining ½ cup of jellied stock. Spoon into cavities of tomatoes. Top each with ¼ slice hard-cooked hen's egg or ½ slice quail or gull egg, and ½ pitted ripe olive. Place the tomatoes between the pointed outer ends of salmon slices. Arrange a row of honeydew balls around the salmon. Brush both tomatoes and honeydew balls with melted jellied stock. Serve with Chantilly Sauce or Green Mayonnaise. Serves 20 to 22. (See illustration, page 37.)

Beef

- Glazed Fillet of Beef (see illustration, page 557)
- Fillet of Beef Rothschild
- Russian-Style Fillet of Beef
- Pickled Tongue Karachi Style (see illustration, page 558)
- Tongue Princesse (see illustration, page 557)

Veal

- Jellied Veal Pot Roast
- Cold Saddle of Veal (see illustrations, page 602)

Ham

- Ham Roulade*
- Ham Glazed with Aspic (see illustration, page 623)
- Ham Villandry (see illustration, page 219)
- Ham Mousse (see illustration, page 626)
- Any other of the more elegant cold ham dishes

⚜ HAM ROULADE

8 large eggs
¾ teaspoon salt
2 cups sifted cake flour
7 tablespoons butter
1½ cups finely ground cooked ham
1½ teaspoons paprika
brandy to taste
1 cup half-set jellied chicken stock
⅔ cup heavy cream

Break eggs into a large bowl; add salt. Place over warm water and beat until the mixture is very thick and lemon-colored. Gently fold in flour. Melt butter, cool, and add it, in a thin stream, to the mixture, and mix lightly to prevent batter from becoming heavy. Pour batter into two buttered, lightly floured pans, 10 by 15 by 1 inch (jelly-roll pans). Spread batter uniformly over the bottom of the pans. Bake in a preheated hot oven (425° F.) for 8 to 10 minutes. Remove from baking pans immediately, roll up as for jelly roll in a slightly moistened cloth, and let stand until cold. Mix ham with paprika, brandy, and the half-set chicken stock. Whip the cream and fold into ham mixture. Unroll the baked sponge layers. Spread with the ham mixture. Roll up, wrap in foil or towel, and chill. Cut into slices ⅓ inch thick. Serves 50 to 60.

Poultry

Assortment of Cold Poultry and Pâtés*
Chaud-froid of Chicken Breasts (see illustration, page 683)
Turkey Breasts Champs Élysées*

⚜ ASSORTMENT OF COLD POULTRY AND PÂTÉS

5-pound cold roast duck
5-pound cold roast chicken
1 pound 5 ounces Foie Gras Mousse
12 peeled, seeded, and quartered tomatoes
3 hard-cooked egg whites
1½ cups clear meat jelly
10 small slices cold chicken
1 quart Waldorf Salad
10 small mushrooms
2-ounce can pimiento
2-pound cold cooked pheasant
2 pounds chilled firm butter
1 cold Pâté of Chicken
10 small Green Peppers à la Grecque
2 cups diced cold cooked chicken
2 cups diced raw mushrooms
¼ cup Vinaigrette Sauce
¼ cup crushed, peeled, and seeded tomato
¼ cup diced gherkins
1 tablespoon tomato catsup
5 to 7 Truffles Surprise
1 large bunch grapes

Remove breast and breast bones from duck and chicken. Discard the breast bones and save the meat of the breasts to use later. Fill the duck carcass with Foie Gras Mousse. Completely cover it with some of the tomato slices. Cut hard-cooked egg whites in crosswise slices and place in a row down the center of the duck. Glaze with melted clear jelly. Chill. Slice duck breast diagonally and place the slices on the 10 slices of cold, cooked chicken, which have been spread thinly with some of the Foie Gras Mousse. Glaze with melted clear jelly. Chill.

Fill chicken carcass with Waldorf Salad, having it piled high in the shape of a dome. Cover with slices of chicken breast. Poach mushroom caps in boiling water 2 to 3 minutes and place in a line down the center of the stuffed chicken, top side up. Garnish with a straight line of pimiento strips. Glaze with clear meat jelly. Chill.

Glaze pheasant with clear meat jelly and chill.

Sculpture butter in the shape of a fowl (see illustration, page 35) and place it on one end of a large platter or tray. Arrange stuffed duck, chicken, and pheasant in front of it. Cut 10 slices cold Pâté of Chicken and place them in a lengthwise row on one side of the tray. Cut green peppers in half and fill with mushroom salad made with the next 6 ingredients. Place them in a row next to the slices of Pâté of Chicken. Garnish the chilled slices of duck breast with tomato slices and a bit of hard-cooked egg white. Put them in a row next to the stuffed peppers. Arrange a row of quartered Truffles Surprise and a row of the remaining tomatoes, quartered and filled with the rest of the Waldorf Salad. Glaze with clear meat jelly. Garnish tray with a bunch of grapes placed between the butter sculpture and the duck. Serves 20 to 30.

⚜ TURKEY BREASTS CHAMPS ÉLYSÉES

15 to 20 slices cooked celeriac (celery root)
5 large raw green peppers, cut in julienne strips
1 cup olive oil or salad oil
⅓ cup wine vinegar
1 teaspoon salt
¼ teaspoon ground black pepper
15 to 20 two-inch tomatoes, peeled and centers removed
2½ cups Waldorf Salad
1¾ cups jellied stock
10 artichoke bottoms
9 to 10 pounds roast turkey breast
30 slices poultry galantine
30 tangerine sections
15 pistachio nuts, halved
7 Truffles Surprise
1 baked 4-inch tart shell
about 55 radish roses

Marinate celeriac and green pepper 2 hours, in separate bowls, in the oil, vinegar, salt, and black pepper. Set aside. Sprinkle inside of tomatoes with salt and black pepper; invert to drain well. Fill cavities with Waldorf Salad and place each on a slice of marinated, well-drained celeriac. Glaze with jellied stock. Chill. Fill artichoke bottoms with well-drained green pepper. Glaze and chill. Slice turkey breasts and place one piece on each slice of poultry galantine. Garnish each slice with a tangerine section and ½ pistachio nut. Glaze with jellied stock and chill. Glaze truffles and chill.

To serve, fill the baked tart shell with Waldorf Salad and place it in the center of a large round tray. Around this arrange, in order given, Truffles Surprise, artichoke bottoms with green peppers, stuffed tomatoes on celeriac slices, slices of poultry galantine and turkey breast, and radish roses. (See illustration, page 35.) Serves 20 to 30.

Game

Glazed Pheasant à la Marie Jeanne (see illustration, page 723)
Saddle of Venison Grand Duchy Style*
Saddle of Venison Renoir*

⚜ SADDLE OF VENISON GRAND DUCHY STYLE

1 saddle of venison, about 6½ pounds
4 slices pineapple
8 truffles
3½ cups jellied stock
24 round slices of poached apples
12 Maraschino cherries
32 fluted and marinated mushrooms
20 cooked artichoke bottoms
2 large raw green peppers, cut into julienne strips and marinated 2 hours in French Dressing
8 baked 2-inch tart shells
3 cups Waldorf Salad
10 slices bread
butter

The venison should be cooked very quickly, 6 to 7 minutes per pound, in a preheated hot oven (450° F.). Cool. Remove meat from the bones and cut it into thin diagonal slices. Replace the slices on the bones so that they overlap. Cut each pineapple slice into 8 wedges and arrange them close together down the center of the sliced meat to stimulate the vertebrae. Garnish each wedge with a bit of truffle. Glaze the whole saddle with melted jellied stock. Chill. Garnish apple slices with ½ cherry and a bit of truffle. Glaze and chill. At the same time glaze 6 of the truffles and mushrooms and chill. Fill artichoke bottoms with marinated green pepper, glaze, and chill. Fill tart shells with Waldorf Salad. Cut bread into 20 rounds, using a 2-inch cooky cutter. Brown on both sides in butter (croutons). Cool. Top with chopped jellied stock.

Coat the bottom of a large rectangular tray with a thin layer of melted jellied stock. When stock is set, place the saddle of venison in the center. Place apple slices down each side, and a truffle flanked with two fluted mushrooms at each end. Place artichoke bottoms filled with green pepper strips on one side of the tray and the jelly-topped croutons on the other. Place salad-filled tarts at each end. Arrange a truffle surrounded by 7 fluted mushrooms in each corner. Serve with Cumberland Sauce, if desired. Serves 18 to 20. (See illustration, page 38, and for another presentation, page 725.)

⚜ SADDLE OF VENISON RENOIR

lardoons (thick strips dry, white, firm pork fat)
1 cup brandy
6 each coriander seeds, whole black peppercorns, and crushed juniper berries (if available)
1 whole clove
½ bay leaf
1 tablespoon chopped parsley
1 small clove garlic
¼ cup olive oil or salad oil
2 fillets of venison
½ pound bacon
1½ pounds mousseline forcemeat made with venison trimmings

Marinate the lardoons 2 hours in brandy, seasonings, and oil. Lard the venison fillets with the lardoons. Rub the outside of the venison lightly with salt and ground black pepper. Set aside. Butter a long mold with a rounded bottom and line it with thin bacon slices. Cover the bottom and sides of the mold with a thick layer of forcemeat, over which place venison and cover with remaining forcemeat. Tap the bottom of the mold several times to spread and settle the forcemeat. Cover with lightly buttered brown paper or foil. Place mold in a pan of hot water. Cook in a preheated moderate oven (350° F.) 35 to 40 minutes. The meat should be undercooked. Cool. Chill at least 6 hours before slicing. Cut into slices, allowing 5 to 6 ounces per serving. Glaze with melted meat jelly. Serve with Waldorf Salad.

Pâtés, Terrines, Galantines, Foie Gras

Any of the more elegant pâtés and terrines
Galantine of Chicken, Duck, or Turkey
Molded Foie Gras Mousse, Modern Style (see illustration, page 724)

Salads

The most decorative, subtlest, and lightest mixed salads

Fruit

Baskets of fruit with a generous selection, elegantly decorated

Desserts

Royal Charlotte (see illustration, page 900)
Charlotte Russe
Oranges Riviera (see illustration, page 38)
Savarins (see illustration, page 901)
Cold Zabaglione
Ices, iced coupes, parfaits, bombes

Pastry and Confectionery

Appropriate cakes
Plain and frosted petits fours
Spun-sugar basket with petits fours (see illustration, page 990)
Croquembouche of tiny cream puffs (see illustration, page 985)
Glacéed fruit
Chocolates

COCKTAIL MIXING AND SERVING

Cocktails are now so much a part of entertaining that this chapter would be incomplete without some suggestions for their preparation and service. The recipes included are for the cocktails most frequently served the world over.

Recipes for the same cocktail may vary widely. The proportion of vermouth to the other ingredients is particularly subject to the taste of the consumer. You may wish to experiment with the recipes that follow, but whatever formula you use, be sure to measure the ingredients accurately. Have glasses chilled if possible. Shake or stir drinks with ice just long enough to chill them thoroughly; otherwise the melting ice will dilute the drink.

Fashions in drinks are constantly changing. New cocktails are invented, others forgotten. At present many people ask for drinks "on the rocks"—that is, with ice cubes in the glass. This applies to Martinis, Manhattans, and various other cocktails which used always to be poured from the beaker or shaker with the ice strained out. Drinks "on the rocks" are usually served in a 4-ounce Old-Fashioned glass instead of a small cocktail glass. Long drinks usually have ice in the glass.

The basic ingredients for cocktails are whisky (Scotch, rye, bourbon), gin, vodka, brandy, liqueurs, vermouths, and fruit juices. A well-stocked bar will also provide Angostura bitters, orange bitters, Worcestershire sauce,

Tabasco, cocktail onions, small green olives, lemons, limes, oranges, and Maraschino cherries.

Cocktails are mixed either in a shaker or in a mixing beaker with a glass rod for stirring and a strainer. Other necessary equipment includes jiggers, measuring cups, droppers, drinking straws (long and short), ice pick, ice crusher, lemon squeezer, and a small sharp knife for cutting the rind of lemons or oranges. ("Peel" in recipes means the outer rind of the fruit, with none of the white part.)

The glasses most often used are: cocktail glasses, 2-ounce and 4-ounce; Old-Fashioned glasses, 4- to 6-ounce; highball glasses, 8-ounce and 10-ounce; Collins glasses, 10-, 12-, and 14-ounce.

⚜ ALASKA

In the shaker:

1/3 yellow Chartreuse
2/3 gin
ice

Stir, strain, and serve in a cocktail glass.

⚜ ALEXANDER

In the shaker:

1 teaspoon fresh cream
1/3 Crème de Cacao
2/3 brandy
ice

Shake and strain into a 4-ounce cocktail glass.

⚜ AMERICANO

In an 8-ounce highball glass:

1 ounce bitter Campari
2 ounces sweet vermouth
ice

Fill with carbonated water; stir slightly. Squeeze a twist of lemon peel over the drink and add the peel.

Assortment of Cold Poultry and Pâtés, page 29 ▲

▼ Turkey Breasts Champs Elysées, page 30

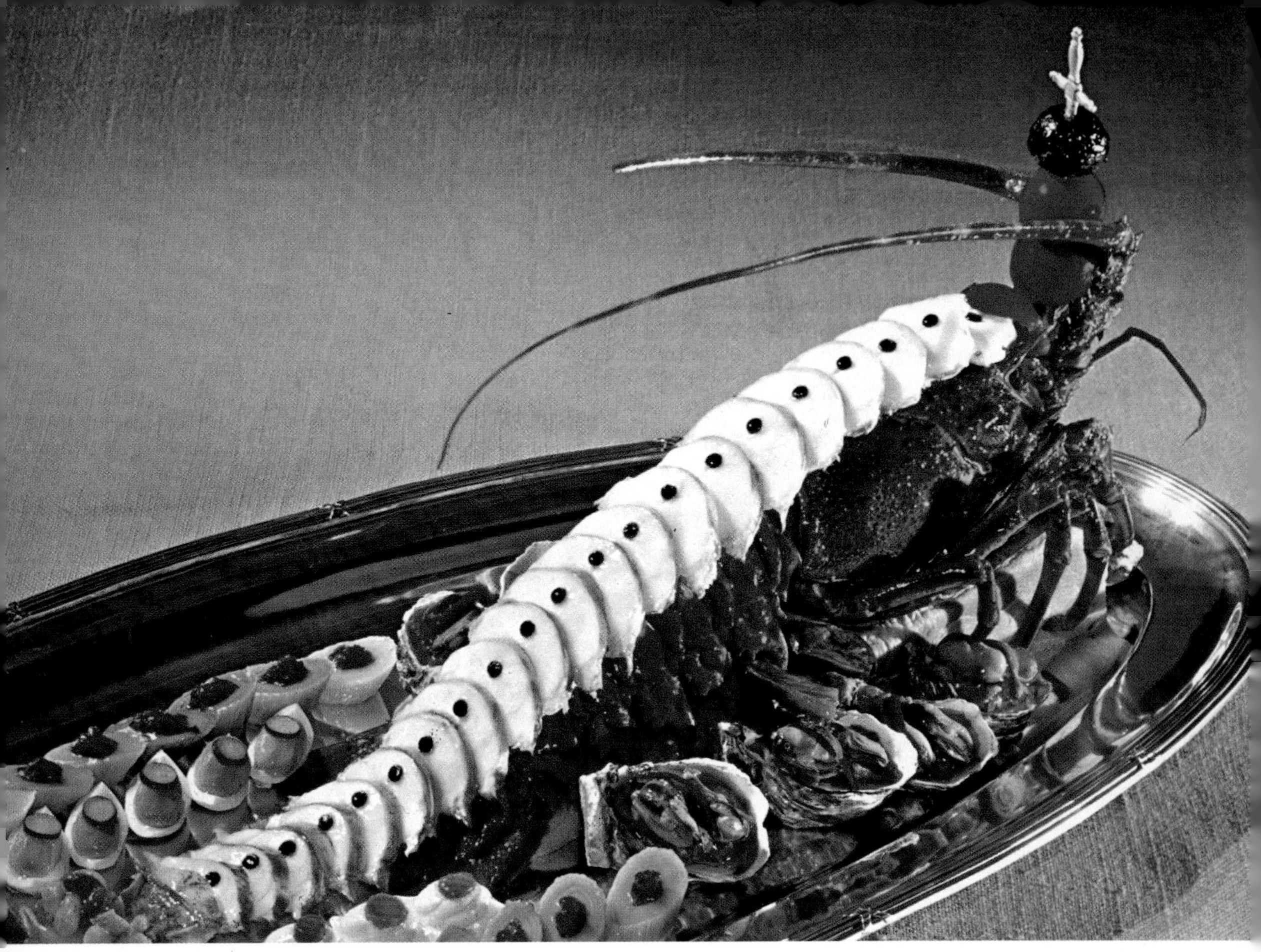

▲ Rock lobster in an artistic presentation (see page 521)

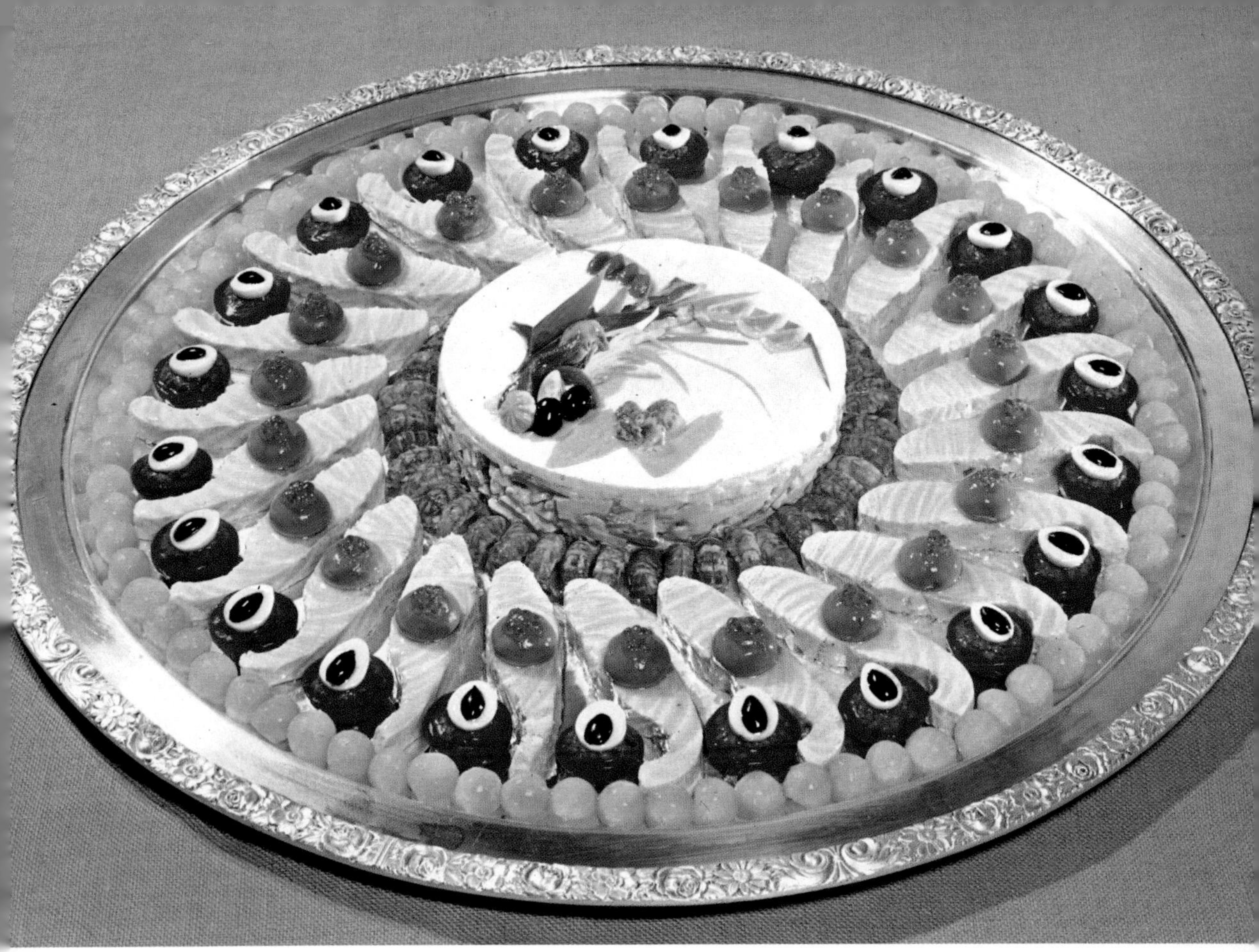

Salmon Steaks Louis XVI, page 27 ▲

▼ A formal cold buffet in a hotel (see pages 26–33)

▲ Saddle of Venison Grand Duchy Style, page 31

Oranges Riviera, page 954 ▼

⚜ BARBOTAGE

In the shaker:

1 teaspoon grenadine
1 ounce lemon juice
1 ounce orange juice
ice

Shake, strain into a 4-ounce cocktail glass, and fill with champagne.

⚜ BELLINI

In a 6-ounce glass:

1 ounce chilled peach juice
chilled dry champagne to fill

To make the peach juice, take 8 ripe peaches, remove the stones, press the peaches through a sieve till only the skin remains. Add the strained juice of 2 lemons, bottle, and keep in the refrigerator. Will keep 2 days.

⚜ BLACK VELVET

½ ice-cold stout
½ chilled champagne

Gently pour simultaneously into a 14-ounce glass.

⚜ BLOODY MARY

In an 8-ounce glass:

dash of lemon juice
2 dashes Worcestershire sauce
1½ ounces vodka
3 ounces tomato juice
ice

Stir well.

⚜ BOURBON COLLINS

See Tom Collins.

⚜ BRANDY EGG NOG

In the shaker:

1 teaspoon sugar
1 egg yolk
1½ ounces brandy
½ cup milk
ice

Shake, strain into a 10-ounce highball glass, and dust the top with grated nutmeg.

⚜ BRANDY FLIP

In the shaker:

½ teaspoon sugar
1 egg yolk
1½ ounces of brandy
ice

Shake and serve in a 4-ounce cocktail glass. Dust top with grated nutmeg.

⚜ BRONX

In the shaker:

2 dashes orange juice
⅙ dry vermouth
⅙ sweet vermouth
⅔ gin
ice

Shake, strain, and serve in a cocktail glass.

⚜ CARDINAL

In the shaker:

⅙ bitter Campari
⅓ dry vermouth
½ gin
ice

Shake, strain into a 4-ounce cocktail glass, and add a twist of lemon peel.

⚜ CHAMPAGNE COCKTAIL

In a champagne glass:

¼ lump of sugar
dash Angostura bitters
dash brandy

Fill with champagne and add a twist of orange peel.

⚜ CUBA LIBRE

In a 10-ounce glass filled with ice:

1½ ounces Bacardi rum

Fill up with Coca-Cola and decorate with a slice of lemon.

⚜ DAIQUIRI

In the shaker:

½ teaspoon simple syrup
juice of ½ lemon
1½ ounces white rum
finely shaved ice

Shake well, strain, and serve in a cocktail glass.

⚜ FROZEN DAIQUIRI

In the shaker:

1½ ounces light rum
juice of ½ lime
1 teaspoon sugar
finely crushed ice

Shake vigorously, or mix in an electric blender. Serve unstrained in a saucer-shaped champagne glass or 4-ounce cocktail glass, with a short straw.

⚜ DUBONNET COCKTAIL

In the mixing beaker:

⅔ Dubonnet
⅓ gin
ice

Stir, strain, and serve in a cocktail glass.

⚜ GIMLET

In the mixing beaker:

¾ dry gin
¼ Rose's sweetened lime juice
ice

Stir, strain, and serve in a cocktail glass. If unsweetened lime juice is used, add 1 teaspoon granulated sugar or simple syrup.

⚜ GIN DAISY

In the shaker:

dash grenadine
juice of ½ lemon
1½ ounces gin

Shake and pour without straining into an 8-ounce highball glass filled with finely crushed ice.

⚜ GIN FIZZ

In the shaker:

1 teaspoon sugar
juice of ½ lemon
1½ ounces gin
ice

Shake, pour into an 8-ounce highball glass, and fill with carbonated water. Fizzes may also be made with brandy or rum.

⚜ GOLDEN FIZZ

In the shaker:

- **1 egg yolk**
- **1 teaspoon sugar**
- **juice of ½ lemon**
- **1½ ounces gin**
- **ice**

Shake, pour into an 8-ounce highball glass, and fill with carbonated water.

⚜ SILVER FIZZ

In the shaker:

- **1 egg white**
- **1 teaspoon sugar**
- **juice of ½ lemon**
- **1½ ounces gin**
- **ice**

Shake, pour into an 8-ounce highball glass, and fill with carbonated water.

⚜ HONEYMOON

In the shaker:

- **juice of 1½ lemons**
- **½ teaspoon honey**
- **1½ ounces rum**
- **½ egg white**
- **ice**

Shake, strain, and serve in a 4-ounce cocktail glass.

⚜ MANHATTAN

In the mixing beaker:

- **1 or 2 dashes Angostura bitters**
- **⅕ sweet vermouth**
- **⅘ bourbon, rye, or blended whisky**

Stir, strain, and serve in a cocktail glass. Add a Maraschino cherry if desired. For a Dry Manhattan, use dry vermouth and omit the cherry.

⚜ DRY MARTINI

In the mixing beaker:

1/5 dry vermouth
4/5 gin
ice

Stir, strain, and serve in a cocktail glass. Add a twist of lemon peel or an olive if desired. A Martini served with 2 or 3 small pearl onions is called a Gibson. Vodka may be used instead of gin in Martinis.

⚜ NEGRONI

In the mixing beaker:

1/3 bitter Campari
1/3 gin
1/3 vermouth, sweet or dry
1/2 slice orange
ice

Stir, strain into an 8-ounce highball glass, and add the zest of a lemon.

⚜ OLD-FASHIONED

In an Old-Fashioned glass, put a small lump of sugar. Shake 2 or 3 dashes of Angostura bitters and a little carbonated water over the sugar and "muddle" until sugar dissolves. Fill glass with ice. Decorate with twist of lemon peel, Maraschino cherry, and 1/2 slice of orange (if desired). Add 1 1/2 ounces of bourbon, rye, Scotch, or rum.

⚜ ORANGE BLOSSOM

In the shaker:

juice of 1/2 orange
1 1/2 ounces gin
ice

Shake, strain, and serve in a 4-ounce cocktail glass.

⚜ PARADISE

In the shaker:

1/2 teaspoon orange juice
1/3 apricot brandy

⅔ gin
ice

Chill and serve in a cocktail glass.

⚜ PINK LADY

In the shaker:
dash grenadine
juice of ½ lemon
1½ ounces gin
ice

Shake, strain, and serve in a 4-ounce cocktail glass.

⚜ PLANTER'S PUNCH

In the shaker:
2 dashes Angostura bitters
juice of ½ lemon or lime
3 ounces rum
ice

Shake vigorously, pour into a 10-ounce Collins glass, and decorate with half a slice of pineapple. Fill with carbonated water.

⚜ PORT OR SHERRY FLIP

In the shaker:
½ teaspoon sugar
1 egg yolk
1½ ounces port or sherry
a few drops brandy
ice

Shake vigorously and serve in a 4-ounce glass. Dust with grated nutmeg.

⚜ ROB ROY

In the mixing beaker:
1 or 2 dashes Angostura bitters
⅔ Scotch
⅓ sweet or dry vermouth

Fill beaker with cracked ice, stir, strain, and serve in a cocktail glass.

⚜ SIDECAR

In the shaker:

½ teaspoon lemon juice
⅓ Cointreau
⅔ brandy
ice

Shake, strain, and serve in a cocktail glass.

⚜ SINGAPORE SLING

In the shaker:

juice of ½ lemon
½ gin
½ cherry brandy
ice

Shake, strain into an 8-ounce highball glass, and fill with carbonated water.

⚜ TOM COLLINS

In a 10-ounce Collins glass:

ice
½ teaspoon sugar or simple syrup
juice of ½ lemon
1½ ounces gin

Add carbonated water and stir. A Collins may also be made with bourbon.

⚜ WHISKY SOUR

In the shaker:

½ teaspoon sugar
juice of ½ lemon
1½ ounces bourbon or rye whisky
ice

Shake vigorously and strain into a 4-ounce cocktail glass which contains a slice of orange and a Maraschino cherry.

⚜ WHITE LADY

In the shaker:

½ teaspoon lemon juice
⅓ Cointreau
⅔ gin
ice

Shake, strain, and serve in a cocktail glass.

·2·

WINES OF THE WORLD

The praise of wine has been sung ever since Noah or Bacchus planted the first vine and pressed out the first grapejuice. Poets—sacred or profane; pagan, Jewish, Christian, and even one Moslem, Omar Khayyam—have sung its excellence and its virtues.

And in spite of the narrow-minded, in spite of prohibitionist propaganda, wine remains the drink of men of taste and men of great heart. (Naturally we exclude the intemperate, who are no more a reason for damning wine than debauchees are for damning love.)

Wine has been loved in France for more than two thousand years, and wine has repaid this affection, for although great vintages exist elsewhere, there is no other country where such a great variety can be found. But if wine is wonderful in itself, it is even more wonderful with the right dishes that bring out its full value. It would be as ridiculous, and sad, to imagine a superb dinner accompanied only by water as to drink a sumptuous and venerable bottle along with a plate of macaroni. In the same way, it would be appalling to serve, for example, a Chambertin with a chocolate cake or a Sauternes with Beef en Daube.

These extremes show the need for harmonizing carefully the flavors of the wine and the food. According to one's taste, one will seek out a wine that will be the best accompaniment to a certain dish, or choose a dish that will best consort with the chosen wine. This is not to say that there may not be some charm in certain discords, as in music. But dissonance is a form of art which must not be confused with a false note, a squawk. That is why, during our promenade among the wines of France, we have added to our description of each wine region a few bars of harmony, of counterpoint, for food and wine.

In addition to describing the wines of France, we have included in this chapter some account of those of other European countries and those of wine-producing countries outside Europe. Since wines the world over fall into the same general categories—red, white, rosé, fortified, still, sparkling, etc.—the advice on serving wines, though using chiefly French examples, can be applied to the wines of other countries as well.

ADVICE ON SERVING WINE

Glasses

Just as sound needs a room built in accordance with the best rules of acoustics in order to spread, vibrate better, and captivate us, so the aroma of a wine must be able to benefit by that olfactory sounding box, the glass. Pouring a great wine into a small glass is like putting a full symphony orchestra on the stage of an intimate theater. A wine glass must be capacious; it must never be filled up. The finer the crystal, the more intimate will be the contact between lips and liquid.

There are various types of glasses. Each French wine-growing region has taken pains to create the shapes best suited to bring out the special qualities of its wines. Here we will confine ourselves to the glasses intended for Bordeaux, Burgundy, and Champagne.

A Bordeaux glass should not be too full-bellied; its curve should have a harmonious line with the top of the bowl slightly narrowed for red wine in order to hold the bouquet captive for a moment. A Burgundy glass, on the other hand, should have long sides (but without being too much like a tankard). This difference is explained by the fact that the aroma of Bordeaux, more vegetable in character, gives the impression of rising in a sheaf, while that of Burgundy, more animal by nature, seems to spread in the round.

For Champagne, a coupe (saucer-shaped glass) should never be used, in spite of the elegance of the shape. It stupidly lets the subtle scent of the wine escape. A flute glass is better, but the ideal is the tulip glass, so called because of its resemblance to the barely opened calyx of the flower.

White wines also have their traditional glasses, in general smaller than those for red wines. A Chablis glass resembles a Bordeaux (claret) glass except in size. Rhine wine (hock) is served in a small goblet with a long stem. In the United States, where traditions regarding the serving of wine are less important, an all-purpose wine glass is becoming popular; its shape most nearly resembles that of the Bordeaux glass.

The Temperature of Wines

How many sins are committed in this area, the worst being to ice white wine and ruin it by the cold, and to serve lukewarm red wine, having put the bottle in a corner of the fireplace, or even placed it in hot water!

Where lies the happy medium between these two equally annoying extremes?

It would be bold indeed—not to say arbitrary—to lay down a precise temperature for every wine. The laws of relativity must be applied. A wine at 70° F. will seem almost lukewarm if served in a room where the temperature is 65°, and almost cold if served in a room at 80°.

One can therefore say that a dry white wine should give an impression of pleasant coolness, but not of cold, not to mention being iced. It should be served at cellar temperature, which is usually 50° to 55°. Champagne can be served colder, at about 45°. The great rich white wines can take the lowest temperature—that is, 40° to 45°.

Important note: The wine cooler should not be stuffed full of ice but filled with very cold water, or water made cold with pieces of ice. When the wine is cool enough, remove it from the cooler.

Light red wines of the type drunk young, such as Beaujolais and Loire wines, are served cool. Though cellar temperature may seem to be rather cold, remember that at table their temperature will quickly rise to about 60°.

It is generally said that red wines should be served *chambré*—that is, at room temperature. True enough, but this does not mean the temperature of the dining room (which is usually about 70°). It means that the wine should be brought up from the cellar early enough to let it take on the temperature of the coolest room in the house.

As a general rule, red wines, especially old ones, must be brought up in advance so that they can rest and any sediment can settle on the bottom of the bottle. If the bottle has to be fetched at the last moment, a wine cradle should be used. This is frequently used without rhyme or reason, especially in restaurants wishing to impress. Its only purpose is to keep the bottle in the horizontal position it has had in its rack, so that the sediment will remain undisturbed on the lower side. A bottle that has been standing upright, therefore, must not be placed in a cradle; this would mix the sediment with the wine, which is precisely what one is trying to avoid. The bottle must be slid gently from the rack into the cradle without turning it and carried carefully upstairs.

The problem of sediment is discussed further in the section on decanting. As regards temperature, red Burgundies should be brought to the table at about 60°; they develop their full bouquet at about 65°.

Red Bordeaux is served at 65°; it reaches its full aroma at about 70°, but it must never be served at this temperature.

Decanting

This is the operation of separating the wine from the sediment or lees. Decanting has its supporters and its opponents. The opponents say that wine is too sensitive, that it suffers trauma, that it is best to pour it from its bottle at table carefully, until the sediment becomes apparent.

On the side of the supporters, there are two cases when decanting should be practiced: for separating old wine from the sediment and for oxydizing certain young wines. The older the wine, the more necessary is it to avoid the aeration brought about by decanting and to postpone this operation to the last moment before the wine is to be drunk. With young wines which one wants to mature artificially by oxydization (and also with wines which have remained "hard" or "aggressive," which do not mellow), decanting should be done in advance, sometimes several hours before serving.

Let us briefly recall the method. Hold the bottle in the right hand by the bottom—not the neck; hold the decanter in the left hand in front of a bright light and pour the wine from the bottle into the decanter as gently as possible, without letting it gurgle. Stop pouring as soon as the first threads of sediment are seen floating toward the bottle neck.

Allowing Wine to Settle

Wine is a living thing; traveling tires it. Let it rest in the cellar for several days—several weeks for venerable bottles—before drinking it. In the same way, if you buy good wine from the grocer, it is best to let it settle for a few days. After the bottle has been in your cellar, it should be brought up in the morning for dinner, and the night before for next day's luncheon.

The Order of Wines during a Meal

In principle, the first wine served with a meal is a dry white wine. This is followed by red, from the youngest to the oldest, from the lightest to the most full-bodied. Sweet white wine is served with dessert. But exceptions are possible. In Bordeaux, for example, Sauternes is served with foie gras (at the beginning of the meal, of course). In this case the Sauternes must be followed by a dry white wine with sufficient body, then a generous red wine.

There are also exceptions to the rule of an order of increasing age. One must not serve a wine of a light year after one of a full-bodied one, simply because it is older. For instance, one would not serve a 1956 after a 1959; one would unhesitatingly do the reverse.

The same applies to the order of registered brands. In theory, one would serve a Pomerol or Saint-Emilion after a Graves or a Médoc. Burgundy follows Bordeaux and Côtes-du-Rhône follows Burgundy. Nevertheless, we might have a very rich, very generous Pomerol, which might harm the subtlety of a Volnay. In this case, with all due respect to the purists, a man of taste would not hesitate; he would serve the Volnay, Burgundy though it is, before the Pomerol, although that comes from the Gironde.

In conclusion, let us point out that the drinking of wine, while it is a matter of knowledge and even more of experience, is above all a matter of taste, in both senses of the word.

The Wines of France

In France, vines are blessed with different climates, Mediterranean, oceanic, and continental; a great variety of soils; and a tradition of viticulture from the early settlements of the Greeks through the development of vineyards and wine-making by monasteries during the Middle Ages, not to mention a multiplicity of ethnic and provincial traditions which have influenced the choice of vines, the methods of cultivation, and the making of the wine itself.

The limits of viticulture follow a line which starts a little above Nantes, north of the Loire; follows the southern limits of Brittany, Normandy, and

Picardy; passes a little to the west of Paris; and reaches the Belgian frontier just north of Champagne. Vines cover an area of about 3,705,000 acres, of which 617,500 acres are vineyards with registered brands. The size of the harvest varies greatly from one year to the next. The 1962 harvest of registered brands was one of the biggest, amounting to 27,742,000 bushels, whereas the 1957 harvest amounted to only 9,793,750 bushels.

Registered Brands

Another element of good fortune for the vines, wines, and wine buyers of France, the most recent and by no means the least important, is due to a legal spirit inherited from the Romans, combined with a countryman's and craftman's pleasure in a good job well done. This is the unique and irreplaceable legislation concerning registered brands (Appellations d'Origine Contrôlées), thanks to which the consumer knows exactly what he is drinking.

The categories are as follows:

Local wines (les vins de pays). The label must bear the words "local wine from the canton of ———." The minimum alcoholic content is 9.5 per cent. These are regional wines, often very pleasant, which one usually drinks locally during one's holidays.

Blended wines (les vins de coupage). The alcoholic content must also be at least 9.5 per cent. These wines are sold under the label and responsibility of the dealer who creates them by mixing and combining wines of different origins (not necessarily French only). They are divided into "ordinary table wines" ("vins de consommation courante") and "choice wines without description of origin" ("vins de marque sans appellation d'origine"), the latter being of higher quality than the former.

Wines bearing a registered brand (les vins d'appellation d'origine contrôlée—A.O.C.). These wines may be recognized by their labels, which must bear the words "*appellation contrôlée.*" (For example, Appellation Margaux contrôlée.) There is only one exception, namely Champagne. These wines are subject to very strict rules of production and vinification, and to a geographic limitation of the area where the vine grows.

Regional wines of superior quality (Vins délimités de qualité supérieure—V.D.Q.S.). These are the regional wines which are not covered by the law on registered brands and for which this category, subject to similar regulations, was subsequently created.

Our region-by-region study will deal only with wines of guaranteed origin (A.O.C. and V.D.Q.S.), since blended wines, whatever their quality, have no specific origin. There is a note on local wines at the end of the section.

BORDEAUX

The town of Bordeaux has given its name to a very important group of vineyards, all lying in the Department of Gironde and flanking the banks of the rivers Garonne and Dordogne and their common estuary, the Gironde. The Bordeaux region offers wine lovers a very complete range, from light red wines to the most full-bodied, from dry white wines to the very sweet. The whole area produces Bordeaux, Bordeaux Supérieur (red and white), and Bordeaux rosé wines.

Médoc. This covers an area 50 miles long and 4 to 8 miles wide, on the left bank of the Garonne. The most famous wines come from the southern part, Haut-Médoc, where one finds the celebrated place names of Margaux, Saint-Julien, Pauillac, Saint-Estèphe, Listrac, and Moulis.

Haut-Médoc wines from good years will age almost indefinitely. In principle, these wines are better not drunk when young. When they have matured they offer an incomparable bouquet, ranging from flowers to truffles, a solid backbone combined with a full-flavored body. When aged they may reach the peak of perfection.

Graves. The vineyard encircles the town of Bordeaux to the north and extends southward along the left bank of the Garonne as far as the Sauternes district.

The red wines resemble those of Médoc, but are perhaps more vigorous; they also age extremely well. The white wines are dry, especially those harvested in the north; they have a typical bouquet and aroma and a great deal of elegance. There are also very popular sweet white Graves, especially from the south of the district.

Saint-Emilion. This district lies northeast of Bordeaux, near the town of Libourne, on the right bank of the Dordogne. Apart from the district of Saint-Emilion proper, there are the neighboring districts of Saint-Georges-Saint-Emilion, Lussac-Saint-Emilion, Montagne-Saint-Emilion, Parsue-Saint-Emilion, Puisseguin-Saint-Emilion, Parsac-Saint-Emilion, and Sables-Saint-Emilion.

An old-fashioned wine cellar ▶

56

Harvesting grapes in western Switzerland

A village wine press ▲

▼ Wines of traditional prestige (Restaurant Lucas Carton, Paris)

▼ A corner for beer

▲ Cocktail preparation and service ▼

The wines are red, generous, and full-bodied, with more roundness than on the Côtes, and more vigor than Graves. They too will mature, but not for as long as Médoc and Graves.

Pomerol. The vines of Pomerol also grow at the gates of Libourne, on the right bank of the Dordogne, and produce a rich, mellow, and fragrant red wine. The neighboring districts of Néac-de-Pomerol and Lalande-de-Pomerol should also be noted.

Sauternes-Barsac. Bordeaux also has the privilege of producing sumptuous sweet white wines, clad in gold, honey-scented. The grapes are harvested almost one by one in successive pickings when they have reached an overripeness as a result of which they are almost candied. This condition is known as "pourriture noble," or noble rot, and is due to the action of a beneficent fungus. The most famous region producing these wines is Sauternes-Barsac, on the left bank of the Garonne, to which should be added Cerons and, on the right bank of the river, opposite, Loupiac and Sainte-Croix-du-Mont.

Other districts. Among red wines, there are the rich wines of Côtes-de-Fronsac and Canon-Fronsac, and those of Bourgeais and Blayais (where white wines are also produced).

Among white wines we have the Entre-Deux-Mers, Graves de Vayres, and Sainte-Foy-Bordeaux.

The first Côtes de Bordeaux, on the right bank of the Garonne, produce popular red and white wine, as do the Côtes de Bordeaux-Saint-Macaire.

Dishes to Accompany Bordeaux Wines

Haut-Médoc, Moulis, Listrac, Saint-Estèphe.	Beef, mutton; grilled meat; feathered game; furred game if not high (wines of sound years); Gruyère-type cheeses.
Margaux, Saint-Julien, Pauillac.	Lamb, veal, poultry, roast or grilled; truffles; fresh game birds; foie gras; Gruyère-type cheeses.
Red Graves.	Same as Médoc: grilled meat, fresh game, Gruyère-type cheeses.
Dry white Graves, first Côtes de Bordeaux (dry).	Oysters, shellfish, fish, and crustaceans, grilled or in a mildly seasoned sauce; caviar.
Mellow white Graves.	As aperitif; foie gras; dessert.

Saint-Emilion and Pomerol.	Beef, mutton; grilled meat or meat in a sauce (duck or chicken with Saint-Emilion), furred or feathered game (Pomerol, or Saint-Emilion of a rich year); lampreys in red wine; cheese; foie gras.
Sauternes-Barsac and sweet white wines.	As aperitif; foie gras; fresh duck liver; fish in fine sauces; desserts (if not too sweet). Some drink these with roast chicken, Roquefort, and ices.

BURGUNDY

The wine-growing area of Burgundy spreads, from north to south, over four departments: Yonne, with Chablis; the Côte-d'Or, divided between the slopes of Nuits and of Beaune; Saône-et-Loire, which includes the Chalons slopes, the Mâcon area, and the north of Beaujolais; and Rhône, which includes almost the whole of Beaujolais.

Chablis. This is the most northerly vineyard of Burgundy. It produces only dry, fresh, elegant, and scented white wines, of a beautiful pale gold with greenish lights. The registered brand covers the great vintage Chablis, first-growth Chablis, Chablis, and Petit Chablis. The department of Yonne also produces a red wine, Yrancy Burgundy, which is excellent in good years.

Côte-de-Nuits. The Côte-de-Nuits starts south of Dijon; it covers a line of rather exposed slopes. From north to south there are the famous parishes of Gevrey-Chambertin, Morey-Saint-Denis, Chambolle-Musigny, Vougeot, Flagey-Echezeaux, Vosne-Romanee, Nuits-Saint-Georges, with their "climats" (the Burgundian name for a place entered in the official register of real estate), some of which—Chambertin, for example—have the right to be registered as brands. The area produces almost entirely heavy red wines, rich and with a full fragrance, sometimes verging on that of game; they mature well.

Côte-de-Beaune. The Côte-de-Beaune borders on the Côte-de-Nuits with the parishes of Aloze-Corton, Pernand-Vergelesse, Chassagne-Montrachet, Puligny-Montrachet, Meursault, Savigny, Beaune, Pommard, Volnay, Santenay. The characteristic of the Côte-de-Beaune is that it produces both red and white wine. The red wines are lighter than those of Nuits, more flexible, with a floral or fruity aroma, a great deal of subtlety and elegance. They also mature well. The white wines are among the greatest of Burgundy and of France. They are dry but mellow, with a very full-blown bouquet, a typical flavor of almond or hazelnut. The most illustrious is Montrachet (and Chassagne-Montrachet, Bâtard-Montrachet, etc.). Meursault and Corton-Charlemagne are also worthy of special mention.

Chalons region. The town of Chalons-sur-Saône has given its name to this region, which is adjacent to the Côte-de-Beaune and with very similar wines. The white wine of Rully and the red wine of Mercurey, when well made, are much appreciated by gourmets. Farther south, the white of Montagny and the red of Givry are not without merit.

Mâcon region. This region gets its name from the town of Mâcon. Under the registered brand of Mâcon it produces very agreeable red, rosé, and white wines. But the ornament of Mâcon is Pouilly-Fuissé and its two brothers, Pouilly-Loché and Pouilly-Vinzelles. These are dry, fragrant, vigorous, and rather full-bodied white wines.

Beaujolais. The actual capital is Villefranche-sur-Saône, but the name of the region is taken from that of the old capital, Beaujeu. Starting in Saône-et-Loire with the parishes of Leynes, Saint-Amour, and Romanèche-Thorins, the region extends into the department of Rhône, to a point north of the city of Lyons.

Beaujolais, Beaujolais Supérieur, and Beaujolais-Villages are, above all, wines to drink cool. They should be tender, fragrant, and smooth.

Apart from the ordinary Beaujolais, there are the vintages, nine in number: Brouilly, Chénas, Chiroubles, Côte-de-Brouilly, Fleurie, Juliénas, Morgon, Moulin-à-Vent, Saint-Amour. Each has its own characteristics, but by and large they are best drunk when young. Some of the Fleurie, Morgon, and, above all, Moulin-à-Vent wines may be allowed to mature, but never as long as a Burgundy from the Côte-d'Or.

Dishes to Accompany Burgundies

Côte-de-Nuits and some Cortons (rich years).	Roast or grilled beef or mutton; stewed meat or meat in a sauce; chicken (Chambertin); hung furred or feathered game; meat pies and terrines, especially of game; all cheeses.
Côte-de-Beaune (red), Mercurey;	Grilled or roast white meats (red

also Givry, Morgon, Fleurie, Moulin-à-Vent; some red Mâcons.	meats for the more full-bodied ones); meat in a sauce (especially if made with Beaune wine); fresh or lightly hung game; soft cheeses if not too ripe; Gruyère-type and pressed cheeses.
Beaujolais, Beaujolais-Villages, and light vintages; rosé from Marsannay.	May accompany a whole meal (even oysters); perfect with cold meat.
Vintage Beaujolais; red Mâcon.	Cold meat and hot pork dishes (regional, especially from Lyons); grilled or roast meat; dishes in a sauce; cheese.
Chablis, Pouilly-Fuissé (or -Loche or -Vinzelles), Rully; and also Montagny, Mâcon, and white Beaujolais.	Oysters, shellfish, grilled fish, crustaceans; fish stews (especially the first three); cold meat, goat cheese (especially the last three).
Meursault, Corton-Charlemagne.	Fish and crustaceans in a sauce (preferably made with the same wine), smoked fish (salmon, trout, eel); terrines; foie gras.
Montrachet, Chevalier-Montrachet, Puligny-Montrachet, etc.	Oysters; caviar; crustaceans and fish, grilled or in a sauce (same wine); foie gras.

CHAMPAGNE

Champagne wine is unlike any other wine. Often imitated, never equaled, it remains unique and irreplaceable.

It is made in accordance with many very strict rules and by means of lengthy and delicate operations and manipulations. The main rule is development of the bubbles by a natural method—that is, in the form of a second fermentation of the wine which must take place in the bottle. This is the "champenoise" ("champagnization") method developed by Dom Perignon and since improved by the shippers in Rheims and Epernay.

The main vineyards of Champagne are the hills of Rheims—Verzenay, Verzy, Mailly, Sillery, Louvois, Beaumont; between the hills and the Marne valley—Bouzy, Ambonnay; the Marne valley—Ay, Cumières, Hautvillers,

Mareuil, Dizy; the Blancs slopes (choice site of the Blanc de Blancs)—Cramant, Avize, Ogar, Mesnil, Vertus.

Blanc de Blancs and Blanc de Noirs. Except in relation to Champagne, these two terms are meaningless. Champagne is the only region where white wine is made from black grapes. "Blanc de Blancs" therefore means white wine made from white grapes (Pinot Chardonnay); "Blanc de Noirs" means white wine made from black grapes (Pinot Noir). Incidentally, most Champagnes, unless the opposite is specifically stated, consist of a mixture of the two.

Brands (vins de marques) and growths (vins de crus). Although there are named growths in Champagne, they do not in general have the importance that a named growth has in Bordeaux or Burgundy. The famous manufacturers blend the various growths (each one has his own secret proportions).

Vintage and nonvintage. Champagne may bear the date of a given year, in which case it is a vintage Champagne. Only the good years are used for vintage Champagne, which must be at least 3 years in bottle. Nonvintage Champagne is a blend of different years and must be at least 1 year in bottle.

Still Champagnes (vins nature de Champagne). These are the red and white wines harvested in the Champagne region, which have remained "still"—that is, have not been subjected to "champagnization." The white wines are fresh, dry, and pleasantly fruity in character. They are mainly harvested on the Blancs slopes. The very elegant Mesnil and the more full-bodied Cramant are well known. The red wines, of which the most esteemed are those of Bouzy and Cumières, are delicate, fruity, and delicious; they are usually drunk young, but in exceptional years (especially 1959) they are heavier in character and may be left to mature.

Dishes to Accompany Champagne

Champagne has been described as the wine for all occasions. Nevertheless, it should not be turned into a maid of all work. It is undeniably a wine for special occasions. It is the perfect accompaniment for the whole of a fine supper, from start to finish.

Blanc de Blancs (extra dry).	Perfect as an aperitif; fish and crustaceans, grilled or cooked with Champagne; caviar; smoked salmon.
Other Champagnes (extra dry).	Luncheons, light meals, for the whole

	of a meal other than the fish. A Blanc de Noirs of a rich year is best with meat (especially red meat and game); foie gras. If you insist on serving Champagne with the dessert choose a medium dry.
Still white Champagne.	Oysters, shellfish, crustaceans, and grilled fish, in a sauce or cooked in a court bouillon (same wine).
Red still Champagne.	Poultry or veal, roasted, grilled, or in a sauce (same wine); fine cold meats.

ALSACE

The Alsatian vineyards are to be found on the eastern slopes of the Vosges, between Strasbourg in the north and Mulhouse in the south. The peculiarity of Alsatian wines, compared with other French wines, is that they bear the name of the grape from which they are made instead of the name of the vineyard or parish. The best-known varieties are:

Chasselas and Sylvaner, which give light, fresh, and fruity wines.

Gray Pinot (wrongly known in Alsace as Tokay), which yields strong and heady wines.

Muscat, famous for its fruity bouquet.

Riesling, which yields first-class wines, elegant, fragrant, dry, and thoroughbred.

Traminer and Gewurztraminer, oily wines, sometimes almost resembling liqueurs, with a strong fragrance; these are wines of the first order.

There are also wines called Zwicker and Edelzwicker, which are blends, often very agreeable ones, of several varieties of grapes.

Dishes to Accompany Alsatian Wines

Chasselas, Sylvaner, Zwicker, Edelzwicker.	As aperitif; cold meat, sauerkraut, shellfish, fish.
Riesling or gray Pinot.	Oysters; crustaceans and fish, grilled or in a sauce (same wine); fresh sal-

	mon; chicken cooked in Riesling; Münster cheese (gray Pinot).
Traminer, Gewurztraminer, or Muscat.	Foie gras; smoked salmon; desserts (if not too sweet).

FRANCHE-COMTÉ (*JURA*)

The old province of Franche-Comté, between Burgundy and Switzerland, produces well-known wines, harvested on the last foothills of the Jura. The most original is the "yellow wine" with a nutty flavor which is the result of a special wine-making process; the most famous of these is Château-Chalon. Another specialty of the region is the "straw wines," made from grapes dried on straw.

The other wines of Franche-Comté or Jura are the red, white, rosé, and yellow Arbois and the wines of Étoile and Côtes-du-Jura.

Dishes to Accompany Jura Wines

Yellow wines.	Will stand up (especially the Château-Chalon) to "difficult" dishes with a strong flavor—for example, duck with orange, shellfish, crustaceans, also game and cheese.
Red wines.	All kinds of meat.
White wines.	Fish and shellfish.
Rosé wines.	Cold meat; throughout a whole meal.

THE LOIRE VALLEY

The name Loire Valley (Val de Loire) groups together the wines harvested on the slopes along the Loire and its tributaries. If one travels down the river from its source to its mouth one finds Pouilly-sur-Loire, Sancerre-Quincy-Reuilly, Touraine, Saumur, Anjou, Muscadet.

The wines of Pouilly-sur-Loire on the right bank of the river, of Sancerre on the left bank, and of Quincy and Reuilly share, with variations caused by different soils, the fruity bouquet, the delicacy, and the elegance of the Sauvignon vine from which they are all made; they are dry and fresh.

The Touraine wines must be divided into red and white. The best known of the white wines, Vouvray, always thoroughbred and fragrant, may be dry, medium dry, or sweet; treated by the "champenoise" method it yields a most agreeable sparkling wine for an aperitif (extra dry) or dessert (medium dry). Let us also mention Montlouis, the neighbor of Vouvray (on the other bank), and the wines of Touraine which are accompanied by the name of the parish of origin. Among red wines there are the well-known violet-scented Chinon wines, and Bourgeuil and Saint-Nicolas-de-Bourgeuil, with a raspberry flavor (also registered as Touraine, accompanied by the name of the parish of origin).

Saumur is notable for dry white wines, thoroughbred, which take fermentation well; the red wine of Saumur-Champigny, very fruity, cousin of those of Chinon and Bourgeuil; and dry rosés.

The white wines of Anjou are famous. Dry or sweet, they all have a remarkable bouquet. The different regions are Coteaux du Layon and the famous Bonnezeaux and Quarts-de-Chaume, wines from which can mature magnificently; Coteaux de la Loire which has drier, crisper wines, including the famous growths of Roche-aux-Moines and Coulée-de-Serrant, of very great quality; Coteaux de l'Aubance. The dry and sweet rosés are also well known (Cabernet rosés).

Muscadet, a very dry, fresh, and smooth wine, sometimes slightly sparkling (on lees) is harvested in the department of Loire-Atlantique. There are two regions—Sevre-et-Maine and Coteaux de la Loire.

Dishes to Accompany Loire Wines

Pouilly-Fumé, Sancerre, Quincy, Reuilly, dry Vouvray, Montlouis, Saumur, dry Anjou, Muscadet.	Oysters, shellfish; grilled or boiled crustaceans; freshwater fish (fresh salmon) or saltwater fish (not fat), grilled or cooked in fish stock or in a sauce (same wine); regional pork specialties (Vouvray rillettes and rillons, sausages); local goat cheeses (Chavignol and Sancerre).
Sweet Anjou and Vouvray.	Dessert or as aperitif (especially mature wines); foie gras.
Sparkling Saumur and Vouvray.	As aperitif; luncheon, light meals (extra dry); dessert (medium dry).

Chinon, Bourgueil, Saumur-Champigny.	White meat, grilled or roasted or in a sauce (chicken cooked in a sauce made with same wine); fish cooked with red wine (eel matelote); local cheeses.

CÔTES-DU-RHÔNE

The vineyards of the Côtes-du-Rhône form terraces on both banks of the river over a distance of 125 miles, from below Lyons to the Rhone delta. The wines differ according to whether they were harvested in the north or in the south. They are therefore divided into two groups:

Northern Côtes-du-Rhône. Elegant, fragrant, heady red wines—Côtes-Rôties, Cornas, Hermitage, Crozes-Hermitage, Saint-Joseph. Dry, fragrant, and aromatic white wines—Condrieu, Château-Grillet, Hermitage, Crozes-Hermitage, Saint-Péray, Saint-Joseph.

Southern Côtes-du-Rhône. Châteauneuf-du-Pape, a strong, full-bodied, luscious red wine. The generous red wines of Gigondas. The very dry, aromatic rosé wines of Tavel, Lirac, Chusclan.

Dishes to Accompany Côtes-du-Rhône Wines

Northern Côtes-du-Rhône red wines.	Beef or mutton; grills; game; cheese.
Northern Côtes-du-Rhône white wines.	Shellfish, crustaceans, grilled fish, fish in a sauce, smoked fish.
Châteauneuf-du-Pape and southern Côtes-du-Rhône red wines.	Beef, mutton; grills; furred game, even when well hung; cheese, even when very ripe.
Tavel, Chusclan.	Cold meat; entrées.

THE MEDITERRANEAN COAST

From Nice to Narbonne, vines have been cultivated for more than 2000 years. These are the wines swollen with the Mediterranean sun. The red wines are generous, full-bodied; the white wines dry, also full-bodied; the rosé wines dry and true to type. There are also liqueur wines, very rich and keeping the fruity aroma of the Muscat grapes from which they are made.

Comté de Nice. Bellet wines (red and white).

Provence. Cassis, Bandol, and the V.D.Q.S. Côtes-de-Provence (red, rosé, and white).

Languedoc. V.D.Q.S. Costières-du-Gard (rósé), Corbières and Minervois (red); A.O.C. Fitou (red).

Frontignan, Lunel, Mireval, Saint-Jean-de-Minervois. Muscats.

Dishes to Accompany Mediterranean Wines

White wines.	Shellfish and crustaceans; bouillabaisse; fish soups; bourride; grilled Mediterranean fish.
Rosé wines.	Pizza; paella; pissaladière; all meats, fish, and vegetables cooked in the local style.
Red wines.	Beef, mutton; grilled meat with herbs; cheese.
Muscat.	As aperitif; above all dessert.

THE CATALAN COAST

The wines of Roussillon and the coast between Argelès and Cerbère are generous and full-bodied wines, of which the best known and most elegant are Banyuls and Banyuls Grand Cru, which can compete on equal terms with the analogous wines of Spain and Portugal. Let us also mention Côtes-d'Agly, Rivesaltes, and Muscat de Rivesaltes.

As regards the dishes to accompany them, these wines are often badly used by being served as an aperitif, which is not their proper place. A Banyuls Grand Cru goes perfectly with foie gras, fresh duck liver, and local dishes (rock lobster stew). Like port, it is a perfect drink at the end of a meal, with cheese or after dessert; it certainly increases a feeling of euphoria by several degrees. We also recommend it with melon.

WINES OF OTHER REGIONS

Outside the major wine-growing regions in France, there are many excellent wines which have their own devotees. They are for the most part drunk locally.

In the southeast, in the Garonne basin exclusive of Bordeaux, there are a number of vineyards. Let us give a special place to Monbazillac, which produces a sweet white wine, similar to Sauternes, fragrant and aromatic.

Among the registered brands worthy of mention are Bergerac (red and white), Montravel (white), Madiran (red), Jurançon (white). Blanquette de Limoux is an excellent white wine which is sparkling by nature, like Gaillac, but which also yields very fine still white wines. Among the regional wines (V.D.Q.S.) are Cahors, Fronton, Rosé du Bearn, Irouléguy, Tursan, etc.

In central France, the Côtes d'Auvergne and Forez (V.D.Q.S.) yield delicate red wines. Let us also mention the wines of the Orléans region. Among registered brands Côteaux-du-Loir and Jasnières are not without merit.

In the southeast, in the Drôme area, there is the Clairette-de-Die, deliciously fruity, and farther south, the Muscat de Beaune-de-Venise. East of Champagne there is Côtes-de-Toul.

Finally we must make special mention of the wines of Savoy, light, fragrant, very pleasant and fresh, sometimes having a slight sparkle. There are Crépy and Seyssel among the registered brands, and among the regional wines (V.D.Q.S.) Abymes, Apremont, Marestal, Montmélian, etc., and the wines of Bugey.

What to eat with these wines? Naturally the regional products and specialties. These are perfect holiday wines. Monbazillac goes perfectly with fish in a fine sauce, with foie gras, and with desserts that are not too sweet.

QUALITY OF FRENCH VINTAGES

(*Revue des vins de France*)

The table on page 70 shows the ratings of French vintages from 1920 to 1962. This edition of ratings, based on 20, has been worked out as the result of many wine tastings.

This classification has a purely relative value. It is given by way of indication, and the grades apply only to the whole of the year's successful wines. They in no way prejudge possible failures of an individual character, due to oenological faults. In the same way they do not, in mediocre years, exclude very honorable wines, even brilliant successes, due to special circumstances.

Table of Vintages, 1920–1962

	Red Bordeaux	*White Bordeaux*	*Red Burgundy*	*White Burgundy*	*Beaujolais*	*Alsace*	*Côtes-du-Rhône*	*Loire region*	*Champagne*
1962	14	13	14	15	16	15	13	13	Vintages:
1961	18	17	18	17	18	17	15	16	1945, 1947,
1960	12	11	7	11	8	13	13	10	1949, 1952,
1959	17	16	16	17	16	18	9	18	1953, 1955,
1958	11	12	10	12	11	12	14	12	1957, 1959
1957	14	15	14	14	13	13	16	12	Nonvintage:
1956	9	10	9	9	10	9	12	9	Individual
1955	16	16	16	14	16	15	15	15	blend by
1954	10	10	10	11	10		13		each shipper
1953	17	16	16	16	18	16	14	17	
1952	15	15	16	15	16	15	16	14	
1951	9	7	8	7		9	9		
1950	15	14	11	16		12	14	12	
1949	17	16	17	12		17	16	16	
1948	15	14	12	11			7	11	
1947	18	18	16	18		19	18	20	
1946	11	9	10	10			14		
1945	20	20	19	14			17	17	
1943	13	16	12	15			15	16	
1942	12	16	12	15			13	12	
1937	14	17	13	15			15	13	
1934	17	16	15	15			15	13	
1933	10	9	17	15			15	14	
1929	18	18	18	18			18	15	
1928	19	16	17	16			15	14	
1926	15	13	12	12			12	12	
1924	16	15	11	11			15	13	
1923	11	12	19	15			16	15	
1921	14	19	13	16			13	18	
1920	16	14	10	11			12	8	

(Table established by *Revue des vins de France;* not to be reproduced)

The years which are not included are those of which the wines can no longer be tasted. The years 1922, 1925, 1927, 1930, 1931, 1932, 1933, 1936, 1938, 1939, 1940, 1941, 1944 have been excluded because they were too mediocre; in fact, they do not have even a historical interest. Ratings are based on a scale of 20, lower numerals indicating lower ratings.

Wines of Other European Countries

A number of other countries in Europe contribute largely to the world's stock of wines. Germany, Austria, Switzerland, Italy, Spain, Portugal, Hungary, and Yugoslavia all have long histories of viticulture and produce notable wines, many of which have long been famous.

GERMANY

The German Federal Republic is the most northerly wine-growing country. Thanks to the exceptional climate of some regions the wines reach a truly remarkable quality.

The Rhineland produces white wines of the first quality (Riesling, Traminer, Gutedel, and Müller-Thurgau stock). The German red wines come from the same region. The Rhenish wines or hocks, such as Ungstein, Deidesheimer, Kallstadt, Forst, Wackenheim, are perfumed, elegant, and very agreeable to drink. The red wine of Bad Dürkheim is very well known.

The wine-growing regions of the Moselle, Saar, and Ruwer valleys produce only white wines. These growths have a world-wide reputation, thanks to their elegant and fruity bouquet and their agreeable freshness.

The wines of Rheinhessen are fruity and characteristic; some are predominantly sweet in taste (Niersteiner, Oppenheimer). Many of the exported German wines are labeled Liebfraumilch. This name is a sign of quality and of recognition of a product coming from Rheinhessen; it does not describe either a region or the product of any given producer. The red wine of Ingelheim has a high reputation.

The wine-growing region of the Nahe river produces thoroughbred wines and wines with a generous bouquet, from the purest Riesling stock.

The wines of the Rheingau and middle Rhine are, with a few exceptions, well-balanced Rieslings. The red wine of Assmannshausen is noteworthy.

The wine-growing regions of Baden produce white wines for everyday consumption and, around the Kaiserstuhl, wines of great quality.

Württemberg is a region of red, fruity, thoroughbred and strong wines.

Franconia, with its capital Würzburg, produces a very well-known white wine known as Steinwein. Its bottles are shaped like goatskin bottles, hence the name Bocksbeutel. These wines have a flavor characteristic of the soil. Klingenberg is a much-appreciated red wine (Burgundy stock).

The Ahr region is famous for its red wines. Its local wines are agreeable, sweet, and smooth. The stock is of Burgundian and Portuguese origin.

Thanks to selected grapes and care in preparation, the wines of the Rhineland, Moselle-Saar-Ruwer, Rheinhessen, the middle Rhine, and the Rheingau are of international standing and exceptional quality.

AUSTRIA

Among the wine-growing regions, lower Austria and the Burgenland should have first mention. In lower Austria, the white stocks of Rheinriesling, Müller-Thurgau, Neuburger, Gruener Weltliner yield full-bodied, fruity wines. These stocks, derived from white Burgundies, are also cultivated in the Burgenland. The red Weltliner stocks yield an aromatic wine.

Ruster-Ansbruch, from the region of Neusiedler Lake, is made from selected, half-dried grapes. It is a wine of pronounced character, closely resembling Tokay.

In the Vienna region, the wines of the Klosterneuburg domain are soft, with a fine bouquet and great value from Burgundian stocks. The fruity wines of Sievering, Nussberg, and Kallenberg are much appreciated.

The Sudbahn region (south of Vienna) yields white wines of notable quality, produce of Riesling, Sylvaner, and Traminer Muscat stocks. Rotgipfler is made of red grapes from Burgundian stock.

Styria produces wines of medium to good quality, products of Rheinriesling, Gutedel, Traminer, and Furmint vines.

SWITZERLAND

The major Swiss vineyards are situated in the sunny valleys of the Rhone, the Rhine, and the Ticino, and on the sheltered, spreading banks of the lakes of Bienne, Constance, Geneva, Lugano, Maggiore, Morat, Neuchâtel, and Zurich. All these regions have mild climates, favorable for the ripening of grapes. The range of the wines of these different regions is very great and varies from one region to the next; it goes from dry pearly white wines to the sweetest; from sparkling rosés and light red wines to the most full-bodied and smoothest.

The cultivation of the vine, the stock, and the nature of the wines vary from one canton to the next. For this reason we distinguish between three groups of vineyards—those of western, eastern, and southern Switzerland.

The vineyards of western Switzerland alone cover more than two-thirds of the area under vines. Soil and climate are particularly favorable to the Chasselas and Fendant (white stock) and the Pinot and Gamay (red stock). In eastern Switzerland the red stock is the commonest, particularly the Pinot Noir. The white stocks of Riesling and Sylvaner yield an appreciated wine. South of the Alps, in Ticino and in the Grisons valley of Mesocco, the old vines, native varieties, yield the Nostrano, a wine with the aroma of the region. All the vineyards are now being planted with Merlot, a new stock originating in Bordeaux, which gives a smooth and velvety wine.

ITALY

". . . No other plant is as interesting. It speaks to those who understand its language, is demanding or confiding; sometimes it sulks and denies itself, but in the end it again shows itself generous. One must always be close to it, never stop studying it. Sometimes it must be treated gently, sometimes artfully, sometimes even roughly, but it must always be served, always be loved and often satisfied. One year it is prodigal, the next miserly. It has charming caprices and diabolical perversities, but it is the Italian plant honored since time immemorial, the plant which yields the wine for our rites and our festivals, for our health, our lively youth, and our smiling old age." Thus Arturo Marescalchi praised this "divine" plant, linked with the actual history of mankind.

Italy was known in ancient times by the name of Oenotria and has produced wine abundantly ever since. A wide variety of vineyards and systems of cultivation and the different character and location of the various wine regions give Italy many qualities of wine. Piedmont, Tuscany, Venetia, Apulia, and Sicily are the regions where production is highest.

Piedmont. Piedmont has a single type of dry white wine, Cortese, a wine for meatless hors d'oeuvre and fish. The fresh and fragrant Moscato, with a white and persistent sparkle, is suitable with desserts. Using the "champenoise" method, the same vineyard produces the medium-dry, fresh, and young Asti Spumante, which is exported all over the world. This region also has the red wines Barbera, Dolcetto, Grignolino, Bonarda, dry Nebbiolo and dry Freisa; and the sparkling Brachetto and Freisa Amabile, all suitable for serving with whole meals and desserts.

The Piedmontese growths also yield some great classic wines to drink with roasts and game, such as the thoroughbred Barolo, the elegant Barbaresco, the full-bodied Gattinara, the savorous Ghemme, and the gentle Carema, all products of the Nebbiolo grape.

Liguria. Liguria does not have a large wine production. Its best-known wines are the slightly bitter and fragrant red Rossese, a good accompaniment to an elegant meal; the white Vermentino, delicately perfumed, served with fish; and, near La Spezia, Cinqueterre–both dry, served with fish, and sweet, served with desserts; the latter is known as Sciacchetra. The white wines of Coronata and the Polcevera valley should also be mentioned; they are served with fish and also throughout a meal.

Lombardy. The great prestige wines of Lombardy are harvested in Valtellina. Grumello, Sassella, and Inferno, suitable for aging, become superb in their maturity. They are drunk with roasts and game. Excellent red and rosé wines, light and fragrant, are produced on the banks of Lake Garda (Moniga). The very distinguished Lugana is the perfect accompaniment to Italian hors d'oeuvre. The left bank of the Po, in the province of Pavia, yields an excellent sparkling Moscato, with a gentle and delicate perfume, and the Pinots and Italian Rieslings, served with fish.

Venetia. The three Venetias offer excellent red and white wines. The tender Terlano and the fruity Traminer, the fine Lago di Caldaro, Santa Maddalena, and Termeno of the province of Bolzano; the fragrant and full-bodied Mezzocorona, Marzemino, and Teroldego, from the province of Trento–all these are wines of superior quality. The region of Gorizia yields excellent white wines, especially at Padua, Treviso, and Conegliano. They include the famous Prosecco, dry, medium dry, or sparkling, and the delicious sparkling Cartizze which is drunk with dessert or between meals. Udine has its lemon-yellow Tocai and its diuretic Verduzzo, which is a beautiful golden yellow. Among the red wines, the Merlot and Cabernet growths, which are very widespread, yield good products suitable for aging. Verona is famous for its white Soave, served with hors d'oeuvre and fish, and for its Bardolino, Valpolicella, and Valpantena, savorous and dry, served with meals.

Emilia. This is the district of light wines, which are produced in the plain, and include the sound, sparkling, and perfumed Lambrusco which blends harmoniously with pork, sausages, and the "zampone" of Modena. Romagna is proud of its white Albana and red Sangiovese, suitable for moderate aging.

Tuscany. This region is rightly celebrated for its Chianti Classico from the Siena vineyards, gentle and harmonious Brunello di Montalcino, and Vino Nobile di Montepulciano, a superb trio to drink with roasts, after suitable maturing in cask. Florence offers the delicate white Pomino and the red Carmignano and Nipozzano, warm and even more highly bred than the classic Chianti itself.

Umbria. The green region of Umbria excels with its dry and soft Orvieto, dear to Pinturicchio, suitable with fish soups and thick soups, while the Marches, in the province of Ancona, offer Verdicchio of the typical straw color, a wine particularly adapted to fish.

Latium. In Latium, the wines "dei Castelli Romani" (of the Roman castles)—Frascati, Velletri, and Marino—are nearly as well known as Rome itself. They are drunk with meals, at room temperature or chilled (50° to 55° F.). At Sperlonga they serve Cecubo, another good wine already known in ancient times.

Abruzzi. The vineyards of Sangiovese and Montepulciano in the Abruzzi yield other good wines to be drunk with meals.

Campagna. The region of Campagna, rich in folklore, presents Aglianico which blends harmoniously with the smoked sausage of the Irpinia region. Other good red and white wines are found at Solopaca: Asprino, of a delicate light green shade, very refreshing, to be drunk throughout the year, and the historic white and red Falerno. In the province of Naples there is the famous Capri Bianco and the delicate wine of Ischia, which goes well with fish and especially with deep-fried dishes. The golden-yellow Lacrima Christi and Gragnano with its aroma of faded violets are also appreciated. Vesuvius also offers a good range of wines, both red and white.

Apulia. In beautiful Apulia, where the olive tree is often wedded to the twisted vine, and where the plain runs into the green hills, red blended wines predominate, while the historic hamlets of Alberobello and Locorotondo produce an excellent white wine suited to whole meals and fish—the very famous Castel del Monte with its delicate aroma of candied fruit; as well as the golden Malvasia, a dry and vigorous wine to serve with flavorsome fish soups, and the exquisite Aleatico to serve with desserts.

Calabria. The strong earth of Calabria offers a good wine, Cirò, bright in color and with a full-bodied aroma, suitable for long aging. Its alcohol content may be as high as 15 per cent; it is served with piquant cheeses or with desserts, and is served at room temperature. The hills of Reggio Calabria yield the Greco di Gerace, a sweet dessert wine. This region has two other wines, Savuto and Pellaro, which after long aging are particularly suitable as an accompaniment to roasts and braised dishes.

Sicily. The southern part of Italy also has a fairly considerable wine production. In Sicily, on the slopes of Mount Etna, at a height of between 1300 and 3300 feet, excellent red and white wines are obtained. In the province of Syracuse an elegant dessert wine is found, obtained from a blend known as Pollio. White, red, and rosé Ciclopi, Val di Lupo, exquisite with fish, and Corvo di Casteldaccia, capable of rivaling the best Chablis of the year, are growths from the Catania region. In the western part of the island lies Marsala, a town made famous in the second half of the eighteenth century by Sir John Woodhouse, who had an inquiring spirit and who made the whole world acquainted with the full-bodied wine which bears the name of the town. Marsala can rival the better-known Madeira, port, and sherry.

Sardinia. On this island, the site of an ancient civilization, the vine has been cultivated since ancient times. The best-known wine of this region is the thoroughbred Vernaccia with a strong perfume and dry aroma, which can be aged for over thirty years. Oliena, bright red in color and strawberry-scented, celebrated by Gabriele d'Annunzio, is the wine to serve with a meal. The blond Malvasia di Cagliari, dry and a little acidulated, with the typical scent of a flowering almond, goes well with rock lobster. Delicate golden Nasco, moss-scented, accompanies desserts. The red Monica is as delicate and thoroughbred as a Malaga. Giro, savorous thanks to its high alcohol content, is recommended for convalescents.

SPAIN

Sherry (*Xérès* in French), although the most famous of Spanish wines outside Spain, accounts for only a small percentage of the country's wine production. The remainder consists of red and white table wines, most of them consumed locally. The total production is about 500 million gallons a year. Spain has about three and a half million acres of vineyards, more than any other country in the world, but because of its arid climate the yield per acre is much lower than in France or Italy, or in California. The major wine regions are Levante, La Mancha, Rioja, and Aragon. The red wines of Levante, Murcia, and Alicante are the most famous; they are produced from Monastrell and Garnacha stocks. The red wines of La Mancha resemble Beaujolais but are stronger. Those of Rioja are full-bodied and smooth and are reminiscent of Bordeaux. The sweet wines of Aragon are excellent.

Sherry, which takes its name from the English pronunciation of Jerez, the town around which it is produced, is a blended fortified aperitif wine, the best as well as the best known of its type. The wines called sherry produced in other countries very seldom reach a quality comparable to the finest Spanish sherries. Sherry is fortified with grape brandy to bring its alcoholic content from the original 13 to 14 per cent by volume to 17 to 20 per cent. It is aged in casks made of American white oak. Sherries are divided into two main categories. The lighter wines, on which flor yeast forms soon after fermentation, become Finos and Amontillados; the heavier ones, with less bouquet and no flor, become Olorosos. The flor is essential to the development of fine dry sherries. The wine is aged for a year or longer and then blended in a solera, which is a collection of casks or barrels arranged to form three or more stages, in which wines of the same type but of different ages are gradually blended. The final result is usually a blend of the end-products of several soleras. All sherries are blends; there is no such thing as a vintage sherry. The labels usually carry a type designation and a brand name, very seldom the name of the district in which the grapes are grown. Sherries are divided by color: *muy palido* (very pale)—most Finos; *palido*—Amontillado; *ambar* (amber)—the medium sherries; *oro* (gold)—the drier Olorosos; *oscuro* (dark)—the sweeter Olorosos or cream sherries; *muy oscuro*—the brown sherries. The darker wines have usually had a concentrate of grape juice added for color.

PORTUGAL

Port is to Portugal as sherry is to Spain—the wine best known outside the country but only a tiny fraction of the total output, which, as in Spain, is chiefly table wines, red, white, and rosé. The export of these is increasing. Some are sold only under brand names but the use of geographical appellations, which are defined by law, is on the rise. Among the wines worthy of mention are Vinho Verde (literally "green wine," but applying to freshness, not color), from the province of Minho in northern Portugal, and Dao, from a mountainous district south of the Douro Valley: both include red, white, and rosé. Colares is a light red wine made of Ramisco grapes grown south of Lisbon, and Bucelas a white, produced just north of Lisbon.

Port, the famous sweet fortified dessert wine especially beloved by the British, takes its name from Oporto, one of the two cities on the Douro River from which, under Portuguese law, all port must be shipped. Only the wine produced in a delimited district of the upper Douro valley can be called port and the name is protected in most countries, though it is used in the United States with a geographic designation (California Port, New York State Port, etc.). The principal grape varieties used for port include Touriga, Bastardo, Tinta Francisca, Tinta Carvalho, Tinta Maderia, Mourisco, and others, all having a high sugar content. When the grapes are partially fermented the juice is put into casks containing high-proof brandy. The best ports are Vintage Ports, unblended wines of great years which require 15 to 50 years in bottle to reach their peak, and Crusted Ports, blended from wines of several good years. Both types form a heavy sediment and must be decanted carefully. Ruby Port and Tawny Port are blended wines, aged in wood; the latter is aged longer and takes on a brownish color.

The island of Madeira, a Portuguese colony in the Atlantic, has been producing the fine wines that bear its name for 400 years; their international reputation began when American clipper ships carried them across the Atlantic in colonial times. In the late nineteenth century the oidium and phylloxera damaged the vineyards of Madeira even more seriously than those of other European wine countries, and the wines have never since reached their former high quality. Madeiras are fortified wines, with an alcoholic content of 17 to 20 per cent. They are aged and blended in soleras, as sherry is, but are made by a different process. The finest aperitif and dessert Madeiras are scarce, but all Madeiras are exceptionally good wines for cooking and are widely so used in France.

Portugal also produces the famous Moscatel de Setubal, another great fortified wine, which is golden in color.

HUNGARY

Hungary's most famous wine is Tokay, one of the great white wines of the world. But the country produces many other wines, 70 per cent of its output being white wines and the remainder red and rosé. Egri Bikaver, considered the finest Hungarian red wine, is a blend of grape varieties including Kadarka and some varieties of French origin. Hungarian wines are usually labeled with a town or district name in adjective form ending in "i" (as Egri–"from Eger"), followed in most cases by the name of the grape. (Bikaver, which means "bull's blood," is an exception.)

True Tokay (spelled Tokaj in Hungarian) comes from the district of Tokaj-Hegyalia on the southern slopes of the Carpathian Mountains in northeast Hungary. The principal grape variety is the Furmint, which is also used in other Hungarian wines. The method of making the wine is unusual. The grapes are harvested as late as possible–that is, when they look like dried currants. The marc resembles a cask of raisins and is no way comparable to ordinary marc. A honeylike liquid with the appearance and density of syrup remains at the bottom of the vat. This is known as essence of Tokay and has a sugar content of 40 to 60 per cent. It ferments very slowly and the alcohol content is not more than 6 to 8 per cent even after several years. Essence of Tokay is produced only in small quantities. After partial fermentation it is mixed with the must, producing a wine of great quality, which keeps exceptionally well.

YUGOSLAVIA

Yugoslavia produces wines from various grape stocks, some of which are said to be directly descended from those of Roman times. The major wine region is in Slovenia, where Traminer, Rheinriesling, and Sauvignon grapes, among others, are grown, producing white wines of remarkable quality, some dry, some sweet. The red wines of Dalmatia and Brazza are tanned, very deep in color, with a high alcoholic content. Refosco and the Istrian Picolit are mellow and fragrant red wines.

Wines Produced Outside Europe

In considering the wines of other continents, it is important to remember that all the newer wine-producing countries were settled by Europeans and are European in culture. Their populations include the descendants of many vignerons, whose traditions and skills traveled with them. The pioneers found in their new homes different soils and different climatic conditions from those they had known, but they also had the advantage of being able, unhampered by restrictions in the use of land, to choose soils and climates best suited to viticulture and to select their own root stocks, either importing them or developing native stocks. In the course of time vines in the new countries have evolved characters of their own, often quite different from those of European vines, and with further development these differences will result in wines great in their own right. At present the wine industries of the newer countries are handicapped by having their wines generally compared with the great and rare European ones, with which they cannot yet compete. But the *vins ordinaires,* the bulk productions of general use, are equal and often superior to those of Europe, and some of the better wines can hold their own with all but the greatest wines of Europe.

The widespread practice of using the geographic designations of the famous European wine districts–Burgundy, Bordeaux, Chablis, Sauternes, Rhine, etc.–as generic or type names for similar wines produced under different conditions and often from different grapes has helped to encourage unfavorable comparisons which might have been partly avoided by a different method of labeling. This has begun to be recognized and a trend toward varietal and geographic names is becoming noticeable.

THE UNITED STATES

When Leif Ericson and his shipmates landed on the eastern shore of North America in about the year 1000, they found such a profusion of wild grapes that they named their discovery Vinland. According to the sagas, they made wine from these grapes, and took both grapes and wine back to Greenland some months later. Six hundred years after that, Captain John Smith found grapes in Virginia and made "neere twentie gallons of wine, which was like our British wine." In 1616 Lord De La Warr, governor of Virginia, suggested to the London Company that wine-making might prove profitable, and French vintners and an assortment of grape cuttings were dispatched to the colony. But the grapes would not grow, and subsequent efforts over more than 200 years were equally doomed to failure. The soil is not suited to *Vitis vinifera*, the species to which all European wine grapes belong, nor could the vines long survive the severe winters of the northeastern part of the continent. In addition, viticulture's worst enemy, the phylloxera, a plant louse indigenous to North America, attacked the imported vines. The native American vines (*Vitis labrusca* and other species), which have tougher roots, are resistant to this pest—one species is even immune—but the wines made from the native grapes did not taste like those of Europe. Since both consumers and vintners wanted the kind of wines they were used to, it was not until the early nineteenth century that a commercial wine industry using the native grapes was developed in the eastern half of the United States.

On the west coast, where soil and climate are more like those of the Mediterranean area, viticulture began in the late 1500s when Cortez, the conqueror of Mexico, ordered extensive planting of vines. The Jesuit fathers who accompanied him carried Spanish colonization, and with it the vine, north into what is now Lower California. The Franciscans, who succeeded the Jesuits, planted vines around a series of missions in California, the first of which was founded at San Diego in 1769. The grapes were a variety of *Vitis vinifera* brought originally from Spain, and while the wine they yielded was not very good, the vines flourished. In the 1830s commercial vineyardists began importing better European stocks which also flourished, and an American wine industry based on *Vitis vinifera* was finally created.

In addition to *Vitis vinifera*, three species of grapes are principally used in American wine-making. *Vitis labrusca*, the species to which the grapes found by Leif Ericson belonged, has furnished more cultivated varieties than any other American species; it provides the basis for the eastern wine industry. *Vitis rotundifolia*, which likes warm soil, flourishes in the central and southern sections of the United States, and *Vitis riparia*, the most widely distributed species and also the most resistant to phylloxera, is used by many growers as a root stock with other varieties. About 1860 American cuttings were taken to Europe for experimental purposes, and both phylloxera and oidium, a damaging fungus of American origin, were accidentally carried along and for two decades wrought enormous havoc in European vineyards. Efforts to repair the damage resulted in the importation of American root stocks resistant to these pests. In themselves these were unsatisfactory but experiments in grafting proved successful and now most European wines are made from grapes grafted onto native American root stocks. This is also the case in California, which was invaded by phylloxera somewhat later.

About 80 per cent of the wine drunk in the United States is produced in California. The Finger Lakes region of New York State is the next largest producer and Ohio the third, both making wine chiefly from native American stocks. Wine is also produced in small quantities in Arkansas, Iowa, Michigan, Virginia, North Carolina, New Jersey, Washington, and Oregon, and the Boordy Vineyard in Maryland is noteworthy for its proprietor's experiments with hybridizing French and American grapes. In North America outside the United States, Canada produces about 6 million gallons a year, chiefly on the Niagara peninsula, where wines similar to those of New York State are made. The climate of Mexico is in general too hot for viticulture, but some grapes are grown and some wine of inferior quality is made.

The American wine industry was less than a hundred years old and was showing remarkable progress when it received a serious setback with the enactment of nationwide Prohibition. In the three decades since repeal, however, it has recouped its losses and both quantity and quality are gaining steadily. The increase in table wines is proportionately greater than that of dessert wines, particularly with New York State wines.

While the industry is subject to a variety of regulations, federal, state, and local, these are by no means as stringent in the areas of labeling and quality control as those of the European wine countries.

Most American wines carry generic names derived from European geographic appellations, or type names such as claret or rosé. However the use of varietal names, particularly for the better-quality wines, is increasing. By American law, a wine cannot bear the name of a grape unless it contains at least 51 per cent of grapes of that name and has the aroma and flavor of the grape; some are made entirely from the grape for which they are named. (In most European wine countries the varieties of grapes grown in the region for which the wine is named are designated by law and varietal names are superfluous.) American wines are also sometimes designated only by class, for example, as "red dinner wine." Most also have a geographic label, indicating the state or district in which they were produced.

In American wine-making it is common practice to blend not only the juices of different varieties of grapes but also those of grapes of the same variety harvested in different years. This is done in Europe with sherry, port, and champagne, although port and champagne of exceptionally good years are not blended and carry a vintage date, which has given rise to the misleading usage of "vintage year" to mean a good year. European table wines, however, are always made entirely of grapes harvested in the year given on the label. Since climatic conditions affecting the quality of the grape crop, particularly in the northern countries, can vary greatly from year to year, the date on the bottle, plus a chart of vintages, can be a valuable guide to the quality of the wine, but in American wine regions climatic variations are too small to affect the harvest. A few American wines do carry a vintage date, which means, as it does with European wines, that they contain only grapes harvested in that year, but generally speaking blending is done to provide uniformity of quality and vintage dates are not used.

California

With soil and climate particularly suited to the cultivation of grapes, California has nearly half of the wineries in the United States and produces about 80 per cent of the wine. Commercial production began with the Mission grape planted by the Franciscans, but in 1831 Jean Louis Vignes, a Frenchman from the Bordeaux region, sent to France for cuttings of grapes of finer quality. The man regarded as most important in the establishment of the California wine industry, however, was a Hungarian nobleman, Agoston Haraszthy, who came to California in 1849 and started vineyards, first in San Diego and then farther north. He is credited with introducing the Zinfandel grape, the origin of which has never been traced but which is still one of the grapes most widely grown in California; it produces a good red table wine with a distinct varietal flavor. Haraszthy was sent to Europe by the governor of California in 1861 to select grape cuttings and returned with some 300 varieties, which were distributed throughout the state. Before 1900 California wines were competing in world markets and winning awards in international competitions.

Today California is producing more than 170 million gallons of wine yearly. Two-thirds of this is fortified wines—sherry, port, Angelica, and Muscatel—chiefly for mass markets, but during the last two decades the proportion of table wines has been increasing. The ordinary red and white table wines compare favorably with European *vins ordinaires* and the better grades can compete with all but the greatest wines of Europe.

Grapes are grown over most of the state, but the principal wine areas are the North Coast counties around San Francisco, where the table wines are made, and the warmer interior valleys, which produce chiefly fortified wines. The best of the champagnes are made by the authentic Champagne process and are excellent, and a few ports and sherries are also of high quality. Some of the highly rated table wines bearing varietal names are: white–Charbonnay and Pinot Charbonnay, Johannisberger Riesling, Pinot Blanc, Traminer; red–Cabernet Sauvignon, Pinot Noir, Gamay Beaujolais; rosé–Grenache and Gamay. Notable producers of fine California wines include, among others, Almadén, Beaulieu, Ficklin, Korbel, Louis M. Martini, Paul Masson, Weibel, Wente Brothers; all are contributing to raising standards of quality in what is potentially one of the truly great vineyard areas of the world.

New York State

The chief wine-producing area of New York State and the most important in the United States outside California is the Finger Lakes region. The lakes temper the extremes of heat and cold, keeping the buds dormant longer in the spring and extending the growing season in the fall, and the soil is particularly suited to the production of cultivated varieties of the native American grape species. Of the four Finger Lakes, only two have vineyards on their shores: Taylor, Pleasant Valley (Great Western)–now a part of the Taylor Company, and Urbana (Gold Seal) are on Lake Keuka, and Widmer's is on Lake Canandaigua. The grape varieties include Delaware, Catawba, Elvira, Ives, Concord, Fredonia, Isabella, Clinton, Diana, Niagara, and other improved varieties of *Vitis labrusca*. The champagnes produced in this region, which represent about half of American champagnes and most of the best, are chiefly made from the Delaware grape. The region also produces red, white, and rosé table wines, sherry and vermouth, and dessert wines. Most of them carry generic or type names but some have varietal names, for example Delaware and Elvira. "New York State" is legally required to appear on the labels.

New York State, in comparison with California, produces a much higher proportion of quality wines in relation to the total output, and the care and technical skills of the vintners have resulted in the development of excellent wines. These wines from native American grapes have a distinctive flavor variously described as "wildness," "foxiness," and sometimes "fruitiness" or "grapiness." The white wines are generally more distinguished than the red, but all should be judged on their native character and not in comparison with European wines or the California wines from European grapes.

Recently wineries in the Finger Lakes area have been experimenting with European-American hybrids, which combine the fruit qualities of European grapes with the disease-resistance of American stocks. Wine from these is being blended with that from native grapes with promising results.

Ohio

Before the Civil War Ohio was America's leading wine-producing state. The first vineyards were planted along the Ohio River. Nicholas Longworth, who went to Ohio in 1830, took with him cuttings of the Catawba grape. His vineyards on the Ohio were the first in America to produce labeled wines sold in competition with imported wines; some of them received medals at European expositions. Later the islands in Lake Erie and the lakeshore around Sandusky were found to provide better conditions for grape growing; the lake helps to protect the vines against frost. Most of Ohio's grapes are now grown in this area. Although relatively less important than it was a hundred years ago, Ohio's wine industry still flourishes, producing several million gallons yearly of table wines, port, sherry, vermouth, champagne, and fruit wines. A fine sauterne and the historic Sweet Catawba are produced on the Isle St. George, where the state's leading vintner, Meier's Wine Cellars, has its vineyards. The Delaware grape, the source of the finest Ohio and New York State white wines, is named for the town of Delaware, Ohio, where it was introduced from New Jersey in 1850.

SOUTH AMERICA

South America produces more than twice as much wine as North America, although only the southern third of the continent has a cool enough climate for viticulture. There are a few vineyards high in the mountains of Peru, but the principal wine countries are Argentina and Chile, with some produced in Uruguay and the southern tip of Brazil. The wines are mainly table wines and are nearly all consumed locally, only Chile exporting an appreciable amount.

Argentina, the largest producer, with more than 400,000 acres of vineyards in the states of Mendoza and San Juan, produces and consumes red, white, and rosé wines at the rate of 200 million gallons a year.

Chile, which produces by far the best wines, has a history of wine-making dating from before 1600. Its modern production began about 1850, when fine French vines and trained French vintners were brought to the country. French methods have been used with success in spite of the very different soil and climatic conditions and some very fine wines produced. Some have varietal names—Cabernet, Semillon, Riesling. Chilean Riesling is the best known wine of export. Others are called Sauternes, Chablis, Borgoña (Burgundy), Rhin (Rhine), and so on. The better grades of still wines usually carry government-controlled labels of *Reservado* or *Gran Vino*. Grape varieties also include Pinot, Sauvignon, Merlot, and other fine wine grapes.

SOUTH AFRICA

The wine-producing areas of South Africa are in the temperate zone, in the same latitude as those of Australia and Chile, and have a climate similar to that of the Mediterranean countries. During the vintage season, rainfall is at its minimum, which allows the grapes to ripen under ideal conditions, without fungus diseases. These conditions are well suited to the production of sweet wines, full-bodied dry red wines, and fortified wines.

The Dutch settlers of South Africa, aided by Huguenot refugees from France, were producing wine as early as the seventeenth century, and Constantia, from the vineyards of that name, near Cape Town, had a greater reputation in Europe in the nineteenth century than any other non-European wine has ever achieved. The district, though now reduced in area as a result of urbanization, still produces light-bodied red table wines of fine quality, from Cabernet, Sauvignon, Schiras, Malbec, and Cinsault vines. The Stellenbosch and Paarl areas also produce excellent wines from the same grape varieties. The percentage of Sauvignon, Pinot, Gamay, and Malbec vines is being increased in the South African vineyards.

Because of the constantly sunny climate, which results in grapes high in sugar content and low in fixed acids, white wine production is at a disadvantage. The wines are high in alcohol, 11 to 12 per cent by volume, but without much bouquet. The best are produced in the Paarl district. The grape types are Riesling, Sauvignon Blanc, Semillon, Clairette Blanche, and Fransdruif or Spanish Palomino.

Paarl and Stellenbosch also produce excellent wines of port character, both vintage and blended, from Cinsault, Schiras, and Teinturier varieties. The Cape district produces a good sweet red wine from red Muscat grapes;

good Muscat wines of robust character, though slightly lacking in finesse and bouquet, are produced in the inland districts of Worcester, Robinson, Montagu, and Bonnievale, and the latter two districts produce wines which are less robust but of fine and delicate bouquet.

South Africa takes pride in its sherries. Flor is indigenous to South Africa as well as to Spain, and many of the sherries blended in soleras. Formulas of production are government controlled. Finos, Olorosos, and brown sherries are made; the grape varieties are Steindruif, Fransdruif, Groendruif, and some Pedro Ximenez.

AUSTRALIA

The only continent entirely in the southern hemisphere, Australia has a small population in relation to its area, which has given its vitriculturists a wide choice in the selection of sites. Good rainfall during the dormant period and a dry, sunny atmosphere at vintage time create excellent conditions for a wide variety of wines. The root stocks were imported from Europe but the differences in soil and climate have resulted in wines of a different character, which are establishing themselves in their own right.

The history of Australian wines began in 1788, when Captain Arthur Phillip planted the first vine. Gregory Blaxland was awarded medals in London for his red wines in 1823 and 1827, and in 1830 James Busby was sent for grape varieties, returning with 20,000 cuttings of more than 600 kinds. Today an established oenological research department, constant revision of cellar manipulation, and great storage cellars insure a constant supply of wines of standard purity and quality.

Wine is produced in five Australian states. The first vines were planted in New South Wales, the oldest state, which now produces red and white table wines, fortified dry red and white wines, sherries, vermouths, wines of port type, muscats, and sparkling wines. Victoria has a larger production of the same kinds of wines. Queensland, the youngest state, in which vines were not planted until 1899, is the smallest producer, and Western Australia the next larger. Both specialize in red and white table wines; Queensland also produces dessert wines and Western Australia a variety of other wines. The largest producer is South Australia, with 73 per cent of the total. The grape varieties include Riesling, Cabernet, Pinots, Shiraz, Verdelho, Malbec, Grenache, Carignan, and Mataró. Australia also produces rosés, both dry and sparkling. European wine names–Chablis, Sauternes, Burgundy, Claret, etc.–are used for wines of these types.

3

THE PRINCIPLES AND BASIC MATERIALS OF COOKERY

The two most important factors in good cooking are the quality of the materials and the skill used in their preparation. In this chapter we first discuss the nature and uses of various basic materials. Methods of cooking are then described in detail, as are methods of preserving food. The final section presents, with recipes, the doughs, stocks, and mixtures which form the foundation of the great French cuisine and lists the classic garnishes which embellish it. The user of this book will find this chapter an important preparation for the recipes in the chapters which follow.

Raw Materials

Every cook can benefit from a knowledge of the nature, sources, food values, and uses of basic materials, both for purchasing, handling, and preparing them, and in planning dishes and menus. The properties and functions of milk and most milk products, fats, cereals, vegetables, fruits, and sweeteners, as well as culinary herbs and spices, are discussed here; similar information on eggs, cheese, fish, shellfish, meats, and poultry is given in later chapters.

MILK AND MILK PRODUCTS

Milk is the product of the mammary glands of animals. Although the cow is the chief source of milk, especially in the United States, other animals, such as the buffalo, camel, goat, llama, reindeer, and sheep, have supplied people of many lands with milk for many centuries.

Milk is very important in the recommended daily food plan. Although not a perfect food, it includes all the nutrients essential to good nutrition (carbohydrates, fats, proteins, minerals, and vitamins). It is such an outstanding source of calcium that two cups of milk or the equivalent in milk products will provide the adult body with its daily calcium requirements. Milk is an excellent source of easily digested, good-quality protein and therefore a good supplement to the incomplete protein contained in such foods as cereals and vegetables. It is low in iron content and in ascorbic acid (vitamin C), but these nutrients can be easily supplemented in the diet by the use of egg yolks and fresh fruits and vegetables. Milk is also a good source of iodine in areas where iodine is present in the water and feed of the milk-producing animals.

Milk is available in the following forms:

Grade A Raw Milk. Unpasteurized, fresh liquid milk containing not less than 3.25 per cent fat, produced under conditions conforming to certain specified sanitary standards.

Certified Milk. To be certified, milk must contain not less than 3.5 per cent butterfat and must conform to standards set up by the American Association of Medical Milk Commissions. The production must be supervised by the local medical society. It may or may not be pasteurized. If desired, it may be homogenized to produce a softer curd. The cost of this milk is twice that of ordinary pasteurized milk.

Pasteurized Milk. Milk that has been heated either to 145° F. for 30 minutes or to 160° F. for 15 seconds and then cooled rapidly to 40° F. or lower to destroy dangerous bacteria.

Homogenized Milk. Milk that has been treated to break up the fat globules into very small, uniformly easily digested particles which remain distributed through the milk instead of rising to the top as cream does in ordinary milk.

Fortified Milk. Milk that has had its vitamin D content augmented either by the addition of vitamin D concentrates directly to the milk, or by other methods.

Skim Milk, Fluid and Powdered. Milk from which cream has been removed to the extent of not more than 1.5 per cent of the butterfat content. Its energy value is only half that of whole milk (making it useful in reducing diets) and it is poorer in the fat-soluble vitamins A, D, E, and K, but it has all the other nutrients contained in whole milk.

Home-Churned Buttermilk. The milk that is left after naturally soured milk has been churned and the butter removed. The composition is similar to that of skim milk.

Commercial or Cultured Buttermilk. Made by adding a lactic-acid culture to skim milk to develop the desired flavor and consistency. It has somewhat more lactic acid but otherwise the composition is practically the same as that of the skim milk from which it was made.

Sour Milk. May be soured naturally or artificially.

Evaporated Milk. Made from homogenized whole milk dehydrated to about one-half of its original volume. When it is diluted with an equal quantity of water the composition is similar to that of whole milk.

Sweetened Condensed Milk. Evaporated sweetened milk. The final product contains 40 per cent sugar, 30 per cent milk solids, and 30 per cent water. It cannot be used as a substitute for milk in cooking. It has good keeping qualities because of its high sugar content.

Dried Whole Milk. Contains all the milk solids. There must not be less than 4 per cent butterfat nor more than 5 per cent moisture.

Nonfat Dried Milk. Skim milk from which all but 5 per cent of the moisture has been removed. Reconstituted dried skim milk approximates fresh skim milk in nutrients, except vitamin C. It keeps better than does dried whole milk.

Clabber. Milk that has soured naturally to the stage where firm curd has formed but not to the point at which the whey separates. It is eaten instead of yoghurt in many parts of the United States.

Yoghurt. A custard-like preparation made from concentrated whole milk fermented by the use of a special culture. It may have fruit flavors or other flavors added. It has the same food value as the milk from which it is made but is more quickly digested because of the fineness of the curd.

Since milk can carry disease-producing bacteria, every precaution should be taken to keep it safe. Sanitary measures for the care of cows and the handling of milk are enforced by law in the United States and some other countries. Pasteurization is used as an added safety factor. Since milk can become recontaminated, it should be handled carefully in the home, kept covered, in its original container, in the coldest part of the refrigerator and used within a few days.

Cream is the part of milk richest in fat globules. It rises gradually to the surface or is separated by centrifugal force. Cream is obtainable commercially in four general types:

Light cream. Generally known as coffee cream; has a minimum fat content of 18 to 20 per cent. It is also used in cream soups, sauces, candies, and frostings.

Heavy cream. Commonly known as whipping cream; has a minimum fat content of 30 to 35 per cent. It is used for whipping, as a seasoning with vegetables, in desserts, and in some salad dressings.

Half-and-half. Contains about 8 per cent butterfat. It is made by adding one part light cream to one part low-fat milk and homogenizing the mixture. It is used for coffee, sauces, soups, and in dishes where a full, rich flavor is desired. It is lower in calories than light or heavy cream.

Cultured sour cream. Light cream to which lactic-acid culture has been added. It usually contains from 18 to 20 per cent butterfat. It gives a tender crumb in baking and to sauces a smoother texture and a slight acid flavor that appeal to many people.

Natural sour cream is light or heavy cream that is allowed to ferment naturally. It is used in the home production of butter.

The other important milk products are butter, discussed under Fats, and cheese, discussed in Chapter 17.

FATS

Solid Fats

Butter is made from either sweet cream or sour cream. According to United States federal law, all commercially produced butter must contain at least 80 per cent milk fat and the cream must be pasteurized. The addition of salt and artificial coloring is optional in both sour- and sweet-cream butters. Salted butter has better keeping qualities than unsalted butter.

Sour-cream butter, as the name implies, is made from sour cream. Farmers making butter for home use usually use unpasteurized cream and let it sour naturally. The commercial producers pasteurize the cream first and then sour it with cultured lactic-acid bacteria. Sour cream churns more quickly, and the flavor of the butter is preferred by most people.

Sweet-cream butter is made from sweet cream. Sweet cream is more difficult to churn, but the delicate flavor of the butter makes it especially desirable to some people for table use and for making certain baked goods. Unsalted sweet-cream butter is known as sweet butter and is gaining in popularity.

Whipped butter is produced by stirring or whipping air or some inert gas into butter to increase its volume and spreadability. In the United States it is usually sold unsalted.

Margarine is used as an alternate to butter. In the United States, margarine is made by churning refined oils of vegetable origin, such as cottonseed, corn, and soybean oils, with pasteurized, cultured skim milk to produce a product similar to butter. Butter-flavored materials, as well as vitamins, may be added during the manufacturing process in order to give margarine flavor and food value equal to those of butter. Salt is optional. Most margarine sold today is artificially colored. United States federal standards for margarine specify not less than 80 per cent fat content.

Lard, one of the oldest of the household fats, is rendered from the fat of the hog. It is nearly 100 per cent fat. The quality of lard is influenced by (1) the feed of the hog, (2) the part of the body from which the fat comes, and (3) the method used to render the fat.

Hogs which are fed on cottonseed meal, peanuts, or soybeans have a softer fat than do those fattened on corn.

Lard rendered from the fat which surrounds the kidneys and abdominal cavity, known as "leaf lard," is harder and is considered to be of better quality than that which comes from other areas. It is kettle-rendered at low temperature and is produced in limited amounts. Most of the lard on the retail market is made from fat from other parts of the hog. This fat is rendered under steam pressure at high temperature and is then refined.

Since natural lard contains some unsaturated fats which have a tendency to become rancid on storage, most of the lard offered for retail sale has been treated to improve its keeping quality. This treatment may consist of pressing out part of the "lard oil" which contains most of the unsaturates, removing the unsaturation by "hydrogenation," adding antioxidants, together with citric acid which increases their effectiveness, and diluting the lard with hydrogenated or unhydrogenated vegetable fats.

Except for some margarines, ordinary lard is the least expensive shortening on the retail market. It is equal, if not superior, to other shortenings for pastry making. It also is suitable for biscuit, other quick breads, and for cakes for which there are special recipes. Lard is also used for frying.

Vegetable shortenings are solidified vegetable oils. The oils most commonly used are those from cottonseed and soybeans, sometimes with varying amounts of other oils, such as corn oil and peanut oil, added. These oils are treated to improve their keeping qualities, color, flavor, texture and over-all baking and cooking performance.

Liquid Fats

Oil is fat that remains liquid at normal temperatures. Olive oil is the oldest of the vegetable oils and the one most used in European cooking. In American homes the vegetable oils most commonly used are made from corn, cottonseed, peanuts, soybeans, and sesame seed; olive oil is used to a lesser extent. In other parts of the world, edible oils are also made from sweet and bitter almonds, coconuts, poppy seed, sunflower seed, and walnuts.

Oils fall into two general types: salad oil and cooking oil. The salad oils most commonly used have been clarified by exposing them to low temperatures for a long time and then filtering off the solids which precipitate; these oils will not solidify or cloud at refrigerator temperatures, while cooking oils may do so. Salad oils also have less tendency to become rancid. They can also be used for cooking purposes.

Olive oil, preferred by connoisseurs for salads, is also widely used in cooking, particularly in the Mediterranean countries and in dishes originating in those areas. The best grade of olive oil is known as pure or virgin olive oil and is cold-pressed from the finest olives. It is greenish-yellow in color, with a fine, distinctive flavor, and keeps well at normal temperatures; it should not be refrigerated. The second grade, known as ordinary olive oil, or simply as olive oil, is extracted by pressure under heat. It is lighter in color than virgin olive oil and becomes rancid more quickly.

CEREALS AND THEIR PRODUCTS

Cereals are the edible, starchy seeds of certain plants of the grass family—barley, corn, oats, rice, rye, wheat, etc. They furnish approximately 80 per cent of the food energy of the world's population. Cereal grains differ in size and shape according to the plant source. However, in general, the structural parts, the food nutrients, and the distribution of the nutrients are similar.

The bran coat, the outer protective covering of the kernel, consists of several cellulose layers which contain minerals, protein, thiamine, and riboflavin. The endosperm is the central portion of the kernel and comprises the greater portion of the grain. It contains chiefly starch but also contains some protein. The embryo or germ, from which the grain sprouts, is found at one end of the kernel. It is comparatively high in fat, and contains some protein, minerals, thiamine, vitamin E, and niacin.

Grain products are deficient in calcium, lack vitamin C, and, with the exception of yellow corn, lack vitamin A.

Wheat

Wheat, the aristocrat of cereals in the Western Hemisphere, is one of the oldest and most respected of cereal grains. Since the wheat plant thrives in both high and low temperatures and does not require much rainfall, it is grown in many parts of the world—in the tropics, the deserts, the northern latitudes, at sea level, and at altitudes of over 8000 feet. However, only the "hard" wheats are grown in the colder regions.

The products for human consumption obtained from wheat are flour and a variety of breakfast foods. Flour, of course, is the most important. There are various flours, each with definite characteristics determined by the protein content of the grain from which it is milled. Protein makes gluten, which forms the framework of doughs. Flour yielding a relatively large amount of gluten has pronounced elastic and cohesive properties and water-absorbing powers. It is called hard or strong flour or bread flour. It is used in the baking industry for making doughs such as yeast doughs in which the leavening action is prolonged.

Flour forming a smaller amount of gluten is less cohesive, less elastic, and absorbs less water. It is suited for making pastry and for making doughs in which the leavening action is rapid, as in cakes and quick breads. This is the most highly refined flour of the mill and is known as soft or weak flour. It is used by the baking industry and by the homemaker.

An intermediate flour known as family or all-purpose flour is made by the skillful blending, before milling, of the wheats from which hard and soft flour are made. This type of flour is found in most households and is suitable for making the majority of baked products.

Graham or wholewheat flour is made from the ground unbolted entire wheat grain.

Semolina is the coarsely ground flour, made from very hard (durum) wheat, high in gluten, which is used for making macaroni, noodles, and spaghetti.

Other wheat products include bulgur wheat, cracked wheat, farina, and wheat germ. Bulgur (or bulghur) wheat, an all-wheat product which originated in the Near East, is parboiled whole wheat that has been dried, partly debranned, and cracked into angular particles. It resembles whole wheat in nutritive value and is used instead of rice in some recipes. Cracked wheat is prepared by cracking cleaned wheat, other than durum, into angular pieces. Farina is made from wheat other than durum, with the germ and bran coat removed. The grain is ground to a granular form and sifted. Its main use is for breakfast foods. Wheat germ is made from the fat-rich embryo of the wheat kernel. The germ is flattened and then sifted out as an oily yellowish flake. It is used mainly to enrich breakfast cereals, breads, and other dishes.

Corn

Corn, which was not known to the civilized world until the discovery of America, stands next to wheat as a cereal used for food in the United States. Although it is used extensively in Italy, other European countries have been slow to accept corn as a staple food. In Europe it is usually known as maize.

For human consumption, in the United States, the dry mature grains of corn are made into breakfast cereals, cornmeal, corn flour (made by milling white cornmeal), cornstarch, corn oil, corn syrup, corn sugar, and hominy. There are two general classes of corn, white corn and yellow corn, the yellow corn having a higher vitamin A content.

"Roasting ears," the immature small green ears of sweet corn, are popular roasted or boiled, as a table vegetable.

Rice

Rice is the food crop of about one-half of the world's population. It is used extensively by the people of China, India, Java, Japan, the Philippines, and to a lesser extent by the people of Europe and the United States. It is eaten largely as boiled rice, with the addition of seasonings if desired. In the United States rice is frequently served instead of potatoes.

Cultivated rice grains are classified according to the length of the grain—

long, medium, and short. Rice is available as brown rice, from which only the husk is removed, and white rice or polished rice, which has both husk and bran layers removed, with a loss of some minerals and vitamins. Brown rice is more nutritious than white, and requires longer cooking. White rice is sold either coated or uncoated. From it are made:

Enriched rice, made by enriching a percentage of the kernels with vitamins or by enriching the mixture used for coating the rice.

Precooked rice, which is a long-grain rice that has been cooked, rinsed, and dried by a patented process. As the name implies, it needs little further preparation.

Converted rice, which has been parboiled by a patented process. Many cooks prefer this type because it cooks more quickly.

Wild rice, which is not a true rice, is not cultivated but is gathered for the market. In the United States it is available in limited quantities at a high price. It is more nutritious than cultivated rice and is becoming popular as a delicacy.

Products obtained from rice include breakfast cereals, such as Rice Crispies, Rice Flakes, and Puffed Rice. Rice flour and rice starch, used as thickening agents, are probably less familiar. There are many varieties of rice grown over the world, each having its own characteristics. Some are superior in flavor and nutritious quality to ordinary white rice, but in the United States they can only be obtained in stores specializing in foods from foreign countries.

Other Cereals

Barley, oats, and rye, in the United States, are less important as foodstuffs for human consumption than as animal fodder. However, they do provide some valuable nutrients.

Oats are made into oatmeal, also called "rolled oats" and "oats." This is made by rolling groats (oats with the hull removed) to form flakes. Quick-cooking oats differ from regular oats only in having thinner flakes. The edible portion of the kernels is cut into small particles which are then rolled thin. Oatmeal is very nutritious, containing more protein than any of the other cereal grains. It is easily digested, therefore valuable in the diets of invalids and infants. It is popular as a breakfast cereal and for making oatmeal cookies and bread. Europeans make oatmeal flour from oats.

Rye is used mainly for making rye flour, which is available in three grades: white, medium, and dark. Since the protein which forms gluten is rather soft and sticky in rye and not as strong as that in hard wheat, wheat flour must be used along with rye flour when making bread. Europeans make greater use of rye flour for bread-making than do Americans.

Barley contains no gluten and cannot be used alone to make acceptable bread. When barley flour is mixed with wheat flour, and, if desired, flours made from other grains, bread of fair quality can be made. Barley flour is used in the diets of invalids and infants. Pearl barley, the polished grain with the bran coat removed, is used for thickening soups. Industrially, barley is used in making malt, which is used in the manufacture of beer and alcohol and also in making beverages and malt syrup used by bakers and confectioners.

The cassava plant, which is grown extensively in the tropics, is the source of tapioca. The starch of the cassava root is made into a dough known as tapioca flour. The moist dough is then forced through a sieve, the size of which determines whether the tapioca is coarse, medium, or fine. The pellets are then subjected to high temperature. This is known as pearl tapioca; it should be soaked one hour before using. Minute tapioca is made by baking the moist tapioca starch in thin sheets and grinding them into fine granules. This tapioca cooks quickly and is preferred by most cooks. Tapioca is chiefly used as a thickening for fruit pies and in puddings.

VEGETABLES

Vegetables form an important part of the world's diet. Generally speaking, they contain few calories, are relatively cheap, and offer plenty of variety to the menu. Fresh vegetables perhaps do more than any other food group except fruit to add appetizing color, texture, and flavor to the diet. As a result of modern methods of agriculture, the ingenuity of scientists, and improved methods of transportation, a variety of vegetables is now available in the retail markets throughout the year in fresh, frozen, canned, dried, and dehydrated forms.

The principal contributions of vegetables to nutrition are minerals, vitamins, and cellulose. Potatoes, corn, dried beans, lentils, peas, and soybeans also provide carbohydrates. Dried beans, lentils, peas, and soybeans also furnish vegetable protein as well as some minerals.

In selecting fresh vegetables, consider the habits and tastes of the family, but remember that the body requires different types of vegetables. Vary your vegetable servings. Consider the use to be made of the vegetable you buy. If it is to be served whole, as a stuffed pepper or tomato, perfection in size and shape is important; but if it is to be cut up, as in a tossed salad, uneven sizes or even a few imperfections that do not affect the interior are permissible. All fresh vegetables, regardless of use, should be crisp, tender, fresh-appearing, and free from bruises, to insure best flavor and more vitamin C. Choose vegetables that have been trimmed the least. Unwilted tops and outside leaves, chopped, make colorful, nutritious, and tasty additions to the salad bowl.

Buy fresh vegetables at the peak of their season, as they are then usually cheaper and also superior in quality and food value. How much to buy at a time depends upon the amount consumed at once, the keeping qualities of the vegetable, storage facilities, and the savings derived from buying in larger amounts.

Care of Vegetables in the Home

Fresh vegetables to be eaten raw should be at their best—fresh, crisp, and tender with all their natural color and flavor. They will retain these properties longer if stored under conditions best suited to each type of vegetable. The ripening process continues after harvesting, unless checked by proper storage conditions. This process impairs the flavor, because of enzyme action changing sugar into starch, as with fresh peas and young sweet corn. Food value and crispness are decreased upon exposure to air and light and by the loss of moisture. As vegetables consist largely of water, evaporation must be kept to a minimum to keep them fresh and palatable. Store vegetables at low temperature and keep them in closed containers of metal, plastic, or pliofilm that permit a little air to circulate.

Vegetables may be classed as perishable, semiperishable, and staple. Vegetables of the first two classes should be refrigerated as soon as possible, after a thorough but quick washing. (Do not soak.) Since dirt and bruises hasten spoilage, trim off all questionable parts. Put them in proper containers and store in the refrigerator. Do not peel or chop until just before using. Pod vegetables, such as young peas and fresh lima beans, retain their freshness and nutrients longer if stored in the pod. If they must be shelled in advance, keep them in a tightly covered jar. Staple vegetables—fully matured roots, bulbs, and seed crops—have better keeping qualities and may be bought in quantity, provided there is suitable storage space, such as a root cellar or a moderately cool basement room away from the furnace. Store dried vegetables in tightly covered jars or cans.

Frozen vegetables should be the last items on the shopping list to be purchased and should be put as soon as possible in a holding cabinet of the proper temperature. A suitable holding temperature for storage for less than a year is 0° F. If vegetables are kept in the freezer compartment of a household refrigerator, check the temperature—if it is as high as 10° F., the vegetables should be eaten within 10 days or 2 weeks for best flavor and nutrition. Frozen vegetables lose vitamin C and palatability continuously during the holding period, but at a rate which is retarded as the temperature decreases.

FRUITS

Fruits, from the botanist's point of view, are the seed-forming parts of plants. They include such fruit-vegetables as cucumbers and tomatoes, cereals, nuts, and legumes. However, the food products most commonly defined as fruits are fleshy and succulent, have a higher acid content than most fruit-vegetables, and when ripe have sufficient sugar to taste sweet.

Fruits vary in nutritive value according to the type. In general, however, they contain cellulose, carbohydrates, traces of protein, minerals, and vitamins, especially vitamin C, and in yellow fruits vitamin A. Ripe fruits are generally easily digested and, because of their appealing flavor and attractive appearance, tempt the appetite.

Buy fruits at the peak of their season, for then they are superior in quality and also cheaper. For immediate consumption, choose firm, ripe fruits. If fruit is to be kept for a few days before using, buy it a little underripe. Do not pinch or poke fruit; it bruises easily and this causes spoilage.

Berries are especially perishable. Keep them dry under refrigeration and do not wash them until ready to use.

Store ripe fruits such as apricots, cherries, grapes, peaches, pears, and plums in the refrigerator in covered containers or in perforated pliofilm bags. Avocados, melons, and pineapples keep best stored at cool room temperature. Ripe fruit should not be kept long, as it spoils quickly. Slightly unripe fruits ripen best in the open air at room temperature, out of the sun.

Bananas, both ripe and green, should be stored above 56° F. since they suffer injury from chilling. They keep best at cool room temperature.

Citrus fruit, if held several weeks at temperatures below 50° to 55° F., will develop pitted skins and discolored flesh. However, all citrus fruit may be held in the household refrigerator a week or two without harmful effects.

Frozen fruits, like frozen vegetables, need a storage temperature of 0° F.

or lower to maintain high quality. If they are to be kept only a few days, store them in the frozen-food compartment of the refrigerator.

Dried fruits keep well in tightly closed containers at room temperature, except in humid weather, when they should be stored in the refrigerator.

The first rule to remember when preparing all fresh fruits, whether they are to be eaten raw or cooked, is to wash them thoroughly to remove all spray residue.

To enjoy fullest flavor and to conserve nutrients, serve fresh fruits raw when possible. Prepare cut or diced fruits just before serving. Fruits which discolor, such as apples, bananas, or peaches, should be mixed with juices from acid fruits such as lemons, limes, oranges, or pineapples, or with ascorbic acid, which may be purchased at the drug store. Eat ripe, fresh fruit without the addition of sugar; most fully ripened fruits do not need it.

SWEETENING AGENTS

Sugars

Usually when we speak of sugar we refer to a white granulated product consisting of 99.5 per cent sucrose, a member of the carbohydrate family obtained by crystallization from the concentrated juice of the sugar cane and sugar beet. Its function as food is only to supply the body with heat and energy; it contains no minerals, vitamins, protein, or cellulose.

White sugar is found in the retail markets in various forms.

Granulated white sugar is the standard product for general use, available to the homemaker in 1-, 2-, 5-, and 10-pound packages. It is also available to commercial users in 100-pound bags.

Superfine granulated sugar is a specially screened, uniformly fine-grained product. It is used in sponge cakes and in other cakes where quick creaming with the fat is desired; for sweetening raw fruit such as berries, peaches, etc.; and in beverages where quick dissolving is preferred.

Confectioners' or powdered sugar is granulated sugar that has been ground or pulverized and screened to give sugar in the powdered form. A little cornstarch is added to prevent caking. It is used in frostings, icings, uncooked candies, for dusting baked products, doughnuts, etc.

Cube sugar is made by compressing moist white granulated sugar into molds. It is cut into cubes or small blocks of 80 to 200 per pound. It is packed in 1- and 2-pound cartons.

Brown sugar is essentially sugar which contains some of the other constituents of cane molasses. (Beet molasses is too bitter for human consumption.) The more molasses it contains the darker its color and the stronger its flavor. Because of its molasses content, it furnishes some minerals not found in white sugar. It is used in cakes, cookies, frostings, candies, sauces, to glaze ham, over breakfast cereals, or whenever a brown-sugar flavor is desired. It is packaged in 1-pound cartons. Recently a granulated brown sugar has been introduced which does not "cake" or dry out as conventional brown sugar does. However, when used in baking it requires adjustments in quantities of other ingredients in recipes. The instructions on the package should be studied before substituting it for conventional brown sugar.

Maple sugar is made by concentrating the sap of the sugar-maple tree to the point of crystallization. Highly prized for its delightful flavor, it is used for candies, frostings, desserts, etc. It is in limited commercial supply and is sold chiefly in gift shops and specialty food stores.

Liquid Sweeteners

Other sweetening agents exist in liquid form. Each is from a different source and has a different chemical composition. These liquid sweeteners are:

- Molasses, a by-product of the manufacture of sugar from sugar-cane juice.
- Sorghum syrup, a product of sorghum cane, resembling molasses; it is popular in the southern part of the United States.
- Corn syrup, a product of corn, available in both light and dark forms.
- Maple syrup, made from the sap of the sugar-maple tree.
- Honey, the nectar of plants, gathered, changed, concentrated, and stored by bees. It is the sweetest and said to be the oldest of all liquid sweeteners. The flavor depends upon the plant source from which the nectar is obtained.

HERBS AND SPICES

Before the beginning of history herbs and spices were already known for their properties of flavoring and enhancing foods; today more and more cooks are learning their uses and appreciating their subtle qualities.

The distinction between herbs and spices is a wavering and uncertain one. Generally speaking, herbs are defined as leaves of plants grown in temperate climates, and spices as various parts of plants grown in the tropics—seeds, roots, fruit, flowers, bark, etc. However, some plants whose seeds are considered spices can be grown in both hot and mild climates and the leaves of some of these can be used as herbs; anise and mustard are examples. In the onion family, the leaves of chives, the leaves and bulbs of spring onions, and the bulbs of garlic and shallots are the parts used in cooking and flavoring. The leaves of herbs can be used fresh or dried; spices are dried and many can be used either whole or in powdered form. In the following lists, the most common culinary use is the criterion for classifying as herb or spice in doubtful cases. The French names, where they differ from the English, are given in parentheses.

Herbs (Plantes Aromatiques)

(Unless otherwise noted, the fresh or dried leaves are the part used.)

NAME AND DESCRIPTION	CULINARY USES
Basil (*Basilic*). Sweet, fragrant.	Soups, sauces, sausages, pâtés, salads; popular in Italian cooking.
Bay leaves (*Laurier*). Strong, pungent; use with discretion.	Meat, poultry, fish, stews.
Borage (*Bourrache*). Fragrant, pronounced cucumber flavor.	Leaves and flowers. Salads and summer drinks.
Burnet, Pimpernel (*Pimprenelle*). Odoriferous, pungent.	Soups, sauces; young leaves as salad.
Chervil (*Cerfeuil*). Mild, aromatic, pleasing shape.	Leaves and stalks. Soups, sauces, salads, decoration of cold dishes.
Chives (*Ciboulettes*). Very mild onion flavor; slender tubular leaves.	Soup, hot or cold, cold sauces, salads, meat, fish, mixed with butter or cream cheese.
Dill (*Aneth*). Fragrant, permeating flavor.	Leaves and seeds. Soups, sauces, crayfish, salads, pickles (seed).
Fennel (*Fenouil*). Mild, fragrant, penetrating, resembles anise.	Leaves: sauces, decoration of cold dishes; seeds: liqueurs, cakes, candies. Stalks and root: as vegetable, in salads.

Garlic (*Ail*). Strong, pungent, penetrating; to be used with discretion.	Sections of bulb, whole, chopped or crushed. Meats, fish, poultry, vegetables, salad dressing.
Horseradish (*Raifort*). Strong, hot, pungent.	Grated root. Sauces, meat dishes, marinades, pickles.
Juniper berries (*Baies de genièvre*). Pleasantly pungent.	Sauerkraut, game, pork, sauces.
Lemon balm (*Citronelle*). Fragrant, lemon smell.	Salads, summer drinks, punch.
Lovage. Celery flavor.	Soups, seafood, meats, salads.
Marjoram (*Marjolaine*). Odoriferous, fragrant. Related to oregano.	Soups, sauces, fish, meat preparations.
Mint (*Menthe*). Mild, fragrant.	Soups, sauces, potatoes, other vegetables, lamb, jelly, vinegars.
Oregano (*Origan*). Related to marjoram, but stronger and more pungent; use with discretion.	Indispensable in Italian cooking, especially pizza; bouquet garni, soups, sauces, fish, meat, potatoes, other vegetables.
Rosemary (*Romarin*). Strong and pungent.	Pork, lamb, mutton, duck, goose, infusions, vinegars, fish soups, sauces, risottos, sausages.
Sage (*Sauge*). Medicinal, aromatic, astringent; bitter if used to excess.	Sausages, fish, pork, goose, duck, brines and marinades.
Savory (*Sarriette*). Rather peppery and piquant. Summer savory is known in some countries as the bean herb. Winter savory is similar but has a stronger aroma.	Green beans, peas, mushrooms, soups, sauces, meats.
Shallots (*Échalotes*). Member of the onion family, but with very delicate flavor.	Bulbs. Many culinary uses, especially fish, meat dishes, poultry, sauces.
Spring onions (*Ciboules*). Also called green onions or scallions. Odoriferous, mildly pungent.	Bulbs and leaves. Peas, salads, egg dishes.
Tarragon (*Estragon*). Fragrant, taste and smell resembling anise.	Soups, sauces, eggs, fish, meat and poultry dishes; mustard, preserves, vinegar; mixed with butter; decoration of cold dishes.
Thyme (*Thym*). Fragrant, pungent.	Most culinary preparations; salads, marinades, vinegar.

Spices (*Épices*)

(Because of the historic interest of the spice trade, the name of the country or region of known or supposed origin follows the name of the spice. Nowadays most spices are grown in the tropical areas of both hemispheres.)

NAME AND DESCRIPTION	CULINARY USES
Allspice (*Toute-épice*). West Indies. Berry with combined flavors of cinnamon, clove, and nutmeg (not a blend of spices).	Whole or ground: meats, gravies, pickles, curry powder, sausages. Ground: cakes, meatloaf, soups, salads.
Anise (*Anis*). Mediterranean origin; grows in temperate or hot climates. Delicate, sweet fragrance, medicinal.	Seeds, whole or ground: soups, meats, pastries, breads, cheese, fruits. Leaves: salads, sauces, shellfish.
Caraway (*Carvi, Cumin des prés*). Origin Asia Minor; grows in temperate climates. Aromatic, distinctive flavor.	Seeds: Austrian specialties, breads, cakes, cheese.
Cardamom (*Cardamome*). India. Pleasantly aromatic, medicinal. Fruits containing 8 to 16 seeds are harvested before they have ripened, then dried in the sun and sometimes bleached.	Seed, whole or ground: curries, syrups, sausages, pastries.
Cayenne pepper (*Poivre rouge*). American tropics. Made from the dried ground pods (with seeds) of small very hot capsicums; not related to black or white pepper. To be used with discretion.	Barbecued or curried meats and poultry, cheese dishes, sauces.
Cinnamon (*Cannells*). Ceylon. Made from the bark of a tree of the laurel family, peeled, dried, and trimmed into quills. Both quills (sticks) and ground cinnamon are used. Delicate, sweet, aromatic.	Beverages, pastries, breads, fruits, preserves.
Cloves (*Clous de girofle*). Indonesia. Flower buds, picked just before	Meats, vegetables, fruit, sauces, marinades and brines, pickles, preserves.

opening and dried in the sun. Used whole or ground. Strong, aromatic, high oil content, medicinal.	
Ginger (*Gingembre*). Southern Asia. Root (rhizome) is used; the young shoots crystallized, preserved; the older roots dried or ground into powder. Very fragrant, pungent, medicinal.	Gingerbread, cakes, pastries, sausages, pickles, curries.
Mace (*Macis*). East Indies. The dried outer shell of the kernel of the fruit of the nutmeg tree, flattened and dried or ground into powder. Fragrant; flavor between nutmeg and cinnamon but stronger. (See Nutmeg.)	Sweet baked goods, preserves, cheese, fruit, soups, sauces, meats, fish, shellfish, potatoes, other vegetables.
Mustard (*Moutarde*). Of Asiatic origin, known for thousands of years. Now grows wild and is cultivated over most of the world. Two varieties, black (dark-brown seeds) and white (yellow seeds) are both used in preparing dry mustard (powder or mustard flour). The powder must be mixed with water to bring out its pungent flavor. Prepared mustards in paste form are widely available commercially; the formula varies with the manufacturer.	Young leaves: salad, or cooked greens. Powder: vinegar, sauces, salad dressings, meats, eggs, pickles. Prepared mustard is used with meats or in sauces.
Nutmeg (*Muscade*). East Indies. Seed or nut found inside the kernel of the fruit of the nutmeg tree (see Mace), dried. Formerly sold whole and grated at home; now available in powdered form. Delicate, pungent.	Cakes, fruit pies, fruits, vegetables, meats, sauces, soups, milk drinks.
Paprika. American tropics. Red powder made from the ripe dried pods of the larger and sweeter varieties of capsicum; the color, flavor, and	Hungarian dishes; as seasoning and decoration for hors d'oeuvre, fish, shellfish, meat, poultry, salads, vegetables.

pungency vary with the exact variety used. Hungarian paprika has a distinctive sweet aroma. Spanish paprika is usually more pungent than American or Hungarian. Rich in vitamin C.	
Pepper (*Poivre*). East Indies. Dried berry of a tropical vine, available whole (peppercorns) or ground. Black peppercorns are the whole berries; white peppercorns are berries from which the outer husks have been removed. White pepper is milder and less pungent, and in Europe is much more popular than black; black pepper is much more used in America than white.	All foods except sweet pastries or desserts. To secure best flavor, either black or white peppercorns should be freshly ground in a pepper mill just before using. Commercially ground pepper loses flavor and is often adulterated. Whole peppercorns are used in soups, stews, sausages.
Poppy seeds (*Pavot*). Europe and Asia Minor. Dried seed of the poppy plant, white to deep blue. Aromatic, flavor resembles walnut.	Breads, cakes, pastries, canapés, vegetables, sauces.
Saffron (*Safran*). Southern Europe and Asia. The dried stamens of a variety of crocus, whole or powdered. Difficulty of harvesting makes saffron the most expensive of spices. Gives attractive yellow color to food. Aromatic, pungent, to be used sparingly.	Soups, sauces, risottos, bouillabaise, curries, pastries, preserves.
Turmeric (*Curcuma*). Tropical Asia and China. Powder made from the dried root of a plant of the ginger family. Color varies from light yellow to orange. Sweet, tangy flavor.	A main ingredient of curry powder; Oriental dishes, fish, shellfish, meats, pickles, sauces.
Vanilla (*Vanille*). Mexico. Pod (bean) of a climbing orchid. Used whole, powdered, or as an extract. The most fragrant of culinary spices.	Pastries, confectionery, ice cream.

Various Methods of Cooking and Their Technology

Cooking is the application of heat, in various forms, to foods of animal and vegetable origin. Cooking makes food more digestible, develops flavor, retards spoilage, and destroys bacteria.

METHODS

In general, methods of cooking are divided into five classes according to the cooking medium: water, steam, air (dry heat), fat, and a combination of two or more of these methods.

Cooking in Water

The terms used to designate the water method of cooking are boiling, parboiling, simmering, poaching, and stewing.

Boiling. Cooking in boiling water (bubbles of steam rise to the surface and break). Pure water boils under standard atmospheric pressure at 212° F. However, it boils at lower temperatures at high altitudes, and mixtures such as sugar syrups boil at higher temperatures. This method is used for the following purposes:

1. To make stock from bones where no meat is present; boiling is necessary to extract the flavor from the bones.
2. To reduce or concentrate meat stock or fish stock by evaporating part of the water. These robust-flavored reduced stocks are used in soups and sauces having meat or fish flavor, in braising, and in glazing.

3. To make vegetables more digestible by softening their cellulose and swelling (gelatinizing) their starch.
4. To cook cereals, pastas, and boiled dumplings, making them more digestible and palatable by softening their cellulose, swelling their starch grains, and developing their flavor.
5. To make sugar syrup, cooked candies and frostings, and meatless sauces and dessert sauces containing starch.

Parboiling. Partial cooking by boiling in water. It is used when another method is employed to complete the process or when strong flavors or water-soluble elements are to be removed and fresh water added to finish cooking.

Simmering. Cooking in very hot water below boiling point (180° to 210° F.). At simmering point tiny bubbles form slowly and break before they reach the surface. This is a slow method, used for making stocks from meats, chicken, or fish, which require long, slow cooking, for cooking tough cuts of meat, tongue, country-cured ham, dried beans and peas, and certain milk and egg dishes requiring slow cooking.

Poaching. Cooking in water or other liquid just below boiling point, either basting the food with the hot liquid or covering with a lid so the steam will perform a self-basting action. Foods which may be cooked by this method are eggs, fish, vegetables, and some raw fruits.

Stewing. Cooking below boiling point in just enough liquid to produce steam. If rapid boiling were to take place, the small quantity of water would evaporate. Foods cooked by this method require long, slow cooking in a saucepan or kettle covered with a tight-fitting lid. This method is used for tough cuts of meat (cut into small pieces), poultry, certain vegetables, and fresh and dried fruits.

Cooking with Steam

Steaming is cooking in moist heat without having the food in direct contact with water. There are three commonly used methods.

Steaming by use of a steamer. Place the food in the perforated inset pan. Place the inset pan in the saucepan containing water. Cover and bring to boiling point. The steam from the boiling water will pass through the perforations and cook the food. This is a long process, and is recommended for cooking vegetables, but not for meats. These steamer pans are designed for this method of steaming and may be purchased in houseware stores over the country.

They are available in various sizes and contain from one to three inset pans for cooking more than one food at one time.

Waterless cooking. Steam is generated by the water that is in the food. No water is added. This method of cooking should be done over very low heat in a heavy-bottomed saucepan having a close-fitting lid. This is an excellent method of cooking mild-flavored vegetables and soft fruits such as plums, berries, and cherries.

Pressure cooker. This method cooks food in a shorter time than does any other method, because the cooking is done in an atmosphere of steam at a temperature higher than the normal 212° F. boiling point. The small amount of water used conserves nutrients and flavor. Foods suitable for cooking at such high pressure are tough meats and poultry, tongue, potatoes, and mature beets that require long cooking. Generally, pressure cooking is not recommended for quick-cooking vegetables since they cook so quickly it is easy to overcook them.

The advantage of steam cooking is that the minerals, vitamins, and flavor of the foods are not destroyed to the extent that they are by boiling in water.

Cooking with Dry Heat

Dry-heat cooking is cooking with air as the medium of heat transfer. The cooking terms used to designate this method are broiling, roasting, and baking.

Broiling. Cooking by dry heat on a grill over an open fire, under the heat unit (broiler) of an electric or gas range, or in a skillet on top of the range (pan-broiling). Broiling is suited to tender, small cuts of meat, such as steaks, chops, cutlets, and ham slices, as well as sausage and other meat patties.

With the broiler method food is placed on the rack in the broiler pan without water. Place the broiler 2 to 5 inches from the source of heat, the distance from the heat depending on the thickness of the cut. Cook meat on one side, then turn and cook on the other side to the desired degree of doneness. Serve at once. By this method, the meat is not grease-soaked since its fat drips through the rack into the broiler pan.

In pan-broiling, meat is put in a skillet and cooked on top of the stove, uncovered, without fat or liquid. Cook slowly, turning occasionally, and pouring off fat as it accumulates. Cook to the desired degree of doneness.

In both methods of broiling, slash the fat around the edges of the meat to prevent curling.

Roasting. Originally, roasting meant cooking meat on a spit over a hot fire, with someone in constant attendance to turn the meat frequently. This method went out of style with the development of ovens, and roasting by dry heat became the vogue. Now with the increased interest in outdoor cooking and the availability of motor-driven spits, this old-fashioned, forgotten method of meat cookery has been revived. It is a simple, tasty way of cooking meat and is also a good method to use for cooking large pieces such as leg of lamb and large chunky roasts, as well as small and large fowls. The size of the spit determines the size and weight of the meat it will accommodate. Consult the directions which come with the equipment to avoid overloading and to obtain best results. Spit-roasting has one disadvantage: the weight loss of the meat due to shrinkage is great.

Oven roasting is still the most generally used method of roasting. It is done in two ways: at constant low temperature (300° to 350° F.); and by searing, which is coagulating the surface of the meat by high heat. Extensive scientific research has proved that low, constant heat gives more juicy and tender meat with less shrinkage. This method has two disadvantages: the cooking time is increased and browning is insufficient. The latter objection may be overcome by increasing the temperature at the end of the roasting period for browning purposes.

The searing method of roasting, still used by French chefs and others, was formerly believed to aid in the retention of meat juices, but experiments have disproved this theory. However, some still prefer the flavor, aroma, and color of roasts cooked by this method. The meat is first seared in a pan over high heat on top of the stove, or placed in a very hot oven (450 to 500° F.) for the first few minutes of the cooking period in order to coagulate the surface protein and for browning. The roasting is then continued at a lower temperature.

Baking. The method used in baking is essentially the same as in roasting, both using dry heat. However, when we speak of roasting, we generally refer to meats (or chestnuts), and when we speak of baking we usually think of breads, cakes, cookies, pies, rolls, and to some extent vegetables and fruits.

When food is baked a crust forms on the parts that are directly exposed to the hot air and on the bottoms and sides where the heat is so intense that it penetrates the pans.

Baking is done at various temperatures, each suited to the particular food being cooked. Therefore it is important to have well-insulated, thermostatically controlled ovens. This is particularly important with products made from batters and doughs, and with pastries, soufflés, and other dishes containing eggs, cheese, etc., where the cooking temperature means the difference between success and failure.

Fresh vegetables and fruits containing enough moisture to prevent drying, such as potatoes, onions, carrots, beets, apples, bananas, and pears, may be baked whole in their skins by direct oven heat, or they may be pared, sliced, and baked in a covered casserole. The casserole serves much the same purpose as the skins in holding in the steam. To prevent baked starchy vegetables from becoming soggy, open the skins when baking is finished to allow the steam to escape.

Cooking in Fat

There are three methods of cooking in fat, or frying: deep-fat frying, pan-frying, and sautéing.

Deep-fat frying. Cooking foods in hot fat deep enough to allow the food to be completely submerged. Foods suitable for deep-fat frying are small units, such as doughnuts, croquettes, fritters, oysters, fish, soft-shell crabs, and some sliced vegetables, such as potatoes, onions, eggplant, and parsnips. The chief advantage of this method over pan-frying is that because of the high temperature the foods will absorb a minimum of fat during cooking.

Fats for deep-fat frying should be flavorless and odorless, such as cottonseed, corn, peanut, and soybean oils, modern vegetable shortenings, or high-grade lard.

In the average home the best utensil for deep-fat frying is a deep kettle made of heavy aluminum or iron, equipped with a frying basket. The surest method of determining the temperature of the fat is to have a deep-fat thermometer clipped to the side of the pan or kettle. If observed closely, it protects against underheating or overheating the fat. If a thermometer is not available, rough tests may be made with a 1-inch cube of bread dropped into the fat. If the cube browns in 40 seconds, the fat is suitable for cooked foods, and if it browns in 60 seconds, the fat is hot enough for uncooked foods.

All foods to be fried in deep fat should be at room temperature, and all excess moisture should be removed to prevent cooling and spattering the fat. Dry raw vegetables, such as potatoes for chips or French fries, thoroughly between clean towels. The food may be first rolled in fine dry cracker crumbs or breadcrumbs, then dipped in egg beaten with milk, using 1 to 2 tablespoons of milk for each egg, and then rolled in crumbs again. Another method is to dip each piece of food in thin batter, using as little as possible in order to give a crisp, delicate crust.

To absorb the excess fat it is important to drain the food on paper towels as soon as it is removed from the hot fat, placing it on the towels in a single layer—never piling pieces of food one on top of another.

Pan-frying. Cooking in a small amount of fat in an uncovered skillet over heat. This differs from pan-broiling in that the fat is permitted to accumulate in the pan and that meat and vegetables may first be floured and crumbed to give a brown, crisp crust.

Sautéing. The French word *sauté* literally means "jumped." This is cooking in a skillet lightly greased to make it possible to "flip" or turn the food without its sticking to the pan. The food is fried lightly and quickly and is turned several times in the process.

Combination Methods of Cooking

Methods of cooking which consist of combinations of two of the methods already described include braising, pot-roasting, à la poele, au gratin, and glazing.

Braising (fricasseeing). These terms represent a method which consists of first sautéing and then cooking in a small amount of liquid in a covered saucepan or Dutch oven (steaming).

Pot-roasting. A form of braising; this is the term applied to cooking large pieces of meat. The meat is first browned and may then either be cooked slowly in a covered pan on top of the range or in the oven. Vegetables are sometimes added near the end of the cooking period, in time for them to be done when the meat has become tender.

À la poele. A term in French cookery applied to a method of pot-roasting meat or poultry which is a combination of pan-frying and steaming. The procedure is as follows:

Brown meat in hot fat over moderately high heat, using the same casserole in which the meat is to be cooked. Remove meat and set aside. Add 2 or 3 sliced carrots and onions and a rib of sliced celery to the casserole. Cover and cook over low heat about 5 minutes without browning. Return meat to casserole. Sprinkle with salt and black pepper and pour melted butter over the top. Cover and cook in a slow oven until meat is done, basting two or three times with pan juices. Remove meat to a warmed platter. Skim from the pan juices all but about 2 tablespoons of fat. Scrape the bottom of the casserole and mash the vegetables into the remaining juice. Heat, season to taste, and strain the sauce into a gravy boat.

Au gratin. This French term designates a dish in which the food is mixed with a sauce, covered with buttered breadcrumbs, and cooked in the oven until the food is done and a brown crust has formed over the top. The sauce should be sufficient to cover the food but not enough to become juicy when it combines with the juices released from the other ingredients. This type of dish may be made with either raw or cooked foods. In the latter, the dish may be browned under the broiler instead of in the oven. This is the authentic method of preparing au gratin dishes.

Another method, which is erroneously labeled au gratin, specifies the use of cheese. It is used mainly for potatoes, vegetables, and various kinds of seafoods and meats, with the addition of cheese. The method of preparation and cooking is the same as that for the authentic au gratin dish, except that the top is sprinkled with grated cheese and the dish may be made either with or without breadcrumbs.

Glazing. This operation, used in French cooking (and in America to some extent), is the application of a coating which gives food a smooth, glossy surface, thereby improving its appearance and usually its flavor. It is applied to both hot and cold dishes.

Materials used for glazing include butter, thick sauces such as Béchamel or Mornay, grated cheese, reduced meat juices acquired in cooking, reduced meat stock, gelatin, jelly, honey, corn syrup, simple sugar syrups, sugar (granulated, brown, and confectioners'), and chocolate. Some of the methods of glazing both hot and cold dishes follow.

Glazing with sauces:

1. Butter sauce. Cover food (such as fillet of sole) heavily with melted butter. Then brown quickly in a very hot preheated broiler, having the dish in a large pan of cold water to prevent the butter from curdling.
2. Thick sauces. Coat the food with a thick sauce, usually Béchamel or Mornay, and sprinkle with grated cheese. Brown quickly in a preheated very hot broiler.
3. Meat juices. Baste meat or poultry (braised or roasted) with reduced juices acquired in cooking and then subject it to intense oven heat.

Glazing with jelly, honey, or syrup:

1. Meat. Mix equal parts jelly, honey, or syrup, and prepared mustard. Spread over meat (usually ham), and bake in a preheated moderate oven (325° to 350° F.) until glazed and browned. If mustard is not desired, replace it with water, using 1 tablespoon to each ½ cup jelly.
2. Cold desserts. Make glaze with water instead of mustard, heat, and use to glaze cold desserts, such as pies and tarts.

Glazing with sugar (one of the simplest forms of glazing):

1. Vegetables. Sprinkle granulated white or brown sugar over vegetables and place in a hot oven to glaze and brown.
2. Cake. Sprinkle white granulated sugar over cake. Bake in a preheated hot broiler (450° F.), leaving door open and watching closely, until sugar melts and forms a brown glaze.
3. Crème Brulée. Sift brown sugar over Crème Brulée (baked custard made with light cream and brown sugar). Then bake in a preheated very slow broiler (250° F.), leaving door open, until sugar melts and forms a smooth caramel topping.

Other glazes are described in various recipes throughout the book.

GENERAL RULES FOR COOKING VEGETABLES AND FRUITS

Fresh Vegetables

Fresh vegetables should be cooked immediately before serving in the smallest amount of water needed to prevent scorching and for the shortest amount of time possible. Use ¼ to 1 inch of water, depending upon the kind of vegetable. Before vegetables are put in, add salt to the water, bring to boiling point, and boil vigorously 2 minutes in order to drive off the free oxygen which is destructive to vitamin C. Then put in the vegetable, cover pan tightly, and quickly bring to boiling point again. Cook only until vegetables are crisp-tender. Most of the water should be absorbed by the vegetables, but if it is not, remove cover and place over low heat until water has evaporated.

Red vegetables, such as beets and red cabbage, take on a bluish tone when cooked in alkaline water. To prevent this add a teaspoon of lemon juice or vinegar to the cooking water. Yellow vegetables are not affected either by the chemical content of the cooking water or by the cooking methods, and are therefore easy to cook. Just one word of caution, don't overcook them or drown them in water.

Green vegetables, if cooked in a tightly covered saucepan the first part of the cooking period, will turn an unattractive brownish-green color. This is caused by trapping a mild, harmless gas given off by the vegetables. To prevent this effect, cook green vegetables uncovered the first 5 minutes, then cover to finish the process. Or cover but lift the lid three or four times during the first part of the cooking period to release any accumulated gas. Spinach is an exception, because it cooks so quickly, needing only the water that clings to the leaves after washing, that the gas does not have time to affect the color.

Vegetables of the cabbage family, onions, and turnips develop a strong flavor and odor if overcooked. Cook such vegetables by any of these methods:

1. Cut vegetables into small pieces and cook in a covered saucepan in a small amount of water until just tender. By this method vegetables cook so quickly that no objectionable flavor develops.
2. For whole vegetables or those cut in large pieces, cook in a moderate amount of water in an uncovered pan. This method produces a milder flavor, but more of the nutrients are lost.
3. Cook in less water (about 1 inch) and uncover during the last half of the cooking period; or leave cover on during the entire cooking time but lift it three or four times to release the gases.

Panned or skillet vegetables. French and Chinese chefs are famous for this simple method which produces crisp-tender vegetables with delicious flavor. Vegetables lending themselves to this method are cabbage, celery, carrots, green beans, potatoes, spinach, and other greens. Shred, slice, or dice vegetables and place in a heavy saucepan or skillet with one or two tablespoons of melted butter or margarine. Mix lightly. Cook, covered, until vegetables sizzle, then reduce heat. Cook only until crisp-tender, stirring once or twice. The French rinse a couple of lettuce leaves in cold water and place them, dripping wet, over the vegetables. Steam is produced by moisture given off by the lettuce.

Baked vegetables. Baking is an excellent method of cooking vegetables to retain minerals and vitamins, especially for those vegetables containing enough water to prevent drying out. When they are cooked whole, the skins hold in the steam, so they remain moist.

To cook in the skin, just wash vegetables and bake until tender. Rubbing skins of potatoes with fat prevents crustiness. Overbaking starchy vegetables, or failure to open skins as soon as vegetables are done, results in sogginess.

Another method is to bake sliced, diced, or shredded vegetables, with seasonings and a very small amount of liquid, in a covered casserole. The cover holds in the steam which prevents the vegetables from becoming too dry.

Frozen Vegetables

Frozen vegetables can be cooked and served in most of the ways used for fresh vegetables. It is unnecessary to thaw most frozen vegetables before cooking. However, corn on the cob and spinach are exceptions. Corn should be completely defrosted, and spinach and other leafy vegetables thawed just enough to separate the leaves before cooking.

Cook frozen vegetables in the smallest amount of water possible—¼ to ½ cup per pint package is the recommended amount. Directions on many of the packages of frozen vegetables specify too much water. It is not necessary to start frozen vegetables in boiling water, because hot water is chilled when the frozen product is added. Frozen vegetables cook in ⅓ to ½ the time of fresh vegetables because of the blanching that takes place when they are prepared for freezing and also because the freezing breaks down the tissues.

Dried Vegetables

The first step in cooking dried vegetables, such as beans, is to wash them thoroughly, changing the water until it is clear. Then rehydrate them by one of these methods:

1. Soak vegetables 5 or 6 hours or overnight in enough cold water to cover generously.
2. Cover vegetable generously with boiling water and boil 2 minutes, then allow to stand for 1 hour before cooking.

   To save nutrients and flavor, cook slowly until done in the water used for soaking, adding more water as necessary.

Many process-dried vegetables, such as onions and potatoes, rehydrate adequately during cooking. Follow the cooking directions on the package for best results.

Fresh Fruits

Although fruit is delicious eaten raw, there are many good reasons for cooking it: to give variety to the menu, to increase keeping qualities, to develop palatability in some fruits, to soften the cellulose, and to cook the starch.

The method of cooking fruits is determined by the product desired. For making purées, sauces, and other products which do not require a definite shape, the fruit is first stewed quickly in a small amount of water to soften it and the sugar is added last. Because exposure of fruits to air, especially when hot, destroys vitamin C, do not strain, mash, or purée until cold. If the fruit must hold its shape after cooking—cooked whole apples or fruits for compotes, for example—cook, without stirring, in sugar syrup. Hard fruits, such as Kieffer pears, should be softened by cooking before adding the sugar. In general, cook fruits a short time in a deep, covered saucepan for retention of flavor and nutrition, using a minimum amount of sugar.

Frozen Fruits

Fruits may be frozen whole, sliced, or crushed, with or without sugar. Generally, they are thawed before using. Frozen berries such as strawberries and raspberries can be served while still slightly frozen unless they are to be cooked. Use frozen fruits as sauces, in frozen desserts, over ice cream, and for making pies, preserves and jams, or in almost any dish in which fresh fruits are used.

Dried Fruits

Tenderized packaged dried fruits are ready for cooking and do not need soaking. However, dried fruits that are not tenderized should be washed and soaked from 30 minutes to several hours in two to four times as much water as fruit. Cook slowly until tender, using the water in which fruit was soaked. Add sugar last.

Methods of Food Preservation

Methods of food preservation are employed to make foods available at all times and places—that is, to enable foods to be processed in season for consumption out of season and to enable shipment of foods from production regions to regions of no production, thereby giving all people a wider selection of foods at a moderate cost. Methods of preserving foods involve storing them, with or without a preliminary treatment, in an environment which will inhibit spoilage.

Causes of food spoilage are:

1. The growth of microorganisms, such as bacteria, yeast, and molds. In order for these microorganisms to grow they need food, favorable moisture content, and favorable temperature. Therefore the processes used to preserve foods must either completely destroy these organisms and prevent others from entering or must inhibit their activity.
2. The action of chemical substances known as enzymes which are normally present in foods of both plant and animal origin. These enzymes cause fruits to ripen, and unless inhibited will eventually cause fresh foods to spoil or decay. Their action can be stopped by heat.

   Methods of preserving foods suitable for home use are drying, canning, freezing, cellar storage, pickling and brining, and preserving with sugar. Complete directions for preserving foods by these methods are given in bulletins issued by the Agricultural Experiment Stations of your state or county.

DRYING

Sun-drying is one of the oldest, simplest, and least expensive forms of food preservation. The process requires very little equipment and because the bulk of the food is greatly reduced, the product requires very little storage space. No sugar, salt, or other preservatives are necessary.

The foods best suited for sun-drying are firm-textured fruits, such as apples, pears, peaches, apricots; and mature vegetables, such as corn, peas, beans, and red peppers. From these foods, water is removed by sun-drying to such an extent that the moisture content is low enough to inhibit the growth of microorganisms. This method of food preservation is practical only in dry climates and during dry seasons, when there is plenty of warm dry air and sunshine.

A process for drying foods commercially is known as artificial dehydration. The food is dried by artificially heated air with carefully controlled conditions of temperature, humidity, and airflow. This method is used for dehydrating fruits, eggs, milk, meat, and vegetables. The advantages of artificial dehydration over sun-drying are many. The process is usually done under more sanitary conditions, the yield of the dried product is greater, the quality is superior, and the process can be used for foods other than fruits and vegetables.

Freeze-drying, a more recently developed process of drying foods, produces a superior product having a greater palatability. However, its high cost has prevented wide usage. This method freezes the food first and then dries it in a vacuum.

All dried foods should be properly stored. They should be protected against dust, insects, and rodents. They should be kept in a dry place, in clean jars or cans with tight-fitting lids, or in covered heavy cardboard or wooden boxes lined with pliofilm or several layers of waxed paper.

CANNING

Canning is one of the most common home methods of preserving foods. The process consists of heating the foods and sealing them in airtight containers. The length of time of the heating process and the degree of heat varies with the type of food and the kind of microorganisms likely to be found in it. The heat destroys the microorganisms and enzymes which cause food spoilage. Sealing the foods in airtight containers prevents organisms from re-entering the foods.

For best results in canning fruits and vegetables, select those of superior quality and process them as soon as possible. A good rule to follow when practical is "two hours from the garden to the can."

Of the three forms of harmful microorganisms in foods (bacteria, yeast, and molds), bacteria are the most difficult to destroy. Therefore any treatment that will kill bacteria will destroy yeast and molds. Some forms of bacteria are resistant to the temperature of boiling water (212° F.) and require higher heat to destroy them. This heat can be obtained by the use of a pressure cooker. Acid fruits are safe when canned by the boiling-water-bath method, but vegetables and nonacid foods, such as meats and poultry, should be processed in a pressure cooker.

FREEZING

Freezing is one of the most modern and easiest methods of food preservation. It is a simple but painstaking process. Freezing does not destroy enzymes and microorganisms present in foods, but it inactivates them. Frozen foods held at the correct temperature are safe and have flavor, color, texture, and nutritive value similar to those of fresh foods. Foods suitable for freezing include most of the common fruits, vegetables that are to be served cooked, fish and shellfish, meats and poultry, baked goods, prepared dishes, and eggs removed from the shells.

Vegetables are best frozen just before they reach full maturity, while fruits should be allowed to reach the fully ripened stage. Both fruits and vegetables should be given special treatment during the process of preparing them for the freezer. Large fruits, when cut, have a tendency to darken and should be treated with ascorbic acid (vitamin C) or with a commercial anti-darkening preparation available at food stores. Vegetables should be scalded or dipped in boiling water from 1 to 8 minutes, the length of time depending on the vegetable, and then quickly dipped in cold water to stop the cooking action. This procedure inhibits the action of enzymes. Both fruits and vegetables must be put into the freezer as soon as possible after harvesting.

In freezing home-slaughtered beef and lamb, rapid freezing is not necessary. In fact, the flavor is enhanced and the meat is tenderer if the meat is held from 5 to 10 days at a temperature of 33° to 40° F. before freezing. Veal and pork should be frozen as soon as thoroughly chilled (from 2 to 3 days). Poultry should be held overnight at a temperature of 32° to 36° F. and then frozen.

Directions for packaging food for home freezing are usually provided by freezer manufacturers or may be obtained from state or county agricultural departments or from the various books available on the subject. When the food is correctly packaged, freeze as quickly as possible. The freezing temperature should be −10° to −15° F., and the holding temperature should never exceed 0° F.

PICKLING AND PRESERVING

Long before canning or modern freezing methods were known, pickling and preserving were widely used.

Pickling is a process of preserving vegetables, fruits, meats, and fish by the use of salt, vinegar, sugar, and spice. In making vegetable pickles it is necessary to remove most of the water from the vegetables so that they will be prepared to absorb the vinegar and seasonings, and so that the water in the vegetables will not dilute the pickling solution. Salt is used as the dehydrating agent. The raw vegetables may be soaked overnight in salt water, or they may be sprinkled with salt and soaked for several hours in a salt solution commonly known as brine. This process is called the quick method and is often used for making pickles or relishes from thinly sliced or chopped vegetables. The long process is another method of making pickles. The vegetables are soaked in brine for as long as 6 weeks to allow the food to ferment and develop an agreeable flavor. Pickles made by the longer process not only have a better flavor, but also a crisper texture, a more attractive color, and better keeping qualities.

Pickles may be made sour by using sufficient vinegar for its flavor to predominate, or sweet by adding sufficient sugar. Spices add flavor and act to some extent as a preservative.

Fruit pickles are generally sweet-sour and flavored with spices. They may be made from peaches, apples, cherries, crab apples, and pears.

Chili sauce, catsup, relishes, and chutney are made with vegetables, fruits, vinegar, sugar, salt, and spices.

Meats and fish may be preserved by pickling and brining. However, these methods of preserving these foods are confined mostly to commercial plants.

Sugar is used to make jelly, jam, marmalade, and preserves from fruits. The combination of heat, sugar, and acid is such as to destroy enzymes and microorganisms. Because of the process by which the fruits have been treated, they do not resemble fresh fruits in texture, but if cooking time and quantity of sugar are reduced to a minimum characteristic color and flavor can be partly retained.

Jelly is made from the juices of fruits containing pectin and acid in the proper proportions with the correct amount of sugar added (generally ¾ cup sugar to 1 cup juice).

Jam is made from crushed fruits cooked with sugar until the mixture is thick. The correct proportion of sugar is ¾ part to 1 part by weight of sugar to 1 part by weight of freshly prepared fruit.

Marmalade is made from pulpy fruits, preferably those containing pectin and acid, using the pulp and having the rind thinly sliced. The pulp and rind are held in suspension throughout the mixture. Citrus fruits are especially suitable for marmalade because of their pectin and acid content. Measure or weigh the cooked pulp and rind and then add an equal amount of sugar.

Preserves are made by cooking small whole fruits such as cherries and berries, or pieces of larger fruits, in sugar syrup until they are clear and somewhat translucent. The amount of sugar varies with the fruit, but usually is ¾ part to 1 part by weight of sugar to 1 part by weight of freshly prepared fruit.

The Bases of Fine French Cookery

The rich variety of the French cuisine is based on a number of different preparations which are used in a great many ways. These preparations include doughs; stocks made with meat, poultry, or fish, and the essences, glazes, and jellies made from stock; the court bouillons used in poaching fish and vegetables; roux for thickening sauces; marinades and brines; forcemeats (farces) and quenelles; and appareils (mixtures that go into the making of dishes). When one knows how to make all these, the preparation of the dishes in the following chapters is greatly simplified. For convenience the recipes are grouped here. Finally, a number of the garnishes which in France traditionally accompany certain dishes are listed and described.

DOUGHS AND BATTERS

The two basic ingredients of all doughs and batters are flour and liquid. When the proportion of liquid to flour results in a mixture thin enough to be stirred with a spoon and either poured or dropped from a spoon, it is a batter. Batters are used for making pancakes, waffles, fritters, cakes, and muffins. Mixtures which are thick enough to roll or knead (too stiff to stir with a spoon or pour) are doughs. Doughs are used for yeast breads, rolls, biscuits, pastry, and some cookies. A dough may be soft (barely stiff enough to handle) or stiff.

With the addition of fat, eggs, salt, leavening agent, fruit, nuts, and flavoring to these two basic ingredients an endless variety of breads, cakes, cookies, pastries, dumplings, and croquettes can be made.

Success in making dishes from batters and doughs requires a good recipe, high-quality ingredients, the proper size of mixing bowl, the proper size of baking pan, and an oven equipped with an accurate thermostat to control the heat. Then it is up to the cook to measure the ingredients accurately, to mix and handle them skillfully, and to bake them for the proper time at the proper temperature, checking the baking to the proper "point" (a French expression) by means of suitable tests. It is important that a beginner be taught to recognize certain characteristics of various finished products so that she may be able to judge her own finished dish.

To insure accurate measurements, standard measuring cups and spoons are important. Only level measurements should be used.

The most commonly used methods of mixing batters and doughs are:

The muffin method. The dry ingredients are sifted together into a mixing bowl. Beaten eggs, liquid, and melted fat are added. The liquid ingredients are then blended with the dry ingredients with varying amounts of stirring, depending on the mixture. For batters such as muffins with minimum amounts of fat and sugar, stir only until ingredients are blended, about 28 strokes. Richer batters may be stirred more.

The cake method. The butter or shortening and sugar are mixed together until fluffy, the eggs are beaten in, usually one at a time, or they may be beaten separately, the yolks being added at this stage and the beaten whites folded in as the last step. Then the dry and liquid ingredients are added alternately, beginning and ending with flour.

The pastry method. The dry ingredients are sifted together into a mixing bowl. The fat is cut into the dry mixture, the liquid is sprinkled over the top and the whole mass is tossed very lightly only until its ingredients are blended. Care must be taken not to stir the dough after the liquid has been added since this would develop the gluten in the flour and would make a tough pastry.

Yeast breads, sponge cakes, cream puffs (choux paste) are mixed by special methods adapted to each. The optimum amount of manipulation varies with the type of product and with the character, proportions, and temperature of the ingredients.

Different types of batters and doughs must be mixed by different methods and to different degrees in order to obtain the texture required for the particular product. Considerable kneading is required to develop the gluten (the protein in flour that gives it the elastic property) in yeast dough. Only a very little kneading is required for biscuit dough. Pastry dough should never be kneaded; it must be handled as little as possible in order to obtain a tender, flaky product.

⚜ FRENCH BREAD

1 envelope active dry yeast
½ teaspoon sugar
1 cup lukewarm water
½ teaspoon salt
2 tablespoons softened shortening or butter
about 3½ cups sifted all-purpose flour

Combine the first 3 ingredients and let stand 5 minutes to soften. Add salt, shortening or butter, and 2 cups of the flour. Turn dough onto a floured pastry board and gradually knead in remaining flour, adding more if needed. Knead dough until it is smooth and satiny. Cover and let it rise until doubled in size. Place dough on a lightly floured board and pound it lightly with a rolling pin to deflate it. Cover and let dough rise 30 minutes in a warm place (80° to 85° F.). Divide the dough in half and shape each half into a roll about 1½ inches in diameter. Place on lightly greased baking sheets, put in a warm place, and let rise until doubled in size. Brush with water and make diagonal slashes in the top with a sharp knife. Place in a preheated hot oven (400° F.) with a shallow pan of hot water in the bottom of the oven. Bake 45 minutes or until the bread is crusty and brown. Makes 2 loaves.

⚜ CROISSANTS

2 envelopes active dry yeast
¼ cup lukewarm water
1½ tablespoons sugar
4 cups sifted all-purpose flour
1½ cups lukewarm milk
1 teaspoon salt
¾ pound (3 sticks) butter
1 egg yolk beaten with 1 tablespoon milk

Soften yeast in lukewarm water with 1 teaspoon of the sugar. Stir in 1 cup of the flour. Shape into a ball, cut a cross (+) in the top, place it in a bowl, cover, and keep in a warm place (80 to 85° F.) to rise until doubled in bulk. Add the remaining sugar and flour and the milk, and salt. Mix well and knead until dough is smooth and elastic. Place dough in a greased bowl, grease the top of the dough, cover, and let rise in a warm place until it has doubled in bulk. Roll the dough into a rectangle ½ inch thick. Wash the butter in cold water, working it well and pressing it in a clean cloth to remove excess water. Spread the butter over the dough and fold the dough into thirds, making three layers. Roll dough out again and fold it into thirds. Wrap it in waxed paper and chill well, preferably overnight. When ready to use, roll the dough out and fold the ends to the center. Roll and fold again twice more. Chill thoroughly, about 1 hour. Divide dough in half and roll each half into a circle ⅛ inch thick. Cut each circle in 18 triangles or wedges. Starting at the wide end, roll the wedges of dough to the tip end, pressing to seal the end. Shape in crescents and place on greased baking sheets. Brush the beaten egg yolk over the tops of the crescents. Cover them with waxed paper and let them rise in a warm place until doubled in bulk. Bake in a preheated hot oven (400° F.) 5 minutes. Reduce heat to 350° F. (moderate) and bake 15 minutes or until crescents are golden brown. Makes 3 dozen.

⚜ BRIOCHE DOUGH

2 envelopes active dry yeast
⅓ cup warm water (110°–115° F.)
2 tablespoons sugar
3½ cups sifted all-purpose flour
1 teaspoon salt
2 large eggs
¾ cup (1½ sticks) butter

Soften yeast in warm water in a small bowl along with 1 teaspoon of the sugar. Stir in ¾ cup of the flour. Cover and let rise is a warm place (80° to 85° F.) for 1 hour or until the mixture has doubled in bulk. In a large mixing bowl, mix together the remaining flour and sugar and the salt. Add the butter, cutting it in until the particles are the size of peas. Blend in the eggs. Add yeast-flour mixture and mix well. Knead on a well-floured board until dough is smooth and satiny, about 8 minutes. Cover and let rise in a warm place until doubled in bulk, about 1 hour. Shape three-fourths of the dough into 24 two-inch balls. Place in greased small tart pans or muffin pans. Shape remaining dough into 24 one-inch balls. Make a depression in the top of each large ball, and place the small ball in it. (This forms the topknot.) Cover and let rise in a warm place until doubled in size. With scissors, make four light slits in the dough of the larger ball around the topknot. Bake in a preheated hot oven (400° F.) 10 to 12 minutes or until golden brown. Makes 3½ dozen rolls. (See illustration, page 976.)

⚜ CHOU PASTE (*Cream-Puff Paste*)

2 cups water
1 cup (2 sticks) butter
¼ teaspoon salt
2 cups sifted all-purpose flour
8 large eggs

Mix the first 3 ingredients together in a 1½-quart saucepan. Bring to boiling point. Remove from heat and stir in all the flour at one time, using a wooden spoon. Beat vigorously. Return to heat and cook until the mixture leaves the sides of the pan and forms a very stiff ball. Remove from heat and beat in eggs one at a time, beating each until it is completely absorbed before adding another. Do not overbeat, as this reduces the volume and the consistency for piping purposes. Squeeze paste from a pastry bag or drop from a tablespoon 2 inches apart onto ungreased baking sheets. Bake in a preheated hot oven (425° F.) 30 to 35 minutes or until golden brown. Do not underbake. Turn off oven heat. Prick puffs with a knife to allow steam to escape, and leave in oven 20 minutes to allow centers to dry out. Cool. Split and fill with creamed mixtures for entrées or with cream fillings, etc., for desserts. Makes 24 large puffs.

To make small hors d'oeuvre puffs, drop the dough from a teaspoon and bake 20 to 25 minutes. This recipe will make 48 small puffs.

⚜ GNOCCHI CHOU PASTE (*For Gnocchi, Quenelles, or Dumplings*)

2 cups milk
½ cup (1 stick) butter
2½ cups sifted all-purpose flour
6 large eggs
¾ cup grated Parmesan cheese
1 cup grated Gruyère cheese

Mix as for Chou Paste, beating the cheese into the warm dough. Let the mixture stand about 10 minutes. Then shape into 1-inch balls. Drop these in boiling stock or boiling salted water (½ teaspoon salt to 1 quart water). Cook until dumplings double in size and rise to the top. Serve hot with Mornay Sauce. Sprinkle with additional grated cheese. Makes 6 servings.

⚜ CHEESE PUFFS

Beat 1 cup grated Parmesan or Swiss cheese into 2 cups warm Chou Paste. Drop the dough from a teaspoon and bake 20 to 25 minutes. Serve hot or cold, with or without filling, as hors d'oeuvre or cocktail accompaniments.

⚜ GNOCCHI BAKED WITH CHEESE

Drain cooked gnocchi and arrange in a buttered baking dish. Sprinkle with an additional ½ cup grated Parmesan cheese and dot with 2 tablespoons butter. Bake in a preheated moderate oven (350° F.) 20 minutes. Serve at once.

⚜ NOODLE DOUGH

3 cups sifted all-purpose flour
4 large eggs, unbeaten

Place flour in a large mixing bowl. Add eggs and mix with the hands until the dough is stiff enough to be gathered into a ball. Knead on a pastry board until all the crumbly particles have been incorporated. This dough should be very stiff; if necessary knead in a little more flour. Divide the dough into thirds. Roll one portion at a time into a very thin sheet with a lightly floured rolling pin. Cover with a clean towel and let stand 30 minutes. Then roll each sheet up as for a jelly roll and cut into wide or narrow strips as desired. Lay out on baking sheets to dry well. Cover. Store in covered containers and use as needed. Makes about 1 pound.

⚜ PUFF PASTRY (*Pâte Feuilletée*)

This dough is also called Puff Paste.

1½ cups (3 sticks) butter
3 cups sifted all-purpose flour
¾ teaspoon salt
2 teaspoons lemon juice
⅔ cup ice water

Cut each stick of butter lengthwise into three strips. Sprinkle waxed paper with an additional 2 tablespoons flour, over which arrange the butter strips. Wrap in waxed paper and refrigerate until ready to use. Mix flour and salt together in a mixing bowl. Combine lemon juice and ice water and stir into the flour, using a circular motion. The dough should be firm, yet slightly sticky. Knead dough 20 minutes. It should be smooth and satiny. Cover dough and let it rest 20 minutes.

Roll dough ¼ inch thick into a 12- by 8-inch rectangle on a well-floured board. Place chilled butter strips side by side on half the dough to within ½ inch of the edges. Fold the remaining half of the dough over the butter. Press edges together firmly with fingertips. Wrap in waxed paper or foil and refrigerate 30 minutes.

Tap dough lightly several times with rolling pin to flatten the butter. Quickly roll out dough on a well-floured pastry board in a 12- by 8-inch rectangle about ¼ inch thick. Be careful not to roll over the edges of the dough until it is 12 inches long; then roll over the edges very gently. Fold both ends of the dough to the center of the rectangle, making sure edges and corners are even. Press edges together firmly. Fold dough in half to make 4 layers. Wrap in waxed paper or foil and refrigerate 30 minutes.

Roll dough again into a rectangle, fold as before, and chill 30 minutes. Repeat 3 more times the rolling, folding, and chilling. The last chilling period should be for 3 hours. (See Culinary Techniques in Pictures.)

Use Puff Pastry for making patty shells, vol-au-vents, pastry horns for cream filling, croissants, palm leaves, and pie crust, according to directions in individual recipes.

⚜ PATTY SHELLS (*Bouchées or Vol-au-Vents*)

Make the recipe for Puff Pastry and divide into thirds. Roll one portion at a time, keeping the others refrigerated until ready to use. Roll paste to ⅛ inch thickness on a well-floured board. For each patty shell, cut three 3-inch pastry circles, using a sharp 3-inch fluted cooky cutter. (For 12 patty shells, 36 circles.) Place 12 of the pastry circles on an ungreased baking sheet. Brush surface of each with 1 egg yolk beaten with 1½ teaspoons cold water. Do not let egg drip on the sides. Using a 2-inch cutter, cut out centers of 12 pastry circles, making a ring as for doughnuts. Place one ring on each of the pastry circles on the baking sheet. Brush with egg yolk. Press a 1½ inch cooky cutter into the centers of remaining 12 pastry circles, but do not cut through it. Place these on top of the first ring. Brush with egg yolk. Bake in a preheated very hot oven (450° F.) for 10 minutes. Reduce heat to moderate (350° F.) and bake 20 minutes or until shells are golden. Remove the indented centers of the top layer with a pointed knife. Return the shells to the 350° F. oven and bake 10 minutes longer to dry out centers. Fill the shells with mixtures such as creamed chicken, shrimp, etc. Garnish tops with removed centers. Makes 12 patty shells.

⚜ CREAM HORNS (*Cornets Feuilletés à la Crème*)

Roll out puff paste on a lightly floured pastry board to ⅛ inch thick and about 30 inches long. Cut into strips about ½ inch wide. This length is for metal horn tubes 5½ inches long. If smaller tubes are desired, use shorter strips of pastry. Beginning at the small end of the horn start wrapping the pastry strips around it, overlapping the edges slightly. Do not pull or stretch pastry. Chill. Brush tops and sides with beaten egg. Sprinkle with granulated sugar, preferably coarse sugar if available. Place horns 1 inch apart on paper-lined baking sheets. Bake in a preheated hot oven (425° F.) for 10 minutes. Reduce heat to moderate (350° F.) and bake until pastry is golden brown. Remove tubes from pastry horns immediately by twisting the tubes to free them from the pastry. Cool. Fill with pastry cream or sweetened whipped cream. Makes 18.

⚜ PLAIN PASTRY DOUGH (*Pâte Brisée*)

For a 9-inch pastry shell:
1 cup sifted all-purpose flour
¼ teaspoon salt
¼ cup (½ stick) butter
1½ tablespoons vegetable shortening
about 3 tablespoons cold water

Sift flour and salt into a mixing bowl. Add butter and vegetable shortening and cut it in until the mixture resembles coarse meal. Add water and blend it in quickly, using a tossing motion. Press the dampened particles together into a ball. Roll into a circle ⅛ inch thick and 2 inches larger than the diameter of the pie plate. Carefully fold the dough in quarters and place it in the pie plate. Unfold and fit it loosely in the plate without stretching or pulling the pastry. Trim the edge of the pastry ½ inch larger than the outside rim of the plate. Flute or crimp edge with fingers or fork. If the filling is to be baked in the shell, bake as directed in each recipe. If the crust is to be filled after it has been baked, prick the bottom and sides of the pastry with a fork. Then fit a smaller pan or bean bag into the pie crust. Bake in a preheated hot oven (425° F.) 12 to 15 minutes, removing the smaller pan or bean bag after the pastry has baked 10 minutes. Bake until golden brown. Makes one 9-inch pie crust. For a 2-crust 9-inch pie, double the ingredients, except use only about 5 tablespoons cold water. Mix and roll as above.

⚜ SWEET PIE PASTRY

1½ cups sifted all-purpose flour
⅓ cup sifted confectioners' sugar
⅛ teaspoon salt
½ cup (1 stick) butter
3 tablespoons milk or cold water

Sift together into a mixing bowl the first 3 ingredients. Add butter and cut it in with a pastry blender until the mixture resembles coarse meal. Add milk or water. Mix lightly to form a dough.

For individual tart shells, divide dough into 8 equal parts. Roll each 1/16 to 1/8 inch in thickness. Fit into tart pans measuring 3 1/2 inches across the top and 2 inches across the bottom. Prick the bottom and sides of pastry with a fork at intervals to prevent blistering. Bake in a preheated moderate oven (350° F.) 15 to 20 minutes. When thoroughly cold, remove tart shells from pans. Fill with pastry cream or fruit fillings. Makes 8 tart shells.

For a 9- or 10-inch pie, roll pastry to 1/8 inch thickness and fit it into a 9- or 10-inch pie plate. Trim dough, turn under and flute edge. Prick bottom and sides with a fork. Bake as for tart shells.

⚜ FRITTER BATTER

1 cup sifted all-purpose flour
½ teaspoon salt
1 large egg, slightly beaten
¾ cup milk
1 tablespoon butter, melted

Sift together flour and salt. Combine egg, milk, and butter, and stir into dry ingredients. Use to cover such vegetables as sliced onions, sliced zucchini squash, cauliflowerets, spinach leaves, and okra; shrimp or other shellfish; Cheddar cheese cubes, for frying. Fry in deep hot fat preheated to 370° F. 3 to 4 minutes. Drain on absorbent paper. Makes approximately 6 portions.

⚜ SWEET FRITTER BATTER

To the flour in Fritter Batter, add 2 tablespoons sugar and 1 teaspoon double-acting baking powder. Use to make fruit fritters.

⚜ BASIC CRÊPE BATTER (*French Pancake Batter*)

1 cup sifted all-purpose flour
½ teaspoon salt
3 large whole eggs, beaten
2 cups milk
2 tablespoons butter, melted

Sift together the flour and salt and set aside. Combine eggs and milk and stir into the flour mixture. Blend in melted butter. Pour 2 tablespoons batter for each crêpe into a hot, lightly greased 6-inch skillet. Brown on the under side. (When crêpes are ready to turn bubbles will form over the top.) Turn and brown the other side. Stack crêpes in an ovenware plate in pancake fashion and place in the oven to keep warm. Makes about 20 crêpes.

STOCKS

The stock pot is the greatest treasure of the French chef, for in it lies the secret of French sauces, soups, aspics, and glazes.

Stocks are made by simmering (not boiling) meat, poultry, or fish, vegetables, herbs, and spices in water for several hours. They are used for braising meats and vegetables and as the liquid for making meat-, poultry-, and fish-flavored sauces, soups, and stews. If stock of stronger flavor is desired, it may be concentrated (reduced) by cooking down to a smaller volume after the bones, meat, and vegetables are removed and the stock strained. In French cooking this essence is used as a flavor-booster to sauces, for making aspics, and for glazing.

The best stocks are made from cracked beef and veal bones; meats such as beef, veal, and poultry; soup vegetables, such as onions, leeks, carrots, celery, and mushroom stems; plus spices and herbs. Starchy vegetables cloud stock and should never be used; nor should strong-flavored vegetables.

All solid particles should be removed by straining the stock through a very fine sieve or through two thicknesses of cheesecloth wrung out in cold water. All fat should be removed, either while still hot or by refrigerating the stock and then lifting off the solidified fat. The clear stock may then be made into soups, sauces, etc.

⚜ PLAIN WHITE STOCK (*Fond Blanc Ordinaire*)

3 pounds shoulder of veal
4 pounds knuckle of veal
4 pounds chicken giblets or backs, necks, and wings
3 tablespoons salt
about 6 quarts of cold water
2 medium-sized carrots
2 medium-large onions
4 leeks
4 ribs celery
large bouquet garni

Bone meat and tie it up with a string. Crack bones, wash chicken parts, and place all in a 12-quart saucepan. Add salt. Add water, having it cover the ingredients by 1 full inch. Bring to boiling point. Skim off and discard scum that has risen to the surface. Peel carrots and onions and add along with celery and bouquet garni. Wash leeks thoroughly and add. Bring to boiling point, partially covered with the lid. Reduce heat and simmer 4 hours or more, never allowing the water to boil. Add more boiling water if water evaporates to the level of the ingredients. Remove meat and bones and cool stock enough that it can be strained. Then strain through two thicknesses of cheesecloth first wrung out in cold water. Refrigerate stock uncovered until fat has hardened on the surface and can be lifted off. If desired, the fat can be removed while the stock is hot. Use for making White Sauce, Velouté Sauce, gravies, aspics, and soups. Makes about 4 quarts.

⚜ WHITE CHICKEN STOCK (*Fond Blanc de Volaille*)

Proceed as for Plain White Stock, but add a 3-pound chicken, or 2 pounds chicken giblets, backs, necks, or wings.

⚜ CLEAR BROWN STOCK (*Brown Stock I*)

5 pounds lean beef soup meat
1 pound rind of salt pork
6 pounds knuckle of veal
2 pounds each beef and veal bones
3 tablespoons butter or meat drippings
2 large carrots
2 medium-large onions
about 7 quarts cold water
3 tablespoons salt
large bouquet garni
1 large clove garlic

Cut meat and pork rind in large pieces. Crack bones. Peel and slice onions. Brown all, including bones, in shortening or suet. Add 2 quarts of the water and the salt. Simmer 1 hour, having the pot partially covered with a lid. Add remaining water, or enough to cover ingredients by 1 full inch. Add bouquet garni and garlic. Simmer 5 or more hours, removing scum from surface from time to time. Remove meat and bones from the stock, strain and skim off fat as described for Plain White Stock. Use in making brown sauces, braising, stews, and in meat jellies. Makes about 4 quarts.

⚜ BROWN STOCK II

3 pounds beef soup meat
3 pounds cracked beef bones
3 pounds cracked veal bones
1 cup sliced carrots
1 cup sliced onion
8½ quarts cold water
3 ribs celery
3 stalks parsley
1 bay leaf
1 tablespoon salt

Cut meat into small pieces and place in a roasting pan with beef bones and veal bones, carrots and onion. Cook in a preheated very hot oven (450° F.) 40 to 50 minutes or until meat and vegetables have browned, turning 2 to 3 times to brown uniformly. Remove pan from oven and drain off and discard fat. Transfer meat, bones, and vegetables to a soup kettle. Pour 1 cup of the water into the roasting pan and heat about ½ minute, scraping all the browned particles from the bottom of the pan. Pour into the soup kettle. Rinse the pan with another cup of water and pour into the soup kettle. Add remaining water and salt. Cover partially, bring to boiling point and simmer 4 to 5 hours. Remove bones and meat from the stock. Strain. Either remove fat while hot or refrigerate and remove solidified fat on the surface. Makes approximately 4 quarts.

⚜ BROWN VEAL STOCK

6 pounds shoulder of veal
⅓ cup shortening
5 pounds knuckle of veal
2 pounds veal bones
2 large carrots
2 medium-large onions
large bouquet garni
7 quarts White Stock
2 teaspoons salt, or salt to taste

Tie up meat with a string and coat it with shortening. Brown on all sides on top of the stove. Crush the bones, peel and slice carrots and onions, and put all in the bottom of a 10-quart saucepan along with the bouquet garni. Top with the browned meat. Cover and let stand 15 minutes. Add 2 quarts of the stock and the salt. Simmer 1 hour, having the pot partially covered with a lid. Add remaining stock. Bring to boiling point; skim off scum from the surface. Reduce heat and simmer 5 hours. Remove meat and bones from the stock, strain and skim off fat as for Plain White Stock. Use for making thin veal gravy, brown sauces, for braising vegetables and red meats, and for making consommé. Makes about 5 quarts.

⚜ THICKENED VEAL STOCK

Cook 2 quarts Brown Veal Stock until it has reduced to one-fourth. Thicken with 1½ tablespoons cornstarch mixed with 3 tablespoons cold Clear Brown Stock. Strain through 2 thicknesses of cheesecloth. Keep hot. Serve as gravy for roasts. Makes about 2 cups.

⚜ TOMATO-FLAVORED VEAL STOCK

Combine 2½ quarts Brown Veal Stock and 1 cup tomato purée. Simmer until the mixture has reduced to 5 cups. Strain through 2 thicknesses of cheesecloth wrung out in cold water. Makes 1¼ quarts.

⚜ STOCK WITH VEAL OR OTHER MEATS

For each ½ pound veal or other meat trimmings cut into small pieces, add 1 medium peeled and diced carrot, 1 medium peeled and diced onion, and brown all in ½ tablespoon butter, sprinkling in 1 tablespoon flour when the meat begins to brown. Cook over moderate heat and stir with a wooden spoon until flour is golden. Then add ½ cup dry white wine and cook until liquid has reduced by one-half. Add 1½ cups meat broth. Simmer, partially covered, 1 hour. Strain through a double thickness of cheesecloth wrung out in cold water. Use in making gravy and as a liquid to dilute the pan juices for small pieces of meat. Makes about 1 cup.

⚜ GAME STOCK

2 pounds each venison and rabbit
4 pounds venison bones, cracked
¼ cup butter or meat drippings
4 medium-sized carrots
1 medium-large onion
4 leeks
4½ quarts water
1 cup sliced mushroom stems
1 tablespoon salt
6 juniper berries (if available)
3 whole cloves
1 small bay leaf

Brown meat and bones in butter or meat drippings. Peel and slice carrots and onions and add to the meat. Wash leeks thoroughly and slice. Add leeks to meat along with remaining ingredients. Cover and simmer 3 hours. Remove meat, bones, and fat and strain as for Plain White Stock. Use in making game sauces and to serve with small pieces of game cooked in butter. If the stock is reduced to one-fourth it may be used to flavor game dishes. Makes about 2½ quarts.

⚜ FISH STOCK

6 pounds fish heads, bones, tails, and fins (pike, haddock, sole, sea perch, whiting, halibut, etc.)
1 medium-large onion
1½ cups sliced mushroom stems
½ cup chopped parsley
1 teaspoon lemon juice
1 tablespoon chopped fresh thyme or 1 teaspoon dried thyme
1 bay leaf
1½ teaspoons salt
2½ quarts cold water
2 cups dry white wine

Wash fish trimmings and place them in an 8-quart saucepan. Peel onion, slice, and add to the pot along with remaining ingredients. Cover partially and slowly bring to boiling point. Reduce heat and skim off scum that has floated to the surface. Simmer 30 minutes. Cool enough to strain. Strain through a double thickness of cheesecloth that has been wrung out in cold water. Refrigerate. Use for poaching or braising fish, for fish stews, fish sauces, etc. Makes about 2 quarts.

This stock can also be made with red wine; use the same amount.

Essences and Glazes

Essences are obtained by boiling down stocks until they are reduced by one-half the volume. The French chef may steep chopped truffles in the stock if it does not have sufficient flavor, while the American cook may add a bouillon cube. Essences are used for poaching fish and for flavoring sauces.

Glazes are progressive and very intensive reductions of clear meat stocks or game stocks. Reduce very slowly over reducing heat. A glaze is ready when it coats the spoon without running off. Glazes are used for coating certain dishes (Chaud-froid of Game, joints of meat, etc.) to improve the flavor and make them look attractive. Glazes are also used, like essences, to lend body to a sauce or a preparation. (See Glazing, pages 113–14.)

Aspics and Jellies

To the French chef an aspic is the whole decorated dish of food coated with or molded in jelly. To the average American cook, however, aspic means stock or consommé (canned or homemade) which stiffens when cold, because it contains either commercial gelatin or natural gelatin obtained from the bones, etc., from which it is made. The French term for this is *gelée*.

The stock for aspic or gelée should be of the same general base as the food which is to be molded or coated. It must be rich enough in gelatin and free enough of suspended solid particles for the finished product to be firm and sparkling clear.

To clarify the stock, remove all traces of fat and have all equipment free from grease. For each quart of cold stock, add 1 beaten egg white and 1 crumbled egg shell. Stir and heat just to simmering point and simmer 15 minutes (never, never boiling). Remove the saucepan from the heat and let stock stand 30 minutes. Strain through a double thickness of cheesecloth wrung out in cold water. The egg white and shell attract all the cloudy particles in the stock, leaving it crystal-clear.

⚜ ASPIC OR GELÉE (*Quick Method*)

- 1½ envelopes (4½ teaspoons) unflavored gelatin
- ⅓ cup water, stock, or dry white wine
- 2 cans (10½ ounces each) consommé or bouillon, or the equivalent in concentrated homemade light stock

Soften gelatin in ⅓ cup cold stock, water, or wine. Heat consommé or bouillon to boiling point, remove from heat, and stir in gelatin. Cool. Use as a base for aspic molds and spoon over Chaud-froid coated foods. Makes approximately 2 ¾ cups.

COURT BOUILLONS

Court bouillons are liquids cooked only a short time with seasonings. Their composition varies with their use—from simple acidulated water (water with vinegar, lemon juice, or wine, and salt) to more highly seasoned preparations of stocks, herbs, spices, and vegetables.

Court bouillons are used as (1) a blanching medium to leech out undesirable flavors, as in some vegetables, in which case the water is discarded; (2) the liquid for cooking and marinating vegetables used on the hors d'oeuvre tray or for garnishing; (3) the liquid for poaching fish and variety meats; (4) a hot marinade for fish; (5) a base for sauces, gravies, chowders, and aspics; (6) bouillon.

⚜ COURT BOUILLON FOR FISH

- ¾ cup diced celery
- ½ cup diced carrots
- ½ cup chopped onion
- 2 tablespoons cooking oil or butter
- 1 cup dry white wine or ¼ cup vinegar or lemon juice
- ½ cup chopped parsley
- 1 tablespoon chopped fresh thyme or 1 teaspoon dried thyme
- 1 bay leaf
- 2 whole cloves
- 1 tablespoon salt
- 3 pounds fish trimmings (heads, bones, tails, and fins) tied in a cheesecloth bag
- 8 whole peppercorns
- 3 quarts cold water

Sauté carrots, celery, and onion in oil or butter in a 4-quart saucepan until vegetables are limp but not browned. Add all remaining ingredients except peppercorns. Cover and slowly bring to boiling point. Reduce heat and simmer (do not boil) 30 minutes. Add peppercorns 10 minutes before cooking time is up. Cool. Remove fish trimmings and strain court bouillon through a double thickness of cheesecloth. Makes approximately 3 quarts.

⚜ POACHED WHOLE FISH

Ask your fish butcher to prepare a 4- or 5-pound fish (salmon, halibut, trout, cod, or striped bass) for cooking whole. Wrap fish in cheesecloth and place it on a rack in a pan long enough to accommodate it. Add strained court bouillon to cover. Bring to boiling point, reduce heat, and simmer 8 to 10 minutes per pound, or until fish is flaky. If fish is to be served cold, shorten the cooking time by 1 to 2 minutes per pound and cool it in the stock. If fish is to be served hot, lay it on a clean towel or napkin on a warm platter so the napkin can absorb the excess liquid. Carefully lift the top skin and cut away the dark flesh. Serve hot with Hollandaise Sauce or any other fish sauce desired, or chill and serve cold with mayonnaise. Makes 6 servings.

⚜ COURT BOUILLON FOR VEGETABLES À LA GRECQUE

Vegetables prepared this way are often served on the hors d'oeuvre tray or are used as a garnish for meat trays or in salads.

½ cup salad oil or olive oil
1 quart cold water
1 medium-sized clove of garlic, crushed
2 celery tops
¼ cup chopped parsley
2 tablespoons chopped shallots or onion
15 coriander seeds
2 teaspoons chopped fresh thyme or ¾ teaspoon dried thyme
¼ teaspoon fennel seeds
8 whole peppercorns
rind of a squeezed lemon

Combine all ingredients except peppercorns and lemon rind in a 3-quart saucepan. Slowly bring to boiling point. Reduce heat and simmer 20 minutes. (Do not boil.) Add peppercorns and lemon rind. Remove from heat and allow this mixture to stand 15 minutes for seasonings to blend. Remove and discard lemon rind. Bring to boiling point again. Add prepared vegetables (see below), the mild-flavored ones first, and bring the liquid to boiling point. Cut off heat and let vegetables cool in the stock, then remove them to a jar or bowl. Add the rest of the vegetables. Cook and cool in the same manner as the first ones. Then either combine the cooked vegetables or put each type of vegetable into a separate jar. Cover with the court bouillon and refrigerate until ready to use.

Vegetables which are suitable for this method of preparation are: julienne carrots, cauliflowerets, artichoke bottoms, sliced cucumbers, celery ribs, fennel ribs, mushrooms, green pepper strips, green beans, leeks, very small white onions, and eggplant strips. To prevent the vegetables from discoloring, mix 3 tablespoons lemon juice with each pound of fresh vegetables prepared for cooking.

ROUX

Roux is used by French cooks as a thickening agent for sauces, soufflés, and croquettes. Roux is made by cooking flour with butter or other fat before adding liquid. This process prevents the finished dish from having a pasty, raw-flour taste and prevents the formation of lumps so often found in incorrectly made sauces.

As a time-saver, make a quantity of roux in advance; measure tablespoon portions onto cooky sheets, flatten, and freeze. Transfer to tightly covered jars and store in the freezer. When ready to use, soften roux in top of double boiler over hot water and proceed as usual for making the sauce, or drop one or more portions of roux into the hot liquid until desired thickness is reached.

There are three general types of roux: white, brown, and blond.

White roux is made by stirring and cooking the butter and flour together until it is bubbly but not browned. The liquid added to it may be milk or light stock (veal, chicken, or fish). This makes a basic white sauce (Velouté or Béchamel).

Brown roux is made like white roux with the following exceptions:

1. The butter and flour are stirred and cooked together until the mixture has turned nut-brown in color but has not burned or scorched.
2. Half again as much flour is used, since browning reduces the thickening power of the flour by converting the starch to dextrin.
3. Beef stock is used as the liquid, and stronger-flavored seasonings may

be added. Brown roux is used to thicken brown sauces such as Espagnole and Demi-Glace.

Blond roux is made the same way as brown roux, except that it is cooked only until its color is pale golden and it is always made with clarified butter (butter that is melted and strained, leaving the milky deposit in the strainer). The liquid is usually light (white) stock (veal, chicken, or fish). It is used in delicately flavored dishes, such as eggs, fish, white meat of chicken, etc.

⚜ BASIC WHITE SAUCES

	PROPORTIONS
Thin sauce or soup	**1 tablespoon each butter (or other fat) and flour to each cup of liquid**
Medium sauce (creamed or scalloped dishes)	**2 tablespoons each butter (or other fat) and flour to each cup of liquid**
Thick sauce (croquettes and soufflés)	**3 to 4 tablespoons each butter (or other fat) and flour to each cup of liquid**

Melt butter or other fat over low heat. Remove from heat and stir in flour. Return to heat and stir and cook until the butter-and-flour mixture is bubbly. Remove from heat and stir in liquid. (Or add previously prepared frozen roux to liquid.) Stir and cook until thickened. Add salt and pepper, using ¼ to ½ teaspoon salt for each cup liquid, the amount depending upon the salt that is in the stock. Add pepper to taste. Makes about 1 cup.

⚜ BROWN SAUCE

Make as for White Sauce, using half again as much flour and cooking longer. Add beef stock and stronger-flavored seasonings.

Béchamel and Velouté sauces are basically the same simple white sauce, the principal difference being that Velouté Sauce is made with white stock (poultry or veal, or with fish stock when it is to be used with a fish dish), while Béchamel Sauce is made either with milk or white stock with the addition of heavy cream. See Chapter 4, Sauces, for recipes.

MARINADES

A marinade is a seasoned liquid, cooked or uncooked, used for steeping certain foodstuffs, such as meat, fish, poultry, and vegetables. Its purpose is to impregnate the food with the flavor of the condiments, to tenderize the less tender cuts of meat, and to increase the keeping quality of the foods. The length of time for marinating depends upon the type of food and the size of the pieces into which it is cut. Small pieces, such as meat for Shish Kebabs, require only a few hours' marinating time, while large cuts, such as thick roasts, may require from 24 hours to 3 or 4 days, with the meat turned frequently to marinate it uniformly.

⚜ UNCOOKED MARINADE FOR MEATS

3 medium-sized carrots, pared and sliced
½ cup sliced onion
3 sliced shallots
6 crushed whole peppercorns
6 crushed juniper berries, if available
½ cup chopped parsley
¾ teaspoon dried thyme or 2 teaspoons chopped fresh thyme
1 teaspoon salt
1 bay leaf
½ cup wine vinegar
2¾ cups dry red or white wine, or beef bouillon
¼ cup salad oil or olive oil

Place meat in bottom of suitable dish with half the carrots, onions, and shallots underneath the meat and the remaining half over the top. Combine all the other ingredients except the oil and pour over the meat. Then pour oil over meat to prevent the top from turning dark. Refrigerate roasts or other large pieces of meat 2 to 3 days, smaller pieces 12 to 24 hours, depending upon size of pieces, turning meat frequently in the marinade. Makes approximately 3¼ cups.

⚜ COOKED MARINADE FOR MEATS

Use the same ingredients as in Uncooked Marinade, increasing the vinegar to ⅔ cup and the wine to 3 cups to allow for evaporation during cooking. Place meat and vegetables in a suitable dish as for Uncooked Marinade. Combine all remaining ingredients except the oil in a 2-quart saucepan, slowly bring to boiling point, and simmer 10 minutes. Pour marinade over the meat first and then pour the oil over it. Steep large pieces of meat such as roasts or leg of lamb 24 hours, smaller pieces 4 to 5 hours, turning meat frequently in the liquid. Makes approximately 3¼ cups.

⚜ MARINADE FOR SMALL PIECES OF VENISON

Sprinkle both sides of venison cutlets, steaks, or chops with salt and ground black pepper, and rub into the meat. Place meat in a suitable dish and pour over it just enough cooking oil or olive oil to cover the top (about ¼ cup for 6 servings). Marinate 1 hour, turning meat twice.

BRINES

⚜ BRINE FOR PICKLING OX TONGUE
(*Saumure pour Langue de Boeuf*)

4 quarts water
1½ cups salt
3½ ounces saltpeter
½ cup sugar
8 whole peppercorns
4 juniper berries, if available
2 tablespoons chopped fresh thyme or 2 teaspoons dried thyme
2 bay leaves

Combine all ingredients in an 8-quart kettle, bring to boiling point, and then cool. To test the liquid for sufficient salt, put a raw egg in its shell in the brine. If it sinks to the bottom, add additional salt until the egg floats to the surface.

Wash a fresh beef tongue, trim, discard excess fat, and prick it with a needle. Then pound it well with a spatula or large spoon to expel the air from the meat. Mix ⅔ cup butchers' salt with ½ ounce saltpeter and rub over the surface of the tongue. Add tongue to the brine solution. Cover and steep in a cool place 8 to 9 days.

⚜ DRY PICKLED TONGUE

Prepare uncooked fresh beef tongue as in preceding recipe and set aside. Mix ½ cup butchers' salt with ¼ cup sugar and 1¾ ounces saltpeter and rub over the surface of the tongue. Mix 1⅓ cups butchers' salt with 1½ ounces saltpeter and sprinkle over the bottom of a glass or earthenware dish, using all the mixture. Place tongue on this mixture and weight it down with a heavy bowl or board. Cover. Let stand for a few days to allow enough liquid to form to cover the tongue. In 6 days, tongue will be half pickled; in 11 to 12 days, tongue will be fully pickled and ready for cooking. Before cooking, soak tongue in water 24 hours, changing water frequently.

⚜ BRINE FOR LARGE PIECES OF MEAT

8 quarts water
1½ pounds (3 cups) butchers' salt
5½ ounces saltpeter
1 pound brown sugar

Combine all ingredients in a 12-quart kettle. Bring to boiling point. To test the liquid for sufficient salt, add a peeled raw potato. If it sinks to the bottom, add additional salt until potato floats to the surface. Cool. Trim a 10- to 11-pound piece of beef (brisket, plate, flank, or rump), prick it deeply with a large needle or ice pick, and place it on a rack in the bottom of an earthenware or enamel brine tub or kettle. Pour in brine. Cover and let stand in a cool place 8 or 9 days. Makes approximately 9 quarts of brine.

FORCEMEATS

Forcemeats (farces) are indispensable to the fine cuisine of the French chef. They are used in a variety of ways: for making quenelles, mousse, mousselines, pâtés, loaves, molds, vol-au-vents, borders, garnishes, canapé spreads, and for stuffing breast of veal or lamb, poultry, game, fish, vegetables, and eggs. For instructions for making forcemeat into quenelles see pages 146–47, also Culinary Techniques in Pictures.

Forcemeats are made of meat, poultry, or lean, close-grained fish (halibut, salmon, pike, cod, or swordfish), finely ground or puréed and mixed with seasonings. (In addition to those given here, recipes for forcemeats appear in other chapters in connection with the dishes in which they are used.)

The preparation of some kinds of forcemeats requires the addition of a Panada, a flour mixture similar to Chou Paste. Panadas act as binding agents in forcemeat mixtures and also give them body. In the past panadas were almost always made of bread, but now a very thick paste made of flour and water or milk is preferred, since quenelles made with this are lighter and more delicate.

⚜ FLOUR PANADA

½ cup water
3 tablespoons butter
¼ teaspoon salt
1 cup sifted all-purpose flour

Mix the first 3 ingredients in a 1-quart saucepan. Bring to boiling point. Remove from heat and beat in all the flour at one time, using a wooden spoon. Continue beating about 1 minute. Return to heat. Stir and cook slowly for 5 minutes or until mixture forms a ball or leaves the sides of the pan. Remove from heat and spread mixture on a buttered plate. Cover with buttered paper to prevent crusting over the top. Refrigerate until thoroughly chilled. Mix with twice-ground meat, chicken, game, or fish as specified in each recipe. Makes 1 cup.

⚜ MILK PANADA

In the recipe for Flour Panada, replace the water with milk.

⚜ EGG PANADA

Use recipe for Milk Panada, and add 1 large whole egg, beating it in well. This panada is used a great deal with fish forcemeats and fish pastries.

⚜ FINE FORCEMEAT FOR QUENELLES (*Chicken, Veal, or Fish*)

1 pound raw boneless white meat of chicken, rump of veal, or firm-textured fish, with gristle and fat removed
½ teaspoon salt
⅛ teaspoon ground black pepper
⅛ teaspoon ground nutmeg
5 tablespoons softened butter
2 egg whites
1 cup chilled Egg Panada
about 6 tablespoons chilled heavy cream

Put meat, chicken, or fish through a food chopper twice, using the finest blade. Add seasonings and beat well. Add soft butter and beat well. Beat in egg whites, one at a time. Beat in chilled Panada, beating vigorously after all of it has been added. Spread the mixture on a buttered plate, cover with buttered paper, and refrigerate until thoroughly chilled. Beat in cream ½ tablespoon at a time, adding only enough for mixture to hold its shape while poaching. Shape into quenelles (see pages 146–47) and poach in simmering stock or water. Makes approximately 18 quenelles.

⚜ GRATIN FORCEMEAT

For stuffing game or as a spread for canapés.

½ pound fat salt pork
1 pound liver (poultry, veal, or game)
½ cup chopped onion or shallots
2 tablespoons chopped parsley
¾ teaspoon salt
½ teaspoon dried thyme, or 1½ teaspoons chopped fresh thyme
¼ teaspoon ground black pepper

Cut salt pork in small dice and cook over low heat until all fat has been rendered. Add liver and onion or shallots to the hot fat. Stir and cook over medium heat until lightly browned. Add seasonings. Stir and cook 1 to 2 minutes. Lift out liver and onion, reserving the fat. Then put liver and onion through a food chopper twice, using the finest blade, or put in an electric blender. (If blender is used, grind one-third of the liver at a time.) Add the reserved fat and beat well with a wooden spoon. Makes about 2 cups.

⚜ MOUSSELINE FORCEMEAT (*Chicken, Fish, or Veal*)

¾ pound boneless breast of chicken or rump of veal, with gristle, skin, and fat removed
¼ teaspoon salt
⅛ teaspoon ground white pepper
2 large egg whites
about 1 cup chilled heavy cream

Put chicken or veal through a food chopper twice, using the finest blade. Add salt and pepper. Gradually beat in egg whites. Put the mixture through a fine sieve. Place bowl on a bed of ice and beat the meat with a wooden spoon until it is thoroughly chilled. Beat in cream, a little at a time. Chill about 2 more hours. Test a small portion in simmering water for correct consistency. If the mixture is too soft, add another egg white. Use for stuffing poultry or game.

The mixture may be shaped with a spoon into the form of large olives. Place these mousselines in a buttered pan. Cover with simmering stock or water. Poach, uncovered, 10 to 15 minutes or until firm, never allowing the water to boil. Transfer with a slotted spoon to a clean towel or cloth to drain. Use to garnish meat or vegetable dishes.

Mousseline Forcemeat may also be made into quenelles or mousse.

⚜ MOUSSE

Pack the Mousseline Forcemeat mixture in buttered individual molds. Place molds in pan of very hot water. Bake in a preheated moderate oven (350° F.)

until mousse is puffed, firm, and begins to pull away from the sides of the molds—40 to 50 minutes.

⚜ QUENELLE FORCEMEAT WITH PANADA

1 pound (2 cups ground) boneless, raw white meat of poultry, veal, or dry, firm-textured fish, with gristle and fat removed
½ teaspoon salt
⅛ teaspoon ground black pepper
⅛ teaspoon ground nutmeg
1 cup cold Flour Panada
½ cup (1 stick) soft butter
2 large whole eggs and 2 large egg yolks

Put poultry, veal, or fish through a meat grinder twice, using the finest blade. Add seasonings and beat well. Add cold Flour Panada and beat it into the meat with a wooden spoon. Beat in butter. Beat in whole eggs and egg yolks, one at a time. Put the forcemeat through a sieve. Test the consistency by shaping a spoonful of the mixture into a small ball or cylinder and poaching it in simmering water. If it disintegrates, beat in 1 or 2 more egg yolks; if the mixture is too dry, beat in a little cream, 1 tablespoon at a time. Test after each addition. Make into quenelles and poach (see pages 146–47).

⚜ SHRIMP FORCEMEAT

For quenelles, mousselines, or mousses, or as a stuffing for fish.

1 pound raw shrimp
1 teaspoon salt
¼ teaspoon ground black pepper
¼ teaspoon ground nutmeg
2 large egg whites
2 cups heavy cream

Peel and devein shrimp and put them through a food chopper twice, using the finest blade. Place the flesh in a mortar or chopping bowl and pound to a paste. (If an electric blender is available, it can take the place of the mortar and pestle and the fine sieve.) Add seasonings and mix well. Gradually beat in egg whites and rub the mixture through a fine sieve unless it has been blended in an electric blender. Place the bowl over cracked ice and gradually work in heavy cream, using a wooden spoon. Test the mixture for consistency before using by putting a 1-inch ball in a small saucepan and pouring in a little hot water. Cook about 2 minutes. If the mixture is too soft, add a little more egg white; if it is too firm work in a little more heavy cream. Test after each addition. Makes approximately 3½ cups.

VARIATIONS

LOBSTER FORCEMEAT

In the recipe for Shrimp Forcemeat, replace shrimp with 1 pound raw lobster meat, using also the lobster coral. Use in the same manner as Shrimp Forcemeat.

FISH FORCEMEAT

In the recipe for Shrimp Forcemeat, replace shrimp with 1 pound raw boneless fish. Use in the same manner as Shrimp Forcemeat.

Preparation of Quenelles

Quenelles, which are made of forcemeat bound with eggs and sometimes with Panada, are of different shapes and sizes and may be shaped in several ways: with spoons, by hand, in molds, or by forcing the mixture through a pastry bag. The size and shaping method depend on the way the quenelles are to be used. They are cooked uncovered in simmering water or stock; if the water is allowed to boil they are likely to split. (See Culinary Techniques in Pictures.)

Spoon method. Wet a soup spoon or dessert spoon and measure out a rounded spoonful of the cold forcemeat. Smooth the top with the inverted bowl of another spoon of the same size which has been dipped in very hot water. Loosen the dumpling from the first spoon and slide it into simmering water or broth. Cook, uncovered, 15 to 20 minutes.

Shaping by hand. Measure out a rounded soup spoon or dessert spoon of forcemeat and roll it with the palms of the hands on a floured board to form 2½-inch cylinders. Simmer as for spoon-shaped dumplings.

In molds. Forcemeat for garnishes may be shaped like large olives, using the spoon method, or it may be cooked in individual flared, round, or boat-shaped molds. First butter molds generously and make a simple design on the bottom of each with bits of truffles, pimiento, or ripe olives. Fill generously with forcemeat, making sure there are no air spaces along the sides. Poach in simmering water as for spoon-shaped quenelles. The quenelles will unmold themselves and float to the surface of the liquid.

With a pastry bag. Place a round ½-inch tube in a large pastry bag and put forcemeat into bag. Pipe small round, or 1½-inch elongated, quenelles onto the bottom of a buttered saucepan or skillet. Cover with simmering water or broth and poach as for spoon-shaped quenelles. To make quenelles for soup, put forcemeat through a pastry bag fitted with a small tube, moving the bag a short distance back and forth to give the quenelles a slight curl. These are sometimes called caterpillar dumplings. Cover with simmering water or stock and cook, uncovered, 12 to 15 minutes. Serve in soup.

APPAREILS (*MIXTURES*)

The French culinary term *appareil* means a simple mixed preparation used in making a dish; for example, *appareil à biscuit* (sponge mixture), *appareil à crème renversée* (custard mixture), *appareil à croquette* (croquette mixture). The following mixtures are frequently used.

⚜ RICH DUXELLES

Duxelles is a cooked mixture resembling hash, made of finely chopped mushrooms, onions, shallots, and ham cooked in butter with the addition of tomato purée. After cooling, it may be stored in a covered jar in the refrigerator to use as needed to add flavor to gravies and sauces.

9 or 10 medium-sized mushrooms
1 tablespoon butter
1 tablespoon chopped shallots
2 tablespoons finely chopped onions
¼ cup minced lean ham
2 tablespoons thick tomato purée
salt to taste
ground black pepper to taste

Wash and finely chop mushrooms and squeeze them in a cloth to extract the moisture. Then cook in butter along with shallots and onions until they begin to brown. Add ham and tomato purée. Cook slowly 7 to 8 minutes or until the moisture has evaporated. Add salt and pepper. Cool. Store in a covered jar in the refrigerator to use as needed. Makes approximately 1 cup.

⚜ MATIGNON

Matignon is a mixture of carrots, celery, onions or shallots, and herbs which are cooked first in butter until they are tender and then in Madeira until most of the liquid has evaporated. Meat, such as thin strips of ham or crumbled crisp bacon, may be added. Matignon may be served with meat or fish dishes or it may be cooked with the meat, as veal roast or fish.

5 small carrots, finely chopped
2 shallots, finely chopped
1 cup thinly sliced onions or shallots
¼ cup finely chopped celery
¼ cup (½ stick) butter
1 tablespoon chopped parsley
¼ teaspoon dried or 1 teaspoon chopped fresh thyme
½ small bay leaf
⅓ cup Madeira
¼ teaspoon salt
¼ teaspoon ground black pepper

Cook vegetables in butter until they are soft. Add remaining ingredients and cook until most of the liquid has evaporated. Serve with meat or fish dishes or cook with roasts or fish. Makes approximately 6 servings.

VARIATIONS

MATIGNON WITH BACON

Replace 2 tablespoons of the butter with 2 tablespoons diced bacon in the recipe for Matignon.

MATIGNON WITH MEAT

Add ½ cup finely chopped ham to the recipe for Matignon. Makes approximately 7 servings.

⚜ MIREPOIX

Mirepoix is a mixture of cooked carrots, celery, and onion, with or without meat, seasoned with herbs. It is used to enhance the flavor of sauces, gravies, meats, fish, and shellfish.

1 carrot
1 rib of celery
1 medium-sized onion
1 tablespoon chopped parsley
1 tablespoon butter
1 small bay leaf
¼ teaspoon dried or 1 teaspoon chopped fresh thyme
1/16 teaspoon minced garlic
salt to taste
ground black pepper to taste

Finely dice vegetables. Cook in butter along with the herbs and garlic 7 to 8 minutes or until the vegetables are soft and browned lightly. Season with salt and pepper. Cool. Store in a covered jar in the refrigerator to use as needed. Makes approximately 1 cup.

VARIATION

MIREPOIX WITH MEAT

Add ¼ cup finely chopped ham or 2 strips crumbled crisp bacon to the Mirepoix mixture. Makes approximately 1¼ cups.

⚜ MONTGLAS (*Salpicon à la Montglas*)

Montglas is made from pickled tongue, mushrooms, truffles, Demi-Glace Sauce, and Madeira. It is used to stuff lamb cutlets, or served in tart shells or very small vol-au-vents.

1 cup julienne pieces pickled tongue
1¼ cups julienne pieces poached mushrooms
¾ cup thick Demi-Glace Sauce
¼ cup Madeira
salt
ground black pepper

Cook the first 4 ingredients together until the mixture is very thick. Add salt and pepper to taste. Use to fill lamb cutlets, tart shells and very small vol-au-vents. If desired, replace Demi-Glace with puréed foie gras. Makes approximately 1½ cups.

⚜ DUCHESS POTATO MIXTURE

Duchess Potatoes are fluffy mashed potatoes into which beaten eggs have been incorporated. They may be served as a dish or put through a pastry bag while hot and formed into cases for serving creamed dishes or into borders or rosettes for decorating a casserole or planked meat or fish. For such uses the potatoes are painted with beaten egg, melted butter, or milk and browned lightly in the oven. Duchess Potatoes are also used for making croquettes.

6 medium-sized potatoes (about 2 pounds)
boiling water
1 teaspoon salt
⅛ teaspoon ground white pepper
¼ teaspoon ground nutmeg
2 whole eggs
2 egg yolks

Peel potatoes and cut into quarters. Cook in a covered saucepan in 1 inch of boiling water with 1 teaspoon salt until soft but still firm. Drain well. Put through a potato ricer or food mill. Beat until potatoes are smooth. Add pepper and nutmeg. Beat whole eggs and egg yolks together until light and foamy and add to potatoes. Whip until fluffy. Put through a pastry bag as desired. Brush with beaten egg, milk, or melted butter. Bake in a preheated very hot oven (450° F.) or under the broiler until browned lightly. Makes 6 servings.

⚜ TOMATO FONDUE

Tomato Fondue is made of very ripe tomatoes, peeled, seeded, quartered or chopped, and cooked in butter with onions, shallots, and crushed garlic until the pulp is firm. The mixture may be seasoned with Hungarian paprika, dried or chopped fresh tarragon, saffron, or chopped sweet green pepper. Tomato Fondue is served as an accompaniment to eggs, fish, meat, and poultry dishes and to fill small baked tart shells.

5 medium-sized tomatoes
¼ cup chopped onions or shallots
1 very small clove of garlic, crushed
2 tablespoons butter
½ teaspoon salt
⅛ teaspoon sugar
1/16 teaspoon ground black pepper
chopped parsley

Peel, seed, and quarter or chop tomatoes. Set aside. Cook onions or shallots and garlic in butter until soft. Add tomatoes and seasonings. Cook over low heat until most of the liquid has evaporated. Serve with eggs, fish, meat, and poultry dishes or in small baked tart shells. Sprinkle with chopped parsley. Makes 6 servings.

GARNISHES

A garnish, to Americans, means a simple decoration or an embellishment for a dish. The garnish may be parsley or other greens, radishes, slices of cucumber, tomato, orange, lemon, or apple, clusters of grapes or berries, slices of chopped hard-cooked eggs, mushroom caps, olives, nuts, whipped cream or mayonnaise put through a decorating tube, a sprinkling of paprika, or any other foods that enhance the appearance of the dish. To the French chef, however, garnish includes not only such items as those, but everything that is served with the principal dish in every course of the meal—from fancy-shaped pastas and vegetables in soup and stews to all such accompaniments as potatoes, stuffings, rice, vegetables, gravies, sauces, butters, and relishes. The garnishes may be placed on the platter or tray with the main dish or served in separate dishes.

A garnish may derive its name from a place, from the man who originated it, from an occasion, in compliment to a person, or from various other sources. The garnish often gives its name to the dish so garnished.

GARNISH	MAIN DISH
Agnes Sorel. Mousseline Forcement made of chicken with slices of sautéed mushrooms, poached, in tartlet molds; round slices of pickled tongue; slices of truffle; Sauce Allemande.	Chicken breasts, poached chicken.
Albuféra. Stuffing of forcement with rice plus coarsely diced truffles and balls of foie gras; puff-pastry tartlets garnished with a salpicon of truffles; mushrooms; quenelles of chicken; bound with Albuféra Sauce; decorated with round slices of pickled tongue; Albuféra Sauce served separately.	Poached chicken.
Algerienne. Sweet-potato croquettes; small seeded tomatoes cooked slowly in oil; light Tomato Sauce to which julienne slices of red pepper have been added.	Roast or sautéed meat.
Alsacienne. Tarts filled with braised sauerkraut with a round slice of ham on top; gravy of the meat juices.	Meats.
Americaine. Sliced lobster tails; Lobster Sauce.	Fish.
Amiral (Admiral). Oysters and mussels Villeroi; fluted mushroom caps; crayfish tails; truffle slices; Sauce Normande enriched with crayfish butter.	Large fish, especially turbot and brill.
Andalouse. Grilled halves of peppers à la Grecque; thick slices of peeled eggplant fried in oil and garnished with Tomato Fondue; chipolata sausages; thickened gravy (Jus Lié).	Meats, chicken.
Argenteuil. White asparagus tips coated with Hollandaise Sauce.	Meat, chicken.
Arlesienne. Slices of eggplant fried in deep fat; peeled, sliced, and sautéed tomatoes; floured and deep-fat-fried onion rings; tomato-flavored Demi-Glace Sauce.	Tournedos (small round slices of beef tenderloin) and noisettes (similar slices of lamb or veal).

Beaugency. Artichoke bottoms with Tomato Fondue, topped with slices of blanched beef marrow; Béarnaise Sauce.	Small pieces of sautéed meat.
Beauharnais. Quarters of sautéed artichoke bottoms; stuffed mushroom caps; Château Potatoes; Béarnaise Sauce.	Small pieces of sautéed or grilled meat.
Belle Hélène. Round flat asparagus croquettes; truffle slices; thickened gravy (Jus Lié).	Tournedos.
Berrichonne (*Berry Style*). Balls of steamed cabbage; whole chestnuts and small glazed onions; small slices of bacon cooked with the cabbage; meat juices thickened with Demi-Glace.	Braised meat.
Bonne Femme. Chopped shallots, sliced mushrooms, and chopped parsley poached with the fish in white wine and fish stock; the stock is reduced and mixed with a white wine sauce enriched with butter, which is poured over the fish to glaze it.	Small fish, fillets of fish.
Bouquetière. Carrots and turnips scooped out with a spoon and glazed; small green beans; peas; flowerets of cauliflower coated with Hollandaise Sauce; Château Potatoes, light gravy.	Roasts and smaller cuts of meat.
Bourguignonne. Diced browned bacon; quartered sautéed mushrooms; small glazed onions; the braising liquid (always made with Burgundy).	Braised beef, ham.
Bruxelloise. Braised endive; Brussels sprouts slowly cooked in butter; Château Potatoes; light Madeira Sauce.	Roasts and smaller cuts of meat.
Cardinal. Sliced lobster tails and claws, truffle slices; Cardinal Sauce.	Fish.
Castilliane (*Castile Style*). Small nests of Duchess Potatoes, filled with diced tomatoes sautéed in olive oil; deep-fat-fried onion rings; the meat juices, reduced and flavored with tomato.	Roasts, small cuts of meat, tournedos, noisettes, poultry.
Catalan. Grilled tomatoes; artichoke bottoms; tomato-flavored Demi-Glace.	Tournedos, noisettes.
Chambord. Quenelles of fish with truffles;	Braised whole fish.

truffles cut into olives; fluted mushroom caps; fried roe; crayfish cooked in court bouillon; heart-shaped croutons fried in butter; sauce made with red wine.	
Chasseur. Mushroom caps filled with onion purée; Duchess Potatoes; sauce made of white wine, Demi-Glace, and herbs.	Roasts, small pieces of sautéed meat.
Chipolata. Small glazed onions and carrots; chestnuts cooked in consommé; diced fried salt pork; chipolata sausages; meat stock reduced with Demi-Glace.	Roasts, poultry.
Choisy. Braised half lettuce; Château Potatoes; buttered meat glaze.	Tournedos, noisettes.
Choron. Artichoke bottoms with green asparagus tips or very small peas cooked in butter; Noisette Potatoes; tomato-flavored Béarnaise Sauce.	Sautéed meat, tournedos.
Clamart. Macaire Potato Cakes; tartlets garnished with French-style peas; thickened veal stock.	Sautéed meat.
Condé. Purée of red beans cooked in red wine with salt pork; meat stock thickened with Demi-Glace.	Braised meat.
Conti. Lentil purée cooked with rectangles of salt pork; the liquid used to braise the meat.	Braised meat.
Demidoff. Slices of onion and half-moons of carrots and turnips cooked in butter; diced celeriac cooked with the bird in a covered casserole; add truffle half-moons last.	Poultry, game birds.
Dieppoise. Shelled shrimp tails; mussels cooked in white wine; White Wine Sauce made with the reduced stock in which the fish was poached.	Small fish, fillets of fish.
Doria. Cucumber cut into olive-shaped pieces cooked slowly in butter; slices of peeled and seeded lemon.	Pan-fried fish.
Dubarry. Cauliflower cooked and shaped into balls, coated with Mornay Sauce, sprinkled with cheese, and browned; meat juices blended with Demi-Glace.	Roasts, tournedos, noisettes.

Financière. Mushroom caps; veal forcemeat quenelles; truffle slices; blanched olives; cockscombs and cocks' kidneys; Sauce Financière.	Roasts, poultry.
Flamande (Flemish Style). Balls of cooked cabbage; glazed carrots and turnips; small boiled potatoes; rectangles of salt pork cooked with the cabbage; stock of the braised meat.	Braised or boiled meat, duck.
Forestière. Morels (or mushrooms) sautéed in butter; diced fried potatoes; diced lean bacon, blanched and fried; Duxelles Sauce blended with the meat juices or with Demi-Glace and reduced.	Roasts, smaller cuts of meat, poultry.
Godard. Veal forcemeat quenelles with chopped truffles and mushrooms; chicken forcemeat quenelles decorated with truffles and pickled tongue; fluted mushrooms; olive-shaped truffles; glazed lamb's sweetbreads; sauce made of champagne boiled with Mirepoix, Demi-Glace, and mushroom essence.	Large roasts, poultry.
Grand Duke. Green asparagus tips bound with butter; truffle slices; crayfish tails; Mornay Sauce.	Fish.
Helder. Artichoke bottoms garnished alternately with buttered asparagus tips, Noisette Potatoes, and coarsely chopped tomatoes; Béarnaise Sauce.	Tournedos, noisettes, sautéed meat.
Henri IV. Artichoke bottoms garnished with very small Noisette Potatoes rolled in melted meat glaze; Béarnaise Sauce.	Tournedos, noisettes.
Hussarde (Hussar Style). Mushroom caps filled with onion purée; Duchess Potatoes; sauce made with white wine, Demi-Glace, and herbs.	Roasted or sautéed meat.
Italienne (Italian Style). Quarters of Italian-style artichokes; triangular macaroni croquettes with a lot of cheese; Sauce Italienne.	Roasts, smaller cuts of meats, poultry.
Jardinière. Carrots and turnips scooped out with a spoon and glazed; peas; green beans	Large and small cuts of meat.

cut into lozenges and flageolets thickened with Beurre Manié; balls of cauliflower coated with Hollandaise Sauce; light veal stock.	
Joinville. Coarsely chopped mushrooms, crayfish tails, and truffles bound with Joinville Sauce; truffle slices; crayfish tails; Joinville Sauce.	Fish.
La Vallière. Artichoke bottoms garnished with green buttered asparagus tips; Château Potatoes; Bordelaise Sauce.	Tournedos, small pieces of sautéed meat.
Lorette. Asparagus tips or peas thickened with Beurre Manié, very small chicken croquettes; truffle slices; veal juices, thickened (Jus Lié).	Tournedos, noisettes.
Maillot. Carrots and turnips scooped out with a spoon and glazed; small glazed onions; braised lettuce; peas, green beans; thickened meat stock.	Braised meat, especially ham.
Maraîchère. Slices of salsify bound with thin Béchamel Sauce; Brussels sprouts cooked in butter; Château Potatoes; juice of the braised meat.	Braised meat.
Maréchale. The food is dipped in melted butter, then in chopped truffles or breadcrumbs mixed with chopped truffles; the garnish consists of truffle slices, green asparagus tips, peas thickened with Beurre Manié.	Sliced veal sweetbreads, lamb chops, chicken breasts.
Marie-Louise. Artichoke bottoms garnished with 3 parts mushroom purée and 1 part onion purée; Madeira Sauce or thickened gravy.	Sautéed meat and poultry.
Mascotte. Artichoke bottoms cooked in butter; potatoes cut into the shape of olives and sautéed in butter; truffle balls; casserole is rinsed with white wine and veal stock.	Tournedos, noisettes, poultry, cooked in a casserole and surrounded by the garnish.
Massena. Artichoke bottoms garnished with thick Béarnaise Sauce; slices of poached beef marrow placed on the meat; Tomato Sauce.	Tournedos, grilled meats, small pieces of sautéed meat.
Mexicaine (*Mexican Style*). Large grilled	Roasts, smaller cuts of

mushroom caps garnished with Tomato Fondue; small grilled peppers; well-seasoned tomato-flavored gravy.	meat, poultry.
Mirabeau. Anchovy fillets placed on the meat; border of blanched tarragon leaves; pitted olives; Anchovy Butter.	Grilled beef or mutton.
Montmorency. Macedoine of vegetables; bunches of green asparagus tips; Madeira Sauce mixed with the meat stock.	Large or small cuts of meat, poultry.
Montreuil. Boiled potato balls coated with Shrimp Sauce, surrounding the fish; the fish coated with White Wine Sauce.	Small fish and fillets of fish.
Murat. The fillets of fish, cut in coarse julienne strips, are sautéed in butter and mixed with diced artichoke bottoms and diced potatoes sautéed in butter; garnished with tomato slices sautéed in butter, chopped parsley, lemon juice; a little meat glaze; Brown Butter (Beurre Noisette).	Fillets of fish.
Nantua. Crayfish quenelles bound with Nantua Sauce; truffle slices; Nantua Sauce.	Fish.
Niçoise I. Tomato Fondue with a chopped clove of garlic and chopped tarragon; anchovy fillets; black olives; peeled, seeded lemon slices; Anchovy Butter.	Fish.
Niçoise II. Tomato Fondue with a little chopped garlic and tarragon; green beans sautéed in butter; Château Potatoes; thickened gravy.	Meats, poultry.
Normande. Oysters and mussels scraped clean and poached; small mushroom caps; peeled shrimp tails; truffle slices; shelled crayfish; small deep-fat-fried gudgeon or smelt; half moons of puff pastry; Sauce Normande.	Fish.
Orientale (*Oriental Style*). Timbales of rice à la Grecque; halved tomatoes cooked slowly in olive oil; sweet-potato croquettes; Tomato Sauce.	Poultry.
Portugaise (*Portuguese Style*). Small tomatoes garnished with Duxelles; Château potatoes; Tomato Sauce.	Meats, poultry.

Princesse. Asparagus tips bound with cream sauce; truffle slices; Allemande Sauce with mushroom essence.	Veal sweetbreads, poultry.
Provençale. Small cooked tomatoes; mushroom caps garnished with Duxelles with a little garlic; Sauce Provençale.	Meats, poultry.
Rachel. Artichoke bottoms each garnished with a large slice of beef marrow and sprinkled with chopped parsley; Bordelaise Sauce.	Tournedos and small cuts of meat.
Regence (Regency Style) I. Spoon-shaped quenelles of whiting forcemeat with crayfish butter; poached oysters; mushroom caps; truffle slices; poached roe; Sauce Normande.	Fish.
Regence (Regency Style) II. Spoon-shaped quenelles of chicken forcemeat; large quenelles of veal forcemeat decorated with truffles; small slices of sautéed foie gras; cockscombs; truffles cut into olive shapes; mushroom caps; Sauce Allemande with truffle essence.	Poultry, veal sweetbreads.
Reine Margot. Stuffing of fine chicken forcemeat and puréed almonds; small chicken forcemeat quenelles finished with pistachio butter; small chicken forcemeat quenelles with crayfish butter; Sauce Suprême mixed with almond milk.	Poached poultry.
Riche. Rock lobster medallions; truffle slices; Victoria Sauce.	Fillets of fish.
Richelieu. Tomatoes and mushroom caps filled with Duxelles; braised lettuce; Château Potatoes; meat juices, lightly thickened.	Roasts, especially beef tenderloin.
Romaine (Roman Style). Tartlets garnished with Roman-style Gnocchi; Spinach Loaf with chopped anchovy baked in brioche molds; Sauce Romaine.	Meats.
Rossini. Medallions of foie gras lightly sautéed in butter; truffle slices; Demi-Glace with truffle essence, or Madeira Sauce.	Tournedos, noisettes.
Saint-Germain. Carrot balls, glazed; small tim-	Meats.

bales of pea purée; small potato croquettes; Béarnaise Sauce; the gravy of the meat.	
Saint-Mande. Base of Macaire Potatoes; fine green beans; peas sautéed in butter; thickened gravy.	Meats.
Sarde. Rice croquettes with saffron; tomatoes stuffed with Duxelles; pieces of hollowed-out cucumber garnished with Duxelles and browned; light Tomato Sauce.	Meats.
Tallyrand. Small pieces of macaroni mixed with butter and with grated cheese to which diced foie gras and truffle have been added; Perigueux Sauce with truffle sticks.	Meat, poultry.
Tortue. Salpicon of veal forcemeat quenelles, mushrooms, truffles, blanched and stuffed olives and gherkins; slices of calves' brains; crayfish; French Fried Eggs; heart-shaped fried croutons; Sauce Tortue.	Calf's head.
Toulousaine (Toulouse Style). Small chicken forcemeat quenelles; small mushroom caps; small slices of calves' and lambs' sweetbreads; cockscombs and cocks' kidneys; truffle slices; Allemande Sauce with mushroom essence.	Poultry, vol-au-vents.
Trouvillaise (Trouville Style). Shrimp tails; poached mussels; small fluted mushroom caps; Shrimp Sauce.	Fish.
Tsarine (Czarina). Cucumber balls braised in butter; fluted mushroom caps; glazed Mornay Sauce.	Fish.
Tyrolienne (Tyrolean Style). Deep-fat-fried onion rings; Tomato Fondue; thickened veal gravy with butter added.	Grilled beef or mutton.
Valois. Large boiled potatoes; poached roe; crayfish; Valois Sauce.	Fish.
Vert-Pré. Potato sticks; watercress; Maître d'Hôtel Butter.	Grilled meat or poultry.
Victoria. Medallions of rock lobster; truffle slices; glazed Victoria Sauce.	Fish.

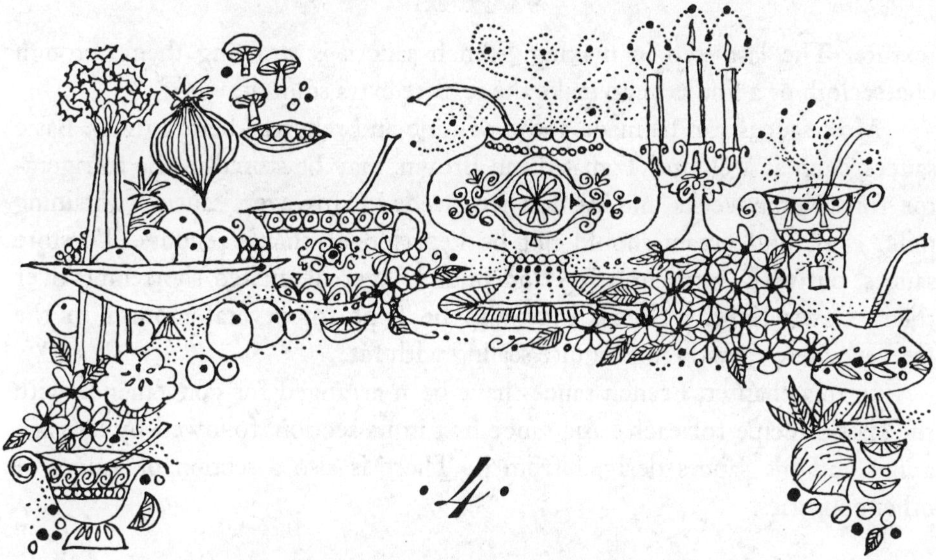

·4·

SAUCES

In France, the term *sauce* is understood to mean any kind of a liquid seasoning, from a simple pan gravy or butter sauce through the great sauces (brown and white), the emulsion types such as Mayonnaise and Hollandaise, to fruit and dessert sauces. Even salad dressing is classed as a sauce.

The *saucier* in French restaurants and hotels is considered second in importance only to the executive chef. He spends considerable time in learning the art of sauce-making. The number of sauces that a *saucier* must master seems enormous, but fortunately it is not as great as it seems, since all sauces stem from a few basic preparations. After he has learned these foundation sauces, he need merely use his ingenuity and imagination to blend skillfully the large number of possible ingredients into an endless number of combinations, using the same methods over and over again.

The ingredients from which sauces are made must be of high quality, for a sauce is only as good as the ingredients from which it is made. Stock is used in most French sauces. Although homemade stock gives the best results, there are also good canned bouillon, consommé, dehydrated beef and chicken bouillon cubes, and meat extract that may be substituted.

In all French sauces, long slow cooking is recommended to produce fine flavor, to cook the starch, if any is used, and to produce a smooth velvety texture. The last step in making French sauces is straining them through cheesecloth or a fine sieve to make the texture extra smooth.

Most sauces can be made ahead of time and reheated before using. Basic sauces, such as Velouté, Tomato, and Brown, may be stored in the refrigerator for several weeks and used when needed. However, sauces containing milk, eggs, and cream should not be kept longer than 24 hours. To store sauces, put them into clean jars and pour a layer of melted shortening over them. Cover tightly. Sauces may also be kept for several months in the freezer where they do not require sealing with fat.

In this chapter, French sauces have been arranged for convenience with the classic recipe for each basic sauce first in its section, followed by its variations and the sauces derived from it. There is also a section of sauces of other countries.

Brown Sauces

The basic sauces are the classic Sauce Espagnole and Brown Sauce. Sauce Espagnole Maigre is basic for brown sauces made with fish stock.

SAUCE ESPAGNOLE AND DERIVATIVES

⚜ SAUCE ESPAGNOLE I (*Classic French Brown Sauce*)

½ cup fat (lard, unsalted beef, veal, or pork drippings)
½ cup flour
8 cups (2 quarts) brown beef stock
1 tablespoon chopped fresh or 1 teaspoon dried thyme
½ cup thick tomato purée or 3 tablespoons tomato paste
1 cup Mirepoix
salt and ground black pepper to taste

Melt fat in a 3-quart saucepan. Blend in flour. Stir and cook until flour has turned the color of a hazelnut, about 10 minutes. Add 6 cups of the stock, mix well, and simmer 4 hours. Strain. Add thyme, tomato purée or paste, and Mirepoix. Add remaining 2 cups stock and continue simmering 2 more hours or until sauce has reduced to about 4 cups, stirring occasionally. Add salt and pepper to taste. Strain. Makes approximately 4 cups.

⚜ SAUCE ESPAGNOLE II (*Quick Method*)

¼ cup (½ stick) butter
½ cup finely chopped onion
½ cup finely chopped carrots
2 tablespoons finely chopped parsley
2 teaspoons chopped fresh or ½ teaspoon dried thyme
½ small bay leaf
4 tablespoons flour
1 cup dry white wine
2½ cups clear brown stock or bouillon
1 tablespoon tomato paste
⅛ teaspoon ground black pepper
salt to taste

Melt butter in a 1½-quart saucepan. Add the next 5 ingredients and stir and cook over low heat 12 minutes, or until vegetables are soft and begin to brown. Remove from heat and blend in flour. Stir and cook over moderate-low heat until the roux turns hazelnut brown. Stir in the wine and stock. Bring to boiling point and simmer 30 to 40 minutes. Add tomato paste and pepper. Add salt to taste if needed. Makes 1½ cups.

⚜ SAUCE BORDELAISE I (*Beef Marrow Sauce*)

1 tablespoon finely chopped shallot or onion
1 tablespoon butter
¾ cup dry red wine
1 cup Sauce Espagnole
⅓ cup diced beef marrow
½ cup brown stock or bouillon
¾ teaspoon lemon juice
¾ teaspoon chopped parsley
1/16 teaspoon ground black pepper

Ask butcher to split the marrow bone so the marrow can be easily removed. Cook shallot or onion in butter until limp. Add wine and reduce the quantity to ¼ cup. Add Sauce Espagnole. Poach marrow gently in hot water 1 to 2 minutes. Remove from water and drain well. Add to the sauce just before serving, along with remaining ingredients. Serve with grilled meats (steaks, chops, etc.) and sweetbreads. Makes approximately 1 cup.

⚜ ROUENNAISE SAUCE

2 cups Bordelaise Sauce
4 uncooked duck livers
dry red wine

Heat Bordelaise Sauce to near boiling point. Chop livers fine and rub through a sieve into the sauce. Heat just enough to cook the livers. Add red wine to desired consistency. Serve with wild and domestic duck. Makes approximately 2⅓ cups.

⚜ SAUCE ITALIENNE I

- 1 teaspoon chopped shallots
- 1 cup peeled and seeded tomatoes
- ¾ cup dry white wine
- ½ cup Sauce Espagnole II (Quick Method)
- 2 tablespoons finely chopped mushrooms
- 1 tablespoon butter
- 2 tablespoons chopped cooked lean ham
- 1 teaspoon chopped parsley
- 1 teaspoon lemon juice
- salt and ground black pepper to taste

Cook shallots and tomatoes in wine until the mixture has reduced by one-half. Stew the mushrooms in the butter and add them with the Sauce Espagnole and the ham. Cook 5 minutes, stirring constantly. Strain. Add parsley and lemon juice. Season to taste with salt and pepper. Use with meats, poultry, fish and leftover meats. Makes approximately 1 cup.

⚜ DEMI-GLACE SAUCE

- 2 cups Sauce Espagnole
- 2 cups brown meat stock
- 2 tablespoons sherry

Combine Sauce Espagnole and meat stock in a 1½-quart saucepan. Simmer until the mixture has reduced to 2 cups. Remove from heat and stir in sherry. Makes 2 cups.

⚜ VENISON SAUCE

- 1 cup dry red wine
- 2 teaspoons sugar
- ¼ cup chopped onion
- 2 cups Demi-Glace Sauce
- 2 tablespoons butter
- 1/16 teaspoon ground black pepper
- dash cayenne

Combine the first 3 ingredients in a 1-quart saucepan. Bring to boiling point and simmer until the quantity is reduced by one-half. Add Demi-Glace and reduce the quantity to 2 cups. Strain. Add remaining ingredients. Use with marinated meats and game. Makes 2 cups.

⚜ SAUCE DIABLE

2 finely chopped shallots
1 cup dry white wine
2 cups Demi-Glace Sauce
dash cayenne
chopped parsley

Cook shallots in wine until the quantity has been reduced by one-half. Stir in Demi-Glace and simmer until the liquid is reduced to 2 cups. Strain. Add cayenne and parsley. Use with broiled chicken and other broiled meats. Makes 2 cups.

⚜ TARRAGON SAUCE I

2 teaspoons chopped fresh or ½ teaspoon dried tarragon
1 cup dry white wine
2 cups Demi-Glace Sauce
1 teaspoon chopped fresh tarragon or parsley

Simmer tarragon in wine for 15 minutes. Strain into Demi-Glace and reduce the quantity to 2 cups. Add 1 teaspoon chopped tarragon or parsley. Use with chicken, fish, and lamb dishes. Makes approximately 2 cups.

BASIC BROWN SAUCE AND DERIVATIVES

⚜ BROWN SAUCE (*Basic*)

¼ cup (½ stick) butter or ¼ cup cooking oil
6 tablespoons flour
2 cups brown stock or canned bouillon
salt and ground black pepper to taste

Melt butter or heat oil in a 1-quart saucepan. Remove from heat and blend in flour. Stir and cook over moderate-low heat until the roux has browned, being careful not to burn. Remove from heat and add stock or bouillon. Stir and cook 2 to 3 minutes or until sauce has thickened. If onion flavor is desired, cook 1 tablespoon finely chopped onion with the butter or oil before adding flour. Makes approximately 1 ¾ cups.

VARIATIONS

MADEIRA SAUCE

Cook 2 cups Brown Sauce until reduced to 1 cup. Add ½ cup Madeira or sherry. Heat only to boiling point. Do not boil. Serve with beef, veal, ham, and poultry. Makes 1 ½ cups.

MUSHROOM SAUCE

Cook ½ cup thinly sliced mushrooms in 1 tablespoon butter until tender. Drain well and add to 1 cup Brown Sauce (or Béchamel Sauce). Cook only until hot. Stir in 1 additional tablespoon butter. Use with chicken, fish, eggs, or roast meats, and in casseroles. Makes approximately 1 cup.

SAUCE TORTUE

Add 1 teaspoon mixed dried herbs (crumbled bay leaf, basil, marjoram, rosemary, and sage) to ⅓ cup boiling Madeira or sherry. Cover and steep 5 minutes. Strain into 2 cups hot Brown Sauce. Heat ½ minute. Add ground black pepper to taste. Use with turtle meat, calf's head, and veal. Makes 2¼ cups.

⚜ SAUCE CHASSEUR

1 cup sliced mushroom stems
2 shallots or 1 small white onion, finely chopped
¼ cup (½ stick) butter
½ cup dry white wine
1 cup Brown Sauce
¾ teaspoon chopped fresh or ⅛ teaspoon dried tarragon
2 tablespoons thick tomato purée
½ teaspoon salt
½ teaspoon chopped parsley
ground black pepper to taste

Cook mushrooms and shallots or onion in the butter until they are tender and the butter has browned. Add wine and cook until the quantity has reduced by one-half. Stir in Brown Sauce, tarragon, tomato purée, and salt. Simmer 5 minutes. Add parsley and black pepper. Makes 1½ cups.

⚜ SAUCE LYONNAISE

⅓ cup finely chopped onion
2 tablespoons butter
½ cup dry white wine
1 cup Brown Sauce
1 teaspoon chopped parsley
salt and ground black pepper to taste

Cook onion in butter until golden brown. Add wine and cook until the quantity has been reduced by one-half. Add Brown Sauce. Stir and cook 10 to 15 minutes. Remove from heat and add parsley. Season to taste with salt and black pepper. Use with meats and vegetables. Makes approximately 1 cup.

⚜ SAUCE ROBERT

⅓ cup finely chopped onion
1 tablespoon butter
½ cup dry white wine
1 tablespoon vinegar
1 cup Brown Sauce
2 tablespoons Tomato Sauce
1 tablespoon prepared mustard
1 tablespoon chopped parsley
1 tablespoon chopped sour pickle
salt and ground black pepper to taste

Cook onion in butter until golden brown. Add wine and vinegar and cook until reduced to three-fourths the original amount. Add Brown Sauce and Tomato Sauce. Simmer 10 minutes. Add mustard, parsley, and pickle. Season to taste with salt and pepper. Use with meats. Makes approximately 1¼ cups.

⚜ SAUCE ROMAINE

2 tablespoons sugar
½ cup vinegar
1 cup Brown Sauce
¼ cup dry white wine
1 tablespoon raisins
1 tablespoon currants
1 tablespoon pine nuts (optional)

Stir and cook 2 tablespoons sugar in a heavy saucepan until it has melted and is golden in color. Add vinegar and cook until the liquid has reduced to a thick syrup. Stir in Brown Sauce. Heat to boiling point. Combine wine, raisins, and currants and cook 1 minute or until fruits are plump. Add to the sauce along with pine nuts if used. Use with beef, ham, tongue, and venison. Makes approximately 1 scant cup.

⚜ JUS LIÉ (*Starch-Thickened Brown Sauce*)

2 tablespoons cornstarch
2 tablespoons cold brown stock or canned bouillon
2 cups cold brown stock or canned bouillon
salt and ground black pepper to taste
¼ cup dry vermouth, sherry, Madeira, or port (optional)

Blend cornstarch with the 2 tablespoons stock or bouillon. Add remaining stock or bouillion. Stir and cook slowly 45 minutes or until of desired thickness. Season to taste. If desired, stir in wine. If canned bouillon is used, simmer it 20 minutes with ½ cup wine (instead of ¼ cup), 2 tablespoons each finely chopped carrots and onions, 1 tablespoon each finely chopped parsley and celery, ½ small bay leaf, and ⅛ teaspoon dried or ½ teaspoon chopped fresh thyme. Use for gravies, and for braising duck, chicken, or ham. Makes 1 ¾ to 2 cups.

⚜ JUS LIÉ TOMATE (*Starch-Thickened Tomato Brown Sauce*)

1 quart Jus Lié
½ cup chopped mushroom stems
6 medium-sized tomatoes, crushed

Combine all ingredients in a 2-quart saucepan. Simmer 30 minutes or until of desired thickness. Strain. Makes approximately 1 quart.

⚜ SAUCE BOURGUIGNONNE I

2 tablespoons minced shallots or onions
2 cups red Burgundy
2 sprigs parsley
1 teaspoon chopped fresh or ¼ teaspoon dried thyme
½ small bay leaf
¼ cup sliced mushroom stems
2 tablespoons flour
2 tablespoons butter

Combine the first 6 ingredients in a 1-quart saucepan. Bring to boiling point, reduce heat, and simmer until the liquid has reduced to 1 cup. Strain. Knead flour with butter and add to the sauce. Cook only long enough to cook the flour and thicken the sauce, 1 to 2 minutes. Use with meat, egg, and snail dishes. Makes 1 scant cup.

⚜ SAUCE DUXELLES I

¼ cup chopped mushroom stems
1 tablespoon finely chopped onion
1 chopped shallot
¼ cup chopped lean cooked ham
1 tablespoon butter
2 tablespoons flour
1 cup brown stock
1 tablespoon chopped parsley
2 tablespoons dry red wine
2 tablespoons tomato purée
salt and ground black pepper to taste

Cook the first 4 ingredients in the butter until golden brown. Blend in flour and stir and cook until browned. Add stock, parsley, wine, and tomato purée. Stir and cook until thickened. Strain. Season to taste with salt and pepper. Use with roasts, poultry, and game. Makes approximately 1 cup.

⚜ SALMIS SAUCE

2 finely chopped shallots
1 tablespoon olive oil or cooking oil
½ small bay leaf
½ teaspoon chopped fresh or ⅛ teaspoon dried thyme
1 tablespoon finely chopped mushroom stems
½ cup dry white or red wine
1 cup game stock
1/16 teaspoon ground nutmeg
dash cayenne
salt and ground black pepper to taste
2 teaspoons currant jelly

Brown shallots in oil. Add the next 4 ingredients and cook slowly 5 to 6 minutes. Add game stock (made from the carcass of cooked game bird) and simmer 15 minutes. Strain. Add seasonings. Stir in jelly just before serving. Use with game birds. Makes approximately ¾ cup.

BROWN SAUCES MADE WITH FISH STOCK

⚜ SAUCE ESPAGNOLE MAIGRE

⅔ cup (1⅓ sticks) butter
1 cup sifted all-purpose flour
8 cups (2 quarts) fish stock
¼ cup chopped onion
½ cup chopped mushroom stems
2 tablespoons butter
½ cup dry white wine

Melt the ⅔ cup butter in a 3-quart saucepan. Heat it until it begins to turn golden. Remove from heat and blend in flour. Stir and cook until the mixture is the color of a hazelnut. Remove from heat and add stock. Mix well. Cook 5 minutes, stirring constantly. Cook onions and mushrooms in the remaining 2 tablespoons butter until they are tender. Add the wine to the mixture. Then mix with the sauce. Simmer until sauce is semitranslucent, 1 to 2 hours, stirring and skimming frequently. The long cooking time makes a better-flavored sauce. Use with fish and egg dishes. Makes approximately 1 quart.

VARIATIONS

SAUCE BORDELAISE II

Cook 2 tablespoons finely chopped shallots and ¼ cup finely chopped mushrooms in 2 tablespoons butter. Drain off liquid and reserve for later use. Add

½ cup dry white wine to shallots and mushrooms. Cook until the liquid is reduced by one-fourth. Add mushrooms and shallot liquid and 2 cups Sauce Espagnole Maigre. Simmer until mixture is reduced to 2 cups. Add an additional 2 tablespoons butter and 1 teaspoon chopped parsley. Makes approximately 2 cups.

SAUCE BOURGUIGNONNE II

Cook 2 tablespoons chopped onion in 1 tablespoon butter until limp. Add 1 sprig or ¼ teaspoon dried thyme, 1 small bay leaf, ½ cup diced mushrooms, and 1 cup dry red wine. Cook until the quantity has been reduced by one-half. Stir in 2 cups Sauce Espagnole Maigre and 2 tablespoons butter. Heat and strain. Makes approximately 2 cups.

SAUCE DUXELLES II

Cook 2 tablespoons chopped shallots in 2 tablespoons each of butter and olive oil (or cooking oil) about 2 minutes. Add ½ cup each dry white wine and fish stock. Cook until the quantity has been reduced by one-half. Add ½ cup Duxelles, 1½ cups Sauce Espagnole Maigre, and ½ cup Tomato Sauce. Stir and bring to boiling point. Reduce heat and simmer 20 minutes. Add 1 tablespoon chopped parsley. Makes approximately 2¼ cups.

SAUCE ITALIENNE II

Cook ¼ cup each finely chopped onion and shallots in 2 tablespoons each of olive oil and butter until limp. Add 1 cup finely chopped mushrooms. Stir and cook 5 minutes. Add ½ cup dry white wine. Simmer until the liquid is reduced by one-half. Add 1½ cups Sauce Espagnole Maigre and ½ cup Tomato Sauce. Simmer 20 minutes. Stir in 1 teaspoon chopped fresh or ¼ teaspoon dried tarragon. Use with fish, cheese, and egg dishes. Makes approximately 2¼ cups.

MATELOTE SAUCE (*Red*)

Reduce ½ cup red wine marinade to one-half the original quantity. Add 2 cups Sauce Espagnole Maigre and cook slowly until the liquid has reduced to 2 cups. Remove from heat and blend in 2 tablespoons butter, 2 teaspoons lemon juice, and a dash of cayenne. Serve with fish dishes. Makes approximately 2 cups.

⚜ SAUCE GENÉVOISE

½ cup chopped onions
½ cup finely diced carrots
6 tablespoons butter
1 bay leaf
1 sprig parsley
1 small sprig fresh or ½ teaspoon dried thyme
2 pounds salmon heads, fins, and tails
2 pounds haddock, halibut, and codfish bones
3 cups dry red wine
fish stock
4 quarts Sauce Espagnole Maigre
1 anchovy, mashed
¼ cup brandy
red wine

Cook onions and carrots in 2 tablespoons butter 10 to 12 minutes or until lightly colored. Add herbs, salmon trimmings, and fish bones. Cover and let stand 30 minutes. Add the 3 cups wine and sufficient fish stock to cover the bones. Cover and simmer 20 minutes. Strain and let stock stand 20 minutes. Bring to boiling point, add Sauce Espagnole Maigre, and cook until the quantity has reduced to 1 quart. Strain. Blend in remaining 4 tablespoons butter, anchovy, and brandy. If sauce is too thick thin with additional red wine. Makes approximately 1 quart.

White Sauces

In spite of the wide diversity that characterizes and confuses the classification of French sauces, Béchamel and Velouté are always conceded to be basic white sauces. All the other white sauces included here have therefore been treated as variations or derivatives of one or the other.

BÉCHAMEL SAUCE AND DERIVATIVES

⚜ BÉCHAMEL SAUCE (*Basic—Medium Thickness*)

4 tablespoons (½ stick) butter
4 tablespoons flour
1½ cups milk or light stock
½ cup heavy cream
1 teaspoon salt, or salt to taste
1/16 teaspoon ground white pepper

Melt butter in a 1-quart saucepan. Remove from heat and stir in flour. Stir and cook over medium-low heat about 1 minute. Remove from heat and add milk or stock. Stir and bring to boiling point. Add cream and seasonings, using only salt and pepper to taste if stock is used. Cook ½ minute. If desired use as a base for other sauces. Makes approximately 2 cups.

VARIATIONS

ECOSSAISE SAUCE I

Cook 2 tablespoons each finely chopped onion, celery, carrots, and string beans in 3 tablespoons butter until vegetables are tender. Mix with 2 cups Béchamel Sauce. Makes approximately 2¼ cups.

MORNAY SAUCE I (*Cheese Sauce*)

Blend 1 cup light stock (veal, poultry, or fish) with 2 cups Béchamel Sauce. Bring to boiling point and stir and cook 3 to 4 minutes. Remove from heat and add 3 tablespoons butter, ½ cup each grated Gruyère and Parmesan cheese. Do not boil after adding cheese. Makes approximately 3 cups.

MORNAY SAUCE II (*Cheese Sauce*)

Blend 1 egg yolk with ¼ cup heavy cream and add to 2 cups hot Béchamel Sauce. Stir and cook ½ minute. Add ½ cup grated Gruyère or Parmesan cheese. Cook only until cheese has melted. Do not boil. Makes approximately 2½ cups.

NANTUA SAUCE (*Crayfish Sauce*)

Blend ¼ cup minced cooked rock lobster with ¼ cup (½ stick) butter. Add 2 cups hot Béchamel Sauce. Stir and cook 2 to 3 minutes. Season to taste with salt and cayenne. Use with shellfish dishes. Makes approximately 2⅓ cups.

SAUCE CARDINAL (*Lobster Sauce*)

Blend ¼ cup minced cooked lobster with ¼ cup (½ stick) butter. Add 2 cups hot Béchamel Sauce made with fish stock. Stir and cook 2 to 3 minutes. Add 1 tablespoon finely chopped truffles and ¼ cup heavy cream. Use with seafood or egg dishes. Makes approximately 2⅓ cups.

SHRIMP SAUCE I

In Sauce Cardinal replace lobster with shrimp. Use with seafood or egg dishes.

CREAM SAUCE MADE WITH FROZEN ROUX

Soften 4 wafers (4 tablespoons) frozen roux (see Roux, pages 138–39) in the top of a double boiler over hot water. Add 2 cups milk. Stir and cook until of desired thickness. Add additional roux if necessary.

SAUCE FRANÇAISE

Cook ½ cup diced mushrooms in ½ cup water and 1 cup fish stock until liquid has reduced by one-half. Strain liquid into 2 cups Béchamel Sauce. Add 1/16 teaspoon each ground mace and minced garlic. Bring to boiling point, stirring constantly. Blend 1 mashed anchovy with 2 tablespoons butter or margarine and stir into the sauce. Season with ground white pepper to taste. Use with egg, cheese, and fish dishes. Makes 2½ cups.

⚜ SAUCE SOUBISE (*Onion Sauce*)

2 cups finely diced onions
1 cup water
2 tablespoons butter
2 cups Béchamel Sauce
½ cup heavy cream
½ teaspoon lemon juice
salt and ground white pepper

Cook onions in water until three-fourths done. Drain; discard water. Then cook onions in butter until they are soft. Add Béchamel Sauce. Stir and cook 2 to 3 minutes. Put through a sieve. Bring to boiling point. Add cream and lemon juice. Season to taste with salt and pepper. Use with egg, lamb, sweetbreads, and some beef dishes. Makes 2 cups.

VELOUTÉ SAUCE AND DERIVATIVES

⚜ VELOUTÉ SAUCE (*Basic—Medium Thickness*)

4 tablespoons (½ stick) butter
4 tablespoons flour
salt to taste
2 cups white stock (veal, poultry, or fish)
ground white pepper to taste

Melt butter in a 1-quart saucepan. Remove from heat and stir in flour. Stir and cook over medium-low heat 1 minute, but do not brown. Remove from heat and add stock. Mix until well blended. Stir and cook until sauce is of medium thickness. Add salt and pepper, the amount of which depends upon the seasonings that are in the stock. If desired, this sauce may be used as a basis for other sauces. Makes approximately 2 cups.

⚜ AURORA SAUCE I (*Sauce Aurore Maigre*)

1½ cups fish Velouté Sauce
½ cup Tomato Sauce
¼ cup (½ stick) butter

Mix Velouté and Tomato sauces in a 1-quart saucepan. Bring to boiling point. Remove from heat and add butter or margarine. Makes approximately 2 cups.

⚜ BRETONNE SAUCE

½ cup celery julienne strips
½ cup mushroom julienne strips
½ cup sliced white portions of leeks
3 tablespoons butter
½ cup fish stock
2 cups fish Velouté Sauce
salt and ground white pepper to taste

Cook vegetables in 2 tablespoons of the butter 3 to 4 minutes over moderate heat. Add fish stock and cook until vegetables are tender. Add to Velouté Sauce along with remaining butter. Season to taste with salt and ground white pepper. Makes approximately 3½ cups.

⚜ CAPER SAUCE (*Sauce aux Câpres Maigre*)

2 cups fish Velouté Sauce
2 tablespoons capers
¼ cup (½ stick) butter
salt and ground white pepper to taste

Heat Velouté Sauce. Remove from heat and blend in capers and butter. Add salt and pepper to taste. Use with fish, egg, and vegetable dishes. Makes approximately 2 cups.

⚜ SAUCE CHIVRY I (*Herb and White Wine Sauce*)

2 tablespoons each chopped parsley, chives, fresh chervil, fresh tarragon
½ cup dry white wine
2 cups Velouté Sauce
¼ cup heavy cream
¼ cup (½ stick) butter
2 tablespoons chopped watercress or spinach

Combine the first 6 ingredients in a 1½-pint saucepan. Cook until the wine is reduced by one-half. Add cream. Blend watercress or spinach with butter and add to the sauce. Season to taste with salt and ground white pepper. If fresh chervil and tarragon are not available, replace them with 1 teaspoon each of dried chervil and tarragon. Makes approximately 2½ cups.

⚜ CURRY SAUCE

¼ cup finely chopped onion
1 tablespoon butter
1 tablespoon curry powder
¼ cup fish stock or chicken stock
1½ cups Velouté Sauce (fish or chicken)
½ teaspoon dried thyme
1/16 teaspoon ground mace
½ cup heavy cream
salt and ground black pepper to taste

Cook onion in butter until limp but not browned. Add curry powder and stir and cook 2 minutes. Add fish or chicken stock (fish stock if used with fish dishes; chicken stock if used with chicken dishes). Bring to boiling point. Remove from heat and stir in Velouté Sauce, thyme, and mace. Bring to boiling point, stirring constantly. Add cream and season to taste with salt and pepper. Use with fish or poultry dishes. Makes approximately 2 cups.

⚜ SAUCE DIEPPOISE (*Shrimp and Mussel Sauce*)

6 cooked, peeled, and deveined shrimps
2 tablespoons butter
1½ cups fish Velouté Sauce
2 tablespoons mussel stock
¾ cup shelled small mussels (cooked in dry white wine)
salt and ground white pepper to taste

Mince and mash shrimps. Mix with butter and add to Velouté Sauce. Beat in the mussel stock. Stir and cook only until hot. Add mussels and heat. Season to taste with salt and pepper. Use with fish dishes. Makes approximately 2⅓ cups.

⚜ SAUCE FINES HERBES

1 tablespoon chopped shallots
1 tablespoon butter
1 tablespoon chopped parsley
1 tablespoon chopped chives
1 teaspoon chopped fresh or ¼ teaspoon dried chervil
2 cups fish Velouté Sauce
½ cup heavy cream
1 teaspoon chopped fresh or ¼ teaspoon dried tarragon
salt and ground white pepper to taste

Cook shallots in butter until they are limp. Add to Velouté Sauce and cream. Heat to boiling point. Strain and add herbs. Season to taste with salt and pepper. Use with fish and egg dishes. Makes 2 cups.

⚜ SAUCE HOMARD (*Lobster Sauce*)

2 cups fish Velouté Sauce
½ cup heavy cream
1 teaspoon paprika
2 tablespoons cooked lobster coral, pounded and minced
¼ cup (½ stick) butter
½ cup diced cooked lobster
salt and ground white pepper to taste

Combine Velouté Sauce, heavy cream, and paprika. Stir and cook over low heat 2 to 3 minutes. Mix lobster coral with butter and add to the sauce along with the diced lobster. Season with salt and pepper to taste. Serve over fish puddings and seafood soufflés. Makes approximately 2 ¼ cups.

VARIATION

SAUCE VICTORIA

Add ½ cup diced mushrooms cooked in 1 tablespoon butter to Sauce Homard (Lobster Sauce). Serve over cheese puddings, fish puddings, and soufflés.

⚜ PARSLEY SAUCE

6 tablespoons coarsely chopped parsley
½ cup hot water
2 cups Velouté Sauce
¼ cup heavy cream
salt and ground white pepper to taste

Blanch 5 tablespoons of the parsley in the hot water. Cover and steep 5 minutes. Cool, strain, and dry in a clean towel. Add the 1 tablespoon remaining parsley to the Velouté Sauce. Bring to boiling point and simmer 3 to 4 minutes. Add dry blanched parsley and cream. Heat ½ minute. Season to taste with salt and pepper. Use with fish, egg, poultry, and vegetable dishes. Makes 2 cups.

⚜ SAUCE RAVIGOTE

½ cup dry white wine
¼ cup wine vinegar
2 cups Velouté Sauce
1 tablespoon minced shallots
2 tablespoons butter
1 tablespoon chopped chives
¼ teaspoon each dried chervil and tarragon
salt and ground white pepper

Combine wine and wine vinegar and cook until the liquid has reduced by one-half. Add to Velouté Sauce. Bring to boiling point. Remove from heat and add shallots, butter, and herbs. Heat ½ minute. Use with egg, fish, and lamb dishes. Makes 2 cups.

⚜ TARRAGON SAUCE II

2 tablespoons chopped fresh or 1 teaspoon dried tarragon
½ cup white wine
2 cups Velouté Sauce (fish or chicken)
¼ cup heavy cream
1 teaspoon chopped fresh tarragon or pinch dried tarragon
salt and ground white pepper

Parboil tarragon in wine. Cool, strain, and mash with ¼ cup of the Velouté Sauce. Rub through a fine sieve, then blend with the cream and the remaining Velouté Sauce. Stir and cook only until hot, add additional tarragon, and salt and pepper to taste. Use with fish, chicken, or egg dishes. The Velouté Sauce should be made with fish stock or chicken stock according to the use for which the Tarragon Sauce is intended.

⚜ VENETIAN SAUCE

½ cup tarragon vinegar
2 tablespoons chopped shallots
1 teaspoon each chopped fresh chervil and tarragon or ¼ teaspoon each dried
2 cups fish Velouté Sauce
1 tablespoon each finely chopped parsley and watercress
¼ cup (½ stick) butter

Cook together vinegar, shallots, chervil, and tarragon until the liquid has reduced to ¼ cup. Strain into Velouté Sauce. Stir and cook 2 to 3 minutes. Blend parsley and watercress with butter and add to the sauce. Heat ½ minute. Use with fish and egg dishes. Makes 2 cups.

Sauce Suprême and Variations

Sauce Suprême is made by adding heavy cream to thick Velouté Sauce, using only enough cream to thin the sauce to the correct consistency. It may be made in a small amount for immediate use, or in a larger quantity and stored in a covered jar in the refrigerator and used as a base for making variations. Use for eggs, fish, poultry, vegetables, and for dishes which are to be gratinéed.

⚜ SAUCE SUPRÊME

Makes about 7½ cups
6 cups Velouté Sauce
about 1½ cups heavy cream
salt
ground white pepper
lemon juice

Makes about 2½ cups
2 cups Velouté Sauce
about ½ cup heavy cream
salt
ground white pepper
lemon juice

Heat sauce to simmering point. Beat in cream, 1 tablespoon at a time, until sauce is of desired consistency. Season to taste with salt, pepper, and lemon juice.

VARIATIONS

SAUCE AMBASSADRICE

Whip ⅓ cup heavy cream and fold into 1 cup Sauce Suprême along with ⅔ cup finely chopped white meat of chicken. Use for egg, poultry, and vegetable dishes.

SAUCE ALBUFÉRA

Add 2 tablespoons concentrated chicken or veal stock to 2 cups Sauce Suprême. Heat to simmering point and stir in 1 tablespoon pimiento purée and a dash of cayenne. Use for sweetbreads and poached or braised poultry. Makes a generous 2 cups.

SAUCE ALEXANDRA

Stir ¼ cup light stock and 1 teaspoon finely chopped truffles into 1 cup Sauce Suprême. Heat. Use for fish and poultry dishes. Makes 1¼ cups.

AURORA SAUCE II

Add 3 tablespoons thick tomato purée or well-reduced Tomato Sauce to 2 cups Sauce Suprême. Heat and stir in 1 tablespoon butter just before using. Use for eggs, fish, or poultry. Makes 2 ¼ cups.

CELERY SAUCE

Cook 1 cup finely chopped celery and a small bouquet garni in 1 cup rich chicken stock or bouillon until celery can be mashed to a pulp. Put through a sieve, or put in the glass container of an electric blender, blend 2 to 3 minutes, and strain. Add to 2 cups Sauce Suprême. Heat to simmering point. Do not boil. Use for broiled and braised poultry. Makes approximately 2⅓ cups.

SAUCE CHIVRY II

Cook 2 teaspoons each chopped fresh chervil, chives, and tarragon and 1 tablespoon chopped watercress in ½ cup rich chicken stock or dry white wine until the liquid is reduced to one-third of the original amount. Add 1 tablespoon cooked spinach and put through a fine sieve. Stir into 2 cups Sauce Suprême. Heat only to boiling point. Use with eggs and poultry. Makes approximately 2 ¼ cups.

SAUCE DUCHESSE

Cook ¼ cup finely chopped mushrooms in 2 tablespoons butter 2 minutes. Add ¼ cup chopped pickled tongue and heat 1 minute. Stir into 2 cups Sauce Suprême. Heat to simmering point. Do not boil. Use with eggs, vegetables, and meats. Makes approximately 1⅓ cups.

SAUCE IVOIRE

To 2 cups hot Sauce Suprême add sufficient chicken glaze or chicken bouillon cubes dissolved in hot water to make an ivory-colored sauce. Use with eggs, sweetbreads, and poultry. Makes 2 cups.

SAUCE À LA REINE

Just before serving, heat 2 cups Sauce Suprême to boiling point. (Do not boil.) Whip ⅓ cup heavy cream and fold into the sauce along with ¼ cup fine julienne strips of white chicken. Use with eggs, poultry, and vegetables. Makes 2 ¾ cups.

RICH TARRAGON SAUCE

Cook ¼ cup chopped fresh tarragon in ½ cup rich chicken stock, dry white wine, or dry vermouth until the liquid is reduced to 3 tablespoons. Put through a sieve into 2 cups Sauce Suprême. Heat. Just before serving stir in 1 teaspoon each chopped parsley and tarragon. (If fresh herbs are not available replace them with dried herbs, using ¼ to ⅓ the specified amount of the fresh.) Use with eggs, fish, chicken, and vegetables. Makes a scant 1 ¼ cups.

Sauce Allemande and Variations

Sauce Allemande is a variation of Sauce Suprême, which in its turn is a derivative of Velouté Sauce. Like other basic sauces, it can be made fresh and used as such, or it may be made up in quantity, stored in a covered jar in the refrigerator, and used as a base for making variations. Since Sauce Allemande is rich with cream and eggs, serve it only with less rich foods such as boiled chicken or poached fish and vegetables. Recipes follow for the basic sauce, in two quantities, and variations.

⚜ SAUCE ALLEMANDE

Makes 5 cups	***Makes 2½ cups***
4 large egg yolks	**2 large egg yolks**
1 cup heavy cream	**½ cup heavy cream**
4 cups Sauce Suprême	**2 cups Sauce Suprême**
4 teaspoons lemon juice	**2 teaspoons lemon juice**

Beat egg yolks lightly with a little of the cream and blend with Sauce Suprême. Stir and cook only to boiling point. Gradually stir in lemon juice and remaining cream. This sauce will curdle if boiled after egg yolks have been added. Serve with boiled chicken, poached fish and vegetables, and as the base for making numerous other sauces.

VARIATIONS

SAUCE POLONAISE

Blend 3 tablespoons grated fresh horseradish with 2 cups Allemande Sauce. Heat only until hot. Stir in ½ teaspoon sugar, 1 tablespoon each chopped parsley, lemon juice, and butter. Thin sauce with stock or bouillon, if necessary, to desired consistency. Heat ½ minute. Use with meat dishes. Makes approximately 2¼ cups.

SAUCE IMPERATRICE

Heat 1⅓ cup Allemande Sauce. Stir in 1 tablespoon chicken glaze and 1 teaspoon finely chopped truffles. Whip ⅓ cup heavy cream and fold into the mixture. Use with fish, chicken, and egg dishes. Makes approximately 2 cups.

SAUCE GASCONNE

Reduce 1 cup chicken or veal stock to ½ cup. Add 1 teaspoon chopped chives, ¼ teaspoon each dried chervil and tarragon, and 2 teaspoons chopped parsley. Strain and reduce the mixture to a near glaze. Add 2 cups Allemande Sauce and heat to boiling point. Blend in anchovy paste to taste. Use with seafood, egg, and vegetable dishes. Makes approximately 2 cups.

SAUCE POULETTE

Cook ½ cup minced mushrooms in 1 tablespoon butter over medium heat until they begin to brown. Add 2 cups Allemande Sauce and bring to boiling point. Remove from heat and stir in 2 teaspoons lemon juice and 1 teaspoon chopped parsley. Serve with fish, brains, eggs, and poultry. Makes approximately 2 cups.

SAUCE REGENCE

Cook ½ cup finely diced mushroom stems in ¾ cup water until mushrooms are tender, about 5 minutes. Strain off the water and place it in a saucepan with ½ cup white Rhine wine. (Discard mushroom stems.) Cook until the liquid is reduced to ½ the original amount. Stir in 2 cups Allemande Sauce, 2 teaspoons finely chopped truffles, and a dash of cayenne. Heat only until hot. Serve with sweetbreads, oven roasts, and braised chicken. Makes approximately 2¼ cups.

SICILIAN SAUCE

Combine ¼ cup each tomato purée, pimiento purée, and chicken stock with 2 cups Allemande Sauce. Mix well. Stir and cook over low heat only until hot. (Do not boil.) Serve with fish and egg dishes. Makes approximately 2½ cups.

Sauce Normande and Variations

⚜ SAUCE NORMANDE

1 tablespoon flour
2 tablespoons (¼ stick) butter, melted
1 cup fish stock, or oyster or mussel liquor
¼ cup mushroom stock
2 large egg yolks
⅓ cup heavy cream
dash cayenne
salt and ground white pepper to taste
1 tablespoon Sauternes (optional)

Blend flour with butter. Stir and cook until it starts to turn golden. Remove from heat and add stocks. Mix well. Bring to boiling point and simmer 10 minutes or until thickened, stirring frequently. Blend egg yolks with cream. Add to the sauce. Heat only until hot (do not boil). Add cayenne and salt and pepper to taste. Strain. Add Sauternes if desired. Use with fish and shellfish. Makes approximately 1 ¼ cups.

VARIATIONS

ANCHOVY SAUCE

To Sauce Normande recipe add 1 teaspoon anchovy paste or 1 finely diced anchovy fillet. Strain. Use with fish.

SAUCE DIPLOMATE

To Sauce Normande recipe add 2 tablespoons finely chopped lobster meat and 1 teaspoon finely chopped truffles. Strain. Use with fish and shellfish.

SAUCE ECOSSAISE II

Cook 1 tablespoon each finely diced carrots, celery, turnips, and leeks or onions in 2 tablespoons butter until vegetables are tender. Blend with Sauce Normande along with 1 teaspoon finely chopped truffles. Strain. Use with fish.

SAUCE NORMANDE WITH OYSTERS

Poach 1 dozen small oysters in their own liquor only until edges curl. Remove oysters and chop fine. Strain liquor and reduce to one-half the original amount. Add to Sauce Normande along with the finely chopped oysters. Add salt and ground white pepper to taste. Strain. Use with fish and oysters. Makes approximately 1 ¾ to 2 cups.

SAUCE JOINVILLE

Add 1 tablespoon each finely chopped cooked shrimp and crayfish and 1 teaspoon finely chopped truffles to Sauce Normande. Strain. Use with shellfish.

SAUCE LAQUIPIÈRE

Add 2 tablespoons sherry and 1 teaspoon finely chopped truffles to Sauce Normande. Strain. Use with fish.

White Wine Sauces with a Fish Velouté Base

⚜ WHITE WINE SAUCE

4 cups fish Velouté Sauce
2 cups fish stock
1 cup (2 sticks) butter
juice of half a lemon
dry white wine

Add fish stock to the Velouté Sauce. Reduce over high heat to 1 quart. Remove from heat; blend in the butter and lemon juice. Add white wine until sauce is of the desired consistency. Strain and butter the surface. Makes approximately 5 cups.

⚜ GLAZED WHITE WINE SAUCE I

4 cups fish stock
2 cups heavy cream
¼ cup (½ stick) butter
juice of half a lemon
dash cayenne
dry white wine

Reduce the stock to a glaze, add cream, and reduce to the consistency of sauce. Remove from heat and allow to cool a little (this is important). Beat in the butter. Stir in lemon juice and cayenne. Add wine until sauce is of desired consistency. Makes about 2 cups.

⚜ GLAZED WHITE WINE SAUCE II

1¾ cups fish Velouté Sauce
⅓ cup fish stock
⅓ cup dry white wine
1 shallot, chopped
2 large egg yolks
1 tablespoon fish stock
¼ cup (½ stick) butter
salt and ground white pepper to taste

Combine the first 4 ingredients in a 1½-quart saucepan. Boil down to one-half the original amount. Mix egg yolks with the 1 tablespoon fish stock and gradually add to the sauce. Stir and cook over low heat ½ minute. Add butter and stir until melted. Season to taste with salt and white pepper. Makes approximately 1¼ cups.

⚜ SAUCE BERCY

4 shallots, chopped
1½ tablespoons butter
1⅓ cups white wine
1⅓ cups fish stock
2⅔ cups fish Velouté Sauce
1 teaspoon lemon juice
1 tablespoon chopped parsley

Cook shallots in butter until they are limp and transparent (do not brown). Add wine and fish stock and boil down to one-third the original amount. Add Velouté Sauce and heat only to boiling point. Remove from heat and add butter, lemon juice, and parsley. Serve with fish. Makes approximately 3 cups.

⚜ SAUCE MARINIÈRE

½ cup mussel liquor
3 large egg yolks
2 cups Bercy Sauce
1 tablespoon butter or margarine
¼ cup (½ stick) butter or margarine
salt and ground white pepper to taste

Reduce mussel liquor to one-half the original amount. Blend egg yolks with Bercy Sauce and add to the mussel liquor with the butter. Season to taste with salt and pepper. Use with fish dishes. Makes approximately 2¼ cups.

⚜ SAUCE COMTESSE

2 cups fish Velouté Sauce
½ cup dry white wine
¼ cup heavy cream
1 anchovy
2 tablespoons butter
1 teaspoon lemon juice

Mix Velouté Sauce with wine in a 1-quart saucepan. Cook until the quantity is reduced by one-third. Add cream. Heat only to boiling point. Mash anchovy to a pulp, blend with butter, and add to the sauce along with lemon juice. Season with salt and pepper to taste. Use with fish and egg dishes. Makes approximately 1 ¾ cups.

⚜ SAUCE GRANDVILLE

¾ cup diced mushrooms
4 tablespoons (½ stick) butter
2 cups fish Velouté Sauce
½ cup dry white wine
1 tablespoon finely chopped truffles
⅓ cup cooked shrimp, peeled and deveined
salt and ground white pepper to taste

Cook mushrooms in 2 tablespoons of the butter and strain the liquid into Velouté Sauce, reserving mushrooms. Add wine, mix well, and cook sauce until it has reduced to 2 cups. Add remaining butter, reserved mushrooms, truffles, and shrimp. Season to taste with salt and ground white pepper. Use with fish puddings, soufflés, and other fish dishes. Makes approximately 2 ¼ cups.

⚜ HUNGARIAN SAUCE (*Sauce Hongroise Maigre*)

½ cup chopped onion
3 tablespoons butter
½ cup dry white wine
2 cups fish Velouté Sauce
2 tablespoons paprika
bouquet garni, small
salt and ground white pepper to taste

Cook onion in butter until limp but not browned. Add wine and reduce the quantity by one-half. Stir in the next 3 ingredients. Simmer 5 minutes. Remove from heat and add remaining butter and salt and pepper to taste. Use with fish or egg dishes. Makes approximately 2 cups.

⚜ MATELOTE SAUCE (*White*)

½ cup sliced mushroom stems
½ cup dry white wine
2 cups fish Velouté Sauce
¼ cup (½ stick) butter
salt and ground white pepper to taste

Cook mushrooms in wine until they are tender and the quantity has been reduced by one-half. Strain into Velouté Sauce. Stir and cook 2 to 3 minutes.

Add butter. Season to taste with salt and pepper. Use with fish and egg dishes. Makes approximately 2 cups.

⚜ SAUCE ORLEANNAISE

¼ cup chopped mushroom stems
½ cup fish stock
2 cups fish Velouté Sauce
¼ cup dry white wine
¼ cup mashed, cooked, minced crayfish
2 tablespoons butter
salt and ground white pepper to taste

Cook mushroom stems in fish stock until stock has reduced to one-half the original amount. Strain into the Velouté Sauce. Add wine. Stir and cook 3 minutes. Stir in crayfish and butter. Season to taste with salt and pepper. Use with seafood dishes and eggs. Makes 2¼ cups.

⚜ SAUCE POMPADOUR

½ cup fish stock
½ cup dry white wine
2 cups fish Velouté Sauce
1 tablespoon truffles, cut into julienne strips
¼ cup cooked, mashed, minced crayfish
2 tablespoons butter
salt and ground white pepper to taste

Cook fish stock and wine together until the liquid is reduced by one-half. Add to Velouté Sauce. Bring to boiling point. Add the next 3 ingredients. Season to taste with salt and pepper. Use with fish dishes. Makes 2½ cups.

⚜ SAUCE SAINT MÂLO

4 shallots
1 tablespoon water
½ cup dry white wine
2 cups fish Velouté Sauce
1 teaspoon powdered mustard
1 tablespoon water
2 tablespoons butter
salt and ground white pepper

Chop shallots, transfer to an electric blender, add 1 tablespoon water, and blend into a purée. Reserve 1 tablespoon and mix the remainder with the wine. Cook until the liquid has reduced by one-half. Add Velouté Sauce. Mix mustard with water and let stand 5 minutes to develop flavor. Then add to the sauce and bring to boiling point. Remove from heat and stir in the remaining 1 tablespoon shallot purée and the butter. Season to taste with salt and pepper. Use with grilled fish. Makes 2 cups.

⚜ SHRIMP SAUCE II

2 cups fish Velouté Sauce
½ cup fish stock
¼ cup heavy cream
¼ cup minced, cooked, peeled, and deveined shrimp
2 tablespoons minced cooked lobster
¼ cup (½ stick) butter
salt and ground white pepper to taste
whole cooked shrimp, peeled and deveined

Combine the first 3 ingredients in a 1½-quart saucepan. Reduce over moderate heat to 2 cups. Remove from heat and stir in minced shrimps, lobster, and butter. Heat only until hot. Season to taste with salt and pepper. Garnish with whole cooked shrimps. Use over seafood dishes. Makes approximately 2½ cups.

Other Types of French Sauces

Certain types of sauces, though equally characteristic of French cookery, have features which distinguish them from the brown sauces and white sauces already described. These include chaud-froid sauces—jellied sauces which can be based on Béchamel, Velouté, or Brown Sauce; tomato sauces; Hollandaise and related cooked emulsion sauces; mayonnaises and other cold emulsion sauces; and various butters and butter sauces.

CHAUD-FROID SAUCES

A classic chaud-froid sauce is actually a jellied white sauce. It is used to coat shapely and elegant cooked cold dishes—fish, chicken, ham, roasts, and other dishes for cold buffets.

The authentic French method of making chaud-froid is by cooking Velouté or Béchamel Sauce, white stock, heavy cream, and jellied veal, chicken, or fish stock (see Jellies) together until the liquid is reduced to the desired consistency and will coat a spoon, the cream and jelly being added to the other ingredients a little at a time (see Chaud-froid Sauce I). The kind of stock and jelly used is determined by the food to be coated. If jelly is not available, a very good and easily made coating sauce can be made by softening 1 envelope unflavored commercial gelatin in ¼ cup dry white wine or dry vermouth (or stock or water) and stirring it into 2 cups hot Velouté or Béchamel Sauce. The sauce is then strained and cooled but not refrigerated.

Another method, used frequently in the United States to make a chaud-froid sauce that looks like the classic French sauce, is to simmer stock or consommé and heavy cream with herbs (parsley, tarragon, thyme, onion, etc.) for about 10 minutes, then stir softened unflavored gelatin into the hot liquid (see Chaud-froid Sauce II).

Chaud-froid may also be made with Brown Sauce. This is especially appropriate for some meat and chicken dishes, and some cooks prefer it because of its appetizing brown color.

To apply a chaud-froid sauce, first thoroughly chill the food, then coat it with the sauce and refrigerate until the coating is almost set (about 2 hours). If the first coat is not thick enough, apply another one and again refrigerate. Decorations are then applied to the food; they may be as simple or as elaborate as desired. Finally coat the whole with a thin layer of clear liquid aspic.

The decorations may be strips of pimiento, eggplant peel, and green sweet pepper, lemon and orange rinds, thinly sliced ham and tongue, sliced hard-cooked eggs and cucumbers, green olives or ripe olives, thin carrot slices, cooked green peas, truffles, mushrooms, chives, and the stems and leaves of herbs. Dip decorations in clear aspic before placing them on the coated food. To make stems and leaves of herbs more pliable for decorative purposes, dip them in boiling water for about ½ minute and dry them well.

Always test the chaud-froid sauce before you start to work with it. Pour a little into a small chilled dish and refrigerate it 10 to 15 minutes. If it does not set in this time, add a little melted softened gelatin and test again.

⚜ CHAUD-FROID SAUCE I (*Classic French Method*)

4 tablespoons flour
4 tablespoons (½ stick) butter, melted
2 cups chicken, veal, or fish stock
2 cups chicken, veal, or fish jelly
¾ cup heavy cream
salt and ground white pepper to taste

Blend flour with butter. Stir and cook 1 minute. Remove from heat and stir in stock (the kind depends upon the food to be coated). Mix well. Stir and cook slowly 10 minutes or until mixture is smooth and thick. Add jelly and cream, a little of each at a time, and reduce until the sauce is of desired consistency and will coat a metal spoon. Add salt and pepper to taste. Strain. Whip the sauce until it is quite cold. Do not refrigerate until it has been spooned over the food. Makes approximately 2½ cups.

⚜ CHAUD-FROID SAUCE II (*With Commercial Gelatin*)

In the preceding recipe, omit the jelly and reduce the amount of cream to ¼ cup. Soften 1 envelope unflavored gelatin in ¼ cup dry white wine or vermouth (or stock or water) and add to the hot sauce. Strain and cool. Makes approximately 2 cups.

⚜ BROWN CHAUD-FROID SAUCE

Use either of the two preceding recipes for Chaud-froid Sauce, making the following changes: (1) Cook flour with butter until the mixture has browned but not burned. (2) Replace light stock with brown stock.

⚜ CHAUD-FROID SAUCE III

1½ cups rich chicken, veal, or fish stock, or canned chicken broth or consommé
1 cup heavy cream
1 small onion, sliced
¼ cup diced carrots
¼ teaspoon dried or 1 teaspoon chopped fresh thyme or tarragon
salt and ground white pepper to taste
1 envelope unflavored gelatin
¼ cup dry white wine, vermouth, stock, or water

Place the first 5 ingredients in a 1½-quart saucepan and bring to boiling point. Reduce heat and simmer until the liquid has reduced to 2 cups. Add salt and pepper to taste. Soften gelatin in wine, stock, or water and add to the sauce. Strain and cool. Makes approximately 2¼ cups.

⚜ GREEN CHAUD-FROID SAUCE

Add 2 tablespoons cooked puréed green herbs (parsley, chervil, tarragon, or thyme) to 2 cups of any of the preceding chaud-froid sauces. Strain and cool.

⚜ CHAUD-FROID À L'INDIENNE

Cook 2 tablespoons chopped onion and 1 teaspoon curry powder in 1 tablespoon butter until onion is limp. Add to each 2 cups of any of the preceding chaud-froid sauces. Strain through a double thickness of cheesecloth or a very fine sieve.

⚜ CHAUD-FROID MADEIRA

Add Madeira (or sherry) to taste to any of the preceding chaud-froid recipes. Strain and cool.

⚜ CHAUD-FROID NANTUA

Add 2 tablespoons crayfish purée to each cup of any chaud-froid sauce. Strain and cool.

⚜ PAPRIKA CHAUD-FROID

Add 1 teaspoon paprika to each cup of any chaud-froid sauce and stir in a dash of cayenne.

⚜ CHAUD-FROID ROSÉ

Add ¼ cup of thick tomato purée to each 2 cups of any chaud-froid sauce, mix well, strain, and cool.

⚜ CHAUD-FROID ROYALE

Add 2 tablespoons truffle purée to each 2 cups of any chaud-froid sauce, mix well, strain, and cool.

⚜ CHAUD-FROID SIBÉRIENNE (*With Saffron*)

Steep ⅛ teaspoon crumbed saffron strands in 1 tablespoon boiling stock or water 10 minutes. Strain into 2 cups of any chaud-froid sauce.

⚜ YELLOW CHAUD-FROID SAUCE

Mix 1 tablespoon cream with 3 large egg yolks and blend with any chaud-froid sauce before removing from heat.

TOMATO SAUCES

⚜ TOMATO SAUCE

½ cup finely diced carrots
¼ cup finely diced celery
¼ cup finely diced onions
1 small clove of garlic, cut in half
3 tablespoons butter or olive oil
4 tablespoons flour
2½ cups diced fresh or canned tomatoes
1½ cups brown stock, or 2 beef bouillon cubes and 1½ cups water
½ bay leaf
¼ teaspoon each dried thyme and oregano or 1 teaspoon each fresh
⅛ teaspoon ground black pepper
1 teaspoon sugar
2 teaspoons salt or salt to taste

Cook the first 4 ingredients in butter or oil until onions are tender but not browned. Remove and discard garlic. Remove from heat and blend in flour. Stir and cook until flour is brown. Add remaining ingredients. Bring to boiling point and boil gently 1 hour or until sauce has thickened, stirring frequently. Run sauce through a sieve. Heat again. Use with fish, shellfish, meat, and vegetables. Makes approximately 2½ cups.

VARIATIONS

SAUCE CREOLE

Cook 1 tablespoon chopped shallots in 1 tablespoon butter until shallots are tender, but not brown. Add ½ cup dry white wine and reduce the original amount by one-third. Add to recipe for Tomato Sauce. Cook ½ cup diced green or red sweet pepper in 2 tablespoons butter or oil until peppers are tender. Add to sauce mixture and cook 10 minutes. Strain through a sieve. Use with fish, shellfish, chicken, and vegetables. Makes approximately 2¾ cups.

TOMATO MEAT SAUCE

Brown ½ pound (1 cup) ground raw chuck in 1 tablespoon bacon drippings or other fat and add to the strained Tomato Sauce. Adjust seasonings. Use with meats, eggplant, or spaghetti. Makes approximately 3¼ cups.

TOMATO SHRIMP SAUCE

To the recipe for Tomato Sauce, add 1 tablespoon chili sauce, 1/4 cup finely chopped green olives, 1/3 cup sautéed chopped mushrooms, and 1/2 cup diced cooked or canned shrimp. Stir and cook 5 minutes. Remove from heat and add 2 tablespoons chopped parsley. Use with fish, spaghetti, or eggplant. Makes approximately 3 cups.

⚜ SAUCE PORTUGAISE

1/3 cup finely chopped onion
1 small clove of garlic
3 tablespoons butter or olive oil
4 medium-sized tomatoes, diced, or 2 cups canned tomtatoes
1 cup fish stock
1/2 bay leaf
1/2 cup thick tomato purée
2 teaspoons chopped fresh or 1/2 teaspoon dried basil
2 teaspoons chopped fresh or 1/2 teaspoon dried thyme
1/2 teaspoon sugar
salt and ground black pepper to taste
2 tablespoons chopped parsley

Cook onions and garlic in 2 tablespoons of the butter or oil until onions are soft. Remove and discard garlic. Add the next 3 ingredients and cook gently 30 minutes or until sauce has thickened. Add tomato purée, herbs, sugar, salt, and pepper. Stir and cook 5 minutes. Strain through a sieve. Add parsley and remaining butter or oil. Use with fish. Makes approximately 2 1/4 cups.

⚜ SAUCE PROVENÇALE

3 chopped shallots
1 small clove of garlic
1/3 cup olive oil or cooking oil
3 pounds (12 small or 9 medium-sized) tomatoes, diced, or 1 quart canned tomatoes
1 cup veal stock
1/2 cup chopped parsley
1 teaspoon sugar
salt and ground black pepper to taste

Cook shallots and garlic in oil until shallots are soft. Remove and discard garlic. Add the next 4 ingredients. Cook gently 40 to 50 minutes, or until sauce has thickened. Season to taste with salt and pepper. Strain through a sieve. Use with eggs, fish, chicken, meat, and vegetables. Makes approximately 3 cups.

HOLLANDAISE AND RELATED SAUCES

⚜ HOLLANDAISE SAUCE

¾ cup (1½ sticks) butter
3 large egg yolks, well beaten
4 teaspoons lemon juice
dash of each salt and cayenne

Break butter into 3 pieces. Put 1 piece into the top of a double boiler. Add egg yolks and lemon juice. Beat with a wire whisk constantly while cooking over hot water (not boiling) until butter is melted. Add the second piece of butter, continue beating and cooking until the mixture thickens, never allowing the water to boil. Then add the last piece of butter. Stir and cook until sauce has thickened. Remove from heat and stir in salt and cayenne. Serve with fish, shellfish, and vegetables. Or, if desired, use as the base for one of the following variations.

Should the Hollandaise mixture curdle, add 1½ tablespoons boiling water, beating constantly, to rebuild the emulsion. Makes ¾ cup.

VARIATIONS

ANCHOVY HOLLANDAISE (*Sauce Arlesienne*)

To ¾ cup Hollandaise Sauce, stir in ½ teaspoon anchovy paste or anchovy paste to taste. Serve over fish, eggs, and vegetables. Makes ¾ cup.

CAVIAR HOLLANDAISE (*Sauce Marquis*)

To ¾ cup Hollandaise Sauce, add a 1-ounce jar of black caviar. Serve over fish, eggs, and asparagus. Makes ¾ cup.

CUCUMBER HOLLANDAISE

To ¾ cup Hollandaise Sauce, add 1½ cups well-drained, finely chopped, peeled cucumbers. Serve with fish and shellfish. Makes approximately 2 cups.

CURRY HOLLANDAISE

To ¾ cup Hollandaise Sauce, add 1 teaspoon curry powder. Serve on fish, shellfish, and eggs. Makes ¾ cup.

SAUCE FIGARO

To ¾ cup Hollandaise Sauce, add 2 tablespoons tomato purée and 1½ teaspoons tomato paste, 1 teaspoon finely chopped parsley, and a dash each of salt and cayenne. Serve with fish. Makes 1 scant cup.

LEMON HOLLANDAISE

To ¾ cup Hollandaise Sauce (made with lemon), add ¼ teaspoon grated lemon rind or lemon rind to taste. Serve over vegetables and fish. Makes ¾ cup.

SAUCE MOUSSELINE

Into ¾ cup Hollandaise Sauce fold ⅓ cup heavy cream, whipped, after the last piece of butter is added. Stir and cook 1 minute over hot water (not boiling). Serve on vegetables and fish. Makes 1 generous cup.

MUSTARD HOLLANDAISE

Replace lemon juice in recipe for Hollandaise Sauce with 1½ tablespoons tarragon vinegar. Mix 1½ teaspoons powdered mustard with 1 tablespoon water and let stand 5 minutes for flavor to develop. Stir into the sauce. Serve with fish, shellfish, chicken, and eggs. Makes ¾ cup.

ORANGE HOLLANDAISE (*Sauce Maltaise*)

To ¾ cup Hollandaise Sauce, add 2 tablespoons orange juice and ½ teaspoon grated orange rind. Serve on asparagus or whole string beans. Makes 1 scant cup.

SAUCE PALOISE

To ¾ cup Hollandaise Sauce, add 1 tablespoon mint infusion at the time the last piece of butter is added. Just before serving, fold in 1 teaspoon chopped fresh mint. Serve with lamb or veal. Makes ¾ cup.

SAUCE VALOIS

To ¾ cup Hollandaise Sauce, add ¾ teaspoon melted beef extract or ¼ beef bouillon cube dissolved in 2 teaspoons boiling water. Serve with eggs and broiled chicken. Makes ¾ cup.

⚜ BÉARNAISE SAUCE

To ¾ cup Hollandaise Sauce, add 1 tablespoon tarragon vinegar and 1 teaspoon each chopped fresh parsley, tarragon, and chervil. (If fresh herbs are not available, use ¼ teaspoon each of the dried herbs.) Serve with broiled or baked fish and meats. Makes ¾ cup.

⚜ SAUCE CHORON

To ¾ cup Béarnaise Sauce, add 1 to 1½ teaspoons tomato purée, and omit herbs. Serve with fish, vegetables, and chicken. Makes ¾ cup.

MAYONNAISE AND OTHER COLD EMULSION SAUCES

⚜ MAYONNAISE

2 large raw egg yolks or 1 large whole egg
½ teaspoon salt or salt to taste
¼ teaspoon paprika
1/16 teaspoon ground white pepper
dash of cayenne
2 tablespoons lemon juice or vinegar
1 cup salad oil

Put eggs and seasonings in a 1-quart bowl. Beat well. Beat in 1 tablespoon of the vinegar. Gradually beat in oil, ½ teaspoon at a time, until ¼ cup is added. Then beat in from 1 to 2 tablespoons oil at a time, beating well after each addition. Add remaining lemon juice or vinegar after ½ cup oil is added. Beat in remaining oil. Use for salads, sandwiches, and sauces. Makes approximately 1¼ cups.

If Mayonnaise curdles when making, add another egg yolk and continue as directed above.

VARIATIONS

COATING MAYONNAISE

Soften 1½ teaspoons unflavored gelatin in cold water. Melt in a pan of hot (not boiling) water and stir into 1 cup Mayonnaise. Use to coat cold dishes where regular Mayonnaise may have a tendency to slip off. This Mayonnaise may also be forced through a decorating tube to make designs on salads and mousses. Makes 1 cup.

SAUCE BERLINOISE

To 1 cup Mayonnaise, add 2 tablespoons red currant jelly and 1 teaspoon grated lemon rind. Beat with a fork. Use with fruit salads. Makes 1 generous cup.

SAUCE DIJONNAISE

Add prepared Dijon mustard to taste to Mayonnaise. Use for egg, meat, poultry, fish, and shellfish salads.

MAYONNAISE ESPAGNOLE

To 1 cup Mayonnaise, add ⅓ cup finely chopped, cooked lean ham, 1 tablespoon paprika, and 1/16 teaspoon minced garlic. Use for meat and egg salads. Makes 1⅓ cups.

GREEN MAYONNAISE (*Sauce Vert*)

To 1 cup Mayonnaise, add 1 tablespoon each finely chopped parsley, watercress, chervil, and tarragon leaves. Add ½ tablespoon sieved, chopped, cooked spinach. Adjust seasonings with a little lemon juice, salt, and ground black pepper to taste. Use with vegetables, eggs, fish, and shellfish. Makes 1 generous cup.

HORSERADISH MAYONNAISE

Blend 1 cup Mayonnaise with 1 tablespoon each well-drained horseradish sauce, black caviar, and chopped fresh parsley. Use for egg or seafood salads. Makes 1 generous cup.

ROQUEFORT MAYONNAISE

To each cup Mayonnaise, add ½ cup finely crumbled Roquefort or Blue cheese and sour cream. Add a dash of cayenne. Use with apple, fruit, celery, cabbage, and potato salads. Makes 2 cups.

⚜ SAUCE AMÉRICAINE (*Lobster Mayonnaise*)

To 1 cup Mayonnaise, add ½ cup puréed cooked lobster, 1 tablespoon each paprika and chopped parsley, and 1 teaspoon powdered mustard soaked in 1 tablespoon water. Use with fish, shellfish, eggs, and vegetables. Makes 1½ cups.

⚜ SAUCE ANTIBOISE

To 1 cup Mayonnaise, add 1 teaspoon anchovy paste (or to taste), ¼ teaspoon dried or ¾ teaspoon chopped fresh tarragon, and 2 tablespoons thick tomato purée. Use with vegetables, fish, and shellfish. Makes 1 generous cup.

⚜ CYPRIOTE SAUCE

Sieve 3 large hard-cooked egg yolks and mix with 1 mashed anchovy and ¼ cup thick Tomato Sauce. Blend with 1 cup Mayonnaise and 1/16 to ⅛ teaspoon ground fennel seed. Use with fish, egg, and vegetable salads. Makes approximately 1½ cups.

⚜ GRIMOD SAUCE

Cut enough truffles in short julienne strips to make 2 tablespoons. Simmer until almost dry in ⅓ cup sherry. Add to 1 cup Mayonnaise. Use with chicken and ham salads. Makes 1 generous cup.

⚜ RAVIGOTE MAYONNAISE

To 1 cup Mayonnaise, add ¼ teaspoon anchovy paste, 1 finely chopped hard-cooked egg white, and 1 tablespoon lemon juice. Cook 2 tablespoons each chopped parsley, fresh chervil, capers, onions, and shallots in ¼ cup dry white wine until all but 1 tablespoon liquid is evaporated. Cool. Add to Mayonnaise mixture. Chill. Use with eggs, fish, and shellfish. Makes a scant 1¼ cups.

⚜ RÉMOULADE SAUCE

1 cup Mayonnaise
2 tablespoons Dijon or Creole prepared mustard
1 tablespoon each finely chopped parsley, celery, capers, and gherkin pickle
1 teaspoon each chopped fresh tarragon and chervil, or ¼ teaspoon each of the dried herbs
1 mashed anchovy

Combine all ingredients. Use for fish, shellfish, and egg salads, for fried or broiled fish. Makes approximately 1⅓ cups.

⚜ RÉMOULADE À L'INDIENNE

Cook 2 tablespoons minced onion and 2 teaspoons curry powder in 1 tablespoon salad oil 2 to 3 minutes and rub through a sieve. Blend with 1 cup Mayonnaise, along with 1 tablespoon chopped capers, 1 tablespoon fresh chives, ¼ teaspoon dried tarragon, ⅛ teaspoon fennel seeds, and ½ teaspoon anchovy paste. Use for fish, shellfish, and eggs. Makes 1 generous cup.

⚜ TARTARE SAUCE I

To 1 cup Mayonnaise, add 1 tablespoon each finely chopped parsley, gherkin pickle, green olives, and capers, and ½ teaspoon paprika. Use for fried or broiled fish, fried oysters, frogs' legs, and scallops. Makes approximately 1¼ cups.

⚜ TARTARE SAUCE II

To 1 cup Mayonnaise, add 1 sieved large hard-cooked egg and 1 teaspoon each chopped parsley and chives. Adjust seasonings to taste with salt and ground black pepper. Serve with grilled or broiled fish and shellfish. Makes 1¼ cups.

⚜ AIOLI SAUCE

1 hot medium-sized cooked potato
1 small clove of garlic
2 large hard-cooked egg yolks
3 large raw egg yolks
3 tablespoons lemon juice
2 cups salad oil
salt and ground white pepper to taste

Mash potato until smooth. Put garlic through a garlic press and add. Put cooked egg yolks through a sieve and add. Mix well. Beat in raw egg yolks. Gradually beat in oil. Add salt and ground white pepper to taste. Use for potato, egg, fish, shellfish, vegetable, and meat salads. Makes approximately 3 cups.

BUTTERS AND BUTTER SAUCES

Special Butters

⚜ BROWN BUTTER (*Beurre Noisette*)

Melt butter over very low heat until it is hazelnut brown. Serve over fish and vegetables. (It is important that this butter be browned over very low heat for best flavor.) To serve over grilled fish, allow 2 teaspoons browned butter per serving. For 6 servings of cooked vegetables, allow ¼ cup browned butter.

⚜ BLACK BUTTER (*Beurre Noir*)

Melt ½ cup (1 stick) butter and cook over moderately low heat until dark brown, being careful not to burn the butter. Remove from heat. Add 2 tablespoons chopped parsley and lemon juice to taste. Use with calf's brains and vegetables. Makes ½ cup.

⚜ CLARIFIED BUTTER

Melt butter over hot water. Pour off the butter and discard the milky sediment left in the bottom of the saucepan or cup. Used for some sauces, as curry sauce, and for some fine pastries.

⚜ THICKENED BUTTER (*Beurre Manié*)

Blend ¾ cup sifted flour with 1 cup (2 sticks) butter. Store in a covered jar in the refrigerator. Use for sauces and gravies. Makes approximately 1½ cups.

Mixed Butters

⚜ ANCHOVY BUTTER

1 tablespoon anchovy paste or 2 canned anchovies, mashed
½ cup (1 stick) butter, softened
lemon juice

Blend anchovies with butter until well mixed. Add lemon juice to taste. Use on broiled or poached fish. Makes ½ cup.

⚜ CAPER BUTTER

Melt ½ cup (1 stick) butter over low heat. Skim off and discard foam. Stir in 1 tablespoon lemon juice, 3 tablespoons capers, and salt and ground white pepper to taste. Serve with calf's brains, vegetables, eggs, and fish. Makes ½ cup.

⚜ GARLIC BUTTER

2 large cloves of garlic
½ cup (1 stick) butter, softened
2 tablespoons chopped parsley (optional)

Boil unpeeled garlic cloves in water to cover for 5 to 6 seconds. Drain off water, peel garlic, and rinse in cold water. Bring to boiling point again in water to cover and boil ½ minute. Remove from water and rinse. Put through a garlic press or pound to a smooth paste in a mortar. Add to butter along with parsley. Season with salt, pepper, and other herbs, if desired. Use on steaks. Makes ½ cup.

⚜ HERB BUTTER

Blend ¼ cup softened butter with any of the following herb combinations:

- 1 teaspoon chopped fresh rosemary or ¼ teaspoon dried rosemary and 1 tablespoon chopped parsley.
- 2 teaspoons chopped fresh thyme or ½ teaspoon dried thyme and 1 tablespoon chopped parsley.
- 2 teaspoons chopped fresh tarragon or ½ teaspoon dried tarragon and 1 tablespoon chopped parsley.
- 2 tablespoons chopped watercress and 1 teaspoon chopped fresh parsley.
- 1 tablespoon chopped parsley and 2 tablespoons chopped chives.

Makes approximately ¼ cup.

⚜ HORSERADISH BUTTER

Push 2 tablespoons grated horseradish through a sieve and blend with ½ cup (1 stick) softened butter. Use for meats. Makes ½ cup.

LOBSTER BUTTER

Break up and pound shells from 2 cooked lobsters, plus any of the creamy parts that may cling to inside of shells. Place in the top part of a double boiler along with 1 cup (2 sticks) butter. Melt slowly over hot water. Strain through a double thickness of cheesecloth. Cool. Store in a covered jar in the refrigerator to use for adding flavor to fish sauces. Makes 1 cup.

MÂITRE D'HÔTEL BUTTER

Blend 2 tablespoons chopped parsley and 1 tablespoon lemon juice into ½ cup (1 stick) softened butter. Season to taste with salt and ground white pepper. Use with chicken and fish dishes. Makes ½ cup.

MUSTARD BUTTER

Mix 2 teaspoons powdered mustard with 1 tablespoon water and let stand 5 minutes to develop flavor. Then blend with ½ cup (1 stick) softened butter. Use with fish, ham, and beef and as butter for canapés.

NUT BUTTER

⅓ cup toasted hazelnuts or almonds
½ cup (1 stick) butter

Put half the nuts at a time into the glass container of an electric blender. Turn on blender and run 4 to 6 seconds or until nuts are very fine. Mix with butter. Use in cream sauces. Makes ¾ cup.

PAPRIKA BUTTER

1 shallot, finely chopped
2 tablespoons butter
1 teaspoon paprika
¼ cup (½ stick) butter, softened

Cook shallots in the 2 tablespoons butter until they are golden. Stir in paprika. Cool. Blend with the remaining ¼ cup butter. Serve with broiled poultry or fish. Makes a generous ¼ cup.

SMOKED SALMON BUTTER

Mince and sieve smoked salmon to make ¼ cup. Then blend with ½ cup (1 stick) softened butter. Stir in ½ teaspoon paprika and a few drops of lemon juice. Use as butter for canapés and in fish sauces. Makes ¾ cup.

⚜ TOMATO BUTTER

Cook 1 small tomato and 1 finely chopped shallot in 2 tablespoons butter until the mixture is almost dry. Put through a sieve and cool. Blend with ½ cup (1 stick) softened butter. Use with fish and white meat of poultry. Makes a generous ½ cup.

Butter Sauces

⚜ BERCY BUTTER

4 shallots, finely chopped
½ cup dry white wine
½ cup (1 stick) butter, softened
lemon juice to taste
salt and ground black pepper to taste

Cook shallots in wine until almost all the liquid has evaporated. Cool. Beat in butter. Season to taste with lemon juice, salt, and pepper. Serve on broiled steaks and chops. Makes a generous ½ cup.

⚜ SAUCE AU BEURRE (*Butter Sauce*)

3 shallots, finely chopped
½ cup dry white wine
½ cup (1 stick) butter, softened

Cook shallots in wine until half the liquid has evaporated. Strain. Reduce until almost all the liquid has evaporated. Cool. Beat in butter. Use to spread on sandwiches, corn on the cob, fish, and steaks. Makes ½ cup.

⚜ CHIVRY BUTTER

4 shallots, chopped
2 tablespoons chopped parsley
1 teaspoon chopped tarragon
2 teaspoons chopped chervil
½ cup (1 stick) butter

Blanch herbs and shallots 5 minutes in hot water to cover. Drain and dry thoroughly with a towel. Rub through a sieve. Cool and blend with butter. Serve with fish. Makes ½ cup.

BUTTER FERMIÈRE

5 large hard-cooked egg yolks
1 cup (2 sticks) sweet butter, softened
salt and ground black pepper to taste
dash cayenne
3 tablespoons dry white wine
lemon juice to taste
1 teaspoon prepared mustard (optional)

Put egg yolks through a sieve and blend with softened butter. Add salt and black pepper to taste, cayenne, wine, lemon juice, and mustard if used. Mix well. Use with fish and vegetable dishes. Makes 1⅓ cups.

BUTTER À L'INDIENNE

Cook 2 tablespoons chopped shallots in 2 tablespoons butter until tender but not browned. Add 1 teaspoon curry powder. Stir and cook 1 minute. Blend in 1 tablespoon Allemande or Béchamel Sauce. Heat ½ minute. Cool and beat in ½ cup (1 stick) softened butter. Use with fish, shellfish, poultry, and egg dishes. Makes ½ cup.

Sauces from Other Countries

A number of sauces developed by cooks outside France are worthy additions to the sauce repertoire. While most of them differ from the classic French sauces, they add interesting variety. For the convenience of the cook, they are divided here into sauces made with stock or wine, those made with oil, and fruit and herb sauces to be served with meat.

SAUCES MADE WITH STOCK OR WINE

FRIED BREAD SAUCE (*English*)

1 shallot, chopped
1 cup soft breadcrumbs
½ cup (1 stick) butter
1½ cups chicken stock
⅓ cup finely diced cooked ham
salt and ground white pepper to taste
lemon juice to taste
1 tablespoon chopped parsley

Cook shallot and breadcrumbs in butter until bread and butter are golden. Add stock and simmer 10 minutes, stirring frequently. Stir in remaining ingredients. Serve with roast game birds or poultry. Makes approximately 1 ¾ cups.

⚜ CAPER SAUCE (*English*)

2 tablespoons flour
2 tablespoons butter, melted
2 cups lamb or mutton stock
1 tablespoon capers (or capers to taste)
salt and ground black pepper to taste

Blend flour with butter. Stir and cook 1 minute. Remove from heat and add stock. Bring to boiling point and simmer 5 minutes, stirring constantly. Add remaining ingredients. Use on boiled lamb or mutton. Makes approximately 1 ½ cups.

⚜ EGG SAUCE (*English*)

4 tablespoons flour
¼ cup (½ stick) butter, melted
1½ cups milk
½ cup light stock
salt and ground white pepper to taste
6 hard-cooked eggs, diced
about ¼ cup heavy cream

Blend flour with butter. Stir and cook 1 minute. Remove from heat and add milk and stock. Bring to boiling point and cook 1 minute, or until thickened, stirring constantly. Add salt and pepper to taste and eggs. Thin to desired consistency with cream. Heat ½ minute. Serve with fish, shellfish, and vegetables. Makes approximately 2 ½ cups.

⚜ GAME PRESERVE SAUCE (*English*)

½ teaspoon whole peppercorns, crushed
2 whole cloves
½ teaspoon dried thyme
1 small bay leaf
½ cup vinegar
2 cups veal stock
1 tablespoon cornstarch
2 tablespoons water
½ cup red currant jelly
⅓ cup each currants and raisins
1 cup water

Place the first 5 ingredients in a 1-quart saucepan. Cook until the liquid is reduced to one-half the original amount. Add veal stock and reduce to one-half. Strain. Mix cornstarch with 2 tablespoons water and add. Cook 1 minute or until thickened. Stir in jelly. Bring currants and raisins to boiling point with 1 cup water. Drain and dry on paper towels. Add to the sauce. Serve with game. Makes approximately 2½ cups.

⚜ BROWN OYSTER SAUCE (*English*)

2 tablespoons flour
2 tablespoons butter, melted
½ cup oyster liquor
1 cup brown stock
12 oysters, chopped
dash cayenne
salt
ground white pepper

Blend flour with butter. Stir and cook until the mixture is light brown. Remove from heat and add oyster liquor and stock. Mix well. Bring to boiling point, stirring constantly. Stir and simmer 10 minutes. Add oysters. Cook 2 to 3 minutes. Add cayenne and salt and pepper to taste. Do not boil after adding oysters. Use for meat puddings, codfish, and grilled meats. Makes approximately 1½ cups.

⚜ SMITANE SAUCE (*Russian*)

½ cup chopped onion
2 tablespoons butter
dash salt
1 cup dry white wine
1 cup sour cream
lemon juice

Cook onions in butter until they are limp. Add salt and wine and cook until wine is reduced to ¼ cup. Add sour cream. Heat but do not boil. Add lemon juice to taste. Use with meats and vegetables. Makes approximately 1¼ cups.

SAUCES MADE WITH OIL

⚜ CAMBRIDGE SAUCE (*English*)

4 hard-cooked egg yolks
2 anchovies
1 tablespoon capers, chopped
1 tablespoon chopped chives
¼ teaspoon dried chervil
¼ teaspoon dried tarragon
1½ cups salad oil
2 tablespoons vinegar
1 tablespoon chopped parsley

Put egg yolks through a sieve. Mash anchovies and capers with herbs and add to the sieved yolks. Mix to a smooth paste. Gradually beat in oil and vinegar as for Mayonnaise. Add parsley. Serve with game, fish, and eggs. Makes approximately 1 1/4 cups.

⚜ RUSSIAN SAUCE

1/2 cup cooked or canned lobster
1 tablespoon black caviar
2 cups Mayonnaise
1 teaspoon A-1 sauce

Mash lobster and caviar to a pulp. Fold into Mayonnaise along with A-1 sauce. Serve with cold fish. Makes 2 1/2 cups.

⚜ TURKISH SAUCE

1 cup fresh breadcrumbs
3 large egg yolks
1 small clove of garlic
1 1/2 cups olive oil or salad oil
1 tablespoon lemon juice or to taste
salt and ground black pepper to taste

Mix breadcrumbs with egg yolk. Put garlic through a press and mix with crumbs. Gradually blend in the oil and lemon juice. Add salt and black pepper to taste. Use with eggs and fish. Makes approximately 1 2/3 cups.

⚜ ZISKA SAUCE (*Hungarian*)

2 teaspoons powdered mustard
1 1/2 tablespoons water
2 tablespoons chopped gherkin pickles
2 teaspoons sugar
salt to taste
1 1/2 cups salad oil
1/2 cup vinegar
black pepper to taste

Mix mustard with water and let stand 10 minutes. Then blend with remaining ingredients. Serve with cold meat. Makes approximately 2 cups.

FRUIT AND HERB SAUCES

⚜ APFELKERN (*Austrian*)

3 medium-sized raw apples, grated
1/4 cup sugar or to taste
1 tablespoon prepared horseradish (or horseradish to taste)
2 teaspoons paprika
dry white wine

Combine the apples, sugar, horseradish, and paprika. Stir in wine until sauce is of desired consistency. Use with pork, duck, and goose. Makes approximately 1½ cups.

⚜ APPLESAUCE (*English*)

4 pounds (12 medium-sized) tart cooking apples
about 1 cup boiling water
1 stick cinnamon, 2 inches long
¾ to 1 cup sugar
dash salt
¼ teaspoon ground nutmeg (optional)

Peel and slice apples. Cook in a covered saucepan with boiling water and cinnamon until apples are tender, stirring occasionally. Remove from heat, mash, and put through a sieve, if desired. Stir in sugar, salt, and nutmeg, if used. Serve with meats, poultry, and as a topping for gingerbread and cake. Makes approximately 6 cups.

⚜ DANISH APPLESAUCE

4 cups cooked sieved tart apples
¼ cup sugar (or sugar to taste)
¼ cup orange juice
1 tablespoon lemon juice
1 tablespoon grated orange rind
1 teaspoon grated lemon rind
sherry

Combine apples, sugar, orange and lemon juices, and orange and lemon rinds. Add sherry until the sauce reaches the desired consistency, stirring sherry in well. Use with game birds, duck, goose, and pork. Makes approximately 4½ cups.

⚜ GOURMET APPLESAUCE (*American*)

2 pounds (6 medium-sized) tart cooking apples
¾ cup orange juice
½ to ¾ cup light brown sugar
2 teaspoons grated orange rind
dash of salt

Peel and slice apples. Place in a 2-quart saucepan with orange juice. Cover and cook until apples are soft. Remove from heat, add sugar, orange rind, and salt. Mash and put through a sieve, if desired. Serve with poultry and meats. Makes approximately 3 cups.

⚜ SANFORD SAUCE (*American*)

2 cups cooked applesauce
1 tablespoon prepared horseradish (or horseradish to taste)
½ cup heavy cream, whipped

Combine applesauce and horseradish. Fold in whipped cream. Serve with duck, goose, and pork. Makes approximately 2 ¾ cups.

⚜ SWEDISH APPLESAUCE

1 pound (3 medium-sized) tart apples
½ cup dry white wine
½ cup Mayonnaise
grated horseradish to taste

Peel and slice apples. Cook in wine in a covered saucepan until apples are tender and sauce is thick. Remove from heat and cool. Fold in Mayonnaise and grated horseradish to taste. Use with pork, duck, and goose. Makes approximately 2 cups.

⚜ CRANBERRY RELISH (*American*)

1 pound raw cranberries
1 medium-sized navel orange
2 cups sugar

Wash cranberries and set aside to drain. Peel the orange, being careful not to include the white bitter portion, and grate the rind. Set aside. Peel off and discard the white portion of the orange. Put peeled orange through a food chopper along with cranberries, using the medium blade. Add orange rind and sugar. Mix well. This relish will keep several weeks in a covered jar in the refrigerator. Use with poultry and meats. Makes approximately 4 cups.

⚜ CRANBERRY SAUCE (*American*)

1 pound raw cranberries
¾ cup water or orange juice
1½ to 2 cups sugar

Wash cranberries and place in a saucepan. Add water or orange juice. Cook, covered, until skins burst, 8 to 10 minutes. Remove from heat and add sugar (the amount depends upon the sweetness desired). Cool. Serve with poultry or meats. Makes approximately 3 ½ cups.

⚜ CUMBERLAND SAUCE (*English*)

1 teaspoon powdered mustard
1 tablespoon water
¼ teaspoon each salt, ground ginger, and cloves
½ cup seedless raisins
1½ cups port
2 teaspoons cornstarch
1½ tablespoons water
¼ cup currant jelly
¼ cup orange juice
2 tablespoons lemon juice
2 teaspoons grated orange rind
1 teaspoon grated lemon rind

Mix mustard with water and let stand while preparing other ingredients. Put the salt, ginger, cloves, and raisins in a saucepan with the port and simmer 8 to 10 minutes. Blend the cornstarch with the 1 ½ tablespoons water and stir into the hot sauce along with the mustard. Stir and cook 2 minutes. Add remaining ingredients. Cook 1 minute. Use with venison and furred game. Makes approximately 1 ¾ cups.

⚜ FENNEL SAUCE (*English*)

⅓ cup finely chopped fennel
½ cup boiling water
½ cup (1 stick) butter, melted

Cook fennel in boiling water ½ minute. Drain and dry with paper towels. Add to butter. Stir and cook 1 to 2 minutes or until butter begins to turn color. Do not brown. Serve with poached mackerel or other poached fish. Makes approximately ½ cup.

⚜ GOOSEBERRY SAUCE (*English*)

4 cans (1 pound) gooseberries or 4 pounds fresh gooseberries
2 cups sugar
½ cup vinegar
¼ teaspoon salt
3 sticks whole cinnamon
½ teaspoon whole allspice
¼ teaspoon whole cloves

Combine the first 5 ingredients in a 3-quart saucepan. Tie allspice and cloves in a cheesecloth bag and add. Cook 30 to 40 minutes, stirring frequently. Remove spices. Cool. Store in a covered jar in the refrigerator. Serve with poultry, meats, and game. Makes approximately 4 cups.

⚜ MINT SAUCE (*English*)

¼ cup water
½ cup vinegar
⅓ cup finely chopped mint leaves
1 tablespoon sugar (or sugar to taste)

Combine all ingredients in a saucepan and heat. Do not boil. Let stand about 30 minutes before serving. Serve with lamb. Makes 1 generous cup.

⚜ ORANGE SAUCE (*English*)

1 cup (8-ounce glass) red currant jelly
¼ cup port
¼ cup orange juice
1 tablespoon lemon juice
1 tablespoon grated orange rind
½ teaspoon grated lemon rind

Break up jelly by beating with a fork. Add port and orange juice and heat only until jelly is melted. Stir in remaining ingredients. Serve with game, chicken, lamb, and veal. Makes approximately 1½ cups.

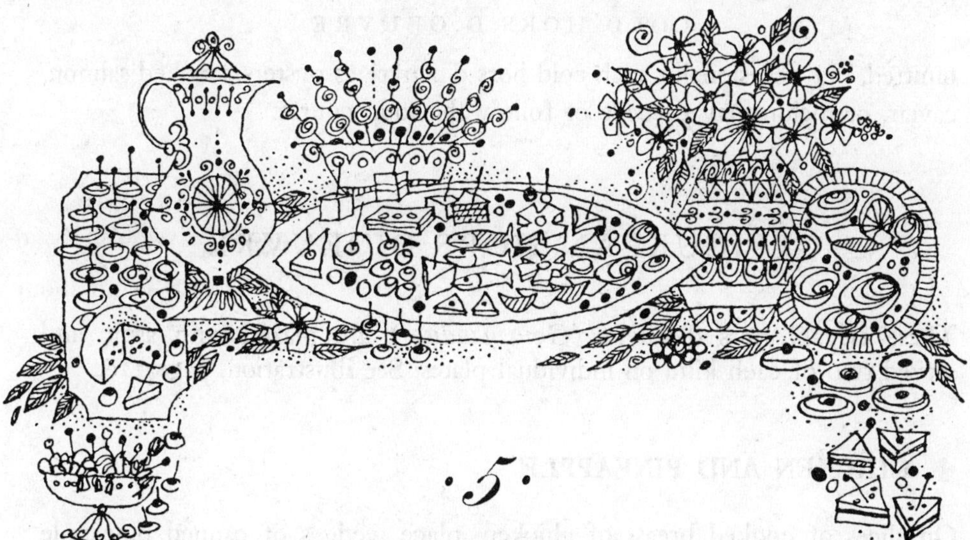

·5·

COLD HORS D'OEUVRE

Nothing is more tempting to the appetite than a well-arranged tray of hors d'oeuvre: the variety of forms, colors, and ingredients delights both the eye and the palate. Remember, however, that these charming frivolities owe their name to the fact that they are "outside" the menu; they should be chosen in relation to the meal that follows. Hors d'oeuvre may be as elaborate or as simple as you choose–many attractive and delicious ones are the result of an ingenious presentation of inexpensive ingredients.

Hors d'oeuvre are here divided into two categories: cold and hot. With the exception of canapés, which may be served either hot or cold, hot hors d'oeuvre are described in the next chapter. Cold hors d'oeuvre may be made of meat, fish, shellfish, chicken, vegetables, cheese, etc., in a wide range of preparations and combinations. Small sandwiches may be served as hors d'oeuvre and also with tea. Other suggestions for hors d'oeuvre will be found elsewhere in this book; see especially Eggs, Shellfish, Foie Gras.

Hors d'oeuvre are usually served only for lunch, very seldom with dinner. When cold hors d'oeuvre are served at dinner, the soup is usually omitted, but occasionally such cold hors d'oeuvre as oysters, smoked salmon, caviar, or melon may precede or follow the soup course.

EPICUREAN HORS D'OEUVRE

These elegant hors d'oeuvre (*Gourmandises*) are glazed with aspic and served two of each kind on individual plates. See illustration, page 226.

⚜ CHICKEN AND PINEAPPLE

On slices of cooked breast of chicken, place wedges of canned pineapple and garnish each with a bit of truffle or black olive. Glaze.

⚜ CORNETS OF HAM

Mix sieved hard-cooked egg yolks with enough softened butter or light or heavy cream to make a smooth consistency. Roll thin slices of cooked ham into cornets and pipe the egg mixture into them with a pastry tube. Garnish each with two half-slices of cucumber and glaze.

⚜ GALANTINE OF CHICKEN

Cut Chicken Galantine into slices ⅛ to ¼ inch thick. Arrange 5 sautéed mushroom slices down the center of each slice. Glaze.

⚜ PORK SLICES

Cut cold tenderloin of pork into slices ¼ inch thick, trimmed into ovals. Garnish each with a pickled caulifloweret and a slice of cucumber pickle. Glaze.

CAVIAR

The roe (eggs) of various species of the sturgeon family is called caviar or black caviar. Salmon roe is called red caviar. The roe is removed as soon as the fish is caught. It is prepared by removing the membrane and cellular tissue and salting the roe slightly.

The best black caviar is of Russian origin, from sturgeon found in the Caspian and Black seas. It is classified by the species of sturgeon from which it comes. Beluga is the Russian name for white sturgeon, the largest of the sturgeon family and the one which produces the finest caviar. Shah is an Iranian sturgeon and Icre Negre a Romanian sturgeon; both produce caviar of fine quality.

Either black or red caviar is served alone as an hors d'oeuvre, or mixed with sour cream and served with Blinis or as a spread for pumpernickel or other dark bread. Black caviar is used as an ingredient in Russian sauces and salad dressings.

With caviar, white wine, champagne, or vodka should be served, never red wine.

FISH AND SHELLFISH HORS D'OEUVRE

A selection of fish and shellfish combinations is shown in the illustration on page 222.

⚜ ANCHOVIES NÎMES STYLE

Cut anchovies in half lengthwise and arrange them in lattice fashion in the center of an hors d'oeuvre dish. Sprinkle with oil from the can and with hard-cooked chopped egg yolk. Garnish with slices of small pickled beets. Allow 3 anchovies per serving.

⚜ NORWEGIAN ANCHOVIES (*Kilkis*)

Serve anchovies in the marinade in which they are canned. Arrange them attractively on an hors d'oeuvre dish. Serve with bread spread with fresh sweet butter. Allow 3 anchovies per serving.

⚜ ANCHOVIES TOULON (*With Potato Salad*)

1 quart potato salad
3 hard-cooked eggs
9 large rolled anchovies
9 green olives, pitted

Mound potato salad in the center of an hors d'oeuvre dish. Slice the hard-cooked eggs in thick rounds, remove the yolks, and place the egg-white rings around the salad. (Reserve the yolks and end slices for other use.) Put an anchovy in the center of each egg-white ring and an olive in the center of each anchovy. Makes 9 servings.

⚜ MIXED FISH HORS D'OEUVRE

Place shredded lettuce in the bottom of an hors d'oeuvre dish. Cut various kinds of poached fish in large dice and coat with mayonnaise seasoned with powdered mustard, cayenne, and lemon juice to taste. Garnish with sliced tomatoes, sliced hard-cooked eggs, and chopped parsley or onions.

⚜ MARINATED FRESH HERRING

¾ cup dry white wine
¾ cup wine vinegar
3 tablespoons chopped onion
⅓ cup thinly sliced carrots
2 sliced shallots
6 peppercorns
1 small bay leaf
¼ teaspoon dried thyme
2 tablespoons chopped parsley
salt to taste
6 fresh herring, cleaned and dressed, with heads removed

Place all ingredients except herring in a small saucepan. Cover and boil slowly 5 minutes. Place the herring in a larger saucepan and pour the sauce over them. Cook 10 minutes, or until herring is flaky, never allowing the sauce to boil. Cool and serve in the marinade. Makes 6 servings.

Fresh mackerel may be marinated in the same way.

⚜ ROLLMOPS

In the recipe for Marinated Herring, replace whole fresh herring with fresh herring fillets. Roll the marinated fillets around gherkins, holding them in place with toothpicks or cocktail picks. Serve in the marinade.

⚜ RUSSIAN HERRING

3 medium-sized apples
1 tablespoon lemon juice
¼ cup finely chopped onion
3 to 4 pickled raw herring
ground black pepper to taste
¼ cup dry white wine
2 tablespoons olive oil or salad oil

Peel, core, and finely dice apples. Add lemon juice and onion. Mix well and mound in the center of an hors d'oeuvre dish. Trim all bones from herring and cut each into 3 lengthwise pieces. Arrange in lattice fashion on the apples. Mix remaining ingredients and sprinkle over apples and fish. Serve as an hors d'oeuvre. Makes 6 servings.

⚜ FILLET OF SMOKED HERRING RUSSIAN STYLE

4 smoked herring fillets
2 ripe firm apples
1 small onion, chopped fine
¼ cup dry white wine
2 to 3 tablespoons olive or salad oil

Dip herring in boiling water and remove skins. Cut fillets in long strips. Set aside. Core the apples but do not peel them. Dice and mix with the chopped onion. Mound in the center of an oval-shaped hors d'oeuvre dish. Garnish with herring strips in lattice fashion. Mix wine and oil and sprinkle over all. Makes 6 servings.

⚜ RED MULLET ORIENTAL STYLE

10 red mullet (4 ounces each), cleaned and dressed
salt and ground black pepper to taste
¼ cup olive oil or salad oil
4 medium-sized tomatoes, peeled, seeded, and diced
1 clove of garlic, crushed
1 teaspoon chopped parsley
⅓ cup dry white wine
2 strands saffron
sliced tomatoes

Roll mullet in flour seasoned with salt and pepper. Brown on both sides in hot oil. Remove fish to an ovenproof dish. Add tomatoes and garlic to the hot oil; stir and cook 5 minutes. Blend in the remaining ingredients; stir and cook slowly 5 minutes. Pour the sauce over the fish. Cook 10 minutes in a preheated moderate oven (350° F.). Chill. Garnish with sliced tomatoes. Makes 10 servings.

⚜ ROCK LOBSTER PARISIENNE

Cover the bottom of an hors d'oeuvre dish with shredded lettuce. Mix 2 cups cooked diced rock lobster with mayonnaise seasoned to taste with lemon juice, powdered mustard, and tomato catsup. Mound in center of dish and garnish with quartered hard-cooked eggs or lettuce hearts. If desired, replace rock lobster with cold poached fish. Makes 6 servings.

VARIATION

ROCK LOBSTER RUSSIAN STYLE

In the preceding recipe, replace the lettuce with mixed-vegetable salad blended with mayonnaise.

⚜ NORWEGIAN SMOKED SALMON

Cut a dressed fresh salmon into 2 lengthwise halves. Rub each side with salt and rub very generously with olive oil or salad oil. Sprinkle with chopped fresh dill, chopped fresh thyme, and 2 small crumbled bay leaves. Place fish in a shallow baking dish and cover with pliofilm or cheesecloth. Refrigerate for 3 days, turning the salmon every day and keeping the dish covered. Remove fish from the dish and wipe dry. Rub very lightly with oil. Smoke 48 hours at a temperature between 64° and 68° F.

To serve smoked salmon, slice salmon very thin and garnish with curly parsley. Serve with horseradish, whipped cream, lemon, and buttered toast. Or the slices may also be shaped into cornets and filled with plain or horseradish butter. Arrange radially on a round dish. Garnish the center with parsley.

In the United States, smoked Nova Scotia salmon, sliced, is available in delicatessen stores and specialty food stores. There are other types of smoked salmon but the Nova Scotia salmon is the best quality. Smoked salmon is also called lox.

⚜ CORNETS OF SMOKED SALMON RUSSIAN STYLE

2 7-ounce cans tuna fish in oil
6 tablespoons softened butter
lemon juice
salt
ground black pepper
12 slices smoked salmon
3 cups mixed cooked vegetables (carrots, peas, potatoes, string beans, and celery)
½ cup mayonnaise
truffles or black olives

Mash tuna fish with the oil in which it was canned and mix with butter. Season to taste with lemon juice, salt, and pepper. Put the mixture through a sieve or blend a little at a time in a blender. Shape salmon slices into cornets, and fill with the tuna-butter mixture, using a teaspoon or a pastry bag with a fluted tube. Chill. Mix vegetables with mayonnaise, adding lemon juice, salt, and pepper to taste. Mound in the center of an hors d'oeuvre dish. Flatten the top and chill. Shortly before serving arrange tuna-filled salmon cornets over the top of the salad, with the small ends pointed toward the center. Garnish with bits of truffle or black olive. If salad is not to be served immediately, glaze it with aspic. Makes 6 to 12 servings. (See illustration, page 222.)

⚜ SARDINES IN OIL

Arrange sardines on one side of a round hors d'oeuvre dish in a fan shape. Serrate the edges of half-slices of lemon, sprinkle with chopped parsley, and place one between each two sardines. On the other side of the dish, put chopped hard-cooked egg yolks and chopped hard-cooked egg whites, chopped onion, and chopped parsley. Serve toast and butter on the side. Allow 3 sardines per serving.

⚜ SARDINES ROVIGO

12 sardines
½ cup Tomato Sauce
ground dried or chopped fresh sage to taste
sweet green pepper cut into small julienne strips
chopped hard-cooked egg white

Drain sardines and place on an hors d'oeuvre dish. Combine Tomato Sauce and sage and spread over sardines. Sprinkle with julienne green-pepper strips and chopped egg white. Makes 6 servings.

⚜ MARINATED SMELTS

18 smelts, cleaned and dressed
flour
salt and ground black pepper to taste
⅓ cup dry white wine
2 tablespoons wine vinegar
3 shallots
1 tablespoon chopped parsley
½ teaspoon powdered mustard mixed with 1 teaspoon water

Roll smelts in flour seasoned with salt and pepper. Brown quickly on both sides in hot oil. In a saucepan combine remaining ingredients. Cover and cook below boiling point 5 minutes. Pour over smelts. Bring to boiling point. Quickly remove from heat and chill in the sauce. Makes 6 to 9 servings.

⚜ TUNA FISH MIREILLE

Mash 1 7-ounce can tuna fish in the oil in which it was canned. Add 2 tablespoons softened butter and mix well. Season to taste with lemon juice, salt, and ground black pepper. Thin to spreading consistency with about 1 tablespoon mayonnaise. Mound on a dish. Stuff large pitted green olives with very thick highly seasoned tomato purée and place around the tuna fish. Serve chilled. Makes 1 cup.

⚜ CREAMED TUNA FISH MIRABEAU

7-ounce can tuna fish in oil
½ cup (1 stick) softened butter
¼ cup mayonnaise
lemon juice
salt and ground black pepper to taste
18 pitted green olives
4 medium-sized tomatoes

Mash tuna fish with the oil in which it was canned. Mix with butter and mayonnaise until smooth. Add lemon juice, salt, and pepper to taste. Mound in the center of an oval dish and smooth over the surface. Decorate the top with olives and make a border of tomatoes cut in eighths. Serve chilled. Makes 8 servings.

COLD PASTRY BOATS, TARTLETS, CANNELONI

Various hors d'oeuvre mixtures are served in small pastry shells, either oval (boats or barquettes) or round (tartlets), or in puff-paste patties or horns. (See illustration, page 223.) For cold mixtures the shells are usually baked in advance; for hot hors d'oeuvre they may be baked with the filling. They can also be filled with fruit or custard and served for dessert. For pastry recipes see Doughs in Chapter 3, pages 123–30.

⚜ CHICKEN BARQUETTES

2 cups finely diced cooked chicken
½ cup thick mayonnaise
¼ teaspoon dried or 1 teaspoon chopped fresh tarragon
¼ teaspoon lemon juice
salt and ground black pepper to taste
aspic
truffle
tarragon or parsley leaves
36 baked boat-shaped tart shells

Combine all ingredients except aspic and garnishes. Spoon into cold baked tart shells or pipe the mixture into the shells with a pastry bag, using a round or star tube. Glaze the tops with aspic. Garnish with slices of truffle and tarragon or parsley leaves. Makes 3 dozen.

⚜ FISH BARQUETTES (*Barquettes Beauharnais*)

1½ cups diced cooked fillet of sole
½ cup diced cooked mussels
½ cup white fish Chaud-froid Sauce
salt and ground black pepper to taste
truffles
crayfish tails or very small cooked shrimp

Combine all ingredients except truffles and crayfish or shrimp. Spoon or pipe the mixture into baked tart shells. Coat with additional Chaud-froid Sauce. Garnish each with a crayfish tail or a shrimp and a bit of truffle. Makes 3 dozen.

⚜ GOOSE-LIVER BOATS (*Barquettes Strasbourgeoises*)

1 cup pâté de foie gras
6 tablespoons softened butter
18 small baked puff-paste boats
aspic
1 truffle or black ripe olive

Blend pâté de foie gras with butter until smooth and creamy. Spoon or pipe into cold pastry boats. Glaze with aspic. Garnish with a small slice of truffle or a bit of black olive. Makes 18.

⚜ ROQUEFORT CHEESE BOATS

6 tablespoons butter
4 ounces Roquefort cheese
½ teaspoon paprika
about 3 tablespoons port
2 tablespoons unsweetened whipped cream
12 baked small pastry boats
½ cup port wine jelly, melted
12 baked boat-shaped tart shells

Mix butter until creamy. Add cheese and paprika and enough wine to make a smooth creamy consistency. Fold in whipped cream. Spoon the mixture into cold baked pastry boats, or pipe it in with a pastry bag, using the star tube. Allow filling to set. Glaze with melted wine jelly. Makes 12.

⚜ SHRIMP BARQUETTES I

2 cups finely diced cooked shrimp
½ cup mayonnaise
½ teaspoon lemon juice
salt and ground black pepper to taste
36 baked boat-shaped tart shells
aspic
hard-cooked egg
chervil or parsley leaves

Combine all ingredients except aspic and garnishes. Spoon into the tart shells. Glaze with aspic. Garnish with hard-cooked egg slices cut into halves and chervil or parsley leaves. Makes 3 dozen.

⚜ TUNA FISH BOATS

7-ounce can white-meat tuna fish
lemon juice
salt
ground black pepper
12 small baked pastry boats
anchovy fillets
aspic

Flake undrained tuna fish and mix it well with the oil with which the tuna is canned. Add lemon juice, salt, and pepper to taste. Spoon or pipe into pastry boats. Garnish each with a long anchovy fillet. Glaze with aspic. Makes 12.

⚜ CHEESE AND OLIVE TARTLETS (*Tartelettes à la Tarnoise*)

½ cup (1 stick) softened butter
6 ounces creamed Gruyère cheese
3 tablespoons finely chopped green olives
1 tablespoon sherry (or sherry to taste)
salt to taste
1 teaspoon paprika
6 small cold baked tart shells
12 slices pimiento-stuffed olives
⅓ cup aspic

Combine butter and cheese. Add olives, sherry, salt and paprika. Mix well. Put the mixture into a pastry bag fitted with a star-shaped tube and pipe into the tart shells. Garnish each with sliced stuffed olives. Glaze with aspic and chill until aspic is set. Makes 6 servings.

Melon-Ball Cocktail, page 232 ▲

▼ Ham Villandry, page 616

▲ Lobster Cocktail, page 231

Lobster Salad in Coconut Shells, page 245 ▼

Tomatoes with various stuffings, pages 240–42;
(below, upper right) Stuffed Artichoke Bottoms, page 237

▲ Cornets of Smoked Salmon Russian Style, page 214

Assorted fish and shellfish hors d'oeuvre, pages 211–16 ▼

Vegetarian hors d'oeuvre ▲

▼ Hors d'oeuvre patties and barquettes, pages 216–18

▲ Assorted canapés, pages 259–61

Assortment of hors d'oeuvre salads, pages 247–49 ▼

Canapés, pages 255–59 ▲

▼ Rich canapés, pages 261–62

▲ Epicurean hors d'oeuvre (Gourmandises), page 210

Avocados with Seafood, page 237 ▼

⚜ CANNELONI WITH CAMEMBERT

Roll puff paste ⅛ inch thick and cut into strips ½ inch wide. Roll strips around small wooden or tin cones or funnels. Brush with beaten egg yolk and milk, using 1 teaspoon milk to each egg yolk. Sprinkle with grated Cheddar cheese. Bake in a preheated hot oven (425° F.) about 12 minutes or until browned. Remove cones while canneloni are still hot. Cool. Fold sufficient whipped cream into soft Camembert cheese to make it fluffy and fill canneloni.

COLD MOLDED MOUSSES

A mousse to be served as a cold appetizer or luncheon dish is a rich velvety-textured molded aspic made of poultry, ham, liver, fish, or shellfish force-meat, enriched with whipped cream and sometimes with softened butter. Wine and other seasonings may be added in just the correct amount to give the mixture a delicate savory flavor.

The mixture may be molded in one large mold or in individual molds. The molds are lined with rich aspic and decorated with truffles, hard-cooked eggs, herb leaves, sometimes olives, and strips of lean cooked ham or tongue.

A mousse is very impressive as an hors d'oeuvre or luncheon main dish, or on a cold buffet or cocktail table.

⚜ CHICKEN MOUSSE

about 3 cups clear chicken aspic
truffles or black olives
hard-cooked egg whites
2 slices pickled tongue
2 cups finely ground poached breast of chicken
1 cup chicken Velouté Sauce
1 cup heavy cream, whipped
salt
ground white pepper
lemon juice
7-ounce can pâté de foie gras
jellied aspic

Coat a 1½-quart mold or 6 to 8 individual molds with aspic and chill until aspic is set. (If aspic does not jell, soften 1 envelope unflavored gelatin in ¼ cup water, melt over hot water, and add to the aspic.) Decorate mold as desired with bits of truffle or black olive and hard-cooked egg whites and pickled tongue cut in fancy shapes. Affix each decoration with a few drops of aspic. Chill until aspic is set. Coat the mold again with another layer of aspic. Chill until aspic is set.

Combine chicken and Velouté Sauce and rub the mixture through a sieve. Gradually add 2 cups of the chicken aspic. Chill until the mixture begins to set. Fold in whipped cream. Season to taste with salt, pepper, and lemon juice. Spoon mousse mixture into the prepared mold or molds until half-filled. Cover with a layer of sliced, chilled pâté de foie gras. Finish filling with remaining mousse mixture. Chill until mousse is firm and ready to serve. Unmold onto a chilled serving plate and garnish with cubes of jellied aspic. Makes 6 to 8 servings.

⚜ FOIE GRAS MOUSSE

about 3 cups clear, well-seasoned chicken aspic
truffles or black olives
hard-cooked egg whites
1½ envelopes unflavored gelatin
¾ cup water
2 cups finely ground cooked foie gras
½ cup heavy cream, whipped
salt and ground white pepper
lemon juice
jellied aspic
watercress

Coat a 1-quart mold or 6 individual molds with chicken aspic. Chill until aspic is set. Decorate with truffles or slices of black olives and egg whites cut in fancy shapes. Affix each decoration to the mold with a few drops of aspic. Chill until aspic is set. Coat the mold again with aspic and chill until set.

Soften gelatin in water. Melt over hot water. Remove from heat and cool to room temperature. Put liver through a fine sieve or blend in an electric blender. Stir in melted gelatin. Fold in cream. Season to taste with salt, pepper, and lemon juice. Turn the goose-liver mixture into the mold or molds, filling a large mold to within ½ inch of the top, smaller molds to within ¼ inch of the tops. Finish filling with chicken aspic. Chill until set and ready to serve. Unmold onto chilled serving plate. Garnish with cubes of jellied aspic and watercress. Makes 6 servings. (See also illustration, page 708.)

⚜ HAM MOUSSE I

1 cup beef or veal aspic
truffles or black olives
hard-cooked eggs
4 cups very finely ground cooked ham
3 tablespoons dry sherry
2 tablespoons tomato purée
2 teaspoons prepared mustard
2 envelopes unflavored gelatin
⅓ cup cold water
1 cup very hot beef or veal stock
salt to taste
¼ teaspoon ground black pepper
1 cup heavy cream, whipped

Coat a 1½-quart mold with aspic and chill until set. Decorate the bottom of the mold with truffles or black olives and sliced hard-cooked eggs. Affix each decoration with a few drops of aspic. Chill until aspic is set. Then coat with another layer of aspic and chill again until set. Combine ham, sherry, tomato purée, and mustard. Mix until well blended. Soften gelatin in cold water. Add hot stock and stir until gelatin is dissolved. Add to the ham mixture along with the salt and pepper. Chill until mixture begins to set. Fold in whipped cream. Turn into the prepared mold. Unmold onto a chilled plate. If desired garnish with small deep baked tart shells filled with vegetable salad and diced jellied aspic. This mousse may also be molded in 6 or 8 individual molds. Makes 6 to 8 servings.

⚜ HUNGARIAN HAM MOUSSE

3 envelopes unflavored gelatin
1½ cups red port wine
3 cups hot beef or veal stock
truffles or black olives
hard-cooked eggs
2 cups finely ground cooked lean ham
½ cup butter
½ cup heavy cream
3 tablespoons tomato purée
1 cup cold thick Béchamel Sauce
1 tablespoon paprika
dash cayenne
salt to taste

Soften gelatin in wine. Add hot stock and stir until gelatin is dissolved. Chill until gelatin is cold. Pour enough gelatin into a 1½-quart charlotte mold or ring mold to coat the bottom and sides. Chill until firm. (Set remaining gelatin aside at room temperature to use later.) Decorate the bottom with truffles and hard-cooked eggs. Affix each decoration with a few drops of gelatin. Chill until set. Coat the mold again with gelatin and chill until set. Blend ham with remaining ingredients. Using a pastry bag with a large round tube, fill mold with the ham mixture, keeping the mousse away from the sides of the mold. Chill until firm. Pour gelatin around the mousse. Chill until set. Chill remaining gelatin until set, then cut into cubes. Unmold mousse onto a chilled serving plate and garnish with the gelatin cubes. Makes 6 to 8 servings.

⚜ SALMON MOUSSE

1½ cups fish aspic
pimiento
hard-cooked egg whites
1 small round of truffle or black olive
1½ firmly packed cups flaked, poached salmon
1 envelope unflavored gelatin
½ cup cold water
¼ cup mayonnaise
¼ cup heavy cream
lemon juice
salt
ground white pepper
cayenne
cubed jellied aspic
watercress

Coat the bottom and sides of a fish-shaped mold with a thin layer of cool, liquid fish aspic. Chill until aspic is set. Outline the mouth, tail, and fins with thin strips of pimiento, and the scales down the back with thin crescents of hard-cooked egg whites. Make the eye with a round piece of black olive or truffle. Affix these garnishes with a few drops of liquid aspic. Chill until aspic is firm. Pour in enough liquid aspic to make a layer ½ inch thick. Chill until firm.

Put salmon through a sieve. Soften gelatin in cold water and set in a pan of hot water to melt. Blend with mayonnaise and cream and add to salmon. Mix well. Season to taste with lemon juice, salt, pepper, and cayenne, and spoon into mold. Chill until firm. Unmold onto a chilled silver or glass platter. Surround fish with aspic cubes. Garnish with watercress. Makes 6 servings.

HORS D'OEUVRE COCKTAILS

"Cocktails" as hors d'oeuvre include seafood, fruit, melon, and other foods served cold with appropriate sauces in glasses or coupes. Like alcoholic cocktails, they are an American invention.

⚜ AVOCADO COCKTAIL

2 slightly underripe avocados
1½ tablespoons salad oil or olive oil
1½ tablespoons wine vinegar
¼ teaspoon salt
⅛ teaspoon ground white pepper
½ cup tomato catsup
1 teaspoon each chopped parsley, chopped chives, and grated horseradish
½ teaspoon finely chopped shallots
½ teaspoon prepared mustard
dash of Tabasco
6 slices hard-cooked egg

Peel avocados, cut into lengthwise halves and remove stones. Cut into slices ¼ inch thick. Combine oil, vinegar, salt, and pepper. Pour over avocados and marinate at least ½ hour in the refrigerator. Drain the marinade from the avocados and blend it with all remaining ingredients except the hard-cooked eggs. Add to avocados, mix lightly, and chill. Serve in chilled coupes or cocktail glasses. Garnish each with a slice of hard-cooked egg and sprinkle with a few drops of tomato catsup. Makes 6 servings.

⚜ CRAYFISH COCKTAIL

½ cup mayonnaise
1 tablespoon tomato paste
2 tablespoons chili sauce
1½ teaspoons each chopped chives and chopped parsley
½ teaspoon onion juice
½ teaspoon Worcestershire sauce
salt
ground black pepper
24 to 28 chilled cooked crayfish
2 diced chilled raw tomatoes
cold hard-cooked egg white
green pepper

Combine all except the last 4 ingredients. Add crayfish, mix lightly and chill. Just before serving, add tomatoes. Spoon into chilled coupes or cocktail glasses. Cut egg white and green pepper into julienne strips and scatter over the top. Makes 4 servings.

The crayfish may be replaced with 1 cup chilled diced lobster, or with 24 chilled medium-sized whole shrimp.

⚜ LOBSTER COCKTAIL I

½ cup thick mayonnaise
2 teaspoons grated horseradish
3 tablespoons tomato catsup
½ teaspoon paprika
½ teaspoon prepared mustard
¾ teaspoon each chopped fresh chervil and tarragon
1 teaspoon each brandy and dry sherry
few drops Tabasco
1 cup chilled cooked lobster in medium-sized chunks
¼ head lettuce
4 large chunks cooked lobster
8 chilled cooked asparagus tips

Combine all ingredients except lobster, lettuce, and asparagus tips. Add medium-sized lobster chunks to half the sauce and chill. Just before serving, shred the lettuce into 4 coupes or cocktail glasses. Divide the lobster mixture equally among the 4 glasses. Garnish each with a large lobster chunk and 2 asparagus tips. Coat with the remaining sauce. Makes 4 servings.

⚜ LOBSTER COCKTAIL II

1 cooked lobster, 1½ pounds
2 tablespoons each mayonnaise and tomato catsup
brandy to taste
2 medium-sized tomatoes, diced
salt
ground black pepper
4 fluted mushrooms

Slice the meat from the lobster tail, dice the meat from the claws, and chill. Combine mayonnaise, catsup, and brandy to taste. Sprinkle lobster claw meat and tomatoes lightly with salt and pepper. Add sauce and mix lightly. Shred lettuce into 4 coupes or cocktail glasses. Divide the lobster-tomato mixture equally among the 4 glasses. Top each with 2 lobster slices and a fluted poached mushroom. Sprinkle lightly with a little brandy and catsup. Makes 4 servings. (See illustration, page 220.)

⚜ OYSTER COCKTAIL

⅓ cup mayonnaise
2 teaspoons grated horseradish
2 tablespoons tomato catsup
lemon juice
Worcestershire sauce
salt
few drops Tabasco
20 large raw oysters
chopped parsley

Combine all ingredients except oysters and parsley. Add 16 of the oysters to the sauce. Chill. Serve in 4 coupes or cocktail glasses. Top each with a whole raw oyster. Garnish with chopped parsley. Makes 4 servings.

MELON COCKTAILS AND HORS D'OEUVRE

⚜ MELON-BALL COCKTAIL

Cut an iced honeydew, cantaloupe, or similar melon in half and remove seeds. Cut melon into small balls with a melon-ball cutter. Pour red or white port wine over the balls, partially covering them. Chill thoroughly. Serve in chilled coupe or cocktail glasses. Garnish with a sprig of mint. If desired, replace port with sherry, Marsala, or Madeira or with rum or gin with sugar and lemon juice to taste. Makes 6 servings. The melon balls can also be served in the halved melon shells, surrounded with cracked ice, on glass plates (see illustration, page 219).

⚜ MELON COCKTAIL WITH WINE

Cut a slice from the stem end of a ripe cantaloupe, honeydew, or other similar melon. Insert a tablespoon in the hole and remove the seeds. Pour in ½ cup red or white port, Madeira, sherry, Marsala, or Tokay. Replace the slice that was cut off. Chill at least 2 hours before serving. To serve, scoop out the pulp with a tablespoon. Serve in well-chilled cocktail glasses. Makes 6 servings.

⚜ SLICED MELON AS HORS D'OEUVRE

Melons are generally eaten either at the beginning of the meal as an hors d'oeuvre, or at the end of the meal as dessert. Some ways of serving melons as an hors d'oeuvre are:

Slice melon (cantaloupe, honeydew, Spanish, etc.) and serve with a slice of lemon or lime.

Slice melon and sprinkle with sherry, Marsala, Tokay, Madeira, Kirsch, or Triple Sec.

Slice melon and sprinkle with ground black pepper or ground ginger.

⚜ MELON AND PARMA HAM

1 large cantaloupe or honeydew melon
sherry
6 thin slices Parma ham

Cut a slice from the stem end of a cantaloupe or honeydew melon. Scoop out the seeds with a spoon and drain well. Using a melon-ball cutter, cut balls from the flesh, leaving the rind intact. Replace the balls. Sprinkle with sherry. Chill 2 hours. To serve, spoon the balls onto silver or glass dishes, each garnished with a thin slice of cooked ham rolled into a cornet. Makes 6 servings.

⚜ MELON WITH PROSCIUTTO

1 large honeydew melon
6 slices prosciutto (Italian ham)
1 lemon or lime

Cut melon in half. Scoop out seeds and drain well. Cut each half into 3 wedges and place each on a serving plate. Drape a thin slice of prosciutto over each. Garnish with a wedge of lemon or lime. Makes 6 servings.

Fresh figs are also often served with prosciutto as an hors d'oeuvre.

OLIVES

Olives, native to the eastern Mediterranean area, are grown throughout the Mediterranean countries, as well as in California, Mexico, and southern Australia. They are marketed in two forms: green olives, harvested before they are fully ripe, specially treated to remove the bitter taste, and then pickled in brine; and ripe olives, harvested after they have ripened, washed several times in water, put into boiling brine, dried, and pickled in oil.

The French cultivate a special variety of olive for the table. Known as *picholines*, they are large, elongated, and reddish-black in color and are preserved in the finest olive oil. As an hors d'oeuvre they are served with a little of their marinade.

Either green or black olives may be stuffed. Choose large olives, hold them upright on a folded towel, and remove stones with a cherry pitter or a hairpin.

⚜ JOINVILLE OLIVES

6 peeled, deveined, cooked large shrimp
2 tablespoons softened salted butter
24 large pitted green or black olives

Pound or grind the shrimp fine, or put them in an electric blender. Mix with the softened butter and fill the olives. Serve as an hors d'oeuvre or use as a garnish for cold fish dishes.

⚜ OLIVES SICILIAN STYLE

½ cup puréed fresh tomatoes
¼ cup puréed red or green sweet pepper
salt and ground white pepper
1½ teaspoons unflavored gelatin
2 tablespoons cold water
9-ounce jar large green olives, stones removed

Combine tomato and pepper purées. Season to taste with salt and pepper. Soften gelatin in cold water in a ramekin; set in a pan of hot water until gelatin melts. Add to the purée. Chill until the mixture begins to set. Fill a decorating tube fitted with a small nozzle with the purée and pipe into the olive cavities. Chill until the purée is set. Serve on an hors d'oeuvre tray or use to garnish salads or cold meat dishes.

VEGETABLES À LA GRECQUE

Vegetables à la Grecque are cooked in water or court bouillon with olive oil, lemon juice, wine, and various herbs and spices added to the cooking liquids. They are usually served cold as hors d'oeuvre, with some of the cooking liquor used as a sauce.

Recipes for various vegetables à la Grecque follow.

⚜ ARTICHOKES

8 very small artichokes
1 teaspoon salt
boiling water to cover
¾ cup boiling water or bouillon
¾ cup dry white wine
¼ cup olive oil
2 tablespoons lemon juice
1 bay leaf
6 whole peppercorns
1 sprig parsley
¼ teaspoon each dried chervil and tarragon

Trim artichokes, cut off the tips of the leaves, wash, and drain well. Place artichokes in a saucepan with salt and enough boiling water to cover them. Cover and cook 10 minutes. Drain off water and add all remaining ingredients. Cover and boil 30 minutes or until artichokes are crisp-tender. Cool in the liquor. Makes 8 servings.

⚜ CELERY

18 celery hearts
½ teaspoon salt
boiling water to cover
¾ cup boiling water or bouillon
¾ cup dry white wine
¼ cup olive oil
2 tablespoons lemon juice
1 small bay leaf
6 whole peppercorns
1 sprig parsley
¼ teaspoon each dried chervil and tarragon

Place celery in a saucepan with salt and enough boiling water to cover it. Cover and boil 3 minutes. Drain off and discard water. Add remaining ingredients. Cover and cook *only* until celery is crisp-tender, 5 to 10 minutes. Cool in liquor. Makes 6 servings.

⚜ FENNEL

In the preceding recipe, replace the celery with ribs of fennel, the large ribs cut in half, lengthwise. Leave a few fennel leaves attached to the ribs. Blanch fennel in salted boiling water 10 minutes. Drain off and discard the water. Finish cooking as in directions for the celery. Makes 6 to 8 servings.

⚜ LEEKS

In the Celery à la Grecque recipe replace celery with the white part of leeks cut into 2- to 3-inch pieces. Proceed as for celery. Makes 6 servings.

⚜ MUSHROOMS

1½ pounds large white mushrooms
1 cup boiling water
¾ cup dry white wine
⅓ cup olive oil
3 tablespoons lemon juice
1 small bay leaf
6 whole peppercorns
¼ teaspoon salt or salt to taste
2 sprigs parsley

Wash mushrooms. Remove stems and save them for soups or sauces. Cut mushroom caps into quarters. Place all other ingredients in a saucepan, cover, and cook slowly 5 minutes. Add mushrooms and cook 6 to 8 minutes over low heat. Cool in liquor. Makes 8 servings.

⚜ ONIONS

1½ pounds small white onions
1 teaspoon salt
boiling water to cover
¾ cup dry white wine
1 cup boiling water
⅓ cup olive oil
3 tablespoons lemon juice
1 small bay leaf
¼ teaspoon salt
6 whole peppercorns

Peel onions and place in a saucepan with the 1 teaspoon salt and boiling water to cover. Cover and cook slowly 10 minutes. Drain off and discard water. Put the remaining ingredients in a saucepan, cover, and cook slowly 5 minutes. Add onions and cook over moderate heat until onions are tender, 12 to 15 minutes. Cool in the liquor. Makes 10 to 12 servings.

STUFFED VEGETABLES AND FRUITS

⚜ STUFFED ARTICHOKE BOTTOMS

12 cooked artichoke bottoms
French dressing
1 cup finely diced cooked crayfish tails or shrimp
⅓ cup finely diced celery
salt
ground black pepper
½ teaspoon curry powder
½ teaspoon lemon juice
¼ cup thick mayonnaise
3 large tomatoes
3 black olives

Marinate artichoke bottoms 2 hours in enough French dressing to cover them. Combine crayfish or shrimp, celery, salt, and pepper. Mix curry powder and lemon juice with mayonnaise and blend with the crayfish or shrimp mixture. Drain artichoke bottoms and fill with the mixture. Peel tomatoes and cut the peels into 36 strips 1¼ inches long and ¼ inch wide and arrange 3 strips over each artichoke. (Save the tomatoes to use in another dish.) Garnish the top of the artichoke with a small piece of black olive. Makes 12 hors d'oeuvre. (See illustration, page 221.)

⚜ AVOCADOS WITH SEAFOOD

2 avocados
lemon juice
½ cup diced cooked lobster
½ cup diced cooked shrimp
⅓ cup diced raw mushrooms
2 teaspoons lemon juice
2 tablespoons olive oil or salad oil
salt
ground black pepper
⅓ cup mayonnaise
1 tablespoon dry sherry
2 teaspoons catsup
2 teaspoons grated horseradish
½ teaspoon powdered mustard
1½ tablespoons unsweetened whipped cream
20 peeled, deveined, and cooked whole shrimp
20 yellow-cheese balls
black olives

Cut avocados in half lengthwise and remove the seed. Scoop out the meat, leaving ¼ inch clinging to the shells. (Reserve the scooped-out portion.) Brush insides of shells with lemon juice to prevent discoloration. Dice the reserved avocado meat and combine with the lobster, shrimp, mushrooms, lemon juice, oil, salt, and pepper. Cover and refrigerate 1 hour. Combine mayonnaise, sherry, catsup, horseradish, mustard, and cream. Blend with the lobster and shrimp mixture. Spoon into the avocado halves. Garnish each with 5 whole shrimp and 5 yellow-cheese balls each topped with a bit of black olive. Makes 4 servings. (See illustration, page 226.)

⚜ CUCUMBER AND HAM HORS D'OEUVRE

- 2 medium-sized cucumbers, oil and vinegar, French dressing
- 2 cups diced cooked ham
- heavy cream
- salt
- ground black pepper
- grated horseradish

Peel cucumbers, cut them into 1-inch lengths, and scoop out the centers, leaving a bottom in each piece. Marinate 1 hour in French dressing. Remove from dressing, invert on a plate, and drain well. Combine ham with enough cream to make a medium thick mixture. Spoon into cucumber cases. Sprinkle with grated horseradish. Makes 6 to 8 servings.

⚜ CUCUMBERS WITH SALMON AND HERRING

- 2 medium-sized cucumbers, oil and vinegar, French dressing
- 1 cup flaked poached salmon
- 2 tablespoons softened butter
- 1 tablespoon heavy cream
- salt and ground white pepper
- ¾ cup poached herring
- 1 hard-cooked egg, diced
- ½ teaspoon wine vinegar
- grated horseradish

Prepare cucumbers as in the preceding recipe. Mash salmon with butter and put the mixture through a coarse sieve. Add salt and pepper to taste. Marinate herring in French dressing, drain well, dice finely, and add to salmon along with egg and vinegar. Mix well and spoon into cucumber cases. Sprinkle with grated horseradish. Makes 6 to 8 servings.

⚜ CUCUMBER STUFFED WITH VEGETABLE SALAD

- 2 medium-sized cucumbers, oil and vinegar, French dressing
- ¼ cup each cooked green peas, diced carrots, diced new potato, green beans
- ⅓ cup diced celery
- 1 tablespoon chopped onion
- salt and ground black pepper
- ¼ cup mayonnaise
- few drops Tabasco
- ½ teaspoon paprika
- parsley

Prepare the cucumbers as in the two preceding recipes. Season vegetables with salt and pepper to taste. Mix mayonnaise with Tabasco and paprika and add to vegetables. Mix lightly. Spoon into cucumber cases. Garnish with sprigs of parsley. Makes 6 servings.

⚜ STUFFED GRAPEFRUIT

- **½ teaspoon ground mustard**
- **1 teaspoon water**
- **¼ cup mayonnaise**
- **½ teaspoon ground ginger**
- **2 large grapefruit**
- **½ pound deveined peeled cooked shrimp**
- **½ cup poached sliced mushrooms**
- **1 small grapefruit**

Mix mustard with water and let stand 10 minutes to develop flavor. Add to mayonnaise along with ginger. Set aside. Cut the large grapefruit into halves. Remove segments, drain, and place in a bowl. Remove membrane from the rinds, leaving the rinds intact. Add shrimp, mushrooms, and mayonnaise to grapefruit segments. Mix lightly and spoon into grapefruit shells. Peel small grapefruit in spiral fashion as one would peel an apple, being sure to cut away all the white portion of the peel from the grapefruit meat. Remove the grapefruit segments, take off the membranes, and place 2 on each serving. Makes 4 servings.

⚜ STUFFED ORANGES

- **4 medium-sized navel oranges**
- **1 red sweet pepper**
- **4 large black olives**
- **1 cup cold cooked rice**
- **¼ cup chopped green onion tops**
- **½ teaspoon curry powder**
- **2 tablespoons oil**
- **2 teaspoons wine vinegar**
- **salt to taste**
- **lettuce**
- **4 large stuffed green olives**

Cut a thick slice from the stem end of each orange. Carefully cut out the segments and remove the membrane, keeping the rind intact. Scrape out the orange cases to remove all seeds and membrane. Notch the edges with scissors or a sharp knife. Cut pepper in half and remove seeds and all pithy tissue. Cut into short, fine julienne strips. Cut the orange sections and olives into fine dice and add to the peppers along with rice and onion tops. Combine curry powder, oil, vinegar, and salt. Pour over the orange and rice mixture and marinate 1 hour. Drain and spoon into the orange cases. Serve on lettuce. Garnish each with a stuffed green olive. Makes 4 servings.

⚜ TOMATOES ANDALUSIAN STYLE

4 medium-sized tomatoes
salt
ground black pepper
3 tablespoons chopped onion
⅓ cup chopped sweet green pepper
2 tablespoons olive oil or salad oil
1 cup cooked rice
mayonnaise
thin green pepper strips and rounds
lettuce

Cut a slice from the stem ends of tomatoes and scoop out the centers, leaving the shells intact. Sprinkle the cavities with salt and pepper and let stand ½ hour. Invert on a plate to drain. Sauté onion and chopped green pepper in oil until vegetables are limp but not browned. Add to rice. Add enough mayonnaise to moisten the mixture. Season to taste with salt and pepper. Chill. Spoon into cavities of tomatoes. Garnish tops with green pepper. Serve on lettuce. Makes 4 servings. (See illustration, page 221.)

⚜ TOMATOES BALTIC STYLE
(*Tomatoes Stuffed with Potatoes and Herring*)

3 medium-sized tomatoes
salt
ground black pepper
wine vinegar
2 small potatoes, cooked and diced
½ cup pickled herring fillets
¼ cup diced unpeeled apple
1 small cucumber pickle
2 tablespoons mayonnaise
1 gherkin

Cut tomatoes in half lengthwise, scoop out the centers, and season the shells to taste with salt, pepper, and vinegar. Let stand ½ hour. Invert on a plate to drain. Combine potatoes, herring, and apple. Dice ½ of the cucumber pickle and add to this mixture along with mayonnaise. Add salt and pepper to taste and mix lightly. Spoon the salad into tomato cavities. Cut remaining cucumber pickle into thin crosswise slices and arrange a few of these on the top of each salad, having them overlapping. Place a round slice of gherkin in the center. Makes 3 servings.

⚜ TOMATOES BEAULIEU (*With Tuna Fish*)

3 medium-sized tomatoes
½ of a 7-ounce can of tuna fish packed in oil
2 tablespoons softened butter
2 tablespoons mayonnaise
lemon juice
salt
ground black pepper
1 hard-cooked egg
3 pitted black olives
lettuce

Prepare tomatoes as in the preceding recipe. Mash tuna fish with the oil, butter, and mayonnaise. Season to taste with lemon juice, salt, and pepper. Spoon into cavities of tomatoes. Chop egg white and egg yolk separately. Sprinkle egg white on one half of each tomato and egg yolk on the other half. Cut olives in half and place one piece in the center of each salad. Serve on lettuce. Makes 3 servings. (See illustration, page 221.)

⚜ TOMATOES BEAUREGARD

6 small tomatoes
stuffing as for Tomatoes Beaulieu
lettuce

Cut a slice from the stem end of each tomato and cut the slices into 4 equal parts. Scoop out centers and season the shells with salt, pepper and vinegar to taste. Let stand ½ hour. Drain well. Fill with Tomato Beaulieu stuffing. Garnish each with 4 pieces of the tomato slices. Serve on lettuce. Makes 3 servings.

⚜ TOMATOES STUFFED WITH CHICKEN

8 small tomatoes
½ cup sliced raw mushrooms
1 cup diced cooked chicken
lemon juice
salt and ground black pepper to taste
¼ cup mayonnaise
¼ sweet green pepper
lettuce or parsley

Prepare whole tomatoes for stuffing as in preceding recipes. Combine mushrooms, chicken, lemon juice, salt, pepper, and mayonnaise. Spoon into tomato cavities, rounding the tops slightly. Cut green pepper into short julienne strips and arrange over tops. Serve on lettuce or parsley. Makes 4 to 8 servings.

⚜ TOMATOES STUFFED WITH CRAYFISH

6 medium-sized tomatoes
salt
ground black pepper
mayonnaise
1½ cups cooked crayfish tails
aspic
6 narrow 1½-inch-long strips sweet green pepper
6 green pistachios

Cut off a slice from the stem end of the tomatoes. Scoop out the centers. Sprinkle cavities with salt and pepper. Let stand ½ hour. Drain well. Put a layer of mayonnaise on the bottom of each tomato and finish filling with cooked crayfish tails. Glaze with aspic. Place a strip of green pepper across the center of each and a half pistachio nut on each side of the pepper strip. Makes 6 servings. (See illustration, page 221.)

⚜ TOMATOES FRIBOURG STYLE
(*Tomatoes Stuffed with Potatoes and Gruyère Cheese*)

6 medium-small tomatoes
salt
ground black pepper
chopped chives
¾ cup diced boiled potatoes
¾ cup diced Gruyère cheese
1 tablespoon chopped onion
mayonnaise

Cut tomatoes in half and scoop out centers. Drain. Sprinkle cavities with salt, pepper, and chopped chives. Combine remaining ingredients and spoon into tomato cavities. Garnish with chopped chives.

⚜ TOMATOES RUSSIAN STYLE

6 medium-sized tomatoes
2 cups Russian Salad
3 to 4 tablespoons mayonnaise
1 sliced hard-cooked egg
parsley

Prepare whole tomatoes for stuffing as in preceding recipes. Mix Russian Salad with mayonnaise and spoon into tomato cavities. Top each with a slice of hard-cooked egg. Serve on a bed of parsley. Makes 6 servings. (See illustration, page 221.)

⚜ TOMATOES STUFFED WITH SHRIMP OR LOBSTER

In the recipe for Tomatoes Fribourg Style, replace crayfish with cooked shrimp or diced cooked lobster. Garnish with cucumber balls. Serve on lettuce. Makes 6 servings. (See illustration, page 221.)

HORS D'OEUVRE SALADS

Salads served as hors d'oeuvre may be made from vegetables, fruit, leftover meat, poultry, fish, and shellfish. The types and varieties to serve are limited only by the imagination of the one preparing them. There are three rules to follow:

1. The salads should be appetizingly fresh in order to stimulate the appetite.
2. No food which appears in the salad hors d'oeuvre should appear in any dish in the main part of the meal. For example, if there are tomatoes in the salad, tomato must not be used in a sauce or in another dish.
3. The salad must be small to prevent dulling the appetite for the rest of the meal.

⚜ BEEF SALAD

Marinate thin slices of leftover beef for 2 hours in oil and vinegar French dressing, a little chopped onion, and parsley. Serve on lettuce. Garnish with gherkins and sliced hard-cooked egg.

⚜ BEET SALAD

Marinate thinly sliced cooked beets in oil and vinegar French dressing. Sprinkle with chopped hard-cooked egg white and chopped parsley. Serve on lettuce.

⚜ RED CABBAGE SALAD

Cut out and discard the thick ribs of the tender inside leaves of red cabbage. Shred enough of the leaves finely to make 4 cups. Dice 3 strips lean bacon and cook until crisp. Add cabbage and ¼ cup dry white wine. Stir and cook until about half done. Season to taste with salt, ground black pepper, ½ teaspoon sugar, 2 tablespoons salad oil or olive oil, and 1 tablespoon wine vinegar. If desired, add 2 tablespoons finely chopped onion. Serve cold. Makes 6 servings.

⚜ WHITE CABBAGE SALAD

Finely shred enough of the heart of tender white cabbage to make 3 cups. Combine 2 tablespoons salad oil or olive oil, 1 tablespoon cider vinegar, ½ teaspoon sugar, ⅛ teaspoon salt or salt to taste, 1/16 teaspoon ground black pepper, and 2 tablespoons finely chopped onion. Pour over cabbage and marinate 1 hour. Serve on lettuce. Garnish with chopped parsley. Or if desired, fry 2 strips of bacon until crisp, add the marinade, heat, and pour over cabbage. Serve cold. Makes 4 to 6 servings.

⚜ CAULIFLOWER SALAD

Cook cauliflowerets only until crisp-tender. Marinate 1 hour in oil and vinegar French dressing. Arrange on an hors d'oeuvre dish, sprinkle with chopped hard-cooked egg yolk, and surround with small tomato slices or marinated cooked French beans.

⚜ CELERY SALAD

Remove the leaves from the center ribs of celery stalks. Cut the ribs into strips 1½ inches long and slice these very thinly lengthwise. Combine ½ cup mayonnaise, 1 tablespoon each capers, finely chopped gherkins, and chopped parsley, and ½ teaspoon Dijon mustard (or mustard to taste). Mix with celery and marinate 1 to 2 hours. Serve on lettuce.

⚜ CUCUMBER SALAD

Peel cucumbers and cut into thin slices. Arrange on hors d'oeuvre dishes, with the slices overlapping. Chill. Just before serving dust lightly with salt and ground black pepper, and sprinkle with oil, vinegar, and chopped parsley.

⚜ EGG SALAD

Cut hard-cooked eggs into slices ¼ inch thick. Arrange them in an hors d'oeuvre dish. Pour Vinaigrette Sauce lightly over them, or cover them with a thin coating of mayonnaise, mixed with powdered mustard, using ½ teaspoon mustard to each ½ cup mayonnaise. Arrange long anchovy fillets over the top in lattice fashion.

⚜ EGG AND TOMATO SALAD

Arrange alternate slices of hard-cooked eggs and tomatoes in an hors d'oeuvre dish. Sprinkle Vinaigrette Sauce over the top. Sprinkle with chopped parsley.

⚜ LOBSTER SALAD IN COCONUT SHELLS

1½-pound lobster, cooked
1 cup thinly sliced raw mushrooms
1 cup 1-inch pieces cooked asparagus
salt to taste
ground black pepper to taste
⅓ cup mayonnaise
2 tablespoons tomato catsup
1 tablespoon brandy
4 dried coconut half-shells
aspic jelly

Cut meat from lobster tails into 8 slices. Remove meat from claws, dice and toss lightly with the next 7 ingredients. Spoon into the 4 coconut shells. Garnish with lobster slices. Glaze with aspic jelly. Chill until aspic is set. Makes 4 servings. (See illustration, page 220.)

⚜ MUSHROOM SALAD

Slice enough well-cleaned white mushrooms to make 2 cups. Immediately marinate 1 hour in dressing made with 3 tablespoons salad oil, 1 tablespoon lemon juice, salt and cayenne to taste, and ¼ teaspoon sugar. Divide into 6 portions, place each on a lettuce leaf, and surround with sliced tomatoes, each topped with a slice of gherkin and a pickled onion. Makes 6 servings.

⚜ POTATO SALAD

1 quart hot potato slices ¼ inch thick
salt
ground black pepper
¼ cup chopped onion
⅓ cup hot beef stock or dry white wine
¼ cup oil and vinegar French dressing
thin mayonnaise
chopped parsley

Combine potatoes, salt, pepper, onion, beef stock or wine, and French dressing. Mix lightly. Marinate several hours or overnight. Before serving, add thin mayonnaise and chopped parsley. Mix lightly to avoid breaking potatoes. Serve on lettuce. Makes 6 to 8 servings.

⚜ POULTRY SALAD

Remove skin from cooked chicken or turkey and cut meat into thin slices. Arrange in a salad bowl on shredded lettuce. Coat with mayonnaise and garnish with anchovy fillets, quartered hard-cooked eggs, and quartered hearts of lettuce.

FISH SALAD

In the recipe for Poultry Salad, replace chicken or turkey with cooked, skinned, and sliced fish.

⚜ RICH POULTRY SALAD

Arrange thin slices of skinned cooked poultry on a bed of shredded lettuce. Coat with thick mayonnaise seasoned to taste with grated horseradish and catsup and thinned to the desired consistency with orange juice and a little brandy. Garnish with quartered hard-cooked eggs, pineapple slices cut in triangles, and half slices of small tomatoes.

⚜ ROCK LOBSTER SALAD IN COQUILLES

Coquilles (scallop shells) are either natural shells or small fireproof dishes made in the shape of shells. They are most often used to cook and serve hot mixtures of fish, shellfish, chicken, etc., but are also sometimes used to serve shellfish salads.

1 small head lettuce
1 pound cooked rock lobster meat
salt and ground black pepper
mayonnaise
1 hard-cooked egg, chopped
capers

Shred lettuce and put into 6 coquilles. Sprinkle rock lobster meat with salt and pepper and arrange it over the lettuce. Cover with a thin layer of mayonnaise and sprinkle with chopped egg and capers. Makes 6 servings.

⚜ MADRID-STYLE SPINACH SALAD

Remove most of the stalks from spinach leaves and cut the leaves into coarse julienne pieces. Blanch quickly in hot water, cool, and squeeze out moisture. Season to taste with salt, ground black pepper, oil and vinegar, using 3 parts oil to 1 part wine vinegar. Serve garnished with hard-cooked eggs. This is a favorite Spanish salad.

⚜ TOMATO SALAD

Peel medium-sized, firm, ripe tomatoes and cut into slices ¼ inch thick. Arrange on hors d'oeuvre dishes so the slices overlap. Dust with salt and ground black pepper and sprinkle with oil and vinegar French dressing. Arrange thin onion rings over the top. Sprinkle with chopped parsley.

Assortment of Hors d'Oeuvre Salads

See illustration, page 224.

⚜ FISH SALAD

Combine diced cold fillet of sole, turbot, or halibut, diced tomatoes, sliced white onions, and bits of truffle or black olives. Mix with Vinaigrette Sauce.

⚜ VENISON SALAD

Combine small slices of cold cooked fillet of venison and sliced mushrooms with mayonnaise.

⚜ VEAL SALAD

Combine diced cold cooked veal and diced celery with mayonnaise mixed with a little catsup. Garnish with paprika.

⚜ CHICKEN AND ASPARAGUS SALAD

Combine diced cold cooked chicken with diced cold cooked asparagus and sliced poached mushrooms and mix with mayonnaise. Garnish each serving with 3 cold cooked asparagus tips.

⚜ ROAST BEEF SALAD DIABLE

Mix diced cold roast beef with diced celery, a little piccalilli, and mayonnaise.

⚜ CHICKEN AND PEACH SALAD

Marinate diced cold boned chicken in Vinaigrette Sauce and combine with sliced fresh peaches and mayonnaise.

⚜ ROAST BEEF AND VEGETABLE SALAD

Mix diced cold roast beef with mixed vegetable salad.

⚜ FRANKFURTER SALAD

Combine sliced cooked frankfurters or Vienna sausages with lightly salted cucumbers and Mustard Mayonnaise. Serve on lettuce with slices of tomato.

⚜ ALSATIAN SALAD

Combine diced Cheddar or Gruyère cheese, sliced sausages, and sliced radishes with mayonnaise.

⚜ ASPARAGUS SALAD

Marinate cold cooked asparagus 1 hour in oil and vinegar French dressing. Combine with julienne strips of ham and pickled tongue. Serve with a little mayonnaise if desired.

⚜ LOBSTER SALAD

Cut cold cooked lobster meat into chunks and combine with diced celery and mayonnaise.

⚜ ARTICHOKE AND SMOKED SALMON SALAD

Marinate cooked artichoke bottoms in oil and vinegar French dressing for 1 hour. Fill with julienne strips of smoked salmon.

⚜ SHRIMP SALAD

Arrange cold cooked shrimp, lightly salted sliced cucumbers, sliced hard-cooked eggs, and sliced tomatoes on lettuce. Sprinkle with French dressing.

⚜ MUSSEL SALAD

Arrange cooked mussels, lightly salted sliced cucumbers, and sliced tomatoes in an hors d'oeuvre dish. Sprinkle with oil and vinegar French dressing.

⚜ CRAYFISH AND ARTICHOKE SALAD

Place crayfish tails on cooked artichoke bottoms marinated in French dressing and top with slices of hard-cooked egg.

SANDWICHES

Sandwiches for hors d'oeuvre, tea, receptions, and cocktail affairs may be simple or elaborate. In any case they should be small, dainty, colorful, and in a variety of shapes. The best bread for preparing sandwiches is firm-textured and a day or two old. The butter should be soft and creamy for easy spreading and the fillings varied. Try to include one or two types of sandwiches that reducers can enjoy, such as the open-faced kind with low-calorie spreads or toppings.

⚜ ANCHOVY SANDWICHES

6 tablespoons softened butter
2 tablespoons mashed anchovies, or anchovy paste
4 thin slices of white or dark bread
2 hard-cooked eggs
parsley, finely chopped

Combine butter and anchovies or anchovy paste. Mix well. Spread on slices of bread from which crust has been trimmed. Chop hard-cooked eggs finely and sprinkle over the top. Cut the sandwiches into triangles and garnish the edges with chopped parsley. Makes 16 sandwiches.

⚜ CAMEMBERT AND APPLE SANDWICHES

softened butter
thinly sliced bread
Camembert cheese
thinly sliced apples
watercress

Butter one side of each slice of bread and spread with soft Camembert cheese. Place apple slices on half the bread and top with remaining bread. Cut in triangles. Garnish the top of each with a leaf of watercress. Allow 3 to 4 little sandwiches per person.

⚜ CAVIAR SANDWICHES

lightly salted butter
thinly sliced bread
black caviar
lemon juice
tiny pickled white onions
finely chopped parsley

Soften butter and spread over one side of slices of bread from which crusts have been trimmed. Then spread lightly with caviar. Sprinkle with a few drops of lemon juice. Cut each slice into 4 squares. Press a tiny pickled onion into the center of each. Garnish the edges with chopped parsley. Allow 3 to 4 little sandwiches per person.

⚜ CHESHIRE AND GRUYÈRE CHEESE SANDWICHES

thinly sliced bread
Dijon prepared mustard
softened butter
sliced Cheshire cheese
sliced Gruyère cheese

Trim crusts from bread and spread with butter. Then spread one side of half the pieces with mustard butter made by blending 1½ teaspoons Dijon mustard with ¼ cup (½ stick) softened butter. Cut the cheese slices to fit the bread and place a piece of each kind on half the slices. Cover with remaining bread. Cut each sandwich into 4 triangles or into 3 to 4 finger strips, the number depending on the width of the bread. Decorate the centers of the sandwiches with a tiny piece of Cheshire cheese cut in the shape of the sandwich. Allow 3 to 4 little sandwiches per person.

⚜ CUCUMBER SANDWICHES

parsley
watercress
softened butter
thinly sliced bread
thinly sliced unpeeled cucumbers
salt and ground black pepper

Finely chop parsley and watercress and mix 1 tablespoon of parsley and 2 tablespoons of watercress with each ½ cup (1 stick) softened butter. Cut the bread into rounds the same size as the cucumber slices. Spread one side of each round with the herb butter and top with a slice of cucumber. Sprinkle very lightly with salt and ground black pepper. Cover with the remaining bread rounds. Place a watercress leaf in the center of each sandwich. Allow 3 sandwiches per person.

⚜ OPEN-FACED CUCUMBER SANDWICHES

Top each round of buttered bread with a thin slice of cucumber. Sprinkle very lightly with salt and ground black pepper. Decorate half the slices with a leaf of watercress and the remainder with a dash of paprika. Allow 3 sandwiches per person.

⚜ EGG AND ANCHOVY SANDWICHES

4 hard-cooked eggs
1½ tablespoons minced celery
¼ teaspoon paprika
1/16 teaspoon ground black pepper
mayonnaise
1/16 teaspoon ground white pepper
thinly sliced bread
softened butter
1 jar rolled anchovies

Remove yolks from hard-cooked eggs and mash them. Reserve whites. Add the next 3 ingredients and enough mayonnaise to moisten. Set aside. Mince egg whites and mix with white pepper and enough mayonnaise to moisten them. Trim crusts from bread and spread with butter. Cut each slice into 4 squares. Spread half of each square with egg-yolk mixture and the other half with the egg white mixture. Top each square with a rolled anchovy. Makes approximately 16 sandwiches.

⚜ FOIE GRAS SANDWICHES

pâté de foie gras
softened butter
ground hazelnuts, almonds, or pistachio nuts
thinly sliced bread

Combine pâté de foie gras with softened butter, using 3 parts pâté to 1 part butter. Add 3 tablespoons ground nuts to each cup of the mixture. Trim crusts from bread and spread half the slices with the pâté mixture. Spread remaining slices with softened butter and put on top. Cut each sandwich into 4 squares or triangles. Allow 3 sandwiches per person.

⚜ HAM OR TONGUE SANDWICHES

thinly sliced bread
softened butter
Dijon prepared mustard
sliced cooked lean ham or cooked tongue
watercress

Trim crusts from bread and spread one side of each slice with mustard butter, using 1½ teaspoons Dijon mustard to ¼ cup (½ stick) softened butter. Cut ham or tongue to fit the bread and place a slice on half the bread. Cover with remaining bread and cut into triangles, squares, or finger strips. Allow 3 sandwiches per person.

OPEN-FACED HAM OR TONGUE SANDWICHES

Place a piece of cooked ham or tongue, cut to fit the bread, on each slice of bread spread with mustard butter. Cut into triangles, squares, or finger strips. Decorate with slices of black or pimiento-stuffed olives. Allow 3 sandwiches per person.

⚜ LETTUCE SANDWICHES

thinly sliced bread
softened butter
finely shredded lettuce
salt
ground black pepper
Dijon prepared mustard

Trim crusts from bread and spread one side of slices with butter. Top each with shredded lettuce and sprinkle lightly with salt and pepper. Cover with remaining slices of bread spread with mustard butter, using 1½ teaspoons Dijon mustard to ½ cup (1 stick) butter. Cut diagonally. Allow 2 sandwiches per person.

⚜ POULTRY SANDWICHES

thinly sliced bread
freshly grated horseradish or horseradish sauce
softened butter
sliced cold cooked chicken, turkey, duck, goose, or game bird
salt
ground black pepper
grapes, cut in half

Cut bread into rounds and spread one side of each with butter mixed with horseradish, using 4 teaspoons grated fresh horseradish or horseradish sauce to ½ cup (1 stick) butter. Top with a slice of poultry cut to fit the bread. Sprinkle lightly with salt and pepper. Garnish with a seeded or seedless grape, cut in half. Allow 3 sandwiches per person.

⚜ RADISH SANDWICHES

thinly sliced bread
softened butter
thinly sliced radishes
salt
parsley

Cut bread into rounds or ovals. Spread one side of each piece with softened butter and on top arrange slices of radishes, having them slightly overlapping. Sprinkle lightly with salt. Decorate the center with a leaf of parsley. Allow 3 sandwiches per person.

⚜ SMOKED SALMON SANDWICHES

thinly sliced bread
softened sweet butter
smoked salmon
gherkin pickle

Trim crusts from bread and spread with softened butter. Cover with smoked salmon cut to fit the bread. Cut in triangles, squares, or finger strips. Decorate the center of each with a slice of gherkin pickle. Allow 3 sandwiches per person.

VARIATIONS

Make Smoked Salmon Sandwiches with any of the following additions.

CURRY POWDER

Mix 1 teaspoon curry powder with each ½ cup (1 stick) butter.

HORSERADISH

Mix 4 teaspoons grated horseradish or horseradish sauce with each ½ cup (1 stick) butter.

HERBS

Mix 2 tablespoons finely chopped parsley and ½ teaspoon ground thyme with each ½ cup (1 stick) butter.

⚜ SAUSAGE SANDWICHES

chopped parsley
crumbled dried rosemary
softened butter
thinly sliced bread
links of cooked pork sausage, 1 inch in diameter
watercress

Combine herbs with butter, using 2 tablespoons chopped parsley and ½ teaspoon finely crumbled rosemary to ½ cup (1 stick) softened butter. Trim crusts from bread and spread one side of each slice with herb butter. Cut sausage into slices ⅛ inch thick, and arrange over half the bread slices. Cover with the remaining bread. Cut into triangles or squares. Decorate the top with a leaf of watercress. Allow 2 to 3 sandwiches per person.

⚜ OPEN-FACED TOMATO SANDWICHES

thinly sliced bread
softened butter
horseradish
tomatoes, sliced
salt
ground black pepper
hard-cooked egg yolk
parsley, or sliced ripe or pimiento-stuffed olive

Cut bread into rounds and spread with horseradish butter, using 4 teaspoons grated horseradish or horseradish sauce to ½ cup (1 stick) butter. Top each with a slice of tomato. Decorate the top with a little sieved hard-cooked egg yolk and a bit of parsley or a slice of ripe or pimiento-stuffed olive. Allow 2 per serving.

⚜ OPEN-FACED PICKLED TONGUE SANDWICHES

thinly sliced bread
softened watercress butter
sliced pickled tongue
watercress

Trim crusts from bread and spread one side of each slice with watercress butter, blending 2 tablespoons finely chopped watercress to ½ cup (1 stick) butter. Cover with slices of pickled tongue. Cut into triangles, squares, or finger strips. Decorate the centers with watercress leaves. Allow 2 to 3 sandwiches per person.

⚜ VEAL SANDWICHES

thinly sliced bread
horseradish sauce
softened butter
sliced cold cooked veal

Trim crusts from bread and spread with horseradish butter, blending 4 teaspoons horseradish sauce with ½ cup (1 stick) butter. Top half the slices with sliced veal cut to fit the bread. Cover with remaining bread. Cut into triangles, squares, or finger strips.

⚜ OPEN-FACED VEAL AND GRAPE SANDWICHES

Spread slices of bread with horseradish butter. Cut into squares. Top each with a slice of veal cut to fit the bread. Top with half a seeded or seedless grape. Allow 2 to 3 per person.

CANAPÉS

Canapés are dainty tidbits served as hors d'oeuvre or as tea or cocktail accompaniments. The base is made from firm-textured day-old white or whole-wheat bread, sliced ¼ to ⅜ inch thick. These slices are cut into squares, triangles, or finger-length strips, or cut with cooky cutters into rounds or other fancy shapes small enough to be eaten gracefully with the fingers. They are either fried in deep fat, sautéed in butter, or toasted in the oven, and then buttered. Shortly before serving, they are spread with various seasoned mixtures or covered with thinly sliced fish, meat, poultry, or cheese cut to fit the bread. Canapés may be garnished with parsley, watercress, truffles, green or black olives, pimiento, mushrooms, hard-cooked eggs, anchovies, etc. They may be served hot or cold. Allow 2 to 3 of any one kind per serving.

⚜ ANCHOVY CANAPÉS

Crustless white bread cut into 2½-by-1½-inch pieces
butter or oil
anchovy paste
softened butter
hard-cooked eggs
anchovy fillets
aspic

Fry bread in butter or oil. Cool. Spread with anchovy paste mixed with butter, using 1 tablespoon anchovy paste for each stick (¼ pound) butter. Garnish one end of each canapé with finely chopped egg white and the other end with sieved hard-cooked egg yolk. Arrange 2 long anchovy fillets in crossed fashion (X) in center of each. Glaze with aspic. (See illustration, page 225.)

⚜ ASPARAGUS CANAPÉS

Cut wholewheat toast into triangles and spread with any desired Herb Butter. Arrange cooked asparagus tips on the triangles, trimming the cut ends to fit the toast. Garnish with strips of pimiento and slices of gherkins. (See illustration, page 225.)

⚜ CAVIAR CANAPÉS (*Canapés au caviar* or *à la Russe*)

Spread 1½-inch rounds of toasted white or wholewheat bread with lightly salted softened butter. Cover with a thin layer of chilled black or red caviar. Cut thin slices of lemon into quarters, remove seeds, and place 1 in the center of each canapé. Allow 3 per serving.

⚜ CHEESE CANAPÉS

Add enough Béchamel Sauce to grated Gruyère cheese to make a smooth spreadable mixture. Season to taste with ground white pepper and paprika. Spread on rectangles of buttered white bread. Brown quickly in a hot oven (425° F.) or under the broiler. Serve hot or cold.

⚜ CHICKEN AND PAPRIKA-BUTTER CANAPÉS (*Canapés à la Hongroise*)

Mix softened butter with enough paprika to give it a delicate pink color. Spread over oval slices of white bread. Mix finely chopped cooked chicken with enough mayonnaise to make a spreadable mixture. Season to taste with salt and black pepper. Spread over the buttered bread. Garnish with very short fine julienne strips of red and green sweet pepper.

⚜ CHICKEN LIVER CANAPÉS

1 pound chicken livers
chicken stock
2 large hard-cooked eggs
¼ cup finely chopped onion
2 tablespoons rendered chicken fat (or butter)
salt and ground black pepper to taste
toast fingers
chopped parsley

Cook livers in hot stock to cover until they have lost their pink color. Remove livers from stock, drain, and put them through a food chopper along with the eggs, using the medium blade. Cook onions in chicken fat (or butter), stirring, until they are soft. Add to the livers. Season to taste with salt and ground black pepper. Mix well. Spread on buttered toast fingers. Sprinkle chopped parsley around the edges. Makes 2 cups.

This mixture may also be piled in mounds on lettuce leaves, sprinkled with diced hard-cooked egg and diced onion, and served with toast rounds or crackers.

⚜ CURRIED-EGG CANAPÉS (*Canapés Bradford*)

Put hard-cooked eggs through a sieve. Mix with enough heavy cream to make the mixture smooth and spreadable. Season to taste with salt, black pepper, curry powder, and lemon juice. Butter toasted 2-inch rounds of white bread and spread with the egg mixture. Top each with a 2-inch slice of tomato and sprinkle with salt and pepper. Garnish with finely chopped gherkins.

⚜ HARD-COOKED-EGG CANAPÉS

Spread rectangular pieces of cold toast with mayonnaise. Cover with slices of hard-cooked eggs, having them overlapping. Garnish the yolks with finely diced gherkins.

⚜ GOOSE-LIVER CANAPÉS (*Canapés à l'Alsacienne*)

Cut ovals of white bread ¼ to ⅜ inch thick. Fry in butter or toast in the oven and then spread with softened butter. Cover with oval slices of chilled goose liver (foie gras) cut to fit the bread. Garnish with a bit of truffle or with sieved hard-cooked egg yolk and chopped parsley. Glaze with aspic. Allow 3 canapés per serving.

⚜ HAM AND CHICKEN OR EGG CANAPÉS (*Canapés Félicia*)

Blend 2 tablespoons prepared mustard with 6 tablespoons softened butter. Spread on rectangles of sautéed white or wholewheat bread. Sprinkle ground cold cooked ham on one half of each rectangle and ground cold cooked chicken or finely chopped hard-cooked egg on the other half.

⚜ CANAPÉS NIÇOIS

Spread rounds of toast or bread fried in butter with Anchovy Butter. Arrange finely chopped tomato in the center and top each with half a black olive. (See illustration, page 225.)

⚜ OYSTER CANAPÉS (*Canapés à l'Ostendaise*)

Cook small soup oysters in oyster liquor over very low heat or over hot water *only* until the edges curl. Remove from liquor, drain, and chill. Coat with mayonnaise mixed with prepared mustard to taste. Chill. Season softened butter with prepared mustard to taste. Spread over 2-inch squares of white bread, top each with an oyster, and encircle with sieved hard-cooked egg yolk.

⚜ ROAST BEEF AND EGG CANAPÉS (*Canapés à la Ménagère*)

Mix equal parts of finely chopped leftover roast beef and finely chopped hard-cooked eggs with enough mayonnaise to make the mixture smooth and spreadable. Season to taste with salt, black pepper, and finely chopped gherkins. Spread on 2-inch squares of sautéed bread. Garnish each with a slice of cherry tomato.

⚜ SMOKED SALMON CANAPÉS (*Canapés à l'Aurore*)

Spread fried, sautéed, or toasted bread with softened butter. Cover with thin slices smoked salmon cut to fit the bread. Garnish with sieved hard-cooked egg yolk. Top each with half of a black olive.

⚜ SARDINE CANAPÉS

Blend 1 tablespoon lemon juice with 6 tablespoons softened butter and spread over rectangle-shaped canapés. Garnish edges with chopped parsley and place a boned sardine down the center of each. Sprinkle with paprika.

SHRIMP CANAPÉS (*Canapés Joinville*)

6 medium-sized cooked shrimp
2 tablespoons butter
salt
lemon juice
6 rounds of bread 2 inches in diameter, sautéed in butter
1 hard-cooked egg yolk
36 tiny cooked shrimp
6 butter curls

Mash or pound the 6 medium-sized shrimp and blend with the butter. Season to taste with salt and a few drops of lemon juice. Spread over rounds of bread sautéed in butter and roll edges of bread in chopped hard-cooked egg. Place 6 tiny shrimp in a circle on each and garnish center with a butter curl. Makes 6 servings. (See illustration, page 225.)

WATERCRESS AND EGG CANAPÉS (*Canapés Parisiens*)

Sauté squares or rounds of white bread in butter and spread with mayonnaise. Sprinkle with chopped watercress and top with sieved hard-cooked egg yolks. Allow 2 or 3 per serving. (See illustration, page 225.)

Assorted Canapés

See illustration, page 224.

ASPARAGUS AND CHICKEN

Cut thin slices cooked white meat of chicken or turkey to fit canapés. Cut cold cooked asparagus tips the length of the bread and arrange over the top of the chicken. Garnish with pimiento strips and sliced olives or pickle. Glaze with aspic.

HERB BUTTER AND TONGUE

Mix equal parts finely chopped watercress and softened butter. Spread over squares of sautéed, fried, or toasted bread. Cover with sliced pickled tongue cut to fit the bread. Garnish with mixed pickle. Glaze with aspic.

⚜ SALAMI AND EGG

Mix 1 part chopped parsley with 2 parts softened butter. Spread over fried, sautéed, or toasted bread. Cover with salami cut to fit the bread. Garnish each with half-slice of hard-cooked egg. Glaze with aspic.

⚜ CHIVE BUTTER AND HAM

Mix softened butter with finely chopped chives to taste. Spread over fried, sautéed, or toasted bread. Cover with thin slices of ham cut to fit the bread. Garnish with cold cooked asparagus tips. Glaze with aspic.

⚜ GALANTINE OF CHICKEN WITH MANDARIN ORANGE SEGMENTS

Spread fried, sautéed, or toasted bread with softened butter. Cover with cold sliced Galantine of Chicken, cut to fit the bread. Garnish with mandarin orange segments. Glaze with aspic.

⚜ GRUYÈRE CHEESE AND ALMOND

Spread fried, sautéed, or toasted bread with softened butter and then with creamed Gruyère cheese. Garnish each with a blanched toasted half almond. Glaze with aspic.

⚜ TARTARE STEAK AND ANCHOVY FILLET

Mix 1 pound ground raw sirloin or tenderloin steak with ½ cup finely chopped onion and salt and ground black pepper to taste. Spread thickly on fried, sautéed, or toasted 2½-inch squares of bread. Make an indentation in the center of each, into which place the yolk of a raw egg, and top with a rolled anchovy. Garnish with capers, small pickled white onions, and chopped parsley.

⚜ MUSTARD BUTTER AND BOILED HAM

Spread fried, sautéed, or toasted bread with mustard butter, using 2 tablespoons prepared mustard to 6 tablespoons softened butter. Cover with thin slices of boiled ham cut to fit the bread. Garnish with a wedge of canned pineapple. Glaze with aspic.

Rich Canapés, Assorted

Spread rectangles of bread, deep-fried, sautéed in butter, or toasted, with the following mixtures. (See illustration, page 225.)

⚜ PÂTÉ DE FOIE GRAS

Spread canapé with pâté de foie gras and decorate with small pieces of tomato arranged in fan shape.

⚜ TURKEY WITH PEACH AND GRAPE

Cut thin slices of turkey breast to fit the canapés and place on top. Garnish each with a small slice of fresh peach and a green seedless grape.

⚜ SMOKED TROUT

Cover canapés with slices of smoked trout cut to fit the bread. Garnish each with ½ teaspoon Tomato Fondue.

⚜ CAVIAR

Spread canapés with caviar and garnish each with ¼ slice of lemon, seeded.

⚜ CRAYFISH OR SHRIMP

Cut pieces of lettuce to fit canapés, place one on each, and arrange crayfish tails or small shrimp on top. Sprinkle lightly with salt and ground white pepper.

⚜ SMOKED SALMON

Cover canapés with slices of smoked salmon cut to fit. Mix 1 part grated horseradish with 3 parts softened butter until creamy and put ½ teaspoon on top of each.

⚜ LOBSTER AND GRAPEFRUIT

Arrange alternate slices of cooked lobster and fresh grapefruit on each canapé and garnish each with a small black olive.

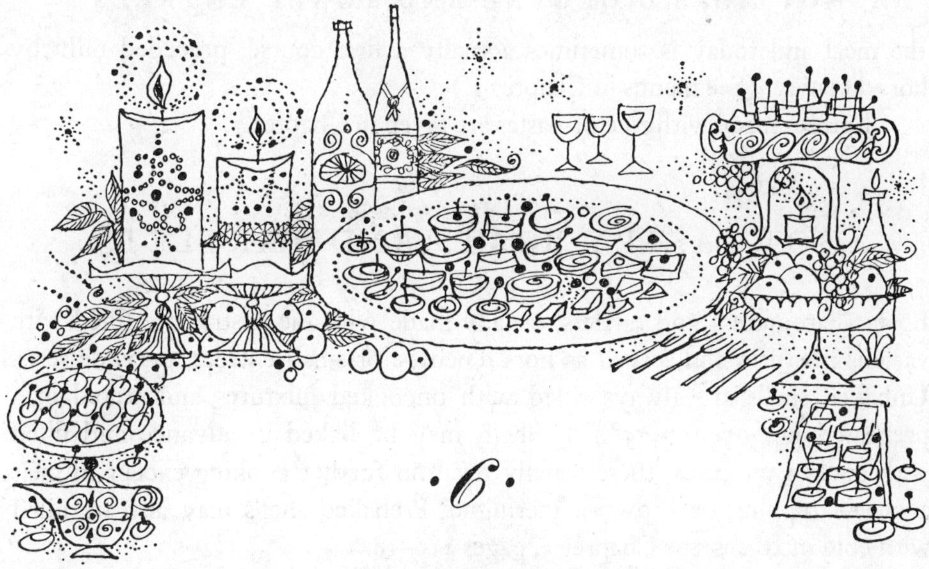

·6·

HOT HORS D'OEUVRE AND SMALL ENTRÉES

From the cook's point of view the only difference between hot hors d'oeuvre and small entrées in most cases is in the size of the individual item. For both, the same variety of mixtures (meat, fish, shellfish, poultry, cheese, vegetables, etc.) are served in tart shells or puff-pastry cases of various shapes and sizes or in small fireproof dishes. Croquettes and cromesquis, mousses, soufflés, quiches, hot deep-fat-fried foods are some of the other preparations which may serve either purpose. When they are to be served as hot hors d'oeuvre, the items are made very small and a selection is placed on individual plates and covered with napkins to keep the food hot. Hot hors d'oeuvre, like cold ones, are usually served at lunch, only occasionally at dinner when the soup course is omitted. When these preparations are served as small entrées, the size of the items and the amounts served are increased, and these dishes may be part of either the lunch or the dinner menu.

While the word *entrée* presumably once meant "first course," it was used in classic French menus to designate the course that followed the remove (relevé), which always followed the fish course. As menus become increasingly simplified, the entrée has gradually moved toward the beginning of the meal and today is sometimes actually a first course, preceded only by hors d'oeuvre. (See menus in Chapter 1.)

Entrées made with rice or pastas are given in Chapter 7.

HOT PASTRY BOATS AND TARTLETS

Boats (barquettes) and tartlets, usually made with pie pastry, are filled with various mixtures and served as hors d'oeuvre or small entrées, or as desserts. Unbaked shells are always filled with uncooked mixtures and baked in a preheated hot oven (425° F.). Shells may be baked in advance and filled with cooked mixtures; these usually need no further cooking except to melt a cheese topping or brown a meringue. Prebaked shells may also be filled with cold mixtures; see Chapter 5, pages 216–18.

⚜ SHRIMP BARQUETTES II

2 cups diced cooked shrimp
1½ cups Mornay Sauce
salt and pepper
12 small baked boat-shaped tart shells
grated Parmesan cheese
12 small whole cooked shrimp, peeled and deveined

Combine diced shrimp with 1 cup of the Mornay Sauce. Adjust seasonings and spoon mixture into tart shells. Coat with remaining Mornay Sauce, sprinkle with grated cheese, and garnish each with a whole shrimp. Put into a hot oven or under the broiler until cheese is melted. Serve hot as an hors d'oeuvre. Makes 12 servings.

⚜ LOBSTER BARQUETTES

1½ cups medium cream sauce
½ cup grated Cheddar cheese
¾ cup finely diced cooked lobster
¼ teaspoon powdered mustard
1 teaspoon water
dash Worcestershire sauce
salt to taste
1/16 teaspoon ground white pepper
18 baked boat-shaped tart shells

Combine the first 3 ingredients. Soak mustard in 1 teaspoon water 5 minutes and add to the mixture along with remaining seasonings. Stir and cook only until hot. Divide the mixture equally among the tart shells. Garnish with bits of truffles, black olives, or sieved egg yolk. Serve hot. Makes 18.

VARIATIONS

SHRIMP BARQUETTES III

Replace lobster in recipe for Lobster Boats with the same amount of finely diced cooked shrimp.

CRABMEAT BARQUETTES

Replace lobster in recipe for Lobster Boats with the same amount of cooked, flaked crabmeat, and add a few drops of lemon juice.

⚜ CADOGAN BOATS (*English*)

1 cup ground cooked ham
2 tablespoons chopped gherkins
½ tablespoon butter
1 cup medium Cheese Sauce
18 baked small boat-shaped tart shells
⅓ cup grated mild Cheddar cheese

Heat ham and gherkins in butter. Put an equal amount in each of the tart shells. Cover with Cheese Sauce. Sprinkle with grated cheese. Place in a preheated very hot oven (450° F.) only until cheese melts. Serve hot, garnished with chopped parsley, if desired. Makes 18.

⚜ CHICKEN AND MUSHROOM TARTLETS (*Tartelettes Marion Delorme*)

unsweetened pastry dough (Pâte Brisée)
1½ cup finely ground cooked chicken (without skin)
1 cup finely ground raw mushrooms
¾ cup Béchamel Sauce
salt, ground black pepper, and lemon juice to taste
2 tablespoons butter
3 large egg yolks, beaten

Line small tartlet molds with thinly rolled pastry and set aside. Combine chicken, mushrooms, Béchamel Sauce, seasonings, and butter. Stir and cook 2 to 3 minutes. Remove from heat, add a little of the hot mixture to the beaten egg yolks, and then add them to the remaining hot mixture. Mix well. Spoon into the tart shells. Place the shells on a baking sheet. Bake in a preheated hot oven (425° F.) 10 to 12 minutes, or until pastry has browned. Serve as a hot hors d'oeuvre, or make larger tarts and serve as a small entrée. Makes 12 tartlets or 6 large tarts.

⚜ MILANESE TARTLETS

unsweetened pastry dough (Pâte Brisée)
½ cup well-drained, finely chopped, cooked macaroni
½ cup grated Gruyère or Cheddar cheese
½ cup ground cooked lean ham
½ cup ground pickled tongue
¼ cup finely chopped raw mushrooms
highly seasoned thick tomato sauce
salt and ground black pepper

Line small tartlet molds with thinly rolled pastry. Prick the pastry generously with a fork to prevent it from puffing. Bake in a preheated hot oven (425° F.) 10 minutes or until browned. Cool. Combine macaroni, cheese, ham, tongue, and mushrooms. Stir in enough tomato sauce to make a spreadable mixture. Add salt and pepper to taste. Stir and cook until hot. Spoon into baked tartlets. Serve very hot as an hors d'oeuvre, or make the tarts larger and serve as an entrée. Makes 12 to 18 tartlets or 6 large tarts.

⚜ RAJAH TARTLETS (*Curried-Shrimp Tartlets*)

1 teaspoon curry powder
1 teaspoon finely chopped onion
1 tablespoon butter
1 cup Béchamel Sauce
¾ cup diced cooked shrimp
few drops of lemon juice
salt to taste
12 baked 1½-inch tart shells
12 small whole mushrooms, sautéed in butter

Stir and cook curry powder and onion in butter 2 to 3 minutes. Add to Béchamel Sauce along with shrimp and lemon juice. Add salt to taste. Heat. Spoon into tart shells. Top each with a mushroom cooked in butter. Serve hot. Makes 12 small tarts.

⚜ ROMANIAN CHEESE TARTS

unsweetened pastry dough (Pâte Brisée)
½ the recipe for Chou Paste (cream-puff pastry)
1⅓ cups grated Gruyère or Cheddar cheese
2 cups thick Béchamel Sauce
3 large egg yolks

Line six 3-inch tart pans with thinly rolled pastry dough and set aside. Mix warm Chou Paste with ⅓ cup of the grated Gruyère or Cheddar cheese, and put the paste into a pastry bag fitted with a small round nozzle. Pipe 3 rings of the cheese paste on top of one another in each unbaked tart shell. Combine Béchamel Sauce and the remaining 1 cup grated cheese. Beat in egg yolks. Stir and cook over low heat *only* until hot. Fill the center of the tarts with this mixture. Bake in a preheated hot oven (400° F.) 20 to 25 minutes, or until the pastry has browned. Serve hot as an entrée. Makes 6 tarts.

⚜ SWISS-CHEESE TARTLETS

unsweetened pastry dough (Pâte Brisée)
¼ cup (½ stick) butter
4 tablespoons flour
½ teaspoon salt
¼ teaspoon powdered mustard
⅛ teaspoon ground white pepper
dash cayenne
2 cups light cream
2 large eggs, beaten lightly
1 cup grated Gruyère or Emmentaler cheese

Line small tartlet molds with thinly rolled pastry. Set aside. Melt butter in a saucepan. Remove from heat and blend in flour. Stir and cook 1 minute. Remove from heat and add cream. Stir and cook until mixture is thick. Blend a little of the hot mixture with the eggs and add to the remaining hot mixture. Add cheese and mix well. Spoon into the unbaked tartlet shells. Place tarts on a baking sheet and bake in a preheated hot oven (425° F.) 15 to 20 minutes, or until crust has browned. Cool 5 to 10 minutes before serving. Serve as a hot hors d'oeuvre, or make the tart shells larger and serve as an entrée. Makes approximately 16 tartlets.

PUFF-PASTE PATTIES, HORNS, ETC.

Patty shells (bouchées), horns (cornets), rolls, and similar preparations are made of puff paste or chou paste and filled. They are sometimes baked in advance and sometimes baked with the filling.

⚜ CHICKEN PATTIES (*Bouchées à la Reine*)

3 cups diced cooked chicken
½ cup sautéed mushrooms
1 small truffle, finely diced (optional)
1¼ cups Sauce Suprême
salt and pepper
8 baked puff-paste patty shells

Combine chicken, mushrooms, truffle (if used), and Sauce Suprême. Adjust seasonings and heat. Fill patty shells and top with the caps removed from the centers of the baked patty shells. (See illustration, page 292.) Makes 4 to 8 servings.

VARIATIONS

MIXED-VEGETABLE PATTIES (*Bouchées Bouquetière*)

Replace the chicken in the preceding recipe with 3 cups diced mixed vegetables. Omit the truffle. Mix with 1¼ cups Béchamel, Mornay, or Suprême Sauce and heat. Serve in puff-paste patty shells, as directed for Chicken Patties.

SHRIMP AND MUSSEL PATTIES

Replace chicken in recipe for Chicken Patties with 2 cups diced cooked shrimp and ½ cup diced poached mussels, and mix with 1¼ cups White Wine Sauce. Heat and serve in 8 baked puff-paste patty shells as previously directed.

LOBSTER PATTIES

Replace chicken in recipe for Chicken Patties with 3 cups diced cooked lobster meat. Mix with 1¼ cups Velouté, Béchamel or Mornay Sauce. Add 2 tablespoons dry sherry. Heat and serve in 8 baked puff paste patty shells.

PATTIES FOR LENT (*Bouchées Quatre-Temps*)

Replace chicken in recipe for Chicken Patties with 1 cup diced cooked fish; ½ cup each diced cooked shrimp and mussels, and ½ cup diced mushrooms sautéed in butter. Mix with 1¼ cups Béchamel Sauce. Adjust seasonings. Heat and serve in 8 baked puff-paste patty shells.

⚜ CORNETS WITH HARD-COOKED EGGS

puff paste
1 egg yolk
2 tablespoons milk
6 diced hard-cooked eggs
½ cup Béchamel Sauce
salt and ground black pepper

Roll puff-paste dough ¼ inch thick and cut into strips ¼ inch wide and 6 inches long. Wrap the pieces around 6 small metal or wooden horn-shaped molds. Brush surface with egg yolk beaten with milk. Place molds 1 inch apart on paper-lined cooky sheets. Bake 10 minutes in a preheated very hot oven (450° F.). Reduce heat to moderate (350° F.) and bake until pastry is golden. Remove the molds from the pastry immediately by twisting them free. Cool. Fill with diced hard-cooked eggs mixed with Béchamel Sauce and seasoned with salt and pepper to taste. Makes 6 servings.

⚜ GOUGÈRE (*Baked Cheese Puff*)

½ recipe for Chou Paste
⅔ cup very finely diced Gruyère cheese
small thin slices of Gruyère cheese

Mix warm Chou Paste with the diced Gruyère cheese. Using a pastry bag and a large round nozzle, pipe a ring on a slightly buttered baking sheet, using all the paste. Cover evenly with thin slices of Gruyère cheese. Bake in a preheated hot oven (425° F.) 20 to 25 minutes. Serve at once. Makes 6 servings.

⚜ CHEESE ROLLS

2 cups grated Cheshire, Cheddar, or other firm cheese
⅔ cup cold thick Béchamel Sauce
2 large egg yolks
puff paste

Mix cheese with Béchamel Sauce and egg yolk. Adjust seasonings. Roll puff paste ¼ inch thick. Cut into lengthwise strips 3 inches wide, and then cut strips into 2-inch lengths, making the pastry for each roll 3 by 2 inches. Spread the filling over each piece of dough to within ¼ inch of the edges. Roll up in jelly-roll fashion and press down the ends to prevent the cheese from seeping out while baking. Place on baking sheet, seam side down. Bake in a preheated hot oven (425° F.) 12 minutes, or until browned. Serve as a hot hors d'oeuvre or small entrée. Makes 6 servings.

⚜ TURKISH CHEESE ROLLS (*Beurrecks*)

4 tablespoons butter
4 tablespoons flour
1¼ cups milk
2 packages (3 ounces each) cream cheese
salt and ground black pepper to taste
noodle dough
1 large egg beaten with 1 tablespoon water
fine dry breadcrumbs
Tomato Sauce (optional)

Melt butter in a saucepan. Remove from heat and blend in flour. Stir and cook 1 minute. Remove from heat and add milk. Stir and cook until the mixture is very thick. Cool until sauce is lukewarm. Add cream cheese, salt, and pepper. If the mixture is too soft to shape, chill until it is manageable. Shape into 1-inch balls and form them into rolls 1½ inches long on a lightly floured board. Roll noodle dough 1/16 inch thick. Cut into 3-by-2-inch pieces. Moisten the dough very lightly and place one cheese roll on each piece. Roll up and pinch the dough together at each end to seal the rolls. Dip in beaten egg and then into breadcrumbs. Fry in deep fat preheated to 375° F. Drain on paper towels. Serve as a hot hors d'oeuvre, or serve as an entrée with Tomato Sauce. Makes approximately 1 dozen.

⚜ TOASTED CHEESE LOGS

½ cup (1 stick) softened butter
½ cup grated Cheddar cheese
½ teaspoon powdered mustard
dash cayenne
2 teaspoons paprika
16 thin slices of white bread

Combine all ingredients except bread. Trim crusts from bread and spread slices with the mixture. Roll up as for jelly roll. Secure edges with toothpicks. Place under the broiler to toast, turning once to brown uniformly. Serve hot as an hors d'oeuvre. Makes 16 logs.

CROUSTADES

Croustades are small cases made from puff pastry or rich pie pastry, or from Duchess Potatoes. They take their name from the main ingredient in the filling.

⚜ SHRIMP CROUSTADES

Cook 1 pound of shrimp in court bouillon 5 minutes, or until the shrimp develop a red color. Remove from heat, peel and devein. Add to 1 cup of hot, thick Béchamel Sauce. Season to taste with salt, ground white pepper, and lemon juice. Spoon into 18 small baked pastry shells. Serve as a hot hors d'oeuvre. Makes 18 tarts.

VARIATION

LOBSTER CROUSTADES

In the recipe for Shrimp Croustades, replace shrimp with 2 cups diced, cooked lobster meat.

⚜ HARD-COOKED-EGG CROUSTADES

8 hard-cooked eggs, peeled and diced
1½ cups hot Béchamel Sauce
dash cayenne
salt and ground white pepper to taste
12 baked 2½-inch puff-pastry or rich pastry cases
chopped parsley

Combine eggs with Béchamel Sauce and cayenne. Season to taste with salt and pepper. Spoon into pastry cases. Sprinkle with chopped parsley. Serve as a hot entrée. Makes 6 servings.

⚜ MUSHROOM CROUSTADES

3 cups sliced mushrooms
2 tablespoons butter
1 cup hot Demi-Glace Sauce
2 tablespoons chopped parsley
¼ teaspoon dried or 1 teaspoon chopped fresh thyme
salt and ground black pepper to taste
12 baked 2½-inch puff-paste or rich pastry cases
2 strips crisp bacon, broken into pieces
fried onion strips

Cook mushrooms in butter 5 minutes, or until they are tender. Add to hot Demi-Glace Sauce. Blend in herbs, salt, and pepper. Stir and cook 2 to 3 minutes. Serve in pastry cases. Garnish with pieces of crisp bacon and strips of onion fried in butter. Makes 6 servings.

SMALL TIMBALES

A timbale was originally a metal mold in which food was cooked. Now timbale cases are made of pastry and may be either precooked or cooked with the filling. They are of various sizes and may be made in various ways. One method, described here, is to make them of batter and use a timbale iron to fry them in deep fat. Timbale irons are available in different shapes: round, diamond-shaped, heart-shaped, etc. For hors d'oeuvre, small entrées, or garnishes, small timbale cases are usually filled with forcemeat, chicken, fish, shellfish, sweetbreads, or mushrooms, bound with a cream sauce. They may also be served with sweet fillings for dessert.

⚜ TIMBALE CASES

1 cup sifted all-purpose flour
½ teaspoon salt
2 eggs, beaten slightly
1 cup milk
1 tablespoon salad oil

Sift flour and salt together. Combine eggs and milk and gradually stir into the flour mixture along with the oil. Beat *only* until batter is smooth. Strain and let stand an hour so that air bubbles can dissipate. When ready to cook timbales, pour some of the batter into a large cup. Dip the timbale iron in deep fat preheated to 360° to 370° F. Drain fat from the iron slightly by passing bottom across a paper towel. Dip the hot iron into the cup of batter, covering only bottom and sides of iron to about ⅛ inch from the top. Lower the batter-covered iron into the hot fat and fry 1 to 1½ minutes or until timbales have delicately browned. Withdraw the iron from the fat, loosen case from the iron with a fork, and drain on paper towel, inverting to drain all fat from the inside. If fat is too cold or too hot, the batter will not cling to the iron. Repeat, adding more batter to the cup as needed, until all the timbales have been fried. Fill with the desired mixture. Makes about 40 cases.

If timbale cases are not to be used immediately, store them in a tightly covered tin box or jar to prevent them from becoming soft. If they soften, place them in a preheated moderate oven (350° F.) for about 5 minutes to become crisp. Do not fill timbale cases until the last minute.

⚜ CHICKEN TIMBALES (*Timbales à la Courtisane*)

12 thin pancakes
3 cups finely ground cooked chicken
1¼ cups Béchamel Sauce
3 large egg yolks
salt and ground black pepper to taste
Soubise Sauce

Butter six 6-ounce custard cups. Cut out circular pieces from pancakes to fit the bottom of the molds and line the bottom of the molds with them. Cut the remaining pancakes into strips long enough and wide enough to line the sides. Mix the chicken with the Béchamel Sauce, and pound and beat well with a wooden spoon. Rub through a sieve. Beat in egg yolks, one at a time, and add salt and pepper. Spoon into the prepared custard cups. Place cups in a pan of hot water. Bake in a preheated moderate oven (350° F.) 30 to 40 minutes. Unmold onto a warm serving plate. Serve with Soubise Sauce. Makes 6 servings.

VARIATION

TIMBALES REGINA

In the preceding recipe, replace 3 cups chicken with 1 cup finely ground raw pike, halibut, or haddock, 1 cup ground raw shrimp, and ½ cup ground raw mussels. Serve with Shrimp Sauce.

⚜ CHICKEN FORCEMEAT TIMBALES

1 small truffle, or 3 pitted black olives
8 round slices of cooked tongue
¾ pound raw chicken breasts
¼ teaspoon salt
1/16 teaspoon ground black pepper
1 large egg white
1 cup heavy cream
1½ cups diced cooked tongue or ham
¾ cup chicken Velouté Sauce
Mushroom Sauce

Butter eight 6-ounce custard cups. Place a slice of truffle (or black olive) in the bottom of each and cover with a larger round of cooked tongue. Set aside. Cut chicken into small pieces and put it through a food chopper twice, using the finest blade. Add salt and pepper, and gradually stir and beat in the egg white. Rub the mixture through a sieve. Put the pan on a bed of cracked ice and work the mixture with a wooden spoon until it is well chilled. Beat in the cream, a little at a time, working it in well after each addition. Line the molds with the forcemeat. Set aside. Mix diced tongue or ham with Velouté Sauce and spoon into the molds. Cover the top with forcemeat. Place cups in a pan of hot water. Bake in preheated moderate oven (350° F.) 30 to 40 minutes, or until a pointed knife inserted in the center comes out clean. Serve with Mushroom Sauce. Makes 8 servings.

VARIATION

VEAL FORCEMEAT TIMBALES

In the preceding recipe replace the chicken breasts with the same amount of raw veal and the chicken Velouté Sauce with veal Velouté Sauce.

⚜ LIVER TIMBALES

4 tablespoons butter
2 tablespoons flour
½ cup milk, or veal stock or chicken stock
½ cup heavy cream
2 large eggs, separated
1 pound chicken livers or calf's liver
1 small onion
¾ teaspoon salt or salt to taste
¼ teaspoon ground black pepper
3 tablespoons Madeira
Mushroom Sauce

Melt 2 tablespoons of the butter in a saucepan. Remove from heat and blend in flour. Stir and cook 1 minute. Remove from heat and stir in milk or stock and cream. Stir and cook until the sauce is of medium thickness. Cool. Beat in egg yolks. Sauté liver in the rest of the butter and put it through a food chopper twice, along with onion, using the finest blade. Add sauce, salt, pepper, and 2 tablespoons of the wine. Beat egg whites until they stand in soft stiff peaks (not too dry) and fold them in. Turn the mixture into 6 well-buttered 6-ounce custard cups. Place cups in a pan of hot water. Cover pan loosely with foil. Bake in a preheated slow oven (325° F.) 40 to 50 minutes, or until a knife inserted in the center comes out clean. Cool a few minutes. Turn onto a warm serving dish. Serve with Mushroom Sauce flavored with the remaining Madeira. Makes 6 servings.

The liver may be replaced with 2 cups ground cooked veal, chicken, ham, fish (haddock, halibut, sole, or pike), crabmeat, lobster, or shrimp.

⚜ MILANESE TIMBALES

unsweetened pastry dough, made with 4 cups flour
1 cup medium-sized macaroni, broken into small pieces
2 tablespoons butter
½ cup sautéed mushrooms
1 cup each diced cooked ham and tongue
½ cup grated Parmesan cheese
1½ cups thick well-seasoned Tomato Sauce

Roll one-third of the pastry at a time ⅛ inch thick. Cut it into circles large enough to line 6-ounce custard cups, pressing the pastry down well against the sides, bottoms, and edges of the cups. Cut off the dough that hangs over the edges and reserve the pieces to use later. Prick the bottom and sides of the pastry generously to prevent it from puffing. Fit waxed paper into the pastry-lined cups and fill them with dried beans or rice to hold the pastry in shape. Bake in a preheated hot oven (425° F.) 10 to 15 minutes, or until the pastry has set and partially baked. Remove the beans or rice and the paper and discard. Continue baking until the pastry has delicately browned. Remove from oven. Roll remaining pastry and trimmings 1/8 inch thick. Using the top of a custard cup, or a large cooky cutter, cut out pastry circles to use as the top crust for the timbales. Cut pastry leaves from remaining pastry, and place 2 on each unbaked crust. Place on ungreased cooky sheet, brush with milk or beaten egg, and bake 10 to 12 minutes, or until golden brown.

Cook macaroni in boiling salted water as directed on the package. Drain well and toss with butter. Add mushrooms, ham, tongue, cheese, and Tomato Sauce. Heat and spoon into pastry cases. Top with the crusts and serve very hot. Makes 6 servings.

⚜ SALMON AND MUSHROOM TIMBALES (*Timbales Beckendorff*)

1 cup medium-sized macaroni broken into small pieces
1½ cups thick Tomato Sauce
3 large egg yolks, lightly beaten
1 cup diced mushrooms
2 tablespoons butter
½ pound smoked salmon, cut in small pieces
fine dry breadcrumbs
Tomato Sauce

Cook macaroni in salted boiling water as directed on the package. Drain, mix with 1½ cups Tomato Sauce, and heat. Blend a little of the hot mixture with the beaten egg yolks and add to the remaining hot mixture. Cook mushrooms in butter 5 minutes, and add to macaroni along with salmon. Mix well. Butter six 6-ounce custard cups and coat them with breadcrumbs. Fill with the macaroni mixture. Place cups in a pan of hot water. Bake in a preheated moderate oven (350° F.) 30 to 40 minutes. Unmold onto a warm serving dish. Serve with Tomato Sauce. Makes 6 servings.

CASSOLETTES

Cassolettes take their name from the small individual fireproof dishes or casseroles in which the food is cooked and served. They may be hors d'oeuvre, small entrées, or desserts.

⚜ CASSOLETTES BOUQUETIÈRE (*Mixed Vegetables*)

4 cups cooked mixed vegetables
1 cup heavy cream
salt and ground black pepper to taste
2 cups Duchess Potatoes
milk
18 cooked asparagus tips

Heat the vegetables in the cream. Season with salt and pepper. Spoon an equal amount into each of 6 cassolette dishes (individual casseroles). Make a border of Duchess Potatoes around the edges. Brush potatoes with a little milk. Cook in a preheated moderate oven (375° F.) until potato is well flecked with brown. Garnish each with 3 asparagus tips. Serve hot as an entrée. Makes 6 servings.

⚜ DEAUVILLE CASSOLETTES (*Lamb*)

2 pounds diced cooked lamb
2 cups Demi-Glace Sauce
1 cup Tomato Fondue
3 hard-cooked eggs

Combine lamb and Demi-Glace Sauce. Heat and spoon into 6 buttered cassolette dishes. Cover with Tomato Fondue. Garnish each with ½ slice of hard-cooked egg. Serve as an entrée. Makes 6 servings.

⚜ FLORENTINE CASSOLETTES (*Spinach*)

2 cups drained, chopped, cooked spinach
1 tablespoon butter
salt and ground black pepper
2 cups diced cooked chicken
¾ cup chicken Velouté Sauce
2 cups Duchess Potatoes
milk

Heat spinach in butter and season with salt and pepper to taste. Divide spinach equally among 6 buttered cassolette dishes, spreading it uniformly over the bottom of the dishes. Combine chicken and Velouté Sauce and spoon into each of the dishes, covering the spinach. Make a border around the edges of the dishes with Duchess Potatoes. Brush potatoes with a little milk. Cook in a preheated moderate oven (375° F.) until potato is well flecked with brown. Serve hot as an entrée. Makes 6 servings.

⚜ JAPANESE-STYLE CASSOLETTES (*Mushroom and Ham*)

2 cups mushrooms, cut in julienne pieces
1 cup cooked ham, cut in julienne pieces
2 tablespoons butter
1 cup Demi-Glace Sauce
2 teaspoons soy sauce
1 tablespoon sake or dry sherry
¼ teaspoon ground ginger
24 hard-cooked quail eggs, or 6 hard-cooked hen's eggs

Cook mushrooms and ham in butter until mushrooms are tender. Add Demi-Glace and cook 2 to 3 minutes, stirring. Season with soy sauce, wine, and ginger. Spoon into 6 cassolette dishes. Peel quail eggs, cut each in half, and arrange 8 halves over each dish, or peel and quarter hen's eggs, and arrange 4 quarters over each serving. Serve as a hot entrée. Makes 6 servings.

⚜ MYLORD CASSOLETTES (*Game and Ham*)

2 cups diced cooked game
1 cup diced cooked ham
¾ cup Salmis Sauce
1 cup fresh breadcrumbs
3 tablespoons butter

Combine game, ham, and Salmis Sauce. Heat and spoon into 6 cassolette dishes. Brown breadcrumbs in butter, and sprinkle over the tops of each. Serve as a hot entrée. Makes 6 servings.

⚜ REGENCY CASSOLETTES (*Chicken*)

3 cups diced cooked chicken
1 truffle, diced (optional)
1½ cups chicken Velouté Sauce
salt and ground black pepper
2 cups Duchess Potatoes
milk
18 cooked asparagus tips

Combine chicken, truffles, and Velouté Sauce. Add salt and pepper to taste. Spoon into each of 6 buttered cassolette dishes. Pipe a border of Duchess Potatoes around the edge of the cassolettes. Brush potatoes with a little milk. Cook in a preheated moderate oven (375° F.) until potatoes are well flecked with brown. Garnish each with 3 cooked asparagus tips. Serve as a hot entrée. Makes 6 servings.

⚜ SULTAN CASSOLETTES (*Game with Chestnut Purée*)

3 cups diced cooked game
½ cup Chestnut Purée
1 cup Salmis Sauce or Game Sauce
1 truffle (optional)
chopped pistachio nuts (optional)

Combine game, chestnut purée, and ½ cup of the sauce. Adjust seasonings. Heat and keep warm in a pan of hot water. Spoon the mixture into small heat-proof cocotte dishes, or individual baked unsweetened pastry shells. Coat each with a little of the remaining sauce. A slice of truffle may be placed on each, or they may be sprinkled with chopped pistachio nuts. Serve as a hot entrée. Makes 6 servings.

⚜ CASSOLETTES SUZANNE

2 cups cooked spinach
2 tablespoons butter
salt and ground black pepper
3 cups diced cooked chicken
½ cup sautéed sliced mushrooms
1⅓ cups Béchamel Sauce
6 truffle slices (optional)
6 pimiento strips (optional)

Put spinach in a sieve and press out excess liquid. Cook spinach in butter 1 to 2 minutes. Season to taste with salt and black pepper. Divide the spinach equally among 6 cassolette dishes. Combine chicken, mushrooms, and 1 cup of Béchamel Sauce. Season to taste with salt and pepper. Spoon an equal amount into each of the cassolettes. Coat lightly with remaining Béchamel Sauce. Heat in a preheated moderate oven (375° F.) 15 minutes. Garnish if desired with a slice of truffle or pimiento strip. Serve as a hot entrée. Makes 6 servings.

COQUILLES

When coquilles, either natural scallop shells or fireproof dishes in the shape of shells, are served with hot food, the shells are first heated and buttered. Then a border of Duchess Potatoes is piped around the edge of each shell, the filling is put in, and the shells are baked.

⚜ COQUILLES OF CALF'S BRAINS MORNAY

3 calf's brains
1 teaspoon salt
1 tablespoon lemon juice or vinegar
1 cup Mornay Sauce
3 cups Duchess Potatoes
1 cup fresh breadcrumbs
3 tablespoons butter, melted
½ cup grated cheese
6 sautéed mushroom caps

Wash the brains, remove membranes, and soak brains ½ hour in cold water. Rinse. Cover with fresh cold water, add salt and lemon juice or vinegar, cover, and simmer 20 minutes. Drain and cool. Cut brains into small pieces and mix with Mornay Sauce. Butter the shells. Pipe a border of Duchess Potatoes around the edge of each. Fill with the brain mixture. Mix the breadcrumbs with the butter and cheese and sprinkle them over the mixture. Bake in a preheated moderate oven (350° F.) 20 minutes or until crumbs are brown. Garnish each with a sautéed mushroom cap. Makes 6 servings.

⚜ COQUILLES OF CHICKEN MORNAY

3 cups Duchess Potatoes
3 cups diced cooked chicken
6 tablespoons grated cheese
3 tablespoons butter, melted
2 cups Mornay Sauce
salt and ground black pepper to taste

Pipe a border of Duchess potatoes around the edges of buttered scallop shells. Set aside. Combine chicken with Mornay Sauce, salt, and pepper. Heat. Spoon the mixture into the prepared scallop shells. Sprinkle with grated cheese and melted butter. Cook in a preheated moderate oven (350° F.) until the top is brown. Makes 6 servings.

⚜ COQUILLES OF GAME DUCHESS

3 cups Duchess Potatoes
2½ cups diced cooked game meat
1 cup diced cooked ham
1 small truffle, chopped
1½ cups Game Sauce
salt and ground black pepper
1 cup soft bread crumbs
3 tablespoons butter, melted

The meat may be rabbit or squirrel or small game birds. Pipe a border of Duchess Potatoes around the edges of 6 buttered scallop shells. Combine game meat, ham, truffles, and Game Sauce. Season with salt and pepper to taste. Heat. Spoon the mixture into the prepared scallop shells. Mix bread-crumbs with melted butter. Sprinkle over the tops. Bake in a preheated moderate oven (350° F.) 20 minutes, or until the top is brown. Makes 6 servings.

⚜ COQUILLES SAINT-JACQUES À LA DIABLE
(*Deviled Scallops in Scallop Shells*)

3 cups Duchess Potatoes
2 pounds (about 1 quart) scallops
5 tablespoons butter
dry white wine to cover (about 2 cups)
2 shallots, chopped
2 cups Béchamel Sauce
½ teaspoon powdered mustard
1 tablespoon water
salt and ground black pepper to taste
dash cayenne
1 cup soft breadcrumbs

Pipe a border of Duchess Potatoes around the edges of 6 buttered scallop shells. Set aside. Place scallops, 2 tablespoons of the butter, wine, and chopped shallots in a saucepan. Bring to boiling point, reduce heat, and simmer 8 to 10 minutes. Remove the scallops. Strain the liquid and simmer it until the quantity has been reduced to one-fourth its original amount. Add 1½ cups of the Béchamel Sauce and strain the mixture through a fine sieve. Blend mustard with water and let it stand 5 minutes, then add it to the sauce along with the rest of the seasonings. Slice scallops and add to the mixture. Heat and spoon into the prepared scallop shells. Coat with remaining Béchamel Sauce. Melt the 3 tablespoons butter that is left and mix with the breadcrumbs. Sprinkle over the tops of the prepared shells and brown under the broiler, or if desired bake in a preheated moderate oven (350° F.) 15 to 20 minutes or until crumbs are brown. Makes 6 servings.

⚜ LOBSTER THERMIDOR IN COQUILLES

3 cups Duchess Potatoes
¼ cup (½ stick) butter
2½ tablespoons flour
½ teaspoon minced shallots
1¼ teaspoon salt
⅛ teaspoon ground white pepper
1¾ cups light cream
2 tablespoons dry sherry
1 tablespoon brandy (optional)
3½ cups cubed cooked lobster meat
⅓ cup grated Cheddar or Gruyère cheese

Pipe a border of Duchess Potatoes around the edges of 6 buttered scallop shells. Set aside. Melt the butter in a saucepan or in the top of a double boiler. Stir in the next 4 ingredients. Stir and cook over low heat or hot water 1 to 2 minutes. Gradually blend in the cream. Cook until the sauce has thickened, stirring constantly. Add sherry, brandy (if used), and lobster. Heat. Spoon into the prepared shells. Sprinkle the tops with grated cheese. Brown lightly under the broiler. Makes 6 servings.

VARIATION

COQUILLES OF SHRIMP

In the preceding recipe replace the lobster with 3 cups cooked shrimp. Omit brandy and sherry and proceed as directed in the recipe.

CROMESQUIS AND CROQUETTES

Cromesquis and croquettes are prepared exactly the same way, except that croquettes are dipped in egg and breadcrumbs before frying, while cromesquis are either wrapped in small thin pancakes or rolled in a slice of uncooked bacon before dipping into frying batter prior to deep-fat frying. They are served as hot hors d'oeuvre or small hot entrées.

⚜ CROMESQUIS FLORENTINE (*Spinach*)

2 cups cooked, drained spinach
1 teaspoon finely chopped onion
1 tablespoon butter
1 cup grated Parmesan cheese
½ cup very thick Béchamel Sauce
salt and ground black pepper
6 thin 4-inch pancakes
fritter batter

Cook the well-drained spinach and the onion in butter 1 to 2 minutes. Add cheese and Béchamel Sauce. Season with salt and pepper to taste. Mix well. Spread over pancakes, and roll up in jelly-roll fashion. Cut each in half. Dip in fritter batter. Fry until brown in deep fat preheated to 375° F. Drain on paper towels. Serve as a hot hors d'oeuvre. Makes 12.

⚜ CROMESQUIS BONNE FEMME (*Beef and Mushrooms*)

2 cups finely diced mushrooms
2 tablespoons finely chopped onion
2 tablespoons butter
3 cups finely diced cooked beef
1½ cups thick Velouté Sauce
3 large egg yolks
salt and ground black pepper
fritter batter

Stir and cook mushrooms and onion in butter 5 minutes. Add beef and Velouté Sauce. Stir and cook until the mixture leaves the sides of the pan. Remove from heat. Mix a little of the hot mixture with the egg yolks, and add the yolks to the hot mixture. Season with salt and pepper to taste. Spread on a buttered baking sheet. Cover lightly and chill. Shape into round croquettes 2 inches long and ¾ inch in diameter. Dip in fritter batter. Fry in deep fat preheated to 375° F. Drain on paper towels. Serve as a hot hors d'oeuvre or as a small entrée. Makes 1½ dozen.

⚜ CROMESQUIS VLADIMIR (*Sole and Crayfish*)

1 pound fillet of sole, poached
12 shelled cooked crayfish tails or 12 small shrimp, diced
1 truffle, chopped (optional)
1 cup Velouté Sauce
salt and ground black pepper
lemon juice
12 thin 3-inch pancakes
2 cups Duchess Potatoes
fritter batter
Sauce Normande

Dice sole finely and mix with the crayfish or shrimp, truffle (if used), and Velouté Sauce. Stir and cook until the mixture leaves the sides of the pan. Season to taste with salt, pepper, and lemon juice. Spread the mixture ¾ inch thick on a buttered baking sheet and chill. Shape into croquettes 2 inches long and ¾ inch in diameter. Spread pancakes with Duchess Potatoes. Place a croquette in the center of each. Roll up, pressing the edges together. Dip in fritter batter and fry in deep fat preheated to 375° F. Drain on paper towel. Serve as a small entrée with Sauce Normande. Makes 6 servings.

⚜ MIXED-VEGETABLE CROMESQUIS

3 cups mixed diced vegetables
1 cup thick Béchamel Sauce
1 cup grated Parmesan cheese
salt and ground black pepper
8 thin 4-inch pancakes
fritter batter

Combine vegetables and Béchamel Sauce. Stir and cook until the mixture leaves the sides of the pan. Add cheese and season to taste with salt and pepper. Spread over pancakes and roll up in jelly-roll fashion. Trim the ends square, and cut each in half. Dip in fritter batter. Fry in deep fat preheated to 375° F. Drain on paper towels. Serve as hot hors d'oeuvre. Makes 16.

⚜ BEEF AND MUSHROOM CROQUETTES

1½ cups finely chopped mushrooms
1 tablespoon butter
3 cups ground boiled beef
¼ cup dry sherry
1 cup thick Béchamel Sauce
2 egg yolks
salt and ground black pepper
fine dry breadcrumbs
1 large egg, beaten

Stir and cook mushrooms in butter 5 minutes. Stir in beef and sherry. Cook until the liquid has evaporated, stirring constantly. Add Béchamel Sauce, mix well, and cook, stirring, until the mixture leaves the sides of the pan. Beat in egg yolks, one at a time. Season with salt and pepper to taste. Spread on buttered baking sheet. Cover loosely and chill. Shape into croquettes 2 inches long and ¾ inch in diameter. Roll in breadcrumbs, then dip in beaten egg, and roll in crumbs again. Let stand 20 minutes to allow crumbs to set. Fry in deep fat preheated to 375° F. Drain on paper towels. Serve as a hot hors d'oeuvre or as a small entrée. Makes 18.

VARIATIONS

HAM AND MUSHROOM CROQUETTES (*Croquettes Montrouge*)

In the recipe for Beef and Mushroom Croquettes, replace beef with the same amount of ground cooked lean ham.

LOBSTER CROQUETTES

In the recipe for Beef and Mushroom Croquettes, replace beef with the same amount of finely diced cooked lobster meat. Season with a dash of cayenne.

ROCK LOBSTER CROQUETTES

In the recipe for Beef and Mushroom Croquettes, replace beef with the same amount of finely diced cooked rock lobster meat.

⚜ CHEESE CROQUETTES

1 cup thick Béchamel Sauce
2 large whole eggs
2 large egg yolks
2 cups grated cheese (Cheddar, Gruyère, or Parmesan)
1/16 teaspoon ground mace
1/8 teaspoon ground white pepper
fine dry breadcrumbs
1 large egg, beaten

Cook Béchamel Sauce over low heat until very thick. Beat in whole eggs and egg yolks, one at a time. Stir and cook over low heat until very thick. Remove from heat; blend in cheese, mace, and pepper. Mix well. Spread on a buttered baking pan. Cover lightly and chill. Shape into croquettes 2 inches long and 3/4 inch in diameter. Roll in breadcrumbs, then dip in beaten egg, and roll again in crumbs. Set croquettes aside for 20 minutes to allow crumbs to set. Brown in deep fat preheated to 375° F. Drain on paper towels. Serve as a hot hors d'oeuvre or small entrée. Makes 12.

⚜ GAME CROQUETTES

1 cup finely chopped mushrooms
1 tablespoon butter
3/4 cup well-reduced Demi-Glace Sauce
3 cups ground cooked lean game meat
1 tablespoon brandy
salt and ground black pepper
fine dry breadcrumbs
1 large egg, beaten
Venison Sauce (optional)

Stir and cook mushrooms in butter 5 minutes. Blend in Demi-Glace Sauce and cook 2 to 3 minutes. Add game and brandy. Season to taste with salt and pepper. Mix well. Spread the mixture on a baking sheet and chill. Shape into croquettes 2 inches long and 3/4 inch in diameter. Roll in breadcrumbs, dip in beaten egg, and roll again in crumbs. Set aside 20 minutes to allow crumbs to set. Brown in deep fat preheated to 375° F. Drain on paper towels. Serve as a hot hors d'oeuvre, or as a small entrée with Venison Sauce. Makes 12.

⚜ OYSTER CROQUETTES

3 cups small soup oysters
1½ cups finely chopped mushrooms
1 tablespoon butter
1 cup thick Béchamel Sauce
2 large egg yolks
dash cayenne
salt to taste
fine dry breadcrumbs
1 egg, beaten
Sauce Normande (optional)

Cook oysters in their own liquor over low heat, only until edges curl. Remove from liquor. Chop finely and set aside. Stir and cook mushrooms in butter 5 minutes. Add Béchamel Sauce. Stir and cook until very thick. Add a little of the hot mixture to the egg yolks, mix well, and stir in. Add oysters, cayenne, and salt. Stir and cook over low heat 2 minutes. Spread on a buttered tray. Cover lightly and chill. Shape into croquettes 2 inches long and ¾ inch in diameter, or into small balls. Roll in breadcrumbs, dip in beaten egg, and roll in crumbs again. Set aside 20 minutes to allow crumbs to set. Brown in deep fat preheated to 375° F. Drain on paper towel. Serve as a hot hors d'oeuvre, or as a small entrée with Sauce Normande. Makes 6 servings.

⚜ FISH BALLS (*English*)

2 cups flaked cooked fish (cod, haddock, tuna, salmon, or turbot)
2 cups mashed potatoes
1 teaspoon grated onion
1 teaspoon dried thyme leaves
2 tablespoons finely chopped parsley
3 eggs
salt and ground black pepper to taste
1 teaspoon lemon juice
fine dry breadcrumbs
fried parsley
lemon wedges
Tomato Sauce

Combine fish, potatoes, herbs, 2 of the eggs, beaten lightly, salt, pepper, and lemon juice. Mix well. Shape into 2-inch balls. Beat the remaining egg with 1 tablespoon water and dip fish balls into it and then roll them in breadcrumbs. Fry until brown in deep fat preheated to 375° F. Drain on paper towels. Serve as an entrée with fried parsley, lemon wedges, and Tomato Sauce. Makes 6 servings. The mixture may also be made into 1-inch balls, fried in the same way, and served as a hot hors d'oeuvre. Makes about 3 dozen small balls.

FRITTERS

⚜ ALMOND FRITTERS

½ cup (1 stick) butter
1 cup boiling water
1 cup sifted all-purpose flour
4 eggs
½ cup grated Gruyère cheese
½ cup cooked lean ham cut into short julienne strips
¼ cup shredded toasted blanched almonds

Add butter to boiling water, and when it is melted add flour all at once. Stir until the dough comes away from the sides of the pan. Beat in eggs, one at a time, beating vigorously after each addition. Stir in cheese, ham, and almonds. Let the dough stand 10 minutes. Drop the mixture, about ½ rounded teaspoonful at a time, into deep fat preheated to 385° F. Cook until fritters are golden brown. Drain on paper towels. Serve hot as a hot hors d'oeuvre. Or drop the batter from a tablespoon and serve the fritters as an entrée with Tartare Sauce. Makes 18 hors d'oeuvre fritters or 6 entrée servings.

VARIATION

PIGNATELLI FRITTERS

In the recipe for Almond Fritters, toss the ham with melted butter before adding it to the mixture.

⚜ CAMEMBERT FRITTERS (*Diablotins à la Normande*)

3 tablespoons butter
3 tablespoons flour
1 cup milk
4 ounces Camembert cheese (without crust)
salt and ground black pepper to taste
fine dry breadcrumbs
1 large egg, beaten with 1 tablespoon water

Melt butter in a saucepan. Remove from heat and blend in flour. Stir and cook 1 minute. Add milk, mix well, and cook until the mixture is quite thick. Add cheese, salt, and pepper, and allow cheese to melt. Mix well. Spread the mixture ¾ inch thick on a buttered baking sheet. Chill. Cut into rounds with a 1½-inch biscuit cutter. Roll in breadcrumbs, dip in beaten egg, and roll in crumbs again. Set aside for 20 minutes to allow crumbs to set. Brown in deep fat preheated to 375° F. Drain on paper towel. Serve as a hot hors d'oeuvre. Makes 12 fritters.

⚜ FISH FRITTERS

Cut poached or braised firm fish fillets into medium-sized pieces. Marinate ½ hour in 3 parts salad oil or olive oil to 1 part lemon juice, with salt and ground black pepper to taste, and chopped parsley. Drain fish well, and dip each piece in fritter batter. Fry in deep fat preheated to 375° F. Drain on paper towel. Serve as a hot entrée, or, if desired, cut into small pieces and serve as a hot hors d'oeuvre. Allow 1½ to 2 pounds of fish for 6 entrée servings.

⚜ OYSTER FRITTERS

2 cups sifted all-purpose flour
2 teaspoons double-acting baking powder
1 teaspoon salt
⅛ teaspoon ground nutmeg
⅛ teaspoon ground black pepper
1/16 teaspoon cayenne
1 tablespoon finely chopped onion
2 large eggs, beaten lightly
½ cup milk
½ cup oyster liquor
1 cup drained fresh or frozen oysters
celery salt (optional)

Sift the first 6 ingredients together into a mixing bowl. Combine the next 4 ingredients and stir into the dry mixture. Chop oysters coarsely and blend with the batter. Drop 1 teaspoon of the batter at a time into deep fat preheated to 375° F. Fry 3 minutes or until browned. Drain on paper towels. Sprinkle with celery salt, if desired. Makes approximately 50.

SAVOURIES

Savouries, in English cookery, are small highly seasoned dishes usually served after the dessert. Many of these, including the ones given here, are equally suitable for serving as hot hors d'oeuvre or small entrées.

⚜ FRIED CAMEMBERT

Beat eggs with water, using 1 tablespoon water with each egg. Into this dip wedges of Camembert cheese. Then roll in fine dry breadcrumbs and in eggs again and roll again in breadcrumbs. Fry in deep fat preheated to 375° F. until browned, about 1 to 2 minutes. Drain on paper towels. Serve on toast. Allow 2 per person.

⚜ CHEESE BALLS

1 cup grated Cheddar cheese
⅓ cup soft breadcrumbs
1 large egg, separated
½ teaspoon prepared mustard
dash cayenne
salt to taste
fine dry breadcrumbs

Combine cheese, soft breadcrumbs, egg yolk, and seasonings. Beat egg white until soft stiff (not dry) peaks form. Fold into the cheese mixture. Shape into 1-inch balls. Roll in fine dry breadcrumbs. Fry in deep fat preheated to 375° F. Drain on paper towels. Serve as a hot hors d'oeuvre. Makes about 12 cheese balls.

⚜ STILTON CHEESE BALLS

1½ cups grated Stilton cheese
½ cup fine dry breadcrumbs
2 tablespoons chopped parsley
1 teaspoon finely chopped chives or onion
about ¼ cup red or white port
fine dry breadcrumbs
1 large egg
1 tablespoon water

Combine the first 4 ingredients. Add wine until the mixture can be shaped. Then shape into 1-inch balls. Roll in breadcrumbs. Dip in egg beaten with the water and roll in crumbs again. Fry until golden in deep fat preheated to 375° F. Drain on paper towels. Serve hot. Makes approximately 24 cheese balls.

⚜ FRIAR'S TOAST

6 thin slices of lean bacon
1 cup grated Cheddar cheese
Worcestershire sauce
6 slices of toast
18 pickled onion rings
6 tablespoons grated Cheddar cheese

Broil bacon until crisp. Crumble and mix with 1 cup cheese and a little Worcestershire sauce. Spread thickly on toast. Top each with 3 slices of onion rings, having them overlapping. Sprinkle with grated cheese. Place under broiler until cheese is melted. Serve hot. Makes 6 servings.

⚜ TARTINES MARQUISE

1 cup grated Gruyère cheese
¾ cup thick Béchamel Sauce
2 egg yolks
white bread, cut into slices ½ inch thick

Combine cheese, Béchamel Sauce, and egg yolks. Mix well. Cut bread into circles with a 2-inch cooky cutter. Spread one side of each piece thickly with the cheese mixture. Smooth the surface. Drop, cheese side down, into deep fat preheated to 375° F. Fry very brown. Remove from fat and drain on paper towels. Serve as a hot hors d'oeuvre. Makes approximately 1½ dozen.

⚜ WELSH RABBIT OR RAREBIT

½ teaspoon powdered mustard
½ teaspoon paprika
1½ teaspoons Worcestershire sauce
dash cayenne
⅓ cup ale or beer
¾ pound shredded Cheshire or Cheddar cheese
6 slices toast, crusts removed

Mix spices and Worcestershire sauce in a saucepan. Add ale or beer, and keep over very low heat until beer is hot. Add cheese. Stir and cook over low heat until cheese is melted. Serve on hot toast. Makes 6 servings.

⚜ CHICKEN LIVERS WITH BACON

chicken livers
salt
ground black pepper
butter
thinly sliced lean bacon
rounds of buttered toast

For each person, allow 1 chicken liver cut into 3 pieces. Season livers lightly with salt and ground black pepper. Wrap each piece in a half slice of bacon. Secure with toothpicks. Brown under the broiler, turning once to crisp the bacon and cook the liver uniformly. Serve on rounds of buttered toast.

⚜ DIANA TOAST (*Chicken Livers and Mushrooms*)

8 chicken livers
¼ teaspoon salt
1/16 teaspoon ground black pepper
1 tablespoon butter
1 cup thick Brown Sauce
3 tablespoons dry sherry or dry vermouth
6 slices buttered toast
6 small mushrooms, sautéed

Cut chicken livers into small pieces and sprinkle with salt and black pepper. Stir and cook in butter until the livers have lost their red color. Blend the wine with the sauce. Add livers. Heat only until hot. Serve on toast as a small entrée, topping each serving with a sautéed mushroom. Makes 6 servings.

⚜ DUTCH TOAST

½ pound smoked fillet of haddock
2 tablespoons butter
¾ cup hot Béchamel Sauce
12 3-inch rounds of toast
sliced hard-cooked eggs

Dice haddock and sauté in butter until it is flaky. Add Béchamel Sauce. Pile in a dome shape on rounds of toast. Garnish as desired with sliced hard-cooked eggs. Makes 12 servings.

⚜ HADDOCK ON TOAST

1 pound fillets of haddock
salt and ground black pepper
about ¼ cup milk
2 tablespoons butter
4 slices toast
paprika

Cut 1 pound of fillet of haddock in 1-inch squares and place them in a well-buttered, shallow baking dish. Sprinkle lightly with salt and ground black pepper and with only enough milk to moisten, about ¼ cup. Dot with 2 tablespoons butter. Bake in a preheated moderate oven (350° F.) 30 minutes or until fish is flaky. Serve on toast, garnished with a dash of paprika. Makes 4 servings.

⚜ HOT HAM AND CHEESE SANDWICHES (*Croque-Monsieur*)

12 thin slices of bread
6 thin slices of Gruyère cheese
6 thin slices cooked ham
clarified butter
parsley
truffle bits, or sliced black olives (optional)

Trim crusts from bread. Place on each of 6 slices 1 slice of cheese and 1 slice of ham. Top with remaining bread. Brown lightly on both sides in clarified butter. Serve hot, cut into squares or if desired whole. Garnish with parsley and bits of truffle or slices of black olive, if desired. Makes 6 large sandwiches or 24 small sandwiches.

⚜ HAM AND CHEESE BROCHETTES (*Brochettes à la Suisse*)

18 squares raw smoked ham, 1¼ by 1¼ by ¼ inches
18 squares Gruyère cheese, 1 by 1 by ¼ inches
2 large eggs, beaten with 2 tablespoons water
fine dry breadcrumbs

Use 6 skewers, 3 to 4 inches long. String 3 ham squares and 3 cheese squares alternately on each skewer. Dip in beaten egg and then roll in breadcrumbs. Fry in deep fat, preheated to 385° F., until browned. They must be fried very quickly to avoid melting the cheese. Drain on paper towels. Serve as a hot hors d'oeuvre. Makes 6 brochettes.

⚜ DERBY TOAST (*Ham and Walnuts*)

walnut halves
1 cup ground ham
½ cup Béchamel Sauce
cayenne
12 2-inch rounds or squares of toast

Heat walnuts in a preheated hot oven (400° F.) only until hot. Combine the next 3 ingredients. Heat. Pile in a dome on rounds or squares of toast. Top each with a toasted walnut half. Makes 12 servings.

⚜ FRIED OYSTERS

2½ dozen large oysters
½ teaspoon salt
¼ teaspoon ground black pepper
2 large eggs
fine dry breadcrumbs

Drain oysters and wipe dry with paper towels or clean tea towels. Add salt and pepper to eggs and beat them lightly. Dip oysters in egg and then roll in breadcrumbs. Let stand about 30 minutes for crumbs to set to the oysters. Fry 2 to 3 minutes or until brown in deep fat preheated to 375° F. Drain on paper towels. Serve hot. Makes 6 servings.

⚜ ANGELS ON HORSEBACK

Sprinkle fresh raw oysters with salt, ground black pepper, and paprika. Wrap each oyster in a half slice of uncooked lean bacon. Secure them with toothpicks. Place in a shallow baking pan and brown slowly in a preheated moderate oven (350° F.) until bacon is crisp. Or, if desired, brown under the broiler, turning once to crisp the bacon on both sides. Serve hot on rounds of buttered toast or serve on toothpicks. Allow 3 oysters per serving.

Vol-au-Vent of Chicken, Modern Style, page 664 ▲

▼ Russian Coulibiac of Salmon, page 472

▲ Chicken Patties, page 267

Quiche Lorraine, page 302 ▼

Croustade of Gnocchi Parisian Style, page 321 ▲

▼ Individual Pizzas, page 318

▲ Ravioli, page 314

Tortellini with Ricotta, page 315 ▼

▼ Green Noodles Bolognese, page 310

Roman Delights, page 310 ▲

▲ Rice à la Grecque, page 323

Milanese Risotto, page 324 ▼

Rice with Cepes, page 323 ▲

▼ Spaghetti Carbonara, page 319

▲ Spaghetti with Clams, page 319

Lasagne (see page 311) ▼

⚜ OYSTER AND MUSHROOM BROCHETTES

18 oysters with liquor
9 slices bacon
18 small mushroom caps
1 large egg, beaten with 1 tablespoon water
fine dry breadcrumbs
salt
dash cayenne
½ cup butter, melted
1 teaspoon lemon juice
chopped parsley

Cook oysters in the liquor over very low heat, or in the top of a double boiler over hot water, *only* until their edges curl. Remove oysters from the liquor and drain them well. Cut bacon slices in half and wrap one piece around each oyster. Use skewers 5 to 6 inches long, and string 3 oysters, alternating with 3 mushrooms caps, on each skewer. Roll in beaten egg and then in fine dry breadcrumbs. Fry in deep fat preheated to 375° F. Drain on paper towels. Sprinkle lightly with salt that has been mixed with a dash of cayenne. Combine butter, lemon juice, and parsley and serve with oysters. Makes 6 servings.

⚜ SHRIMP FRIED IN BATTER

2 pounds medium-sized raw shrimp
2 tablespoons lemon juice or cognac
1 teaspoon Worcestershire sauce
dash cayenne
fritter batter
Tartare Sauce or wedges of lemon

Peel and devein shrimp, leaving the tails attached. Marinate 2 to 3 hours in lemon juice or cognac, and seasonings. Dip shrimps a few at a time in the fritter batter, holding them by the tails. (Do not dip tails in batter.) Fry in deep fat preheated to 375° F. until golden brown. Drain on paper towels. Serve with lemon wedges or Tartare Sauce as a hot hors d'oeuvre or an entrée. Makes 6 servings.

⚜ BREADED FRIED SHRIMP

30 raw jumbo shrimp
½ teaspoon salt
1/16 teaspoon ground black pepper
dash cayenne
2 tablespoons water
2 large eggs
fine dry breadcrumbs
parsley fried in deep fat
lemon wedges

Peel and devein shrimp. Set aside. Beat seasonings and water with eggs. Dip shrimp into the mixture, roll in breadcrumbs, and fry until browned in deep fat preheated to 375° F. Serve with deep fat-fried parsley and wedges of lemon. Makes 6 servings.

⚜ SCOTCH WOODCOCK

6 large eggs
¼ cup milk or light cream
salt to taste
⅛ teaspoon ground black pepper
1 tablespoon butter
6 slices of toast
anchovy fillets
capers

Beat eggs lightly with cream or milk, salt and black pepper. Heat butter in a skillet. Add eggs. Stir and cook over low heat until eggs are soft-firm. Pile on buttered toast. Top with anchovy fillets in lattice pattern and place a caper in each square. Reheat in a preheated moderate oven (350° F.) Serve hot. Makes 6 servings.

MOUSSES

⚜ BAKED CHICKEN MOUSSE WITH SAUCE SUPRÊME

3 cups diced cooked chicken
1 cup Sauce Suprême
2 tablespoons dry sherry
3 large eggs, separated
½ teaspoon salt
¼ teaspoon ground white pepper
1 cup heavy cream, whipped

Put chicken through a food chopper twice, using the finest blade. Mix with ½ cup of the Sauce Suprême, sherry, beaten egg yolks, salt, and pepper. Beat egg whites with a dash of salt until they stand in soft stiff peaks, being careful not to overbeat them. (The tips of the peaks should droop slightly when the egg beater is lifted from the whites.) Fold beaten whites into the chicken mixture alternately with the whipped cream. Turn into 8 buttered 6-ounce custard cups and place them in a pan of hot water. Bake in a preheated slow oven (325° F.) 40 to 50 minutes or until a pointed knife inserted in the center comes out clean. Unmold onto a warm serving dish. Coat with hot Sauce Suprême. Garnish with watercress. Serve as a hot entrée. Makes 8 servings.

⚜ CHICKEN MOUSSE FLORENTINE

chicken breast weighing ¾ pound
¼ teaspoon salt
⅛ teaspoon ground white pepper
1 unbeaten egg white
1 cup heavy cream
2 cups hot chicken stock
2 pounds fresh spinach or 2 packages (10 ounces each) frozen cooked spinach
⅛ teaspoon ground nutmeg
salt and ground black pepper to taste
2 tablespoons butter
1 cup Mornay Sauce
½ cup grated cheese

Remove skin, gristle, and bones from chicken breast, and save them for making stock. Dice the chicken breast and put the meat through a food chopper, using finest blade. Add salt, pepper, and egg white. Pound and beat the mixture thoroughly with a wooden spoon, and then rub it through a fine sieve into a bowl. Set the bowl in a pan of ice water, and stir the mixture with a wooden spoon until it is thoroughly chilled. Work in the cream, a little at a time, using a wooden spoon. Shape the mixture into 1½-inch balls or ovals on a floured board. Place them in a buttered saucepan. Pour in hot chicken stock. Bring just to boiling point and poach *very gently* over low heat 15 minutes, or until mousseline quenelles are firm. Meanwhile drain and press out all excess water in the spinach. Heat spinach with nutmeg, salt, pepper, and butter. Spread on the bottom of a baking dish. Arrange the mousselines over it and cover with Mornay Sauce. Sprinkle with cheese and brown in a preheated hot oven (400° F.). Serve as an entrée. Makes 6 servings.

⚜ CHICKEN MOUSSELINES WITH NOODLES

Mix and poach chicken mousseline quenelles as directed in the preceding recipe. Cook 1 cup julienne strips sweet red or green pepper in 3 tablespoons of butter. Add ½ pound cooked medium-wide noodles and mix lightly. Spread over the bottom of a baking dish. Arrange mousselines over the noodles and cover with 1 cup Mornay Sauce. Sprinkle with ½ cup grated cheese. Brown in a preheated hot oven (400° F.). Serve as an entrée. Makes 6 servings.

SAVORY CUSTARD DISHES

⚜ QUICHE LORRAINE

plain pastry for 9-inch pie plate
1 tablespoon bacon drippings
1 cup thinly sliced onions
1½ cups cubed Gruyère or Emmentaler cheese
4 slices crisp bacon
4 eggs, beaten lightly
1 cup each heavy cream and milk, or 2 cups light cream
½ teaspoon salt
¼ teaspoon each ground nutmeg and ground white pepper

Line a 9-inch pie plate with pastry and bake 5 minutes. Cook onions in bacon drippings until they are transparent. Cover bottom of pastry with cheese, onion, and crumbled bacon. Combine remaining ingredients and pour over the onion and cheese. Bake in a preheated, very hot oven (450° F.) for 10 minutes, then reduce heat to moderate (350° F.) and bake 15 to 20 minutes, or until a knife inserted in the center comes out clean. Serve as a hot hors d'oeuvre or as an entrée. (See illustration, page 292.) Makes one 9-inch quiche.

⚜ ONION QUICHE

plain pastry, using 1 cup flour to line a 9-inch pie plate
1 cup sliced onions
2 tablespoons bacon drippings
4 large eggs
1 tablespoon flour
½ teaspoon salt
¼ teaspoon powdered mustard
¼ teaspoon ground nutmeg
dash cayenne
2 cups light cream
2 teaspoons butter, melted
2 strips crisp bacon

Line a 9-inch plate with plain pastry and set aside. Cook onions in bacon drippings until they are transparent. Set aside. Beat eggs lightly. Combine flour, salt, mustard, and cayenne, and add to eggs. Beat only enough to blend. Stir in cream and melted butter. Spread onions over the bottom of the pastry. Pour in the egg and cream mixture. Bake in preheated moderate oven (375° F.) for 40 minutes, or until custard is set. Serve as an entrée. Garnish each serving with ⅓ strip crisp bacon. Makes 6 servings.

VARIATION

LEEK QUICHE

In the recipe for Onion Quiche, replace onions with the same amount of sliced white part of leeks.

⚜ CHEDDAR CUSTARD TARTS

1½ cups finely diced Cheddar cheese
24 unbaked 1½-inch tart shells
4 large eggs
1 tablespoon flour
½ teaspoon salt
½ teaspoon powdered mustard
1/16 teaspoon ground mace
dash cayenne
1 cup milk
1 cup light cream
1 tablespoon butter, melted

Divide cheese equally among the tart shells. Set aside. Beat together the next 6 ingredients, then stir in milk, cream, and butter. Strain the mixture and divide equally between the tart shells. Bake in a preheated moderate oven (375° F.) 30 minutes, or until custard is set. Serve hot. Makes 24 tarts.

⚜ CHEDDAR CUSTARD PIE

Pour the Cheddar Custard mixture into an unbaked 9-inch pie shell. Bake in a preheated moderate oven (375° F.) 45 minutes or until custard is set. To test, insert a pointed knife in the center of the custard. If it comes out clean, the custard is done. Makes 6 servings.

⚜ CHEESE PUDDING

6 slices bread
½ pound Gruyère or Cheddar cheese, cut into thin slices
3 large eggs
½ teaspoon salt
½ teaspoon powdered mustard
dash cayenne
2½ cups milk

Remove crusts from bread and cut the slices in half. Arrange them over the bottom of a 10-by-6-by-2-inch baking dish. Cover with cheese slices. Beat eggs until frothy. Add salt, spices, and ½ cup of the milk. Heat remaining milk and blend with eggs. Pour over bread and cheese. Bake in a preheated slow oven (325° F.) 1 hour or until custard is set. Makes 6 servings.

SOUFFLÉS

CHEESE SOUFFLÉ

¼ cup (½ stick) butter
4 tablespoons flour
¼ teaspoon salt
1 cup (¼ pound) grated Gruyère or Cheddar cheese
1 cup milk
4 large eggs, separated
dash cayenne
¼ teaspoon cream of tartar

Melt butter in a saucepan. Remove from heat and blend in flour and salt. Stir and cook 1 minute. Remove from heat and stir in milk. Cook until the sauce is of medium thickness, stirring constantly. Stir in cheese. Beat egg yolks until they are thick and lemon-colored. Add a little of the hot sauce to the egg yolks and then stir the yolks into the remaining hot mixture. Add cayenne. Beat egg whites until they are foamy. Add cream of tartar and beat until the whites stand in soft stiff peaks. Gently fold into the mixture. Butter the bottom (not the sides) of a 1½-quart soufflé dish and pour in the mixture. Place the dish in a pan of hot water. Bake in a preheated slow oven (325° F.) 1¼ hours, or until soufflé is well puffed and browned. Serve immediately. Makes 6 servings.

CHICKEN SOUFFLÉ

3 tablespoons each butter and flour
½ cup each light cream and chicken stock
4 large eggs, separated
½ teaspoon salt
⅛ teaspoon ground white pepper
2 cups finely chopped cooked chicken
1 teaspoon lemon juice
¼ teaspoon cream of tartar

Melt butter in a saucepan. Remove from heat and blend in flour. Stir and cook 1 minute. Remove from heat and add cream and chicken stock. Stir and cook over low heat until the sauce is smooth and is of medium thickness. Beat egg yolks until thick and lemon-colored, mix with a little of the sauce, and add to the sauce along with salt, pepper, chicken, and lemon juice. Beat egg whites until they are foamy. Add cream of tartar and continue beating until the whites stand in soft, stiff peaks. Carefully fold into the mixture. Butter *only* the bottom of a 1½-quart soufflé dish and empty the mixture into it. Place the dish in a pan of water. Bake in a preheated slow oven 1½ hours, or until the soufflé is well puffed and browned. Serve immediately. Makes 6 servings.

⚜ HAM SOUFFLÉ

In the preceding recipe use 1 cup milk instead of ½ cup each light cream and chicken stock. Replace chicken with 2 cups ground cooked lean smoked ham. Add ½ teaspoon powdered mustard at the time salt and pepper are added. Proceed as directed.

⚜ LOBSTER SOUFFLÉ

3 tablespoons each butter and flour
1 cup milk
4 eggs, separated
¾ teaspoon salt
⅛ teaspoon ground white pepper
½ teaspoon powdered mustard
2 cups finely chopped lobster meat
1 teaspoon lemon juice
¼ teaspoon cream of tartar

Melt butter in a saucepan. Remove from heat and blend in flour. Stir and cook until the sauce is of medium thickness. Beat egg yolks until thick and lemon-colored. Add a little of the hot sauce to the egg yolks and then stir the yolks into the remaining hot mixture. Blend in salt and spices. Purée lobster meat in a blender with a little of the hot sauce and lemon juice, or put it through a food mill. Add to the remaining sauce. Beat egg whites until foamy. Add cream of tartar and continue beating until the whites stand in soft, stiff peaks. Carefully fold into the mixture. Butter *only* the bottom of a 1½-quart soufflé dish and empty the mixture into it. Place the dish in a pan of hot water. Bake in a preheated slow oven (325° F.) 1½ hours or until the soufflé is well puffed and browned. Serve immediately. Makes 6 servings.

VARIATION

SHRIMP OR CRABMEAT SOUFFLÉ

In the preceding recipe, replace the lobster with 2 cups finely diced cooked shrimp or finely flaked cooked crabmeat. Proceed as directed.

⚜ POTATO SOUFFLÉ

½ cup light cream
1 teaspoon salt
¼ teaspoon ground black pepper
⅛ teaspoon ground nutmeg
2 cups thick mashed potatoes
3 tablespoons grated Parmesan cheese
4 eggs, separated
¼ teaspoon cream of tartar

Add cream and seasonings to potatoes. Stir and cook over low heat until the mixture is hot. Remove from heat and blend in cheese. Beat in egg yolks, one at a time, beating well after each addition. Cool. Beat egg whites until they are foamy. Add cream of tartar and beat again until the whites stand in soft stiff peaks when the egg beater is withdrawn. Carefully fold into the potatoes. Butter the bottom (not sides) of a 1-quart soufflé dish, and pour in the mixture. Place the dish in a pan of hot water and bake in a preheated slow oven (325° F.) 1 hour or until the soufflé is well puffed and lightly browned. Serve at once. Makes 6 servings.

⚜ SPINACH SOUFFLÉ

¼ cup (½ stick) butter
4 tablespoons flour
1 cup milk
½ teaspoon salt
⅛ teaspoon ground nutmeg
1/16 teaspoon ground black pepper
2 teaspoons lemon juice
1 cup grated Cheddar cheese
1 cup finely chopped, well-drained, cooked spinach
4 large eggs, separated
¼ teaspoon cream of tartar

Melt butter in a saucepan. Remove from heat and blend in flour. Stir and cook 1 minute. Remove from heat and add milk. Stir and cook until sauce is of medium thickness. Add seasonings, lemon juice, cheese, and spinach. Mix well. Beat egg yolks until they are thick and lemon-colored, then blend a little of the hot mixture with the eggs and add to the remaining hot mixture. Beat egg whites until they are foamy, add cream of tartar and continue beating until soft stiff peaks form when the beater is withdrawn. (Do not beat too dry.) Fold beaten whites into hot mixture and turn into a 1½-quart soufflé dish. Place dish in a pan of hot water and bake in a preheated slow oven (325°) 1½ hours or until the soufflé is well puffed and lightly browned. Serve at once. Makes 6 servings.

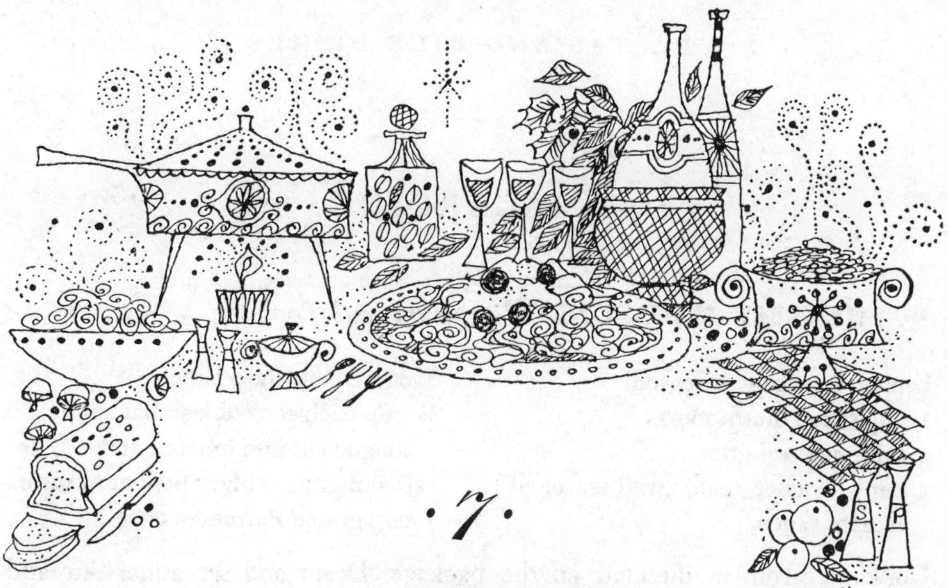

·7·

PASTAS AND RICE DISHES

This chapter includes entrées and main dishes made with cereal products as their main ingredient (see Cereals, pages 93–97).

Macaroni, noodles, and spaghetti, collectively known as pastas, are bland-flavored products made from wheat flour. They are similar in texture and flavor, differing chiefly in shape. Macaroni and spaghetti are usually bought in packaged form. Noodles of many shapes are also available in packages, but some of the recipes in this chapter call for homemade Noodle Dough (see page 127).

Gnocchi are dumplings made either with semolina or Chou Paste. Polenta is made with cornmeal.

Rice, although a different grain with somewhat different flavor and nutritive values, is used in many of the same ways as the pastas. Both can be combined with meat, poultry, fish, or eggs, and the same sauces can frequently be used with either. It is traditional to serve rice with Oriental foods, noodles with German or other Middle European specialties, and macaroni, noodles, or spaghetti with Italian dishes.

MACARONI

⚜ MILANESE MACARONI (*With Ham and Tongue*)

½-pound package macaroni
1 cup sliced mushrooms
2 tablespoons butter
1 cup (8-ounce can) well-seasoned tomato sauce
1 cup Demi-Glace Sauce
½ cup each cooked lean ham and tongue cut into julienne strips
salt and ground black pepper to taste
1 cup grated Parmesan cheese

Cook macaroni as directed on the package. Drain and set aside. Stir and cook mushrooms in butter for 5 minutes, or until they are soft. Add tomato sauce and Demi-Glace Sauce, ham and tongue. Heat. Add macaroni, salt, and pepper. Bring to boiling point. Remove from heat and carefully blend in cheese. Serve hot. In Italy, the cooked, well-drained macaroni is tossed lightly with butter and placed in a dish. A depression is made in the center and filled with the sauce. Makes 6 servings.

⚜ NEAPOLITAN MACARONI (*With Beef and Cheese*)

½ pound macaroni
3 tablespoons butter or olive oil
⅓ cup finely chopped onion
2 cups diced cooked lean beef
1½ cups tomato sauce
½ teaspoon each dried, or 2 teaspoons each chopped fresh basil and oregano
1 tablespoon chopped parsley
salt and ground black pepper to taste
1 cup grated Parmesan cheese

Cook macaroni as directed on the package. Drain well, toss lightly with 2 tablespoons of the butter or oil, and set aside. Cook onion in the remaining 1 tablespoon of butter (or oil) until it is transparent. Add beef, tomato sauce, and herbs. Simmer 5 minutes. Add salt and pepper. In a well-buttered 10-by-6-by-2-inch baking dish, put layers of the ingredients in this order: sauce, macaroni, Parmesan cheese. Repeat until all ingredients are used. Bake in a preheated moderate oven (350° F.) 30 minutes, or until browned. Makes 6 servings.

⚜ SOUTH ITALIAN MACARONI (*With Eggplant and Cheese*)

½ pound macaroni
3 tablespoons butter or olive oil
12 slices eggplant 2½ inches in diameter, or 8 slices 4 inches in diameter, peeled and cut ½ inch thick
salt and ground black pepper
flour
about 1 cup olive oil or salad oil
⅓ cup chopped onion
2 cups (2 cans, 8 ounces each) tomato sauce
1 tablespoon chopped parsley
1 teaspoon dried basil leaves
1 cup grated Parmesan cheese
12 thin 1-inch squares Mozzarella cheese
3 tablespoons butter, melted

Cook macaroni as directed on the package. Drain well. Toss lightly with 2 tablespoons of the butter or oil and set aside. Sprinkle eggplant slices lightly with salt and pepper, roll in flour, and brown in hot oil (eggplant absorbs a great deal of oil when frying). Drain on paper towels. Cook onion in remaining butter or oil until it is transparent. Add tomato sauce, parsley, and basil. Heat; stir in salt and pepper to taste. Save ½ cup of the sauce to use later. Add macaroni to remaining sauce and mix lightly. In a well-buttered 9-by-9-by-2-inch baking dish, layer the ingredients in this order: macaroni, fried eggplant, Parmesan cheese. Repeat, using remaining macaroni, eggplant and Parmesan cheese. Cover with the ½ cup reserved sauce. Top with Mozzarella cheese squares and sprinkle with melted butter. Bake in a preheated moderate oven (350° F.) 30 minutes, or until cheese has melted and browned. Serve hot as an entrée. Makes 6 to 8 servings.

NOODLES

⚜ NOODLES WITH ALMONDS AND POPPY SEEDS

1 box (½ pound) noodles, or ½ pound homemade noodles (see Noodle Dough)
boiling water
1 teaspoon salt
¼ cup (½ stick) butter
1 tablespoon poppy seeds
½ cup sliced toasted almonds

Cook noodles until tender in a large amount of boiling water with salt added. Drain well. Melt butter, add poppy seeds, stir and cook 1 to 2 minutes or until butter begins to brown. Add to drained noodles along with almonds. Toss lightly. Makes 6 servings.

⚜ GREEN NOODLES

4 cups sifted all-purpose flour
1 teaspoon salt
¾ cup well-drained spinach purée
2 large eggs, well-beaten

Sift flour and salt togther into a mixing bowl. Make a well in the center into which put spinach and eggs. Mix well to form a stiff dough, adding a little water if mixture is too dry. Divide the dough into 3 equal parts and roll one part at a time. Roll out very thin into a rectangle on a lightly floured board. Roll the sheet of thin dough tightly in jelly-roll fashion and cut into narrow strips. Arrange on a board or pan and dry until very brittle. Use as needed.
To cook Green Noodles: Cook in a large quantity of rapidly boiling water until they are tender, 4 to 5 minutes. Drain well. Toss over low heat with 1 cup (2 sticks) of melted butter, 1 cup grated Parmesan cheese, and ⅛ teaspoon ground white pepper. Makes 6 servings.

⚜ GREEN NOODLES BOLOGNESE (*Tagliatelli Verdi alla Bolognese*)

½ cup finely chopped onion
1 small clove of garlic, finely chopped
2 tablespoons olive oil or butter
½ pound ground lean beef
1 cup chopped mushrooms
1-pound can (2 cups) Italian plum tomatoes
2 tablespoons tomato paste
½ teaspoon sugar
½ teaspoon dried thyme leaves
salt and ground black pepper to taste
½-pound cooked green noodles
3 tablespoons butter

Cook onion and garlic in hot oil or butter, until onion is transparent. Add beef and cook until lightly browned. Add mushrooms and cook 3 minutes. Stir in tomatoes, tomato paste, and seasonings. Bring to boiling point, reduce heat, and simmer 15 minutes, stirring frequently. Drain noodles and toss lightly with butter. Then mix lightly with the sauce. Makes 6 servings. (See illustration, page 295.)

⚜ ROMAN DELIGHTS

½-pound package noodles
1 cup Béchamel Sauce
1 cup grated Parmesan cheese
¼ teaspoon grated nutmeg
2 large eggs, beaten with 2 tablespoons water
fine dry breadcrumbs
2 cups diced cooked lean ham

2 cups veal gravy or Béchamel Sauce
salt and ground black pepper to taste
fresh parsley or parsley fried in deep fat

Break noodles into 1-inch pieces and cook according to package directions. Drain them well and mix with Béchamel Sauce, cheese, and nutmeg. Spread on a large oiled tray, or jellyroll pan, in a layer 2½ inches thick. Cool completely. Make noodle patty shells by cutting rounds from the noodles mixture with a 2½-inch cooky cutter. Cut centers out of these rounds with a 1¼-inch cooky cutter, being careful not to cut through the bottom; remove the smaller rounds and leave them intact. Roll both the cases and the lids in beaten eggs and then in breadcrumbs. Let them stand a few minutes to dry the crumbs. Fry in deep fat preheated to 375° F. Drain on paper towels. Heat ham with veal gravy or Béchamel Sauce, and spoon into the noodle cases. Cover the filled noodle cases with the fried noodle lids. Garnish with fresh parsley or parsley fried in deep fat. Makes 6 servings. (See illustration, page 295.)

⚜ LASAGNE CASALINGA

½ cup chopped onion
1 clove garlic, minced
4 tablespoons olive oil or salad oil
¼ cup grated carrot
¼ cup finely chopped celery
½ pound ground chuck
1 cup chopped raw mushrooms
1 cup water or beef stock
2 tablespoons tomato paste
1 tablespoon flour
¼ cup Marsala
½ teaspoon sugar
salt
ground black pepper
2 cups cream sauce
2 tablespoons chopped parsley
½ pound lasagne noodles
1½ cups grated Parmesan cheese
6 tablespoons butter, melted

Cook onion and garlic in oil until onion is transparent. Add carrot and celery, and cook 2 to 3 minutes. Add meat and mushrooms and cook over moderate heat until meat begins to brown. Stir in 1 cup water or beef stock and the tomato paste. Cover and cook 30 minutes. Blend flour with wine and add. Stir and cook 1 to 2 minutes, or until sauce has thickened. Stir in sugar, salt, pepper, cream sauce, and parsley. Set aside. Cook noodles as directed on package. Drain well. In a 10-by-6-by-2-inch baking dish put layers of the ingredients in this order: meat sauce, lasagne noodles, grated Parmesan cheese, and melted butter. Repeat until all ingredients are used. Bake in a preheated moderate oven (350° F.) 30 minutes, or until lasagne is hot and the top has browned. Serve as a hot entrée. Makes 6 servings. (See illustration, page 298, for a variation of this, using green lasagne noodles.)

⚜ LASAGNE LIGURIAN STYLE (*With Sausage and Mushrooms*)

½ cup finely chopped onion
1 small clove garlic, minced
2 tablespoons olive oil or salad oil
1 cup diced mushrooms
1 pound sausage meat
1 cup (8-ounce can) tomato sauce
1 cup Italian plum tomatoes
½ teaspoon sugar
1½ cups Béchamel Sauce
⅓ cup dry white wine
1 teaspoon dried or 1 tablespoon chopped fresh basil leaves
2 tablespoons chopped parsley
salt and ground black pepper to taste
1 pound lasagne noodles
1½ cups grated Parmesan cheese

Cook onions and garlic in hot oil 3 to 4 minutes, or until onions are transparent. Add mushrooms and sausage meat and brown very lightly. Add tomato sauce, plum tomatoes, and sugar. Simmer 20 minutes or until the sauce has thickened. Stir in Béchamel Sauce, wine, basil, parsley, salt, and pepper. Simmer 10 minutes. Cook noodles according to package directions; or, if desired, make your own noodles, using the noodle recipe in this book. Drain noodles well. In a 12-by-8-by-2-inch baking dish, put layers of the ingredients in this order: sauce, cooked noodles, grated Parmesan cheese. Repeat until all ingredients are used. Bake in a preheated moderate oven (350° F.) 30 minutes, or until browned. Makes 10 servings.

NOODLE DOUGH WITH FILLINGS

⚜ CANNELONI

Canneloni are made by poaching squares or rectangles of thinly rolled noodle dough and rolling them around a filling, then dotting the rolls with butter, sprinkling with grated cheese, adding a sauce if desired, and browning in the oven. (An imitation of Canneloni is made by filling thin crêpes; see recipe, page 130.) Fillings for Canneloni are made of various cheeses, meat, poultry, fish, shellfish, or vegetables. They should be fresh, delicately seasoned, and blended with a sauce compatible with the main ingredient. The same fillings can be used for Ravioli.

Make the recipe for Noodle Dough (page 127). Divide dough into 3 equal parts. Roll one part at a time into paper-thin strips 4 inches wide. Straighten the edges by trimming them with scissors or a sharp knife. Cut the strips into pieces 6 inches long by 4 inches wide. Drop 4 pieces at a time into rapidly boiling water, reduce heat, and simmer 8 to 10 minutes. Remove from water with a perforated spoon or skimmer. Drain well. Spread the cooked strips of dough between two moist towels and let stand while preparing the filling.

Noodle Dough with Fillings

Prepare any of the following fillings according to directions and spread in the center of each cooked strip of dough. Roll the long way, pinch at ends to hold filling in, and place side by side, seam side down, in a buttered baking dish. Cover with desired sauce and sprinkle with ½ cup Parmesan cheese. Dot with butter. Bake in preheated moderate oven (375° F.) 20 minutes or place under broiler to brown. Serve hot as an entrée. Makes 6 servings.

FILLINGS FOR CANNELONI

CHEESE

2 cups Ricotta cheese
1¾ cups grated Parmesan cheese
¾ cup finely diced Mozzarella cheese
⅓ cup cream sauce
1 large egg, beaten
salt and ground black pepper to taste
1 cup well-seasoned tomato sauce
4 tablespoons (½ stick) butter

Combine Ricotta cheese with 1¼ cups of the grated Parmesan cheese, the Mozzarella cheese, cream sauce, egg, salt, and pepper, and mix well. Shape the filling into 12 rolls 5 inches long. Place one roll in the center of each of 12 strips of cooked noodle dough, roll, and place in buttered baking dish. Cover with tomato sauce, sprinkle with remaining ¼ cup Parmesan cheese, and dot with butter. Bake as in directions for Canneloni.

CHICKEN AND CHICKEN LIVERS

7 chicken livers
¼ cup chopped onion
7 tablespoons butter
3 cups diced cooked chicken
½ teaspoon dried thyme leaves
salt and ground black pepper
2 large eggs, beaten
2 cups Béchamel Sauce
¼ cup grated Parmesan cheese
Mushroom Sauce (optional)

Sauté chicken livers with onion in 3 tablespoons of the butter. Put the mixture through a food chopper along with the chicken. Season with thyme, salt, and pepper. Add beaten eggs and 1 cup of the Béchamel Sauce and mix. Spread on centers of pieces of cooked noodle dough, roll, and place in baking dish. Cover with remaining 1 cup Béchamel Sauce, sprinkle with Parmesan cheese, and dot with remaining 4 tablespoons butter. Bake as in directions for Canneloni. Serve with Mushroom Sauce if desired.

VEAL AND CHICKEN LIVERS

In the recipe for Chicken and Chicken Livers, replace chicken with 3 cups cooked diced lean veal.

HAM AND SPINACH

2 large eggs, beaten
1 cup minced ham
1 cup well-drained, finely chopped cooked spinach
½ cup fresh breadcrumbs
¼ cup heavy cream
1 cup grated Parmesan cheese
1 tablespoon chopped parsley
2 tablespoons minced onion
salt and ground black pepper to taste
about 1 cup Béchamel Sauce
4 tablespoons (½ stick) butter

Combine beaten eggs, ham, spinach, breadcrumbs, cream, ½ cup of the Parmesan cheese, parsley, onion, salt, and pepper. Mix well. Spread on strips of cooked noodle dough, roll, and place in buttered baking dish. Cover with Béchamel Sauce, sprinkle with remaining ½ cup Parmesan cheese, and dot with the butter. Brown as directed for Canneloni.

⚜ CRÊPES STUFFED WITH HAM AND CHEESE

12 very thin crêpes, 4 inches in diameter
2 large eggs, beaten
1 cup finely diced Mozzarella cheese
1½ cups grated Parmesan cheese
2 cups ground cooked lean ham
½ teaspoon powdered mustard
salt and ground black pepper to taste
1½ cups Béchamel Sauce
4 tablespoons (½ stick) butter

Make pancakes, using recipe for Crêpe Batter on page 130. Set aside. Combine eggs, Mozzarella cheese, 1 cup of the Parmesan cheese, ham, seasonings, and ¼ cup of the Béchamel Sauce. Mix well. Put 2 tablespoons of this mixture on the center of each pancake. Roll up. Cover the bottom of a baking dish with the remaining Béchamel Sauce, over which arrange the stuffed pancakes. Sprinkle with remaining Parmesan cheese and dot with butter. Bake in a preheated moderate oven (375° F.) 20 minutes, or until browned. Serve hot as an entrée. Makes 6 servings.

⚜ RAVIOLI

Noodle Dough
filling
melted butter
grated Parmesan cheese

Make Noodle Dough, using the recipe on page 127. Divide dough in half and roll each half on a lightly floured board to the same size and shape as the board, as thin as possible without breaking the dough. Prepare one of the following fillings (or one of the Canneloni fillings). Drop the filling from a teaspoon, in small mounds, 2 inches apart, on one sheet of dough. Cover with the second sheet, and with the index finger press dough firmly around each mound. Cut the dough between the mounds with a pastry cutter or a sharp-pointed knife. Boil the squares in hot broth or water about 12 minutes or until the dough is thoroughly cooked but not mushy. Serve with melted butter and grated Parmesan cheese. (See illustration, page 294, also Culinary Techniques in Pictures.)

FILLINGS FOR RAVIOLI

VEAL AND SPINACH

1 cup finely ground cooked veal
1 cup sieved, chopped cooked spinach
½ cup cracker crumbs
¼ cup grated Parmesan cheese
¼ cup cream sauce or heavy cream
½ teaspoon dried marjoram leaves
1 tablespoon chopped parsley
1 teaspoon minced onion
salt and ground black pepper to taste

Combine all ingredients and mix well. This filling can also be used for Canneloni.

CHICKEN AND SPINACH

In the preceding recipe replace the veal with the same amount of ground cooked chicken, and the marjoram with ½ teaspoon ground nutmeg.

⚜ TORTELLINI WITH RICOTTA

2 cups ground, cooked chicken breast
1⅓ cups Ricotta cheese
¼ cup grated Parmesan cheese
4 large egg yolks
2 large egg whites
¼ teaspoon ground nutmeg
½ teaspoon grated lemon rind
salt and ground pepper to taste
Noodle Dough
2 quarts chicken broth

Combine all ingredients except the Noodle Dough and the broth, mix well, and set aside. Roll Noodle Dough on a lightly floured board into thin sheets. Cut it into 2-inch squares. Put 1 teaspoon of filling on each square of dough. Fold the square in half and press edges firmly together. Cook the tortellini in chicken broth for 15 to 18 minutes, or until the dough is thoroughly cooked but not mushy. Drain well and sprinkle with additional Parmesan cheese and Brown Butter. Makes 8 to 10 servings. (See illustration, page 294.)

PIZZAS

A pizza is an Italian pie with a filling of vegetables, cheese, anchovies, etc., cooked in oil. The dough differs from Noodle Dough in being made with yeast.

⚜ PIZZA I (*Rich Pastry*)

1 envelope active dry yeast
½ cup lukewarm water
1 teaspoon sugar
¾ cup hot water
⅓ cup shortening
¼ cup sugar
1 teaspoon salt
1 large egg
about 5 cups sifted all-purpose flour

Combine yeast, water, and sugar and let stand 5 minutes. Mix hot water, shortening, sugar, and salt in a large bowl. Stir to melt shortening and to dissolve sugar. Cool to lukewarm. Blend in yeast and egg. Gradually add enough flour to make a soft dough. Knead until dough is smooth and satiny. Place in a greased bowl, turning the dough to bring the greased side to the top. Cover and let rise in a warm place (80° to 85° F.) about 1 hour, or until the dough has doubled in size. Divide the dough in 2 equal parts. Cover and let it rest 10 minutes. Place each ball of dough on a greased cooky sheet and roll into a 15-by-12-inch rectangle. Chill until ready to spread with filling.

PIZZA FILLING I

¼ cup finely chopped onion
½ cup finely chopped sweet green pepper
½ clove garlic, minced
2 tablespoons olive oil or salad oil
2 cups well-drained canned tomatoes
1 teaspoon salt
1 teaspoon oregano leaves
½ teaspoon ground black pepper
½ teaspoon sugar
Spanish sausage (chorizos)
pimiento-stuffed green olives, sliced
Mozzarella cheese, sliced
anchovy fillets
grated Parmesan cheese

Cook onion, green pepper, and garlic in oil until onion is transparent. Add oil, tomatoes, and seasonings. Stir and cook slowly 10 minutes, or until the sauce has thickened. Cool. Spread over the pizza dough. Top each portion with any or all of the following: cooked thinly sliced sausage, olives, thin slices Mozzarella cheese, anchovies. Sprinkle with grated Parmesan cheese. Bake in a preheated hot oven (400° F.) 15 to 20 minutes, or until the crust is brown and the edges crisp. Cut into 2-by-1-inch pieces if the pizza is to be served as a hot hors d'oeuvre; cut into larger pieces if it is to be served as an entrée. Makes 2 pizzas, 12 by 15 inches.

PIZZA II (*Traditional Pastry*)

1 envelope active dry yeast
1 cup lukewarm water
½ teaspoon sugar
½ teaspoon salt
about 3¼ cups sifted all-purpose flour

Combine yeast, water, and sugar, and let stand 5 minutes. Add salt and 2 cups of the flour. Turn the dough onto a floured board and gradually knead in the remaining flour. Knead until the dough is smooth and satiny. Cover and let the dough rise until it has doubled in size. Place dough on a lightly floured board and pound lightly with a rolling pin to deflate it. Cover and let dough rise 30 minutes. Roll and stretch the dough to ¼-inch thickness and fit it into a 12-inch lightly oiled pizza pan. (There will be a small piece of dough left, which may be made into rolls or a smaller pizza.) Chill until ready to spread with filling.

PIZZA FILLING II

¼ cup finely chopped onion
⅛ teaspoon finely chopped garlic
5 tablespoons olive oil or salad oil
2 cups drained canned Italian plum tomatoes
2 tablespoons tomato paste
1½ teaspoons dried oregano leaves
½ teaspoon salt
½ teaspoon sugar
⅛ teaspoon ground black pepper

TOPPINGS

½ pound Mozzarella cheese, thinly sliced
2-ounce can anchovy fillets
¼-pound Italian sausage, sliced
4-ounce can sliced buttered mushrooms, or ½ cup sliced fresh mushrooms cooked in butter
½ cup grated Parmesan cheese

Cook onion and garlic in 2 tablespoons hot olive oil until onion is transparent. Break up tomatoes with a fork and add to onion along with tomato paste and seasonings. Stir and cook 5 minutes. Cool. Spread over the unbaked pizza crust. Arrange Mozzarella cheese slices over the top. Place anchovies, sausage, and mushrooms over the cheese in any desired pattern. Sprinkle with ¼ cup of the Parmesan cheese. Drizzle with remaining 3 tablespoons olive oil. Bake in a preheated hot oven (400° F) 25 to 30 minutes, or until crust is brown and the edges crisp. Sprinkle with remaining Parmesan cheese and serve hot. Makes one 12-inch pie.

⚜ INDIVIDUAL PIZZAS

Make the Pizza dough by either of the preceding recipes. Roll it in 4-inch circles ¼-inch thick on a lightly oiled baking sheet. Spread with either Pizza Filling and proceed as directed in whichever Pizza recipe used; or top only with sliced Mozzarella cheese, grated Parmesan cheese, and sliced black olives. (See illustration, page 293.) Makes 5 individual pizzas.

SPAGHETTI

⚜ SPAGHETTI WITH ANCHOVY SAUCE

1 tablespoon finely chopped onion
1 small clove garlic
½ cup olive oil
1 can (2 ounces) anchovies
⅛ teaspoon ground black pepper
½ teaspoon paprika
1 tablespoon chopped parsley
½ pound spaghetti, cooked as directed on the package
3 tablespoons butter
pimiento strips

Cook onion and garlic in hot oil until onion is transparent. Remove and discard garlic. Dice anchovies and heat in the oil 5 minutes, or just long enough for the oil to absorb the flavor of the anchovies. Add seasonings and cook ½ minute. Drain spaghetti and toss with butter. Pour anchovy sauce over the spaghetti. Garnish with pimiento strips. Makes 6 servings.

⚜ SPAGHETTI WITH ARTICHOKE SAUCE

To the preceding Anchovy Sauce, add 5 chopped, canned artichoke hearts (or cooked fresh or frozen artichoke hearts) along with the seasonings. Cook 3 to 4 minutes. Serve over ½ pound cooked spaghetti.

⚜ SPAGHETTI CARBONARA (*With Ham*)

¼ cup (½ stick) butter, melted
2 cups cooked ham, in julienne strips
1 cup heavy cream
3 large egg yolks
salt and ground black pepper to taste
½ pound spaghetti, cooked as directed on the package

Melt butter in a saucepan. Add ham and ¾ cup of the cream. Cook over low heat until cream has reduced by one quarter the original amount. Blend remaining ¼ cup cream with egg yolks and add to hot mixture. Stir and cook ½ minute over low heat. Add salt and pepper. Pour over well-drained cooked spaghetti. Toss lightly with 2 forks. Serve as a hot entrée. Makes 6 servings. (See illustration, page 297.)

⚜ SPAGHETTI WITH MUSSELS OR CLAMS

¼ cup finely chopped onion
1 clove garlic, finely chopped
2 cups (1-pound can) canned tomatoes
6-ounce can tomato paste
1½ cups hot water
½ teaspoon sugar
salt and ground black pepper to taste
2 cups mussel or clam liquor (bottled clam juice may be used)
½ teaspoon each dried basil and oregano
2 cups chopped mussels or clams
3 tablespoons butter
⅓ cup chopped parsley
1 pound spaghetti, cooked as directed on the package

Cook onion and garlic in hot oil until onion is transparent. Add tomatoes, tomato paste, water, sugar, salt, and pepper. Bring to boiling point, reduce heat, and simmer 40 minutes, or until the sauce has thickened. Add mussel or clam liquor and herbs. Simmer (do not boil) 2 to 3 minutes. Five minutes before serving add mussels or clams and simmer. Stir in butter and parsley. Serve one-half the sauce over well-drained, cooked spaghetti and the remainder in a sauceboat. Makes 8 to 10 servings. (See illustration, page 298.)

⚜ NEAPOLITAN SPAGHETTI (*With Tomato Meat Sauce*)

¾ cup chopped onion
1 clove garlic
¼ cup olive oil or salad oil
1 pound ground chuck
½ cup finely chopped green pepper
7 cups canned Italian plum tomatoes
1 teaspoon sugar
1 bay leaf
6-ounce can tomato paste
1 teaspoon dried or 1 tablespoon chopped fresh basil
salt and ground black pepper to taste
1 pound spaghetti, cooked as directed on the package
grated Parmesan cheese

Cook onion and garlic in hot oil until onions are transparent. Remove and discard garlic. Add beef and green pepper, and cook until meat begins to brown. Add tomatoes, sugar, and bay leaf. Cover and simmer 2 hours. Stir in tomato paste, basil, salt, and pepper. Cook, uncovered, 15 minutes, stirring occasionally. Serve over well-drained cooked spaghetti. Sprinkle with Parmesan cheese. Makes 12 servings.

⚜ GNOCCHI ROMAN STYLE

4 cups milk
½ teaspoon salt
⅛ teaspoon ground nutmeg
1 cup fine semolina or farina
3 large egg yolks, beaten
6 tablespoons melted butter
1 cup grated Parmesan cheese
1 cup grated Gruyère cheese
paprika

Heat together the first 3 ingredients in the top of a double boiler. Slowly add semolina or farina, stirring constantly from the bottom of the pan to prevent lumping. Stir and cook the mixture 15 to 20 minutes over hot water or until it is thick and smooth. Beat a little of the hot mixture into the egg yolks and then beat them into the remaining hot mixture, beating fast to prevent the eggs from setting before they are thoroughly mixed with the semolina or farina. Stir and cook over hot water 1 minute or until thickened. Spread the mixture about ½ inch thick in a well-buttered 11-by-7-by-1½-inch baking dish. Cool and chill. Cut into 2-inch squares or into fancy shapes with cooky cutters. Brush tops with melted butter. Sprinkle with grated cheese and paprika. Bake in a preheated moderate oven (350° F.) 30 minutes or until cheese is melted. Makes 6 to 8 servings.

⚜ CHEESE GNOCCHI PARISIAN STYLE

½ recipe for Chou Paste
¾ cup grated Gruyère cheese
½ teaspoon salt
1 cup medium-thick Béchamel Sauce
¾ cup grated Gruyère cheese
2 tablespoons butter, melted

Mix warm Chou Paste with cheese. Shape into 1-inch balls and poach 10 minutes in simmering (not boiling) salted water. Remove gnocchi from water and drain well. Add to hot Béchamel Sauce and simmer 5 to 6 minutes. Remove saucepan from heat and carefully fold in ½ cup of the cheese. Put mixture in a buttered baking dish, sprinkle with remaining cheese and melted butter, and bake in a preheated moderate oven (350° F.) 20 minutes. Serve as an entrée. Makes 6 servings.

⚜ CROUSTADE OF GNOCCHI PARISIAN STYLE

2 cups grated Gruyère cheese
½ recipe for Chou Paste
2½ cups Béchamel Sauce
plain pastry for 9-inch pie, using 1 cup flour
2 tablespoons butter, melted

Mix 1 cup of the cheese with warm Chou Paste. Shape into 1-inch balls and poach in boiling salted water. Remove the balls from water and drain. Add to 2 cups of the Béchamel Sauce. Stir in ¾ cup of remaining grated cheese. Line a 9-inch pie plate with pastry and add cheese mixture. Spread with remaining ½ cup Béchamel Sauce and sprinkle with melted butter and the remaining ¼ cup cheese. Bake the pie 10 minutes in a preheated, very hot oven (450° F.); reduce heat to 375° F. and continue baking 30 to 40 minutes. Serve as an entrée. Makes 6 servings. (See illustration, page 293.)

POLENTA

⚜ POLENTA (*Cornmeal Mush*)

4 cups water
1 teaspoon salt
1 cup yellow or white cornmeal

Mix half the water and the salt in the top part of a double boiler and bring to boiling point over direct heat. Blend remaining water and cornmeal and add to the boiling water. Reduce heat and stir and cook until the mixture boils. Place the pan over boiling water, cover and cook 45 to 50 minutes, stirring frequently to prevent lumping. Serve hot with butter and, if desired, with grated Parmesan or Gruyère cheese. Makes approximately 4 cups.

⚜ GENOA-STYLE POLENTA

Add 1 cup grated Parmesan, Cheddar, or Gruyère cheese to the hot Polenta. Turn the mixture into a well-buttered 1-quart mold or an 8- or 9-inch square baking pan. Let stand 25 minutes in a warm place. Turn out onto a serving dish and pour ¼ cup (½ stick) melted and browned butter over the Polenta. Makes approximately 4 cups.

⚜ SHALLOW-FRIED POLENTA

Turn Genoa-Style Polenta into a well-buttered 11-by-7-by-1½-inch pan. Let stand until cold. Cut into squares or diamonds and fry until golden brown in hot butter. Makes 8 to 10 servings.

RICE DISHES

⚜ RICE PILAF

1 cup long-grain converted raw rice
water to cover
4 tablespoons butter or 2 tablespoons chicken fat and 2 tablespoons butter
2 tablespoons chopped onion
2¼ cups boiling chicken stock
1 teaspoon salt
1 teaspoon lemon juice
1 cup cooked peas
1 cup sautéed mushrooms
⅛ teaspoon ground black pepper

Soak rice in water to cover 30 minutes. Drain well. Cook in 2 tablespoons butter or chicken fat along with onion until rice is dry and begins to stick to the bottom of the pan. Add chicken stock, salt, and lemon juice. Cover and cook without stirring 12 to 15 minutes or until rice is tender and has absorbed all the water. Add peas, mushrooms, black pepper, and remaining 2 tablespoons butter. Mix lightly with a fork, being careful not to mash the starch grains. Makes 6 servings.

⚜ CREOLE RICE

1 cup long-grain converted raw rice
⅓ cup (⅔ stick) butter
½ teaspoon salt
2⅓ cups hot water

Place rice, one-half the butter, salt, and hot water in a 1-quart casserole. Cover and cook in a preheated moderate oven (350° F.) 18 to 20 minutes or until rice is tender. Remove lid. Break remaining butter in small pieces and scatter over the top. Allow to stand 5 minutes. Separate grains with a fork. Makes 6 servings.

⚜ RISOTTO (*Savory Rice*)

1 cup long-grain converted raw rice
¼ cup finely chopped onion
⅓ cup butter
½ teaspoon salt
2⅓ cups chicken stock

Soak rice in water to cover 30 minutes. Drain well. Cook onion in half the butter until onion is soft. Add rice and remaining butter. Stir and cook until rice is well coated with the butter and begins to stick to the bottom of the pan. Add salt and stock. Cover and cook 12 to 15 minutes. Remove from heat and let stand covered 5 to 10 minutes or until ready to serve. Makes 6 servings.

VARIATION

CURRIED RICE

To the recipe for Risotto, add 2 teaspoons curry powder and cook it with the onion.

⚜ RICE À LA GRECQUE

¼ cup chopped onion
½ clove garlic, crushed
2 tablespoons butter
2 tablespoons olive oil or salad oil
1 cup converted rice
½ cup sliced mushrooms
1 cup diced lean ham
½ cup diced cooked tongue
¼ cup diced red pickled pepper or pimiento
1 small bay leaf
1 teaspoon salt
¼ teaspoon ground black pepper
2½ cups hot bouillon or veal stock
1 cup shelled raw peas

Cook onion and garlic in butter until onion is transparent. Add oil, heat, and then add rice. Stir and cook until rice is dry and sticks to the bottom of the pan. Put into a 2-quart casserole and add all remaining ingredients except peas. Cover and cook in a preheated moderate oven (375° F.) 20 minutes. Add peas and mix by tossing the rice lightly with a fork. Cover and cook 10 minutes longer. Serve as a hot entrée. Makes 6 to 8 servings. (See illustration, page 296.)

⚜ RICE WITH MUSHROOMS OR CEPES

2 tablespoons chopped onion
2 tablespoons olive oil or salad oil
4 tablespoons butter
1 cup converted long-grain rice
1 cup mushrooms or cepes
2 cups hot bouillon or stock
⅓ cup dry white wine
1 teaspoon salt
¼ teaspoon ground white pepper
¾ cup or more grated Parmesan cheese

Cook onion in oil until transparent, blend in 2 tablespoons of the butter, and add the rice. Stir and cook until rice is dry and begins to stick to the bottom of the pan. Add mushrooms or cepes, bouillon or stock, wine, salt, and pepper. Cover and cook 15 minutes. Add remaining 2 tablespoons butter and the cheese and toss lightly with a fork. Cover and let stand 15 minutes. Serve hot. Makes 6 servings. (See illustration, page 297.)

⚜ MILANESE RISOTTO (*Rice with Saffron*)

2 tablespoons finely chopped onion
5 tablespoons butter
1 cup converted rice
¼ teaspoon crumbled saffron strands
2 cups chicken stock or beef stock
½ teaspoon salt
⅛ teaspoon ground white pepper
½ cup or more grated Parmesan cheese

Sauté onion in 1 tablespoon of butter. Blend in 2 more tablespoons of the butter and add rice. Stir and cook until rice is dry and sticks to the bottom of the pan. Mix saffron with a little of the stock and add to the remaining stock. Bring stock to boiling point and pour over rice. Add salt and pepper. Cover and cook over low heat 15 minutes. Dot with remaining 2 tablespoons butter and sprinkle with Parmesan cheese. Serve hot. Makes 6 servings. (See illustration, page 296.)

⚜ PORTUGUESE RICE

1 cup raw long-grain converted rice
¼ cup chopped onions
1 small clove garlic, crushed
¼ cup (1 stick) butter
1 red or green sweet pepper
1 cup canned or cooked tomatoes
1½ cups boiling beef stock
1 teaspoon salt
¼ teaspoon ground black pepper
1 small bay leaf

Soak rice in water to cover 30 minutes. Cook onion and garlic in half the butter until onions are limp and transparent. Finely chop green or red pepper and add. Stir and cook about 2 minutes. Drain rice well and add to the onions and pepper along with the rest of the butter. Stir and cook until rice is dry. Add remaining ingredients. Turn into a buttered 1½-quart casserole. Cover and cook in a preheated moderate oven (350° F.) 20 to 25 minutes or until rice is barely soft and all the liquid has been absorbed. Makes 6 servings.

⚜ SHRIMP RISOTTO

1 pound raw shrimp
1 small onion, sliced
2 tablespoons chopped celery
½ clove of garlic
2 tablespoons olive oil or salad oil
1 cup dry white wine
2 cups hot water
1 teaspoon salt
2 tablespoons finely chopped onion
4 tablespoons (½ stick) butter
1 cup converted rice
¼ teaspoon ground black pepper
⅓ cup grated Parmesan cheese

Shell, peel, and devein shrimp. Reserve, separately, both the shrimp and the shells. Cook sliced onion, celery, and garlic in hot oil until onion is transparent. Remove and discard garlic. Add the shrimp shells and the wine. Simmer 10 minutes. Add hot water and salt. Cover and simmer 30 minutes. Strain the stock and skim. Set aside. Cook the 2 tablespoons chopped onion in 1 tablespoon of the butter until onion is transparent. Add 2 more tablespoons of butter, the shrimp, and the rice. Stir and cook over low heat until rice is dry and begins to stick to the pan. Add 2 cups of the strained shrimp stock and the pepper. Pour mixture into a 6-cup casserole, cover, and cook in a preheated moderate oven (350° F.) 30 minutes, or until all liquid has been absorbed and the rice is tender. Sprinkle with Parmesan cheese and dot with remaining 1 tablespoon butter. Serve as a hot entrée. Makes 6 servings.

⚜ PAELLA (*Spanish*)

2½ pounds chicken breasts and thighs
1¼ pounds lean pork, cut in 1-inch pieces
1¼ pounds fish (fillet of haddock or perch)
2½ tablespoons salt
1 teaspoon ground black pepper
⅓ cup olive oil or salad oil
1 cup finely chopped onions
1¼ teaspoons crumbled saffron strands
6 cups chicken stock
1¾ cups chopped green pepper
3½ cups diced fresh tomatoes
2¼ cups converted rice
1⅓ cups peeled and deveined raw shrimp
1¼ cups fresh raw peas
10 clams, steamed
10 mussels, steamed
10 artichoke hearts, cooked
pimiento

Rub chicken, pork, and fish with salt and black pepper. Brown each in hot oil in a heavy skillet. Set aside. In the same skillet, cook onions until they are soft. Add saffron and stock and bring to boiling point. In a 6-quart casserole or roasting pan, combine stock, green pepper, tomatoes, and rice, and place chicken, pork, and fish on top. Cover with foil. Bake in a preheated slow oven (325° F.) 1 hour. Add shrimp and peas and mix lightly with a fork. Cover and bake 25 minutes. Garnish with hot steamed clams and mussels and with artichoke hearts and pimiento, if desired. Makes 10 to 12 servings.

⚜ WILD RICE

1 cup raw wild rice
3 cups water
1 teaspoon salt
1 tablespoon butter

Wash rice and soak it 30 minutes in water to cover. Drain off water and rinse in cold water. Bring water, salt, and butter to boiling point in a 2-quart saucepan. Add rice. Cover and cook without stirring 30 minutes or until rice grains are barely tender. If rice has not absorbed all the water, drain it off and keep rice hot over low heat or hot water, or in a slow oven. Makes 6 servings.

Cooked wild rice may be tossed with 1 cup sautéed mushrooms or ¼ cup blanched, slivered, and toasted almonds.

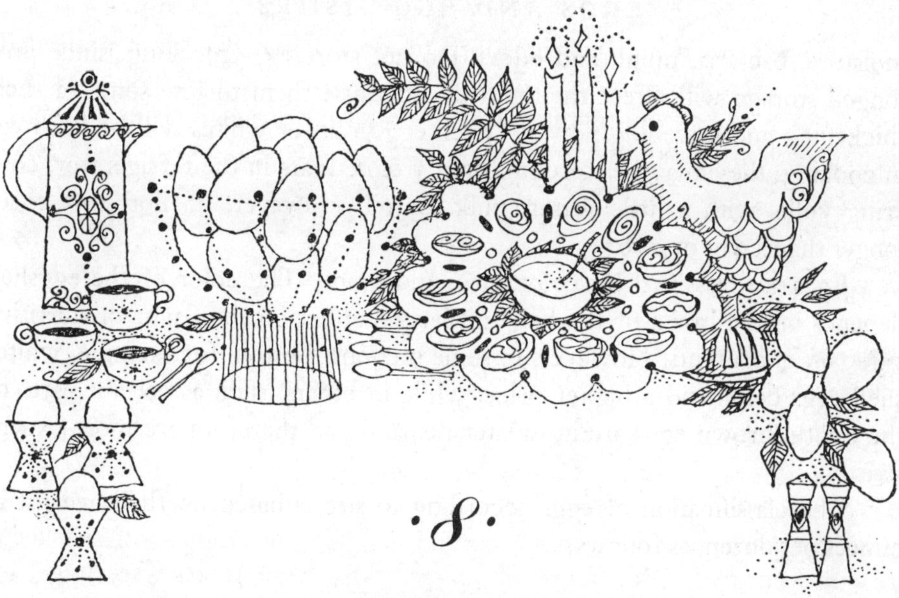

8

EGGS AND EGG DISHES

Eggs of various kinds (birds', fishes', turtles') are consumed as food in every part of the world. Hens' eggs, however, are the most commonly used, and in this book the term egg refers to a hen's egg unless another kind of egg is specified.

The egg is a staple food which can be prepared in so many ways that it may be served at any meal of the day, although the United States is one of the few countries in which eggs are commonly served for breakfast.

Eggs make a significant contribution to the nutrient content of our diet. They are an important source of good-quality protein, easily digested emulsified fat, iron, vitamin A, and riboflavin, and are one of the few food sources of vitamin D. In addition, they contain some thiamin, calcium, and phosphorus and traces of other minerals. One large egg yields 80 calories, 60 of which are from the yolk. Nutritionists recommend that the average person eat from 4 to 7 eggs per week, including those used in cooking.

When eggs are brought home from the market they should be put into the refrigerator at once. Do not wash the shells until just before using eggs. Washing removes the thin protective film that seals the pores and keeps out moisture, bacteria, mold, and odors. Do not store eggs too long, since prolonged storage will affect their flavor and cause them to lose some of their thickening and leavening power. Often egg yolks or whites will be left over in cooking; these may be stored in tightly closed jars in the refrigerator, covering yolks with a little water, milk, or oil. However, do not store them longer than a day or two.

Eggs are classified by color, size, and grade. The color of the eggshell depends on the breed of the hen and has no effect on the flavor or nutritive value of its contents. However, in some sections, Boston, for example, white-shell eggs command a higher price, while in others, such as certain parts of the South, brown eggs are in greater demand and therefore are more expensive.

The classification of eggs according to size is based on their weight in ounces per dozen, as follows:

SIZE	WEIGHT (*ounces per dozen*)
Jumbo	30
Extra large	27
Large	24
Medium	21
Small	18
Pullet (peewee)	15

The United States Department of Agriculture has set up standards for the freshness of eggs. Most states require that eggs be labeled in accordance with those standards, with or without modifications. The three marketable grades, listed in order of decreasing quality, are AA (fresh, fancy quality), A, and B. The top grades, because of their fine flavor and appearance, are recommended for cooking in the shell, poaching, and frying. Grade B eggs are satisfactory for scrambling and in dishes cooked with other ingredients. The grading is done by candling. An older egg will have a larger air space, a thinner (less viscous) white, a larger and flatter yolk, and a more prominent germ spot.

Eggs may be cooked in a variety of ways—poached, fried, scrambled, soft- or hard-cooked in the shell, etc.—and in any of these ways may be served alone or in combination with other foods. One fundamental rule applies to all forms of egg cookery: cook with low to moderate heat, never high heat, and for exactly the length of time specified in the recipe. A properly cooked egg has a tender white and a smooth yolk.

In addition, eggs form an important ingredient in many kinds of cooking—in sauces, mixtures, soufflés, custards, cakes, etc. Heat coagulates the protein in eggs, thus making it possible for them to serve the following functions in cookery:

Thickening agent. For custards, puddings, sauces, soufflés, etc. Two yolks or two whites are equal to one whole egg in thickening power.

Binding agent. To hold ingredients together in mixtures, such as meatloaf, croquettes, etc., and also to hold a coating of breadcrumbs, flour, or cornmeal to the surface of foods for frying.

Strengthening agent. To increase the rigidity of cell walls and crusts in doughs and batters.

Clarifying agent. As a magnet to attract and agglomerate particles which cloud broths or stocks.

Emulsifying agent. To blend dissimilar liquids into a stable mixture, as melted butter and lemon juice in Hollandaise Sauce. Heat is not essential in forming an emulsion; for example, eggs emulsify the oil and vinegar in mayonnaise.

Leavening agent. Air beaten into egg whites expands when heated. The whites are thus stretched and set or coagulate to form a light porous product, as in sponge cake.

Glazing agent. Eggs beaten with a little water and brushed over the surface of bread, rolls, etc., before baking create an attractive shiny crust.

In addition, eggs improve the flavor, texture, color, and richness of such foods as cakes, puddings, and ice cream.

When eggs are used as a thickening agent, the following rules should be observed:

1. Beat whole eggs only enough to blend the egg yolks with the whites. Overbeating incorporates too much air with the result that the foam floats over the surface of the mixture that is to be thickened.
2. As a safeguard against curdling when combining eggs with hot liquids or mixtures, such as sauces or cream-pie and cake fillings, stir a small portion of the hot mixture, a little at a time, into the eggs. Then gradually stir the eggs into the remainder of the hot liquid.
3. To prevent egg mixtures from curdling during surface cooking, use a double boiler and keep the water in the bottom part just below the boiling point. For oven cooking, set the dish in a pan of hot water and cook at 325° to 350° F. Remove egg mixture (whether surface-

cooked or oven-baked) from the heat promptly when done. For soft custards, cook only until the mixture coats a metal spoon, remove from heat immediately, and replace the hot water in the bottom of the boiler with cold water. For baked custards, cook only until a pointed knife inserted in the center comes out clean. Remove from oven and hot water and set dish on a rack to cool.

4. In making dishes in which flour, tapioca, potato starch, or cornstarch is used in combination with eggs, as for cream-pie filling or tapioca pudding, first combine the starchy element with sugar and liquid and cook thoroughly before adding eggs. Since starches need longer cooking than do eggs, this method guards against producing a curdled mixture.

When egg whites are used as a leavening agent, several important facts must be kept in mind:

1. The leavening power of egg whites depends upon the amount of air beaten into them and the amount retained while preparing the food. Egg whites at room temperature beat more easily and give a greater volume than do those at refrigerator temperature.
2. A small amount of salt added to the egg whites aids in producing a stiff foam. However, excessive stiffening of the walls surrounding the air cells is undesirable, because the lack of elasticity will cause the cell walls to break rather than to stretch, resulting in a loss of air which means smaller volume.
3. The addition of an acid (such as cream of tartar in angelfood cakes and lemon juice in sponge cakes), after egg whites have been beaten *only* until foamy, results in large volume, more stable foam, and a whiter or lighter cake.
4. Beating a portion of the sugar into egg whites after considerable volume is obtained produces a stronger foam without decreasing the volume and also decreases the danger of overbeating.

For best results, beat eggs *only* until soft, stiff peaks form—not until they are dry and stiff. They should be moist and glossy. The following tests are helpful in determining the correct stiffness of beaten egg whites:

The beaten egg whites should flow very slowly when the bowl is partially inverted.

"Tails" or peaks should form when the egg beater is withdrawn from the egg whites. For angelfood cakes the peaks may curve at the tips rather than standing straight and stiff.

Air cells should be as fine and uniform in size as is possible to obtain without beating to a dry state.

If eggs are beaten insufficiently, the foam structure will be coarse and uneven and will not be strong enough to hold other ingredients such as sugar and flour.

Combine beaten egg whites with other ingredients using a folding motion (not stirring). Mix only enough to blend the ingredients thoroughly.

The leavening power of egg whites is also affected by the cooking temperature. If the temperature is too high, the protein coagulates before the air bubbles have fully expanded, and the result is a heavy product with the outside portion overdone before the center is set.

POACHED EGGS

⚜ HOW TO POACH EGGS

Pour into a skillet enough water to cover the eggs, and add ¼ teaspoon vinegar for each cup water. Heat water to just below boiling point. Break 1 egg at a time into a saucer and slip into the water. When all are in, reheat water to simmering point. Cover, remove from heat, and let stand 3 to 5 minutes, until eggs are of desired firmness. For breakfast, sprinkle with salt and ground black pepper and serve on buttered toast. The eggs may be trimmed before serving (see Culinary Techniques in Pictures). They should always be trimmed before being used in hot or cold egg dishes for entrées.

Hot Poached-Egg Dishes

Firm poached eggs and eggs soft-cooked in the shell 5 to 6 minutes can be used interchangeably in the following recipes and in those for Cold Soft-Cooked-Egg Dishes (pages 342–45).

⚜ POACHED EGGS ARCHDUKE STYLE

2 tablespoons butter
3 tablespoons flour
¾ cup chicken stock
¼ cup heavy cream
¼ teaspoon salt
1 pound chicken livers
1 small truffle (optional)
3 tablespoons butter or chicken fat
salt and ground black pepper to taste
fried croutons, fried bread, or buttered toast
4 to 8 hot poached eggs
chopped parsley

Melt the 2 tablespoons butter in a 3-cup saucepan. Remove from heat and blend in flour. Stir and cook until the mixture is golden brown. Remove from heat, add stock and cream, and mix well. Cook until of medium thickness, stirring constantly. Add salt and set aside. Sauté livers in the 3 tablespoons butter or chicken fat over moderate heat until they are tender. Sprinkle with salt and pepper. Serve over croutons or toast. Top each serving with 1 or 2 poached eggs. Reheat sauce ½ minute or only until hot and spoon over eggs. Sprinkle with parsley. Serve at special breakfasts, luncheon, or supper. Makes 4 servings.

⚜ POACHED EGGS ARGENTEUIL

48 cooked large asparagus tips
8 baked tart shells
8 hot poached eggs
¾ cup cooked diced asparagus stalks
1 cup cream sauce
watercress

Put 6 asparagus tips in each of the tart shells and place a hot poached egg on top. Mix diced asparagus with Cream Sauce, adjust seasonings, and spoon over eggs. Garnish with crisp watercress. Makes 4 servings.

⚜ EGGS AURORA

8 hot poached eggs
4 slices sandwich-size bread fried in butter, or buttered toast
salt and ground black pepper to taste
½ cup Velouté Sauce
2 tablespoons heavy cream
2 teaspoons thick tomato purée
hard-cooked egg yolk, sieved

Place 2 poached eggs on each of 4 slices toast. Sprinkle with salt and pepper to taste. Combine Velouté Sauce, cream, and tomato purée, heat, and spoon over eggs. Sprinkle with sieved hard-cooked egg yolk. Makes 4 servings. (See illustration, page 354.)

⚜ POACHED EGGS WITH BACON

8 hot poached eggs
16 thin slices bacon
salt and ground black pepper to taste
8 teaspoons melted bacon drippings or melted butter

Arrange 2 poached eggs on each 4 slices of bacon. Sprinkle with salt and pepper to taste. Spoon 2 teaspoons bacon drippings or melted butter over each. Serve for breakfast. Makes 4 servings.

⚜ POACHED EGGS BAYARD

8 medium-sized firm tomatoes
salt and ground black pepper to taste
8 teaspoons butter
8 thin slices grilled bacon
8 hot poached eggs
¾ cup Tomato Sauce

Cut a slice from the stem end of each tomato and discard. Scoop out centers and invert tomatoes on a plate to drain well. Sprinkle inside of each with salt and pepper and put in 1 teaspoon butter. Bake in shallow pan in a preheated moderate oven (350° F.) until tomatoes are soft, yet firm enough to retain their shape. Insert a slice of cooked bacon in each and top with a hot poached egg. Heat Tomato Sauce and spoon over the top. Serve as a main dish for breakfast, lunch, or supper. Makes 4 servings.

⚜ POACHED EGGS BEAUGENCY

8 hot poached eggs
8 large cooked artichoke bottoms
salt and ground black pepper to taste
¾ cup Béarnaise Sauce
8 slices poached beef marrow

Place a poached egg on each artichoke bottom. Sprinkle with salt and pepper. Coat each with Béarnaise Sauce. Serve for lunch or supper. Makes 4 servings. (See illustration, page 350.)

⚜ POACHED EGGS BONVALET

8 hot poached eggs
8 thick round slices of bread fried in butter
¾ cup chicken Velouté Sauce
1 teaspoon tomato purée
½ teaspoon tomato paste
1 teaspoon chopped parsley
⅓ cup Béarnaise Sauce
8 slices truffle (optional)

Place a hot poached egg on each of 8 slices of fried bread. Cover with chicken Velouté Sauce. Mix tomato purée, tomato paste, parsley, and Béarnaise Sauce. Spoon around each serving. Garnish with a slice of truffle, if desired. Serve for lunch or supper. Makes 4 servings.

⚜ POACHED EGGS BURGUNDY STYLE
(*Oeufs Pochés à la Bourguignonne*)

1 teaspoon chopped shallots
¼ teaspoon dried thyme or 1 teaspoon chopped fresh thyme
2 cups dry red wine
8 fresh eggs
1 tablespoon flour
1½ tablespoons soft butter
½ cup thinly sliced mushrooms poached in water
salt and ground black pepper to taste
4 slices bread, sandwich-size

Add shallots and thyme to wine, cover, bring to boiling point, and boil 5 to 6 minutes. Break eggs, one at a time, into a saucer and slide into the hot wine. Bring wine to simmering point. Cover, remove from heat, and let stand 3 to 5 minutes. Remove eggs from wine with a slotted spoon. Keep warm. Strain the wine. Blend flour with butter and add to wine. Stir and cook until the sauce is of medium thickness. Add mushrooms and salt and pepper. Fry bread in butter or toast it and spread with butter. Top each slice with 2 poached eggs. Cover with wine-mushroom sauce. Serve for lunch or supper. Makes 4 servings.

VARIATION

POACHED EGGS BUDAPEST STYLE

Cook 2 pounds fresh spinach or 1½ packages (10-ounce) frozen spinach, season, and put in a mound in the center of a baking dish. Poach 6 eggs in wine and make wine sauce as directed for Burgundy-Style Poached Eggs. Put each egg on a half slice of fried bread or toast and arrange around the spinach. Cover with wine sauce. Meanwhile, cook ½ pound small whole mushrooms (caps and attached stems) in 1 inch hot salted water for 5 minutes or until tender. Drain, mix with ½ cup Demi-Glace Sauce, and pile on top of the spinach. Garnish with paprika. Makes 6 servings. (See illustration, page 352.)

⚜ POACHED EGGS CARDINAL (*With Lobster*)

1¾ cups diced cooked lobster
2½ cups Béchamel Sauce
salt and ground black pepper to taste
½ teaspoon lemon juice
6 baked 2½-inch tart shells
6 hot poached eggs
1 teaspoon minced truffle (optional)
2 tablespoons heavy cream

Combine 1½ cups of the lobster, 2 cups of the Béchamel Sauce, salt, pepper, and lemon juice. Heat. Spoon into tart shells. Top each with a poached egg and sprinkle with salt and pepper. Mince the remaining ¼ cup lobster, mix with the rest of the Béchamel Sauce, and add truffle and cream. Heat and spoon over eggs. Makes 6 servings.

⚜ CHARTRES-STYLE POACHED EGGS

2 cups veal stock
8 hot poached eggs
8 baked 2-inch tart shells
¾ teaspoon dried or 1 tablespoon fresh tarragon, chopped
fresh tarragon leaves or parsley

Cook veal stock until reduced by one-third. Place a poached egg in each of the 8 baked tart shells. Add chopped tarragon to veal stock and spoon over eggs. Garnish with fresh tarragon leaves or parsley. Makes 4 servings.

⚜ POACHED EGGS CHASSEUR

1 pound chicken livers
2 tablespoons butter
salt and ground black pepper to taste
6 baked 2½-inch tart shells
6 hot poached eggs
¾ cup Chasseur Sauce
chopped parsley

Sauté chicken livers in butter, add salt and pepper to taste, and spoon an equal amount into each of 6 baked tart shells. Top each with a poached egg and sprinkle with salt and pepper. Coat with hot Chasseur Sauce. Garnish with chopped parsley. Makes 6 servings.

⚜ POACHED EGGS DAUMONT

⅓ cup (⅔ stick) butter
5 tablespoons flour
1¾ cups chicken stock
½ cup heavy cream
1½ cups finely diced cooked chicken
salt and ground black pepper to taste
6 baked 2½-inch tart shells, or 6 slices of toast
6 hot poached eggs
6 slices truffle, or crisp watercress

Melt butter in a 1½-quart saucepan. Remove from heat and blend in flour. Stir and cook 2 to 3 minutes. Remove from heat and stir in chicken stock and cream. Cook until the sauce is of medium thickness, stirring constantly. Add 1 cup chicken sauce to 1¼ cups diced chicken. Add salt and pepper to taste. Spoon into tart shells or over toast. Top each with a poached egg. Chop the remaining ¼ cup chicken very fine and blend with the remaining sauce. Spoon over eggs. Garnish with a truffle slice or watercress leaves. Makes 6 servings.

⚜ ENGLISH-STYLE POACHED EGGS

8 hot poached eggs
4 slices sandwich-size bread fried in butter or buttered toast
salt and ground black pepper to taste
⅓ cup grated Cheshire or Cheddar cheese
¼ cup clarified butter
watercress

Put 2 eggs on each slice fried bread or toast. Sprinkle with salt, pepper, and 4 teaspoons grated cheese. Heat clarified butter until golden brown and spoon 1 tablespoon over each serving. Garnish with watercress. Makes 4 servings.

⚜ POACHED EGGS FLORENTINE

1½ packages (15-ounce) frozen or 2 pounds fresh spinach, cooked
6 tablespoons butter
6 hot poached eggs
¾ cup Mornay Sauce
¼ cup grated cheese
¼ cup fine dry breadcrumbs

Drain cooked spinach well and sauté in 2 tablespoons of the butter. Place spinach in a shallow 1-quart baking dish. Arrange poached eggs over the top. Coat with Mornay Sauce. Sprinkle with cheese and breadcrumbs. Melt remaining butter and pour over the top. Place in a preheated very hot oven (450° F.) for 5 minutes or until well browned. Serve as a luncheon or supper dish. Makes 6 servings.

⚜ POACHED EGGS GRAND DUKE STYLE

8 hot poached eggs
8 slices buttered toast
salt and ground black pepper
8 crayfish tails
8 slices of truffle (optional)
¾ cup Mornay Sauce
1½ pounds cooked asparagus

Poached Eggs

Place poached eggs on toast and arrange them in a round ovenproof dish. Put a crayfish tail between each two eggs and a truffle slice on each egg. Coat with Mornay Sauce. Place under the broiler to glaze, watching carefully to prevent burning. Pile cooked buttered asparagus in the center of the dish. Serve for lunch. Makes 4 servings.

⚜ HOLLANDAISE POACHED EGGS

¾ pounds boneless salmon
⅓ to ½ cup heavy cream
½ teaspoon lemon juice
salt and ground black pepper to taste
8 puff-paste shells or 8 baked 2-inch tart shells
8 hot poached eggs
¾ cup Hollandaise Sauce

Tie salmon in cheesecloth and place in a pan of simmering water. Cover and cook below boiling point until salmon is flaky, 5 to 6 minutes. Remove from cloth and mash fine. Add enough cream to make the mixture a creamy consistency. Add lemon juice and salt and pepper to taste. Heat. Spoon an equal amount into each of the shells and top with a poached egg. Coat with Hollandaise Sauce. Serve for lunch or supper. Makes 4 servings.

⚜ POACHED EGGS À L'INDIENNE

2 tablespoons minced onion
6 tablespoons butter
1 teaspoon curry powder
2 tablespoons flour
¾ cup chicken stock
½ cup milk or light cream
salt and ground black pepper to taste
1 cup rice
2 cups boiling water
1 teaspoon salt
6 hot poached eggs

Stir and cook onions in 3 tablespoons of the butter for 3 minutes. Add curry powder. Stir and cook 3 more minutes. Remove from heat and blend in flour. Stir and cook 2 to 3 minutes. Remove from heat and add stock and milk or light cream. Cook until of medium thickness, stirring constantly. Meanwhile, soak rice for 30 minutes in enough water to cover it. Drain well. Melt remaining 3 tablespoons butter in a 1½-quart saucepan. Add rice. Stir and cook only until rice begins to stick to the bottom of the pan. Pour in 2 cups boiling water. Add salt. Cover and cook without stirring 12 to 15 minutes. Arrange eggs in a circle on a round serving platter. Fill center with rice. Coat eggs with the curry sauce. Serve hot as a luncheon or supper dish. Makes 6 servings.

⚜ POACHED EGGS JOINVILLE

3 tablespoons butter
3 tablespoons flour
¾ cup fish stock
¾ cup milk or light cream
salt and ground black pepper to taste
½ teaspoon lemon juice
½ cup finely chopped cooked shrimp
8 hot poached eggs
8 buttered toast points
8 cooked, peeled, and deveined whole shrimp

Melt butter in a 1½-quart saucepan. Remove from heat and blend in flour. Stir and cook 2 to 3 minutes. Remove from heat and add stock and milk or cream. Mix well. Cook until sauce is of medium thickness, stirring constantly. Add salt, pepper, lemon juice, and chopped shrimp. Heat. Place poached eggs on toast points and arrange them on a warmed platter. Coat eggs with the shrimp sauce and pour remaining sauce around them. Garnish each egg with a whole shrimp and dust with paprika. Serve hot as a luncheon or supper dish. Makes 4 servings. (See illustration, page 352.)

⚜ POACHED EGGS MIGNON

1 cup cooked green peas
16 peeled deveined cooked shrimp
2 tablespoons butter
salt and ground black pepper to taste
8 large cooked artichoke bottoms
8 hot poached eggs
1 cup hot Shrimp Sauce
8 truffles or slices sautéed mushrooms

Heat together peas, shrimp, and butter only until hot. Add salt and black pepper. Spoon onto artichoke bottoms, and top each with a poached egg. Cover with Shrimp Sauce. Garnish with either a truffle or mushroom slice. Serve for lunch or supper. Makes 4 servings.

⚜ MISS HELYETT'S POACHED EGGS

6 large, firm, ripe tomatoes
salt and ground black pepper to taste
16 peeled and deveined cooked shrimp
½ cup drained sautéed mushrooms
1½ cups Béchamel Sauce
¼ cup finely chopped cooked shrimp
1 tablespoon heavy cream
6 hot poached eggs
6 slices truffles or sautéed mushrooms

Cut a slice from the stem end of each tomato. Scoop out centers and sprinkle inside with salt and pepper. Invert on a plate to drain. Combine shrimp, mushrooms, and 1 cup of the Béchamel Sauce. Adjust seasonings. Spoon into tomato cups and top each with a poached egg. Mix together remaining ½ cup Béchamel Sauce, finely chopped shrimp, and cream. Spoon over eggs. Garnish with a slice of truffle or sautéed mushroom. Makes 6 servings.

⚜ MONSEIGNEUR POACHED EGGS (*With Hake or Codfish*)

½ pound poached hake or codfish
3 tablespoons soft butter
1 cup Béchamel Sauce
6 baked 2½-inch tart shells, or 6 slices of toast
6 hot poached eggs
parsley

Flake fish finely and mix with the butter and ⅓ cup Béchamel Sauce. Spoon into tart shells or onto toast. Top each with a poached egg. Sprinkle with salt and black pepper. Coat with remaining Béchamel Sauce. Garnish with parsley. Makes 6 servings.

⚜ POACHED EGGS MORNAY

8 poached eggs
4 slices sandwich-size fried bread or buttered toast
salt and ground black pepper to taste
¾ cup Béchamel Sauce
4 tablespoons grated cheese
2 tablespoons fine dry breadcrumbs
3 tablespoons melted butter
watercress

Place 2 poached eggs on each of 4 slices of fried bread or toast. Arrange on a baking sheet. Sprinkle with salt and pepper. Coat with Béchamel Sauce. Combine cheese and breadcrumbs and sprinkle over the top. Drizzle with melted butter. Place in a preheated very hot oven (450° F.) to melt cheese, 4 to 5 minutes, being careful not to overcook eggs. Garnish with watercress. Makes 4 servings.

⚜ EGGS ORIENTAL STYLE

4 tablespoons (½ stick) butter
4 tablespoons flour
1 cup chicken stock
1 cup milk
salt and black pepper to taste
½ cup finely diced chicken
6 large cooked artichoke bottoms
6 hot poached eggs
2 teaspoons finely chopped onion
¾ teaspoon curry powder
1 tablespoon peanut oil or clarified butter
pimiento strips
1 tablespoon catsup
½ pound broiled fillet of sole or haddock
2 green peppers
3 truffle slices

Melt butter in a 1-quart saucepan. Remove from heat and blend in flour. Stir and cook 2 to 3 minutes. Add chicken stock and milk. Stir and cook until the sauce is of medium thickness. Add salt and pepper to taste. Combine chicken with ½ cup of the sauce and spoon into artichoke bottoms. Arrange in a circle on a platter. Top each with a poached egg. Cook onion and curry powder in oil or clarified butter until onions are limp. Add to half of the remaining sauce. Spoon over 3 of the eggs and garnish them with pimiento. Mix catsup with the rest of the sauce and spoon over the 3 remaining eggs. Garnish each of them with a truffle slice. Fill center of platter with broiled fillet of sole or haddock and green peppers that have been cut into strips and fried in peanut oil. Serve as a luncheon or supper dish. Makes 6 servings. (See illustration, page 351.)

⚜ EGGS PERIGORD STYLE

8 hot poached eggs
8 round pieces of fried bread, or 8 baked 2-inch tart shells
2 cups Basic Brown Sauce
½ cup Madeira or sherry
8 truffle slices

Place a poached egg on each piece of fried bread or in each tart shell. Meanwhile, cook Brown Sauce slowly until it is reduced to 1 cup. Add wine, mix well, heat, and spoon over eggs. Top each with a slice of truffle. Makes 4 servings. (See illustration, page 351.)

⚜ POACHED EGGS POLISH STYLE

2 medium-sized tomatoes
4 tablespoons butter
salt and ground black pepper
8 puff-paste patty shells
8 hot poached eggs
¾ cup Sauce Suprême
3 tablespoons fine dry breadcrumbs

Peel tomatoes, squeeze out seeds, and sauté in 1 tablespoon of the butter. Add salt and pepper to taste. Spoon into patty shells. Top each with a poached egg; coat with hot Sauce Suprême. Fry breadcrumbs in remaining butter. Sprinkle over eggs. Serve as a luncheon or supper dish. Makes 4 servings.

⚜ POACHED EGGS REGINA

½ pound poached fillet of sole or flounder
½ cup diced cooked shrimp
½ cup sautéed mushrooms
¾ cup Shrimp Sauce
salt and ground black pepper to taste
8 hot poached eggs
8 baked 2-inch tart shells
¾ cup Sauce Normande
truffles cut in julienne strips, or buttered mushroom slices

Flake fish and mix with shrimp, mushrooms, and Shrimp Sauce. Season to taste with salt and black pepper. Spoon into tart shells. Top each with a poached egg. Coat with hot Sauce Normande. Garnish with truffles or mushrooms. Serve as a luncheon or supper dish. Makes 4 servings.

⚜ POACHED EGGS À LA REINE

1 cup diced cooked chicken
2¼ cups Sauce Suprême
salt and ground black pepper to taste
8 puff-paste patty shells
8 hot poached eggs
8 truffle slices, or parsley

Combine chicken and 1 cup of the sauce. Heat and add salt and pepper. Spoon into patty shells. Top each with a poached egg. Heat remaining sauce and spoon over eggs. Garnish with truffle slices or parsley. Serve for luncheon or supper. Makes 4 servings. (See illustration, page 353.)

⚜ POACHED EGGS ROSSINI

8 round 2-inch slices of foie gras
2 tablespoons butter
8 round 2-inch slices of toast
8 hot poached eggs
1 cup veal stock
2 tablespoons Madeira
8 truffle slices, or watercress

Cut foie gras with a round scalloped 2-inch cooky cutter. Sauté in butter. Place one slice on each round of buttered toast, and top with a poached egg. Heat stock until reduced to ½ cup and add Madeira. Spoon over eggs. Garnish with truffle slices or watercress. Serve for lunch or supper. Makes 4 servings.

⚜ POACHED EGGS VILLEROI

8 cold poached eggs
1 raw egg, beaten
fine dry breadcrumbs
deep fat for frying
¾ cup Tomato Sauce
fried parsley

Dip one egg at a time in beaten egg and roll in breadcrumbs. Let stand 30 minutes for crumbs to set. Fry in deep fat, preheated to 375° F., until browned—2 to 3 minutes. Drain on paper towels. Serve hot with Tomato Sauce. Garnish with fried parsley. Serve for lunch or supper. Makes 4 servings.

SOFT-COOKED EGGS

⚜ HOW TO SOFT-COOK EGGS IN THE SHELL

Place eggs in a saucepan with enough water to cover them to a depth of about 1 inch. Cover, bring to boiling point, remove from heat, and let stand 3 to 5 minutes, allowing the longer time for a larger number of eggs or for firmer consistency.

Serve soft-cooked eggs for breakfast or make them into hot or cold dishes for lunch or supper or for a buffet. If soft-cooked eggs are to be peeled, let stand 5 to 6 minutes and then plunge into cold water.

Cold Soft-Cooked-Egg Dishes

In these recipes, as in those for Hot Poached-Egg Dishes (pages 331–41), medium soft-cooked eggs (5 to 6 minutes) and firm poached eggs can be used interchangeably.

⚜ EGGS IN ASPIC COLINETTE

6 cold poached eggs
⅔ cup Chaud-froid Sauce
2 cups aspic
18 peeled, deveined, cooked shrimp
aspic slices cut ¼ inch thick
7 thin slices of truffle
½ pound cooked salmon
3 to 4 tablespoons heavy cream
salt and pepper to taste
1 to 2 teaspoons lemon juice
smoked salmon
parsley

Trim edges of the egg whites to shape eggs uniformly. Coat the eggs with Chaud-froid Sauce and chill until coating is set. Coat the inside of a 9-inch ring mold with aspic and chill until aspic is almost set. Decorate the bottom of mold with shrimp and truffle slices and place Chaud-froid-coated eggs on top. Finish filling the mold with aspic. Chill until aspic is firm. Just before serving, unmold the ring onto a large serving plate and surround with half slices of aspic. Meanwhile, flake the salmon and blend with cream, salt, pepper, and lemon juice. Chill until ready to serve, then spoon into the center of the ring. Garnish with smoked salmon wedges and a truffle slice. Serve at once, for a buffet or lunch or supper. Makes 6 servings. (See illustration, page 348.)

⚜ EGGS IN ASPIC À LA JEANNETTE

6 cold poached eggs
1½ cups half-set aspic
⅔ cup Chaud-froid Sauce
⅔ cup foie gras purée
¼ cup (½ stick) softened butter

Trim edges of the egg whites to shape eggs uniformly. Coat with Chaud-froid Sauce. Place an egg in each of 6 custard cups and chill until coating is set. Finish filling cups with half-set aspic, but do not cover the top of the eggs. Combine foie gras and butter. Using a pastry bag and a fluted tube, garnish each dish with a fluted ring of the mixture. Chill until ready to serve. Garnish the top of each egg with a bit of sliced truffle. Serve for lunch, supper, or for a buffet. Makes 6 servings. (See illustration, page 350.)

⚜ EGGS IN ASPIC WITH PARMA HAM

6 cold medium soft-cooked eggs
3 cups aspic
6 thin slices of truffle
tarragon or parsley leaves
6 thin slices cooked ham

Peel eggs and set aside. Coat the insides of 6 small oval-shaped molds with aspic and chill them until aspic is almost set. Decorate the bottom of the mold with truffle slices and tarragon or parsley leaves. Wrap each egg in a slice of ham and place one in each mold. Finish filling the molds with half-set aspic. Chill until aspic is firm. There will be some aspic remaining; chill this until set and reserve. To serve, unmold eggs onto a cold serving plate, arranging them in a circle. Chop firm aspic and spoon it around the eggs. Serve for a buffet, lunch, or supper. Makes 6 servings. (See illustration, page 348.)

⚜ EGGS CARMEN

1 cup sliced onions
2 tablespoons butter
2 tablespoons flour
1 cup milk
salt and ground black pepper to taste
1 tablespoon unflavored gelatin
2 tablespoons cold water
¼ cup heavy cream
12 cold medium soft-cooked eggs
2 each green and red sweet peppers
chopped aspic
French dressing

Pour enough boiling water over onions to cover them and let stand 5 minutes. Pour off water and drain onions well. Then cook them in the butter until they are soft. Remove from heat and blend in flour. Stir and cook 1 minute. Remove from heat and add milk. Stir and cook until the sauce is of medium thickness. Meanwhile, soften gelatin in cold water, add to the hot sauce and mix well. Put sauce through a sieve, pushing as much of the onion through as possible, or blend a few seconds in an electric blender. Add cream. Peel soft-cooked eggs and coat with the sauce. Chill until the coating is almost firm. Decorate top of each with 3 small green and 3 small red diamond-shaped pieces of sweet pepper. Arrange in a cold serving dish. Surround with chopped aspic. Fill center of the dish with thin green pepper sticks marinated 30 minutes in French dressing. Serve for lunch or supper. Makes 6 to 12 servings. (See illustration, page 349.)

⚜ EGGS CASINO

⅓ cup Coating Mayonnaise
1 tablespoon tomato purée
1 to 2 drops red food coloring (optional)
18 eggs, soft-cooked in the shells and cooled
1 hard-cooked egg
¾ cup finely chopped cold cooked chicken
3 tablespoons mayonnaise
salt and ground black pepper to taste
6 cold baked pastry barquettes
12 cold cooked asparagus tips
12 slices cold cooked ham
½ truffle, sliced, or 12 slices of black olives

Combine Coating Mayonnaise and tomato purée. If a deeper color is desired, add 1 to 2 drops red food coloring. Peel the soft-cooked eggs. Coat 6 of them with the Coating Mayonnaise mixture. Using the white and yolk of the hard-cooked egg, make a design on the top of each to simulate a daisy. Chill until set. Mix the chicken with mayonnaise and salt and pepper to taste. Spoon the mixture into the baked barquettes. Place 2 asparagus tips and a tomato-mayonnaise-coated egg on each. Garnish the ends of the asparagus tips with a bit of Coating Mayonnaise. Arrange the barquettes in the center of a platter. Fold the ham slices in quarters and arrange 6 folded slices in a circle at each end of the platter. Decorate the remaining 12 soft-cooked eggs with a bit of truffle or a slice of black olive and place one on each slice of ham. (See illustration, page 347.)

⚜ EGGS FROU-FROU

24 cold crisply cooked asparagus tips
1 cup cold cooked peas
1 cup cold cooked green beans, cut into 1-inch pieces
1¼ cups thick mayonnaise
salt and ground black pepper to taste
12 cold poached eggs
2 hard-cooked egg yolks, sieved

Combine all vegetables with 1/3 cup of the mayonnaise. Season with salt and pepper to taste. Pile in the center of a serving dish. Trim the edges of the egg whites to shape eggs uniformly and coat each with mayonnaise. (If desired, use Coating Mayonnaise.) Sprinkle eggs with sieved hard-cooked egg yolks and arrange them around the salad. Serve for lunch or supper. Makes 6 to 12 servings.

⚜ EGGS TARTARE

4 medium-sized tomatoes
salt and ground black pepper to taste
2 cups mixed cooked vegetables (peas, diced carrots, string beans in 1-inch pieces)
2/3 cup mayonnaise
6 cold poached eggs
2 tablespoons chopped parsley
2 tablespoons chopped gherkins
lettuce

Cut 3 of the tomatoes in half, scoop out the centers, and drain well. Dice the centers, drain well, and reserve. Sprinkle tomato halves with salt and pepper. Combine the cold cooked vegetables and the tomato centers with 1/4 cup of the mayonnaise and salt and pepper to taste. Trim edges of the egg whites to shape eggs uniformly. Coat the eggs with mayonnaise. Place one on each tomato half. Sprinkle with chopped parsley and gherkins. Line a serving plate with lettuce, over which arrange salad-filled tomatoes. Garnish the center of the plate with the remaining whole tomato. Makes 6 servings. (See illustration, page 349.)

⚜ VIRGINIA CLUB EGGS (*With Corn and Tomatoes*)

6 cold medium soft-cooked or poached eggs
2 cups well-drained canned whole-kernel corn or whole corn kernels cut from ears of cooked corn
2/3 cup mayonnaise
salt and ground black pepper to taste
watercress
3 medium-sized tomatoes
6 black olives

Peel eggs and set aside to cool. Mix corn with 1/4 cup of the mayonnaise. Season to taste with salt and pepper, put on a serving plate, and chill. Just before serving, coat eggs with mayonnaise and place them on the corn. Arrange 6 small bunches watercress on the plate. Peel tomatoes, cut them in half, and place 1 on each bunch of watercress. Garnish with black olives. Serve cold for a buffet, lunch, or supper. Makes 6 servings.

HARD-COOKED EGGS

Properly prepared, hard-cooked eggs are firm enough to slice but still tender; they will be appetizing in appearance. Long cooking at high temperatures makes egg whites tough and rubbery, produces hard spots in the yolks, and causes the green discoloration which forms between the yolk and the white. This discoloration is harmless but unattractive; it results from chemical action between the sulfur in the white and the iron in the yolk. Cooling eggs promptly in cold water helps to avoid it.

⚜ HOW TO HARD-COOK EGGS IN THE SHELL

Place eggs in a saucepan with sufficient water to cover them to a depth of about 1 inch. Cover, bring to boiling point, remove from heat, and let stand 20 minutes. Cool eggs immediately in cold water.

Use hard-cooked eggs in hot or cold entrées and main dishes, hors d'oeuvre, sandwiches, salads, and as garnishes.

Hot Hard-Cooked-Egg Dishes

⚜ HARD-COOKED EGGS AURORA

10 hard-cooked eggs
2 cups Béchamel Sauce
salt and ground black pepper to taste
½ cup hot Tomato Sauce

Slice 8 of the eggs and add to the Béchamel Sauce. Put the yolks of two of the remaining 2 eggs through a sieve and set aside. Slice the 2 remaining whites and add to the Béchamel Sauce. Season to taste with salt and pepper. Put the mixture in a buttered 1-quart casserole and brown in a preheated moderate oven (325° F.). Sprinkle with sieved egg yolks. Serve Tomato Sauce separately. Serve as a luncheon or supper dish. Makes 6 servings.

Eggs Casino, page 344 ▲

▼ Stuffed hard-cooked eggs, pages 360–61

▲ Eggs in Aspic with Parma Ham, page 343

Eggs in Aspic Colinette, page 342 ▼

Eggs Tartare, page 345 ▲

▼ Eggs Carmen, page 343

▲ Eggs in Aspic à la Jeannette, page 343

Poached Eggs Beaugency, page 333 ▼

Eggs Oriental Style, page 339 ▲

▼ Eggs Perigord Style, page 340

▲ Poached Eggs Budapest Style, page 334

Poached Eggs Joinville, page 338 ▼

Omelette Arlésienne, page 379 ▲

▼ Poached Eggs à la Reine, page 341

▲ Eggs Aurora, page 332

Omelette Chasseur, page 381 ▼

⚜ HARD-COOKED EGGS WITH BÉCHAMEL SAUCE

1½ cups Béchamel Sauce
2 tablespoons butter
8 hard-cooked eggs
salt and ground black pepper to taste
6 slices toast or baked patty shells
parsley

Combine Béchamel Sauce and butter. Heat until butter is melted. Slice eggs and add. Season with salt and pepper. Heat, without boiling, only until hot. Serve on toast or in patty shells. Garnish with parsley. Makes 6 servings.

⚜ BERCHERON HARD-COOKED EGGS (*With Potatoes*)

10 hot hard-cooked eggs
3 hot boiled potatoes of medium size, peeled
salt and ground black pepper to taste
1¾ cups Béchamel Sauce
chopped parsley

Slice eggs and potatoes while they are hot. Sprinkle with salt and pepper and arrange them in a serving dish in alternate layers with Béchamel Sauce, having the potatoes as the bottom layer and the sauce as the top layer. Sprinkle with chopped parsley. Makes 6 servings.

⚜ HARD-COOKED EGGS À LA BOULANGÈRE

2 tablespoons chopped onion
1 tablespoon butter
1 cup hot Béchamel Sauce
salt and ground black pepper to taste
6 rolls, 6 inches long
parsley

Sauté onions in butter and add to Béchamel Sauce. Heat. Slice eggs and add. Season with salt and pepper. Heat, without boiling. Remove the insides of the rolls and fill with the egg mixture. Garnish with parsley. Makes 6 servings.

⚜ BRETON HARD-COOKED EGGS (*With Leeks and Mushrooms*)

1 small onion, sliced
¼ cup sliced leeks
1 tablespoon butter
3 tablespoons stock
½ cup sautéed mushrooms
1 cup Béchamel Sauce
salt and ground black pepper to taste
10 hard-cooked eggs

Cook onion and leeks in butter until they are soft. Add stock and cook 1 minute. Stir in mushrooms and blend with Béchamel Sauce. Heat, without boiling. Season with salt and pepper. Pour one-third of the mixture into a serving dish. Slice eggs, saving 1 of the yolks, and arrange over the sauce.

Cover with remaining sauce. Put the reserved egg yolk through a sieve and sprinkle on top. Serve as a main dish for lunch or supper. Makes 6 servings.

⚜ HARD-COOKED EGGS WITH ONION

1 medium-sized onion
2 tablespoons butter
1½ cups Béchamel Sauce
10 hard-cooked eggs
salt and ground black pepper to taste
6 baked patty shells or 6 slices toast

Peel onion and slice thinly. Sauté in butter until soft. Add to Béchamel Sauce and cook slowly 5 minutes. Slice eggs and add. Heat, without boiling, 1 minute. Season to taste with salt and pepper. Serve in patty shells or on toast. Makes 6 servings.

⚜ HARD-COOKED EGGS IN POULETTE SAUCE

1 cup sliced mushrooms
2 tablespoons butter
1 cup Poulette Sauce
1 tablespoon lemon juice or to taste
10 hard-cooked eggs
2 tablespoons chopped parsley
salt and ground black pepper to taste
6 baked patty shells or 6 slices toast
paprika

Sauté mushrooms in butter and add to poulette sauce. Stir in lemon juice. Slice eggs and add along with parsley to the mixture. Season to taste with salt and pepper. Serve in patty shells or on toast. Garnish with paprika. Makes 6 servings.

⚜ HARD-COOKED-EGG TARTLETS

Mix finely diced hard-cooked eggs with only enough Poulette or Béchamel Sauce to bind the mixture. Season to taste with salt, ground black pepper, and thyme, parsley, rosemary, or tarragon. Spoon the mixture into tiny baked tart shells or puff-paste patty shells or puffs. Serve hot as an hors d'oeuvre.

⚜ EGG CROMESQUIS

10 hard-cooked eggs
2 raw eggs, lightly beaten
1¾ cups Béchamel Sauce
salt and ground black pepper to taste
Tomato Sauce (optional)

BATTER

1 cup sifted all-purpose flour
1 teaspoon double-acting baking powder
½ teaspoon salt
1 egg, lightly beaten
¾ cup milk
1 tablespoon butter, melted

Finely dice hard-cooked eggs. Add raw eggs, Béchamel Sauce, salt, and pepper. Stir and cook in a saucepan until mixture is very thick. Chill. Make batter by sifting together into a bowl the flour, baking powder, and salt; then combine lightly beaten egg with milk and add to dry ingredients along with the melted butter. Mix well. Form the chilled egg mixture into 1-inch balls. Dip them in the batter and fry until browned in deep fat preheated to 375° F. Drain on paper towels. These can be fried ahead of time and heated in a 350° F. oven just before serving. Serve hot as an hors d'oeuvre, with Tomato Sauce as a dip if desired. Makes about 4 dozen.

⚜ HARD-COOKED-EGG CUTLETS

Make the egg and Béchamel Sauce mixture as for Egg Cromesquis. Chill. Shape into cutlets. Dip in fine dry breadcrumbs and then into beaten egg (1 egg beaten with 1 tablespoon water), and in breadcrumbs again. Let stand 20 minutes for crumbs to set. Fry until browned in deep fat preheated to 375° F. Drain on paper towels. Press a piece of macaroni into the end of each cutlet to simulate the bone and dress it with a paper frill. Place on a warmed serving dish with a cooked vegetable, such as asparagus, peas, or spinach. Serve for lunch or supper. Makes 6 servings.

⚜ HARD-COOKED-EGG RISSOLES

Make the egg and Béchamel Sauce mixture as for Egg Cromesquis. Do not chill. Make short pastry dough, using 3 cups flour and roll one-third of the dough at a time on a lightly floured board to ⅛-inch thickness. Cut into circles with a 2-inch cooky cutter. Place 1 teaspoon of the egg mixture on each round. Fold over the pastry and crimp edges with a fork. Bake in a preheated hot oven (400° F.) 5 to 8 minutes, or fry until browned in deep fat preheated to 375° F. Drain on paper towels. Serve as a hot hors d'oeuvre. These may be made ahead of time and heated in the oven (350° F.) just before serving. Makes approximately 4 dozen.

Hot Stuffed Eggs

⚜ STUFFED EGGS AURORA

9 hard-cooked eggs
4 tablespoons softened butter
⅓ cup Tomato Sauce
¾ cup Béchamel Sauce
salt and ground black pepper to taste

Cut eggs into lengthwise halves. Remove yolks and put them through a sieve. Add 2 tablespoons of the butter, 1 tablespoon of the Tomato Sauce and ¼ cup of the Béchamel Sauce. Season to taste with salt and pepper. Stuff into the egg whites and place them in a buttered baking dish. Melt remaining 2 tablespoons butter and pour over the eggs. Bake in a preheated moderate oven (350° F.) 8 minutes. Combine remaining Tomato and Béchamel sauces, heat, and pour over eggs. Serve for lunch or supper. Makes 6 servings.

⚜ STUFFED EGGS CHIMAY

9 hard-cooked eggs
6 tablespoons softened butter
1 tablespoon Béchamel Sauce
¼ cup Mornay Sauce
½ cup finely chopped mushrooms
salt and ground black pepper to taste
¼ cup fine, dry breadcrumbs
¼ cup grated Cheddar or Parmesan cheese

Cut eggs into lengthwise halves. Remove yolks and put them through a sieve. Blend with Mornay and Béchamel sauces. Sauté mushrooms in 2 tablespoons of the butter and mix with the yolks. Season with salt and pepper. Stuff into the egg whites. Arrange them on a buttered baking dish. Melt remaining butter, mix with breadcrumbs and cheese, and sprinkle over eggs. Place in a preheated moderate oven (350° F.) to brown. Serve hot for lunch or supper. Makes 6 servings.

⚜ HUNGARIAN-STYLE STUFFED EGGS

9 hard-cooked eggs
4 tablespoons finely chopped onion
4 tablespoons butter
1 teaspoon paprika
salt and ground black pepper to taste
4 firm medium-sized tomatoes
lemon juice to taste
½ cup heavy cream

Cut eggs into lengthwise halves. Remove yolks and put them through a sieve. Cook onions in butter until they are soft and blend half of them with the yolks. Reserve the remaining onions and butter. Add ½ teaspoon of the paprika to the yolk mixture and season with salt and pepper to taste. Stuff the egg whites and set aside. Cut tomatoes into slices ½ inch thick. Sauté them in the reserved butter and onion. Place tomato slices in the bottom of a baking dish, and arrange the stuffed eggs on top. Bake in a preheated moderate oven (350° F.) 5 minutes. Add lemon juice and the remaining paprika to the cream and pour over eggs. This is a good luncheon or supper dish. Makes 6 servings.

Cold Hard-Cooked-Egg Dishes

Cold hard-cooked eggs may be used for making hors d'oeuvre, entrées, salads, sandwiches, and garnishes. They should be well seasoned and presented in an attractive, colorful manner.

When cold salad-like egg mixtures are served in pastry tart shells or on other pastry crusts, coat the inside of the shell with a thin layer of mixed butter and mayonnaise, using two-thirds butter and one-third mayonnaise. Then chill the pastry. This prevents the pastry from becoming soggy.

⚜ SLICED HARD-COOKED EGGS WITH MAYONNAISE

Allow 1 egg per serving. Split hard-cooked eggs in half lengthwise or cut in thick crosswise slices. Coat with mayonnaise. Arrange on a serving dish and garnish with chopped parsley. Serve as an hors d'oeuvre or on a meat, fish, or vegetable salad plate.

⚜ HARD-COOKED EGGS MIMOSA

1 cup mixed cooked green peas and diced carrots
½ cup finely diced celery
¾ cup finely diced cooked ham
¾ cup flaked cooked lobster
⅓ cup mayonnaise
salt and ground black pepper to taste
16 baked 2-inch tart shells
8 hard-cooked whole eggs
2 hard-cooked egg yolks
chopped parsley

Combine cooked vegetables, celery, ham, lobster, mayonnaise, salt, and pepper. Chill. Coat the bottom of tart shells with the butter-mayonnaise mixture and chill. Shortly before serving, fill the tart shells one-half full with the salad mixture. Cut hard-cooked eggs in half lengthwise and place one on each tart. Coat lightly with mayonnaise. Put the 2 hard-cooked egg yolks through a sieve and sprinkle over eggs. Garnish with chopped parsley. Chill a few minutes for mayonnaise to set. Serve on a buffet table or on a meat, fish, or vegetable salad plate. Makes 16 tarts.

Cold Stuffed Eggs

⚜ HERB-STUFFED EGGS

6 hard-cooked eggs
4 tablespoons softened butter
½ cup chopped, cooked, well-drained spinach
⅛ teaspoon each dried tarragon and dried chervil
2 tablespoons finely chopped watercress
¼ cup mayonnaise
1 cup half-set aspic
tarragon, watercress, or parsley leaves

Cut eggs in half lengthwise. Remove yolks and put them through a sieve. Add softened butter and mix well. Heat spinach with herbs 1 minute. Then cool and put spinach through a sieve, squeezing out as much of the liquid as possible. Reserve 2 tablespoons of this purée for later use. Mix remaining purée with egg-yolk mixture. Stuff the egg whites. Mix the reserved spinach purée with mayonnaise and brush over eggs. Garnish with tarragon, watercress, or parsley leaves. Coat with the half-set aspic. Spread the remaining aspic over a serving platter and chill until set, then arrange the eggs on top. Makes 6 servings. (See illustration, page 347.)

⚜ STUFFED EGGS ROSCOFF

6 hard-cooked eggs, peeled
1 cup finely diced cooked lobster
½ cup mayonnaise
salt and ground black pepper to taste
about ¼ cup Coating Mayonnaise
1 cup cold cooked mixed vegetables
lettuce

Cut eggs in half lengthwise and remove yolks, leaving the whites intact. Reserve both yolks and whites. Combine lobster, ⅓ cup of the mayonnaise, and salt and pepper to taste. Spoon the mixture into the cavities of the egg whites, mounding it over the tops. Then coat the stuffed eggs thinly with Coating Mayonnaise. Chill until mayonnaise is set. Combine the cooked vegetables with the remaining mayonnaise and salt and pepper to taste. Arrange lettuce on the bottom of a serving dish. Spoon the vegetable mixture into the center and surround it with the stuffed eggs. Chop the hard-cooked egg yolks and sprinkle them over the eggs. Makes 6 servings. (See illustration, page 347.)

⚜ STUFFED EGGS STRASBOURG STYLE (*With Foie Gras*)

6 hard-cooked eggs
3½ ounces foie gras purée
chopped truffles
2 cups aspic

Cut eggs in half lengthwise. Remove yolks and put them through a sieve. Add foie gras purée and mix well. Stuff the egg whites. Sprinkle with chopped truffles. Serve on a bed of chopped aspic. Makes 6 servings. (See illustration, page 347.)

⚜ STUFFED EGGS TOULONNAISE

Spread a serving dish generously with mayonnaise and set it aside. Cut peeled hard-cooked eggs in half lengthwise and place them, cut side down, in the mayonnaise-coated dish. Cut anchovy fillets into narrow strips and arrange them over the eggs in any pattern desired. Garnish the dish with parsley. Allow 1 egg per serving. (See illustration, page 347.)

⚜ ASSORTED COLD STUFFED EGGS

12 hard-cooked eggs
¾ cup (1½ sticks) softened butter
⅓ cup mayonnaise
stuffings
1 cup aspic

Cut eggs into crosswise halves and cut a thin slice from each end so halves will stand upright, reserving end slices to use later. Remove yolks, keeping whites intact, and put yolks through a sieve, then mix with butter and mayonnaise. Divide this mixture into 4 equal parts and mix 1 part with each of the following 4 stuffings. Using a pastry bag and a large, round, smooth tube, fill 6 egg-white halves with each of the stuffing mixtures. Chill all the stuffed eggs, then coat them lightly with aspic. Serve on a buffet table or to garnish a platter of meat, fish, or vegetable salad. Makes 8 to 12 servings.

STUFFINGS

DUCK-LIVER STUFFING

2 duck livers, sautéed
salt and ground black pepper
chopped parsley, dried chervil, dried tarragon, chopped fresh chives
Madeira
1 small truffle

Slice livers thinly, trim slices into 6 medallions slightly smaller in diameter than the eggs, and set them aside. Purée the trimmings in a sieve or blender and mix with 1 part of the egg-yolk mixture. Season to taste with salt, pepper, herbs, and Madeira. Fill 6 egg-white halves. Decorate the top of each with a liver medallion and a small slice of truffle. Save remainder of truffle.

CRAYFISH STUFFING

12 cooked crayfish tails
salt and pepper
herbs as in Duck-Liver Stuffing
brandy
chili sauce

Mash 6 of the crayfish tails and mix with 1 part of the egg-yolk mixture. Chop remainder of truffle very fine and add. Stir in salt, pepper, herbs, brandy, and chili sauce to taste. Fill 6 egg-white halves with mixture and garnish each with a crayfish tail.

CAVIAR STUFFING

black or red caviar
salt and pepper
herbs as in Duck-Liver Stuffing

Mix 1 part of the egg-yolk mixture with caviar, salt, pepper, and herbs to taste. Fill 6 egg-white halves with the mixture and garnish each with a bit of caviar.

ANCHOVY STUFFING

6 anchovy fillets
pepper
herbs as in Duck-Liver Stuffing
slices of egg white
6 slices pimiento-stuffed green olive

Mash the anchovy fillets and blend with 1 part of the egg-yolk mixture. Dice the reserved slices of egg white very fine and add. Mix well. Add pepper and herbs to taste. (Do not add any salt.) Fill 6 egg-white halves and garnish each with a slice of stuffed olive.

FRIED EGGS

Fried eggs are cooked over surface heat. Any of the following methods may be used. See also French Fried Eggs, pages 366–68. Allow 1 or 2 fried eggs per serving.

⚜ FRIED EGGS I

Heat butter, bacon drippings, or other fat in a skillet, using only enough to grease the bottom of the pan. Break eggs into a saucer, one at a time, and then slip them into the pan. Sprinkle with salt and ground black pepper. Cover pan tightly and cook over very low heat 2 to 3 minutes or until the egg whites are firm and the yolks are covered with a film of coagulated white.

⚜ FRIED EGGS II

Prepare pan and eggs as for Fried Eggs I, and pour in 1 to 2 tablespoons hot water. Cover pan tightly and steam over very low heat until eggs are cooked as desired.

⚜ FRIED EGGS III

Prepare pan and eggs as for Fried Eggs I. Cook over very low heat until eggs have cooked underneath, 1 to 2 minutes. Turn eggs over and cook on the other side about 1 minute.

⚜ ANCHOVY FRIED EGGS

12 coiled anchovy fillets
butter
8 eggs
ground black pepper to taste

Dice 4 of the anchovy fillets and scatter them over the bottom of a hot buttered skillet. Break the eggs over the anchovies. Cover and cook *only* until egg whites are firm and yolks are covered with a film of coagulated white. Transfer from skillet to a warmed serving dish. Surround with remaining coiled anchovy fillets. Sprinkle eggs with black pepper to taste. Do not add salt. Serve for lunch or supper.

⚜ FRIED EGGS BERCY (*With Sausage and Tomatoes*)

8 hot fried eggs
salt and ground black pepper to taste
8 small hot cooked sausages
½ cup hot Tomato Sauce
chopped parsley

Sprinkle eggs with salt and black pepper to taste and arrange in a serving dish. Place sausages between the eggs and surround with Tomato Sauce. Sprinkle chopped parsley over the sauce. Serve for lunch or supper.

⚜ FRIED EGGS WITH BLACK BUTTER

8 hot fried eggs
4 tablespoons (½ stick) butter
dash each salt and ground black pepper
1 teaspoon vinegar

Arrange fried eggs in a serving dish. Brown the butter in a saucepan, add a dash each of salt and pepper, and pour over eggs. Pour the vinegar into the saucepan, heat, and pour over eggs. Serve for breakfast, lunch, or supper.

⚜ FRIED EGGS CHASSEUR

½ pound chicken livers
3 tablespoons butter
½ cup Demi-Glace Sauce
8 fried eggs
salt and ground black pepper to taste
chopped parsley

Sauté livers in butter until centers have cooked. Heat Demi-Glace, add livers and set aside to keep warm. Arrange fried eggs on a serving dish, sprinkle with salt and pepper, and top with chicken livers. Sprinkle with chopped parsley. Serve for special breakfasts, lunch, or supper.

⚜ FRIED EGGS WITH HAM

8 slices ham
8 eggs
salt and ground black pepper to taste

Cook ham in a skillet over surface heat until it has browned underneath. Turn, top each slice with a raw egg, and sprinkle with salt and pepper. Cover and cook over low heat until whites are firm and the yolks are covered with a film of coagulated white. Serve for breakfast, lunch, or supper.

⚜ JOCKEY CLUB FRIED EGGS (*With Veal Kidneys and Truffles*)

4 veal kidneys
3 tablespoons butter
salt and ground black pepper to taste
½ truffle
½ cup Demi-Glace Sauce
8 fried eggs
8 slices buttered toast
4 ounces foie gras purée
watercress

Trim fat and membrane from kidneys. Place in a bowl with ½ teaspoon salt and enough cold water to cover them. Soak 2 hours. Remove from water, wipe dry, and cut into crosswise slices. Melt butter in a skillet, add kidneys, salt and pepper, and truffle. Stir and cook until kidneys are tender. Add Demi-Glace, heat, and set aside to keep warm. Cut fried eggs round with a large cooky cutter or trim them round with a knife. Place each egg on a slice of buttered toast. Spread with foie gras purée. Arrange in a ring around a serving dish. Fill center with the hot kidney mixture. Garnish with watercress. Serve for special breakfast, lunch, or supper.

⚜ FRIED EGGS MIREILLE

8 chicken livers
4 tablespoons butter
salt and ground black pepper to taste
12 slices firm tomatoes
8 fried eggs
Madeira Sauce

Sauté chicken livers in 2 tablespoons of the butter. Set aside to keep warm. Sauté tomatoes in remaining butter. Sprinkle both livers and tomatoes with salt and pepper. Arrange eggs and tomato slices alternately on a serving dish. Garnish each serving with chicken livers. Surround with Madeira Sauce. Serve for lunch or supper.

⚜ FRIED EGGS MISTRAL

4 firm tomatoes
2 tablespoons butter
8 hot fried eggs
8 pitted olives

Cut tomatoes in half and sauté them in butter. Arrange fried eggs on a serving dish. Place a tomato half between each 2 eggs. Garnish with olives. Serve for lunch or supper.

⚜ PORTUGUESE-STYLE FRIED EGGS

4 firm tomatoes
2 tablespoons butter
8 hot fried eggs
salt and ground black pepper to taste
chopped parsley

Slice tomatoes and sauté in butter. Arrange eggs on a serving dish, with tomatoes placed between eggs. Sprinkle with salt and pepper. Garnish with chopped parsley. Serve for breakfast, lunch, or supper.

⚜ FRIED EGGS VICTORIA

1¼ cups cooked lobster
½ chopped truffle sautéed in butter
2 cups hot cream sauce
salt and ground black pepper to taste
8 hot fried eggs

Combine 1 cup of the lobster and the truffle with 1½ cups cream sauce. Chop the remaining ¼ cup lobster very fine, blend it with the rest of the cream sauce, and adjust seasonings. Arrange eggs in a ring on a serving dish and coat each with the lobster-truffle sauce. Spoon the creamed lobster in the center of the dish. Serve for lunch or supper.

French Fried Eggs

Eggs that are to be cooked by this method must be absolutely fresh in order to retain their shape and appetizing appearance. In addition to being served in the ways that follow, they are also often used to garnish meat or poultry dishes—Chicken Marengo, for example. Allow 1 or 2 eggs per serving.

⚜ HOW TO FRENCH FRY EGGS

Heat 1 cup cooking oil in a small skillet until very hot. Break one egg at a time into a saucer and salt the white lightly. Holding the pan at a slight angle, slide the egg into the hot oil. Turn it over at once with a wooden spoon to prevent the white from bubbling. Gently press the white down with the spoon, and when the underneath side is browned, turn the egg over to brown the other side and to aid the egg in retaining its oval shape. The white must be firm and the yolk remain soft. Remove egg from skillet, drain on a paper towel, and keep warm while cooking the rest of the eggs. Cook only 1 egg at a time.

⚜ FRENCH FRIED EGGS WITH BACON OR HAM

8 French fried eggs
8 slices crisp bacon or 8 small slices grilled ham or Canadian bacon
salt to taste
ground black pepper to taste
bacon or ham drippings or melted butter
chopped parsley
fried bread or buttered toast

Place a French fried egg on each slice of bacon, ham, or Canadian bacon. Sprinkle with salt, pepper, bacon or ham drippings or melted butter, and parsley. Serve with fried bread or buttered toast for breakfast, lunch or supper. Makes 4 to 8 servings.

⚜ BORDEAUX-STYLE FRENCH FRIED EGGS

1 clove garlic
2 tablespoons chopped parsley
3 tablespoons cooking oil
8 firm tomatoes
8 cepes or whole mushroom caps
2 tablespoons butter
8 hot French fried eggs
salt and ground black pepper to taste
fried parsley

Split garlic and place it in an 8-inch skillet along with chopped parsley and oil. Heat 1 to 2 minutes. Cut tomatoes in half and place them in the hot oil, cut side down, and cook 1 minute (do not overcook). Discard garlic. Sauté cepes or mushroom caps in butter only until they are tender. Arrange tomatoes in a ring on a serving dish and top each with a sautéed cepe or mushroom cap. Place hot fried eggs in the center of the dish and sprinkle with salt and pepper. Garnish with fried parsley.

⚜ FRENCH FRIED EGGS CAVOUR

½ cup long-grain rice
8 firm tomatoes
salt and ground black pepper to taste
8 teaspoons cooking oil
3 tablespoons butter
2 tablespoons chopped onion
1 cup boiling water
½ teaspoon salt
¼ cup Tomato Sauce
8 French fried eggs
veal stock, thickened

Soak rice in water to cover for 30 minutes. Meanwhile scoop out centers of tomatoes, sprinkle cavities with salt, pepper, and 1 teaspoon oil. Bake in a preheated moderate oven (350° F.) 10 minutes or until tomatoes are soft but retain their shape. Drain rice well and cook in butter along with the onion until rice is dry and begins to stick to the bottom of the pan. Add 1 cup boiling water and ½ teaspoon salt, cover, and cook 12 to 15 minutes or until rice is almost tender. Add Tomato Sauce and let stand 5 minutes. Stuff the tomatoes with the rice, and arrange them on a serving dish. Top each with a hot French fried egg. Serve accompanied with veal gravy in a sauceboat.

⚜ PROVENÇAL-STYLE FRENCH FRIED EGGS

1 teaspoon salt
¼ teaspoon ground black pepper
1 cup fine, dry breadcrumbs
8 large slices of peeled eggplant cut ½ inch thick
1 egg beaten with 1 tablespoon water
cooking oil or shortening
8 firm tomatoes
1 tablespoon butter, melted
salt and ground black pepper to taste
8 French fried eggs
parsley

Combine salt, black pepper, and breadcrumbs and roll eggplant slices in the mixture. Then dip them in beaten egg and roll again in breadcrumbs. Let stand 20 minutes for crumbs to set. Brown eggplant slices on both sides in hot cooking oil or melted shortening. Drain on paper towels. Set aside in a warm place. Cut tomatoes in half and place them on a baking sheet, cut side up. Brush with melted butter and sprinkle with salt and pepper. Broil 5 to 6 minutes. Arrange eggplant slices in a circle on a serving dish. Place a broiled tomato on each. Put fried eggs in the center of the dish. Sprinkle with salt and pepper. Garnish with parsley. Serve for lunch or supper.

⚜ FRENCH FRIED EGGS SAINT BENOÎT

1 pound dried salt codfish
1 small clove garlic
½ cup heavy cream
½ cup olive oil or salad oil
⅛ teaspoon ground white pepper
8 French fried eggs
salt and ground black pepper to taste
French bread

Soak codfish in enough water to cover it for 8 hours, changing the water 5 times. Drain off water and rinse well. Place fish in a saucepan with enough cold water to cover it. Bring the water to boiling point, reduce heat, and simmer 10 to 15 minutes, or until fish falls apart. Drain well. Remove and discard skin and bones. Break meat into small pieces and mash to a pulp. Place in a saucepan. Mash garlic and add. Heat only slightly. Then, over moderately low heat, blend in cream and oil, adding 1 teaspoon each at a time, as in making mayonnaise. The mixture should be white and creamy. Add white pepper. Place fish mixture in the center of a serving dish. Surround with French fried eggs. Sprinkle eggs with salt and black pepper. Serve with French bread for special breakfasts, lunch, or supper.

⚜ FRENCH FRIED EGGS WITH TOMATO SAUCE

8 French fried eggs
salt and ground black pepper
fried parsley
1 cup hot Tomato Sauce

Arrange the eggs around the edge of a serving dish and sprinkle them with salt and pepper. Pile fried parsley in the center. Serve hot Tomato Sauce in a sauceboat.

EGGS EN COCOTTE

A cocotte is a small round or oval dish in which food is cooked and served—a ramekin or individual casserole. It may be made of fireproof china, tempered glass, earthenware, porcelain, cast iron, copper, or stainless steel. The food cooked and served in such dishes is usually called "en cocotte."

⚜ HOW TO COOK EGGS EN COCOTTE

The dishes should be warmed and buttered before the eggs are put in. Break 1 egg into each dish and place the dishes in a shallow pan of hot water. Cook over surface heat 2 to 3 minutes, never allowing the water to boil. Cover the dishes with foil or a baking sheet and finish cooking in a preheated slow oven (325° F.)—about 3 or 4 minutes. The whites should be firm and the yolks soft. Allow 1 egg per serving.

A tablespoon of heavy cream or of concentrated veal stock or chicken stock may first be put in each dish. Add eggs and sprinkle with salt and pepper. Cook as described above but cook in the oven only 3 minutes.

⚜ COLBERT EGGS EN COCOTTE (*With Chicken*)

2 cups finely ground leftover chicken
1 tablespoon chopped parsley
¼ teaspoon dried thyme leaves
about ¼ cup light cream
6 eggs
¼ cup (½ stick) butter
1 tablespoon each lemon juice and liquid meat glaze

Combine chicken, parsley, thyme, and enough cream to make chicken of spreading consistency. Spread over the bottoms and sides of 6 buttered cocotte dishes. Break 1 egg into each. Cook as in basic recipe 3 minutes over low surface heat and 5 minutes in the oven. Combine remaining ingredients and put an equal amount on each serving.

⚜ FLORENTINE EGGS EN COCOTTE

10-ounce package frozen spinach
2 tablespoons butter
6 eggs
salt and ground black pepper to taste
6 tablespoons warmed heavy cream
6 tablespoons grated Cheddar or Parmesan cheese

Cook and season spinach according to package directions. Drain well and sauté in butter 2 to 3 minutes. Spread over bottoms and sides of 6 buttered cocotte dishes. Break 1 egg into each. Sprinkle with salt and pepper. Cook as in basic recipe 3 minutes over surface heat. Pour 1 tablespoon cream over each egg, then sprinkle each with 1 tablespoon grated cheese. Cover and cook 5 minutes in a preheated slow oven (325° F.).

⚜ PARIS-STYLE EGGS EN COCOTTE

1 cup each finely ground leftover cooked chicken and roast beef
¼ cup finely chopped sautéed mushrooms
1 tablespoon chopped truffles (optional)
½ cup cream sauce
salt and ground black pepper to taste
6 eggs
6 tablespoons Demi-Glace Sauce

Combine chicken, beef, mushrooms, truffles (if used), and cream sauce. Season to taste with salt and pepper. Spread over bottoms and sides of 6 buttered cocotte dishes. Break 1 egg into each. Sprinkle with salt and pepper. Cook as in basic recipe 3 minutes over surface heat and 5 minutes in the oven. Heat Demi-Glace and put a spoonful on each serving.

⚜ PARSLEY EGGS EN COCOTTE

2 sprigs parsley
1 cup concentrated veal stock
1 teaspoon cornstarch
1 tablespoon tomato purée
6 eggs
salt and ground black pepper to taste

Simmer parsley sprigs in veal stock 5 minutes. Strain. Mix cornstarch with tomato purée and add to veal stock. Stir and cook 1 to 2 minutes or until the cornstarch has cooked. Then put 2 tablespoons of the mixture into each of 6 buttered cocotte dishes. Break 1 egg into each. Sprinkle with salt and pepper. Cook as in basic recipe 3 minutes over surface heat and 3 minutes in the oven. Garnish with chopped parsley.

Fresh tarragon may be used instead of parsley in this recipe.

⚜ SHEPHERDESS EGGS EN COCOTTE (*With Lamb and Mushrooms*)

1 cup ground leftover roast lamb
1 cup sautéed finely chopped mushrooms
about ½ cup cream sauce
6 eggs
salt and ground black pepper to taste

Combine lamb, mushrooms, and cream sauce. Spread over the bottom and sides of 6 buttered cocotte dishes. Break 1 egg into each. Sprinkle with salt and pepper. Cook as directed in basic recipe but cook 5 minutes in the oven. (When eggs cooked en cocotte are combined with meat they must be cooked longer, because the heat penetrates more slowly.)

MOLDED EGGS

⚜ MOLDED EGGS I

Butter the insides of 6-ounce custard cups generously. Then, if desired, sprinkle with minced cooked ham, crumbled crisp bacon, fine dry breadcrumbs, chopped truffles or mushrooms, or chopped herbs. Break 1 egg into each cup. Sprinkle with salt and ground black pepper to taste. Place cups in a pan of hot water, having the pan three-fourths full. Simmer over surface heat 2 to 3 minutes. Then cook in a preheated slow oven (325° F.) only until whites are set enough to retain the shape of the mold when unmolded. To unmold, run a spatula or knife around the edge of the mold and turn out the egg onto a serving dish. Garnish with parsley or watercress. The whites of these eggs should be just firm enough to retain the shape of the mold; the yolks should be soft as in poached or soft-cooked eggs, never firm or hard-cooked. Allow 1 to 2 eggs per person.

⚜ MOLDED EGGS II

Another method of preparing molded eggs is with scrambled eggs. Use an equal number of scrambled eggs and beaten raw eggs. Mix lightly, turn into a buttered 6-ounce custard cup, and cook in a preheated slow oven (325° F.) until the outside has set, but the center is still soft. Allow 2 eggs per serving.

⚜ NEAPOLITAN MOLDED EGGS

7 large eggs
1 tablespoon butter
1¼ cups grated Parmesan cheese
salt and ground black pepper to taste
2 tablespoons Tomato Sauce
⅔ cup Demi-Glace Sauce

Scramble 5 of the eggs very lightly in butter. Add ¾ cup of the Parmesan cheese, the 2 remaining raw eggs, salt and pepper to taste. Mix well. Spoon into well-buttered 6-ounce custard cups. Set cups in a pan of hot water and bake in a preheated slow oven (325° F.) 10 minutes or *only* until eggs are set. Turn out onto a buttered oven-proof platter. Sprinkle with remaining cheese. Combine Tomato and Demi-Glace sauces and pour over eggs. Cook in a preheated very hot oven (450° F.) until glazed. Serve for special breakfasts, lunch, or supper. Makes 4 servings.

⚜ MOLDED EGGS NINETTE

7 large eggs
1 tablespoon butter
salt and ground black pepper to taste
20 peeled, deveined, cooked shrimp
4 slices buttered toast
3 tablespoons whipped cream
½ cup Hollandaise Sauce

Scramble 5 of the eggs very lightly in the butter. Add salt and pepper. Dice 16 of the shrimp and mix with the cooked eggs, along with the remaining 2 raw eggs, beaten lightly. Spoon into well-buttered 6-ounce custard cups. Set cups in a pan of hot water in a preheated slow oven (325° F.) and cook only until eggs are set. Turn out onto a buttered oven-proof platter. Fold whipped cream into Hollandaise Sauce, heat, and spread over eggs. Garnish with remaining whole shrimp. Serve for lunch or supper. Makes 4 servings.

⚜ EGG LOAF FARM STYLE

1 cup creamy cottage cheese
3 tablespoons soft butter
½ cup finely chopped cooked ham
⅓ cup heavy cream
5 large eggs, beaten lightly
salt and ground black pepper to taste
¾ cup cream sauce

Drain cheese and press it in clean cheesecloth to extract all the whey. Turn into a bowl, add the butter, and mix well. Stir in ham, cream, salt and pepper to taste, and eggs. Mix well. Pour into a well-buttered 1-quart casserole, set in a pan of hot water in a preheated slow oven (325° F.) and bake 30 minutes, or *only* until the mixture has set. Turn out onto a serving dish. Coat with hot cream sauce. Serve for lunch or supper. Makes 6 servings.

SCRAMBLED EGGS

⚜ HOW TO SCRAMBLE EGGS

Break eggs into a bowl. Add milk or light cream in the following proportions: For Creamy Scrambled Eggs, add 1 tablespoon milk or light cream for each egg; for Dry Scrambled Eggs, add ½ tablespoon milk or light cream for each egg. Beat the mixture *only* until yolks and whites are blended. If flecks of the whites are preferred in scrambled eggs, omit milk or cream and beat the eggs very slightly. Season to taste with salt and ground black pepper. Pour the mixture into a heated skillet in which a small amount of butter or other fat has been melted. Stir and cook slowly until the eggs are set, but still moist (soft-firm). Scrambled eggs may also be cooked in a little butter in the top of a double boiler over simmering water (not boiling). Allow 1 to 2 eggs per person.

⚜ SCRAMBLED EGGS WITH ARTICHOKE BOTTOMS

3 cooked artichoke bottoms
2 tablespoons butter
8 large eggs
⅓ cup light cream
salt and ground black pepper to taste

Dice artichoke bottoms and sauté in the butter in an 8-inch skillet. Beat egg lightly; add cream, salt and pepper. Pour into the skillet over artichokes. Stir and cook over low heat until eggs are soft-firm. Serve for lunch or supper. Makes 4 servings.

⚜ SCRAMBLED EGGS WITH ASPARAGUS TIPS

tips from ½ pound fresh asparagus
2 tablespoons butter
8 large eggs
⅓ cup light cream
salt and pepper to taste

Wash asparagus and cut tips in ½-inch pieces. Place in a saucepan with ½ inch boiling water and ½ teaspoon salt. Cover and cook 5 minutes or *only* until crisp tender. Remove from water, drain well, and sauté in 1 tablespoon of the butter in an 8-inch skillet. Beat eggs lightly; add cream, salt, and pepper. Add remaining butter to the asparagus and heat until butter is melted. Add egg mixture. Stir and cook until eggs are soft-firm. Serve for lunch or supper. Makes 4 servings.

⚜ SCRAMBLED EGGS CHASSEUR

½ pound chicken livers
2 tablespoons butter
½ cup sautéed sliced mushrooms
¾ cup cream sauce
salt and ground black pepper to taste
8 eggs, scrambled with ⅓ cup milk or light cream
chopped parsley

Cook livers in butter until they are no longer pink. Remove from heat and dice the livers. Add the mushrooms, cream sauce, and salt and pepper to taste. Put the mixture in the center of a warmed serving dish and spoon the scrambled eggs around it. Garnish with chopped parsley. Serve for breakfast, lunch, or supper. Makes 6 servings.

⚜ SCRAMBLED EGGS WITH CHEESE

8 large eggs
⅓ cup light cream
½ cup grated Cheddar or Gruyère cheese
salt and ground black pepper to taste
1 tablespoon butter
8 slices Cheddar or Gruyère cheese

Beat eggs lightly; add cream, grated cheese, salt, and pepper. Melt butter in an 8-inch skillet. Pour in egg mixture. Stir and cook over low heat until eggs are soft-firm. Serve over slices of cheese. Makes 4 servings.

⚜ SCRAMBLED EGGS CLAMART

8 large eggs
⅓ cup light cream
¾ cup tiny French peas (petits pois)
salt and ground black pepper to taste
1 tablespoon butter
1 cup cream sauce

Beat eggs lightly; add cream, peas, and salt and pepper. Melt butter in an 8-inch skillet, add eggs, and cook until eggs are soft-firm, stirring constantly. Serve with cream sauce for lunch or supper. Makes 6 servings.

⚜ SCRAMBLED EGGS WITH CRAYFISH

1 cup peeled crayfish tails
3 tablespoons butter
8 large eggs
⅓ cup light cream
salt and ground black pepper to taste

Cook crayfish in 2 tablespoons of the butter over moderately low heat until they are tender. Beat eggs lightly and add crayfish, cream, salt, and pepper. Melt the remaining butter in an 8-inch skillet. Pour in eggs. Stir and cook over low heat until eggs are soft-firm. Serve hot. Makes 6 servings.

⚜ SCRAMBLED EGGS WITH CROUTONS

8 large eggs
⅓ cup light cream
salt and ground black pepper to taste
1 tablespoon butter
30 white-bread croutons fried in butter

Beat eggs lightly; add cream and salt and pepper to taste. Melt butter in an 8-inch skillet. Pour in eggs. Stir and cook over low heat until eggs begin to set. Add croutons. Continue cooking until eggs are soft-firm. Serve on a warmed platter for breakfast, lunch or supper. Makes 6 servings.

⚜ SCRAMBLED EGGS GEORGETTE

1 cup peeled crayfish tails
2 tablespoons butter
8 large eggs
⅓ cup light cream
salt and ground black pepper to taste
6 large baked potatoes with centers scooped out
parsley

Sauté crayfish tails in butter in an 8-inch skillet. Beat eggs lightly; add cream, salt, and pepper. Pour into the skillet over crayfish tails. Stir and cook until eggs are soft-firm. Heat the potato shells and fill with egg mixture. Garnish with parsley. Serve for lunch or supper. Makes 6 servings.

⚜ SCRAMBLED EGGS WITH KIDNEYS

4 veal kidneys
1 teaspoon chopped shallot or onion
4 tablespoons butter
¾ cup diced raw tomatoes
salt and ground black pepper to taste
8 large eggs
⅓ cup light cream
1 cup Madeira Sauce

Soak kidneys 2 hours in enough cold water to cover, adding ¾ teaspoon salt. Remove from water, wipe dry, and cut into crosswise slices, removing all fat and membrane. Sauté shallot or onion in 2 tablespoons of the butter 2 minutes, then add kidneys and cook briskly 5 to 8 minutes. Set aside; keep warm. Sauté tomatoes in 1 tablespoon of the butter. Add salt and pepper to taste. Set aside; keep warm. Scramble the eggs with cream, salt, and pepper in the remaining 1 tablespoon butter, adding tomatoes just before eggs are set. Make a ring of scrambled eggs in a warmed serving dish. Add Madeira Sauce to kidney mixture, heat, and spoon into the center of the dish. Serve for special breakfasts, lunch or supper. Makes 6 servings.

⚜ SCRAMBLED EGGS MAGDA

1 teaspoon powdered mustard
1 tablespoon water
8 large eggs
⅓ cup light cream
¼ cup chopped parsley
½ cup grated Cheddar cheese
salt and ground black pepper to taste
3 tablespoons butter
12 cubes of white bread

Mix mustard with water and let stand 5 minutes. Beat eggs lightly. Add mustard, cream, parsley, cheese, salt, and pepper. Melt 1 tablespoon of the butter in an 8-inch skillet. Pour in egg mixture. Stir and cook over low heat until eggs are soft-firm. Fry bread cubes in remaining butter and scatter over eggs. Serve for breakfast, lunch, or supper. Makes 4 servings.

⚜ SCRAMBLED EGGS WITH MORELS

¾ cup sliced morels
1 tablespoon bacon drippings
1 tablespoon butter
8 large eggs
⅓ cup light cream
salt and ground black pepper
2 strips crisp bacon

Sauté morels in bacon drippings and butter in an 8-inch skillet. Beat eggs lightly; add cream and salt and pepper. Pour into the skillet over the morels. Crumble bacon and add. Stir and cook over low heat until eggs are soft-firm. Serve for lunch or supper. Makes 4 servings.

⚜ SCRAMBLED EGGS WITH MUSHROOMS

1 cup thinly sliced mushrooms
2 tablespoons butter
8 large eggs
¼ cup light cream or milk
salt and ground black pepper to taste

Sauté mushrooms in butter until they have browned. Beat eggs lightly, add cream or milk, and mix *only* until blended. Pour the mixture into the skillet over the mushrooms. Add salt and pepper. Stir and cook over low heat until eggs are soft-firm. Serve for breakfast, lunch, or supper. Makes 6 servings.

⚜ PORTUGUESE-STYLE SCRAMBLED EGGS

2 cups diced raw tomatoes
3 tablespoons butter
salt and ground black pepper to taste
8 large eggs
⅓ cup light cream
2 tablespoons chopped parsley

Sauté tomatoes in 2 tablespoons of the butter until most of the liquid has evaporated. Set aside; keep warm. Scramble the eggs with cream, salt, and pepper in remaining butter. Arrange scrambled eggs in a ring in a warmed serving dish. Fill center with sautéed tomatoes. Sprinkle with chopped parsley. Makes 4 servings.

⚜ SCRAMBLED EGGS WITH SHRIMP

8 large eggs
⅓ cup light cream
½ pound peeled, deveined, cooked shrimp
salt and ground black pepper to taste
2 tablespoons butter

Beat eggs lightly; add cream, shrimp, and salt and ground black pepper to taste. Melt butter in an 8-inch skillet. Add mixture and cook until eggs are soft-firm, stirring constantly. Serve for special breakfasts, lunch, or supper. Makes 6 servings.

OMELETTES

There are three basic types of omelettes: French (plain), American (puffy), and Italian (pancake or *frittata*). The French or plain omelette is made with whole eggs beaten only enough to blend the whites with the yolks, with no additional liquid. The American or puffy omelette is made by beating the whites and yolks separately with 1 tablespoon water to each egg. The Italian frittata is made with whole eggs beaten lightly, usually mixed with meat or vegetables, and cooked in a little oil, first on one side and then on the other, pancake-style. French and American omelettes are folded.

A variety of other foods, sauces, etc., may be added to omelettes, either cooked with the eggs or used as a filling. Mixtures added to frittatas are always cooked with the eggs. Fillings may be added to French or American omelettes after the omelette is cooked but just before it is folded. (See recipes on pages 379–86.)

⚜ FRENCH OMELETTE (*Plain*)

4 large eggs
½ teaspoon salt
dash ground black pepper
about 1½ tablespoons butter

Beat eggs only until the whites and yolks are mixed. Add salt and pepper and stir only until ingredients are blended. Melt butter in an 8- or 9-inch skillet. Pour in egg mixture. Cook over moderately low heat. As omelette cooks, lift the edges and turn them toward the center so the uncooked mixture flows under the cooked portion. Cook only until the bottom is light brown and the top is set. Make a crease across the center with a spatula or the back of a knife. Fold half the omelet over the other half. Serve immediately on a warmed platter. Serves 2. If desired, a filling may be spread on one side of the omelette just before it is folded or a sauce served over it.

PUFFY OMELETTE AMERICAN STYLE

A puffy omelette should have fine, uniform air cells throughout and a soft, puffy, moist texture. It should have a tender, light golden-brown crust. Overcooking or cooking at too high temperature causes the bottom to become tough and heavy, and the omelette may fall and be tough and dry.

6 large eggs
¾ teaspoon salt
⅓ cup water
¼ teaspoon ground black pepper
1½ tablespoons butter

Separate eggs, placing whites and yolks in separate bowls. Add salt and water to the egg whites. Beat until soft, stiff, moist (not dry) peaks form. Add pepper to the egg yolks and beat them until they are thick and lemon-colored. Fold egg yolks into beaten egg whites. Meanwhile, melt butter in an 8- or 9-inch skillet. Pour in omelette mixture. Cook over low surface heat 5 to 6 minutes or until omelette is puffy and light brown on the bottom, lifting omelette at the edges with a spatula to judge the color. Bake in a preheated slow oven (325° F.) 12 to 15 minutes or *only* until a knife inserted in the center of the omelette comes out clean. Make a crease across the center with the back of a knife or with a spatula. Fold half of the omelette over the other half. Serve promptly on a warmed platter. If desired, a filling may be added just before folding. Makes 4 generous servings.

ITALIAN OMELETTE (*Frittata*)

5 large eggs
½ to ¾ teaspoon salt
dash of ground black pepper
¼ teaspoon dried thyme or 1 teaspoon finely chopped fresh thyme
1 tablespoon chopped parsley
1 cup diced cooked vegetables, ham, or seafood
1½ tablespoons olive oil or cooking oil

Beat eggs with a fork only until the whites and yolks are mixed. Add seasonings, herbs, and vegetables, ham, or seafood. Heat oil in an 8- or 9-inch skillet. Pour in the mixture. Cook over moderately low heat until the bottom of the frittata is set and the top is creamy like scrambled eggs. Have another skillet of the same size greased and hot, and turn the frittata by placing the second skillet over the first as though it is to be used as a cover. Reverse the position of the skillets so the uncooked side falls into the second skillet. Cook 1 to 2 minutes. Serve on a warmed plate, cut into pie-shaped wedges. The amount of salt used depends upon the amount that is in the filling. Other ingredients may be substituted for the vegetables, ham, or seafood. Makes 4 servings.

Fillings, Additions, and Sauces for Omelettes

Any of the following combinations can be used with French Omelettes or Puffy Omelettes American Style. Only those which are added before cooking the eggs are suitable for Italian Omelettes. Each of the following is sufficient for 4 servings.

AGNÈS SOREL

1 cup sliced mushrooms
2 tablespoons butter
½ cup ground or minced cooked chicken
sliced cooked tongue

Sauté mushrooms in butter. Add chicken and cook only until hot. Spread on one side of cooked omelette, before folding. Garnish with sliced cooked tongue.

ARCHDUKE

6 raw chicken livers
2 tablespoons butter
1 cup medium Brown Sauce
salt and ground black pepper to taste
sliced truffles

Slice chicken livers, sauté in butter, and add to Brown Sauce. Add salt and pepper to taste. Heat. Fill cooked omelette, fold, and garnish top with sliced truffles.

ARLÉSIENNE

1 clove garlic
¼ cup each diced green pepper and diced onion
2 tablespoons olive oil or cooking oil
1½ cups peeled, diced, raw eggplant
2 cups diced raw tomatoes, or 1½ cups canned broken tomatoes
½ teaspoon sugar
salt and ground black pepper to taste
½ cup hot Tomato Sauce (optional)

Sauté garlic, onion, and green pepper in oil until they are limp. Remove and discard garlic. Add eggplant, tomatoes, and sugar. Stir and cook until eggplant is soft and most of the liquid has evaporated. If necessary, thicken the mixture by adding 1 to 2 tablespoons fine, dry breadcrumbs. Season to taste with salt and pepper. Reserve ½ cup of mixture; use the rest to fill cooked omelette. Fold omelette and garnish top with the reserved ½ cup of the eggplant-tomato mixture. If desired, pour Tomato Sauce around the omelette. Serve as a luncheon or supper dish. (See illustration, page 353.)

WITH ASPARAGUS TIPS

1 cup diced cooked asparagus
12 cooked asparagus tips
3 tablespoons butter, melted
thin slices of cooked ham

Fill cooked omelette with drained diced cooked asparagus. Place omelette on a warm platter and make a lengthwise incision down the center. Heat asparagus tips in butter and place them in the incision. Serve hot on a warmed platter with thin slices of cooked ham.

BOHEMIAN STYLE

¾ cup sliced mushrooms
1½ tablespoons butter
⅓ cup diced cooked ham
1 cup stewed tomatoes
1 tablespoon tomato paste
½ teaspoon sugar
1 small truffle
salt and ground black pepper to taste
½ cup Tomato Sauce

Sauté mushrooms in butter until they are tender. Add all remaining ingredients except Tomato Sauce. Stir and cook over moderate heat until the liquid is reduced. Reserve ½ cup of mixture, fill omelette with remainder, and fold. Pour reserved sauce over the top. Surround with a ring of Tomato Sauce.

BOULOGNE STYLE

2 pairs roe: shad, carp, or flounder
1 tablespoon finely chopped shallots or onion
1 tablespoon parsley
2 tablespoons butter
1 teaspoon lemon juice
dash ground nutmeg
salt and ground black pepper to taste
melted Herb Butter

Poach roe in boiling water to cover for 5 minutes. Remove from water and drain. Cook shallots or onions and parsley in butter 1 to 2 minutes. Remove membrane from roe and discard, break up roe with a fork and add to the butter mixture along with lemon juice. Stir and cook over low heat 5 minutes. Add nutmeg, salt, and ground black pepper. Fill omelette. Serve with melted Herb Butter. If desired, replace fresh roe with 1 cup canned roe.

CHASSEUR

½ pound chicken livers
½ cup sliced mushrooms
3 tablespoons butter or bacon drippings
½ cup chopped onion
salt and ground black pepper to taste
¼ cup Demi-Glace Sauce
chopped parsley

Sauté chicken livers and mushrooms in butter or bacon drippings over moderately low heat until livers are no longer pink. Remove from heat, cool, and chop livers medium-fine. Sauté onions 2 to 3 minutes in the same skillet. Add livers and mushrooms, salt, black pepper, and Demi-Glace. Spread two-thirds of the mixture on one side of the omelette, over which fold the other half. Place omelette on a warmed platter and make a lengthwise incision down the center. Fill with the remaining liver mixture. Sprinkle with chopped parsley. (See illustration, page 354.)

CHEESE

Mix ½ cup shredded Cheddar cheese with the eggs before cooking.

CHEVREUSE

6 cooked artichoke bottoms
1 cup diced asparagus
1 tablespoon chopped truffles
6 truffle slices

Combine artichokes, asparagus, and chopped truffles with the eggs before cooking. Garnish with truffle slices.

CLAMART

1 cup little French peas (petits pois)
1½ tablespoons butter
salt and ground black pepper to taste

Heat peas in butter. Add salt and pepper to taste. Spoon two-thirds of the peas onto one side of the omelette. Fold. Place the omelette on a warmed platter and make an incision down the center. Fill with remaining peas.

WITH CROUTONS

Fry 1 ¼ cups ½-inch bread cubes in 3 tablespoons butter. Use 1 cup as filling for omelette and ¼ cup for garnish.

FARM STYLE

1 cup chopped cooked ham
1 tablespoon chopped parsley

Mix ham and parsley with the eggs before the omelette is cooked. Do not fold omelette, but serve flat on a warmed round platter.

FINES HERBES

2 tablespoons chopped parsley
1 tablespoon chopped chives
¼ teaspoon each dried chervil and tarragon

Combine herbs with eggs before cooking.

FLORENTINE

1 cup cooked spinach
2 tablespoons butter
salt and ground black pepper to taste

Chop spinach and drain well. Sauté 1 or 2 minutes in butter. Season to taste with salt and pepper. Add to eggs before cooking.

LYONNAISE

1 cup sliced onions
2 tablespoons butter
1 tablespoon chopped parsley

Cook onions in the butter until they are soft. Add parsley and cook ½ minute. Blend with the eggs before cooking.

MEXICAN

1 cup sliced mushrooms
¼ cup diced green or red sweet pepper
2 tablespoons butter
salt and ground black pepper to taste
¾ cup stewed tomatoes seasoned to taste with salt and ground black pepper

Cook mushrooms and sweet peppers in butter until they are tender. Season to taste with salt and pepper. Use to fill omelette. Place omelette on a warmed platter and make lengthwise incision down the center of the top. Fill with stewed tomatoes.

MUSHROOM

1 cup sliced mushrooms
2 tablespoons butter
parsley
3 small whole mushrooms sautéed in butter

Sauté sliced mushrooms in butter 3 to 5 minutes until tender. Combine mushrooms, butter, and parsley with the eggs before cooking the omelette. Garnish with whole mushrooms.

NORMANDY STYLE

1½ dozen small (soup) oysters
oyster liquor
1 cup Sauce Normande
salt and ground black pepper to taste

Put oysters in enough oyster liquor to cover them. Cook in a saucepan over low heat or in the top of a double boiler over hot water only until edges curl. Remove from liquor, drain, and mix with ⅓ cup of Sauce Normande. Add salt and pepper to taste. Fill omelette and serve on a warmed platter surrounded with remaining sauce, or serve sauce in a separate bowl.

PARMENTIER

2 tablespoons butter
1 cup diced cooked potatoes
salt and ground black pepper to taste
8 slices crisp bacon
chopped parsley

Melt butter in a 10-inch skillet. Add potatoes and cook over moderate heat until browned. Sprinkle with salt and pepper to taste. Pour egg mixture for either French or Puffy Omelette over potatoes. Cook omelette, fold, and serve on a warmed platter, garnished with crisp bacon and sprinkled with chopped parsley.

FOR THE PRIEST

2 pairs roe: shad, carp, or flounder
½ cup tuna fish
1 finely chopped shallot
4 tablespoons (½ stick) butter
salt and ground black pepper to taste
chopped parsley and chives

Poach roe in boiling water 5 minutes. Remove from water, cool, remove and discard membrane, and break up roe with a fork. Add tuna fish and shallot and cook in butter 3 to 4 minutes, over moderately low heat. Season to taste with salt and pepper. Turn out mixture onto the bottom of a warm platter and place the omelette on top. Sprinkle with parsley and chives.

PRINCESS

cooked tips from 1½ pounds fresh asparagus
½ cup Velouté Sauce
truffle slices

Combine asparagus tips with Velouté Sauce. Fill cooked omelette and fold. Garnish with sliced truffles.

PORTUGUESE STYLE

3 ripe tomatoes
3 tablespoons olive oil, cooking oil, or butter
1 tablespoon finely chopped onion
¼ teaspoon sugar
salt and ground black pepper to taste
1 tablespoon chopped parsley
Tomato Sauce (optional)

Peel tomatoes, squeeze out seeds, and chop the pulp rather coarsely. Cook in oil or butter along with onion and sugar until the mixture is of medium thickness. Add salt and pepper to taste; add parsley. Fill cooked omelette and fold it. If desired, surround the omelette with Tomato Sauce or serve it in a separate bowl.

À LA REINE

1 cup finely diced cooked chicken
2 tablespoons butter
¾ cup Sauce Suprême
watercress

Heat chicken in butter only until hot. Spread on cooked omelette just before folding. Serve omelette on a warmed platter surrounded with a ring of hot Sauce Suprême or serve sauce in a separate bowl. Garnish with watercress.

ROSSINI

½ cup cooked foie gras
1 tablespoon finely diced truffle
truffle slices
½ cup Demi-Glace Sauce with truffle essence

Add foie gras and diced truffles to eggs before cooking. Cook as for French or Puffy Omelette and fold. Garnish as desired with truffle slices and surround with a ring of Demi-Glace Sauce.

SAVOY STYLE

1 cup sliced cooked potatoes
2 tablespoons butter
⅓ cup shredded Gruyère cheese
¼ cup heavy cream
salt and pepper to taste
chopped parsley

Sauté potatoes in butter, add cheese, cream, salt, and pepper. Add to the uncooked omelette mixture and cook as in previous directions. Do not fold. Turn out onto a warmed round plate. Garnish with chopped parsley.

SHRIMP

4 tablespoons butter
1 tablespoon flour
1 cup milk or ½ cup each shrimp stock and light cream
¾ teaspoon salt
ground black pepper and lemon juice to taste
1 pound peeled and deveined cooked shrimp
1 tablespoon butter

Melt 2 tablespoons of the butter in a 1½-quart saucepan. Blend in flour. Stir and cook 1 to 2 minutes. Remove from heat and add milk or shrimp stock and cream. Stir and cook until sauce is of medium thickness. Divide shrimp into three equal quantities. Chop one-third fine and add to the sauce along with one-third of the whole shrimp. Mix well and heat. Fill omelette with one-half of this mixture. Place omelette on a warmed platter and make a lengthwise incision down the center of the top. Sauté remaining one-third whole shrimp in the rest of the butter and place in the incision. Surround the omelette with the remaining shrimp sauce or serve it in a separate bowl.

TUNA FISH

½ cup tuna fish canned in oil
2 anchovy fillets
3 tablespoons butter, melted
watercress

Drain oil from the tuna fish, flake it with a fork, and add to beaten eggs before cooking. Cook as in previous directions, fold, and place on a warmed platter. Mince anchovy fillets, mix with melted butter, and pour over omelette. Garnish with watercress.

WITH TRUFFLES

2 small truffles, finely diced
truffle slices

Mix diced truffles with beaten eggs. Cook as in previous directions, fold, and serve on a warmed platter. Garnish the top with sliced truffles as desired.

VICTORIA

½ cup finely diced lobster
1 cup Béchamel Sauce
⅓ cup coarsely flaked lobster

Combine finely diced lobster and Béchamel Sauce. Add ⅓ cup of this sauce to the coarsely flaked lobster. Heat and spread on the omelette just before folding. Serve on a warmed platter surrounded with a ring of the remaining hot lobster sauce or serve sauce in a separate bowl.

VOSGES STYLE

3 slices crisp bacon
⅓ cup shredded Gruyère cheese
2 tablespoons heavy cream

Break bacon into bits and mix with cheese and cream. Add to eggs before cooking the omelette.

·9·

SOUPS

In a meal of several courses, soup comes first except when it is preceded by cold hors d'oeuvre. The soup can therefore be regarded as an indication of the gastronomic pleasures to come. Even a simple meal is enhanced if it begins with a good soup.

Soups may be classified as either clear soups (consommés); cream soups and thickened soups, with or without vegetables; and vegetable soups.

Good soup can be made from comparatively modest materials, but all soups must be well seasoned; an insipid soup without character spoils the appetite for the courses to follow. A good homemade soup requires time and trouble, but the results are worthwhile. The recipes in this chapter provide detailed instructions for the preparation of a great many different kinds of soups, including French regional soups and soups of other countries which have the greatest international popularity.

In serving soup it is especially important that hot soup be piping hot and cold soup really cold. The soup tureen and the soup plates or cups used to serve hot soup should always be warmed beforehand. Nowadays cups are commonly used for consommés and fine cream soups; very small cups are available for serving turtle soup and other rich exotic soups. Cold soups and jellied consommés are always served in cups.

BASIC SOUPS

⚜ GRAND MARMITE

2 pounds lean soup meat
1 shinbone of beef, cracked
2½ quarts cold water
2 teaspoons salt
2 leeks
1 cup diced turnip
1 cup sliced carrots
1 large onion studded with 2 whole cloves
1 rib of celery
1 clove of garlic
½ bay leaf
6 whole peppercorns
1 tablespoon chopped fresh or 1 teaspoon dried thyme

Place meat and shinbone in 6-quart saucepan. Add water and salt. Cover and bring to boiling point. Skim. Add all remaining ingredients except thyme. Simmer 3½ hours. Add thyme 10 minutes before cooking time is up. Cool. Remove meat and bones. Strain broth through 2 thicknesses of cheesecloth or through a very fine sieve. Makes approximately 2 quarts broth.

⚜ POT AU FEU

10 pounds beef shinbones
1½ pounds lean soup meat
4½ quarts cold water
2½ teaspoons salt
2½ cups diced carrots
3 leeks
1 cup diced turnip
1 cup diced celery
1 large onion studded with 4 whole cloves
1 bouquet garni
1 pound chicken giblets

Crack bones and put them in a 8-quart saucepan. Cut meat into 2-inch pieces and add to the bones. Add water and salt. Cover and bring to the boiling point. Skim. Add remaining ingredients. Bring to boiling point and skim again. Simmer 3 hours. Cool. Remove meat and bones. Skim off all fat before serving. Serve hot. This is an excellent broth for preparing consommé. Makes 3 quarts of broth.

POT AU FEU WITH CABBAGE

To hot Pot au Feu, add 3 cups shredded cabbage, cover, and cook 5 minutes. Serve with finger-length strips of bread which have been sprinkled with broth from the pot and then with grated Gruyère cheese and toasted in the oven.

⚜ CONSOMMÉ (*Clear Soup*)

1 pound ground lean beef
2 egg whites
1 leek, shredded
1 carrot, grated
2 quarts stock from Basic Broth
1 tablespoon chopped fresh or 1 teaspoon dried thyme or chervil

Mix beef with egg white, leek, and carrot. Skim off all fat from the broth and mix with the beef and vegetables. Cover. Slowly bring to boiling point, stirring frequently. Simmer gently for 50 minutes. Add herbs 10 minutes before cooking time is up. Cool. Remove meat. Strain through 2 thicknesses of cheesecloth or through a very fine sieve. Serve hot. Makes 3½ pints.

⚜ CHICKEN BROTH

1 pound lean ground chuck
1 carrot, grated
1 leek (the white part) shredded
1 egg white
3 pounds chicken backs and necks
4½ cups Basic Broth
salt to taste
ground black pepper to taste

Mix meat with vegetables and egg white. Place in a 4-quart saucepan. Cook chicken backs and necks in the oven (375° F.) until they begin to brown. Drain off fat and discard. Add backs and necks to the other ingredients. Add broth. Cover and bring to boiling point. Reduce heat and simmer 1 hour. Strain through 2 thicknesses of cheesecloth or through a very fine sieve. Add salt and pepper to taste. Serve hot. Makes 3½ pints.

⚜ FISH BROTH

1½ pounds pike or whiting, minced
½ cup shredded white part of leeks
1 cup finely chopped mushroom stems
¼ cup finely chopped parsley
2 egg whites
2 cups dry white wine
1 quart fish stock
salt to taste
ground white pepper to taste

Thoroughly mix the first 6 ingredients together and put into a 4-quart saucepan. Add fish stock. Mix well. Cover. Slowly bring to boiling point. Reduce heat and simmer 30 minutes. Cool. Strain through 2 thicknesses of cheesecloth or through a very fine sieve. Serve hot, seasoned to taste with salt and pepper. Makes 3½ pints.

⚜ GAME BROTH

1 pound lean meat from furred game (deer, rabbit, etc.)
1 cup finely chopped mushroom stems
1 egg white
4½ pints game stock
whole carcasses of small game or 3 pounds bone from deer
1 teaspoon chopped fresh or ¼ teaspoon dried rosemary
salt to taste
ground black pepper to taste

Put the meat through a food chopper and mix with mushroom stems and egg white. Put into a 4-quart saucepan. Brown carcasses or bones in a moderate oven (375° F.) and add to the meat, along with game stock. Cover. Slowly bring to boiling point. Reduce heat and simmer 1 hour. Add rosemary 10 minutes before cooking time is up. Cool. Remove meat and bones. Strain through 2 thicknesses of cheesecloth or through a very fine sieve. Add salt and pepper to taste. Serve hot. Makes 3½ pints of broth.

⚜ PETITE MARMITE

2 pounds chicken backs and necks
1 pound plate beef
1 pound beef ribs
1 medium-large onion
1 rib of celery
2 quarts beef broth
1 cup thinly sliced carrots
1 cup diced turnip
½ cup sliced celery
1 cup shredded cabbage

Lightly brown chicken pieces in a moderate oven (375° F.). Drain off fat and discard. Put chicken in a 4-quart saucepan. Add beef, ribs, onion, celery rib, and beef broth. Cover. Slowly bring to boiling point. Skim. Reduce heat and simmer 1½ hours. Remove and discard onion and celery. Remove chicken, beef, and ribs from the stock. Pick meat from chicken bones and beef ribs and cut plate beef into ½-inch squares. Set aside. Skim the broth, bring it to boiling point, and add carrots, turnip, and sliced celery. Cover and cook 15 minutes or until vegetables are tender. Add cabbage and meat. Cover and cook 5 minutes or until cabbage is crisp-tender. Adjust seasonings. Serve in an earthenware casserole with toast. Makes 6 servings.

CONSOMMÉS

⚜ CONSOMMÉ AURORA

3 tablespoons quick-cooking tapioca
½ cup tomato purée
2 quarts chicken consommé
1 cup julienne strips white chicken meat

Combine the first 3 ingredients in a 3-quart saucepan. Cover and cook until tapioca is transparent. Add chicken and bring to boiling point. Adjust seasonings. Serve hot. Makes 8 servings.

⚜ CONSOMMÉ BASQUE STYLE

2 quarts consommé
⅓ cup julienne strips sweet green pepper
½ cup diced, peeled, seeded tomatoes
⅓ cup cooked rice
1 teaspoon chopped fresh or ¼ teaspoon dried chervil
chopped parsley

Pour consommé into 3-quart saucepan. Add green pepper and tomato. Cover and cook 5 minutes or until pepper is crisp-tender. Add rice and chervil. Cook 2 to 3 minutes. Adjust seasonings. Serve hot, sprinkled with chopped parsley. Makes 8 servings.

⚜ CONSOMMÉ BRUNOISE

Brunoise, in French cookery, means vegetables finely diced or shredded and cooked in butter.

1½ cups shredded carrots
1½ cups shredded turnip
1 cup thinly sliced celery
¼ teaspoon sugar
2 tablespoons butter
1 cup hot consommé
hot consommé for 8 to 10 servings

Cook the vegetables with the sugar in butter in a covered saucepan over low heat, stirring frequently, until vegetables are wilted. Add 1 cup consommé, cover, and cook until celery is tender. Add 1 tablespoon of mixture to each serving of hot consommé and adjust seasoning. Makes enough for 8 to 10 servings. If desired, a thick soup may be made from these ingredients, increasing the quantities as required.

⚜ CONSOMMÉ CELESTINE

Cut 2 to 3 small paper-thin crêpes into julienne strips and put them in the bottom of soup plates. Pour in hot consommé. Sprinkle with chopped fresh chervil or parsley. This quantity is enough for 4 to 6 servings.

⚜ CONSOMMÉ CHIFFONNADE (*With Lettuce and Sorrel*)

¼ medium-size head lettuce, shredded
½ cup sorrel (sourgrass) leaves
1 tablespoon butter
dash salt
hot consommé for 8 servings

Cook lettuce and sorrel in butter with salt very quickly, about 1 to 2 minutes. Put in the bottom of soup plates and pour in hot consommé. If desired add 3 small quenelles to each serving. Garnish with plucked leaves of chervil or parsley. Serve hot. Makes 8 servings.

⚜ CONSOMMÉ WITH DIABLOTINS

¾ cup Béchamel Sauce
½ cup grated Parmesan cheese
dash of cayenne
16 slices French bread
hot consommé for 8 servings

Combine Béchamel Sauce, cheese, and cayenne and spread over one side of each slice of French bread. Toast in the oven or under the broiler and serve hot with consommé, 2 slices to a serving.

⚜ CONSOMMÉ WITH FOUR FILLETS

Cut cooked white meat of chicken, pickled tongue, poached mushrooms, and truffles into short julienne strips. Measure ½ cup of each and add to 1½ quarts hot consommé. Serve hot, garnished with chopped parsley. Makes 6 servings.

⚜ CONSOMMÉ MOSAIC

1 cup each diced carrots and turnip
½ cup each diced green beans and green peas
1 diced small truffle (optional)
1 cup bouillon, or 1 cup boiling water and 1 beef bouillon cube
½ cup diced pickled tongue
1 diced hard-cooked egg white
1½ quarts consommé

Place vegetables, truffle, and bouillon (or water and bouillon cube) in a saucepan. Cover and cook until vegetables are tender, 8 to 10 minutes. Add remaining ingredients. Bring to boiling point. Adjust seasonings. Serve hot in soup plates. Makes 6 servings.

⚜ CONSOMMÉ MOUSSELINE

2 tablespoons quick-cooking tapioca
2 quarts boiling consommé
3 egg yolks
½ cup heavy cream

Sprinkle tapioca into boiling consommé. Cover and cook until tapioca is transparent. Beat egg yolks with cream and gradually stir into the hot consommé. Serve hot in soup plates. Makes 8 servings.

⚜ CONSOMMÉ WITH OXTAILS (*Hochepot*)

2 pounds oxtail
1 pound knuckle of veal
3 quarts water
3 teaspoons salt
1 cup diced carrots
½ cup diced turnips
3 leeks
1 large onion studded with 3 whole cloves
1 pound ground chuck
1 tablespoon butter
3 tablespoons arrowroot or cornstarch

Cut oxtail into slices and place them in an 8-quart saucepan. Add veal, water, and salt. Cover. Slowly bring to boiling point. Skim. Add carrots, turnips, leeks or scallions, and whole onion with cloves. Cover and simmer 4 hours. Lightly fry ground chuck in butter. Mix arrowroot or cornstarch with the beef and then mix with the stock. Cover and cook 1 hour. Remove meat from the stock, cut the meat from the bones, and then dice it. Strain broth through 2 thicknesses of cheesecloth or through a fine sieve. Remove all fat and scum. Add diced meat to the broth and bring to boiling point. Serve in soup plates. Makes 6 to 8 servings.

⚜ CONSOMMÉ WITH PASTA

Break ¼ pound fine noodles or fine spaghetti into 2 quarts boiling consommé. Cover and cook 10 minutes or until pasta is tender. Adjust seasonings. Serve hot in soup plates. Makes 8 servings.

⚜ CONSOMMÉ WITH PEARL BARLEY

Add 2 tablespoons pearl barley to 1 cup boiling water. Cover and cook 3 minutes. Drain off water and add blanched barley to 2 quarts boiling consommé. Cover and cook until barley is tender. Serve hot in soup plates. Garnish with chopped parsley. Makes 6 to 8 servings.

⚜ CONSOMMÉ PRINTANIER

¼ cup each diced carrots and turnips
½ cup green beans, cut into ⅜-inch pieces
½ cup green peas
1½ quarts consommé
chopped chervil or parsley

Cook each vegetable separately in ½ inch boiling water, 8 to 10 minutes. Drain off water and add vegetables to boiling consommé. Bring back to boiling point. Adjust seasonings. Serve hot. Garnish with chopped chervil or parsley. Makes 6 servings.

⚜ CONSOMMÉ WITH PROFITEROLES

Profiteroles are little puffs or eclairs of Chou Paste piped through a pastry bag and baked. Besides being served with consommé, they may be filled after baking with various savory or sweet mixtures and served as a garnish or a dessert. For this recipe cheese is mixed with the Chou Paste.

2 cups warm Chou Paste
1 cup grated Parmesan cheese

Mix the cheese with the Chou Paste and with a pastry bag with a small round tube pipe the mixture into tiny balls onto lightly buttered baking sheets. Bake in a preheated hot oven (425° F.) 15 to 20 minutes, or until puffs are golden. Turn off oven, prick puffs with a knife to allow the steam to escape, and leave them in the oven 20 minutes to dry the centers. Put 2 or 3 profiteroles in each soup plate, pour consommé over them, and serve at once. Makes about 24 profiteroles.

⚜ CONSOMMÉ WITH RICE

Sprinkle ¼ cup uncooked rice into 1½ quarts boiling consommé. Cover and cook 12 to 15 minutes or until rice is tender. Adjust seasonings. Serve hot in soup plates. Garnish with finely grated carrots. Makes 6 servings.

⚜ CONSOMMÉ WITH ROYALE

Royale is a custard made from the following ingredients, which is used to garnish thin or thick soups.

4 large eggs
½ cup cold beef or veal stock
3 cups hot consommé
salt and ground white pepper to taste
chopped parsley

Beat eggs lightly and blend in cold stock. Add 3 cups hot consommé. Season to taste with salt and pepper. Pour into a lightly buttered 8- or 9-inch square pan. Place pan in a large pan of hot water and bake in a preheated slow oven (325° F.) 30 to 40 minutes or until a knife inserted in the center comes out clean. Cool completely. Cut into cubes or small fancy shapes. Carefully place in soup plates. Pour in hot consommé. Sprinkle with chopped parsley. Makes enough for 6 to 8 servings.

⚜ CONSOMMÉ MIMOSA

1 tablespoon quick-cooking tapioca
½ cup green beans, cut into short julienne strips
1½ quarts boiling consommé
1 cup diced Royale
1 hard-cooked egg white
1 hard-cooked egg yolk

Sprinkle tapioca and beans into boiling consommé, cover, and cook until tapioca is transparent. Adjust seasonings. Carefully put diced Royale in soup plates, along with egg white cut into strips. Pour in hot consommé. Put egg yolk through a sieve and sprinkle over each serving. Serve at once. Makes 6 servings.

⚜ CONSOMMÉ XAVIER

¼ cup milk
2 large eggs
1/16 teaspoon salt
½ cup sifted all-purpose flour
½ teaspoon chopped fresh or ⅛ teaspoon dried chervil
2 quarts consommé

Beat milk, eggs, and salt together. Gradually stir in flour and chervil. Pour this mixture through a coarse strainer into boiling consommé. Beat well with a wire whisk. Serve at once. Makes 8 servings.

Cold Consommés

In the summer, or for cold buffets, consommé is usually served cold. The consommé should be well seasoned and rich enough to jelly when chilled. If you have any doubt that it will set, add 1 envelope plain gelatin to each quart of hot consommé. Serve very cold in chilled consommé cups.

⚜ CONSOMMÉ MADRILÈNE

1½ pounds ground chuck
green top of 1 leek, coarsely chopped
1 tablespoon chopped fresh or 1 teaspoon dried chervil
2 egg whites
5 pounds cracked beef bones
2 quarts cold water
2 teaspoons salt
4 whole peppercorns
5 medium-sized tomatoes, peeled, seeded, and crushed
¾ cup julienne strips sweet green pepper
1 tablespoon butter

Combine chuck, leek top, chervil, and egg whites. Mix well. Place in a saucepan with bones, 1½ quarts cold water, salt, and black pepper. Cover. Slowly bring to boiling point. Skim. Add 4 of the tomatoes and simmer 2 hours. Cool. Remove bones. Strain. Skim off fat and scum. Add the remaining crushed tomato. Cook green peppers in butter until they are soft. Add to the broth. Bring to boiling point. Adjust seasonings. Chill until broth is jellied. Break up the jelly coarsely with a fork. Serve in cold consommé cups with a wedge of lemon. Makes 6 servings.

⚜ CONSOMMÉ WITH TARRAGON

In the recipe for Consommé Madrilène, omit chervil and add 1 tablespoon chopped or 1 teaspoon dried tarragon 5 minutes before cooking time is up. Strain stock and skim off all fat. Chill until jellied. Break up coarsely with a fork. Serve in cold consommé cups. Garnish with chopped parsley.

⚜ CONSOMMÉ WITH WINE

To 10 parts Chicken Broth, add 1 part wine—Madeira, Marsala, port, or sherry—and mix well. Chill until jellied.

CREAM SOUPS

⚜ CREAM OF BARLEY SOUP

4 tablespoons butter
5 tablespoons flour
5 cups beef stock
3 tablespoons pearl barley, cooked separately in bouillon
2 egg yolks
¾ cup milk
¼ cup heavy cream
salt and ground black pepper to taste

Melt butter in a 2-quart saucepan. Remove from heat and blend in flour. Stir and cook until the mixture is golden. Remove from heat and add beef stock. Cook until the mixture is slightly thickened. Add cooked barley. Blend egg yolks with milk and add to the soup. Cook 5 minutes. Add cream and heat. Season to taste with salt and pepper.

⚜ CREAM OF RICE SOUP

4 tablespoons butter
3 tablespoons cream of rice
5 cups beef or veal bouillon
¾ cup milk
2 egg yolks
⅓ cup heavy cream
salt and ground black pepper to taste

Melt butter in a 2-quart saucepan. Blend in cream of rice. Stir and cook 1 minute. Add 1 cup of the bouillon. Bring to boiling point, stirring constantly. Add remaining bouillon. Cook gently 25 minutes. Add milk and heat. Beat egg yolks with cream and add. Cook 1 minute. Season to taste with salt and pepper. Serve hot. Makes 6 to 8 servings.

⚜ ANDALUSIAN CREAM SOUP

1 medium-sized onion
4 tablespoons butter
3 medium-sized potatoes
3 medium-sized tomatoes
1 cup beef marrow
1½ quarts beef or veal stock
salt and ground black pepper to taste
½ cup heavy cream
½ cup cooked rice

Peel and slice onion and cook in butter until slices are transparent. Peel potatoes and cut in small dice and cut tomatoes into quarters, then add to onions. Stir and cook 5 minutes. Add marrow, stock, salt, and pepper. Bring to boiling point and simmer 5 minutes. Stir in cream and rice. Cook 1 minute. Serve hot in soup plates. Makes 6 to 8 servings.

⚜ CREAM OF ARTICHOKE SOUP (*Crème à la Châtelaine*)

5 tablespoons butter
2 tablespoons flour
3½ cups stock
4 raw artichoke bottoms
2 egg yolks
1 cup milk
⅓ cup heavy cream
salt and ground white pepper to taste

Melt 3 tablespoons of the butter in a 2-quart saucepan. Remove from heat and blend in flour. Stir and cook 1 minute. Remove from heat and add stock.

Stir and cook until the mixture has slightly thickened. Slice artichoke bottoms and cook them until soft in the remaining 2 tablespoons butter. Add to soup. Simmer 20 minutes. Strain through a fine sieve. Beat egg yolks with milk and add. Heat 1 minute. Add cream, salt, and pepper. Serve hot. Makes 6 to 8 servings.

⚜ CREAM OF ASPARAGUS SOUP

4 tablespoons butter
2 tablespoons cornstarch
5 cups stock
1 pound fresh asparagus
2 egg yolks
⅓ cup milk
salt and ground white pepper to taste
⅓ cup heavy cream

Melt butter in a 2-quart saucepan. Remove from heat and blend in cornstarch. Stir and cook 1 minute. Remove from heat, add stock, and mix well. Bring to boiling point, stirring frequently. Wash and trim asparagus. Cut off tips and cook them in ½ inch of boiling water in a separate saucepan. Cut remaining asparagus in ½-inch pieces, cook in additional stock until tender, and add to the soup. Beat egg yolks with milk, add to soup, and bring it to boiling point. Stir in salt, pepper, cream, and asparagus tips. Heat. Serve hot. Makes 6 to 8 servings.

⚜ CALCUTTA CREAM SOUP

4 medium-sized onions
4 tablespoons butter
2 teaspoons curry powder
4 cups Cream of Rice Soup
1 cup milk
¾ cup cooked rice

Slice onions, blanch in boiling water, drain well, and cook until soft in butter. Dust with curry powder, stir, and cook over low heat until browned. Add Cream of Rice Soup. Simmer 5 minutes. Add milk, rice, and cream and heat 1 minute. Serve hot. Makes 6 servings.

⚜ CREAM OF CARROT SOUP

5 medium-sized carrots, peeled and thinly sliced
½ cup water
½ teaspoon each salt and sugar
1 tablespoon chopped onion
¼ cup (½ stick) butter
4 tablespoons flour
1 cup veal or chicken stock
1¼ cups milk
2 egg yolks
salt and ground white pepper to taste
½ cup heavy cream
grated carrot

Place sliced carrots, water, salt, and sugar in a saucepan. Cover and cook slowly 15 minutes or until carrots are soft. Cook onion in butter until onion is soft, remove from heat, and blend in flour. Stir and cook 1 minute. Remove from heat and stir in stock, 1 cup of the milk, and the carrots. Cook 10 minutes over moderately low heat, stirring frequently. Mix egg yolks with the rest of the milk and add to the soup. Heat. Strain through a fine sieve or blend in a blender, a little at a time. Add salt, pepper, and cream. Cook only until soup is hot enough to serve. Serve in soup plates, garnished with a little grated carrot. Makes 6 servings.

⚜ CREAM OF CAULIFLOWER SOUP

1 medium-sized cauliflower
4 cups boiling veal stock or water
⅓ cup raw rice
½ cup finely chopped onion
¼ to ½ teaspoon curry powder
1 tablespoon butter
salt and ground white pepper to taste
⅓ to ½ cup heavy cream

Break cauliflower into flowerets and place them in a saucepan with the boiling veal stock or water. (If water is used add ½ teaspoon salt.) Cover, bring to boiling point, and cook 12 to 15 minutes or until cauliflower is tender. Remove cauliflower from stock (or water) and put rice in. Sauté onions and curry powder in butter until onions are soft and add to the stock. Cover and cook slowly 15 minutes or until rice is soft. Rub the mixture through a sieve or blend in a blender, a little at a time. Chop cauliflower fine and add it to the soup. Heat 1 to 2 minutes. Add salt, pepper, and cream just before serving. Makes 6 servings.

VARIATION

CREAM OF TURNIP SOUP

Replace cauliflower in the preceding recipe with 2¾ cups diced turnips. Garnish with fried bread cubes.

⚜ CREAM OF CELERY SOUP

2 cups chopped celery or celery root
¼ cup chopped onion
6 cups chicken stock
3 tablespoons butter
3 tablespoons flour
2 egg yolks
½ cup milk
½ cup heavy cream
salt and ground white pepper to taste
chopped parsley

Cook celery and onion in stock until celery is very soft. Strain through a sieve or blend in a blender, a little at a time. Melt butter in a 2-quart saucepan. Remove from heat and blend in flour. Stir and cook 1 minute. Remove from heat and stir in strained celery mixture. Stir and cook 10 minutes. Mix egg yolks with milk, add to the soup, and bring to boiling point. Turn off heat immediately. Add cream, salt, and pepper. Serve at once, garnished with chopped parsley. Makes 6 servings.

⚜ CREAM OF CHICKEN SOUP

4 tablespoons (½ stick) butter
4 tablespoons all-purpose flour or rice flour
5 cups chicken stock
⅓ cup chopped celery
1 small onion, chopped
¼ cup chopped parsley
1 cup julienne strips cooked chicken
2 egg yolks
½ cup milk
salt and ground black pepper to taste
½ cup heavy cream

Melt butter in a 2½ quart saucepan. Remove from heat and blend in flour. Stir and cook 1 minute. Remove from heat, add chicken stock, celery, onion, and parsley. Cover and bring to boiling point. Reduce heat and simmer 25 minutes. Strain. Skim off fat, if necessary. Add chicken. Mix egg yolks with milk, add to the soup, and bring to boiling point. Turn off heat. Add salt, pepper, and cream. Serve at once. Makes 6 servings.

⚜ CREAM OF CORN SOUP

2½ cups finely cut fresh raw corn kernels
1 cup boiling water
2 tablespoons finely chopped onion
3 tablespoons butter
3 tablespoons flour
1½ cups veal or chicken stock
1½ cups milk
salt and ground white pepper to taste
½ cup heavy cream
chopped chives

Run a sharp knife down the center of each row of corn, splitting the kernels in half. Cut off the tips from the kernels and then cut the remainder of the kernels from the cobs. Scrape the cob well, getting out all the milk. Cook corn in the boiling water 5 to 6 minutes. Set aside. Sauté onion in butter until transparent. Remove from heat and blend in flour. Stir and cook 1 minute. Add corn, stock, and milk. Cook 5 minutes, stirring frequently. Add salt, pepper, and cream. Heat. Serve hot with chopped chives sprinkled over the top. Makes 6 servings.

⚜ CREAM OF LETTUCE SOUP

1 large head of Romaine or iceberg lettuce
¼ cup finely chopped onion
white part of 1 leek, chopped fine
1½ cups (1½ pounds) shelled green peas
3 tablespoons butter
5 cups chicken stock
3 tablespoons all-purpose flour or rice flour
¾ cup milk
salt and ground black pepper to taste
½ cup heavy cream

Shred lettuce fine, saving 1½ cups for garnish. Cook remaining lettuce slowly in a covered saucepan, without water, until lettuce has wilted. Set aside. Cook onion, leek, and peas in butter over very low heat until soft, adding a little water if necessary. Put vegetables through a sieve or blend them in a blender, a little at a time. Add the purée to the stock. Blend the flour with the milk until smooth and add. Bring to boiling point, reduce heat, and simmer 2 to 3 minutes. Add salt, pepper, and cream. Serve hot, garnished with the reserved shredded lettuce. Makes 6 servings.

⚜ CREAM OF MUSHROOM SOUP

3 tablespoons butter
3 tablespoons flour
⅛ teaspoon powdered mustard
1 teaspoon salt
dash cayenne
4 cups rich chicken stock
3 cups (about ¾ pound) chopped mushrooms
½ cup heavy cream
⅓ cup dry sherry
6 tablespoons whipped cream
paprika
toasted blanched almonds, shredded

Melt butter in a 3-quart saucepan. Remove from heat and blend in flour mixed with the seasonings. Stir and cook 1 minute. Remove from heat and add stock and mushrooms. Cover and simmer 30 minutes. Strain through 2 thicknesses of cheesecloth or through a fine sieve. Add cream and heat. Stir in sherry. Serve hot with each serving garnished with 1 tablespoon whipped cream, a dash of paprika, and shredded toasted almonds. Makes 6 servings.

⚜ PORTUGUESE CREAM SOUP (*Tomato Soup with Rice*)

2 slices bacon, cut into small pieces
1 cup diced carrots
½ cup chopped onion
4 tablespoons flour
5 cups veal stock
8 medium-sized tomatoes, quartered, or 4 cups canned tomatoes
1 teaspoon sugar
2 sprigs parsley
salt and ground black pepper to taste
¼ cup heavy cream
cooked rice

Cook bacon with carrots and onions until bacon has browned, remove from heat, and blend in flour. Stir and cook 1 minute. Add stock, tomatoes, sugar, and parsley. Cover and cook 30 minutes over low heat. Strain through a sieve, pushing as much as possible of the vegetables through. Stir in salt and pepper. Bring to boiling point. Add cream. Put 1 tablespoon cooked rice in each soup bowl and fill with hot soup. Serve at once. Makes 8 servings.

⚜ CREAM OF VEGETABLE SOUP

4 tablespoons (½ stick) butter
2 tablespoons flour
5 cups veal stock
4 medium-sized tomatoes, or 2 cups canned tomatoes
1½ cups diced potatoes
1 cup diced turnips
1½ cups diced carrots
1 cup green beans cut into ½-inch pieces
salt and ground black pepper to taste
½ teaspoon sugar
chopped parsley

Melt 2 tablespoons of the butter in a 2½-quart saucepan. Remove from heat and blend in flour. Stir and cook 1 minute. Remove from heat, add stock, mix well, and bring to boiling point. Add tomatoes and potatoes. Cook slowly 30 minutes. Cook turnips in a separate saucepan in enough boiling salted water to cover them. Cook carrots and beans together until tender with ½ teaspoon salt and 1 inch boiling water. Strain soup through a fine sieve, pushing as much as possible of the tomatoes and potatoes through. Add salt, pepper, and sugar. Bring to boiling point. Stir in remaining butter. Drain vegetables and add. Serve hot, garnished with chopped parsley. Makes 6 servings.

SOUPS WITH A VEGETABLE-PURÉE BASE

⚜ DRIED-BEAN SOUP

2 cups dried beans (pea-beans, navy, or marrow beans)
7 cups boiling water
1 ham bone
1 carrot, quartered
1 large onion, sliced
3 sprigs parsley
4 whole cloves
6 whole peppercorns
2 teaspoons salt (or salt to taste)
1 cup milk
3 tablespoons butter
½ teaspoon ground black pepper
¼ cup heavy cream

Wash beans, add 4 cups of the water, and bring to boiling point. Boil 2 minutes. Remove from heat and soak 1 hour. Add remaining boiling water and next 7 ingredients. Cover and cook slowly 2 hours or until beans are very soft. Remove the ham bone. Pour the soup through a sieve, pushing as much of the vegetables through as possible. Add the milk and butter. Heat. Stir in black pepper and cream just before serving. Makes 8 servings.

VARIATIONS

POTAGE PAULETTE

Garnish each serving of Dried Bean Soup with lettuce and a few sorrel leaves cooked in butter or bacon drippings only until lettuce is wilted. Sprinkle with chopped chervil or parsley.

RED BEAN SOUP (*Potage Condé*)

Make Dried Bean Soup with red kidney beans. Garnish each serving with crumbled crisp bacon and fried bread cubes.

⚜ CARROT SOUP WITH RICE (*Potage Crécy*)

½ cup diced onions
2 strips bacon cut into squares
4 cups sliced carrots
1½ quarts bouillon
⅓ cup uncooked rice
salt and ground black pepper to taste
2 tablespoons butter
¼ cup heavy cream
6 tablespoons cooked rice

Lightly fry onion with diced bacon until onion is soft. Add carrots, bouillon, and rice. Cover and cook 20 minutes. Put through a sieve. Bring to boiling point and add salt, pepper, butter, and cream. Sprinkle 1 tablespoon cooked rice over each serving. Makes 6 servings.

⚜ GARBURE SOUP

2 medium-sized carrots
2 medium-sized turnips
3 medium-sized potatoes
4 tablespoons (½ stick) butter
1 cup hot beef stock, or 1 cup hot water and 1 teaspoon salt
2 cups shredded cabbage
1 cup cooked dried beans
2 cups diced fresh tomatoes or 1½ cups canned tomatoes
1 egg
1 cup grated Parmesan or Cheddar cheese
6 slices French bread

Peel carrots, turnips, and potatoes and slice thin. Place in a saucepan with 2 tablespoons of the butter. Heat and toss for 3 minutes. Add hot beef stock or water. (If water is used, add 1 teaspoon salt.) Cover and cook until vegetables are tender, adding cabbage 5 minutes before the other vegetables are done. Heat beans with tomatoes and put them through a sieve along with the other vegetables, pushing as much of the vegetables through as possible. Thin to desired consistency with stock. Adjust seasonings. Add remaining butter and heat. Beat egg, mix with cheese, and spread over slices of French bread. Toast in a very hot oven or under the broiler. Place a piece in each soup plate, pour hot soup over it, and serve immediately. Makes 6 servings.

⚜ LEEK AND POTATO SOUP (*Potage Parmentier*)

white part of 2 leeks
6 tablespoons butter
5 cups veal or chicken stock
4 medium-sized potatoes
1 small ham bone
1 cup milk
salt to taste
¼ teaspoon ground black pepper
½ cup heavy cream
ground mace

Shred leeks and cook them in 2 tablespoons of the butter until they are limp. Add stock. Peel and slice potatoes and add to the soup pot along with ham bone. Cover, bring to boiling point, reduce heat, and cook slowly 1 hour. Remove ham bone. Put soup through a strainer, pushing as much of the potatoes and leeks through as possible. Add milk, salt, and pepper. Bring to boiling point. Stir in remaining butter and cream just before serving. Serve hot, garnished with a dash of ground mace. Makes 6 servings.

⚜ LENTIL SOUP

1½ cups (½ pound) lentils
5 cups water
4 slices bacon
½ cup sliced carrots
½ cup diced green sweet peppers
1 cup sliced onion
1 cup diced tomatoes or ¾ cup canned tomatoes
3 tablespoons butter
3 tablespoons flour
2 cups beef or ham stock
salt to taste (1 to 2 teaspoons)
2 tablespoons wine vinegar
½ teaspoon ground black pepper
fried bread cubes

Wash lentils and put in a 2½-cup saucepan with water. Cover, bring to boiling point, reduce heat, and cook slowly 1 hour. Cut bacon into small pieces and cook until it is crisp. Add all the vegetables to the bacon and drippings and sauté over low heat about 5 minutes. Add to the lentils. Melt butter in the bacon skillet, remove from heat, and blend in flour. Stir and cook 1 minute. Remove from heat and add stock; mix well and add to the lentil pot. Add salt and vinegar. Mix well. Bring to boiling point, stirring constantly. Reduce heat, cover, and cook about 35 minutes, stirring frequently. Add black pepper. Serve hot with fried bread cubes. Makes 6 servings.

⚜ PEA SOUP WITH CREAM (*Potage Chantilly*)

1½ cups (1½ pounds) shelled green peas
½ teaspoon salt
boiling water
4 tablespoons all-purpose flour or rice flour
3¼ cups stock
3¼ cups milk
salt
ground black pepper
2 tablespoons bacon drippings or butter
½ cup heavy cream
2 strips crisp bacon (optional)

Cook peas with salt in 1 inch of boiling water 5 minutes or until they are soft. Drain off water and reserve ⅓ cup of the peas to use as a garnish. Put remaining peas through a sieve or blend them in a blender. Mix flour with ½ cup of the stock until the mixture is smooth, then add to the remaining stock along with the milk. Stir and cook 5 to 6 minutes. Stir in pea purée, salt, pepper, and bacon drippings or butter. Bring to boiling point. Stir in cream just before serving. Put 1 tablespoon of the reserved cooked peas in each soup bowl and finish filling with soup. If desired, garnish with crumbled crisp bacon. Makes 6 servings.

⚜ SPLIT-PEA SOUP (*Potage Saint-Germain*)

2 cups (1 pound) green split peas
2 quarts cold water
1 rib celery
1 carrot, peeled and quartered
1 large onion, sliced
1 small ham bone or ¼ pound bacon rind
4 cups beef or veal stock
salt to taste
½ teaspoon ground black pepper
2 tablespoons butter
½ cup heavy cream

Wash peas, add water, and soak overnight in the refrigerator. Add vegetables and ham bone or bacon rind. Cover and bring to boiling point. Simmer 2 to 3 hours or until peas are very soft and mixture is thick. Remove ham bone or bacon rind. Force soup through a sieve. Add stock. Bring to boiling point and cook 5 minutes. Add salt and pepper. Stir in butter and cream just before serving. Makes 6 to 8 servings.

VARIATIONS

POTAGE FONTANGES

Garnish Split Pea Soup with shredded lettuce and a few sorrel leaves cooked until wilted in a little butter.

POTAGE LAMBALLE

Thin Split-Pea Soup to the desired consistency with beef or veal stock or milk. Add 1 teaspoon quick-cooking tapioca for each cup of soup to be served. Cook, covered, until tapioca is transparent.

⚜ WATERCRESS SOUP

white parts of 3 leeks or scallions
1 small onion
2 tablespoons butter
3 medium-sized potatoes, peeled and sliced thinly
3 cups chicken stock
1 cup milk
1 bunch watercress
salt and ground black pepper to taste
1 cup heavy cream
watercress leaves

Slice leeks and onions and sauté in butter until they are golden. Add potatoes and stock. Cover, bring to boiling point, reduce heat, and simmer 30 minutes.

Pour soup through a strainer, rubbing as much of the potatoes and onion through as possible, or purée in a blender, a little at a time. Add milk, stir, and cook 5 minutes. Cook watercress in ½ cup boiling water in a covered saucepan until it is limp. Force it through a sieve or purée in a blender. Add to soup and heat. Add salt, pepper, and cream. Serve hot or chilled. Garnish with watercress leaves. Makes 6 servings.

FISH SOUPS

The best French chefs prefer the more delicately flavored fish, such as cod, hake, haddock, halibut, pike, sole, and eel, for making fish soups. The fish should be cooked below boiling point and only until the meat is flaky and falls from the bones. These soups have a fish Velouté base.

⚜ STOCK FOR FISH SOUPS

3 shallots, sliced
¾ cup sliced onion
4 stalks parsley
1 cup mushroom stems
2 ribs of celery
1 small bay leaf
2 teaspoons salt
2 quarts cold water
3 pounds fish heads, bones, and trimmings (sole, turbot, hake, whiting, cod, pike, etc.)
1½ cups dry white wine
10 white peppercorns

Place the first 7 ingredients in the bottom of a 4-quart saucepan. Add fish trimmings, water, and wine. Cover, slowly bring to boiling point, reduce heat and simmer 30 minutes. Add peppercorns after stock has cooked 20 minutes. Remove and discard bones. Skim. Strain stock through 2 thicknesses of cheesecloth or through a fine sieve. Makes approximately 2 quarts.

⚜ VELOUTÉ BASE FOR FISH SOUPS

¼ cup (½ stick) butter
¾ cup sifted all-purpose flour (rice flour is traditionally used)
5 cups fish stock

Melt butter and gradually stir in flour. Cook, stirring, until the roux begins to brown. Add stock and mix well. Stir and cook until the stock is smooth and has slightly thickened. Simmer (do not boil) 20 minutes. Skim if necessary and strain through a fine sieve. Makes approximately 4½ cups.

⚜ FISH SOUP

1¼ pounds chopped raw fish (pike, halibut, or whiting)
2 egg whites
¼ cup finely chopped parsley
½ cup finely chopped mushroom stems
6 cups fish stock
1½ cups dry white wine

Combine fish, egg whites, parsley, and mushrooms. Add fish stock and wine. Mix well. Bring to boiling point, reduce heat and simmer gently 10 minutes. Strain and skim off all fat and scum. Serve hot. Makes 6 servings.

⚜ POTAGE JACQUELINE

7 cups fish Velouté Base
½ cup cooked diced carrots
2 egg yolks
½ cup heavy cream
½ cup cooked peas
1⅓ cups cooked rice

Heat Velouté Base only to boiling point. Mix egg yolks with cream and add. Mix well. Stir in vegetables and rice. Heat 1 minute. Makes 8 servings.

⚜ LOBSTER SOUP (*Potage Cardinal*)

3 cups fish Velouté Base
2 cups Béchamel Sauce
½ cup tomato purée
⅓ cup cooked lobster meat and coral
⅓ cup softened butter
salt and pepper to taste
chunks cooked lobster

Combine Velouté Base, Béchamel Sauce, and tomato purée in a 2-quart saucepan. Heat. Pound and mash lobster and coral, blend with butter, and add to the soup. Adjust seasonings. Serve hot, garnished with chunks of cooked lobster. Makes 6 servings.

⚜ MUSSEL SOUP (*Potage Dieppoise*)

5 cups fish Velouté Base
1½ cups cooking liquor from the mussels
2 egg yolks
1 cup heavy cream
6 tablespoons diced cooked carrots
6 tablespoons cooked peas
6 tablespoons cooked rice
18 poached mussels

Combine Velouté Base and cooking liquor from the mussels. Heat, but do not boil. Combine egg yolks and cream and add to the soup. Mix well and cook *only* until hot. In each soup bowl place 1 tablespoon each of the carrots, peas, and rice, and 3 mussels. Pour soup over these and serve at once. Makes 6 servings.

⚜ OYSTER SOUP

1 cup sliced mushrooms
2 tablespoons butter
½ teaspoon lemon juice
6 cups fish Velouté Base
18 small (soup) oysters in liquor
2 egg yolks
⅓ cup heavy cream
salt and ground black pepper to taste

Cook mushrooms in butter and lemon juice until tender. Add to Velouté Base. Stir and cook until hot. Heat oysters in their own liquor only until edges curl, and add. Blend egg yolks with cream and add. Cook about ½ minute. Add salt and pepper. Serve hot. Makes 6 servings.

⚜ PROVENÇAL FISH SOUP

2 pounds conger eel
1½ cups coarsely chopped onions
4 tablespoons (½ stick) butter
6 cups cold water
salt
white part of 1 leek
1 clove garlic, crushed
2 tablespoons olive oil or salad oil
3 medium-sized tomatoes
1/16 teaspoon crushed saffron
bouquet garni
½ teaspoon grated dried orange peel
ground black pepper
French bread

Skin the eel and remove and chop all bones. Brown the bones with the onions in 2 tablespoons butter. Add water and 1½ teaspoons salt. Cover, bring to boiling point, and simmer 30 minutes. Strain and set aside. Slice leek into julienne strips and cook, with the garlic, in the remaining 2 tablespoons butter and the oil until leek is transparent. Cut eel into 1-inch strips, add to leek, and brown lightly. Peel, seed, and dice tomatoes. Add to the strained stock along with saffron, bouquet garni, and orange peel. Cover and simmer 20 minutes. Adjust salt. Remove bouquet garni. Garnish with chopped parsley and serve hot with thin slices of French bread. Makes 6 servings.

⚜ REGENCY SOUP

1 pound whiting
7 cups fish Velouté Base
⅔ cup heavy cream
croutons

Clean, wash, and trim the whiting. Add to Velouté Base. Cook until the fish falls off the bones. Remove and discard bones. Strain through a fine sieve, pushing as much of the fish through as possible. Add cream, heat, and adjust seasonings. Serve hot with croutons. Makes 6 servings.

FRENCH REGIONAL SOUPS

The recipes which follow are for soups served in the provincial towns and country regions of France. They are both healthful and economical.

⚜ CABBAGE SOUP

2 pounds pickled pork (such as pigs' feet)
½ pound salt pork
2 quarts cold water
4 medium-sized potatoes, peeled and cubed
2 medium-sized turnips, peeled and cubed
2 large carrots, peeled and sliced ¼-inch thick
1 cup sliced leeks or onions
½ pound pork sausage
1 small head cabbage, quartered
salt and black pepper to taste

Wash the pickled pork and the salt pork. If meat is very salty, soak in cold water 1 hour. Drain off and discard water. Place the meat in a stock pot with cold water to cover generously. (Do not add salt.) Bring to boiling point, reduce heat, and cook slowly 1 hour. Add potatoes, turnips, carrots, leeks (or onions), and sausage. Cover, bring to boiling point, reduce heat and simmer 30 to 40 minutes, or until vegetables are tender. Brown the sausage and add. Add cabbage 15 minutes before cooking time is up. Add salt and pepper. Serve as a main-dish soup with some of the meat in each serving. Makes 6 to 8 servings.

VARIATION

VOSGES-STYLE CABBAGE SOUP

In the recipe for Cabbage Soup, replace the pickled pork with the same quantity of ham.

⚜ SOUP CHEVRIÈRE

2 cups green beans in 1-inch pieces
1 cup sliced carrots
½ cup chopped onion
6 cups beef stock
1 cup milk
salt and ground black pepper to taste
2 tablespoons butter
croutons
chopped chervil or parsley

Cook all the vegetables in 2 cups of the boiling beef stock until tender and rub them through a sieve. Combine remaining stock and milk and add to the vegetable purée. Heat. Add salt and pepper to taste. Add butter. Serve with croutons as a main-dish soup, garnished with chopped chervil or parsley. If desired, replace the green beans with 1 cup cooked dried beans. Makes 6 servings.

⚜ FARM-STYLE SOUP

1 cup shredded carrots
1 cup shredded turnip
½ cup chopped onion
½ cup chopped white part of leeks or scallions
2 tablespoons butter
7 cups beef, veal, or chicken stock
1 cup cooked dried beans
salt and ground black pepper to taste
thin slices toasted rye bread

Cook all the raw vegetables together in butter 3 to 4 minutes. Add stock and cook slowly 30 minutes or until vegetables are tender. Add cooked beans and cook 5 minutes. Season with salt and pepper. Serve over thin slices of rye toast as a main-dish soup. Makes 8 servings.

⚜ GARLIC SOUP BONNE FEMME

2 leeks or 3 scallions, sliced thin
3 cloves garlic, crushed
olive oil or salad oil
2 cups peeled, seeded, diced tomatoes
1½ cups diced potatoes
1/16 teaspoon crumbled saffron
5 cups boiling water
salt and ground black pepper to taste
sliced French bread
grated Cheddar or Parmesan cheese

Cook leeks or scallions with crushed garlic in hot oil until tender. Add vegetables, saffron, and water. Cover and cook slowly until vegetables are tender. Add salt and black pepper. Brush bread slices with oil, sprinkle with cheese, and toast in a very hot oven until golden brown. Serve the soup as a main dish with the toasted bread. Makes 6 to 8 servings.

⚜ SOUP MARAÎCHÈRE

1 cup chopped onions
1 cup sliced celery
½ cup diced turnip
½ cup diced potato
3 tablespoons butter
6 cups boiling stock
½ cup fine noodles or spaghetti, broken into 2-inch pieces
2 cups shredded cabbage
1 cup each shredded spinach and lettuce
½ cup shredded sorrel (sourgrass), if available
1¾ cups milk
salt and ground black pepper
chopped chives or chervil

Cook the first 4 vegetables in the butter in a covered saucepan over low heat until they are about half done. Add stock and noodles or spaghetti. Cover and cook until vegetables and pasta are tender. Add remaining vegetables. Cover and cook 5 minutes. Stir in milk, salt, and pepper. Heat. Serve as a main-dish soup, garnished with chopped chives or chervil. Makes 8 servings.

⚜ ONION SOUP WITH CHEESE

4 large onions
3 tablespoons butter
1 tablespoon flour
2 quarts brown stock
salt and ground black pepper
6 to 8 thin slices French bread
softened butter
6 to 8 thin slices Gruyère cheese

Peel and slice onions and sauté in 3 tablespoons butter until they are soft and golden but not browned. Add flour; stir and cook 1 minute. Add stock and simmer 10 to 15 minutes. Stir in salt and pepper to taste. Spread French bread with softened butter and cover each slice with a slice of cheese. Toast under the broiler until cheese is melted. Use individual soup bowls with covers. Place 1 slice in each and pour the hot soup over it. Cover and let stand 5 or 6 minutes before serving. Makes 6 to 8 servings.

VARIATION

ONION SOUP "GRATINÉE"

Make the preceding recipe with 1 additional tablespoon flour. Pour the soup into an ovenproof tureen, sprinkle generously with grated Gruyère or Parmesan cheese, and place the tureen in a preheated very hot oven (450° F.) until cheese melts. Sprinkle with plenty of ground black pepper. Place a slice of toasted French bread with Gruyère cheese in each soup plate, pour soup over it, and serve at once. Makes 6 to 8 servings.

⚜ PISTOU SOUP

Pistou soup is made of various vegetables and vermicelli, with a binding agent of egg, oil, pounded garlic and herbs, and thick tomato purée.

1 cup diced onion
white part of 1 leek or scallion, sliced
2 tablespoons butter
1 cup green beans cut into ½-inch pieces
1 cup diced potatoes
1½ cups diced tomatoes or 1 cup canned tomatoes
6 cups beef stock
½ cup vermicelli, broken into 1-inch pieces
salt and ground black pepper to taste
2 cloves garlic
2 teaspoons chopped fresh or ½ teaspoon dried basil
1 teaspoon each chopped fresh or ¼ teaspoon each dried thyme and sage
2 egg yolks
¼ cup olive oil or salad oil
2 tablespoons tomato purée
½ cup grated Cheddar or Gruyère cheese

Cook onion and leeks in butter until they are transparent. Add vegetables and stock. Cover and bring to boiling point. Reduce heat and cook 30 minutes or until vegetables are soft. Add vermicelli after 15 minutes. Season with salt and pepper. Pound garlic with herbs. Add egg yolks. Gradually beat in oil as in making mayonnaise. Add tomato purée slowly, beating constantly. Put this mixture in a soup tureen, and stir in soup gradually to prevent cooking the egg yolks. Sprinkle with grated cheese. Serve as a main-dish soup. Makes 6 to 8 servings.

⚜ PUMPKIN SOUP

1 tablespoon finely chopped onion
1 tablespoon butter
1½ cups mashed cooked pumpkin
4 cups hot chicken stock
1½ tablespoons flour
1½ teaspoons salt
¼ teaspoon ground ginger
⅛ teaspoon ground mace
1½ cups top milk or light cream
2 large eggs, beaten
chopped chives or parsley

Sauté onion in butter until onion is soft, about 2 minutes, and mix with pumpkin in the top of a double boiler or saucepan. Blend flour with spices and mix with ⅓ cup of the milk or cream until smooth. Stir into the pumpkin mixture.

Combine remaining milk or cream with the beaten eggs and add to the pumpkin. Cook, stirring frequently, over hot water or low heat 5 to 10 minutes or until hot. Serve hot, garnished with chopped chives or parsley. Makes 6 servings.

⚜ POTAGE THOURIN

Thourin soup is served in all parts of France but is especially favored in the southern part of the country.

3 cups finely chopped onion
3 tablespoons butter
2 tablespoons flour
4 cups milk
4 large egg yolks
1 cup heavy cream
salt and ground black pepper to taste
French bread

Cook onions in butter, stirring until they are soft and golden, but not brown. Remove from heat and blend in flour. Stir and cook 1 minute. Add milk. Mix well and simmer 25 minutes, stirring frequently, never allowing the milk to boil. Blend egg yolks with ¼ cup of the cream, and add to the soup. Stir and simmer 5 minutes. Add remaining cream, salt, and ground black pepper. Heat. Serve with thinly sliced French bread toasted in the oven. Makes 6 servings.

SOUPS FROM OTHER COUNTRIES

⚜ BORSCH (*Ukrainian Beet Soup*)

2 medium-sized carrots
6 medium-sized beets
1 rib of celery
1 parsley root
white part of 2 leeks
3 tablespoons fat skimmed from bouillon, or 3 tablespoons butter
2 quarts cold water
1½ pounds beef brisket
½ pound lean salt pork
6 whole peppercorns
1 bay leaf
2 teaspoons salt
2 cups shredded cabbage
1 teaspoon vinegar
chopped fresh dill
thick sour cream

Peel carrots and beets and cut both carrots and 4 of the beets into julienne strips. Slice celery, parsley root, and leeks thinly. Heat the vegetables in bouillon fat or butter. Mix well. Add water, beef, peppercorns, bay leaf, and salt. Cover, bring to boiling point, reduce heat, and simmer 1½ to 2 hours, or until meat is tender. Remove meat, slice, and put into a soup tureen. Add cabbage to the soup and cook 10 to 12 minutes. Grate the 2 remaining beets and press in cheesecloth to squeeze out all the juice. Add vinegar to beet juice and mix with the soup. Pour soup in the tureen over the meat. Sprinkle with chopped dill. Serve with sour cream in a sauceboat. A browned duck is sometimes cooked with this soup. Borsch may also be served cold. Makes 8 servings.

⚜ BOTVINIA (*Russian Cold Soup*)

1 cup chopped sorrel (sourgrass), if available
3 cups each finely shredded spinach and young tender beet tops
salt
5 cups light beer or dry white wine
½ teaspoon sugar
salt and ground black pepper to taste
1 cup julienne strips raw peeled cucumber
chopped parsley

Cook sorrel (if available), spinach, and beet tops with ¼ teaspoon salt, and with only the water that clings to the leaves, in a covered saucepan until vegetables are wilted and soft. Put through a sieve, pushing as much of the vegetables through as possible. Add beer or wine, and season with sugar, salt, and pepper. Chill. Put 2 tablespoons cucumber in each soup bowl, and pour chilled soup over it. If desired, place 2 ice cubes in each serving. Sprinkle with chopped parsley. This soup is usually accompanied by a small piece of salmon or sturgeon, without skin or bone, served in a separate dish with a little grated horseradish mixed with vinegar. Makes 6 servings.

⚜ ENGLISH CHICKEN BROTH

4-pound chicken
6 cups cold water
2 teaspoons salt
1 rib celery, sliced
white part of 2 leeks, sliced
4 whole peppercorns
2 cups diced carrots
1 cup diced turnips
¼ cup rice

Place chicken, water, and salt in a 6-quart saucepan. Cover. Slowly bring to boiling point and simmer 1½ hours, or until chicken is tender, adding vegetables and rice after 1 hour. Lift chicken from the stock pot, remove skin, cut meat into pieces, and put into the soup bowls. Adjust seasonings in the soup, and pour into the bowls. Serve hot. Makes 6 servings.

CHICKEN GIBLET SOUP (*English*)

4 each chicken necks and gizzards
8 chicken wings
4 tablespoons butter
¼ cup flour
6 cups rich chicken stock
1 small carrot, diced
½ cup chopped onion
1 rib celery, sliced
1 cup cooked rice
salt and ground black pepper to taste

Cut chicken necks and gizzards in half and disjoint the wings. Brown the pieces lightly in butter. Remove from heat and sprinkle flour lightly over chicken, then brown lightly. Add stock, carrots, and onion. Cover and simmer 1 hour. Cook celery separately in water. To serve, put chicken in a tureen with celery and cooked rice. Season the soup stock with salt and pepper. Pour into the tureen over the chicken, celery, and rice. Makes 6 servings.

COCKALEEKIE (*Scottish*)

4 cups sliced white part of leeks
2 cups boiling water
1½ teaspoons salt
2 tablespoons butter or chicken fat
2 cups rich chicken stock
2½ cups boiling water
4 peppercorns
2 cups cooked white chicken meat cut in thin strips
18 dried prunes, soaked and cooked until tender in stock

Cook leeks in boiling water with salt 5 minutes, or until leeks are soft. Add chicken stock, water, and peppercorns. Cover and bring to boiling point. Add chicken. Adjust seasonings. Serve hot, with 3 prunes added to each serving. Makes 6 servings.

CREOLE CHICKEN GUMBO SOUP (*American*)

3-pound chicken
3 tablespoons salad oil
1 cup sliced onion
2 cups sliced okra (fresh, frozen, or canned)
3 cups canned tomatoes
5 cups water
2 teaspoons salt
½ teaspoon sugar
½ teaspoon ground thyme
½ teaspoon ground black pepper
1 cup cooked rice

Cut chicken into frying-size pieces and brown lightly in oil. Remove chicken from the skillet. Cook and stir onion and okra in the hot oil remaining in the skillet until onion is transparent. Add tomatoes and water. Return chicken to the skillet. Add salt and sugar. Cover and cook 30 to 40 minutes or until chicken is tender. Add thyme 5 minutes before cooking time is up. Adjust salt and add black pepper and rice. Serve hot as a main-dish soup. Makes 6 servings.

⚜ GAZPACHO ANDALUZ (*Spanish Cold Soup*)

4 large tomatoes
1 cucumber, sliced
1 medium-sized onion, sliced
1 medium-sized sweet green pepper, sliced
2 cloves garlic
3 eggs, beaten
dash cayenne
¼ cup vinegar
½ cup olive oil
1 cup thick tomato juice
salt and ground black pepper to taste
1 cup bread cubes
1 cup diced cucumber
¾ cup diced green sweet pepper
½ cup chopped onion
chopped parsley

Put the tomatoes, sliced cucumber, onion, green pepper, and 1 clove garlic through a food mill, or purée them, a little at a time, in an electric blender. Add beaten eggs, cayenne, vinegar, ¼ cup oil, tomato juice, salt, and pepper. Mix well and chill. Crush remaining clove garlic, add to remaining ¼ cup oil, and brown the bread cubes in this oil. Add to the soup along with diced cucumber, diced green pepper, and chopped onion just before serving. Sprinkle chopped parsley on each serving. Makes 8 servings.

⚜ MAGYAR GULYAS LEVES (*Hungarian Goulash Soup*)

1 pound lean shoulder of beef, cut into 1-inch pieces
1 cup sliced onion
2 tablespoons lard or other shortening
1 teaspoon salt
2 tablespoons caraway seed, crushed
2 cups diced fresh tomatoes or 1½ cups canned tomatoes
2 cups diced sweet green pepper
2 cups diced potatoes
5 cups water
1 teaspoon marjoram leaves
½ teaspoon ground black pepper
¼ pound noodles, cooked

Cook beef and onions in lard or shortening, until meat begins to brown. Add salt and caraway seed. Cover and cook the mixture 20 minutes in its own juice. Add tomatoes and peppers with about ¼ cup water. Cover and cook until meat is three-quarters done, adding a little water to the pot as it is needed to prevent the mixture from cooking too dry. Add potatoes and 5 cups water. Cover and cook until potatoes and meat are done—about 30 minutes. Adjust salt. Add marjoram and black pepper. Heat 1 to 2 minutes. Add noodles and serve as a main-dish soup. Makes 6 servings.

⚜ MILLE-FANTI (*Italian Bread Soup*)

- 4 cups fresh breadcrumbs
- 1 cup grated Parmesan cheese
- 3 eggs, beaten
- 5 cups rich bouillon
- salt and ground black pepper to taste
- ground nutmeg

Combine breadcrumbs and cheese. Blend in eggs. Stir in bouillon. Beat well with a wire whisk to prevent lumping. Cook slowly 7 to 8 minutes, stirring frequently. Add salt and pepper. Sprinkle a dash of nutmeg over each serving. Makes 6 servings.

⚜ MINESTRONE (*Italian Vegetable Soup*)

- ¼ pound lean salt pork, diced
- 1 quart rich beef stock
- 1 cup each diced potatoes, carrots, and turnips
- ¼ cup raw rice
- 1 cup sliced onion
- ½ cup each green peas and lima beans
- ¼ small head cabbage, shredded
- ¼ pound spinach, shredded
- white part of 1 leek or scallion, shredded
- ½ cup diced celery
- 1 cup sliced zucchini
- 4 medium-sized fresh tomatoes, diced, or 3 cups canned tomatoes
- 2 tablespoons tomato paste
- 2 tablespoons chopped parsley
- ½ teaspoon each sage and ground black pepper
- salt to taste
- grated Parmesan cheese

Cook salt pork in water to cover in a covered saucepan 30 minutes. Add stock and bring to boiling point. Add potatoes, carrots, turnips, and rice. Cover and cook 10 minutes. Add remaining ingredients. Slowly bring to boiling point and cook until soup is very thick and vegetables are tender. Serve as a main-dish soup. Sprinkle with grated Parmesan cheese. Makes 8 servings.

⚜ MULLIGATAWNY SOUP (*Indian*)

- 8 pounds chicken necks and backs
- 1 quart cold water
- 2 teaspoons salt
- ½ cup each sliced mushroom stems, celery, and carrots
- 2 tablespoons chopped parsley
- 1 small clove garlic, quartered
- ½ cup chopped onion
- 1 tablespoon curry powder
- 2 tablespoons butter
- 4 teaspoons flour
- ½ cup heavy cream
- 1 cup cooked rice

Put the chicken necks and backs with water, salt, vegetables, and garlic into a large stock pot, cover, and slowly bring to boiling point. Reduce heat and simmer 1 hour. Remove chicken backs and necks from the stock. Strain stock, rubbing as much of the vegetables through as possible, and set aside. Cook onion and curry powder in butter until onion is transparent. Remove from heat and stir in flour. Stir and cook 1 minute. Add stock, mix well, and cook 7 to 8 minutes. Strain stock again through a fine sieve. Add cream and heat thoroughly. Pick chicken from bones and add a little to each soup bowl, along with 2 tablespoons cooked rice. Pour soup into bowls. Serve hot. Makes 6 servings.

⚜ OLLA-PODRIDA (*Spanish Stock Pot*)

1 cup chick peas
3 cups cold water
2 pounds brisket of beef
1 pound shoulder of lamb or mutton stew meat
¼ pound lean salt pork
2 pigs' feet
1 ham bone or ½ pound raw ham
3 quarts cold water
2 teaspoons salt
½ pound Chorizos (Spanish garlic sausage)
3-pound chicken
1 cup sliced carrots
1 cup sliced white part of leeks or scallions
2 cups diced potatoes
2 cups shredded cabbage
½ cup sliced onion
3 cloves garlic
bouquet garni
ground black pepper
2 cups shredded lettuce

Wash chick peas and soak overnight in cold water, in the refrigerator. Combine chick peas, beef, lamb or mutton, salt pork, pigs' feet, and ham bone or ham with cold water and salt. Cover and bring to boiling point. Reduce heat and simmer 2 hours. Add sausage and chicken. Cook, covered, 30 minutes. Add all vegetables except lettuce and cook slowly 30 minutes. Remove all meat and chicken from the pot, and keep warm in a little stock. Add black pepper to the stock and adjust the salt. Add lettuce and cook 1 to 2 minutes. Do not strain. Serve soup in a tureen. Put meat and chicken on a platter and pass it to let each person serve himself. Makes 8 to 10 servings.

⚜ ENGLISH OXTAIL SOUP

2½ pounds oxtail
beef suet
1 cup sliced onion
2 cups sliced carrots
2 tablespoons flour
2 quarts beef bouillon or stock
1 cup sliced white part of leeks or scallions
½ teaspoon each, dried basil, marjoram, rosemary, and sage
8 tablespoons port

Cut oxtail into 2-inch pieces. Brown the pieces in suet, along with onion and carrots. Sprinkle with flour. Stir and cook until flour has browned. Add bouillon or stock and leeks or scallions. Cover and simmer 2 hours. Strain the soup. (It should be gelatinous and full-bodied.) Steep all the herbs together 10 minutes in 1 cup boiling bouillon or stock from the pot. Strain into the soup. Put a few pieces of oxtail in each soup bowl and pour soup over them. Add 1 tablespoon port to each serving. Makes 8 servings.

⚜ ARAN SCALLOP SOUP (*Irish*)

2 slices lean bacon
1 cup thinly sliced potatoes
2 tablespoons butter
6 scallops
hot water to barely cover scallops
2½ cups fish stock
1 tablespoon each chopped parsley and fresh thyme
½ cup beef marrow
2 cups diced fresh tomatoes or 1½ cups canned tomatoes
salt and ground black pepper to taste
½ cup cream
2 tablespoons rusk crumbs
dash of ground mace

Cook bacon until crisp. Remove from the drippings and reserve for later use. Add potatoes and butter to bacon drippings. Blanch scallops in hot water over low heat until they are flaky. Drain off the scallop stock and add it to the potatoes along with fish stock. Add herbs. Cover and cook slowly until potatoes are tender, 15 to 20 minutes. Dice scallops and add, along with the marrow and tomatoes. Cover and cook slowly another 15 minutes, never allowing the soup to boil. Add salt and pepper. Stir in cream and rusk crumbs just before serving. Sprinkle with ground mace. Crumble the reserved bacon and sprinkle over the top. Makes 6 servings.

⚜ SCHTCHI RUSSKI (*Russian Cabbage Soup*)

1 cup each sliced onion, carrots, white part of leeks or scallions
1 cup diced celery
1 bay leaf
6 whole peppercorns
5 cups beef stock
3 cups sliced cabbage
salt and ground black pepper to taste
1 pound boiled brisket, cut into cubes
sour cream

Place onions, carrots, leeks or scallions, celery, bay leaf, peppercorns, and stock in an 8-quart saucepan. Cover, slowly bring to boiling point, and cook gently 20 minutes. Add cabbage and cook 10 to 12 minutes. Add salt and black pepper. Put some beef cubes in each soup bowl and pour the hot soup over them. Serve with sour cream in a sauceboat. Makes 6 servings.

⚜ SCOTCH BROTH

1 pound lean lamb or mutton stew meat
2 quarts mutton stock
bouquet garni
½ cup pearl barley
1 cup each diced carrots, turnips, celery, and onion
2 cups shredded cabbage
salt and ground black pepper to taste
chopped parsley

Cut meat into 1-inch cubes and place in an 8-quart saucepan with stock and bouquet garni. Cover, bring to boiling point, and skim. Sprinkle in the barley. Simmer, covered, 1½ hours. Add carrots, turnips, celery, onions, and parsley. Cover and cook 30 minutes. Add cabbage, cover, and cook 10 to 12 minutes. Add salt and pepper. Serve hot as a main-dish soup. Garnish with chopped parsley. Makes 8 to 10 servings.

⚜ STRACCIATELLA ALLA ROMANA (*Italian Consommé with Eggs*)

2 large eggs, beaten
3 tablespoons fine, soft breadcrumbs
3 tablespoons grated Parmesan cheese
1 teaspoon grated lemon rind
3 cups hot bouillon
salt and ground black pepper

Combine eggs, bread crumbs, cheese, and lemon rind. Mix well. Gradually beat in hot bouillon and bring to boiling point, stirring constantly. Reduce heat and cook slowly until soup thickens slightly. (Do not boil.) Serve hot with salt and black pepper to taste. Makes 3 servings.

⚜ ZUPPA ALLA PAVESE (*Italian Consommé Pavia Style*)

For each serving, fry a slice of bread in oil or butter, and place it in an oven-proof bowl. Break 1 raw egg over the bread. Pour 1 cup hot, well-seasoned, concentrated consommé over the egg. Sprinkle with grated Parmesan cheese. Cook in a preheated hot oven (400° F.) only until egg is set, 5 to 10 minutes. Serve at once.

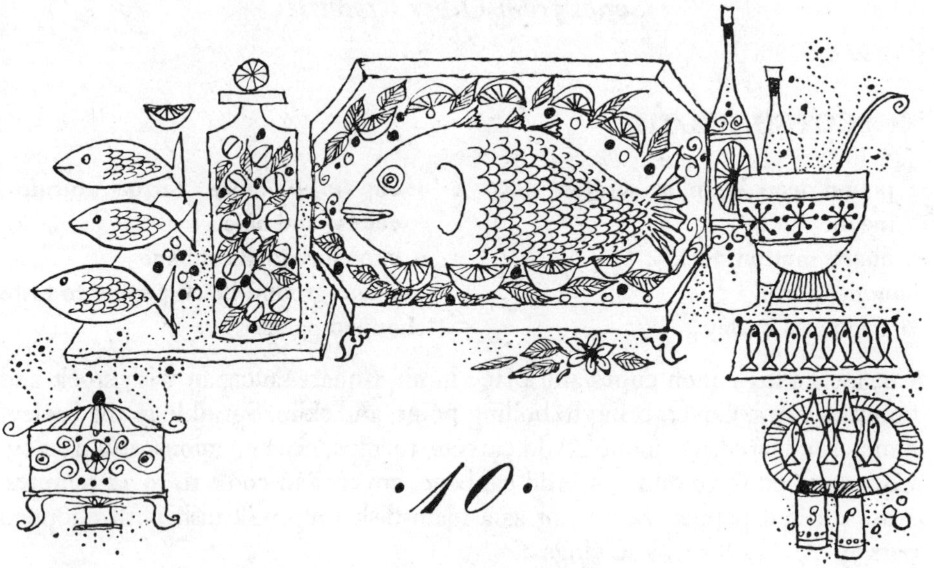

·10·

FISH

Freshwater fish have always been caught for food in lakes and rivers, and men have gone down to the sea in ships in search of saltwater fish for thousands of years. The process of drying, salting, and smoking marine fish to preserve it has long been known, and since the beginning of the nineteenth century the canning process has enabled people in inland cities to consume appreciable quantities of canned salmon, sardines, and other fish. The common use of fresh saltwater fish at a distance from the sea, however, is very recent. Only with the development of refrigeration for fishing boats, railway cars, and trucks has it become, as it is today, an important article of diet in areas far from the oceans. While the variety of freshwater fish is not so great, some of the most delicious fish come from rivers and lakes, and since they can usually be bought alive, their freshness is assured.

Fish offers the same high quality of protein as does meat, and in about the same proportions. Its fat content in most cases is considerably lower than that of meat; while different kinds of fish differ in amount of fat, practically all have less fat than medium beef. The white-meat fish, such as cod, haddock, and halibut, have a fat content ranging from less than 2 per cent to 5 per cent or less. Oily, darker-meat fish, such as salmon, turbot, mackerel, etc., can contain up to 20 per cent fat, thereby resembling beef. The fat content of fish varies with the season, being lowest in the spring at spawning time. Fish has a higher percentage of mineral matter than does meat, and shellfish contains almost twice as much as other kinds of fish. Fish is one of our very few sources of iodine, besides containing copper, iron, and calcium, in amounts varying considerably with the variety of fish. Vitamins A and D are found in fish-liver oils and in the flesh of fat fish. Salmon contains vitamin G. Fish does not appear to contain significant amounts of vitamin C.

Even when refrigerated, fish should not be kept more than 24 hours. Its delicate structure, together with the activity of its enzymes, causes it to spoil quickly. It should be kept tightly covered to prevent its odor from contaminating other foods.

When selecting fresh fish in the market, the following points should be considered:

The eyes should be clear, bright, and bulging.

The gills should be free from odors or slime, and reddish-brown in color.

The scales should be bright-colored, with characteristic sheen, and should adhere tightly to the skin.

The flesh should be firm and elastic; it should spring back when pressed and not separate from the bones.

The odor should be fresh and in no way objectionable.

Frozen fish must be solidly frozen; it should be kept at a constant temperature of 0°F. Before cooking, defrost in the refrigerator or under cold running water.

Amount to buy. Allow ½ pound of dressed fish per person—this means fish that has been scaled and eviscerated and has usually had the head, tail, and fins removed. If fish is purchased in steaks, fillets, or sticks, allow ⅓ pound per serving. With whole fish, allow about 1 pound per serving, or 5 pounds for 6 people, of fish as it comes from the water. Before whole fish is cooked, it must be scaled and eviscerated. If desired, the head and fins may be removed and the fish cut into serving-size portions. Fish to be baked is left whole. Very small fish, such as smelts, are usually cooked with only the entrails removed.

For the preparation of various kinds of fish for cooking, see Culinary Techniques in Pictures.

BASIC METHODS OF COOKING FISH

⚜ FISH STOCK

2 tablespoons (¼ stick) butter
4 pounds fish head bones, and fins
2 cloves of garlic
1 cup each sliced onion, carrots, and scallions or leeks
2 ribs celery, cut into quarters
1 bay leaf
¼ teaspoon peppercorns
2 teaspoons salt
1 teaspoon dried thyme leaves

Melt butter in a large soup kettle. Wash fish heads, bones and fins, and add to the kettle along with water to cover, and all remaining ingredients except thyme. Bring to boiling point, reduce heat, and simmer, with cover ajar, for 30 minutes. Strain. This stock will keep in the refrigerator 1 week. If desired, freeze it in containers and defrost it as needed. Makes 3 quarts stock. (See also page 134.)

⚜ BROILED FISH (*Grilled Fish*)

This method is suitable for fresh (and defrosted-frozen) fish fillets, fish steaks, and small whole fish.

Cut the fish into serving-size pieces. Small fish such as whiting and butterfish, should be split and left whole. Sprinkle both sides with salt and ground black pepper. Place fish on a preheated greased broiler rack. Brush with melted butter, using 4 tablespoons for each 2 pounds fish. Sprinkle with lemon juice. Place in the broiler 4 inches from the source of heat. Broil 5 to 8 minutes. Turn carefully, brush the other side with butter, sprinkle with lemon juice, and broil 5 to 8 minutes or until fish is flaky. Transfer carefully to a platter, garnish, and serve immediately. Makes 6 servings.

⚜ PAN-FRIED FISH (*À la Meunière*)

2 pounds dressed fish
1 tablespoon salt
¼ teaspoon ground black pepper
1 large egg, lightly beaten
⅓ cup milk
½ cup cornmeal, flour, fine dry breadcrumbs, or cracker crumbs
2 tablespoons each butter and shortening
lemon juice

Cut fish into serving-size pieces. Rub both sides with salt and pepper. Combine egg and milk, dip fish into the mixture, then roll it in flour, cornmeal, breadcrumbs or cracker crumbs, or pancake mix. Fry in hot butter and shortening over moderate heat, turning carefully to brown both sides, until fish has browned and is flaky. Cooking time is about 10 minutes, depending upon the thickness of the fish. Drain on paper towels and serve immediately, sprinkled with lemon juice. Makes 6 servings.

⚜ OVEN-FRIED FISH

2 pounds fish fillets or steaks
1½ teaspoons salt
¼ teaspoon ground black pepper
milk
flour or fine dry breadcrumbs
¼ cup (½ stick) butter, melted

Cut fish into serving-size pieces. Add salt and pepper to the milk and mix well. Dip the fish into the milk and then roll it in flour or breadcrumbs. Place fish in a well-buttered baking pan. Spoon melted butter over the fish. Place pan on the top rack of preheated very hot oven (500° F.). Bake 10 to 12 minutes or until the fish flakes when tested with a fork. Serve at once on a warm platter, plain, or with a sauce. Makes 6 servings.

⚜ DEEP-FAT-FRIED FISH

2 pounds fillets, steaks, or pan-dressed fish
1 teaspoon salt
¼ teaspoon ground black pepper
1 egg, beaten lightly with 1 tablespoon water or milk
1 cup fine dry breadcrumbs or cracker crumbs or batter

Cut fish into serving-size pieces. Sprinkle both sides with salt and pepper. Dip fish into the beaten egg and then roll in crumbs or dip in batter. Place a layer of fish in a frying basket, lower basket into deep fat preheated to 375° F., and fry 3 to 6 minutes or until fish is golden brown. Remove fish from fat and drain on paper towels. Serve immediately. Makes 6 servings.

BATTER FOR FRYING FISH

1 large egg
½ teaspoon salt
½ cup milk
½ cup sifted all-purpose flour

Beat egg, salt, and milk together. Add flour all at one time, mix, and beat until smooth. Use as a coating for fish, shellfish, chicken, vegetables, etc., for pan frying, or deep-fat frying. Makes enough batter for 6 servings.

⚜ POACHED FISH

2 pounds fish fillets or steaks
2 quarts boiling fish stock, or 2 quarts boiling water with 3 tablespoons salt

Cut fish into serving-size pieces. Place in a wire basket (deep-fat-frying basket), or place on a plate and tie plate in a piece of cheesecloth. Lower the fish into the boiling stock, or salted water, reduce heat, and simmer (never boil) 10 minutes, or until fish is flaky when tested with a fork. Carefully remove fish to a warm platter. Garnish attractively with parsley or watercress, lemon, tomato or unpeeled cucumber slices. Serve with Herb Butter; Curry or Tarragon Sauce; or Hollandaise, Béarnaise, Rémoulade, or Tartare Sauce. Makes 6 servings.

⚜ STEAMED FISH

3½ to 4 pounds dressed whole fish, or 2 pounds fish steaks or fillets
salt
ground black pepper
water

Sprinkle fish with salt and pepper. Wrap in a piece of cheesecloth and tie the ends. Place a rack or trivet in a Dutch oven or saucepan. Pour in hot water to level of the rack. Place fish on the rack. Cover saucepan or Dutch oven tightly. Steam whole fish 30 minutes, steaks or fillets 12 minutes, or until fish flakes when tested with a fork. Open cheesecloth and carefully transfer fish to a warm platter. Remove skin and bones, if desired. Serve with Egg Sauce, Herb Butter, or Chivry Sauce. Makes 6 servings.

⚜ BAKED FISH

3- to 4-pound fish, dressed
1½ teaspoons salt
¼ teaspoon ground black pepper
¼ cup (½ stick) butter, melted
bacon (optional)

Rub a dressed fish inside and out with salt and pepper. Place fish in a buttered baking pan. Brush with melted butter and lay 1 to 2 slices of bacon over the top, if desired. Bake in a preheated moderate oven (350° F.) 40 to 50 minutes, or until fish is flaky when tested with a fork. If fish seems dry while baking, baste with melted butter or pan drippings. Serve immediately, plain, or with Herb Butter or Hollandaise, Béarnaise, Tartare, or Chivry Sauce. Makes 6 servings.

⚜ PLANKED FISH

Fish suitable for baking or broiling may be planked. An advantage of this method of preparation is that the cooked fish may be brought to the table and served without transferring it to a platter. The plank, made from a piece of well-seasoned ash, hickory, or oak about 1½ inches thick, should be grooved around the edge and have several grooves cut into the surface to hold the juices from the fish or the basting liquor. These planks are available in housewares departments of hardware and department stores. If you are unable to obtain a plank, an oven-proof platter may be used. Put the plank in a cold oven and preheat it with the oven. Remove the plank and oil it thoroughly, then place the fish on it. Proceed as directed in the recipe you plan to use.

3- to 4-pound dressed fish
1½ teaspoons salt
¼ teaspoon ground black pepper
¼ cup (½ stick) butter, melted
seasoned Duchess Potatoes
seasoned cooked vegetables (peas, carrots, cauliflower, onions, tomatoes, etc.)

Rinse the fish and wipe dry. Sprinkle inside and out with salt and pepper. Brush with melted butter. Place on a hot oiled plank or oven-proof platter. Bake in a preheated hot oven (350° F.) until the fish flakes when tested with a fork. Remove from oven and quickly pipe a border of Duchess Potatoes around the fish. Brown potatoes lightly under broiler heat. Remove from broiler and arrange two or more kinds of cooked vegetables around the fish. Garnish with parsley, radishes, etc. Serve at once from the plank. Makes 6 servings.

BASS (*Bar*)

There are many varieties of bass, both marine and freshwater. It is a delicately flavored fish, which lends itself to numerous methods of preparation—poaching, broiling, frying, and baking whole, with or without a stuffing.

⚜ POACHED BASS WITH CHIVRY SAUCE

Allow 2 pounds boned fish, or 3½ to 4 pounds undressed fish, for 6 servings. Cut fish into serving-size pieces, or, if they are very small, remove heads and leave fish whole. Poach according to recipe for Poached Fish. Remove fish from poaching liquid, drain, and arrange on a warm platter. Garnish with parsley. Serve with Chivry Sauce and boiled potatoes.

⚜ BAKED BASS

Allow 3½ to 4 pounds for 6 servings. Bake according to recipe for Baked Fish. Serve with Herb Butter or a sauce. (See illustration, page 440.)

⚜ BASS BAKED IN FOIL (*Bar en Papillote*)

This is an American version of Daurade en Papillote (see illustration, page 439). Daurade is not an American fish and the greased paper used by French cooks for this type of dish is generally replaced in America by foil.

½ pound sliced mushrooms
1 teaspoon chopped shallot or onion
4 tablespoons (½ stick) butter
1 cup thick cooked tomatoes
salt
ground black pepper
¼ teaspoon sugar
5-pound dressed striped bass
2 tablespoons oil
¼ cup dry white wine
1 tablespoon lemon juice
18 black olives
¾ pound ready-to-cook shellfish

Cook mushrooms and shallot or onion in 2 tablespoons of the butter until all the liquid has evaporated. Add tomatoes, salt and pepper to taste, and sugar. Cook 2 to 3 minutes, stirring constantly. Sprinkle fish with salt and pepper. Heat remaining 2 tablespoons butter and the oil in a long baking pan, add fish, and cook in a preheated moderate oven (375° F.) 20 minutes or until fish is golden. Spread the mushroom-tomato mixture over a long piece of foil the length and width of the fish. Cook the remaining ingredients together over low heat 5 minutes and spoon the mixture over the fish. Bring both ends of the foil up over the fish and make a lengthwise drugstore fold over it. Turn up the ends, folding them 3 times. Place fish on a baking sheet and cook in a preheated hot oven (400° F.) 10 to 12 minutes or until the steam has inflated the foil. Transfer the foil-wrapped fish to a platter and serve it in the foil, turning it back. Makes 6 servings.

BRILL (*Barbue*)

Brill is a flat sea fish similar in shape to turbot, but smaller and more elongated. It is more abundant in European seas than in the Atlantic Ocean. However, the Atlantic brill is of greater gastronomical value. The flesh is very delicate, light, and moist, resembling sole. It may be poached, baked, boned and stuffed, fried, or used in combination with other fish and shellfish.

⚜ BRILL THEODORA

Cook 3½ pounds dressed brill in 1½ cups dry white wine as directed for Brill in White Wine. Mix together 3 tablespoons each butter and flour to make a roux. Strain the wine in which fish was cooked into a saucepan. Add the roux and cook until of desired sauce consistency. Season to taste with salt and ground white pepper. Mix ⅓ cup of this sauce with 1 tablespoon tomato purée. Transfer fish to a warm platter, coat with wine sauce, and decorate in lattice pattern with the tomato sauce. Garnish with shrimp croquettes. Makes 6 servings.

⚜ BRILL IN WHITE WINE

3½ to 4 pounds dressed brill
salt
1 small onion, thinly sliced
bouquet garni
½ cup dry white wine
White Wine Sauce

Rub brill inside and out with salt. Place in a well-buttered baking dish with onion and bouquet garni, and pour wine over it. Cover and bake in a preheated moderate oven (350° F.) 30 minutes or until fish flakes when tested with a fork. Baste two or three times with the wine in the dish. Carefully transfer fish to a warm platter. Serve with White Wine Sauce, using the wine in which fish was cooked as part of the liquid for the sauce. Makes 6 servings.

⚜ FILLETS OF BRILL CHAUCHAT

2½ pounds brill fillets
salt
1½ cups fish stock
2 tablespoons each flour and butter
ground white pepper to taste
2 egg yolks
2 tablespoons heavy cream or cold fish stock
6 servings boiled potatoes
2 tablespoons soft breadcrumbs
2 tablespoons butter, melted

Rub both sides of fish with salt and place it in a well-buttered baking dish. Add fish stock. Cover and bake in a preheated moderate oven (350° F.) 20 minutes or until fish flakes when tested with a fork. Blend flour with butter to make a roux. Strain stock in a saucepan, add roux, stir, and cook until the mixture begins to thicken. Season to taste with salt and pepper. Mix egg yolks with cream or stock and add to the sauce. Stir and cook ½ minute over low heat. Carefully transfer fish to a warm platter and arrange potatoes around it. Sprinkle fish and potatoes with cheese, coat with sauce, sprinkle with cheese again, then with breadcrumbs and melted butter. Brown in a very hot oven (450° to 500° F.). Serve at once. Makes 6 servings.

CARP (*Carpe*)

This freshwater fish is of Asiatic origin and was first introduced in Europe in the seventeenth century and in the United States in 1875. It is now widely distributed. In France carp weighing up to 16 pounds are found; in the United States the average market weight is from 2 to 7 pounds. The same cooking methods are suitable for all varieties.

⚜ DEEP-FAT-FRIED CARP WITH RÉMOULADE SAUCE

3 pounds dressed carp
salt
ground black pepper
flour
1 large egg beaten with 1 tablespoon water
fine dry breadcrumbs
fried parsley
lemon slices
¾ cup Rémoulade Sauce

Split carp lengthwise and remove as many of the bones as possible. Rub fish lightly with salt and pepper. Roll in flour and dip in beaten egg and then in crumbs. Fry until browned in deep fat preheated to 375° F. Drain on paper towels. Serve on a warmed platter garnished with fried parsley and lemon slices. Pass Rémoulade Sauce in a separate dish. Makes 6 servings. Bercy Sauce may be served instead of Rémoulade Sauce.

⚜ CARP POLISH STYLE

3 pounds dressed carp
salt
pepper
4 tablespoons butter
1 cup sliced onions
2 sprigs parsley
1 bay leaf
½ teaspoon dried or 1½ teaspoons chopped fresh thyme
2 whole cloves
¼ teaspoons coriander seeds
carp roe
1½ cups light ale or beer
¾ cup dry red wine

½ teaspoon sugar
1 tablespoon wine vinegar
3 tablespoons gingerbread or gingersnap crumbs
2 tablespoons each raisins and sliced blanched almonds
6 servings of boiled potatoes

Cut carp into 6 portions and rub lightly with salt and pepper. Set aside. Melt 2 tablespoons of the butter in a skillet. Add onion, herbs, and spices and lay fish and lightly salted roe on top. Add beer, wine, sugar, and vinegar. Bring to boiling point, reduce heat, sprinkle with gingerbread or gingersnap crumbs and cook 10 to 12 minutes, or until the fish flakes when tested with a fork. Transfer fish to a serving platter. Strain the cooking liquor. Add the remaining 2 tablespoons butter and the raisins and almonds. Bring to boiling point. Adjust seasonings and pour the sauce over the fish. Serve with boiled potatoes. Makes 6 servings.

⚜ CARP BAKED IN BEER

6 tablespoons butter
1 cup sliced onions
½ cup diced celery
3 pounds dressed carp
salt
ground black pepper
1 cup light ale or beer
2 stalks parsley
2 tablespoons gingerbread or gingersnap crumbs
carp roe
1 teaspoon lemon juice

Melt 2 tablespoons of the butter in a baking dish, add onion and celery, and mix well. Rub fish lightly with salt and pepper and lay over vegetables. Add beer and parsley. Sprinkle gingerbread or gingersnap crumbs over the top. Cover and cook in a preheated slow oven (325° F.) 30 to 40 minutes or until the fish flakes when tested with a fork. Transfer fish to a warmed platter and keep it warm. Reduce the stock by one-half and strain. Meanwhile, slice carp roe, sprinkle lightly with salt, pepper, and lemon juice, and cook in 2 more tablespoons of the butter over moderately low heat 5 minutes or until done. Arrange the roe around the fish. Add remaining butter to the reduced stock, heat, adjust seasonings, and pour over the fish. Garnish with parsley. Makes 6 servings.

⚜ CARP BAKED IN FOIL (*Carpe en Papillote*)

1 whole carp (6 to 7 pounds)
oil
butter
½ cup dry white wine
12 ounces mixed shellfish (crabmeat, lobster, shrimp)
1 cup thick cooked tomatoes
20 olives
lemon juice to taste
salt and ground black pepper to taste

Make incisions in the fish along the sides to shorten the cooking time. Fry lightly in 1 tablespoon each oil and butter, and then cook 20 minutes in a preheated moderate oven (350° F.). Add wine and cook over low heat until the liquid has reduced to three-fourths its original amount. Add the shellfish, cooked tomatoes, olives, lemon juice, salt, and pepper. Cook in a preheated hot oven (400° F.) 10 minutes. Spread a large square of aluminum foil with butter, place the shellfish in the center, and place the bream or carp on top. Bring the edges of the foil over the top of the fish and fold them over as in making a drugstore fold. Press the foil together at the ends. Place the package in an oiled baking pan and bake in a very hot oven (450° F.) until the package is inflated by the interior steam. Serve at the table in this package. Makes 10 servings.

Fish or meat *en papillote* is baked in a package made by folding oiled or buttered paper around the food and folding the edges to seal it. In America foil is more commonly used (see Bass Baked in Foil).

⚜ CARP QUENELLES SAXONY STYLE

Carp bones, skins, and heads
1 pound boned raw carp
½ teaspoon salt
⅛ teaspoon each ground white pepper and nutmeg
2 unbeaten egg whites
2 cups heavy cream
¾ cup ale or beer
fish stock
¼ cup (½ stick) butter, melted
2 tablespoons gingerbread or gingersnap crumbs
chopped parsley
cooked rice or boiled potatoes

Make stock from carp bones, skins, and heads. Set aside. Put carp through a food chopper, using the finest blade. Add seasonings. Pound and beat the fish vigorously with a wooden spoon, beating in the egg whites. Rub the mixture through a sieve into a bowl and set the bowl in a pan of cracked ice. Gradually beat and pound in cream. Beat vigorously 2 to 3 minutes and set aside. Heat ½ cup of the beer or ale with enough fish stock barely to cover the dumplings. Melt butter in a shallow skillet. Make quenelles, shaping them into ovals with 2 tablespoons. Gently slide them into the buttered skillet, a few at a time. Pour in the hot beer and stock. Bring to boiling point and simmer 5 minutes. (Do not boil.) Soften gingerbread or gingersnap crumbs in remaining ¼ cup beer or ale, add to the poaching sauce and continue cooking the quenelles over low heat 5 more minutes or until done, turning them several times to cook them uniformly. Transfer them to a bowl, cover with the sauce, and sprinkle with chopped parsley. Serve with rice or boiled potatoes. Makes 6 servings.

⚜ CARP ROE DIPLOMAT STYLE

1 pound carp roe
3 tablespoons butter
1 teaspoon lemon juice
½ teaspoon salt
6 large croustades or puff-paste cases
1 cup Nantua Sauce
6 truffle slices or 6 small sautéed mushroom caps

Carp roe is a much-esteemed delicacy. First soak the roe in cold water for 1 hour. Melt butter in a skillet; add lemon juice and salt. Drain roe, arrange in the skillet, and cook over moderately low heat 5 to 10 minutes or until done. Slice roe and put in toasted, buttered bread cases (croustades) or baked puff-paste cases. Fill with Nantua Sauce. Garnish each with a truffle slice or a sautéed mushroom cap. Serve very hot. Makes 6 servings.

⚜ COLD POACHED BLUE CARP

1 dressed carp, 3½ pounds
fish stock
aspic
scalloped lemon halves
parsley
1 cup Béchamel Sauce
1 tablespoon well-drained prepared horseradish
¼ teaspoon prepared mustard

Poach the whole fish in fish stock (see general directions for poaching fish). Transfer fish to a cold platter. Brush with almost set aspic. Chill until aspic is set. Garnish with scalloped lemon halves and parsley. Mix Béchamel Sauce with horseradish and mustard and serve with the fish. Or, if desired, serve mayonnaise. Makes 6 servings.

⚜ COLD CARP WITH RAISINS

2 dressed carp, 2 pounds each
⅓ cup chopped onion
2 shallots, chopped
4 tablespoons olive oil or salad oil
2 tablespoons flour
1½ cups dry white wine
1½ cups water
bouquet garni
1 teaspoon salt
4 peppercorns
⅛ teaspoon crumbled saffron
⅓ cup each raisins and currants

Cut carp into crosswise slices, 2 inches thick. Set aside. Cook onions and shallots in 2 tablespoons of the oil until they begin to turn golden brown. Remove skillet from the heat and blend the flour into the oil. Stir in wine and water. Add bouquet garni, salt, peppercorns, remaining oil, and fish. Simmer 30 minutes or until the fish flakes when tested with a fork. Remove fish from the stock and arrange on a long platter in the shape of a carp. Reduce stock to three-fourths of the original quantity. Add saffron, mix well, and strain over fish. Pour hot water over raisins and currants. Drain and sprinkle around fish. Chill until sauce has slightly jellied. Makes 6 servings.

COD, HADDOCK, AND HAKE
(*Cabillaud, Églefin, Colin*)

These three saltwater fish are members of the same family and may be used interchangeably in most recipes. They may be poached, baked, deep-fat-fried, dipped in crumbs or flour and sautéed in butter, broiled, made into croquettes, used in chowders, or served with sauces. These fish are also available in dried salted form. In France, where dried cod is very popular, it is called *morue;* dried hake is called *merluche.* (See also Whiting.)

⚜ BROILED COD

Cut cod steaks into slices ½ to ¾ inch thick. Rub both sides with salt and ground black pepper and brush with butter. Place on a preheated greased grill. Broil as in directions for Broiled Fish. Serve with lemon wedges and Anchovy or Maître d'Hôtel Butter. Allow 2 pounds fish for 6 servings.

⚜ DEEP-FAT-FRIED COD WITH TARTARE SAUCE

Cut cod steaks ½ inch thick, or use cod fillets. Dip in egg and fine dry bread-crumbs and fry in deep fat. (See Deep-Fat-Fried Fish.) Arrange fish on a warmed platter. Garnish with parsley. Serve with Tartare Sauce, separately. Allow 2 pounds fish steaks for 6 servings.

⚜ DEEP-FAT-FRIED COD FILLETS

Dip fish in ½ cup milk seasoned with 1 teaspoon salt and ¼ teaspoon ground black pepper. Roll in flour and fry very crisp in deep fat preheated to 375° F. Drain on paper towels. Serve with lemon wedges and fried parsley. Allow 1½ to 2 pounds for 6 servings.

Vol-au-Vent of Fillets of Sole La Vallière, page 489 ▲

▼ Fillets of Sole Venini, page 487

▲ Fillets of Sole Herriot, page 484

Paupiettes of Sole Daumont, page 487 ▼

Fillets of Sole Monte Carlo, page 485 ▲

▼ Fillets of Sole Paillard, page 486

▲ Poached Cod English Style, page 443

Fillets of Sole Murat, page 485 ▼

Daurade en Papillote (see page 428) ▲

▼ Poached Slices of Turbot, page 500

440

▲ Baked Bass, page 428

Mixed Fried Fish (see page 456) ▼

Cold Cod Russian Style, page 446 ▲

▼ Cold Red Mullet Niçoise, page 454

▲ Fillets of Sole Floralies, page 490

Mold of Rolled Fillets of Sole in Aspic, page 491 ▼

⚜ COD WITH EGG SAUCE

2 pounds cod fillets or steaks
6 servings boiled potatoes
4 hard-cooked eggs
1½ cups Béchamel Sauce
1 tablespoon chopped parsley
salt
ground black pepper

Cut fish into 6 servings. Poach in fish stock (see Poached Fish). Drain fish well and arrange on a warmed platter, encircled with potatoes. Chop 3 of the hard-cooked eggs and add to the Béchamel Sauce. Stir in the parsley. Season to taste with salt and pepper. Serve over the fish. Slice the remaining hard-cooked egg and arrange the slices as a garnish over the top of the fish. Makes 6 servings.

⚜ POACHED COD ENGLISH STYLE

2 pounds fresh cod
boiling fish stock, or salted water with
1 tablespoon vinegar
1 lemon; parsley
6 tablespoons butter, melted
6 servings boiled potatoes

Poach cod in boiling stock or salted water to which 1 tablespoon vinegar has been added. (See Poached Fish.) Drain fish well. Carefully transfer to a warmed platter. Garnish with parsley and lemon slice. Serve garnished with melted butter and accompanied by boiled potatoes. Makes 6 servings. (See illustration, page 438.)

⚜ COD MISTRAL

2 pounds cod steaks, cut ½-inch thick
1 teaspoon salt
¼ teaspoon ground black pepper
oil or shortening
5 medium sized tomatoes
1 cup sliced mushrooms
½ cup dry white wine
1 small clove garlic, crushed
½ cup fresh breadcrumbs
3 tablespoons butter, melted

Cut fish into 6 servings. Rub both sides with salt and pepper. Roll in flour and fry over moderate heat in oil or shortening until browned on both sides. Place in a baking dish. Peel and seed tomatoes and dice coarsely. Mix with mushrooms, wine, garlic, salt, and pepper to taste. Bring to boiling point and pour over fish. Mix breadcrumbs with butter and sprinkle over the top. Cook in a preheated moderate oven (350° F.) 30 minutes or until crumbs are brown. Serve hot as an entrée. Makes 6 servings.

⚜ COD PARMENTIER

4 medium-sized cooked potatoes
1½ pounds cold leftover cod or other fish
1 cup sliced mushrooms
4 tablespoons butter
salt and ground black pepper to taste
2 tablespoons tomato purée
1 cup Béchamel Sauce
2 hard-cooked egg yolks, sieved

Slice potatoes and arrange, overlapping, in a ring inside a round shallow baking dish. Flake cod, hake, haddock, or other leftover fish and place in the center of the dish. Cook mushrooms in 2 tablespoons of the butter and spread them thinly over the fish. Sprinkle with salt and pepper. Blend the tomato purée with the Béchamel Sauce and spread over the mushrooms. Dot with the remaining butter. Cook in a preheated moderate oven (350° F.) 25 to 30 minutes or until the top is well flecked with brown. Sprinkle the top with sieved egg yolk and serve hot. Serve as a hot entrée. Makes 6 servings.

⚜ BAKED COD PARISIENNE

1 whole 5-pound dressed codfish
fish stock
anchovy fillets
1 cup fine fresh breadcrumbs
4 tablespoons (½ stick) butter, melted
Clam or Mussel Sauce

Marinate fish in fish stock overnight. Simmer very gently for 30 minutes or until fish flakes when tested with a fork. Remove from heat and carefully transfer fish to a cold heatproof platter. Quickly remove skin from fish. Make an incision along the backbone ¼ inch deep and insert anchovy fillets. Mix breadcrumbs with butter and sprinkle over fish. Brown in a preheated moderate oven (375° F.) 20 minutes. Serve with Clam or Mussel Sauce. Makes 6 servings.

⚜ COD FILLETS FLORENTINE

1½ pounds cod fillets
2 pounds fresh spinach, or 2 packages (10 ounces each) frozen spinach, cooked
2 tablespoons butter
½ teaspoon sugar
⅛ teaspoon ground nutmeg
salt and ground black pepper to taste
1½ cups Mornay Sauce
3 tablespoons dry white wine
¼ cup grated Parmesan or Cheddar cheese
2 tablespoons butter, melted

Poach fish fillets in stock (see Poached Fish). Drain cooked spinach well and heat with butter. Add seasonings. Place spinach in the bottom of a well-buttered baking dish and arrange fish over it. Stir and cook Mornay Sauce with wine 2 to 3 minutes, then pour over fish, covering it entirely. Sprinkle with cheese and melted butter. Cook in a preheated hot oven (425° F.) 10 to 15 minutes or brown under broiler heat. Makes 6 servings.

⚜ PORTUGUESE-STYLE COD FILLETS

1½ to 2 pounds cod fillets
1 teaspoon salt
¼ teaspoon ground black pepper
⅓ cup olive oil or salad oil
⅓ cup chopped onion
4 medium-sized tomatoes, peeled, seeded, and diced
1 small clove garlic, crushed
½ cup dry white wine
½ teaspoon sugar
salt and pepper to taste
chopped parsley

Mix fish fillets with salt, pepper, and 3 tablespoons of the oil. Place in a baking dish. Stir and cook onions, tomatoes, garlic, and remaining oil in a saucepan 5 to 6 minutes, or until tomatoes are soft and have thickened. Add wine and season lightly with salt, pepper, and ½ teaspoon sugar. Pour over fish. Bake in a preheated moderate oven (350° F.) 25 minutes. Serve hot as an entrée, sprinkled with chopped parsley. Makes 6 servings. Any fish fillets may be prepared in this way.

⚜ DRIED CODFISH BENEDICTINE

1 pound dried codfish
2 medium-sized hot boiled potatoes, drained
6 tablespoons butter
about ½ cup milk
salt and ground white pepper to taste
½ cup heavy cream, whipped

Soak codfish in cold water for 12 hours, changing the water 5 times. Drop fish in boiling water, reduce heat, and simmer 10 to 15 minutes, or until fish is tender. Remove from water, drain, flake, and mash finely with boiled and well-drained potatoes. Mix and mash until the mixture is smooth. Heat 4 tablespoons (½ stick) of the butter and milk together, and add to the fish and potatoes along with seasonings. Stir and beat until the mixture is fluffy. Fold in whipped cream. Put into a well-buttered baking dish in a mound. Dot with remaining butter. Bake in a preheated hot oven (400° F.) 20 minutes or until browned. Serve hot. This mixture is sometimes used to fill tart shells and barquettes or used as a garnish. Makes 6 servings.

⚜ BISCAY-STYLE DRIED CODFISH

1 pound dried codfish
flour
¼ cup salad oil or olive oil
6 medium-sized tomatoes, peeled, seeded, and quartered
1 small clove garlic, crushed
½ teaspoon sugar
salt and ground black pepper to taste
chopped parsley

Soak codfish in cold water 12 hours, changing the water 5 times. Drain off water and wipe fish dry. Roll in flour. Brown on both sides in very hot oil. Transfer fish to a warmed platter. In the same skillet and oil, cook tomatoes and garlic until tomatoes form a sauce. Add seasonings and pour the sauce over the fish. Sprinkle with chopped parsley. Makes 6 servings.

⚜ DRIED CODFISH MÉNAGÈRE

1 pound dried codfish
fish stock or water
3 tablespoons butter
½ cup thinly sliced onions
2 tablespoons flour
1 cup milk
salt and ground white pepper to taste
5 medium-sized raw potatoes, peeled and sliced

Soak codfish in cold water 12 hours, changing the water 5 times. Poach in stock or water as in recipe for Dried Codfish Benedictine. Set aside to keep warm. Melt butter in a skillet, add onion, toss lightly, and sprinkle with flour. Stir and cook without letting the flour brown. Add milk, salt, and pepper; stir and cook over low heat 10 minutes. Arrange potatoes uniformly over the bottom of a well-buttered baking dish and place well-drained poached fish on top. Cover completely with sauce. Place in a preheated moderate oven (350° F.) 20 to 30 minutes. Makes 6 servings.

⚜ COLD COD RUSSIAN STYLE

2 pounds dressed cod, all in 1 piece with the skin
1 tablespoon vinegar
½ teaspoon salt
18 cooked, peeled, and deveined shrimp
18 truffle slices, or small sautéed mushroom caps
aspic jelly
6 timbales of Russian Salad
anchovy fillets
parsley
lemon wedges

Place fish in boiling water, reduce heat, add vinegar and salt, cover and simmer 15 minutes or until the fish flakes when tested with a fork. Drain water from the fish and remove the skin from upper half of the sides and from the back of the fish. (See illustration, page 441.) Chill. Place on a cold platter. Alternate shrimp and truffle slices or mushroom caps on top of fish in a row down the center. Glaze with aspic jelly. Arrange 3 salads on the platter on each side of the fish. Decorate each salad with anchovy fillets. Garnish the platter with parsley and lemon wedges. Makes 6 servings.

⚜ POACHED HADDOCK WITH MELTED BUTTER

2 pounds fillet of haddock
2 quarts boiling water
3 tablespoons salt
6 servings boiled potatoes
½ cup (1 stick) butter
2 tablespoons each lemon juice and chopped parsley
¼ teaspoon ground black pepper

Cut fish into 6 serving-size pieces and poach as given in the recipe for Poached Fish (page 426). Arrange fish on a warmed platter with boiled potatoes. Combine remaining ingredients and serve separately as a sauce. Makes 6 servings.

⚜ POACHED SMOKED HADDOCK (*English*)

Cut the haddock into halves lengthwise. Cut the halves into serving-size pieces. Place the portions in a skillet. Cover with milk or with equal amounts of milk and water. Bring to boiling point, reduce heat, and simmer 7 to 10 minutes. Remove from the milk and serve for breakfast with melted butter. Allow ¼ pound of haddock for each serving. Smoked haddock is a very popular breakfast dish in England.

⚜ SMOKED HADDOCK WITH EGG SAUCE

2 tablespoons each flour and butter
1 cup milk
½ teaspoon salt
⅛ teaspoon ground black pepper
½ teaspoon lemon juice
2 hard-cooked eggs, diced
Poached Smoked Haddock
chopped parsley

Melt butter in a 3-cup saucepan. Remove from heat and blend in flour. Stir and cook 1 minute. Remove from heat and add milk. Mix well. Cook until the sauce is medium thick. Add seasonings and eggs. Serve on Poached Smoked Haddock. Sprinkle with chopped parsley. Makes 4 servings.

⚜ FILLETS OF HAKE BERCY

1 shallot, chopped
2½ pounds boned hake
½ cup fish stock
½ cup dry white wine
2 tablespoons butter
½ cup heavy cream
1 tablespoon lemon juice

Butter a baking dish generously and sprinkle with chopped shallot. Cut fish into 6 serving-size pieces and arrange in the dish. Pour in stock and wine. Dot with butter. Cover and simmer 8 minutes or until the fish flakes when tested with a fork. Drain the cooking liquor into a saucepan. Add cream and cook until the liquid has reduced by one-fourth. Blend in lemon juice and parsley. Arrange fish on a heat-proof platter and cover with the sauce. Glaze under broiler heat. Makes 6 servings.

⚜ FILLETS OF HAKE BRETONNE

½ cup each diced carrots, leeks, onions, and celery
1 cup sliced mushrooms
¼ cup (½ stick) butter
salt
2½ pounds boned hake
½ cup each dry white wine and fish stock
1 cup Velouté Sauce
½ cup heavy cream
1 tablespoon or more lemon juice
ground white pepper to taste

Place vegetables and butter in a saucepan with ½ teaspoon salt. Cover tightly and cook slowly 10 minutes or until vegetables are tender. Cut fish into 6 serving-size pieces, rub both sides lightly with salt, and arrange in a buttered baking dish. Add wine, fish stock, and vegetables. Cover and cook in preheated moderate oven (350° F.) about 25 minutes—only until fish flakes when tested with a fork. Drain fish liquid into a saucepan. Add Velouté Sauce and cream. Cook to sauce consistency. Strain and add lemon juice and pepper. Adjust the salt. Place fish on a heat-proof platter, cover with the sauce, and glaze under broiler heat. Makes 6 servings.

EEL (*Anguille*)

Eels are elongated snakelike fish which ascend rivers but return to the ocean to breed. Both the European and American species are important as food fish, although eels are more popular in Europe than in the United States.

⚜ BROILED EEL WITH TARTARE SAUCE

2 pounds eel
1 cup dry white wine
1 tablespoon chopped onion
parsley
½ teaspoon salt
4 whole peppercorns
1 egg, beaten with 1 tablespoon water
fine dry breadcrumbs
¼ cup olive oil or salad oil
fried parsley
Tartare Sauce

Cut eel into pieces 2 inches long and place in a skillet. Add wine, onion, 1 stalk parsley, salt, peppercorns, and enough boiling water to cover eel. Simmer 10 to 15 minutes or until eel flakes when tested with a fork. Remove from water and cool. Dip eel in beaten egg, roll in crumbs, and arrange on preheated, oiled broiler pan. Cook in the broiler, 4 inches from the source of heat until browned, turning to brown both sides. Serve with fried parsley and Tartare Sauce. Makes 6 servings.

⚜ DEVILED EEL

2 pounds cooked eel, cut into 6 portions
1 egg beaten with 1 tablespoon water
fine dry breadcrumbs
salt and ground black pepper to taste
dash cayenne
1 cup Sauce Diable
fried parsley

Dip eel in beaten egg, roll in breadcrumbs, and fry in deep fat preheated to 375° F. until browned. Drain on paper towels. Mix together salt, pepper, and cayenne and sprinkle over fish. Serve with Sauce Diable. Garnish with fried parsley. Makes 6 servings.

⚜ EEL DUTCH STYLE

2 pounds eel
⅓ cup sliced onion
parsley
1 teaspoon vinegar
4 whole peppercorns
½ teaspoon salt
boiling water
lemon slices
¼ cup (½ stick) butter, melted
6 portions of boiled potatoes

Cut eel into serving pieces. Place in a skillet and add onion, 2 stalks parsley, vinegar, peppercorns, salt, and enough boiling water to cover eel. Simmer 10 to 15 minutes or until eel flakes when tested with a fork. Transfer to a serving platter and garnish with parsley and lemon slices. Serve with melted butter and boiled potatoes. Makes 6 servings.

⚜ GREEN EEL (*Belgian*)

2 eels, 1½ pounds each
6 tablespoons butter
sorrel (sourgrass)
parsley
fresh chervil
1 sprig each savory and sage
⅓ cup dry white wine
½ teaspoon salt
⅛ teaspoon ground black pepper
3 egg yolks
2 tablespoons lemon juice
1 teaspoon potato flour or cornstarch

Skin, clean, and wash eel and cut it into pieces. Melt butter in a skillet. Add eel. Chop herbs rather fine and scatter a medium-thick layer over the eel. Cover and cook 5 minutes over moderate heat. Add wine and enough water to cover the eel and herbs. Sprinkle with salt and pepper. Cover and simmer 20 to 25 minutes. Blend egg yolks with lemon juice and potato flour or cornstarch and then mix in a little of the eel liquor. Add to the eel and simmer (do not boil) 1 minute. Place the eel in a tureen and pour the unstrained herb sauce over it. Cool. This dish is eaten cool or lukewarm. Makes 6 servings.

HERRING (*Hareng*)

Herring, which are exceedingly abundant in the North Atlantic, are sold fresh, salted, smoked, dried, or pickled. In America young herring are extensively canned and sold as sardines. Fresh herring are firm and fleshy, with a pleasant taste.

⚜ DEVILED GRILLED HERRING

6 dressed herring (heads removed), weighing ¾ to 1 pound each
salt and ground black pepper
prepared mustard
fine dry breadcrumbs
salad oil or olive oil
chopped parsley
Ravigote Sauce

Rub herring lightly with salt and pepper inside and out. Brush the outside thinly with prepared mustard. Roll in fine dry breadcrumbs. Drizzle lightly with oil. Place in the broiler 5 inches from source of heat and cook until the fish flakes when tested with a fork, turning to brown both sides. Or if desired, fry in oil or shortening over surface heat. Serve sprinkled with chopped parsley, and pass Ravigote Sauce in a separate dish. Makes 6 servings.

⚜ GRILLED HERRING MAÎTRE D'HÔTEL

Prepare 6 small herring as in the recipe for Deviled Grilled Herring, omitting the prepared mustard, and grill as directed. Melt ½ cup (1 stick) butter, add 2 tablespoons lemon juice, 1 tablespoon chopped parsley, salt and ground black pepper to taste. Serve over grilled fish. Makes 6 servings.

⚜ FRIED HERRING

6 dressed herring (heads removed), weighing ¾ to 1 pound each
salt
ground black pepper
flour
6 tablespoons butter
2 tablespoons salad oil or olive oil
chopped parsley
6 lemon wedges

Rub herring lightly with salt and pepper inside and out. Roll in flour. Brown on both sides in half the butter and all the oil, adding more butter and oil as the fish cooks if necessary. Arrange the fish on a warmed platter. Brown the remaining 3 tablespoons butter and pour over the fish. Sprinkle with chopped parsley. Serve with lemon wedges. Makes 6 servings.

MACKEREL (*Maquereau*)

A fatty and savory saltwater fish, mackerel is greenish-blue on the back and silvery underneath. It is eaten fresh, salted, smoked, or pickled.

⚜ FILLETS OF MACKEREL MIREILLE

3 pounds mackerel, dressed and filleted
salt
ground black pepper
flour
olive oil or salad oil
1 cup sliced mushrooms
1 shallot, chopped
1 tablespoon chopped onion
1/16 teaspoon minced garlic
¼ teaspoon salt
6 small tomatoes
chopped parsley

Rub the fillets lightly with salt and pepper, roll in flour, and brown on both sides in hot oil. Place fish on a warmed platter and keep warm. Pour 2 tablespoons fresh oil in the skillet, heat, and add mushrooms, shallot, onion, garlic, and ¼ teaspoon salt. Stir and cook 5 minutes, or until mushrooms are tender. Pour over fish. Peel and seed tomatoes and fry in oil in the same skillet. Sprinkle with salt and pepper to taste, and place around the fish. Garnish with chopped parsley. Makes 6 servings.

⚜ VENETIAN-STYLE FILLETS OF MACKEREL

3 pounds mackerel, dressed and filleted
salt
ground black pepper
1 cup dry white wine
¼ cup tarragon vinegar
1 tablespoon each flour and butter
1 tablespoon tomato purée
¼ teaspoon each dried chervil and tarragon
6 servings boiled potatoes

Rub the fillets lightly with salt and pepper and place them in a buttered baking dish. Pour in ½ cup of the wine. Cover and cook in a preheated moderate oven (350° F.) 25 minutes or until the fish flakes when tested with a fork. Drain the wine from the baking dish into a saucepan. Add vinegar and boil until the liquid has been reduced to one half its original quantity. Add remaining ½ cup white wine. Blend together 1 tablespoon each, flour and butter, and add to the sauce along with tomato purée, herbs, and salt and pepper to taste. Stir and cook 2 to 3 minutes. Arrange fish on a warm platter, cover with sauce, and sprinkle with chopped parsley. Serve with boiled potatoes. Makes 6 servings.

⚜ FRIED MACKEREL

Score the mackerel across the thickest part of the flesh. Rub lightly with salt and ground black pepper, roll in flour, and fry as in recipe for Pan-Fried or Oven-Fried Fish. Allow 1 dressed mackerel weighing 1 pound for each serving. Fillets of mackerel may be fried in the same ways.

MULLET

The red mullet, called *rouget* in France because of its color, is one of the most highly prized Mediterranean fish and is so delicate in flavor that it should always be prepared in the simplest way. Since it has no gall, it does not need to be cleaned. It is sometimes called *bécasse de mer* (sea woodcock), because its insides, like those of woodcock, can be eaten. On the Côte d'Azur it is taken fresh from the water, wiped without removing the scales, floured, and grilled —a method of preparation esteemed by connoisseurs. The gray mullet (*muge, mulet*) belongs to a different family, of which the gray mullet and the striped mullet are the commonest varieties; the American mullet, a very important food fish in the southern United States, is a striped mullet. One of the most popular ways of preparing mullet is to grill it and serve it with Maître d'Hôtel Butter.

⚜ FRIED RED MULLET

Allow ¾ pound to 1 pound per serving. Prepare as in recipes for Fried Fish.

⚜ RED MULLET EGYPTIAN STYLE

6 red mullet
salt
ground black pepper
flour
3 to 4 tablespoons olive oil or salad oil
6 medium-sized tomatoes, peeled, seeded, and diced
½ clove garlic, mashed
½ teaspoon sugar
1 tablespoon chopped parsley
½ cup fresh breadcrumbs
2 tablespoons butter

Clean mullet, if desired. Season with salt and pepper, flour lightly, and brown quickly on both sides in hot oil in a skillet. Cook tomatoes with the garlic to a pulp. Add sugar and parsley. Season to taste with salt and pepper. Spread one half of the mixture over bottom of a baking dish. Top with fried mullet. Cover with the remaining tomatoes. Sprinkle with breadcrumbs and dot with butter. Cook in a preheated hot oven (425° F.) about 10 minutes, or until crumbs are brown. Garnish with chopped parsley. Makes 6 servings.

⚜ RED MULLET MONTE CARLO

6 red mullet, ½ to ¾ pound each
1 tablespoon anchovy paste
6 tablespoons butter
6 slices toast
6 tablespoons butter, melted
2 tablespoons chopped parsley
1 tablespoon lemon juice
French fried potato sticks

Dress red mullet if desired, or leave it undressed. Broil as in the recipe for Broiled Fish. Mix 1 tablespoon anchovy paste with 6 tablespoons butter and spread on 6 slices of hot toast. Place fish on the toast. Combine melted butter, parsley, and lemon juice and spoon over fish. Garnish with French fried potato sticks. Makes 6 servings.

⚜ COLD RED MULLET NIÇOISE

2 dressed red mullet (1 pound each) with heads attached
salt and ground black pepper to taste
⅓ cup sliced onions
1 cup dry white wine
tomato slices
lemon slices
lemon juice
salad oil or olive oil
½ lemon
1 black olive
parsley

Sprinkle fish lightly with salt and pepper and set aside. Place onions on the bottom of a skillet and lay fish on top. Pour in wine, bring to boiling point, reduce heat, cover, and simmer 8 to 10 minutes, or until the fish flakes when tested with a fork. Chill in the wine stock. Transfer the fish to a cold platter, reserving the stock to use later. Surround with alternate, overlapping slices of tomatoes and lemons. Reduce the reserved stock to one half the original amount. Season to taste with salt, pepper, lemon juice, and oil. When stock begins to set (jelly), spoon it over the fish. Chill. Notch the edge of ½ lemon, garnish with a black olive, and place between the heads of the fish. (See illustration, page 441.) Makes 4 servings.

⚜ GRAY MULLET IN ASPIC

Cook small mullet in water seasoned with vinegar and salt as directed for Cold Codfish Russian Style. Cool in the stock. Transfer fish to a cold platter. Season aspic to taste with tarragon, and when it is about half set brush it over the fish. Garnish the platter with peeled whole medium-sized tomatoes and parsley. Chill. Allow ½ pound fish for each serving.

PERCH (*Perche*)

A popular freshwater fish, perch resembles trout and can be cooked in many of the same ways, although the flesh is less delicate. Small perch are usually fried in deep fat; medium-sized are filleted and pan-fried in butter; large ones may be stuffed and cooked like shad.

⚜ DEEP-FAT-FRIED PERCH

Soak dressed small perch 10 minutes in ½ cup milk with ½ teaspoon salt added. Roll in flour. Fry until golden in deep fat preheated to 375° F. Drain on paper towel. Garnish with parsley and lemon. Allow 3 small perch per person.

⚜ DORPAT PERCH (*Russian*)

1 dressed perch, 3½ to 4 pounds
1 small onion, sliced
1 stalk parsley
1 small bay leaf
½ teaspoon dried or 2 teaspoons chopped fresh thyme
1 teaspoon salt
4 peppercorns
1 tablespoon vinegar
1½ cups grated hard-roll crumbs
½ cup (1 stick) butter
2 hard-cooked eggs, chopped
chopped parsley

Place perch in a large saucepan, add onion, parsley, bay leaf, thyme, peppercorns, and vinegar and hot water to cover. Bring to boiling point, reduce heat, and simmer 12 to 15 minutes or until the fish flakes when tested with a fork. Transfer fish to a warmed platter. Fry hard-roll crumbs in half the butter, add chopped eggs, and spoon over fish. Melt remaining butter and pour over fish. Sprinkle with chopped parsley. Makes 6 servings.

⚜ FILLETS OF PERCH MEUNIÈRE

Rub fillets lightly with salt and ground black pepper. Roll in flour and fry until golden in butter or oil over moderate heat, turning to brown both sides. Transfer fillets to a warm platter, sprinkle with chopped parsley and garnish with lemon. (See illustration, page 460.) Allow ⅓ pound per person.

⚜ MARINATED SMALL PERCH

6 dressed perch, ½ pound each, or other small freshwater fish
salt
ground black pepper
flour
1 rib celery
1 small carrot, peeled
1 small onion, grated
3 tablespoons olive oil or salad oil
1 cup dry white wine
¼ cup wine vinegar
1 small bay leaf
½ teaspoon slivered lemon peel

Sprinkle fish lightly with salt and pepper inside and out. Roll in flour. Fry in oil until browned on both sides. Cut celery and carrot into julienne strips and cook slowly in oil in a saucepan with the grated onion until tender. Add wine, vinegar, bay leaf, and lemon peel. Cover and simmer 30 minutes. Pour over the fish and cool. Makes 6 servings. Any small freshwater fish may be prepared in this way. (See illustration, page 466.)

⚜ MIXED FRIED FISH (*Friture de la Mediterranée*)

This dish, which the Italians call *fritto misto*, appears very frequently on the menus of restaurants along the Riviera. It is a platter of assorted fried fish, usually shrimp, red mullet, and squid (see illustration, page 440). The fish are dipped in flour, batter, or breadcrumbs and egg, and deep-fat fried in very hot olive oil. The squid must be precooked for 30 minutes to 1 hour, or until tender; other fish and shrimp are fried raw. The same type of dish can be made in the United States with shrimp, perch, and smelts (or other small fish, such as sunfish, trout, or whiting).

18 peeled and deveined raw shrimp
18 smelts (or more if desired)
6 dressed small perch, or other small fish
salt and ground black pepper
flour, or Fritter Batter, or fine dry breadcrumbs and 2 beaten eggs
fried parsley
lemon halves
potato chips, Soufflé Potatoes, or French Fried Potatoes

Sprinkle shrimp and fish with salt and pepper. Dredge with flour, or dip in Fritter Batter, or roll in breadcrumbs, dip in beaten egg, and roll again in breadcrumbs. Fry in deep fat preheated to 370° F., until golden brown—about 4 or 5 minutes. Drain on paper towels. Serve garnished with fried parsley, lemon halves, and either potato chips, Soufflé Potatoes, or French Fried Potatoes. Makes 6 servings.

PIKE (*Brochet*)

Pike is a large freshwater fish with firm white flesh of fine flavor. The best-known species in the United States are common pike, muskellunge, and pickerel.

⚜ PAN-FRIED OR DEEP-FAT-FRIED PIKE

6 pickerel pike, 12 inches long
1 tablespoon salt
½ teaspoon ground black pepper
1 large egg, lightly beaten with
⅓ cup milk
½ cup cornmeal, flour, fine breadcrumbs, or cracker crumbs
2 tablespoons butter or shortening
parsley

Dress pike and remove and discard heads. Rub salt and pepper over both sides of the fish. Dip fish into egg and milk mixture, then roll in cornmeal, flour, breadcrumbs, or cracker crumbs. Fry in hot butter or shortening over moderate heat until the fish have browned nicely on both sides and flake when tested with a fork—about 10 minutes. Drain the fish on paper towels. Transfer them to a warm platter and garnish them with parsley. Makes 6 servings.

Pike prepared in this way may also be fried in deep fat. Place 2 fish at a time in a wire deep-fat-frying basket and lower into deep fat preheated to 375° F. Fry 3 to 6 minutes or until fish is golden brown. Remove the fish from the fat and drain it on paper towels. Serve immediately. Allow 1 fish per serving.

⚜ PIKE WITH CAPER SAUCE

2 pounds boned pike
2 quarts fish stock or salted water
parsley
Caper Sauce

Cut pike into slices ½ inch thick. Place the pieces in a wire basket (deep-fat-frying basket) or on a plate. If a plate is used, tie plate with the fish on it in a piece of cheesecloth. Lower basket or plate into boiling stock or salted water. Reduce heat and simmer (never boil) 10 minutes, or until the fish flakes when tested with a fork. Carefully remove fish to a warm platter. Garnish with parsley and serve with Caper Sauce. If desired, the pike may be served with mayonnaise or Mousseline Sauce instead of Caper Sauce. Makes 6 servings.

⚜ PIKE MANON

1 dressed 4-pound pike
fish stock
10 small cooked, peeled, deveined shrimp
6 baked 2-inch pastry shells
2 cups shrimp salad
6 truffle slices or black olive slices
parsley
18 cooked cold asparagus tips, marinated in French dressing

Cook pike in fish stock until it barely flakes. Remove from heat and cool fish in the stock. Transfer fish to a board and remove the skin from the back only, leaving head and tail attached. Place the pike on its belly on a long platter. Arrange a row of shrimp down the back of the fish, holding them in place with toothpicks. Fill pastry cases with shrimp salad. Garnish with truffle or black olive slices and parsley, and arrange around fish. Place asparagus tips at each end of the platter. Makes 6 servings.

⚜ BLANQUETTE OF PIKE

2½ pounds dressed boned pike
salt
¼ cup (½ stick) butter
2 tablespoons flour
½ cup dry white wine
½ cup hot water
12 small white onions, parboiled
½ pound small mushroom caps
2 tablespoons chopped parsley
2 egg yolks
⅓ cup heavy cream

Cut pike into slices ¾ inch thick and sprinkle salt over each side. Cook in butter without browning. Sprinkle fish with flour and cook 1 to 2 minutes. Add the next 5 ingredients. Cover and simmer 10 to 15 minutes or until onions are tender. Transfer fish and vegetables to a serving dish. Keep warm. Blend egg yolks with cream, add to the sauce, mix well, and cook slowly 1 to 2 minutes. Adjust salt and pour the sauce over the fish and vegetables. Serve hot. Makes 6 servings.

⚜ COLD PIKE

1 dressed pike, 3½ to 4 pounds
fish stock
tarragon leaves
sliced truffles or hard-cooked egg whites
aspic
2 cups mixed cooked vegetable salad
6 baked 2-inch tart shells or tomato cases (scooped-out tomatoes)
Green Mayonnaise

Put pike in a saucepan with barely enough fish stock to cover it. Slowly bring to boiling point and simmer until almost flaky when tested with a fork. Remove fish from the heat and let it cool in the stock. Then transfer fish to a board and remove all the skin except that on the head. Place the fish on a cold platter, decorate with taragon leaves and sliced truffles or hard-cooked egg whites. Glaze lightly with aspic. Spoon salad into cold baked tart shells or tomato cases. Coat lightly with aspic and arrange on the platter around the fish. Serve with Green Mayonnaise. Makes 6 servings.

▼ Trout Renato, page 495

Trout with Almonds, page 493 ▲

▲ Fillets of Perch Meunière, page 455

Pike Quenelles Lyonnaise, page 468 ▼

▼ Trout Mâcon Style, page 495

Salmon Mousseline Chantilly, page 478 ▲

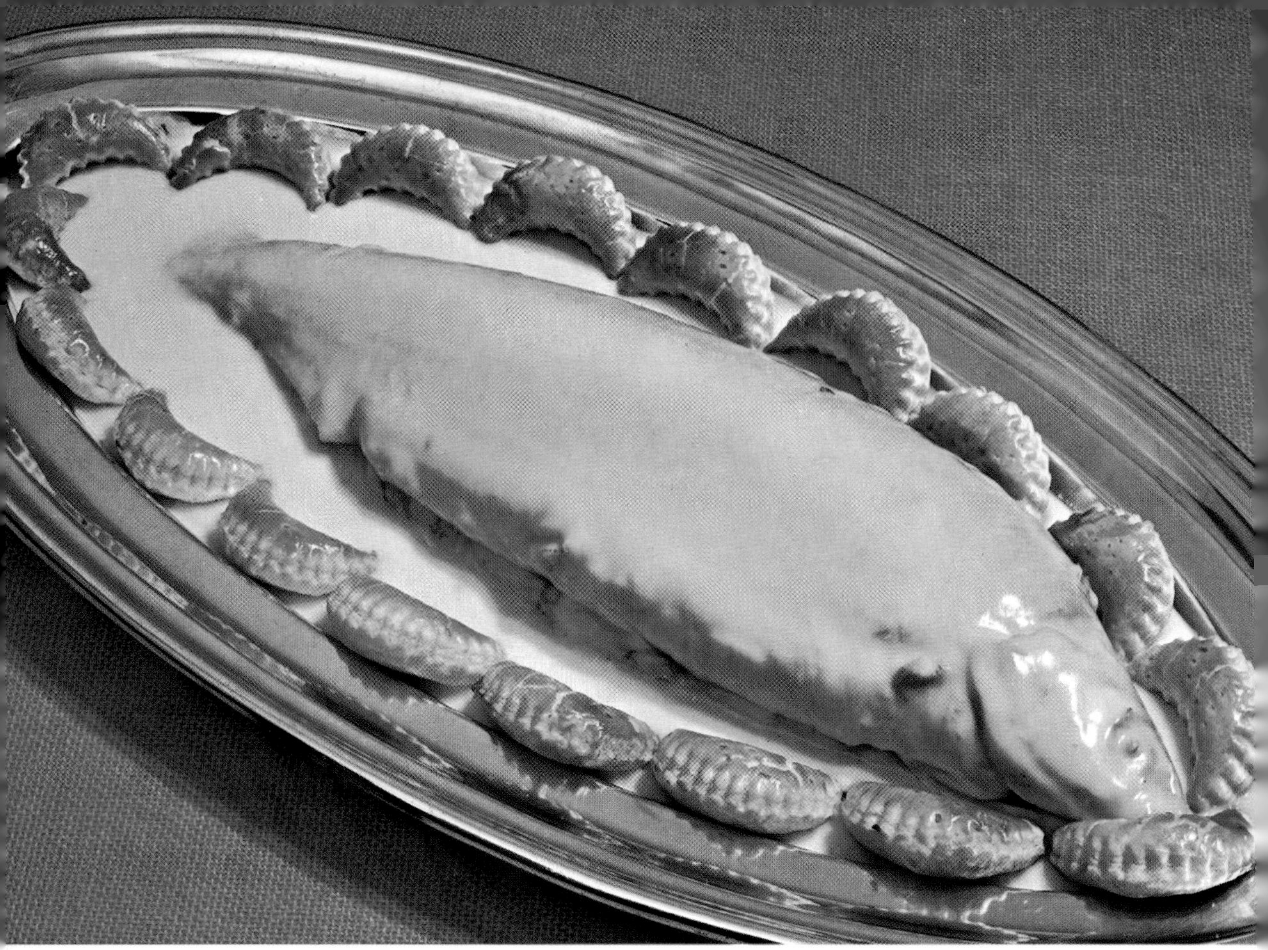

▲ Whitefish in White Wine, page 503

Grilled Salmon Steaks, page 469 ▼

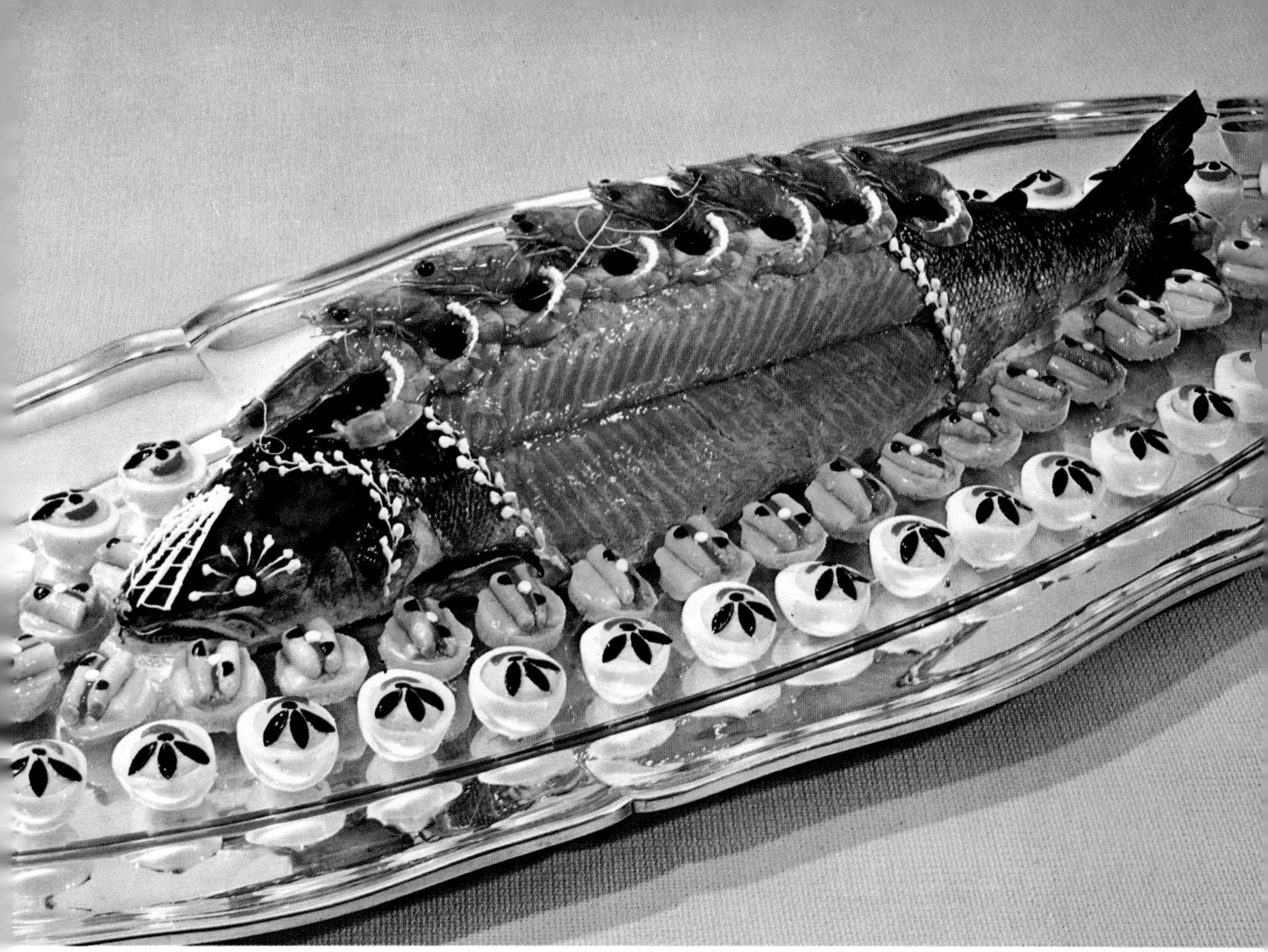

Cold Steamed Whole Salmon, page 473 ▲

▼ Salmon Moscow Style, page 471

▲ Glazed Trout Vladimir, page 497

Glazed Trout Andréa, page 496 ▼

▼ Cold Salmon with Shrimp, page 475

Cold Trout Palace Hotel Style, page 497 ▲

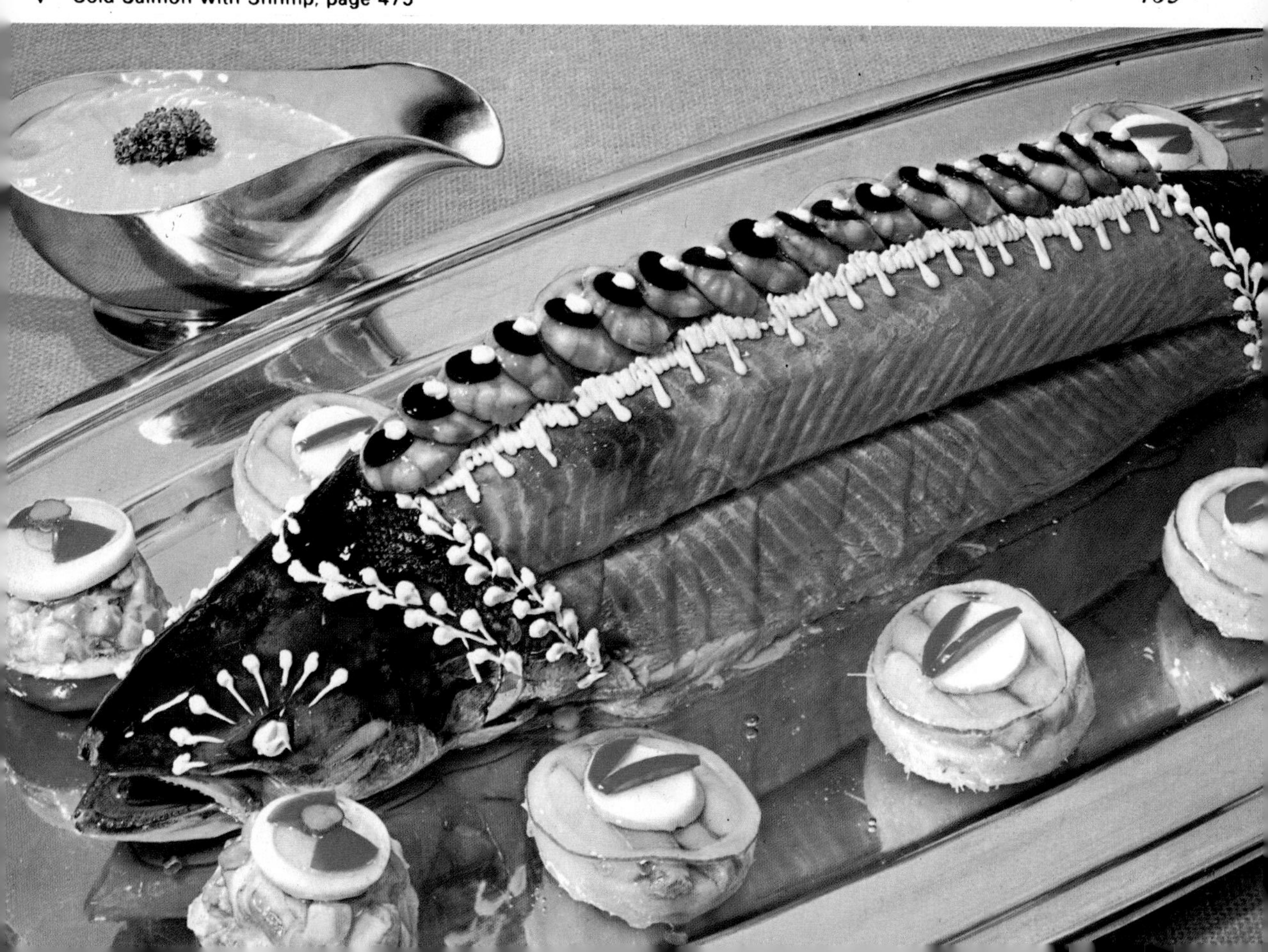

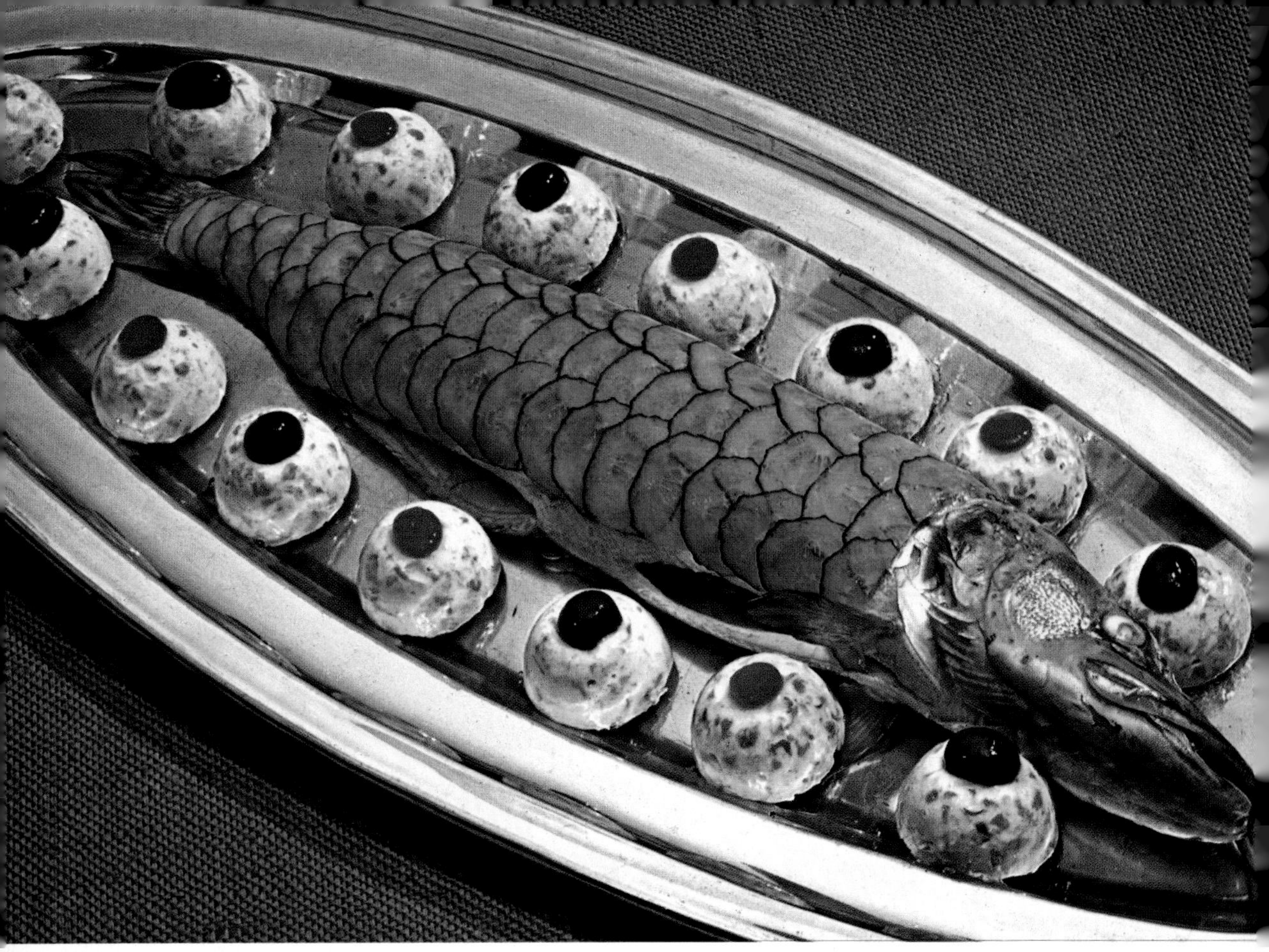

▲ Glazed Pike Riga, page 467

Marinated Small Perch, page 455 ▼

⚜ GLAZED PIKE RIGA

1 dressed 4-pound pike with head and tail
fish stock
aspic
4 small cucumbers, sliced
3 cups shrimp salad
¼ cup finely chopped green and red sweet peppers
pimiento circles
sliced truffles or black olive halves

Cook the pike in enough fish stock to cover it until fish is almost flaky. Remove fish from heat and cool it in the stock. Transfer fish to a board, and remove skin from one side of the back *only*. Set aside. Coat the bottom of a long platter with aspic. Chill until aspic is set. Lay the fish in the center of the platter. Arrange small unpeeled cucumber slices down the back of the fish to simulate scales. Coat with aspic. Combine shrimp salad and green and red sweet peppers and ¼ cup aspic. Mold in small (1½-inch) timbales and chill. Unmold and arrange on the platter around the fish. Garnish half the mold with pimiento circles and the remaining half with truffle slices or black olive halves. Makes 6 servings. (See illustration, page 466.)

⚜ PIKE MOUSSE WITH SAUCE FINES HERBES

1 pound boned pike (reserve bones and trimmings)
1 cup very thick Béchamel Sauce
salt and ground black pepper to taste
1 teaspoon lemon juice
1 whole egg and 2 egg yolks
½ cup heavy cream
1 small onion, sliced
1 stalk parsley
3 peppercorns
water
½ cup dry white wine
2 tablespoons flour
2 tablespoons softened butter
2 egg yolks
1 tablespoon chopped parsley
¼ teaspoon dried chervil
sautéed mushroom caps (optional)
cooked shrimp (optional)

Put pike through a food chopper 3 times, using the finest blade. Mix with Béchamel Sauce and rub through a sieve. Add salt, pepper, egg and 2 egg yolks, and cream, and mix well. Turn into a well-buttered 1-quart mold, set mold in a pan of hot water, and cook in a preheated slow oven (325° F.) 1 hour or until a knife inserted in the center of the mold comes out clean.

Meanwhile make stock with the reserved pike bones and trimmings, onion, parsley stalk, peppercorns, 1½ cups water, and the wine. Cook 30 minutes. Strain. Reduce stock to 1 cup. Blend flour and softened butter and add. Stir in ½ cup water and stir and cook until mixture is slightly thickened. Beat 2 egg yolks with 2 tablespoons water and add. Cook ½ minute or until of desired consistency. Add chopped parsley and chervil. Unmold the mousse onto a serving plate and spoon the sauce over it. Garnish with sautéed mushroom caps and cooked shrimp if desired. Makes 6 servings.

⚜ PIKE MOUSSE NEMOURS

Prepare pike mousse as in preceding recipe. Unmold onto a round serving plate, surround with Potato Croquettes, and serve with Shrimp Sauce. Makes 6 servings.

POTATO CROQUETTES

Mix together 3 cups hot riced potatoes, 3 tablespoons butter, ½ cup finely diced cooked shrimp, 1 tablespoon chopped parsley, ¾ teaspoon salt, ⅛ teaspoon ground black pepper and 2 egg yolks. Shape into 12 croquettes of equal size. Coat croquettes with flour. Beat 2 eggs with 2 tablespoons water. Dip the croquettes in egg and then roll them in fine dry breadcrumbs. Fry them until golden in deep fat preheated to 375° F. Drain on paper towels. Makes 12 croquettes.

SHRIMP SAUCE

Stir and cook 1 tablespoon finely chopped onion in 2 tablespoons butter 1 minute. Remove from heat and blend in 2 tablespoons flour. Stir and cook 1 minute. Add ¾ cup each milk and fish stock. Mix well. Stir and cook 2 to 3 minutes or until of sauce consistency. Add 1 teaspoon chopped parsley, dash of grated nutmeg, salt and black pepper to taste, ⅓ cup finely diced shrimp, add 1 tablespoon butter. Makes 1¼ cups sauce.

⚜ PIKE QUENELLES LYONNAISE

1 cup dry crumbs of French bread
1 cup hot milk
1 pound raw boneless pike
fish stock from pike bones, head, and skin (optional)
1 teaspoon salt

⅛ teaspoon ground black pepper
$\frac{1}{16}$ teaspoon ground nutmeg
1 cup (2 sticks) butter, softened
2 whole eggs and 2 egg yolks
Nantua Sauce
½ pound cooked, peeled, and deveined shrimp

Combine breadcrumbs and hot milk and mix to form a smooth paste. If mixture is too wet, stir and cook over low heat 2 to 3 minutes. Spread the paste on a plate and chill till firm. (This is a bread panada.) Put pike through a food chopper twice, using the finest blade. Add salt, pepper, and nutmeg. Mix with softened butter, working it in with a wooden spoon. Add the panada and mix until smooth. Beat in the whole eggs and the egg yolks one at a time. Adjust seasonings. Shape scant tablespoons of the mixture into balls on a lightly floured board. Arrange quenelles in a buttered skillet, add boiling fish stock or boiling water to cover, and cook 10 to 12 minutes over low heat, never allowing the liquid to boil. Remove to a serving dish, coat with Nantua Sauce, and garnish with the shrimp. Makes 6 servings. (See illustration, page 460.)

SALMON (*Saumon*)

Both European and American salmon inhabit coastal seas and ascend rivers to spawn. One of the delicious food fish, salmon is characterized by its orange-pink color, which varies with the species and the season. It is a large fish, which may be prepared whole, in large pieces cut from the center of the body, or in steaks. Salmon trout (*truite salmonée*), also called European sea trout, has flesh of similar color and also spawns in rivers. It is not found in North America, but since it is prepared in many of the same ways as salmon some recipes calling for either salmon or salmon trout are included here. See also Trout; Whitefish.

⚜ GRILLED SALMON STEAKS

6 salmon steaks
oil
Herb or Anchovy Butter

Wipe the salmon dry with a clean cloth and brush with oil. Arrange the steaks on an oiled preheated broiler rack and place them under broiler heat, having the thermostat set at Broil. Cook quickly on both sides. Reduce heat to moderate (350° F.) and cook until the backbone can be removed easily with the tip of a knife. Serve with Herb or Anchovy Butter. Makes 6 servings. (See illustration, page 462.)

⚜ DANISH-STYLE SALMON STEAKS

1 shallot, finely chopped
2 tablespoons wine vinegar
¼ cup fish stock
½ cup (1 stick) unsalted butter
ground white pepper
anchovy paste
6 salmon steaks
6 servings boiled potatoes

Cook shallot, vinegar, and stock until the liquid has been reduced to 2 tablespoons. Beat in butter, a small piece at a time. Continue beating until the butter is melted and the sauce is thick and foamy. Beat in pepper and anchovy paste to taste. Set aside.

Poach salmon steaks in fish stock. Drain well. Serve with boiled potatoes and the sauce in a sauceboat. Makes 6 servings.

⚜ SALMON STEAKS FOYOT

6 salmon steaks
salt
ground black pepper
Noisette Potatoes
½ cup Béarnaise Sauce
1 tablespoon meat glaze

Rub salmon lightly with salt and pepper. Brown on both sides in shortening or butter. Arrange on a platter and encircle with Noisette Potatoes (potato balls, shaped with a French melon-ball cutter, browned in butter on all sides, and sprinkled with salt and pepper). Make Foyot Sauce by combining Béarnaise Sauce and meat glaze. Serve over fish. Makes 6 servings.

⚜ SLICED SALMON DORIA

6 slices salmon or salmon trout, ½ pound each
salt and ground black pepper
flour
4 tablespoons (½ stick) butter
lemon juice
¼ cup browned butter
2 cucumbers, 6 inches long

Sprinkle slices lightly with salt and pepper. Roll in flour and brown on both sides in butter over moderate heat. Transfer fish to a platter. Sprinkle with lemon juice and browned butter. Meanwhile cut cucumbers in half; remove and discard seeds. Cut cucumbers into lengthwise strips and then cut the strips into 1-inch pieces. Cook 2 to 3 minutes in butter. Serve with the fish. Makes 6 servings.

⚜ SALMON SLICES MAÎTRE D'HÔTEL

6 slices salmon or salmon trout, ½ pound each
salad oil or clarified butter
½ cup butter
1 teaspoon chopped parsley
1½ tablespoons lemon juice
salt and ground black pepper

Wipe slices dry, dip in oil or clarified butter, and place on a preheated grill. Grill under broiler heat 3 minutes on each side. Reduce the heat and lower the grill. Cook until the fish flakes when tested with a fork. Transfer fish to a warmed platter and set aside to keep warm. Meanwhile melt the butter in a saucepan and add the remaining ingredients. Serve the butter over the fish. Makes 6 servings.

⚜ SALMON MOSCOW STYLE

2 center pieces of salmon, 1 pound each
court bouillon
aspic
peeled cooked shrimp
anchovies
24 small baked tart shells
1½ cups cooked vegetable salad
caviar
mayonnaise
grated horseradish or horseradish sauce

Place salmon in a skillet with barely enough court bouillon to cover. Bring to boiling point, reduce heat, and simmer 10 to 12 minutes or until the fish flakes when tested with a fork. Do not allow the stock to boil. Cool in the stock. Transfer fish to a platter and glaze with aspic. Garnish with shrimp and anchovies and glaze with aspic. Fill 12 of the tart shells with vegetable salad. Fill the remaining tart shells with caviar. Glaze all the tarts with aspic and arrange on the platter around the fish. Season mayonnaise to taste with grated horseradish or horseradish sauce and serve with the salmon. Makes 6 servings. (See illustration, page 463.)

⚜ SALMON WITH MOUSSELINE SAUCE

1 dressed salmon or salmon trout, 3½ to 4 pounds
fish stock
parsley
lemon wedges
6 portions cooked potatoes
Hollandaise Sauce
whipped cream

Place fish in a baking pan and pour in enough cold fish stock to cover it. Slowly bring the stock to boiling point, reduce heat, and simmer until the fish flakes when tested with a fork. Remove the skin very carefully and transfer fish to a platter. Garnish with parsley and lemon slices. Put equal parts of Hollandaise Sauce and whipped cream in the top of a double boiler. Stir and cook over hot water until sauce is very hot. Serve in a sauceboat. Makes 6 servings.

⚜ SALMON REGENCY STYLE

1 dressed salmon or salmon trout, 3½ to 4 pounds
1¾ cups court bouillon
1¾ cups Velouté Sauce
3 large egg yolks
½ cup finely chopped cooked crayfish or shrimp
¼ cup (½ stick) butter
6 small fish quenelles
1 cup sautéed small mushroom caps

Place the fish in a saucepan large enough to accommodate it. Pour in court bouillon. Bring to boiling point, reduce heat, and simmer until the fish flakes when tested with a fork. Transfer fish to a platter and set aside to keep warm. Reduce the court bouillon to one half and mix 1½ cups of the Velouté Sauce with it. Blend egg yolks with the remaining ¼ cup Velouté Sauce and add to the bouillon. Stir and cook ½ minute. Add crayfish or shrimp, butter, fish quenelles, and mushrooms. Heat and pour over fish. Makes 6 servings.

⚜ RUSSIAN COULIBIAC OF SALMON

1½ ounces marrow from the backbone of a sturgeon
1 pound fresh salmon
¾ cup farina
beef broth
Brioche Dough or Puff Paste
½ teaspoon salt
⅛ teaspoon ground black pepper
3 hard-cooked eggs, sliced
½ tablespoon chopped parsley
½ tablespoon chopped fresh dill or ¼ teaspoon dill seed
2 tablespoons chopped onion
6 tablespoons butter
1 raw egg, beaten
sour cream
stalks of parsley
1 whole tomato

Soak sturgeon marrow in cold water overnight. Cover and cook slowly 5 hours or until marrow is soft. Cool, and cut into thin slices, and set aside. Poach salmon (see directions for Poached Fish), cool, remove skin and bones, and flake the salmon. Set aside. Cook farina—in Russia buckwheat groats are used—as directed on the package, but replace the water with beef broth. Cool. Roll out Brioche Dough or Puff Paste ¼ inch thick in a 12- by 8-inch rectangle. Spread one-half of the cooked farina down the center of the rectangle of dough and place one-half of the sturgeon marrow on top. Sprinkle the flaked salmon with salt and black pepper and scatter it over the marrow, using it all. Arrange the egg slices over the salmon and sprinkle them with the chopped parsley and dill. Sauté the onion in 1 tablespoon of the butter and scatter it over the egg slices. Cover the egg slices with the rest of the sturgeon marrow and spread the remaining farina over it. Turn the two sides of the dough up, bringing it over the filling and having the edges overlap down the center. Turn up the dough at the ends and place the roll, seam side down, on a lightly buttered baking sheet. Roll the trimmings of the dough ¼ inch thick, cut it into narrow strips, ¼ to ½ inch wide, and arrange them in lattice fashion over the roll. Cut a hole in the center of the top to allow for the escape of steam. Brush the surface with beaten egg. Cover the roll with a clean towel, set it in a warm place (80 to 85° F.), and let the dough rise for 30 minutes. Bake in a preheated hot oven (400° F.) 30 minutes or until browned. Remove from oven. Melt remaining butter and pour it through a funnel into the hole in the top of the crust. Transfer the roll to a serving platter and garnish the platter with stalks of parsley and the whole tomato. Cut the roll into slices and serve with sour cream. Makes 8 to 10 servings. (See illustration, page 291.)

⚜ COLD STEAMED WHOLE SALMON

5- to 6-pound whole salmon
salt
ground black pepper
1 small bay leaf
1 small onion, quartered
¼ cup sliced celery
¼ cup sliced carrots
½ stalk parsley
3 cups aspic
thick mayonnaise
34 cooked artichoke bottoms
68 cooked asparagus tips, 1½ inches long
French Dressing
2 truffles or 8 black olives
2 pimientoes
34 Deviled Hard-Cooked Egg halves
8 cooked crayfish or shrimp

Ask your fish butcher to remove scales and eviscerate the salmon, leaving the head, tail, and fins attached. Sprinkle the inside of the body cavity with salt and pepper and fill it with the next 5 ingredients. Close opening with skewers or toothpicks. Rub salt and pepper over the skin of the fish, wrap it in a large piece of cheesecloth, tie at each end, and place it on a rack in a 17¼- by 11½- by 2¼-inch roasting pan. Pour in boiling water until it just reaches the top of the rack. Cover and steam over surface heat or in a preheated moderate oven (375° F.) 30 to 50 minutes (the time depends upon the size of the fish) or only until the fish flakes when tested with a fork. Remove from heat and cool. Discard the celery, onion, etc. stuffed in the cavity. Strip off and discard the skin from the middle portion of the salmon's body and coat the whole fish with aspic. (See illustration, page 463.) Chill until the aspic is set. Pour a thin layer of aspic over the bottom of a long fish platter and chill until aspic is set. Transfer fish to the platter and decorate the head and the lines on the body where the unskinned portion meets the skinned portion with thick mayonnaise put through a pastry tube fitted with a thin nozzle. Meanwhile marinate the cooked artichoke bottoms and cooked asparagus tips in French Dressing. Arrange 2 asparagus tips on each artichoke bottom, garnish with bits of truffle or black olive and pimiento, and coat with aspic. Chill until aspic is set and arrange on the platter around the fish. Decorate halves of Deviled Hard-Cooked Eggs with bits of truffle or olive and pimiento, coat with aspic, and chill until aspic is set. Place eggs on the platter around the artichoke bottoms and asparagus. If crayfish are used as a garnish, leave heads attached, dip crayfish in aspic, and place them along the lengthwise center of the back. If crayfish is not available, cooked deveined shrimp may be used. Serve for a cold buffet. Makes 12 to 15 servings.

⚜ SALMON "PORTE-BONHEUR"

1 dressed 3½ pound salmon
court bouillon
1 tomato
1 truffle
2 or 3 black olives
6 hard-cooked eggs
mayonnaise

Cut salmon into 6 slices, leaving head and tail attached to their respective pieces. Place the slices in a skillet with enough court bouillon barely to cover them. Bring to boiling point, reduce heat, and simmer 10 to 12 minutes or until the fish flakes when tested with a fork. Remove fish from stock. Cut the slices in half, skin, and place the pieces on a platter. Make a design on each half and on the head and tail with bits of tomato and truffle or black olive. Cut peeled hard-cooked eggs in half and place halves between the fish slices. Serve cold with mayonnaise. Makes 6 servings.

⚜ COLD SALMON D'ORSAY

4 cups aspic
1 poached salmon or salmon trout, 3½ to 4 pounds
18 peeled cooked shrimp
3 hard-cooked eggs
caviar
3 medium-sized tomatoes, cut in half
Green Mayonnaise

Coat the bottom of a tray with a layer of aspic ½ inch thick. Chill. Remove the skin from the back of the fish and place fish on the bed of jellied aspic. Garnish the top with a row of peeled cooked shrimp. Coat shrimp and fish with aspic. Cut hard-cooked eggs in half, remove yolks, fill cavities with caviar, and place around the fish on the tray, alternating with tomato halves. Coat with aspic. Serve Green Mayonnaise separately. Makes 6 servings.

⚜ COLD SALMON RUSSIAN STYLE

1 dressed salmon or salmon trout, 3½ to 4 pounds
fish stock
3 cups fish aspic
hard-cooked eggs
green pepper
black olives
watercress or parsley
6 baked 2-inch pastry tart cases
Russian Salad
mayonnaise

Carefully poach salmon trout in fish stock. Remove from heat and allow fish to cool in the stock. Drain, skin, and place on a large cold tray. Decorate as desired with hard-cooked eggs, green pepper, black olives, watercress or parsley. Coat with aspic. Fill tart cases with Russian Salad, coat with aspic, and arrange on the tray. Fill the spaces with diced aspic. Serve with mayonnaise. Makes 6 servings.

⚜ COLD SALMON WITH SHRIMP

1 dressed salmon or salmon trout, 3½ to 4 pounds
fish stock
aspic
about 18 peeled cooked shrimp
18 slices of truffle or black olive slices
1 envelope unflavored gelatin
¼ cup water
1 cup mayonnaise
6 medium small tomatoes
1 cup mixed cooked vegetable salad
4 hard-cooked eggs
2 gherkin pickles
6 baked 1½-inch pastry tart shells
24 one-inch cooked asparagus tips
⅓ cup thick Velouté Sauce
6 thin slices cucumber
mayonnaise

Poach the fish (with head attached) in fish stock, and allow it to cool in the stock. Coat a long platter with aspic and chill until aspic is set. Remove fish from the stock, drain well, and remove the skin. Place fish on the aspic-coated platter. Arrange a row of cooked shrimp down the center of the back. Garnish each shrimp with a slice of truffle or black olive. Soften gelatin in the ¼ cup water and set in a pan of hot water to melt. Add to mayonnaise, mix well, and put the mixture through a pastry bag, using a small nozzle, to decorate the fish around the head and around the shrimp. Cut tomatoes in half and scoop out the centers. Drain well and fill with vegetable salad. Top with a slice of hard-cooked egg and garnish with a little red tomato and a slice of gherkin pickle. Coat with aspic. Fill tart shells with cooked asparagus tips. Cover with thick Velouté Sauce. Top each with a thin slice of cucumber and a slice of hard-cooked egg. Garnish with bits of tomato. Coat with aspic. Arrange the tomatoes and tart shells around the fish. Serve the mayonnaise separately in a sauceboat. Makes 6 to 8 servings. (See illustration, page 465.)

⚜ SALMON SOUFFLÉ DIVA

1 pound peeled and deveined cooked shrimp
¾ cup heavy cream
¾ cup Béchamel Sauce
salt
ground black pepper
1 cup flaked cooked salmon
2 tablespoons butter
lemon juice
4 large egg yolks
2 large egg whites
unsweetened unbaked Plain Pie Pastry

Line 6 individual tart pans, or one 9-inch pie plate, with pie pastry. Trim, turn over edges, and flute. Store in the refrigerator until ready to use. Combine shrimp, ⅓ cup of the cream, ¼ cup of the Béchamel Sauce, salt and pepper to taste. Set aside. Pound and beat the salmon with a wooden spoon. Work in butter and remaining cream and Béchamel Sauce. Mix well, stir, and heat until the mixture forms a paste. Season with salt, pepper, and lemon juice to taste. Beat in egg yolks. Beat egg whites until they stand in soft peaks and fold into the salmon mixture. Cover the unbaked pastry shells with the shrimp mixture. Finish filling the shells with the Salmon Soufflé. Bake in a preheated hot oven (425° F.) 10 minutes, then reduce heat and bake 30 minutes, or until pastry is brown and the filling is well puffed in the center and soft-firm. Makes 6 servings.

⚜ SALMON CUTLETS POJARSKY

1¼ pounds boned, skinned salmon
2 cups soft breadcrumbs
½ cup milk
4 eggs
6 tablespoons softened butter
1 teaspoon lemon juice
salt and ground black pepper to taste
6 servings cooked vegetables (peas, carrots, green beans, etc.)

Chop salmon very fine or put through a food chopper, using the finest blade. Soak breadcrumbs in milk, squeeze dry, and add crumbs to the salmon. Beat in 2 of the eggs. Add 3 tablespoons of the butter and the lemon juice. Mix well. Season to taste with salt and pepper. Shape the mixture into 6 large or 12 small cutlets on a floured board. Beat the 2 remaining eggs with 2 tablespoons of water and dip cutlets into the beaten egg, then roll in fine dry breadcrumbs. Cook slowly until browned in the rest of the butter, adding it as needed. Arrange cutlets in a ring on a warmed dish. Toss cooked vegetables, such as peas, carrots, green beans, etc., in butter and spoon into the center of the dish. Makes 6 servings.

⚜ SALMON KEDGEREE (*English*)

1 pound (2 cups) diced leftover cooked salmon, without skin or bones
2 tablespoons water
4 tablespoons butter
3 tablespoons chopped onion
1 cup raw rice
2 cups boiling water
1 teaspoon salt
1 tablespoon curry powder
3 cups Béchamel Sauce (made with fish stock)
2 hard-cooked eggs
2 hard-cooked egg yolks, sieved
chopped parsley

Cook salmon in water and half the butter until water has evaporated. Melt remaining butter in another saucepan, add onions, and cook until onions are transparent. Meanwhile soak rice in water to cover for ½ hour. Drain rice well and add to butter and onion. Stir and cook until rice is dry and begins to stick to the pan. Add water and salt. Cover and bring to boiling point. Reduce heat and cook 12 to 15 minutes. Blend curry powder with Béchamel Sauce. Add fish and chopped hard-cooked eggs. Mix lightly. Fill a serving dish with alternating layers of rice and fish mixture, beginning and ending with fish. Sprinkle sieved, hard-cooked egg yolks over the top. Garnish with chopped parsley. Makes 6 servings.

⚜ SALMON MOUSSE

1 quart aspic
1 cup flaked leftover cooked salmon
½ cup (1 stick) softened butter
⅓ cup heavy cream
¼ cup thick Béchamel Sauce
lemon juice
salt
ground black pepper

Pour a ¼-inch layer of aspic in an 8-inch square pan. Chill until firm and reserve for later use. Coat the bottom and sides of a 1-quart charlotte mold or ring mold with aspic. Chill until almost firm. Decorate as desired with sliced hard-cooked eggs, bits of tomato, green pepper, and truffles or black olives. Cover with a thin layer of aspic and chill until firm and ready to use. Let remaining aspic stand at room temperature until ready to use later. Blend finely flaked salmon with softened butter until smooth. Gradually beat in cream and Béchamel Sauce. Season to taste with lemon juice, salt, and pepper. Turn into the prepared mold. Finish filling the mold with the liquid aspic. Chill until the mousse is set and ready to use. Unmold on a round serving plate. Cut triangles from the firm aspic and arrange on the plate around the mold. Makes 6 servings.

⚜ SALMON MOUSSELINE CHANTILLY

1¼ pounds boned raw salmon
2 large egg whites
1¾ cups heavy cream
1 teaspoon salt
¼ teaspoon ground black pepper
dash cayenne
Hollandaise Sauce
whipped cream
2 tablespoons shrimp butter or crayfish butter
6 whole cooked shrimp or crayfish tails
2 cups cooked buttered mushroom caps
chopped chervil or parsley

Put salmon through a food chopper, using the finest blade. Pound and beat the salmon with a spoon. Set the bowl in a pan of cracked ice. Gradually beat in egg whites, using a wooden spoon. Gradually beat in cream. Add salt, pepper, and cayenne. Spoon into well-buttered custard cups, place cups in a pan of hot water, and bake in a preheated moderate oven (350° F.) 40 to 50 minutes or until a knife inserted in the center comes out clean. Unmold the timbales onto a serving dish. Combine equal parts of Hollandaise Sauce and whipped cream, and season with 2 tablespoons shrimp butter or crayfish butter. Serve over the timbales. Garnish each with a shrimp or a crayfish tail. Fill center of the dish with mushrooms. Sprinkle with chopped chervil or parsley. Makes 6 servings. (See illustration, page 461.)

⚜ SALMON LOAF VALOIS

1¼ pounds boned raw salmon
1 egg and 3 egg yolks
¾ cup Béchamel Sauce
⅓ cup heavy cream
1 teaspoon salt
¼ teaspoon ground black pepper
½ teaspoon dried or 1½ teaspoons chopped fresh thyme
parsley
Béarnaise Sauce

Put salmon through a food chopper, using the finest blade. Pound and beat the salmon with a wooden spoon. Beat in whole egg and egg yolks. Stir in Béchamel Sauce, cream, salt, pepper, and thyme. Put through a sieve. Spoon into buttered custard cups. Place cups in a pan of hot water and bake in a preheated moderate oven (350° F.) 40 to 50 minutes, or until a knife inserted in the center comes out clean. Turn the loaf out onto a platter and garnish with parsley. Serve Béarnaise Sauce in a sauceboat. Makes 6 servings.

SHAD (*Alose*)

Shad resembles herring but is larger. The fish go up the rivers to spawn in the spring; the flavor of shad caught soon after spawning is especially delicious. Shad roe is highly prized.

⚜ GRILLED SHAD ENGLISH STYLE

3½ to 4 pounds dressed shad
salad oil
½ teaspoon salt
¼ teaspoon ground black pepper
2 strips bacon
2 tablespoons butter, melted
buttered boiled potatoes for 6 servings
lemon wedges
parsley

Score the fish, oil slightly, rub with salt and pepper, and roll in flour. Place it on 2 strips of bacon in a baking dish and bake in a preheated slow oven (325° F.) 40 to 50 minutes or until fish is flaky when tested with a fork.

Baste with melted butter and place under the broiler 4 inches from the source of heat to brown. Transfer shad to a serving platter and pour the pan juices over it. Serve with buttered boiled potatoes. Garnish with lemon wedges and parsley. Makes 6 servings.

⚜ SHAD WITH SORREL

¼ cup olive oil or salad oil
2 tablespoons lemon juice
1 small bay leaf
¼ teaspoon dried or 1 teaspoon chopped fresh thyme
1 tablespoon chopped parsley
½ teaspoon salt
⅛ teaspoon ground black pepper
3½ to 4 pounds dressed shad
3 pounds sorrel (sourgrass)
2 tablespoons butter
salt and ground black pepper to taste

Combine oil, lemon juice, and seasonings. Pour over shad and marinate for 2 hours. Broil on a hot broiler 4 inches from the source of heat for 12 to 15 minutes, turning carefully to brown both sides. Fish is done when it is flaky when tested with a fork. Wash sorrel and cook it, using only the water that clings to the leaves, until it is very soft. Drain, press out all the water possible, and rub through a sieve. Add butter, salt, and pepper. Serve over shad. Makes 6 servings.

SOLE

The true European sole is considered the finest of the flat fish. It is found in most European waters but not in American waters, and though it is sometimes imported it is not commonly available in the United States, where the fish known as "sole" are usually flounder or other flat fish. Other fish which can be filleted and poached in the same way as sole include whiting, pollack, dab, and freshwater trout. For technique of filleting, see Culinary Techniques in Pictures.

⚜ SOLE MEUNIÈRE

Allow 1 sole, weighing ½ pound, per person. Fry as directed for Fried Fish. Place on a warm platter. Serve very hot, with wedges of lemon. (For technique of serving, see Culinary Techniques in Pictures.)

⚜ DEEP-FAT-FRIED SOLE

Allow 1 sole, weighing ½ pound, per person. Fry in deep fat as directed for Deep-Fat-Fried Fish. Serve very hot on a warm platter, garnished with fried parsley and lemon slices.

⚜ DEEP-FAT-FRIED SOLE WITH LEMON

Allow 1 sole, weighing ½ pound, per serving. Dip fish in lightly salted milk, roll in flour and shake off surplus. Fry until golden brown in deep fat preheated to 375° F. Drain on paper towels. Sprinkle salt and pepper lightly on both sides of fish. Put a handful of thoroughly dried washed parsley in the hot fat and remove it immediately with a perforated spoon or skimmer. Arrange this around the fish as a garnish, along with lemon slices.

⚜ SOLE À L'ANGLAISE

This name is applied to three methods of cooking sole.

1. Broil sole as directed in the recipe for Broiled Fish. Serve with melted butter or Maître d'Hôtel Butter and boiled potatoes.
2. Simmer sole in equal parts milk and lightly salted water 8 minutes, or until the fish flakes when tested with a fork. Serve with melted butter and boiled potatoes.
3. Dip serving-size pieces of sole in egg beaten with water (1 tablespoon water to each egg), roll in fine dry breadcrumbs, and brown in butter. Serve with soft Maître d'Hôtel Butter.

Allow 2 pounds fillets for 6 servings.

⚜ SOLE SAINT-GERMAIN

6 dressed sole, ½ pound each
salt
ground black pepper
flour
½ cup (1 stick) butter, melted
fine dry breadcrumbs
12 small (1½ inches in diameter) parboiled potatoes

Wipe sole dry. Sprinkle lightly with salt and pepper, dip in flour, in ¼ cup of the melted butter, and then in breadcrumbs. Press the fish down well with a spatula. Place on buttered broiler rack and sprinkle with 3 tablespoons melted butter. Cook in a broiler 4 to 5 inches from source of heat until browned, turning to brown both sides. Or, if desired, bake in a well-buttered baking dish in a preheated moderate oven (350° F.) 25 minutes or until fish has browned. Roll potatoes in remaining butter. Arrange in a baking pan and bake in a moderate oven (350° F.) 25 minutes or until browned. If fish is baked, the potatoes may be baked at the same time. Transfer fish to a warmed platter, and place potatoes around fish. Serve Béarnaise Sauce separately. Makes 6 servings.

⚜ SOLE BERCY

2 shallots, chopped
¼ cup chopped parsley
¼ cup dry white wine
¼ cup fish stock
2 pounds fillet of sole
salt and ground white pepper to taste
1 tablespoon lemon juice
3 tablespoons butter

Sprinkle chopped shallots and parsley over the bottom of a well-buttered baking dish. Add wine and stock. Rub both sides of sole fillets lightly with salt and pepper, and arrange over shallots. Sprinkle with lemon juice and dot with butter. Cook, uncovered, in a preheated moderate oven (350° F.) 20 minutes, basting twice with the pan liquid. Place under broiler heat to brown. Arrange on a warm platter and garnish with parsley and lemon wedges. Makes 6 servings.

⚜ SOLE COLBERT

6 sole, weighing ½ pound each
1 cup milk
½ teaspoon salt
flour
2 eggs beaten with 2 tablespoons water
fine, dry breadcrumbs
½ cup softened butter
½ teaspoon chopped parsley
⅛ teaspoon dried tarragon or ½ teaspoon chopped fresh tarragon
½ teaspoon melted beef extract, or 1 teaspoon beef bouillon
salt and ground black pepper to taste

Split the sole along the side from which the skin has been removed. Raise the fillets so that the backbone can be loosened. Cut or break the backbone in 2 or 3 places so that it can be removed easily after cooking. (If your fish butcher knows how to do this, ask him to do it for you.) Soak the sole 10 minutes in milk to which salt has been added, roll in flour, dip in beaten egg, and then roll in fine dry breadcrumbs. Fry in deep fat preheated to 375° F. until fish has browned. Drain on paper towel. Remove the backbone. Combine remaining ingredients, shape into ½-inch balls, and place in the backbone cavity. Serve on a platter. Makes 6 servings. (See Culinary Techniques in Pictures.)

⚜ SOLE MORNAY

6 sole, ½ pound each
salt and ground black pepper
1½ cups dry white wine
1 cup Mornay Sauce
¼ cup grated Cheddar or Gruyère cheese

Sprinkle sole lightly with salt and pepper. Heat wine in a skillet, add fish, and simmer 8 to 10 minutes or until fish flakes when tested with a fork. Transfer sole to a buttered heatproof platter. Reduce the wine to one half its original amount, add to Mornay Sauce, and spread over fish. Sprinkle with grated cheese. Brown under broiler heat. Makes 6 servings.

⚜ FILLETS OF SOLE WITH ALMONDS

6 fillets of sole
salt and ground pepper to taste
6 tablespoons butter
¼ cup slivered blanched almonds
lemon wedges
parsley

Sprinkle sole fillets lightly with salt and pepper. Sauté in butter over moderate heat until lightly browned. Transfer fish to a warm platter and set aside in a warm place. In the butter that is left in the skillet, cook almonds until golden. Pour almonds and butter over the fillets of sole. Garnish with lemon wedges and parsley. Makes 6 servings.

⚜ FILLETS OF SOLE BONNE FEMME

6 sole fillets, weighing ½ pound each
salt and ground black pepper
1 shallot, minced
¼ finely chopped mushrooms
½ cup hot fish stock
½ cup hot dry white wine
1 small bay leaf
2 tablespoons chopped parsley
½ teaspoon dried thyme leaves
18 small mushroom caps
2 tablespoons butter
1 tablespoon flour
1 tablespoon butter

Sprinkle fillets of sole lightly with salt and pepper. Arrange in the bottom of a well-buttered baking dish and sprinkle with shallots and mushrooms. Add stock, wine, bay leaf, parsley, and thyme. Cover and bake in a preheated moderate oven (350° F.) 15 to 20 minutes or until the fish flakes. Drain the liquid into a small saucepan. Cook until the liquid has been reduced to 1 cup. Transfer fish to a heatproof platter. Cook mushroom caps in butter about 5 minutes and place 3 on each serving of fish. Blend the flour with the butter and add to the reduced liquid. Bring to boiling point and cook 2 minutes, stirring constantly. Pour the sauce over the fillets, covering them completely. Place the dish under the broiler just until the top is glazed. Makes 6 servings.

⚜ BURGUNDY-STYLE FILLETS OF SOLE

3 sole fillets, 1 pound each
salt and ground black pepper
2 shallots, finely chopped
1 cup dry red Burgundy
½ cup Demi-Glace Sauce
1 tablespoon flour
3 tablespoons butter
24 small glazed onions
24 small mushroom caps sautéed in butter

Sprinkle fish lightly with salt and pepper and place it in a well-buttered baking dish. Add shallots and wine. Cover and simmer 8 to 10 minutes or until the fish flakes when tested with a fork. Drain off the cooking liquor, strain into a saucepan, and cook until the quantity has reduced to one half the original amount. Add Demi-Glace Sauce and cook ½ minute. Blend flour with 2 tablespoons of the butter. Mix with the sauce and stir and cook 1 minute. Add the rest of the butter. Transfer fillets to a platter and cover with the sauce. Garnish with onions and mushroom caps. Makes 6 servings.

⚜ FILLETS OF SOLE HERRIOT

3 sole fillets, 1 pound each
salt and ground black pepper
1 shallot, chopped
2 tablespoons lemon juice
¾ cup fish stock
⅔ cup dry white wine
1 tablespoon flour
4 tablespoons butter
18 Fish Quenelles
12 small artichoke hearts, quartered
1 truffle (optional)
1 cup Lobster Sauce

Sprinkle sole lightly with salt and pepper. Fold fillets and place in a buttered baking dish. Sprinkle with shallots and lemon juice. Add fish stock. Cover and simmer 8 to 10 minutes or until the fish flakes when tested with a fork. Drain cooking liquid into a small saucepan and cook until it has reduced to ⅓ cup. Add wine. Blend flour with 2 tablespoons of the butter and mix with the sauce. Stir and cook 1 to 2 minutes. Add quenelles. Set aside to keep warm. Sauté artichoke hearts in remaining butter until they are tender but not mushy. Season to taste with salt and pepper. Arrange fish fillets down the center of a platter, having them overlap. Top each with a slice of truffle. Cover with Lobster Sauce. Garnish with quenelles at one end of the platter and artichokes at the other. Makes 6 servings. (See illustration, page 436.)

⚜ FILLETS OF SOLE MONTCALM

2 pounds fillets of sole
salt
ground white pepper
½ cup dry white wine
¾ cup Hollandaise Sauce
6 medium-sized boiled potatoes
⅓ cup diced cooked shrimp
⅔ cup fish Velouté Sauce

Sprinkle fillets lightly with salt and pepper. Simmer in wine in a covered saucepan 8 to 10 minutes or until the fish flakes when tested with a fork. Transfer fish to a warmed platter and set aside in a warm place. Reduce the wine stock to one half the original amount and blend with the Hollandaise Sauce. Arrange potatoes on a platter around the fish and coat them with the sauce. Mix shrimp with fish Velouté Sauce and spread over fish. Makes 6 servings.

⚜ FILLETS OF SOLE MONTE CARLO

2 pounds fillets of sole
salt
ground black pepper
flour
¼ cup olive oil or salad oil
2 tablespoons mashed anchovy fillets or 1 tablespoon anchovy paste
½ cup (1 stick) butter, melted
6 whole anchovy fillets

Cut fillets into 6 servings. Sprinkle lightly with salt and pepper. Roll in flour. Fry in hot oil over moderate heat until fillets have browned on both sides. Transfer to a warmed platter. Combine mashed anchovies or anchovy paste and melted butter and pour over fish. Garnish as desired with whole anchovy fillets. Makes 6 servings. (See illustration, page 437.)

⚜ FILLETS OF SOLE MURAT

2 pounds fillets of sole
1 teaspoon salt
¼ teaspoon ground black pepper
½ cup milk
flour
¼ cup oil or shortening
5 medium-sized potatoes, peeled and diced
6 tablespoons butter
shortening
6 raw artichoke bottoms
3 firm ripe tomatoes, thickly sliced
chopped parsley

Cut sole into lengthwise halves. Add ½ teaspoon salt and ⅛ teaspoon pepper to the milk, dip fish in seasoned milk, and roll it in flour. Fry in oil or shortening until crisp and brown. Set aside in a warm place. Parboil potatoes 2 to 3 minutes, drain off water, toss in 2 tablespoons of the butter, and cool. Fry potatoes until brown in shortening, using as little as possible. Set aside in a warm place. Dice artichoke bottoms, and cook in butter. Mix lightly with potatoes and fish, and put all into a serving dish. Fry tomatoes in butter and arrange on top of the dish. Sprinkle lightly with salt, pepper, and chopped parsley. Makes 6 servings. (See illustration, page 438.)

⚜ FILLETS OF SOLE PAILLARD

1 pound whiting
2 unbeaten egg whites
½ cup heavy cream
salt and ground black pepper to taste
12 crayfish
dry white wine
6 fillets of sole
1½ cups fish Velouté Sauce
1 cup sliced mushrooms, sautéed in butter
6 thin slices truffle (optional)

Purée the whiting in an electric blender with 2 tablespoons of the cream, or put it through a food chopper, using the finest blade. Stir and beat fish with a wooden spoon, beating in the egg whites. Set the bowl in a pan of ice water. Gradually beat the cream into the fish. Beat well. Season to taste with salt and pepper. Cook the crayfish in a little dry white wine until they turn red, about 5 minutes. Peel crayfish and remove the meat from the shells. Empty the heads, reserving 6 heads for decoration. Reserve the crayfish meat. Wipe the sole fillets dry, spread with a layer of the whiting forcemeat, and fold them over in half. Arrange fillets down the center of a heatproof platter and place a crayfish head at the pointed end of each. Fill the space in between them with remaining forcemeat to hold the heads in place. Pour in ½ cup of the wine in which the crayfish was cooked. Cover and bake 15 to 20 minutes in a preheated moderate oven (350° F.). Drain the wine from the platter into a small saucepan, and cook until it has reduced to ⅓ cup. Mix with ½ cup of the Velouté Sauce. Heat, adjust seasonings, stir in butter, and spoon over the cooked rolled fillets. Combine the remaining Velouté Sauce, cooked crayfish tails, and mushrooms. Add salt and pepper to taste and pour the mixture around the fillets. Garnish each serving with a thin slice of truffle if desired. Makes 6 servings. (See illustration, page 437.)

⚜ FILLETS OF SOLE VENINI

10½ pounds sole
1 quart cold water
⅓ cup chopped onion
⅔ cup dry white wine
salt
9 tablespoons butter
¼ cup Béchamel Sauce
⅓ cup heavy cream
30 peeled raw deveined shrimp
¾ cup Tomato Sauce
2 tablespoons brandy

Fillet the sole. Put the bones, skins, and heads in a saucepan with 1 quart cold water, onion, ⅓ cup of the wine, and 1 teaspoon salt. Cover, bring to boiling point, reduce heat, and simmer 30 minutes. Strain and reduce the stock to 3 cups. Poach the sole fillets in the fish stock and the remaining wine until the fish flakes when tested with a fork. Arrange the fillets, overlapping, around the bottom of a serving dish and keep them warm. Strain the cooking liquor into a saucepan and reduce to half. Add 4 tablespoons butter and bring liquid to boiling point. Beat in Béchamel Sauce and simmer to sauce consistency. Stir in cream and 3 tablespoons butter and beat with a whisk. Keep warm. Cook shrimp in 2 tablespoons butter in a skillet until shrimp turns red. Remove shrimp and keep them warm. Add Tomato Sauce to the skillet and cook 5 minutes. Add brandy and adjust seasonings. Cover the sole with the Béchamel Sauce mixture. Arrange the shrimp in a circle inside the circle of sole fillets in the dish and pour the Tomato Sauce in the center. Makes 10 servings. (See illustration, page 435.)

PAUPIETTES OF SOLE DAUMONT

3 pounds whiting
1 cup heavy cream
4 unbeaten egg whites
salt
ground black pepper
2 pounds fillets of sole
18 crayfish or shrimp
1 cup crayfish or shrimp stock
½ cup dry white wine
¼ cup finely chopped mushrooms
2 cups Béchamel Sauce
¼ cup (½ stick) butter
1 tablespoon flour
2 quarts Herbed Steamed Mussels

Purée whiting in an electric blender with 4 tablespoons of the cream, or put the fish through a food chopper, using the finest blade. Stir and beat in the egg whites, using a wooden spoon or an electric mixer. Set the bowl in a pan of ice water. Gradually beat in the remaining cream. Beat well. Season to taste with salt and pepper. Cut fillets of sole into 12 pieces of uniform size and shape, dry them, spread each with a layer of forcemeat (whiting mixture), and fold each over in half. Arrange the fillets in a ring in a buttered baking dish. Put crayfish or shrimp in a saucepan, cover with water, and add ½ teaspoon salt. Bring to boiling point, reduce heat, and simmer 5 minutes, or until the crayfish or shrimp turn red. Drain off water, reserving it for later use. Peel the crayfish or shrimp and set aside. Add wine to crayfish or shrimp stock, heat, and pour over the fillets. Add mushrooms. Cover and bake in a preheated moderate oven (350° F.) 15 to 20 minutes or until the fish flakes when tested with a fork. Drain off the stock, strain it through a fine sieve, reduce it to ½ cup, and add Béchamel Sauce. Mash 6 of the crayfish or shrimp very fine and blend with the butter and flour. Add to the sauce and cook until of desired thickness. Pour over fillets of sole. Place a crayfish or shrimp between each pair of fillets. Remove the steamed mussels from their shells and put them in the center of the dish. Makes 6 servings. (See illustration, page 436.)

⚜ PAUPIETTES OF SOLE

1⅓ cups mushrooms, finely chopped
3 tablespoons butter
⅓ cup each chopped onion, chives, and parsley
salt and ground black pepper to taste
6 fillets of sole
2 eggs, beaten
½ cup milk
Fritter Batter
fine dry breadcrumbs
4 to 6 tablespoons butter
3 tablespoons flour
1 cup dry white wine
1 cup heavy cream
⅓ cup grated Parmesan cheese

Cook mushrooms in butter 5 minutes. Add onion, chives, and parsley, and cook 2 to 3 minutes or until vegetables are soft enough to spread. Add salt and pepper. Sprinkle fish lightly with salt and pepper and spread uniformly with the cooked mushroom mixture. Roll up in jelly-roll fashion and fasten the seams with toothpicks. Beat eggs with milk and dip the fish rolls into the mixture. Then dip them in Fritter Batter, roll in breadcrumbs, and set aside for 10 minutes for coating to dry. Brown on all sides in butter. Transfer to a warm platter and set aside in a warm place. Blend flour with the butter that was left in the skillet. Stir and cook 1 minute. Add wine. Stir and cook until sauce is smooth and thickened. Add cream, mix well, and heat. Pour the sauce into the platter around the fish. Sprinkle with Parmesan cheese and brown under the broiler heat. Makes 6 servings.

⚜ VOL-AU-VENT OF FILLETS OF SOLE LA VALLIÈRE

8 fillets of sole, 3 ounces each
1 cup whiting forcemeat
½ cup fish stock
½ cup dry white wine
1 cup sautéed sliced mushrooms
1 cup peeled, deveined cooked shrimp
8 crayfish tails
1 cup cooked mussels
3½ cups Nantua Sauce
1 large (8-inch) hot Puff Pastry case (vol-au-vent)
8 truffle slices, or 8 pitted black olives

Beat the fillets lightly with a spatula. Spread each with a layer of whiting forcemeat, fold in half, and poach in stock and wine until the fish flakes when tested with a fork, 8 to 10 minutes. Combine mushrooms, shrimp, crayfish, mussels, and Nantua Sauce. Adjust seasonings. Place the hot vol-au-vent on a serving plate. Fill with the shellfish and mushroom mixture, arrange the fillets over the top, slightly overlapping, and garnish each with a truffle slice or black olive. Serve very hot. Makes 8 servings. (See illustration, page 435; see also Classic Vol-au-Vent in Culinary Techniques in Pictures.)

⚜ COLD FILLETS OF SOLE WITH VEGETABLE SALAD

4 sole fillets, ½ pound each
salt
ground black pepper
3 tablespoons lemon juice
¼ cup chopped onions
¾ cup mayonnaise
2 teaspoons unflavored gelatin
⅓ cup dry white wine
1 cup each cooked peas, diced cooked carrots, diced cooked potatoes, and diced raw celery
Chaud-froid Sauce
chervil leaves
aspic

Fold fillets. Trim them uniformly and place them in a buttered baking dish. Sprinkle with salt, pepper, lemon juice, and wine. Cover and bake in a preheated moderate oven (350° F.) 25 to 30 minutes or until the fish flakes when tested with a fork. Transfer fish to a flat surface and cool under slight pressure. Combine vegetables with salt, pepper, and lemon juice to taste. Soften gelatin in 3 tablespoons cold water, set in a pan of hot water to melt, mix with the mayonnaise, and add to the salad. Mix lightly and turn the salad into a flat round dish. Chill. Arrange sole fillets on a wire rack and coat with Chaud-froid Sauce. Before the sauce sets, decorate each fillet with a chervil leaf dipped in liquid aspic. Chill until the coating is set. Coat with semi-liquid aspic and chill until the aspic is set. Turn out the vegetable salad into the center of a large round serving plate and arrange the fillets over it with the tips pointing toward the center. Fill in between the fillets with chopped aspic. Surround the salad with diced aspic. Makes 8 servings.

⚜ FILLETS OF SOLE IN ASPIC

2 pounds fillets of sole
salt
ground black pepper
lemon juice
1 cup dry white wine
1 truffle, sliced
aspic
Mayonnaise or Ravigote or Green Mayonnaise

Cut sole fillets into uniform servings. Sprinkle with salt, pepper, and lemon juice. Place in the bottom of a skillet, add wine, bring to boiling point, reduce heat, and simmer 8 to 10 minutes or until the fish flakes when tested with a fork. Cool the fillets in the stock under slight pressure. Trim edges uniformly and place fish on a platter. Garnish with truffles, coat with almost-set aspic, and chill. Surround with chopped aspic. Serve with a cold sauce—plain mayonnaise or Ravigote or Green Mayonnaise. Makes 6 servings.

⚜ FILLETS OF SOLE FLORALIES

12 fillets of sole (4 pounds)
fish stock
Chaud-froid Sauce
pimiento
green sweet pepper, or cucumber pickle
3 cups aspic
4 cups macédoine of cooked vegetables
4 firm ripe tomatoes
thick mayonnaise
13 black olives
gherkins, sliced
1 lemon

Fold fillets, trim them uniformly, and poach in fish stock according to directions for Poached Fish. Transfer fish to a flat surface, cover with foil, and place a large plate on the foil in order to give a little pressure to the fish as it cools. Place a wire cooling rack on a baking sheet and arrange the cold sole fillets on the rack. Coat with Chaud-froid Sauce. Before the sauce sets, simulate flowers on each fillet with small pieces of pimiento. Make stems and leaves with thin slices of green pepper or pickle. Chill. Glaze with aspic. Chill again until aspic is set. Pour a thin layer of aspic on a large serving plate and chill until aspic is firm. Turn the cooked vegetables into the center of the tray and spread them to form a circle. Place the fillets of sole on the vegetables forming a ring with the small ends pointed inward. Encircle with sliced tomatoes. Using a pastry bag and a leaf nozzle, pipe enough thick mayonnaise around the macédoine of vegetables to cover the edges and a portion of the tomato slices. Place black olives between the large ends of the fillets. If desired, decorate the center of the dish with a lemon cut and decorated to resemble a white tulip; this is made by cutting off and discarding the yellow portion of the peel, leaving the white part intact, and cutting 6 deep notches in the bud end half of the lemon to make it resemble the petals of a tulip. Garnish the center of the lemon with 3 lengthwise slices of black olive and a piece of pimiento. Serve cold. Makes 12 servings. (See illustration, page 442.)

⚜ MOLD OF ROLLED FILLETS OF SOLE IN ASPIC

4 fillets of sole, ¾ pound each
lemon juice
salt
ground black pepper
1 cup dry white wine
1 cup fish stock
1½ quarts fish aspic
2 truffles (or 2 pimientoes if truffles are not available)
3 cups cold cooked macédoine of vegetables

Trim fish fillets to uniform shape. Sprinkle with lemon juice, salt, and pepper to taste. Roll up in jelly-roll fashion. Hold ends in place with toothpicks. Heat wine and fish stock in a saucepan, add fish rolls, and simmer 12 to 15 minutes or until the fish flakes when tested with a fork. Cool rolls in poaching liquid, transfer to a plate, and chill 1 to 2 hours. Cut rolls in slices ½ inch thick and decorate centers with ½-inch disks of truffle or pimiento dipped in aspic. Chill until aspic is set. Coat the bottom and sides of a 1½-quart mold with 2 layers of aspic, chilling each layer until set. Dip the slices of rolled fillet of sole in aspic and arrange them in the bottom and on the sides of the mold, reserving the leftover slices for later use. Chill again until aspic is set. Season the vegetables with salt and pepper to taste, mix them with 1 cup of the aspic, chill until the aspic begins to set, and put in the center of the mold. Chill until firm and ready to serve. Chill remaining aspic until firm. Just before serving, unmold the dish onto a serving plate. Chop aspic, spoon it onto the plate around the mold, and arrange the reserved slices of rolled fillet of sole on the chopped aspic. Serve mayonnaise in a separate bowl. Makes 8 to 10 servings. (See illustration, page 442.)

STURGEON (*Esturgeon*)

Sturgeon is a large fish which lives in the sea but migrates up river to spawn. Those caught in fresh water in the spring are preferred. The sturgeon meat has no particular flavor, and it is sought mainly because of its rarity. However, the sturgeon roe, caviar, is a highly prized delicacy.

Sturgeon may be prepared in the same way as veal, which it resembles in appearance after cooking. It is often cut into thick steaks, larded and braised and served with vegetables in the same way as Fricandeau of Veal. Sturgeon is also served with sauces, such as Curry, Hongroise, Velouté, and Mushroom.

⚜ BRAISED STURGEON

2½ pounds sturgeon
thin narrow strips fat salt pork (lardoons)
salt
ground black pepper
butter
1 large carrot
1 medium-sized onion
1 cup dry white wine

Remove skin and bones from sturgeon and lard one side with lardoons. Sprinkle lightly with salt and pepper. Brown on both sides in butter. Peel and slice carrot and onion and add. Pour in wine. Cover and braise in a preheated slow oven (325° F.) 25 to 30 minutes or until sturgeon flakes when tested with a fork. Transfer sturgeon and vegetables to a warmed platter. Reduce the braising stock to one-fourth the original amount. Pour over fish. Makes 6 servings.

⚜ SLICED STURGEON

2½ pounds sturgeon
salt
ground black pepper
flour
6 tablespoons butter
lemon juice
chopped parsley

Remove skin and bones from the sturgeon and cut into slices weighing about 4 ounces each. Sprinkle lightly with salt and pepper. Roll the pieces in flour and brown on both sides in 3 tablespoons of the butter. Remove fish to a warm platter. Sprinkle with lemon juice. Melt remaining butter and pour over the fish. Garnish with chopped parsley. Makes 6 servings.

TROUT (*Truite de Rivière*)

Freshwater trout, which are related to salmon, are found in brooks, rivers and lakes in North America. There are many varieties, all delicious, though trout caught in mountain streams is particularly prized. Char is a related species, found in deep lakes. Recipes calling for salmon or salmon trout can usually be used for freshwater trout.

⚜ TROUT WITH ALMONDS

1 teaspoon salt
1 cup milk
6 dressed trout, ½ pound each
flour
butter
⅓ cup sliced blanched almonds

Add salt to milk and dip trout into it. Roll in flour. Brown on both sides in butter over moderate heat. Transfer trout to a warm platter. Put 2 more tablespoons butter in a skillet. Add almonds and stir and cook until almonds are brown. Pour over the cooked trout. Makes 6 servings. (See illustration, page 459.)

⚜ FRIED TROUT

In the recipe for Trout with Almonds, omit the almonds and serve the browned trout with sizzling browned butter. Sprinkle with lemon juice. Garnish with parsley and lemon wedges. Allow 1 trout (½ pound) per serving.

⚜ GRENOBLE-STYLE FRIED TROUT

Fry trout as directed in Trout with Almonds. Omit the almonds. Top each trout with a slice of lemon and sprinkle generously with capers. Pour browned butter over the top. Allow 1 trout (½ pound) per serving.

⚜ TROUT MANTUA STYLE

Fry 6 trout, ½ pound each, as directed in Trout with Almonds. Omit the almonds. Meanwhile cook 1 teaspoon chopped shallots and 2 peeled, seeded, chopped tomatoes in ¾ cup Marsala until tomatoes are soft and the sauce is reduced to half its original amount. Cook 3 tablespoons finely chopped mushrooms in 1 tablespoon butter and add. Stir in 2 tablespoons finely chopped cooked lean ham, and salt, pepper, and lemon juice to taste. Serve over fish. Sprinkle with chopped parsley. Makes 6 servings.

⚜ TROUT VAUCLUSE STYLE

Fry trout as directed in Trout with Almonds, using oil instead of butter. Sprinkle with lemon juice and garnish with parsley and lemon wedges. Makes 6 servings.

⚜ TROUT GLAZED IN RED WINE

1 medium-sized onion, sliced
salt
ground black pepper
6 dressed trout, ½ pound each
1¾ cups dry red wine
2 tablespoons flour
2 tablespoons butter
heart-shaped fried white-bread croutons

Scatter onion slices over the bottom of a large baking dish. Sprinkle salt and pepper lightly over trout and arrange them over the onions. Pour wine over the fish. Bring to boiling point, reduce heat, and cook until the fish flakes when tested with a fork. Drain the wine into a small saucepan. Blend flour with butter and add to the wine. Mix well and cook ½ minute. Pour over trout. Quickly glaze under broiler heat. Serve on a platter garnished with heart-shaped fried white-bread croutons. Makes 6 servings.

⚜ HUSSAR-STYLE TROUT

3 tablespoons chopped onion
6 tablespoons butter
1 cup sliced onion
3 cups soft breadcrumbs
½ cup milk
¼ teaspoon dried thyme leaves
1 tablespoon chopped parsley
⅛ teaspoon ground black pepper
salt to taste
1 egg, beaten
6 dressed trout, ½ pound each
¾ cup dry white wine
1 tablespoon flour

Cook chopped onion in 2 tablespoons of the butter until onion is transparent. Transfer the cooked onion to a mixing bowl. In the same skillet add 2 more tablespoons of the butter and the sliced onion. Cook until onions are transparent, then place them in the bottom of a baking pan. Soak crumbs in milk, squeeze them dry, fluff them with a fork, and add to the chopped onion. Stir in seasonings and beaten egg. Spoon into the body cavities of trout. Close openings with toothpick. Place fish on the cooked onion slices in the baking pan. Sprinkle with salt and pepper. Pour in wine. Place in a preheated moderate oven (350° F.) and bake 25 to 30 minutes or until the fish flakes when tested with a fork. Pour off stock into a saucepan and boil down to one-half. Blend flour with remaining 2 tablespoons butter and add to the stock. Mix well and cook ½ minute. Season with salt and pepper to taste. Pour over trout. Glaze quickly under broiler heat. Makes 6 servings.

⚜ TROUT MÂCON STYLE

6 dressed trout, ½ pound each
1¾ cups red wine
2 cups sliced onion
7 tablespoons butter
bouillon
½ teaspoon salt
¼ teaspoon sugar
2 cups small mushroom caps
1 rounded teaspoon meat glaze
1 tablespoon flour

Place trout in a baking pan. Pour in wine. Bake in a preheated moderate oven (350° F.) 30 minutes, or until the trout flakes when tested with a fork. Set aside to keep warm. Brown the onion in 3 tablespoons of the butter. Add enough bouillon to cover the onion more than half. Add salt and sugar. Simmer until the liquid has evaporated and onions are glazed. Set aside to keep warm. Sauté mushrooms in 3 tablespoons of the butter until they are tender. Drain the wine from the trout into a saucepan and boil it down to a little less than half. Add meat glaze. Blend flour with the remaining 1 tablespoon butter and add to the stock. Mix well and boil up 3 or 4 times. Adjust seasonings. Transfer trout to a platter and pour the sauce over it. Pile mushrooms at one end of the platter and onions at the other end (see illustration, page 461). Makes 6 servings.

⚜ TROUT RENATO (*Italian*)

6 dressed boned trout, ½ pound each
salt
ground black pepper
6 teaspoons capers
6 anchovy fillets, diced
¼ cup olive oil or salad oil
1 cup dry white wine
6 servings steamed potatoes
1 whole large tomato, peeled
lemon slices, cut in half
black olives

Open trout flat like a book and sprinkle lightly with salt and pepper. Scatter 1 teaspoon capers and 1 diced anchovy on each. Fold the tail toward the head.

Pour oil and wine in a skillet and add trout. Cover, bring to boiling point, reduce heat and simmer 10 minutes or until the fish flakes when tested with a fork. Transfer trout to a round serving dish and keep hot. Reduce the cooking stock. Season to taste with salt and pepper and pour over fish. Serve with steamed potatoes. Cut a whole tomato, peeled, into 6 wedges and place it in the center of the dish in its original shape. Sprinkle with chopped parsley. Place lemon slices around the edge of the dish. Garnish with black olives. Makes 6 servings. (See illustration, page 459.)

⚜ GLAZED TROUT ANDRÉA

6 trout, ½ pound each
1 cup dry white wine
1 cup fish stock
½ teaspoon dried or 2 teaspoons chopped fresh tarragon
radishes
whole tarragon leaves and stems
6 baked 2-inch pastry tart shells
1½ cups Shrimp Mousse
6 peeled cooked shrimp
parsley

Ask the fish butcher to clean the trout through the gills without cutting open the stomach. Cut off fins, remove scales, and wash. Place the fish in a large buttered baking pan. Add wine, stock, and tarragon. Bake in a preheated slow oven (325° F.) 25 to 30 minutes or until the fish flakes when tested with a fork. Remove fish from the oven and cool it in the stock. Transfer fish to a large platter. Set aside. Make aspic from the stock, using the recipe in this book. Garnish the fish with sliced radishes, tarragon leaves, and stems. Coat lightly with semiliquid aspic. Chill until aspic is set. Fill the baked tart shells with Shrimp Mousse; garnish each with a whole shrimp. Coat with aspic. Chill until set. Just before serving arrange the tart shells on the tray with the fish. Garnish with parsley. Makes 6 servings. (See illustration, page 464.)

⚜ TROUT IN ASPIC

8 trout, ½ pound each
salt
ground black pepper
½ teaspoon dried thyme or 2 teaspoons chopped fresh thyme
1 small bay leaf
1 small onion, sliced
1 cup dry white wine
2 cups fish aspic
¼ pound cooked shrimp
blanched tarragon leaves or parsley or watercress

Cook the trout in seasonings and wine as in the recipe for Glazed Trout Andréa. Cool in the stock. Arrange trout on a large platter that has been coated thinly with aspic and coat the trout with aspic. Decorate as desired with peeled shrimp and blanched tarragon leaves, parsley, or watercress. Makes 6 servings.

Red wine may be substituted for white wine in this recipe, and the fish decorated with truffles and small balls of turnip and carrot instead of the shrimp and herbs.

⚜ COLD TROUT PALACE HOTEL STYLE

8 trout, ½ pound each
court bouillon
30 cooked crayfish tails, or 30 cooked shrimp (leave tails attached to 16 shrimp)
1 cup diced cooked asparagus tips
1 cup cooked green beans
3 peeled, seeded, diced tomatoes
salt, ground black pepper
¼ cup olive oil or salad oil
1½ tablespoons vinegar
2 cups liquid fish aspic
fresh dill or parsley
Vinaigrette Sauce

Remove the 2 fillets from each trout, leaving them attached to the head. Roll each fillet around a medium-small potato on either side of the head, giving the appearance of a pair of lorgnettes. Poach and cool in court bouillon to cover. Reserve 16 crayfish tails or shrimp with tails attached. Dice the remainder and mix with the asparagus tips, beans, tomatoes, salt and pepper to taste, oil, and vinegar. Marinate 1 hour. Drain the marinade from the vegetables and add aspic. Chill until the mixture begins to set. Drain the trout well and arrange them on a large tray. Fill the openings in the poached trout with the salad jelly mixture and brush the trout with semiliquid aspic. Chill until set. Fill the center of the tray with crayfish tails or shrimp with tails attached. Garnish with fresh dill or parsley. Serve with Vinaigrette Sauce in a separate dish. Makes 8 servings. (See illustration, page 465.)

⚜ GLAZED TROUT VLADIMIR

1 dressed trout (or salmon trout), 3½ to 4 pounds
fish stock
fish aspic
8 large hard-cooked eggs
½ cup (1 stick) softened butter
¼ cup mayonnaise
salt
ground black pepper
spinach purée or green food coloring
tomato purée or red food coloring
Green Mayonnaise

Poach trout in fish stock. Remove from heat and allow fish to cool in the stock. Remove skin and chill the fish. Cut out the fillets, slice them, and replace them with the rest of the fish in the original shape on a large tray. Coat with aspic. Peel eggs, cut in half, and remove yolks. Rub the yolks through a sieve, blend with butter, add mayonnaise, and season to taste with salt and pepper. Divide the mixture into two equal parts. Add spinach purée or green food coloring to one half, and tomato purée or red food coloring to the remaining half, until the mixtures reach the desired colors. With pastry bags or decorators' tubes, pipe the egg-yolk mixtures into the cavities of the egg whites, filling half the cavities with red and half with green. Brush with aspic. Place the stuffed egg halves on the tray around the fish. Decorate the top of the fish with green and red rosettes, using the rest of the egg-yolk mixtures. Garnish the tray at each end with a notched lemon half. Chill. Serve with Green Mayonnaise in a separate bowl. Makes 6 servings. (See illustration, page 464.)

TUNA (*Thon*)

The tuna (tunny) is a large fish, widely distributed in warm or temperate seas; many species are found in the Pacific. Tuna is eaten fresh and is also popular in the United States in canned form, usually canned in oil.

⚜ GRILLED TUNA MAÎTRE D'HÔTEL

Sprinkle thick slices of tuna lightly with salt and ground black pepper. Dip in flour, shake off surplus, and cook until browned in oil or shortening over moderate heat, turning to brown both sides. Blend 2 tablespoons lemon juice and 1 teaspoon chopped parsley with ½ cup (1 stick) softened butter. Season with a little salt and ground black pepper. Serve over fish. Allow ⅓ pound of fish per serving.

⚜ TUNA BORDEAUX STYLE

1½ pounds tuna
salt and ground black pepper
2 tablespoons oil
4 tablespoons butter
½ cup thinly sliced onion
2 shallots, chopped
5 medium-sized tomatoes, peeled, seeded, and quartered
⅓ cup Demi-Glace Sauce
⅓ cup dry white wine
2 cups quartered mushrooms
chopped parsley

Rub tuna fish lightly with salt and pepper. Brown on both sides in oil and 2 tablespoons of the butter. Add onions, shallots, tomatoes, Demi-Glace, wine, and salt and pepper to taste. Cover and cook over moderate heat until the fish flakes when tested with a fork. Transfer fish to a platter. Set aside in a warm place. Return the skillet to the heat and cook the sauce until the quantity is reduced by one fourth its original amount. Meanwhile sauté mushrooms in remaining 2 tablespoons butter and add to the sauce. Heat ½ minute. Pour over fish. Sprinkle with chopped parsley. Makes 6 servings.

⚜ TUNA MÉNAGÈRE

2 pounds tuna, cut ½ inch thick
salt and ground black pepper to taste
4 tablespoons (½ stick) butter
⅓ cup chopped onion
⅓ cup each wine and water
3 tablespoons tomato purée
2 tablespoons lemon juice
1½ cups sliced mushrooms cooked in butter, or 1 cup diced, peeled, and seeded tomatoes cooked in butter

Place fish in a saucepan, cover with cold water, bring to boiling point, reduce heat, and simmer 4 to 5 minutes. Remove fish from the water, drain, season lightly with salt and pepper, and brown on both sides in 2 tablespoons butter. Melt remaining butter in a casserole. Add onion, mix well, sprinkle with flour, and stir and cook 1 minute. Add wine and water. Cook until the sauce has reduced by one-fourth its original quantity. Stir in tomato purée and lemon juice. Add the tuna fish, cover, and cook in a preheated moderate oven (350° F.) 15 minutes or until the fish flakes when tested with a fork. Transfer fish to a platter. Set aside in a warm place. Add mushrooms or tomatoes to the sauce and bring to boiling point. Adjust seasonings and pour around fish. Makes 6 servings.

TURBOT

The turbot is a large European flat fish with very delicate flesh. Various large American flat fishes, including halibut and large flounder, are sometimes called turbot, though they are not of the same species; halibut can be substituted for turbot in these recipes. For the preparation of turbot for cooking, see Culinary Techniques in Pictures.

⚜ GRILLED TURBOT MAÎTRE D'HÔTEL

Cut 2 pounds turbot into serving-size pieces. Sprinkle lightly with salt and ground black pepper. Roll in flour and brush with salad oil. Place on preheated oiled broiler pan and broil 4 inches from the source of heat 5 to 8 minutes. Turn fish carefully and brush again with oil. Cook 5 to 8 minutes or until the fish flakes when tested with a fork. Blend 2 tablespoons lemon juice and 1 tablespoon chopped parsley with ½ cup (1 stick) butter. Serve on the fish. Makes 6 servings.

⚜ DEEP-FAT-FRIED TURBOT WITH TARTARE SAUCE

2 pounds turbot
½ cup milk
½ teaspoon salt
¼ teaspoon ground black pepper
flour
Tartare Sauce

Cut fish into serving-size pieces. Dip in milk seasoned with salt and pepper and then in flour. Fry until browned in deep fat preheated to 375° F. Drain on paper towels. Serve with Tartare Sauce. Makes 6 servings.

⚜ POACHED SLICES OF TURBOT

4 slices (1 pound, 5 ounces) turbot
Fish Stock or boiling salted water
1 whole onion
1 each whole clove and bay leaf
parsley
lemon wedges
tomatoes
Hollandaise Sauce

Poach fish in Fish Stock or boiling salted water as directed in recipe for Poached Fish, adding onion, clove, and bay leaf. Garnish with parsley and lemon wedges and serve with tomatoes and Hollandaise Sauce in separate dishes. Makes 4 servings. (See illustration, page 439.)

⚜ TURBOT AIDA

2 pounds turbot
salt and ground black pepper to taste
1½ pounds cooked fresh spinach or 2 packages (10 ounces each) frozen spinach
ground nutmeg to taste
1 cup Mornay Sauce
1 teaspoon paprika
¼ cup grated Cheddar cheese
fine dry breadcrumbs
¼ cup (½ stick) butter

Fillet the turbot. Make stock from the bones and strain the stock. Cut each fillet in half, sprinkle lightly with salt and pepper, and cook 8 to 10 minutes in the strained stock. Remove fish and reserve. Drain out all the liquid from the cooked spinach. Season spinach with salt, pepper, and ground nutmeg to taste. Cook the fish stock almost to a glaze, add Mornay Sauce and paprika, and adjust seasonings. Spread spinach in the bottom of a well-buttered baking dish. Top with the fish and cover with the sauce. Sprinkle with cheese and dot with butter. Cook in a preheated very hot oven (450° F.) 10 minutes or until browned. Makes 6 servings.

⚜ TURBOT AU GRATIN

Duchess Potatoes
1 cup sliced mushrooms
3 tablespoons butter
2 cups Mornay Sauce
1½ cups flaked cooked turbot
salt and ground black pepper to taste
⅓ cup grated Cheddar or Gruyère cheese
½ cup fresh breadcrumbs

Using a pastry bag and a star-shaped nozzle, pipe a high border of Duchess Potatoes around the top of a casserole. Brown lightly in the oven. Sauté mushrooms in 1 tablespoon of the butter and add to Mornay Sauce along with the fish. Add salt and pepper. Turn into the baking dish inside the potato ring. Sprinkle with grated cheese and breadcrumbs. Dot with the remaining 2 tablespoons butter. Bake in a preheated very hot oven (350° F.) 10 minutes or until browned. Makes 6 servings.

WHITEFISH (*Lavaret*)

Whitefish is the name given to a dozen or more species of freshwater fish related to the salmon and trout families which are found chiefly in northern lakes. The largest American species, common in the Great Lakes, attains a length of about 2 feet. The back is olive-tinted and the underside white. Lavaret is a European species; it resembles féra, which is a lake fish belonging to the salmon family, in the delicacy and flavor of its flesh. Féra is cooked in the same ways as whitefish or salmon. North American landlocked salmon can be prepared by the same methods.

⚜ GRILLED WHITEFISH

Sprinkle dressed whitefish lightly with salt and ground black pepper. Dip in flour, brush with olive oil or salad oil, and place on an oiled preheated grill. Cook under broiler heat until the fish flakes when tested with a fork, turning to brown both sides. Transfer fish to a platter. Sprinkle with browned butter, capers, and chopped parsley. Or, if desired, omit browned butter and capers, and serve with Béarnaise Sauce. Allow 1 fish (½ pound dressed fish) per serving.

⚜ FRIED FILLETS OF WHITEFISH

6 whitefish, ½ pound each
salt
ground black pepper
flour
shortening or oil
lemon juice
browned butter
chopped parsley
lemon slices

Cut the fish with a sharp knife down the back. Cut off heads and remove bones. Wash and wipe dry. Sprinkle lightly with salt and pepper. Dip in flour and cook in shortening or oil until golden brown on both sides. Arrange fish on a warmed platter. Sprinkle with lemon juice. Pour sizzling hot browned butter over the fish. Sprinkle with chopped parsley. Garnish with lemon slices. Makes 6 servings.

⚜ WHITEFISH COLBERT

6 whitefish, ½ pound each
1 egg, beaten
¾ teaspoon salt
⅛ teaspoon ground black pepper
fine dry breadcrumbs
butter and oil
6 tablespoons butter, melted
1 tablespoon chopped parsley
1 teaspoon chopped fresh thyme

Remove heads from fish. Split the fish down the back (do not open along the belly) and remove the bones in such a way that the fillets remain attached. Keep the fish opened flat. Wash and dry the fish, flour them, dip in beaten egg seasoned with salt and pepper, and roll in breadcrumbs. Let fish stand 10 minutes for crumbs to dry. Fry in equal parts butter and oil until browned on both sides. Combine the melted butter and the herbs and serve over fish. Makes 6 servings.

⚜ WHITEFISH IN WHITE WINE (*Féra au Vin Blanc*)

4-pound whitefish
salt
ground black pepper
1 shallot, chopped
½ cup dry white wine
1 cup Velouté Sauce
lemon juice to taste
1 tablespoon butter
Puffed Crescents

Ask your fish butcher to scale and eviscerate fish, leaving head, tail, and fins attached if desired. Sprinkle with salt and pepper. Scatter chopped shallot over the bottom of a baking dish and put fish on top. Heat wine and pour over fish. Cover the dish with foil and cook in a preheated moderate oven (350° F.) until the fish flakes when tested with a fork. Transfer fish to a warmed platter. Reduce the liquid around the fish to ¼ cup and blend it with the Velouté Sauce. Heat, add lemon juice, salt, and pepper to taste, and stir in the butter. Pour the sauce over the fish. Arrange Puffed Crescents around the edge of the platter. Makes 6 servings. (See illustration, page 462.)

PUFFED CRESCENTS

With a scalloped crescent cooky cutter, cut crescents from Puff Paste rolled ⅓ inch thick. Place on a baking sheet and bake in a preheated hot oven (400° F.) 10 minutes or until crescents have puffed and browned.

⚜ WHITEFISH FILLETS LUCERNE STYLE (*Filets de Féra à la Lucernoise—Swiss*)

12 fillets of whitefish, or landlocked salmon, 3 ounces each
2 cups sliced mushrooms
1½ cups peeled, seeded, diced tomatoes
1 teaspoon salt
¼ teaspoon ground black pepper
⅛ teaspoon ground nutmeg
¼ teaspoon each dried thyme, marjoram, and sage
½ cup dry white wine
1 cup Velouté Sauce
1 egg yolk
¼ cup heavy cream
medallions of baked pastry (optional)

Place the fillets, overlapping, in a well-buttered baking dish. Cover with mushrooms and tomatoes. Sprinkle with salt, pepper, nutmeg, and herbs. Add wine. Cover and cook in a preheated slow oven (325° F.) 30 to 40 minutes or until the fish flakes when tested with a fork. Transfer fillets to a serving dish. Strain the stock into a saucepan, mix with Velouté Sauce, and simmer 1 to 2 minutes. Blend egg yolk with cream and add. Cook ½ minute. Spoon over the fillets. If desired, garnish with medallions of baked pastry. Makes 6 servings.

WHITING (*Merlan*)

The European whiting is caught mainly in the Baltic Sea and the English Channel. Various American food fishes, including the silver hake, are also called whiting.

⚜ DEEP-FAT-FRIED WHITING IN A RING

Dress the whiting, remove the eyes, and with scissors cut off all the fins except the tail fin. With a smooth, firm motion remove the skin on both sides of the fish by pulling it toward the tail. Sprinkle fish lightly with salt and ground black pepper. Stick the tail in the fish's mouth and secure with toothpicks. This forms a circle. Dip fish in egg beaten with water (1 tablespoon to 1 egg), then roll in fine dry breadcrumbs. Fry until browned in deep fat preheated to 375° F. Drain on paper towels. Remove toothpicks. Serve on a platter and garnish with fried parsley and lemon slices. Pass Tomato Sauce in a separate bowl. Allow 1 fish (½ pound) per serving.

⚜ WHITING COLBERT

6 whiting, ½ pound each
½ teaspoon salt
¼ teaspoon ground black pepper
1 cup cold boiled milk
flour
2 eggs beaten with 2 tablespoons water
fine dry breadcrumbs
½ cup (1 stick) softened butter
½ cup chopped parsley
⅛ teaspoon dried or ½ teaspoon chopped fresh tarragon
½ teaspoon melted beef extract, or 1 teaspoon beef bouillon

Split whiting along the backbone and lift out the bones. Add salt and pepper to the milk and pour over fish. Soak 10 minutes. Remove fish from milk and drain well. Roll in flour, dip in beaten egg, and roll in breadcrumbs. Fry in deep fat preheated to 375° F. until fish has browned. Drain on paper towels. Blend together the remaining ingredients. Serve on fish. Makes 6 servings.

⚜ ENGLISH-STYLE WHITING

Prepare and cook whiting as directed for Whiting Colbert. Transfer to a platter and serve with melted butter and boiled potatoes. Allow 1 fish (½ pound) per serving.

⚜ DIEPPE-STYLE WHITING

4 dressed whiting, ½ pound each
salt
ground black pepper
¾ cup dry white wine
¾ cup fish stock
2 shallots, chopped
½ pound cooked shrimp
½ pound steamed mussels (without shells)
1 tablespoon each flour and butter
chopped parsley

Sprinkle fish lightly with salt and pepper. Simmer in a covered skillet in wine and fish stock with the shallots 8 to 10 minutes or until the fish flakes when tested with a fork. Transfer fish to a platter and garnish with shrimp and mussels. Blend flour with butter, add to the liquid in which the fish was cooked, and mix well. Stir and cook 1 to 2 minutes. Adjust seasonings and spread over fish, shrimp, and mussels. Sprinkle with chopped parsley. Makes 4 servings.

⚜ WHITING AU GRATIN

1½ cups chopped raw mushrooms
2 tablespoons oil
3 shallots, chopped
⅓ cup dry white wine
1 cup Demi-Glace Sauce
2 tablespoons chopped parsley
2 tablespoons tomato purée
6 dressed whiting, ½ pound each
¼ cup fine dry breadcrumbs
¼ cup (½ stick) butter

Cook mushrooms and shallots in oil 5 minutes. Add wine and simmer until most of the liquid has evaporated. Stir in Demi-Glace Sauce, parsley, and tomato purée and bring to boiling point. Cover the bottom of a baking dish with a little of the sauce. Sprinkle whiting lightly with salt and pepper, and place over the sauce. Spread the fish with the remaining sauce. Sprinkle with breadcrumbs and dot with butter. Bake in a preheated moderate oven (350° F.) 30 minutes or until crumbs have browned. Garnish with chopped parsley and lemon wedges. Makes 6 servings.

⚜ BAKED WHITING

6 whiting, ½ pound each
2 shallots, chopped
salt and ground black pepper to taste
½ cup dry white wine
chopped parsley
3 tablespoons fine dry breadcrumbs
3 tablespoons butter

Split the fish and remove the backbones. Set aside. Sprinkle chopped shallots over the bottom of a buttered baking pan. Season fish lightly with salt and pepper, fold them into their original shape, place them over the shallots, and pour the wine over them. Sprinkle with parsley and breadcrumbs. Dot with butter. Bake in a preheated moderate oven (350° F.) 25 minutes or until crumbs have browned and the fish flakes when tested with a fork. Makes 6 servings.

⚜ WHITING FILLETS ORLY

Carefully fillet 6 whitings, ½ pound each. Add 1 teaspoon salt, ¼ teaspoon ground black pepper, 2 tablespoons each, chopped parsley and lemon juice, and marinate 1 hour. Dip fish in Fritter Batter and fry until browned in deep fat preheated to 375° F. Drain on paper towels. Serve with Tomato Sauce. Makes 6 servings.

FISH STEWS

Bouillabaisse and other regional fish stews are among the greatest examples of fish cookery. Since they all contain a variety of fish (and sometimes shellfish), they are grouped together.

⚜ BOUILLABAISSE MARSEILLE STYLE

2 cups chopped onions
white part of 2 leeks, sliced
1 clove garlic, mashed
½ cup olive oil
1 cup diced carrots
2 stalks parsley
1 bay leaf
4 or 5 medium-sized tomatoes, peeled, seeded, and diced, or 1 cup tomato purée
rind of ½ orange, dried
½ cup sliced fresh fennel or ¼ teaspoon fennel seed
1 tablespoon salt

1 pound each red snapper, perch, cod, bass, and eel, and 2 pounds Spanish mackerel, all sliced 1 inch thick
2½ pounds whole lobsters or lobster tails, shells included
2 quarts water
¼ teaspoon crumbled saffron
1 teaspoon dried or 1 tablespoon chopped fresh thyme
½ teaspoon ground black pepper
2 cups dry white wine
12 slices French bread, cut ¼ inch thick

In a large kettle, cook onions, leeks, and garlic in hot oil until onions are transparent. Add carrots, parsley, bay leaf, tomatoes, orange rind, fennel or fennel seed, salt, fish, lobster, and water. Cover and bring to boiling point. Reduce heat and simmer 15 minutes. Add saffron, thyme, pepper, and wine. Simmer 8 to 10 minutes. Adjust seasonings. To serve, remove fish and lobster to a serving dish. Pour the broth into soup plates over French bread. Serve fish in a separate dish. Makes approximately 12 servings.

⚜ BOUILLABAISSE PROVENÇALE

This regional dish is made with eel and a variety of fish, such as bass, cod, flounder, haddock, perch, and red snapper, and always includes dried orange peel.

1 cup sliced onion
white part of one leek, sliced
1 clove garlic, crushed
½ cup olive oil or salad oil
2 ribs celery, sliced
1 rib fennel, sliced or ¼ teaspoon whole fennel seed
2 stalks parsley
rind of ¼ orange, dried
1 pound each eel, cod, haddock, bass, red snapper, and perch or flounder, all cut into 2-inch pieces
1½ quarts cold water
2 teaspoons salt
1 bay leaf
3 egg yolks
6 to 8 ¼-inch-thick slices French bread toasted

Cook onion, leek, and garlic in hot oil until onion is transparent. Add celery, fennel or fennel seed, parsley, orange peel, fish, water, salt, and bay leaf. Cover and bring to boiling point. Reduce heat and simmer 25 minutes. Remove fish with a perforated spoon or skimmer. Beat egg yolks with a little of the stock and add them to the rest of the stock. Heat 1 minute. Adjust seasonings. Put some of the fish and a slice of toasted French bread in each soup plate and fill with hot fish stock. Makes 6 to 8 servings.

⚜ PAUCHOUSE (*Freshwater Fish Stew*)

4 pounds freshwater fish (eel, carp, perch, pike)
2 small onions, sliced
bouquet garni
4 peppercorns
salt
¼ pound salt pork, diced
1 clove garlic, finely chopped
2 cups dry white wine
fish stock
⅓ cup brandy
2 cups sliced mushrooms
4 tablespoons butter
3 egg yolks
¼ cup heavy cream

Have the fish dressed at the fish market, saving the heads for stock. Cook fish heads 30 minutes with one of the onions, bouquet garni, peppercorns, 1 teaspoon of salt, and enough cold water barely to cover them. Cool. Strain and set aside. Cut fish into 6 portions, rub lightly with salt, and set aside. Brown diced salt pork with garlic in a large skillet. Add fish, wine, and enough stock barely to cover the fish. Cook until hot. Heat brandy, pour over the fish, and ignite. Cover and cook slowly until the fish flakes. Sauté mushrooms and the remaining onion in 2 tablespoons of the butter. Arrange the cooked fish over the mushrooms. Reduce the stock by one-half. Blend the flour with the remaining butter and add. Stir and cook 1 minute. Beat egg yolks with cream, add, and cook slowly 1 minute. Pour sauce over the fish and heat (do not boil). Serve in timbales or patty shells, accompanied with slices of French bread, rubbed with garlic and dried in the oven. Makes 6 servings.

⚜ WATERZOI (*Flemish*)

4½ pounds dressed fish (carp, eel, pike, trout, etc.)
salt
ground black pepper
2 cups sliced celery
¼ cup chopped parsley
½ cup (1 stick) butter
2 or 3 grated rusks
brown bread, thinly sliced

Cut fish into serving-size pieces. Sprinkle lightly with salt and pepper. Set aside. Scatter celery and parsley over the bottom of a well-buttered skillet and arrange the fish on top. Pour in hot water to cover. Dot with butter. Bring to boiling point, reduce heat, and simmer 10 minutes. Transfer fish to a warm serving dish and keep hot. Reduce the stock by one-half the original quantity. Thicken only to sauce consistency with grated rusks. Pour over fish. Serve very hot with thinly sliced brown bread and butter. Makes 6 servings.

11

SHELLFISH, FROGS' LEGS, AND SNAILS

The term *shellfish* covers various saltwater and freshwater crustaceans and mollusks. The marine crustaceans most popular as food are lobsters, rock lobsters (also called spiny lobsters or sea crayfish), crabs, and shrimp. The freshwater crayfish is also a crustacean. The mollusks include oysters, clams, mussels, and scallops. *Seafood*, a term often used to designate shellfish, can also refer to saltwater fish; it is used to describe shellfish cocktails and dishes made of various shellfish (and sometimes fish) in combination. The corresponding French term is *fruits de mer*.

Frogs are amphibians; only the legs are edible.

Snails, the only edible land mollusk, are extremely popular in France, where certain varieties are specially fed for the market; in the United States, however, they can usually be obtained only by being imported in cans.

Shellfish, like fish, provide protein of the same quality as that of meat and in about the same proportion. The fat content of white-meat shellfish is only about 2 to 5 per cent; that of lobster may be as high as 20 per cent. Shellfish is especially high in mineral matter, containing almost twice as much as other fish (see introduction to Chapter 10). Oysters are a good source of vitamin G and also contain some vitamin B.

For additional recipes for the various kinds of shellfish, see Chapters 5, 6, and 7.

CRABS (*Crabes*)

Crabs are designated as hard-shell or soft-shell, according to the condition of the shells. Hard-shell crabs are available throughout the year but are more plentiful during the summer months. Soft-shell crabs are crabs which are molting—that is, they are throwing off the hard shells, leaving soft ones underneath. They are available from May to October.

Fresh crabmeat can be purchased by the pound or half-pound. Before it is used, the tendons should be removed and the meat flaked. One pound of fresh crabmeat makes about 3 cups. Crabmeat is also available frozen or in cans.

⚜ BOILED HARD-SHELL CRABS

Wash crabs in plenty of cold water and scrub with a brush. Rinse well in cold water. Plunge the crabs head first into enough rapidly boiling water to completely cover them. Add 1 tablespoon of salt to 1 quart of water. Boil 15 to 20 minutes or until the shells turn red. Drain and hold under running cold water. Drain again and let them cool, resting on the claws. Break off the claws and legs close to the body. Crack claws with a nutcracker and remove the meat. Break off the tail or pointed apron. With both hands, pull the upper and lower shells apart, beginning at the tail. Wash away loose matter under running cold water. Remove membranous covering along the edges. Using a pointed knife, remove the meat between the sections and the cartilage. Keep the pieces whole if possible. Save roe and liver to garnish crabmeat salad. Six crabs make about 1 cup of meat.

⚜ BOILED SOFT-SHELL CRABS

Wash crabs in cold water several times. Place the live crabs on a board, face down. With scissors, make an incision straight across the crabs just back of the eyes and cut out the face. Lift the pointed ends of the shells and scrape out the spongy portion. Turn crabs on their backs and cut off their tails. Wash thoroughly under cold running water. Plunge the cleaned crabs in enough boiling water to cover them. Add 1 teaspoon salt to 1 quart of water. Cover and boil 15 minutes. Drain. Serve hot or cold with lemon slices or Herb Butter or mayonnaise. Allow 2 crabs per person.

⚜ DEEP-FAT-FRIED SOFT-SHELL CRABS

12 soft-shell crabs
salt
ground black pepper
flour
2 large eggs beaten with 2 tablespoons water
fine dry breadcrumbs or cracker crumbs

Prepare crabs for cooking as in preceding recipe. Sprinkle crabs with salt and pepper and roll in flour. Beat eggs with water. Dip floured crabs into eggs, and then roll them in fine breadcrumbs or cracker crumbs. Fry in deep fat preheated to 370° F. until golden brown. Drain on paper towels. Serve hot. Makes 6 servings.

⚜ CRAB MORNAY

meat of 8 medium-sized cooked crabs, or 1⅓ cups cooked crabmeat
2 cups Mornay Sauce
salt to taste
ground black pepper to taste
1 teaspoon lemon juice
½ cup grated Cheddar cheese
4 tablespoons butter
1 cup soft breadcrumbs

Add the crabmeat to Mornay Sauce. Stir in salt, pepper and lemon juice. Spoon into 6 well-buttered crab shells or coquilles. Sprinkle with grated cheese. Melt butter, add breadcrumbs, mix well, and sprinkle over the cheese. Bake in a preheated moderate oven (350° F.) 30 minutes or until crumbs are brown. Makes 6 servings.

⚜ CRAB WITH RICE PILAF

4 cups cooked Rice Pilaf
meat of 8 medium-sized crabs or 1⅓ cups cooked crabmeat
2 cups Shrimp Sauce
salt and ground black pepper to taste
1 teaspoon lemon juice
parsley

Pack Rice Pilaf into an oiled 1-quart ring mold, place mold in a pan of hot water, and bake in a preheated moderate oven (375° F.) 30 to 40 minutes or until hot. Combine crabmeat, Shrimp Sauce, salt, pepper, and lemon juice and heat only until hot. Unmold Rice Pilaf onto a round serving dish and pile the crabmeat mixture in the center of the ring. Garnish with parsley. Makes 6 servings.

⚜ COLD CRAB ENGLISH STYLE

1 teaspoon English-style powdered mustard
1 tablespoon water
1 cup mayonnaise
6 medium-sized crabs, cooked
2 large hard-cooked eggs, chopped
chopped parsley

Soak mustard in water 5 minutes and blend with mayonnaise. Remove meat from crabs, dice, and add to mayonnaise. Spoon the mixture into the crab shells, or into coquilles. Sprinkle with hard-cooked eggs. Garnish with chopped parsley. Chill and serve. Makes 6 servings.

LOBSTER (*Homard*)

Although American and European lobsters belong to different species, the same methods of preparation can be used for both. Lobsters should be bought alive. They may be killed by severing the spinal cord with a sharp pointed knife at the point where the tail joins the body, or by plunging them briefly into rapidly boiling water. Lobster boiled 20 to 30 minutes (according to size) in boiling water or court bouillon may be served with hot melted butter or with mayonnaise, or used in the preparation of more elaborate lobster dishes.

⚜ LOBSTER À L'AMÉRICAINE

Since this is strictly a French dish, characteristic of Provence in its preparation, the origin of its name is a mystery. According to some authorities, it was probably once "à l'Amoricaine," from the old name for Brittany, Amorica, and was miscopied.

2 live lobsters, 1½ pounds each
¼ cup olive oil or salad oil
salt
¼ cup finely chopped onions or shallots
1 small clove of garlic, finely chopped
2 tablespoons butter
2 pounds (6 medium-sized) fresh tomatoes
¼ cup chopped parsley
1 teaspoon chopped fresh or ¼ teaspoon dried tarragon
1 small bay leaf
¾ cup dry white wine, fish stock, or water
2 to 3 tablespoons tomato paste
cayenne
salt and ground white pepper to taste
¼ cup warmed brandy

Sever the spinal cord at the base of the lobster's neck. Remove the tail section from the body and cut it into 3 or 4 crosswise slices. Cut the body section in half lengthwise, clean it, and reserve the coral and liver to use in the sauce. Heat the oil. Season the lobster meat with salt and cook it in the hot oil until the shells turn red and the meat is seared. Remove the meat from the shells and reserve. Save shells to use in sauce to give it more flavor. Cook shallots or onions and garlic in butter until onions are limp. Peel, seed, and dice tomatoes and add to onions. Stir in herbs and the wine, stock, or water. Cover and simmer 30 minutes. Add tomato paste, cayenne, salt and pepper to taste. Pour brandy over lobster meat and ignite. Transfer lobster meat and shells to the sauce, cover, and simmer 30 minutes. Just before serving remove shells and blend in liver and coral. Makes 6 servings.

⚜ LOBSTER BORDEAUX STYLE

2 lobsters, 2 pounds each
6 tablespoons butter
¼ cup chopped shallots
1 clove garlic, crushed
⅓ cup warmed brandy
1 cup dry white wine
1½ cups fish stock
1½ cups Sauce Espagnole
1½ cups Tomato Sauce
1 teaspoon dried or 1 tablespoon chopped fresh tarragon
1 teaspoon dried or 1 tablespoon chopped fresh chervil or parsley
salt and ground black pepper to taste
parsley

Cut up the lobsters as directed for Lobster à l'Américaine. Cook them in a skillet in 4 tablespoons of the butter until shells begin to turn red. Add shallots and garlic. Stir and cook until shallots are transparent. Pour in the brandy and ignite. Add wine, fish stock, Sauce Espagnole, and Tomato Sauce. Mix well. Cook uncovered 20 minutes. Transfer the lobster to a serving dish and keep hot. Reduce the cooking liquid to half. Stir in the remaining 2 tablespoons butter, herbs, and salt and pepper. Simmer 1 minute. Pour the sauce over the lobster. Garnish with parsley. Makes 6 to 8 servings.

⚜ LOBSTER CREOLE

2 lobsters, 2 pounds each
well-salted fish stock
3 tablespoons butter
2 cups Curry Sauce
3 cups cooked rice

Cook lobsters in fish stock. Cut in half, remove meat, and cut it into collops. (Reserve claws.) Heat the collops lightly in butter. Add Curry Sauce and simmer 5 minutes. Arrange rice in a border in a serving dish. Spoon lobster meat and a little of the sauce in the center. Serve remaining sauce in a separate bowl. Garnish with lobster claws. Makes 6 to 8 servings.

⚜ LOBSTER À L'INDIENNE

2 cooked lobsters, 1½ pounds each
1¾ cups Sauce à l'Indienne
salt and ground black pepper
4 cups hot cooked rice
¼ cup (½ stick) butter

Remove meat from lobsters, cut into nice slices, and heat 2 to 3 minutes in butter. Add the sauce and heat. Season to taste with salt and pepper. Meanwhile, toss rice lightly with butter. Place it in a preheated moderate oven (350° F.) to dry, about 10 minutes. Spoon rice into an oiled 1-quart ring mold. Turn out onto a serving dish. Fill center with lobster and a little of the sauce. Serve remaining sauce in a separate dish. Makes 6 servings.

⚜ LOBSTER NEWBURG

2½ cups lobster meat
3 tablespoons butter, melted
⅓ cup Madeira or sherry
4 large egg yolks
1 cup light cream
dash each cayenne and nutmeg
½ teaspoon paprika
salt to taste
1 tablespoon cognac or tomato paste (optional)

Put lobster and butter in the top of a double boiler and cook over low direct heat until the meat is tender. Add wine and cook until almost all the liquid has evaporated. Blend egg yolks with ¼ cup of the cream and add to the lobster. Stir in remaining cream and cook over hot water (not boiling) until the sauce is of medium thickness. Remove from heat and add seasonings. If desired add cognac or tomato paste. Serve on toast, topped with a little of the lobster coral. Makes approximately 6 servings.

Rock Lobster Bouquetière ►

Rock lobster in modern presentations (top, see page 522)

Crayfish in Court Bouillon, page 525 ▲

▼ Lobster Thermidor, page 519

▲ Scampi Thermidor, page 523

Brochettes of Shrimp, page 524 ▼

⚜ LOBSTER THERMIDOR

3 lobsters, 1¼ pounds each
fish stock
2 shallots, chopped
3 tablespoons butter
½ cup dry white wine
½ teaspoon powdered mustard
2 cups Mornay Sauce
salt
ground black pepper
1 tablespoon whipped cream
½ cup grated Parmesan cheese

Boil lobsters in fish stock 5 minutes, reduce heat and simmer 15 minutes or until lobster turns red. When lobsters are cool enough to handle, remove meat from the claws and bodies, keeping the bodies intact. Dice the meat and set aside. Cook shallots in butter until they are transparent, add wine, and reduce to one-fourth its original quantity. Soak mustard 5 minutes in 1 tablespoon water and add, along with Mornay Sauce. Stir and cook only to heat the ingredients. Add salt and pepper to taste. Mix the lobster meat with two-thirds of the sauce. Put a little of the remaining sauce in each of the shells and fill them with the lobster mixture. Blend whipped cream with the remaining sauce and spread over the tops. Sprinkle with Parmesan cheese. Brown under broiler heat. Instead of using lobster shells, this may be served in a casserole or in coquilles. Makes 6 servings. (See illustration, page 517.)

⚜ LOBSTER ASPIC

3½ pints fish aspic
2 truffles or 6 large black olives
6 hard-cooked eggs
meat from 2 cooked lobsters, 1½ pounds each
watercress

Coat the inside of a 1½-quart mold with fish aspic. Chill until set. Decorate the bottom with alternating slices of truffle or olive and slices of hard-cooked eggs. Arrange thin slices of lobster tails, each decorated with a slice of truffle or olive, vertically against the side of the mold. Coat with cold liquid aspic. Chill until set. Repeat with a second row of sliced lobster tails and coat with aspic. Chill until aspic is set. Continue until the mold is full. Chill until ready to serve. To unmold, flash dip the mold in very hot water and turn out on a round serving plate. Shake the mold to release the aspic. Garnish with watercress. Makes 6 to 8 servings.

⚜ LOBSTER MEDALLIONS NIÇOISE

2 cooked lobsters, 1 pound each
12 tomato slices
1 quart aspic
6 pitted green or black olives
1½ cup cold cooked diced potatoes
1 cup cold cooked green beans cut into 1-inch pieces
1 small tomato, diced
4 anchovy fillets, diced
2 teaspoons unflavored gelatin
3 tablespoons cold water
⅓ cup mayonnaise
ground black pepper
12 baked 3-inch tart shells

Cut 12 medallions 1½-inch thick from lobster tails. Reserve the remaining lobster for salads, etc. Dip tomato slices in aspic and place one on each lobster medallion. Decorate with half of a pitted olive, round side up, and glaze with aspic. Chill until aspic is set. Combine potatoes, beans, diced tomato, and anchovies. Soften gelatin in cold water. Set in a pan of hot water to melt. Blend with mayonnaise and add to the vegetables. Season to taste with pepper. Spoon into the tart shells, smooth lightly, and coat with aspic. Chill until set. Chill remaining aspic until set. To serve, put a lobster medallion on top of each filled tart shell, arrange the tart shells on a serving plate, and surround them with chopped aspic. Garnish the center of the plate with parsley. Makes 6 servings.

⚜ LOBSTER MEDALLIONS WINDSOR STYLE

1 cooked lobster, weighing 2 pounds
8 slices large pimiento-stuffed olives
3 cups aspic
2 cups diced celeriac or celery
whites of 2 hard-cooked eggs, diced
½ cup finely diced green or red sweet pepper
1 tablespoon wine vinegar
3 tablespoons olive oil or salad oil
½ teaspoon salt
⅛ teaspoon ground black pepper
1 teaspoon curry powder
½ cup mayonnaise
8 baked 2-inch pastry tart shells

Cut lobster tail into 8 good slices and top each with an olive slice. Glaze with aspic, chill, and reserve. Cook celeriac or celery 1 minute in boiling water, drain, and rinse in cold water. Dice the meat from the lobster claws and the tail trimmings. Add to the celeriac or celery along with egg whites and pepper. Combine vinegar, oil, and seasonings. Mix lightly with the salad. Marinate 1 hour in the refrigerator. Save out ⅓ cup aspic. Chill the remaining aspic until set. Drain salad, adjust seasonings, mix with mayonnaise, and fill tart shells to the top edge. Glaze with aspic. Chill. Just before serving, top each with a lobster medallion and place on a large serving plate. Surround with chopped jellied aspic. Makes 8 servings.

⚜ COLD LOBSTER SOUFFLÉ

2 lobsters, 1¼ pounds each, cooked and cooled in court bouillon
1 cup fish Velouté Sauce
1 teaspoon lemon juice
dash cayenne
¼ cup brandy
salt
ground white pepper
3 cups liquid aspic
1 cup heavy cream, whipped

Extend the height of a 1½-quart soufflé dish 1 or 2 inches with a band of foil or white paper, folded to a width of 3 or 4 inches and long enough to reach around the dish. Tie the band in place with a string, and pin or staple the seam together. Set dish aside. Remove meat from lobster shells, keeping the flesh intact so that 6 nice slices can be cut from it. Purée the remaining lobster meat in an electric blender a little at a time, with some of the Velouté Sauce. Or, if desired, chop the meat fine, mix with a little Velouté Sauce, and rub the mixture through a sieve. Add lemon juice, cayenne, brandy, and remaining sauce. Add 2½ cups of the aspic. Season with salt and pepper to taste. Chill until the mixture begins to set. Fold in whipped cream. Turn into the prepared soufflé dish. Smooth and flatten the top. Chill until firm and ready to use. Remove the paper band from the dish. Arrange lobster and truffle slices alternately over the top of the soufflé. Coat with aspic. Chill. Coat again with aspic. Chill. Serve cold. Makes 8 servings.

ROCK LOBSTER (*Langouste*)

Rock lobsters resemble the larger lobsters but lack the large claws of the latter and have less flavor. They can be prepared in the same ways. Cold rock lobster is often featured in cold buffets; for preliminary preparation see Culinary Techniques in Pictures and for presentations see illustrations, pages 36, 515, and 516.

⚜ ROCK LOBSTER BOUQUETIÈRE

1 lobster, weighing 2½ pounds, cooked and cooled in court bouillon
truffles
pimiento
4 cups aspic
2 teaspoons unflavored gelatin
3 tablespoons cold water
½ cup mayonnaise
4 cups mixed cooked vegetables
salt
ground black pepper
3 hard-cooked eggs

Remove the tail from the lobster and take out the meat without damaging the shell. Reserve the shell, claws, and feelers. Cut the lobster meat into medallions and decorate them with truffle and pimiento. Glaze with aspic. Chill. Soften gelatin in cold water, set over hot water to melt, blend with the mayonnaise, and add to cooked vegetables. Season to taste with salt and pepper. Turn onto a serving plate and shape into a dome. Chill. Save out ½ cup aspic; pour remaining aspic into small molds and chill until set. Slice eggs, garnish with truffles and pimiento, glaze with aspic, and chill.

To serve, arrange lobster medallions over the dome of salad. Unmold aspics and place them around one-half of the salad. Then place egg slices around the aspic molds. Decorate the dish with the lobster tail, claws and feelers as illustrated on page 515. Glaze the shells with aspic and chill a few minutes to set the glaze. Makes 6 servings. (See illustration, page 515.)

⚜ ROCK LOBSTER IN A MODERN PRESENTATION

1 cooked rock lobster, weighing 2½ pounds
1 small truffle (or black olives)
1 small piece of pimiento
6 small molds of jellied Russian Salad
6 tomato slices
6 halves of Deviled Eggs
18 cooked asparagus tips, 2 inches long
French dressing
6 long anchovies
radish roses
parsley

Remove the meat from the tail of the lobster without damaging the shell. Cut the meat into medallions and decorate each with a bit of truffle or black olive and a bit of pimiento. Glaze with aspic. Chill. Arrange on a tray. Unmold the salads and place on the tray. Top each tomato slice with a Deviled Egg half and place on the tray. Marinate asparagus tips 1 hour in French dressing, drain, and arrange in bundles of three on the tray. Place a long anchovy across the center of each bundle. Garnish tray with radish roses and parsley. For additional garnish, stand the shell on a bed of parsley on one corner of the tray. (See illustration, page 516.) Makes 6 servings.

SHRIMP (*Crevettes*)

There are many varieties of edible shrimp, ranging in size from the very tiny ones popular in the Scandinavian countries to a southern United States form which averages only a dozen to the pound. Large shrimp are sometimes called prawns, but the name prawn properly applies to a different crustacean

(French *langoustine;* Italian *scampi*). Prawns are prepared in the same ways as shrimp, and either can be used in many of the same ways as crayfish.

⚜ FRIED SHRIMP

1½ pounds raw shrimp, peeled and deveined
½ cup olive oil or salad oil
salt, dash cayenne
Creole Rice
parsley

Fry shrimp quickly in hot oil. Drain on paper towels. Season with salt and a little cayenne. Serve with Creole Rice. Garnish with parsley. Makes 6 servings. (See other Fried Shrimp recipes in Chapter 6.)

⚜ SHRIMP À L'INDIENNE

⅓ cup chopped onion
3 tablespoons butter
about 2 teaspoons curry powder
1½ pounds raw shrimp, peeled and deveined
1 cup Velouté Sauce
Rice à l'Indienne

Cook onion in butter over low heat until transparent. Blend in curry powder. Stir and cook 1 minute. Add shrimp, stir, and cook until shrimp turns red, adding more butter if necessary. Add Velouté Sauce and bring to boiling point (do not boil). Serve over Rice à l'Indienne. Makes 6 servings.

⚜ SCAMPI THERMIDOR (*Italian*)

1 cup Béchamel Sauce
¾ cup milk
1 cup heavy cream
⅓ cup grated Parmesan cheese
1 teaspoon powdered mustard
1 tablespoon water
6 tablespoons butter
¼ cup olive oil or salad oil
2½ pounds cooked scampi or shrimp, peeled and deveined
¼ cup warmed brandy
12 thin slices truffle (optional)
½ cup grated Parmesan cheese

Combine Béchamel Sauce, milk, cream, and cheese in a 1-quart saucepan. Stir and cook 3 to 4 minutes over medium low heat or until sauce has thickened. Soak the mustard in the water 5 minutes and add to the sauce. Stir in 3 tablespoons of the butter. Strain. Put the remaining 3 tablespoons butter and the oil in a skillet. Heat and add scampi or shrimp. Stir and cook 4 minutes. Add brandy and ignite. Heat ½ minute. Add sauce, and truffle slices, if used. Turn into a heatproof serving dish. Sprinkle with Parmesan cheese.

Brown under broiler heat. If desired, replace truffles with ½ cup sautéed mushrooms. Makes 6 servings. (See illustration, page 518.)

⚜ BROCHETTES OF PRAWNS OR SHRIMP

24 medium-large prawns or shrimp
salt
ground black pepper
flour
lemon wedges
butter or Herb Butter
parsley
notched lemon halves

Peel and devein the prawns or shrimp; remove tails. Rinse in cold water and wipe dry. Sprinkle lightly with salt and pepper. Roll in flour and thread 4 on each of 6 short skewers. Fry until browned in deep fat preheated to 375° F. Drain on paper towels. Serve hot with plain butter or Herb Butter and a lemon wedge for each serving. Garnish with parsley and notched lemon halves. Makes 6 servings. (See illustration, page 518.)

⚜ BROCHETTES OF SCAMPI OR SHRIMP "SAVOIA BEELER" (*Itálian*)

24 peeled raw scampi or shrimp
24 small mushroom caps
24 slices raw lean ham
24 squares Mozzarella cheese, 1 by 1 by ½ inch
½ teaspoon dried thyme
½ cup (1 stick) butter, melted
3 cups plain cooked rice or Rice Pilaf
1 tablespoon lemon juice

Wipe scampi or shrimp and sprinkle with salt and pepper. Thread on each of 12 skewers 2 each of the following: shrimp or scampi, mushroom, ham slice folded in four, and cheese. Add thyme to butter and brush over the skewered food. Place skewers in a shallow pan. Cook in a preheated moderate oven (350° F.) 10 to 15 minutes, basting 2 times with butter. Carefully remove the skewers and arrange the scampi, etc. in a ring in a round dish. Fill the center with a mound of plain cooked rice or Rice Pilaf. Sprinkle scampi or shrimp with lemon juice. Makes 6 servings.

⚜ PRAWNS BELLVILLE

3 pounds prawns or shrimp
court bouillon
cooked-vegetable salad
chopped parsley
mayonnaise

Cook prawns or shrimp in court bouillon 5 minutes, or until they turn pink. Remove from the stock and when cool enough to handle, peel and devein, leaving the tails attached. Fill a large goblet or round bowl with cooked vegetable salad and hang the shrimp by the tails around the edges. Sprinkle the salad with chopped parsley. Serve mayonnaise separately. Makes 6 servings.

CRAYFISH (*Écrevisses*)

Crayfish (also called crawfish) are small freshwater crustaceans that look like miniature lobsters. They are rare in the northeastern part of the United States but readily obtainable in the South and West. They are interchangeable with shrimp in many recipes. Other recipes for crayfish appear in Chapters 5 and 6.

⚜ CRAYFISH IN COURT BOUILLON (*Écrevisses à la Nage*)

1 cup each sliced celery and carrots
1 onion, sliced
1 shallot, sliced
2 stalks parsley
½ bay leaf
¼ teaspoon peppercorns
½ teaspoon dried thyme
3 to 4 pounds bones and heads of any white-fleshed fish
2 quarts cold water
1 teaspoon salt
1 cup dry white wine
6 to 8 crayfish per person

Place all ingredients except crayfish into a 6-quart saucepan. Bring slowly to the boiling point, reduce heat, and simmer, uncovered, 25 minutes. Remove and discard fish bones. Strain stock through cheesecloth into a saucepan. Bring to a boiling point. Wash crayfish thoroughly. Remove the intestinal tract by inserting a knife tip under the intestine in the middle of the tail and pulling the intestine out gently, holding it between the knife and one finger. Immediately throw the crayfish into the boiling court bouillon to prevent the body liquids from escaping through the body opening. Cover and simmer 5 to 10 minutes or until the crayfish turn red. Serve in a tureen as one would serve soup. (See illustration, page 517.) Makes 6 to 8 servings.

OYSTERS (*Huitres*)

Oysters have been used as food since prehistoric times; both the ancient Celts and the American Indians ate them in abundance. While the true oyster-fancier insists that they are properly appreciated only when eaten raw, there are many delicious ways of cooking them.

⚜ OYSTERS ON THE HALF SHELL

Allow 6 raw oysters per person. Open the shells at the last minute, leaving each oyster on the deep half of the shell. Arrange on a bed of cracked ice. Serve as an hors d'oeuvre with a dish of lemon juice and freshly ground black pepper.

⚜ OYSTERS FLORENTINE

20 oysters with liquor
1 cup drained cooked spinach
5 tablespoons butter
⅓ cup Béchamel Sauce
1/16 teaspoon ground nutmeg
salt, ground black pepper
¾ cup Mornay Sauce
¼ cup grated Cheddar cheese
lemon wedges

Cook oysters in their own liquor over very low heat or over hot water *only* until the edges curl. Cook spinach until dry in 2 tablespoons of the butter. Add Béchamel Sauce, nutmeg, and salt and pepper to taste. Put 1 teaspoon spinach in the bottom of each well-cleaned oyster shell. Top each with an oyster. Coat with Mornay Sauce and sprinkle with cheese. Melt remaining 3 tablespoons butter and drizzle over the tops. Serve hot with lemon wedges. Makes 4 servings.

⚜ OYSTERS MORNAY

20 to 24 oysters in liquor
¾ cup Béchamel Sauce
1 large egg yolk
½ cup grated Gruyère cheese
salt
ground black pepper
lemon juice

Cook oysters in their own liquor over very low heat or over hot water *only* until edges curl. Drain off the liquor and add ¼ cup to the Béchamel Sauce. Beat in egg yolk and ¼ cup of the cheese. Season to taste with salt, pepper, and lemon juice. Place 1 teaspoon sauce in each of 4 heatproof dishes and add 5 to 6 oysters. Cover with sauce. Sprinkle with remaining cheese. Brown quickly under broiler heat. Serve at once. Makes 4 servings.

⚜ OYSTERS VILLEROI

24 oysters with liquor
1 cup Béchamel Sauce
2 large egg yolks
1 cup fine dry breadcrumbs

Cook oysters in own liquor over very low heat *only* until edges curl. Drain off liquor and add ¼ cup to Béchamel Sauce. Beat in egg yolks. Dry the oysters between paper towels. Dip them into the sauce and roll them in fine dry breadcrumbs. Let them stand a few minutes to dry the crumbs. Fry in butter until golden brown on both sides. Serve at once. Makes 4 to 6 servings.

CLAMS (*Palourdes*)

Many varieties of clams are known and eaten; the two most common on the Atlantic Coast of North America are round or hard clams and long or soft clams. The small hard clams are eaten raw in the same way as oysters and they can also be cooked in some of the same ways as oysters or mussels. Large hard clams are used in chowders and stews. Soft clams are usually steamed or fried in deep fat.

MUSSELS (*Moules*)

It is essential that mussels be absolutely fresh; to insure freshness the shells must be tightly closed. As a safety measure, test the mussels by attempting to slide the two halves of the shells across each other. Discard any that slide, even slightly.

⚜ HOW TO WASH MUSSELS

Put the mussels in a colander and hold them under running cold water to rinse off all the loose dirt and mud. Then scrub the shells with a stiff brush and scrape them with a knife to remove all the seaweed, slime, and dirt that has adhered to the shells. Rinse well under running cold water. With scissors trim off the beard which protrudes from the closed shell. Soak mussels 2 hours in cold water to rid the interior of possible sand and to get rid of some of the salty flavor. Then put mussels in a colander and rinse again under cold running water.

⚜ STEAMED MUSSELS

Mussels should be cooked only until the shells open. This requires about 8 to 10 minutes. Put mussels in a large kettle with only enough water or wine to create steam. Add a little parsley and freshly ground black pepper. Cover the kettle tightly and cook over high heat 8 to 10 minutes or *only* until shells open, shaking the kettle occasionally up and down and sideways to cook all the mussels uniformly. Transfer mussels to another pan and cover tightly to keep hot. Strain the broth through a very fine sieve or through 2 thicknesses of cheesecloth.

To serve, put mussels in a soup plate, heat the broth, and pour it over them. With the fingers or an oyster fork, pick the mussels out of the shells and discard shells in a dish provided for that purpose. Provide each guest with a soup spoon for drinking the broth, a large napkin, and a finger bowl or a finger towel wrung out in hot water for cleaning the fingers. Allow 1 quart of mussels per person when served steamed.

⚜ HERBED STEAMED MUSSELS

⅓ cup olive oil or salad oil
1 clove of garlic
½ cup chopped parsley
1 teaspoon dried or 1 tablespoon chopped fresh oregano
dash cayenne
3 quarts scrubbed and thoroughly cleaned mussels
salt
ground black pepper

Heat together in a large kettle the first 5 ingredients. Add mussels and mix until the shells are well coated with oil. Cover the kettle and steam until all the shells open, 8 to 10 minutes. Season the sauce with salt and pepper to taste. Serve the mussels in their shells and the sauce together in soup plates. Makes 3 servings.

⚜ MUSSELS FRANCILLON

3 quarts scrubbed and cleaned mussels
1 cup dry white wine
¾ cup mayonnaise
¼ teaspoon powdered mustard
1 teaspoon water
3 medium-large cooked potatoes

Cook the mussels in the wine 8 to 10 minutes, or until all the shells open. Remove the mussels, trim off and discard beards, and allow mussels to cool. Reduce the stock to almost the thickness of syrup. Cool and blend with mayonnaise. Soak the mustard in the water 5 minutes and add to mayonnaise. Remove mussels from shells, blend with the mayonnaise mixture, and place in the center of an hors d'oeuvre dish. Slice the potatoes and arrange them around the mussels. Makes 4 servings.

⚜ MUSSELS MARINIÈRE

4 to 5 quarts scrubbed, thoroughly cleaned mussels
1 cup dry white wine
3 shallots, sliced
1 stalk parsley
½ teaspoon dried thyme
3 whole peppercorns
chopped parsley

Put mussels in a large kettle with wine, shallots, parsley, thyme, and peppercorns. Cover and steam over low heat 8 to 10 minutes, or until all the shells open. Transfer mussels to soup plates. Strain stock, heat ½ minute, and pour over the mussel. Sprinkle with chopped parsley. Makes 4 to 5 servings.

⚜ MUSSELS IN POULETTE SAUCE

3 quarts mussels
1 shallot, chopped
1 stalk parsley
1 cup dry white wine
1 cup fish Velouté Sauce
2 egg yolks
¼ cup heavy cream
salt
ground black pepper

Cook thoroughly cleaned mussels, shallot, and parsley in the wine 8 to 10 minutes, or until all the shells open. Drain off the liquor. Let it stand a few minutes and strain through 2 thicknesses of cheesecloth. Blend with Velouté Sauce and egg yolks. Remove mussels from the shells, beard them, and add to the sauce along with the cream. Stir and cook 1 minute, or *only* until hot. Add salt and pepper to taste. Serve in baked pastry shells or bread cases, or over toast points or cooked rice. Makes 6 servings.

⚜ MUSSELS VILLEROI

3 to 4 quarts cooked mussels
2 lightly beaten egg yolks
2 cups thick Velouté Sauce
⅛ teaspoon ground black pepper
2 tablespoons water
2 whole eggs
fine dry breadcrumbs

Remove mussels from their shells, remove beards, and dry the mussels. Blend egg yolks with Velouté Sauce. Stir and cook over very low heat (do not boil) until sauce has thickened and reduced to 1½ cups. Beat whole eggs with pepper and water. Dip mussels in the sauce and let stand 1 to 2 minutes. Dip them in beaten eggs and then roll them in crumbs. Dip in egg and crumbs again and fry until brown in deep fat preheated to 375° F. Drain on paper towels. Serve as a main dish, or use to garnish other seafood dishes. Makes 6 servings.

SCALLOPS (*Pétoncles*)

In France scallops are called *coquilles Saint-Jacques*, from the fact that in the Middle Ages the shells were brought back by pilgrims to the shrine of St. James of Compostella. They are sold in their shells and the shells are used to cook and serve various seafoods and other foods (see recipes in Chapter 6). In the United States scallops are usually marketed without the shells. The small bay scallops are tenderer and of better flavor than the larger sea varieties. Scallops may be broiled or fried and are often combined with other seafood.

FROGS' LEGS

The bull frog or bellowing frog native to the United States is about twice the size of the European frog (French *grenouille*). Only the legs of frogs are eaten and even the large ones contain no more than a tidbit of meat. The meat resembles chicken in texture and is regarded as a delicacy. About 6 frogs' legs should be allowed for a serving.

Frogs' legs may be obtained ready to cook, fresh or frozen. If you prepare them yourself, cut off the hind legs close to the frog's body. Wash the legs in cold water and strip off the skin as you would pull off a glove. Cut off the feet and soak the legs 2 hours in very cold water, changing the water often, then drain and dry thoroughly.

⚜ FRIED FROGS' LEGS

Dip the legs in milk and dredge in flour seasoned with salt and ground black pepper. Pan-fry in hot shortening or oil 8 to 10 minutes, until browned on all sides. Serve in the same way as southern fried chicken.

⚜ FROGS' LEGS FRITTERS

36 prepared frogs' legs
2 tablespoons lemon juice
⅓ cup olive oil or salad oil
1 tablespoon chopped parsley
1 teaspoon salt
¼ teaspoon ground black pepper
1 recipe Fritter Batter
fried parsley
lemon slices

Marinate frogs' legs 1 hour in lemon juice, oil, and seasonings. Wipe the legs dry, dip in Fritter Batter, and fry until brown in deep fat preheated to 375° F. Drain on paper towels. Serve as an entrée or as a hot hors d'oeuvre. Garnish with fried parsley and lemon slices.

⚜ FROGS' LEGS WITH FINE HERBS

Fry frogs' legs in very hot butter until browned on all sides. Toss with chopped parsley and a little lemon juice.

⚜ FROGS' LEGS IN POULETTE SAUCE

36 frogs' legs
5 tablespoons butter
½ cup finely chopped mushrooms
2 shallots, finely chopped
3 tablespoons flour
1 cup chicken stock
¼ cup light cream
salt to taste
½ cup sherry
1 teaspoon lemon juice
4 tablespoons chopped parsley

Cook frogs' legs slowly in half the butter, without letting them brown, until they are tender, remove from the skillet, and keep them hot. Add the remaining butter to the skillet. Stir in mushrooms and shallots. Cook, stirring frequently, over low heat 5 minutes, or until shallots are transparent. Add stock and cream. Stir and cook until sauce has thickened. Blend in salt, sherry, and lemon juice. Add frogs' legs and bring to boiling point once. Serve sprinkled with chopped parsley.

SNAILS (*Escargots*)

Although fresh snails are rarely available in the United States, canned snails imported from Europe may be purchased in specialty shops and in gourmet sections of supermarkets and department stores. The package usually consists of two compartments: a can of snails and a box containing an equivalent number of snail shells. Serving instructions are given on the package. Allow 12 snails to a serving.

⚜ SNAILS IN BURGUNDY OR WHITE WINE

3 cups Burgundy or dry white wine
1 teaspoon finely chopped shallot or onion
½ cup softened butter
¼ cup finely chopped parsley
½ teaspoon minced garlic
salt and ground black pepper to taste
6 dozen canned snails and shells

Boil the wine with shallot or onion until the wine is reduced by one-half. Strain. Blend butter with parsley, garlic, salt, and pepper. Pour about ½ to 1 teaspoon wine in each shell, insert a snail, and top with a little of the herbed butter (Snail Butter). Bake in a preheated very hot oven (450° F.) 10 minutes. Serve hot.

⚜ SNAILS IN CHABLIS

2 cups Chablis
1½ teaspoons finely chopped shallot
⅓ cup meat glaze
6 dozen canned snails and shells
Snail Butter (see recipe for Snails in Burgundy)

Boil wine with shallot until the wine is reduced to ⅔ cup. Add meat glaze and pour the liquid into the snail shells, filling them about half full. Insert a snail and top with a little of the Snail Butter. Bake in a preheated very hot oven (450° F.) 10 minutes.

⚜ SNAILS SPANISH STYLE

½ cup chopped onion
½ cup short julienne strips green sweet pepper
1 cup chopped raw ham
1 clove garlic, crushed
¼ cup olive oil or salad oil
6 dozen canned snails, drained
salt
ground black pepper
2 tablespoons chopped parsley

Cook onion, green pepper, ham, and garlic in oil 2 to 3 minutes. Add drained snails. Season to taste with salt and pepper. Sauté until snails start to brown. Add parsley and toss lightly. Serve very hot in a deep dish. The snails must be highly seasoned.

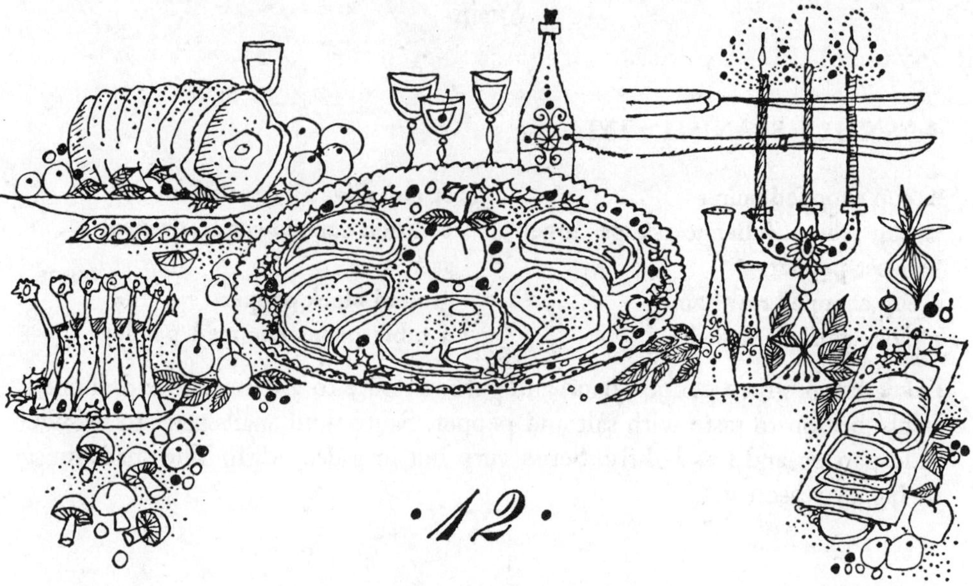

·12·

MEATS

The broad term "meat" may be used to refer to the flesh of any animal, bird, fish, or shellfish; in this chapter, however, only beef, veal, lamb, mutton, and pork, with the so-called variety meats of each, are discussed. The most favored meat in England and the Americas is beef; in France and Italy, veal; in Greece and the Near East lamb; in Australia and Scotland mutton.

Since meat is one of the most expensive of foods, it should be purchased with thrift and knowledge, and cooked with care. Within any type of meat the various cuts differ in tenderness, flavor, and price, depending on the part of the animal from which the cut is taken, the animal's age and sex, and the method used to fatten it.

All cuts of plump lamb and pork are tender. Leg of lamb and leg of pork ("ham" when cured) are very popular, but in these and other animals the tenderer cuts generally come from the rib and loin sections, which make up about one-fourth of the carcass. The cuts of beef from these sections, which are the most expensive cuts, are steaks–porterhouse, T-bone, sirloin, tenderloin, rib–and oven roasts–rib and tenderloin (fillet). The remaining three-quarters of the carcass consists of the less tender, less expensive cuts, which in beef are steaks–chuck, shoulder, round, flank; pot roasts–arm, blade, round, rump, chuck, briskets; and stew meat–brisket, neck, shank, flank, heel of round. In the smaller animals the same principles apply, but the steaks are generally called chops and various other cuts also given different names.

The housewife should be able to recognize the different cuts in order to purchase meat suited to the method planned for preparing it. While methods of cutting meat and names of cuts vary from country to country and even in different sections of the same country, the general principles are the same. The tender portions are separated from the less tender, and the chunky pieces from the thin ones. This is important because methods of cooking vary with the different types of cuts.

Variety meats, called offal in Great Britain and *abats de boucherie* in France, are the parts of the meat animal not included among the regular cuts—organs, head, feet, tail, etc. Since methods of cooking these vary according to the part rather than the type of animal from which it comes, recipes for them are grouped together at the end of this chapter.

Meat should be so cooked as to be tender, juicy, flavorful, and attractive in appearance. Here are a few simple general rules:

Do not wash meat.

Use a method of cooking suited to the chosen cut.

The preparation of meat for cooking may require a certain amount of trimming. Save the trimmings to use in stews or to grind for meat balls, patties, or meat loaf. Save bones to add flavor to stocks, soups, and stews.

Cook chunky cuts longer than slender cuts of the same weight.

Always cook pork and veal well done.

In France meat is usually roasted at higher temperatures than are commonly used in the United States. For methods, see Roasting, page 51.

Beef

Fillet of beef, usually called the tenderloin in the United States, is the long teardrop-shaped muscle that lies along the backbone inside the loin. It is the tenderest and also the most expensive cut. Cow's tenderloin is sometimes preferred to that from steer because it has a thinner layer of fat (the fat layer serves as an insulator against the oven heat and a thicker layer prolongs the cooking time). Cow's tenderloin is also less expensive, since the short loin of the steer is the source of the porterhouse and T-bone steaks so popular in America and if the tenderloin has been removed the remainder of the short loin has to be sold as strip steak at a lower price. The remaining meat of the cow is made into various kinds of processed meats.

In America the term *filet mignon* tends to be applied to any cut from the tenderloin. In France, however, different names are assigned to various portions of the fillet. Authorities seem to agree that the thick middle portion (the choicest part) should be called chateaubriand, but they differ in regard to the names of other cuts. Some call the larger-diameter rear end filet mignon and the smaller front end tournedos, with the extreme front tip removed and reserved for such dishes as Beef Stroganoff. Others call the rear end the tenderloin butt, or "bifteck," then, proceeding in order toward the front, chateaubriand, filet steak, tournedos, and filet mignon. Still others say that the name is determined only by the thickness of the slice, a thick slice being a filet mignon and a thin one a tournedos. The usual thickness of the various cuts is 2 to 3 inches for chateaubriand, 1½ to 2 inches for filet mignon, and 1 inch for tournedos. Any of these may be sliced at an angle to make the slices look larger.

There are three principal ways of serving fillet of beef. The entire tenderloin may be roasted in one piece, with the tip curled under the heavier portion, and the meat sliced at the table; the chateaubriand portion may be roasted whole and sliced at the table, with the other sections sliced before cooking; or the entire tenderloin may be sliced before being cooked. Fillet of beef makes an elegant company roast because it is sure to be tender, cooks in a short time, and is easy to serve. Filet mignon is often served on American airliners, both because it is popular and because its small round shape fits the serving dishes.

When purchasing a fillet roast it is wise to order a few days in advance, since most markets do not keep fillets in stock. The size to buy depends on the number of servings desired. Allow ½ pound to a serving. A whole fillet weighs 4 to 6 pounds and any that is left over is delicious served cold, but it is also possible to buy half a fillet. Ask the butcher to trim off the fat and connective tissue and either lard the meat or tie thin strips of fat salt pork or beef suet around it. The suet from around the kidneys has a better flavor than the fat from the tenderloin. Fillet of beef should be roasted for a short time at a high temperature (see Roast Fillet of Beef) and allowed to stand 15 to 20 minutes after it comes out of the oven to make carving easier.

Next to the tenderloin, the sirloin and rib cuts of beef are considered most desirable. There is a French cut called the entrecôte, which is not usually available in the United States; it is the boneless meat between the ribs, and is about 1 inch thick. The American cuts that come closest to this in tenderness and flavor are sirloin without the tenderloin, or rib steak with or without bone. The other less tender cuts of beef require longer cooking and more seasoning, but they are equally nutritious and less expensive.

⚜ ROAST FILLET OF BEEF

Trim the fat and connective tissue from a beef fillet roast and lard it with larding pork, or tie thin strips of fat salt pork or beef suet around it. If a meat thermometer is used, insert it in the thickest part of the roast. Place the roast in a preheated very hot oven (450° F.). Cook a 4- to 6-pound roast 45 to 60 minutes (10 minutes per pound for very rare meat; 12 to 13 minutes per pound for pink or medium-rare meat). Cook a 2- to 3-pound roast 45 to 50 minutes, or to 140° F. on a meat thermometer. Serve with the pan juices or spread with meat glaze or beef extract. Allow about ½ pound to a serving.

⚜ FILLET OF BEEF BOUQUETIÈRE

2 to 3 pounds fillet of beef
about 2 tablespoons oil or shortening
1 cup sliced carrots
½ cup sliced onions
½ cup sliced celery
salt
ground black pepper
½ cup (1 stick) butter
1 cup brown stock
4 to 6 cooked potatoes
1 small head cooked cauliflower
2 cups each cooked green beans and cubed turnips
sherry or cognac (optional)

Ask the butcher to lard the roast for you. Brown it on all sides in hot fat in a Dutch oven. Remove the meat and set aside. Add carrots, onions, and celery. Cover and cook 5 minutes over low heat without browning the vegetables. Return the roast to the casserole. Sprinkle with salt and pepper. Melt half the butter (¼ cup) and pour over meat. Cover and cook in a preheated very hot oven (450° F.) about 40 minutes. Shortly before the meat is done, remove the cover to finish browning. Transfer meat to a platter and let it stand in a warm place 15 to 20 minutes. Skim and discard the fat from the pan juices. Add the brown stock, strain, bring to boiling point, and simmer to reduce the quantity by one-fourth. If the sauce needs it, thicken with 1 tablespoon flour blended with 1 tablespoon butter. Bring to boiling point. Stir in sherry or cognac to taste, if desired. Serve with the meat. Toss the hot cooked vegetables in butter and arrange them on the platter around the meat. Serve hot. Makes 4 to 6 servings.

VARIATION

FILLET OF BEEF JARDINIÈRE

Cook the beef fillet as directed for Fillet of Beef Bouquetière, and use the same vegetables. Cut potatoes and turnips in strips or cut them into balls with a melon-ball cutter. Divide cauliflower into flowerets and coat them lightly with Hollandaise Sauce.

⚜ FILLET OF BEEF GIRONDINE

2 to 3 pounds fillet of beef
1 cup Demi-Glace Sauce
6 artichoke bottoms
4 tablespoons (½ stick) butter
1 pound mushrooms
2 tablespoons cooking oil
salt
ground black pepper

Cook the beef fillet as directed for Fillet of Beef Bouquetière. Transfer the meat to a platter. Keep warm. Add Demi-Glace to pan drippings and bring to boiling point. Strain and keep warm. Cut artichoke bottoms in quarters and simmer in half the butter. Cut mushrooms in thick slices and cook in the remaining 2 tablespoons butter and the oil 5 minutes, or until tender. Season artichokes and mushrooms to taste with salt and pepper, and arrange around the platter. Coat with the sauce, and serve remaining sauce separately. Makes 4 to 6 servings.

⚜ ROAST FILLET OF BEEF WITH MADEIRA SAUCE

2 to 3 pounds fillet of beef
1 cup Brown Sauce
⅓ cup Madeira
1 pound mushrooms
3 tablespoons butter
salt and ground black pepper to taste

Roast the beef fillet according to the directions for Roast Fillet of Beef. Transfer meat to a platter and keep warm. Mix the Brown Sauce and the wine with the pan drippings. Bring to boiling point. Skim off and discard fat. Meanwhile, remove mushroom caps from the stems (save stems for other uses) and sauté caps in butter until all the moisture has evaporated and the caps are tender. Add salt and pepper. Place around the meat and coat with the sauce. Serve remaining sauce separately. Makes 4 to 6 servings.

⚜ FILLET OF BEEF RICHELIEU

3½ pounds fillet of beef
¼ cup chopped onion
3 tablespoons butter
2 cups chopped mushroom stems
⅔ cup Demi-Glace Sauce
1 tablespoon tomato purée
about ¾ cup fine dry breadcrumbs
salt and ground black pepper
8 medium-sized firm ripe tomatoes
24 sautéed mushroom caps
8 servings Braised Lettuce
parsley

Roast the beef according to directions on page 537, and let it stand a short time in a warm place before carving. Sauté the onions in 1 tablespoon of the butter until they are limp. Add the chopped mushroom stems and stir and cook 5 minutes. Add the Demi-Glace, tomato purée and enough of the breadcrumbs to make a smooth mixture. Season to taste with salt and pepper. Cut a slice from the top of each tomato and scoop out the insides, leaving the shells intact. Sprinkle the cavities with salt and pepper and fill them with the mushroom mixture. Melt the remaining butter, mix with the rest of the breadcrumbs, and sprinkle them over the tomatoes. Bake them in an 8- by 8- by 2-inch baking pan in a preheated moderate oven (325° F.) 25 minutes or until crumbs are brown. To serve: Slice the roast and arrange the slices, overlapping, down the center of a warmed platter. Garnish the dish with the stuffed tomatoes, sautéed mushroom caps, Braised Lettuce, and parsley. Makes 8 servings. (See illustration, page 551).

⚜ FILLET OF BEEF WELLINGTON

4-pound fillet of beef
1 cup (1 stick) butter
salt
ground black pepper
½ cup each sliced celery and onion
1 cup sliced carrots
⅓ cup chopped parsley
1 bay leaf
½ teaspoon crumbled dried rosemary
1½ teaspoons chopped fresh rosemary
pâté de foie gras
Plain Pie Pastry, made with 2 cups flour, or Puff Pastry
milk
1 cup veal stock
¼ cup additional pâté de foie gras
1 truffle or ¼ cup mushrooms, chopped

It is unnecessary to lard the roast for this dish. Spread the meat generously with butter. Sprinkle with salt and pepper. Spread all the vegetables, bay leaf, and rosemary over the bottom of a shallow baking pan, and place the roast on them. Cook in a preheated very hot oven (450° F.) 40 to 50 minutes. Remove roast from the oven and cool completely. When roast is cold spread pâté de foie gras over the entire surface. Roll pastry ⅛ inch thick and wrap it around the roast. Trim the edges of the pastry, moisten with water, and seal by pressing the edges together. If desired, decorate with strips of pastry cut ½ inch wide and laid in lattice fashion over the crust. Place in a baking pan, seam side down. Brush the crust with milk (or with an egg yolk beaten with 1 teaspoon milk). Prick the crust in a few places to allow the steam to escape. Bake in a preheated hot oven (425° F.) 15 to 20 minutes, or until browned. Transfer to a platter and keep warm. Add veal stock, ¼ cup pâté de foie gras, and chopped truffle or mushrooms to the roasting pan. Simmer 10 to 15 minutes or until of sauce consistency. Slice the beef and serve with the sauce in a separate bowl. Makes 6 servings. (See illustration, page 551.)

⚜ FILLET OF BEEF ROTHSCHILD

3 pounds cold roast fillet of beef
½ pound foie gras purée
1 small truffle
1 cup port-flavored aspic

Roast fillet of beef the day before and chill. Cut into slices ¼ inch thick. Spread one side of each slice with foie gras purée. Arrange the slices on a long dish, overlapping them. Place a slice of truffle on each. Cover with half-set aspic. Chill. Serve cold. Makes 6 servings.

⚜ RUSSIAN-STYLE FILLET OF BEEF

3 pounds cold roast fillet of beef
3½ cups port-flavored aspic
sliced tomatoes
1 cup Tartare Sauce

Roast the beef the day before and cut it into slices ¼ inch thick. Place slices, in an upright position, in a 9- by 5- by 3-inch loaf pan. Fill with half-set aspic, tilting the pan so the aspic will run between the slices, coating them well. Chill until aspic is firm and ready to serve. Turn out onto a platter. Garnish with sliced tomatoes. Serve with Tartare Sauce. Makes 6 servings.

⚜ GLAZED FILLET OF BEEF

3-pound roast fillet of beef
1 quart aspic flavored with port
20 truffle slices
¼ pound pickled or smoked beef tongue
¾ pound pâté de foie gras
¼ pound (1 stick) softened butter

Roast the fillet of beef the day before, keeping it underdone. Coat bottom and sides of a 9- by 5- by 3-inch loaf pan with aspic. Chill until almost set. Decorate the bottom with slices of truffle and beef tongue cut into julienne pieces. Cover with half-set aspic. Chill until aspic is firm. Combine pâté de foie gras with butter, mixing well. Slice cold fillet of beef about ¼ inch thick. Spread both sides with the pâté-and-butter mixture, and place the slices in an upright position in the mold. Fill with half-set aspic. Refrigerate until firm and ready to serve. Turn out onto a platter and, if desired, garnish with additional aspic cut into cubes. Makes 8 servings. (See illustration, page 557.)

⚜ FILLET OF BEEF CHARLEMAGNE

¼ cup (½ stick) butter
2 finely chopped shallots, or 2 tablespoons chopped onion
½ pound finely chopped mushroom caps or stems
1 tablesoon chopped parsley
½ teaspoon salt
ground black pepper to taste
1 cup Tomato Sauce
2 pounds leftover roast fillet of beef
Béarnaise Sauce

Melt butter in a 1½-quart saucepan. Add shallots or onions and mushrooms. Stir and cook until the moisture has evaporated. Season with parsley, salt, and pepper, and add to Tomato Sauce. Slice beef and arrange the slices in a baking dish with mushroom-tomato sauce between the slices. Cover with Béarnaise Sauce. Cook under broiler heat until glazed. Makes 4 to 6 servings.

⚜ GRILLED CHATEAUBRIAND

Chateaubriand, which is cut from the middle of the fillet, is the tenderest and most flavorful of all beefsteaks.

1 chateaubriand steak, 2½ to 3 inches thick
salt to taste
butter

Sprinkle both sides of meat lightly with salt. Spread generously with butter and broil about 6 minutes in a preheated broiling oven. Transfer steak to a pan, reduce broiler heat to 350° F., and cook about 15 minutes if rare steak is desired, 20 minutes for medium-rare. Serve with Béarnaise Sauce and Pommes Soufflés or French Fried Potatoes. Makes 2 servings. (See illustration, page 555; also Culinary Techniques in Pictures.)

⚜ BROILED FILET MIGNON

4 filet mignon steaks, 1½ to 2 inches thick
salt
melted butter
ground black pepper
Béarnaise Sauce

Sprinkle meat lightly on both sides with salt and brush both sides with melted butter. Broil 3 inches from the source of heat in a preheated broiling oven

6 minutes on each side, or until cooked as desired, brushing with melted butter. Sprinkle with black pepper and serve with Béarnaise Sauce. Makes 4 servings.

⚜ BROILED TOURNEDOS

Allow 1 tournedos to a serving. Tie string around them to hold them in shape. Sprinkle both sides of tournedos with salt and spread with butter. Broil on each side 3 minutes for rare, and 4 to 5 minutes for medium rare, in a preheated broiler oven. Or, if desired, pan-broil or sauté tournedos over surface heat, cooking the same length of time as for oven broiling. Add stock or wine to the frying residue, cook until thickened, and serve it as a sauce over the steaks. Remove the strings before serving. Transfer to a hot platter and garnish with broiled small mushroom caps, cooked carrots cut into quarters, buttered artichoke hearts, topped with asparagus tips, and watercress. (See illustration, page 555.)

⚜ BROILED TOURNEDOS WITH BÉARNAISE SAUCE

Broil the tournedos as in the preceding recipe. Cut pieces of white bread to fit them and fry it in butter. Put each steak on a slice of fried bread and top with a ring of very thick Béarnaise Sauce. Garnish with boiled potatoes and watercress. Allow 1 per serving.

⚜ TOURNEDOS WITH BONE MARROW

6 tournedos
2 shallots, finely chopped
½ cup dry red wine
1 cup Brown Sauce
6 slices poached bone marrow
chopped parsley

Broil steaks as in the recipe for Broiled Tournedos. Cook the shallots in the wine until liquid is reduced to one-quarter the original quantity. Stir in Brown Sauce and simmer 4 to 5 minutes or until sauce is of desired thickness. Transfer steaks to a platter and cover with the sauce. Top each with a slice of poached bone marrow. Sprinkle with chopped parsley. Makes 6 servings.

⚜ TOURNEDOS CHORON

6 tournedos
6 fried rounds of white bread cut to fit the steaks
½ cup Béarnaise Sauce
1 tablespoon tomato paste
6 cooked artichoke bottoms
boiled or French fried potato balls

Broil steaks as for Broiled Tournedos. Place each on a round of fried bread and arrange on a hot platter. Keep hot. Combine Béarnaise Sauce and tomato paste, put a teaspoonful on each artichoke bottom, and place them on the platter around the steaks. Garnish with boiled or French fried potato balls. Makes 6 servings.

⚜ TOURNEDOS CLAMART

6 tournedos
6 rounds white bread cut to fit the meat and fried in butter stock
6 baked tart shells
1½ cups buttered cooked green peas
6 ends of cooked carrots 1½ inches long
French fried potato balls

Broil steaks as for Broiled Tournedos. Place each on a round of fried bread and place them on a hot platter. Keep hot. Fill tart shells with buttered cooked peas. Garnish each with a carrot and place around the meat. Serve Dauphine Potatoes in a separate dish. Makes 6 servings. (See illustration, page 554.)

⚜ TOURNEDOS COLBERT

6 tournedos
6 round flattened chicken croquettes
6 small French Fried Eggs
6 truffle slices, or 6 mushroom caps sautéed in butter

Sauté or broil steaks as in Broiled Tournedos. Place each on a round chicken croquette. Top with a fried egg and garnish with a truffle slice or sautéed mushroom cap. Makes 6 servings.

⚜ TOURNEDOS HENRI IV

18 tiny new potatoes
6 tablespoons butter
1 teaspoon salt
ground white pepper
6 tournedos
6 rounds bread cut to fit meat and fried in butter
6 cooked large artichoke hearts
¾ cup Béarnaise Sauce

Scrape new potatoes, wash, and dry. Cook, covered, very slowly in butter with the salt added, about 30 minutes or until potatoes are tender. Meanwhile broil steaks as for Broiled Tournedos. Place each tournedos on a slice of fried bread and place them on a platter. Pile 3 potatoes on each artichoke heart and arrange on the platter around the steaks. Pass Béarnaise Sauce in a sauceboat. Makes 6 servings.

⚜ TOURNEDOS MASSENA

2 shallots, finely chopped
2 tablespoons finely chopped onion
1 tablespoon butter
1 teaspoon flour
¼ cup bouillon
¾ cup dry white wine
1 tablespoon brandy
1 truffle, finely chopped
6 tournedos
6 rounds of white bread fried in butter
12 slices poached bone marrow
6 large cooked artichoke bottoms
½ cup Béarnaise Sauce

Cook shallots and onion in butter until transparent. Blend in flour. Stir and cook until browned. Add bouillon. Mix well and set aside. In another saucepan heat wine. Warm brandy, ignite, and add to wine; then add wine and brandy to the first mixture. Cover and simmer over very low heat 20 minutes, stirring frequently. Strain. Add truffle and cook 2 to 3 minutes. Broil tournedos as for Broiled Tournedos. Place each on a round of fried bread and arrange them on a hot platter. Top each with 2 slices poached marrow and coat with the sauce. Fill artichoke bottoms with Béarnaise Sauce and arrange on the platter around the meat. Serve at once. Makes 6 servings. (See illustration, page 556.)

⚜ TOURNEDOS ROSSINI

½ pound fat goose liver
1 truffle
¼ cup Madeira
6 tournedos
6 rounds white bread cut to fit the steaks and fried in butter
¾ cup Demi-Glace Sauce
1 tablespoon butter

Cut goose liver in 6 thick slices. Cut truffle in 6 thin slices. Marinate liver and truffle in Madeira in a covered dish 1 to 2 hours. Broil or sauté tournedos as in Broiled Tournedos. Place each on a fried round of bread. Keep hot. Drain marinade into pan drippings, add truffle slices and Demi-Glace, and simmer 4 minutes. Fry liver in butter, place a slice on each tournedos, and pour sauce over them. Top each with a truffle slice. Serve at once. Makes 6 servings. (See illustration, page 556.)

⚜ BEEF STROGANOFF

2 pounds beef fillet
salt
ground black pepper
4 tablespoons (½ stick) butter
½ cup sliced onion
1 tablespoon flour
1 cup hot canned consommé or beef stock
1 teaspoon prepared mustard
¼ cup sour cream

Cut meat across the grain into strips 2 by ½ by ½ inches. Sprinkle lightly with salt and pepper and refrigerate 2 hours. Melt 2 tablespoons of the butter in a heavy skillet. Put in just enough meat and onion to cover the bottom. Brown quickly on all sides. Transfer meat to a platter and keep it warm. Discard onions. Repeat until meat and onions are all used. In a saucepan melt 2 tablespoons butter. Blend in flour. Stir in consommé or stock. Mix quickly and thoroughly until sauce is smooth and begins to thicken. Add mustard. Blend in sour cream and heat 2 to 3 minutes. Adjust seasonings. Add meat and toss lightly. Serve at once. If desired, replace beef fillet with boneless sirloin or porterhouse steak. Makes 6 servings.

⚜ ROAST BONED LOIN OF BEEF

This is a roast made from the sirloin after the tenderloin has been removed. Fat, bones, and sinews have been trimmed away.

Tie thin slices of larding pork or beef suet around the roast to cover it completely. Place a prepared 4- to 5-pound roast in a preheated very hot oven (450° F.) for about 10 minutes. Reduce heat to moderate (350° F.) and cook 10 minutes per pound for medium-rare. Remove the larding pork or suet 20 to 25 minutes before cooking time is up, so that the meat will brown. Let the meat rest 20 minutes before carving. Transfer roast to a platter. Make pan gravy in the roasting pan. Makes 8 to 10 servings.

⚜ BEEFSTEAK

Allow ⅓ pound sliced sirloin or rump steak, cut between ¼ and ½ inch thick, per serving. Flatten the meat slightly with a mallet or a heavy spatula, being careful not to flatten it too thin. Sprinkle lightly with salt and pepper. Fry in a hot heavy skillet 2 minutes, or until blood begins to seep out of the top side, then turn and cook 2 more minutes, or until browned. Serve with Herb Butter and French Fried Match Stick Potatoes.

⚜ PEPPER STEAK

about 2 pounds sirloin steak
salt to taste
1 tablespoon white peppercorns, coarsely crushed
2 tablespoons melted butter
⅓ cup brandy
2 tablespoons Demi-Glace Sauce

Cut steak into 4 servings. Rub salt lightly into both sides of the meat. Dip meat into the crushed pepper, pressing the pepper into both sides with the hand. Fry the steaks in a heavy skillet in melted butter to desired doneness, turning to brown both sides. Transfer steaks to a hot platter and keep hot. Add brandy to the skillet and bring to boiling point. Add Demi-Glace, mix with a wooden spoon, and bring to boiling point once. Pour over the steaks. Serve at once. Makes 4 servings.

⚜ FONDUE BOURGUIGNONNE (*Swiss*)

2 pounds sirloin steak
1½ cups cooking oil
salt and ground black pepper
assorted cold sauces (mayonnaise, Aurora, mustard, Rémoulade, Vinaigrette, catchup, etc.)

Cut the raw meat into 1½-inch cubes. Skewer the cubes, using wooden skewers. (Do not use forks or metal skewers.) Heat oil in a heatproof dish and place in the center of the table on a hotplate, or over an alcohol lamp. The guests dip their own pieces of skewered meat into the hot oil and cook them as desired (rare, medium, or well-done). Provide salt, pepper in pepper mills, and a selection of sauces, each in a separate bowl. The pieces of meat are removed from the skewers and speared with forks for dipping into the desired sauce. Makes 6 servings.

⚜ ENTRECÔTE WITH MUSHROOMS

2 entrecôte steaks (or sirloin or rib steaks), 1 pound each, cut 1 inch thick
5 tablespoons butter
2 tablespoons oil
½ pound blanched mushrooms (save liquid)
½ cup Demi-Glace Sauce
salt and ground black pepper
parsley

Trim any excess fat from steaks and make a small incision around them, in the layer of gristle between the fat and the meat. This prevents the steak from curling. Dry meat thoroughly. Heat 3 tablespoons of the butter and the 2 tablespoons oil in a skillet. When the butter foam begins to subside, add steaks and sauté each side 3 to 4 minutes, regulating the heat so that the fat will not burn. The steak is medium rare when bubbles of red juice begin to appear on the surface. Transfer steaks to a hot platter and keep hot. Skim off and discard fat from the pan juices, and add a little of the liquid used for blanching mushrooms to the pan. Mix well. Cook ½ minute. Stir in Demi-Glace and mushrooms, mix well, and then add remaining 2 tablespoons butter. Bring to boiling point. Adjust seasonings. Sprinkle steaks with salt and pepper and cover them with mushroom sauce. Garnish with parsley. Makes 6 servings. (See illustration, page 553.)

⚜ ENTRECÔTE MIRABEAU

2 entrecôte steaks (or sirloin or rib steaks), 1 pound each, cut 1 inch thick
melted butter or oil
salt
ground black pepper
anchovy fillets
pimiento-stuffed olives, sliced
pitted green olives
watercress

Trim and flatten the steaks. Brush with melted butter or oil, and sprinkle lightly with salt. Place in a preheated broiler oven 3 inches from the source of heat. Broil 5 minutes on each side for rare meat; 7 to 8 minutes for medium-rare, and 10 minutes for well-done. Sprinkle with ground black pepper. Transfer to a hot platter. Dip anchovy fillets in oil and place in lattice fashion over the top of the steaks. Put slices of pimiento-stuffed olives in the squares. Garnish platter with pitted green olives and watercress. Serve with Soufflé Potatoes or French Fried Potatoes. Makes 4 servings. (See illustration, page 554.)

⚜ ENTRECÔTE LYONNAISE

3 cups sliced onions
3 tablespoons butter
salt
ground black pepper
1 teaspoon wine vinegar
1 tablespoon meat glaze
¼ cup dry white wine
4 entrecôte steaks (or sirloin or rib steaks), ⅓ pound each and 1 inch thick
chopped parsley

Fry onions in butter until golden brown. Season with salt and pepper to taste. Add vinegar, meat glaze, and wine. Simmer 2 to 3 minutes.

Grill steaks as directed in the recipe for Entrecôte Mirabeau. Transfer steaks to a hot platter, pour onions over them. Sprinkle with chopped parsley. Serve at once. Makes 4 servings.

⚜ ONE-MINUTE ENTRECÔTE

Cut entrecôte steaks very thin, or flatten the thicker ones. Sprinkle both sides lightly with salt and ground black pepper. Fry very quickly, about 2 minutes on each side, in a little butter and oil (in equal amounts), or in rendered beef suet. Serve at once with Herb Butter. Allow 1 steak per serving.

⚜ STEAK VIENNESE STYLE (*Wiener Rostbraten*)

6 entrecôte steaks (or sirloin or rib steaks), 1 pound each, cut ½ inch thick
salt
ground black pepper
3 tablespoons lard or shortening
1 teaspoon paprika
¾ cup bouillon
¾ cup sour cream

Flatten the steaks slightly. Sprinkle with salt and pepper and brown in about 2 tablespoons lard or shortening in a large skillet. Transfer meat to a platter and keep warm. In the same skillet brown onions in an additional tablespoon lard or shortening. Place half the onions in a 1½-quart casserole, put steaks on top, and cover with remaining onions. Sprinkle lightly with salt, pepper, and paprika. Add bouillon. Cover and cook in a preheated slow oven (325° F.) 1 hour or until meat is tender. Transfer meat to a serving dish. Stir sour cream into the pan drippings and onions. Heat, adjust seasonings, and serve over meat. Serve with mashed potatoes. Makes 6 servings.

⚜ BEEF À LA MODE (*French Pot Roast*)

12 lardoons (long strips fat salt pork)
salt
ground black pepper
1 tablespoon chopped parsley
1 clove garlic, minced
4-pound round or beef roast
⅛ teaspoon ground nutmeg
3 tablespoons shortening or salad oil
¼ cup warmed brandy
1 cup dry red wine
1 cup beef stock
1 calf's foot (if available)
12 small carrots, pared
18 small white onions
3 tablespoons butter
1 tablespoon potato starch or cornstarch
3 tablespoons water

Roll lardoons in salt, pepper, parsley, and garlic, and with a larding needle lard the meat. Rub the outside of the meat with salt, pepper, and nutmeg. Brown it on all sides in hot shortening or oil in a Dutch oven. Pour warmed brandy over the meat and ignite. Add wine, beef stock, and calf's foot (if used). Cover and cook in a preheated slow oven (325° F.) 1½ hours. Brown carrots and onions in butter over low heat and add to the meat. Cover and cook 1 more hour, or until meat and vegetables are tender. Skim off and discard all fat from the gravy. Transfer meat to a warmed platter. Surround with vegetables. Blend starch with water and add to the gravy. Bring to boiling point, strain, and spoon some over the meat. Serve the remainder in a sauceboat. Garnish meat with parsley. Makes 6 to 8 servings.

⚜ BEEF À LA MODE IN ASPIC

4 to 5 pounds eye round of beef
6 lardoons (strips fat salt pork)
salt
ground black pepper
½ teaspoon ground mace
½ cup brandy
2 to 3 tablespoons rendered beef suet or bacon fat
2 calf's feet
3 cups dry white wine
1 large onion
5 carrots
2 shallots, chopped
2 ribs celery, sliced
parsley
1 bay leaf
3 whole cloves
12 small onions, peeled, halved, and cooked
6 cooked whole string beans
parsley

Lard the beef with the lardoons, or ask the butcher to do it for you. Sprinkle with salt, pepper, and mace. Place meat in a bowl, pour brandy over it, and marinate 3 to 4 hours, turning meat occasionally. Remove beef (reserve marinade), wipe dry, and brown on all sides in hot fat in a heavy saucepan. Transfer meat to another pan and keep warm. Split the calf's feet and parboil 10 mintues in hot water. Remove from water, dry, chop into coarse pieces, and brown in the same saucepan in which the beef was browned. Pour in the reserved marinade. Cook 3 to 4 minutes, scraping up all the browned bits from the bottom of the saucepan. Add wine. Peel the large onion, cut in half, and add. Peel 2 of the carrots, quarter, and add, along with the celery, 2 stalks parsley, bay leaf, and cloves. Return meat to the saucepan, cover, and simmer 4 hours or until meat is tender, turning occasionally. Transfer meat and calf's feet to another bowl and cool. Slice meat and set aside. Cut meat from the calf's feet and slice it into julienne pieces. Set aside. Skim off and discard fat from the stock and strain the stock through a fine sieve. Pour enough of the stock into a mold or large pan, about 2 inches deep, to coat the bottom and sides. (Reserve remaining stock.) Chill until coating is almost set.

Meanwhile peel the small onions, cut in half, and cook in water until tender. Peel remaining carrots, leave whole, and cook separately until tender. Cool. Cut 2 inches from the small ends of carrots. Split and arrange them in the center bottom of the mold to simulate a daisy. Finish covering the bottom with the rest of the carrots, sliced, the onions, and the string beans. (See illustration, page 558.) Cover with semiliquid aspic from stock. Chill until firm. Finish filling mold with sliced beef and meat cut from the calf's feet. Pour in enough of reserved stock to cover the meat and fill the mold. Chill until firm and ready to serve. Unmold on a platter. Garnish with parsley. Makes 8 to 10 servings.

⚜ SAUERBRATEN BERLIN STYLE

1 clove garlic
½ cup sliced onion
2 carrots, sliced
1 rib celery, diced, or ¼ cup diced celeriac
¼ cup chopped parsley
1 bay leaf
8 peppercorns
1½ cups wine vinegar
1 teaspoon salt
3 to 4 pounds round of beef
⅓ cup olive oil or salad oil
1 lemon, sliced
2 tablespoons shortening or oil
1 cup beef stock
¾ cup sour cream

Combine the first 9 ingredients and bring to boiling point. Place beef in a bowl and pour the marinade and then the oil over it. Top with lemon slices. Cover and marinate in the refrigerator 3 days, turning meat occasionally.

Remove meat and vegetables from marinade. Reserve marinade. Dry meat with paper towels and brown on all sides in shortening or oil in a Dutch oven or a heavy 4-quart saucepan, along with the vegetables. Add marinade and beef stock. Cover and cook in a preheated slow oven (325° F.) 2½ to 3 hours, or until meat is tender. Transfer meat to a serving dish and keep warm. Strain stock and reduce to one-half the original quantity. Stir in sour cream and heat. Adjust seasonings. Cut meat into slices and serve with the gravy, Red Cabbage with Apples, and mashed potatoes. Makes 6 to 8 servings.

⚜ SPOON BEEF (*Boeuf à la Cuillere*)

3 pounds top round steak, cut 1 inch thick
salt
ground black pepper
flour
1 to 2 tablespoons shortening or oil
½ to 1 cup water or dry white wine
1 cup diced carrots
½ cup chopped onion
1/16 teaspoon minced garlic
1 tablespoon tomato paste

Rub the steak lightly on both sides with salt and pepper. Dredge meat lightly in flour and brown slowly on both sides in shortening or oil in a heavy skillet. Add water or wine, vegetables, and garlic. Cover. Cook over low surface heat or in a preheated moderate oven (325° F.) 1 to 1½ hours or until meat is so well done that it will fall apart when you attempt to slice it. Transfer meat to a platter. Add tomato paste to the gravy, adjust seasonings, strain, and pour over meat. Makes 6 servings.

Fillet of Beef Wellington, page 539 ▲

▼ Fillet of Beef Richelieu, page 539

▲ Italian Braised Beef, page 560

Braised Rump of Beef, page 559 ▼

Salt Brisket of Belle Flamande, page 563 ▲

▼ Entrecôte with Mushrooms, page 546

▲ Entrecôte Mirabeau, page 547

Tournedos Clamart, page 543 ▼

▼ Broiled Tournedos, page 542

Grilled Chateaubriand, page 541 ▲

▲ Tournedos Massena, page 544

Tournedos Rossini, page 544 ▼

▼ Tongue Princesse, page 640

Glazed Fillet of Beef, page 540 ▲

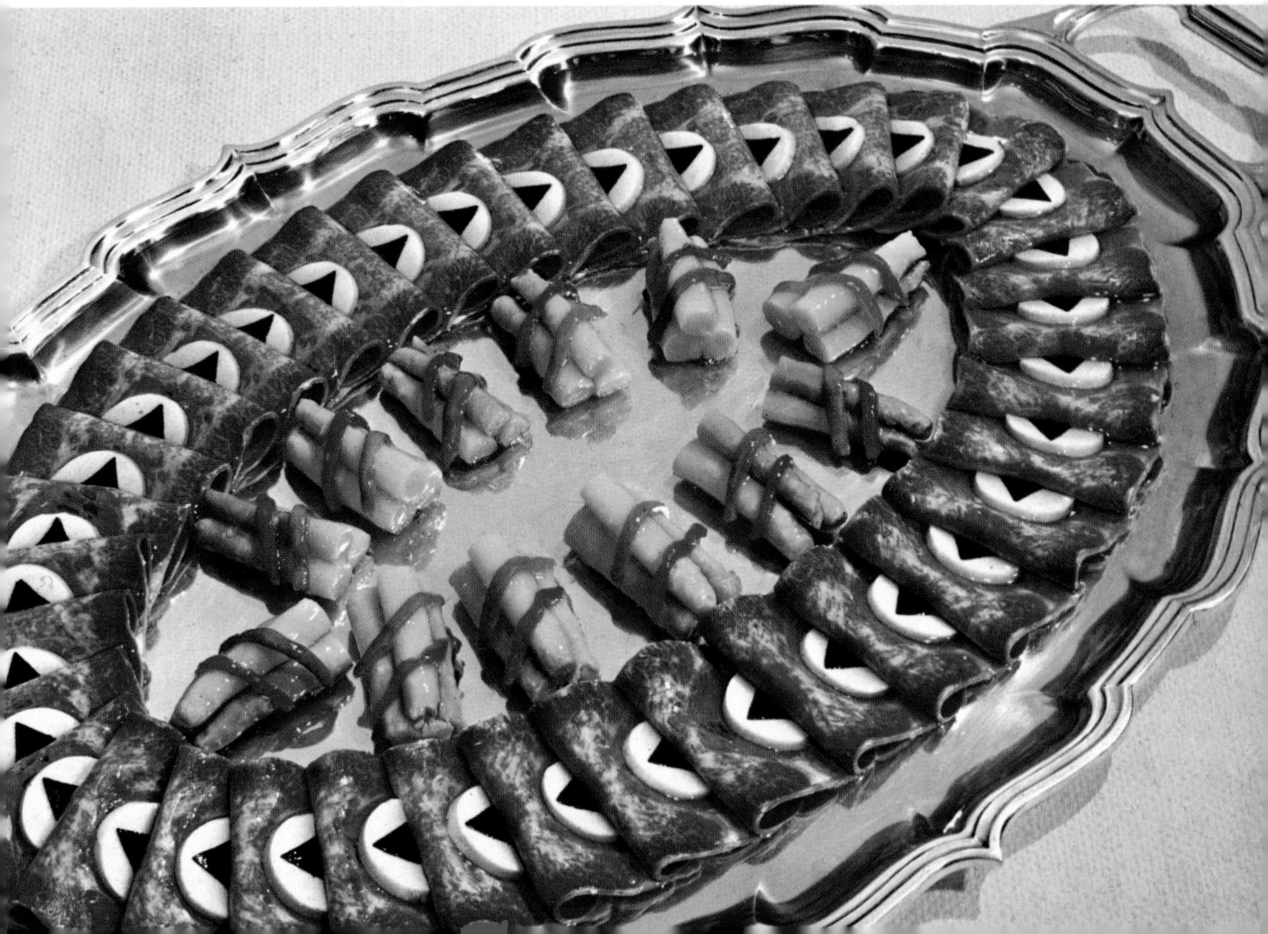

▲ Beef à la Mode in Aspic, page 549

Pickled Tongue Karachi Style, page 639 ▼

⚜ BEEF BOURGUIGNONNE

2½ pounds boneless beef (rump or chuck)
flour
3 tablespoons olive oil or salad oil or shortening
1 clove garlic, finely chopped
1¾ cups Burgundy
hot water
1 small bay leaf
1½ teaspoons salt
3 stalks parsley
2 strips bacon
½ cup coarsely chopped onion
1 tablespoon tomato paste
¼ teaspoon ground black pepper
18 medium-sized mushroom caps
2 tablespoons butter

Cut beef into large cubes and roll them in flour. Brown on all sides in hot oil or shortening. Add garlic and fry with the meat 1 minute. Turn into a 2-quart casserole. Add wine and enough hot water barely to cover the meat, along with bay leaf, salt, and parsley. Cover and cook in a preheated slow oven (325° F.) 2 hours. Dice bacon and fry briefly, then add onions and cook until they have browned lightly and bacon is crisp. Add both to the meat and cook ½ hour or until meat is tender. Add tomato paste and black pepper. Stir until blended. Cook another 10 minutes. Cook mushroom caps in butter and arrange over top of casserole. Serve hot. Makes 6 servings.

⚜ BRAISED RUMP OF BEEF

3 pounds boneless rump or other lean roast
salt
ground black pepper
2 tablespoons lard or shortening
½ cup sliced onions
½ cup sliced carrots
2 cups dry white wine, stock, or water
1 cup Demi-Glace Sauce
2 stalks parsley
1 rib celery, quartered
6 braised potatoes
12 braised carrots
½ pound braised white onions

Ask your butcher to lard the roast with strips of fat salt pork. Rub the outside of the meat with salt and black pepper and brown it on all sides in lard or shortening along with the sliced onions and carrots. Pour off the excess fat, add wine, stock, or water, and cook the meat, uncovered, until the liquid has reduced to one-half the original amount. Pour the Demi-Glace over the meat. Add parsley and celery. Cover and cook slowly 2½ to 3 hours, turning the meat 3 or 4 times. Transfer meat to a warmed platter and keep it warm until ready to serve. Skim off excess fat from the cooking liquid and discard. Strain the liquid and if it is not thick enough, boil it a few minutes to reduce it to desired consistency. Slice the meat, having the slices overlapping on the platter. Garnish with the braised vegetables. Decorate the platter, if desired, with watercress. Makes 6 to 8 servings. (See illustration, page 552.)

⚜ ITALIAN BRAISED BEEF (*Manzo Brasato*)

3 pounds boneless rump or other lean roast
2 whole carrots
2 ribs celery
1 cup red wine
½ cup salad oil or olive oil
½ teaspoon sage
½ teaspoon rosemary
½ cup chopped onions
½ cup chopped carrots
½ cup chopped celery
¼ cup tomato purée
1 cup water
flour (optional)
8 braised onions
8 braised potatoes

Have the butcher lard the meat and roll it the long way, rolling it around the whole carrots and the ribs of celery (see illustration, page 552). Make a marinade with the red wine, ⅓ cup of the oil, and the sage and rosemary, and marinate the meat in this for 48 hours. Remove the meat, reserving the marinade. Brown the meat on all sides in the remaining oil, adding the chopped vegetables to the pan a few minutes before the meat is all browned. Pour the marinade over the meat and cook uncovered until the liquid is reduced by one-half. Add the tomato purée and 1 cup water. Cover and cook slowly 2½ to 3 hours, turning the meat 2 or 3 times. Remove the meat to a warm serving platter and keep it warm. Skim off the excess fat from the cooking liquid, strain the liquid, and thicken with a little flour if necessary. Arrange the braised onions and potatoes on the platter around the meat. Serve the gravy separately. Makes 6 to 8 servings.

⚜ DAUBE À LA MARSEILLE

3 pounds shoulder or rump of beef, cut into large cubes
lardoons (strips of fat salt pork)
2½ cups dry red wine
1 cup brandy
1 cup sliced carrots
1½ cups sliced onions
1 clove garlic
6 peppercorns
½ teaspoon salt
2 stalks parsley
3 tablespoons olive oil or salad oil
¼ pound pork rinds
1 cup diced, peeled, seeded tomatoes or ¾ cup canned tomatoes
1 dozen pitted black olives

Lard each cube of meat with a lardoon. Add wine, brandy, carrots, onions, garlic, peppercorns, and parsley. Pour oil over the top. Cover and marinate in the refrigerator overnight. Wash pork rinds in hot water, rinse, cut into 1-inch squares, and put them in the bottom of a Dutch oven. Place the meat on the pork rinds and pour in the marinade. Add tomatoes and olives. Cover tightly and cook in a slow oven (325° F.) 2 to 3 hours. If desired, use a whole piece of meat without cubing it. The method of cooking is the same but the cooking time may need to be increased ½ hour. Makes 6 servings.

⚜ BEEF BIRDS

6 thin large slices of beef (6 inches square)
salt
ground black pepper
6 strips bacon
6 thin slices raw ham
2 tablespoons shortening
1 cup sliced carrots
½ cup sliced onion
⅓ cup dry white wine
2 cups diced fresh tomatoes or 2½ cups canned tomatoes

Sprinkle both sides of meat slices lightly with salt and pepper. Place a strip of bacon and a slice of ham on each. Roll up and tie with strings or fasten with skewers. Brown on all sides in shortening with carrots and onions. Pour off fat. Add wine and cook 1 to 2 minutes. Add tomatoes, cover, and cook over slow heat 1 hour or until meat is tender. Transfer meat to a serving dish and remove strings or skewers. Strain the gravy and skim off fat, adjust seasonings, and serve over meat. Garnish with any desired vegetables. Makes 6 servings.

VARIATIONS

BEEF BIRDS PROVENÇALE

In the recipe for Beef Birds replace the bacon and ham with ¾ pound sausage meat mixed with 2 tablespoons chopped parsley and 1/16 teaspoon finely chopped garlic. Add 12 pitted green olives to the gravy.

BEEF BIRDS MILANESE

In the recipe for Beef Birds Provençale, omit the garlic and the olives. Serve with boiled macaroni cooked as directed on the package. These may also be served with Risotto.

⚜ EXETER BEEFSTEAK PIE (*English*)

2 pounds round steak
salt
ground black pepper
6 tablespoons flour
½ cup chopped parsley
2 cups sliced onions
4 hard-cooked eggs
Puff Pastry or Plain Pastry
water or stock
milk

Cut steak into thin 2-inch pieces. Sprinkle lightly with salt and pepper, roll in flour, and put half the meat into a buttered casserole with half the parsley and onion. Peel eggs, cut in half, and place over meat. Repeat, using remaining meat, parsley, and onion. Pour in enough water or stock to cover the meat. Top with puff pastry rolled 1/4 inch thick, or plain pastry rolled 1/8 inch thick. Trim, turn, and flute the edge. Cut 2 or 3 vents in the pastry to allow for the escape of steam. Brush crust with milk. Bake in a preheated hot oven (450° F.) 10 minutes. Reduce heat to 350° and continue cooking 30 to 40 minutes, or until meat is tender. Makes 6 servings.

⚜ BEEFSTEAK AND MUSHROOM PIE (*English*)

2 pounds round steak
salt
ground black pepper
1 cup finely chopped onion
1/4 cup finely chopped parsley
3 cups finely chopped mushrooms
flour
Puff Pastry or Plain Pastry
hot water or beef stock

Cut meat into 12 thin slices. Sprinkle lightly with salt and pepper. Combine onions, parsley, and mushrooms. Sprinkle with salt, pepper, and flour. Mix well and spread an equal amount on each of the meat slices. Roll up, then roll in flour and place in an 8-by-8-by-2-inch baking pan. Pour in enough hot water or hot beef stock to come almost to the top of the meat. Cover with puff pastry rolled 1/4 inch thick or plain pastry rolled 1/8 inch thick. Trim, turn under, and flute edge. Cut 2 or 3 vents to allow for escape of steam. Bake in a preheated very hot oven (450° F.) 10 minutes. Reduce heat to moderate (350° F.) and cook 40 minutes, or until meat is tender and pastry is brown. Makes 6 servings.

⚜ ROMANIAN MEAT BALLS WITH HERBS

1 pound lean beef, ground
3/4 pound lean pork, ground
1/2 cup finely chopped onion
1 1/2 teaspoon salt
1/8 teaspoon ground black pepper
2 tablespoons each finely chopped chervil, dill, parsley, spinach, tarragon, and watercress, mixed
1/4 pound (1 stick) butter
3/4 cup Demi-Glace Sauce
1/2 cup sour cream

Combine the first 5 ingredients. Shape into 1 1/2-inch balls and roll in the mixture of herbs. Cook in butter over low heat until done; do not allow meat balls to brown. Add Demi-Glace and cook 3 to 4 minutes. Serve sour cream in a separate bowl. Makes 6 servings.

⚜ HAMBURGER STEAK (*Beefsteak Haché à l'Allemande*)

For each serving:
- **⅓ pound ground lean beef**
- **1 teaspoon finely chopped onion**
- **1 egg yolk**
- **salt and ground black pepper to taste**
- **butter**

Mix meat with onion, egg yolk, salt, and pepper. Shape into a steak ½ inch thick. Brown on both sides in butter, keeping the inside slightly underdone, if desired. Pour the browned frying butter over the top.

⚜ SALT BRISKET OF BEEF BELLE FLAMANDE

- **3 to 4 pounds corned beef**
- **cold water**
- **6 each medium-sized carrots, potatoes, and turnips, quartered**
- **heart of 1 head of cabbage**
- **6 servings green beans, cooked in a separate saucepan**
- **chopped parsley**
- **½ pound sausage, cooked**
- **Vincent Sauce**

Place beef, with cold water to cover, in a Dutch oven. Bring to boiling point and skim. Cover and simmer (do not boil) for 4 hours or until meat is tender. Add carrots, potatoes, and turnips 20 minutes before cooking time is up, and cabbage 10 minutes before meat is done.

To serve, slice enough meat for one meal and put it on a hot platter, arranging vegetables and sausage around the meat. Sprinkle vegetables with chopped parsley. (See illustration, page 553.) Serve Vincent Sauce separately. Makes 6 servings of sliced corned beef with vegetables, and enough beef for hash for another meal.

VINCENT SAUCE

Blanch equal amounts of parsley, watercress, and chives in hot water. Drain well and purée. Add 2 tablespoons purée to each ½ cup mayonnaise. Mix well. Stir in the chopped white of 1 hard-cooked egg. Serve with corned beef.

Veal

Veal is the meat from calves up to 1 year of age. It contains very little fat, and for that reason should never be broiled. It should always be cooked well done. The age and weight of the calf determines the color of the meat but does not affect the flavor or eating qualities. The meat is fine in grain, fairly firm, velvety in texture, and grayish-pink in color. The bones are porous and are red at the ends.

The flavor of veal is more delicate than that of any other meat and harmonizes with the flavors of many other foods. Both the French and the Italians have created world-famous veal dishes.

⚜ ROAST LOIN OF VEAL

5-pound boned veal loin roast
salt
ground black pepper
thin strips salt pork
mushrooms (optional)

Sprinkle veal with salt and pepper. Cover with thin strips of salt pork. Put roast on a rack, fat side up. Cook, uncovered, in a preheated moderate oven (375° F.) 18 to 20 minutes per pound, or to 180° F. on the meat thermometer if one is used. Add a little water to the pan if the fat tends to scorch. Transfer meat to a hot platter and keep warm while making the gravy. Make gravy from pan drippings, adding sautéed mushrooms if desired. Makes 10 to 12 servings.

⚜ ROAST BONED LOIN OF VEAL WITH KIDNEYS (*Rognonade de Veau Rôti*)

Have the butcher cut a 5-pound boned loin of veal with the kidneys attached and roast it as directed for Roast Loin of Veal. Make gravy from pan drippings. Serve with sautéed fluted mushrooms. Makes 10 to 12 servings. (See illustration, page 592.)

⚜ VEAL RIB ROAST WITH VEGETABLES

1 veal rib roast, allowing 2 ribs per serving
salt
ground black pepper
cooked vegetables: carrots, cauliflower, potatoes, and tomatoes
chopped chives

Ask the butcher to remove the backbone for easier carving. Sprinkle meat lightly with salt and pepper, and wrap it in buttered paper or foil. Roast on a spit or in a preheated slow oven (325° F.) 1 hour. Remove the paper or foil and continue cooking until the meat is golden brown. (Allow total cooking time of 30 minutes per pound.) Transfer roast to a warm platter. Serve with buttered cooked vegetables. Sprinkle potatoes with chopped chives. Allow 2 ribs per serving. (See illustration, page 592.)

⚜ ROAST VEAL NIVERNAISE

3 pounds rolled rump veal roast
lardoons (long strips fat salt pork)
salt and ground black pepper
1 cup brown stock
1 tablespoon flour
¼ cup water or stock
3 tablespoons butter
2 cups turnips, cut in the shape of large olives
30 small white onions
½ pound whole string beans
6 broiled whole tomatoes

Ask the butcher to lard the roast. Rub salt and pepper over the surface of the meat, and place it on a rack in a heavy saucepan or Dutch oven. Cook meat, uncovered, in a preheated very hot oven (500° F.) 10 to 15 minutes, or until browned. Reduce heat to 325° F. (slow). Add brown stock, cover, and cook 40 minutes per pound, or until meat is tender. Transfer meat to a warm platter, and keep hot. Blend flour with water or stock until smooth and add to the gravy. Stir and cook until gravy has thickened slightly. Strain. Cook turnips, onions, and beans separately, drain, and toss with the butter. Slice the meat and arrange the vegetables and the broiled tomatoes on the platter around the roast. Serve gravy separately in a gravy boat. Makes 6 servings. (See illustration, page 591.)

⚜ JELLIED VEAL POT ROAST

4 pounds rolled rump veal roast
lardoons (long strips fat salt pork)
salt
ground black pepper
butter
1½ cups aspic
12 medium-small carrots
2 small white turnips
12 small white onions
½ pound string beans

Ask the butcher to lard the roast. Sprinkle surface of roast with salt and pepper. Put it in a Dutch oven over moderate heat and brown on all sides in butter, adding it as needed. Drain the butter from the pan. Slip a rack under the meat. Add aspic, not more than 1 cup at a time. Cover and cook slowly until meat is tender, adding remaining aspic as needed. Peel carrots and turnips and cut into large julienne pieces. Brown in butter along with onions. After meat has cooked 1 hour, add these vegetables to the meat. Cover and cook until meat and vegetables are tender. Cook string beans in a separate saucepan and add to the veal at the last moment. If liquid tends to evaporate too fast, add more aspic. Place veal and vegetables in a deep bowl. Skim fat from the aspic and pour into the bowl over meat and vegetables. Chill. Serve in the jellied aspic. Makes 6 to 8 servings.

⚜ ROAST SADDLE OF VEAL

Saddle of veal is rarely cooked in private homes, since it is too large and heavy. It is, rather, a *pièce de résistance* for special occasions and banquets in hotels and restaurants.

Ask the butcher to trim and lard a saddle of veal. Fold the long ends under and tie in place with strings. Sprinkle with salt and ground black pepper. Place on a rack in a large baking pan. Cook in a preheated slow oven (325° F.) 30 minutes per pound. Make gravy from pan drippings and veal stock. Thicken it with cornstarch, using 1 teaspoon for each cup of stock. (See illustration, page 591.)

⚜ COLD SADDLE OF VEAL

cold Roast Saddle of Veal
6 hard-cooked eggs
20 thin slices truffle
small baked pastry tart shells
marinated cold cooked asparagus tips
pimiento strips
1 medium-sized tomato
1 ripe olive
parsley

For roasting saddle of veal, see the preceding recipe. Slice as much of the roast as needed and place it in its original shape on a large tray. Peel and slice hard-cooked eggs, cover the yolks with truffle slices, and arrange the egg slices in a row in the center of the roast for two-thirds of its length. Finish the row with baked tart shells filled with asparagus tips and garnished with pimiento strips. Fill additional baked pastry tart shells with asparagus tips and arrange them on the tray. Cut a slice, ½ inch thick, from the top of the tomato. Scoop out the center and notch the edge, making a tomato cup. Place a peeled hard-cooked egg in the cup. Top egg with a ripe olive, using a toothpick to hold it in place. Stand it on one end of the roast. Garnish tray with parsley. (See illustrations, page 602, for this and another presentation.)

⚜ VEAL MEDALLIONS WITH MUSHROOMS

6 medallions of veal tenderloin, cut ¾ inch thick
salt
ground black pepper
6 tablespoons butter
1 cup veal gravy
6 large fluted mushroom caps sautéed in butter
chopped parsley

Sprinkle veal with salt and pepper. Sauté in butter over moderately low heat until browned and thoroughly done, adding butter as needed. Place chops in a serving dish, and cover with hot veal gravy. Top each with a sautéed mushroom cap. Garnish with chopped parsley. Serve with boiled potatoes. Makes 6 servings. (See illustration, page 598.)

⚜ FILLET OF VEAL IN A PASTRY CRUST
(*Filet de Veau en Croûte*)

¾ pound mushrooms
3 tablespoons butter
¼ teaspoon salt
⅙ teaspoon ground black pepper
2 pounds Puff Pastry
2½ pounds fillet of veal
10 ounces goose-liver purée
1 egg yolk
1 tablespoon milk
watercress
2 notched lemon halves
Sherry Sauce

Wash and slice the mushrooms and sauté them in the butter. Add the salt and black pepper and set them aside to cool. Roll Puff Pastry ¼ inch thick, 2 inches longer than the veal fillet, and wide enough to wrap around it and overlap about 1 inch. (The length and width of the pastry depends upon the length and width of the fillet.) Place the fillet in the center of the pastry and spread the top and sides with goose-liver purée. Drain the mushrooms and spread them over the top of the fillet. Bring the sides of the pastry over the top of the fillet, overlapping it about 1 inch to form a flat seam. Pull the ends of the pastry up over the ends of the fillet and press flat against the meat to seal the ends tightly. Cut 2 or 3 slits in the pastry to allow for the escape of steam. Roll the remaining pastry about ⅛ inch thick, cut it into leaves, crescents, diamonds, or other desired shapes, and place them over the pastry for decoration. Place the pastry-covered fillet in a lightly buttered baking pan. Beat the egg yolk with the milk and brush over the pastry. Place the pan in a preheated hot oven (400° F.). Bake 1 hour or until the pastry has browned and the veal is tender. If the pastry tends to brown too much, cover it with foil or brown paper. Transfer the fillet to a warmed serving platter. Garnish with watercress and lemon halves. Cut the fillet into slices ½ inch thick. Serve with Sherry Sauce. Makes 6 servings. (See illustration, page 593.)

⚜ SAUTÉED VEAL CHOPS (*Noisettes de Veau Sautées*)

Noisettes are small round steaks of veal or lamb from the loin or rib, cut 1½ to 2 inches thick, corresponding to tournedos of beef. Loin or kidney chops can be substituted for noisettes in the United States, where the cut is not available.

6 loin or kidney veal chops
¾ teaspoon salt
⅛ teaspoon ground black pepper
12 fresh sage leaves or ½ teaspoon dried sage
flour
about ½ cup (1 stick) butter
½ cup dry white wine

Rub chops with seasonings. Dredge in flour. Brown on both sides, over moderate heat, in butter, adding it as needed. If fresh sage is used, place 2 leaves on each chop, or sprinkle with dried sage. Add wine, cover, and simmer 15 minutes. Transfer chops to a hot platter. If any butter is left, add it to the cooking liquid. Heat and strain over chops. Serve with French fried or boiled potatoes. Makes 6 servings. (See illustration, page 599.)

⚜ VEAL CHOPS MOLIÈRE

6 veal chops
salt
ground black pepper
butter
6 cauliflowerets
boiling water
3 medium-sized tomatoes
mayonnaise
1 slice cooked tongue or ham
1 hard-cooked egg white

Sprinkle chops with salt and pepper and fry them in butter until brown on both sides. Add butter as needed. Cool chops under a weight to flatten them. Cook cauliflowerets in 1 inch boiling water and ½ teaspoon salt until barely tender, about 5 minutes. Cool and chill. Peel and cut tomatoes in half and scoop out centers. Sprinkle with salt and pepper and place a caulifloweret in each. Cover carefully with mayonnaise. Chill until ready to serve. Cut tongue or ham and egg white into small daisy-petal shapes and arrange them in daisy fashion on each chop. (See illustration, page 599.) Glaze with aspic and chill. Cut tongue or ham into ½- to ¾-inch disks and place one on each caulifloweret. Cut truffle slices into four-leaf-clover shapes and place one on each disk of ham or tongue. Coat a round tray with aspic and chill until aspic is set. Place chops on the tray, having the bone ends toward the center. Place a piece of parsley in the center, partially covering the ends of the bones. Arrange tomatoes and cauliflowerets between the chops near the rim of the tray. Makes 6 servings.

⚜ VEAL CHOPS IN WHITE WINE (*Grenadins de Veau*)

6 veal loin or kidney chops, boned
¾ teaspoon salt
⅛ teaspoon ground black pepper
flour
about ½ cup (1 stick) butter
½ cup dry white wine
6 slices bread fried in butter

Rub chops with salt and pepper. Dredge in flour. Brown on both sides, over moderate heat, in butter, adding it as needed. Add wine, cover, and simmer 15 minutes. Cut slices of bread to fit the chops and fry in butter. Serve the chops on the bread on a hot platter. Garnish with vegetables as desired: cauliflower, green beans, peas, carrots, etc. Makes 6 servings.

⚜ VEAL CUTLETS CHENONCEAUX

6 veal cutlets, 6 ounces each
salt
ground black pepper
¼ pound (1 stick) butter
12 slices pickled or boiled beef tongue
½ cup sherry
6 teaspoons slivered, toasted, blanched almonds
Macaire Potatoes

Sprinkle cutlets lightly with salt and pepper. Brown on both sides in butter, adding it as needed. Transfer cutlets to a platter and keep hot. In the same skillet heat the tongue in the butter that is left, adding more if necessary. Place 2 slices on each cutlet. Pour sherry into the skillet. Mix with pan drippings, bring to boiling point, and boil 1 to 2 minutes. Pour over meat. Sprinkle with almonds. Serve with Macaire Potatoes. Makes 6 servings. (See illustration, page 596.)

⚜ VEAL CUTLETS FOYOT (*With Onions and Cheese*)

2 cups sliced onions
2 tablespoons butter
6 veal cutlets
salt
ground black pepper
1 cup grated Gruyère or Cheddar cheese
½ cup fine dry breadcrumbs
4 tablespoons (½ stick) butter
½ cup dry white wine
¾ cup veal stock

Cook onions in butter until they are transparent. Place half in the bottom of a baking pan. Sprinkle cutlets with salt and pepper, put on top, and cover with remaining onions. Mix cheese with breadcrumbs and sprinkle over onions. Dot with butter. Combine wine and stock and pour over the top. Bake in a preheated slow oven (325° F.) 1 hour. Makes 6 servings.

⚜ VEAL CUTLETS MILANESE

6 veal cutlets
1 egg, beaten
½ teaspoon salt
⅛ teaspoon ground black pepper
3 tablespoons olive oil or salad oil
½ cup grated Cheddar cheese
½ cup fine dry breadcrumbs
3 tablespoons butter
6 medium-sized cold boiled potatoes
chopped parsley

Beat the egg with salt, pepper, and 1 tablespoon of the oil. Dip cutlets in egg; then roll in breadcrumbs mixed with cheese, pressing into the meat. Fry over moderately low heat in equal parts of oil and butter, adding it as needed, until meat is thoroughly cooked and browned on both sides.

Slice cold potatoes. Sprinkle with salt and pepper and brown in butter. Serve with the cutlets, sprinkling with chopped parsley. Makes 6 servings. (See illustration, page 594.)

⚜ WIENER SCHNITZEL (*Viennese Veal Cutlets*)

2 pounds veal cutlets
1 egg, beaten
2 tablespoons flour
6 tablespoons fine dry breadcrumbs
1 teaspoon salt
¼ teaspoon ground black pepper
4 tablespoons (½ stick) butter
6 thin lemon slices

Cut veal into 6 serving-size pieces. Dip in beaten egg, then in flour mixed with breadcrumbs, salt, and pepper. Brown on both sides in butter, adding it as needed. Transfer veal to a hot platter and top each cutlet with a lemon slice. Makes 6 servings.

⚜ VEAL CUTLETS WITH WATERCRESS

4 veal cutlets
salt
ground black pepper
2 tablespoons butter, melted
3 tablespoons softened butter
1 tablespoon chopped parsley
1 tablespoon chopped watercress
watercress
Straw Potatoes

Sprinkle both sides of cutlets with salt and pepper and rub it in. Brush with melted butter. Brown on both sides over moderately slow heat, being sure to cook veal thoroughly. Meanwhile blend softened butter with chopped parsley and chopped watercress. Chill and shape into a cylinder. Cut 4 slices and place one on each cutlet. Transfer cutlets to a platter. Garnish with watercress. Serve with Straw Potatoes. Makes 4 servings. (See illustration, page 593.)

⚜ JELLIED VEAL CUTLETS

4 veal cutlets, 6 ounces each
salt
ground black pepper
butter
4 cups liquid aspic
8 small carrots
12 small white onions
2 medium-sized tomatoes
chervil leaves or parsley

Trim cutlets to make them of uniform size. Sprinkle with salt and pepper. Brown on both sides in butter over moderate heat. Place cutlets in an 8- by 8- by 2-inch ovenproof dish. Pour ⅓ cup of the aspic over them. Brown carrots and onions in butter, and place them over the cutlets. Top each cutlet with half a tomato, and chervil or parsley leaves. Pour remaining aspic over the cutlets and vegetables. Chill until aspic is set and the dish is ready to be served. Serve in the baking dish. Garnish with parsley or chervil leaves. Makes 4 servings.

⚜ VEAL SCALOPPINE VALDOSTANA (*Italian*)

2 pounds veal steak, cut into 6 thin uniform scallops
salt
ground black pepper
1 egg, beaten
3 tablespoons olive oil or salad oil
3 tablespoons butter
½ pound mushrooms, sliced
6 thin slices Gruyère or Cheddar cheese
Stuffed Eggplant
Stuffed Tomatoes
Browned Potatoes

Flatten steaks to ¼-inch thickness with a mallet. Sprinkle with salt and pepper, dredge in flour, dip in beaten egg, and brown on both sides in the oil and 2 tablespoons of the butter. Transfer veal to an 11- by 7- by 1½-inch baking dish. Add remaining butter and mushrooms. Stir and cook 3 to 4 minutes and spoon over scallops. Top each scallop with a slice of Gruyère or Cheddar cheese. Cook in a preheated hot oven (400° F.) 10 minutes, or until cheese has melted. Serve with Stuffed Eggplant, Stuffed Tomatoes, and Browned Potatoes. Makes 6 servings.

⚜ VEAL SCALOPPINE WITH MARSALA (*Italian*)

2 pounds veal steaks, cut into 6 thin uniform scallops
salt
ground black pepper
flour
3 tablespoons olive oil or salad oil
3 tablespoons butter
¼ cup veal or chicken broth
¼ cup Marsala

Pound steaks to ¼ inch thickness with a mallet. Sprinkle with salt and pepper, dredge in flour, and fry quickly in oil. and butter. Add stock and half the wine. Cover and simmer 10 minutes. Transfer meat to a hot platter. Pour remaining wine into the skillet and reduce the liquid by one-half the original quantity. Adjust seasonings and pour over the meat. Makes 6 servings.

⚜ SALTIMBOCCA ALLA ROMANA (*Italian*)

2½ pounds veal sirloin steaks, cut ¼ inch thick
salt
ground black pepper
6 slices raw ham
6 fresh sage leaves or dried sage
flour
2 tablespoons olive oil or salad oil
3 tablespoons butter
⅓ cup dry white wine
buttered diced potatoes
chopped parsley

Cut steaks into 12 pieces of equal size. Flatten with a mallet and sprinkle lightly with salt and pepper. Place on each of 6 steaks 1 ham slice, 1 sage leaf or a sprinkling of dried sage, and another veal steak (sandwich fashion). Hold in place with half-toothpicks. Dredge with flour. Brown in a heavy skillet in 2 tablespoons oil and 2 tablespoons of the butter. Transfer to a hot platter and keep warm. Put remaining 1 tablespoon butter and the wine in the skillet. Bring to boiling point and boil ½ minute. Strain over the meat. Serve with buttered diced potatoes sprinkled with parsley. Makes 6 servings. (See illustration, page 594.)

⚜ BREADED VEAL CUTLETS (*Escalopes de Veau à l'Anglaise*)

4 veal scallops
salt
ground black pepper
fine dry breadcrumbs
1 egg
1 tablespoon water
butter
8 grapefruit sections
chopped parsley
watercress

Sprinkle scallops with salt and pepper. Roll in breadcrumbs, dip in egg beaten with water, and roll in crumbs again. Fry over moderate heat in butter, adding it as needed, until brown on both sides. Transfer scallops to a hot platter. In the same skillet, brown 2 more tablespoons butter and pour over meat. Garnish with grapefruit sections, chopped parsley, and watercress. Makes 4 servings. (See illustration, page 598.)

⚜ SCALLOPS OF VEAL ZINGARA

Zingara is a garnish for small cuts of meat. It is made of shredded ham, tongue, mushrooms, and truffles, bound with Demi-Glace Sauce flavored with tomato and tarragon.

6 veal scallops
salt
ground black pepper
flour
butter
½ cup Demi-Glace Sauce
1 teaspoon tomato paste
¼ cup Madeira
½ cup shredded cooked or pickled beef tongue
½ cup shredded cooked ham
½ cup shredded poached mushrooms

Sprinkle veal with salt and pepper. Dredge in flour. Brown on both sides over moderate heat in butter, adding it as needed. Transfer meat to a hot platter and keep warm. Combine next 3 ingredients in a saucepan, mix well, and heat. Stir in remaining ingredients and heat. Use as a garnish for the top of the scallops. Make gravy from the pan drippings and veal stock. Thicken it with cornstarch, using 1 teaspoon for each cup of stock. Makes 6 servings. (See illustration, page 597.)

⚜ STUFFED BREAST OF VEAL

3 to 4 pounds boned breast of veal
salt
ground black pepper
½ cup finely chopped onion
½ clove garlic, crushed
½ pound sausage meat

2 cups soft breadcrumbs
2 tablespoons minced parsley
½ teaspoon dried, or 1½ teaspoons chopped fresh marjoram
2 tablespoons butter
¼ cup water or bouillon
1 teaspoon cornstarch
1 tablespoon water

Ask the butcher to cut a pocket in the veal. Sprinkle inside and out lightly with salt and pepper. Cook onions and garlic with sausage until sausage begins to brown. Add breadcrumbs, herbs, and salt and pepper to taste. Mix well and stuff lightly into the pocket of the breast of veal. Close openings with skewers and lace tightly with a string. Dredge meat with flour and brown on all sides in butter in a Dutch oven. Add water or bouillon, cover, and simmer 2 hours or until meat is tender. Transfer meat to a platter and keep hot. Thicken drippings with cornstarch mixed with 1 tablespoon water. Bring gravy to boiling point. Serve over the sliced veal. Makes 6 to 8 servings.

⚜ STUFFED BREAST OF VEAL NAPLES STYLE

4 pounds boned breast of veal
salt
ground black pepper
½ pound ground veal
¼ cup finely chopped onion
½ clove garlic, crushed
5 tablespoons butter
2 cups soft fine breadcrumbs
2 cups finely chopped raw spinach
½ teaspoon dried thyme leaves
2 eggs
¼ cup cooked or canned tomatoes
1½ cups veal stock
2 teaspoons cornstarch
1½ tablespoons water

Ask the butcher to cut a pocket in the breast of veal. Sprinkle inside and out with salt. Brown veal, onion, and garlic in 2 tablespoons of the butter. Add 2 more tablespoons of the butter, the breadcrumbs, spinach, thyme, eggs, and tomato. Mix well. Add salt and pepper to taste. Spoon into the pocket of the veal breast. Close opening with skewers and lace with a string. Place veal in an open baking pan. Rub top of veal with remaining 1 tablespoon butter. Roast in a preheated slow oven (325° F.) 2½ hours or until meat is thoroughly cooked, basting occasionally with melted butter. Let the meat rest 10 to 15 minutes. Remove skewers and string and transfer meat to a warm platter. Add veal stock to the roasting pan. Scrape up the browned bits from the bottom and boil the stock 2 to 3 minutes. Blend cornstarch with water and add to the stock. Bring to boiling point and boil ½ minute. Adjust seasonings. Slice meat and serve with the sauce. Makes 6 to 8 servings.

⚜ GARNISHED RIBLETS OF VEAL (*Tendrons de Veau Garnis*)

Tendron of veal is sliced breast of veal with the bone. In the United States this cut is called riblets.

3 pounds veal riblets
salt
ground black pepper
flour
lard
½ cup sliced onions
1 cup sliced carrots
veal stock or water
20 small boiled onions
6 small cooked new carrots
1½ cups each cooked green peas and green beans cut into 1-inch pieces
4 tablespoons (½ stick) butter

Sprinkle riblets with salt and pepper and dredge in flour. Brown on both sides in 2 tablespoons lard over moderate heat. Transfer to another pan and keep hot. In the same skillet cook onions and carrots, adding more lard as needed. Sprinkle with salt and pepper and place in the bottom of an 11- by 7- by 1½-inch baking dish. Top with browned riblets. Add enough veal stock or water to half cover the meat. Cook in a preheated slow oven (325° F.) 1 hour or until meat is tender, basting frequently. Remove meat to a platter and keep hot. Skim off and discard fat from the gravy. If necessary add a little more stock to the gravy and thicken with about 1½ teaspoons cornstarch mixed with 2 tablespoons water. Stir and cook until gravy is transparent. Pour over the meat. Toss hot cooked onions with 1 tablespoon of the butter and scatter over the veal. Mix carrots, peas, and beans lightly with remaining butter. Serve with the veal in a separate dish. Makes 6 servings. (See illustration, page 596.)

⚜ BLANQUETTE OF VEAL

2¼ pounds shoulder or breast of veal
water
1 large onion
2 stalks parsley
6 peppercorns
2 teaspoons salt
1 clove garlic
12 small white onions, peeled
4 carrots, peeled and quartered
2 tablespoons flour
2 tablespoons butter
2 large egg yolks
½ cup heavy cream
½ pound small mushroom caps, sautéed in butter

Cut meat into 2-inch pieces and parboil 5 minutes in a saucepan in water to cover. Drain. Add the large onion, parsley, peppercorns, salt, and garlic, with water to cover (about 4 cups). Bring to boiling point, reduce heat, and simmer 1½ hours or until veal is tender. Add small onions and carrots 30 minutes before cooking time is up. Using a perforated spoon, transfer meat, carrots, and onions to a serving dish and keep hot. Strain stock and reduce to about two-thirds. Blend the flour with the butter, add to the broth, bring to boiling point, and cook 1 minute. Beat egg yolks lightly with cream and stir into the broth. Stir and heat until sauce thickens. (Do not boil.) Adjust seasonings. Pour over the meat, carrots, and onions. Garnish with mushroom caps. Serve with rice or boiled potatoes. Makes 6 servings.

⚜ VEAL MARENGO

2½ pounds shoulder of veal
salt
ground black pepper
butter
olive oil or salad oil
1½ tablespoons flour
1 small clove garlic, crushed
⅓ cup dry white wine
bouillon or water
2 stalks parsley
1 tomato or ½ cup canned tomato, drained
24 small white onions
½ pound mushrooms
12 to 16 toast points
chopped parsley

Cut meat into 2-inch pieces. Sprinkle with salt and pepper and brown in a Dutch oven in 2 tablespoons each butter and oil, adding it as needed. Sprinkle with flour; stir and cook until flour has browned. Add garlic and wine and cook until most of the wine has evaporated. Pour in enough bouillon or water barely to cover the meat. Add parsley, cover, and cook in a preheated slow oven (325° F.) 1 hour or until meat is tender. Meanwhile peel and seed tomato and mix with a little oil, or if canned tomatoes are used drain well, pick out seeds, and mix tomatoes with oil. Peel onions and cook in a little bouillon. When meat is tender, transfer it to a casserole, strain gravy over meat, and add tomatoes, onions, and raw mushrooms. Put casserole back into 325° oven, cover, and cook 30 minutes. Fry toast points in hot oil. Transfer contents of casserole to a serving dish and garnish with toast points and chopped parsley. Makes 6 to 8 servings. (See illustration, page 597.)

⚜ VEAL WITH YOGURT (*Turkish*)

2 pounds boneless veal blade or arm steak, cut ¼ inch thick
salt
ground black pepper
4 tablespoons (½ stick) butter
¾ cup sliced onions
18 small mushroom caps
1 tablespoon flour
⅓ cup heavy cream
⅓ cup water
½ cup yogurt
2 teaspoons paprika

Cut veal into strips 1 inch wide. Sprinkle with salt and pepper, and sauté in a heavy skillet in 2 tablespoons of the butter. Remove meat to another pan and keep hot. In the same skillet put 1 additional tablespoon butter, the onions, and the mushrooms. Sprinkle lightly with salt and pepper. Stir and cook until lightly browned. Transfer to the meat dish. Melt the remaining butter in the skillet, blend in flour, and brown lightly. Add cream and water, mix well, and bring to boiling point, stirring constantly. Remove from heat. Beat the yogurt and gradually pour into the skillet, along with the paprika. Heat but do not boil. Add meat, onions, and mushrooms. Adjust seasonings. Heat and serve in a hot dish. Serve with rice, if desired. Makes 6 servings.

⚜ VEAL ROLLS MORANDI (*Italian*)

1½ pounds veal steak, cut ½ inch thick
salt
ground black pepper
12 thin slices raw ham
12 thin slices truffle
12 thin slices Gruyère cheese
about 2 tablespoons butter
¾ cup Marsala
¼ cup veal stock
6 rolls of braised lettuce
6 servings Rice à la Grecque

Flatten steak with a mallet, cut into 12 pieces of equal size, and sprinkle them lightly with salt and pepper. Place on each a slice of ham, truffle, and cheese. Roll up and secure ends with toothpicks, or tie rolls with string. Brown on all sides in butter. Heat wine until reduced one-half and pour over rolls along with the veal stock. Cover and simmer 10 minutes, or until meat is well done. Arrange on a serving dish with braised lettuce around a mound of Rice à la Grecque. Makes 6 servings. (See illustration, page 595.)

⚜ PAUPIETTES OF VEAL À LA GRECQUE

Paupiettes are thin slices of meat spread with a stuffing, rolled, and tied (see Culinary Techniques in Pictures).

6 thin veal scallops
salt
ground black pepper
1 cup chopped onions
5 tablespoons butter
2¼ cups soft breadcrumbs
2 tablespoons chopped parsley
½ teaspoon dried thyme
salt and pepper
6 thin slices raw ham
1 small onion, sliced
1 small carrot, sliced
1 cup veal stock
Rice à la Grecque
2 teaspoons cornstarch
2 tablespoons water

Sprinkle scallops with salt and pepper. Cook onions in 3 tablespoons of the butter until they are limp. Add next 3 ingredients and salt and pepper to taste. Spread over the meat. Cover each scallop with a thin slice of raw ham. Roll up and tie with strings at both ends. Cook lightly, along with sliced onion and carrot, in remaining 2 tablespoons butter. Add veal stock. Cook in a preheated slow oven (325° F.) 1 hour, basting occasionally with the veal stock. Arrange paupiettes on a mound of Rice à la Grecque. Skim fat from gravy. Blend cornstarch with water, add to gravy, bring to boiling point, and pour over the paupiettes. Makes 6 servings.

⚜ VEAL KNUCKLES MILANESE (*Osso Buco alla Milanese*)

6 leg-round steaks, with the round bone included
salt
ground black pepper
flour
2 tablespoons olive oil or salad oil
3 tablespoons butter
1 carrot, sliced
1 rib celery, sliced
¼ cup diced onion
1 small clove garlic, crushed
½ cup tomato purée
½ cup dry white wine
1 cup veal stock
2 tablespoons chopped parsley
½ teaspoon grated lemon rind
2 teaspoons cornstarch
2 tablespoons water

Sprinkle steaks with salt and pepper, and dredge in flour. Brown meat on both sides in a heavy skillet in equal parts oil and butter, adding more as needed. Add vegetables, garlic, and remaining 1 tablespoon butter. Stir and cook until vegetables have lightly browned. Add tomato purée and wine. Cover and simmer until the liquid has reduced to one-half the original quantity. Pour in stock, cover, and simmer until veal is tender. Add parsley and lemon rind. Adjust seasonings. Blend cornstarch with water, add to gravy, and bring to boiling point. Turn into a serving dish. Serve with cooked rice or Risotto. Makes 6 servings. (See illustration, page 595.)

Lamb and Mutton

Lamb is the flesh of young sheep and mutton that of older sheep, the dividing line being set at an age of approximately one year. The meat of the young animal is more tender and juicy and has a milder flavor than that of the older animal. About 93 per cent of the sheep sold in the United States is lamb, mutton being available only on special order. In Europe, however, people appear to like the characteristic flavor of sheep's meat, and mutton, particularly that in the yearling class, is popular and available. In lamb, the sex of the animal appears to make little difference. In the meat of older animals, however, sex influences the flavor, so that mutton from wethers ranks higher than that from ewes or rams. The color of the meat is a good indication of the age of the animal. Young lamb has bright pinkish flesh and reddish bones. As the age of the animal increases its flesh becomes darker in color and its bones and fat become lighter.

⚜ ROAST LEG OF LAMB OR MUTTON BOULANGÈRE

6- to 7-pound leg of lamb or mutton
salt
ground black pepper
8 medium-sized potatoes, quartered
4 medium-sized onions, sliced
1 tablespoon cornstarch
2 cups lamb or mutton stock, or water

Trim off all but a thin layer of fat from the roast. Rub it with salt and pepper and place on a rack, fat side up, in a baking pan. Roast, uncovered, using one of the following methods:

French Two-Temperature Method. Cook meat in a preheated very hot oven (450° F.) 15 minutes, then reduce heat to 350° F. (moderate). For medium-rare, cook 10 to 12 minutes per pound; for well-done, cook 13 to 15 minutes per pound.

American Low-Temperature or One-Temperature Method. Cook meat in a preheated slow oven (325° F.). For medium-rare cook 30 minutes per pound, or to 175° F. on the meat thermometer; for well-done, cook 35 minutes per pound or to 180° F. on the thermometer.

Parboil potatoes 5 to 7 minutes in boiling water to cover. Drain and add to the roasting pan along with sliced onions about 45 minutes before cooking time is up. Transfer meat and vegetables to a hot platter and keep warm. Skim off and discard fat from pan drippings. Blend cornstarch with a little of the stock or water and add to the roasting pan along with remaining stock or water. Stir and cook until gravy has thickened, scraping all the browned bits from the bottom of the pan. Serve with the roast. Makes 8 to 10 servings. (See illustration, page 604.)

⚜ ROAST LEG OF MUTTON OR LAMB WITH MINT SAUCE

Roast a 6- or 7-pound leg of mutton or lamb as directed in the preceding recipe. Serve with Mint Sauce. Serve vegetables separately.

MINT SAUCE

Combine 1 cup water, ½ cup vinegar, ¼ cup finely chopped fresh mint leaves. Cook until liquid has reduced to one-half. Strain. Add ½ cup water, lemon juice to taste (2 to 4 tablespoons), and 2 to 3 tablespoons sugar. Chill. Add ¼ cup chopped fresh mint leaves just before serving. Makes about 1 cup.

⚜ ROAST LOIN OF LAMB WITH PARSLEY

1 loin lamb roast, allowing 2 to 3 ribs per serving
salt
ground black pepper
¼ teaspoon powdered mustard
¼ cup finely chopped parsley
½ cup fine dry breadcrumbs
watercress
Grilled Whole Tomatoes
asparagus tips

Ask the butcher to saw across the ribs close to the backbone so the roast can be carved easily. Sprinkle roast with salt, pepper, and mustard, and stand it on the ribs in a large shallow pan. Cook in a preheated slow oven (325° F.) 35 minutes per pound or until the meat thermometer registers 180° F. After the meat has been in the oven for three-fourths of the cooking time, mix the parsley with the breadcrumbs and sprinkle over the roast. Continue cooking until meat is done. Transfer roast to a hot platter. Garnish with watercress, Grilled Whole Tomatoes, and asparagus tips. Allow 2 to 3 ribs per serving. (See illustration, page 603.)

⚜ SADDLE OF LAMB FRENCH STYLE

Saddle of lamb is not generally available in the United States but can usually be obtained by placing a special order with the butcher.

1 saddle of lamb roast
salt
ground black pepper
3 cups Duchess Potatoes
2 eggs, beaten with 2 tablespoons water
fine dry breadcrumbs
parsley

Ask the butcher to saw across the ribs close to the backbone so the roast can be carved easily. Sprinkle the meat with salt and pepper and stand it on the ribs in a large shallow pan. Cook in a preheated slow oven (325° F.) 35 minutes per pound, or until the meat thermometer, if one is used, registers 180° F.

Transfer the roast to a hot platter. In the meantime, shape Duchess Potatoes into cylindrical croquettes 2½ inches long and 1½ inches in diameter. Dip in eggs beaten with the water, and then roll in breadcrumbs. Fry until brown in deep fat preheated to 375° F. Drain on paper towels. Place on the platter on either side of the roast. Garnish the platter with parsley. Allow 2 to 3 ribs per serving. (See illustration, page 605; also Culinary Techniques in Pictures.)

⚜ LAMB CHOPS CYRANO

In France, rib lamb chops are called *côtelettes;* in England they are known as cutlets.

12 rib lamb chops
salt
ground black pepper
2 tablespoons butter
12 precooked artichoke bottoms
12 small slices fried goose liver (foie gras)
12 truffle slices, or 12 sautéed mushroom caps
Chateaubriand Sauce

Sprinkle chops with salt and pepper and brown on both sides in butter. Heat artichoke bottoms in butter and place a chop on each. Top each with a slice of fried goose liver, coat lightly with Chateaubriand Sauce, and decorate with a truffle slice or a sautéed mushroom. Makes 6 servings. (See illustration, page 606.)

CHATEAUBRIAND SAUCE

Simmer ¾ cup dry white wine with 1 finely chopped shallot, ¼ bay leaf, and ⅛ teaspoon ground thyme until wine is slightly reduced. Add 2 tablespoons meat glaze or meat extract, and reduce by one-fourth the original amount. Add 2 tablespoons butter, ¼ teaspoon dried tarragon or 1 teaspoon fresh tarragon, 2 teaspoons chopped parsley, dash cayenne. Season with salt and pepper to taste.

⚜ ITALIAN-STYLE LAMB CHOPS

12 rib lamb chops
salt
ground black pepper
2 large eggs beaten with 2 tablespoons water
1 cup fine dry breadcrumbs
1 cup grated Parmesan cheese
6 tablespoons butter
¾ pound tiny zucchini
1½ pounds cooked asparagus tips
2 tablespoons browned butter

Trim excess fat from lamb chops and rub them with salt and pepper. Dip in eggs beaten with water and then in breadcrumbs mixed with Parmesan cheese. Pan-fry in butter, adding it as needed. Peel zucchini and cut into slices ¼ inch thick. Sprinkle with salt and pepper. Dip in beaten egg and then in breadcrumb-cheese mixture. Pan-fry in butter, adding it as needed. Place lamb chops and fried zucchini on a hot platter, having the chops and slices of squash overlapping in a circle. Place asparagus tips in the center and pour browned butter over them. Sprinkle with grated Parmesan cheese. Serve hot. Makes 6 servings.

⚜ LAMB CHOPS MADELON

12 rib lamb chops
salt
ground black pepper
2 tablespoons butter
1 cup finely chopped leftover chicken or veal
1 cup sautéed chopped mushrooms
1 cup Béchamel Sauce
1 cup soft breadcrumbs
¼ cup (½ stick) butter, melted
Madeira Sauce

Sprinkle lamb chops with salt and pepper and brown in butter only on one side. Place chops in a 13- by 9- by 2-inch baking dish. Combine chicken or veal, mushrooms, and Béchamel Sauce. Adjust seasonings and put a heaping tablespoonful of the mixture on each chop. Mix the breadcrumbs with the butter and sprinkle over the tops. Bake in a preheated moderate oven (350° F.) 25 minutes or until crumbs are brown. Serve with Madeira Sauce. Makes 6 servings.

⚜ LAMB CHOPS MONTMORENCY

8 rib lamb chops
salt
ground black pepper
2 eggs, beaten
fine dry breadcrumbs
3 tablespoons butter
12 cooked asparagus tips
4 large cooked artichoke bottoms
½ cup Béchamel Sauce
small potatoes, browned

Sprinkle lamb chops with salt and pepper. Dip in beaten egg and then in breadcrumbs. Brown on both sides in butter. Arrange chops on a hot platter, overlapping. Place 3 asparagus tips on each of 4 artichoke bottoms. Cover with Béchamel Sauce and place on the platter around the chops. Serve with browned small potatoes. Makes 4 servings. (See illustration, page 604.)

⚜ LAMB CHOPS SAINT-MICHEL

12 rib or loin lamb chops
salt and ground black pepper
flour
4 tablespoons butter
½ cup finely chopped onion
boiling water
6 parboiled artichoke bottoms, quartered
1 cup Béchamel Sauce
6 baked pastry tart shells

Sprinkle chops with salt and pepper, dredge in flour, and brown on both sides in 3 tablespoons of the butter. Arrange on a hot platter and keep warm. Meanwhile, parboil onion 2 to 3 minutes in boiling water to cover, then drain well. Cook in butter along with artichoke bottoms 2 to 3 minutes (do not brown). Add to Béchamel Sauce. Spoon the mixture into baked tart shells. Arrange these on the platter around the chops. Notch the edge of half of a lemon and place on the platter as a garnish. Makes 6 servings. (See illustration, page 606.)

⚜ PAN-FRIED NOISETTES OF LAMB OR MUTTON

Noisettes are slices from the boned rib or loin of lamb or mutton (or veal), trimmed into little round steaks, cut 1½ to 2 inches thick. All excess fat is cut off and discarded. Their weight varies from 2½ to 3 ounces. This cut is not generally available in the United States but may be obtained by placing a special order with the butcher.

Rub a heated heavy skillet with a little butter, or with some of the fat trimmed from the steaks. Lay noisettes in the skillet and cook over moderate heat until well browned on one side. Pour off any fat that accumulates in the pan. Turn steaks to brown the other side. Sprinkle with salt and ground black pepper. Cut slices of bread to fit the noisettes, fry in butter, and place one under each chop. Transfer to a hot platter. Serve with potatoes, creamed asparagus tips in artichoke bottoms or in baked pastry shells, buttered peas, or other vegetables. Garnish with parsley. If pan gravy is desired, add 1 tablespoon hot water for each chop to the skillet. Bring to boiling point. Season to taste with salt and ground black pepper. Allow 1 to 2 steaks per serving. (Chops may be cooked the same way; see illustration, page 605.)

⚜ MUTTON LOIN CHOPS OR NOISETTES NIÇOISE

4 medium-sized potatoes
2 tablespoons olive oil or salad oil
4 tablespoons (½ stick) butter
6 loin mutton or lamb chops (or noisettes)
salt
ground black pepper
2 shallots, chopped
1 clove garlic, crushed
2 medium-sized tomatoes
⅓ cup pitted black olives
2 tablespoons diced anchovy fillets
chopped parsley (optional)
Tomato Veal Gravy

Pare and cube potates and fry in the oil and half the butter. Drain potatoes on paper towels and keep warm. Sprinkle lamb or mutton chops with salt and pepper and fry in the same skillet and fat in which potatoes were fried. Transfer chops to another dish and keep warm. In the same skillet and the same fat, cook shallots and garlic about 1 minute. Drain off and discard fat. Chop tomatoes coarsely and add to the shallots and garlic. Bring to boiling point, reduce heat, and simmer 5 minutes or until tomatoes are cooked. Add olives and anchovies, adjust seasonings, add potatoes, and toss together. Turn out onto a platter and arrange the chops over the mixture. If desired, sprinkle with chopped parsley. (See illustration, page 603.) Serve with Tomato Veal Gravy in a separate bowl, and buttered green beans or another green vegetable. Makes 6 servings.

⚜ EPIGRAMMES OF LAMB OR MUTTON SAINT-GERMAIN

Epigrammes are slices of breast of lamb or mutton, or chops or cutlets, dipped in beaten egg and breadcrumbs and broiled or fried.

3½ pounds breast of lamb or mutton
water
bouquet garni
1 carrot, sliced
1 rib celery, sliced
1 medium-sized onion, sliced
6 peppercorns
3 whole cloves
1 teaspoon salt
1 egg
fine dry breadcrumbs
Lamb Sauce

Place meat in a Dutch oven or heavy saucepan. Pour in enough water barely to cover the meat. Add the next 7 ingredients. Cover, bring to boiling point, and simmer 1½ hours or until meat is tender. Transfer meat to a board, pull out bones, cover with foil, top with a heavy weight, and cool. Cut into heart-shaped cutlets, dip in egg beaten with 1 tablespoon water, and then in breadcrumbs. Broil, pan-fry, or fry in deep fat preheated to 375° F. Serve with Lamb Sauce. Makes 6 to 8 servings.

LAMB SAUCE

Melt 2 tablespoons butter in a 1-quart saucepan. Remove from heat and blend in 2 tablespoons flour. Return to heat; stir and cook 1 minute. Remove from heat and add 2 cups strained lamb stock. Bring to boiling point and cook 3 to 4 minutes, or until the sauce has thickened slightly. Adjust seasonings.

⚜ STUFFED BREAST OF LAMB

2 slices bread
water
½ pound pork sausage
2 tablespoons chopped onion
1 tablespoon chopped parsley
1 egg, beaten
3 pounds boned breast of lamb
salt
ground black pepper
½ cup sliced onion
½ cup sliced celery
½ cup sliced carrots
½ cup water
1 cup brown gravy or brown stock
¼ cup catsup

Soak bread in water, squeeze dry, and fluff with a fork. Mix with sausage, onion, parsley, and egg. Spread over lamb. Roll up in jelly-roll fashion and tie with a string at each end. Sprinkle with salt and pepper. Brown the roll in a heavy skillet or Dutch oven. Put the vegetables in the pan around the meat. Pour in ½ cup water, cover, and cook in a preheated slow oven (325° F.) 2 hours, or until meat is fork tender. Transfer meat to a hot platter and keep hot. Add gravy or stock to the pan drippings and cook until reduced to one-half the original quantity. Strain, add catsup, boil 1 minute, and serve in a sauceboat. Makes 6 servings.

⚜ STUFFED BREAST OF LAMB OR MUTTON FLORENTINE

3-pound boned breast of lamb
salt
ground black pepper
2 pounds fresh or 1½ packages (10 ounces each) frozen spinach
5 tablespoons butter
2 diced fresh or 1 cup well-drained canned tomatoes
dash of sugar
½ cup lamb stock or water
6 cups Dauphine Potatoes
1 cup Demi-Glace Sauce

Flatten breast of lamb with a mallet or with the side of a heavy knife. Sprinkle with salt and pepper. Set aside. Cook spinach, drain, chop, toss with 2 tablespoons of the butter, and season to taste with salt and pepper. Spread one-third of it over breast of lamb. Heat tomatoes with only 1 tablespoon butter until hot. Season to taste with salt, pepper, and a dash of sugar and spread over spinach. Roll up the breast in jelly-roll fashion. Hold in place with strings tied near each end. Brown the lamb roll in remaining 2 tablespoons butter in a Dutch oven. Add stock or water. Cover and cook in a preheated slow oven (325° F.) 1½ hours or until meat is tender, adding more stock or water if needed. Transfer lamb to a hot platter, and cut into as many slices as needed. Spoon remaining spinach onto the platter around lamb and surround with Dauphine Potatoes. Keep hot. Add Demi-Glace to pan drippings and bring to boiling point. Adjust seasonings and strain. Serve separately. Makes 6 servings.

⚜ CREOLE LAMB STEW

2½ pounds boned shoulder of lamb cut into 1½-inch cubes
3 tablespoons butter
1½ cups chopped onions
2 to 3 teaspoons curry powder
3 tablespoons flour
3 cups bouillon
1 teaspoon salt
2 stalks parsley
½ cup grated fresh coconut
½ teaspoon ground black pepper
3 cups cooked rice

Trim off and discard excess fat from lamb. Brown meat on all sides in butter in a Dutch oven. Add onions and curry powder. Stir and cook until onions are limp. Sprinkle with flour; stir and cook until flour has browned. Add bouillon, salt, and parsley. Cover and cook slowly in a preheated slow oven (325° F.) 1¼ hours. Remove parsley, add coconut, and cook ½ hour or until meat is tender. Skim off fat, add pepper, and adjust seasonings. Serve with cooked rice. Makes 6 servings.

⚜ HUNGARIAN PAPRIKA LAMB

2½ pounds boned shoulder of lamb
⅓ cup diced fat salt pork
1 cup sliced onions
1 small clove garlic, crushed
2 teaspoons paprika
2 large green sweet peppers
¼ cup tomato purée
1 cup water
2 teaspoons salt
dash cayenne
1½ cups sour cream
3 cups cooked rice

Trim off fat and cut lamb into 1½-inch cubes. Set aside. Fry salt pork with onions until lightly browned. Add lamb and garlic and brown lightly. Stir in paprika. Cut green peppers into strips ½ inch wide and add to meat, along with tomato purée, water, and salt. Cover and cook slowly 1¾ hours or until meat is very tender and the water has evaporated. Stir in cayenne and sour cream, and heat only until hot. Serve with cooked rice. Makes 6 servings.

⚜ LAMB KORMA (*India*)

Korma is a dry curry, made with meat marinated in yogurt.

2 pounds boneless leg of lamb
¾ cup yogurt
2½ teaspoons salt
1 teaspoon ground cumin seeds
1½ teaspoons ground turmeric
½ teaspoon ground cardamon
¼ cup peanut oil (or ghee)
1½ cups chopped onion
1 clove garlic, crushed
1 teaspoon powdered mustard
1 teaspoon ground ginger
½ teaspoon ground cinnamon
½ teaspoon ground black pepper
¼ to ½ teaspoon cayenne
⅛ teaspoon ground cloves
1 cup water
1 teaspoon lemon juice
2 tablespoons grated fresh or packaged flaked coconut

Trim off and discard excess fat from lamb. Cut meat into 1-inch pieces. Mix with the next 5 ingredients and marinate for 2 or more hours. Brown in 1 tablespoon peanut oil or ghee (clarified butter). Pour off excessive fat. In another skillet, cook onions and garlic until golden in remaining oil or ghee. Add next 6 ingredients, stir and cook 2 minutes. Add lamb, cover tightly, and simmer 20 minutes. Pour in 1 cup water and mix well. Cover and simmer 30 minutes, or until lamb is tender, adding water if needed. Stir in lemon juice and coconut just before serving. Serve over rice. Makes 6 servings.

⚜ STEWED LAMB WITH PEAS

2½ pounds boneless shoulder of lamb, cut into 1½-inch cubes
3 tablespoons flour
6 tablespoons butter
bouillon
1 teaspoon salt
2 stalks parsley
2 tablespoons tomato purée
12 small white onions
2 cups cooked green peas
½ teaspoon ground black pepper

Trim off and discard fat from lamb. Dust the meat with flour and brown on all sides in 3 tablespoons butter in a Dutch oven. Add enough bouillon to come halfway to the top of the meat. Add the next 3 ingredients. Cover and cook in a preheated slow oven (325° F.) 1 hour. Brown onions in remaining 3 tablespoons butter and add to the meat. Cover and cook ½ hour or until meat and onions are tender. Remove and discard parsley. Add cooked peas and pepper. Adjust seasonings. Serve hot. Makes 6 servings.

⚜ STEWED LAMB WITH RICE

2½ pounds boneless shoulder of lamb cut into 1½-inch cubes
3 tablespoons flour
4 tablespoons butter
1 cup chopped onions
1 clove garlic, mashed
4 cups bouillon
1½ teaspoons salt
2 stalks parsley
¾ cup long-grain white rice

Trim off and discard fat from the lamb. Dust the meat with flour and brown on all sides in 3 tablespoons of the butter. Add onions and garlic and cook until onions are limp. Stir in the next 3 ingredients. Cover and cook in a preheated slow oven (325° F.) 1¼ hours. Remove and discard parsley. Stir and cook rice in the remaining butter 2 to 3 minutes. Add to the stew, cover and cook 20 minutes or until rice is tender and has absorbed all the liquid. Add more bouillon if the stew tends to be too dry. Makes 6 servings.

⚜ ROMANIAN LAMB STEW WITH VEGETABLES

2½ pounds boned shoulder of lamb
1 cup sliced onions
6 tablespoons olive oil or salad oil
2 medium-sized green sweet peppers
1 small eggplant (½ pound)
2 small yellow summer squash (½ pound)
½ pound green beans
1½ cups sliced okra
2 medium-sized tomatoes, sliced
2 teaspoons salt
1 teaspoon paprika
dash cayenne

Trim off and discard excess fat from lamb. Cut meat into 1-inch cubes and brown with onions in 2 tablespoons of the oil. Set aside. Cut green peppers into strips ½ inch wide. Peel and dice eggplant. Dice unpeeled squash. Cut beans into 1-inch pieces. Brown all vegetables except tomatoes in oil. Put into a 2-quart casserole in this order: lamb, vegetables and tomatoes, sprinkling each layer lightly with salt, paprika, and cayenne mixed together. Repeat, using remaining meat and vegetables. Cover casserole and cook in a preheated moderate oven (350° F.) 1 hour or until meat is tender. Bring to the table in the casserole. Makes 6 to 8 servings.

⚜ KEUFTES (*Turkish Lamb Sausage*)

5 slices white bread
water
1½ pounds ground lamb or mutton
2 eggs
1½ teaspoons salt
¼ teaspoon ground black pepper
1/16 teaspoon ground cinnamon
1/16 teaspoon finely chopped garlic
2 tablespoons olive oil or salad oil

Trim crusts from bread. Break bread into pieces and soak in enough water to cover until bread is wet. Squeeze bread dry and fluff with a fork. Add to meat along with all the remaining ingredients except the oil. Mix well. Divide the mixture into 18 pieces of equal size. Form, on waxed paper, into little sausage-shaped rolls 1 inch in diameter. Fry in oil until browned on all sides. Serve very hot. Makes 6 servings.

Pork

The fresh pork normally found in the markets comes from hogs 6 to 12 months of age and is quite tender. It is most plentiful and cheapest in late fall and early winter. It must be thoroughly cooked in order that its rich flavor may be fully developed and to destroy a little parasite, *Trichinella spiralis*, often embedded in the muscle tissue of hogs. If such infected meat is eaten by humans, it may cause a condition known as trichinosis.

Pork also is available as salt pork and as cured or smoked ham and bacon. A great deal of pork is made into sausage.

FRESH PORK

⚜ ROAST LOIN OF PORK

5-pound center-cut loin pork roast
1½ teaspoons salt
¼ teaspoon ground black pepper
¼ teaspoon ground ginger
1 tablespoon cornstarch
2 cups water
Parsley Potatoes
Buttered Green Peas

Ask the butcher to saw through the bone of the loin in several places to make carving easier. Combine seasonings and sprinkle over the meat. Place meat on a rack in the roasting pan, fat side up. Cook in a preheated moderate oven (350° F.) 30 minutes per pound, or until the meat thermometer registers 185° F. Transfer roast to a hot platter, and let it rest 15 minutes in a warm place. This will make the meat easier to carve. Pour off and discard the fat from the pan drippings. Blend cornstarch with 2 cups water and add to the roasting pan. Bring to a boil, stirring and scraping the browned particles from the bottom of the pan. Adjust seasonings. Garnish the roast with Parsley Potatoes and Buttered Green Peas. Makes approximately 10 servings.

⚜ ROAST STUFFED SUCKLING PIG

12- to 15-pound suckling pig
1½ teaspoons salt
¼ teaspoon ground black pepper
¼ teaspoon ground ginger
Liver and Pork Stuffing
3 tablespoons butter, melted
2 cups boiling water
gravy
1 small apple
2 Maraschino cherries

Wash pig under running water, drain, and wipe dry with paper towels. Mix salt, pepper, and ginger and rub the inside of the pig with this mixture. Fill the cavity loosely with Liver and Pork Stuffing. Close opening with skewers and lace tightly with a string. Wipe the skin and rub with the melted butter. Place a small block of wood in the pig's mouth to brace it for the apple which will be inserted when the pig is cooked. Place pig, in kneeling position, on a rack in a large shallow pan. Pour 2 cups boiling water in the pan and cover pig with foil. Roast in a preheated slow oven (325° F.) 5 to 6 hours, basting every 45 minutes with the hot water that is in the pan. Add more water if needed. Remove pig to a large hot platter. Replace wooden block with a small red apple. Insert a large red cherry in each eye socket. Place parsley in or around the pig's ears. If desired, follow the American custom and place a necklace of whole cranberries around the pig's neck. Serve with gravy, a vegetable, applesauce or cranberry sauce, and a salad. Makes 12 to 15 servings.

LIVER AND PORK STUFFING for Roast Stuffed Suckling Pig

½ pound suckling pig's liver
½ cup water
½ pound ground lean pork
1 cup chopped onion
8 tablespoons (1 stick) butter
1 cup diced celery
1 cup diced mushrooms
2½ teaspoons dried or 2½ tablespoons chopped fresh thyme
3 tablespoons minced parsley
½ teaspoon ground black pepper
1 tablespoon salt
2 quarts (8 cups) toasted bread cubes (croutons)

Slice liver and cook in water in a covered saucepan until it is tender. Put through a food chopper, using the fine blade. Set aside. (Reserve the cooking water.) Cook pork in 1 tablespoon of the butter until pork loses its pink color, in a kettle large enough for mixing the stuffing. Add onion and remaining butter. Stir and cook until onions are limp. Add celery and mushrooms, stir, and cook 5 minutes. Add liver, the cooking water, and remaining ingredients. Mix well. Spoon loosely into the body cavity of the pig. Makes sufficient stuffing for a 12- to 15-pound pig.

Roast Veal Nivernaise, page 565 ▲

▼ Roast Saddle of Veal, page 566

▲ Veal Rib Roast with Vegetables, page 565

Roast Boned Loin of Veal with Kidneys, page 564 ▼

▼ Fillet of Veal in a Pastry Crust, page 567

Veal Cutlets with Watercress, page 571 ▲

594

▲ Saltimbocca alla Romana, page 572

Veal Cutlets Milanese, page 570 ▼

Veal Rolls Morandi, page 577 ▲

▼ Veal Knuckles Milanese, page 578

▲ Garnished Riblets of Veal, page 574

Veal Cutlets Chenonceaux, page 569 ▼

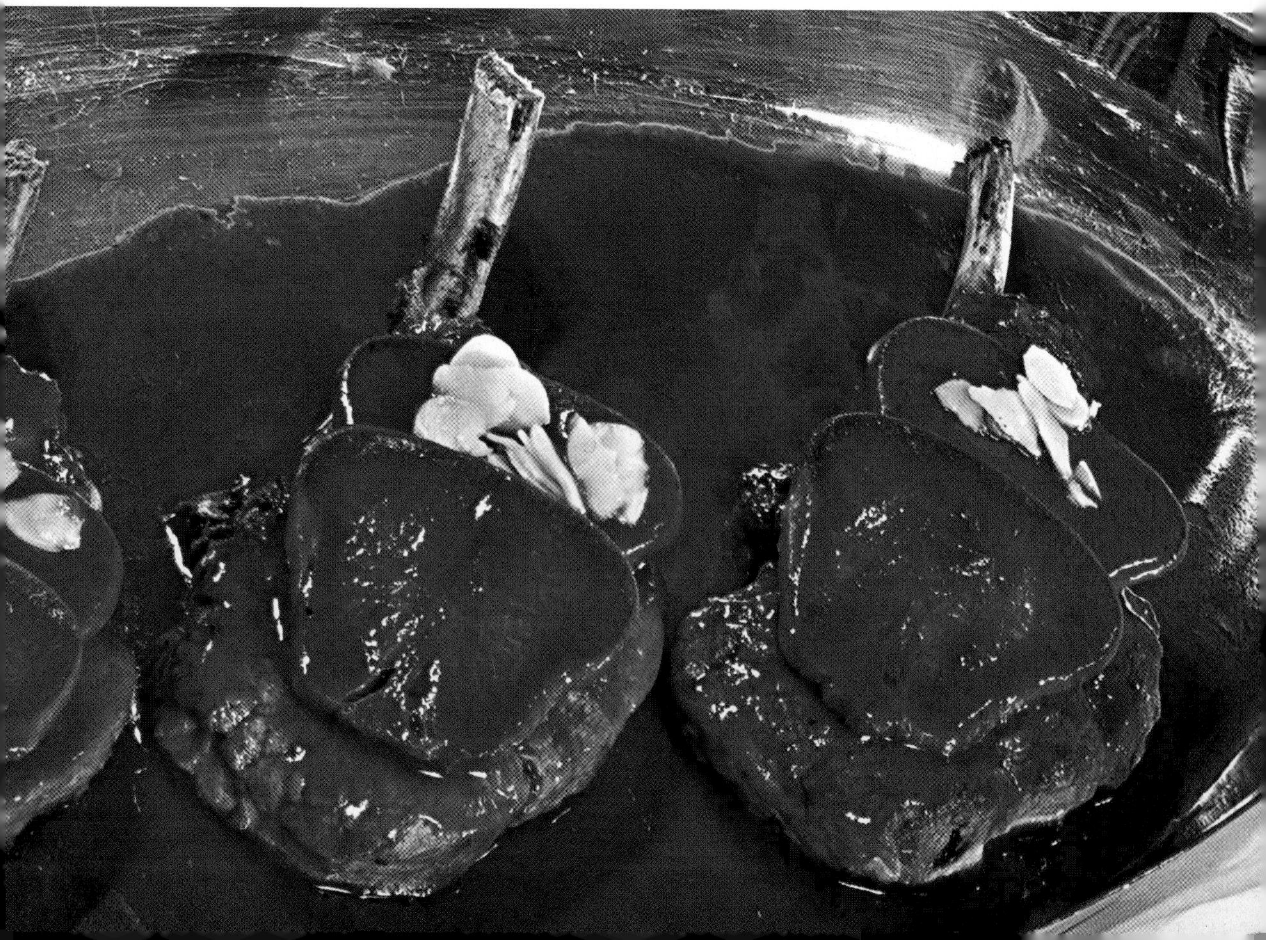

Veal Marengo, page 576 ▲

▼ Scallops of Veal Zingara, page 573

▲ Breaded Veal Cutlets, page 573

Veal Medallions with Mushrooms, page 567 ▼

Sautéed Veal Chops, page 568 ▲

▼ Veal Chops Molière, page 568

▲ Sliced Sweetbreads Graziella, page 638

Braised Sweetbreads Comtesse, page 637 ▼

Calf's Brains in Black Butter, page 621 ▲

▼ Veal Kidneys Bordelaise, page 630

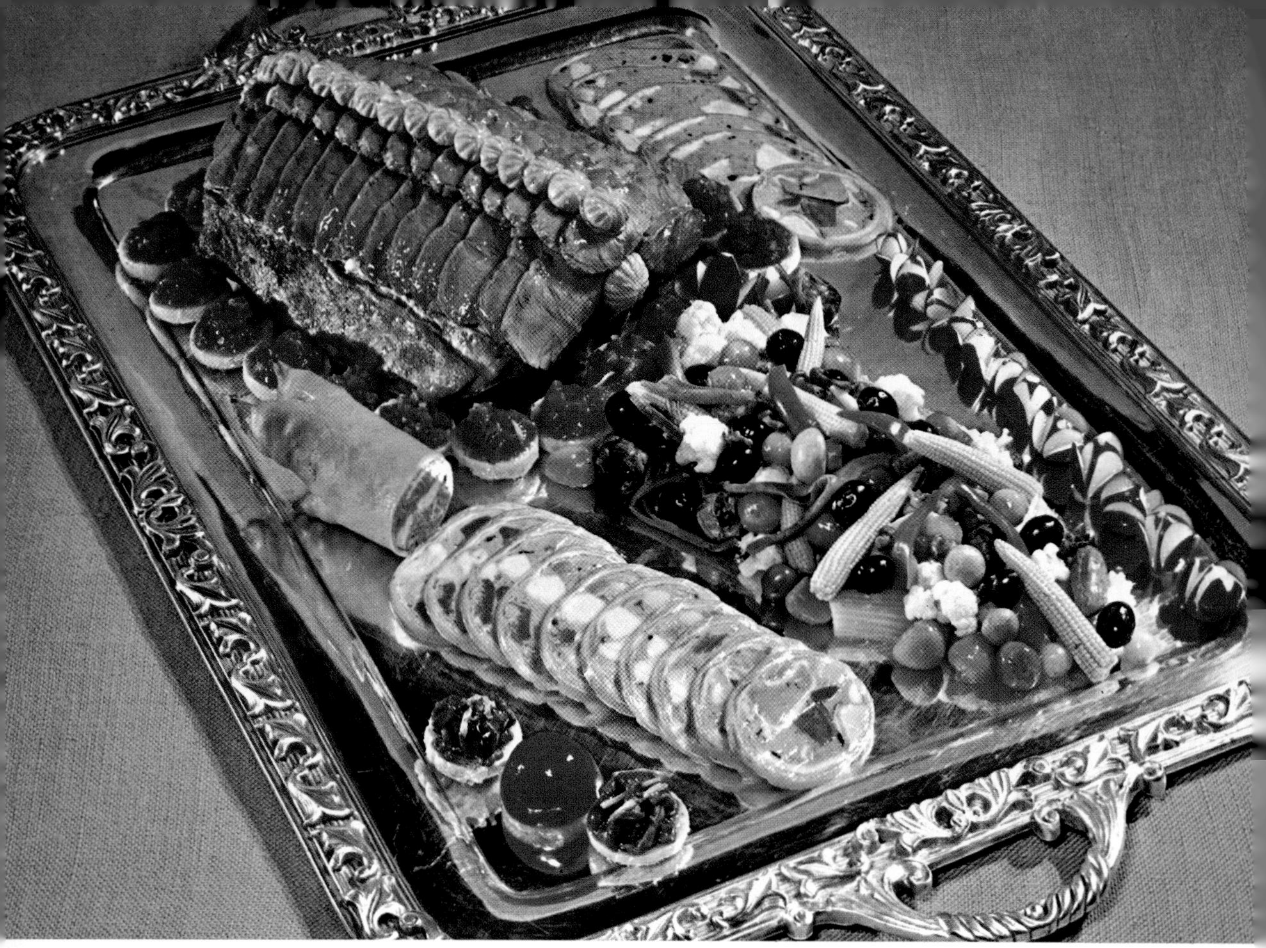

Cold Saddle of Veal (see page 566)

Mutton Noisettes Niçoise, page 584 ▲

▼ Roast Loin of Lamb with Parsley, page 580

▲ Saddle of Lamb French Style, page 580

Roast Leg of Lamb Boulangère, page 579 ▼

Lamb Chops Montmorency, page 582 ▲

▼ Pan-Fried Mutton Chops (see page 583)

▲ Lamb Chops Saint-Michel, page 583

Lamb Chops Cyrano, page 581 ▼

⚜ LOIN OF PORK BELLE FERMIÈRE

3½ to 4 pounds cured boneless loin of pork, cooked
plain pastry, using 3 cups flour
6 medium-sized carrots, cooked
4 medium-sized turnips, cooked
2 pounds red cabbage, cut into wedges, cooked
1 cup cooked spinach
6 slices bacon, cooked
1 tomato
parsley

Cool cooked roast and trim off fat if the layer is thick. Roll three-quarters of the pastry ⅛ inch thick in an oblong large enough to cover the meat and allow 3 inches in length and 2 inches in width to overlap. Place the cold loin in the center of the dough. Bring the dough from the two sides to the top, overlapping about ¾ inch. Then bring the two ends to the top of the loin, pressing the edges together. Place the roll on an ungreased cooky sheet, seam side down. Roll the remaining dough ⅛ inch thick. Cut strips ¼ inch wide and place them in lattice fashion over the roll. Bake in a preheated hot oven (425° F.) 10 to 15 minutes. Reduce heat to 350° F. (moderate) and continue baking until pastry is brown. Cut off a few slices and place on a tray. Garnish with buttered cooked carrots and turnips cut into short strips, small wedges of buttered cooked red cabbage, rolls of buttered spinach wrapped in strips of cooked bacon. Decorate one end of the tray with a tomato nested in fresh parsley. Makes approximately 8 to 10 servings. (See illustration, page 624.)

⚜ PORK TENDERLOIN WITH APPLE BRANDY

2 pork tenderloins
1 teaspoon salt
¼ teaspoon ground black pepper
⅛ teaspoon ground cumin seeds
butter
2 tablespoons apple brandy
¾ cup light cream
1 tablespoon meat glaze
½ pound cooked noodles

Cut the pork tenderloins into slices about ½ inch thick, weighing approximately 2 ounces each. Flatten slices with a mallet or the flat side of a meat cleaver. Mix seasonings and rub over meat. Brown in butter in a heavy skillet over low heat. Cook slowly until meat is well done. Transfer meat to a hot platter. Add apple brandy to the skillet, swirl it around the bottom, heat, and ignite. Add cream and meat glaze and simmer to reduce the liquid by one-quarter the original amount. Pour over tenderloins. Serve with buttered noodles. Makes 6 servings.

⚜ PORK CHOPS WITH APPLES

6 rib pork chops, cut ¾ inch thick
salt
ground black pepper
3 tablespoons butter
2 large tart baking apples
1 cup veal gravy (optional)

Trim off and discard excess fat and sprinkle pork with salt and pepper. Brown in a heavy skillet over moderately low heat in 1 tablespoon of the butter. Transfer chops to a 12- by 7½- by 2-inch baking dish. (Reserve unwashed skillet for later use.) Wash and core apples, and cut in crosswise slices ½ inch thick. Place one slice on each chop. Melt 2 tablespoons butter and brush over apples. Bake in a preheated moderate oven (350° F.) ½ hour or until chops and apples are tender, basting apples with butter twice. Transfer the chops to a hot platter. If desired, add 1 cup veal gravy to the skillet, bring to the boiling point, strain, and serve separately in a sauceboat. Makes 6 servings.

⚜ PORK CHOPS BONNE FEMME

6 pork chops, cut ½ to ¾ inch thick
salt
ground black pepper
flour
butter
12 small parboiled new potatoes
2 strips bacon, diced
30 small glazed onions
parsley

Trim off and discard excess fat from pork chops. Sprinkle with salt and pepper and dredge in flour. Brown on both sides in lard or shortening over moderately low heat. Reduce heat and cook slowly until well done. Transfer chops to a hot platter. Keep warm. Finish cooking potatoes in 1 tablespoon butter with the diced bacon. Place on platter with the chops, along with glazed onions. Dress the end bones of the chops with paper frills. Sprinkle chops with chopped parsley and garnish the platter with sprigs of parsley. Makes 6 servings. (See illustration, page 624.)

⚜ PORK CHOPS WITH BRUSSELS SPROUTS

6 rib pork chops
salt and ground black pepper
1 egg, beaten with 1 tablespoon water
fine dry breadcrumbs
4 tablespoons lard or shortening
1 quart basket Brussels sprouts
boiling water
2 teaspoons salt
3 tablespoons butter, browned

Trim off and discard excess fat and sprinkle chops with salt and pepper. Dip in egg beaten with water and then roll in crumbs. Fry in lard or shortening over moderately low heat until golden brown on each side. Meanwhile, wash and trim Brussels sprouts and soak 20 minutes in 1 quart cold water and 1 teaspoon salt. Drain off water and rinse in cold water. Place in a saucepan with ½ inch boiling water and 1 teaspoon salt. Bring to boiling point and cook, uncovered, 5 minutes. Drain off the water. Sauté parboiled sprouts in browned butter until they are done. Sprinkle lightly with salt and pepper. Transfer chops to a hot platter and place the sautéed Brussels sprouts around them. Makes 6 servings.

⚜ PORK CHOPS ITALIAN STYLE

6 pork chops
salt
ground black pepper
butter
½ pound medium-wide noodles
⅛ teaspoon ground nutmeg
Sauce Italienne

Trim off and discard excess fat from pork chops. Rub salt and pepper into the meat on both sides. Brown chops over low heat in butter, adding it as needed. Cook slowly until pork is well done. Cook noodles as directed on the package. Drain. Add 2 tablespoons butter and the nutmeg to the noodles and toss lightly. Transfer the chops to the center of a hot platter and arrange the noodles around them. Spoon Sauce Italienne over the chops. Makes 6 servings.

⚜ PORK CHOPS NORMANDE

6 pork chops
salt
ground black pepper
2 tablespoons butter
1 cup light cream
lemon juice to taste
tart applesauce, or sautéed sliced apples

Trim off and discard excess fat from pork chops. Rub salt and pepper into the meat on both sides. Brown chops over low heat in butter, adding butter as needed. Cook slowly until pork is well done. Transfer chops to a hot platter and keep hot. Add the cream to the skillet and simmer until the quantity is a reduced by one-quarter the original amount. Season the sauce to taste with lemon juice, salt, and pepper. Pour over chops. Serve with tart applesauce or sliced apples sautéed in butter. Makes 6 servings. (See illustration, page 625.)

⚜ PORK CHOPS WITH SAUCE ROBERT

6 loin pork chops
salt
ground black pepper
butter
Sauce Robert
Noisette Potatoes

Trim off and discard excess fat from pork chops. Rub with salt and pepper. Brown chops over low heat in butter, adding it as needed. Cook slowly until chops are well done. Transfer meat to a hot platter and cover with Sauce Robert. Serve with Noisette Potatoes. Makes 6 servings.

NOISETTE POTATOES

Peel potatoes and with a French melon-ball cutter scoop out balls about the size of hazelnuts. Fry in a heavy skillet in butter. Season with salt and ground black pepper to taste. Allow 6 balls per serving.

⚜ RAGOUT OF PORK

2 pounds boneless lean shoulder of pork
2 tablespoons butter
2 tablespoons flour
2 stalks parsley
5 peppercorns
1 small clove garlic, crushed
2 teaspoons salt
3 cups water
18 small white onions
4 carrots
3 turnips
3 potatoes
¼ teaspoon ground black pepper

Trim off and discard excess fat from pork. Cut the meat into 1½-inch cubes and brown in butter in a Dutch oven. Sprinkle with flour and stir and cook until flour has browned. Add parsley, peppercorns, garlic, and 3 cups water. Cover, bring to boiling point, and simmer 1½ hours. Peel all the vegetables. Leave onions whole, slice carrots thickly, quarter turnips and potatoes, and add vegetables to the stew. Cover and cook ½ hour, or until vegetables are tender. Add black pepper and adjust salt. If gravy tends to be too thin, thicken it with a little cornstarch blended with water. Makes 6 to 8 servings.

⚜ PORK SATÉ (*Indonesian*)

2 pounds lean pork
¼ cup soy sauce
1 tablespoon brown sugar
2 tablespoons minced onion
3 tablespoons lemon juice
1 small clove garlic, crushed
2 tablespoons ground coriander
½ teaspoon ground black pepper
⅛ teaspoon cayenne
1 teaspoon salt
¼ cup ground Brazil nuts or unblanched almonds
olive oil or salad oil, or melted butter

Cut away and discard excess fat. Cut lean pork into 1½-inch cubes. Combine all remaining ingredients except oil or butter. Pour over meat, mix well, and marinate about 4 hours or overnight. String meat on skewers and cook over slow-burning charcoal about 25 to 30 minutes or until meat is browned on all sides and is well-done, basting with oil or melted butter and turning frequently. Serve hot. Makes 6 servings.

⚜ SPARERIBS ORIENTAL STYLE

4 to 5 pounds spareribs
2 tablespoons honey
¼ cup Madeira wine
⅓ cup soy sauce
½ cup water
1 tablespoon minced onion
1 small clove garlic, crushed
1½ teaspoons salt
½ teaspoon ground ginger
¼ teaspoon ground black pepper

Cut meat between the ribs, but do not cut all the way through. Place meat in a long dish. Combine remaining ingredients, pour over meat, and marinate 4 to 5 hours or overnight. Turn meat occasionally to marinate uniformly. Remove meat from marinade, reserving the liquid. Place meat on a rack in a large baking pan. Bake in a preheated moderate oven (350° F.) 1½ hours or until meat is tender, basting frequently with the marinade. If desired, cook on a spit or on a rack over slow-burning charcoal about 1¼ hours, basting frequently. Makes 6 servings.

⚜ GARNISHED SAUERKRAUT (*Choucroute Garnie*)

Bacon rinds
2½ pounds sauerkraut
6 slices bacon
6 frankfurters
1½ pounds pickled spareribs, cooked ham, or goose
1 stalk of parsley
2 medium-sized carrots, sliced
2 whole medium-sized onions
2 whole cloves
1 cup dry white wine

Line a 2-quart casserole with bacon rinds. Wash sauerkraut and squeeze it well by hand. Place half of it in the casserole. Blanch bacon and frankfurters in boiling water, drain, and place over the sauerkraut. Put the remaining sauerkraut on top. Cut spareribs, ham, or goose into serving-size pieces, and place over the sauerkraut along with the parsley and carrots. Stud each onion with a clove and add. Pour in wine. (Do not add salt.) Cover and cook in a preheated slow oven (325° F.) 1½ hours. To serve, place sauerkraut and meat in the center of the dish and arrange bacon, frankfurters, and carrots around it. Serve boiled potatoes in a separate dish. Makes 6 servings.

SAUSAGE

⚜ FRIED SAUSAGE WITH CABBAGE

12 links pork sausage
boiling water
1 head (2 pounds) cabbage
½ teaspoon sugar
½ teaspoon salt
ground black pepper

Prick sausage with a fork, and arrange in a 10- by 6- by 2-inch baking pan. Pour in 2 tablespoons water. Cook in preheated hot oven (400° F.) 30 minutes or until sausages are brown. (Reserve fat.) Meanwhile, chop cabbage coarsely and cook with the sugar and salt in ½ inch boiling water in a covered saucepan 8 to 10 minutes, or only until cabbage is crisp-tender. Toss lightly with pepper to taste and 2 tablespoons of the sausage fat. Serve cabbage in a shallow dish with sausage around it. Makes 6 servings.

⚜ PORK SAUSAGE IN WHITE WINE

12 links pork sausages
⅓ cup dry white wine
¾ cup Demi-Glace Sauce
6 portions mashed potatoes
cooked peas, string beans, or spinach

Prick sausage with a fork, place in a baking pan, and pour in wine. Bake in a preheated hot oven (400° F.) 30 minutes, or until sausages are thoroughly cooked. Drain the wine into a saucepan, add Demi-Glace, and bring to boiling point. Skim off fat. Transfer sausage to a platter and pour the sauce over it. Serve with mashed potatoes and one or more green vegetables. Makes 6 servings.

⚜ CHORIZOS (*Spanish Sausage*)

3 pounds lean pork
¼ cup vinegar
3 teaspoons salt
¾ teaspoon crushed hot red pepper
1½ teaspoons freshly ground black pepper
1½ teaspoons dried orégano
¼ teaspoon ground allspice
1½ yards sausage casing (or cloth bags)

Put meat through a meat grinder, using the coarse blade. Add remaining ingredients and mix well. Fill the sausage casing, using the attachment to the grinder known as a sausage stuffer, or pack it in thin cloth bags about 2 inches wide and 10 to 12 inches long. When ready to use, turn back the casing and cut in slices ¼ to ½ inch thick. Store sausage in refrigerator or other cold place. It will keep for several weeks. This sausage may be fried or used in any recipe specifying chorizos sausage. Makes 3 pounds.

⚜ RILLETTES TOURS STYLE (*Potted Pork*)

Rillettes are made of lean and fat pork cut into fine dice, cooked slowly in lard, and seasoned with salt, black pepper, and herbs. The mixture is then cooled and ground very fine or pounded in a mortar. Rillettes are made commercially all over France, the most highly esteemed being those of Tours and Le Mans.

3 pounds boneless shoulder butt of pork
about 1 cup boiling water
1 bay leaf
3 whole cloves
½ teaspoon dried marjoram
½ teaspoon dried sage
¼ teaspoon dried rosemary
1 teaspoon coarsely ground black pepper
1½ teaspoons salt

Cut pork, both lean and fat, into ½-inch dice. Place in a saucepan with the next 3 ingredients. Cook slowly, stirring occasionally, until water has evaporated. Continue cooking until the fat dice begin to brown, but not until the meat is dry. Remove from heat and transfer meat to a strainer. Set the strainer over the saucepan in which the meat was cooked until most of the fat has drained out of the meat. Reserve fat. Remove and discard bay leaf and cloves. Put meat through a food chopper, using the finest blade, or chop very fine and pound in a mortar or wooden bowl. Gradually blend in all the fat except 1 cup, add the herbs, salt, and pepper, and mix well. Pack the meat mixture into small jars or crocks, and pour a layer of the remaining fat, ½ inch thick, over the top. Cover jars with lids. Store in the refrigerator until ready to use. To serve, remove fat layer from the top and spread the mixture on toast, crusty rolls, or crackers. Makes approximately 2 pounds.

HAM

⚜ BRAISED HAM

8- to 10-pound boiled ham
whole cloves
1½ cups Madeira, Marsala, port, sherry, or champagne
confectioners' sugar
Demi-Glace Sauce

Place the ham in a roasting pan just big enough to fit it. Remove skin and trim the fat layer if it is thick. Score the fat and stud it with whole cloves. Pour wine or champagne over the ham. Cover and cook in a preheated moderate oven (350° F.) ½ hour. Remove cover, baste with cooking liquid, and sprinkle lightly with confectioners' sugar. Cook 25 to 30 minutes more, or until the sugar forms a light glaze. Transfer ham to a platter and keep hot. Let the ham rest 20 to 30 minutes before carving. Skim off and discard fat from the cooking liquor. Add Demi-Glace to the pan liquid and cook until the sauce has reduced to the desired consistency, stirring occasionally. Adjust seasonings. Serve with the ham. Makes 16 to 20 servings. (See illustration, page 623.)

⚜ MEDALLIONS OF HAM CÉZANNE

6 thin slices ham
¼ cup chopped onion
4 tablespoons butter
1 cup diced raw mushrooms
2 tablespoons chopped parsley
1 cup Mornay Sauce
salt
ground black pepper
6 baked 4-inch rounds of pastry
½ cup well-drained, chopped cooked spinach
grated Gruyère or Parmesan cheese
6 wide pieces celery 2 inches long, braised
6 slices beef marrow
Sauce Bordelaise

Cut medallions from the ham slices with a 4-inch cookie cutter. Save trimmings. Cook onions in 2 tablespoons of the butter until limp; add mushrooms and parsley and cook until mushrooms are tender. Add ½ cup ham trimmings and blend with all but 2 tablespoons of the Mornay Sauce. Season to taste with salt and pepper. Spread over baked pastry rounds. Top each with a ham medallion. Mix spinach with reserved 2 tablespoons Mornay Sauce, using only enough to bind the spinach, and spoon about ½ teaspoon onto the center of each medallion. Brush with melted butter, sprinkle with grated cheese, and put under broiler until cheese is melted. Transfer medallions to a warm platter and keep them warm. Top each piece of celery with a piece of beef marrow, cover with Sauce Bordelaise, and arrange around the medallions. Makes 6 servings. (See illustration, page 625.)

⚜ MEDALLIONS OF HAM POLIGNAC

12 slices baked ham
½ pound foie gras purée or pâté de foie gras
¼ cup (½ stick) softened butter
2 truffles, or 8 black olives
3 pints Madeira-flavored aspic
1 quart Russian Vegetable Salad

Cut medallions from the ham slices with a 3-inch cookie cutter. Save trimmings. Blend foie gras purée or pâté with the softened butter, spread on 6 of the ham rounds, and cover each with another ham round. Garnish the center of each "sandwich" with a slice of truffle or black olive and glaze with half-set aspic. Coat a large round tray with melted aspic and chill until firm. Put the Russian Salad in a mound in the center of the tray. Garnish with slices of truffle or black olive and small rounds of ham cut from the trimmings from the large medallions. Coat with liquid aspic and chill until set; there will be some aspic left. Chill remaining aspic until firm. Just before serving, dice the firm aspic, spoon it onto the tray around the salad, and arrange the ham-and-foie-gras sandwiches in a circle on top of the aspic around the edge of the tray. Serve at once. Makes 6 servings. (See illustration, page 626.)

⚜ HAM GLAZED WITH ASPIC

10- to 12-pound cold cooked ham
1 quart Madeira-flavored aspic
3 hard-cooked egg whites
2 tomatoes, finely chopped
2 truffles, finely chopped
watercress

Peel the rind from a cold cooked ham, and trim the fat if the layer is very thick. Saw the end of the shank bone smooth. Place the ham on a tray, rounded side up. Slice the top thinly, cutting down to the bone. Slip the long, thin blade of a sharp knife between the bone and the slices to loosen them so they may be served easily. Glaze the remaining ham with half-set aspic. Put the hard-cooked egg whites, well-drained tomatoes, and truffles in separate bowls and mix each with a little half-set aspic. Use to decorate the ham in any desired pattern. Chill until aspic is set. Serve on a large tray and garnish with watercress. Makes about 20 servings. (See illustration, page 623.)

⚜ HAM VILLANDRY

3½ quarts aspic
40 disks of truffles or slices of black olives
40 medallions of pickled tongue
Puff Pastry (page 127)
1¾ pounds cold cooked ham
¼ pound softened butter
ground black pepper
toasted chopped hazelnuts or almonds
40 small pineapple wedges
1½ pounds cooked smoked fillet of pork, sliced
40 cold cooked asparagus tips
6 small tomato cases
1½ quarts mixed vegetable salad
12 fluted mushrooms, cooked
6 cooked marinated round celeriac bottoms

Coat a large tray with aspic and chill it until aspic is set. Pour aspic into 40 2-ounce molds, making a layer ¼ inch thick. Chill until aspic is set. Decorate the bottom of each with a disk of truffle and a medallion of pickled tongue. Finish filling the molds with aspic. Chill until aspic is set.

Roll Puff Pastry ⅛ inch thick and cut it to the shape of a small ham (9 by 6 inches). Place it on a baking sheet, prick the top well, and bake as directed for Puff Pastry. Cool and set aside. Cut 30 thin slices of ham and cut each into a medallion with a round 2½-inch cooky cutter. Make ham purée from the trimmings, grinding the ham fine and mixing it with the butter and black pepper to taste. Make sandwiches with each 2 ham slices with the purée as filling. Roll the edges in chopped nuts. Decorate the top of each sandwich with 2 pineapple wedges. Coat with aspic and chill until aspic is set. Roll a slice of pork around each asparagus tip. Coat with aspic and chill until aspic is set. Fill tomato cases with vegetable salad and coat them with aspic. Chill until aspic is set.

Place the baked Puff Pastry in the center of the aspic-coated tray, and heap the remaining vegetable salad on top. Use a spatula to shape it to resemble a ham. Cover the salad completely with neatly arranged slices of pork. Place a row of fluted mushrooms down the center. Coat with aspic and chill until aspic is set. Surround the simulated ham with ham-medallion sandwiches. Invert the stuffed tomatoes on the celeriac bottoms. Unmold the small aspic molds and arrange around the edges of the tray. Arrange the tomatoes, pork-asparagus rolls, and remaining sandwiches on the tray. Makes approximately 20 servings. Serve at a cold buffet. (See illustration, page 219.)

⚜ COLD HAM ALSATIAN STYLE

3 pints port-flavored aspic
1 truffle, or 6 to 8 black olives
12 slices cooked ham
6 slices cooked goose liver

Pour about ½ cup liquid aspic into a chilled, lightly oiled 1½-quart mold. Swirl the mold around so as to coat the bottom and sides completely. Chill until aspic is almost set. Decorate the bottom and sides as desired with thin slices of truffle or black olives, lightly pushing the slices into the aspic to hold them in place. Pour in another ½ cup of aspic, swirling the mold so as to cover the truffles or olives completely. Chill until aspic is set. Fill the mold with alternate layers of sliced cooked ham and sliced goose liver and chill. Chill remaining aspic until it begins to set, then pour enough into the mold to cover the ham and liver completely. Chill until firm and ready to serve. Chill remaining aspic. Unmold onto a tray. Cut jellied aspic into cubes and spoon it onto the tray around the mold. Serve at once. Makes 6 to 8 servings.

⚜ HAM À LA ROTHSCHILD

½ pound pâté de foie gras, or foie gras purée
¼ cup (½ stick) softened butter
12 slices baked ham
1 truffle
2 cups port-flavored aspic

Blend pâté de foie gras or foie gras purée with butter. Spread over one side of each ham slice. Arrange the slices, overlapping, on a platter. Decorate with slices of truffle. Glaze with half-set aspic. Chill until aspic is set. Makes 6 servings.

⚜ HAM MOUSSE

3 envelopes unflavored gelatin
¾ cup water
⅓ cup (⅔ stick) butter
5 tablespoons flour
2¼ cups milk
1 cup mayonnaise
¾ cup heavy cream
¾ teaspoon salt
⅛ teaspoon ground white pepper
4½ cups or more finely diced ham

Soften gelatin in cold water and set aside. Melt butter in a saucepan. Remove from heat and blend in flour. Stir and cook 1 minute. Remove from heat, add milk, and mix well. Cook until thickened, stirring frequently. Remove from heat. Add softened gelatin. Combine mayonnaise, ¼ cup cream, salt, and pepper and add to the sauce. Chill until mixture begins to set. Fold in ham. Whip remaining cream and gently fold into the mousse. Turn mousse into a lightly oiled 10- by 10- by 2-inch pan. Chill until firm. Makes 12 servings.

⚜ HAM MOUSSE FOR A COLD BUFFET

12 slices baked lean ham, cut ¼ inch thick
½ pound pâté de foie gras, or foie gras purée
1 cup Chaud-froid Sauce
1 recipe Ham Mousse
2 each red, green, and yellow sweet peppers
⅓ cup julienne strips of celery or celeriac
Vinaigrette Dressing
1 quart sherry-flavored aspic
6 tomatoes, peeled

Trim ham slices into pear-shaped pieces 3½ inches long and 2½ inches wide at the widest part. Cut 3 triangles from the trimmings and reserve; reserve remaining trimmings to add to the Mousse. Top each slice with a dome-shaped mound of pâté de foie gras or foie gras purée. Chill. Cover with Chaud-froid Sauce and chill again. Cut 1 pepper of each color into julienne strips and marinate these and the celery or celeriac (in 2 separate bowls) in Vinaigrette Dressing.

Make Ham Mousse according to the preceding recipe. When mousse is firm, unmold and carve it into the shape of a small ham. Cover with Chaud-froid Sauce and brush the shank end with a little meat glaze. (See illustration, page 626.) Chill. Coat the 3 triangles of ham with Chaud-froid Sauce and chill, glaze with aspic and chill again, and arrange in a collar below the simulated shank bone. Chill. Decorate the pear-shaped slices with strips cut from the remaining red and green peppers and the "ham" with medallions made from the red and yellow peppers. Glaze with semi-liquid aspic and chill until firm. Cut tomatoes in half, remove seeds, drain, and top with the marinated celery or celeriac and pepper strips. Glaze a large platter with aspic and chill until firm. Place the "ham" in the center, with 3 pear-shaped slices at each end and 2 tomato halves at each side. Use the remaining pear-shaped ham slices and tomato halves to replenish the platter as required. Makes 12 servings.

⚜ CHESSBOARD HAM MOUSSE

1 recipe Ham Mousse
2 cups sherry aspic
truffles
hard-cooked egg whites
12 small baked plain pastry tart shells
Russian Vegetable Salad

Make the recipe of Ham Mousse. Coat a lightly oiled 10- by 10- by 2-inch pan with sherry aspic, swirling the pan to coat the bottom and sides completely. Chill until aspic is almost set. Cover the bottom in chessboard pattern with squares of truffles and hard-cooked egg whites. Decorate the sides of the pan with egg-white crescents. Cover with another thin layer of aspic. Chill until firm. Fill the pan with mousse. Chill until the mousse is firm. Fill baked pastry shells with Russian Vegetable Salad. Coat with aspic. Chill until aspic is firm.

To serve, unmold the mousse on a tray and surround it with salad-filled pastry shells. Garnish with fancy shapes cut from firm aspic. Makes 12 servings.

Variety Meats

Variety meats, which are organs and other parts of animals which are not classified as regular cuts, contribute important nutrients, since they all contain the same food elements found in lean meats, and some, especially liver, are superior sources of vitamins and minerals. Most variety meats, though not all, are also economical. The methods of preparation vary according to the physical structure. Some require precooking.

BRAINS

Brains are obtained from veal, beef, lamb, and pork, veal brains being the most popular (and most expensive). However, there is very little difference in the tenderness or flavor of brain from these various sources. Brains are delicate and perishable. If they are not to be used as soon as purchased, they should be precooked in simmering water as described below, refrigerated in a covered container, and used within 24 hours. Frozen brains are also obtainable. They should be kept frozen until ready to use. To thaw, drop them in hot water.

Veal brains weigh approximately ½ pound each; beef brains approximately ¾ pound each; lamb and pork brains approximately ¼ pound each. Allow 1 pound for each 4 servings.

⚜ HOW TO PRECOOK BRAINS

Soak brains 15 to 20 minutes in cold salted water (1 teaspoon salt to 1 quart water). Rinse under running water and drain. Drop brains in boiling salted acidulated water (1 teaspoon salt and 1 tablespoon lemon juice or vinegar to 1 quart water). The acid helps to retain their shape and whiteness. Cover, reduce heat, and simmer 15 to 20 minutes (do not boil). If brains are not to be served immediately, refrigerate in a covered jar with the membrane on and use within 24 hours. When ready to use, remove membrane with a pointed knife.

For some methods of cooking, and if brains are used soon after purchasing, precooking is unnecessary. Precooked brains may be prepared according to the following recipes.

⚜ FRIED BRAINS

Cut brains in thick slices and fry in browned butter.

⚜ SAUTÉED BRAINS

Dip thick slices of brains in beaten egg, then in fine dry breadcrumbs. Sauté in hot oil or shortening until browned on both sides.

⚜ BRAIN FRITTERS

Dip slices of brains in Fritter Batter and fry in deep fat preheated to 375° F. Drain on paper towels. Serve with Tomato Sauce.

⚜ COQUILLE OF BRAINS

Put sliced or diced brain in coquilles, or in individual casseroles. Cover with Mornay Sauce or Sauce Italienne, sprinkle with buttered soft breadcrumbs, and brown in a hot oven.

⚜ BROILED BRAINS

Brush brains generously with melted butter. Broil 10 to 15 minutes, until browned, in the broiler oven, turning to brown both sides. Serve with Black Butter, or with crisp bacon and grilled tomatoes.

⚜ CALF'S BRAINS IN BLACK BUTTER
(*Cervelle de Veau au Beurre Noir*)

4 calf's brains
cold water to cover
boiling water to cover
2 tablespoons lemon juice
1 teaspoon salt
ice-cold water
flour
1 cup (2 sticks) butter
4 teaspoons capers (optional)
2 tablespoons vinegar
chopped parsley (optional)

Soak the brains in the cold water for 1 hour. Drain and put them in boiling water to cover. Add the lemon juice and salt. Bring to boiling point, reduce heat, and simmer 15 minutes. Drain, cover the brains with ice water, and let stand until brains are cold, then remove brains from the water and wipe them dry with a clean towel. Roll brains in flour and sauté them in 4 tablespoons of the butter, adding it as needed. When brains have nicely browned, transfer them to a warmed platter, sprinkle with capers, if desired, and keep warm. Add remaining butter to the skillet. As the butter begins to brown, remove the skillet from the heat, add the vinegar, and give the skillet a few good shakes to mix the vinegar with the butter. Heat the butter and vinegar to the foaming point and pour over the brains. If desired sprinkle with chopped parsley. Serve at once. Makes 4 servings. (See illustration, page 601.)

⚜ BRAINS AND EGGS, SCRAMBLED

Finely chop 1 veal brain (precooked or raw). Cook in a little melted butter. Add 4 beaten eggs and 2 tablespoons milk. Stir and cook over moderately low heat until eggs are set. Season to taste with salt and black pepper. Serve on toast garnished with chopped parsley. Makes 4 servings.

HEAD

⚜ CALF'S HEAD VINAIGRETTE

meat from 1 calf's head, including tongue and brains
cold water to cover
2 quarts water
2 whole onions
4 whole cloves
½ teaspoon peppercorns
2 teaspoons salt
1 bay leaf
1 large leek
a few green celery leaves
4 stalks parsley
2 carrots, sliced
Vinaigrette Sauce

Place the calf's head, tongue, and brains in a large saucepan, cover with cold water, and let stand 2 hours. Place all remaining ingredients except the Vinaigrette Sauce in a large saucepan and bring to boiling point. Add the meat from the calf's head and simmer it 35 minutes. Add the tongue and simmer 1 hour or until tongue is tender. Then add the brains and simmer 20 minutes. Transfer the brains to a bowl to cool. Cool the tongue and meat in the broth. Remove the skin and membrane from the brains. Dice the brains and reserve. Take the tongue and meat out of the broth. Remove the gristle and skin from the tongue. Slice both tongue and meat and arrange the slices on a platter. Add the diced brains to the Vinaigrette Sauce and serve over the slices. Allow ½ pound calf's head per serving.

⚜ HEAD CHEESE

This is called Pressed Meat in some southern sections of the United States.

1 calf's head or pig's head
water
dry white wine
2 teaspoons salt
1 carrot, sliced
3 ribs celery, sliced
3 stalks parsley
4 shallots, quartered
1 clove garlic
1 large onion, quartered
5 whole cloves
5 whole allspice
¼ teaspoon peppercorns
1 bay leaf
dash cayenne
⅛ teaspoon ground nutmeg
¾ teaspoon dried sage

Ask the butcher to clean the head, removing snout and reserving the brains and tongue. Place the well-washed head and the tongue in a large kettle. Cover with equal parts of water and wine. Add salt. Tie the next 10 ingredients in a cheesecloth bag and add. Bring to boiling point and skim the surface. Reduce heat, cover and simmer 4 hours or until meat falls off the bones. Remove the tongue from the water after it has cooked 1½ hours or is tender. Remove the root portion and skin and cut the tongue into 1-inch pieces. Pour a little stock over the tongue and set it aside. Remove the head from the stock and trim off the rind. Cut the meat into 1-inch pieces and add to the pieces of tongue. Set aside. Simmer the brains in a little of the cooking water, covered, 15 minutes or until they are done. Lift from the cooking water, cut into pieces, and add to tongue and meat. Add cayenne, nutmeg, and sage. Mix well. Pack the meat into a 9½- by 5- by 3-inch loaf pan. Pour in ¾ cup of the cooking liquid. Cover with foil and place a weight on top to keep the meat submerged in the stock. Cool and refrigerate at least 2 days before using. Serve sliced and well chilled. Makes 1 loaf 9½ by 5 by 3 inches.

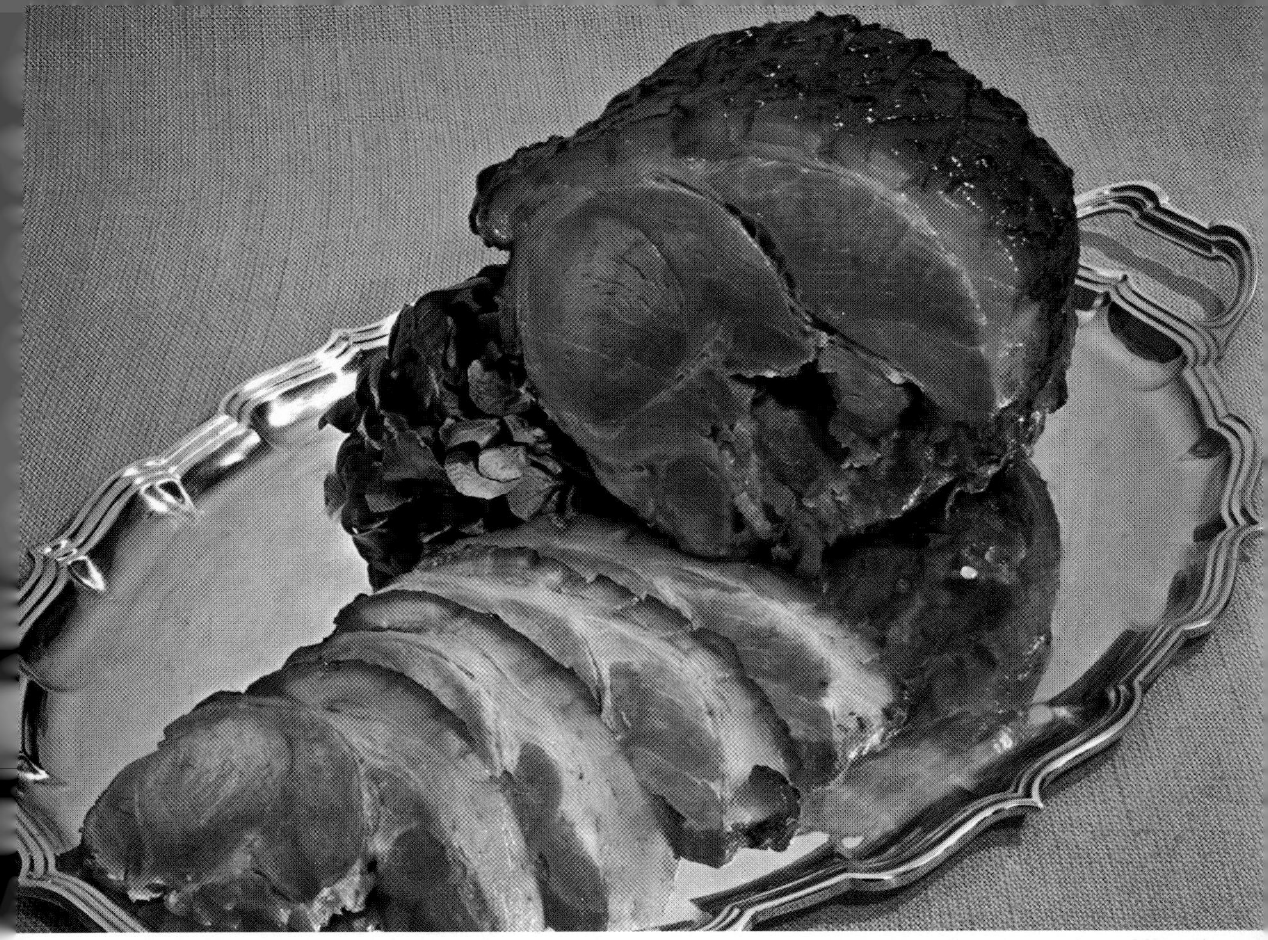

Braised Ham, page 614 ▲

▼ Ham Glazed with Aspic, page 615

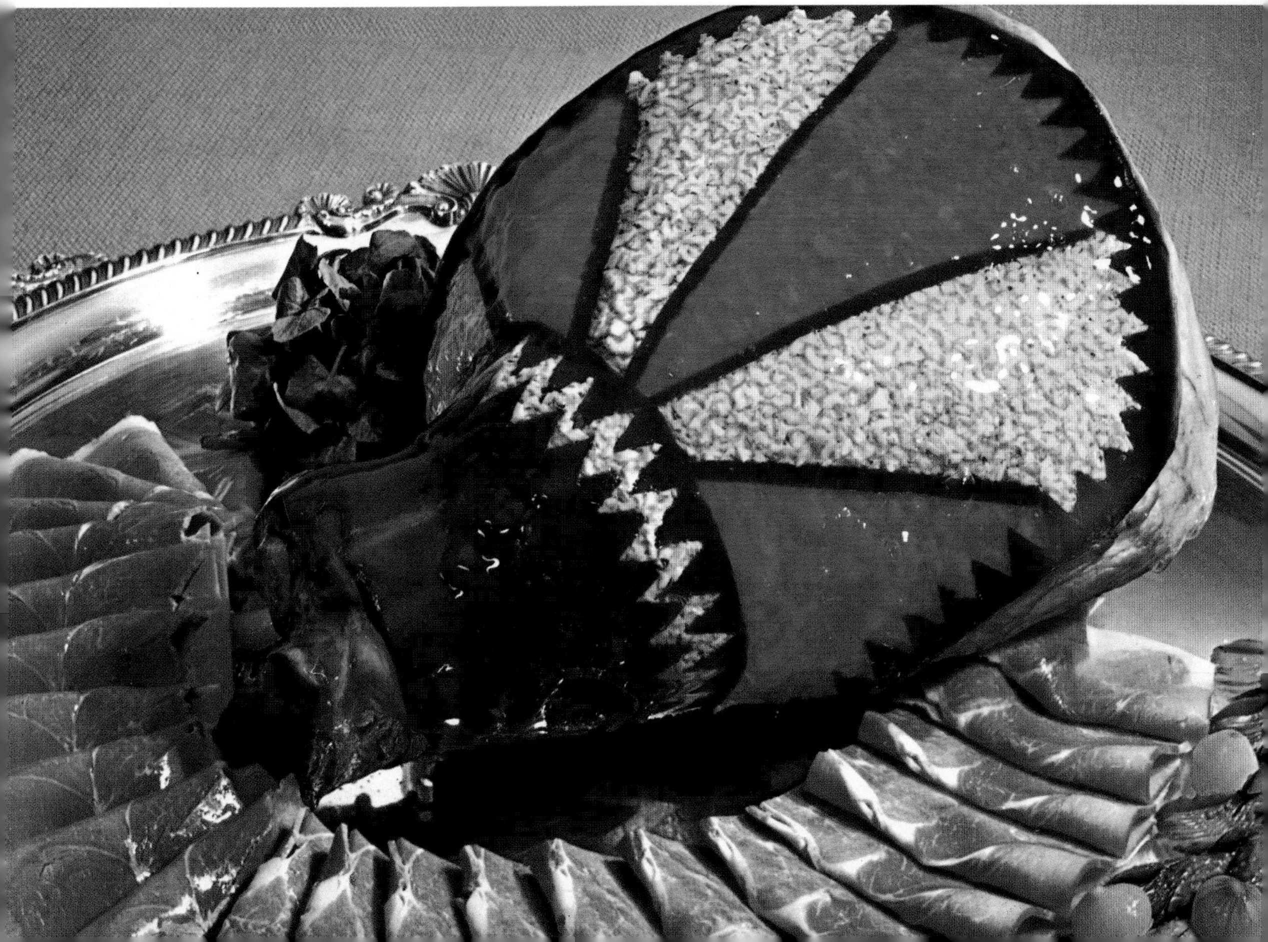

▲ Loin of Pork Belle Fermière, page 607

Pork Chops Bonne Femme, page 608 ▼

Medallions of Ham Cézanne, page 614 ▲

▼ Pork Chops Normande, page 609

▲ Ham Mousse for a Cold Buffet, page 618

Medallions of Ham Polignac, page 615 ▼

HEART

The heart is a muscular organ of the animal's body that receives considerable exercise. Therefore, it is one of the less tender variety meats. It is firm-textured with very little waste. Veal heart, due to its delicate flavor and tenderness, is preferred to heart of lamb, pork, or beef. Beef heart is the least desirable and the largest, usually weighing 3½ to 4 pounds.

When buying heart, allow, for 6 servings, 2 pounds beef heart and 1½ pounds of veal, lamb, or pork heart.

To prepare heart for cooking, wash it and cut out the arteries and veins at the top of and inside the heart. Soak in sour milk or in water to which a little vinegar has been added. This helps to tenderize the tissues. To cook heart, use one of the following methods:

Cooking in liquid. Cover the heart with water, adding 1 teaspoon salt for each quart water. Simmer until tender. Cook beef heart 3 to 3½ hours; veal, pork, or lamb heart, 2½ hours.

Braising. Brown heart in a little fat. Add a small amount of water or other liquid. Add salt and pepper. Cover tightly and cook slowly over surface heat or in a moderate oven (350° F.) from 1½ to 2½ hours for veal, lamb, or pork hearts; 2½ to 3½ hours for beef hearts.

Veal heart is tender enough to slice thinly and sauté.

⚜ STUFFED BEEF HEART

1 beef heart
2 slices salt pork
2 cups soft breadcrumbs
½ cup diced onion
1½ teaspoons salt
¼ teaspoon ground black pepper
½ teaspoon ground thyme
1 tablespoon chopped parsley
3 tablespoons flour
½ cup boiling water

Prepare beef heart for cooking as previously directed. Dice the salt pork and fry until crisp in a Dutch oven. Set aside. Combine breadcrumbs, onion, ¼ teaspoon salt, ⅛ teaspoon pepper, the thyme, and the parsley. Stuff into the cavity of the heart. Close opening with skewers and lace with twine. Sprinkle heart with remaining salt and pepper, dredge with flour, and brown in the rendered salt pork. Add water, cover, and simmer over surface heat or cook in a preheated moderate oven (350° F.) 2½ to 3 hours, adding more water if needed. Makes 6 servings.

⚜ STUFFED VEAL HEARTS

In the recipe for Stuffed Beef Hearts, replace beef heart with 2 veal hearts. Cook 2 to 2½ hours.

⚜ SAUTÉED CALF'S HEART

2 calf's hearts, 1 pound each
salt
ground black pepper
flour
about 3 tablespoons butter
assorted cooked vegetables

Cut hearts into thin slices, sprinkle with salt and pepper, and dredge in flour. Fry over moderate heat in butter, adding it as needed. Serve with buttered boiled onions, string beans, and sautéed potatoes, or with other vegetables if desired. Makes 6 servings.

⚜ LAMB HEART CASSEROLE

3 lamb hearts
flour
2 tablespoons butter or bacon drippings
½ cup sliced onion
1 small clove garlic, crushed
½ cup chopped celery
2 cups canned tomatoes
1 small bay leaf
½ teaspoon sugar
1 teaspoon salt
¼ teaspoon ground black pepper
chopped parsley

Prepare hearts for cooking as previously directed. Cut them in half, dredge with flour, and brown on all sides in butter or bacon drippings. Add onion and garlic and cook until onions are limp. Turn the mixture into a casserole and add all remaining ingredients except the parsley. Cover and cook in a preheated moderate oven (350° F.) for 2 to 2½ hours or until hearts are tender, adding a little water if needed. Sprinkle with chopped parsley. Makes 6 servings.

⚜ BRAISED PORK HEARTS

3 pork hearts
1 teaspoon salt
⅛ teaspoon ground black pepper
flour
3 tablespoons olive oil or salad oil
¾ cup sliced onions
½ cup boiling water
½ teaspoon dried thyme

Prepare pork hearts for cooking according to previous directions. Cut hearts in quarters, rub with salt and pepper, and dredge with flour. Brown all sides in oil. Add onions and cook until they are limp. Pour in ½ cup boiling water. Cover and simmer 2 to 2½ hours or until hearts are tender, adding thyme 30 minutes before cooking time is up. Makes 6 servings.

KIDNEYS

The size, flavor, and tenderness of a kidney is largely determined by the type and the age of the animal from which it comes. In general, the kidneys from small young animals are more delicate in flavor than those from larger older animals. For example, veal kidney which makes 1 serving or lamb kidney which requires 2 to make a serving is more tender and has a more delicate flavor than a kidney from a steer, which is large enough to make 4 servings. Pork kidneys have a stronger flavor.

Veal, lamb, or pork kidney should be cooked for only a short time over medium heat. Beef kidney needs to be cooked slowly in moist heat until tender.

⚜ SAUTÉED KIDNEYS

Allow 1 veal kidney or 2 lamb kidneys per serving. Remove the membrane from the kidneys and split them in half lengthwise, or slice ¼ inch thick. Cut out the fat and the white veins. Sauté in hot bacon fat or melted butter 10 to 15 minutes, turning frequently. Season to taste with salt, ground black pepper, and a little sherry. Serve on toast for lunch or supper with scrambled eggs.

⚜ SAUTÉED KIDNEYS AND MUSHROOMS

¾ cup finely chopped onion
2 tablespoons butter
3 veal kidneys
salt
ground black pepper
1½ tablespoons flour
½ pound sliced mushrooms
3 tablespoons water
2 tablespoons sherry

Sauté onions in butter until transparent. Meanwhile remove the membrane from kidneys and cut them into thin slices. Sprinkle with salt, pepper, and flour. Add kidneys and mushrooms to onions. Stir and cook until kidneys are lightly browned. Simmer, uncovered, 10 to 12 minutes. Add 3 tablespoons water and cook until thickened. Stir in sherry. Serve on toast or rice. Makes 6 servings.

⚜ BROILED KIDNEYS

4 lamb kidneys or 2 veal kidneys
French Dressing, or ¼ cup melted butter
8 broiled buttered mushroom caps
4 grilled tomatoes
8 slices crisp bacon
parsley

Remove membrane and cut each kidney in half. Pour a little French Dressing in a bowl and dip kidneys into this, or, if preferred, dip them into melted butter. If butter is used, sprinkle kidneys with salt and pepper. Place kidneys on a baking sheet and broil for 7 or 8 minutes 3 inches from the source of heat. Turn and broil 5 minutes or until kidneys are browned. Serve hot with broiled buttered mushroom caps, grilled tomatoes, and crisp bacon. Garnish kidneys with parsley. Makes 4 servings.

⚜ VEAL KIDNEYS BORDELAISE

6 veal kidneys
2 tablespoons butter
2 tablespoons oil
3 cups sliced mushrooms
1 cup dry red wine
2 shallots, finely chopped
1 cup Brown Sauce
6 slices blanched marrow
chopped parsley

Remove the outer membrane from kidneys and split them in half, lengthwise, or slice them ¼ to ½ inch thick crosswise. Remove fat and veins. Wash and dry. Fry in a heavy skillet in half the butter and half the oil 10 to 15 minutes, turning frequently. Sauté mushrooms separately in remaining butter and oil and mix with the kidneys. Transfer to a serving dish and keep hot. Add wine and shallots to the skillet juices and cook until the liquid has almost evaporated. Add Brown Sauce, bring to boiling point, and pour over kidneys and mushrooms. Garnish with slices of blanched marrow and chopped parsley. Makes 6 servings. (See illustration, page 601.)

⚜ BEEF KIDNEY RAGOUT

1 beef kidney
water to cover
3 tablespoons vinegar
salt and ground black pepper
flour
2 tablespoons butter
1 tablespoon olive oil or salad oil
¾ cup sliced onion
1 clove garlic, finely chopped
1 small bay leaf
½ cup beef stock
½ cup dry red wine
1 teaspoon dried or 1½ teaspoons chopped fresh thyme

Remove the membrane and soak the kidney 2 hours in water to cover, with the vinegar. Drain off water and wipe kidney dry. Cut into thin slices and sprinkle with salt and pepper. Dredge with flour and brown in butter and oil. Add onion, garlic, and bay leaf. Stir and cook 5 minutes. Add beef stock and wine. Cover and cook 20 minutes. Add thyme 5 minutes before cooking time is up. Adjust seasonings. Serve with boiled potatoes or buttered noodles. Makes 4 servings.

⚜ STEAK AND KIDNEY PIE

1 pound round steak, cut 1 inch thick
3 veal kidneys or 6 lamb kidneys
5 tablespoons flour
1½ teaspoons salt
⅛ teaspoon ground black pepper
¼ teaspoon ground ginger
2 tablespoons butter
2 tablespoons shortening
1 teaspoon prepared mustard
2 cups sliced onion
1¼ cups beef stock or 1 can (10½ ounces) beef bouillon
2 cups water
unsweetened pie pastry, made with 1 cup flour, or Puff Pastry

Cut steak into 1-inch cubes. Wash kidneys and remove the membranes, fat, and tubes. Cut kidneys into quarters. Combine flour and seasonings and dredge kidneys, reserving flour that is left. Brown kidneys in butter and shortening. Remove from heat and add the reserved flour, the mustard, onions, stock or bouillon, and water. Cover, bring to boiling point, reduce heat, and simmer 1 hour. Turn the beef and kidney mixture into a 10- by 6- by 2-inch baking dish. Cover with unsweetened pie pastry or puff pastry. Trim, turn under, and flute edges. Cut 2 or 3 gashes in top of crust to allow for escape of steam. Bake in a preheated hot oven (425° F.) 40 minutes or until browned. Serve hot as an entrée for lunch or supper. Makes 6 servings.

LIVER

All kinds of liver are highly nutritious. Calf's liver is the most popular, since it is the tenderest and has the mildest flavor. Baby beef or yearling liver is nearly as tender as calf's liver; steer liver has a stronger flavor and requires longer cooking. Lamb and pork liver have a less desirable flavor but may be cooked in any of the same ways.

⚜ CALF'S LIVER EN BROCHETTE

24 pieces calf's liver cut into 1½-inch squares, ¼ inch thick
butter
24 pieces lean bacon cut in 1½-inch squares
fine dry breadcrumbs
2 eggs beaten with 2 tablespoons water
salt
ground black pepper
Herb Butter

Fry liver lightly in butter. Dip bacon in hot water and drain well. Thread liver and bacon alternately on short skewers. Roll in breadcrumbs, dip in eggs beaten with water, and roll in crumbs again. Fry in deep fat preheated to 375° F. Drain on paper towels and sprinkle lightly with salt and pepper. Serve with Herb Butter. Makes 6 servings.

⚜ CALF'S LIVER ENGLISH STYLE

6 slices calf's liver
flour
4 tablespoons butter
salt
ground black pepper
2 tablespoons bacon drippings
chopped parsley
6 slices crisp bacon
watercress
6 boiled potatoes

Remove tubes from liver, dredge in flour and brown on both sides in butter. Sprinkle with salt and pepper. Transfer liver to a platter. Add bacon drippings to the skillet, blend with the cooking butter, heat, and pour over liver. Sprinkle with chopped parsley. Garnish with crisp bacon, watercress, and boiled potatoes. Makes 6 servings.

⚜ CALF'S LIVER BERCY

6 slices calf's liver
salt
ground black pepper
flour
7 tablespoons butter
2 shallots, chopped
⅓ cup dry white wine
1 teaspoon chopped parsley

Sprinkle liver with salt and pepper and dredge in flour. Brown on both sides in 3 tablespoons of the butter. Let the remaining butter soften. Cook shallots in wine until most of the liquid has evaporated. Cool. Blend the parsley with the softened butter and add to the cooled shallots. Season to taste with a little salt and pepper. Pour the sauce over the browned liver, heat, and serve. Makes 6 servings.

OXTAIL

⚜ BRAISED OXTAIL

4 pounds oxtail, disjointed
salt
flour
¼ cup shortening or lard
12 small white onions
1¼ cups sliced carrots
1 clove garlic
1¼ cups beef stock
1¼ cups dry white wine
1 small bay leaf
2 stalks parsley
1 cup sliced mushrooms
1 tablespoon butter
¼ teaspoon ground black pepper
chopped parsley

Sprinkle oxtail with salt and dredge in flour. Brown in shortening or lard in a Dutch oven. Add onions, carrots, and garlic to the pan and cook until browned. Add stock, wine, bay leaf, and parsley. Sprinkle with ½ teaspoon salt. Cover and cook in a preheated slow oven (325° F.) 3 to 4 hours or until meat is done. Sauté mushrooms in butter and add to the oxtails the last 30 minutes of cooking. Stir in black pepper. Serve hot, sprinkled with chopped parsley. Makes 6 servings.

⚜ OXTAIL BOURGEOISE STYLE

3 oxtails
salt
flour
¼ cup shortening or lard
beef broth
Burgundy
4 whole cloves
1½ dozen small white onions
1½ dozen small potatoes
1 dozen small carrots, quartered
1 clove garlic
¼ cup chopped parsley
1 leek, if available
½ teaspoon peppercorns
12 small mushrooms
½ teaspoon dried sage leaves
chopped parsley

Wash oxtails and cut each into 6 pieces, or ask the butcher to cut them for you. Sprinkle with salt and dredge in flour. Brown on all sides in shortening or lard in a Dutch oven. Drain off fat. Pour in equal parts of broth and wine, enough barely to cover the oxtails. Stick the cloves in one of the onions and add it, along with the rest of the onions and the potatoes, carrots, garlic, parsley, leek, and peppercorns. Cover and cook in a preheated slow oven (325° F.) 3 to 4 hours or until done. About ½ hour before the oxtails are done, slice mushroom stems and add along with the mushroom caps and sage. Adjust seasonings. Serve hot, sprinkled with chopped parsley. Makes 6 to 8 servings.

PIGS' FEET

⚜ PIGS' FEET (*Trotters*)

Place cleaned pigs' feet in a saucepan with water to cover, 1 teaspoon salt, 1 each sliced carrot and onion, 2 stalks parsley, and 2 whole cloves. Cover, bring to boiling point, reduce heat, and cook slowly 2½ hours. Serve plain, with a sauce, or dip the pigs' feet in melted butter, roll in fine dry breadcrumbs, and fry. Allow 1 pig's foot per serving.

⚜ PIGS' FEET SAINTE-MENEHOULD

6 pigs' feet
water
1 cup dry white wine
1 carrot, sliced
1 medium-sized onion, sliced
2 stalks parsley
coarsely ground black pepper
¼ cup (1½ stick) butter, melted
fine dry breadcrumbs
6 portions mashed potatoes
6 portions cooked green peas

Split pigs' feet, tie back together, and place in a large saucepan. Add water to cover. Add the next 5 ingredients. Cover, bring to boiling point, and simmer until the feet are tender. Remove from the stock and pull out the bones. Spread the feet between 2 boards and place a weight on top. Let stand in a cool place until the next day. Sprinkle with pepper, dip in melted butter, and roll in breadcrumbs, pressing them down. Fry in a heavy skillet in butter until browned on both sides. Serve with mashed potatoes and green peas. Makes 6 servings.

⚜ BAKED PIGS' FEET WITH TRUFFLE SAUCE

Prepare pigs' feet as for Pigs' Feet Sainte-Menehould and let stand overnight. Place them in a buttered 13- by 9- by 2-inch baking dish. Cook in a preheated slow oven (325° F.) 1 hour or until the feet have browned. Transfer the feet to a platter and pour Truffle Sauce around them. Serve with any vegetables desired. Allow 1 pig's foot per serving.

SWEETBREADS

Sweetbreads are the delicate edible thymus glands of young beef, calves, and lambs. They are prenatally developed, and when the calf or lamb is taken off milk, they begin to disappear. Beef sweetbreads, therefore, come from very young beef.

Sweetbreads consist of two parts, the heart sweetbread and the throat sweetbread, connected by membrane and tubing. The heart sweetbread, as the name indicates, is near the heart. It is round in shape and is the more desirable. The less desirable throat sweetbread is located near the throat. It is elongated and less regular in shape, one side having a thick piece of tough cartileginous skin which must be removed before cooking. This operation usually breaks the sweetbread into pieces.

Calf's sweetbreads are the most delicate in flavor; consequently they are the most popular and the highest in price. They are white and tender.

Lamb sweetbreads are also white, tender, and delicate in flavor. While they are not considered as choice as those from calves, they are preferable to beef sweetbreads. They may be prepared in the same manner as calf's sweetbreads.

All sweetbreads are prepared for cooking in the same way as brains (see How to Precook Brains, page 620).

⚜ SWEETBREADS IN CREAM SAUCE

3 pairs calf's or lamb's sweetbreads
salt
ground black pepper
flour
4 tablespoons (½ stick) butter
½ cup heavy cream
brandy
lemon juice
1 cup sliced poached mushrooms

Soak sweetbreads according to the directions in How to Precook Brains. Poach in simmering water 8 minutes. Cool, trim, and slice ½ inch thick. Sprinkle the slices lightly with salt and pepper and roll in flour. Cook in a skillet in butter until done, turning to brown both sides. Transfer sweetbreads to a hot platter and keep hot. Add the cream to the skillet and mix well with the pan residue. Simmer until the sauce is slightly thick. Season to taste with salt, pepper, brandy, and lemon juice. Add mushrooms, heat, and pour sauce over sweetbreads. Makes 6 servings.

⚜ SWEETBREADS FLORENTINE

3 pairs calf's or lamb's sweetbreads
salt
ground black pepper
flour
6 tablespoons (¾ stick) butter
1½ packages (10-ounce) frozen or 2 pounds fresh spinach, cooked
dash ground nutmeg
1 cup Mornay Sauce
⅓ cup grated Parmesan cheese

Soak sweetbreads according to the directions in How to Precook Brains. Poach in simmering water or stock 8 minutes. Cool, trim, and slice ½ inch thick. Sprinkle slices lightly with salt and pepper and roll in flour. Cook in butter, using 2 tablespoons, until done, turning to brown both sides. Sauté well-drained frozen or fresh spinach in 1 tablespoon of the butter. Season to taste with salt, pepper, and nutmeg. Spread in a buttered 8- by 8- by 2-inch baking dish. Arrange sweetbreads over the spinach. Cover with Mornay Sauce. Sprinkle with grated cheese. Dot with the remaining 3 tablespoons butter. Brown under broiler heat 4 inches from the source of heat. Makes 6 servings.

⚜ BROILED SWEETBREADS WITH HAM

3 pairs calf's sweetbreads
salt
ground black pepper
½ cup (1 stick) butter, melted
1 cup fine dry breadcrumbs
6 slices broiled ham
6 slices buttered toast
6 mushroom caps sautéed in butter

Soak and precook sweetbreads in water or stock according to the directions in How to Precook Brains. Drain, cool in ice water, and remove connective tissue and outer covering. Split sweetbreads and season with salt and pepper. Dip in melted butter and roll in breadcrumbs. Sprinkle with more melted butter. Broil 4 inches from the source of heat until well browned, about 5 minutes on each side. Place a slice of broiled ham on each of 6 slices buttered toast. Top each with a sweetbread and a sautéed mushroom cap. Makes 6 servings.

⚜ SWEETBREADS IN PASTRY CASES

3 pairs veal sweetbreads
4 tablespoons (½ stick) butter
4 tablespoons flour
2 cups sweetbread broth
1 cup milk
1 cup diced cooked ham
salt
ground white pepper
6 baked Puff-Pastry or Plain-Pastry cases
parsley

Soak sweetbreads and cook in water or stock according to the directions in How to Precook Brains, saving the sweetbread broth. Cool the cooked sweetbreads in ice water. Remove connective and covering tissue and cut sweetbreads into cubes. Set aside. Melt the butter in the top of a double boiler. Remove from heat and blend in flour. Stir and cook over direct heat 1 minute. Remove from heat and add stock and milk. Stir and cook over boiling water until sauce has thickened. Add sweetbreads and ham. Season to taste with salt and pepper. Serve in pastry cases. Garnish with parsley. Makes 6 servings.

⚜ BRAISED SWEETBREADS COMTESSE

3 pairs calf's or lamb's sweetbreads
¼ cup sliced onion
½ cup sliced carrots
3 tablespoons butter
1 tablespoon flour
½ cup dry white wine
1 cup veal or chicken stock
salt and ground black pepper to taste
2 tablespoons sherry
1 teaspoon cornstarch
Braised Lettuce
Veal Quenelles
truffle slices

Soak and precook sweetbreads according to the directions in How to Precook Brains. Remove all connective and covering tissue. Cook onion and carrots in butter until onions are golden. Sprinkle with flour. Add sweetbreads, wine, stock, salt, and pepper, and heat to simmering. Cover and bake in a preheated moderate oven (350° F.) 20 minutes. Remove cover and bake 10 minutes more. Place sweetbreads in the center of a hot platter. Mix sherry with the cornstarch and add to the pan liquids. Mix well and heat until the sauce has thickened slightly and is transparent. Pour over sweetbreads. Serve with Braised Lettuce and Veal Quenelles garnished with truffle slices. Makes 6 servings. (See illustration, page 600.)

⚜ SLICED SWEETBREADS GRAZIELLA

3 pairs calf's or lamb's sweetbreads
salt
ground black pepper
flour
5 tablespoons butter
6 rounds fried bread
3 firm ripe tomatoes
chopped onion
6 sautéed mushroom caps
6 tablespoons Madeira Sauce

Soak sweetbreads according to the directions in How to Precook Brains. Cool, trim, and slice ½ inch thick. Sprinkle with salt and pepper to taste, and roll in flour. Cook in 4 tablespoons of the butter until sweetbreads are done and browned on both sides. Place each slice on a round of fried bread and place on a hot platter. Keep hot. Cut tomatoes in half. Sprinkle with salt and ground black pepper to taste and with chopped onion. Dot with remaining 1 tablespoon butter and broil in the broiler oven until tomatoes are brown. Remove from oven. Top each with a sautéed mushroom cap. Cover with Madeira Sauce and place on the platter around the sweetbreads. Serve with potatoes. Makes 6 servings. (See illustration, page 600.)

TONGUE

Beef tongue (called ox tongue in England) is the most commonly used. Calf's and lamb's tongues are not readily available in American markets; if obtainable, they may be braised or served in ragouts. Cooked ready-to-serve tongue and pickled tongue can be obtained in jars or cans.

⚜ BROILED TONGUE WITH MADEIRA SAUCE

3- to 4-pound smoked beef tongue
cold water
bouquet garni
3 whole cloves
1 medium-sized onion
1 clove garlic
½ cup sliced carrots
5 peppercorns
1 small bay leaf
Madeira Sauce

Soak tongue in cold water overnight. Put tongue in a 6-quart kettle and cover with cold water. Add remaining ingredients. Bring to boiling point and simmer 3 hours or until tongue is tender. Cool in the broth for ½ hour. Cut off the tongue root or muscle and peel off the skin. Slice diagonally and serve with Madeira Sauce. Makes 6 to 8 servings.

If tongue is to be served cold, let it cool in the stock before it is trimmed and skinned.

BEEF TONGUE SAINT-GERMAIN

1 hot cooked smoked beef tongue (3 to 4 pounds)
1¾ cups Madeira Sauce
3 cups cooked green peas, puréed
⅛ teaspoon sugar
salt and ground black pepper to taste
2 tablespoons butter

Slice hot tongue and arrange it in overlapping slices down the center of a platter. Coat with Madeira Sauce. Serve remaining sauce in a separate dish. Heat pea purée. Add seasonings and butter. Serve separately. Makes 6 to 8 servings.

TONGUE WITH ORANGE SAUCE

3 tablespoons butter
3 tablespoons flour
1 cup tongue stock
1 cup orange juice
1 tablespoon grated orange rind
½ teaspoon grated lemon rind
2 tablespoons sherry
1 teaspoon currant jelly
3-pound cooked beef tongue

Melt 2 tablespoons of the butter in a 1-quart saucepan. Remove from heat and blend in flour. Stir and cook 1 minute. Remove from heat and add tongue stock and orange juice. Mix well and simmer until sauce has reduced to 1½ cups, stirring frequently. Add orange and lemon rinds, sherry, and jelly. Stir and cook ½ minute. Strain and stir in remaining butter. Serve over sliced tongue. Makes 6 servings.

PICKLED TONGUE KARACHI STYLE

5 cups aspic
4½ pounds pickled tongue
6 hard-cooked eggs, sliced
24 slices cucumber pickle
1 teaspoon unflavored gelatin
1 tablespoon cold water
½ cup mayonnaise
1 cup cooked rice
⅓ cup diced sweet red pepper
2 shallots, finely chopped
1 banana, diced
curry powder to taste
10 baked tartlet shells
2 cucumber pickles, 2 inches long
½ medium tomato

Coat a large platter with aspic and chill until aspic is set. Cut the tongue in thin slices and set aside. Garnish each egg slice with a slice of cucumber pickle and place one on each slice of tongue. Border the aspic-lined tray with tongue slices, having them overlapping, showing half of each egg slice. Coat the slices with aspic and chill. Soften the gelatin in cold water, melt it over hot water, and add to the mayonnaise. Combine with the next 4 ingredients and curry powder to taste. Spoon the mixture into the baked tartlet shells. Garnish the top of each with 3 narrow strips of cucumber pickle and a bit of tomato. Arrange the tartlets inside the tongue slices. Chill remaining aspic, dice, and spoon it into the center of the tray. Makes 10 servings. (See illustration, page 558.)

⚜ TONGUE PRINCESSE

2½ cups aspic
36 asparagus tips, cooked
¼ cup French Dressing
pimiento
cucumber pickle
1 pickled ox tongue
whites of 6 hard-cooked eggs
1 truffle, or 6 large pitted black olives

Coat a large platter with aspic and chill until aspic is set. Marinate the cooked asparagus tips 1 hour in French Dressing. Remove asparagus from the marinade, drain well, and arrange in bundles of 3 tips in the center of the aspic-coated platter. Cut pimiento and pickle into narrow strips and drape one of each across each asparagus bundle. Coat with aspic. Chill until aspic is set. Cut the tongue into thin slices. Fold each slice in half and decorate as desired with the whites of hard-cooked eggs and truffle slices or sliced black olives. Arrange tongue slices on the aspic-coated tray around the asparagus, coat them with aspic, and chill until aspic is set. Makes 12 servings. (See illustration, page 557.)

TRIPE

Tripe is the walls of the stomachs of cud-chewing animals. There are three kinds: plain tripe from the smooth first stomach; honeycomb tripe from the second stomach (this is considered the best variety and is called honeycomb because it is full of pockets on one side and smooth on the other); and the type called the "need," which comes from the fourth stomach (sometimes called the rennet stomach).

Beef tripe is the most popular. However, pork and sheep tripe are also used in some places. Sheep tripe, called Haggis, is used in Scotland, and pork tripe is used in the southern part of the United States. Both France and Italy are famous for their tripe dishes.

To make tripe "from scratch" is a long and laborious task. Precooked fresh tripe is available in the markets today, but it needs further cooking. Pickled tripe is also available but must be soaked several hours before using. Canned tripe, ready to heat, is also available. A real connoisseur of tripe would use only the fresh precooked tripe.

⚜ TRIPE À LA MODE DE CAEN

This is the most popular tripe dish in France.

3 pounds precooked fresh tripe
2 calf's feet
2 medium-sized onions, sliced
2 large carrots, sliced
2 ribs celery, sliced
2 leeks, sliced
2 stalks parsley
¼ pound chopped beef-kidney suet
1 teaspoon dried or 1 tablespoon chopped fresh thyme
1 bay leaf
2 cloves garlic
6 peppercorns
3 whole cloves
1 blade mace
1 teaspoon salt
¼ cup brandy
½ cup hard cider
beef stock or water

Wash tripe and cut into 2-inch squares. Set aside. Wash and split calf's feet. Set aside. In a 3-quart earthenware casserole put all the ingredients, in this order: vegetables, tripe, calf's feet, suet, seasonings. Pour in brandy, cider, and enough beef stock or water barely to cover the ingredients. Cover the casserole and seal it with a roll of dough made by mixing 2 cups flour with enough cold water to make a very stiff paste. Bring the liquid to boiling point. Put the casserole into a preheated slow oven (300° F.) and cook 10 to 12 hours or overnight. (Never open the casserole or disturb the tripe while it cooks.) Transfer the tripe to another casserole. Remove calf's feet, pick off meat, discard bones, and return meat to the casserole. Skim off fat from the liquid and discard. Strain the stock over the tripe. Heat. Serve very hot from the casserole, accompanied by boiled or baked potatoes. Makes 8 servings.

⚜ TRIPE À LA POULETTE

3 pounds precooked fresh tripe
2 large onions, sliced
2 large carrots, sliced
2 stalks parsley
1 bay leaf
6 peppercorns
½ teaspoon salt
water
1 cup sliced mushrooms
5 tablespoons butter
1 tablespoon flour
½ cup each tripe stock and beef stock
2 egg yolks
½ cup heavy cream
¼ cup sherry
5 mushroom caps, cooked in butter

Wash tripe and cut into 1-inch pieces. Place in a saucepan with onions, carrots, seasonings, and water barely to cover. Cover and simmer 3 hours. Remove tripe and strain the stock. Sauté tripe and mushrooms in 3 tablespoons of the butter until mushrooms are tender, being careful not to brown the tripe. In a 1-quart saucepan, melt remaining 2 tablespoons butter. Remove from heat and blend in flour. Stir and cook 1 minute. Remove from heat and add tripe and beef stocks. Stir and cook until sauce thickens. Mix egg yolks with cream and add to the sauce. Cook, stirring, until it reaches desired consistency. (Do not boil.) Add sherry. Heat ½ minute and serve over tripe and mushrooms. Adjust seasonings. Garnish with mushroom caps. Makes 8 servings.

·13·

POULTRY

The term poultry is used to designate all domesticated birds used as food—chicken, turkey, duck, goose, guinea fowl, and pigeon. Chicken is the most popular. The French term *volaille* means poultry or bird; it is also used in a general way for chicken.

CHICKEN

Because of its flavor, versatility, and ease of cooking, chicken has been a favorite dish all over the world for many centuries. It can be prepared in innumerable ways and combined with a wide variety of other foods to make dishes which can be proudly served for any occasion.

Chickens are classified by age, sex, and weight. The kinds available, with their dressed, cleaned, ready-to-cook weights, are:

Broiler-fryer (*poulet de grain* and *poulet de reine*)	About 9 weeks old, 1½ to 3 pounds (broilers usually 1½ to 2½; fryers 2 to 3)

Roasting chicken (*poulet gras* or *poularde*)	3½ to 6 pounds
Capon (*chapon*)—castrated male	4 to 8 pounds
Fricassee chicken or fowl (*poule de l'année*)	2½- to 5-pound mature bird

⚜ HOW TO TRUSS CHICKEN OR TURKEY

Just before roasting a chicken or turkey, rub the crop and body cavities with salt and pepper. The bird may be stuffed or not. If stuffing is used, spoon it into the body cavities loosely, to allow room for expansion during cooking. Stuff neck first. Pull the neck skin to the back, fold the ends of the skin under neatly, and pin it to the back skin with a skewer. Turn the turkey breast side up. Lift each wing and fold the tip under and press it against the back—akimbo style. This method eliminates the need of skewers for holding the wings in place and gives the birds a base on which to rest in the roasting pan and serving platter. Now put the stuffing into the body cavity loosely. Close the opening of the body cavity by inserting 3 or 4 skewers through the skin at the edge of one side of the opening, having them pass over the opening through the skin on the opposite side. Then draw the edges of the skin together by crisscrossing a string around the skewers as in lacing shoes. Tie the ends of the string together at the bottom of the opening and fasten to the tail piece. Press drumsticks and thighs closely against the body of the bird, tie the ends of the drumsticks together with a string, and fasten it to the tail piece. If the bird is not stuffed and there is a band of skin across the opening to the body cavity, push the ends of the legs under it. This holds the legs in place. Remove all skewers and strings before serving.

⚜ ROAST CHICKEN WITH OYSTER DRESSING (*American*)

4- to 5-pound roasting chicken
salt
ground black pepper
Oyster Dressing
softened butter
parsley
radishes

Wash and dry chicken. Sprinkle inside of body and crop cavities with salt and pepper. Fill with Oyster Dressing. Close cavities with skewers and lace tightly with twine. Sprinkle skin with salt and pepper and rub with butter. Place chicken on a rack in a shallow baking pan. Bake in a preheated slow oven (325° F.) 3½ hours, basting with butter and pan drippings occasionally. If breast, wings, and legs tend to brown too much, cover these parts with foil. Remove from oven, put on a warmed platter, and let stand in a warm place 20 minutes before carving. Garnish with parsley and radishes. Serve with gravy made from pan drippings. Makes 6 to 8 servings. (For carving roast chicken see Culinary Techniques in Pictures.)

OYSTER DRESSING

2 cups diced bread, toasted
¼ cup (½ stick) butter, melted
1 teaspoon salt
¼ teaspoon ground black pepper
½ teaspoon dried thyme
¼ cup chicken broth
2 tablespoons minced onion
¼ cup finely diced celery
1 cup well-drained oysters

Combine all ingredients except oysters and mix lightly. Pick over oysters and remove all bits of shell. Chop and add. Mix well, using a fork. This amount will stuff a 4- to 5-pound chicken.

⚜ COLD CAPON ASTOR STYLE

5-pound roasted capon
4 cups semiliquid aspic
3 cups Waldorf Salad
8 halves of walnut meats
16 Maraschino cherries
⅓ cup Cumberland Sauce
2 bananas, diced
8 baked tart shells
grated orange rind
8 apple slices
8 mandarin orange slices

Remove the breast from a cold roast capon, cut it into 8 lengthwise slices, and trim the slices into oval shapes. Blend ¼ cup of the aspic with Waldorf Salad and spoon it into the body cavity of the capon. Smooth it over with a spatula and place a row of walnut halves down the center. Repeat with a row of Maraschino cherry halves on each side. Glaze with aspic. Chill until aspic is set. Blend Cumberland Sauce with 2 tablespoons semiliquid aspic and add diced bananas. Spoon into cold baked 2-inch tart shells. Sprinkle with grated orange rind. Chill. Top each slice of breast with a slice of apple. Garnish with a segment of mandarin orange. Glaze with aspic. Coat a rectangular tray with a thin layer of aspic. Chill until aspic is set. Place the capon in the center of the tray and arrange the tart shells and the slices of breast on the tray around the capon. Garnish the tray with cubed aspic. Makes 8 servings.

⚜ CHICKEN ANDALUSIAN STYLE

4-pound whole ready-to-cook chicken
water to cover
1¼ teaspoons salt
2 egg yolks
3 tablespoons dry sherry
⅓ cup heavy cream
1 cup Velouté Sauce
2 teaspoons lemon juice
1/16 teaspoon ground white pepper
12 small slices Fried Eggplant
¾ cup Tomato Fondue
3 skinned cooked red or green sweet peppers, halved
Rice à la Grecque

Wash chicken and leave whole. Cook in water to cover with 1 teaspoon of the salt until it is tender but still holds its shape—40 to 50 minutes. Combine egg yolk, sherry, cream, Velouté Sauce, lemon juice, the remaining ¼ teaspoon of the salt, and the pepper. Bring to boiling point, but do not boil. Transfer chicken to a warmed platter and cover with the sauce. Top Fried Eggplant with Tomato Fondue and arrange on the platter. Stuff cooked green or red peppers with Rice à la Grecque and place on the platter. Makes 6 servings. (See illustration, page 681.)

⚜ HARLEQUIN CHICKEN

4-pound ready-to-cook chicken
2 tablespoons olive oil or salad oil
2 carrots, sliced
2 ribs celery, sliced
⅓ cup sliced onion
1 teaspoon salt
¼ teaspoon ground black pepper
¼ cup (½ stick) butter, melted
2 envelopes unflavored gelatin
½ cup cold water
1 cup pâté de foie gras
⅔ cup heavy cream, whipped
1 cup finely ground cooked or pickled tongue
2 cups Chaud-froid Sauce
1 tablespoon thick tomato purée
1 truffle
2 slices cooked tongue
12 baked tart shells (optional)

Brown chicken in hot oil in a Dutch oven over moderately high heat. Remove and set aside. Cook vegetables in the Dutch oven, over low heat, about 5 minutes without browning them, then return the chicken to the pot. Sprinkle with salt and pepper and pour melted butter over the top. Cover and cook in a preheated slow oven (325° F.) 1 hour or until chicken is done, basting 2 to 3 times with pan juices. Cool chicken.

Soften 1 envelope of the gelatin in ¼ cup cold water and melt over hot water (not boiling). Beat pâté de foie gras and blend in melted gelatin. Fold in half the cream. Stuff into the body cavity of the cold cooked chicken, filling one side. Make tongue mousse with the ground tongue, remaining gelatin, water, and cream. Stuff into the other side of the chicken's body cavity. Chill.

Divide Chaud-froid Sauce into two parts. Coat the side of the chicken filled with liver mousse with plain white Chaud-froid Sauce. Stir tomato purée into the other half of the sauce and coat the side of the chicken filled with tongue mousse. Slice truffles and cut into ¾-inch circles. Cut in half and place a row lengthwise down the center of the pink side of the chicken. Repeat on the white side of the chicken with tongue circles, same size and shape. Chill.

If desired, fill 6 small baked tart shells with pâté de foie gras mousse and 6 with tongue mousse. Coat half with white Chaud-froid Sauce and the remainder with pink Chaud-froid Sauce. Chill. Place on the platter around the chicken. Makes 6 servings. (See illustration, page 684.)

⚜ GLAZED CHICKEN MUGUETTE

4-pound ready-to-cook fat chicken
2 tablespoons butter
2 tablespoons olive oil or salad oil
1 carrot, peeled and sliced
1 medium-sized onion, peeled and sliced
1 rib, celery, sliced
1½ teaspoons salt
½ teaspoon ground black pepper
1 envelope unflavored gelatin
¼ cup water
2 cups finely ground cooked lean ham
1 cup ground goose liver
¼ cup (½ stick) softened butter
½ cup heavy cream, whipped
2 cups Chaud-froid Sauce
¼ cup tomato purée
aspic

Brown chicken in butter and oil in a Dutch oven over moderately high heat. Remove chicken and set aside. Put vegetables into Dutch oven, cover, and cook over low heat 5 minutes without browning. Return chicken to Dutch oven. Sprinkle with salt and pepper. Cover and cook in a slow oven (325° F.) 1½ hours or until chicken is done, basting occasionally with pan drippings. Remove chicken and allow to cool. Remove breast and breastbone from the cold cooked chicken. Soften gelatin in cold water, melt over hot water (not boiling), and add to ham and goose liver. Mix well. Add butter and salt and pepper to taste. Fold in whipped cream. Spoon it into the cavity of the cooked chicken. Cover chicken with Chaud-froid Sauce mixed with tomato purée. Chill until set. Decorate the breast with tarragon leaves or green pepper strips and whipped cream to simulate lily of the valley. Simulate the flower pot with a piece of tomato. Cut the breast that was removed into nice slices. Coat with Chaud-froid Sauce. Decorate with lily of the valley design and glaze with aspic. Chill. Arrange chicken on one end of tray and the breasts on the other end. Surround with cubed aspic. Makes 8 servings.

⚜ CHICKEN WITH CHAMBERTIN OR RIESLING

3- to 4-pound whole chicken, or 3 to 4 pounds chicken parts
2 teaspoons salt
½ teaspoon ground black pepper
2 tablespoons olive oil or salad oil
3 tablespoons butter
½ pound small mushroom caps
12 small white onions
2 shallots, chopped
½ cup Chambertin or Riesling
½ cup heavy cream
chopped parsley

Wash chicken and cut into 12 serving-size pieces, or, if desired, purchase 12 meaty pieces of chicken (legs, thighs, and breasts) weighing 3 to 4 pounds. Rub pieces with salt and pepper and brown on all sides in oil and butter, adding more as needed. Wash mushroom caps and add to the chicken. Peel onions and add. Cover and cook in a preheated slow oven (325° F.) 30 to 40 minutes, or until chicken is tender. Transfer chicken and vegetables to a warm serving dish and keep warm. Put shallots in the chicken pan and cook 1 to 2 minutes; do not brown. Add wine and simmer until reduced to half. Stir in cream and cook until sauce is creamy. Pour over chicken. Sprinkle with chopped parsley. Makes 6 servings. (See illustration, page 682.)

⚜ CHAUD-FROID CHICKEN LAMBERTYE

Truss a fat hen or capon and place it in a large saucepan with enough well-seasoned rich chicken stock to cover it. Cover the saucepan, bring the stock to boiling point, reduce heat and cook slowly about 1½ hours or until chicken is tender. (The cooking time depends upon the size and the age of the chicken.) Uncover the saucepan and cool the chicken in the stock. Transfer chicken to a pastry board or other flat surface and wipe it dry with paper towels. Make a circular incision around the breast and remove it. Fill the chicken's cavity with Foie Gras Mousse, rounding the top nicely to re-form the shape of the chicken. Cut the chicken breast into slices and place them over the mousse. Coat the whole chicken with white Chaud-froid Sauce and chill it until sauce has set. Then coat with aspic and chill again until aspic is firm. Decorate as desired with shapes cut from truffles or cold cooked tongue. Glaze with aspic again and chill. If desired cut cooked ham slices in oval-shaped pieces the size of a goose egg. Cover each with a dome of Foie Gras Mousse. Coat with white Chaud-froid Sauce and chill until sauce has set. Decorate as desired with shapes cut from truffles or cold cooked tongue and coat them with aspic. Chill until aspic is set. Cover the bottom of a large serving tray with chopped jellied aspic and arrange the chicken and the simulated eggs on the aspic. Makes approximately 6 servings. For a more fanciful presentation, see illustration, page 685.

⚜ DEVILED SPRING CHICKEN (*Poulet de Grain à la Diable*)

In England chickens of this size are sometimes called asparagus chicken, because the chickens reach this weight at about the time fresh asparagus comes in season in the spring.

1 ready-to-cook young chicken, 1½ to 2 pounds
½ teaspoon salt
⅛ teaspoon ground black pepper
dash cayenne
¼ teaspoon powdered mustard
3 tablespoons fine dry breadcrumbs
3 tablespoons butter
4 strips crisply fried bacon
parsley
Sauce Diable

Cut chicken in half lengthwise, trim off the vertebrae, and spread chicken out flat. Pull out any bones that can be easily removed. Beat chicken with a mallet or the flat side of a cleaver. Sprinkle with salt and pepper. Place in a buttered baking pan in a preheated very hot oven (450° F.) and cook 20 minutes or until about half done. Remove from oven. Mix cayenne and mustard with breadcrumbs, sprinkle over chicken, and dot with butter. Place under broiler heat for about 10 minutes to finish cooking. Transfer to a warmed platter and top with strips of crisp bacon. Garnish platter with parsley. Serve Sauce Diable in a sauceboat. Makes 2 servings. (See illustration, page 676; also Culinary Techniques in Pictures.)

⚜ SAUTÉED CHICKEN PORTUGUESE STYLE

3- to 3½-pound ready-to-cook young chicken
salt
ground black pepper
6 tablespoons butter
½ cup dry white wine
1½ cups small mushrooms
1 tablespoon chopped onion
½ teaspoon sugar
1 cup drained canned tomatoes
3 Mushroom-Stuffed Tomatoes
chopped parsley

Cut chicken into serving-size pieces and rub with salt and pepper. Melt 4 tablespoons of the butter and dip chicken pieces in it. Place in a baking dish and pour the wine over. Cook in a preheated moderate oven (350° F.) 1 hour or until tender, basting frequently. Remove from oven and let cool in the cooking liquid. Sauté mushrooms and onion in the remaining 2 tablespoons butter. Add sugar and tomatoes and season with salt and pepper to taste. Cook 5 minutes. Heat the chicken in the cooking liquid and remove to a warmed platter. Cover with the mushroom and tomato mixture. Arrange Mushroom-Stuffed Tomatoes on the platter and garnish the platter with chopped parsley. Makes 6 servings. (See illustration, page 680.)

⚜ SAUTÉED CHICKEN FORESTIÈRE

3- to 4-pound ready-to-cook young chicken, cut in serving pieces
1½ teaspoons salt
½ teaspoon ground black pepper
½ pound morels or mushrooms
6 tablespoons butter
½ cup dry white wine
¾ cup Demi-Glace Sauce
chopped parsley

Rub chicken with salt and black pepper and set aside. Wash and slice morels or mushrooms and cook in 2 tablespoons of the butter, draining off liquid as it forms in the pan and reserving it. Add 2 tablespoons butter. Add chicken and brown on both sides, continuing to cook the morels or mushrooms all the while, adding remaining butter as needed. Transfer chicken and morels or mushrooms to a warmed platter and keep hot. Pour wine and Demi-Glace into the skillet. Stir and cook until the liquid has thickened to sauce consistency. Adjust seasonings and pour over chicken. Sprinkle with chopped parsley. Makes 6 servings. (See illustration, page 678.)

⚜ CHICKEN STANLEY

3-pound ready-to-cook chicken, cut into serving pieces
2 cups sliced onions
¼ cup (½ stick) butter
1 teaspoon curry powder
1½ cups sliced mushrooms
1 cup heavy cream
dash cayenne
1½ teaspoons salt
1 tablespoon lemon juice
1 truffle, sliced
half-moon-shaped biscuits or croissants (optional)

Cook the chicken and onions in the butter about 15 minutes. Add the curry powder and cook 3 to 4 minutes. Add the mushrooms and cook 3 to 4 minutes more. Add next 4 ingredients. Cover and cook in a preheated moderate oven (350° F.) 30 minutes or until chicken is tender. Turn into a warmed platter. Garnish with sliced truffles. If desired, serve with half-moon-shaped rich biscuits or croissants. Makes 6 servings. (See illustration, page 677.)

MUSHROOM-STUFFED TOMATOES

- ¼ pound mushrooms (caps and stems)
- 2 tablespoons chopped onion
- 1 tablespoon butter
- 2 shallots, finely chopped
- salt and ground black pepper to taste
- 1/16 teaspoon ground nutmeg
- 3 medium-sized tomatoes
- ½ cup buttered soft breadcrumbs

Wash mushrooms and chop very fine. Put them in a cloth and squeeze or extract all the liquid possible. Lightly brown onion in butter. Add mushrooms and shallots. Stir and cook over a moderately high heat to evaporate all moisture left in the mushrooms. Season with salt, pepper, and nutmeg. Cut tomatoes in half. Scoop out centers, sprinkle cavities with salt and pepper, and invert on a plate to drain. Fill with the mushroom mixture. Sprinkle with breadcrumbs. Brown in a preheated hot oven (400° F.) 10 to 12 minutes. Makes 6 servings.

⚜ VIENNESE FRIED CHICKEN

- 2½-pound ready-to-cook chicken
- 4 chicken livers
- 2 teaspoons salt
- ¼ teaspoon ground black pepper
- 2 eggs, beaten
- ½ cup fine dry breadcrumbs
- 4 lemon slices
- parsley

Cut chicken into quarters, wash, and wipe dry. Sprinkle chicken and chicken livers with salt and pepper and dip in beaten egg and then in breadcrumbs. Fry chicken pieces in deep fat preheated to 350° F. until browned, then fry chicken livers. Drain on paper towels. Put on a warmed platter and garnish with lemon slices and parsley. Serve a quarter of chicken and a chicken liver to each person. Makes 4 servings.

⚜ CHICKEN FRICASEE

- 4-pound ready-to-cook fricasee chicken
- 1 teaspoon salt
- flour
- 3 to 4 tablespoons butter
- 2 cups chicken broth
- 1 carrot, peeled and sliced
- 1 rib celery, sliced
- 1 sprig parsley
- 5 peppercorns
- 1 small bay leaf
- 12 peeled whole white onions
- ¼ pound mushrooms
- ½ teaspoon dried marjoram
- ¼ teaspoon dried rosemary
- 2 egg yolks
- ⅓ cup heavy cream
- 1 teaspoon lemon juice
- heart-shaped croutons

Wash chicken and cut into 12 pieces (include neck and gizzard). Rub with salt and dredge in flour. Brown lightly over moderate heat in butter, adding butter as needed. Heat broth to simmering in a large saucepan and add chicken, along with the next 5 ingredients. Cover and simmer 45 minutes or until chicken is tender. Transfer chicken to a warmed platter and keep hot. Strain stock and return it to the saucepan. Add onions, cover, and cook until onions are tender, about 30 minutes. Wash mushrooms, chop stems, and leave caps whole. Add to the broth 5 minutes before cooking time is up. Return chicken to saucepan, add herbs, and cook 5 minutes. Blend egg yolks with cream, add to the broth, and heat 1 minute. Add lemon juice. Adjust salt. Put chicken in a serving dish, pour sauce over it, and garnish with heart-shaped croutons. Makes 6 servings.

⚜ CHICKEN PILAF ORIENTAL STYLE

3-pound ready-to-cook chicken
salt
ground black pepper
6 tablespoons butter
½ cup chopped onions
1 cup long-grain converted rice
2½ cups hot chicken stock or water
¼ teaspoon crumbled saffron strands
1 large sweet green pepper, cut into strips
2 quartered, peeled, and seeded tomatoes
¼ teaspoon ground black pepper

Cut chicken into 11 pieces (omit gizzard) and rub with salt and pepper. Brown on both sides over moderate heat in 4 tablespoons of the butter, along with the onions. Meanwhile soak rice 30 minutes in cold water to cover. Drain and cook in remaining 2 tablespoons butter until it begins to stick to the bottom of the pan. Add to the chicken, along with 1 teaspoon salt and the remaining ingredients. Turn into a 2-quart casserole. Cover and bake in a preheated moderate oven (350° F.) 20 to 25 minutes, or until chicken and rice are tender and the rice has absorbed most of the liquid. Serve with the chicken arranged over the rice. Makes 6 servings. (See illustration, page 678.)

⚜ BROWNED BREASTS OF CHICKEN
(*Suprêmes de Volaille à Brun*)

3 boned chicken breasts
salt
ground black pepper
⅓ cup butter

Skin and halve chicken breasts and remove wing tips but not the main wing bones. Sprinkle with salt and black pepper and dredge lightly in flour. Cook in butter in a heavy skillet until chicken is browned, 20 to 25 minutes, adding butter as needed. Makes 6 servings. (See Culinary Techniques in Pictures.)

⚜ CHICKEN BREASTS WITH CURRY SAUCE
(*Suprêmes de Volaille à l'Indienne*)

1 recipe for Browned Breasts of Chicken
3 cups fluffy cooked rice
1½ cups Curry Sauce

Prepare the recipe for Browned Breasts of Chicken. Arrange the cooked breasts in a crown on a heated platter. Fill center with rice. Heat Curry Sauce and spoon over the breasts. Makes 6 servings.

⚜ POACHED BREASTS OF CHICKEN
(*Suprêmes de Volaille à Blanc*)

This is really baked, not poached, but since it is not browned the chicken looks like poached chicken.

3 boned chicken breasts
salt
ground black pepper
¼ cup (½ stick) butter, melted
½ lemon
chopped parsley

Skin and halve the chicken breasts and remove wing tips but not the main wing bones. Sprinkle with salt and ground black pepper and dip in melted butter. Arrange breasts in an 11- by 7- by 1½-inch baking dish. Sprinkle with the juice of ½ lemon. Bake in a preheated very hot oven (450° F.) 10 to 12 minutes or until breasts are tender but not browned. Sprinkle with chopped parsley. Makes 6 servings.

⚜ CHICKEN BREASTS FLORENTINE

1 recipe Poached Breasts of Chicken
1½ pounds spinach, cooked
4 tablespoons (½ stick) butter
1/16 teaspoon ground nutmeg
⅛ teaspoon ground black pepper
salt to taste
Mornay Sauce
½ cup grated Parmesan cheese

Make the recipe for Poached Breasts of Chicken. Toss the spinach with 2 tablespoons of the butter and the seasonings and spread it over the bottom of an 11- by 7- by 1½-inch baking dish. Put the cooked chicken breasts on top. Spread with Mornay Sauce, sprinkle with the cheese, and dot with bits of butter, using the remaining 2 tablespoons. Place under broiler heat to warm and melt cheese. Makes 6 servings.

⚜ BREASTS OF CHICKEN WITH MUSHROOMS

1 recipe Poached Breasts of Chicken
12 mushroom caps
2 tablespoons butter
salt
ground black pepper
1½ cups Allemande Sauce

Make the recipe for Poached Breasts of Chicken. Wash mushroom caps and remove stems. Sauté the caps in butter and arrange 2 on each chicken breast. Place the breasts on a warmed platter. Set aside to keep warm. Drain the butter that was left in the pan in which chicken was cooked into the liquid left from sautéeing mushrooms. Add the Allemande Sauce. Heat and spoon over chicken. Makes 6 servings.

⚜ BREASTS OF CHICKEN WITH BRANDY

3 boned chicken breasts
salt
ground black pepper
½ teaspoon dried or 1½ teaspoon chopped fresh thyme
¼ cup (½ stick) butter
¼ cup brandy
1 cup heavy cream
1¼ teaspoons paprika
toast points
cooked asparagus tips
1 truffle, chopped (optional)

Skin and halve chicken breasts and remove wing tips but not the main wing bone. Sprinkle with salt, pepper, and thyme and dredge in flour. Cook breasts in a heavy skillet in butter, adding the butter as needed, *only* until lightly browned (not cooked through the center). Heat brandy, pour over chicken, and ignite. Add cream, cover, and simmer 15 minutes, turning the breasts once. Add paprika and adjust seasonings. Arrange the breasts in a warmed platter and surround with toast points. Garnish with asparagus tips. Strain sauce over the chicken and asparagus. Sprinkle with chopped truffle, if desired. Makes 6 servings.

⚜ CHICKEN KIEV

3 boned chicken breasts, with or without wing bones attached
salt
ground black pepper
½ cup (1 stick) butter
6 teaspoons chopped chives
flour
2 eggs, lightly beaten
about 1 cup soft breadcrumbs

Cut chicken breasts in half and place each between pieces of waxed paper. Pound until they are thin with a mallet or the flat side of a cleaver, being careful not to break through the meat. Remove and discard waxed paper. Sprinkle with salt and pepper. Cut butter into 6 pieces of equal length and width. Freeze or chill until very firm. Place one piece in the middle of each chicken breast. Sprinkle each with 1 teaspoon chopped chives. Roll up envelope style, sides and ends overlapping. (It is not necessary to tie or pin the meat in place with skewers.) Dredge rolls in flour, dip in beaten egg, and roll in crumbs. Refrigerate at least one hour so crumbs will adhere. Fry 2 rolls at a time in deep fat preheated to 370° F. until browned. Drain on paper towels. Serve at once. Makes 6 servings.

⚜ CHICKEN BREASTS MARYLAND STYLE

3 boned chicken breasts
salt
ground black pepper
flour
2 eggs, lightly beaten
about 1 cup soft breadcrumbs
3 tablespoons olive oil or salad oil
3 tablespoons butter
6 slices ham
6 Fried Bananas
6 Corn Croquettes
6 Grilled Whole Tomatoes
Horseradish Sauce

Cut chicken breasts in half. Remove wing tips but not the main wing bone. Sprinkle with salt and pepper, dredge in flour, dip in eggs and roll in crumbs. Fry until browned in oil and butter. Fry ham. Arrange chicken and ham on a warmed platter. Garnish with Fried Bananas, Corn Croquettes and Grilled Tomatoes. Serve with Horseradish Sauce. Makes 6 servings. (See illustration, page 675.)

FRIED BANANAS

Peel 6 bananas. Cut in half lengthwise or leave whole. Brush with lemon juice and cook in butter over low heat 3 to 4 minutes. Sprinkle with 1 tablespoon sherry. Makes 6 servings.

CORN CROQUETTES

Combine 1 cup corn cut off the cob, or 1 cup well-drained whole-kernel canned corn, chopped, with ⅓ cup Béchamel Sauce. Season to taste with salt and ground black pepper. Chill. Shape into 6 flat round croquettes. Dip in beaten egg and roll in fine dry breadcrumbs. Let stand 20 minutes for crumbs to adhere. Fry in shallow fat or in deep fat preheated to 375° F. Makes 6 croquettes.

GRILLED WHOLE TOMATOES

Make 4 or 5 crisscross cuts in the bud ends of 6 whole medium-sized tomatoes. Sprinkle each with salt and ground black pepper, and top with ½ pat of butter. Cook 3 to 4 minutes under broiler heat. Makes 6 servings.

⚜ BREASTS OF CHICKEN SANDEMAN

3 boned breasts of chicken
salt
ground black pepper
6 tablespoons butter
¼ cup brandy or whisky
1 cup heavy cream
1 tablespoon meat glaze
2 tablespoons sherry
1 canned pimiento

Skin and halve chicken breasts and remove wing tips but not the main wing bone. Sprinkle with salt and pepper. Cook breasts in a heavy skillet in 2 tablespoons of the butter until browned. Transfer chicken to a warmed platter. Add brandy or whisky to the skillet, heat, and ignite. Pour in cream and meat glaze and simmer about 5 minutes. Add sherry, heat, and pour over chicken. Garnish the center with pimiento cut in julienne strips. Serve rice in a separate bowl. Makes 6 servings. (See illustration, page 679.)

⚜ BREASTS OF CHICKEN SPANISH STYLE

2 chicken breasts
salt
ground black pepper
8 tablespoons (1 stick) butter
1 cup long-grain converted rice
water to cover
½ cup chopped onion
¼ teaspoon crumbled saffron
¼ cup each sliced red and green sweet peppers
1 cup raw green peas
2½ cups chicken stock
2 tablespoons flour
1½ cups chicken or veal stock
1½ cups Tomato Fondue

Rub chicken breasts with salt and pepper. Melt 3 tablespoons of the butter and brush some of it over the chicken. Place chicken in a buttered baking pan and bake in a preheated moderate oven (350° F.) 50 minutes, or until breasts are tender, basting frequently with melted butter. Meanwhile, soak rice 30 minutes in water to cover. Drain off water and cook rice in 2 tablespoons of the butter until it is dry and sticks to the bottom of the pan. Add

2 more tablespoons butter and the chopped onion. Stir and cook until onions are limp. Add saffron, ½ teaspoon salt, green and red peppers, peas, and chicken stock. Cover and cook 12 to 15 minutes. Slice chicken breasts into 6 servings and place on a warmed platter. Melt the remaining 1 tablespoon butter in the chicken pan drippings. Blend in flour. Stir and cook 1 minute. Remove from heat and add chicken or veal stock. Stir and cook until sauce has slightly thickened. Season to taste with salt and pepper and spoon over chicken. Serve remaining sauce in a separate dish. Garnish the dish with the rice mixture and Tomato Fondue. Serve hot. Makes 6 servings. (See illustration, page 677.)

⚜ STUFFED CHICKEN BREASTS

3 breasts of chicken, boned and halved
salt
ground black pepper
1½ cups chicken or veal forcemeat with panada

Place chicken breasts between waxed paper and pound until thin with a mallet or the flat side of a cleaver, being careful not to split the breasts. Remove waxed paper. Sprinkle breasts with salt and pepper and place ¼ cup forcemeat in the middle of each breast. Roll up in envelope style. (Do not tie or pin with skewers.) Place rolls in a generously buttered baking dish and top each with a pat of butter. Cover and cook in a preheated moderate oven (350° F.) 35 minutes, basting with pan juices, and with additional butter if chicken tends to be dry. Remove cover and cook 15 minutes or until breasts are golden brown. Makes 6 servings.

VARIATION

STUFFED CHICKEN BREASTS WITH WINE

In recipe for Stuffed Chicken Breasts, baste chicken with ½ cup dry white wine during the first 35 minutes of cooking.

⚜ CHICKEN BREASTS WITH SAVORY STUFFING

3 chicken breasts, boned and halved
salt
ground black pepper
Savory Stuffing
3 tablespoons butter
1 cup chicken stock
1½ teaspoons cornstarch
2 tablespoons dry white wine
¼ cup heavy cream

Place chicken breasts between waxed paper and pound until thin with a mallet or the flat side of a cleaver, being careful not to split the breasts. Remove waxed paper. Sprinkle breasts with salt and pepper and place ¼ cup Savory Stuffing in the middle of each breast. Roll up envelope style, overlapping the sides and ends of meat. Sprinkle both sides with salt and pepper and dredge in flour. Brown on all sides in butter over moderate heat. Arrange chicken breasts in a buttered 11- by 7- by 1½-inch baking dish and pour chicken stock over them. Cover and bake in a preheated moderate oven (350° F.) 30 minutes, basting with chicken stock that is in the baking dish. Remove cover and bake 15 to 20 minutes. Mix cornstarch with wine and thicken the stock that is left in the pan. Add cream and heat. Adjust seasonings. Serve over chicken. Makes 6 servings.

SAVORY STUFFING

Combine 2 cups soft white breadcrumbs with ¼ teaspoon each dried savory, thyme, and marjoram, ⅛ teaspoon ground black pepper, ¼ teaspoon salt, 1 tablespoon each finely chopped onion and parsley, ¼ cup butter, melted, and 3 tablespoons water or chicken stock. Makes enough for 6 servings.

⚜ CHICKEN AND HAM ASPIC MERCÉDÈS

1½ quarts chicken aspic
1 3-pound chicken, poached and boned
baked ham slices
salt to taste
⅛ teaspoon ground white pepper
1 cup heavy cream, whipped
1 or 2 truffles or large black olives
aspic triangles
2 hard-cooked egg whites

Coat the inside of a 1½-quart mold with liquid aspic and chill until set. Cut chicken in crosswise slices about ¼ inch thick. Trim an equal number of ham slices to the same size. Set aside. Reserve trimmings. From remaining chicken, cut enough in small pieces to make 2 cups when added to ham trimmings. Put through a food chopper, using the finest blade, and add to 2 cups of the chicken aspic. Add salt and pepper. Chill until mixture begins to set. (If mousse does not set, add 1 envelope unflavored gelatin, softened in ¼ cup cold water and melted over hot water.) Fold in whipped cream. Decorate the center of the bottom of the mold with truffles and hard-cooked egg whites cut in petal shapes. Using a pastry bag, pipe the mousse on enough ham and chicken slices to surround the egg and truffle decoration, and place them mousse side up, alternating ham and chicken slices. Chill until set. Pour in a layer of aspic and chill. Arrange alternating chicken and ham slices topped with aspic around the sides of the mold. Finish filling mold with half-set aspic. Chill until firm and ready to use. Unmold on a large tray. Garnish with aspic triangles. Makes 8 servings. (See illustration, page 686.)

⚜ CHAUD-FROID OF CHICKEN BREASTS

3 boned chicken breasts
water
½ teaspoon salt
1 quart white Chaud-froid Sauce
1 truffle, or 2 large black olives
1 quart aspic
6 Cucumber Cups Filled with Ham Salad
1 tomato cup filled with ham salad

Poach chicken breasts in simmering water, with salt, until they are tender, 30 to 40 minutes. Cool. Remove skins from the breasts, cut in half, and trim the meat into uniform ovals. Coat breasts with half-set Chaud-froid Sauce and chill until the sauce is set. Decorate each oval as desired with truffle or olive cutouts. Glaze with half-set aspic. Chill until set. To serve, arrange the ovals of chicken breasts on a serving dish and surround with diced aspic, or, if desired, fill cucumber cups with ham salad and place on the tray. Garnish center of tray with a tomato filled with salad. Makes 6 servings. (See illustration, page 683.)

⚜ CHICKEN CUTLETS

1 cup soft breadcrumbs
½ cup milk
3 cups ground raw chicken breasts
1 teaspoon salt
¼ teaspoon ground white pepper
½ teaspoon dried or 1½ teaspoons chopped fresh thyme
½ cup (1 stick) butter
¼ cup heavy cream
flour
about 4 tablespoons butter

Soak bread in milk 15 minutes. Drain and squeeze out the excess milk. Fluff the crumbs with a fork and mix well with the next 6 ingredients. Divide the mixture into 6 equal portions and mold into shapes resembling chicken breasts. (Chill mixture before shaping if it seems too soft.) Dredge in flour and brown, over moderate heat, in butter, adding butter as needed. Makes 6 servings.

⚜ CURRIED CHICKEN

1⅓ cups chopped onion
1 clove of garlic, crushed
¼ cup peanut oil or ghee
1 teaspoon turmeric
1 teaspoon ground cumin seeds
½ teaspoon ground ginger
½ teaspoon ground black pepper
½ teaspoon ground mustard seeds
3 teaspoons ground coriander seeds
⅛ to ¼ teaspoon ground red pepper
1 stick cinnamon, 2 inches long
3 pounds chicken legs and breasts
3 teaspoons salt
1 cup hot water
1 teaspoon lemon juice
3 to 4 cups fluffy hot rice

Stir and cook onions and garlic in hot oil or ghee (clarified butter) 2 to 3 minutes. Add turmeric and cook over moderately low heat about 10 minutes, or until onions are very soft, stirring constantly to prevent the turmeric from scorching. Add remaining spices and stir, and cook 2 to 3 minutes. Rub chicken with 2 teaspoons of the salt, add to onion mixture, and cook over moderate heat 10 to 15 minutes, or until chicken is lightly browned. Add remaining salt and 1 cup hot water. Cover and cook 50 minutes, or until chicken is tender and the gravy thickens. Remove the cover the last 5 minutes of cooking period. Remove and discard the cinnamon stick. Stir in lemon juice just before serving. Serve with hot fluffy rice. Makes 6 servings.

⚜ ANGLO-INDIAN CHICKEN CURRY

1 cup chopped onion
1 small clove garlic, mashed
¼ cup butter or peanut oil
1 teaspoon ground turmeric
1 teaspoon ground ginger
1½ teaspoons ground cumin
½ teaspoon ground black pepper
½ teaspoon ground cardamom
¼ teaspoon ground red pepper
3 pounds chicken legs and breasts
2 cups water
1½ teaspoons salt
2 tablespoons ground coriander
¼ cup Coconut Milk (or ¼ cup undiluted evaporated milk)
1 teaspoon lemon juice
Rice à l'Indienne
¼ cup toasted sliced blanched almonds

Stir and cook onions and garlic in butter or peanut oil until the onions are wilted. Add the next 6 ingredients. Stir and cook 10 minutes over moderate heat. Add chicken, a few pieces at a time, and brown lightly on all sides, adding more oil if needed. Add water, salt, and coriander. Cover and cook 30 minutes or until chicken is tender. The sauce should be well reduced; if it is not, remove cover and cook slowly until the sauce has thickened. Add coconut milk or evaporated milk and lemon juice just before serving. Heat but do not boil. Serve on Rice à l'Indienne. Garnish with toasted almonds. Makes 6 servings.

RICE À L'INDIENNE

- 1 cup rice
- water to cover
- 2 tablespoons butter
- ¼ cup chopped onion
- ½ small bay leaf
- 1-inch piece of stick cinnamon
- 5 peppercorns
- 3 little black seeds from a cardamom seed pod
- 2¼ cups chicken stock

Soak rice 30 minutes in water to cover. Drain and cook in butter, without browning, until the rice is dry and sticks to the bottom of the pan. Add onion and cook until limp. Add remaining ingredients. Cover and cook slowly over direct heat about 12 minutes, or in a preheated moderate oven (350° F.) 15 to 17 minutes. The rice is done when it has absorbed all the stock and every grain separates. Remove spices before serving. Serve with curry. Makes 6 servings.

COCONUT MILK

Heat a whole coconut in a very slow oven (275° F.) half an hour. Punch holes in the eyes, drain out coconut water, crack the shell, and remove the coconut meat with a pointed paring knife. Trim off the brown coat. Grate coconut meat or put it through a food chopper and soak 1 cup in 1 cup boiling water ½ hour. Strain through cheesecloth, squeezing out all the liquid. Makes 1 cup of coconut milk.

⚜ CHICKEN MARENGO

- about 3½ pounds chicken legs and breasts
- 2 teaspoons salt
- ½ teaspoon ground black pepper
- flour
- ¼ cup olive oil or salad oil
- 3 tablespoons butter
- 1 cup chicken stock or water
- 12 small white onions, peeled
- ½ cup sliced green pepper
- 1 cup well-drained Italian canned tomatoes, or 4 peeled, seeded, and quartered fresh tomatoes
- ½ cup pitted black olives
- ⅛ teaspoon ground allspice
- ¼ pound sliced mushrooms
- ½ cup dry white wine

Rub chicken with 1 teaspoon of the salt and black pepper. Dredge in flour. Brown in 1/4 cup oil and 2 tablespoons butter. Add the next 6 ingredients. Cover and simmer 45 minutes or until chicken is tender. Sauté mushrooms in remaining 1 tablespoon butter and add to chicken along with wine 5 minutes before cooking time is up. Adjust seasonings. Serve with rice. Makes 6 servings.

⚜ TUSCAN FRIED CHICKEN (*Italian*)

3 pounds chicken legs and breasts
2 teaspoons salt
½ teaspoon ground black pepper
2 large eggs, beaten
¾ cup fine dry breadcrumbs mixed with ¾ cup grated Parmesan cheese
⅓ cup olive oil or salad oil
6 lemon slices
parsley

Wash chicken parts and wipe dry. Rub with salt and pepper. Dip in beaten eggs and then in mixture of breadcrumbs and cheese. Fry in hot olive oil or salad oil until chicken is browned on all sides and is tender. Serve garnished with lemon slices and parsley. Makes 6 servings.

⚜ CHICKEN AND RICE VALENCIANA (*Spanish*)

2½ pounds chicken thighs, drumsticks, and breasts
½ pound lean pork, cubed
4 tablespoons olive oil or salad oil
¾ cup chopped onions
1 small clove garlic, crushed
1½ cups long-grain converted rice
3 tablespoons butter or olive oil
3 tablespoons salt
½ teaspoon ground black pepper
½ teaspoon crumbled saffron
4 cups chicken stock
½ pound cooked lobster chunks
12 sautéed frogs' legs (optional)
8 artichoke bottoms, quartered
parsley
1 pimiento or 1 tomato

Brown chicken and pork in 1 tablespoon oil in a heavy skillet over moderate heat. Transfer to a 9- by 13- by 2-inch baking dish. Add onions and garlic. Meanwhile, soak rice 30 minutes in water to cover, drain, and cook in remaining 3 tablespoons oil until rice is dry and sticks to the bottom of the pan. Add to the baking dish. Add seasonings to chicken stock and pour over chicken, pork, and rice. Cover and cook in a preheated slow oven (325° F.) for 1 hour. Add lobster, frogs' legs (if used), peas, and artichoke bottoms. Mix *very lightly* with the rice, tossing with a fork. Cover and bake 15 minutes. Garnish with parsley and pimiento or tomato strips. If this dish tends to be too dry, add a little stock. Makes 8 servings.

⚜ CHICKEN ARCHDUKE STYLE

6 chicken legs with thighs (about 3 pounds)
2 teaspoons salt
½ teaspoon ground black pepper
¼ cup (½ stick) butter
⅓ cup white port
⅓ cup brandy
½ cup Béchamel Sauce
½ cup heavy cream
6 truffle slices
6 servings cooked asparagus tips
1 tablespoon butter, melted
6 strips pimiento

Rub the chicken legs with salt and half the pepper. Cook them in the butter in a heavy skillet, without browning, about 15 to 20 minutes. Cover and cook in a preheated moderate oven (350° F.) until chicken is tender. Transfer chicken to a warmed platter and keep hot. Pour port and brandy in the skillet and cook 2 to 3 minutes. Add Béchamel Sauce and cream. Stir and cook until the sauce has thickened slightly. Add remaining pepper and adjust salt. Spoon over chicken. Garnish with truffle slices. Pour melted butter over asparagus and arrange it in serving-size portions on the platter around the chicken. Garnish asparagus with pimiento. Makes 6 servings. (See illustration, page 683.)

⚜ STUFFED CHICKEN LEGS REGENCY STYLE
(*Ballottines de Volaille à la Regence*)

6 large chicken legs (drumsticks)
2 cups Quenelle Forcemeat with Panada
½ cup julienne strips boiled tongue or pickled tongue
stock made from chicken bones and veal bones
2 tablespoons butter
2 tablespoons flour
¼ cup heavy cream
salt
ground black pepper
6 sautéed artichoke bottoms
½ cup sautéed mushrooms
6 pitted green olives
Madeira Sauce
6 truffle slices

Bone the chicken legs or have the butcher do it for you. Stuff them with Quenelle Forcemeat and tongue strips. Wrap each leg separately in cheesecloth. Make a rich stock from the chicken bones and veal bones. Simmer the stuffed chicken legs in the stock, allowing 18 minutes per pound of chicken. Set aside and keep warm. Melt the butter in a saucepan, remove from heat, and blend in flour. Stir and cook 1 minute, remove from heat, and add ¾ cup of the stock in which the chicken legs were cooked. Cook until sauce has thickened, stirring constantly. Add the cream and salt and pepper to taste. Reserve. Fill the artichoke bottoms with the mushrooms. Top each with a pitted olive that has been rinsed in boiling water and mask with Madeira Sauce. Arrange artichoke bottoms in the center of a serving platter. Unwrap the chicken legs, place them at the ends of the platter, spoon Madeira Sauce over them, and put a truffle slice on each. Makes 6 servings. (See illustration, page 679.)

⚜ VOL-AU-VENT OF CHICKEN, MODERN STYLE

Puff Pastry (see page 127)
2 eggs, beaten

Chicken Ragout

Make a double recipe of Puff Pastry. Roll one-fourth of the dough into a 10-inch circle ⅛ inch thick. Cut out a 9-inch circle, using a round 9-inch cake pan as a guide. (Save all the trimmings of the dough to use later.) Place the dough on a baking sheet and prick it all over with a fork to permit it to rise uniformly. Make a ball of paper 6 inches in diameter, wrap it in tissue paper or foil, and tie it with string. (For this and the following procedures, see Culinary Techniques in Pictures.) Place the ball in the center of the circle of dough. Brush the edges of the dough with water. Roll one-half of the remaining dough into a 13-inch circle ⅛ inch thick and cut it into a 12-inch circle, using a 12-inch plate as a guide. Fit the dough over the paper ball and press the edges down well all around the circle. Brush the entire surface with beaten egg. Roll one-half of the remaining dough ⅛ inch thick. Cut out strips ½ inch wide and long enough to reach across the top of the dome and to the edges on both sides. Roll the rest of the dough into a 10-inch circle. Cut out a 9-inch circle, from which cut a ring 1 inch wide. Place this ring around the dome. Roll all the reserved trimmings of the dough ⅛ inch thick and cut into circles, crescents, and rings, using scalloped cooky cutters and a pastry cutter. Place these cutouts as desired on the puff-paste dome and around the edge. Prick the paste with a fine needle in several places. Brush the entire surface with beaten egg.

Bake the vol-au-vent in a preheated hot oven (400° F.) 20 to 25 minutes. If the puff paste tends to brown too much, cover it with foil or brown paper. Remove the vol-au-vent from the oven and cool. Using a sharp-pointed knife, cut around the edge of the dome, being careful not to cut the base crust. Carefully lift up the dome and set it aside. Remove and discard the paper ball. Fill the center of the vol-au-vent with Chicken Ragout. Cover with the baked puff paste dome. For a more fanciful presentation see illustration, page 291. Makes 8 servings.

CHICKEN RAGOUT

- 2 cups sliced mushrooms
- 1 tablespoon finely chopped onion
- 2 tablespoons butter
- 3 cups cubed cooked chicken
- 2 tablespoons chopped parsley
- 2 cups Mornay Sauce
- ½ truffle, diced (optional)
- salt to taste
- ground black pepper to taste

Sauté mushrooms and onion in butter 5 minutes. Add the remaining ingredients. Stir and cook the mixture until it is hot. Serve on rice or in patty shells or use to fill a large vol-au-vent. Makes 8 servings.

⚜ CHICKEN SUKIYAKI (*Japanese*)

- 2 cups green onions, cut into 1-inch pieces
- 1 cup white meat from broiler-size chicken, cut into thin julienne strips
- 1 tablespoon chicken fat or butter
- 1 tablespoon soy sauce
- 2 tablespoons sugar
- 2 cups sliced celery
- 1 cup thinly sliced water chestnuts
- 1 cup thinly sliced bamboo shoots
- 1 cup sliced mushrooms
- ¼ pound young whole spinach leaves
- 2 squares bean curd (optional)
- rice wine, sherry, or chicken broth

Cook onions and chicken in chicken fat or butter about 5 minutes over high heat. Sprinkle with soy sauce and sugar. Toss. Add all remaining ingredients except wine or broth. Toss. Reduce heat to moderate. Cook 4 to 5 minutes, adding wine or broth as needed to prevent the ingredients from becoming too dry. There should be very little liquid in the pan. Serve hot with fluffy cooked rice. Makes 4 servings.

⚜ CHICKEN QUENELLES ISABELLA

- 2½ cups Chicken Forcemeat with Panada
- chicken or veal stock, or slightly salted water
- croutons
- 2 tablespoons butter
- 2 tablespoons flour
- ¾ cup chicken stock
- ¼ cup heavy cream
- ½ teaspoon salt
- dash ground white pepper
- ½ teaspoon meat extract
- 2 tablespoons chopped cooked tongue
- 1 small truffle, finely chopped

Pass forcemeat through a fine sieve and shape into quenelles, either with tablespoons, by rolling on a floured board, or by filling buttered small barquette molds (oval-shaped tart pans) with the forcemeat. Poach 15 to 20 minutes in a deep skillet containing 3 to 4 inches barely simmering slightly salted water, or chicken or veal stock, never allowing the liquid to boil. Remove quenelles from the liquid and drain well. Arrange on croutons the same size and shape as the quenelles. Meanwhile, melt the butter in a 3-cup saucepan, remove from heat, and blend in flour. Stir and cook 1 minute. Add stock and cook 2 minutes or until thickened. Blend in cream, salt, pepper, and meat extract. Heat and spoon over quenelles. Sprinkle with chopped tongue and truffle. Makes 6 servings. (See illustration, page 680.)

⚜ CHICKEN QUENELLES IN TARRAGON SAUCE

1 recipe for Chicken Quenelles Isabella, omitting tongue and truffles
½ teaspoon dried or 1½ teaspoons chopped fresh tarragon
12 slices sautéed mushrooms
tarragon or parsley leaves

Make the recipe for Chicken Quenelles Isabella, and place the quenelles on croutons as directed. Arrange on a warmed platter. Make the sauce as directed, season it with tarragon, and spoon over quenelles. Decorate each with a mushroom slice and a cross of tarragon or parsley leaves. Makes 6 servings.

⚜ GIBLETS WITH MUSHROOMS

½ cup sliced onions
3 cups sliced mushrooms
¼ cup (½ stick) butter
½ pound raw chicken livers or turkey livers
½ pound cooked chicken or turkey gizzards and hearts
salt and ground black pepper to taste
½ cup dry white wine
5 slices toasted white bread
parsley

Sauté onions and mushrooms in butter until vegetables are tender, stirring frequently. Cut chicken livers in half, or turkey livers in quarters, and add. Slice gizzards and hearts and add. Stir and cook 3 to 4 minutes. Season to taste with salt and pepper. Add wine and cook 3 minutes. Serve on toast. Garnish with parsley. Makes 6 servings.

⚜ GIBLETS WITH RICE

½ pound chicken or turkey gizzards and hearts
1 cup chopped onion
4 tablespoons (½ stick) butter
1 stalk parsley
2¾ cups chicken stock, or 2 chicken bouillon cubes and 2¾ cups boiling water
1 cup raw long-grain converted rice
1¼ teaspoons salt
chopped parsley

Cut gizzards and hearts into small dice and cook with onions in 2 tablespoons of the butter until browned. Add parsley, stock, or bouillon cubes and water, and cook slowly 30 minutes or until giblets are tender. Meanwhile, soak rice 30 minutes in water to cover. Drain and cook in remaining 2 tablespoons butter until rice is dry and sticks to the bottom of the pan. Add to giblets along with salt. Cover and cook 12 to 15 minutes. Turn off heat and let stand 5 or 10 minutes or until rice has absorbed all liquid. Sprinkle with chopped parsley. Makes 6 servings.

TURKEY

Turkey, traditional in the United States for Thanksgiving Day dinner, and also for Christmas and New Year's Day, is now available, fresh and frozen, the year around. It is trussed, stuffed, and roasted in the same way as chicken, and young turkeys may also be broiled. When buying turkey, if the ready-to-cook weight is less than 12 pounds, allow ¾ pound to 1 pound per serving; if it is over 12 pounds, allow ½ to ¾ pound. Cold turkey yields more servings per pound than hot turkey. In France turkeys are known as *dindon* (turkey cock), *dinde* (hen turkey), and *dindonneau* (young turkey); recipes usually call for *dindonneau*, and if *dinde* is specified, a young and small bird is usually meant. The larger turkeys are more commonly served in America, but small turkeys are becoming more popular. French and American methods of roasting turkey differ (see Roast Turkey). Either method may be used for turkey, capon, or large chickens. To make carving easier, allow turkey to stand 20 to 30 minutes after it comes out of the oven.

⚜ ROAST TURKEY

To prepare turkey, see How to Truss Chicken or Turkey, page 644. If turkey is stuffed, see the following recipes, or use any other preferred stuffing. Roast according to either of the following methods:

French Two-Temperature Method. Lay the bird on its side on a rack in a roasting pan. Spread generously with melted butter and lay thin slices of salt pork over the breast. Roast, uncovered, in a preheated hot oven (425° F.) for 15 minutes; turn on the other side and roast 15 minutes longer. Reduce heat to moderate (350° F.) and cook until turkey is done, turning from side to side and basting with pan drippings every 20 minutes, and allowing 20 minutes per pound total cooking time. Place the bird on its back for the last 15 minutes of cooking. If the pan drippings tend to burn, add a little water to the pan but be careful not to add enough to create steam. To test for doneness, pierce the thigh with a fork: if the juice runs out clear without a trace of pink the bird is done.

American One-Temperature Method. Place turkey breast side up on a rack in a roasting pan. Spread with softened butter or shortening. Cut 3 or 4 thicknesses of cheesecloth large enough to cover the bird, wring them out in hot water in which butter or shortening has been melted, and spread over the turkey. Put turkey in a preheated slow oven (325° F.) and roast according to the following timetable:

6 to 8 pounds	3 to 4 hours
8 to 12 pounds	4 to 5 hours
12 to 16 pounds	5 to 6 hours
16 to 20 pounds	6 to 7½ hours
20 to 25 pounds	7½ to 8½ hours

If a meat thermometer is used, when it registers 190° to 195° F., the turkey should be done. If the breast and legs brown too fast, cover these parts with foil. To test for doneness, move a leg joint up and down; if it moves easily or breaks, the turkey is done. Another test is to wrap a piece of paper around one's index finger and press the fleshy part of the drumstick; if it feels soft, the turkey is done. (See illustration, page 675.)

BASIC AMERICAN BREAD STUFFING

1 cup chopped onions
1 cup (2 sticks) butter
2½ quarts (10 cups) toasted soft breadcrumbs or bread cubes (croutons)
3 teaspoons poultry seasoning
¼ cup chopped parsley
¾ teaspoon ground black pepper
¾ cup turkey stock, or 1 chicken bouillon cube and ½ cup hot water

Cook onions in butter until they are limp. Add all the remaining ingredients and mix lightly but well. Stuff and truss turkey and roast according to American One-Temperature Method for Roast Turkey. Makes enough stuffing for a 12- to 15-pound bird.

MUSHROOM STUFFING

To the preceding recipe, add ½ pound chopped mushroom caps and stems. Cook with the onions.

OYSTER STUFFING

Mix 1 cup finely chopped oysters, well drained, with other ingredients for Basic American Bread Stuffing.

SAUSAGE STUFFING

Crumble ½ pound sausage meat and brown in a skillet. Drain off fat. Add sausage to other ingredients for Basic American Bread Stuffing.

CORNBREAD STUFFING

This is a favorite stuffing in the southern part of the United States.

1½ cups chopped onions
1 cup (2 sticks) butter
½ cup finely chopped celery
4 cups toasted breadcrumbs or bread cubes (croutons)
8 cups toasted cornbread crumbs
⅓ cup chopped parsley
5 teaspoons rubbed sage
2½ teaspoons salt, or salt to taste
¾ teaspoon ground black pepper
1 cup turkey stock, or 1 chicken bouillon cube and 1 cup hot water

Cook the onions in the butter until they are limp. Mix with all the other ingredients. Stuff and truss turkey and roast according to American One-Temperature Method for Roast Turkey. Makes enough stuffing for a 15-pound turkey.

CHESTNUT STUFFING

2 pounds chestnuts
2 pounds sausage meat
3 cups soft breadcrumbs
1 teaspoon salt
1 teaspoon poultry seasoning
¼ cup cognac

Cut gashes in the convex side of chestnuts with a sharp-pointed knife. Place chestnuts in a saucepan with water to cover and bring to boiling point. Remove from heat (do not drain off water). Remove chestnuts, one at a time, from the water and peel off shells and inner skins while nuts are hot. Cook in chicken stock to cover ½ hour, or until chestnuts are barely soft. Drain and chop. Add to remaining ingredients. Mix lightly but well. Stuff and truss turkey and roast according to either method for Roast Turkey. Makes enough stuffing for an 8- to 10-pound bird.

LIVER AND MUSHROOM STUFFING

- 1 turkey liver
- 6 chicken livers
- 2 tablespoons chopped parsley
- 3 shallots, chopped
- ½ cup chopped mushrooms
- ½ cup chopped onion
- ⅓ cup chopped celery leaves
- 4 cups soft breadcrumbs
- 1 teaspoon salt
- ½ teaspoon ground black pepper
- 3 tablespoons turkey fat or butter, melted
- ¼ cup cognac

Put the first 8 ingredients through a food chopper twice, using the finest blade. Add the next 4 ingredients and mix well. Stuff and truss turkey and roast according to either method for Roast Turkey. Makes enough stuffing for a 10-pound bird.

⚜ BRAISED TURKEY

- 5- to 6-pound ready-to-cook young turkey
- salt
- ground black pepper
- 5 tablespoons butter
- 1 cup boiling chicken stock, or 2 chicken bouillon cubes and 1 cup boiling water
- 1 tablespoon flour
- 1 cup sour cream
- cooked rice

Sprinkle turkey with salt and pepper and brown on all sides in 3 tablespoons of the butter in a Dutch oven. Place turkey on a trivet in the Dutch oven. Add stock, or bouillon cubes and water, along with the neck, heart, and gizzard. Cover and bring to boiling point. Reduce heat and simmer 2 to 2½ hours or until turkey is tender. Remove turkey to a warmed platter and keep warm. Just before serving, garnish platter with parsley. Cut meat from turkey. Chop gizzard and heart and add to the cooking liquid. Blend flour with the remaining 1 tablespoon butter and add. Mix well. Stir and cook 1 minute. Add sour cream and heat (do not boil). Adjust salt and pepper. Serve with turkey on rice. Makes 8 servings.

⚜ BROILED YOUNG TURKEY

5- to 6-pound young turkey
3 tablespoons butter, or salad oil
1 teaspoon salt
¼ teaspoon ground black pepper
½ teaspoon sugar
chopped parsley

Ask the butcher to split the turkey into 2 lengthwise halves and remove the backbone. Fold the wings under the back. Place the turkey, skin side down, in a buttered or oiled broiler pan. Brush well with melted butter or oil. Mix salt, pepper, and sugar and sprinkle over the turkey. Place the broiler pan 9 inches from the source of heat. (If the oven is a gas oven, set thermostat at 350° F.) Broil 40 minutes, brushing with melted butter, oil, or pan drippings. Turn and cook 40 to 50 minutes or until turkey is done, basting 2 to 3 times with pan drippings. To test for doneness, twist the drumstick. If it moves easily, the turkey is done. To serve, cut each half into 4 pieces. Makes 8 servings.

⚜ TURKEY BREAST MERCURE

5 cups mixed cooked vegetables
⅓ cup mayonnaise
2¼ cups semiliquid aspic
salt and pepper to taste
6 slices raw turkey breast, about ¼ inch thick
3 tablespoons butter
½ cup dry white wine
½ cup chicken consommé
1 truffle
1 small tomato or pimiento
1 hard-cooked egg white
2 pounds chilled butter
6 small baked tart cases

Combine the vegetables with the mayonnaise and ¼ cup of the aspic and add salt and pepper to taste. Put 4 cups of the mixture into a 1-quart cone-shaped mold and chill until set. Reserve remaining mixure. Cook turkey slices in 3 tablespoons butter in a tightly covered saucepan over low heat for 5 minutes. Add wine, cover, and simmer 15 minutes; then add consommé, re-cover, and simmer 15 minutes more. Cool in the cooking liquid. Remove turkey slices, cut in uniform long narrow triangle shapes (reserving the trimmings), and garnish each slice with bits of truffle, tomato or pimiento, and hard-cooked egg white. Coat with aspic and chill until set.

Coat a large platter with a thin layer layer of aspic and chill. From the chilled butter model the heads and forelegs of two kneeling horses (see illustration, page 686), leaving an oval shape between for the vegetable mold. Unmold it and place in the center, surrounding it with the triangles of turkey breast, points upward, and top the center with a half tomato or slice of pimiento, strips of egg white, and a truffle slice. Coat the whole with a thin film of aspic and chill. Fill the tart cases with the remaining vegetable mixture. Garnish the tops with small triangles of turkey cut from the trimmings and with bits of truffle and tomato or pimiento. Cover with aspic and chill. Arrange tart cases at the sides of the sculpture. Keep the whole chilled until ready to serve. Makes 6 servings.

⚜ TURKEY AND VEGETABLE PLATTER
(*Suprêmes de Dindonneau Garnis*)

Arrange slices of cold breast of turkey and small precooked link sausages or Vienna sausages on a platter. Surround with hot vegetables, such as Duchess Potatoes, Boiled Brussels Sprouts, Braised Chestnuts, and yellow Turnip Balls with Salt Pork (include the slices of salt pork). (See illustration, page 676.)

DUCK

Domesticated duck has more dark meat and fat than chicken or turkey and a smaller proportion of meat in relation to bone. The average ready-to-cook weight of duck on the American market is 4 to 5 pounds; in Europe the weight ranges from 3½ to 6 pounds, depending on the breed. Duck may be roasted (stuffed or unstuffed), braised, or fricasseed. Very young duckling may be fried. Stuffings suitable for duck are fruit—apples, prunes, oranges, or grapes—or potatoes, rice, sauerkraut, or bread with fruit added. Since duck has a large amount of fat, it is an efficient self-baster and no basting is required during cooking. The excess fat that accumulates in the roasting pan should be spooned or siphoned off and may be saved for cooking purposes.

Only young ducks should be cooked; French recipes usually specify *caneton* (duckling) rather than *canard* (duck).

For wild duck, see Chapter 14.

⚜ ROAST DUCK

4-pound ready-to-cook duck
salt
ground black pepper
2 teaspoons cornstarch
1½ cups chicken or veal stock

Wash duck, dry, and place on a rack in a baking pan. Truss and roast in a preheated slow oven (325° F.) 1½ hours or until duck is tender. Transfer duck to a warmed platter and keep it hot. Pour off fat from the pan drippings. Blend cornstarch with stock and add to pan drippings. Stir and cook 2 minutes or until sauce has thickened. Adjust seasonings. Serve in a separate sauceboat. Makes 4 servings.

⚜ DUCK BIGARADE

4-pound ready-to-cook duck
2 tablespoons sugar
¼ cup vinegar
½ cup veal stock
½ cup Demi-Glace
1 tablespoon lemon juice
1 cup orange juice
2 tablespoons julienne strips orange rind
8 orange slices

Wash and dry duck. Place on a rack in a baking pan. Cook in a preheated slow oven (325° F.) 1½ hours. Transfer duck to another pan to keep warm. Skim off and discard fat from pan drippings. Stir and cook sugar in a very small saucepan until it is melted, being careful not to burn it. Add vinegar, mix well, and add to pan drippings along with next 4 ingredients. Simmer 5 minutes. Add orange rind. Cut duck into long thin slices and arrange on a warmed platter. Garnish with orange slices. Serve sauce in a sauceboat. Makes 4 servings.

⚜ DUCK WITH CHIPOLATAS

Chipolatas are little sausages stuffed in sheep's intestines. If these are not available, use other small sausages.

4-pound ready-to-cook duck
24 small whole white onions, peeled
1½ cups Demi-Glace Sauce
½ pound mushrooms
12 chipolata sausages
salt
ground black pepper
½ pound braised chestnuts

Wash duck and wipe dry. Place in a rack in a pan in a very hot oven (450° F.) 15 minutes, or until browned. Remove duck from the pan and fry onions in the pan drippings. Drain off fat and add Demi-Glace. Return duck to the pan. Cover and cook in a preheated moderate oven (350° F.) 40 minutes. Add mushrooms and sausage and cook 10 minutes. Remove from heat and transfer duck, sausage, onions, and mushrooms to a warmed platter. Skim off fat from pan drippings and discard and season the drippings to taste with salt and pepper. Spoon over duck. Garnish with braised chestnuts. Serve any remaining sauce in a separate dish. Makes 4 servings.

⚜ DUCKLING WITH FIGS

2 dozen fresh figs
port
4-pound ready-to-cook duck
salt
ground black pepper
2 tablespoons butter, melted
2 tablespoons brandy

Wash figs and soak in wine to cover in a covered jar for 24 hours. Wash duck and wipe dry. Sprinkle with salt and pepper. Place duck in a casserole with melted butter. Bake, uncovered, in a preheated slow oven (325° F.) ½ hour. Drain off fat. Add the marinating wine, reserving the figs. Return duck to oven and continue cooking for 1 hour or until duck is tender, basting with wine occasionally. Skim off fat and discard. Add figs and cook 10 minutes. Transfer duck to a warmed platter, and place figs around it. Add brandy to pan drippings, heat, and spoon over duck. Serve remaining sauce in a sauceboat. Serve with rice, green beans, or peas. Makes 4 servings.

⚜ DUCK NIÇOISE

4-pound ready-to-cook duck
salt and ground black pepper
1 small clove garlic, crushed
6 medium-sized tomatoes, peeled, seeded, and quartered, or 2 cups drained canned whole tomatoes
½ cup pitted green olives
2 tablespoons chopped parsley
½ cup dry white wine
¼ cup brandy
¼ cup bouillon
½ teaspoon sugar

Wash and dry duck and rub with salt and pepper. Truss and place on a rack in a roasting pan. Cook in a preheated slow oven (325° F.) 1½ hours or until duck is browned. Put duck on a warm platter and keep it warm. Drain excess fat from the pan. Add all the rest of the ingredients to the pan drippings. Stir and cook 10 minutes or until most of the liquid has evaporated. Adjust seasonings. Spoon sauce onto platter around the duck. Makes 4 servings. (See illustration, page 681.)

Chicken Breasts Maryland Style, page 655 ▲

▼ Roast Turkey, page 668

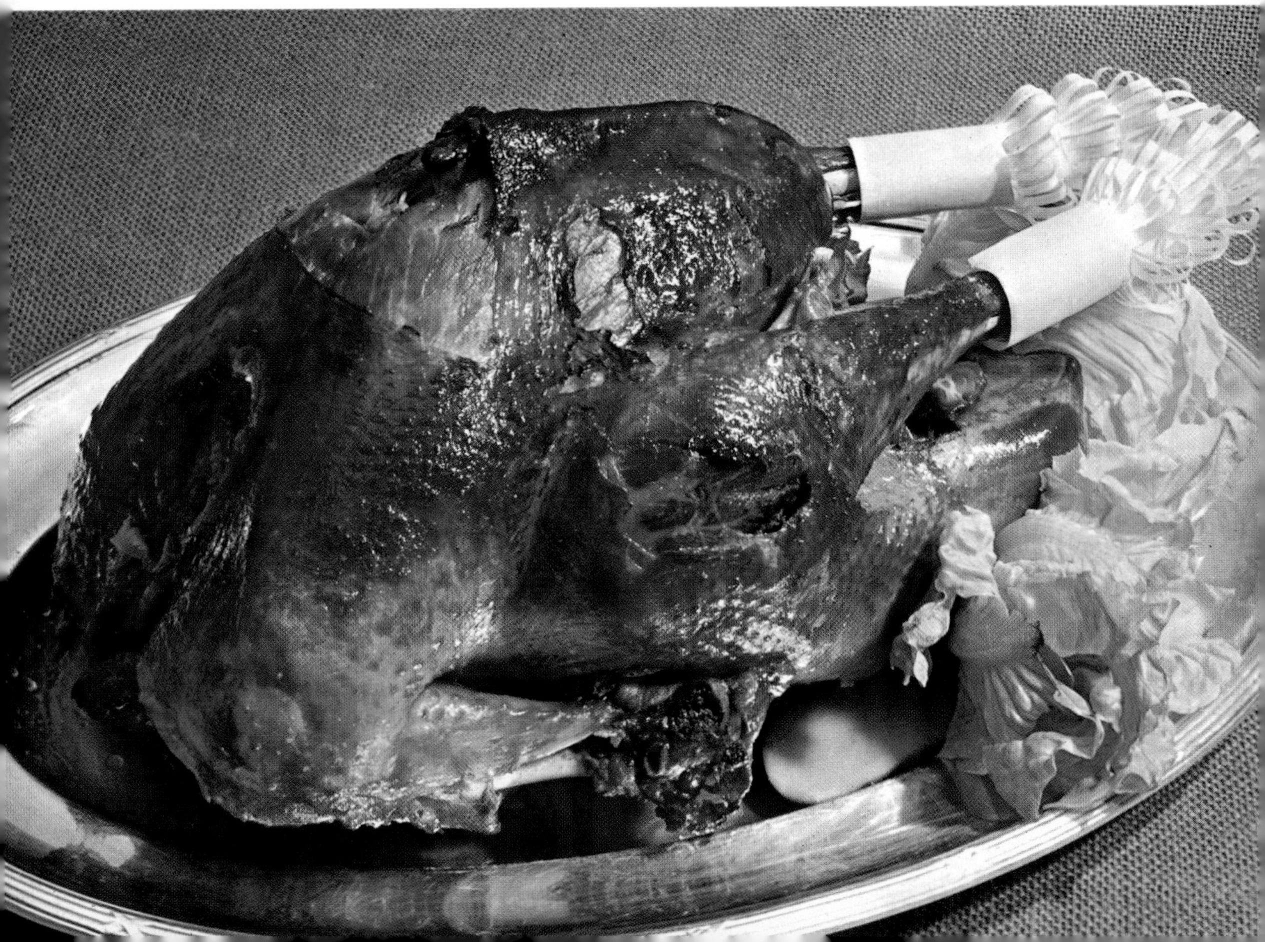

▲ Deviled Spring Chicken, page 649

Turkey and Vegetable Platter, page 672 ▼

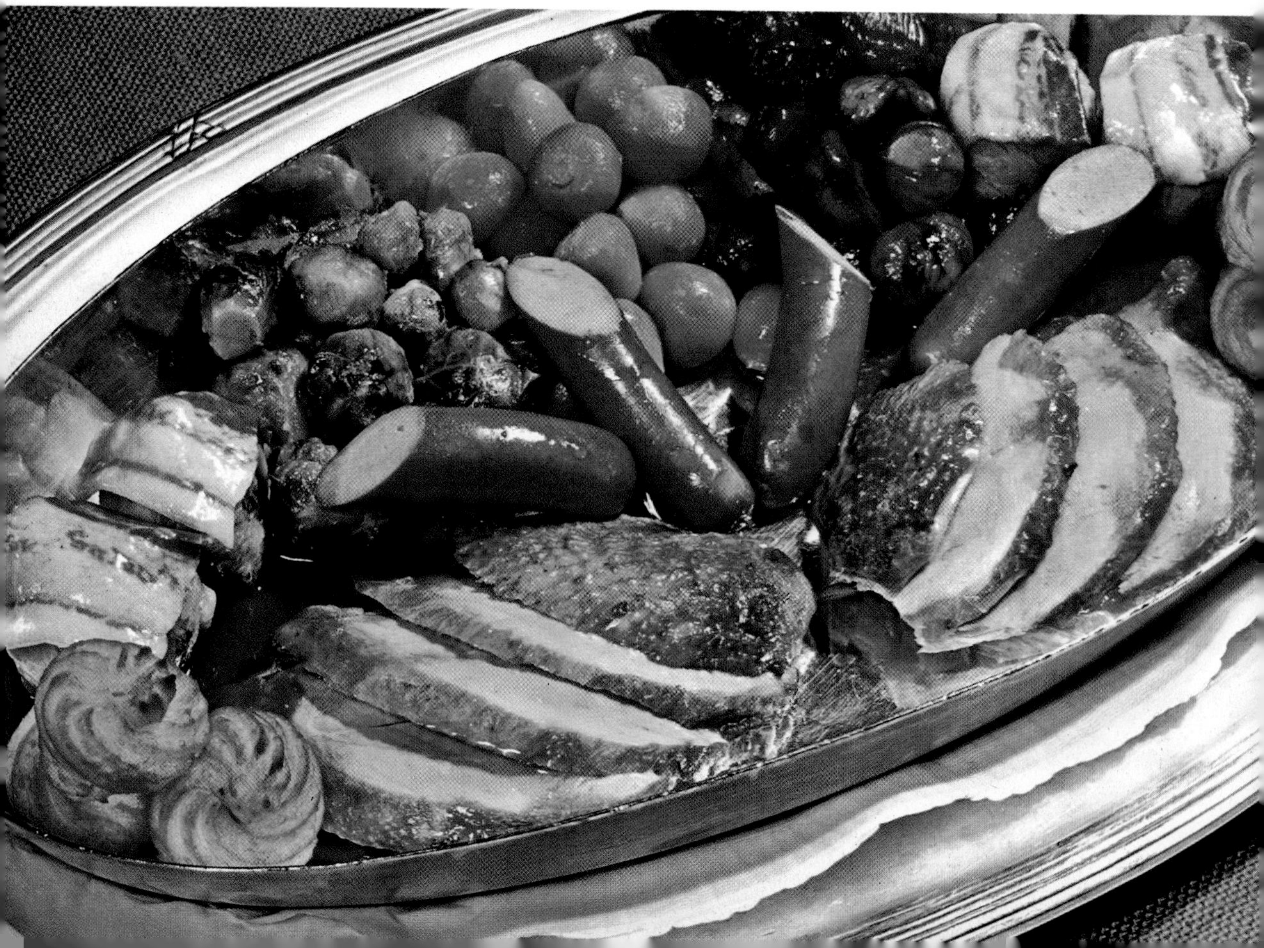

Breasts of Chicken Spanish Style, page 656 ▲

▼ Chicken Stanley, page 650

▲ Sautéed Chicken Forestière, page 650

Chicken Pilaf Oriental Style, page 652 ▼

Stuffed Chicken Legs Regency Style, page 663 ▲

▼ Breasts of Chicken Sandeman, page 656

▲ Sautéed Chicken Portuguese Style, page 649

Chicken Quenelles Isabella, page 665 ▼

▼ Duck Niçoise, page 674

Chicken Andalusian Style, page 646 ▲

▲ Pigeons with Little Peas, page 700

Chicken with Chambertin, page 648 ▼

▼ Chaud-froid of Chicken Breasts, page 659

Chicken Archduke Style, page 663 ▲

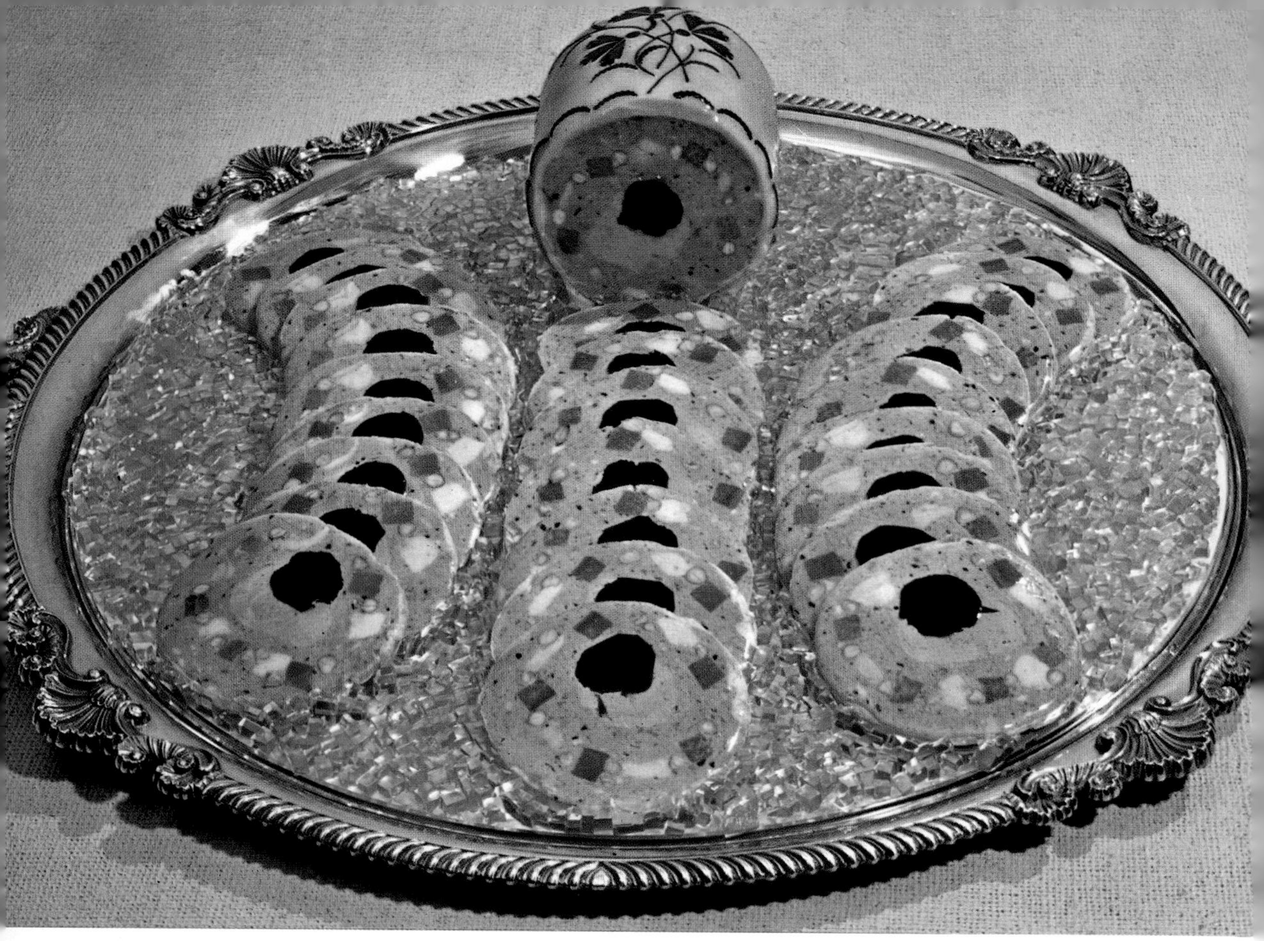

▲ Galantine of Chicken, page 742

Harlequin Chicken, page 646 ▼

▼ Stuffed Duck Charles Vaucher, page 690

Chaud-froid Chicken Lambertye, page 648 ▲

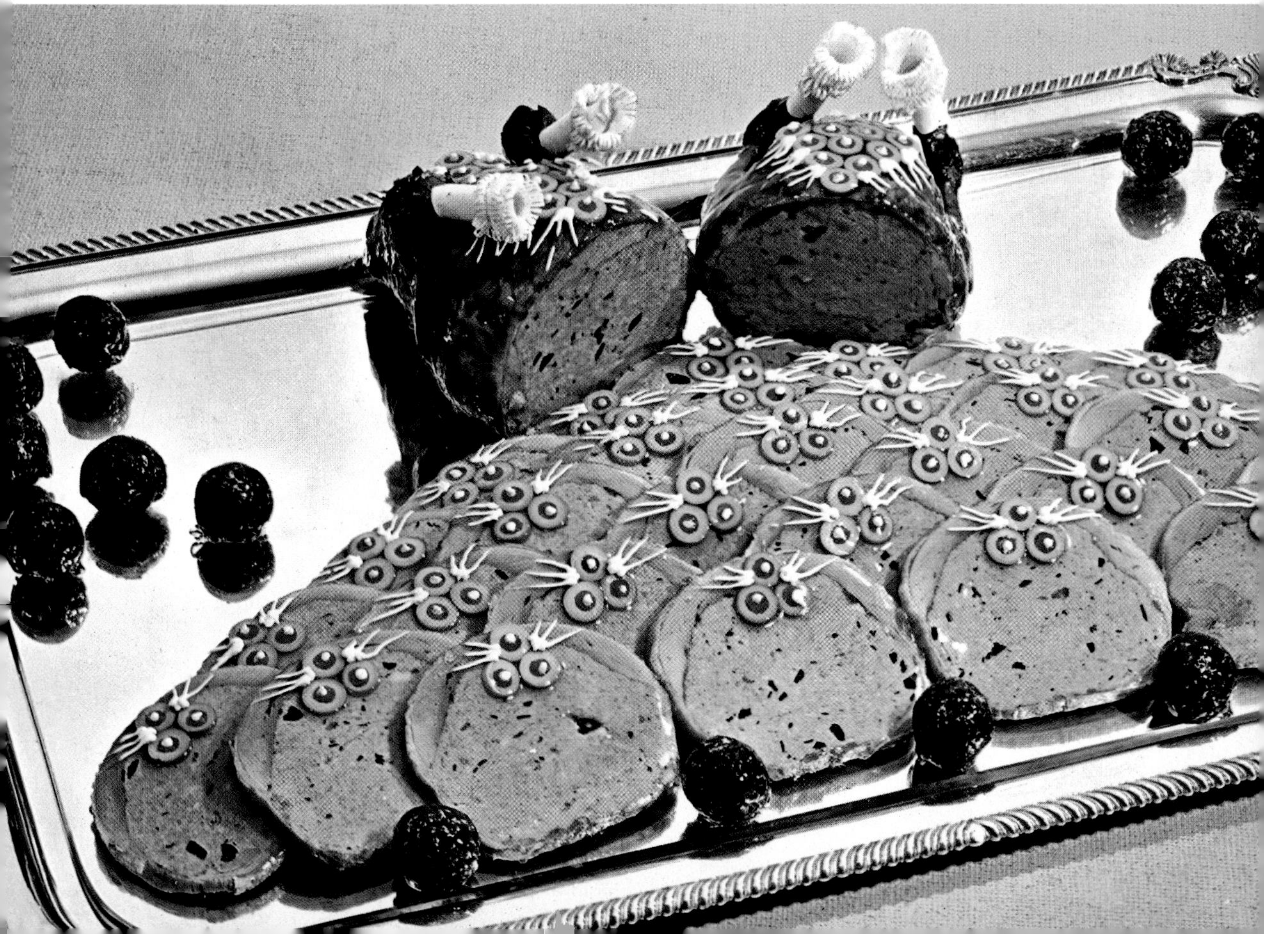

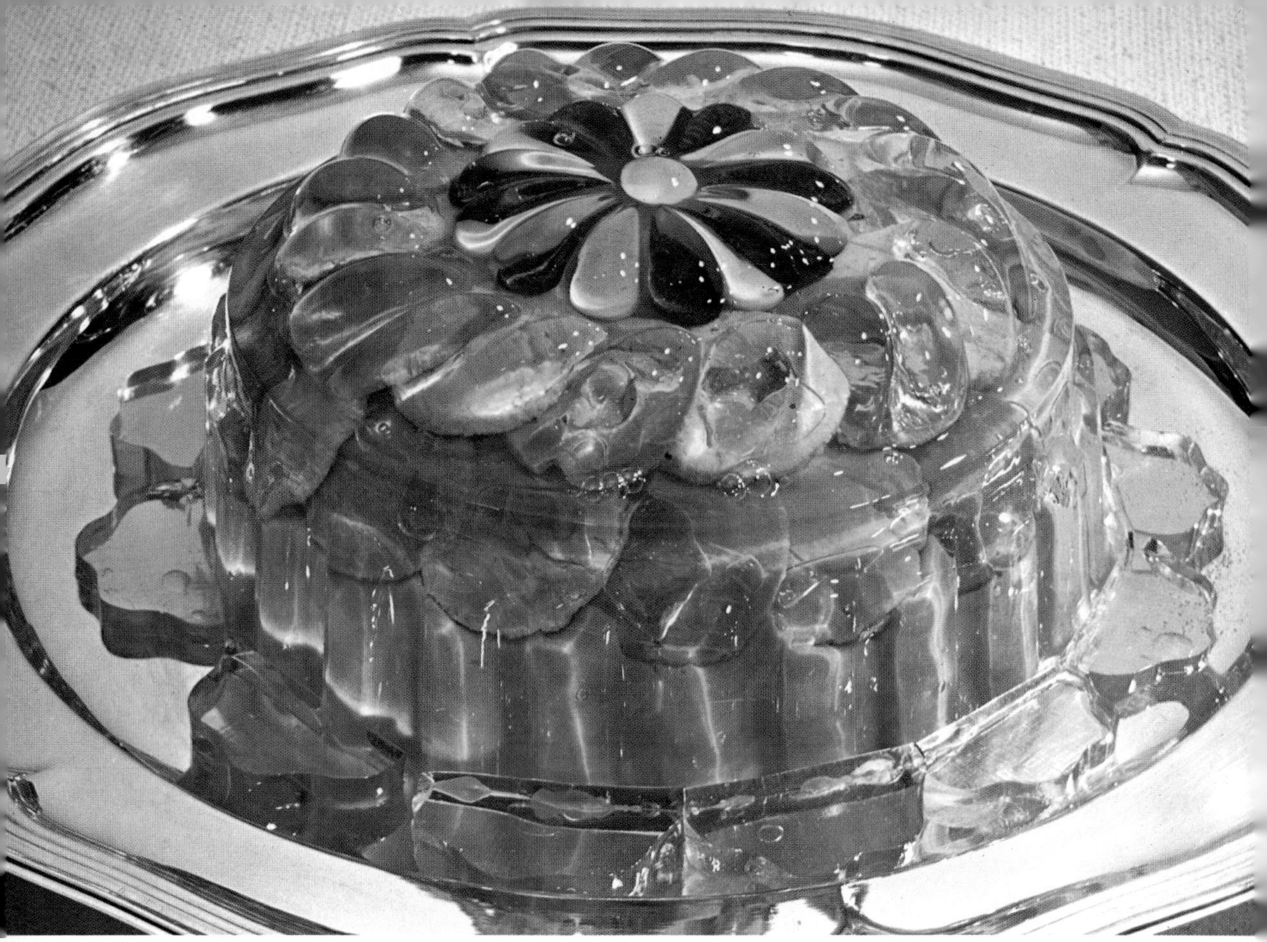

▲ Chicken and Ham Aspic Mercédès, page 658

Turkey Breast Mercure, page 671 ▼

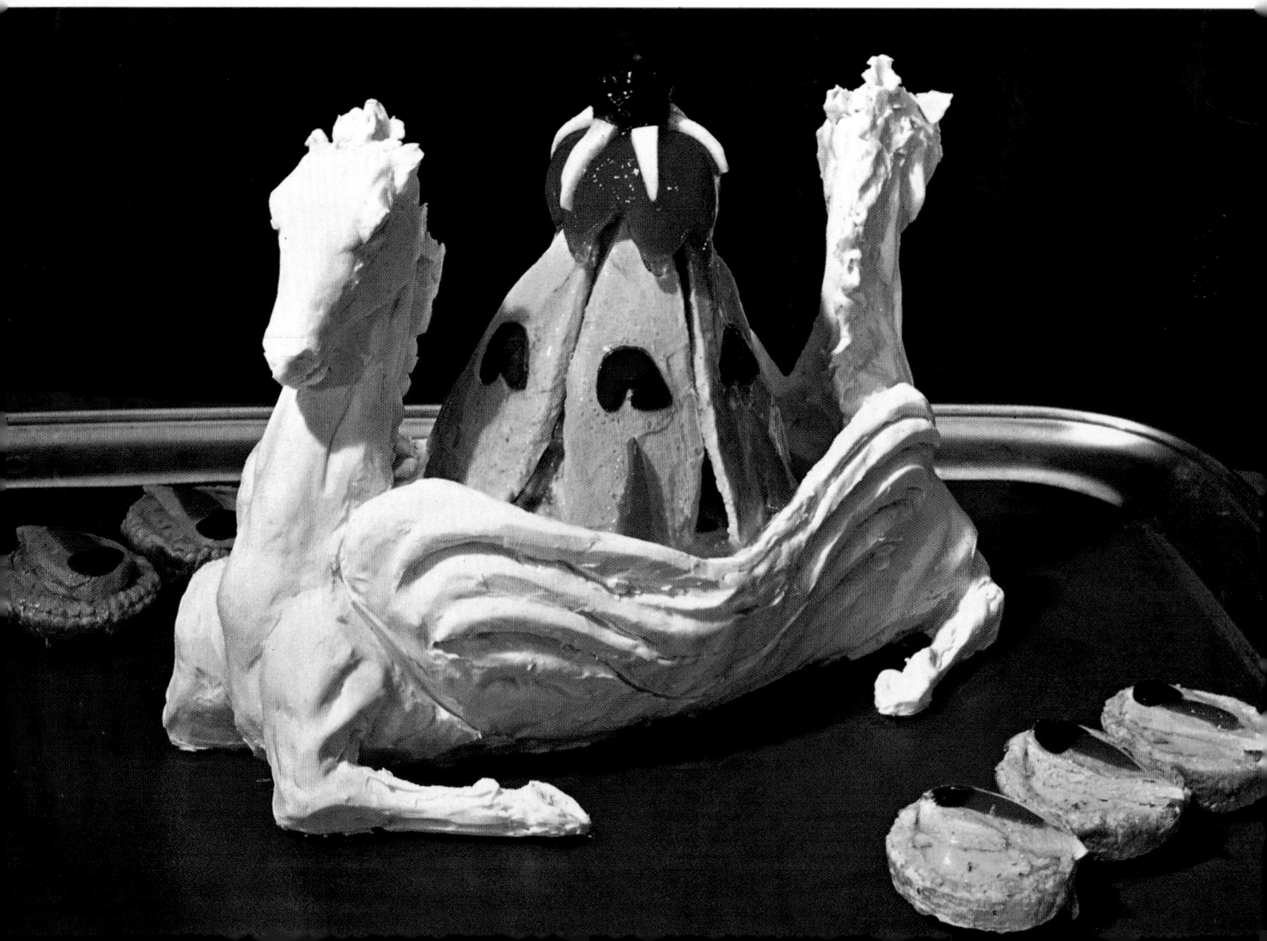

⚜ DUCKLING MISTRAL

4-pound ready-to-cook duck
½ pound chicken livers
1 duck liver
4 tablespoons (½ stick) butter
2 shallots, chopped
1 pound mushrooms
1 teaspoon salt
½ teaspoon ground black pepper
¼ cup Madeira
salt
ground black pepper
3 tablespoons bacon drippings
1 carrot, peeled and sliced
1 onion, peeled and sliced
1 rib celery, sliced
½ cup chicken or veal stock
1½ cups Demi-Glace Sauce
1 truffle, sliced
½ cup pimiento-stuffed green olives

Wash duck, dry, and set aside. Dice chicken livers and duck liver coarsely and brown them in 2 tablespoons of the butter. Add shallots. Chop half the mushrooms and add, along with salt, black pepper, and wine. Cover and simmer 5 minutes. Drain and put the mixture through a sieve or food mill. Season to taste with salt and pepper. Rub inside of duck's body cavity with salt and pepper and stuff with liver purée mixture. Close openings with skewer and lace tightly with twine. Brown the duck on all sides in a casserole in 2 tablespoons of the bacon drippings. Remove duck and add vegetables. Cover and cook 5 minutes without browning. Return duck to casserole. Sprinkle with salt and pepper. Melt remaining butter and pour over duck. Cover and cook in a preheated oven (325° F.) 1 hour or until duck is tender. Transfer duck to a warmed platter and keep warm. Add stock and Demi-Glace to the casserole. Bring to boiling point and boil 5 minutes. Skim off excess fat and discard. Spoon a little of the sauce over the duck. Serve remaining sauce separately in a sauceboat. Decorate breast of duck with slices of truffle and 4 poached mushroom caps. Slice remaining mushrooms, sauté in butter, and spoon onto the platter around duck. Garnish with stuffed green olives. Makes 4 servings.

⚜ DUCK WITH ORANGE SAUCE (*Canard à l'Orange*)

4- to 5-pound ready-to-cook duck
1½ teaspoons salt
¼ teaspoon ground black pepper
1 tablespoon butter
1 tablespoon flour
1 cup white stock
½ cup dry white wine
2 medium-sized oranges
water
2 tablespoons sugar
2 tablespoons water
1½ cups orange juice
2 tablespoons lemon juice

Truss the duck and rub the skin and the body cavity with 1 teaspoon of the salt and the black pepper. Place it on a rack in a roasting pan and put it in a preheated very hot oven (450° F.). Roast 20 minutes or until duck is golden brown, turning it to brown all sides. Transfer the duck to another pan. Remove the rack. Pour off and discard all but 1 tablespoon of the fat. Add the butter to the roasting pan and heat until it is melted. Blend in the flour. Stir and cook over medium-low heat until the roux is light brown. Add the stock, wine, and remaining ½ teaspoon salt. Stir and cook until the sauce has thickened slightly. Add the duck to the sauce. Cover and cook in a preheated moderate oven (350° F.) 1 hour or until duck is tender. Cut the peel (zest) from the oranges, being careful not to include the bitter white portion. Cut the peel into very fine strips, place them in water to cover, and boil 3 minutes. Drain and set aside. Cut off and discard the white bitter portion from the oranges, cut them into slices, and set aside. Transfer duck to a warm platter and keep it warm. Skim off and discard all excess fat from the sauce. Cook until the sauce has reduced to 1 cup. Cook the sugar and water in a small saucepan until the syrup is straw-color, then add to the sauce. Stir in the orange juice and lemon juice. Bring the sauce to boiling point and boil 1 minute. Add the orange peel and additional salt if needed. Carve the duck into 4 servings and place it on a warmed platter, spooning some of the sauce over it. Serve the remaining sauce in a sauceboat. Garnish the platter with the orange slices. Makes 4 servings.

⚜ DUCK AND ORANGES IN ASPIC

4 envelopes unflavored gelatin
1 cup orange juice
3 cups chicken stock
salt to taste
⅛ teaspoon ground black pepper
1 tablespoon vinegar
½ teaspoon dried tarragon or 2 teaspoons chopped fresh tarragon
2 egg whites, stiffly beaten
2 egg shells, crushed
about 1 pound sliced cooked cold duck
6 slices truffle (optional)
2 cooked carrots, sliced
3 to 4 medium-sized mushrooms, poached and sliced
12 orange sections
watercress

Soften the gelatin in the orange juice and set aside. Place the next 7 ingredients in a 2-quart saucepan. Bring to boiling point over medium heat, stirring constantly. Remove from heat, add softened gelatin, and let the mixture stand 10 minutes. Strain it through a fine sieve lined with a layer of cheesecloth. Pour 2 cups of the aspic into a lightly oiled 2-quart mold and chill until firm. Let the remaining aspic stand at room temperature until the aspic in the mold is set. Then chill the remaining aspic until it almost reaches the point of setting. Arrange the sliced duck, truffles (if used), carrots, mushrooms, and orange sections in an attractive pattern over the aspic in the mold. Cover carefully with the almost-set aspic. Chill until the aspic is firm and you are ready to serve the dish. Unmold onto a serving tray and garnish with watercress. Makes 6 servings.

⚜ BRAISED DUCK WITH PEAS

4-pound ready-to-cook duck
2 tablespoons butter
4 slices salt pork
24 small white onions
½ cup chicken or veal broth
1½ cups Demi-Glace Sauce
bouquet garni
1 teaspoon salt
½ teaspoon ground black pepper
2 cups shelled fresh green peas or thawed frozen peas

Wash duck and wipe dry. Brown on all sides in butter in a Dutch oven. Transfer duck to another pan. Fry salt pork in the Dutch oven. Add onions and cook until they begin to color. Drain off fat. Add broth, Demi-Glace, bouquet garni, salt, and pepper. Return duck to the Dutch oven, cover, and cook over low heat 1 hour or until duck is tender. Add peas and cook 10 minutes. Transfer duck and vegetables to a serving dish. Serve the sauce separately in a sauceboat. Makes 4 servings.

⚜ CASSEROLE OF DUCK WITH CHAMBERTIN

4-pound ready-to-cook duck
1 teaspoon salt
½ teaspoon ground black pepper
2 tablespoons olive oil or salad oil
2 tablespoons butter
½ pound small white onions
½ pound mushrooms
1 cup Chambertin wine
1 shallot, chopped
½ cup heavy cream

Wash duck, dry, and cut into quarters. Sprinkle with salt and pepper and brown on all sides in oil and butter in a casserole. Add onions. Cover and cook in a preheated moderate oven (350° F.) 40 minutes. Wash mushrooms, remove stems, and add caps to the duck. Cover and cook 10 minutes, or until duck is tender. Transfer duck, onions, and mushrooms to a platter. Skim off excess fat and discard from the pan drippings. Add wine and shallot. Simmer until the liquid has been reduced by one-half of its original volume. Stir in cream. Heat sauce and spoon over the duck. Sprinkle with chopped parsley. Serve remaining sauce in a sauceboat. Makes 4 servings.

⚜ ROMANIAN DUCKLING WITH PICKLED CUCUMBERS

4-pound ready-to-cook duck
1 teaspoon salt
¼ cup butter or lard
1 cup chopped onion
1 teaspoon salt
1½ cups thin Demi-Glace Sauce
1 tablespoon tomato purée
¼ teaspoon ground black pepper
4 pickled cucumbers, 3 inches long
½ cup sour cream

Cut duck into quarters and rub with salt. Brown in butter or lard in a heavy skillet over moderate heat. Add onion after one side of the duck has browned and cook as the other side browns. Drain off fat if an excess accumulates in the pan. Add next 4 ingredients. Cover and cook over low heat until duck is tender, about 50 minutes. Peel pickled cucumbers, flute by running the tines of a fork down the side, cut into quarters, remove seeds, cut into slices, and add to duck. Cook 10 to 15 minutes. If sauce tends to be too thick, add a little bouillon. Adjust seasonings. Arrange in a serving dish. Serve sour cream separately. Makes 4 servings.

⚜ STUFFED DUCK CHARLES VAUCHER

2 ready-to-cook ducks, 4 pounds each
3 pounds boneless lean shoulder of pork
1 cup dry white wine
¼ cup cognac
½ teaspoon poultry seasoning
½ teaspoon dried rosemary
1 teaspoon salt
½ teaspoon ground black pepper
2 truffles
2 cups brown stock made from duck bones
green olives stuffed with pimiento and almonds
hard-cooked egg whites
aspic
½ pound foie gras purée

Split the ducks lengthwise along the back without breaking the skin and remove all bones except those in the drumsticks (or have the butcher do this for you). Remove the meat, being careful to keep the skin intact. Cut the meat into cubes and discard excess fat. Make brown stock with the bones. Cut the pork into cubes, trimming off and discarding excess fat. Mix the next 6 ingredients, pour over the duck meat and pork, and marinate 24 hours. Then remove meat from marinade, drain, and put it through a food chopper twice, using the finest blade. Dice 1 truffle and add, mixing well. Stuff the duck skins with the mixture, forming them into their original shape. Sew up the openings. Braise in 2 cups of the brown stock for 2 hours, keeping the heat very low to prevent steam from bursting the skins. Cool and then chill. Slice the front half of each duck thinly. Decorate the rear halves and the slices of duck with slices of stuffed olive and thin strips of hard-cooked egg white. Coat with aspic and chill. Chop remaining truffle very fine. Shape the foie gras purée into 1-inch balls and roll them in chopped truffle. Place the duck halves on one side of a chilled tray and decorate the ends of the drumsticks with paper frills. Arrange the slices of duck in front and garnish the tray with foie gras balls. Serve cold. Makes 15 or more servings. (See illustration, page 685.)

⚜ GLAZED DUCKLING MARIVAUX

4-pound ready-to-cook duck
2 cups aspic
1 cup cooked green peas
½ cup cooked diced carrots
½ cup cooked diced potatoes
¼ cup diced celery
3 tablespoons mayonnaise
salt
ground black pepper
½ pound pâté de foie gras
6 tablespoons softened butter
1 truffle
lettuce

Roast the duck, keeping it slightly underdone. Cool. Remove the breast, cut it into long thin slices, and mask with aspic. Chill. Remove breastbone. Combine vegetables, mayonnaise, and salt and pepper to taste, and spoon into the breast cavity. Mask with semiliquid aspic. Mix pâté de foie gras with butter and fill small molds (duck-shaped molds if available). Chill until firm. Unmold and decorate with sliced truffle. Mask with aspic. Cover the bottom of a tray with aspic and chill until set. Place the duck in center of the tray and arrange duck slices and molded pâté de foie gras around it. Garnish with lettuce. Makes 6 servings.

GOOSE

Goose is the Christmas bird of many European countries, just as turkey is the favored Christmas bird in America. Goose (French *oie*) may be roasted, braised, and otherwise cooked in the same manner as duck.

Since goose older than 10 months is apt to be tough, select a younger bird, weighing from 6 to 10 pounds, for roasting. It may be roasted stuffed or unstuffed. If a stuffing is used, allow ½ cup per pound of goose. Braising is the recommended method of cooking a goose weighing over 10 pounds.

During cooking, the goose gives off much fat. The Europeans save this fat for use in cooking. It is especially good for seasoning vegetables, such as sauerkraut, potatoes, and fresh vegetables of the cabbage family. Cooks of some countries use it in cookies.

Allow 1 to 1½ pounds ready-to-cook goose per serving.

⚜ ROAST GOOSE WITH CHESTNUT STUFFING

2 pounds chestnuts
water to cover
chicken stock
1 pound bulk sausage meat
½ teaspoon dried thyme leaves
½ teaspoon dried marjoram leaves
¼ cup cognac
8- to 10-pound ready-to-cook goose
goose fat or chicken fat
1 cup hot water
2 teaspoons cornstarch
salt and black pepper to taste
watercress or parsley

Using a pointed sharp knife, slit the shells of chestnuts on the convex side. Place in a saucepan, cover with water, and bring to boiling point. Remove pan from heat (do not drain off water), remove chestnuts one at a time from the water, and peel off shells and inner skins while nuts are hot. Cook in chicken stock to cover ½ hour or only until they are barely tender. Drain chestnuts and mix lightly with sausage meat, thyme, marjoram, and cognac. Stuff into the body and crop cavities of the goose. Close openings with skewers and lace tightly with twine. Truss. Rub body of goose with goose fat or chicken fat. Place goose on a rack in a large baking pan. Pour 1 cup hot water into pan. Roast in preheated slow oven (325° F.) 3½ to 4 hours or until goose is tender and browned, adding more water to the pan as it evaporates. Siphon off the fat that accumulates in the pan. Transfer goose to a warmed platter. Keep warm. Blend cornstarch with 1½ cups chicken stock or water and add to pan drippings. Cook, stirring in all the brown bits from the bottom of the pan. Season to taste with salt and pepper. Garnish goose with watercress. Serve gravy in a sauceboat. Makes 8 to 10 servings.

⚜ DANISH ROAST GOOSE

8-pound ready-to-cook goose
salt
ground black pepper
2 tablespoons lemon juice
2 cups chopped dried prunes
2 cups sliced tart cooking apples
2 cups stock made from giblets
1½ tablespoons flour
2 tablespoons softened butter
¼ cup red currant jelly (optional)

Wash goose and dry thoroughly inside and out. Rub inside of cavity with salt, pepper, and 1 tablespoon lemon juice. Plump prunes in hot water, remove pits, and chop. Peel, core, and slice apples. Mix with prunes and stuff into the body cavity of the goose. Close opening with skewers and lace tightly with twine. Truss. Rub the skin with salt, pepper, and remaining lemon juice. Place on a rack in a roasting pan. Cook in a preheated slow oven (325° F.) about 3½ hours or until the leg joint moves easily and the flesh is soft. Remove goose from the oven, transfer to a large warmed platter, and let stand in a warm place 30 minutes before carving. Drain fat from roasting pan and add giblet stock. Blend flour with butter and add. Mix well. Stir and cook 2 minutes or until sauce has thickened. The Danish cook adds red currant jelly to the sauce. Serve in a sauceboat. Makes approximately 8 servings.

⚜ ROAST GOOSE ENGLISH STYLE

8- to 10-pound ready-to-cook goose
salt
3 cups chopped onion
3 tablespoons butter
1½ one-pound loaves white bread
milk
2 eggs, beaten
2 teaspoons rubbed sage
ground black pepper
½ teaspoon ground mace
3 tablespoons flour
2 cups stock
watercress
applesauce

Wash goose and wipe dry. Rub inside of body cavity with salt. Set aside. Sauté onions in butter. Cut bread into cubes, add milk to cover, and soak until bread has absorbed most of the milk. Squeeze dry and fluff crumbs with a fork. Add sautéed onions, 1 teaspoon salt, beaten eggs, sage, pepper, and mace. Mix well and stuff into the body cavity and crop of the goose. Close openings with skewers and lace with twine. Truss. Place goose on a rack in a baking pan. Bake in a preheated slow oven (325° F.) 3½ to 4 hours. Transfer goose to a warmed platter and keep warm. Skim off and discard excess fat from pan drippings. Blend flour with stock and add to pan drippings. Stir and cook until thickened. Add salt and pepper to taste. Serve in a sauceboat. Garnish goose with watercress. Serve with applesauce in a separate sauceboat. Makes 8 to 10 servings.

⚜ ROAST GOOSE WITH APPLE STUFFING (*German*)

1 cup chopped onion
½ cup (1 stick) butter
1 quart peeled diced apples
1 quart cooked chestnuts, chopped
1½ cups diced cooked potatoes
1 goose liver, chopped
1 cup dark raisins
⅓ cup chopped parsley
1½ teaspoons salt, or salt to taste
½ teaspoon ground black pepper
1 teaspoon rubbed sage
1 teaspoon ground nutmeg
dash ground cloves
8- to 10-pound ready-to-cook goose
1 cup hot water
2½ tablespoons flour
2 cups broth made from giblets

Cook onion in 2 tablespoons of the butter until limp. Add remaining butter and next 4 ingredients; pour boiling water over raisins, drain, and add along with next 6 ingredients. Mix well. Wash and dry goose. Sprinkle inside of body and neck cavities with salt. Stuff, close openings with skewers, and lace tightly with twine. Truss goose and place on a rack in a large baking pan. Pour 1 cup hot water into the roasting pan. Cook in a preheated slow oven (325° F.) 3½ to 4 hours, or until goose is tender and brown, basting frequently with the liquid in the pan. Add more water to the pan as it evaporates. Siphon off the fat as it accumulates in the pan. Transfer goose to a warmed platter. Blend flour with a little of the giblet broth and add to the pan drippings. Stir and cook until slightly thickened, scraping all the brown bits from the bottom of the pan. Season with salt and pepper to taste. Makes 8 to 10 servings.

⚜ BRAISED GOOSE LYONNAISE

6- to 7-pound ready-to-cook goose
salt
⅓ cup dry white wine
1¾ cups Demi-Glace Sauce
20 small white onions, peeled
3 tablespoons butter
20 peeled chestnuts
½ pound raw mushrooms
½ pound chipolatas or other small sausages

Wash goose and wipe dry. Rub inside of body and neck cavities with salt. Truss. Place in a roasting pan. Cook in a preheated very hot oven (450° F.) 20 to 25 minutes to brown. Pour off fat. Add wine and Demi-Glace. Cook onions in butter until they begin to brown. Place in the roasting pan around the goose, cover, reduce heat to 325° F., and cook 1½ hours. Add chestnuts and continue cooking 30 minutes. Wash mushrooms and add along with sausages. Continue to cook until goose is tender. Transfer goose and vegetables to a warmed platter. Skim off fat from the pan sauce and discard. Adjust seasonings and serve sauce in a sauceboat. Makes 6 to 7 servings.

⚜ FRICASSEED GOOSE GIBLETS

neck, wing tips, gizzard, and heart of goose
salt
2 cups water or chicken bouillon
2 medium-sized potatoes
8 small white onions
½ cup sliced celery
½ cup sliced carrots
¼ teaspoon ground black pepper
2 tablespoons chopped parsley
2 tablespoons flour, or 2 egg yolks
¼ cup heavy cream

Cut neck into 3 parts and wing tips into 2 parts each; cut gizzard and heart into slices ¼ inch thick. Put in a saucepan with water or bouillon and 1 teaspoon salt, cover, bring to boiling point, reduce heat, and simmer 1 hour or until meat is tender. Remove from stock and cut the meat from the neck and wing bones. Strain the stock. Peel and dice potatoes; peel onions, leaving them whole. Add potatoes, onions, celery, and carrots to the stock, cover, and cook 20 minutes or until vegetables are tender. Return the goose meat and giblets to the stock. Add black pepper, chopped parsley, and salt to taste. Blend the flour or egg yolks with the cream, add, and cook 1 minute to thicken. Makes 4 servings.

⚜ CASSOULET OF GOOSE TOULOUSAINE

2⅓ cups (1 pound) dried white beans (Great Northern)
5 cups boiling water
2 medium-sized onions
2 whole cloves
1 carrot, cut in half
1 small clove garlic, crushed
1 stalk parsley
1 rib celery
¼ cup finely diced salt pork
¼ pound garlic pork sausage
2 teaspoons salt
2 tablespoons goose or duck drippings or cooking oil
¾ pound cubed boneless lean pork
¾ pound cubed boneless lean lamb
4 shallots, chopped
1 cup diced, peeled, seeded tomatoes
½ cup tomato sauce
1 tablespoon chopped parsley
½ cup dry white wine (optional)
½ teaspoon ground black pepper
1 to 1½ pounds sliced roast goose or duck
1 cup soft breadcrumbs
2 tablespoons butter, melted

Wash the beans, add the boiling water, cover, and boil 2 minutes. Remove from heat and soak in the cooking water 1 hour. Stud 1 of the onions with the 2 cloves and add to the beans. Add the next 7 ingredients. Bring to boiling point, uncovered. Skim off the foam from the surface, cover, and simmer 30 minutes. Remove the sausage and reserve. Cover the pan and continue to simmer the beans 30 minutes longer. Heat the goose or duck drippings or cooking oil in a skillet, add the pork and lamb, and sauté over moderate heat 10 to 15 minutes or until meat has browned. Transfer the meat to the bean mixture, leaving the fat in the skillet. Chop the remaining onion and add to the fat along with the chopped shallots. Cook over moderate heat 5 minutes or until onion is lightly browned, stirring constantly. Then add the tomatoes, tomato sauce, chopped parsley, and wine (if used). Stir and cook 5 minutes, then add to the bean mixture. Cover and simmer 1 hour, or until beans are tender, adding more boiling water if the beans tend to cook too dry. Remove and discard the whole onion, carrot, parsley stalk, and celery. Add the black pepper and additional salt to taste. (If you have any leftover goose or duck gravy, add it to the beans.) Fill a 2-quart earthenware casserole with alternating layers of beans, sliced goose or duck, and the reserved garlic sausage, having beans as the bottom and top layers. Combine the breadcrumbs with the melted butter and sprinkle over the beans. Bake in a preheated moderate oven (350° F.) 40 minutes or until the crumbs are brown. Makes 6 to 8 servings.

GUINEA FOWL

Guinea fowl (French *pintade*) is native to Africa and was known to the Romans as Numidian or Carthage hen. It is now raised in many parts of the world. The flesh is delicate, resembling that of pheasant, to which the guinea fowl is related. Fully grown guinea fowl can be prepared in any way suitable for chicken.

⚜ ROAST GUINEA HEN

2 ready-to-cook guinea hens, 2 pounds each
2 teaspoons salt
1 teaspoon ground black pepper
2 medium-sized onions
2 ribs celery, sliced
2 carrots, peeled and quartered
2 stalks parsley
softened butter
8 thin strips of salt pork

Wash guinea hens and wipe dry. Rub the body cavities with some of the salt and pepper. Put 1 each of the vegetables into the body cavity of each guinea hen. Close openings with skewers and lace tightly with twine. Truss. Rub the skin of the hens with remaining salt and pepper and with softened butter. Place birds, breast side down, on a rack in a shallow baking pan. Place 2 salt pork strips across the back of each bird. Bake, uncovered, in a preheated moderate oven (350° F.) 45 minutes. Turn the birds over and place 2 salt pork strips across the breast of each. Bake 45 to 50 minutes or until the birds are tender. Serve with gravy made from pan drippings. Makes 4 to 6 servings.

⚜ GUINEA FOWL MACARTHUR

2 young guinea fowl
2 teaspoons salt
½ teaspoon ground black pepper
3 tablespoons olive oil or salad oil
3 tablespoons butter
2 tablespoons brandy
½ cup dry white wine
1 cup diced fresh pineapple
1½ cups Demi-Glace Sauce
dash cayenne
¼ cup toasted slivered blanched almonds
Saffron Rice Pilaf

Cut guinea fowl into serving-size pieces as for fried chicken. Rub guinea fowl with salt and pepper and brown in oil and butter in a heavy saucepan over moderate heat. Transfer to a warmed platter. Pour brandy into pan drippings and ignite. Add wine and reduce to one-half the original quantity. Add pineapple and simmer 2 to 3 minutes. Stir in Demi-Glace and cayenne and cook 5 minutes. Pour sauce over guinea fowl and sprinkle with almonds. Serve with Saffron Rice Pilaf. Makes 8 servings.

⚜ FRIED BREASTS OF GUINEA HEN

breasts of young guinea hens
salt
ground black pepper
butter or salt pork drippings
buttered mushroom caps
flour
chicken stock or water
cream

Allow 1 breast per serving. Rub breasts with salt and pepper. Fry in butter or salt pork drippings in a heavy skillet over moderate heat until browned and tender. Transfer to a warmed platter and garnish with buttered mushroom caps. Blend flour with pan drippings, using 1½ tablespoons flour for each cup of stock or water used. Stir and cook until flour has browned. Remove from heat and add stock or water. Cook until sauce has thickened, stirring constantly. Add cream and salt and pepper to taste. Heat ½ minute. Serve in a sauceboat.

⚜ GUINEA FOWL WITH LICHEE NUTS

3 ready-to-cook small young guinea fowl
½ cup sherry
¾ cup chicken stock
¾ cup Demi-Glace Sauce
¼ cup orange juice
½ teaspoon ground ginger
½ teaspoon ground coriander
dash ground cloves
salt
⅓ cup lichee nuts
½ pound cooked buttered noodles

Roast guinea fowl as directed in recipe for Roast Guinea Hen. Remove breasts and legs. Bone the legs. Add a little sherry to the breasts and legs and keep warm. (Save the rest of the fowl for another meal.) Pour the remaining sherry and the chicken stock into the roasting pan and scrape the pan thoroughly with a wooden spoon. Reduce to half the volume over moderately high heat. Stir in Demi-Glace, orange juice, and spices. Bring to boiling point. Remove from heat, strain, and add salt if needed. Add half of the lichee nuts. Arrange guinea legs and breasts on a platter and add sauce to cover. Sprinkle remaining lichee nuts over the top. Serve with buttered noodles. Serve remaining sauce separately in a sauceboat. Makes 6 servings.

⚜ SAUTÉED GUINEA FOWL À L'AFRICAINE

2 young guinea fowl
2 teaspoons salt
½ teaspoon ground black pepper
flour
6 tablespoons butter
2 tablespoons olive oil or salad oil
⅓ cup dry white wine
1 teaspoon tomato paste
¾ cup hot water
8 slices sweet potatoes
4 bananas, peeled
lemon juice

Cut guinea fowl into serving-size pieces as for fried chicken, season with salt and pepper, and dredge with flour. Brown lightly in 2 tablespoons each butter and oil in a heavy skillet over moderate heat. Add wine, tomato paste, and water. Cover and cook 20 minutes. Place sweet potato slices in a buttered baking pan, sprinkle with salt, and dot with 2 tablespoons of the butter. Cover and cook until tender. Cut peeled bananas in thick diagonal slices, sprinkle with lemon juice, and sauté in remaining 2 tablespoons butter. Arrange pieces of guinea fowl on a platter, with sweet potatoes and bananas around them. Skim off and discard fat from pan in which guinea fowl was cooked, reduce pan liquid to sauce consistency, and pour over guinea fowl. Makes 8 servings.

PIGEON AND SQUAB

Very young pigeons are called squabs. The average weight is about 1 pound and they are tender and delicious. French recipes usually specify *pigeonneau* (squab). Allow 1 squab or pigeon per serving.

⚜ BROILED PIGEON

6 ready-to-cook young pigeons (or squabs)
salt
ground black pepper
¼ cup (½ stick) butter, melted
buttered toast
watercress

Split pigeons from the back without separating the halves and flatten them with the broad side of a cleaver. Sprinkle with salt and pepper. Brush with melted butter. Arrange pigeons skin side down on a buttered broiler rack. If the broiler is thermostatically controlled, set thermostat at 350° F.; if it is not, as in an electric broiler, place the pigeons 7 or 8 inches from the source of heat. Broil 15 to 20 minutes on one side, brush both sides of pigeons again with melted butter, turn and cook 15 minutes or until skin is brown and crisp and pigeons are well done. Serve on buttered toast. Garnish with watercress. Makes 6 servings.

⚜ SAUTÉED PIGEON

Split ready-to-cook pigeons or squabs in lengthwise halves. Sprinkle with salt and pepper. Brown on both sides in butter in a heavy skillet over moderate heat. If squabs brown before they are well done, lower heat and cook until done. Allow 1 bird per person.

⚜ ROAST PIGEON

4 young pigeons
2 tablespoons lemon juice
salt
ground black pepper
12 chicken livers, cut in halves
4 tablespoons butter
⅔ cup finely chopped mushrooms
½ cup ground lean cooked ham
⅓ cup chopped blanched almonds or chopped chestnuts
½ teaspoon dried thyme
8 thin slices fat salt pork

Rub the inside of the body cavities with lemon juice, salt, and pepper. Cook chicken livers in 2 tablespoons butter until just barely done. Transfer to a wooden bowl and chop fine. In the same skillet, sauté mushrooms in remaining butter. Add to livers along with ham, almonds or chestnuts, and thyme. Season to taste with salt and pepper. Stuff lightly into the body cavities of pigeons. Close openings with skewers and lace tightly with twine.

Tie legs of each pigeon together. Rub skin with lemon juice, salt, and pepper. Place pigeon on a rack, breast side up, in a shallow baking pan. Cover breasts with thin slices fat salt pork. Roast in a preheated slow oven (325° F.) 1 hour or until pigeons are done, basting occasionally with pan drippings. Serve hot or cold, garnished with watercress. Makes 4 servings.

⚜ PIGEONS WITH LITTLE PEAS

4 ready-to-cook pigeons (or squabs)
salt
ground black pepper
4 tablespoons (½ stick) butter
6 thin slices salt pork
chopped parsley
⅓ cup dry white wine
1 cup Demi-Glace Sauce
20 small white onions
1½ teaspoons cornstarch
¼ cup chicken stock or water
3 cups buttered cooked little peas

Rub the skin and inside of the body cavities of the pigeons with salt and pepper. Brown them lightly in the butter in a heavy skillet over moderate heat. Remove the birds, reserving the butter, and place them breast side up in a large casserole. Place a thin slice of salt pork over the breast of each and sprinkle with chopped parsley. Dice remaining salt pork and add it to the casserole. Pour the butter that was left in the skillet over the pigeons. Add wine, Demi-Glace, and onions. Cover and cook in a preheated slow oven (325° F.) 40 minutes or until pigeons and onions are tender. Transfer pigeons to a serving platter and arrange the onions around them. Skim off and discard excess fat from the pan liquid. Blend cornstarch with chicken stock and add to the liquid. Stir and cook 2 to 3 minutes or until the sauce is slightly thick. Serve the sauce in a sauceboat. Accompany with buttered peas in a separate dish. Makes 4 to 8 servings. (See illustration, page 682.)

⚜ PIGEONS WITH TURNIPS AND ONIONS

6 young pigeons
salt
ground black pepper
2 tablespoons butter
1 tablespoon olive oil or salad oil
1 cup Demi-Glace Sauce
2 tablespoons tomato purée
12 small white onions, peeled
3 medium-sized white turnips
chopped parsley

Sprinkle pigeons with salt and pepper. Brown on all sides in 1 tablespoon each butter and oil in a heavy deep skillet. Add next 3 ingredients. Peel turnips, cut them to resemble large olives, brown in remaining butter, and add to pigeons. Cover, bring to boiling point, reduce heat, and simmer 30 to 40 minutes, or until pigeons and vegetables are done. Skim excess fat off the gravy, and adjust seasonings. Serve in a large deep dish. Sprinkle with chopped parsley. Makes 6 servings.

⚜ SQUABS ON FRIED CROUTONS

6 squabs
salt
ground black pepper
2 tablespoons butter, melted
6 thin strips salt pork
6 pigeon livers
¼ pound purée of foie gras
6 slices bread fried in butter
½ cup chicken stock
½ cup dry white wine
2 tablespoons brandy
2 teaspoons flour
1 tablespoon softened butter

Rub the skin and the inside of body cavities of squabs with salt and pepper. Brush the skin with melted butter. Place squabs on a rack in a shallow baking pan. Place a strip of salt pork over the breast of each squab. Cook in a preheated slow oven (325° F.) 1 hour or until squabs are done. Cook pigeon livers in melted butter until they are barely done. Chop fine, mix with the purée of foie gras, and adjust seasonings. Spread the mixture over one side of each slice of fried bread, and top each with a roasted squab. Skim off fat from the roasting pan drippings. Add stock, wine, and brandy. Blend flour with softened butter and add. Mix well. Stir and cook until sauce is slightly thickened. Serve in a sauceboat to spoon over squab. Makes 6 servings.

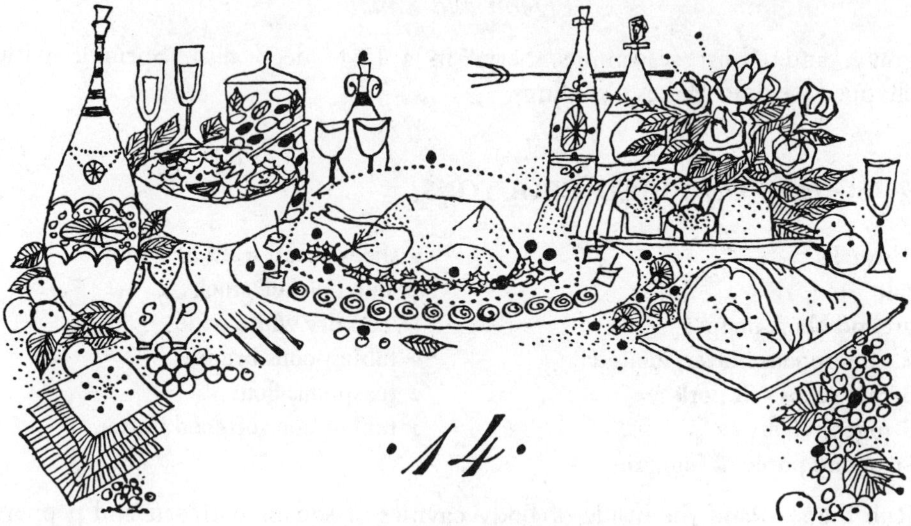

·14·

GAME

The term game (French *gibier*) is applied generally to wild birds and animals which are hunted and to their flesh used as food. Game is more strongly flavored than the flesh of domesticated animals and birds. The "gamy" taste is highly regarded by many people and as strongly disliked by others; game should not be wasted on the latter. The meat is usually lean, and larding is a necessary part of its preparation. In the United States, as in Great Britain, most game can be hunted only during legally specified periods.

Game can usually be frozen satisfactorily. Pluck or skin and eviscerate the game. Make sure it is thoroughly clean and dry. Cool overnight. Wrap in freezer paper (moisture-proof and vapor-proof). Store in a freezer at 0° F. or lower.

If venison is to be frozen, have the local butcher or the butcher at the freezer locker cut the carcass into steaks, roasts, etc. Wrap it correctly in freezer paper and store it in a freezer at 0° F. or lower.

Game Birds

The kinds of game birds available vary in different parts of the world and in different sections of the United States. However, all can be roasted in the same way and other methods of preparation also used for different birds.

WILD DUCK (*Canard Sauvage*)

Wild duck is one of the most popular of game birds. Mallard, the commonest species, is the ancestor of the domesticated duck. There are many other species of wild duck and related waterfowl, all cooked in the same ways.

⚜ ROAST WILD DUCK

1½-pound ready-to-cook wild duck
½ teaspoon salt
1/16 teaspoon ground black pepper
1 medium-sized carrot, sliced
1 rib celery, sliced
1 small white onion, sliced
3 juniper berries (optional)
2 slices fat salt pork
½ cup dry white wine

Sprinkle surface of duck and body cavity with salt and pepper. Stuff the cavity with the next 4 ingredients. Close opening with skewers and lace tightly with twine. Truss. Place duck on a rack in a shallow roasting pan. Cover breast with salt pork slices. Roast 40 minutes in a preheated very hot oven (450° F.), basting frequently with wine. If well-done duck is desired, roast 10 to 20 minutes longer. Remove skewers and twine. Cut duck into serving-size pieces and place on a heated platter. Makes 2 servings.

⚜ BROILED WILD DUCK

1½ pound ready-to-cook wild duck, halved
¼ cup (½ stick) butter, melted
½ teaspoon salt
ground black pepper
2 tablespoons currant jelly, melted

If desired, rub entire duck with about 1 tablespoon baking soda and rinse well. Combine butter, salt, and pepper and brush over the entire surface of the duck. Place duck on a broiler rack, skin side down. Broil 6 inches from broiler heat; or, if a gas broiler, set thermostat to 400° F. and broil 10 to 15 minutes, depending on desired doneness, brushing occasionally with the melted butter mixture. Turn duck and broil 10 to 15 minutes longer, brushing with butter mixture. Transfer duck to a heated platter and brush with melted currant jelly. Makes 2 servings.

⚜ ROAST MARINATED WILD DUCK

3 wild ducks (1½ pounds each)
salt
ground black pepper
lemon juice
port to cover
1 bay leaf
3 whole cloves
1 small onion, sliced
1 carrot, sliced
1 rib celery, sliced
sliced fat salt pork
Marinade Sauce

Thoroughly clean ducks and let them hang for 2 days. Rub them inside and out with salt, pepper, and lemon juice. Truss. Put the ducks in a deep dish and cover with port. Add the next 5 ingredients. Marinate 24 hours. Remove ducks from marinade, reserving it. Place ducks on a rack in a shallow roasting pan. Cover breasts with slices of salt pork. Roast in a preheated very hot oven (450° F.) 40 minutes, basting with the marinade 3 times. If well-done duck is desired, roast 10 to 20 minutes longer. Cut duck into serving-size pieces and serve with Marinade Sauce. Makes 6 servings.

MARINADE SAUCE

1¼ cups strained marinade
1 teaspoon minced shallot
1 stalk celery
⅔ cup orange juice
½ teaspoon lemon juice
1 tablespoon flour
1 cup veal or chicken stock
dash cayenne
½ teaspoon grated orange rind
salt to taste

Combine the first 5 ingredients and cook until the liquid has been reduced to half its original volume. Strain. Blend flour with stock and add to the sauce along with remaining ingredients. Simmer 5 minutes. Serve over duck. Makes approximately 1½ cups.

GROUSE

Grouse, of which there are various species, is highly prized in England and the United States. In France, where it is known as *gelinotte,* it is much less common and the meat is inferior to that of the English and American species. Grouse, partridge, and pheasant can all be prepared in many of the same ways; see the following recipes for Partridge and Pheasant.

⚜ ROAST GROUSE

ready-to-cook grouse
salt
ground black pepper
melted butter
slices of salt pork
½ cup hot water
1 tablespoon butter
2 or 3 juniper berries (optional)

Allow 1 bird per serving. Rub the skin with salt and pepper and with melted butter. Place slices of salt pork across the breast. Roast, uncovered, in a preheated very hot oven (450° F.) 10 to 20 minutes. Remove from oven, place on a warmed platter, and keep warm. Add ½ cup hot water to the roasting pan, bring to boiling point, and simmer until liquid is reduced to half. Add 1 tablespoon butter and, if desired, 2 or 3 juniper berries, which can be bought in drug stores or health food stores. Serve over grouse. Grouse may also be served with Breadcrumb Sauce.

BREADCRUMB SAUCE

2 cups milk
2 whole shallots
2 whole cloves
¼ teaspoon salt
1/16 teaspoon ground black pepper
1 cup fresh breadcrumbs
1½ tablespoons butter

Combine the first 5 ingredients in a saucepan. Bring to boiling point, reduce heat, and simmer 5 to 6 minutes. Strain. Add breadcrumbs and butter. Serve over grouse or other birds. Makes 2 cups.

PARTRIDGE

In French, young partridges are *perdreaux*, older ones *perdrix.*

⚜ PARTRIDGES ON CANAPÉS

4 ready-to-cook partridges
salt
ground black pepper
½ cup (1 stick) butter
4 slices bread
4 partridge livers
1 truffle (optional)
¼ pound foie gras
1 tablespoon chopped parsley
2 tablespoons brandy
4 Baked Whole Tomatoes
parsley

Truss partridges. Rub the skin with salt and pepper and spread with softened butter. Place on a rack in a large roasting pan and cook in a preheated slow oven (325° F.) 45 minutes or until partridges are tender. Drain the butter from the roasting pan into a skillet, and fry the bread, adding remaining butter as needed. Remove bread, and in the same skillet and butter sauté the partridge livers. Chop livers and the truffles, if used, and mix with foie gras and parsley. Spread on the fried bread. Arrange on a round tray. Place a partridge on each slice of bread, with the feet pointing toward the center of the tray. Rinse the roasting pan with brandy and pour over partridges. Garnish tray with Baked Whole Tomatoes and parsley. Makes 8 servings. (See illustration, page 722.)

BAKED WHOLE TOMATOES

Place medium-sized whole tomatoes in a baking pan and bake in a preheated moderate oven (350° F.) 20 minutes or until tomatoes are soft. Allow 1 tomato per serving.

⚜ PARTRIDGES TITANIA

2 ready-to-cook partridges
salt
ground black pepper
4 slices bacon
¼ cup sliced carrots
¼ cup sliced celery
1 small onion, sliced
½ cup (1 stick) butter, melted
segments from 2 oranges
1 cup green grapes
¼ cup orange juice
¼ cup chicken stock

Truss partridges, rub skin with salt and pepper, and lay bacon slices over the breasts. Place vegetables on the bottom of a Dutch oven and lay partridges on the vegetables. Spoon 2 tablespoons melted butter over each partridge. Cover and cook in a preheated slow oven (325° F.) 45 minutes or until partridges are tender. Remove the birds to an ovenproof platter. Surround with orange segments and grapes. Remove and discard the vegetables in the Dutch oven and add orange juice and stock. Boil 1 to 2 minutes. Pour over the partridges and return them to the oven for 5 minutes. Serve at once. Makes 4 servings. (See illustration, page 722.)

PHEASANT (*Faisan*)

⚜ BRAISED PHEASANT WITH WILD RICE

2- to 3-pound ready-to-cook pheasant
salt
ground black pepper
⅓ cup sliced celery
½ small white onion
1 cup chicken stock, or 1 chicken bouillon cube and 1 cup water
2 servings celery hearts
1 cup cooked wild rice

Rub pheasant inside and out with salt and pepper. Stuff celery and onion into the body cavity. Put bird in a large saucepan or Dutch oven. Add stock. Cover, bring to boiling point, and simmer 45 minutes or until bird is tender. Add celery hearts to the saucepan 10 minutes before cooking time is up. Serve the bird with Braised Celery Hearts and Wild Rice. Makes 2 servings.

⚜ CASSEROLE OF PHEASANT

2- to 3-pound ready-to-cook pheasant
salt
ground black pepper
1 tablespoon butter
2 tablespoons olive oil or salad oil
4 slices fat salt pork
1½ cups sliced mushrooms
¼ pound small white onions, peeled
¼ cup Madeira
chopped parsley

Sprinkle the pheasant inside and out with salt and pepper. Brown on all sides in butter and oil. Cover the breast of the pheasant with salt pork. Place bird in a casserole, cover, and cook in a preheated moderate oven (350° F.) 20 minutes per pound, or until pheasant is tender. The meat should be a little on the pink side, otherwise it becomes dry. Add mushrooms and onions when pheasant is half done. Sprinkle them with salt and pepper. When pheasant and vegetables are done, add Madeira and cook 3 to 4 minutes over moderate heat, stirring. Serve in the casserole, sprinkled with parsley. Or transfer pheasant to an oval platter, arrange mushrooms on one side and onions on the other, and garnish with fried bread. Makes 2 servings. (See illustration, page 723.)

VARIATION

PHEASANT AUGE VALLEY STYLE

Cook pheasant as in the recipe for Casserole of Pheasant but omit mushrooms and onions. When pheasant is done, add ¾ cup cream and cook 5 minutes over moderately low heat. Stir in ½ teaspoon lemon juice. Serve hot, with applesauce in a separate dish. Instead of the applesauce, 2 peeled, cored, and quartered tart apples may be added to the casserole 10 minutes before cooking time is up. Makes 2 servings.

⚜ GLAZED PHEASANT À LA MARIE-JEANNE

1 ready-to-cook 3-pound pheasant
2 tablespoons butter
2 tablespoons olive or salad oil
1 cup game or brown stock
1 cup Demi-Glace Sauce
3 pints aspic
salt
ground black pepper
½ pound chestnuts, cooked
1 pound foie gras (fat goose liver)
10 walnut halves, peeled
2 to 3 truffles
12 cashew nuts, halved and grilled
green seedless grapes

The day before serving, brown pheasant in butter and oil in a heavy saucepan. Add stock, cover, and cook 1 hour or until pheasant is tender. Cool. Make a Chaud-froid Sauce, using the pan juices, the Demi-Glace, and 1 cup of the aspic. Adjust seasonings. Remove the breast and bones from the pheasant and set the breast aside. Put chestnuts through a food chopper twice, using the finest blade. Poach foie gras in simmering water, put through the food chopper, and mix with chestnuts. Rub through a sieve. Fill the cavity left by the removal of the breast. Cut breast into strips and lay them over the top of the foie gras mousse. Cover lightly with Chaud-froid Sauce and decorate with a row of walnut halves in the center and a row of sliced truffles on each side. Glaze with aspic. Line small molds with aspic and chill until aspic has set. On the bottom of each of 8 molds put 3 bits of truffle and 3 cashew nut halves in a design, fill molds with remaining mousse, cover with aspic, and chill. Put half of a green seedless grape and several small slices of pheasant breast in the bottom of each remaining mold, fill with the rest of the sauce, cover with aspic, and chill until set. Arrange pheasant on a large oval tray. Turn out the molds and arrange them around the pheasant. Makes 6 to 8 servings. (See illustration, page 723; also Culinary Techniques in Pictures.)

⚜ ROAST PHEASANT

2- to 3-pound ready-to-cook pheasant
salt
ground black pepper
1 slice of lemon
4 slices fat salt pork
melted butter
Madeira Sauce (optional)

Sprinkle pheasant inside and out with salt and pepper. Place the lemon slice in the body cavity. Truss. Cover the breast with the slices of salt pork. Cut cheesecloth large enough to cover the bird completely, soak it in melted butter, and spread over the pheasant. Place covered bird on a rack in a shallow baking pan. Roast in a preheated moderate oven (350° F.) 30 minutes per pound, or until bird is done, basting occasionally with melted butter. Transfer pheasant to a warmed platter. In the roasting pan, make Madeira Sauce or pan gravy (see following recipe) and serve with the bird. Makes 2 servings.

MADEIRA SAUCE FOR ROAST PHEASANT

Add to the roasting pan 1 cup chicken stock, or 1 chicken bouillon cube dissolved in 1 cup boiling water. Cook over moderate heat, scraping all the browned bits from the bottom of the pan. Blend 1½ tablespoons of the stock with 2 tablespoons softened butter and add gradually to pan, stirring constantly. Add 3 tablespoons Madeira and stir. Chop the pheasant liver and add along with salt and pepper to taste.

For plain pan gravy, use 1¼ cups stock and omit the wine.

⚜ SALMIS OF PHEASANT

1 pheasant
2 tablespoons olive oil or salad oil
¼ cup chopped onion
1 shallot, chopped
¼ small clove garlic, crushed
1½ tablespoons flour
⅔ cup dry white or red wine
1 stalk parsley
4 peppercorns
½ bay leaf
½ teaspoon salt
1 cup canned tomatoes
8 mushroom caps
2 tablespoons butter
2 slices toast
pâté de foie gras

Roast pheasant (preferably an older bird) underdone the day before. Cool in the roasting pan. The day the dish is to be served, remove the bird from the pan, put the oil in the pan, and add onion. Stir and cook until onion is golden. Add the next 3 ingredients; stir and cook 1 minute. Add wine, parsley, peppercorns, bay leaf, and salt. Stir and cook until thickened. Add tomatoes. Meanwhile cut breasts and legs from the pheasant, remove and discard skin, and slice meat. Then cut up the carcass and add to the sauce along with the leg bones. Cover and simmer 1 hour. Place the slices of meat in a skillet and strain sauce over them. Cook over low heat until hot. Sauté mushroom caps in butter and arrange over the meat. Serve on toast spread with pâté de foie gras. Makes 2 servings.

QUAIL (*Caille*)

⚜ BROILED QUAIL

ready-to-cook quail
salt
ground black pepper
softened butter
toast
pâté de foie gras (optional)
Sauce for Game
parsley

Allow 1 quail per serving. Split dressed quail and sprinkle with salt and ground black pepper. Spread with softened butter. Place the bird, skin side down, on a preheated broiler pan. Broil 5 to 6 minutes. Turn and broil 5 to 6 minutes longer or until quail is tender and browned. Serve on toast spread with butter or pâté de foie gras. Serve with Sauce for Game. Garnish with parsley.

SAUCE FOR GAME

For each serving, blend 1 teaspoon flour with 1/4 cup chicken stock, and pour into the broiler pan. Stir and cook 1 minute or until sauce has thickened, scraping all the browned bits from bottom of the pan. Add 1 tablespoon light cream and salt and pepper to taste. Serve over quail.

⚜ QUAILS À LA BONNE-MAMAN

3 carrots, peeled
3 ribs celery
3 small white onions
5 tablespoons butter
salt and ground black pepper
6 ready-to-cook quails
3/4 cup veal stock
chopped parsley

Cut carrots and celery into short julienne pieces. Slice onions thinly. Simmer in 1 tablespoon butter until almost done. Season with salt and pepper to taste. Sprinkle quails, inside and out, with salt and pepper. Brown in remaining 4 tablespoons butter. Add to vegetables along with stock. Cover and simmer 10 minutes. Sprinkle with chopped parsley. Makes 6 servings.

If this dish is to be served cold, the stock should be rich enough to jelly; or 1½ teaspoons unflavored gelatin softened in 2 tablespoons cold water may be added to the stock.

⚜ ROAST QUAIL

ready-to-cook quail
salt
ground black pepper
butter
slices fat salt pork
½ cup water
1 tablespoon dry sherry

Allow 1 quail per serving. Rub quail, inside and out, with salt and pepper, then rub with softened butter. Cover breast with 2 slices salt pork and place bird in a buttered shallow roasting pan. Roast, uncovered, 20 minutes, or until done, in a preheated very hot oven (450° F.). If the bird has not browned sufficiently, place under the broiler for a few minutes to brown. Transfer bird to serving dish. Add water to the pan. Stir and cook 1 to 2 minutes, scraping the browned bits from bottom of the pan. Add sherry and season to taste with salt and pepper.

⚜ QUAIL TURKISH STYLE

1 cup raw long-grain converted rice
2 tablespoons olive oil or salad oil
2 cups boiling chicken stock
salt
6 ready-to-cook quails
ground black pepper
¼ cup (½ stick) butter
¾ cup Tomato Sauce
1 tablespoon chopped onion

Soak rice 30 minutes in water to cover. Drain and cook in oil until rice is dry and begins to stick to the pan. Add stock and ½ teaspoon salt. Cover and bring to boiling point, reduce heat, and simmer 6 minutes. Meanwhile, sprinkle quails inside and out with salt and pepper. Brown quickly in butter and add to the rice. Cover and cook 10 minutes, or until rice is tender. Combine Tomato Sauce and onion in a small saucepan. Rinse the skillet in which the quails were browned with ¼ cup chicken stock and add to Tomato Sauce. Stir and cook 2 to 3 minutes. Spoon over quails. Makes 6 servings.

⚜ QUAILS IN WINE

6 ready-to-cook quails
salt
ground black pepper
3 tablespoons butter
½ cup diced carrots
2 tablespoons diced onion
2 tablespoons diced green pepper
½ cup diced mushrooms
2 medium-sized pieces orange peel
1 tablespoon flour
1 cup chicken stock
½ cup dry white wine

Sprinkle quails with salt and pepper, and brown them lightly in butter. Transfer to a buttered casserole. To the skillet in which the quails were browned, add the next 4 ingredients. Blanch orange peel in hot water, drain, and add to the vegetables. Cook slowly for 5 to 6 minutes. Add flour and mix well. Gradually stir in stock. Stir and cook until sauce has thickened. Season with salt and pepper to taste. Simmer 10 minutes. Pour wine over the quails and cook in a preheated moderate oven (350° F.) 10 to 15 minutes. Add the vegetable sauce. Cover and cook 25 minutes or until birds are tender. Makes 6 servings.

WILD TURKEY

The largest of American upland game birds, wild turkey is found only in North America. The average weight of the young hen turkeys is about 8 pounds, of young toms about 12 pounds.

⚜ BRAISED WILD TURKEY

1 ready-to-cook wild turkey
salt
ground black pepper
thick slices fat salt pork
1 medium-sized onion, sliced
1 carrot, sliced
3 stalks parsley
1 rib celery, sliced
1 bay leaf
3 cups chicken stock, or 3 chicken bouillon cubes and 3 cups boiling water
1 teaspoon dried thyme
1 tablespoon cornstarch
2 tablespoons water

Rub salt and pepper over turkey and inside body and crop cavities. Stuff if desired. Truss and cover the breast with salt pork slices. Place on a rack in a roasting pan and roast in a preheated very hot oven (450° F.) until bird is well browned, 15 to 20 minutes. Remove and discard fat that has dripped into the bottom of the roasting pan. Add the next 6 ingredients. Cover, bring to boiling point, reduce heat, and simmer 2 to 3 hours, or until bird is tender, adding more stock if needed. Stir in thyme 10 minutes before cooking time is up. Transfer bird to a heated platter. Strain the sauce and thicken it with 1 tablespoon cornstarch mixed with 2 tablespoons water. Serve with applesauce or cranberry sauce, wild rice, or corn fritters. Allow about 1 pound of turkey per serving.

⚜ ROAST WILD TURKEY

Dress, stuff, and truss as for domestic turkey. Cover breast with fat salt pork slices, or spread the body generously with butter and cover with a clean cloth or 3 thicknesses of cheesecloth (large enough to drape over the bird) that has been lightly wrung out in hot water and butter or shortening, using 1 stick butter or ½ cup shortening to 1½ cups hot water.

Roast in a preheated slow oven 25 minutes per pound. Allow 1 pound per serving. Serve with wild rice, hominy, applesauce or cranberry sauce.

WOODCOCK (*Bécasse*)

Woodcock is regarded in France as the choicest of game birds. The American woodcock belongs to a different but related species.

⚜ ROAST WOODCOCK

ready-to-cook woodcock
salt
ground black pepper
melted butter
slices of salt pork
½ cup hot water
1 tablespoon butter
2 or 3 juniper berries (optional)
toast

Allow 1 bird per serving. Rub ready-to-cook woodcock with salt and pepper. Rub the skin with melted butter. Place slices of salt pork across the breast. Roast, uncovered, in a preheated very hot oven (450° F.) 10 to 15 minutes. Remove from oven and place it on a warmed platter and keep warm. Add ½ cup water to the roasting pan. Bring to boiling point and simmer until the liquid has reduced to half. Add 1 tablespoon butter and, if desired, 2 or 3 juniper berries. (Juniper berries are available in health food stores and drug stores.) Serve on toast with the sauce.

⚜ WOODCOCK STRASBOURG STYLE

2 cold roasted woodcocks, a little underdone
¼ pound poached goose liver
Brown Chaud-froid Sauce flavored with game
1 truffle or black olive
2½ cups game aspic

Remove breasts from the cold woodcocks. With scissors cut out the breastbone. Fill the cavity with goose liver. Cut the breasts diagonally in 3 slices and replace them in the original position over the cavities of the birds. Coat the birds completely with Brown Chaud-froid Sauce. Chill. Garnish with slices of truffle or black olive. Mask with game aspic. Chill the woodcocks and the remaining aspic until set. Coat a platter with chilled aspic and place the birds on it. Break up the jellied aspic with a fork and spoon it onto the platter around the birds. Makes 4 servings.

⚜ BREAST OF WOODCOCK DIPLOMAT

3 roasted woodcocks, a little underdone
¾ pound poached goose liver
salt
ground black pepper
2 truffles or large black olives, sliced
2½ cups game aspic

When woodcocks are cold, remove skin and cut out the breasts and slice them. Remove the meat from the legs and put it through the food chopper twice, using the finest blade. Blend with the goose liver and season to taste with salt and pepper. Spread a layer over the bottom of a 10- by 6- by 2-inch dish. Cover with sliced woodcock breasts and spread with remaining gooseliver mixture. Garnish the top with slices of truffle or black olive. Cover completely with cold but still liquid game aspic. Chill until set. Serve sliced on a chilled tray. Makes 6 servings.

Furred Game

Of the smaller game animals, hare and rabbit are most common. Squirrel, which is hunted in many parts of the United States, is cooked in the same ways as young rabbit. Deer are becoming increasingly prevalent in the

United States as a result of having been protected, and deer hunting, in the limited legal season, increasingly popular.

HARE AND RABBIT

Although hare (French *lièvre*) is larger and has a wilder, gamier flavor, hare and rabbit may be cooked in the same ways. Both are at their best at the age of 7 to 8 months, when they are tender and plump and have reached full maturity. The age of a rabbit or hare can be determined from examining its ears and legs. When the animal is young, its ears are soft, easily torn, and loose in their skins, and its legs are easily broken. The French name for rabbit is *lapin*, but a young rabbit is a *lapereau*. Domesticated rabbit can be cooked in the same ways as wild rabbit or hare.

⚜ BRAISED RABBIT

2 ready-to-cook rabbits, 1 pound each
1½ teaspoons salt
½ teaspoon ground black pepper
3 slices fat salt pork
1 small onion, sliced
1 clove garlic, crushed
1 cup undrained canned tomatoes
½ teaspoon dried basil
½ teaspoon dried oregano
¼ cup claret or port
chopped parsley

Cut rabbit into serving-size pieces. Mix well with salt and pepper. Fry salt pork until crisp, remove slices and drain on paper towels. In the salt pork fat, brown the rabbit on all sides. Add crumbled salt pork along with next 3 ingredients. Cover and bring to boiling point, reduce heat, and simmer 45 minutes or until rabbit is tender. Add herbs and wine 10 minutes before cooking time is up. Serve in a heated platter. Garnish with chopped parsley. Makes 6 servings.

⚜ HASENPFEFFER

1 large ready-to-cook hare or jack rabbit, about 4 pounds
1½ cups wine vinegar
1 cup water
1 cup claret
2 cups sliced onion
2 teaspoons salt
1 teaspoon powdered mustard
1 teaspoon ground black pepper
1 tablespoon mixed pickling spice
flour
¼ cup (½ stick) butter
1 tablespoon sugar
1 cup sour cream

Cut rabbit into serving-size pieces. Let it marinate 48 hours in the next 8 ingredients in the refrigerator. Remove rabbit from marinade, wipe dry, dredge in flour, and brown in butter in a heavy saucepan. Strain marinade and pour over rabbit. Cover, bring to boiling point, reduce heat, and simmer 45 minutes or until tender. Transfer rabbit to a heated platter. Add sugar to the broth and correct salt and pepper. Blend ⅓ cup flour with a little water, add to the broth, and stir and cook 1 to 2 minutes. Just before serving, add sour cream, and heat but do not boil. Pour over rabbit. Serve with Potato Dumplings or buttered noodles. Makes 6 servings.

⚜ JUGGED HARE (*Civet de Liévre*)

4½-pound hare
2½ cups dry red wine
⅓ cup fat rendered from salt pork
2 tablespoons flour
¼ cup brandy
water
1 tablespoon tomato purée
1 stalk parsley
1 clove of garlic, crushed
1 teaspoon salt
¼ teaspoon ground black pepper
20 small white onions, peeled
½ pound mushrooms (caps and stems)
⅓ cup heavy cream

Clean the hare, reserving the liver and blood. Cut hare into pieces and marinate 48 hours in red wine. Reserve the marinade. Wipe the pieces dry and brown over high heat in 3 tablespoons of the salt pork fat. Sprinkle with flour and let it brown. Add brandy, heat, and ignite. Add red wine marinade and an equal amount of water and the next 5 ingredients. Cover, bring to boiling point, reduce heat and simmer 20 minutes. Brown onions in remaining salt pork fat and add to the hare. Simmer 45 minutes. Wash mushrooms and add. Cover and cook 15 minutes or until hare is tender, adding the diced liver 5 minutes before cooking time is up. Mix the hare's blood with a few spoonfuls of the sauce and stir into the mixture. Remove parsley. Add cream and heat (do not boil). Adjust salt and turn into a deep dish, heaping the mushrooms in the center. Makes 6 to 8 servings. (See illustration, page 719.)

VARIATION

JUGGED HARE WITH CHESTNUTS

Make the recipe for Jugged Hare, replacing the mushrooms with 1 pound of chestnuts, scored, peeled, and cooked in the oven until done.

⚜ JUGGED HARE GERMAN STYLE

2½ pounds hare forelegs
1½ teaspoons salt
¼ teaspoon ground black pepper
3 tablespoons bacon drippings
1 cup claret or port
2½ cups Demi-Glace Sauce
¾ cup hare's blood
½ pound small white onions
¼ cup (½ stick) butter
½ pound mushrooms
stewed apples

Mix hare forelegs with salt and black pepper. Brown on all sides in bacon drippings. Add wine and reduce the quantity to one-half. Add Demi-Glace, cover, and simmer until hare is tender. Transfer meat to a heated serving dish. Thicken the sauce with the hare's blood. Heat but do not boil. Adjust salt and pepper. Meanwhile, parboil onions, sauté in half the butter, and arrange in the dish with hare. Quarter the mushrooms, cook in remaining butter until tender, and arrange around the serving dish. Strain the sauce over the rabbit. Serve with stewed apples. Makes 6 servings.

⚜ MARINATED ROAST HARE OR RABBIT

2 ready-to-cook young hares or rabbits
½ cup water
½ cup brandy
2 tablespoons olive oil or salad oil
2 small onions, sliced
½ cup sliced carrots
1 clove garlic, crushed
2 stalks parsley
1 bay leaf
1 teaspoon salt
½ teaspoon poultry seasoning
¼ teaspoon ground black pepper
⅔ cup peeled green grapes
2 hare livers

Place hares or rabbits in a deep dish. Add the next 11 ingredients and marinate in the refrigerator 2 days, turning rabbits in the marinade occasionally. Place the rabbits along with marinade in a casserole or Dutch oven. Cover and cook in a preheated moderate oven (350° F.) 1½ hours or until rabbits are tender, basting frequently with marinade. Transfer rabbits to a warmed serving dish. Add grapes to the cooking liquid. Sauté livers in butter, mash and add. Bring sauce *only* to boiling point. Pour around the hare. Makes 6 servings.

⚜ SADDLE OF HARE (*Râble de Lièvre*)

The saddle is the back of the hare from the first ribs to the legs. It should be roasted medium-rare. (*Continued*)

2 ready-to-cook saddles of hare, 1½ pounds each
salt
ground black pepper
slices fat salt pork, or lardoons
olive oil or salad oil

Rub the saddles of hare with salt and pepper. Cover with slices of salt pork or lard with narrow strips of salt pork (lardoons). Pour enough oil into a roasting pan to cover the bottom generously. Heat in a preheated very hot oven (450° F.) until the oil is smoking, then put in the meat. Roast from 18 to 20 minutes. Transfer meat to a board and carve as illustrated in Culinary Techniques in Pictures. Makes 6 servings.

⚜ SADDLE OF HARE DIANE

2 ready-to-cook saddles of hare, 1½ pounds each
salt
ground black pepper
slices of salt pork or lardoons
olive oil or salad oil
watercress (optional)
Chestnut Purée
Sauce Diane

Rub saddles of hare with salt and pepper. Cover with slices of salt pork or lard with narrow strips of salt pork (lardoons). Pour enough oil into a roasting pan to cover the bottom generously. Heat in a preheated very hot oven (450° F.) until oil is smoking, then put in the meat. Roast 18 to 20 minutes. Transfer meat to a heated platter. If desired, chop the salt pork and garnish the top, or garnish with watercress. Serve with Chestnut Purée and Sauce Diane. Makes 6 servings. (See illustration, page 719.)

CHESTNUT PURÉE

1 pound shelled and cooked chestnuts
2 tablespoons butter
salt and ground black pepper to taste
heavy cream

Put chestnuts through a food chopper, using the finest blade. Then force through a sieve. Add butter, salt, and pepper. Thin with heavy cream to consistency desired. Makes approximately 1½ cups.

VENISON

Venison is the meat of any kind of deer. Like beef, it should be aged for a period of 2 to 4 weeks before cooking. Since the meat lacks fat, venison roasts should be larded with strips of fat salt pork or covered with slices of salt

Jugged Hare, page 716 ▲

▼ Saddle of Hare Diane, page 718

▲ Medallions of Venison Madame Lacroix, page 730

Saddle of Venison with Mushrooms, page 729 ▼

Venison Cutlets with Mandarin Oranges, page 728 ▲

▼ Venison Steaks with Cherries, page 729

▲ Partridges Titania, page 706

Partridges on Canapés, page 706 ▼

Casserole of Pheasant, page 707 ▲

▼ Glazed Pheasant à la Marie-Jeanne, page 708

▲ Pâté of Hare, page 737

Molded Foie Gras Mousse, Modern Style, page 747 ▼

Cold Veal and Ham Loaf, page 735 ▲

▼ Saddle of venison for a cold buffet (see page 32)

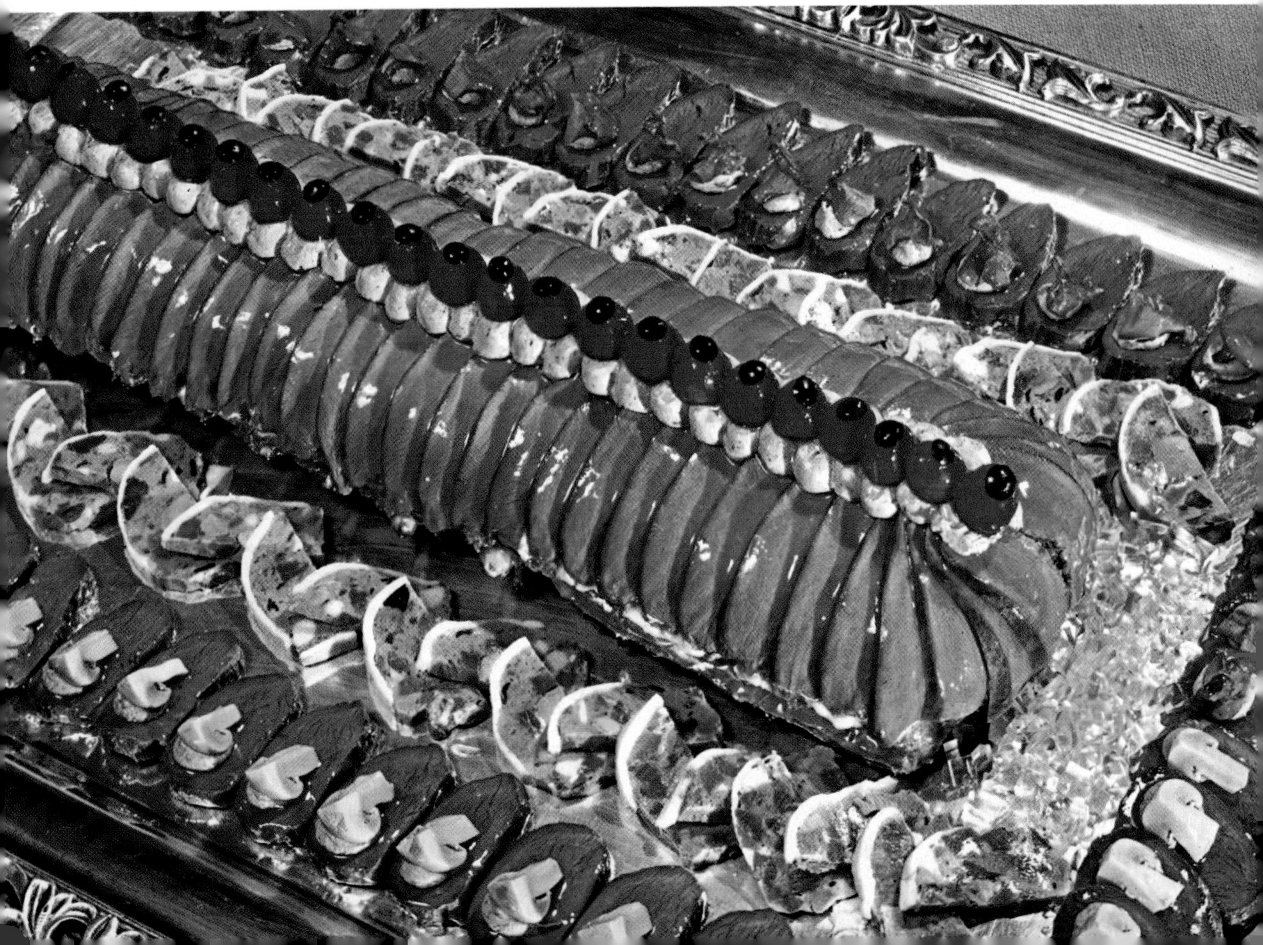

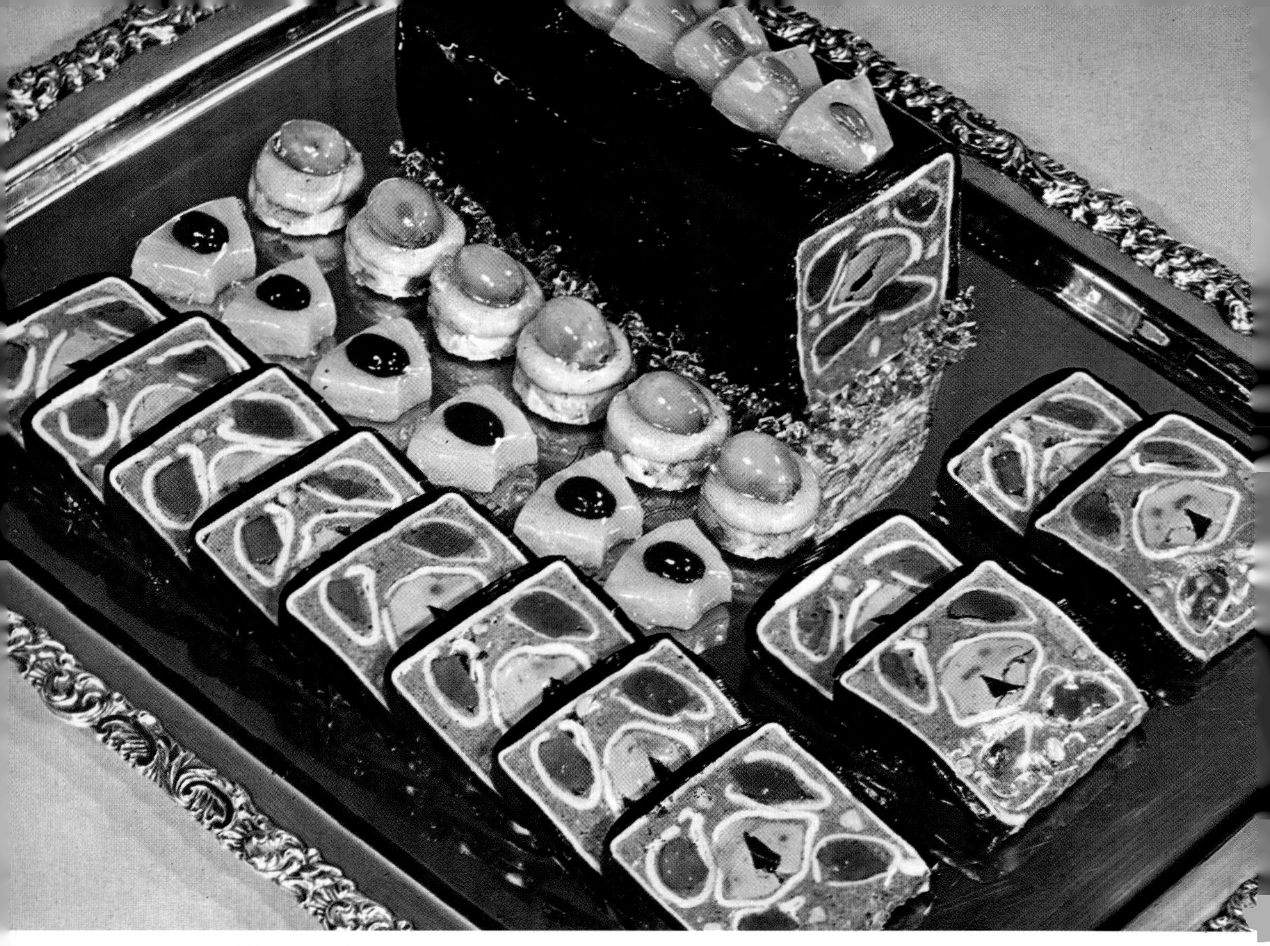

▲ Truffled Venison Pâté, page 738

Chicken Pâté, page 736 ▼

pork, and venison steaks should be cooked in a generous amount of butter or oil. The less tender cuts of venison should always be marinated. The tender saddle of young venison, however, should not. Saddle should be cooked only to the rare stage. A saddle weighing 5 to 6 pounds will cook in 45 minutes to 1 hour in a very hot oven (450° F.)

⚜ ROAST VENISON

6- to 7-pound leg of venison
2 cups Burgundy or claret
1 cup beef bouillon
1 medium-size onion, sliced
1 clove garlic, crushed
1 bay leaf
3 juniper berries (optional)
1 teaspoon salt
6 slices fat salt pork

If the lower part of the leg is used, remove the shank bone. Place meat in a large bowl and refrigerate for 24 hours in the next 7 ingredients. Remove meat from marinade and skewer and tie it into a compact shape. Strain marinade and reserve. If meat thermometer is used, insert it in the thickest part of the muscle. Place the meat on the rack of a shallow roasting pan. Arrange salt pork slices over the top. Roast, uncovered, in a preheated very hot oven (450° F.) 20 minutes. Reduce heat to 325° F. (slow) and cook 15 to 18 minutes per pound, or to an internal temperature of 140° F. for very rare, 150° F. for medium-well-done. Baste meat occasionally with marinade while it is cooking. Transfer meat to a heated platter. Remove and discard fat from pan drippings. Strain and serve hot with the roast, or serve with Sauce Poivarde. Makes 10 to 12 servings.

⚜ ROAST VENISON WITH COOKED MARINADE

6- to 7-pound leg of venison
4 cups water
1½ cups wine vinegar
½ cup chopped onions
½ cup sliced carrots
¼ cup chopped parsley
1 clove garlic, crushed
3 teaspoons salt
10 peppercorns
1 bay leaf
1 teaspoon dried thyme
salt pork slices

If the lower part of the leg is used, remove the shank bone. Place the meat in a large bowl. Put all remaining ingredients except salt pork in a saucepan, bring to boiling point, reduce heat, and simmer 30 minutes. Pour over venison. Cover and refrigerate 24 hours or longer. Remove meat from marinade, skewer, and tie in a compact shape. Insert a meat thermometer if one is used.

Arrange salt pork slices over the top and place meat on a rack in a shallow roasting pan. Roast, uncovered, in a preheated very hot oven (450° F.) 20 minutes. Reduce heat to 325° F. (slow) and cook 15 to 18 minutes per pound, or to an internal temperature of 140° F. for very rare, 150° F. for medium-well-done. Transfer meat to a heated platter. Serve with Sauce Poivarde. Makes 10 to 12 servings.

⚜ ROAST SADDLE OF VENISON

5- to 6-pound saddle of venison
salt
ground black pepper
slices of fat salt pork
½ pound mushrooms, fluted
Cream Pan Sauce

Wipe meat with a damp cloth. Rub with salt and pepper. If a meat thermometer is used, insert it in the thickest part of the meat, not touching a bone. Place meat on a rack in a shallow roasting pan. Cover top with slices of salt pork. Place in a preheated very hot oven (450° F.) and cook, uncovered, 45 minutes to 1 hour, or until the internal temperature is 140° F. for very rare, 150° F. for medium-well-done. About 15 minutes before meat is done, add fluted mushrooms that have been simmered 5 minutes in a little water. Remove meat to a preheated platter. (Do not wash roasting pan.) Garnish with the mushrooms, new potatoes parboiled and sautéed in butter, and chestnuts cooked until tender and sautéed lightly in butter. Serve with Cream Pan Sauce. Makes 6 to 8 servings.

CREAM PAN SAUCE FOR VENISON

1 shallot, finely chopped
2 tablespoons butter
2 teaspoons flour
1½ cups heavy cream
salt and ground black pepper to taste

Remove and discard fat from the venison roasting pan. Add shallots, butter, and flour. Mix well. Stir and cook about 2 minutes. Remove from heat and add cream. Mix well. Stir and cook until sauce thickens. Add salt and pepper. Serve over roast venison. Makes enough for 6 to 8 servings.

⚜ VENISON CUTLETS WITH MANDARIN ORANGES

12 venison cutlets
salt
ground black pepper
4 tablespoons (½ stick) butter
1 tablespoon cognac
¼ cup mandarin orange juice
1 to 2 tablespoons currant jelly
½ cup mandarin orange sections

Sprinkle cutlets with salt and pepper, and sauté them in butter, browning both sides. Transfer meat to a heated platter and keep hot. Add cognac, mandarin orange juice, and jelly to the pan drippings. Mix well, bring to boiling point, and cook 1 minute. In a small saucepan heat mandarin orange sections in their own juice. Place them in the center of the platter. Spoon the sauce over the meat. Serve at once. Makes 6 servings. (See illustration, page 721.)

⚜ VENISON STEAKS WITH CHERRIES

12 small round venison steaks (medallions), 2 ounces each
butter
¾ cup pitted Bing cherries
1-inch piece of stick cinnamon
¼ cup dry sherry
2 teaspoons cornstarch
1 tablespoon water

Pan-broil meat in butter in a skillet over surface heat as desired. Keep warm. Place cherries, cinnamon, and sherry in a saucepan, bring to boiling point, reduce heat, and simmer 2 to 3 minutes. Strain, reserving cherries. Remove cinnamon. Blend cornstarch with water and add to the cherry juice. Bring to boiling point and boil 1 minute. Transfer meat to a heated round platter and arrange in a circle. Put cherries in the center. Pour sauce over steaks and cherries. Serve at once. Makes 6 servings. (See illustration, page 721.)

⚜ SADDLE OF VENISON WITH MUSHROOMS

1 saddle of venison
salt
ground black pepper
slices fat salt pork
butter
½ cup brown stock
½ cup Demi-Glace Sauce
½ cup heavy cream
½ cup chopped onions
3 cups sliced mushrooms
3 cups sliced cepes (optional)
6 to 8 servings boiled potatoes
chopped parsley

Wipe meat with a damp cloth and rub with salt and pepper. If a meat thermometer is used, insert it in the thickest part of the meat, not touching a bone. Place meat on a rack in a shallow roasting pan. Cover top with slices of fat salt pork. Cook in a preheated very hot oven (450° F.) 45 minutes to 1 hour, or until the internal temperature is 140° F. for very rare, 150° F. for medium-rare. Baste several times with melted butter while cooking. Transfer meat to a heated platter and keep warm. Remove and discard fat from pan drippings. Add brown stock and boil 3 minutes. Add Demi-Glace and cream.

Cook until the sauce has reached desired consistency. Adjust salt and pepper. Brown onions in 1 tablespoon butter, add mushrooms, and 2 tablespoons butter. Stir and cook until mushrooms are done. Sauté cepes, if used, in 2 tablespoons butter. Arrange onions and mushrooms and cepes on the platter around the roast. Spoon sauce over the meat. Cut salt pork in julienne strips and sprinkle along the top as a garnish. Serve remaining sauce in a sauceboat. Serve potatoes in a separate dish. Sprinkle with chopped parsley. Makes 6 to 8 servings. (See illustration, page 720.)

⚜ STUFFED VENISON STEAKS
(*Noisettes de Chevreuil Farcies à la Duxelles*)

These steaks are cut either from the loin fillet or from the topside of the leg. They are cut fairly thick, averaging 2½ to 3 inches.

6 large venison steaks
salt
ground black pepper
5 tablespoons butter
Duxelles
flour
2 eggs, beaten
1 cup fine dry breadcrumbs
2 tablespoons olive oil or salad oil

Rub steaks with salt and pepper and fry in 3 tablespoons of the butter over high heat, keeping them very underdone. Cool slightly. Cut the steaks open but not through (like cutting a biscuit). Fill with thick Duxelles, using a pastry bag. Press the top slightly, dredge in flour, dip in beaten eggs, and roll in fine dry breadcrumbs. Fry until golden brown on both sides in remaining 2 tablespoons butter and 2 tablespoons oil. Makes 6 servings.

⚜ MEDALLIONS OF VENISON MADAME LACROIX

1 cup rice
6 tablespoons butter
2 tablespoons chopped onions
2 tablespoons chopped candied ginger
½ teaspoon salt
2 cups hot bouillon
6 steaks cut from the fillet saddle of venison
salt
ground black pepper
6 large sautéed mushroom caps
¼ cup heavy cream
1 cup Sauce Poivarde
1 tablespoon currant jelly
green and red pepper relish

Cook rice 30 minutes in enough water to cover it. Drain and cook rice in 2 tablespoons of the butter until it is dry and begins to stick to the bottom of the pan. Cook onions in 1 tablespoon of the butter until they are limp; add them to rice. Add ginger and bouillon. Cover, bring to boiling point, reduce heat, and simmer 12 to 15 minutes. Remove rice from heat and let it stand about 5 minutes. Fry steaks in remaining 3 tablespoons butter, browning both sides. Sprinkle with salt and pepper. To serve, place rice in a mound in the center of a heated round serving platter, and arrange steaks around it. Top each steak with a mushroom cap sautéed in butter. Rinse skillet with cream, add Poivarde Sauce and jelly, and cook 1 to 2 minutes. Pour a little over the steaks. Serve remaining sauce in a sauceboat. Garnish top of rice with green and red pepper relish. Makes 6 servings. (See illustration, page 720.)

⚜ VENISON STEW HUNGARIAN STYLE

2 pounds boneless venison
3 tablespoons flour
2 teaspoons salt
3 tablespoons fat rendered from salt pork
¾ cup onion rings
1 clove garlic, crushed
3 cups beef or veal stock
6-ounce can tomato paste
½ teaspoon ground black pepper
3 teaspoons paprika
dash cayenne
1 cup sour cream

Cut venison into 1½-inch cubes. Dredge in flour mixed with salt, pressing it in well. Brown meat in salt pork fat. Add onions and garlic. Stir and cook until onions are limp. Add stock. Cover, bring to boiling point, reduce heat, and simmer 2 hours or until meat is tender. Add tomato paste and cook 10 minutes. Add remaining ingredients. Heat but do not boil. Serve with buttered noodles, boiled new potatoes, and red cabbage cooked with apples. Makes 6 servings.

WILD BOAR

Only very young tender boar should be cooked. It must be marinated and cooked well done. Any of the recipes for venison (except those for saddle of venison, which is not marinated) may be used for preparing young tender wild boar.

⚜ YOUNG WILD BOAR CUTLETS

12 cutlets of young wild boar
¾ cup dry white wine
½ cup wine vinegar
1 small onion, sliced
1 carrot, sliced
1 stalk parsley
1 small bay leaf
6 peppercorns
½ teaspoon dried thyme
½ teaspoon salt
12 lardoons
3 tablespoons olive oil or salad oil
3 tablespoons butter

Trim cutlets neatly and marinate 24 hours in the next 9 ingredients. Wipe dry. Lard each cutlet with a narrow strip of fat salt pork (lardoon). Brown on each side in hot oil and butter. Cook in a preheated moderate oven (350° F.) 20 minutes or until meat is thoroughly cooked. Serve with wild rice and currant jelly. Makes 6 servings.

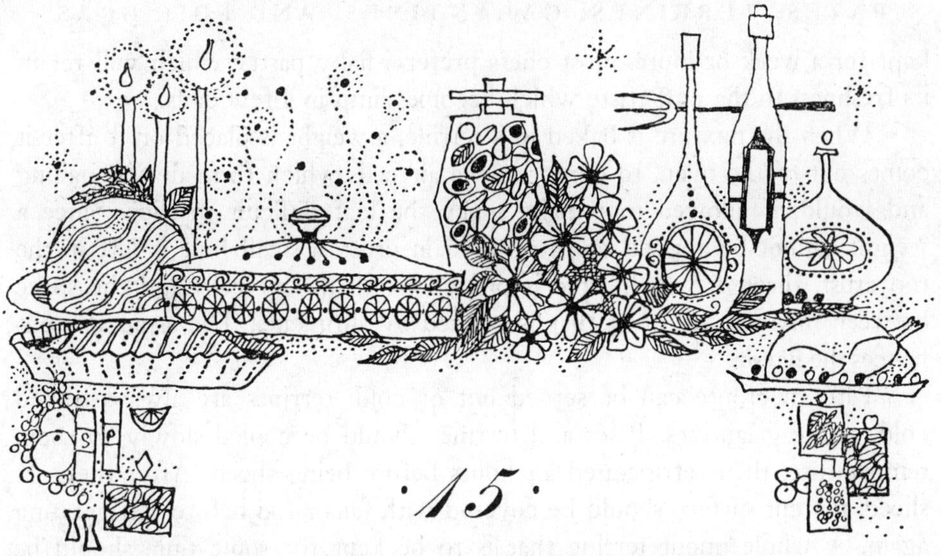

15

PÂTÉS, TERRINES, GALANTINES, AND FOIE GRAS

Pâtés, terrines, and galantines play an important role in the diet of the French people, in everyday meals as well as in those served on important occasions. In French *haute cuisine* these dishes are indispensable.

Terrines and pâtés are made of the same mixtures, which may consist of pork, veal, fowl, liver, game, or fish finely ground and seasoned with wine, brandy, or both, and with herbs and spices. When the mixture is baked in an earthenware dish (terrine) which has been lined with slices of salt pork, the result is called a terrine. The same mixture baked in a pastry crust makes a pâté en croûte. When the same kind of mixture is used to stuff a boned fowl or breast of veal, which is then rolled in a cloth, cooked in stock, and glazed with aspic, the result is a galantine.

Pâté mixtures may be plain or fancy. Plain pâtés are made of ground meat mixtures seasoned and cooked as previously described. Fancy pâtés have strips of ham, tongue, veal, pork, or fowl, and pieces of truffle if available, sandwiched between layers of the ground mixture to form an attractive mosaic pattern when the pâté is sliced. When a crust is used, it may be made either of rich flaky pastry or of yeast-raised puff paste. Since pâtés can be kept for a week or more, most chefs prefer a flaky pastry which will retain its freshness to the puff paste which becomes limp in a few days.

When the mixture is baked in a terrine, a weight is placed on it after it comes out of the oven, to compress the air cells which form during baking and would, if allowed to remain, make the loaf difficult to slice. Since a weight cannot be applied to pâté baked in crust, a small hole is left in the top crust, through which aspic is poured to fill the air cells and the space between mixture and crust that is created by shrinkage. The aspic also enhances the flavor.

Pâté en croûte can be served hot or cold; terrines are always served cold, as are galantines. Pâtés and terrines should be cooled slowly to room temperature, then refrigerated 24 hours before being sliced. After they are sliced, the cut surface should be covered with fat or foil before refrigerating again. A whole uncut terrine that is to be kept for some time should be completely covered with a thick layer of fat. Pork fat melted and cooled is usually preferred for this purpose.

Because foie gras is also characteristic of French *haute cuisine*, recipes for this delicacy are included in this chapter.

PÂTÉS EN CROÛTE

⚜ PASTRY FOR PÂTÉ EN CROÛTE

4 cups sifted all-purpose flour
1 teaspoon salt
1 cup (2 sticks) butter
1 cup lard
1 egg, beaten
about ½ cup water

Sift flour and salt together into a mixing bowl. Add butter and lard and cut in until the dough reaches coarse crumb consistency. Sprinkle in enough water to make a dough that is manageable. Chill at least 2 hours.

⚜ HOW TO LINE A PÂTÉ MOLD

Use a loaf pan or mold 9½ by 5 by 3 inches. Roll out pastry ¼ inch thick, then imprint the pan on the pastry 4 times (see Culinary Techniques in Pictures). Cut off one of the imprints, set aside, and cover with a cloth. Butter the pan and flour lightly. Fit the pastry into the pan, pressing it firmly into the corners with a piece of pastry dough or with the fingers. Trim the edges evenly, leaving a ½-inch border. Fill with forcemeat as specified in the recipe you are making, packing it in well. Press the edges of the pastry inward upon the filling. Roll the reserved piece of pastry ⅛ inch thick, cut it to fit the top of the pan, moisten the under edges, and lay it over the filling. Crimp the edges with a pastry crimper or with a fork. Decorate the top as desired with pastry leaves or flowers made from leftover dough. With a fork prick the crust in several places. Make a small hole in the center, into which insert a funnel of waxed paper or foil to provide space for fat to rise during baking and to allow for escape of steam. Beat 1 egg with 1 tablespoon milk and brush the top crust with the mixture.

⚜ HOW TO BAKE AND COOL PÂTÉ

Bake pâté in a preheated moderate oven (350° F.) 30 to 35 minutes per pound. The pâté is done when the fat which rises in the funnel is perfectly clear. If crust tends to brown too much, cover with foil or buttered brown paper.

Remove pâté from the oven and pour aspic through the funnel to fill air spaces and the space between the filling and crust formed during baking. Cool slowly to room temperature, then refrigerate at least 24 hours. To serve, turn out on a tray and cut into slices.

⚜ COLD VEAL AND HAM LOAF
(*Pâté de Veau et Jambon en Croûte*)

¾ pound lean veal
¾ pound lean ham
¾ cup port or claret
½ cup sliced carrots
¼ cup sliced onion
5 peppercorns
¼ teaspoon poultry seasoning
1 bay leaf
½ pound diced fat salt pork
2 pounds finely ground lean veal
1 tablespoon chopped parsley
2 shallots, finely chopped
1½ teaspoons salt
⅓ cup heavy cream
2 large eggs, beaten
Pastry for Pâté en Croûte
2 chopped truffles (optional)
pistachio nuts
1 egg, beaten with 1 tablespoon milk
sherry-flavored aspic

Slice ham and veal 1 inch thick and cut in strips 4 inches long. Add the next 6 ingredients and marinate in the refrigerator overnight. Put the next 7 ingredients in a bowl and mix well. Make Pastry for Pâté en Croûte. Line the pan or mold as directed in How to Line a Pâté Mold. Spread a layer of the forcemeat 1 inch thick over the bottom of the pastry-lined pan. Press 3 strips each marinated ham and veal onto the forcemeat, laying them lengthwise 3 abreast. Strew chopped truffles in between the strips if desired, and sprinkle with pistachio nuts. Repeat with another layer of forcemeat and another of veal and ham strips, truffles, and pistachio nuts. Cover with remaining forcemeat. Top with pastry, brush with beaten egg, bake, add aspic, and cool, according to directions in How to Bake and Cool Pâté. To serve, turn out onto a tray and slice. Garnish the tray with jellied aspic broken up with a fork, and with grilled or raw stuffed tomatoes. Makes approximately 15 servings. (See illustration, page 725.)

⚜ CHICKEN PÂTÉ

Use the recipe for Veal and Ham Loaf, replacing the ham with chicken. Following previous directions, make Pâté Pastry, line the pâté pan or mold, fill with layers of forcemeat and of sliced chicken and veal, bake, and cool. Serve sliced on a tray garnished with aspic broken up with a fork, and with cheese and black olive canapés and chicken and grape canapés. If desired, remove crust from the top and sides of the loaf and coat with Chaud-froid Sauce. Chill and coat with clear aspic. Chill. Place a row of halved pitted black olives and pistachio nuts down the center. Makes approximately 15 servings. (See illustration, page 726.) Duck may be used instead of chicken.

⚜ SALMON PÂTÉ

2 pounds raw salmon, boned and skinned
1 teaspoon salt
¼ teaspoon ground black pepper
¼ teaspoon ground nutmeg
2 large egg whites
2 cups heavy cream
Pastry for Pâté en Croûte
1 egg, beaten with 1 tablespoon milk

Put 1 pound of the raw salmon through a food chopper twice, using the finest blade. Add half the salt, half the pepper, and the nutmeg. Gradually beat in the egg whites, beating vigorously with a wooden spoon, or mix in an electric mixer. Place the mixing bowl in a pan of cracked ice and gradually beat in the heavy cream.

Make pastry for Pâté en Croûte and line a pâté mold or loaf pan, following previous instructions. Spread the pastry-lined bottom with a layer of salmon forcemeat 1 inch thick. Sprinkle remaining salt and pepper over the rest of the salmon and place half of it in the mold over the forcemeat layer.

Cover with a layer of forcemeat. Repeat, using remaining salmon and forcemeat, having forcemeat as the top layer. Top with pastry and bake according to previous instructions, but *do not add aspic* after removing the pâté from the oven. Cool slowly to room temperature and refrigerate at least 24 hours. To serve, unmold on a tray and slice. Makes approximately 15 servings. Sole or trout may be used instead of salmon.

⚜ PÂTÉ OF WILD RABBIT OR HARE

3- to 4-pound ready-to-cook rabbit or hare
boneless lean fresh pork
boneless lean veal
2 tablespoons olive oil or salad oil
¼ cup chopped parsley
¼ cup sliced onions
½ cup sliced carrots
1 clove garlic, quartered
¾ cup dry white wine
2 tablespoons cognac
1 pound fat fresh pork
1 teaspoon salt
½ teaspoon poultry seasoning
1 onion, sliced
4 stalks parsley
Pastry for Pâté en Croûte
2 truffles, chopped (optional)
1 egg, beaten with 1 tablespoon milk
port-flavored game aspic

Remove the sinews from the dressed rabbit or hare, if this has not been done. Cut the meat from the loin and the tender part of the legs into narrow slices. Weigh this meat and add equal amounts of lean fresh pork and lean veal, also cut in narrow strips. Add the next 5 ingredients, ¼ cup of the wine, and 1 tablespoon of the cognac to the rabbit, pork, and veal strips, and marinate in the refrigerator overnight.

Cut the rest of the rabbit meat from the bones and put it, along with the liver and heart, ¾ pound lean fresh pork, and the fat fresh pork, through a food chopper twice, using the finest blade. Add the remaining ½ cup wine and 1 tablespoon cognac, the salt, and the poultry seasoning and mix well. Cover with slices of onion and the 4 stalks of parsley. Cover bowl tightly and refrigerate overnight. When ready to bake the pâté, remove and discard the onion and parsley, drain the marinade from the sliced meat into the forcemeat, and mix well.

Make pastry for Pâté en Croûte and line a loaf pan or mold according to previous directions. Spread a layer of forcemeat 1 inch thick over the bottom. Lay half the strips of rabbit, pork, and veal on the forcemeat. Sprinkle with chopped truffle, if used. Repeat with another layer of forcemeat and then the remaining strips of meat and chopped truffle. Cover with the remaining forcemeat. Following previous directions, top with pastry, bake, add aspic, and cool. To serve, turn pâté out on a tray, slice, and garnish tray with jellied aspic, broken up with a fork. Or, if desired, remove crust and coat pâté with half-set aspic, smoothing the aspic with a spatula dipped in hot water. Chill until set. Garnish the top with a row of orange segments, each topped with a pistachio nut; glaze with aspic and chill. Decorate the tray with tomato halves topped with mayonnaise. Makes approximately 15 servings. (See illustration, page 724.)

⚜ TRUFFLED VENISON PÂTÉ

1¾ pounds boneless venison
¼ pound fatback
¼ pound goose liver
1 large truffle (optional)
3 tablespoons cognac
1/16 teaspoon ground black pepper
¼ teaspoon dried thyme
1 small bay leaf
2 teaspoons salt
1 pound boneless lean fresh pork
½ pound fat salt pork
2 shallots, finely chopped
⅓ cup heavy cream
2 large eggs, beaten
Pastry for Pâté en Croûte
pistachio nuts
1 egg beaten with 1 tablespoon milk
game aspic flavored with port

Slice ¾ pound of the venison, the fatback, and the goose liver 1 inch thick and cut into strips 4 inches long (cut the goose liver strips the length of the liver). Dice truffle, if used. Marinate with the cognac, pepper, thyme, bay leaf, and ½ teaspoon salt for 4 hours.

Put the remaining 1 pound venison, the fresh pork, and the salt pork through a food chopper twice, using the finest blade. Add remaining salt, shallots, cream, and beaten eggs and mix well.

Make pastry for Pâté en Croûte and line a loaf pan or mold, following previous directions. Spread a layer of forcemeat 1 inch thick on the bottom. Spread half the marinated strips of venison, fatback, and goose liver over it and sprinkle with half the truffle (if used) and with pistachio nuts. Repeat with another layer of forcemeat and then the remaining venison, fatback, goose liver, truffle, and pistachio nuts. Cover with the remaining forcemeat. Following previous directions, top with pastry, bake, add aspic, and cool.

To serve, turn out on a tray, slice, and garnish tray with jellied aspic, broken up with a fork. Or, if desired, cut off the crust and coat the pâté with half-set aspic. Smooth the aspic with a spatula dipped in hot water. Chill until set. Garnish the top with a row of pineapple wedges, each topped with a pistachio nut and glazed with aspic. Decorate the tray with Chicken and Grape Canapés and with additional pineapple wedges topped with black olive halves and glazed with aspic. Makes approximately 15 servings. (See illustration, page 726.)

TERRINES

⚜ HOW TO BAKE AND COOL A TERRINE

Use a terrine mold or other earthenware casserole that has a tight-fitting cover. Line the bottom and sides with thin slices of salt pork. After filling with the desired mixture, cover completely with thin slices of salt pork and lay a bay leaf on top. Cover with the lid and tie 2 thicknesses of foil over it. Place mold in a pan of hot water, having the water about halfway up the sides of the mold, and place in a preheated oven to bake. Add more hot water to the pan as it evaporates. For temperatures and baking times, see individual recipes.

The terrine is done when the mixture shrinks from the sides of the mold. Take it out of the oven, remove the mold from the pan of water, and take off the lid. Remove and discard the salt pork from the top, as well as the bay leaf. Weight the top of the terrine with a heavy plate or a wooden block cut to fit the mold. Cool slowly to room temperature—several hours or overnight. Chill in the refrigerator 12 to 24 hours, keeping the weight on top.

⚜ HOW TO UNMOLD AND SERVE A TERRINE

While the pâté can be served directly from the terrine without unmolding, it may also be unmolded by dipping the dish quickly into very hot water, loosening the edges with a spatula, and inverting the dish on a platter. The slices of salt pork are then removed and the excess fat wiped off. The pâté may then be sliced or returned to the mold for serving. Or it may be returned to the mold and aspic flavored with sherry, Madeira, or port poured over it. It is then chilled again until aspic is firm, then turned out onto a platter and sliced.

⚜ CHICKEN-LIVER TERRINE (*Terrine de Chagny*)

1 pound raw chicken livers
¾ pound pork sausage
3 tablespoons sherry wine
1½ tablespoons cognac
½ teaspoon dried thyme
¾ teaspoon salt
2 large eggs, well beaten
thin slices fat salt pork
1 bay leaf
sherry (optional)

Chop chicken livers very fine and mix with the next 5 ingredients. Beat in the eggs and continue beating the mixture with a wooden spoon until well blended. Line the bottom and sides of a 1½-quart terrine mold or casserole with thin slices of salt pork and fill with the mixture. Following directions in How to Bake and Cool a Terrine, cover, seal, bake in a preheated hot oven (400° F.) 1½ hours, cool, and refrigerate. If desired, pour a little sherry over the pâté before refrigerating. Serve from the mold or unmold and slice (see How to Unmold and Serve a Terrine). Makes 10 to 12 servings.

⚜ PORK-LIVER TERRINE

1½ pounds pork liver
milk
½ pound boneless lean veal
½ pound fatback, cubed
1 tablespoon flour
2 medium-sized eggs
1 teaspoon chopped parsley
½ teaspoon salt
½ teaspoon dried thyme
¼ teaspoon dried marjoram
2 tablespoons finely chopped onion
1 finely chopped shallot
thin slices fat salt pork
1 bay leaf
aspic flavored with claret or port (optional)

Cut liver into cubes and soak 1 hour in milk to cover. Drain liver, rinse with cold water, and wipe dry. Put liver, veal, and fatback through a food chopper, using the finest blade. Add flour and mix about 5 minutes with a wooden spoon, or blend in an electric mixer. Beat in eggs, one at a time. Add the next 6 ingredients. Mix well.

Line the bottom and sides of a heavy 1½-quart casserole or terrine mold with slices of salt pork and pack in the pâté mixture. Following previous directions, cover, seal, and bake in a preheated moderate oven (350° F.) 1½ hours; open, cool, refrigerate, and unmold. Return the pâté to the casserole. Either serve it from the casserole, or pour aspic flavored with claret or port over the pâté, chill again, and then turn out onto a tray and slice. Garnish with parsley and black olives. Makes 12 to 15 servings.

⚜ LIVER PÂTÉ

2 pounds pork, lamb, or beef liver
milk
¾ pound lean raw pork
¾ pound fat raw pork
2 teaspoons chopped parsley
¼ teaspoon ground thyme
¼ teaspoon ground marjoram
½ teaspoon salt
2 finely chopped shallots or 2 tablespoons chopped onion
1½ tablespoons flour
2 large eggs
thin slices of salt pork

Cut the liver into small pieces. Add milk to cover and soak 1 hour or more. Drain liver, rinse in cold water, and dry well. Put both fat and lean pork through a food chopper twice, using the finest blade. Add the next 6 ingredients, stir, and beat 5 to 6 minutes. Beat in eggs, one at a time, mixing well. Line a 9½- by 5- by 3-inch loaf pan with thin slices of salt pork. Put in the pâté mixture and pack it in well. Cover top with salt pork slices and cover pan with 2 thicknesses of foil, tying it down. Following previous directions, bake in a preheated moderate oven (350° F.) 1¾ hours; open, cool, and refrigerate. Unmold according to previous directions, slice, and serve. Makes a 9½- by 5- by 2½-inch loaf.

⚜ PORK AND VEAL TERRINE

1¼ pounds boneless lean veal
¼ pound boneless lean ham
¼ cup cognac
¼ teaspoon salt
⅛ teaspoon ground black pepper
¼ teaspoon dried thyme
¼ teaspoon ground nutmeg
1 tablespoon finely chopped shallot or onion
2 truffles, finely chopped (optional)
¾ pound lean fresh pork
½ pound fat salt pork
2 large eggs, beaten
¼ teaspoon ground ginger
½ teaspoon poultry seasoning
1 clove garlic, crushed
thin strips fat salt pork
1 bay leaf
aspic flavored with sherry or Madeira (optional)

Slice ½ pound of the veal and the ham ¼ inch thick and cut into strips 4 inches long. Marinate 2 to 3 hours in the cognac, along with the salt, pepper, nutmeg, shallot or onion, and 1 chopped truffle (if used). Put fresh pork, ½ pound salt pork, and remaining ¾ pound of veal through a food chopper twice, using the finest blade. Add the next 4 ingredients. Drain the marinade from the veal and ham strips and add. Mix well.

Line the bottom and sides of a 2-quart terrine mold or casserole with strips of salt pork. Put one-third of the meat mixture on the bottom. Cover with half the veal and ham strips. Sprinkle with chopped truffle (if used). Repeat with the second third of the meat mixture and the remaining veal and ham strips and truffle. Cover with the rest of the meat mixture. Following previous directions, cover, seal, and bake in a preheated moderate oven (350° F.) 1½ hours, or until the pâté shrinks from the sides of the mold and the juices are clear yellow with no trace of pink; open, cool, refrigerate, and unmold. Return the pâté to the terrine. Serve it from the mold, or pour aspic flavored with sherry or Madeira over it and chill again, then turn it out on a tray and slice. Garnish the tray if desired with parsley and diced jellied aspic. Makes approximately 20 servings.

GALANTINES

Galantines were originally made only of chicken, but now other fowls are also used, as well as breast of veal.

⚜ HOW TO ROLL AND COOK A GALANTINE

Generously butter a large clean cloth or several thicknesses of cheesecloth and spread on a flat surface. Lay the skin of the fowl on the cloth with the outside down and spread with other ingredients as directed in the individual recipes. By lifting the edge of the cloth and pulling gently, carefully shape the arrangement into a firm roll, drawing the edges of the skin together to form a sausage-shaped roll. Sew the skin together along the length of the roll and at the ends. Wrap the roll tightly in the cloth, making sure it is smooth and even, and tie it in the middle and at the ends with string.

Place the roll and other ingredients as specified in a large kettle and pour in stock to cover. Cover the kettle, bring to boiling point, reduce heat, and simmer according to individual recipes. Let the galantine cool in the stock, then remove it, unroll, and roll again in a clean cloth. Weight it with a heavy plate and let stand for 2 hours or longer.

Make a clear aspic from the stock in which the galantine was cooked. Remove the cloth and the threads with which the skin was sewed. Glaze the roll with Chaud-froid Sauce and the aspic, or with the aspic alone. Chill until firm and cut in thin slices for serving.

Galantines may be served at a cold buffet or as a first course accompanied with buttered toast.

⚜ GALANTINE OF CHICKEN

6-pound ready-to-cook roasting chicken
1 calf's foot (optional)
2 pounds veal shank
½ pound boneless lean pork
½ pound boneless lean veal
½ pound salt pork, cubed
3 tablespoons cognac, sherry, or Madeira
1½ teaspoons salt
¼ teaspoon ground mace
1 teaspoon ground thyme
½ cup heavy cream
¼ pound fatback
¼ pound cooked tongue or ham
1 truffle, chopped (optional)
⅓ cup pistachio nuts
1 stalk parsley
1 carrot
½ cup sliced onions
½ cup sliced celery
Chaud-froid Sauce (optional)

Have the butcher bone the chicken (or bone it yourself). Make a rich stock from the chicken bones, veal shank, and the calf's foot if available. Reserve.

Split the boned chicken down the whole length of the back and open it out flat, skin side up. Starting at the back, with a sharp knife carefully cut the skin away from the meat, removing the skin in one piece. Be careful not to pierce the skin. Trim skin at the legs and wings, leaving enough to cover the openings. Cut the meat of the breast and the tenderloin under the breast and that of the drumsticks into thin slices and set aside. Put the remaining chicken meat and the lean pork and the veal through a food chopper twice, using the finest blade. Add the next 6 ingredients and mix well.

Place the chicken skin, outside down, on a buttered cloth (see preceding directions) and spread it with the meat mixture. Cut fatback and tongue into strips and arrange them in alternate layers over the meat. Sprinkle chopped truffle (if used) between the slices. Sprinkle with pistachio nuts. Cover with the slices of chicken.

Following the preceding directions, make the arrangement into a roll and place it, with the parsley, carrot, onions, and celery, in a large kettle. Pour in stock to cover. Cover the kettle, bring to boiling point, reduce heat, and simmer 1¼ hours. Cool, glaze, chill, and slice, according to preceding directions. Makes approximately 8 servings. (See illustration, page 684.)

⚜ GALANTINE OF TURKEY

Use the recipe for Galantine of Chicken, but replace the chicken with a 12- to 15-pound turkey and double all the other ingredients. Increase the simmering time to 1¾ hours. Makes 12 to 15 servings.

⚜ GALANTINE OF DUCK

4- to 5-pound ready-to-cook duck
1 calf's foot (optional)
2 pounds veal shank
¾ pound veal cutlets
¼ cup cognac or sherry
¾ pound boneless lean veal
½ pound boneless lean pork
¼ pound fatback
1½ teaspoons salt
¼ teaspoon ground black pepper
¾ teaspoon poultry seasoning
⅓ cup heavy cream
1 finely chopped truffle (optional)
¼ cup pistachio nuts
½ cup sliced carrots
½ cup sliced onions
2 stalks parsley
2 whole cloves
8 peppercorns
Chaud-froid Sauce (optional)

Have the butcher bone the duck and reserve the carcass and the liver. Make a rich stock from the duck carcass, veal shank, and the calf's foot if available. Reserve the stock.

Detach the meat from the skin as in Galantine of Chicken. Cut the breast and leg meat into thin strips, removing and discarding sinews. Cut the veal cutlets into strips 4 inches long and 1 inch wide. Marinate the strips of veal and the strips of duck meat in cognac or sherry for 2 hours. Put the remaining duck meat, the duck liver, the boneless veal and pork, and the fatback through a food chopper twice, using the finest blade. Drain the cognac or sherry from the veal strips into the ground meat, add seasonings and cream, and mix well.

Lay the duck skin, outside down, on a buttered cloth (see previous instructions) and spread with the meat mixture. Over this lay the marinated strips of veal and duck. Sprinkle with chopped truffle (if used) and pistachio nuts.

Following the previous directions, make the arrangement into a roll and place it in a kettle, along with the carrots, onions, parsley, cloves, and peppercorns. Pour in stock to cover. Cover the kettle, bring to boiling point, reduce heat, and simmer 1½ hours. Cool, glaze, chill, and slice, according to the previous directions. Makes 6 to 8 servings.

GALANTINE OF VEAL

3½ pounds breast of veal
salt
ground black pepper
1 teaspoon poultry seasoning
½ teaspoon crumbled dried rosemary
1¾ pounds sausage
¾ pound lean ham, sliced
3 tablespoons pistachio nuts
1 carrot, sliced
⅓ cup sliced onion
1 rib celery, sliced
2 pounds veal shank
Chaud-froid Sauce (optional)

Ask the butcher to bone the veal and reserve the bones. Make a rich stock from the bones and reserve it.

Spread the meat out flat on a buttered cloth (see previous directions) and sprinkle it with salt, pepper, and herbs. Spread the sausage over the veal, leaving a 1-inch border all around. Cut the ham into strips 4 inches long and 1 inch wide and arrange these in rows down the length of the veal. Sprinkle with pistachio nuts.

Following the previous directions, make the meat into a roll and place it, with the vegetables and veal shank, in a large kettle. Pour in hot stock to cover. Cover the kettle, bring to boiling point, reduce heat, and simmer 2 hours. Cool, glaze, chill, and slice, according to previous directions. Makes 12 to 15 servings.

FOIE GRAS

Literally translated, foie gras means "fat liver." In cookery, however, the term is used for the livers of geese (and sometimes of ducks) which have been fattened by special feeding. The finest foie gras comes from geese raised in Alsace and southwestern France, but excellent livers are exported by Austria, Czechoslovakia, and Hungary. Foie gras is internationally regarded by gourmets as one of the greatest delicacies of the table.

Raw foie gras, which is available in Europe only during a limited season, cannot be obtained in America. Foie gras purée or pâté is imported in cans or jars. Livers of ordinary geese can sometimes be obtained on special order from very specialized stores in some areas.

⚜ SCALLOPS OF FOIE GRAS LUCULLUS

1 pound raw foie gras or goose liver
¼ teaspoon salt
1/16 teaspoon ground black pepper
¼ cup sherry
12 slices truffle
flour
8 tablespoons (1 stick) butter
¾ cup Demi-Glace Sauce
12 2-inch rounds bread

Cut foie gras diagonally into 12 fairly thick slices. Season with salt and pepper and marinate 2 hours in the sherry, along with the truffle slices. Remove foie gras slices from the marinade, wipe dry, dredge in flour, and sauté in 3 tablespoons of the butter, browning both sides. Combine the Demi-Glace with wine and truffles and cook slowly for a few minutes. Fry the rounds of bread in the remaining butter. Put a slice of foie gras on each round and cover with the sauce, being careful to get a truffle slice on top of each. Makes 6 servings.

⚜ FRIANDISES OF FOIE GRAS

Plain Pastry (using 2 cups flour), or Puff Paste
1½ cups (10 ounces) foie gras purée, or foie gras puréed with butter
1 egg yolk, beaten with 1 teaspoon milk

Roll pastry to ⅛ inch thickness on a lightly floured board. Cut into rounds with a 2-inch cooky cutter. Top the center of each with a heaping ½ teaspoon purée. Moisten the edges slightly and fold the dough over. Crimp edges with a fork and brush with egg yolk beaten with the milk. Bake in a preheated hot oven (400° F.) 5 to 8 minutes or until browned. Serve as a hot hors d'oeuvre. Makes approximately 4 dozen.

⚜ SMALL ECLAIRS WITH GOOSE-LIVER PURÉE
(*Carolines au Foie Gras*)

Make small eclairs with Chou Paste (page 126). Cool. Make an opening and with a pastry bag and round ¼-inch tube fill them wtih foie gras purée. If desired, coat the eclairs with white or light brown Chaud-froid Sauce. Or serve plain. Serve as an hors d'oeuvre. Allow 3 to 4 per person.

⚜ FOIE GRAS IN ASPIC

1 whole foie gras or goose liver, cooked
semiliquid chicken aspic
6 slices truffles
Melba toast
watercress or parsley

Place whole cooked goose liver on a chilled tray. Cover the liver with several layers of aspic, chilling after each layer is applied. On each side of the liver place 3 truffle slices. Mask again with several layers of aspic, chilling after each layer. Chill until serving time. Slice and serve on Melba toast. Garnish with watercress or parsley. Makes 6 servings.

⚜ TRUFFLES SURPRISE

1 pound foie gras or goose liver, poached in sherry
½ cup (1 stick) butter, softened
truffles, or truffle peel, finely chopped
1 cup sherry-flavored aspic

Purée the poached liver and blend in the softened butter. Cool and chill. Shape into walnut-size balls and roll them in finely chopped truffles or finely chopped truffle peel until well coated. Dip in aspic and chill until set. Arrange in a pyramid on a tray or use to garnish cold meat, poultry, or game dishes. Makes 6 servings.

⚜ SMALL MOLDS OF FOIE GRASS IN WINE ASPIC

1 quart Madeira- or port-flavored aspic
2 truffles, sliced
8 two-inch cubes foie gras or goose liver
parsley

Coat 8 4-ounce molds with aspic and chill. Place a truffle slice in the bottom of each and put a 2-inch cube of foie gras on top. Fill the molds with aspic. Chill until set. Chill remaining aspic. Just before serving unmold in a circle on a chilled tray. Break up chilled aspic with a fork and spoon it around the molds. Garnish with parsley and slices of remaining truffle. Makes 8 servings.

⚜ JELLIED FOIE GRAS LOAF (*Pain de Foie Gras en Gelée*)

1 large foie gras or goose liver
1 cup port
3 truffles
1 tablespoon meat glaze
2 large egg yolks
¼ cup (½ stick) butter, softened
¼ cup hazelnuts, chopped
salt and ground black pepper
4 cups aspic

Poach goose liver in port with truffles the day before and let it cool in the wine. Pour off the stock, skim off fat, and boil the stock down with the meat glaze until only 2 tablespoons remain. Place in a small bowl and beat with egg yolks, as in beating Hollandaise Sauce. Blend in softened butter. Pound hazelnuts, or put them through an electric blender, and add. Put goose liver through a sieve or an electric blender and mix thoroughly with the egg and nut mixture. Slice 2 of the truffles and add. Season to taste with salt and pepper. Line a 1-quart mold with aspic. Chill until set. Slice remaining truffle and arrange in the bottom and around the sides of the mold. Coat again with aspic. Chill until set. Then pack in the liver mixture. Chill until set. Finish filling the mold with aspic. Chill until set. Chill remaining aspic until set. Unmold the loaf onto a chilled tray. Break up additional aspic with a fork and spoon it around the loaf. Makes 1-quart mold.

⚜ MOLDED FOIE GRAS MOUSSE, MODERN STYLE

3½ pints chicken aspic
2 truffles
2 envelopes unflavored gelatin
¾ cup water
3 cups purée of foie gras
½ cup heavy cream, whipped

Place a pâté mold or a 9½- by 5- by 3-inch loaf pan in a pan of cracked ice. Pour in chicken aspic and roll the pan from side to side to coat evenly with aspic. Cut ½-inch circles from truffles and arrange them in a row ½ inch apart down the lengthwise center of the mold. Affix each circle with a few drops of aspic and let it stand a few minutes to set.

Soften the gelatin in ¾ cup water in a small bowl. Place over hot water (not boiling) to melt. Force foie gras purée through a fine sieve. Stir in melted gelatin. Fold in whipped cream. Pack the foie gras mixture into the mold or pan, filling it half full. Cut truffles into small pieces and place a row lengthwise down the center of the pâté. Pack in remaining foie gras, filling the mold or pan to within ½ inch of the top. Chill until the mousse is set. Finish filling the mold with cool but still liquid aspic. Chill until aspic is firm.

To serve, unmold the mousse on a large tray. Cut into slices ¼ inch thick. Decorate the tray with jellied aspic broken up with a fork. Makes approximately 15 servings. (See illustration, page 724.)

·16·

VEGETABLES

Vegetables are grown all over the world, except in the arctic and antarctic zones, but the United States and France probably produce more different varieties than does any other country. Methods of vegetable cookery in these two countries differ to some extent. Since the American housewife is especially concerned with preserving the nutritive value of vegetables, she uses very little water and usually cooks them a shorter time. The French housewife, on the other hand, is interested primarily in flavor and appearance and therefore does not hesitate to soak, blanch, mash, squeeze, trim, or carve vegetables if these processes will produce a more flavorful and attractive result. If a vegetable is not being served immediately, one of her culinary tricks is to blanch it first in boiling water, then quench in cold water, and finish the cooking just before serving time. If a vegetable is cooked ahead of time, instead of setting it aside to keep warm, she cools it and reheats it later; with this method the vegetable does not overcook and the color is brighter.

For general instructions on cooking vegetables, see Various Methods of Cooking and Their Technology in Chapter 3, pages 114–17.

ARTICHOKES (*Artichauts*)

⚜ WHOLE ARTICHOKES

Allow 1 large artichoke or 2 small ones to a serving. Wash artichokes, cut off stems even with the base, and remove and discard tough outer leaves. Cut off and discard the top third of each artichoke; if any prickly ends of leaves are left, trim them off. Stand artichokes upright in a saucepan just large enough for them to fit snugly, or tie a string around each one to hold it in shape. To prevent discoloration, rub lemon juice over the cut surfaces or fasten a thin slice of lemon onto the base of each artichoke with a toothpick or small skewer. Pour in boiling water to cover and add 1 teaspoon salt. Cover and cook 40 minutes to 1 hour, or until artichokes are tender. They are done when a leaf will pull out easily. Remove strings, if used, and place artichokes upside down to drain. Using a sharp knife, remove the prickly choke in the center that covers the heart; this is discarded. Serve hot artichokes with melted butter, Hollandaise or Mousseline Sauce, or one of the following:

Lemon Butter. Melt ½ cup (1 stick) butter and add 1½ tablespoons lemon juice and a dash of ground black pepper.

Parsley Butter. Melt ½ cup (1 stick) butter and add 2 tablespoons chopped parsley, 1 teaspoon lemon juice, and a dash of ground black pepper.

⚜ ARTICHOKES WITH VINAIGRETTE SAUCE

Cook artichokes as in preceding recipe. Arrange them on a serving platter and put a large sautéed mushroom cap in the opening of each. Garnish platter with parsley and wedges of tomato. Serve Vinaigrette Sauce in a sauceboat. Either hot or cold artichokes may be served with Vinaigrette Sauce. (See illustration, page 759.)

⚜ ARTICHOKES MIREILLE

12 small artichokes
½ cup olive oil or salad oil
1 cup hot chicken bouillon
12 small white onions
4 medium-sized tomatoes
½ teaspoon salt
⅛ teaspoon ground black pepper
¼ teaspoon sugar
chopped parsley

Artichokes

Cut off the stems and tops of artichokes and trim off the tips of the leaves. Wash well. Put in a casserole with oil, bouillon, and onions. Peel tomatoes, quarter, and add. Sprinkle with salt, pepper, and sugar. Cover casserole and bake in a preheated hot oven (425° F.) 40 minutes or until vegetables are tender. Sprinkle with chopped parsley and serve from the casserole. Makes 6 servings.

⚜ ARTICHOKES ROMAN STYLE

12 small or 6 large artichokes
lemon
salt
1 clove of garlic
½ cup chopped parsley
½ cup chopped mint leaves
1 teaspoon salt
6 peppercorns
⅓ cup olive oil or salad oil
2 cups dry white wine
⅔ cup chicken or veal stock

Prepare artichokes for cooking as instructed for Whole Artichokes. Scoop out the choke with a pointed teaspoon. Finely chop garlic, mix with chopped parsley and mint, and stuff into the centers of the artichokes. Stand artichokes in an upright position in a saucepan or flameproof casserole just big enough for them to fit snugly, or tie a string around each to hold them in shape. Skewer a thin slice of lemon on the base of artichokes to prevent discoloration. Add salt, peppercorns, and oil. Cover and cook over moderate heat 10 minutes. Add wine and stock. Cover and cook in a preheated moderate oven (375°F.) 40 to 60 minutes, or until the leaves pull out easily and the sauce is well reduced. Makes 6 servings.

⚜ SAUTÉED ARTICHOKE BOTTOMS

6 large artichokes
lemon juice
1 tablespoon flour
1 quart water
1 teaspoon salt
2 tablespoons butter

Wash artichokes and cut off stems even with the base. Trim the bottoms and rub them with lemon juice to prevent discoloration. Using a sharp knife, cut off leaves about ½ inch from the base. Cut each artichoke into 6 pieces. Mix flour with a little of the water in a 1½-quart saucepan. Add remaining water, salt, and 1 teaspoon lemon juice. Bring to boiling point and add artichoke pieces. Cover and cook over moderate heat 30 minutes, or until artichokes are tender. Drain them well. Remove and discard the prickly chokes. Brown the butter lightly in a skillet. Add artichoke bottoms and sauté a few minutes on each side. Serve hot. Makes 6 servings.

⚜ ARTICHOKE BOTTOMS ARGENTEUIL

6 cooked large artichoke bottoms
4 to 5 tablespoons butter
2 tablespoons flour
1 cup milk, or ¾ cup stock and ¼ cup heavy cream
salt
ground black pepper
1½ pounds asparagus tips, cooked
chopped parsley

Prepare and boil artichoke bottoms as for Sautéed Artichoke Bottoms. Cook in 2 to 3 tablespoons butter a few minutes, but do not brown. Meanwhile, melt 2 tablespoons butter in a 2-cup saucepan. Remove from heat and blend in flour. Stir and cook 1 minute. Remove from heat and add milk or stock and cream. Stir and cook until sauce is of medium thickness. Add salt and pepper to taste. Drain cooked asparagus tips and blend with the sauce. Turn into the center of a serving dish and arrange cooked artichoke bottoms around the edge. Sprinkle asparagus with chopped parsley. If desired, fill the artichoke bottoms with the creamed asparagus and place under the broiler to brown. Makes 6 servings. (See illustration, page 762.)

⚜ ARTICHOKE BOTTOMS COLBERT

6 cooked large artichoke bottoms
flour
⅛ teaspoon ground black pepper
2 eggs, beaten
fine dry breadcrumbs
10 tablespoons butter (1¼ stick) or more
½ teaspoon lemon juice
1 teaspoon chopped parsley
½ teaspoon chopped fresh or ⅛ teaspoon dried tarragon
½ teaspoon meat glaze or melted beef extract

Prepare and boil artichoke bottoms as for Sautéed Artichoke Bottoms, drain well, and remove chokes. Mix flour with black pepper and dredge pieces of cooked artichoke bottoms. Dip in beaten eggs and then roll in breadcrumbs. Fry in 2 to 3 tablespoons butter, browning all sides. Drain on paper towels and transfer to a serving dish. Melt remaining butter, add all other ingredients, mix, and pour over artichoke bottoms. Serve hot. Makes 6 servings.

⚜ STUFFED ARTICHOKE BOTTOMS

6 large artichokes
lemon juice
boiling water
salt
6 teaspoons pâté de foie gras
6 tablespoons sautéed chopped mushrooms
6 teaspoons butter
ground black pepper to taste
¼ cup Madeira wine or consommé

Wash artichokes and cut off stems even with the base. Cut off leaves ½ inch above the bottom; if there are any prickly tips left on, trim off tips. Rub lemon juice over the cut surface to prevent discoloration. Place in a saucepan, pour in boiling water to cover, and add 1 teaspoon salt and 1 teaspoon lemon juice. Cover and cook 30 to 40 minutes, or until the bottoms are tender. Drain well. Remove the chokes from the centers. In the center of each artichoke bottom put 1 teaspoon pâté de foie gras and 1 tablespoon sautéed mushrooms. Dot each with 1 teaspoon butter. Sprinkle with salt and pepper. Pour the Madeira or consommé over the tops of all. Bake in a preheated hot oven (400° F.) 15 to 20 minutes. Makes 6 servings.

⚜ ARTICHOKE BOTTOMS STUFFED WITH MUSHROOMS

1 cup Mushroom Purée
¼ cup Béchamel Sauce
1 large egg, separated
salt
ground black pepper
6 cooked large artichoke bottoms
¼ cup grated Parmesan cheese
3 tablespoons butter, melted

Combine Mushroom Purée, Béchamel Sauce, egg yolk, and salt and pepper to taste. Mix well and bring to boiling point. Remove from heat and let cool while beating egg white. Beat egg white until it stands in soft stiff peaks and fold it into the mushroom mixture along with 2 tablespoons of the grated Parmesan cheese. Stuff into the bottoms of cooked artichokes. Arrange in a buttered baking dish. Sprinkle tops with remaining cheese and with the melted butter. Bake in a preheated moderate oven (350° F.) 30 minutes or until the mushroom stuffing has puffed and browned. Serve hot. Makes 6 servings. (See illustration, page 762.)

⚜ ARTICHOKE BOTTOMS STUFFED WITH SPINACH
(*Fonds d'Artichauts à la Florentine*)

6 large artichokes
½ cup well-drained cooked spinach
3 tablespoons butter
salt
ground black pepper
2 tablespoons flour
1 cup milk or stock
2 egg yolks
¼ cup heavy cream
2 tablespoons grated Parmesan cheese

Prepare and cook artichoke bottoms as for Stuffed Artichoke Bottoms. Drain well and remove chokes. Combine spinach, 1 tablespoon butter, and salt and pepper to taste. Spoon into the cooked artichoke bottoms. Meanwhile, melt 2 tablespoons butter in a 3-cup saucepan. Remove from heat and blend in flour. Stir and cook 1 minute. Remove from heat and add milk or stock. Stir and cook until sauce has thickened. Beat egg yolks lightly, mix with cream, and add to the sauce. Stir and cook over low heat 1 to 2 minutes. Add ½ teaspoon salt and a dash of ground black pepper. Spoon over stuffed artichokes. Sprinkle with Parmesan cheese. Brown under broiler heat.

Other cooked vegetables such as peas, carrots, mushrooms, asparagus tips, or green beans, or a mixture of vegetables, tossed in a little butter, may be used in place of spinach. Makes 6 servings. (See illustration, page 762.)

ASPARAGUS (*Asperges*)

⚜ HOW TO COOK ASPARAGUS

To peel or not to peel asparagus is a question in the minds of many. The French method is to peel the spears, tie them in serving-size bundles, and cook them 10 to 18 minutes, or only until barely tender, in a large amount of boiling salted water, using 1½ teaspoons salt to 1 quart water. Then the asparagus is drained immediately and placed on a dish covered with a clean towel or put in a special asparagus dish equipped with a rack to permit thorough draining. Asparagus may be served hot or cold with various sauces. Peeled asparagus cooks more quickly than the unpeeled. The spears can be eaten down to the butt end and they retain their natural green color and texture. (See Culinary Techniques in Pictures.)

The American cook uses one of two methods of cooking asparagus, neither of which specifies peeling. Select firm, crisp stalks, with moist cut ends and compact closed tips. If possible, select spears of uniform thickness so that they will all finish cooking at the same time. Break the asparagus at the point where the stalk becomes tender, remove scales, and wash thoroughly. Tie the spears in serving-size bundles and stand them in the bottom part of a double boiler, tip ends up. Add ½ teaspoon salt and boiling water to a depth of 2 inches. Cover with the inverted top part of the double boiler. Boil 15 to 20 minutes. By this method the tips are not overcooked before the ends are done.

The second method is to lay cleaned asparagus in a skillet, add ½ teaspoon salt, and pour in boiling water to a depth of 1 inch. Bring to boiling point, uncovered, and cook 5 minutes. Cover and cook 5 to 10 minutes; the time depends upon the size and natural tenderness of the asparagus. Remove from the water with a slotted pancake turner.

Asparagus cooked by any of these methods may be served with melted butter, Brown Butter, Egg Butter, Almond Butter, Maître d'Hôtel Butter, Mustard Butter, or with Antiboise, Béarnaise, Caper, or Mousseline Sauce. (See Chapter 4.)

⚜ ASPARAGUS MILANESE

2½ pounds asparagus, cooked
½ cup grated Cheddar or Parmesan cheese
2 tablespoons butter
chopped parsley
Brown Butter (optional)

Arrange cooked asparagus in overlapping rows in a shallow baking dish, having the tips visible. Sprinkle with grated cheese and dot with butter. Cook in a preheated hot oven (400° F.) 10 to 15 minutes to melt cheese and brown. Sprinkle with chopped parsley. If desired, serve Brown Butter in a sauceboat to spoon over the asparagus. Makes 6 servings.

⚜ ASPARAGUS POLISH STYLE

2½ pounds asparagus, cooked
2 hard-cooked eggs, chopped
chopped parsley
6 tablespoons butter
¼ cup fine dry breadcrumbs

Arrange cooked asparagus in overlapping rows in a shallow serving dish, having the tips visible. Sprinkle with chopped eggs and parsley. Melt butter in a small skillet or saucepan, add breadcrumbs, and stir and fry until crumbs are brown. Sprinkle over asparagus and serve immediately. Makes 6 servings.

⚜ ASPARAGUS WITH WHITE WINE

2½ pounds asparagus, cooked
⅓ cup butter, melted
½ cup dry white wine
salt
ground black pepper
½ cup grated Parmesan cheese

Arrange cooked asparagus in a shallow baking dish and pour melted butter and wine over it. Sprinkle lightly with salt and pepper and with grated Parmesan cheese. Place in a preheated hot oven (425° F.) 10 to 15 minutes or until cheese browns lightly. Makes 6 servings.

BEANS

⚜ GREEN BEANS IN CREAM SAUCE (*Haricots Verts à la Crème*)

1 pound green beans
1 teaspoon salt
¼ teaspoon sugar
boiling water
2 tablespoons butter
½ cup heavy cream
dash ground black pepper

Wash beans, cut off tips, split lengthwise, and cut into 2-inch pieces. Place in a saucepan with salt, sugar, and boiling water, filling the pan to a depth of 1 inch. Bring to boiling point and cook, uncovered, 5 minutes. Cover and cook 10 to 12 minutes, or only until beans are crisp-tender. Drain off excess water. Shake the pan over low heat 1 to 2 minutes to dry the beans. Add butter and mix well. Then add cream and pepper. Cook until the cream has thickened slightly. Makes 6 servings.

⚜ GREEN BEANS MAÎTRE D'HÔTEL

1 pound green beans
1 teaspoon salt
¼ teaspoon sugar
boiling water
Béchamel Sauce
chopped parsley

Combine beans in salt, sugar, and boiling water as instructed in the recipe for Green Beans in Cream Sauce. Drain and shake the pan over low heat 1 to 2 minutes. Add Béchamel Sauce and heat. Turn into a serving dish. Sprinkle with chopped parsley. Makes 6 servings.

⚜ GREEN BEANS À LA PAYSANNE

1 pound green beans
10 small new potatoes
1 teaspoon salt
½ teaspoon sugar
boiling water
3 tablespoons butter
1/16 teaspoon ground black pepper

Wash beans and remove tips. Cut beans into pieces 1 inch long and place in a saucepan. Wash and scrape new potatoes and cut into quarters. Add to beans along with salt and sugar. Pour in boiling water to a depth of 1 inch.

Bring to boiling point, uncovered, and cook 5 minutes. Cover and cook 10 to 12 minutes or until beans are crisp-tender and potatoes are done. Drain off water and shake pan over low heat 1 to 2 minutes. Melt butter in a small saucepan and cook until it is golden brown. Pour over beans, add pepper, toss lightly, and serve immediately. Makes 6 servings.

⚜ PORTUGUESE-STYLE GREEN BEANS

¼ pound salt pork
1 pound green beans
2 medium-sized tomatoes
¾ cup bouillon
½ teaspoon salt
½ teaspoon sugar
⅛ teaspoon ground black pepper

Dice salt pork fine and put it in the bottom of a flameproof 1½-quart casserole. Wash green beans, cut off tips, cut beans into 1-inch pieces, and place in the casserole over the pork. Peel, seed, and cube tomatoes. Scatter over beans. Add bouillon, salt, sugar, and pepper. Bring to boiling point over surface heat. Cover and cook in a preheated moderate oven (350° F.) 30 minutes, or until beans are tender. Sprinkle with chopped parsley. Serve hot. Makes 6 servings.

⚜ BROAD BEANS

2 cups shelled young broad beans, or lima beans
boiling water
1 teaspoon salt
½ teaspoon sugar
2 tablespoons butter
¼ cup heavy cream (optional)
⅛ teaspoon ground black pepper

Wash beans and place them in a saucepan. Add boiling water to a depth of 1 inch, along with salt and sugar. Cover, bring to boiling point, and cook 20 minutes, or until beans are tender. Drain and toss with butter and, if desired, with cream. Add pepper. Adjust salt.

⚜ RED BEANS IN WINE (*Haricots Rouges au Vin*)

2 cups dried red kidney beans
4 cups cold water
1 teaspoon salt
½ cup chopped onions
1 tablespoon butter
¼ pound lean salt pork
¼ teaspoon ground black pepper
2 tablespoons flour
1 cup dry red wine

Wash beans and soak 2 hours in enough cold water to cover them. Drain and add the 4 cups cold water. Cover, bring to boiling point, and cook 2 hours or until beans are tender. Add salt. Cook onions in butter until they are limp. Dice salt pork, add to onions, and cook until onions and pork are lightly browned. Add pepper, sprinkle with flour, and add wine. Mix lightly. Simmer 10 minutes. Adjust salt. Makes 6 servings.

⚜ DRIED BEANS BRETON STYLE

2 cups dried beans
4 cups cold water
1 teaspoon salt
½ cup chopped onions
3 tablespoons butter
1 cup thick Tomato Sauce
⅛ teaspoon ground black pepper
chopped parsley

Wash beans and soak 2 hours in enough cold water to cover. Drain the beans and add the 4 cups cold water. Cover and cook 2 hours or until beans are tender. Add salt. Cook the onions in the butter until they are limp. Add them to the beans along with Tomato Sauce and pepper. Mix lightly and cook 5 to 10 minutes over moderately low heat. Adjust salt. Sprinkle with chopped parsley. Serve hot. Makes 6 servings.

⚜ DRIED BEANS IN CREAM SAUCE

2 cups dried beans
4 cups cold water
1 teaspoon salt
½ cup chopped onions
1 cup diced carrots
3 tablespoons butter
3 tablespoons chopped parsley
¾ cup heavy cream
¾ cup thin Béchamel Sauce

Wash beans and soak 2 hours in enough cold water to cover them. Drain. Add the 4 cups cold water, cover, bring to boiling point, and cook 2 hours, or until beans are tender. Add salt. Cook onions and carrots in the butter until carrots are soft. Add to the beans along with the parsley, cream, and Béchamel Sauce. Mix lightly and cook 10 minutes. Adjust the salt. Makes 6 servings.

⚜ FLAGEOLET BEANS

Flageolet beans, fresh and dried, may be prepared in the same ways as other fresh and dried beans.

Artichokes with Vinaigrette Sauce, page 750 ▲

▼ Boiled Leeks, page 785

▲ Tuscan-Style Stuffed Eggplant, page 781

Eggplant Carlton, page 781 ▼

Peppers Stuffed with Meat, page 793 ▲

▼ Vegetables Mediterranean Style, page 816

▲ Milanese Stuffed Zucchini, page 814

Assorted vegetables (see pages 749–58, 767–94, 805–17) ▼

Eggplant Provençale, page 780 ▲

▼ Duchess Tomatoes, page 809

▲ Braised Celery Hearts, page 775

Sautéed Cepes Italian Style, page 789 ▼

Ratatouille Niçoise, page 817 ▲

▼ Cardoons with Beef Marrow, page 771

▲ Assorted potatoes (see pages 795–805)

Italian Stuffed Baked Potatoes, page 797 ▼

BROCCOLI (*Choux Brocolis*)

⚜ HOW TO COOK BROCCOLI

Allow 2 pounds of broccoli for 6 servings. Wash broccoli and cut off the tough portion of the stems. Place broccoli in a saucepan in 1 inch of boiling water and add 1 teaspoon salt for each 6 portions. Bring to boiling point, uncovered, and boil 5 minutes. Cover and cook 10 minutes, or only until broccoli is tender. Drain. Serve with melted butter or with Brown Butter, or Anchovy, Almond, Maître d'Hôtel, Mustard, or Tomato Butter, or Anchovy Sauce, Béarnaise, Caper, Mornay, or Vinaigrette Sauce.

BRUSSELS SPROUTS (*Choux de Bruxelles*)

⚜ BRUSSELS SPROUTS ENGLISH STYLE

1½ pounds Brussels sprouts
boiling water
2 teaspoons salt
1 teaspoon sugar
⅛ teaspoon ground black pepper
2 tablespoons butter

Wash and trim Brussels sprouts. Soak 20 minutes, with 1 teaspoon salt, in enough cold water to cover them. Drain and rinse in cold water. Place in a saucepan, pour in boiling water to a depth of 1 inch, and add 1 teaspoon each salt and sugar. Bring to boiling point, uncovered, and boil 5 minutes. Cover and cook 10 minutes, or until Brussels sprouts are barely tender. Drain off excess water. Toss lightly with the pepper and butter. Makes 6 servings. If desired, serve with grated Parmesan cheese, or with Anchovy, Béarnaise, Caper, Egg, Hollandaise, or Mornay Sauce.

⚜ FRIED BRUSSELS SPROUTS

1½ pounds Brussels sprouts, cooked
ground black pepper
6 tablespoons butter
chopped parsley

Sprinkle cooked Brussels sprouts with pepper. Fry in butter, turning to brown all sides. Sprinkle with chopped parsley. Serve immediately. Makes 6 servings.

⚜ BRUSSELS SPROUTS AU GRATIN

1½ pounds Brussels sprouts, cooked
2 cups Béchamel Sauce
1 tablespoon butter, melted
½ cup grated Cheddar or Parmesan cheese

Mix cooked Brussels sprouts with 1⅓ cups of the Béchamel Sauce. Turn into a 1-quart casserole. Cover with remaining sauce. Sprinkle with melted butter and cheese. Brown in a preheated very hot oven (450° F.). Serve hot. Makes 6 servings.

CABBAGE (*Choux*)

⚜ BRAISED CABBAGE

1 head (1½ pounds) cabbage
1 cup sliced carrots
1 cup sliced onions
4 slices lean salt pork
1 teaspoon salt
⅛ teaspoon ground black pepper
½ teaspoon sugar
1 cup stock or bouillon

Remove and discard damaged leaves from cabbage. Cut cabbage into 6 wedges and remove cores. Place carrots and onions in a buttered 2-quart casserole. Cover with salt pork and then with cabbage wedges. Combine seasonings with bouillon and pour over cabbage. Cover and cook in a preheated moderate oven (350° F.) 30 to 40 minutes, or only until cabbage is barely tender. Makes 6 servings.

⚜ CABBAGE AU GRATIN

1 head (1½ pounds) cabbage
½ teaspoon salt
½ teaspoon sugar
boiling water
1½ cups Béchamel Sauce
⅛ teaspoon ground black pepper
½ cup grated Cheddar cheese

Remove and discard the damaged leaves from cabbage and cut the head into quarters. Cut out the stalk and shred cabbage coarsely. Place in a saucepan with salt and sugar. Pour in boiling water to a depth of 1 inch. Bring to boiling point, uncovered. Cover and cook 5 to 8 minutes or only until cabbage is barely tender. Drain off excess water. Add 1 cup of the Béchamel Sauce and black pepper. Adjust salt. Turn into a shallow baking dish. Spoon the remaining Béchamel Sauce over the top. Sprinkle with grated cheese.

Place in a preheated hot oven (400° F.) to melt and brown the cheese. Makes 6 servings.

⚜ WHOLE STUFFED CABBAGE

1 large (2-pound) head cabbage
salt
boiling water
3 slices bread
milk
½ pound pork sausage
¼ cup chopped onion
2 tablespoons butter
2 tablespoons chopped parsley
½ clove garlic, crushed
⅛ teaspoon ground black pepper
1 large egg, beaten
1 slice of salt pork
beef stock or consommé
¼ cup buttered breadcrumbs

Remove and discard the damaged outer leaves from cabbage. Scoop out the center and reserve it for slaw or salad. Place the head and 1 teaspoon salt in a deep saucepan and add boiling water to cover the head completely. Bring to boiling point, uncovered, and boil 10 minutes. Remove cabbage, rinse in cold water, and invert in a bowl to drain thoroughly.

Crumble bread and soak it in enough milk to cover until bread is thoroughly wet. Squeeze dry and fluff with a fork. Crumble sausage and brown it over moderate heat. Drain off fat and add the sausage to the bread. Cook onion in butter until limp and add to the bread along with salt to taste. Add the next 4 ingredients. Mix well. Stuff mixture into the cavity of the cabbage. Tie salt pork around the cabbage with twine and place cabbage in a saucepan. Pour in stock or consommé to a depth of 1 inch. Cover and cook over moderately low heat 30 minutes. Transfer cabbage to a baking pan, sprinkle with buttered breadcrumbs, and brown in a preheated hot oven (400° F.). Remove string and salt pork and transfer the cabbage to a serving dish. Makes 6 servings.

⚜ DOLMAS (*Stuffed Cabbage Leaves Turkish Style*)

12 large outside cabbage leaves
½ cup chopped onions
olive oil or salad oil
2 cups minced cooked lamb
1 cup cooked rice
¼ cup (½ stick) softened butter
½ teaspoon dried oregano
¼ teaspoon ground cumin
¼ teaspoon ground black pepper
1 teaspoon salt
½ small clove garlic, crushed
½ cup sliced carrots
½ cup sliced onion
1 cup beef, veal, or mutton stock
¼ cup tomato purée
12 thin lemon slices
lemon juice

Pour boiling water over cabbage leaves and let them stand 10 minutes, or until leaves are pliable. Remove leaves from water, spread out on a clean towel, and with scissors cut out the thick ribs. Cook onions until limp in 2 tablespoons oil, and combine with the next 8 ingredients. Put a rounded tablespoon of the stuffing on each cabbage leaf. Fold the edges of the leaf over the filling, roll securely, and fasten with toothpicks. Place 2 tablespoons oil and the carrots, and sliced onions in the bottom of a baking dish and arrange the cabbage rolls, seam side down, on top. Bake in a preheated moderate oven (350° F.) 15 to 20 minutes, or until cabbage begins to brown. Blend stock with tomato purée and pour over the dolmas. Cover and cook 25 to 30 minutes in a 350° F. oven. Transfer dolmas to a serving dish and garnish each with a lemon slice. Reduce the stock to half the original amount and season to taste with lemon juice. Serve over dolmas. Makes 6 servings.

⚜ RED CABBAGE WITH APPLES (*Chou Rouge aux Pommes*)

1 head (1½ pounds) red cabbage
2 to 3 tablespoons wine vinegar
½ teaspoon salt
2 medium-sized onions
3 medium-sized apples, sliced
1 cup water or bouillon
1½ tablespoons flour
2 tablespoons butter
½ teaspoon sugar
⅛ teaspoon ground black pepper
dash of clove

Remove and discard the damaged outer leaves from cabbage head. Shred cabbage fine, mix with vinegar and salt, and let stand 30 minutes. Slice onions thickly, place them in the bottom of a 1½-quart casserole, and cover with half the cabbage. Add the apples. Top with remaining cabbage. Pour in water or bouillon. Place a plate upside down on the cabbage to weight it down. Cover and cook in a preheated moderate oven (350° F.) 1 hour or until done; or cook slowly over surface heat. Blend the last 5 ingredients and add 10 minutes before cooking time is up. Serve hot. Makes 6 servings.

⚜ RED CABBAGE LIMOUSIN STYLE

6 cups coarsely shredded red cabbage
2 cups shelled chopped chestnuts
½ teaspoon salt
⅛ teaspoon ground black pepper
½ teaspoon sugar
1 cup beef stock or consommé

Fill a greased 2-quart casserole with alternating layers of cabbage and chestnuts, beginning and ending with cabbage. Combine remaining ingredients and pour over cabbage. Cover and cook in a preheated moderate oven (350° F.) 40 minutes, or until cabbage and chestnuts are tender. Serve hot. Makes 6 servings.

⚜ RED CABBAGE WITH RICE

½ cup long-grain converted rice
water
¼ cup (½ stick) butter
½ cup chopped onions
4 cups coarsely shredded red cabbage
¼ cup red currant jelly
2 tablespoons light brown sugar
¼ teaspoon salt
⅛ teaspoon ground black pepper
1¼ cups hot chicken or veal stock

Soak rice 30 minutes in enough water to cover it. Drain and cook in half the butter until rice is dry and sticks to the bottom of the pan. Cook onions in the remaining butter until limp. Add to rice along with cabbage. Combine remaining ingredients and pour over cabbage and rice. Mix well. Cover and cook in a preheated moderate oven (350° F.) 30 minutes, or until rice is tender and cabbage crisp-tender. Makes 6 servings.

⚜ RED CABBAGE IN RED WINE

1 cup thinly sliced onions
4 slices lean salt pork, diced
1½ teaspoon flour
4 cups coarsely shredded red cabbage
½ teaspoon salt
1/16 teaspoon ground black pepper
½ cup dry red wine

Cook onions with diced salt pork until the onions begin to wilt. Sprinkle with flour and stir and cook until onions and pork have browned lightly. Add cabbage, salt, and pepper and mix well. Cover and cook in a preheated moderate oven (350° F.) ½ hour or until done. Bring wine to boiling point, pour over cabbage, and cook 10 minutes. Makes 6 servings.

CARDOONS (*Cardons*)

The cardoon is a thistlelike plant related to the artichoke, which grows in the Mediterranean area. Only the stems are eaten.

⚜ CARDOONS WITH BEEF MARROW

2 cardoons
lemon juice
2 quarts boiling water
1 tablespoon flour
1½ tablespoons lemon juice
2 whole cloves
1 carrot, peeled
1 medium-sized onion
1 small bay leaf
2 teaspoons salt
Madeira Sauce or Mornay Sauce
sliced beef marrow, poached

Remove and discard the tough outside stalks of the cardoons. Separate the other stalks from the hearts (as in preparing celery). Wash the stalks, scrape off the strings, and cut stalks into 3- to 3½-inch lengths, leaving the hearts whole. Rub cardoons with lemon juice and place them in a 3-quart saucepan. Add boiling water. Blend flour with lemon juice and add to the water. Stir in the next 5 ingredients. Cover and cook 2 hours. Drain and rinse in hot running water. Transfer cardoons to a serving dish. Cover with Madeira Sauce or Mornay Sauce. Garnish with slices of beef marrow poached 5 minutes in simmering water. Makes 6 servings. (See illustration, page 765.)

CARROTS (*Carottes*)

⚜ CARROTS CHANTILLY

1 pound young tender carrots
½ teaspoon salt
½ teaspoon sugar
boiling water
⅓ cup Béchamel Sauce
⅓ cup heavy cream
ground black pepper to taste
2 cups hot cooked peas
2 tablespoons butter

Wash and scrape carrots. Cut into 2-inch pieces. Place in a saucepan with salt and sugar. Pour in boiling water to a depth of 1 inch. Cover, bring to boiling point, and cook 10 minutes, or only until carrots are crisp-tender. Drain and add Béchamel Sauce and cream and cook until the sauce is very creamy. Add black pepper and adjust salt. Turn carrots into the center of a serving dish. Toss peas with butter, season to taste with salt and pepper, and turn them into the dish around the carrots. Makes 6 servings.

⚜ CARROTS IN CREAM SAUCE

1 pound young tender carrots
3 tablespoons butter, melted
salt
ground black pepper
½ teaspoon sugar
⅓ cup heavy cream

Wash carrots, trim both ends, and leave whole. Blanch in boiling water 5 minutes. Rinse under running cold water and slip off the skins. Place in a skillet with melted butter. Sprinkle with salt, pepper, and sugar. Simmer 5 minutes. Add cream, cover, and cook until carrots are tender. Makes 6 servings.

⚜ GLAZED CARROTS

3 dozen young tender carrots
2 tablespoons sugar
½ teaspoon salt
¼ cup (½ stick) butter
boiling water
chopped parsley

Wash and scrape carrots. Leave whole if small, or cut in lengthwise halves if medium-sized or large. Place them in a saucepan with the next 3 ingredients and enough boiling water barely to cover them. Cook, uncovered, until carrots are crisp-tender and the liquid is reduced to a syrupy consistency, giving the carrots an attractive glaze. Turn into a serving dish and sprinkle with parsley. Makes 6 servings.

⚜ CARROT PUDDING

12 medium-sized carrots, cooked
2 tablespoons minced onion
3 tablespoons minced green pepper
3 tablespoons butter
1½ tablespoons flour
1½ tablespoons sugar
1¼ cups hot milk
salt
ground white pepper
1 large egg
½ cup buttered soft breadcrumbs

Mash carrots and set aside. Cook onion and green pepper in 2 tablespoons of the butter until onion begins to turn golden. Add remaining butter, flour, and sugar. Stir and cook 1 minute. Add hot milk, mix well, and cook until the sauce has thickened slightly, stirring constantly. Add to carrots. Season to taste with salt and pepper. Beat in egg. Turn into a buttered 1½-quart casserole. Sprinkle with buttered breadcrumbs. Bake in a preheated moderate oven (350° F.) 30 to 40 minutes, or until a knife inserted in the center comes out clean. Serve hot. Makes 6 servings.

⚜ CARROTS VICHY I

2 dozen young tender carrots
½ teaspoon salt
1 teaspoon sugar
2 tablespoons butter
boiling water
ground white pepper to taste
chopped parsley

Peel carrots, slice thinly, and place in a saucepan with salt, sugar, and butter. Add boiling water to a depth of ½ inch. Cover, bring to boiling point, and cook 5 to 6 minutes, or only until carrots are barely tender and the water has evaporated. Add pepper and parsley. Makes 6 servings.

⚜ CARROTS VICHY II

2 dozen young tender carrots
¼ cup chopped onions
2 tablespoons butter
½ teaspoon salt
1 teaspoon sugar
boiling water
chopped parsley

Peel carrots, slice thinly, and place in a saucepan with the next 4 ingredients. Add enough boiling water barely to cover them. Cover, bring to boiling point, and boil rapidly until about half done. Remove cover and cook until all the liquid has evaporated. Transfer to a serving dish. Sprinkle with parsley. Makes 6 servings.

CAULIFLOWER (*Chou-Fleur*)

⚜ BOILED CAULIFLOWER

1 large head cauliflower
boiling water
1 teaspoon salt
½ teaspoon sugar

Cut off and discard the coarse leaves surrounding the cauliflower head, leaving only the young tender leaves that adhere to the head. Wash the cauliflower well and soak it 20 minutes in cold water with 1 teaspoon salt per quart of water. Drain and rinse under running cold water. Place in a deep saucepan and pour over enough boiling water barely to cover. Add salt and sugar. Bring to boiling point, uncovered, and boil 5 minutes. Cover and cook 20 minutes, or until cauliflower is barely tender. Drain. Serve with melted butter and ground black pepper to taste, or serve with Anchovy, Béarnaise, Caper, Cream, Egg, Hollandaise, Mornay, or Mousseline Sauce (see Chapter 4). Makes 6 servings.

⚜ CAULIFLOWER AU GRATIN

1 large head cauliflower
2 tablespoons butter
2 tablespoons flour
¼ cup heavy cream
¾ cup chicken or veal stock
4 tablespoons grated Parmesan cheese
4 tablespoons Gruyère cheese
½ teaspoon salt
1/16 teaspoon ground black pepper

Cook cauliflower as instructed in the recipe for Boiled Cauliflower. Meanwhile, melt butter in a 1-quart saucepan. Remove from heat and blend in flour. Stir and cook 1 minute. Remove from heat and add cream and stock.

Stir and cook until the sauce is of medium thickness. Add 2 tablespoons of each kind of cheese and the salt and pepper. Pour ¼ cup sauce in the bottom of a casserole and put in the cooked cauliflower, rounded side up. Cover with remaining sauce. Sprinkle with the rest of the cheese. Brown in a preheated hot oven (400° F.). Makes 6 servings.

⚜ CAULIFLOWER MILANESE

1 large cauliflower
1 teaspoon salt
½ teaspoon sugar
boiling water
ground black pepper
½ cup grated Parmesan cheese
6 tablespoons butter

Wash cauliflower and break into flowerets. Place in a saucepan with salt and sugar, and add boiling water to a depth of ½ inch. Bring to boiling point, uncovered, and cook 5 minutes. Cover and cook 8 to 10 minutes, or only until barely tender. Transfer the flowerets to a buttered shallow baking dish. Sprinkle with Parmesan cheese. Melt half the butter and sprinkle over the cheese. Brown in a preheated very hot oven (450° F.). Dot with the remaining butter. Makes 6 servings.

⚜ CAULIFLOWER POLISH STYLE

1 large head cauliflower
2 hard-cooked eggs, chopped
2 tablespoons chopped parsley
½ cup soft breadcrumbs
6 tablespoons butter

Cook whole cauliflower head as instructed in the recipe for Boiled Cauliflower. Remove from water and drain well. Place in a serving dish, rounded side up. Sprinkle with chopped hard-cooked eggs and parsley. Brown breadcrumbs in a skillet in half the butter; sprinkle on cauliflower. Melt remaining butter and pour over cauliflower. Serve at once. Makes 6 servings.

CELERY AND CELERIAC

⚜ BRAISED CELERY HEARTS

3 stalks celery
½ cup sliced carrots
¼ cup onion slices
boiling stock or water
½ teaspoon salt
1 tablespoon butter
½ cup Demi-Glace Sauce

Remove outside ribs from the stalks of celery and cut off tops. Save these for soup, stock and stew. Do not separate the celery ribs forming the heart. Split hearts lengthwise, parboil them 5 minutes, and then put them in cold water. Spread the ribs apart and hold them under cold running water to rinse out any dirt that might be lodged between the ribs. Spread carrot and onion slices over the bottom of a baking dish and place the celery hearts on top, all lying in the same direction. Pour in boiling stock or water to a depth of ½ inch. Sprinkle celery with salt and dot with butter. Cut a piece of waxed paper the size of the baking dish, making a small hole in the center, and place it over the top. Bring liquid to boiling point, cover, and bake in a preheated hot oven (400° F.) 1 hour or until celery is tender. Remove celery to a serving dish. Bring cooking liquid to boiling point and cook until stock has reduced to ½ cup. Add Demi-Glace and cook 3 to 4 minutes. Pour over celery. Makes 6 servings. (See illustration, page 764.)

⚜ CELERY À LA MENAGÈRE

2 stalks celery
2 medium-sized onions
2 tablespoons butter
1 cup sliced carrots
2 medium-sized tomatoes
½ teaspoon salt
⅛ teaspoon ground black pepper
¼ teaspoon sugar
½ cup bouillon

Remove and discard the big outer ribs of celery stalks. Cut the remaining ribs into 2-inch pieces. Set aside. Peel onions, cut into slices ¼ inch thick, and brown lightly in butter along with carrots in an ovenproof dish. Place celery over the top. Peel, seed and quarter tomatoes and arrange over celery. Sprinkle with salt, pepper, and sugar. Add bouillon. Cover and cook in a preheated moderate oven 40 minutes or until celery is tender. Serve with veal. Makes 6 servings. (See illustration, page 762.)

⚜ CELERY WITH PARMESAN CHEESE

4 cups celery cut into 1-inch pieces
boiling chicken or veal stock, or boiling water and ½ teaspoon salt
2 tablespoons butter
½ cup grated Parmesan cheese
dash ground white pepper

Place celery in a saucepan and pour in stock or water to a depth of ½ inch. Add salt if water is used. Cover, bring to boiling point, and cook 10 minutes, or only until celery is crisp-tender. Drain, add butter, half the cheese, and pepper. Toss. Serve with remaining cheese sprinkled over the top. Makes 6 servings.

⚜ BOILED CELERIAC

Celeriac (*céleri-rave*), also called celery root, is a variety of celery with a large edible root. It is sliced and either served raw with salt, pepper, and vinegar or cooked in various ways.

To boil celeriac, trim off leaves and root fibers, pare root, and slice ½ inch thick, or cut into dice. Pour in boiling water to a depth of ½ inch and add ½ teaspoon salt. Cover and cook 15 minutes, or until the vegetable is tender. Drain and serve with melted butter, Hollandaise Sauce, or Béchamel Sauce. Allow 3 to 4 roots for 6 servings.

⚜ CELERIAC FRITTERS

celeriac
boiling water
salt
flour
egg beaten with 1 tablespoon milk
fine dry breadcrumbs
Tomato Sauce

Peel celeriac and cut into slices ½ inch thick. Place in a saucepan with boiling water and salt, adding ½ teaspoon salt for each 2 cups water. Cover and boil until celeriac is soft, being careful not to overcook. Drain well. If slices are very large, cut them into halves or quarters. Dredge in flour, dip in egg beaten with milk, and roll in breadcrumbs. Fry until brown in deep fat preheated to 375° F., or shallow-fry in butter. Serve with Tomato Sauce. Allow 3 to 4 roots for 6 servings.

CHESTNUTS (*Marrons*)

⚜ HOW TO PEEL CHESTNUTS

Four methods of peeling chestnuts follow.

Skillet. Slit each chestnut with a sharp knife and put them in a skillet with enough oil to coat them. Stir and cook over moderate heat about 10 minutes. When cool enough to handle, remove shells and skins with a sharp knife.

Oven. Slit chestnuts and coat them with oil as in the Skillet method. Bake in a preheated very hot oven (450° F.) 20 minutes. Cool. Remove shells and skins with a sharp knife.

Deep-Fat. Cut all around the chestnuts with a sharp knife. Place a few of them at a time in a wire basket, or sieve, and immerse them in deep fat preheated to 375° F. until the peel opens of its own accord. Drain chestnuts well on paper towels. When cool enough to handle, remove peels.

Boiling. Slit each shell and place in boiling water to cover. Boil 20 minutes. Drain and cool. Peel off shells.

⚜ BRAISED CHESTNUTS

2 pounds chestnuts, peeled
boiling beef, chicken, or veal stock
ground black pepper to taste
2 tablespoons butter

Place chestnuts in a saucepan. Add stock to a depth of 1 inch. Cover, bring to boiling point, reduce heat, and simmer 10 to 15 minutes, or until just tender. Add pepper and butter. Toss and serve. Makes 6 servings.

VARIATION

CREAMED CHESTNUTS

Braise chestnuts as in the recipe for Braised Chestnuts. Drain. Omit butter. Mix with 1½ cups Béchamel Sauce.

⚜ CHESTNUT PURÉE

2 pounds chestnuts, peeled
1 slice celeriac, or ¼ cup sliced celery
boiling bouillon, or boiling water and ½ teaspoon salt
2 tablespoons butter
stock, milk, or heavy cream

Place chestnuts and celeriac or celery and 1 inch boiling bouillon or water in a saucepan. Add salt if water is used. Cover. Bring to boiling point and cook 15 to 20 minutes, or until chestnuts are soft enough to put through a sieve or food mill. Add butter. Thin with stock, milk, or cream to consistency desired. Serve hot. Makes 6 servings.

CORN (*Maïs*)

⚜ CORN ON THE COB

Remove the outer husks from ears of tender corn. Pull back the inner husks and remove the silk. Return the inner husks to their original position. Place the ears in a saucepan with enough boiling water to cover them. Bring the water to boiling point and cook the corn 5 to 8 minutes or only until the milk in the kernels is set. Or, if desired, remove all the husks before cooking.

To serve, remove all the husks if corn was cooked with the husks attached. Place the ears in a deep platter. Melt ¼ pound butter for each 8 or 10 ears, add ¼ teaspoon salt and ground black pepper to taste. Pour over the corn. Allow 1 to 2 ears for each person.

⚜ SWEET CORN IN CREAM SAUCE

Boil young tender corn on the cob 5 minutes in enough boiling water to cover it. Remove from water and when ears are cool enough to handle, cut off the kernels with a sharp knife. Simmer kernels 1 to 2 minutes in melted butter, using 2 tablespoons to 1 cup corn kernels. Then blend with Béchamel Sauce, using ⅓ cup to 1 cup corn. Season to taste with salt and ground black pepper. Allow 2 cups corn kernels for 6 servings.

CUCUMBERS (*Concombres*)

⚜ CUCUMBERS IN BUTTER

3 cucumbers
salt
boiling water
¼ cup (½ stick) butter, melted
⅛ teaspoon ground black pepper
1 tablespoon lemon juice
chopped parsley

Peel cucumbers, cut them into quarters lengthwise, and then cut each quarter into 1-inch pieces. Place in a saucepan with ½ teaspoon salt and boiling water to cover. Cover and simmer 3 minutes. Drain. Pour melted butter into a 1-quart flameproof casserole and add cucumbers. Sprinkle with ¼ teaspoon salt and ⅛ teaspoon pepper. Cover and cook over very low heat 15 to 20 minutes. Sprinkle with lemon juice and chopped parsley. Serve in the casserole. Makes 6 servings.

VARIATION

CREAMED CUCUMBERS

Prepare cucumbers as in the recipe for Cucumbers in Butter. When they are about three-fourths done, add 1 cup hot cream. Finish cooking them in the cream. Omit the lemon juice. Sprinkle with chopped parsley.

EGGPLANT (*Aubergines*)

⚜ EGGPLANT BOSTON STYLE

3 medium-small eggplants
½ cup olive oil or salad oil
⅓ cup Béchamel Sauce
1 egg, beaten lightly
salt
ground black pepper
1 cup grated Gruyère cheese
⅓ cup heavy cream

Wash eggplants and cut them in lengthwise halves. Cut the meat crosswise several times with a knife without piercing the skin. Pour the oil into a baking pan large enough to accommodate the eggplants and heat. Place the eggplant halves, cut side down, in the hot oil and bake until the meat can be easily scooped out, leaving the shell intact. Chop the eggplant meat and mix well with Béchamel Sauce, egg, salt and pepper to taste, and half the cheese. Stuff the shells with this mixture, sprinkle with remaining grated cheese, and place in a baking pan. Brown in a preheated hot oven (400° F.). Salt the cream lightly, and just before serving pour a little over the top of each eggplant half. Makes 6 servings.

⚜ EGGPLANT PROVENÇALE

2 pounds eggplant
salt
flour
½ cup olive oil or salad oil
6 medium-sized tomatoes
ground black pepper
1 small clove garlic, crushed
chopped parsley (optional)

Wash eggplant, peel, cut into large dice, and sprinkle with ½ teaspoon salt. Let stand 20 minutes. Wipe the salt off the eggplant, dredge in flour, and sauté in ¼ cup hot oil. In the meantime, peel, quarter, and seed tomatoes. Sauté them quickly in remaining hot oil in another saucepan. When both vegetables are done, toss them together and season to taste with salt and pepper and crushed garlic. Cook the vegetables together 5 minutes. Sprinkle with chopped parsley, if desired. Makes 6 servings.

The eggplants may be cut in half lengthwise, the meat removed, and the shells reserved. When the eggplant and tomatoes have been tossed together, the mixture is divided and put into the shells, which are then baked in a preheated moderate oven (350° F.) for 5 minutes. (See illustration, page 763.)

⚜ EGGPLANT CARLTON

3 medium-sized eggplants
2 medium-sized tomatoes
¼ pound Gruyère or Cheddar cheese, diced
2 tablespoons minced onion
salt and ground black pepper to taste
olive oil or salad oil
¼ cup hot water

Wash eggplants and tomatoes. Cut eggplant in lengthwise halves, scoop out the meat, and cut it into small dice. Peel, seed, and dice tomatoes, and mix with eggplant and cheese. Add salt and pepper to taste. Stuff the eggplant shells with the mixture and sprinkle with oil. Pour ¼ cup each oil and hot water into a baking pan large enough to accommodate the eggplant. Put in eggplant and bake in a preheated moderate oven (350° F.) 40 minutes or until eggplant is done. Transfer eggplant to a platter. Serve hot. Makes 6 servings. (See illustration, page 760.)

⚜ EGGPLANT PIEDMONT STYLE

3 medium-small eggplants
½ cup olive oil or salad oil
½ cup chopped onion
¼ cup (½ stick) butter
3 medium-sized tomatoes
1 cup cooked rice
¼ teaspoon crumbled saffron
¼ cup hot beef or veal stock
salt
ground black pepper
½ cup grated Parmesan cheese

Wash eggplants, peel, and cut in half lengthwise. Scoop out and reserve the meat, being careful to leave shell ¼ inch thick. Cook eggplant halves in oil in the oven without allowing them to become too soft. Cook the onion until limp in half the butter. Add the reserved eggplant meat. Peel, seed, and dice tomatoes and add to eggplant and onion, along with rice. Dissolve saffron in hot stock and add. Season to taste with salt and pepper. Cook 2 to 3 minutes. Stuff the mixture into the eggplant shells. Sprinkle with grated Parmesan cheese and dot with remaining butter. Bake in a preheated very hot oven (450° F.) until tops have browned. Makes 6 servings.

⚜ TUSCAN-STYLE STUFFED EGGPLANT (*Italian*)

6 small eggplants
2 tomatoes, coarsely chopped, and 6 slices tomato
¼ cup soft breadcrumbs
1 teaspoon salt
⅛ teaspoon ground black pepper
½ pound Mozzarella or other soft white cheese
¼ cup chopped onions
2 tablespoons olive oil or salad oil
1 recipe Eggplant Provençale (optional)

Wash eggplants, cut them in halves lengthwise, and scoop out the meat, leaving the shells intact. Divide meat into two equal portions. Chop one portion and mix with the coarsely chopped tomatoes, the breadcrumbs, ¼ teaspoon salt, and ⅛ teaspoon pepper. Stuff into the shells, filling them about half full. Place a thin slice of cheese on each. Cook onions in the oil until limp. Chop remaining eggplant and add, with remaining salt and pepper. Stir and cook about 5 minutes. Finish filling eggplant shells with this mixture. Cut tomato slices in half and put a half slice on each stuffed eggplant half. Cover with remaining cheese, sliced thin. Arrange on a large baking sheet and bake in a preheated moderate oven (350° F.) 30 mintues. If desired, make 1 recipe Eggplant Provençale. When the stuffed eggplants are cooked, arrange them around the edge of a large round serving tray and pile the Eggplant Provençale in the center. (See illustration, page 760.) Makes 6 to 12 servings.

ENDIVE

The white bleached heads of Belgian endive, used in the United States principally for salad, are popular in France and some other European countries as a cooked vegetable. Endive may be braised, gratinéed with cheese, or served with a sauce. This plant, which has the botanical name *Chicorium endivia*, is called chicory in England.

⚜ BRAISED ENDIVE

12 medium-sized heads endive
5 tablespoons butter
½ teaspoon salt
⅛ teaspoon black pepper
1 teaspoon sugar
1 tablespoon lemon juice
½ cup boiling water
chopped parsley

Trim off and discard the base and any wilted leaves of endive. Wash heads one at a time under cold running water. Arrange the heads in the same direction in 2 layers in a generously buttered flameproof casserole, dotting each layer with 2 tablespoons butter, and sprinkling with salt, pepper, sugar and lemon juice. Pour in boiling water. Cut a piece of waxed paper the size of the casserole, cut a small hole in the center, and lay over the endive. Bring the water to boiling point, reduce heat, and simmer 45 minutes. Remove endive to a serving dish. Reduce the liquid to about ½ cup, add remaining 1 tablespoon butter, and pour the sauce over endive. Sprinkle with parsley. Serve hot. If desired, this dish may be cooked in a preheated moderate oven (350° F.) 45 minutes. Makes 6 servings.

VARIATIONS

ENDIVE WITH BROWN BUTTER

Cook Braised Endive as in preceding recipe but instead of thickening the cooking liquid to make a sauce, brown 2 tablespoons butter and pour over the endive. This recipe uses 6 tablespoons butter in all, instead of 5 as in preceding recipe.

ENDIVE FLEMISH STYLE

Cover Braised Endive with 1 cup hot Demi-Glace Sauce.

ENDIVE AU GRATIN WITH HAM

Spread ⅔ cup Béchamel or Mornay Sauce in a casserole. Wrap each head of Braised Endive in a thin slice of boiled ham and arrange over the sauce in two layers. Cover with 1⅓ cups Béchamel or Mornay Sauce. Sprinkle with grated Gruyère, Swiss, or Cheddar cheese. Put casserole in a preheated hot oven (425° F.), or under broiler heat, having the oven control set to 375° F., until cheese is lightly browned. Makes 6 servings.

JERUSALEM ARTICHOKES (*Topinambours*)

Jerusalem artichokes are tubers of firm consistency that resemble globe artichokes in flavor, although they are an entirely different vegetable.

To prepare them, peel the tubers carefully and drop them in cold water immediately to prevent discoloration. Then blanch briefly in boiling water, drain, and simmer in butter until tender. Season to taste with salt and ground black pepper. Or, if desired, serve with Béchamel Sauce.

Large Jerusalem artichokes may be sliced, blanched, dipped in Fritter Batter, and fried in hot deep fat. They may also be cooked in boiling water until tender, drained, and puréed. The sliced cooked tubers may be chilled and put into vegetable salads.

⚜ JERUSALEM ARTICHOKES BAKED WITH CREAM

18 Jerusalem artichokes
1 teaspoon salt
boiling water
2 tablespoons butter
ground black pepper
heavy cream

Wash and peel Jerusalem artichokes and cut them into olive shapes, dropping them in cold water as they are peeled to prevent discoloration. Place them in a saucepan with salt and enough boiling water to cover them. Cover, bring to boiling point, and cook 15 minutes. Drain off water and discard. Turn tubers into a buttered baking dish. Dot with butter. Sprinkle with pepper. Pour in enough heavy cream to barely cover and bake in a preheated hot oven (425° F.) 20 to 25 minutes. Makes 6 servings.

KOHLRABI (*Choux-raves*)

Kohlrabi is a member of the cabbage family with an edible turnip-shaped stem and a cabbagelike leaf. When the leaves are young and tender they may be used in salads. The tuberous stems may be stuffed; boiled and served with butter, cream sauce, or Hollandaise Sauce; made into an au gratin dish; or served cold with Vinaigrette Sauce. They may also be cooked in the same ways as turnips or celeriac. In France they are sometimes made into sauerkraut.

⚜ BOILED KOHLRABI

Cut the leaves off the kohlrabi. (If the leaves are young and tender, reserve them for use in salads.) Wash and pare the kohlrabi and cut into ½-inch cubes, or slice ¼ inch thick. Place in a saucepan with salt and 1 inch boiling water, using ½ teaspoon salt to 2 cups water. Cover, bring to boiling point, and cook 25 minutes or until barely tender. Drain. Season to taste with salt and pepper and toss with butter. Allow 1 medium-sized kohlrabi per serving; use 2 tablespoons butter for 6 servings.

LEEKS (*Poireaux*)

⚜ BOILED LEEKS

4 bunches leeks
½ teaspoon salt
boiling water
3 tablespoons butter
ground black pepper
chopped parsley

Cut off and discard the green tops and whiskers from the root ends of leeks. Remove one or two layers of their white skin. Wash them in lukewarm water and rinse under cold running water to make sure all sand is removed. Drain. Place leeks in a saucepan with salt. Pour in boiling water to a depth of 1 inch. Cover and cook 15 to 20 minutes, or until barely tender. Drain well. Add butter and pepper to taste. Cover and let stand 2 to 3 minutes or until butter melts. Transfer to a serving dish and sprinkle with chopped parsley. Serve as a vegetable. Makes 6 servings. (See illustration, page 759.)

VARIATION

CREAMED LEEKS ON TOAST OR FRIED BREAD

Arrange 5 cooked leeks on each piece of toast or fried bread, and spoon Velouté Sauce or Béchamel Sauce over them. Garnish each serving with chopped parsley.

⚜ BRAISED LEEKS

4 bunches leeks
½ cup sliced carrots
⅓ cup sliced onion
½ cup coarsely chopped celery tops
¼ cup diced salt pork
¼ teaspoon salt
1/16 teaspoon ground black pepper
¼ teaspoon ground nutmeg
½ teaspoon ground thyme
2 to 3 cups rich beef stock or bouillon
2 tablespoons flour
3 tablespoons butter
⅔ cup buttered soft breadcrumbs

Prepare leeks for cooking as in recipe for Boiled Leeks. Cover the bottom of a well-buttered baking dish with carrots, onions, celery tops, and salt pork, and arrange leeks on top. Sprinkle with the seasonings and pour in enough stock or bouillon barely to cover the leeks. Cut a piece of waxed paper the size of the baking dish, make a tiny hole in the center, and place over the leeks. Cover and cook in a preheated moderate oven (350° F.) 35 to 40 minutes, or until leeks are tender and have absorbed most of the stock. Remove and discard the waxed paper. Blend flour with butter and add to 1¼ cups rich beef stock or bouillon. Stir and cook until sauce has thickened. Pour over leeks. Sprinkle with buttered crumbs. Brown under the broiler with oven control set to 400° F. Makes 6 servings.

LENTILS (*Lentilles*)

Lentils can be prepared in any way suitable for dried beans.

⚜ LENTILS LORRAINE STYLE

The Lorraine region is renowned for its cooking, especially of substantial dishes.

2 cups dried lentils
4 cups cold water
2 medium-sized onions
1 medium-sized carrot
1 stalk parsley
3 tablespoons butter
3 slices lean salt pork, diced
1 small clove garlic, crushed
2 teaspoons salt
⅛ teaspoon ground black pepper
1½ tablespoons flour

Wash lentils and soak 1 hour in cold water. Peel and dice onions and carrots. Add half the onions, all the carrots, and the parsley to the lentils and the water in which they have soaked. Cover, bring to boiling point, reduce heat, and simmer 1½ hours or until lentils are almost tender, adding more water if needed. Remove and discard parsley. Sauté remaining chopped onion in 1 tablespoon of the butter, along with the diced salt pork. Add to the lentils. Stir in garlic, salt, and pepper. Blend flour with remaining butter, add to lentils, and cook 10 minutes. Serve hot. Makes 6 servings.

LETTUCE (*Laitue*)

⚜ BOILED LETTUCE WITH HAM

2 medium-small heads lettuce
½ teaspoon salt
2 tablespoons bacon or ham drippings
1 small onion, sliced
¼ cup sliced carrots
boiling water or stock
6 slices fried, boiled, or baked ham
1 tablespoon flour
1½ tablespoons butter
2 tablespoons Madeira wine

Remove and discard wilted outside leaves from the lettuce. Wash the lettuce well under cold running water. Cut each head into 3 wedges and place them in a deep 10-inch skillet with the next 4 ingredients. Pour in boiling water or stock to a depth of 1 inch. Cover and simmer 1 hour. Transfer lettuce wedges to a round serving dish, arranging them in a ring, alternating with slices of ham the same size. Keep warm. Reduce the cooking liquid to 1¼ cups. Blend the flour with the butter, add to the liquid, and mix well. Pour in wine. Stir and cook 1 to 2 minutes, or until sauce has thickened. Adjust the salt. Pour over lettuce. Makes 6 servings.

MUSHROOMS (*Champignons*)

For directions for making fluted mushrooms, see Culinary Techniques in Pictures.

⚜ MUSHROOMS IN CREAM SAUCE

1½ pounds small mushrooms
2 tablespoons butter, melted
1 tablespoon lemon juice
1 cup Béchamel Sauce
¼ cup heavy cream
salt to taste
ground black pepper to taste

Remove stems from mushrooms and save for sauces and soups. Wash mushroom caps and simmer them 5 minutes in butter and lemon juice. Add Béchamel Sauce, cream, salt, and pepper. Simmer until mushrooms are tender and sauce has thickened. Makes 6 servings.

GRILLED MUSHROOMS

12 large mushroom caps
½ cup olive oil or salad oil
½ teaspoon salt
firm butter

Wash mushroom caps and drain well. Pour oil into a baking pan and heat it in a very hot preheated oven (450° F.). Add mushrooms and stir to coat them thoroughly with oil. Sprinkle with salt. Return the pan to the oven and cook 10 minutes, or until the mushrooms are done. Remove mushrooms from the oven and fill the cavities with firm butter. Serve at once. Makes 6 servings.

MUSHROOMS IN HERB SAUCE

1½ pounds mushrooms
2 tablespoons chopped onions
4 tablespoons (½ stick) butter
1 teaspoon salt
⅛ teaspoon ground black pepper
1 tablespoon flour
¼ cup heavy cream
½ teaspoon dried chervil or 1½ teaspoons chopped fresh chervil
chopped parsley

Remove stems from mushrooms and reserve for other use. Wash the caps and set aside. Cook onions until limp in half the butter. Add mushroom caps and cook over medium low heat 10 minutes. Add salt and pepper. Blend flour with remaining butter and add to the mushrooms along with cream and chervil. Mix well and cook slowly 1 to 2 minutes or until the sauce thickens. Turn into a serving dish. Sprinkle with chopped parsley. Makes 6 servings.

MUSHROOM PURÉE

2½ pounds mushrooms
3 tablespoons butter
1 tablespoon lemon juice
salt
ground black pepper
½ to ¾ cup very thick hot Béchamel Sauce

Wash mushrooms thoroughly, leaving stems attached, and put them through a food mill or an electric blender, puréeing a few at a time. Melt butter in a saucepan. Add puréed mushrooms and lemon juice. Stir and cook until the moisture has all evaporated. Season with salt and pepper to taste, and add hot Béchamel Sauce. Heat, but do not boil. Serve as an accompaniment to meat dishes, or to fill tartlets, barquettes, or artichoke bottoms. Makes 6 servings.

⚜ RUSSIAN STEWED MUSHROOMS

1½ pounds mushrooms or boletus
3 tablespoons butter
¾ teaspoon salt or salt to taste
¼ teaspoon fennel seed, or 1 teaspoon chopped fresh fennel
¼ teaspoon dill seed or 1 teaspoon chopped fresh dill
2 tablespoons chopped chives
⅛ teaspoon ground black pepper
4 tablespoons sour cream

Wash mushrooms. Slice and place in a 10-inch skillet with butter and next 4 ingredients. Stir and cook until mushrooms are tender. Transfer mushrooms to a serving dish. Cook the liquid until it has reduced to three-fourths the original amount. Add pepper and sour cream. Heat about 1 minute. Pour over mushrooms. Serve immediately. Makes 6 servings.

⚜ SAUTÉED MUSHROOMS OR CEPES ITALIAN STYLE

1½ pounds mushrooms or cepes
2 small cloves garlic
½ cup olive oil
½ cup chopped parsley

Wash the mushrooms or cepes and cut them in thin slices. Brown the garlic very lightly in the oil and remove. Put mushrooms or cepes into the oil and sauté 3 minutes or until limp. Add half the parsley and sauté 1 minute longer. Remove to a serving dish and sprinkle with remaining parsley. Makes 6 servings. (See illustration, page 764.)

OKRA (*Gombos*)

⚜ HOW TO COOK OKRA

Wash okra and cut off the stems. Leave the pods whole. Place in a saucepan with ½ teaspoon salt. Pour in boiling water to a depth of ½ inch. Bring to boiling point, uncovered, and cook 5 minutes. Cover and cook 5 minutes, or only until okra is tender. Drain off and discard water. Add 2 tablespoons butter to the saucepan. Simmer 2 to 3 minutes. Sprinkle with black pepper. Serve hot. Allow 5 medium-sized pods per serving.

ONIONS (*Oignons*)

⚜ SMALL GLAZED ONIONS

1½ pounds small white onions
½ cup boiling water
½ cup chicken or veal stock
2 tablespoons butter
1 tablespoon sugar

Drop unpeeled onions into rapidly boiling water and let them stand about 10 seconds, or just long enough to loosen the skins from the onions. Drain and hold a few seconds under cold running water. Cut off a thin slice from the bottom and the top. Then slip off the outside skin and the first layer of onion with the fingers. Cut a cross (+) in the root end of the onion to prevent the onion from bursting. Place onions in a saucepan with boiling water, stock, 1 tablespoon of the butter, and the sugar. Bring to boiling point, reduce heat, and simmer, uncovered, 15 minutes, or until the onions are tender and all the liquid has evaporated. Add the remaining 1 tablespoon butter. Shake and cook over low heat until onions take on a glaze. Makes 6 servings.

⚜ DEEP-FAT-FRIED ONIONS

4 large mild onions
½ cup milk
½ cup flour
½ teaspoon salt
⅛ teaspoon ground black pepper

Peel onions, wash, and cut into slices ¼ inch thick. Separate the rings, dip them in milk and then in flour seasoned with salt and pepper. Place a few rings at a time in a wire basket or large sieve and immerse in deep fat preheated to 375° F. Fry until onions are golden brown. Remove from fat and turn out onto paper towels to drain. Serve hot. Makes 6 servings.

⚜ STUFFED ONIONS

6 large Spanish onions
boiling water to cover
salt
2 tablespoons butter or olive oil
1 small clove garlic, crushed
½ teaspoon dried marjoram
1 cup chopped leftover meat
½ cup cooked rice
ground black pepper
6 tablespoons buttered soft breadcrumbs
6 teaspoons grated Parmesan cheese

Peel onions and parboil 10 minutes in boiling water to cover, with ½ teaspoon salt. Remove the centers and set the onion shells aside. Chop centers and cook in butter or oil, along with the garlic, until onions begin to turn golden. Add marjoram, meat, and rice. Stir and cook 2 minutes. Season to taste with salt and pepper. Stuff mixture into the onion shells. Top each with 1 tablespoon buttered crumbs and 1 teaspoon grated Parmesan cheese. Place in a 9- by 9- by 2-inch baking pan. Pour in stock or bouillon to a depth of 1 inch. Cook in a preheated hot oven (400° F.) 30 to 40 minutes, or until tops are brown. Serve each onion in an individual serving dish and pour a little of the stock around it. Makes 6 servings.

PEAS (*Pois*)

Green peas in France are eaten when they are still small and are known as *petits pois*.

⚜ PEAS BONNE FEMME

3 pounds green peas, shelled
¼ pound lean salt pork
2 tablespoons butter
¼ cup chopped onion
1½ tablespoons flour
½ cup stock or water
½ teaspoon salt
12 small whole white onions

Wash peas and set them aside to drain. Rinse salt pork in hot water and cut into dice. Place in a 1½-quart saucepan with butter and chopped onion. Stir and cook until onions and pork have browned lightly. Sprinkle with flour, mix well, and stir and cook 1 minute. Add stock or water and salt. Mix well, bring to boiling point, and add whole onions. Cover and cook 10 minutes. Add peas and continue cooking until onions and peas are tender, about 10 minutes. Makes 6 servings.

⚜ PEAS FRENCH STYLE

3 pounds green peas, shelled
3 tablespoons butter
6 small white onions
6 lettuce leaves, shredded
1 stalk parsley
¼ teaspoon dried chervil
1 teaspoon sugar
½ teaspoon salt
¼ cup water
½ teaspoon flour
1/16 teaspoon ground black pepper

Place peas in a sieve, wash under cold running water, and set aside to drain. Melt 2 tablespoons of the butter in a saucepan. Add peas and the next 7 ingredients. Cover, bring the water to boiling point, reduce heat, and simmer only until peas are barely tender and only 2 to 3 tablespoons of water remain in the pan (20 to 25 minutes). Remove and discard parsley. Blend flour with the remaining 1 tablespoon butter and add to the liquid along with the pepper. Shake the pan and cook until the liquid has thickened slightly. Makes 6 servings.

⚜ PEAS WITH MINT

3 pounds green peas, shelled
2 tablespoons minced fresh mint leaves
1 tablespoon salt
boiling water
2 tablespoons butter
dash ground black pepper
6 whole fresh mint leaves

Wash peas and place them in a 1½-quart saucepan with minced mint leaves and salt. Pour in boiling water to a depth of ½ inch. Bring to boiling point, cover, and boil briskly 5 minutes or until almost done. Drain off water, add butter, cover, and simmer 3 to 4 minutes, or until peas are tender. Add pepper and toss lightly. Turn into a serving dish and garnish with 6 whole fresh mint leaves. Makes 6 servings.

⚜ PEAS À LA PAYSANNE

3 pounds green peas, shelled
4 tablespoons (½ stick) butter
12 small white onions, peeled
12 small young carrots, peeled
12 very small new potatoes, scraped
2 stalks parsley
2 teaspoons sugar
1 teaspoon salt
½ cup boiling water
2 medium-small heads of lettuce
1 teaspoon flour
1/16 teaspoon ground black pepper

Wash peas and set them aside to drain. Melt 3 tablespoons of the butter in a saucepan. Add peas and the next 7 ingredients. Remove and discard wilted outside leaves from the lettuce. Cut each head into 3 wedges and tie them at each end and in the center with twine to hold them in shape. Place over the vegetables. Cover, bring the water to boiling point, reduce heat, and simmer only until vegetables are done, 20 to 25 minutes. Remove and discard parsley. Transfer vegetables to a serving dish. Remove twine from lettuce. Blend flour with remaining 1 tablespoon butter and add it to the cooking liquid. Stir and cook 1 to 2 minutes, or until thickened. Add pepper. Serve over the vegetables. Makes 6 servings.

⚜ SPLIT-PEA PURÉE (*Purée de Pois Cassés*)

2 cups split peas
4 cups cold water
¼ pound lean salt pork
½ cup diced onions
½ cup diced carrots
½ teaspoon salt, or salt to taste
⅛ teaspoon ground black pepper
2 tablespoons butter

Wash peas and place them in a saucepan with cold water. Dice salt pork, brown, and add to the peas along with onions and carrots. Soak 1 hour. Do not drain. Cover, bring to boiling point, reduce heat, and simmer 1½ hours. Add salt and cook 30 minutes, or until peas are well done. Stir in pepper and butter. This purée should be very thick. Makes 6 servings.

PEPPERS (*Poivrons*)

⚜ PEPPERS STUFFED WITH MEAT

6 medium-sized green or red sweet peppers
boiling water
salt
½ cup chopped onion
1 small clove of garlic, crushed
1¼ pounds pork sausage
2 cups cooked rice
3 tablespoons chopped parsley
⅛ teaspoon ground black pepper
¾ cup beef or veal stock
¾ cup soft breadcrumbs
3 tablespoons olive oil or salad oil
¾ cup hot water, stock, or tomato juice
1½ cups hot Tomato Sauce

Wash peppers, cut off the tops, and remove seeds and pith. Parboil peppers 5 minutes in boiling water to cover with ½ teaspoon salt. Remove from water and invert on a pan to drain. Cook onion, garlic, and sausage together until sausage browns. Add next 4 ingredients and salt to taste. Mix. Stuff the mixture into well-drained peppers. Arrange peppers in an oiled baking dish. Mix breadcrumbs with oil and sprinkle over tops of peppers. Pour a little hot water, stock, or tomato juice into the pan around the peppers. Bake in a preheated moderate oven (350° F.) 40 to 50 minutes, or until crumbs are brown. Transfer peppers to a serving dish. Add Tomato Sauce to the pan liquid, heat, and pour around peppers. Makes 6 servings. (See illustration, page 761.)

⚜ PEPPERS STUFFED WITH RICE

6 medium-sized green or red sweet peppers
boiling water
salt
½ cup chopped onion
1 small clove garlic, crushed
1 tablespoon olive oil or salad oil
1 cup peeled, seeded, and diced tomatoes
2 cups cooked rice
1 cup bouillon
¼ teaspoon ground black pepper

Wash peppers, cut off the tops, and remove seeds and pith. Parboil peppers 5 minutes in boiling water to cover with ½ teaspoon salt. Remove peppers from the water and invert on a pan to drain. Cook onion and garlic in oil until onions are limp. Add tomatoes, rice, ½ cup of the bouillon, black pepper, salt to taste, and oil. Mix lightly and stuff into peppers. Arrange peppers in a baking dish. Pour remaining bouillon into the pan around the peppers. Cover and bake in a preheated moderate oven (350° F.) 40 minutes, basting occasionally with the bouillon. Serve hot. Makes 6 servings. (See Culinary Techniques in Pictures.)

⚜ SPANISH STUFFED PEPPERS

6 large green or red sweet peppers
salt
boiling water
½ cup chopped onions
about 5 tablespoons olive oil or salad oil
2 cups finely diced ham
1 cup cooked rice
1 teaspoon capers
½ small clove garlic, crushed
⅛ teaspoon ground black pepper
2 tablespoons chopped parsley
8-ounce can tomato sauce
½ cup water or bouillon

Wash peppers and cut a slice from the stem ends, saving the slices. Remove seeds and pith. Place peppers and the slices cut from the stem ends in a saucepan with ½ teaspoon salt and enough boiling water to cover. Cover and parboil 5 minutes. Remove peppers from water and drain well. Sauté onions in 2 tablespoons of the oil. Add ham, rice, capers, garlic, pepper, parsley, and salt to taste. Stuff the mixture into the peppers. Replace top slices and brush peppers with oil. Arrange peppers in a baking pan. Combine 2 tablespoons oil, tomato sauce, and water or bouillon, and pour into pan around peppers. Bake in a preheated moderate oven (350° F.) 45 minutes or until peppers are done. Transfer peppers to a serving dish. Season pan sauce to taste with salt and pepper and serve in a sauceboat. Makes 6 servings.

POTATOES (*Pommes de Terre*)

⚜ POTATOES ANNA

6 cups thinly sliced potatoes
½ cup (1 stick) butter
1 teaspoon salt
⅛ teaspoon ground black pepper

Peel potatoes, then wash, wipe dry, and slice thin. Pat slices dry between clean towels. Butter the bottom and sides of an 8- by 8- by 2-inch baking pan generously. Sprinkle potatoes with salt and pepper and arrange them over the bottom and around the sides of the pan, having the slices slightly overlapping. Finish filling pan with layers of potatoes. Melt remaining butter and heat until it has browned very lightly. Pour over potatoes. Bake in a preheated hot oven (425° F.) 40 to 50 minutes or until potatoes are tender when tested with a pointed knife. Turn potatoes out onto a large heatproof serving plate. Place under broiler heat to brown. Serve hot. Makes 6 to 8 servings.

VARIATION

POTATOES VOISIN

In the recipe for Potatoes Anna, sprinkle grated cheese between the layers of potatoes.

⚜ POTATOES BADEN STYLE

2 pounds hot boiled potatoes
2 tablespoons butter
2 eggs, separated
¼ cup milk
salt to taste
⅛ teaspoon ground black pepper
½ cup grated Cheddar cheese

Put potatoes through a sieve and mix with the butter. Beat egg yolks, blend with milk, and add to potatoes along with the next 3 ingredients. Mix well. Beat egg whites until they stand in soft stiff peaks, and carefully fold into the potatoes. Turn into a buttered 1½-quart casserole, reserving 1 cupful. Put the reserved potatoes into a pastry bag fitted with a fluted nozzle and pipe a border of potatoes around the edge of the casserole. Bake in a preheated moderate oven (350° F.) until potatoes have puffed like a soufflé and browned over the top. Makes 6 servings.

⚜ POTATOES BOULANGÈRE

6 medium-large potatoes
6 medium-sized onions
1 teaspoon salt
¼ teaspoon ground black pepper
1 cup boiling bouillon, or beef or veal stock

Peel potatoes and onions. Slice potatoes ½ inch thick and onions ¼ inch thick. Mix together along with salt and pepper, and put into a well-buttered 2-quart baking dish. Pour in bouillon or stock. Cover and cook 15 minutes in a preheated hot oven (400° F.). Remove cover and continue cooking until the liquid has evaporated and the vegetables begin to roast. Serve hot with beef, veal, or pork roasts. Makes 6 servings.

⚜ CHÂTEAU POTATOES

2 pounds potatoes
1 teaspoon salt
cold water
3 tablespoons butter
⅛ teaspoon ground black pepper
chopped parsley

Peel potatoes and cut them in the size and shape of large olives. Place them in a saucepan with salt and enough cold water to cover them. Bring the water to boiling point and cook 1 to 2 minutes. Drain and cool in cold water. Drain and dry thoroughly. Heat butter in a skillet. Add potatoes, a few at a time, and sauté until golden. Sprinkle with pepper and parsley. Makes 6 servings.

⚜ POTATO CHIPS

Peel potatoes, cut them into balls about 1 inch in diameter, and slice thin. Place a few slices at a time in a wire basket or medium-large sieve and fry in deep fat preheated to 375° F. about 1 minute, or until golden. Drain on paper towels. Allow 1 medium-sized potato per serving. (See illustration, page 766.)

⚜ DAUPHINE POTATOES

½ cup butter
1 cup water
2 teaspoons salt
1 cup sifted all-purpose flour
4 large eggs
2½ pounds (7 to 8 medium-sized) potatoes
1 teaspoon ground nutmeg
⅛ teaspoon ground black pepper

Place first 3 ingredients in a 1-quart saucepan, bring to boiling point, and add all the flour at one time. Stir, and cook over low heat 1 to 2 minutes, or until the mixture leaves the sides of the pan and forms a ball. Cool slightly. Beat in one egg at a time. (This is chou paste.) Peel potatoes, boil, and mash until fluffy (do not add milk or butter). Add to chou paste and mix well. Shape mixture into 1-inch balls, or drop it from a tablespoon, or put it into a pastry bag and pipe 2-inch lengths. Fry in deep fat preheated to 375° F. 2 to 3 minutes or until browned. Drain on paper towels. Makes 6 to 8 servings. (See illustration, page 766.)

VARIATION

LORETTE POTATOES

Make the recipe for Dauphine Potatoes, adding ½ cup grated Gruyère or Cheddar cheese to the mashed potatoes.

⚜ DUCHESS POTATO RINGS

Prepare Duchess Potatoes (see page 149). Put the mixture into a pastry bag fitted with a rosette nozzle and pipe it into 3-inch rings on a buttered baking sheet. Bake in a preheated very hot oven (450° F.) 10 minutes or until browned. Allow 1 or 2 per serving. (See illustration, page 766.)

⚜ ITALIAN STUFFED BAKED POTATOES

6 medium-sized baking potatoes
salt to taste
ground black pepper to taste
about ¼ cup milk
about ¼ cup heavy cream
2 tablespoons butter, melted
grated Parmesan cheese

Wash and dry potatoes. Bake in a preheated hot oven (400° F.) until potatoes are soft. Cut off a thick lengthwise slice from each potato. Scoop out potatoes, leaving shell, about ¼ inch thick, intact. Place potato shells in the oven to dry and crisp. Mash the scooped-out portion of the potatoes, add salt, pepper, and enough milk and cream to give a fluffy consistency. Put into a pastry bag and pipe into the shells, rounding them over the tops. Brush with melted butter and sprinkle with Parmesan cheese. Brown in a preheated very hot oven (400° F.), or place under the broiler to brown. Makes 6 servings. (See illustration, page 766.)

⚜ LYONNAISE POTATOES

2 pounds (6 medium) potatoes
¼ cup (½ stick) butter
½ pound onions
salt
ground black pepper
chopped parsley

Cook potatoes in their jackets until they are done. Peel, slice, and fry slices in hot butter until browned. Peel onions, slice thin, and sauté in a separate skillet. Add to the potatoes. Sprinkle with salt and pepper and mix lightly. Turn into a serving dish. Sprinkle with chopped parsley. Makes 6 servings.

⚜ MACAIRE POTATOES

6 large baking potatoes
½ teaspoon salt
⅛ teaspoon ground black pepper
6 tablespoons butter

Wash potatoes and bake in a preheated hot oven (400° F.) until done. Remove from oven, cut in half, and scoop out the flesh. Add salt, pepper, and half the butter and mash coarsely with a fork. Heat 2 tablespoons of the remaining butter in a skillet, add potatoes in 6 pancake-size portions, and press them down to the thickness of pancakes. Brown on both sides, adding remaining butter as needed. Serve hot. Makes 6 servings.

⚜ MAÎTRE D'HÔTEL POTATOES

6 medium-large potatoes
¾ cup bouillon
salt
ground black pepper
¼ teaspoon ground nutmeg
2 tablespoons butter
⅓ cup milk
chopped parsley

Cook potatoes in their jackets until they are done. Peel, slice thin, and place in a 10-inch skillet. Add bouillon, salt and pepper to taste, nutmeg, and butter. Bring to boiling point and cook, uncovered, 5 minutes. Add milk and simmer (do not boil) until the sauce is creamy and has slightly thickened. Turn into a serving dish. Sprinkle with chopped parsley. Makes 6 servings.

⚜ MATCHSTICK POTATOES

Peel potatoes and cut them into strips the size of matchsticks. Wash in cold water, drain, and dry thoroughly between clean towels. Put a few potatoes at a time in a wire basket or medium-large sieve and immerse in deep fat preheated to 370° F. Fry 2 to 3 minutes or until browned. Drain on paper towels. Sprinkle with salt and serve hot. Allow 1 medium-large potato per serving. These are also called shoestring potatoes or straw potatoes. (See illustration, page 766.)

⚜ POTATOES MONT D'OR

6 medium-sized potatoes
1 teaspoon salt
boiling water
2 tablespoons butter
¼ teaspoon grated nutmeg
⅛ teaspoon ground black pepper
3 eggs, beaten
½ cup thin slices Gruyère or Cheddar cheese
¼ cup grated Gruyère or Cheddar cheese

Wash, peel, and quarter potatoes. Put them in a saucepan with salt. Pour on boiling water to a depth of 1 inch. Cover, bring to boiling point, and cook until potatoes are soft. Drain well and put through a potato ricer or coarse sieve. Add butter, nutmeg, pepper, and beaten eggs and mix well. Stir in sliced cheese. Turn the mixture into a heatproof serving dish and mound over the top. Sprinkle with grated Gruyère or Cheddar cheese. Brown in a preheated hot oven (400° F.). Makes 6 servings.

⚜ NOISETTE POTATOES

With a French melon-ball cutter, cut pared potatoes into balls the size of hazelnuts. Fry in butter until golden. Cover and keep in a warm place until ready to serve.

⚜ POTATO OLIVES

Cut pared potatoes into oval shapes the size of olives, using a French oval-shaped scoop. Fry in butter until golden. Cover and keep in a warm place until ready to serve. Allow 4 medium-sized potatoes for 6 servings.

⚜ POTATOES PAYSANNE

12 small onions
¼ pound lean salt pork
2 tablespoons butter
1 tablespoon flour
1½ cups bouillon or beef stock
2 pounds (6 medium-sized) potatoes
ground black pepper to taste
salt
chopped parsley

Peel onions and put into a 10-inch skillet. Cut salt pork into strips ½ inch wide and add to onions along with butter. Cook over medium heat until onions are golden, stirring occasionally. Sprinkle flour over onions; stir and cook until flour has browned lightly. Add bouillon or stock and mix well. Peel potatoes and add. Cover and cook 25 minutes, or until potatoes are tender. Season to taste with pepper and salt. Turn into a serving dish and sprinkle with chopped parsley. Makes 6 servings.

⚜ ROESTI (*Browned Sliced Potatoes; Swiss*)

6 medium-sized potatoes, baked
about ¼ cup (½ stick) butter
salt
ground black pepper

Cool the baked potatoes. Peel them and cut them into fine strips. Fry in a shallow skillet in butter, adding it as needed. When the underneath side has browned, slip a spatula under the potatoes and slide them onto a large plate or thin lid with the unbrowned side up. Invert the skillet over the unbrowned side and turn plate and skillet over, letting the potatoes fall back into the skillet with the browned side up. Continue to cook, adding more butter if needed, until the potatoes have browned. Sprinkle lightly with salt and pepper. Makes 6 servings.

⚜ SNOW POTATOES

6 medium-large potatoes
¼ cup (½ stick) butter
1 teaspoon salt
boiling water

Peel potatoes, cut them in large pieces, and put them in a saucepan. Add butter and salt. Pour in boiling water to a depth of ¼ inch. Cover and bring to boiling point. Remove cover and cook until potatoes are soft and all the water has evaporated. Put potatoes through a potato ricer or a coarse sieve. Serve hot. Makes 6 servings.

⚜ SOUFFLÉ POTATOES

Peel baking potatoes of uniform size and trim the surface so that they will be smooth and regular. Cut potatoes into long narrow slices a scant ⅛ inch thick. Or, if desired, cut them into long pointed ovals a scant ⅛ inch thick. For best results use a potato slicer. Wash the potatoes in cold water and dry them thoroughly.

Fill a deep-fat frying kettle half full of cooking oil or salad oil, or rendered beef suet. Preheat to 275° F. Drop a few slices of potatoes at a time into the hot fat. With a large perforated spoon raise the slices, one at a time, from the hot fat for a few seconds and return them to the kettle until they begin to puff, about 7 to 8 minutes. Using a sieve, remove the potatoes from the hot fat, drain them on paper towels, and cool them at least 5 minutes. The second frying may follow immediately, or if desired, the potatoes may be finished later in the day or even chilled and finished the next day. The potatoes will deflate but will puff again in the second frying.

For final frying, preheat fat to 400° F. Put a few slices at a time into a wire basket or medium-large sieve and lower it into the hot fat. Potatoes will puff into small oval-shaped balloons. Turn the puffs to brown them on all sides. Remove from the fat and drain them on paper towels. Sprinkle with salt and serve immediately.

Allow 2 pounds large potatoes for 6 servings.

⚜ POTATOES YVETTE

1 pound (3 medium-sized) potatoes
½ cup (1 stick) butter
½ teaspoon salt
1/16 teaspoon ground black pepper

Wash potatoes, peel, cut in julienne strips, and rinse under cold running water. Drain well and dry thoroughly between clean towels. Melt butter in a shallow 9-inch skillet. Add potatoes, sprinkle with salt and pepper, mix with the butter, and spread over the bottom of the skillet. Cook until potatoes are brown on the underside. Press potatoes down slightly with a spatula. Slip the spatula under the potatoes and slide them onto a large plate or thin flat lid with the unbrowned side up. Then invert skillet over the unbrowned side, and turn plate and skillet over, letting the potatoes drop into the skillet, with the browned side up. Continue cooking until potatoes are brown. Serve at once. Makes 3 servings.

⚜ NEW POTATOES WITH BACON

18 small white onions, peeled
2 tablespoons butter, melted
2 slices lean bacon
1 cup bouillon
2 tablespoons tomato purée
18 small new potatoes
½ teaspoon salt
⅛ teaspoon ground black pepper
chopped parsley

Cook onions in melted butter until they are lightly browned. Dice bacon, add to onions, and cook until browned. Add bouillon and tomato purée and cook 3 to 4 minutes. Scrape potatoes and add to onions along with salt. Cover and cook 20 minutes, or until potatoes and onions are tender. Add pepper. Serve hot, sprinkled with chopped parsley. Makes 6 servings.

⚜ NEW POTATOES WITH HOLLANDAISE SAUCE

2 pounds small new potatoes
boiling water
1 teaspoon salt
ground white pepper
¾ cup Hollandaise Sauce

Scrape potatoes and rinse under cold running water. Place in a saucepan with 1 inch boiling water and salt. Cover, bring to boiling point, and boil 15 to 20 minutes, or until potatoes are tender. Drain and season with pepper to taste. Serve with Hollandaise Sauce. Makes 6 servings.

⚜ POTATO CROQUETTES

2 pounds (6 medium-sized) potatoes
boiling water
1 teaspoon salt
¼ teaspoon ground black pepper
3 whole eggs and 2 egg yolks
flour
fine dry breadcrumbs

Peel and quarter potatoes. Cook until soft in a covered saucepan with 1 inch boiling water and the salt. Drain potatoes well and put them through a ricer or food mill. Add pepper. Beat 2 of the whole eggs and the egg yolks together until light and foamy and add to potatoes. Whip the mixture until fluffy. Sprinkle a pastry board lightly with flour and shape the potatoes into pear-shaped croquettes or into balls, using 2 rounded tablespoons of the mixture for each croquette. Beat the remaining egg slightly. Dip croquettes in beaten egg and then roll them in breadcrumbs. Let them stand about 20 minutes and then fry in deep fat preheated to 375° F. Drain on paper towels. If croquettes are pear-shaped, stick a 1-inch piece of spaghetti in the small end of each to simulate a pear stem. Serve hot. Makes 6 servings. (See illustration, page 766.)

VARIATION

POTATO CROQUETTES WITH ALMONDS

Make the recipe for Potato Croquettes. Form the mixture into pear-shaped croquettes or balls, dip them into beaten egg, and then roll them in thin blanched almond shavings. Fry in deep fat preheated to 375° F. until browned. Drain on paper towels.

⚜ POTATO CROQUETTES WITH CURRANTS

½ cup dried currants
1 recipe for Potato Croquettes
1 large egg, beaten
½ cup chopped blanched almonds

Place currants in a sieve and steam them over boiling water until they are plump. Cool and dry thoroughly between towels. Make the recipe for Potato Croquettes and stir in currants. Shape mixture into cakes 2½ inches in diameter and ½ inch thick. Dip cakes in beaten egg and then roll them in finely chopped almonds. Let stand 20 minutes. Fry in deep fat preheated to 375° F. until browned. Drain on paper towels. Serve with game. Makes 6 servings.

⚜ POTATO FRITTERS

3 cups Duchess Potatoes (see page 149)
1 cup Chou Paste
salt and ground black pepper to taste

Combine the Duchess Potatoes and the Chou Paste, mix well, and add salt and pepper if needed. Put the mixture in a pastry bag with a plain tube and pipe it in rings on buttered paper or buttered foil. Holding the paper or foil by a corner, slide it into deep fat preheated to 375° F. The rings will slip off and the paper or foil is then taken out. Fry the rings 2 or 3 minutes, or until puffed and brown. Makes about 24 rings. (See Culinary Techniques in Pictures.)

⚜ POTATO GNOCCHI

The potatoes should be dry and mealy.

1 pound (3 medium-sized) potatoes
3 large egg yolks
½ teaspoon salt
1 cup sifted all-purpose flour
1½ cups grated Gruyère, Cheddar, or Parmesan cheese
¼ cup (½ stick) butter, melted

Boil potatoes in their jackets, then peel and mash until smooth. Beat in egg yolks and salt. Continue beating until potatoes are fluffy. Stir in flour, butter, and ½ cup of the cheese. Shape into 1½-inch balls on a lightly floured board. Flatten them slightly. Poach about one-fourth of the balls at a time in 2 quarts boiling water for 5 minutes. As they are cooked, arrange them in layers in a buttered 1½-quart casserole, sprinkling grated cheese between the layers and over the top. Dribble with melted butter. Bake in a preheated hot oven (400° F.) 10 to 15 minutes, or until top is browned. Makes 6 servings.

⚜ POTATO DUMPLINGS WITH CHEESE (*Knepfes au Fromage*)

Make the recipe for Potato Gnocchi. Shape the mixture into balls and fry in butter until golden brown. Serve sprinkled with grated Gruyère, Cheddar, or Parmesan cheese. Makes 6 servings.

⚜ POTATO PANCAKES (*Subrics de Pommes de Terre*)

Potato pancakes should be cooked as soon as they are mixed to prevent the batter from turning dark.

⅓ cup all-purpose flour
1½ pounds potatoes
1 tablespoon grated onion
1 teaspoon salt
⅛ teaspoon ground black pepper
1 large egg, unbeaten
1 tablespoon chopped parsley (optional)
olive oil, salad oil, or butter

Turn flour into a mixing bowl. Peel the potatoes and grate over the flour, using a fine grater. Add onion, salt, pepper, egg, and parsley if desired. Mix quickly and well. Grease a heavy-bottomed 9- or 10-inch skillet with oil or butter and heat until hot. Drop 1 heaping tablespoon of the mixture at a time on the hot skillet. Fry until pancakes are brown on the underside. Turn and brown the other side, adding more oil or butter as needed. Drain on paper towels. Serve hot as a vegetable with roasts. Makes approximately 15 pancakes.

⚜ POTATO SOUFFLÉ

2 cups mashed potatoes
½ cup hot milk
¾ teaspoon salt
¼ teaspoon ground black pepper
1 tablespoon minced onion
½ teaspoon powdered mustard
2 teaspoons water
¾ cup grated Gruyère or Cheddar cheese
1 large whole egg
2 large eggs, separated

Combine smooth mashed potatoes with the next 4 ingredients. Beat until fluffy. Mix mustard and water and let stand 5 minutes. Add to potatoes along with the cheese. Beat whole egg and egg yolks together and add to potato mixture. Mix well. Beat the 2 egg whites until they stand in soft stiff peaks, and carefully fold into the potatoes. Butter *only* the bottom of a 1-quart casserole and put in the mixture. Bake in a preheated moderate oven (350° F.) 1 hour, or until the soufflé is well puffed and the top is flecked with brown. Serve at once. Makes 6 servings.

SALSIFY (*Salsifis*)

Salsify, of which the root is the edible portion, is also called oyster plant.

⚜ DEEP-FAT-FRIED SALSIFY

White Court Bouillon for Vegetables
2 pounds salsify
2 tablespoons chopped parsley
2 tablespoons lemon juice
1 tablespoon olive oil or salad oil
½ teaspoon salt
⅛ teaspoon ground black pepper
Fritter Batter
Fried Parsley

Make court bouillon according to the following recipe and set aside. Wash and scrape salsify, dropping them into the court bouillon as they are scraped to prevent discoloration. Remove and cut into 3-inch pieces. Bring court bouillon to boiling point, return the salsify to the court bouillon, and cook about 5 minutes. Transfer salsify to a bowl, add the next 5 ingredients, mix well, and marinate 30 minutes. Drain. Dip pieces of salsify in Fritter Batter, and fry until brown in deep fat preheated to 375° F. Drain on paper towels. Makes 6 servings.

WHITE COURT BOUILLON FOR VEGETABLES

Mix 2 tablespoons flour with ½ cup water to a smooth paste. Add 4 cups water, mix, and strain through a fine sieve. Add 1 teaspoon salt, 1½ tablespoons lemon juice, and 2 tablespoons raw chopped beef suet. Boil 3 to 4 minutes.

⚜ SALSIFY WITH HERBS (*Salsifis sauté aux fines herbes*)

2 pounds salsify
White Court Bouillon for Vegetables
¼ cup (½ stick) butter
2 teaspoons chopped fresh thyme, or ½ teaspoon dried thyme
salt to taste
ground black pepper to taste
2 tablespoons chopped pars'

Wash, scrape, and cut salsify and cook in White Court Bouillon for Vegetables, as instructed in the recipe for Deep-Fat-Fried Salsify. Rinse well in water. Sauté in hot butter. Toss with thyme, salt, and black pepper. Turn into a serving dish and sprinkle with chopped parsley. Makes 6 servings.

SORREL (*Oseille*)

Sorrel is also called sour grass. The young leaves are used in salad.

⚜ BUTTERED SORREL

Wash 2 pounds sorrel, changing the water several times. Shred fine. Melt 3 tablespoons butter in a 2-quart saucepan, add sorrel, cover, and cook until wilted, using only the water that clings to the leaves. Remove cover and shake the pan over moderately low heat until all liquid has evaporated. Season to taste with salt and pepper and ½ teaspoon sugar. Add a little heavy cream if sorrel is too acid. Makes 6 servings.

SPINACH (*Epinards*)

⚜ CREAMED SPINACH WITH HARD-COOKED EGGS

2 pounds fresh spinach, or 2 packages (10 ounces each) frozen spinach
4 tablespoons (½ stick) butter
1¼ teaspoon salt
½ teaspoon sugar
¼ teaspoon ground black pepper
¼ teaspoon ground nutmeg
1 teaspoon lemon juice
1 teaspoon chopped onion
2 tablespoons flour
½ cup chicken or veal stock
½ cup milk or light cream
2 hard-cooked eggs

If frozen spinach is used, cook according to package directions. If fresh spinach is used, wash it thoroughly in several waters, drain, and place it in a saucepan. Cover and cook, without adding water, over moderately low heat *only* until spinach is wilted. Remove cover, press out water from spinach, and shake the pan over moderately low heat to evaporate liquid. Chop spinach fine and heat with 2 tablespoons of the butter 2 to 3 minutes. Stir. Season with the next 5 ingredients. Melt remaining butter in a small saucepan, add onion, and cook only until wilted. Remove from heat and blend in flour. Stir and cook 1 minute. Remove from heat and add stock and milk or cream. Stir and cook 4 to 5 minutes, or only until sauce has thickened. Add salt to taste, if needed. Pour over spinach and mix lightly. Transfer spinach to a serving dish. Cut peeled hard-cooked eggs into quarters or eighths and arrange over the top. Makes 6 servings.

⚜ SPINACH LOAF (*Pain d'Epinards*)

2 pounds fresh spinach, or 1½ 10-ounce packages frozen spinach
1 cup soft breadcrumbs
¼ cup (½ stick) butter
1 tablespoon minced onion
5 tablespoons flour
1½ cups spinach liquid and milk
2 eggs, separated
1 teaspoon sugar
1 teaspoon salt
½ teaspoon dried thyme, or 1½ teaspoons chopped fresh thyme
½ teaspoon ground black pepper
2 hard-cooked eggs, sliced
Velouté Sauce (optional)

If frozen spinach is used, cook according to package directions. If fresh spinach is used, wash it thoroughly in several waters, drain, and place it in a saucepan. Cover and cook, without adding water, over moderately low heat *only* until spinach is wilted. Press out the water, draining it into a cup, and reserve. Chop spinach fine, add breadcrumbs, and set aside. Melt butter in a 1-quart saucepan, add onion and stir and cook until wilted. Remove from heat and blend in flour. Stir and cook 1 minute. Measure spinach liquid and add milk to make 1½ cups. Add to the butter and flour. Stir and cook until the sauce is thick. Add to spinach and crumbs. Beat egg yolks lightly and add, along with the next 4 ingredients. Mix well. Beat egg whites until they stand in soft stiff peaks, and fold into the mixture. Turn into a buttered 9- by 5- by 3-inch loaf pan. Bake in a preheated moderate oven (375° F.) 1 hour, or until a knife inserted in the center comes out clean. Let stand in the pan 10 minutes. Unmold onto a serving platter and garnish with sliced hard-cooked eggs. To serve, cut in ½-inch slices. If desired, serve Velouté Sauce in a separate bowl. Spinach Loaf may also be served with Cheese Sauce. Makes approximately 8 servings.

TOMATOES (*Tomates*)

⚜ TOMATOES ALGERIAN STYLE

8 medium-large tomatoes
olive or salad oil
salt
ground black pepper
1 medium-sized eggplant
¼ to ⅓ cup olive oil or salad oil
1 small clove garlic, crushed

Wash tomatoes, cut them in half, and scoop out the centers, leaving the shells intact. (Save centers for salad.) Sprinkle the cavities with oil, salt, and pepper. Place shells in a baking pan and cook in a preheated moderate oven (350° F.) 10 to 15 minutes, being sure that they do not lose their shape. Wash eggplant, peel, and cut into slices ½ inch thick. Sprinkle with salt and set aside for 30 minutes. Wipe salt and moisture from eggplant and fry in hot oil, browning both sides. Chop the cooked eggplant fine. Cook garlic in a little oil about 2 minutes and add to eggplant. Season to taste with salt and pepper. Stuff into the tomato shells. Arrange in a baking pan and heat 5 to 10 minutes in a preheated moderate oven (350° F.). Makes 8 servings.

⚜ TOMATO AND EGGPLANT CASSEROLE
(*Tomatoes à la Mode d'Avignon*)

2 medium-sized eggplants
salt
flour
⅓ cup olive oil or salad oil
6 medium-sized tomatoes, or 2 cups canned tomatoes
1 small clove garlic, crushed
1 teaspoon sugar
2 tablespoons fine dry breadcrumbs
⅛ teaspoon ground black pepper
1 cup soft breadcrumbs
3 tablespoons butter, melted
½ cup grated Parmesan cheese (optional)

Wash and peel eggplant and cut into crosswise slices ½ inch thick. Sprinkle with salt and set aside for 30 minutes. Wipe salt off the slices, dredge them in flour, and fry in oil, browning both sides. If fresh tomatoes are used, wash, peel, seed, and dice them, and cook in 1 tablespoon oil, along with the garlic, sugar, pepper, and salt to taste. Add dry breadcrumbs. If canned tomatoes are used, add seasonings, heat, and add dry breadcrumbs. Arrange alternating layers of fried eggplant slices and cooked tomatoes in a 10- by 6- by 2-inch baking dish, having eggplant on the bottom and tomatoes on the top. Blend soft breadcrumbs with melted butter and sprinkle over the top. If desired, sprinkle with grated Parmesan cheese. Bake in a preheated moderate oven (375° F.) 25 minutes, or until crumbs are brown. Makes 6 servings.

⚜ TOMATOES MIREILLE

1 medium-sized eggplant
salt
flour
about ⅓ cup olive oil or salad oil
6 medium-sized tomatoes
1 small clove garlic, crushed
2 tablespoons chopped parsley
½ teaspoon dried basil, or 2 fresh basil leaves
½ teaspoon sugar
1/16 teaspoon ground black pepper

Wash eggplant, peel, and slice ¼ inch thick. Sprinkle the slices with salt and set aside for 30 minutes. Wipe salt off the slices and dredge them in flour. Sauté in oil, browning both sides. Keep warm. Wash, peel, quarter, and seed tomatoes and cook them 5 to 8 minutes in a separate saucepan in 1 tablespoon of the oil along with the garlic, parsley, basil, and sugar. Add black pepper and salt to taste. Arrange fried eggplant slices in a circle in a round serving plate. Pour the cooked tomatoes into the center. Sprinkle with additional chopped parsley, if desired. Makes 6 servings.

⚜ DUCHESS TOMATOES

6 medium-sized tomatoes
salt and ground black pepper
Duchess Potatoes made from 1 pound (4 medium) potatoes
¼ cup grated Parmesan cheese
1 tablespoon melted butter

Wash and dry tomatoes and cut in half. Scoop out the centers and sprinkle the cavities lightly with salt and pepper. Invert on a tray to drain well. Fill a pastry bag with Duchess Potatoes and pipe into the tomatoes, heaping them over the top. Sprinkle with Parmesan cheese. Brush with melted butter. Brown in a preheated very hot oven (450° F.). Makes 6 servings. (See illustration, page 763.)

⚜ TOMATOES STUFFED WITH MEAT

6 medium-large tomatoes
salt
ground black pepper
2 slices bread, crumbled
water
½ cup chopped onion
2 tablespoons butter
1½ cups finely chopped cooked beef, veal, or mutton
2 tablespoons chopped parsley
1 small clove garlic, crushed
1 cup soft breadcrumbs
½ cup grated Cheddar, Gruyère, or Parmesan cheese
olive oil or salad oil

Wash tomatoes, cut into halves, and scoop out centers. Reserve ½ cup of the centers for use in the stuffing and save the rest for salads, etc. Sprinkle inside of the tomato shells with salt and pepper and drain them well. Soak bread in water about 5 minutes, squeeze it dry, and fluff it with a fork. Cook onions in butter until they are limp. Add bread, ½ cup tomato centers, meat, parsley, garlic, and salt and pepper to taste. Stuff into the tomato shells. Sprinkle tops with breadcrumbs, grated cheese, and a few drops of oil. Arrange in a baking pan and bake in a preheated moderate oven (350° F.) 30 to 40 minutes or until done. Makes 6 servings.

⚜ MUSHROOM-STUFFED TOMATOES (*Tomates à la Hussarde*)

6 medium-large tomatoes
½ cup chopped onions
2 tablespoons olive oil, salad oil, or butter
½ cup soft breadcrumbs
1 cup chopped cooked ham
1½ cups finely chopped mushrooms
2 tablespoons chopped parsley
salt
ground black pepper
parsley leaves

Wash tomatoes, cut into halves, and scoop out centers. (Save centers for soups, sauces, salads, etc.). Sprinkle inside of tomato shells with salt and pepper and drain them well. Cook onions in oil or butter, add breadcrumbs, stir, and cook 1 minute. Add next 3 ingredients and salt and pepper to taste. Mix well and cook 2 to 3 minutes. Stuff into tomato shells. Sprinkle the top of each with a little oil. Arrange tomatoes in a large baking dish. Bake in a preheated moderate oven (350° F.) 30 minutes or only until tomatoes are hot through. Garnish each with a leaf of parsley. Makes 6 servings.

⚜ TOMATOES PORTUGUESE STYLE

8 medium-large (3 pounds) tomatoes
2 tablespoons olive oil or salad oil
2 shallots, chopped
1 small clove garlic, crushed
1 teaspoon meat extract
½ teaspoon sugar
salt to taste
ground black pepper to taste
½ cup soft breadcrumbs
chopped parsley

Wash tomatoes. Peel or not, as desired. Remove seeds and sauté tomatoes in hot oil 5 to 8 minutes. Add the next 7 ingredients and cook 1 minute. Turn into a serving dish and sprinkle with chopped parsley. Makes 6 servings.

⚜ TOMATOES STUFFED WITH SPINACH

6 medium-sized firm tomatoes
½ teaspoon salt
1 pound spinach
2 tablespoons butter
¾ teaspoon salt
⅛ teaspoon ground black pepper
1 tablespoon minced onion
¼ cup soft breadcrumbs
Hollandaise Sauce

Wash tomatoes, cut into crosswise halves, and scoop out centers. (Save centers for sauces, soup, etc.) Sprinkle tomato cavities with salt. Invert tomatoes on a tray to drain well. Wash spinach and cook with butter in a covered saucepan until spinach wilts. Remove spinach from heat and chop medium-fine. Add the next 4 ingredients, mix well, and stuff into the tomato cavities. Place tomatoes in an 11- by 7- by 1½-inch baking pan. Bake in a preheated moderate oven (350° F.) 25 to 30 minutes. Serve with Hollandaise Sauce. Makes 6 servings. (See illustration, page 762.)

TURNIPS (*Navets*)

⚜ TURNIPS IN CREAM SAUCE

2½ pounds turnips
salt
boiling water
¼ cup (½ stick) butter
2 tablespoons flour
¾ cup beef or veal stock
¼ cup light cream
⅛ teaspoon ground black pepper

Wash, peel, and slice turnips. Place in a saucepan with 1 teaspoon salt. Pour in boiling water to a depth of 1 inch. Bring to boiling point and cook, uncovered, 5 minutes. Cover and cook 15 to 20 minutes or until turnips are tender. Drain off water. Toss turnips lightly in 2 tablespoons of the butter. Melt remaining butter in a saucepan, remove from heat, and blend in flour. Stir and cook 1 minute. Remove from heat and add stock and cream. Cook until of medium thickness, stirring constantly. Add salt to taste and 1/8 teaspoon pepper. Pour over turnips and cook 1 to 2 minutes over low heat. Makes 6 servings.

⚜ GLAZED TURNIPS

2½ pounds turnips
½ teaspoon salt
boiling water
1 cup beef bouillon or stock
3 tablespoons butter
1 tablespoon sugar
⅛ teaspoon ground white pepper
chopped parsley

Wash, peel, and slice turnips. Place in a saucepan with the salt and enough boiling water to cover them. Bring to boiling point and boil, uncovered, 5 minutes. Drain off water. Add boiling bouillon or stock. Cover and cook 10 minutes. Remove cover and cook until all but 2 to 3 tablespoons of the liquid has evaporated. Add 2 tablespoons butter and the sugar. Shake the pan over medium low heat until turnips are glazed. Add remaining 1 tablespoon butter and the pepper. Toss lightly. Sprinkle with chopped parsley. Serve around a roast. Makes 6 servings.

⚜ STEWED TURNIPS

2½ pounds turnips
2 to 3 tablespoons shortening
2 tablespoons flour
½ cup chopped onions
1 cup bouillon or beef stock
⅛ teaspoon ground black pepper
salt
1 tablespoon butter

Wash and peel turnips and cut in crosswise slices 1/4 inch thick. Brown slices on both sides in hot shortening. Sprinkle with flour and onions. Cook over medium low heat until onions are limp, stirring frequently. Add bouillon or stock. Cook, uncovered, 5 minutes. Add pepper, salt to taste and butter. Makes 6 servings.

⚜ STUFFED TURNIPS

6 medium-sized round turnips
salt
boiling water
¾ pound pork sausage
1 teaspoon minced onion
2 tablespoons butter, melted
½ cup soft breadcrumbs

Select purple-top turnips. Trim off the tap root and cut a slice from the top, leaving a border of purple around the top. Scoop out centers, leaving a shell ¼ inch thick. Reserve the centers. Place shells in a saucepan with ½ teaspoon salt and boiling water to cover. Bring to boiling point, uncovered, and boil 5 minutes. Transfer to a baking pan and set aside. Place turnip centers in a saucepan. Pour in ½ inch boiling water. Cover and cook until soft. Drain and mash. Crumble sausage in a skillet, brown lightly, and add to turnips. Add salt to taste and mix well. Stuff into turnip shells. Combine butter and breadcrumbs and sprinkle over top of turnips. Bake in a preheated moderate oven (350° F.) 30 minutes, or until tops are brown. Makes 6 servings.

⚜ YELLOW TURNIP BALLS WITH SALT PORK

4 thin slices salt pork
1½ cups water
1 pound yellow turnips
½ teaspoon salt
½ teaspoon sugar
2 tablespoons butter
dash ground black pepper

Cook salt pork in water in a covered saucepan for 15 minutes. Peel turnips, cut into balls with a French melon-ball cutter and add to the salt pork. Add salt and sugar. Cook, uncovered, 15 to 20 minutes or until turnips are tender. Drain off water and toss the turnip balls lightly with butter and black pepper. Serve with the salt pork. Makes 4 servings.

ZUCCHINI (*Courgettes*)

This long slender green squash, which looks like a cucumber, is known in the United States by its Italian name, zucchini, and also as Italian squash; in England it is called baby marrow and sometimes courgette. Zucchini does not need to be peeled before cooking.

⚜ FRIED ZUCCHINI

Select small zucchini, wash, and cut in lengthwise slices ½ inch thick. Sprinkle with salt and let stand 15 minutes. Dry the slices with a towel, dredge them in flour, and fry until brown in deep fat preheated to 375°. Drain on paper towels and serve immediately. Allow 3 or 4 slices per serving.

⚜ ZUCCHINI FRITTERS

3 small zucchini
salt
1 cup sifted all-purpose flour
1 egg, beaten lightly
¾ cup milk
1 tablespoon butter, melted

Wash zucchini and cut into crosswise slices ½ inch thick. Sprinkle with salt and let stand 15 minutes. Drain and wipe dry with a clean towel. Meanwhile, sift flour with ½ teaspoon salt into a mixing bowl. Add egg, milk, and butter and mix well. Dip zucchini slices in the batter, one by one, and fry until browned in deep fat preheated to 375° F. Drain on paper towels. Serve hot. These fritters may be fried ahead of time and heated in the oven just before serving. Makes 6 servings.

⚜ MILANESE STUFFED ZUCCHINI (*Italian*)

5 small zucchini
⅓ cup chopped onion
¼ cup (1 stick) butter
1 cup Béchamel Sauce
¼ pound bitter-almond macaroons
salt
ground black pepper
grated Parmesan cheese

Wash zucchini, cut in lengthwise halves, and cook 6 minutes in 1 inch boiling water and ½ teaspoon salt. Drain off hot water and rinse with cold water. Invert zucchini on a tray to drain well. Scoop out centers, being careful not to damage the skins. Chop centers. Cook onion in 2 tablespoons of the butter until limp. Mix with zucchini. Stir and cook the mixture 3 minutes. Add Béchamel Sauce and simmer 1 to 2 minutes. Heat macaroons in a preheated slow oven (300° F.) 10 minutes. Cool. Roll a few at a time in a paper or plastic bag with a rolling pin to form fine crumbs. Mix the crumbs with the zucchini mixture. Season to taste with salt and pepper. Put mixture in a pastry bag fitted with a star tube and pipe into the zucchini shells. Sprinkle with grated Parmesan cheese. Brown in a preheated very hot oven (450° F.). Makes 10 servings. (See illustration, page 762.)

⚜ ZUCCHINI STUFFED WITH MUSHROOMS

6 small zucchini
salt
chopped mushrooms
½ small clove garlic, crushed
3 tablespoons olive oil or salad oil
2 tablespoons chopped parsley
ground black pepper
1 cup soft breadcrumbs
grated Parmesan cheese
Tomato Sauce

Cut zucchini in half lengthwise. Make small cuts about ¼ inch deep and ½ inch wide all around the edge and a few in the cut surface. Sprinkle with salt and allow to stand 15 minutes. Drain, wipe off the salt and fry in deep fat preheated to 350° F. Drain on paper towels. Scoop out centers, being careful not to break the skins. Measure the scooped-out centers and then measure an equal amount of mushrooms. Cook mushrooms and garlic in 1 tablespoon oil until mushrooms are tender. Add to the scooped-out zucchini, along with parsley. Season to taste with salt and pepper. Stuff the mixture into the zucchini shells. Mix breadcrumbs with 2 tablespoons oil and sprinkle over the tops. Sprinkle with grated Parmesan cheese. Brown in a preheated moderate oven (375° F.). Serve Tomato Sauce in a sauceboat. Makes 6 servings.

⚜ STUFFED ZUCCHINI, ORIENTAL STYLE

⅓ cup finely chopped onions
4 to 5 tablespoons olive oil or salad oil
½ cup finely diced sweet green peppers
½ cup raw rice
1 cup chicken or veal stock
½ teaspoon salt
¼ teaspoon ground black pepper
1 clove garlic, crushed
4 medium-sized tomatoes
1 cup diced cooked lamb
6 small zucchini squash
grated Parmesan cheese
1 cup soft breadcrumbs
2 tablespoons butter, melted

Cook onions until limp in 2 tablespoons oil. Add green peppers and rice and stir and cook 3 to 4 minutes. Add the next 4 ingredients. Peel, seed, and cube tomatoes and add. Cover, bring to boiling point, reduce heat, and simmer 12 to 15 minutes. Add lamb and set aside. Wash zucchini, cut in half lengthwise, and remove and discard seeds. Place zucchini, cut side down, in a baking pan. Pour 2 to 3 tablespoons oil in the pan. Bake in a preheated hot oven (400° F.) 10 minutes or until about half done. Remove from the oven. Carefully scoop out the centers and add them to the rice and lamb. Spoon the mixture into the zucchini shells, mounding it over the top. Sprinkle with grated cheese. Blend breadcrumbs and butter and sprinkle over squash. Arrange in baking pan and bake in a preheated moderate oven (350° F.) 20 minutes or until crumbs are brown. Makes 6 servings.

⚜ ZUCCHINI VAUCLUSE STYLE

3 small zucchini
salt
flour
olive oil or salad oil
4 medium-sized tomatoes
1 small clove garlic, crushed
2 tablespoons chopped parsley
¼ teaspoon sugar
⅛ teaspoon ground black pepper
½ teaspoon dried oregano
1 cup soft breadcrumbs

Wash, peel, and cut zucchini in lengthwise quarters. Sprinkle with salt and let stand 15 minutes. Wipe off salt, dredge in flour, and fry in shallow hot oil, turning to brown all sides. Place zucchini side by side in rows in a 10- by 6- by 2-inch baking dish. Peel, seed, and dice tomatoes, and cook 5 minutes in 2 tablespoons hot oil, adding salt to taste, garlic, parsley, sugar, pepper, and oregano. Spread over zucchini. Mix breadcrumbs with 2 tablespoons oil and sprinkle over the tomatoes. Cook in a preheated hot oven (350° F.) 30 minutes or until crumbs are brown. Makes 6 servings.

⚜ VEGETABLES MEDITERRANEAN STYLE (*Italian*)

6 small zucchini
6 very small eggplants
48 tomato slices
salt
ground black pepper
olive oil or salad oil
6 thin slices Cheddar cheese
4 medium-sized whole tomatoes
½ cup cooked peas
1 cup cooked rice
2 tablespoons chopped onion
1 teaspoon oregano

Wash zucchini and eggplant and cut 4 deep incisions, reaching to the center, in one side of each. Insert a tomato slice in each incision. Arrange eggplant and squash in separate oiled baking dishes. Sprinkle each with salt, pepper, and oil. Top each zucchini with a slice of cheese. Bake zucchini 10 to 15 minutes, eggplant 20 to 25 minutes, in a preheated moderate oven (350° F.). Cut 3 of the tomatoes in half and scoop out centers. Dice ½ cup of the centers and reserve for use in this recipe. (Save the rest for later use.) Drain tomato cups and sprinkle with salt and pepper. Combine remaining ingredients and stuff into tomato cups. Place in an oiled baking dish. Cut a thin slice from the top of the remaining whole tomato, sprinkle tomato with salt, pepper, and oil, and place it in the baking dish with the stuffed tomatoes.

Bake 10 to 15 minutes in a 350° F. oven. Arrange vegetables in a large oval serving dish with squash placed in the middle in spoke fashion, the small ends pointed toward the center of the dish. Place eggplant and stuffed tomatoes alternately around the squash, and the whole tomato in the center of the dish. Makes 12 servings. (See illustration, page 761.)

⚜ RATATOUILLE NIÇOISE

2 small zucchini
1 small eggplant
4 medium-sized tomatoes
2 red or green sweet peppers
½ cup sliced onions
¼ cup salad oil
1 clove garlic, crushed
½ teaspoon sugar
¼ teaspoon ground black pepper
salt to taste
chopped parsley

Cut zucchini and eggplant into slices ⅛ inch thick. Peel and dice tomatoes. Remove seeds and pith from peppers and cut them into strips. Sauté onions in oil until they begin to turn golden. Add tomatoes and cook 1 minute, then add remaining vegetables, garlic, and seasonings. Cover, bring to boiling point, and cook 1 to 2 minutes. Remove cover and cook until all the liquid has evaporated, stirring occasionally. Turn into a serving dish and sprinkle with parsley. Makes 6 servings. (See illustration, page 765.)

17

SALADS

There are two general classes of French salads: those made with fresh raw greens and combination (composed) salads.

Green leafy salads may be made of head lettuce, Romaine or cos lettuce, chicory, endive, escarole, or other salad greens, singly or in combination. The greens must be carefully washed and drained and must be absolutely dry before the dressing is put on. They are best when tossed with French Dressing (Sauce Vinaigrette) to which herbs, spices, chopped hard-cooked eggs, and other ingredients may be added. These salads are light enough to be served with a roast or an entrée.

Combination salads may be a mixture of cooked or uncooked vegetables or they may include a variety of other ingredients—meat, poultry, fish, shellfish, game, or fruit. The main ingredients must be neatly cut, never chopped beyond recognition, and well seasoned and artistically arranged. Combination salads may accompany a cold dish at dinner, be served as hors d'oeuvre, or, if hearty enough, be served as a main dish. Recipes for hors d'oeuvre salads are given in Chapter 5. Combination salads are very often made with mayonnaise or similar dressings; for recipes for these see Chapter 4.

⚜ ANDALUSIAN SALAD

2 cups cold cooked rice
3 tablespoons French Dressing
1 tablespoon finely chopped onion
2 tablespoons chopped parsley
a very small bit of crushed garlic
2 medium-sized sweet green peppers
3 medium-sized tomatoes, quartered
chopped chervil
paprika

Toss rice lightly with the next 4 ingredients and arrange in a mound in the center of a serving dish. Wash, seed, and skin green peppers and cut them into julienne strips. Arrange in clusters around the rice, alternating with quartered tomatoes. Sprinkle rice with chopped chervil and paprika. Makes 6 servings.

⚜ SALAD ARGENTEUIL

2 cups finely diced cooked potatoes
½ cup finely diced cooked carrots
½ cup cooked peas
⅓ cup mayonnaise
salt
ground black pepper
12 cooked asparagus tips, 2 inches long
2 tablespoons French Dressing
shredded lettuce
3 hard-cooked eggs, quartered

Mix vegetables lightly with mayonnaise. Season to taste with salt and pepper. Arrange in a mound in a serving dish. Marinate asparagus tips in French Dressing and arrange them over the top. Surround with shredded lettuce and quarters of hard-cooked eggs. Makes 6 servings.

⚜ ARTICHOKE SALAD À LA GRECQUE

12 small tender artichokes
lemon juice or lemon slices
boiling water
12 small tender carrots
12 small white onions, peeled
2 cups water
¾ cup wine vinegar
¼ cup lemon juice
⅓ cup olive oil or salad oil
1 teaspoon salt
1 small bay leaf
6 peppercorns
6 coriander seeds
1 tablespoon chopped fresh thyme or 1 teaspoon dried thyme
18 small mushroom caps
black olives
pimiento-stuffed green olives

Cut off and discard the top third of each artichoke. Pull off and discard all tough outer leaves. Trim off prickly ends of the leaves. Cut stems even with the base and rub lemon juice over the cut surfaces, or skewer a thin slice of lemon with a toothpick or a small skewer onto the base of each artichoke, to prevent discoloration. Place artichokes in a saucepan with enough boiling water to cover them generously. Bring to boiling point and cook 5 minutes. Add carrots and onions. Bring to boiling point and cook 5 minutes. Drain vegetables and set them aside. Place next 6 ingredients in a 1½-quart saucepan. Tie spices in a cheesecloth bag and add to the vinegar mixture. Bring mixture to boiling point and pour over blanched vegetables. Cover and cook slowly 25 minutes. Wash mushroom caps and add to hot mixture. Continue cooking 10 minutes, or until all the vegetables are done. Cool vegetables in marinade. Remove and discard the spice bag. Cut artichokes into quarters and remove and discard the chokes. Slice carrots thickly. Transfer vegetables to a salad bowl. Arrange onions and black and green olives around the edge and on top. Chill and serve as an hors d'oeuvre. Makes 6 servings. (See illustration, page 831.)

⚜ SALAD BEATRICE

1½ pounds green beans, cooked
¼ cup French Dressing
3 medium-large tomatoes
watercress
2 hard-cooked egg yolks, chopped

Mix cold cooked green beans with French Dressing. Turn into a serving dish. Slice tomatoes, place the slices on small bunches of watercress, and arrange them around the beans. Sprinkle with chopped egg yolk. Makes 6 servings.

⚜ SALAD BEAUCAIRE

2 cups coarse julienne strips celeriac
salt
2 cups thinly sliced celery
2 medium-sized potatoes, cooked
⅓ cup mayonnaise
ground white pepper
1 medium-sized beet, cooked
2 medium-sized tomatoes, sliced
1 truffle, chopped (optional)

Blanch the celeriac in enough boiling water to cover, with ½ teaspoon salt added. Drain and rinse under cold running water and drain again. Dry and add to celery. Dice potatoes finely and add to celery along with mayonnaise and salt and pepper to taste. Mix lightly but thoroughly. Turn into a salad bowl and shape into a mound. Cut beet into long narrow strips and arrange them in pairs around the mound. Arrange sliced tomatoes, overlapping, in a circle in the top center of the salad. Top tomatoes with a heart of lettuce. If desired, sprinkle chopped truffle around the sides of the mound. Makes 6 servings. (See illustration, page 831.)

⚜ SALAD BELLE HÉLÈNE

4 cups coarse julienne strips celeriac
boiling water
salt
2 hard-cooked egg yolks, chopped
1 raw egg yolk
¾ cup olive oil or salad oil
1 teaspoon wine vinegar
ground white pepper
1 teaspoon chopped chervil or parsley
6 slices cooked beets
1 large truffle, or 6 large black olives
6 English walnut halves

Blanch celeriac in enough boiling water to cover with ½ teaspoon salt added. Drain and rinse under cold running water. Drain again and dry between clean towels. Set aside.

Make a type of mayonnaise by gradually beating the oil and vinegar into the cooked egg yolks and the raw egg yolk. Add salt and pepper to taste and chervil or parsley. Add to celeriac and mix well but lightly. Turn into a salad bowl and shape the mixture into a mound. Cut beet slices into crescents and arrange around the salad. Slice truffles or olives and arrange them around the salad over the center of each beet crescent. Garnish the top of the salad with a circle of walnut halves. Makes 6 to 8 servings. (See illustration, page 832.)

⚜ CHICORY AND DANDELION SALAD WITH BACON

Chicory and Belgian endive are related though very different-looking plants, of which the nomeclature is badly confused. The salad plant with crisp curly green and white leaves is called endive in England and *chicorée* in France and is usually known as chicory in the United States, while the plant known as endive in the latter two countries is called chicory in England; and in Belgium, where it is widely grown (hence Belgian endive), it is called *chicorée de Bruxelles*. To confuse the situation further, the two names are sometimes reversed, both in the United States and in England. See Endive in Chapter 16, page 782.

6 slices bacon, or thin slices salt pork, diced
2 tablespoons wine vinegar
ground black pepper
1 quart washed and dried chicory
1 quart washed and dried dandelion greens

Cook bacon or salt pork until lightly browned. Drain off and discard half the drippings. Add vinegar and black pepper to bacon and remaining drippings. Heat ½ minute. Mix the greens in a salad bowl and toss lightly but well with the bacon and bacon drippings. Serve immediately. Makes 6 servings.

⚜ SALAD MARGUERITE

2 cups diced cooked potatoes
1 cup small cooked cauliflowerets
1 cup cooked green beans, cut into 1-inch pieces
1 cup cooked asparagus tips
9 tablespoons French Dressing
salt
ground black pepper
mayonnaise
3 hard-cooked eggs

Put each vegetable in a separate bowl and mix with French Dressing, using 3 tablespoons for the potatoes and 2 tablespoons each for the other vegetables. Marinate for 1 hour. Season vegetables with salt and pepper to taste. Put the potatoes into a salad bowl and arrange the other vegetables in separate layers on top of the potatoes. Cover the top layer completely with mayonnaise. Make a large daisy for the center of the top and smaller daisies in a circle around the mound of salad by cutting strips of hard-cooked egg whites to simulate the petals and mixing the mashed egg yolks with a little mayonnaise to make the centers. Makes 8 servings.

⚜ SALAD MERCÉDÈS

4 cups creamy white centers of chicory
2 hard-cooked eggs
⅓ cup olive oil or salad oil
2 tablespoons lemon juice
½ teaspoon salt
⅛ teaspoon ground black pepper
2 tablespoons chopped parsley
1 tablespoon chopped fresh chervil or 1 teaspoon dried chervil
1½ cups julienne celery strips
1½ cups julienne strips cooked beets
1 cup orange sections

Tear chicory into small pieces and place it in a salad bowl. Chop eggs finely and mix with the next 6 ingredients. Pour over endive and toss lightly. Wipe the sides of the salad bowl. Arrange celery and beets in alternating nests in a circle over the top of the chicory. Place orange sections in the center. Makes 6 servings.

⚜ SALAD MIMOSA I

1 cup cooked green beans, cut into 1-inch pieces
1 cup diced cooked potatoes
1 cup diced cooked carrots
1 cup diced cooked turnips
1 cup cooked green peas
mayonnaise
ground black pepper
1 hard-cooked egg
chopped parsley
truffles or black olives, chopped
shredded raw beets

Mix each vegetable separately with 2 tablespoons of mayonnaise and salt and pepper to taste. Mound each vegetable separately in one salad bowl. Sprinkle the beans with chopped egg white; the potatoes with chopped egg yolk; the carrots with chopped parsley; the turnips with chopped truffles or black olives; the peas with shredded beets. Makes 8 to 10 servings.

⚜ SALAD MIMOSA II

In France, a small crust of bread rubbed with garlic is usually mixed with salad greens to impart a delicate flavor of garlic to the salad. This is called a *chapon*. It is removed before serving.

½ head Romaine or cos lettuce
½ head iceberg lettuce
1 head Boston lettuce
chapon
salt
freshly ground black pepper
⅓ cup French Dressing
3 hard-cooked egg yolks

Wash, drain, and dry all the lettuce thoroughly. Tear into bite-size pieces, place them in a salad bowl with the chapon, and sprinkle with salt and pepper to taste. Add French Dressing and toss. Remove and discard the chapon before serving. Sprinkle with hard-cooked egg yolk rubbed through a coarse sieve. Makes 6 to 8 servings.

⚜ MIXED VEGETABLE SALAD (*Salade Macédoine*)

1 cup cooked green beans, cut into 1-inch pieces
1 cup cooked diced carrots
½ cup cooked diced turnips
½ cup cooked green peas
1½ cups cooked diced potatoes
2 cooked artichoke bottoms, diced
½ cup mayonnaise
salt
ground black pepper
2 medium-sized beets, cooked
2 hard-cooked eggs, sliced

Combine the first 7 ingredients. Season to taste with salt and pepper. Turn mixture into a salad bowl and round it over the top. Peel and slice beets. Arrange beet slices and hard-cooked egg slices over the top as desired. Makes 8 to 10 servings.

⚜ WALDORF SALAD

2 cups diced celery
2½ cups diced raw apples
1 teaspoon lemon juice
dash salt
½ cup mayonnaise
½ cup hazelnuts or English walnuts

Blanch celery in boiling water 1 minute. Drain and rinse in cold water. Add to apples along with lemon juice and salt and let the mixture stand 1 hour. Add mayonnaise and mix well. Turn into a salad bowl. Slice nuts and sprinkle them over the top. Makes 6 servings.

⚜ SALAD NIÇOISE

2 cups diced cold cooked potatoes
2 cups cold cooked green beans, cut into 1-inch pieces
⅓ cup French Dressing
salt
ground black pepper
clove of garlic
3 tomatoes, quartered
3 hard-cooked eggs, quartered
6-ounce can tuna fish chunks
pitted ripe olives
6 to 12 anchovy fillets

Toss the potatoes and beans with the French Dressing and season them to taste with salt and pepper. Rub the inside of a salad bowl with a cut clove of garlic. Turn potatoes and beans into the bowl. Decorate the salad with quartered tomatoes interspersed with quartered hard-cooked eggs, chunks of tuna fish, olives, and anchovy fillets. Makes 6 servings. (See illustration, page 832.)

⚜ PARISIAN SALAD

1 cup diced cooked carrots
1 cup cooked green beans, cut into 1-inch pieces
½ cup cooked green peas
1 cup diced cooked lobster meat
⅓ to ½ cup mayonnaise
1 teaspoon lemon juice
salt
freshly ground black pepper
½ medium-large tomato
2 hard-cooked eggs, sliced
4 lettuce hearts

Combine the first 6 ingredients. Add salt and pepper to taste. Turn the mixture into a salad bowl and round it over the top. Place the tomato half in the center and top it with a slice of hard-cooked egg. Wash and thoroughly dry lettuce hearts, split them into lengthwise halves, and arrange them in a circle over the top of the salad, alternating with slices of hard-cooked egg. Makes 8 servings.

⚜ SALAD RACHEL

½ pound mushrooms, poached
6 artichoke bottoms, cooked
½ pound asparagus
6 tablespoons olive oil or salad oil
6 teaspoons wine vinegar
salt and freshly ground black pepper
3 tablespoons brandy
3 tablespoons port

Slice mushrooms and artichoke bottoms thinly and set them aside in separate bowls. Cut asparagus, except the heads, into small pieces and cook, with the heads, until crisp-tender. Drain all the water from asparagus and turn into a small bowl. Marinate each vegetable separately in 2 tablespoons oil, 2 teaspoons wine vinegar, 1/8 teaspoon salt, dash pepper, 1 tablespoon brandy, and 1 tablespoon port. Arrange all the vegetables in separate mounds in a salad bowl. Garnish the top of each mound with an asparagus head. Makes 6 servings.

SALAD DRESSINGS

The true basic salad dressing (*assaisonnement*) of France is Sauce Vinaigrette, which consists of a mixture of 3 parts olive oil and 1 part good wine vinegar seasoned with salt and pepper and sometimes with mustard and herbs. To this base other ingredients, such as capers, anchovies, olives, etc., may be added to create a wide variety of interesting dressings. The use of garlic in French salad dressings is usually confined to southern France.

The recipes for mayonnaise and related dressings used in combination salads appear in Chapter 4.

⚜ BASIC FRENCH DRESSING (*Sauce Vinaigrette*)

2 tablespoons wine vinegar, or 1 tablespoon wine vinegar and 1 tablespoon lemon juice
6 tablespoons light olive oil, or good salad oil
1/4 teaspoon salt
1/8 teaspoon freshly ground black pepper
1/4 teaspoon powdered mustard soaked in 1/2 teaspoon water (optional)
1 tablespoon chopped parsley and/or other fresh herbs, such as chervil, chives, basil, tarragon, thyme, marjoram, or 1 teaspoon dried herb (optional)

Place vinegar, or vinegar and lemon juice, oil, salt, pepper and, if desired, mustard soaked in water for 5 minutes, in a small mixing bowl. Beat vigorously with a rotary beater or French wire whip. If fresh herbs are used, add them just before tossing the dressing with the salad. Add dried herbs along with salt and pepper. Makes approximately 1/2 cup.

VARIATIONS

ANCHOVY DRESSING

To ½ cup Basic French Dressing made without salt, add 1 anchovy fillet, finely chopped, 1 teaspoon minced shallots, and 1 tablespoon minced chives. Mix well. Use with salad greens, endive, celery, or cold cooked vegetables. Makes about ⅔ cup.

LORENZO DRESSING

To 1½ cups Basic French Dressing add ¼ cup chili sauce, ⅓ cup finely chopped watercress leaves, and 2 teaspoons finely chopped onion. Mix well and let stand 30 minutes before using. Makes a generous 2 cups.

NEW ORLEANS DRESSING

To ½ cup Basic French Dressing add 1 teaspoon Dijon prepared mustard and ½ teaspoon Worcestershire sauce. Mix well and let stand at least 30 minutes before using. Makes a generous ½ cup.

VINAIGRETTE NIÇOISE

To ½ cup Basic French Dressing made without salt, add 1 teaspoon each capers, chopped anchovies, and chopped green olives, and 1 small clove garlic, quartered. Mix well and let stand at least 30 minutes. Remove garlic before using. Makes a generous ½ cup.

ROQUEFORT VINAIGRETTE DRESSING

Beat 1 tablespoon finely crumbled Roquefort cheese with 2 tablespoons heavy cream. Mix thoroughly with ½ cup Basic French Dressing made without salt. Makes a generous ⅔ cup.

RUSSIAN VINAIGRETTE DRESSING

To ¼ cup Basic French Dressing add 1 tablespoon mayonnaise, 1 teaspoon chili sauce, and 1 teaspoon ground ginger. Beat vigorously with a rotary beater. Serve on head lettuce or with cooked vegetable salads. Makes a scant ⅓ cup.

⚜ ITALIAN DRESSING

⅓ cup white wine vinegar
2 teaspoons honey
⅓ cup coarsely chopped tomatoes
1/16 teaspoon mashed garlic
1 teaspoon salt
¼ teaspoon ground black pepper
1 cup olive oil or salad oil

Combine the first 6 ingredients. Gradually beat in oil. Makes approximately 1⅔ cups.

⚜ RAVIGOTE DRESSING

1 teaspoon chopped capers
1 teaspoon minced shallots, or green onion
1 hard-cooked egg, finely chopped
1 tablespoon minced parsley or other finely chopped fresh herb such as chervil, tarragon, or chives
1 cup Basic French Dressing
salt to taste
ground black pepper to taste

Stir the first 4 ingredients into the French Dressing. Add salt and pepper to taste. Serve over vegetables, poached fish, poached calves brain, hot or cold boiled beef or chicken, and pigs' feet. Makes approximately 1¼ cups.

⚜ RÉMOULADE FRENCH DRESSING (*Vinaigrette à la Rémoulade*)

1 cup light olive or salad oil
⅓ cup wine vinegar
½ teaspoon salt
⅛ teaspoon freshly ground black pepper
2 anchovy fillets, finely chopped
2 teaspoons capers, chopped
1 small clove garlic, crushed

Combine all ingredients in a mixing bowl and beat vigorously with a rotary beater or French wire whip. Toss with salad greens, mix with cold cooked vegetables for salads, or serve over tomatoes and seafood salads. Makes approximately 1⅓ cups.

⚜ SOUR-CREAM DRESSING (*Crème Acidulée*)

1 egg yolk
¼ cup sour cream
½ cup Basic French Dressing
1 teaspoon lemon juice or lemon juice to taste
1 tablespoon chopped fresh dill, or 1 teaspoon dried dill weed
1 tablespoon chopped parsley

Beat egg yolk and cream together in a bowl. Then gradually beat in French dressing as in making mayonnaise. Add lemon juice, dill, and parsley. Serve over cold or hot fish, cold egg or vegetable dishes. Makes approximately ¾ cup.

⚜ SPANISH CREAM DRESSING (*Crème Espagnole*)

2 teaspoons sugar
2 teaspoons Dijon prepared mustard
2 tablespoons lemon juice
salt to taste
1 cup heavy cream, whipped

Combine the first 4 ingredients and fold into cream. Makes approximately 1¾ cups.

⚜ THERMIDOR DRESSING

2 teaspoons chopped fresh or ¼ teaspoon dried tarragon
2 teaspoons Dijon prepared mustard
2 tablespoons lemon juice
1 cup heavy cream, whipped

Combine the first 3 ingredients and gradually fold into cream. Makes approximately 1¾ cups.

·18·

CHEESE

Cheese is made from the curd of whole, partly skimmed, and skimmed milk, with or without the addition of cream.

History does not tell us when, where, or by whom the first batch of cheese was made, but it does tell of its use by the Jews, Greeks, and Romans and of its very early use by the nomadic tribes of Asia and Africa. Because cheese is a food in which many nutrients can be stored in a very small space for a considerable time without spoilage, it would naturally be used as a food by those without fixed habitation.

In the early days of cheese-making, much of the cheese was made by stock-raising peoples to use the surplus milk. The milk-producing animals were buffaloes, camels, cows, goats, reindeer, and sheep. Today most cheese is made from cows', goats', or sheep's milk. Cheese is made in some form in every country of the world, each country, and often different districts within a country, having its own special cheeses. The list of cheeses includes more than 400 varieties. Cheeses of the same general type are known under a variety of names, both in the same country and in different countries. For example, French Roquefort, Danish Blue, Italian Gorgonzola, and English Stilton are all blue-mold cheeses; except for Roquefort, which is a product of sheep's milk, they are made from cows' milk.

CHEESE

Cheese is the casein of milk with varying amounts of butterfat and whey. Factors affecting the differences in cheeses are: the source of milk (cow, goat, or sheep); the butterfat content of the milk (whole, partly skimmed, skimmed); the agent used to coagulate the milk (acid or rennet); the amount of whey removed from the curd; and the treatment and final curing process. Cheese manufacturers must take every precaution to prevent the use of unsuitable milk. They give farmers advice on the breed of cows, the food fed to the cows, and the sanitary handling of milk. All milk is tested for purity and for butterfat and casein content as it comes from the farms. Usually milk that is high in butterfat is also high in casein.

One of the first steps in cheese-making is to coagulate the milk in order to separate the curd from the whey (liquid). This may be brought about by allowing the milk to sour naturally or by adding a lactic-acid starter, or may be induced artificially by the addition of rennet, an enzyme found in the fourth stomach of the calf. When rennet is used the milk must be slightly acid. It is from the rennet-coagulated curd that most commercial cheeses are made.

The curd is separated from most of the whey by means of a press, the degree of separation being determined by the type of cheese desired (soft or hard). The softer cheeses have a greater liquid content than the harder varieties. The curd is seasoned and pressed into shapes characteristic of the particular cheese being produced.

For Roquefort, Gorgonzola, Blue, and Stilton cheeses, the curd is inoculated with a pure culture of blue mold (*Penicillium roquefortii*) which penetrates during the curing process.

The Swiss cheeses, Emmentaler and Gruyère, owe their flavor and their holes to the addition of an organism which produces certain gases during the early stages of the ripening process while the cheese is soft and elastic. This bacteria must be very carefully controlled to prevent bad flavor and the formation of holes of undesirable size.

Cheese is allowed to ripen or cure in natural caves or in storerooms with controls that regulate the temperature and humidity. The time of aging depends upon the type of cheese desired. The longer the aging time the sharper the cheese. Cheddar and Parmesan are two cheeses that require a long ripening period, while Limburger, Camembert, and Brie are ripened for a short time in a moist atmosphere. Changes which occur during the ripening process affect the flavor, texture, and cooking qualities. They also affect the ease with which cheese may be blended with other ingredients in cooking.

Unripened cheeses, such as cottage cheese, ricotta, and Norwegian

Salad Beaucaire, page 820 ▲

▼ Artichoke Salad à la Grecque, page 819

▲ Salad Belle Hélène, page 821

Salad Niçoise, page 824 ▼

French cheeses (see page 837) ▲

▼ Swiss cheeses (see pages 837–38)

▲ Italian cheeses (see page 838)

Cheeses of northern Europe (see page 839) ▼

Primost, require no aging. The whey is drained from the curd, the curd is salted, and the product is sold for immediate use. This freshly made cheese is known in Germany as Schmierkase and in Switzerland as Schabriziger.

Cheeses in general may be divided into the following classes:

Soft

Unripened: cottage, cream, United States Neufchâtel, Primost, ricotta

Ripened: Brie, Camembert, Liederkranz, Limburger, French Neufchâtel

Semihard

Ripened by blue mold: Bel Paese, Danish and other Blue cheeses, Gorgonzola, Roquefort, Stilton, Wensleydale

Ripened by bacteria: Brick, Münster

Ripened by bacteria and surface microorganisms: Port du Salut, Oka, Trappist

Hard

Ripened with gas bubbles: Emmentaler, Gruyère

Ripened by bacteria without gas bubbles: Cheddar, Edam, Gouda, Provolone

Very hard

Ripened by bacteria: American Cheddar, Parmesan, Romano, Sapsago, Spolen

Processed or pasteurized cheese, which is produced in large quantities in the United States, is made by blending several lots of cheeses of a specific variety in proportions that will assure a desirable finished product. The cheese is ground and an emulsifying agent added; then the cheese is melted. The emulsifying agent is required to produce a uniform blend without separating the fat. The cheese is then put into molds, which may be jars, glasses, or foil-lined boxes, and the packages are heat-sealed. Since the heat destroys bacteria and enzymes, further ripening is prevented. Processed cheeses have good spreading and cooking qualities. Their flavor depends upon the flavor of the cheeses from which they are made.

The nutritive value of cheese varies with the method used for separating the curd from the whey, with the amount of water removed, and with the kind of milk from which the cheese is made.

Cheese made by using lactic acid as the coagulation agent (natural souring process or the addition of a lactic-acid starter) loses more calcium from the whey than does cheese made by the addition of rennet, because the lactic acid changes the calcium to a soluble form. Cheese made from milk that is coagulated by the use of rennet is therefore an excellent source of calcium as well as a good source of phosphorus and sulfur. In cheeses using either agent to coagulate the milk the iron content is quite well retained.

Since milk contains fat-soluble vitamin A, cheeses made from whole milk are an important source of this vitamin. Milk also contains water-soluble vitamins B, G, and some C, but much of these tend to be lost with the whey. Consequently, the softer cheeses retain more of the water-soluble vitamins than do the hard dry ones.

Cheese is high in protein and fat and is a highly concentrated food. A pound of cheese made from whole milk contains as much butterfat as 4 quarts of milk and as much protein as 2⅘ quarts. Cheese contains no roughage and is well utilized by the body. The discomfort sometimes experienced after eating cheese may be in part a result of irritation of the stomach by volatile acids and by certain products of enzymic action on the protein during the ripening process. Then, too, some individuals do not tolerate high fat content in any food. Many times the distress occurs when cheese is eaten after an already adequate meal. In France cheese is served before the dessert, and not after it as it is in England and the United States.

Soft, perishable cheeses, such as cottage cheese and cream cheese, should be purchased only in quantities that are likely to be consumed in a short period, as one buys milk. They should be well wrapped or placed in closed containers and refrigerated away from strong odors.

Semihard cheeses, such as Port du Salut, Münster, Brick, and Roquefort, may be purchased in larger quantities, enough to last for two or more weeks if kept well wrapped and refrigerated. About two hours before serving, remove cheese from the refrigerator and let it stand at room temperature to release the flavor. For appearance, cut away any mold that has formed. (It harms neither you nor the cheese.) Slice only the amount of cheese that can be used at the time.

Hard cheeses, such as Swiss, Parmesan, and Romano, may be purchased in larger quantities if the quantity is all in one piece. Cut off only as much as is needed at a time. This prevents the cheese from drying out. Keep it well wrapped in the refrigerator or another cool place. If the cheese has a tendency to dry out, wrap it in a cloth wrung out in vinegar and keep it damp.

Processed cheese may be kept in its original container in the refrigerator, well wrapped to keep out the air.

There is one fundamental principle to follow when cooking with cheese—one which applies to all protein cookery. Use low to moderate heat and cook as short a time as possible. If cheese dishes are cooked at a high temperature for a long time the fat separates and the protein becomes stringy and hard, causing the formation of a tough rubbery curd which tends to harden in cooling.

CHEESES OF VARIOUS COUNTRIES

Even to list all the fine cheeses of the world would require more space than is available here. The following paragraphs include only a sampling of some of the most famous, classified according to the country of origin.

France

No country in the world has a greater variety of cheeses than France, where practically every rural section produces its own local cheese. Probably the most famous is Roquefort, known for 200 years and called the king of cheeses. Only cheese actually made in the village of Roquefort is legally entitled to the name, but there are other fine French Bleu cheeses, some of them made from cows' milk. Other classic French cheeses are Brie, a ripened soft cheese of which there are several varieties, and Camembert, another ripened soft cheese made from whole milk. Camembert was either invented or perfected in the late eighteenth century by Madame Harel, a farmer's wife, a statue of whom was erected in the market square of the village of Camembert. Today this cheese is made all over France. Port du Salut, a creamy yellowish whole-milk cheese first made by Trappist monks in the monastery of Port du Salut, is now made by Trappist monks all over the world. Among the many other fine French cheeses are Angelot, Cachat, Cantal, Chabichou, Dauphin, Feuille de Dreux, Gervais, Gournay, Pont-l'Evêque, Saint-Remi, and Troô. (See illustration, page 833.)

Switzerland

The best-known of the Swiss cheeses are Emmentaler and Gruyère. The former is a hard cheese made of whole milk, named for the Emme valley in the canton of Berne but made in all parts of Switzerland where there is highland pasture. Emmentaler is creamier and less pungent than Gruyère. It has a straw-colored rind and fairly large "eyes" or holes. True Gruyère is made only in western (French) Switzerland. Originally made from semi-skimmed or wholly skimmed milk, it is now also made from whole milk, especially when intended for export. It is made in factories near the pastures and is the cheese used in fondue. Crème de Gruyère is a processed cheese with a mild flavor. Schabeizer, which has been made in the canton of Glarus for 500 years, is a small piquant cheese, with a greenish color caused by the addition of dried clover and wild herbs. Vacherin, made in Jura and Franche-Comté, is a soft cheese with a liquid center rather like thick cream. Tomme is a hard cheese, with several varieties. (See illustration, page 833.)

Italy

There are many excellent Italian cheeses. Southern Italy, because of its hot climate, specializes in hard cheeses, such as Romano and those of the Provolone family, which have excellent keeping qualities, particularly when smoked. Caciocavallo, made near Naples, is molded in the shape of gourds and straddled on sticks to dry; it may also be smoked. This cheese has been known from Roman times. Parmesan is the name given for export to various hard cheeses made of skim milk in Lombardy and Romagna. These cheeses are especially suitable for grating and keep a very long time. Gorgonzola, named for a village near Milan, is a blue-mold cheese, similar to Roquefort but made of whole cows' milk. Bel Paese is a delicate soft cheese of fine flavor. Mozzarella, a soft, very slightly ripened cheese, is especially suited to pizzas. (See illustration, page 834.)

Great Britain

The oldest of English cheeses is Cheshire, sometimes mistakenly called "Chester" on the Continent, and often referred to as the "twelfth-century cheese." It is crumbly, with a slightly salty taste caused by salt deposits under the pastures. Cheddar was originally made in the Cheddar district of Somerset. When properly aged it is mellow and flaky, with a deep orange color. Wensleydale and Stilton are blue-mold cheeses. Stilton is made from whole milk with the addition of cream and is marked with gray and green streaks. It is improved by being soaked in port or sherry. Dunlop, made in Scotland, is pure white unless artificially colored and has a texture similar to that of Cheddar. Caerphilly is a famous Welsh cheese, soft and creamy with a slightly sour taste.

Northern European Countries

Holland's best-known cheeses are Edam and Gouda. Edam, made from partly skimmed milk, is put up in slightly flattened balls weighing about 5 pounds, which are bright red on the outside and orange-yellow within. Gouda, similar in taste and texture, is made from whole milk and is put up in flatter and larger pats weighing about 20 pounds. Both are available in the United States in smaller pats, weighing 1 pound or less.

Germany produces Geheimratskäse, which is similar to Gouda, and Tilsiter, a semihard cheese. Best known are its soft cheeses, Limburger, Steinbuscher, and Romadur.

Danish Blue, resembling Roquefort but made of cows' milk, and the Norwegian Oka, Primost, and Gjeltöst, a hard brown cheese made of goats' milk, are among the better known of the many fine cheeses made in the Scandinavian countries. (See illustration, page 834.)

The United States

Most of the cheese produced and consumed in the United States is of the Cheddar type. Much of it is made in Wisconsin, New York State, and Vermont, but cheese is produced in nearly every state of the Union. The first cheese factory was established in 1851 in Oneida County, New York, by a farmer named Jesse Williams, who found that his cheeses brought premium prices and began buying milk for his cheese-making from neighboring farmers. In 15 years New York State had about 500 cheese factories. Today much of New York State's milk is sold in large cities as fluid milk and Wisconsin has become the leading state in cheese production.

In addition to Cheddar, however, American cheese manufacturers now produce many European types of cheese, although there are some differences in the manufacturing process. All American cheeses are made from cows' milk, while some European cheeses are made from sheep's milk or goats' milk. American-made cheeses are not usually aged as long as European varieties are. The care and storage space involved in aging represents an expense that many American cheese manufacturers are not willing to underwrite, since the average American consumer is no such connoisseur of cheese as his European counterpart. Nevertheless, more than a billion pounds of various varieties of cheese are made in the United States each year.

CHEESE IN THE MENU

Cheese or cheese dishes may be served at almost any stage of a meal. (The Dutch and the Scandinavians serve it for breakfast.) A cheese tray often accompanies cocktails, and many delicious hors d'oeuvre and entrées are made with cheese (see recipes in Chapter 5). Grated cheese is an ingredient of many dishes and a popular garnish, and cheese is also important in sauces. A cheese course may precede or follow the dessert course, according to national custom. The practice—common in Europe—of serving cheese and fresh fruit instead of an elaborate dessert is gaining favor in the United States. Some suggested American combinations of cheese, fruit, and appropriate wines are:

Red Delicious or McIntosh apples, sharp Cheddar or Brie, port
Fresh pears, Camembert, tawny port
Nectarines, Blue cheese, sweet sherry
Golden Delicious apples, Port du Salut, Pink Catawba
Tangerines, Roquefort, Tokay
Oranges, Bel Paese, Sauternes
Concord or Tokay grapes, Gouda, rosé wine
White grapes, Roquefort, pink champagne
Fresh peaches, Camembert, sparkling Burgundy
Ripe persimmons, Emmentaler or Gruyère, champagne or sparkling Burgundy

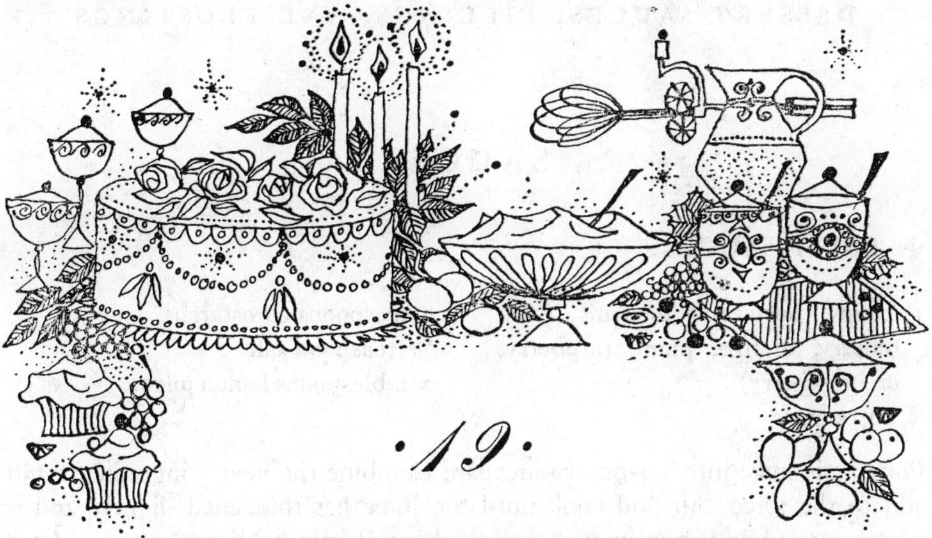

·19·

DESSERT SAUCES, FILLINGS, AND FROSTINGS

The purpose of a dessert sauce is to provide complementary flavors and qualities to enhance the basic dish. A simple dessert requires a sauce that contrasts sharply in flavor and richness, while a rich dessert is improved by the addition of a light delicate sauce of a mild flavor. Certain substantial desserts—steamed puddings, mince pie, apple dumplings—call for a bland but rich butter sauce and Hard Sauce is commonly used for these. Some of the simple sauces—Custard, Lemon, or Orange Sauce, for example—can be made into fluffy sauces by adding whipped cream or beaten egg whites. Stewed fruits spiked with brandy, rum, sherry, or a liqueur make a party dessert of plain cake or simple puddings, while chilled Custard Sauce, which can be kept in reserve in the refrigerator, will dress up not only cake or pudding but stewed or poached fruits and some fresh fruits.

For convenience, a number of sauces, pastry creams, frostings, and other dessert preparations are grouped in this chapter; others are given in connection with dessert recipes in Chapters 20–22. Basic pastry doughs not included in Chapters 20–22 are to be found in Chapter 3, pages 123–30.

SAUCES

⚜ FRUIT SAUCE

1½ cups unsweetened fruit juice (cherry, orange, plum, raspberry, or strawberry)
⅓ cup sugar
2 teaspoons cornstarch
1/16 teaspoon salt
2 tablespoons lemon juice

Pour fruit juice into a 1-quart saucepan. Combine the next 3 ingredients and add to the juice. Stir and cook until the juice has thickened slightly and is transparent. Add lemon juice and cook about ½ minute. Serve over puddings or plain cake. Makes approximately 1⅔ cups sauce.

⚜ APRICOT SAUCE I

½ pound dried apricots
water
½ cup sugar
1/16 teaspoon salt
Kirsch, cognac, or apricot brandy to taste

Wash and cook apricots in water as directed on the package. Put the cooked apricots through a food mill, or purée them, about ¾ cup at a time, in an electric blender. Add sugar and salt. Stir and cook 4 to 5 minutes over moderate heat. Add Kirsch, cognac, or apricot brandy to taste. Serve over puddings or plain cake.

To store: Turn the sauce into a jar and add 1 to 2 tablespoons Kirsch, cognac, or apricot brandy. Cover tightly and place in the refrigerator.

Makes approximately 1½ cups sauce.

⚜ APRICOT SAUCE II

1½ cups apricot jam
½ cup water
2 tablespoons sugar
1/16 teaspoon salt
1 tablespoon apricot brandy, Kirsch, or cognac

Combine the first 4 ingredients in a 1-quart saucepan. Mix well. Heat to boiling point, stirring constantly. Stir and cook over low heat 5 to 8 minutes. Strain. Stir in apricot brandy, Kirsch, or cognac. Serve hot or cold over puddings, vanilla ice cream, or plain cake.

To store: Turn the sauce into a jar and add 1 to 2 tablespoons apricot brandy, Kirsch, or cognac. Cover the jar tightly and place in the refrigerator.

Makes approximately 1 ¾ cups sauce.

⚜ BING CHERRY SAUCE

1 cup liquid from a No. 2½ can of Bing cherries
1 tablespoon cornstarch
1/16 teaspoon salt
2 cups drained Bing cherries
½ teaspoon vanilla extract
1 teaspoon lemon juice

Combine the first 3 ingredients in a 1-quart saucepan. Stir and cook until the sauce has thickened and is transparent. Remove from heat. Add remaining ingredients and mix well. Cool and serve over plain cake, puddings, and ice cream. Makes approximately 2 ½ cups sauce.

⚜ SHERRY CRANBERRY SAUCE (*American*)

1 pound (4 cups) raw cranberries
1 cup dry sherry
1¾ cups sugar
dash salt

Wash cranberries and place in a saucepan with the sherry. Cover and cook 8 to 10 minutes, or until only the skins pop. Add the sugar and salt, mix well, and cook 1 minute. Serve as a dessert sauce, or with meat or poultry. Makes approximately 3 ½ cups sauce.

⚜ LEMON SAUCE

½ cup sugar
1 tablespoon cornstarch
1/16 teaspoon salt
1 cup water
2 tablespoons lemon juice
1 teaspoon grated lemon rind
2 tablespoons (¼ stick) butter
¼ teaspoon vanilla extract

Combine the first 3 ingredients in a 1-quart saucepan. Add the water. Stir and cook until the mixture has thickened and is clear. Remove from heat and stir in the remaining ingredients. Serve over plain cake, puddings, etc. Makes approximately 1 ¼ cups sauce.

⚜ LEMON MOUSSELINE SAUCE

Make Lemon Sauce and cool it. Fold in 1 cup whipped heavy cream. Serve on cake and cold puddings, etc.

⚜ LINGONBERRY SAUCE

Lingonberries are grown in the arctic regions, and in Minnesota and New England.

2 cups raw lingonberries
¾ cup sugar
¼ cup water
dash salt

Wash lingonberries and place them in a 1-quart saucepan with remaining ingredients. Bring to boiling point and cook 10 minutes. Serve as a sauce for Dessert Crêpes or over puddings. Makes approximately 2 cups sauce.

VARIATION

APPLE-LINGONBERRY SAUCE

Make Lingonberry Sauce, increasing the sugar to 1 cup. While sauce is hot, add 1 cup grated raw apples. Serve as a dessert sauce, or with meat or poultry. Makes approximately 2 ¾ cups sauce.

⚜ ORANGE SAUCE

½ cup sugar
1 tablespoon cornstarch
1/16 teaspoon salt
1 cup orange juice
1 tablespoon grated orange rind
1 teaspoon grated lemon rind
2 tablespoons (¼ stick) butter
¼ teaspoon vanilla extract

Combine the first 3 ingredients in a 1-quart saucepan. Add the orange juice. Stir and cook until the mixture has thickened and is clear. Remove from heat and stir in the remaining ingredients. Serve over plain cake, puddings, sweet waffles, etc. Makes approximately 1 ¼ cups sauce.

⚜ PINEAPPLE SAUCE

2 tablespoons sugar
2 tablespoons cornstarch
⅛ teaspoon salt
20-ounce can crushed pineapple
1 tablespoon butter
½ teaspoon grated lemon rind
1½ teaspoons vanilla extract

Combine the first 3 ingredients in a 1-quart saucepan. Add pineapple and mix well. Stir and cook over moderate heat until the sauce has thickened.

Remove from heat and add remaining ingredients. Serve over plain cake. Makes approximately 2 cups sauce.

⚜ PINEAPPLE-RUM SAUCE

⅓ cup sugar
1 tablespoon cornstarch
⅛ teaspoon salt
1 cup pineapple juice
¼ teaspoon grated lemon rind
2 tablespoons light or dark rum, or rum to taste
2 tablespoons butter

Combine the first 3 ingredients in a 1-quart saucepan. Gradually stir in pineapple juice. Stir and cook until the sauce is of medium thickness. Remove from heat and add remaining ingredients. Makes 1 generous cup.

⚜ FRESH RASPBERRY SAUCE

2 cups fresh raspberries
2 to 3 tablespoons sugar
1 teaspoon lemon juice
¼ teaspoon vanilla extract

Crush the raspberries and put them through a sieve. Add sugar, lemon juice, and vanilla extract. Mix well. Serve over ice cream, plain cake, and puddings. Makes approximately 1½ cups sauce.

⚜ FRESH STRAWBERRY SAUCE

1 cup fresh strawberries, crushed
2 tablespoons sugar
1 cup fresh strawberries, sliced
¼ teaspoon vanilla extract
Kirsch to taste (optional)

Combine crushed strawberries and sugar. Fold in sliced strawberries and vanilla extract, and Kirsch, if used. Serve over ice cream, cake, puddings, Bavarian Creams, and other cream desserts. Makes 2 cups sauce.

⚜ BRANDY SAUCE

1 large egg, separated
about ¾ cup sifted confectioners' sugar
dash salt
½ cup heavy cream, whipped
3 tablespoons apricot brandy or peach brandy

Beat the egg white until it stands in soft stiff peaks. Gradually beat in sugar. Add salt and egg yolk and beat well. Fold in whipped cream and brandy. Chill until the sauce is cold. Serve over hot or cold puddings or plain cake. Makes approximately 1½ cups sauce.

⚜ CREAM AND BRANDY SAUCE

1 cup heavy cream
½ cup apricot brandy or peach brandy

Whip the cream until it stands in soft stiff peaks. Fold in the brandy. Makes approximately 3 cups sauce.

⚜ BUTTERSCOTCH SAUCE

1¼ cups light brown sugar
⅔ cup light corn syrup
¼ cup (½ stick) butter
⅓ cup heavy cream
⅓ cup milk
1 teaspoon vanilla extract

Combine the first 3 ingredients in a 1-quart saucepan. Mix well. Stir and cook over moderate heat until boiling point has been reached. Continue cooking until a candy thermometer shows 230° F., or until ½ teaspoon of the mixture dropped in cold water forms a very soft ball. Remove from heat and add remaining ingredients. Mix well. Serve over ice cream or plain cake.

To store: Turn the sauce into a jar. Cover tightly and refrigerate. If the sauce stiffens on standing, add 1 to 2 tablespoons of hot water to it and mix well.

Makes approximately 2 cups sauce.

⚜ CHOCOLATE SAUCE

1 square (1 ounce) unsweetened chocolate
1 cup sugar
¼ cup light corn syrup
1/16 teaspoon salt
⅓ cup water
2 tablespoons butter
1 teaspoon vanilla extract

Melt chocolate over hot water. Remove from heat, add the next 4 ingredients, and mix well. Stir and cook over low heat 4 to 5 minutes, or until the sauce has thickened. Remove from heat and add butter and vanilla extract. Serve over ice cream, puddings, or plain cake.

To store: Turn the sauce into a jar. Cover tightly and refrigerate. If this sauce stiffens on standing, stir in 1 to 2 tablespoons hot water.

Makes approximately 1 ¼ cups sauce.

⚜ COFFEE SAUCE

1½ cups sugar
1 teaspoon instant coffee
⅛ teaspoon salt
¾ cup boiling water
⅓ cup light corn syrup
1 tablespoon butter
1 teaspoon vanilla extract

Combine the first 5 ingredients in a saucepan. Stir and cook 10 minutes, or until the mixture has thickened slightly. Add butter. Cool. Add vanilla extract. Makes 1⅔ cups.

⚜ CUSTARD SAUCE (*Crème à l'Anglaise*)

2 cups milk
2 large whole eggs
⅓ cup sugar
¼ teaspoon salt
1 teaspoon vanilla extract, or ½ teaspoon almond extract

Heat 1 ¾ cups of the milk until tiny bubbles appear around the edges (do not boil). With a fork beat the eggs lightly, and add to them the remaining ¼ cup cold milk, the sugar, and the salt. Mix well. Stir in hot milk. Stir and cook over low heat or hot water only until the custard coats a metal spoon. Remove from heat and stir in vanilla or almond extract. Strain through a sieve. Serve over plain cake, puddings, or cooked fruits. Makes approximately 2 cups sauce.

VARIATIONS

COCONUT CUSTARD SAUCE

Add ¼ cup flaked coconut to Custard Sauce.

TIPSY CUSTARD SAUCE

To Custard Sauce add apricot or peach brandy, sherry, Kirsch, or other liqueur to taste. Bourbon is a popular flavoring for Custard Sauce in the southern part of the United States.

RICH CUSTARD SAUCE

In Custard Sauce replace 1 cup of the milk with 1 cup heavy cream and replace the 2 whole eggs with 4 large egg yolks. Mix 1 teaspoon cornstarch with the sugar.

CHOCOLATE CUSTARD SAUCE

Add 1 square (1 ounce) unsweetened chocolate to the hot Custard Sauce. Stir until chocolate is melted.

⚜ FOAMY EGG SAUCE

¼ cup (½ stick) softened butter
1 cup sifted confectioners' sugar
1 large egg, well beaten
1 tablespoon hot water
dash salt
1¼ teaspoons vanilla extract

Stir butter until fluffy in the top of a 1-quart double boiler. Gradually blend in sugar. Beat in egg, hot water, and salt. Stir and cook over hot water (not boiling) until mixture is glossy and smooth. Remove from heat and add vanilla extract. Serve over plain cake or puddings. Makes approximately 1 cup sauce.

VARIATIONS

CHOCOLATE FOAMY SAUCE

Melt 1 square (1 ounce) unsweetened chocolate and blend with the butter, sugar, and egg in Foamy Egg Sauce. Omit the 1 tablespoon hot water.

LEMON FOAMY SAUCE

Add 1 teaspoon grated lemon rind and 2 teaspoons lemon juice to Foamy Egg Sauce.

ORANGE FOAMY SAUCE

Replace the 1 tablespoon hot water in Foamy Egg Sauce recipe with 1 tablespoon orange juice. Add 1 tablespoon grated orange rind.

TIPSY FOAMY SAUCE

Replace the 1 tablespoon hot water in Foamy Egg Sauce with 1 tablespoon brandy, rum, sherry, or liqueur.

⚜ GRAND MARNIER SAUCE

4 large egg yolks
½ cup sugar
¾ cup heavy cream
1 cup scalded milk
¼ teaspoon salt
½ teaspoon vanilla extract
3 tablespoons Grand Marnier

Place the egg yolks in the top part of a 1-quart double boiler and beat them until they are light. Gradually beat in the sugar. Stir in the cream, milk, and salt. Stir and cook over hot (not boiling) water until the mixture coats a metal spoon. Remove the sauce from the heat and beat in vanilla extract and Grand Marnier. Serve as a dessert sauce. Makes approximately 2 cups.

⚜ HARD SAUCE

½ cup softened sweet butter
1 to 1¼ cups sifted confectioners' sugar
1 tablespoon brandy, rum, or liqueur

Stir butter until it is fluffy. Gradually beat in sugar and brandy, rum, or liqueur. Serve over warm puddings. Makes approximately 1 cup sauce.

VARIATIONS

COFFEE HARD SAUCE

Make Hard Sauce, replacing brandy, rum, or liqueur with 1 tablespoon strong coffee infusion. Add ½ teaspoon vanilla extract.

ORANGE HARD SAUCE

Make Hard Sauce, replacing brandy, rum, or liqueur with 1 tablespoon orange juice. Add 1 teaspoon grated orange rind and ¼ teaspoon grated lemon rind.

⚜ JELLY SAUCE

Put an 8-ounce glass of jelly into a small saucepan. With a fork, break up the jelly and mix with 3 tablespoons hot water. Stir the mixture over low heat until the jelly has melted and blended with the water. Makes 1 generous cup.

⚜ SABAYON SAUCE

Sabayon Sauce is an adaptation of the Italian dessert, Zabaglione. It may be served hot over hot puddings and soufflés or served chilled with Ladyfingers as a dessert.

4 large egg yolks
⅔ cup sugar
1 cup white wine or Marsala
1 tablespoon Kirsch or rum

Place egg yolks and sugar in top part of a 1½-quart double boiler and beat with a wire whip until the mixture is light and fluffy. Gradually stir in white wine or Marsala. Cook over hot (not boiling) water, stirring constantly, until the mixture is thick and creamy. (Cooking too long or at too high a temperature causes the mixture to curdle.) Beat in Kirsch or rum. Makes approximately 1⅔ cups.

⚜ VANILLA SAUCE

½ cup sugar
4 teaspoons cornstarch
¼ teaspoon salt
1 cup water
2 tablespoons butter
2 tablespoons heavy cream
1 teaspoon vanilla extract

Combine the first 3 ingredients in a 1-quart saucepan. Mix well. Add water. Stir and cook 5 minutes, or until the sauce is clear and has thickened. Remove from heat and stir in butter. Add the cream and vanilla extract. Serve over plain cake or puddings. Makes approximately 2 cups.

VARIATIONS

VANILLA-BOURBON SAUCE

Add 2 tablespoons Bourbon to Vanilla Sauce.

LEMON-VANILLA SAUCE

Omit the cream in the Vanilla Sauce recipe and add 1½ tablespoons lemon juice and 1 teaspoon grated lemon rind.

VANILLA-RUM SAUCE

Add 2 tablespoons rum to Vanilla Sauce.

⚜ VANILLA CREAM SAUCE

¼ cup sugar
2 teaspoons cornstarch
⅛ teaspoon salt
2 large egg yolks
1½ cups milk
1½ teaspoons vanilla extract
½ cup heavy cream, whipped

Combine the first 3 ingredients in a 1-quart saucepan, or in the top of a double boiler. Add egg yolks and mix well. Stir in the milk. Cook, stirring constantly, over low heat or over hot water until the custard coats a metal spoon. Remove from heat and cool completely. Fold in vanilla extract and whipped cream. Makes approximately 2½ cups.

⚜ WHIPPED CREAM TOPPING

1 cup heavy cream
¼ cup confectioners' sugar, or 2 tablespoons granulated sugar
1 teaspoon vanilla extract

Place all ingredients in a mixing bowl and beat mixture until it stands in soft stiff peaks. Makes approximately 2 cups.

VARIATIONS

COFFEE WHIPPED CREAM

Mix 1 teaspoon instant coffee with the sugar in Whipped Cream Topping.

MOCHA WHIPPED CREAM

Mix 1 teaspoon instant coffee and 1 tablespoon cocoa with the sugar in Whipped Cream Topping.

COCONUT WHIPPED CREAM

Fold ¼ cup flaked coconut into Whipped Cream Topping.

ORANGE WHIPPED CREAM

Fold 2 tablespoons grated orange rind and ¼ teaspoon grated lemon rind into Whipped Cream Topping.

⚜ WHIPPED CREAM WITH ALMONDS AND KIRSCH

3 tablespoons sifted confectioners' sugar
dash salt
½ cup heavy cream
1 tablespoon shredded blanched almonds
2 tablespoons Kirsch or Kirsch to taste

Put the first 3 ingredients in a bowl and beat the mixture until it stands in soft peaks. Fold in almonds and Kirsch. Serve on fruit or plain cake. Makes approximately 1 cup.

CREAMS

⚜ CHANTILLY CREAM

1 cup heavy cream
1½ to 2 tablespoons sifted confectioners' sugar
½ teaspoon vanilla extract

Beat the cream until it stands in soft peaks. Fold in the sugar and vanilla extract. This cream may be flavored to taste with rum, brandy, Kirsch, Cointreau, or other liqueur if desired. Makes 2 cups.

⚜ FRENCH PASTRY CREAM (*Crème Pâtissière*)

½ cup sugar
4 tablespoons cornstarch
1/16 teaspoon salt
2 cups milk
4 large egg yolks
1½ teaspoons vanilla extract

Combine first 3 ingredients in the top of a double boiler, or in a 1-quart saucepan. Add ¼ cup of the milk and mix well. Heat 1½ cups milk and gradually add to the mixture, stirring constantly. Stir and cook over moderate direct heat until the mixture is very thick. Beat egg yolks, blend with remaining ¼ cup of milk, and add to the cooked mixture. Cook over hot water or very low heat, stirring constantly, until the cream is about as thick as mayonnaise. Remove from heat and add vanilla extract. Cool completely before using, stirring occasionally to prevent a crust from forming. Makes 2 cups or filling for 8 tarts.

VARIATIONS

CHOCOLATE PASTRY CREAM

Make French Pastry Cream, adding 2 squares (2 ounces) melted unsweetened chocolate to the cooked cornstarch, sugar, and milk mixture. Continue as directed in the recipe.

COFFEE PASTRY CREAM

In the recipe for French Pastry Cream, blend 2 teaspoons instant coffee with the sugar, cornstarch, and salt. Continue as directed in the recipe.

MOCHA PASTRY CREAM

Follow the recipe for Chocolate Pastry Cream, adding 2 teaspoons instant coffee along with the chocolate.

CREAM SAINT-HONORÉ

Soften 2 teaspoons unflavored gelatin with 2 tablespoons cold water, and stir into 2 cups of hot French Pastry Cream (or Chocolate or Coffee Pastry Cream). Beat 4 egg whites until they stand in soft stiff peaks but are not dry, then beat in ¼ cup of sugar, 1 tablespoon at a time, and fold the mixture into the hot cream.

⚜ ALMOND PASTRY CREAM

1 cup blanched almonds
½ cup sifted confectioners' sugar
3 tablespoons softened butter
2 large egg yolks
1 tablespoon Kirsch or rum

Put almonds through a food chopper twice, using the finest blade. Add sugar and mix well. Set aside. Mix butter until creamy, then beat in one egg yolk at a time and the Kirsch or rum. Blend into the almond mixture. Makes approximately 1 ¼ cups.

⚜ FRANGIPANE CREAM

2 cups milk
3-inch piece vanilla bean, or 1 teaspoon vanilla extract
5 tablespoons flour
¾ cup sugar
dash of salt
2 large whole eggs
2 large egg yolks
2 tablespoons butter
4 macaroons, crumbled (see Macaroon Crumbs, page 864)

Heat milk, with vanilla bean (if used), only until milk is hot. Combine the next 3 ingredients in a 1 ½-quart saucepan. Add whole eggs and egg yolks. Mix well. Gradually stir in hot milk. Cook over moderately low heat until boiling point is reached, stirring vigorously. Cook 2 more minutes, without boiling, stirring constantly. Remove saucepan from heat and discard the vanilla bean. (If vanilla bean was not used, add 1 teaspoon vanilla extract now.) Add butter and Macaroon Crumbs. Mix well. Cool, stirring occasionally to prevent a skin from forming over the top of the cream. Makes 2 cups cream.

⚜ THICK CUSTARD FILLING

½ cup sugar
2 tablespoons cornstarch
1 tablespoon flour
dash of salt
3 large egg yolks
1 cup light cream
1 cup milk
1 teaspoon vanilla extract

Combine the first 4 ingredients in a saucepan or the top of a double boiler. Beat in egg yolks and ¼ cup of the cream. Heat the remaining cream with the milk only until hot. (Do not boil.) Add to the sugar and egg mixture. Stir and cook over low heat or hot water (not boiling) until the custard is very thick. Cool before using, stirring frequently to prevent a skin from forming over the top. Use as a filling for cakes, pastries, etc. Makes 2 cups filling.

⚜ SWEET CHESTNUT PURÉE

This may be purchased in specialty food stores.

1 pound chestnuts
1 cup hot milk
2-inch piece vanilla bean
½ cup sugar
¼ cup water
dash salt
1 tablespoon soft butter

Shell and peel chestnuts (see directions on pages 777–78). Chop coarsely and cook them, along with the vanilla bean, in hot milk 20 to 30 minutes, or until chestnuts are very soft. Remove vanilla bean. Force chestnuts through a ricer, or purée them in an electric blender. Put sugar, water, and salt in a small heavy saucepan. Stir and cook slowly until the mixture begins to boil. Cover and cook rapidly 3 minutes, or until the steam has washed off any sugar crystals which may have formed around the sides of the pan. Cook, without stirring, until a soft ball forms when a little of the syrup is dropped in cold water (or to 234° F. on a candy thermometer). Blend the syrup with the chestnut purée, beating vigorously until a thick paste is formed. Cool to lukewarm and stir in the butter. Store in a tightly covered jar in the refrigerator and use as needed. Makes ¾ to 1 cup of purée.

CAKE FROSTINGS AND FILLINGS

⚜ BUTTER-CREAM FILLING AND FROSTING (*Crème au Beurre*)

This frosting is rich, creamy, and not excessively sweet. It is easier to make with an electric mixer, since a lot of beating is required. If all the frosting is not used at one time, store remainder in a covered jar in the refrigerator for use on another cake.

½ cup sugar
1/16 teaspoon cream of tartar
2 tablespoons water
2 egg yolks
8 tablespoons (1 stick) butter
1½ teaspoons vanilla extract

Combine the first 3 ingredients in a 3-cup saucepan. Bring to boiling point over medium-low heat, stirring constantly to dissolve the sugar. Cook rapidly, without stirring, until a candy thermometer shows 244° F., or until the syrup spins a long thread. Cool syrup about 1 minute. Beat egg yolks in a bowl with a small bottom (or in the smaller bowl of the electric mixer) until they are very thick and lemon-colored. Gradually beat in the syrup, beating well after each addition. Beat in 1 tablespoon of the butter at a time. Add vanilla extract and beat well until the frosting is cool. Chill until medium stiff and beat again with a spoon. Chill until of spreading consistency. Use as frosting and filling for cakes, or as filling for pastries. Cakes or pastries frosted or filled with this frosting must be stored in a cool place. Makes 2 cups.

VARIATIONS

CHOCOLATE BUTTER-CREAM FILLING AND FROSTING

Put 2 squares (2 ounces) unsweetened chocolate in a cup and set in a pan of hot water over low heat. When it is melted, stir it into Butter-Cream Filling and Frosting along with the vanilla extract.

COFFEE BUTTER-CREAM FILLING AND FROSTING

Replace the water in the recipe for Butter-Cream Filling and Frosting with 3 tablespoons strong coffee. Or beat in 1 teaspoon instant coffee along with the vanilla extract.

KIRSCH BUTTER-CREAM FILLING AND FROSTING

Add 1 tablespoon Kirsch, or Kirsch to taste, to Butter-Cream Filling and Frosting along with the vanilla extract.

MINT BUTTER-CREAM FILLING AND FROSTING

Add 2 tablespoons Crème de Menthe, or Crème de Menthe to taste, to Butter-Cream Filling and Frosting along with the vanilla extract.

MOCHA BUTTER-CREAM FILLING AND FROSTING

To Coffee Butter-Cream Filling and Frosting, add 1 square (1 ounce) melted unsweetened chocolate.

PRALINE BUTTER-CREAM FILLING AND FROSTING

Add ¼ cup Praline Powder and Kirsch to taste to Butter-Cream Filling and Frosting along with the vanilla extract.

RUM BUTTER-CREAM FILLING AND FROSTING

Add 2 tablespoons dark rum, or rum to taste, to Butter-Cream Filling and Frosting along with the vanilla extract.

RUM-CHOCOLATE BUTTER-CREAM FILLING AND FROSTING

Add 1 square (1 ounce) melted unsweetened chocolate to Rum Butter-Cream Filling and Frosting.

⚜ UNCOOKED BUTTER-CREAM FILLING AND FROSTING

This recipe and its variations may be used if desired in any recipe calling for Butter-Cream Filling and Frosting.

3 egg yolks
¼ cup granulated sugar
1 teaspoon vanilla extract
½ cup (1 stick) softened butter
½ cup (1 stick) firm butter (not hard)

Place the first 3 ingredients in an electric blender and blend until well mixed. Add the softened butter a little at a time and blend until well mixed. Blend in the firm butter, a small piece at a time, until the mixture is creamy and thick. Makes approximately 1 ¼ cups.

Any of the following additions may be made if desired, before adding the butter. Chill if the mixture becomes soft.

CHOCOLATE

Add 1 square (1 ounce) melted and cooled unsweetened chocolate.

COFFEE

Add 1 teaspoon instant coffee, or instant coffee to taste.

LEMON

Add 1 teaspoon each lemon juice and grated lemon rind.

LIQUEUR OR BRANDY

Add 1 tablespoon Cointreau, Grand Marnier, Kirsch, or cognac.

NUTS

Add ¼ cup finely ground almonds, hazelnuts, pecans, or walnuts.

ORANGE

Add 1 tablespoon each grated orange rind and frozen concentrated orange juice.

⚜ WALNUT-RUM BUTTER CREAM

2 tablespoons rum
1¼ cups finely ground walnuts
1 large egg white
¼ cup sugar
¾ cup softened sweet butter

Mix rum with walnuts and set them aside. Break egg white into the top of a double boiler, place over boiling water, and gradually beat in sugar. Continue beating until the meringue is the consistency of heavy cream. Beat in butter, 1 tablespoon at a time. Stir in walnuts. Use as filling for cakes. Makes approximately 1½ cups.

⚜ BUTTER FILLING AND FROSTING

2 tablespoons flour
⅓ cup granulated sugar
¾ cup water
3 egg yolks
2 teaspoons vanilla extract
½ cup (1 stick) butter
1 cup sifted confectioners' sugar

In a 1-quart saucepan combine flour and granulated sugar. Add water and mix well. Stir and cook over moderate heat until the mixture is very thick. Remove saucepan from the heat. Beat egg yolks in a bowl with a small bottom, gradually beat in about 2 tablespoons of the hot mixture, and then beat egg yolks into the remaining hot mixture. Stir and cook over low heat until the mixture is very thick. Remove from heat and beat in the vanilla extract and the butter, 1 tablespoon at a time. Gradually beat in confectioners' sugar. Continue beating until sugar is thoroughly blended. Chill the frosting. Beat 5 minutes or until frosting is thick and fluffy. Use as a filling or as a frosting for cakes. This filling will keep several days if stored in a tightly covered jar in the refrigerator. Makes 2 cups.

VARIATIONS

CHOCOLATE BUTTER FILLING AND FROSTING

Add 2 squares (2 ounces) unsweetened chocolate to the hot Butter Filling and Frosting along with the vanilla extract. Stir and beat until chocolate is melted. Continue as directed in the recipe.

CHOCOLATE-RUM BUTTER FILLING AND FROSTING

Beat 2 tablespoons dark rum (or other rum), or rum to taste, into Chocolate Butter Filling and Frosting. Continue as directed in the recipe for Butter Filling and Frosting.

COFFEE BUTTER FILLING AND FROSTING

In the recipe for Vanilla Butter Filling and Frosting replace the water with ¾ cup coffee infusion. Continue as directed in the recipe.

MINT BUTTER FILLING AND FROSTING

Beat 2 tablespoons Crème de Menthe into Butter Filling and Frosting. Continue as directed in the recipe.

MOCHA BUTTER FILLING AND FROSTING

Add 1 square (1 ounce) unsweetened chocolate and 1 teaspoon instant coffee to the hot Butter Filling and Frosting. Stir and beat until chocolate is melted. Continue as directed in the recipe.

RUM BUTTER FILLING AND FROSTING

Beat 2 tablespoons dark rum, or rum to taste, into Butter Filling and Frosting. Continue as directed in the recipe.

⚜ UNCOOKED BUTTER FROSTING

This can be substituted for the cooked Butter Filling and Frosting.

¼ cup (½ stick) softened butter
2½ cups sifted confectioners' sugar
1 teaspoon vanilla extract
1 large egg white

Stir butter until it is creamy. Blend in 1 cup of the sugar and the vanilla extract. Beat well. Beat egg white until it stands in soft stiff peaks. Gradually beat the remaining sugar into the egg white and fold into the butter and sugar mixture. Makes enough frosting for top and sides of 2 8-inch cake layers.

FONDANT CAKE ICING

1 cup cooked Fondant (see page 1036)
1 to 2 tablespoons liquid (water, simple syrup, maple syrup, strong coffee, orange juice, or lemon juice)
flavoring to taste (almond extract, vanilla extract, any liqueur, or grated orange or lemon peel)
1 teaspoon egg white (optional)

Warm the Fondant in a heavy-bottomed saucepan over *very* low heat, or in the top of a double boiler over hot (not boiling) water, stirring constantly. (Be very careful not to overheat.) Add the liquid gradually, using only enough to thin the Fondant to pouring consistency while keeping it thick enough to mask the cake. Add desired flavoring. To give more sheen to the icing, if desired, add the unbeaten egg white just before using the icing. Brown-Sugar Fondant (page 1037) may be treated in the same way. Makes enough icing for the top and sides of an 8- or 9-inch cake. (For Fondant Frosting for Petits Fours, see page 1013.)

EASY CARAMEL FILLING

1 cup white granulated sugar
1 cup brown sugar
½ cup milk
½ cup (1 stick) butter
1½ teaspoons vanilla extract
½ cup chopped nuts (optional)

Combine the first 4 ingredients in a 1½-quart saucepan. Mix well. Stir and cook until mixture begins to boil. Cook, without stirring, exactly 2 minutes over moderate heat. Remove from heat, add vanilla extract, and beat until filling is of spreading consistency. Add nuts, if desired, just before the filling is stiff enough to spread. Makes filling for 2 8-inch layers.

CHOCOLATE CREAM FROSTING

¼ cup (½ stick) butter
1 square (1 ounce) unsweetened chocolate
2 to 2½ cups sifted confectioners' sugar
2 to 3 tablespoons milk
1 teaspoon vanilla extract

Brown butter lightly in a saucepan large enough for mixing the frosting. Add chocolate and stir until it has melted. Add sugar and milk alternately until frosting is smooth and stiff enough to hold its shape when the spoon is raised. Stir in vanilla extract. Spread frosting over the top of an 8-inch-square cake, or put it through a cake-decorating tube to decorate Petits Fours and other cakes. Makes enough frosting for the top of an 8-inch-square cake.

⚜ COFFEE CREAM FROSTING

2 teaspoons instant coffee
3 tablespoons softened butter
1 pound sifted confectioners' sugar
5 to 6 tablespoons sour cream
1 teaspoon vanilla extract

Blend instant coffee with the butter. Add sugar alternately with sour cream, using only enough cream to make a frosting that is of smooth spreading consistency. Stir in vanilla extract. Makes approximately 2 cups of frosting.

⚜ ROYAL ICING (*Glace Royale*)

3 large egg whites
about 2 cups sifted confectioners' sugar
½ teaspoon cream of tartar

Beat the egg whites with ⅔ cup of the sugar until the mixture is creamy. Add the cream of tartar. Gradually beat in the remaining sugar. If the frosting is to be used for spreading it should have the consistency of heavy cream. If it is to be used for decorating purposes (put through a cake-decorating tube) it should stand in stiff peaks. Since this frosting thickens as it is beaten, beating it with an electric beater saves time and energy. Add additional sugar if necessary to make the icing the consistency desired. Makes approximately 2 cups icing.

GLAZES AND OTHER DESSERT PREPARATIONS

⚜ CARAMEL

Melt 1 cup sugar in a small heavy saucepan over low heat, stirring constantly with a wooden spoon. Remove from heat and add 1 cup of water. Return to heat and simmer until the syrup is thick and smooth. This syrup may be stored in a covered jar and kept to use as needed. Makes approximately ¾ cup.

⚜ CARAMEL GLAZE

Melt 1 cup of sugar in a small saucepan over low heat. Add 1½ tablespoons butter and stir until the mixture is golden brown. Makes enough glaze for the top of a 9- or 10-inch cake.

⚜ CARAMEL SYRUP

1 cup sugar
½ cup hot water
½ teaspoon vanilla extract

Melt sugar in a heavy skillet or saucepan over moderately low heat, stirring constantly. Remove from heat and add the hot water. At this point the sugar will form hard lumps. Stir and cook until all the lumps have dissolved. Remove from heat. Cool. Stir in vanilla extract. Serve over pancakes, or as a sauce for ice cream, puddings, or cold desserts. Makes approximately ¾ cup.

⚜ CHOCOLATE GLAZE

6 squares (6 ounces) semisweet chocolate
¼ cup light corn syrup
3 tablespoons water
2½ tablespoons sweet butter

Break the chocolate into small pieces and set it aside. Place the remaining ingredients in a small saucepan. Stir and cook the mixture over moderate heat until boiling point has been reached. Remove from heat and stir in chocolate. Continue stirring the mixture until the chocolate has completely melted. Use this glaze to frost-glaze cakes, cookies, and Petits Fours. Makes approximately ¾ cup.

⚜ GLAZING SYRUP

2 cups sugar
⅔ cup water
⅛ teaspoon cream of tartar
dash salt

Combine all ingredients in the top part of a double boiler. Stir and cook until boiling point has been reached. Cook, without stirring, until a candy thermometer shows 300° F., or until a little of the mixture dropped in cold water separates into threads. Remove pan from the heat and quickly set it in a pan of cold water to prevent further cooking. Then set pan containing mixture over hot water to prevent syrup from hardening. Use for glazing nuts and for glazing other confections. Makes approximately 1¼ cups.

⚜ SUGAR SYRUP WITH RUM, COGNAC, OR LIQUEUR

HEAVY

(Makes approximately 3 cups)

1½ cups sugar
2 cups water
½ cup rum, cognac, Kirsch, Cointreau, or other liqueur

LIGHT

(Makes approximately 3¼ cups)

1 cup sugar
2 cups water
½ cup rum, cognac, Kirsch, Cointreau, or other liqueur

Combine sugar and water in a 1½-quart saucepan. Mix well and bring to boiling point. Cool to lukewarm and add rum, Kirsch, or other liqueur. Use as directed in specific recipes in this book. This syrup may be stored in a covered jar in the refrigerator to use as needed.

⚜ VANILLA SUGAR

Bury a vanilla bean in 5 pounds of granulated sugar in a canister equipped with a tight-fitting lid. Store at least 1 week before using. Replenish the sugar as it is used. Vanilla sugar may be used in any recipe specifying sugar and vanilla extract or vanilla bean. Makes 5 pounds vanilla sugar.

Vanilla beans impart a much better vanilla flavor than is provided by vanilla extract, which is often adulterated. The beans, which are imported from Madagascar, Mexico, and other tropical countries, are not easily obtained in the United States, although they can sometimes be found in specialty food stores. Information on where to obtain vanilla beans can be secured from L. A. Champon and Company, Inc., 230 West 41st Street, New York, N.Y. 10036. If vanilla beans are unavailable, any recipe which specifies them can be made with pure vanilla extract, using ½ teaspoon for each 1 inch of vanilla bean.

⚜ VANILLA SYRUP

¾ cup sugar
2 cups water
dash of salt
2-inch piece vanilla bean, or 1 teaspoon vanilla extract

Combine the sugar, water, salt, and vanilla bean (if used) in a 1-quart saucepan and mix well. Bring to boiling point and boil 2 minutes. Remove the vanilla bean, if used, or add the vanilla extract now if vanilla bean was not used. Makes 2 ¼ cups.

⚜ CHOCOLATE CURLS

Let a square of chocolate stand at room temperature until warmed. Using a vegetable parer or a sharp paring knife, shave thin curls from the top of the square.

⚜ HOW TO MELT CHOCOLATE FOR DECORATING PURPOSES

Melt semisweet chocolate over warm water (not hot). Cool it until chocolate is stiff enough to be piped through a decorating tube. A little sifted confectioners' sugar may be added if the chocolate is too thin.

⚜ MACAROON CRUMBS

Heat macaroons in a preheated moderate oven (350° F.) for 10 minutes. Remove from oven and cool. Place the macaroons in a plastic bag or paper bag and roll into crumbs with a rolling pin.

⚜ PRALINE POWDER

1 cup sugar
1 cup blanched almonds
½ teaspoon vanilla extract

Put the sugar and almonds in a heavy skillet. Stir and cook over moderate heat until the sugar is well caramelized. Add the vanilla extract. Turn out onto a buttered platter and cool until the mixture hardens, then break it into pieces and put them in a plastic bag or paper bag. With a heavy rolling pin roll and pound the pieces to powder. Store in a tightly closed container. Use as needed. Makes approximately 1 cup.

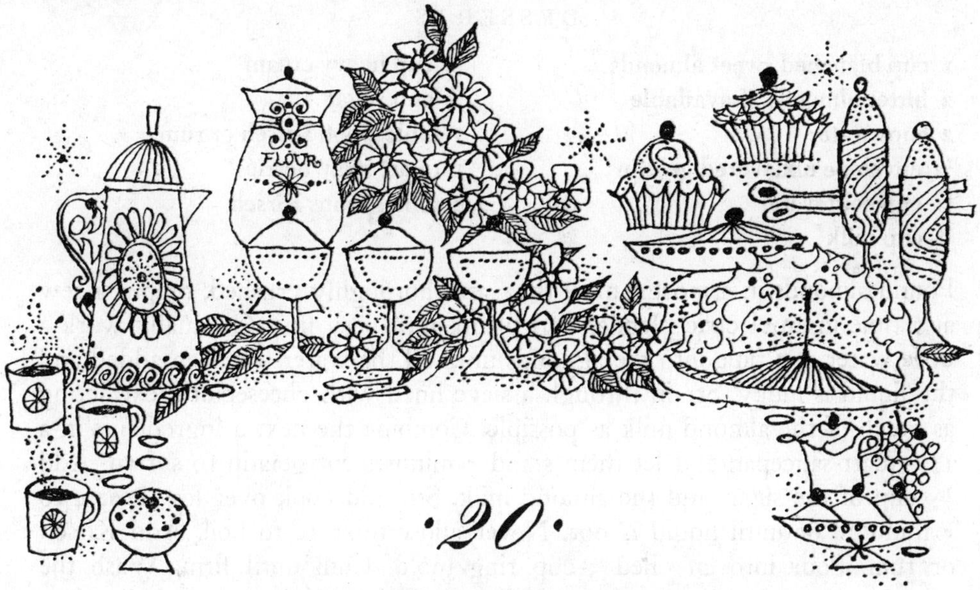

·20·

DESSERTS

Dessert, unless it is followed by cheese, is the last course of a luncheon or dinner. This sweet course rounds out the meal, from the standpoint of good nutrition as well as of pleasure. It satisfies the palate and its attractive appearance adds to the enjoyment of the meal.

The type of dessert served is determined by the rest of the menu. A hearty meal should end with a light dessert, while after a light meal a richer, heavier dessert is welcome.

This chapter includes all kinds of desserts (*entremets*) except cakes, pastries, and desserts in which fruit is the principal element. Fruit desserts are in Chapter 21, cakes and pastries in Chapter 22.

CREAMS AND CUSTARDS

⚜ BLANCMANGE (*Blanc-manger*)

Blancmange, a favorite dessert of the French gourmet, is always made with almond milk and thickened with gelatin, cornstarch, or arrowroot (not with flour).

1 cup blanched sweet almonds
2 bitter almonds, if available
2 cups water
½ envelope unflavored gelatin
¼ cup cold water
½ cup milk
½ cup heavy cream
⅔ cup sugar
1 tablespoon Kirsch or rum
1 quart strawberries
2 tablespoons Kirsch

Pound almonds in a mortar until they are thoroughly crushed, or put a few at a time in an electric blender and blend until very fine. Gradually work a little water at a time into the almonds until all the water has been added and the liquid is milky. Strain through a sieve lined with cheesecloth, extracting as much of the almond milk as possible. Combine the next 4 ingredients in a 1½-quart saucepan and let them stand 5 minutes for gelatin to soften. Add ½ cup of the sugar and the almond milk. Stir and cook over low heat 4 to 5 minutes, or until liquid is hot. Never allow mixture to boil. Add Kirsch or rum. Pour into an oiled 3-cup ring mold. Chill until firm. Wash the strawberries and reserve a few whole unhulled ones to use as decoration. Slice remaining berries, sprinkle with remaining sugar and 2 tablespoons Kirsch, and marinate at least 30 minutes. Just before serving, unmold the Blancmange on a serving plate. Fill center with sliced strawberries. Decorate dish with whole unhulled berries. Makes 6 servings.

VARIATIONS

CHOCOLATE BLANCMANGE

Prepare Blancmange, adding to the hot liquid 1½ squares (1½ ounces) unsweetened chocolate melted in a custard cup in a pan of hot water. Replace Kirsch with 2 teaspoons vanilla extract, or heat a 3-inch piece vanilla bean with the liquid mixture. Continue as instructed in the recipe. Serve with Chantilly Cream.

HAZELNUT BLANCMANGE

In the Blancmange recipe, replace the almonds with fresh hazelnuts. Continue as directed in the recipe.

LIQUEUR BLANCMANGE

Prepare Blancmange with either almonds or hazelnuts, and add 2 tablespoons Cointreau, Curaçao, Kirsch, Maraschino, or any other liqueur desired.

⚜ CRÈME BRÛLÉE

3 cups light cream
2-inch piece vanilla bean, or 1 teaspoon vanilla extract
6 large egg yolks
6 tablespoons sugar
½ cup light brown sugar

Heat the cream, with the vanilla bean (if used), in the top of a double boiler until bubbles form around the edge. Beat the egg yolks with the sugar and slowly beat in the hot cream. Beat vigorously. Return the mixture to the top of the double boiler and cook it over hot water (not boiling) until the custard coats a metal spoon, being careful not to overcook it. Add vanilla extract (if vanilla bean was not used). Strain the custard into a 10- by 6- by 1½-inch baking dish decorative enough to be brought to the table. Cool. Refrigerate 6 to 8 hours. Before serving, sift the brown sugar to remove the lumps and sprinkle it uniformly over the top of the custard. Set the oven regulator to 250° F. (very slow) and preheat 5 minutes. Place the dish under the broiler 4 inches from the source of heat. Leave the door open and broil 3 to 4 minutes or until the sugar melts and forms a smooth glaze. Watch closely to prevent burning. Chill again. Serve from the dish in which the Crème was glazed. Makes 6 servings.

⚜ CARAMEL CRÈME BRÛLÉE

1 cup granulated sugar
1 tablespoon water
2 cups light cream
2-inch piece vanilla bean, or 1 teaspoon vanilla extract
4 large eggs, lightly beaten
½ teaspoon salt
¼ cup light brown sugar

In a small saucepan over low heat, melt ½ cup of the granulated sugar, stirring constantly to prevent burning. Add the water and stir and cook until all the lumps disappear. Pour the syrup into a 10- by 6- by 1½-inch baking dish decorative enough to bring to the table, coating the bottom of the dish completely. Set the dish aside to cool. Heat the cream, with vanilla bean (if used), in the top of a double boiler over hot water until bubbles form around the edge. Combine the remaining ½ cup granulated sugar, the eggs, the salt, and the vanilla extract (if vanilla bean was not used) in a mixing bowl. Gradually beat in the hot cream. Beat vigorously. Strain the mixture into the prepared baking dish and place the dish in a pan of hot water. Bake in a preheated slow oven (325° F.) 40 minutes, or until a knife inserted in the center comes out clean. Remove the dish from the water and cool. Refrigerate 4 to 5 hours or overnight. Before serving, sift the brown sugar uniformly over the top of the Crème. Set oven control to 250° F. (very slow) and preheat 5 minutes. Place the dish under the broiler 4 inches from the source of heat. Broil 3 to 4 minutes or until the brown sugar melts and forms a glaze. Watch carefully to prevent burning. Cool. Refrigerate 3 to 4 hours or until well chilled. Serve from the dish in which the Crème was baked. Makes 6 servings.

⚜ ORANGE HARLEQUIN CREAM (*Crème à l'Orange Arlequin*)

1 envelope unflavored gelatin
¼ cup cold water
½ cup sugar
2 tablespoons cornstarch
⅛ teaspoon salt
¾ cup hot water
¾ cup dry white wine
¾ cup strained orange juice
2-inch piece vanilla bean, or 1 teaspoon vanilla extract
6 large egg yolks
1 cup heavy cream, whipped
Royal Icing
shaved semisweet chocolate
pistachio nuts
¾ cup white wine jelly

Soften gelatin in cold water and set aside. Combine sugar, cornstarch, and salt in a 1½ quart saucepan or top part of a double boiler. Add the next 3 ingredients and the vanilla bean (if used). Mix well. Cook over moderate heat until liquid has thickened. Beat egg yolks, stir in a little of the hot mixture into them, and then add them to the remaining hot mixture. Cook over hot water (not boiling) or very low heat about 4 minutes, stirring constantly. Remove custard from heat and strain it into a bowl. Add softened gelatin and the vanilla extract (if vanilla bean was not used). Mix well. Chill in a pan of ice water until mixture begins to set. Fold in whipped cream. Pour into a glass bowl and chill until the cream is set. Decorate with Royal Icing, shaved semisweet chocolate, and pistachio nuts. Heat wine jelly until about half melted and spread it over the frosting and nuts. Makes 6 to 8 servings.

⚜ SHERRY CUSTARD

1 envelope unflavored gelatin
¼ cup cold water
½ cup sugar
1½ tablespoons cornstarch
1 cup milk
2-inch piece of vanilla bean, or 1 teaspoon vanilla extract
3 large egg yolks
⅓ cup sweet sherry
¾ cup heavy cream, whipped
⅛ teaspoon salt
2 large egg whites
Chantilly Cream

Soften gelatin in cold water and set aside. Combine ⅓ cup of the sugar and cornstarch in a 1½-quart saucepan or top of a double boiler. Add milk and vanilla bean (if used). Stir and cook over moderate heat until thickened. Beat egg yolks, stir a little of the hot mixture into them, and then add them to the remaining hot mixture. Cook over hot water (not boiling) or very low heat, about 4 minutes, stirring constantly. Remove from heat and strain into a bowl. Add softened gelatin, vanilla extract (if vanilla bean was not used), and sherry. Chill in a pan of ice water until the custard begins to set. Fold in whipped cream. Meanwhile, add salt to egg whites and beat until they stand in soft stiff peaks. Beat the remaining sugar into the egg whites and fold into mixture. Pour into champagne glasses and decorate each with Chantilly Cream. Makes 6 servings.

⚜ PRALINE FLOATING ISLAND (*Île Flottante Pralinée*)

1/16 teaspoon salt
4 large egg whites
½ cup sugar
¾ teaspoon vanilla extract
6 tablespoons Praline Powder
Custard Sauce
whole toasted blanched almonds

Add salt to egg whites and beat them until stiff. Beat in sugar, 1 tablespoon at a time. Beat in vanilla extract and Praline Powder. Butter a 1-quart round mold and sprinkle lightly with granulated sugar, or coat it with caramel. Fill with the meringue. Place the mold in a pan of hot water and bake in a preheated very slow oven (275° F.) 25 to 35 minutes, or until the meringue is firm. Cool. Unmold it in a glass bowl and pour Custard Sauce around it. Decorate with whole toasted almonds. Makes 6 servings.

⚜ MOLDED CHESTNUT PURÉE

1 pound chestnuts
2 large eggs
½ cup sugar
¼ teaspoon salt
1 square (1 ounce) unsweetened chocolate
2 cups milk
4 tablespoons cognac
1½ teaspoons vanilla extract
1 cup heavy cream, whipped
2 tablespoons confectioners' sugar

Cut a slit in the pointed ends of the chestnuts. Cover chestnuts with boiling water and boil 35 to 40 minutes. Drain off water and cool the chestnuts until they can be handled. Remove the brown inner skin. Purée chestnuts, a few at a time, in an electric blender or put them through a food mill. Break the eggs into the top of a double boiler and gradually beat in the sugar. Add salt, chocolate, and milk. Mix well. Stir and cook over hot water (not boiling) until the chocolate is melted and the mixture coats a metal spoon. Add 2 tablespoons of the cognac and the vanilla extract to the chestnut purée. Add the purée to the cooked mixture. Cool. Pour the mixture into a well-buttered 8-inch tube cake pan. Chill overnight or until cake is firm. Unmold onto a serving plate. Fold the remaining cognac and the confectioners' sugar into the whipped cream. Spread over the cake as a frosting. Makes 8 to 10 servings.

⚜ SABAYON WITH STRAWBERRIES

6 large eggs, separated
⅔ cup sugar
¾ cup sweet sherry
¼ teaspoon salt
2 cups sliced strawberries
8 whole unhulled strawberries

Combine egg yolks and sugar in the top of a 1½-quart double boiler. Beat with a rotary beater until sugar and egg yolks are well blended. Beat and cook over hot water (not boiling) until the mixture is fluffy and has thickened. (The water in the bottom of the double boiler should never boil. This is important.) Gradually beat in sherry and continue beating until mixture is the consistency of thick cream. Cool quickly and chill. Just before serving, add salt to egg whites and beat them until stiff but not dry. Fold into the custard and turn it into a crystal bowl. Arrange the sliced strawberries over the top and garnish with whole unhulled strawberries. Makes 8 servings.

⚜ ZABAGLIONE GRITTI (*Italian*)

2 teaspoons unflavored gelatin
3 tablespoons cold water
9 large egg yolks
9 tablespoons sugar
1 cup Marsala
Chantilly Cream
6 glacé cherries
unsweetened chocolate

Soften the gelatin in the cold water and melt over hot water. Beat egg yolks in the top of a double boiler and gradually beat in sugar and wine. Place the mixture over hot water and beat vigorously with a wire whisk until the custard is quite foamy and begins to thicken. Add the softened gelatin and continue beating as the mixture cools. Pour into serving dishes and chill. Just before serving garnish each serving with a dollop of Chantilly Cream, a glacé cherry, and a few shavings of unsweetened chocolate. Makes 6 servings. (See illustration, page 902.)

Bavarian Creams

A Bavarian Cream is made with soft custard, gelatin, whipped cream, and any desired flavoring, such as vanilla, coffee, chocolate, etc. It is usually molded, sometimes with macaroon crumbs, ladyfingers, or chunks of sponge cake soaked in a liqueur, sherry, or rum. Nuts and fruit may also be added. These ingredients must be folded in after the mixture is thick enough to hold them in suspension so that the added ingredients will be evenly distributed throughout the custard to give the finished dessert a smooth, uniform texture. If the cream has become too firm before these ingredients are added, place the bowl in a pan of warm water and stir until cream is soft.

Rub the dry mold lightly with oil, or rinse it in cold water, before pouring in the gelatin mixture. Chill for several hours or overnight, until the dessert is firm. Just before serving, loosen edges with a small spatula and turn the dessert out onto a serving plate. If the dessert does not slip out of the mold readily, flash dip it in very hot water, or wrap the mold in a cloth wrung out in water as hot as the hands can stand.

⚜ JELLIED SOFT CUSTARD (*Crème à l'Anglaise Collée*)

This is the basis of all Bavarian Creams.

1 envelope unflavored gelatin
¼ cup cold water
2-inch piece vanilla bean
1 cup milk
3 large egg yolks
½ cup sugar
dash salt

Soften gelatin in cold water and set aside. Add vanilla bean to milk and heat only until hot, stirring to prevent a skin from forming over the surface. Beat eggs lightly in the top part of a double boiler, or in a 1-quart saucepan. Gradually beat in sugar. Add salt. Gradually add hot milk, including the vanilla bean. Stir and cook the custard over hot water (not boiling) or over very low heat until custard coats a metal spoon. Remove from heat. Remove vanilla bean, rinse it, and save it for use in another dessert. Strain custard into a bowl and stir in softened gelatin. Cool the cream, stirring occasionally to prevent a skin from forming over the surface. Makes 4 servings.

If a vanilla bean is not available, Jellied Soft Custard may be made without it, and 1 teaspoon vanilla extract added to Bavarian Creams or other desserts using Jellied Soft Custard; the vanilla extract should be added to the cream just before it is whipped.

⚜ VANILLA BAVARIAN CREAM (*Bavarois à la Vanille*)

1 recipe Jellied Soft Custard
1 cup heavy cream, whipped
Fruit Sauce

Prepare Jellied Soft Custard. Chill in a bowl of ice water or in the refrigerator until the mixture begins to thicken and hold its shape. Fold in whipped cream. Turn into an oiled 1-quart mold. Chill until firm and ready to serve. Unmold onto a serving plate and serve with Fruit Sauce. Makes 6 to 8 servings.

VARIATIONS

CHERRY BAVARIAN CREAM

Prepare Vanilla Bavarian Cream and fold in ½ cup pitted brandied cherries and 2 tablespoons Kirsch along with the whipped cream. Continue as instructed in the recipe. Unmold onto a serving plate and decorate with glacé cherries and angelica.

CHOCOLATE BAVARIAN CREAM

Prepare Vanilla Bavarian Cream, adding 2 squares (2 ounces) unsweetened chocolate to the hot custard, and stirring until chocolate is melted and well mixed. Continue as directed in the recipe. Serve with rum-flavored whipped cream.

COFFEE BAVARIAN CREAM

Prepare Jellied Soft Custard, heating 1 tablespoon instant coffee with the milk. Continue as directed in the recipe for Vanilla Bavarian Cream. Unmold the dessert on a serving plate and serve with Chantilly Cream.

BAVARIAN CREAM DIPLOMAT

Fill an oiled 6-cup mold with alternate layers of Vanilla Bavarian Cream and finely chopped mixed candied fruit, using ½ cup and 12 Ladyfingers broken into pieces and sprinkled with 3 tablespoons Kirsch. Chill until set. Just before serving, unmold onto a serving plate. Garnish with glacé cherries, angelica, and whipped cream.

BAVARIAN CREAM WITH LIQUEURS

Prepare Vanilla Bavarian Cream. Before folding in the whipped cream, add 3 tablespoons of one of the following: Benedictine, Chartreuse, Cointreau, Crème de Menthe, Curaçao, Kirsch, rum, sherry, etc. Continue as instructed in the recipe. Just before serving, unmold onto a serving plate and decorate with candied or glacé fruit and/or whipped cream put through a decorators' tube.

PISTACHIO BAVARIAN CREAM

Prepare Vanilla Bavarian Cream, adding ¼ cup finely ground or chopped pistachio nuts and 2 tablespoons Kirsch along with the gelatin. Continue as instructed in the recipe. Unmold onto a serving plate, serve with Chantilly Cream, and sprinkle with pistachio nuts.

⚜ GINGER BAVARIAN CREAM

1 envelope unflavored gelatin
¼ cup cold water
¼ cup sugar
⅛ teaspoon salt
2 large egg yolks
1 cup milk
1 cup heavy cream, whipped
2-inch piece vanilla bean, or 1 teaspoon vanilla extract
2 tablespoons syrup drained from preserved ginger
¼ cup finely diced preserved ginger
strips of preserved ginger
angelica

Soften the gelatin in the cold water and set aside. Combine the next 3 ingredients in the top of a double boiler, or 1-quart saucepan. Mix well. Heat milk with vanilla bean (if used) and gradually stir into the sugar and egg mixture. Stir and cook over hot water (not boiling), or over very low heat, 12 to 15 minutes, or until custard coats a metal spoon. Remove from heat. Strain and stir in softened gelatin and the ginger syrup. Chill until the custard begins to thicken, stirring occasionally. Fold in ginger, vanilla extract (if vanilla bean was not used), and whipped cream; turn into an oiled 1-quart mold. Chill until set and ready to serve. Unmold onto a serving plate. Decorate with strips of preserved ginger and angelica. Makes 6 servings.

VARIATION

NESSELRODE BAVARIAN CREAM

In Ginger Bavarian Cream, replace ginger syrup and chopped preserved ginger with ¼ cup syrup drained from glacéed chestnuts and ¼ cup finely chopped glacéed chestnuts. Flavor with 1 to 2 tablespoons rum, if desired. Decorate with whipped cream, glacéed chestnuts, and glacéed cherries.

⚜ ORANGE BAVARIAN CREAM

1 envelope unflavored gelatin
½ cup orange juice
½ cup sugar
4 large egg yolks
⅛ teaspoon salt
1½ cups milk
2-inch piece vanilla bean, or 1½ teaspoons vanilla extract
1 tablespoon grated orange peel
1 teaspoon grated lemon peel
1½ cups heavy cream, whipped
orange sections
glacéed cherries

Soften the gelatin in the orange juice and set aside. Combine the next 3 ingredients in the top of a double boiler or 1-quart saucepan and mix well. Heat milk with the vanilla bean (if used) and gradually stir it into egg and sugar mixture. Stir and cook over hot water (not boiling) or over very low heat 12 to 15 minutes, or until custard coats a metal spoon. Remove from heat and strain into a bowl. Add softened gelatin and mix well. Add orange and lemon peel. Mix well. Chill until mixture begins to thicken. Fold in 1 cup of the whipped cream, adding vanilla extract if vanilla bean was not used. Turn into an oiled 6-cup mold. Chill until the Bavarian is set and ready to serve. Turn out onto a large plate. Decorate with remaining whipped cream, orange sections, and glacéed cherries. Makes 8 servings.

Cold Soufflés and Dessert Mousses

These so-called soufflés are not actually soufflés but light molded gelatin desserts, often containing fruit.

⚜ COLD MOCHA SOUFFLÉ

2 envelopes unflavored gelatin
½ cup cold water
½ square (½ ounce) unsweetened chocolate
3 squares (3 ounces) semisweet chocolate
2 tablespoons strong coffee
4 large whole eggs
3 large egg yolks
½ cup sugar
1½ teaspoons vanilla extract
2 tablespoons rum or brandy
1¼ cups heavy cream, whipped
shaved semisweet chocolate, or chocolate decorettes

First prepare the soufflé dish. Fold a 26-inch piece of foil in half lengthwise and tie it around the outside of a 1-quart soufflé dish as a collar. This extends the capacity of the dish. Set aside.

Soften the gelatin in the cold water and place it in a pan of hot water (not boiling) to melt. Set aside to cool slightly. Melt the chocolate with the coffee over hot water (not boiling). Beat whole eggs and egg yolks with sugar in an electric beater about 15 minutes, or beat vigorously by hand over hot water. Add the melted gelatin, chocolate, vanilla extract, and rum or brandy, and mix well. Whip ¾ cup of the cream and fold it into mixture. Pour the mixture into the prepared soufflé dish. Chill until soufflé is firm. Remove foil collar and carefully press shaved semisweet chocolate, or chocolate decorettes, around the exposed sides of the soufflé. Whip remaining ½ cup cream, put it into a pastry bag with a fluted nozzle, and make rosettes over the top of the soufflé. Makes 6 to 8 servings.

⚜ COLD APRICOT SOUFFLÉ

2 envelopes unflavored gelatin
¼ cup cold water
2 tablespoons lemon juice
4 large whole eggs
3 large egg yolks
½ cup sugar
1 cup apricot purée (made from dried or canned apricots)
1 tablespoon cognac
½ teaspoon vanilla extract
1 cup heavy cream
2 teaspoons confectioners' sugar

Prepare a 1-quart soufflé dish as directed in the recipe for Cold Mocha Soufflé. Set aside. Soften the gelatin in the cold water and lemon juice and place it in a pan of hot water (not boiling) to melt. In a mixing bowl combine whole eggs, egg yolks, and sugar and beat in an electric beater, or beat by hand over hot water, until eggs are thick and lemon-colored. Drain the apricot purée well and add it to the egg mixture along with the cognac, vanilla extract, and melted gelatin. Mix well. Whip ⅔ cup of the cream and fold it into the mixture. Pour the mixture into the prepared soufflé dish. Chill until the soufflé is firm and spongy. Remove the foil band. Add the confectioners' sugar to the remaining cream and beat until soft peaks form. Press the cream through a pastry bag fitted with a fluted nozzle to decorate the top of the soufflé. Makes 6 to 8 servings.

⚜ COLD LEMON SOUFFLÉ

1½ envelopes unflavored gelatin
⅓ cup cold water
4 large eggs, separated
½ cup lemon juice
¼ teaspoon salt
1 cup sugar
1 teaspoon grated lemon rind
1 teaspoon vanilla extract
1⅓ cups heavy cream
2 teaspoons confectioners' sugar
toasted blanched almonds, slivered
6 to 8 fresh whole strawberries

Prepare a 1-quart soufflé dish as directed in the recipe for Cold Mocha Soufflé. Set aside.

Soften the gelatin in the cold water. Set aside. In the top of a double boiler combine egg yolks, lemon juice, salt, and ½ cup of the sugar. Stir and cook over hot water (not boiling) until mixture is of custard consistency. Stir in gelatin, lemon rind, and vanilla extract, and turn into a 2-quart mixing bowl. Cool. Beat egg whites until they stand in soft stiff peaks, then gradually beat in the remaining ½ cup sugar. Continue beating until mixture stands in stiff peaks. Whip 1 cup of the cream until it stands in soft peaks. Pile both the egg whites and the cream over the lemon custard and gently fold them into the mixture. Pour into the prepared soufflé dish. Chill until firm and spongy. Remove the foil band. Combine the remaining ⅓ cup of cream and the confectioners' sugar and whip until the cream stands in soft peaks. Spread it over the top of the soufflé. Sprinkle with toasted blanched almonds. Arrange whole unhulled fresh strawberries around the edges. Makes 6 to 8 servings.

⚜ COLD ORANGE SOUFFLÉ

1½ envelopes unflavored gelatin
¼ cup cold water
1 tablespoon lemon juice
4 large eggs, separated
½ cup orange juice
¼ teaspoon salt
¾ cup sugar
½ teaspoon grated lemon rind
1 tablespoon grated orange rind
1 tablespoon Triple Sec
1⅓ cups heavy cream
2 teaspoons confectioners' sugar
mandarin orange sections

Prepare a 1-quart soufflé dish as directed in the recipe for Cold Mocha Soufflé. Set aside.

Soften gelatin in cold water and lemon juice. Set aside. In the top of a double boiler combine egg yolks, orange juice, salt, and ½ cup of the sugar. Stir and cook mixture over hot water (not boiling) until it is of custard consistency. Stir in gelatin, lemon rind, orange rind, and Triple Sec. Turn the mixture into a mixing bowl. Cool. Beat egg whites until they stand in soft stiff peaks, then gradually beat in remaining ¼ cup of sugar. Continue beating until the mixture stands in stiff peaks. Whip 1 cup of the cream until it forms soft peaks. Pile both the egg whites and the cream over the orange custard and gently fold them into the mixture. Pour into the prepared soufflé dish. Chill until soufflé is firm and spongy. Remove the foil band. Combine the remaining ⅓ cup of cream and the confectioners' sugar and beat until cream stands in soft peaks. Press the whipped cream through a cake decorator's tube fitted with a fluted nozzle to decorate the top of the soufflé. Garnish with mandarin orange sections. Makes 6 to 8 servings.

⚜ CHOCOLATE MOUSSE (*Mousse au Chocolat*)

6 squares (6 ounces) semisweet chocolate, or one 6-ounce package semisweet chocolate pieces
¼ teaspoon salt
2 tablespoons water
4 large eggs, separated
2 teaspoons vanilla extract
¾ cup heavy cream
1½ teaspoons sugar

Combine the first 3 ingredients in the top part of a double boiler. Place over hot water and stir until chocolate is melted. Beat egg yolks until light and lemon-colored, then gradually beat in melted chocolate. Stir in vanilla extract. Beat egg whites until they stand in soft stiff peaks, then fold them into the mixture. Whip ½ cup of the cream and fold it in. Spoon the mousse into a decorative serving dish or into sherbet glasses and chill until ready to serve. Garnish with the remaining ¼ cup of cream, whipped and sweetened with sugar to taste. Makes 6 to 8 servings.

⚜ STRAWBERRY MOUSSE

1 quart strawberries
12 tablespoons sugar
1/16 teaspoon salt
3 large egg whites
½ teaspoon vanilla extract
½ cup heavy cream

Wash and hull strawberries. Save out 6 for use as a garnish. Crush the remaining strawberries and mix with 5 tablespoons of the sugar. Set aside. Add salt to egg whites and beat them until they stand in soft, stiff peaks. Gradually beat in 6 tablespoons of the sugar. Fold in the strawberry purée and the vanilla extract. Turn into a glass bowl and chill. Just before serving, add the remaining 1 tablespoon sugar to the cream and beat it until it stands in soft peaks. Pipe the cream through a pastry bag, or spoon it, as desired, over the top of the Strawberry Mousse. Decorate with the reserved 6 whole unhulled strawberries. Makes 6 servings.

⚜ RASPBERRY MOUSSELINE

1 quart fresh raspberries
1 tablespoon lemon juice
¾ cup sugar
2 envelopes unsweetened gelatin
½ cup cold water
1 teaspoon vanilla extract
1½ cups heavy cream, whipped
whole raspberries, or whole unhulled strawberries
ladyfingers (optional)

Crush raspberries and put them through a sieve. Add lemon juice and sugar. Stir until sugar has completely dissolved. Soften the gelatin in the cold water in a custard cup. Set in a pan of hot water (not boiling) to melt. Then add to the raspberry purée along with the vanilla extract. Place the bowl in a pan of cracked ice and stir until raspberries begin to thicken. Fold in the whipped cream. Rinse a 1½-quart mold in cold water and pour in the raspberry cream. Chill several hours or overnight, or until the cream is firm. To serve, unmold onto a large chilled serving plate and garnish the top with whole raspberries or strawberries. If desired, split ladyfingers and arrange them around the sides of the mold. Makes 8 servings.

⚜ STRAWBERRY MOUSSELINE

In the recipe for Raspberry Mousseline replace the raspberries with strawberries. Continue as directed in the recipe. Makes 8 servings.

Baked Custards

⚜ BAKED VANILLA CUSTARD (*Crème Renversée à la Vanille*)

3 cups milk
3-inch piece vanilla bean, or 2 teaspoons vanilla extract
4 whole eggs
4 egg yolks
½ cup sugar
⅛ teaspoon salt
⅓ cup heavy cream, whipped (optional)

Scald milk, with vanilla bean (if used), and let cool slightly. Beat whole eggs and egg yolks together, and beat in sugar and salt. Add a little of the hot milk to the eggs and then add them to the remaining milk. Mix well, adding vanilla extract if vanilla bean was not used. Strain into a lightly buttered 1½-quart casserole, or into 8 lightly buttered custard cups. Place casserole or cups in a pan of hot water. Bake in a preheated slow oven (325° F.) 50 to 60 minutes, or until a knife inserted in the center comes out clean. Cool. Serve topped with whipped cream, if desired. Makes 8 servings.

VARIATIONS

BAKED COFFEE CUSTARD

Make the recipe for Baked Vanilla Custard, replacing ¾ cup of the milk with ¾ cup strong coffee infusion. Continue as directed in the recipe. Makes 8 servings.

BAKED PRALINE CUSTARD

Make the recipe for Baked Vanilla Custard, adding 3 tablespoons Praline Powder to the hot mixture. Mix well. Continue as directed in the recipe. Makes 8 servings.

⚜ BAKED CARAMEL CUSTARD

1 cup sugar
½ cup water
Baked Vanilla Custard
Chantilly Cream

Heat sugar in a heavy skillet until it melts. Gradually stir in water. At this point the sugar will lump. Cook until all lumps have melted. Pour the caramel syrup into a 6-cup ring mold and tilt the mold until all the inside is coated. (Or coat the inside of 8 custard cups.) Chill a few minutes for caramel to set. Make the recipe for Baked Vanilla Custard and pour it into the 6-cup mold or the custard cups. Place mold or cups in a pan of hot water and bake in a preheated slow oven (325° F.) 50 to 60 minutes, or until a knife inserted in the center of the custard comes out clean. Cool. If the ring mold is used, turn it out onto a serving plate and set a bowl of Chantilly Cream in the center. If custard cups are used, serve from the cups or unmold onto individual serving dishes. Top with Chantilly Cream. Makes 8 servings.

⚜ BAKED CHOCOLATE CUSTARD

3 cups milk
3-inch piece vanilla bean, or 2 teaspoons vanilla extract
3 squares (3 ounces) unsweetened chocolate
4 large whole eggs
4 large egg yolks
½ cup sugar
⅛ teaspoon salt
½ cup Chantilly Cream

Heat milk, with vanilla bean (if used). Melt chocolate over hot water and gradually stir in ½ cup of the hot milk. Beat whole eggs and egg yolks together and beat in sugar and salt. Add a little of the hot milk to the eggs and then add them to the remaining hot milk. Stir in the chocolate and milk mixture and add vanilla extract if vanilla bean was not used. Strain into a lightly buttered 6-cup casserole, or into 8 lightly buttered custard cups. Place casserole or cups in a pan of hot water. Bake in a preheated slow oven (325° F.) 50 to 60 minutes, or until a knife inserted in the center of custard comes out clean. Cool. Serve with Chantilly Cream. Makes 8 servings.

⚜ BAKED COCONUT CUSTARD

2 cups milk
2-inch piece vanilla bean
3 large eggs, beaten
¼ cup sugar
¾ cup flaked coconut or grated fresh coconut
grated nutmeg

Heat 1¾ cups of the milk with the vanilla bean. Combine beaten eggs, sugar, and the remaining ¼ cup of milk. Add to the hot milk. Stir in coconut. Turn into a buttered 1-quart casserole. Sprinkle the top with grated nutmeg. Place the casserole in a pan of hot water. Bake in a preheated slow oven (300° F.) 1 hour, or until a knife inserted in the center of the pudding comes out clean. If vanilla bean is not available, add 1½ teaspoons vanilla extract along with the eggs and sugar. Makes 6 servings.

⚜ BAKED LEMON CUSTARD (*English*)

2 teaspoons grated lemon rind
3-inch piece vanilla bean, or 2 teaspoons vanilla extract
3 cups milk
6 large eggs
½ cup sugar

Heat lemon rind and vanilla bean (if used) with 2⅔ cups of the milk. Beat eggs until foamy, then gradually beat in the sugar and the remaining ⅓ cup milk. Add to the hot mixture. Add vanilla extract (if vanilla bean was not used). Strain into a buttered 1-quart mold. Place mold in a pan of hot water. Bake in a preheated slow oven (325° F.) 1 hour or until a knife inserted in the center comes out clean. Serve warm or cold. Makes 6 servings.

Petits Pots de Crème

Petits Pots de Crème are rich custards baked and served in small individual ceramic pots designed especially for this purpose.

⚜ PETITS POTS DE CRÈME À LA VANILLE

2 cups light cream
3-inch piece vanilla bean, or 1½ teaspoons vanilla extract
6 egg yolks
½ cup sugar
⅛ teaspoon salt
Chantilly Cream (optional)

Heat 1¾ cups of the cream with the vanilla bean (if used). Beat egg yolks until light and lemon-colored. Gradually beat in sugar and salt and the remaining ¼ cup of cream and the vanilla extract (if vanilla bean was not used). Gradually beat in the hot cream. Strain mixture into crème pots or custard cups. Place them in a baking pan. Pour in hot water to depth of 1 inch. Cover the pots with crème pot covers or foil. Bake in a preheated slow oven (325° F.) 20 to 25 minutes, or until a knife inserted in the center comes out clean. Cool and chill before serving. Garnish with Chantilly Cream, if desired. Makes 6 servings.

VARIATIONS

PETITS POTS DE CRÈME AUX AMANDES

Make the recipe for Petits Pots de Crème à la Vanille. Put ⅓ cup blanched almonds through a food chopper, using the finest blade. Mix well with 2 tablespoons Kirsch and add to the uncooked custard mixture just before pouring it into the baking pots or cups. Bake as directed in the recipe. Makes 6 servings.

PETITS POTS DE CRÈME AU CAFÉ

Make the recipe for Petits Pots de Crème à la Vanille, but heat 1½ teaspoons of instant coffee with the cream and vanilla bean. Continue as directed in the recipe. Makes 6 servings.

PETITS POTS DE CRÈME AU CRÈME DE CACAO

Make the recipe for Petits Pots de Crème à la Vanille, and add 2 tablespoons Crème de Cacao to the sugar and eggs along with the ¼ cup of cold cream. Continue as directed in the recipe. Makes 6 servings.

PETITS POTS DE CRÈME PRALINÉE

Make the recipe for Petits Pots de Crème à la Vanille. Add 3 tablespoons sifted Praline Powder to the hot cream and mix well. Continue as directed in the recipe. Chill. Garnish with Chantilly Cream sprinkled with Praline Powder. Makes 6 servings.

⚜ PETITS POTS DE CRÈME CARACAS

2 cups light cream
4-inch piece vanilla bean, or 3 teaspoons vanilla extract
4 squares (4 ounces) semisweet chocolate
6 egg yolks
¼ cup sugar
⅛ teaspoon salt
2 tablespoons rum
Chantilly Cream

Combine 1 ¾ cups of the cream and the vanilla bean (if used) in a saucepan. Heat, add chocolate, and stir until chocolate is melted and thoroughly blended with the cream. Beat egg yolks until light and lemon-colored. Gradually beat in sugar and salt. Add the remaining ¼ cup cold cream and rum. Mix well. Stir in the hot cream and the vanilla extract (if vanilla bean was not used). Strain into little crème pots or custard cups. Arrange them in a baking pan. Pour hot water into the pan to a depth of 1 inch. Cover pots with crème pot covers or with foil. Bake in a preheated slow oven (325° F.) 20 to 25 minutes, or until a knife inserted in the center comes out clean. Cool and chill. If desired, serve with Chantilly Cream that has been flavored to taste with a little rum. Makes 6 servings.

VARIATION

PETITS POTS DE CRÈME AU CHOCOLAT

Make the recipe for Petits Pots de Crème Caracas, omitting the rum. Continue as directed in the recipe. Makes 6 servings.

CHARLOTTES

Charlottes are cylindrical-shaped desserts consisting of an outer shell of bread or cake and a cold or hot filling. Hot charlottes were made much earlier than cold charlottes.

To make a cold charlotte, line a charlotte mold or a spring-form pan with Ladyfingers or strips of sponge cake or Génoise. Pour into it a filling consisting of Jellied Soft Custard, Bavarian Creams, French Pastry Cream, or ice cream, with or without fruits or nuts. Chill until firm. Then unmold onto a serving plate and garnish with whipped cream and glacéed or candied fruit, or small fresh fruit, such as strawberries. Serve cold.

For hot charlottes, the mold is lined with butter-soaked bread strips and filled with sweetened very thick stewed fruit. The fruit may or may not be flavored with liqueur or rum. The charlotte is baked and then turned out onto a serving plate. Unless the stewed fruit is very thick the charlotte is apt to collapse at this point. Apple Charlotte was the first of the hot charlottes, but they have since come to be made from other fruits, such as apricots, pears, peaches, plums, and quinces.

⚜ APPLE CHARLOTTE

firm-textured bread, sliced ¼ inch thick
1 cup (2 sticks) butter, melted
6 to 8 large cooking apples
¼ cup water
¼ cup (½ stick) butter
½ cup sugar, or sugar to taste
¼ teaspoon salt
1 tablespoon lemon juice
½ teaspoon vanilla extract
½ cup apricot marmalade or jam
¼ cup dark rum
2 tablespoons sugar

For best results, use bread 2 to 3 days old. Remove crusts. Cut 1 slice of bread into 4 semicircles and dip them in the melted butter. Sauté until golden brown on each side, adding a little more butter if needed. Fit them into the bottom of a 6-cup charlotte mold or deep casserole. Cut bread slices in strips 1¼ inches wide, enough to line the inside of the mold. Dip them in melted butter and fit them, overlapping, around the inside sides of the mold. Trim off all protruding ends. Peel, quarter and core apples and cut into thin slices. Place them in a pan with ¼ cup water and ½ stick butter. Cover and cook over very low heat until apples are soft and all the water has evaporated. Add next 4 ingredients. Mix well. Heat again if apples seem watery; they should be thick enough to remain in a solid mass in a spoon. Turn the mixture into the prepared mold. Dip in melted butter enough bread strips to cover the top and arrange them over the mold. Pour all remaining butter over the top of the mold. Place the mold on a baking sheet in order to catch any butter that drips over the sides and to prevent the bottom from browning too much. Bake in a preheated hot oven (400° F.) 40 minutes, or until top is browned. Remove from the oven and let stand 20 minutes before removing from the mold. Place marmalade, rum, and sugar in a saucepan, bring to boiling point, and cook 1 minute. Serve spooned over the warm Apple Charlotte. Makes 6 to 8 servings.

⚜ CHOCOLATE CHARLOTTE

12 Ladyfingers, or 12 strips of sponge cake
½ cup milk
4 squares (4 ounces) semisweet chocolate
7 tablespoons sugar
2 envelopes unflavored gelatin
½ cup water
4 large eggs, separated
2 tablespoons Praline Powder, or 1 tablespoon rum
⅛ teaspoon salt
1 cup heavy cream, whipped

Line a 7-inch spring-form pan, or 1-quart bowl, with waxed paper and then with split Ladyfingers or sponge cake strips. Set aside. Heat the milk in the top of a double boiler. Add chocolate, stir, and heat until chocolate is melted and smooth. Add 4 tablespoons of the sugar. Soften the gelatin in the water and add to the hot milk. Beat egg yolks lightly. Stir in a little of the hot milk and gradually add to the remaining hot mixture. Stir and cook over hot water (not boiling) until custard coats a metal spoon, 10 to 12 minutes. Remove from heat and blend in the Praline Powder or rum. Cool, stirring occasionally, until custard begins to thicken. Add salt to the egg whites and beat them until they stand in soft stiff peaks, then beat in 2 tablespoons of the sugar. Carefully fold into the custard. Whip ½ cup of the cream and fold into mixture. Turn into the prepared pan or bowl. Chill until firm. Just before serving, unmold and decorate with the rest of the cream beaten with remaining 1 tablespoon sugar and put through a pastry tube fitted with a rosette nozzle. Makes 6 servings.

⚜ CHARLOTTE MALAKOFF

12 Ladyfingers
½ cup fine granulated sugar
½ cup (1 stick) softened butter
½ cup finely ground blanched almonds
4 tablespoons Kirsch
1½ teaspoons vanilla extract
2½ cups heavy cream
1 tablespoon confectioners' sugar

Oil a 1-quart charlotte mold and cover the bottom with a piece of waxed paper cut to fit it. Split the Ladyfingers and arrange vertically around the sides of the mold. Gradually blend sugar into butter and beat the mixture until it is fluffy. Add almonds, Kirsch, and vanilla extract. Whip 2 cups of the cream, fold into the mixture, and turn it into the prepared mold. Chill several hours or overnight. If the ladyfingers extend beyond the top of the charlotte, trim them even with it. Unmold onto a serving plate. Remove waxed paper. Whip the remaining ½ cup of cream with confectioners' sugar and put through a pastry bag fitted with a rosette tube to decorate the top. Makes 6 to 8 servings.

⚜ PEACH CHARLOTTE

12 Ladyfingers
1 envelope unflavored gelatin
¼ cup cold water
1 cup crushed fresh peaches
2 teaspoons lemon juice
¾ cup sugar
2 large egg yolks
1 large whole egg
⅛ teaspoon salt
¾ cup milk
2-inch piece vanilla bean, or 1 teaspoon vanilla extract
1½ cups heavy cream
1 tablespoon confectioners' sugar
Raspberry Purée

Line bottom and sides of a lightly oiled charlotte mold with split ladyfingers and set aside. Soften gelatin in water and set aside. Combine peaches with lemon juice and ¼ cup of the sugar and set aside. Beat egg yolks and whole egg in the top of a double boiler or in a 1-quart saucepan. Beat in remaining ½ cup sugar, the salt, milk, and vanilla bean (if used). Cook over hot water (not boiling) or very low heat until the custard coats a metal spoon. Strain through a fine sieve into a bowl. Stir in softened gelatin. Chill in a pan of ice water until the custard begins to thicken and set. Whip 1 cup of the cream and fold it into the custard along with the peaches. If vanilla extract is used instead of vanilla bean, add it with the peaches and cream. Turn into the prepared mold and refrigerate until charlotte is firm and ready to serve. Unmold onto a serving dish. Decorate with remaining ½ cup cream, whipped with confectioners' sugar and put through a pastry bag fitted with a star tube. Serve with Raspberry Purée. Makes 6 servings.

RASPBERRY PURÉE

Crush 2 cups fresh raspberries and put them through a sieve. Add a dash of salt, 1 teaspoon lemon juice, ½ teaspoon vanilla extract, and ⅓ cup of sugar, or sugar to taste. Makes approximately 1 cup.

⚜ CHARLOTTE ROYALE

1 15½- by 10½- by 1-inch Jelly-Roll Sponge Cake Layer
Charlotte Cream
Petits Fours

Make the sponge cake layer and line a charlotte mold as directed in the following recipe. Fill the mold with Charlotte Cream and chill as directed in the Charlotte Cream recipe. Unmold onto a cake plate, surround with Petits Fours, and serve. Makes 8 to 10 servings. (See illustration, page 900.)

JELLY-ROLL SPONGE CAKE LAYER

4 large eggs
¾ teaspoon double-acting baking powder
¼ teaspoon salt
¾ cup sugar
1 teaspoon vanilla extract
¾ cup sifted cake flour
apricot jam
currant jelly
confectioners' sugar

Place the first 3 ingredients in a mixing bowl and set the bowl *over* a pan of hot water (not in it). Beat with a wire whip or rotary beater until the eggs are foamy. Gradually beat in the sugar and continue beating until the mixture is very thick. Beat in vanilla extract. Remove bowl from over the hot water. Add flour all at once and carefully fold it into the mixture. Line a lightly greased 15½- by 10½- by 1-inch jelly-roll pan with waxed paper (or brown paper) cut to fit. Grease the paper. Pour the batter into the pan and spread it uniformly over the bottom. Bake in a preheated hot oven (400° F.) 12 to 13 minutes, or until cake springs back when touched in the middle with index finger. Turn cake upside down on a clean dish towel that has been dusted with confectioners' sugar. Quickly remove paper, trim off browned edges, and set cake aside to cool. Cut cake in half and put the 2 layers together with red currant jelly. Spread apricot jam over the top layer. Let layers stand 1 hour or more so that they will hold together.

Line a charlotte mold with the cake as follows: cut the cake into 1- by 10-inch strips as needed—the number used depends on the diameter of the mold. (Save leftover cake for making Petits Fours.) Place the first strip, cut side against the mold, across the center bottom, having the strip extend up both sides, dividing the mold in half. Cut the second strip in half and butt one end of each against the first strip in the center bottom of the mold to make a cross, dividing the mold into quarters. Cut 2 more strips of cake in half, pointing one end of each, and place this end in the center of each of the four sections. This divides the mold into eighths. Fill in remaining space with as many half strips of cake as needed to cover the bottom and sides completely, shaping the ends that are placed in the center so that they will fit snugly.

CHARLOTTE CREAM

¾ cup mixed glacéed fruit
½ cup Maraschino liqueur
2 envelopes unsweetened gelatin
½ cup water
4 eggs
⅓ cup sugar
1/16 teaspoon salt
3-inch piece vanilla bean, or 2 teaspoons vanilla extract
1½ cups milk
1½ cups heavy cream, whipped

Soak the glacéed fruit in Maraschino liqueur until ready to use. Soften the gelatin in the water and set aside. Beat egg yolks in the top of a double boiler or in a 1-quart saucepan. Gradually beat in sugar. Add salt, vanilla bean (if used) and milk. Stir and cook over hot water or very low heat until mixture coats a metal spoon. Remove from heat and strain the custard into a mixing bowl. Add the glacé fruit and the vanilla extract (if vanilla bean is not used). Chill in a pan of ice water until the custard begins to set. Fold in whipped cream. Pour into a sponge-cake-lined mold (see preceding recipe). Chill until the Charlotte Cream is firm and ready to serve.

PETITS FOURS FOR CHARLOTTE ROYALE

Cut the sponge cake that was left from lining the mold into small cakes of any desired shape. Cover tops and sides with a thin layer of Apricot Glaze, and let stand 30 minutes or more for the glaze to set. Then frost with Coffee Fondant Frosting for Petits Fours (see page 1013). Decorate as desired with Chocolate Cream Frosting put through a cake-decorating tube.

⚜ CHARLOTTE RUSSE

1 small round cooky
18 Ladyfingers
1 envelope unflavored gelatin
¼ cup cold water
4 large egg yolks
½ cup sugar
2-inch piece of vanilla bean
1 cup milk
1 cup heavy cream, whipped
Chantilly Cream

In a 1-quart charlotte mold or a 1-quart bowl, place a small round cooky in the center bottom. Finish covering bottom of mold with ends of ladyfingers cut into triangles, placing them close together and radiating them from the round cooky in the center to simulate the petals of a daisy. Place remaining Ladyfingers (full size) upright and close together around the sides of the mold. Set aside.

Soften gelatin in cold water and set aside. Beat egg yolks in the top of a double boiler or 1-quart saucepan and gradually add the sugar. Mix well. Heat vanilla bean with milk and gradually beat the milk into the eggs and sugar, stirring rapidly. Stir and cook over hot water (not boiling) or very low heat until the custard coats a metal spoon. Remove from heat and strain into a bowl. Chill in a pan of ice water until mixture begins to thicken and set. Fold in whipped cream and pour into the prepared mold. Chill until firm and ready to serve. Unmold onto a serving dish and decorate with Chantilly Cream that has been put through a pastry bag fitted with a star tube. Makes 6 servings.

⚜ MARQUISE ALICE

1 envelope unflavored gelatin
¼ cup cold water
1 cup milk
½ cup sugar
¼ teaspoon salt
2 eggs, separated
1½ teaspoons vanilla extract
3 tablespoons Praline Powder
¾ cup heavy cream, whipped
12 Ladyfingers
6-ounce glass red currant jelly
Chantilly Cream

Soften the gelatin in the cold water and set aside. Beat the milk, ¼ cup of the sugar, the salt, and the egg yolks together in a saucepan or in the top of a double boiler. Stir and cook over very low heat, or over hot water (not boiling), until the custard coats a metal spoon. Stir in softened gelatin. Strain the custard into a mixing bowl. Add vanilla extract. Chill until custard begins to set. Beat egg whites until they stand in soft peaks, then gradually beat in the remaining ¼ cup sugar. Fold into the gelatin mixture. Fold in whipped cream.

Meanwhile, split the Ladyfingers, sprinkle them with Kirsch, and arrange a layer over the bottom and around the sides of a 7-inch spring-form pan. Add half the gelatin mixture and put a layer of Kirsch-sprinkled Ladyfingers over it. Pour in the remaining gelatin mixture. Chill until firm and ready to serve. Remove the sides from the spring-form pan and place the dessert on a serving plate. Spread Chantilly Cream over the top. Put the currant jelly into a plastic bag, cut a small hole in one corner, and pipe parallel lines of jelly over the cream. A very pretty decoration can be made by lightly drawing the point of a knife across the lines at intervals. Makes 8 servings.

MERINGUES

A meringue is a foam made from egg white, sugar and air, plus salt and flavoring. To the American cook, the word meringue generally means the topping for a pie, which is a soft meringue. However, to the French cook, it more often means a hard meringue (Swiss meringue) used as the base or bowl for a dessert. Hard meringues require more sugar and more beating than do soft meringues and are baked at a lower temperature for a longer time. Hard meringue is usually piped through a pastry bag or shaped with the bowl of a large spoon to form shells for tarts and pies or layers for meringue cakes. After hard meringues have been baked and cooled, they are filled with fruit, ice cream, pastry cream, whipped cream, or a combination of whipped cream and fruit. Hard meringue shells may be made several days before using and stored in a tightly closed container in a dry place.

Italian meringue is still another type, which is made by beating hot sugar syrup into stiffly beaten egg whites. It is not as stiff as hard meringue and does not require baking, since the egg whites are cooked by the hot sugar syrup. However, if desired, it may be browned lightly in a slow to moderate oven. Italian meringue is used to frost cakes, is spread over pastry fillings, and is added to certain types of sherbets to give them a fluffier, lighter texture.

⚜ SOFT MERINGUE (*Pie Topping*)

¼ teaspoon salt
3 large egg whites
¼ teaspoon cream of tartar
6 tablespoons sugar
½ teaspoon vanilla extract

Add salt to egg whites and beat them until they are foamy. Add cream of tartar and beat until the egg whites stand in soft peaks. Gradually beat in sugar and vanilla extract. Continue beating until the egg whites stand in stiff peaks. Spread the meringue over the top of any pie specifying meringue topping, and seal it to the inside edges of the crust. Bake in a preheated slow oven (325° F.) 15 minutes. Cool on a cooling rack away from drafts. Makes meringue for a 9-inch pie.

⚜ ITALIAN MERINGUE

1 cup sugar
¼ teaspoon cream of tartar
½ cup water
1/16 teaspoon salt
3 large egg whites
1½ teaspoons vanilla extract

Combine the sugar and cream of tartar in a 1-quart saucepan. Add the water. Stir and cook slowly until sugar has dissolved and water begins to boil. Cover and boil 3 minutes, or until the steam has washed down any crystals that may have formed on the sides of the pan. Remove cover and boil rapidly, without stirring, to 242° F. on a candy thermometer, or until syrup spins a thread 6 to 8 inches long. Add the salt to the egg whites and beat them until they stand in stiff peaks. Using an electric or rotary beater, gradually beat in the hot syrup. Add the vanilla extract and continue beating until the meringue stands in very stiff peaks. Use as a pie or pudding topping, to frost cakes, and to make sherbets and frozen parfaits. Makes approximately 2½ cups.

VARIATIONS

CARAMEL ITALIAN MERINGUE

In Italian Meringue recipe replace white sugar with brown sugar.

CHOCOLATE ITALIAN MERINGUE

Add 2 squares (2 ounces) melted and cooled unsweetened chocolate to Italian Meringue just before serving.

COFFEE ITALIAN MERINGUE

In Italian Meringue recipe replace water with coffee infusion.

FRUIT ITALIAN MERINGUE

Fold ¾ cups puréed fruit (peaches, raspberries, strawberries, cooked apples) into Italian Meringue just before using.

JAM ITALIAN MERINGUE

Fold ¾ cup apricot, berry, or peach jam into Italian Meringue just before using.

MINT ITALIAN MERINGUE

Fold ⅓ cup crushed cream mints into Italian Meringue just before using.

NUT ITALIAN MERINGUE

Fold ½ cup finely chopped almonds, pecans, pistachios, or walnuts into Italian Meringue just before using.

PEPPERMINT ITALIAN MERINGUE

Fold ½ cup crushed peppermint candy into Italian Meringue just before using.

⚜ HARD MERINGUE (*Swiss Meringue*)

¼ teaspoon salt
¼ teaspoon cream of tartar
4 large egg whites
1 cup fine granulated sugar
½ teaspoon vanilla extract

Add salt and cream of tartar to egg whites. Beat with an electric beater at high speed until the whites are stiff enough to hold their shape. Beat in the sugar, 2 tablespoons at a time, at low speed. Beat the whites until they stand in very stiff peaks and are shiny and moist. This is very important for making successful meringues.

INDIVIDUAL MERINGUE SHELLS

Make the recipe for Hard Meringue. Mark 12 three-inch circles on a piece of brown paper. Butter the paper lightly and dust it with cornstarch. Using a pastry bag, spread each circle with a layer of the meringue mixture ¼ inch thick. Build a border with more meringue to a height of 1½ inches, leaving the center unfilled. Place paper on a cooky sheet. Bake in a preheated very slow oven (250° F.) 1¼ hours. Turn off heat and cool in the oven ½ hour. Remove from the oven. When cold, remove to a tin box and cover tightly. Use as needed for cream fillings, fruits, and ice cream. Makes 12 3-inch shells.

MERINGUE PIE SHELL

Make the Hard Meringue recipe, using only 2 egg whites and half the quantities of the other ingredients. Using a round 9-inch layer cake pan as a guide, mark a 9-inch circle on brown paper. Butter it lightly and dust with a little cornstarch. Spread the circle with a layer of meringue ¼ inch thick. Build a border with remaining meringue to a height of 1½ inches. Place paper on a cooky sheet. Bake in a very slow oven (250° F.) 2 hours. Cool in the oven ½ hour. Remove from oven and cool. Remove the shell from the paper. Fill with a cream filling, fruit, or ice cream. Makes one 9-inch meringue shell.

MERINGUE CAKE LAYERS

Make the Hard Meringue recipe. Using an 8-inch layer cake pan for a guide, trace two 8-inch circles on each of 2 large pieces of brown paper. Butter lightly and dust with a little cornstarch. Spread each circle with a layer of meringue about ⅓ inch thick. Bake as directed for the Meringue Pie Shell. Spread cream fillings and fruit and ice cream mixtures between the layers. Makes 4 8-inch layers.

FILLINGS FOR HARD MERINGUES

LIME CREAM

4 large egg yolks
½ cup sugar
1/16 teaspoon salt
¼ cup lime juice
¼ teaspoon grated lime rind
½ cup heavy cream, whipped
½ teaspoon vanilla extract

Beat the egg yolks in the top of a double boiler. Gradually beat in sugar and salt. Add lime juice and mix well. Stir and cook over hot water (not boiling) until mixture is thick and smooth. Remove from heat and cool. Fold in remaining ingredients. Pile the mixture in 6 Individual Meringue Shells or in a 9-inch Meringue Pie Shell. Makes 6 servings.

LEMON CREAM

Make the recipe for Lime Cream, replacing the lime juice with lemon juice, and the ¼ teaspoon grated lime rind with ½ teaspoon grated lemon rind. Continue as directed in the recipe. Makes 6 servings.

PEACH CHANTILLY CREAM

2 cups diced peaches
½ cup sifted confectioners' sugar
⅛ teaspoon salt
2 cups heavy cream
2 teaspoons vanilla extract

Combine peaches, ¼ cup of the sugar, and the salt. Whip cream until almost stiff and then gradually beat in the remaining ¼ cup sugar and the vanilla extract. Fold in the peaches. Use as a filling for Meringue Shells. Makes 8 servings.

RASPBERRY CHANTILLY CREAM

In the recipe for Peach Chantilly Cream, replace diced peaches with the same amount of whole fresh raspberries. If desired, flavor to taste with Kirsch or cognac. Makes 8 servings.

STRAWBERRY CHANTILLY CREAM

In the recipe for Peach Chantilly Cream, replace diced peaches with the same amount of sliced strawberries. If desired, flavor to taste with Kirsch or cognac. Makes 8 servings.

VANILLA WHIPPED-CREAM FILLING

1½ teaspoons unflavored gelatin
1½ tablespoons cold water
1 cup heavy cream
2 tablespoons sugar
1 teaspoon vanilla extract
Chocolate Curls (optional)

Soften the gelatin in the cold water in a custard cup and place the cup in a pan of hot water to melt the gelatin, stirring frequently. Combine the cream and sugar and beat until the cream stands in soft stiff peaks. Fold in the melted gelatin and the vanilla extract. Makes enough filling for 8 Individual Meringue Shells or 4 Meringue Cake Layers. After filling the meringues, garnish the tops, if desired, with Chocolate Curls.

COFFEE WHIPPED-CREAM FILLING

In the recipe for Vanilla Whipped-Cream Filling, mix 2 tablespoons strong coffee with the melted gelatin, replacing the vanilla extract, and fold into the whipped cream.

⚜ FRUIT IN MERINGUE NESTS

1 recipe Hard Meringue
2 cups diced peaches, sliced strawberries, or whole raspberries
⅓ cup confectioners' sugar
1 teaspoon vanilla extract
2 tablespoons Kirsch (optional)
⅔ cup Chantilly Cream (page 852)

Butter the bottoms of 6 2½-inch muffin pans and line them with unglazed brown or white paper cut to fit. Make the recipe for Hard Meringue and pipe or spoon the mixture into the muffin pans, filling them. Bake in a preheated very slow oven (250° F.) 1 to 1¼ hours. Remove the meringues from the pans while warm and scoop out the soft centers from the underside. Cool. Combine fruit, sugar, vanilla extract and Kirsch, if used. Marinate 30 minutes. Just before serving, fill the meringue nests with the fruit. Place on a serving plate with tops of meringues up. Top with Chantilly Cream. Makes 6 servings.

⚜ MERINGUES GLACÉES

12 Individual Meringue Shells 3 inches in diameter
6 scoops ice cream (any desired flavor)
1 tablespoon confectioners' sugar
Kirsch or Cointreau to taste
½ cup heavy cream

Press a meringue shell on each side of a scoop of ice cream, using 2 shells per serving. Combine the last 3 ingredients and beat until the cream stands in peaks. Put the cream in a pastry bag fitted with a fluted nozzle and decorate edges of shells with a fluted design of whipped cream. Makes 6 servings.

⚜ MERINGUE CAKE

4 Meringue Cake Layers
⅓ cup sugar
2 cups raspberries, sliced strawberries, or sliced peaches
1½ teaspoons vanilla extract
2 tablespoons Kirsch (optional)
1 cup heavy cream
raspberries, whole unhulled strawberries, or diced peaches

Make the Meringue Cake Layers and set them aside. Combine the sugar, fruit, vanilla extract, and Kirsch (if used). Set aside to marinate 30 minutes. Whip the cream until it stands in stiff peaks, being careful not to overbeat it. Save 1 cup of it for decorating the cake. Fold the fruit into the remaining cream and spread it between the Meringue Cake Layers in layer-cake fashion. Color the reserved 1 cup whipped cream with red or yellow food coloring to harmonize with the fruit in the filling. Spread it over the top and sides of the cake. There should be some left. Put remaining cream in a pastry bag fitted with a rosette nozzle and pipe rosettes over the top and sides of the cake as desired. Garnish the plate with raspberries, whole unhulled strawberries, or diced peaches, using the fruit that was used in the filling. Makes 8 servings.

⚜ MERINGUE VACHERIN

1/16 teaspoon salt
6 large egg whites
1½ cups sifted confectioners' sugar
1½ teaspoons vanilla extract
8-inch Sweet Pie Pastry Layer
Strawberry Chantilly Cream
8 whole unhulled fresh strawberries

On each of 2 pieces of brown paper, cut to fit a cooky sheet, mark 2 8-inch circles, using an 8-inch cake pan as a guide. Lay the sheets of paper on 2 well-buttered cooky sheets and press down well so that the butter will seep through the papers and grease the cooky sheets. Sprinkle the papers lightly with cornstarch. Set aside.

Add the salt to the egg whites and beat them stiff but not dry. Sift 1¼ cups of the sifted confectioners' sugar over them all at one time, add the vanilla extract, and with a rubber spatula gently fold in sugar and vanilla extract. Fill a pastry bag fitted with the largest nozzle (¾- to 1-inch diameter) with meringue, and pipe it into 4 rings or wreaths, using the marked circles as a guide. Sift remaining ¼ cup sifted confectioners' sugar lightly over the wreaths. Reserve leftover meringue mixture. Bake in a preheated very slow oven (250° F.) about 1 hour, or until meringues are dry. Turn off heat and let meringues remain in the oven ½ hour. With a damp cloth moisten the paper on the bottom of the meringues, strip off the paper, and invert the meringues to allow them to dry. Using reserved meringue mixture, put the meringue wreaths together in layer-cake fashion, on a heatproof plate. Trim the edges smooth with a sharp knife, and cover the top and sides with the meringue mixture. Put the rest of the meringue mixture in a pastry bag fitted with a rosette nozzle and pipe rosettes as desired around the top and sides, reserving any leftover meringue. Return meringue wreath to a preheated slow oven (275° F.) and bake 40 to 45 minutes, or until dry. Cool. Just before serving, spread the bottom of the meringue wreath with a little leftover meringue and fit it onto a baked 9-inch Sweet Pie Pastry Layer. Fill center with Strawberry Chantilly Cream. Garnish with whole uncapped strawberries. Makes 8 servings.

SWEET PIE PASTRY LAYER

Make the recipe for Sweet Pie Pastry (page 129). Roll the dough in a circle between ⅛ and ¼ inch thick. Using a round 9-inch cake pan as a guide, cut a 9-inch circle from the pastry and transfer it to a cooky sheet. Prick the pastry all over with a fork to prevent it from puffing out of shape as it bakes.

Bake in a preheated moderate oven (350° F.) 15 to 20 minutes. If the pastry begins to puff after cooking, about five minutes, prick it again in 5 or 6 places. Remove from heat and cool.

⚜ SNOW EGGS (*Oeufs à la Neige*)

1/16 teaspoon salt
4 large egg whites
3/4 cup sugar
2 cups milk
2 tablespoons sugar
2-inch piece vanilla bean, or 1½ teaspoons vanilla extract
4 egg yolks
whole unhulled strawberries, or whole raspberries
1 cup crushed strawberries or raspberries
sugar to taste

Add the salt to the egg whites and beat them until they are stiff. Gradually beat in the sugar, beating well after each addition. (To test for stiffness, rest an egg on the meringue. If the egg does not sink, the egg whites have been beaten enough.) Heat the milk, sugar, and vanilla bean (if used) in a shallow saucepan. Bring to boiling point and reduce heat to simmering. (If vanilla bean was not used, add vanilla extract.) Using a soup spoon, shape the meringue into ovals the size and shape of an egg, and drop them into simmering milk. After poaching 2 minutes, turn them carefully with a fork and poach 2 more minutes. (If the meringue eggs are cooked longer they will collapse.) Remove the meringue eggs from the milk with a perforated spoon and drain them on a dry cloth or paper towels. Set aside. Reserve the milk. Beat the egg yolks well. Strain the hot milk and gradually beat it into the egg yolks. Stir and cook over hot water or very low heat until the custard begins to thicken. Remove from heat and chill.

To serve, strain the custard into a glass bowl, and float the meringue eggs on it. Garnish with unhulled whole strawberries, or whole raspberries. Combine crushed strawberries or raspberries with sugar to taste and serve in a separate bowl. Makes 6 servings.

⚜ SNOW EGGS WITH CHOCOLATE CUSTARD (*Oeufs à la Religieuse*)

2 cups milk
3-inch piece vanilla bean
½ cup sugar
¼ teaspoon cornstarch
1/8 teaspoon salt
4 large egg yolks
2 squares (2 ounces) unsweetened chocolate
6 Snow Eggs
Praline Powder

Heat 1¾ cups of the milk with the vanilla bean until hot. Combine sugar, cornstarch, and salt in the top of a double boiler or in a saucepan. Add egg yolks and mix well. Stir in the remaining ¼ cup cold milk. Then add the hot milk and stir and cook over hot water or low heat until custard coats a metal spoon. Add the chocolate and stir until it is melted. Cool. Make the Snow Eggs, according to the preceding recipe, and place them in a glass bowl. Strain the chocolate custard over them and sprinkle with Praline Powder. Makes 6 servings.

⚜ MON RÊVE

6 Snow Eggs
custard for Snow Eggs
1½ cups heavy cream
½ cup Chocolate Sauce
2 tablespoons Praline Powder
Kirsch to taste

Make the Snow Eggs and custard according to the recipe for Snow Eggs. Cool the custard. Whip the cream and fold the cold Chocolate Sauce and the Praline Powder into it. Turn it into a serving bowl and shape it into a smooth dome. Arrange the Snow Eggs on top. Add Kirsch to the cooled custard and pour it over. Makes 6 servings.

PUDDINGS

⚜ APPLE PUDDING

¾ cup (1½ sticks) softened butter
2 large egg yolks
2 large whole eggs
2 tablespoons flour
17 (6 ounces) almond macaroons
2 cups sweetened applesauce
1/16 teaspoon salt
1 teaspoon vanilla extract
whipped cream
confectioners' sugar

Beat the butter until fluffy. Beat in the egg yolks and whole eggs, one at a time. Stir in the flour. Break the macaroons into fine pieces, mix with the applesauce, salt, and vanilla extract, and blend with the butter and egg mixture. Turn into 7 buttered 6-ounce custard cups. Place them in a pan of hot water. Bake in a preheated moderate oven (350° F.) 50 minutes or until puddings are firm. Cool 10 minutes. Turn out into dessert dishes. Sweeten whipped cream with confectioners' sugar to taste and serve it as desired over the puddings. Makes 7 servings.

⚜ BREAD-AND-BUTTER PUDDING

2 cups bread cut in small dice
3 to 4 tablespoons butter
1¾ cups hot milk
¼ cup finely chopped glacéed orange peel
¼ cup currants or raisins
1 teaspoon grated lemon rind
1 teaspoon vanilla extract
3 large eggs, separated
½ cup sugar
1 cup sweet sherry
1 tablespoon sugar
3 tablespoons apricot jam

Sauté the diced bread in butter, adding more butter as needed. Add the sautéed bread to the hot milk. Stir in the next 4 ingredients. Beat the egg yolks, gradually beat in ¼ cup of the sugar, and carefully blend with the milk and bread mixture. Beat the egg whites until they stand in soft stiff peaks, and beat into them the remaining ¼ cup sugar. Fold into the mixture. Turn into a buttered 1-quart mold. Place the mold in a pan of hot water. Bake in a preheated slow oven (325° F.) 1 hour, or until a knife inserted in the center of the pudding comes out clean. Let the pudding stand 20 to 30 minutes before unmolding it onto a serving dish. Combine the last 3 ingredients in a small saucepan. Bring to boiling point and cook 2 minutes. Serve over the pudding. Makes 6 servings.

⚜ BREAD PUDDING FRENCH STYLE
(*Pouding au Pain à la Française*)

2 cups milk
2-inch piece vanilla bean, or 1 teaspoon vanilla extract
2½ cups soft breadcrumbs
½ cup sugar
2 whole eggs
3 large eggs, separated
Sabayon Sauce or Vanilla Sauce

Scald the milk, with the vanilla bean (if used). Add breadcrumbs. Beat ¼ cup of the sugar with the whole eggs and the 3 egg yolks and carefully blend with the milk and breadcrumbs. Rub the mixture through a sieve. Add vanilla extract (if vanilla bean was not used). Beat the 3 egg whites until they stand in soft stiff peaks; gradually beat in the remaining ¼ cup sugar. Fold into the custard mixture and turn it into a buttered 1-quart mold. Place the mold in a pan of hot water. Bake in a preheated slow oven (325° F.) 50 to 60 minutes, or until a knife inserted in the center comes out clean. Let the pudding stand 20 to 30 minutes before unmolding it. Serve warm with Sabayon Sauce or Vanilla Sauce. Makes 6 servings.

Saxon Soufflé Pudding, page 928 ▲

▼ Apple Fritters, page 945

▲ Baked Alaska, page 939

Charlotte Royale, page 886 ▼

Royal Soufflé Pudding, page 929 ▲

▼ Babas and Savarins, pages 997–98

▲ Zabaglione Gritti, page 870

Saint-Honoré Cake, page 992 ▼

Almond Cake, page 967 ▲

▼ Apricots Condé, page 914

▲ Baskets of fresh fruit (see page 942)

Pineapple Croûte, page 998 ▼

Mixed Fruits in Champagne, page 964 ▲

905

▼ Pears Fioretta, page 959

▲ Lattice-Top Apple Tart, page 1026

Orange Tart, page 1028 ▼

Strawberry Tart, page 1028 ▲

▼ Apple Meringue Tart, page 1026

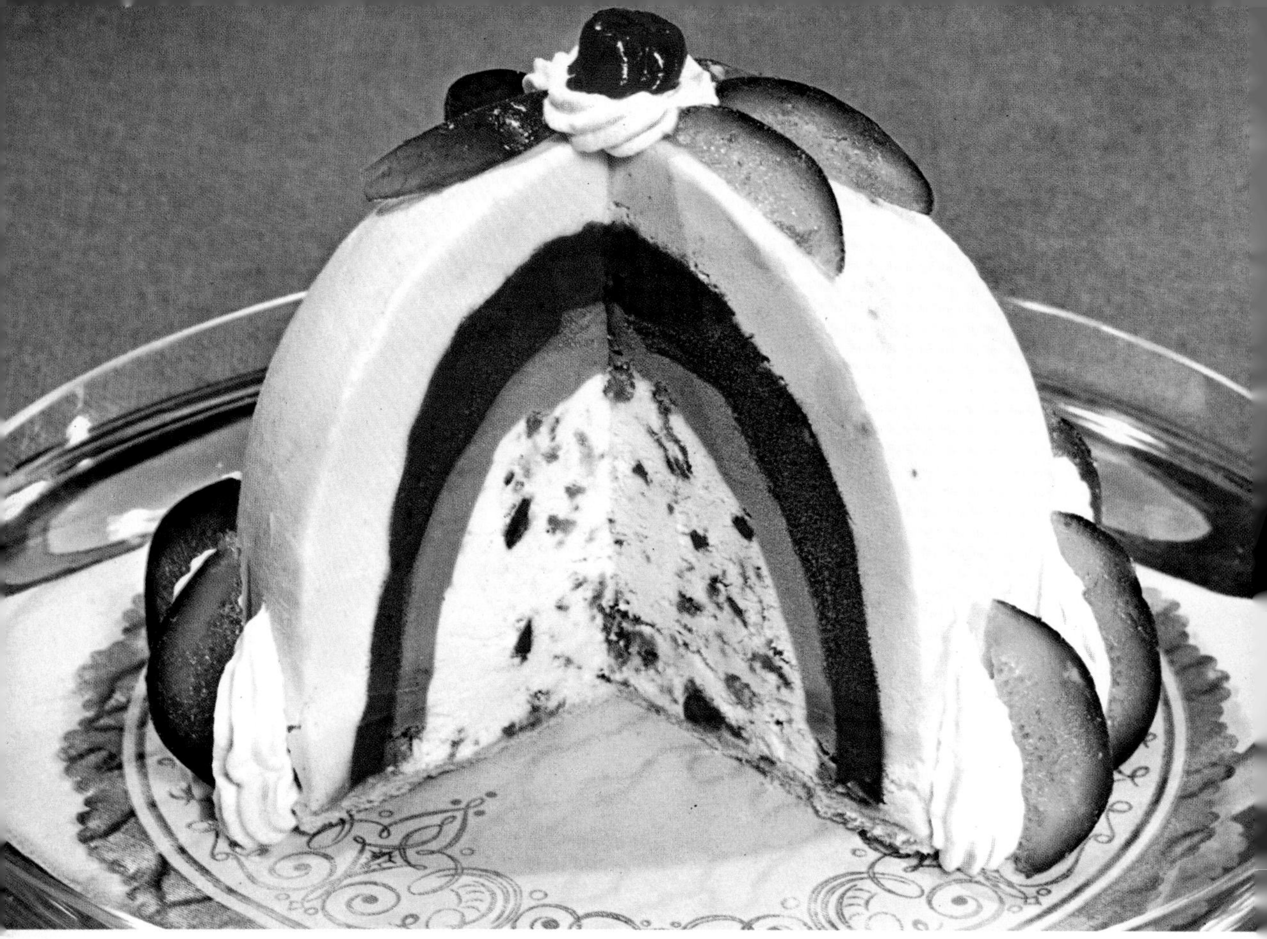

▲ Neapolitan Cassata, page 940

Assorted fruit barquettes (tartlets), pages 1030–34 ▼

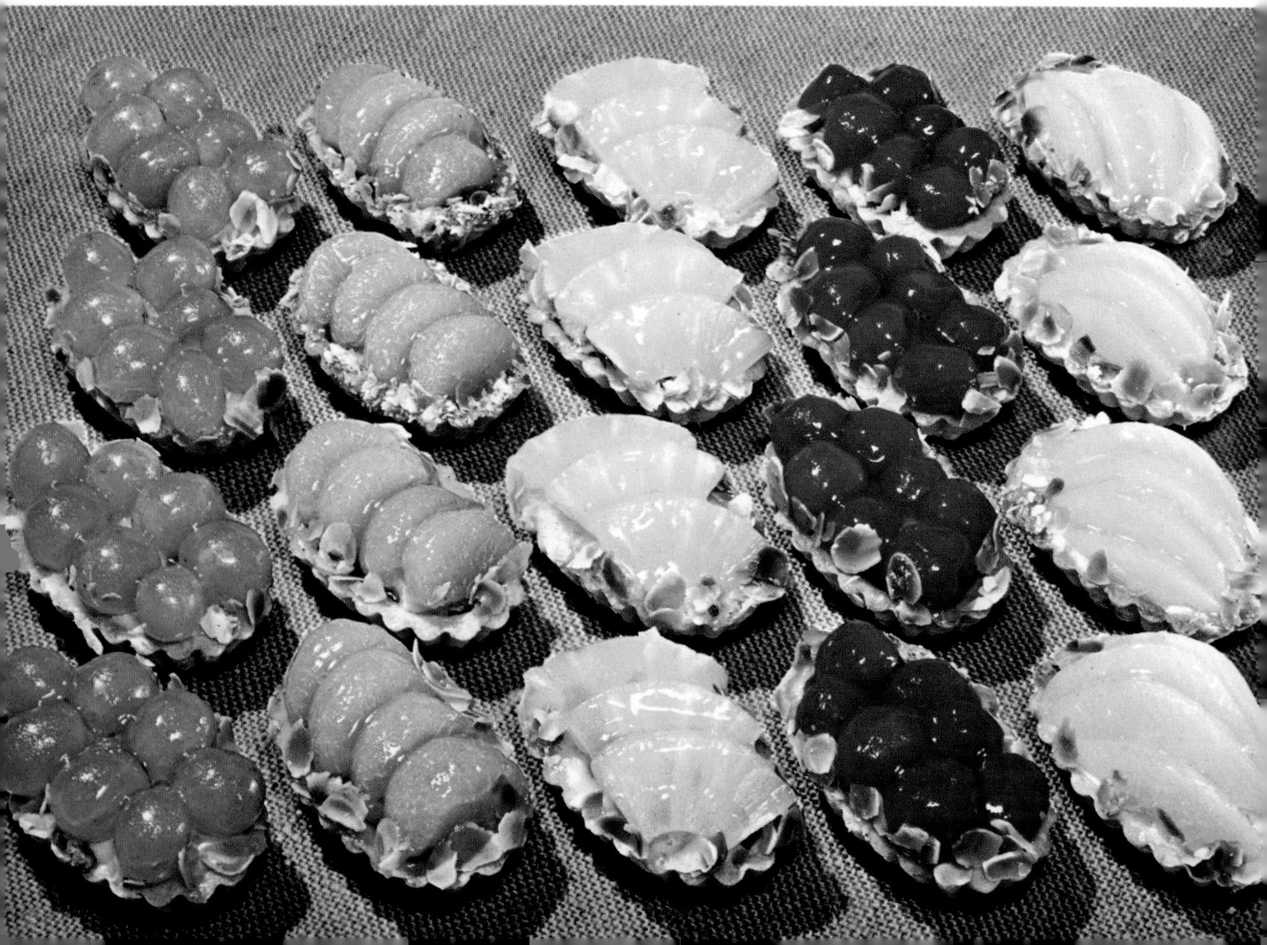

Frosted Lemons, page 940 ▲

▼ Mocha Parfait, page 936

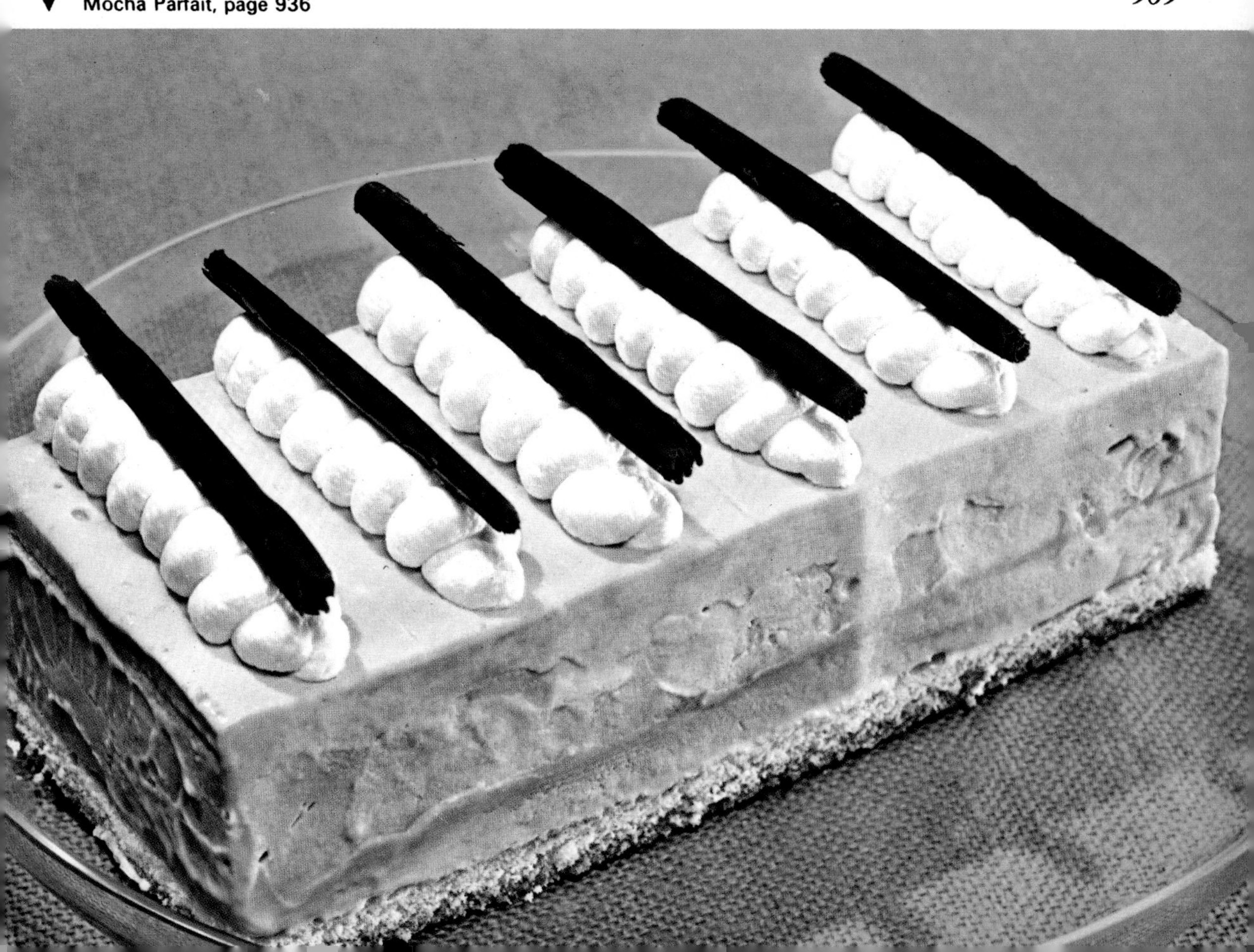

▲ Bombe Diane, page 938

Frozen Tourte with Assorted Fruits, page 941 ▼

⚜ ENGLISH ROLYPOLY JAM PUDDING

¼ pound beef suet
2 cups sifted all-purpose flour
2 teaspoons double-acting baking powder
½ teaspoon salt
about ½ cup water
marmalade or apricot, strawberry, gooseberry, raspberry, or plum jam
jam sauce

Put beef suet through the food chopper, using the finest blade, or chop it fine with a knife. Sift the next 3 ingredients together. Add the suet and mix well. Gradually add enough water to the mixture to make a soft stiff dough that can be rolled. Knead about 20 seconds. Roll dough ¼ inch thick on a lightly floured board. Spread the dough with marmalade or apricot, strawberry, gooseberry, raspberry, or plum jam. Roll up in jelly-roll fashion. Moisten the edge and press down to seal thoroughly. Rinse a clean towel in cold water and wrap it around the roll. Tie the roll tightly at both ends and tie again in the middle. Place it in a large saucepan containing enough boiling water to cover it generously. Cover and boil 2½ hours, adding more water as needed. Or, if desired, bake the roll on a lightly greased baking sheet in a preheated moderate oven (350° F.) 1 hour or until browned. Cut into slices ½ inch thick and serve with a jam sauce. Makes 6 servings.

⚜ ENGLISH PLUM PUDDING

½ pound (1¼ cups) chopped pitted dates
½ pound (1¼ cups) glacéed lemon peel
½ pound (1¼ cups) chopped glacéed orange peel
1 pound (2½ cups) chopped glacéed citron
15-ounce package dried currants
15-ounce package seedless raisins
15-ounce package seeded raisins
1 cup slivered blanched almonds
2 cups apricot or peach brandy
2 cups sifted all-purpose flour
½ cup light brown sugar
1 teaspoon ground cinnamon
1 teaspoon ground ginger
1 teaspoon ground nutmeg
¼ teaspoon ground cloves
1 teaspoon salt
1 cup fine dry breadcrumbs
1 pound beef suet
4 large eggs, well beaten
6-ounce glass red currant jelly
2 or 3 lumps sugar
brandy or rum
Hard Sauce, Chantilly Cream, or Sabayon Sauce

Soak fruit and almonds in brandy for 4 days. Sift together into a large mixing bowl flour, sugar, spices, and salt. Add breadcrumbs and mix well. Put beef suet through a food chopper, using the finest blade, and mix well with the flour mixture. Add the brandied fruit and almonds, the beaten eggs, and the jelly. Mix well. Turn the dough into 2 greased and floured 2-quart molds. Cover with the lids, or with 2 layers of heavy-duty foil tied tightly to hold it in place. Place the molds in large kettles and pour in enough boiling water to come halfway up the sides of the molds. Cover the kettles and boil 4 hours from the time the water starts to boil. Remove from water and cool. Store the puddings in a cool place for at least a month before serving. If desired, wrap puddings in cloth wrung out in sherry, rum, or brandy. Before serving, steam the pudding for 1½ to 2 hours in the mold in which it was cooked. Unmold onto a serving plate. Soak 2 to 3 lumps of sugar in brandy or rum and heat ¼ cup brandy or rum. Ignite and quickly pour over the pudding. Bring the pudding to the table flaming. Serve with Hard Sauce, Chantilly Cream, or Sabayon Sauce. Makes two 2-quart puddings (10 servings each).

⚜ TAPIOCA PUDDING

3 cups milk
2-inch piece vanilla bean, or 1½ teaspoons vanilla extract
2 large eggs, separated
½ cup sugar
¼ teaspoon salt
¼ cup quick-cooking tapioca
½ teaspoon grated lemon rind
sliced bananas, whole raspberries, sliced strawberries, canned crushed pineapple, or applesauce (optional)
⅓ cup heavy cream
2 teaspoons sugar

Heat 2¾ cups of the milk, with the vanilla bean (if used). Beat the egg yolks and add the remaining ¼ cup milk, ¼ cup of the sugar, and the salt. Mix well. Add to the hot milk along with the tapioca. Stir and cook over very low heat until the mixture has thickened and the tapioca is transparent, 10 to 15 minutes. Remove from heat and remove vanilla bean if used. Beat egg whites until they stand in soft stiff peaks, then beat in the remaining ¼ cup of sugar. Fold into the hot mixture along with the lemon peel and the vanilla extract (if the vanilla bean was not used). If desired, fold in sliced bananas, whole raspberries, sliced strawberries, well-drained canned crushed pineapple, or applesauce. Combine the cream and the 2 teaspoons sugar and beat until cream stands in soft stiff peaks. Serve over pudding. Makes 6 servings.

⚜ RHUBARB TAPIOCA PUDDING

6 cups diced rhubarb
2 tablespoons quick-cooking tapioca
1 teaspoon grated lemon peel
¼ teaspoon salt
1½ teaspoons vanilla extract
6 tablespoons butter
2½ cups soft breadcrumbs
2 teaspoons sugar
⅓ cup heavy cream

Combine the first 5 ingredients and set aside. Melt the butter in a saucepan. Add breadcrumbs and mix well. Fill a buttered 1½-quart casserole with alternate layers of breadcrumbs and the rhubarb mixture, having breadcrumbs as the bottom and top layers. Cover and bake in a preheated hot oven (400° F.) 25 minutes. Remove cover and bake the pudding 10 minutes, or until crumbs are brown. Combine sugar and cream and beat until the cream stands in soft stiff peaks. Serve over warm pudding. Makes 6 servings.

RICE DESSERTS

⚜ RICE CONDÉ

¾ cup long-grain rice
hot water
½ teaspoon salt
3 cups milk
¾ cup sugar
2-inch piece vanilla bean, or 1 teaspoon vanilla extract
4 large egg yolks
2 tablespoons butter
2 tablespoons heavy cream
glacéed cherries
angelica
Apricot Sauce II

Place rice in a 1½-quart saucepan and add enough hot water to cover it. Soak 30 minutes. Drain off all the water from the rice. Add the next 3 ingredients and the vanilla bean (if used), cover, and cook 20 to 25 minutes or until rice is tender but not mushy. Remove and discard vanilla bean, or if vanilla extract is to be used add it now. Beat the egg yolks until they are light and foamy and add them to the rice. Add the butter and cream. Mix well, being careful not to crush the rice. Heat 1 to 2 minutes or only enough to cook the egg yolks. Turn the mixture into a 5-cup mold. Let stand until the mixture takes the shape of the mold. Unmold onto a serving platter. Garnish as desired with glacéed cherries and angelica. Serve with Apricot Sauce II. Makes 6 to 8 servings.

⚜ APPLES CONDÉ

¾ cup sugar
2 cups water
2-inch piece vanilla bean
3 medium-sized tart apples
2 tablespoons rum
½ cup long-grain rice
2 cups milk
1-inch piece vanilla bean, or ½ teaspoon vanilla extract
¼ teaspoon salt
¼ cup sugar
3 large egg yolks
1 tablespoon butter
glacéed cherries
angelica
Apricot Sauce

Combine sugar, water, and vanilla bean in a saucepan large enough for poaching apples. Bring to boiling point and simmer 5 minutes. Peel, halve, and core apples. Add them to the syrup and cook, uncovered, until apples are tender when pierced with a toothpick but still hold their shape. Add rum and let apples stand in the syrup until ready to use them. Soak the rice 30 minutes in enough hot water to cover. Drain well. Add the milk, with vanilla bean (if used), salt, and sugar. Cover and cook over very low heat 20 to 25 minutes, or until rice is tender but not mushy. Beat the egg yolks until light and foamy, and gradually stir them into the rice, along with the vanilla extract (if vanilla bean was not used) and butter. Press the rice into a round mold or pan 8 inches in diameter and 2 inches deep, and let stand until the rice takes the shape of the mold. Unmold onto a warmed platter. Remove the apples from the syrup, drain them well, and arrange them over the top of the rice. Garnish with glacéed cherries and angelica. Serve warm with Apricot Sauce. Makes 6 servings.

VARIATIONS

APRICOTS CONDÉ

Use the recipe for Apples Condé, replacing the apples with 9 poached apricots, or with 18 canned apricot halves. Garnish with glacé cherries and citron. Makes 6 servings. (See illustration, page 903.)

PEACHES CONDÉ

Use the recipe for Apples Condé, replacing the apples with peaches. Makes 6 servings.

PINEAPPLE CONDÉ

Use the recipe for Apples Condé, replacing the apples with thin slices of fresh pineapple, or with canned sliced pineapple. Serve with Apricot Sauce flavored with rum to taste. Makes 6 servings.

⚜ PRALINE CONDÉ

Use the recipe for Rice Condé, but reduce the amount of sugar to ⅓ cup and add ¼ cup Praline Powder. Continue as directed in the recipe. When ready to serve the condé, unmold it onto a serving plate and sprinkle it with toasted slivered blanched almonds. Serve with Chantilly Cream. Makes 6 to 8 servings.

⚜ APRICOTS COLBERT

24 poached apricot halves
Vanilla Syrup
3 cups Rice Condé
flour
2 eggs, beaten
2 tablespoons water
fine dry breadcrumbs
confectioners' sugar
Apricot Sauce

Poach the apricot halves in Vanilla Syrup only until they are firm-tender. Remove from syrup, drain well, and dry with paper towels. Prepare the rice as instructed in the recipe for Rice Condé and spoon it into the centers of 12 of the apricot halves. Cover each with one of the remaining apricot halves. Roll them in flour. Beat the eggs with the water. Dip the floured apricots into beaten eggs, roll in breadcrumbs, and fry 2 to 3 minutes (or until browned) in deep fat, preheated to 375° F. Drain on paper towels. Sprinkle with confectioners' sugar. To serve, place 3 apricots in each individual dessert dish and spoon Apricot Sauce over them. Serve warm. Makes 8 servings.

⚜ ORANGE RICE MOLD (*Riz à la Maltaise*)

1½ cups long-grain rice
3½ cups hot milk
½ teaspoon salt
2-inch piece vanilla bean, or 1½ teaspoons vanilla extract
⅔ cup sugar
2 teaspoons grated orange rind
½ teaspoon grated lemon rind
½ cup orange juice
1 cup heavy cream, whipped
2 cups orange sections
¼ cup Grand Marnier

Soak rice in enough water to cover it for 30 minutes. Drain well. Add the rice to the hot milk along with salt and vanilla bean (if used). Cover and simmer (do not boil) 30 minutes. Remove from heat and let the rice stand 10 minutes with cover on. Remove vanilla bean, if used, or add vanilla extract if vanilla bean was not used. Stir in sugar, orange and lemon rind, and orange juice. Fold in whipped cream. Pour into a lightly oiled 9-inch ring mold. Chill several hours or overnight. To serve, unmold onto a chilled serving plate and fill center with orange sections marinated in Grand Marnier. Makes 8 servings.

⚜ PEARS À L'IMPÉRIALE

½ cup mixed glacéed fruit
3 tablespoons Kirsch
½ cup long-grain rice
2 cups milk
¼ teaspoon salt
3 tablespoons sugar
2-inch piece vanilla bean, or 1½ teaspoons vanilla extract
6 large halves of pears, poached in Vanilla Syrup
½ cup red currant jelly
1 teaspoon cornstarch
2 teaspoons water

Marinate the glacéed fruit in 2 tablespoons of the Kirsch while preparing the other ingredients. Soak the rice for 30 minutes in enough hot water to cover. Drain well and add the milk, salt, sugar, and vanilla bean (if used). Cover and cook over low heat 20 to 25 minutes, or until rice is tender but not mushy. Remove vanilla bean, or, if vanilla bean was not used, fold in vanilla extract, along with the marinated glacéed fruit. Turn this mixture into a shallow serving bowl. Arrange the poached pear halves over the top. Melt the jelly in a small saucepan, blend the cornstarch with the water, add to the jelly, and stir and cook about 1 minute. Add the remaining Kirsch. Spoon the sauce over the pears, covering them completely. Serve warm. Makes 6 servings.

⚜ PEARS MARIE-ANNE

6 medium-small pears
½ cup sugar
2 cups water
1 teaspoon lemon juice
1/16 teaspoon salt
2-inch piece vanilla bean, or ½ teaspoon vanilla extract
2 tablespoons Kirsch
1 8-inch round Génoise layer
½ cup long-grain rice
Soft Meringue, using 2 egg whites
glacéed cherries
angelica

Wash and peel the pears, leaving them whole with stems attached. Combine the sugar, water, lemon juice, salt, and vanilla bean (if used) in a saucepan. Bring to boiling point and simmer 5 minutes. Add the pears and cook 10 minutes, or until pears are tender when pierced with a toothpick. Add Kirsch and set aside. Cook the rice as directed in the recipe for Apples Condé. Place the Génoise in the bottom of an ovenproof bowl and spoon the cooked rice over it, shaping it in the form of a pyramid, leaving space around the edge of the cake to place the pears in upright position later. Cover the rice with Soft Meringue forced through a pastry bag fitted with a star nozzle. Place the bowl in a very slow oven (275° F.) 25 to 30 minutes, or until meringue is dry. Drain the pears well and wipe dry with paper towels. Arrange them on the cake around the pyramid of rice in the space provided for them. Decorate as desired with glacéed cherries and angelica. Makes 6 servings.

⚜ PINEAPPLE WITH RICE, SINGAPORE STYLE

¾ cup long-grain rice
4 cups milk
½ cup sugar
½ teaspoon salt
2-inch piece vanilla bean, or 1½ teaspoons vanilla extract
2 envelopes unflavored gelatin
½ cup cold water
1 cup heavy cream, whipped
½ cup sugar
1 cup water
3 cups fresh pineapple wedges
¼ cup Maraschino
Apricot Jam Sauce

Wash the rice and add it to the milk. Stir in the sugar and salt, and add the vanilla bean (if used). Cover and cook slowly 20 to 25 minutes, or until rice is very soft and creamy. Push the rice through a sieve. Soften the gelatin in ½ cup cold water and add to the hot rice. Add vanilla extract (if vanilla bean was not used), and stir until gelatin has melted. Chill until the rice begins to set. Fold in the whipped cream and turn into a lightly oiled 6-cup ring mold. Chill until cream is firm, 5 to 6 hours, or overnight. Meanwhile, combine ½ cup sugar and 1 cup water in a saucepan, bring to boiling point, reduce heat, and simmer 3 to 4 minutes. Add the pineapple, cover, and cook slowly 10 minutes. Remove from heat and cool in the syrup. Drain off syrup and add Maraschino. Marinate at least 1 hour. To serve, unmold the rice cream onto a large chilled serving plate or tray. Fill the center with the marinated pineapple wedges. Serve with Apricot Jam Sauce flavored to taste with some of the Maraschino in which the pineapple was marinated. Makes 8 servings.

⚜ RICE À L'IMPÉRATRICE

½ cup finely chopped glacéed fruit
3 tablespoons Kirsch
½ cup long-grain rice
3 cups milk
¼ teaspoon salt
3-inch piece vanilla bean, or 1½ teaspoons vanilla extract
1½ teaspoons unflavored gelatin
2 tablespoons water
¼ cup sugar
2 large egg yolks
½ cup heavy cream, whipped
glacéed cherries
angelica
½ cup red currant jelly

Combine the glacéed fruit and 2 tablespoons of the Kirsch and marinate while preparing the rest of the ingredients. Soak the rice in hot water 30 minutes. Drain well. Add 2 cups of the milk, the salt, and the vanilla bean (if used). Cover and cook 20 to 25 minutes, or until rice is tender but not mushy. If rice becomes too dry before it has finished cooking, add a little more milk. Soften the gelatin in the water. Combine the sugar and egg yolks and mix well. Stir in the remaining 1 cup milk. Stir and cook over low heat or hot water (not boiling) until custard coats a metal spoon. Add the gelatin and stir until it is dissolved. Strain the custard into the rice. Mix well and chill until the mixture begins to set. Fold in the marinated fruit, the vanilla extract (if vanilla bean was not used), and the whipped cream. Turn the mixture into a lightly oiled 1-quart mold. Chill until the rice mixture is set. Unmold onto a serving plate. Decorate as desired with glacéed cherries and angelica. Whip the jelly with the remaining 1 tablespoon Kirsch and serve over the dessert. Makes 6 servings.

⚜ CHESTNUT FROU-FROU

Rice à l'Impératrice
Almond Wafer Cornets
2 tablespoons thick Sweet Chestnut Purée
½ teaspoon vanilla extract
½ cup heavy cream, whipped
Chantilly Cream

Prepare and mold Rice à l'Impératrice as directed in the recipe. Make Almond Wafer Cornets. Fold Sweet Chestnut Purée and vanilla extract into the whipped cream and pipe it into the cornets, using a pastry bag with a star nozzle. Unmold the Rice à l'Impératrice onto a large serving plate. Fill the center with Chantilly Cream and surround the mold with the filled Almond Wafer Cornets. Makes 8 servings.

⚜ STRAWBERRY RICE CREAM (*Fraises à l'Impératrice*)

Replace the glacéed fruit in the recipe for Rice à l'Impératrice with 1½ cups sliced strawberries. Marinate them in 3 tablespoons Kirsch. Continue as directed in the recipe. When the cream is unmolded on a serving plate decorate it with the whole unhulled strawberries. Omit the currant jelly and serve with whipped cream flavored to taste with sugar and Kirsch. Makes 8 servings.

HOT DESSERT SOUFFLÉS

A hot dessert soufflé is a light, airy baked sweet dish prepared with a base of butter, milk, flour, egg yolks, sugar, and flavoring, made fluffy by steam formed from liquid that is in the mixture and by air beaten into the egg whites. The three standard methods of preparation are:

Béchamel Sauce or Cream Sauce method. Make a Béchamel Sauce or Cream Sauce, starting with a cooked roux. Cool slightly and beat in egg yolks. Carefully incorporate stiffly beaten egg whites.

Bouille method. Mix flour, milk, and sugar together and cook until the mixture has thickened. Cool slightly and beat in butter and egg yolks. Then gently fold in the stiffly beaten egg whites. This method is preferred by some because it requires less butter and makes a lighter soufflé.

French Pastry Cream (Crème Pâtissière) method. This is the method commonly used in the better restaurants and hotels, where a supply of French Pastry Cream is usually kept on hand and a soufflé can thus be prepared in a short time. The egg yolks are beaten into the pastry cream and the stiffly beaten egg whites are then folded into the mixture.

No matter which method of preparation is used, the size of a soufflé depends upon the amount of air beaten into the egg whites and upon maintaining this air during the baking period. Therefore, it is essential that the egg whites be beaten correctly and that they be folded into the cooked mixture carefully. If the egg whites are beaten insufficiently, too little air is enclosed in the egg-white foam and the air cells do not expand sufficiently during the baking, with the result that the soufflé will be smaller and less stable than it should be. If the egg whites are overbeaten, the cell walls will lose their elasticity and break; the egg whites will have a dry, lumpy appearance; and the soufflé will collapse.

⚜ HOW TO BEAT EGG WHITES FOR A SOUFFLÉ

To beat egg whites to the greatest volume and stability, have them at room temperature, make sure that they are free of fat in any form (for example, particles of egg yolk or grease on the beater or bowl), and beat them with a fine wire whip. Although a rotary beater or an electric beater may be used, it is difficult for them to incorporate as much air into the egg whites as can be incorporated by beating by hand with a fine wire whip. The result will be a smaller soufflé.

Two ingredients which may be added to egg whites to increase their stability are cream of tartar and sugar. Add ¼ teaspoon cream of tartar to 4 to 6 egg whites after they have been beaten until foamy. Continue beating until they glisten and stand in soft peaks when the beater is raised. Then beat in 1 tablespoon sugar (reserved from the total amount specified in the recipe) and continue beating until the egg whites stand in sharp, stiff, moist-looking peaks when the beater is withdrawn. The addition of these ingredients permits the air bubbles to swell along with the expansion of the air they contain.

Fold the egg whites into the soufflé mixture as soon as they have been beaten sufficiently. First mix 2 tablespoons of the beaten whites into the soufflé preparation to thin it so that the remaining whites can be folded in more easily. Then, using a rubber spatula and a light folding motion, *never stirring*, fold in the remaining egg whites. This operation should be done quickly and with a light hand. If a few particles of foam are not fully incorporated this will not interfere with the success of the soufflé.

⚜ HOW TO PREPARE A SOUFFLÉ DISH

Soufflés may be baked in a charlotte mold (a cylindrical metal mold commonly used in France), or in a straight-sided ovenproof casserole. The charlotte mold is usually tall enough to accommodate the soufflé after it has baked, but the average casserole will need to have its sides extended with a collar made of 2 thicknesses of foil or brown paper folded to a width of 6 inches and tied around the dish so it will extend 4 inches above the top of the dish. (As the soufflé bakes it will puff and rise up the sides of the collar. Remove the collar after the soufflé has baked.) Butter the bottom and sides of the dish and the inside of the collar generously and sprinkle with granulated sugar. Spoon the soufflé mixture into the dish, filling it three-fourths full.

⚜ HOW TO GIVE A SOUFFLÉ A "TOP HAT"

Smooth the top of the soufflé. Using a knife with a rounded tip, the tip of a teaspoon, or the index finger, trace a circle ½ inch deep around the top of the soufflé 1 inch from the edge. The crust will break at this point and form a taller center. This permits the soufflé to rise evenly.

⚜ HOW TO BAKE A SOUFFLÉ

There are two methods of baking soufflés—the French method and the low-temperature method now favored in the United States.

French Method (bake at a moderately high temperature for a short time). Place the soufflé in a preheated hot oven (400° F.) and immediately set the oven control to 375° F. (moderate). Bake a 1½-pint mold 20 minutes; a 1½-quart mold 30 to 35 minutes; a 2-quart mold 45 minutes. The center of a soufflé baked at this temperature is rather soft and creamy. The soufflé will collapse in a few minutes; therefore serve it *immediately*.

Low-Temperature Method (bake at a low temperature for a longer time). Place the soufflé dish in a pan of hot water. Bake in a preheated slow oven (325° F.) 1 to 1½ hours, or until a knife or a cake tester inserted in the center of the soufflé comes out clean. A soufflé baked by this method will have a firmer and more stable center and it will hold its voluminous puff until it can be brought to the table. Serve it at once.

⚜ HOW TO SERVE A SOUFFLÉ

Serve the soufflé in the dish in which it was baked. Break the top with a fork and with a fork and spoon (holding them vertically) spread it apart, using the same technique as for tearing an angel-food cake into slices with two forks. Each serving should include some of the center and some of the bottom, top, and side crusts.

⚜ HOT VANILLA SOUFFLÉ I

3 tablespoons flour
¾ cup milk
7 tablespoons sugar
4 large egg yolks
2 tablespoons butter
2½ tablespoons vanilla extract
¼ teaspoon salt
5 large egg whites
¼ teaspoon cream of tartar

Prepare a 1½-quart soufflé dish or casserole according to previous directions and set aside. In a saucepan combine the flour and ¼ cup of the milk and mix until the mixture is smooth. Beat in remaining milk and 6 tablespoons of the sugar. Stir and cook until the mixture is very thick. Remove the saucepan from the heat and beat mixture vigorously for 2 minutes. Beat in egg yolks one at a time. Beat in butter and vanilla extract. Transfer the mixture to a large mixing bowl. Set aside. Add salt to egg whites and beat them until they are foamy. Add cream of tartar and continue beating until the egg whites glisten and stand in soft peaks when the beater is raised. Add the remaining 1 tablespoon sugar and beat until the egg whites stand in sharp stiff peaks. Stir 2 tablespoons of the beaten whites into the soufflé mixture. Carefully fold in remaining beaten egg whites. Spoon the mixture into the prepared casserole or soufflé dish. Trace a circle around the top of the soufflé (see How To Give a Soufflé a "Top Hat"). Bake by either the French Method or the Low-Temperature Method (see previous directions). Serve immediately with Cream and Brandy Sauce, Lemon Sauce, or Chocolate Sauce. Makes 6 servings.

VARIATIONS

HOT ALMOND SOUFFLÉ

Make Hot Vanilla Soufflé, adding ½ cup finely ground toasted blanched almonds and ¼ teaspoon almond extract to the cooked mixture just before folding in the beaten egg whites.

HOT COFFEE SOUFFLÉ

Make Hot Vanilla Soufflé, blending 1 tablespoon instant coffee with the flour.

HOT MACAROON SOUFFLÉ

Make Hot Vanilla Soufflé, adding ½ cup macaroon crumbs to the cooked mixture just before folding in the beaten egg whites.

⚜ HOT VANILLA SOUFFLÉ II

5 large eggs, separated
2 tablespoons sugar
½ cup French Pastry Cream
¼ teaspoon vanilla extract
¼ teaspoon salt
¼ teaspoon cream of tartar
Sabayon Sauce or Cream and Brandy Sauce

Prepare a 1½-quart soufflé dish or casserole according to previous directions and set it aside. Beat egg yolks well, then beat in 1 tablespoon of the sugar. Add French Pastry Cream and vanilla extract. Mix well. Add salt to the egg whites and beat them until they are foamy. Add cream of tartar and continue beating until the egg whites glisten and stand in soft peaks. Add the remaining 1 tablespoon sugar and continue beating until the egg whites stand in sharp stiff peaks. Stir 2 tablespoons of the egg whites into the mixture. Carefully fold in the remaining egg whites. Spoon the mixture into the prepared soufflé dish or casserole. Trace a circle around the top (see previous directions). Bake by either the French Method or the Low-Temperature Method (see previous directions). Serve immediately with Sabayon Sauce or Cream and Brandy Sauce. Makes 6 servings.

⚜ HOT CHOCOLATE SOUFFLÉ

2 squares (2 ounces) unsweetened chocolate
3 tablespoons butter
¼ cup flour
1 cup milk, scalded
6 tablespoons sugar
3 large eggs, separated
2 teaspoons vanilla extract
¼ teaspoon salt
¼ teaspoon cream of tartar
Vanilla Sauce or Chantilly Cream

Prepare a 1-quart soufflé dish or casserole according to previous directions and set it aside. Melt the chocolate in a 1-quart saucepan over hot water (not boiling). Add the butter and stir over hot water until it has melted. Blend in the flour. Stir and cook over low heat 1 minute to form a roux. Remove from heat and stir in the hot milk and 5 tablespoons of the sugar. Stir and cook mixture until it is very thick. Remove the saucepan from heat and beat the mixture 1 minute. Beat in egg yolks, one at a time, and vanilla extract. Stir and cook about ½ minute. Transfer the mixture to a large mixing bowl. Add the salt to egg whites and beat them until they are foamy. Add the cream of tartar and beat them until they glisten and stand in soft peaks. Add the remaining 1 tablespoon sugar and continue beating until the egg whites stand in sharp stiff peaks. Stir 2 tablespoons of the beaten egg whites into the cooked mixture. Carefully fold in the remaining egg whites. Spoon the mixture into the prepared soufflé dish or casserole. Trace a circle around the top (see previous directions). Bake by either the French Method or the Low-Temperature Method (see previous directions). Serve immediately with Vanilla Sauce, Rum Sauce, or whipped cream. Makes 5 servings.

VARIATION

HOT CHOCOLATE-RUM SOUFFLÉ

Add 1 to 2 tablespoons rum to the Hot Chocolate Soufflé mixture along with the vanilla extract.

⚜ HOT LEMON SOUFFLÉ

2 tablespoons butter
2 tablespoons flour
½ cup water
¾ cup sugar
¼ cup lemon juice
4 large eggs, separated
1 tablespoon grated lemon rind
½ teaspoon vanilla extract
¼ teaspoon salt

Prepare a 1½-quart soufflé dish or casserole according to previous directions and set aside. Melt the butter in a 1-quart saucepan. Remove from heat and blend in the flour. Stir and cook 1 minute to form a roux. Add the water. Reserve 1 tablespoon sugar to beat with the egg whites and add the rest to the mixture. Mix well. Stir and cook until the mixture is very thick. Add lemon juice, mix well, and cook 1 to 2 minutes, stirring constantly. Remove from heat. Beat the egg yolks, beat in a little of the hot mixture, and then stir into the remaining hot mixture. Add lemon rind and vanilla extract. Transfer the mixture to a large mixing bowl. Set aside. Add salt to egg whites and beat them until they glisten and stand in soft peaks. Then beat in the reserved 1 tablespoon sugar. Continue beating until the egg whites stand in sharp stiff peaks. Stir 2 tablespoons of the beaten egg whites into the cooked mixture. Carefully fold in the remaining egg whites. Spoon the mixture into the prepared soufflé dish or casserole. Trace a circle around the top of the soufflé (see previous directions). Bake by either the French Method or the Low-Temperature Method (see previous directions). Serve immediately, with whipped cream. Makes 6 servings.

⚜ HOT ORANGE SOUFFLÉ

¼ cup (½ stick) butter
⅓ cup flour
1 cup orange juice
2 tablespoons lemon juice
6 tablespoons sugar
4 large eggs, separated
1 tablespoon grated orange rind
1 teaspoon grated lemon rind
½ teaspoon vanilla extract
¼ teaspoon salt
Foamy Sauce or whipped cream

Prepare a 1½-quart soufflé dish or casserole according to previous directions and set it aside. Melt the butter in a 1-quart saucepan. Remove from heat and blend in the flour. Stir and cook 1 minute to form a roux. Add orange juice, lemon juice, and 5 tablespoons of the sugar. Mix well. Stir and cook until the mixture is very thick. Remove from heat. Beat the egg yolks, beat in a little of the hot mixture, and then stir into the remaining hot mixture. Add orange rind, lemon rind, and vanilla extract. Transfer the mixture to a large mixing bowl. Set aside. Add salt to the egg whites and beat them until they glisten and stand in soft peaks. Then beat in the remaining 1 tablespoon sugar. Continue beating until egg whites stand in sharp stiff peaks. Stir 2 tablespoons of the beaten egg whites into the cooked mixture. Carefully fold in the remaining egg whites. Spoon mixture into the prepared soufflé dish or casserole. Trace a circle around the top (see previous directions). Bake by either the French Method or the Low-Temperature Method (see previous directions). Serve immediately with Foamy Sauce or whipped cream. Makes 6 servings.

⚜ HOT GRAND MARNIER SOUFFLÉ

2 tablespoons butter
2 tablespoons flour
½ cup light cream
½ cup sugar
4 large egg yolks
1 tablespoon grated orange rind
¼ teaspoon salt
5 large egg whites
¼ teaspoon cream of tartar
6 Ladyfingers or 6 macaroons
¼ cup Grand Marnier

Prepare a 1½-quart soufflé dish or casserole according to previous directions and set it aside. Melt the butter in a 1-quart saucepan. Remove from heat and blend in the flour. Stir and cook 1 minute to form a roux. Add the cream. Reserve 1 tablespoon of the sugar to beat with the egg whites and add the remaining sugar. Mix well. Stir and cook until the mixture is very thick. Remove from heat. Beat the egg yolks, beat in a little of the hot mixture, and then stir into the remaining hot mixture. Stir and cook 1 minute over low heat. Add orange rind. Transfer the mixture to a large mixing bowl and set it aside. Add the salt to the egg whites and beat them until they are foamy. Add cream of tartar and continue beating until the egg whites stand in soft peaks. Beat in the reserved 1 tablespoon of sugar. Continue beating until the egg whites stand in sharp stiff peaks. Stir 2 tablespoons beaten egg whites into the cooked mixture. Carefully fold in the remaining beaten egg whites. Spoon half the mixture into the prepared soufflé dish or casserole. Dip the Ladyfingers or macaroons in Grand Marnier and place them over the top, then spoon the remaining soufflé mixture over them. Trace a circle around the top of the soufflé and bake by either the French Method or by the Low-Temperature Method (see previous directions). Serve immediately with whipped cream flavored to taste with Grand Marnier. Makes 6 servings.

If desired, replace the Grand Marnier in this recipe with Cointreau or Triple Sec. Or omit the orange rind and dip the Ladyfingers in Crème de Cacao or other liqueur.

⚜ HOT BANANA SOUFFLÉ

3 large firm ripe bananas
lemon juice
⅓ cup sugar
1 tablespoon cornstarch
¼ teaspoon salt
½ teaspoon grated lemon rind
¾ cup milk
3 large eggs, separated
3 tablespoons butter
1 teaspoon vanilla extract
heavy cream, whipped
sugar
ground nutmeg

Peel the bananas, slice them, and dip them in lemon juice to prevent discoloration. Combine the next 4 ingredients. Add the milk and mix well. Stir and cook over medium heat until mixture has thickened. Beat the egg yolks, beat in a little of the hot mixture, and then mix with the remaining hot mixture. Stir in the butter and vanilla extract. Fold in the bananas. Beat the egg whites until they stand in soft stiff peaks and fold them into the mixture. Butter only the bottom of a 1½-quart soufflé dish and turn the mixture into it. Place the dish in a pan of hot water. Bake in a preheated slow oven (325° F.) 1½ hours, or until the soufflé is soft-firm in the center when pressed with the index finger. Serve with whipped cream sweetened to taste with sugar. Garnish the cream with a dash of ground nutmeg. Makes 6 servings.

⚜ HOT FRUIT SOUFFLÉ

Make the Hot Vanilla Soufflé. Mix 1 cup crushed strawberries, peaches, or apricots with 1 tablespoon Kirsch or Kirsch to taste and 2 tablespoons sugar. Add to the soufflé mixture just before folding in the beaten egg whites. Bake as previously directed. Serve with the following Fruit Sauce, made with the same or a different fruit.

FRUIT SAUCE

Combine 1 cup coarsely crushed strawberries, peaches, or apricots with 1 tablespoon Kirsch and 2 tablespoons currant jelly, melted. Mix. Makes a scant 1 ¼ cups.

Soufflé Puddings

Soufflé puddings are popular with French housewives. They are made with a Chou Paste base and will puff again if reheated after they become cold. The baked, unmolded, cold pudding should be placed in a pan of hot water and baked in a preheated moderate oven (350° F.) 30 to 40 minutes, or until it has puffed.

⚜ CHOCOLATE SOUFFLÉ PUDDING

2 squares (2 ounces) unsweetened chocolate
6 tablespoons butter
⅔ cup sifted all-purpose flour
⅔ cup milk, heated
6 tablespoons sugar
2 teaspoons vanilla extract
4 large eggs, separated
¼ teaspoon salt
¼ teaspoon cream of tartar
Vanilla-Rum Sauce

Melt the chocolate in a 1-quart saucepan over hot water (not boiling). Add the butter and stir until butter is melted. Gradually blend in the flour. Stir in the hot milk, a little at a time, mixing well after each addition. Stir and cook over low heat until the mixture leaves the sides of the pan clean and forms a ball. Remove from the heat. Beat in 5 tablespoons of the sugar and the vanilla extract. Continue beating until the mixture is creamy. Stir and cook about 1 minute. Transfer the mixture to a large mixing bowl. Add the salt to the egg whites and beat them until they are foamy. Add the cream of tartar and continue beating until the egg whites glisten and stand in soft peaks. Add the remaining 1 tablespoon sugar. Continue beating until the egg whites stand in sharp stiff peaks. Stir 2 tablespoons of the beaten whites into the cooked mixture. Carefully fold in the remaining egg whites. Butter a 5-cup ring mold generously, sprinkle it with sugar, and spoon the soufflé mixture into it. Place the mold in a pan of hot water. Bake in a preheated moderate oven (350° F.) 45 to 50 minutes, or until the pudding has puffed and a toothpick inserted in the center comes out clean. Unmold onto a serving plate and serve immediately. Serve with Vanilla-Rum Sauce. Makes 6 servings.

⚜ SAXON SOUFFLÉ PUDDING

¾ cup milk
2-inch piece vanilla bean, or 1½ teaspoons vanilla extract
3 tablespoons butter, melted
6 tablespoons flour
4 large eggs, separated
6 tablespoons sugar
1/16 teaspoon salt
Custard Sauce, Kirsch-flavored Apricot Sauce, or White Wine Sabayon Sauce

Heat milk, adding vanilla bean if it is used. Combine butter and flour and mix until flour is well blended, forming a thick roux. Remove vanilla bean from milk and pour in all the milk at one time. Stir, beat, and cook mixture over low heat until it pulls away from the sides of the pan. Use a wire whisk during the first part of the cooking period, and then use a wooden spoon, beating vigorously. (This mixture is similar to Chou Paste.) Transfer the dough to a 2-quart mixing bowl, and while it is still hot beat in the egg yolks, one at a time, being sure that each yolk is thoroughly incorporated before adding another. Beat in vanilla extract (if vanilla bean was not used) and 5 tablespoons of the sugar, one at a time. Add salt to egg whites and beat them until they stand in soft stiff peaks, then beat in remaining 1 tablespoon sugar and continue beating until egg whites stand in sharp stiff peaks. Stir 2 tablespoons of the beaten egg whites into the dough mixture to thin it a little so that the egg whites can be folded in more easily. Now fold in remaining egg whites carefully, avoiding a beating or stirring motion. Butter a 1½-quart soufflé dish or a mold with a tube in the center, and sprinkle the bottom and sides lightly with sugar. Pour in the soufflé mixture. Place mold in a pan of hot water. Bake the soufflé in a preheated moderate oven (350° F.) 50 to 60 minutes, or until a cake tester or toothpick inserted in the center comes out clean. Let stand a few minutes before unmolding, then unmold onto a round serving plate. Serve with Custard Sauce, Kirsch-flavored Apricot Sauce, or White Wine Sabayon Sauce. Makes 6 servings. (See illustration, page 899.)

⚜ ROYAL SOUFFLÉ PUDDING

1 15½- by 10½- by 1-inch Jelly-Roll Sponge Cake
1½ cups apricot jam or red currant jelly
1 recipe Saxon Soufflé Pudding
glacéed cherries
Apricot Sauce flavored with Madeira or Muscatel

Bake Jelly-Roll Sponge Cake and while it is still warm spread it with a thin layer of apricot jam or red currant jelly. Roll it up quickly and let it stand wrapped in a clean towel for at least 1 hour. Cut the roll into slices ½ inch thick and arrange them on the bottom and around the sides of a buttered 1½-quart mold. Make the recipe for Saxon Soufflé Pudding and pour the mixture over the jelly-roll slices. Place mold in a pan of hot water and bake in a preheated moderate oven (350° F.) 50 to 60 minutes, or until a cake tester or toothpick inserted in the center comes out clean. Cover the soufflé with brown paper or foil if it tends to brown too much. Take the soufflé out of the oven, run a small spatula around the inside rim of the mold, and place a round platter upside down over the soufflé. Holding the mold and platter together firmly, invert them. Tap the platter lightly on the table and remove the mold. Decorate the top of the pudding with glacéed cherries. (For a more elaborate presentation, see illustration, page 901.) Serve with Apricot Sauce flavored to taste with Madeira or Muscatel. Makes 8 servings.

FROZEN DESSERTS

Frozen desserts, deservedly popular, range from simple fruit ices made with a sugar syrup to such elaborate preparations as Baked Alaska. Commercially made ice creams and ices, so good and so easily obtainable everywhere in the United States, may be used in many of these recipes.

Ices

⚜ LEMON ICE

1 envelope unflavored gelatin
4½ cups cold water
2 cups sugar
⅛ teaspoon salt
1 cup lemon juice
1 tablespoon grated lemon rind
1 teaspoon vanilla extract

Soften the gelatin in ¼ cup of the water. Combine the sugar, remaining 4 cups water, and the salt in a saucepan. Bring to the boiling point and boil, uncovered, for 5 minutes. Remove from heat and cool 2 to 3 minutes. Add the softened gelatin and cool the mixture to lukewarm. Stir in the remaining ingredients. Pour the mixture into 2 freezer trays or into an 8- by 2-inch square baking pan and freeze until the mixture is a firm mush. Turn the mixture into a large mixing bowl and beat with an electric beater until the mixture is fluffy, starting with the beater at low speed and increasing the speed to the highest as the mixture softens. (Do not beat long enough to melt the mixture.) Return the mixture to the trays or pan and freeze until firm, stirring the mixture twice while it is freezing. If the ice is frozen too hard to serve, let it stand 15 to 20 minutes at room temperature to soften. Makes 1½ quarts.

⚜ ORANGE ICE

1 envelope unflavored gelatin
¼ cup water
2 cups sugar
4 cups water
2 cups orange juice
¼ cup lemon juice
¼ cup Cointreau or Triple Sec
1 teaspoon grated lemon rind
dash salt

Soften the gelatin in cold water and set it aside. Combine the sugar and water in a saucepan, bring to boiling point, and boil 5 minutes. Cool slightly and add the softened gelatin. Cool 10 minutes. Stir in the remaining ingredients. Strain and pour the mixture into two freezer trays. Freeze until the mixture is mushy, then turn it into a bowl and beat it with an electric beater until smooth and fluffy. Return the ice to the freezer trays and freeze until firm, stirring twice without removing it from the trays. Before serving, let the ice stand at room temperature 15 to 20 minutes to soften. Makes 1¾ quarts.

⚜ RASPBERRY ICE

1 envelope unflavored gelatin
¼ cup cold water
1½ cups sugar
3½ cups water
½ cup apricot brandy or peach brandy
⅛ teaspoon salt
2 cups raspberry purée
2 tablespoons lemon juice
½ teaspoon grated orange rind

Soften the gelatin in the cold water and set it aside. Combine the sugar and the 3½ cups water in a 2-quart saucepan, bring to boiling point, and boil gently 5 minutes. Cool slightly and add the softened gelatin. Add the remaining ingredients and strain. Pour the mixture into 2 freezer trays and freeze it until it is a firm mush. Turn it into a large mixing bowl and beat with an electric beater until it is fluffy. Return the mixture to the freezer trays and freeze until it is firm, stirring it twice in the trays. If the ice is frozen so hard that it is difficult to serve, let it stand 15 to 20 minutes at room temperature to soften. Makes 2 quarts.

⚜ STRAWBERRY ICE

Use the recipe for Raspberry Ice, but replace the raspberries with 2 cups strawberry purée. Makes 2 quarts.

Sherbets

⚜ CANTALOUPE SHERBET

1 envelope unflavored gelatin
5 tablespoons lemon juice
1⅔ cups sugar
2 cups water
3 tablespoons Kirsch
2 cups mashed very ripe cantaloupe
¼ teaspoon grated lemon rind
dash salt
2 large egg whites, unbeaten
½ teaspoon vanilla extract

Soften the gelatin in the lemon juice and set it aside. Combine the sugar and water in a 1½-quart saucepan, mix well, bring to boiling point, and cook without stirring 5 minutes. Remove from heat and cool slightly. Stir in gelatin and Kirsch. Pour the mixture into 2 freezer trays, place them in the freezer, and freeze to a firm mush. Turn the mixture into a large bowl. Add remaining ingredients and beat the mixture with an electric beater until it is fluffy. Return it to the freezer trays, freeze it to a firm mush, stir without removing from the trays, and then freeze until firm. Remove the sherbet from the freezer and let it stand 20 minutes at room temperature before serving. Makes 2 quarts.

VARIATION

HONEYDEW SHERBET

In the Cantaloupe Sherbet recipe replace cantaloupe with ripe honeydew. Makes 2 quarts.

⚜ LEMON SHERBET

1 envelope unflavored gelatin
½ cup cold milk
1 cup sugar
⅓ cup lemon juice
1½ cups milk
¾ teaspoon vanilla extract
dash salt
2 large egg whites, unbeaten

Soften the gelatin in the ½ cup cold milk and place it over hot water (not boiling) to melt. Combine the next 4 ingredients and stir until the sugar is dissolved. Add the melted gelatin and pour the mixture into a freezer tray. Freeze until the mixture is almost firm. Turn it into a mixing bowl, add the salt and egg whites, and beat with an electric beater until the mixture is fluffy. Return the mixture to the freezer tray and freeze until firm. Remove the sherbet from the freezer and let it stand at room temperature about 20 minutes to soften before it is served. Makes 1 quart.

Ice Creams

The old-fashioned crank freezer made a smoother ice cream than can usually be achieved by modern methods, but with the prevalence of refrigerators and the availability of commercial ice creams that method of making ice cream is practically extinct. The following recipes result in an excellent smooth ice cream.

⚜ VANILLA ICE CREAM

1¼ cups sugar
¼ teaspoon salt
3 teaspoons vanilla extract
2 cups milk
2 cups heavy cream

Combine the first 4 ingredients in order and stir until the sugar is dissolved. Add the cream and mix well. Pour the mixture into 2 freezer trays or into an 8- by 2-inch square baking pan. Freeze until the mixture is a firm mush. Turn it into a large mixing bowl and beat with an electric beater until the mixture is fluffy, starting with the beater at low speed and increasing the speed to the highest as the mixture softens. (Do not beat so long that the mixture melts.) Return the mixture to the trays or pan and freeze until the ice cream is firm, stirring once before it is completely frozen. Makes 1½ quarts.

VARIATIONS

GINGER ICE CREAM

Add 2¼ teaspoons powdered ginger and mix it with the sugar before adding the milk. Or, if desired, use ¼ cup chopped candied ginger and 2 tablespoons of syrup drained from the ginger and fold into the beaten mixture just before returning it to the trays for freezing.

PISTACHIO ICE CREAM

Fold ¼ to ⅓ cup finely ground pistachio nuts into the beaten mixture just before returning it to the trays for freezing.

FRUIT ICE CREAM

Mix 1 cup coarsely crushed strawberries, peaches, or apricots with 2 tablespoons sugar and 1 tablespoon Kirsch. Fold into the beaten mixture just before returning it to the trays for freezing.

Frozen Mousses

⚜ HONEYDEW MOUSSE

1 envelope unflavored gelatin
¼ cup cold water
2 cups mashed ripe honeydew
½ cup sugar
1 tablespoon lemon juice
½ teaspoon vanilla extract
1 cup heavy cream, whipped

Soften the gelatin in the cold water and set it aside. Combine the next 3 ingredients and cook only until the mixture is hot and the sugar has dissolved. Stir in the softened gelatin. Chill until the mixture begins to thicken. Fold in the vanilla extract and whipped cream. Turn the mixture into a freezer tray and freeze until it is firm. Remove the mousse from the refrigerator and let it stand 10 minutes at room temperature before serving. Makes 1 quart.

VARIATIONS

CANTALOUPE MOUSSE

Use the recipe for Honeydew Mousse, replacing the honeydew with 2 cups mashed ripe cantaloupe. Makes 1 quart.

PEACH MOUSSE

Use the recipe for Honeydew Mousse, replacing the honeydew with 2 cups mashed ripe peaches. Makes 1 quart.

⚜ STRAWBERRY MOUSSE

2 cups (1 pint) fresh strawberries
¾ cup sugar
1½ teaspoons vanilla extract
⅛ teaspoon salt
1 tablespoon Kirsch or Kirsch to taste
1 cup heavy cream, whipped

Wash and hull the strawberries, crush them, and mix with the next 4 ingredients. Fold in whipped cream. Turn the mixture into a freezer tray and freeze until firm. Remove mousse from the freezer 20 minutes before serving to soften slightly. Makes 6 servings.

Parfaits

⚜ ANGEL PARFAIT

⅔ cup sugar
¾ cup water
3 large egg whites
2 cups heavy cream, whipped
1½ teaspoons vanilla extract

Combine the sugar and water in a 1-quart saucepan. Stir and cook until boiling point is reached. Cover and cook 3 minutes. Remove cover and continue to cook, without stirring, to 234° F. on a candy thermometer, or until ½ teaspoon syrup forms a soft ball when dropped in cold water. Beat the egg whites until they stand in soft stiff peaks, then gradually beat in the hot syrup. Continue beating until mixture is cool. Fold in the cream and vanilla extract. Pour into a 9- by 9- by 2-inch pan or into 2 freezer trays. Freeze without stirring until firm. This may be frozen in a crank-type freezer if desired. Makes 1½ quarts.

⚜ ANISETTE PARFAIT

1¼ cups sugar
1 cup water
dash salt
8 large egg yolks, beaten
2 tablespoons anisette
2½ cups heavy cream
2 tablespoons confectioners' sugar
glacéed cherries

Combine the first 3 ingredients in a 1½-quart saucepan. Stir and cook the mixture until boiling point is reached. Cook, without stirring, to 234° F. on a candy thermometer, or until ½ teaspoon of the syrup forms a soft ball in cold water. Remove the saucepan from the heat and cool until the syrup stops bubbling. Pour the syrup in a fine stream into the beaten egg yolks, beating all the while. Place the bowl in cracked ice and beat the mixture until it is quite cold. Beat in the anisette. Whip 2 cups of the cream until stiff and fold into the beaten egg mixture. Rinse a 5-cup mold with cold water and fill it with the parfait. Freeze until firm, 4 to 5 hours. To serve: Turn the mold out onto a serving plate. Add confectioners' sugar to the remaining ½ cup cream and beat until stiff, then put it in a pastry bag and pipe a design over the top and sides. Decorate with glacéed cherries. Makes 1¼ quarts parfait.

⚜ COFFEE PARFAIT

1 cup sugar
¾ cup strong coffee infusion
¼ teaspoon salt
3 large egg whites
1½ teaspoons vanilla extract
2 cups heavy cream, whipped

Combine the sugar and coffee in a 1-quart saucepan. Bring to boiling point, stirring all the time. Continue boiling rapidly, without stirring, about 5 minutes or until mixture reaches the soft-ball stage (234° F.) on a candy thermometer. Remove syrup from the heat and cool about 1 minute. Meanwhile, add the salt to the egg whites and beat until they stand in soft stiff peaks. Pour the hot syrup in a fine stream over the beaten egg whites, beating the mixture all the while. Add the vanilla extract and continue beating until mixture is thick and cool. Fold in the whipped cream. Turn the mixture into 2 freezer trays, or into a 9- by 9- by 2-inch baking pan. Freeze without stirring until mixture is firm. Makes 1½ quarts.

VARIATION

COFFEE-RUM PARFAIT

Make Coffee Parfait and fold 2 to 3 tablespoons dark or light rum into the mixture along with the whipped cream.

⚜ MINT PARFAIT

1 cup sugar
¾ cup water
¼ teaspoon salt
3 large egg whites
2 tablespoons Crème de Menthe, or to taste
2 cups heavy cream, whipped
a few drops green food coloring

Combine the sugar and water in a 1-quart saucepan. Bring to the boiling point, stirring all the while, and boil rapidly, without stirring, about 5 minutes, or until mixture reaches the soft-ball stage (234° F.) on a candy thermometer. Remove from heat and cool about 1 minute. Meanwhile, add the salt to the egg whites and beat until they stand in soft stiff peaks. Pour the hot syrup in a fine stream over the beaten egg whites, beating the mixture all the while. Continue beating until mixture is thick and cool. Beat in the Crème de Menthe. Fold in the whipped cream and food coloring. Turn the mixture into 2 freezer trays, or into a 9- by 9- by 2-inch baking pan. Freeze until firm, without stirring. This mixture may also be flavored with vanilla, cognac, Kirsch, rum, etc. Makes 1½ quarts.

⚜ MOCHA PARFAIT

1 9- by 5- by 1-inch layer of Génoise or Jelly-Roll Sponge Cake
Heavy Sugar Syrup flavored with rum
1 pint chocolate ice cream, softened
3 tablespoons rum
1 pint Coffee Parfait, softened
2 tablespoons sugar
1½ teaspoons instant coffee
1 teaspoon vanilla extract
1 cup heavy cream
shaved sweetened or unsweetened chocolate, or chocolate cigarettes

Line the bottom and sides of a 9- by 5- by 3-inch loaf pan with heavy waxed paper, having the paper extend 2 to 3 inches above the top of the pan. Place the cake in the bottom of the pan and sprinkle it with the rum-flavored Sugar Syrup. Freeze for 1 hour. Combine the chocolate ice cream with the rum, spread over the cake, and freeze until firm. Spread Coffee Parfait over the chocolate layer and freeze until it is firm. The day before or several hours before serving, remove the mold from the pan by running a metal spatula around the sides between the paper and the pan. Lift the mold up by the waxed paper, place it on a serving tray, and remove paper. Add the sugar, instant coffee, and vanilla extract to the cream and whip until the cream stands in soft stiff peaks. Spread the cream over top and sides of the mold. Put the remaining whipped cream into a pastry bag fitted with a plain or rosette nozzle, and pipe crosswise rows of rosettes over the top of the mold. Garnish with shaved chocolate or with chocolate cigarettes, which can be obtained in specialty candy shops. Cut into 1-inch slices. Makes 9 servings or one 9- by 3-inch mold. (See illustration, page 909.)

⚜ PEACH PARFAIT CHANTILLY

1 pint vanilla ice cream
1⅓ cups heavy cream
⅔ cup toasted slivered almonds
4 to 5 medium-sized ripe peaches, sliced
2 teaspoons confectioners' sugar
3 drops vanilla extract

Remove the ice cream from the freezer and let it stand at room temperature until it begins to soften. Beat 1 cup of the cream and fold it into the ice cream along with ½ cup of the almonds. Turn the mixture into 2 ice-cube trays and freeze until the ice cream is soft-firm. Spoon into parfait glasses, alternating with sliced peaches. Combine the remaining cream, the sugar, and the vanilla extract. Beat the mixture until it stands in soft peaks. Serve as a topping over the parfait. Sprinkle with the remaining almonds. Makes 8 servings.

Fruit Sundaes (Coupes Glacées)

These combinations of ices or ice creams with fruit (usually marinated in a liqueur and sometimes with Chantilly Cream) are traditionally served in silver or crystal coupes or in short-stemmed saucer-shaped champagne glasses, usually as a luncheon dessert. The following recipes represent only a few of the many possible variations.

⚜ FROU-FROU SUNDAE

Fill each coupe or glass half-full with Vanilla Ice Cream. Cover the ice cream with chopped fresh peaches which have been marinated in Curaçao. Garnish with Chantilly Cream and top each serving with a glacéed cherry.

⚜ COUPE JACQUES

Put a large spoonful of Lemon Ice in the bottom of each coupe or glass. Add a spoonful of any desired fresh fruit or combination of fruits marinated in Kirsch. Fill with Strawberry Ice Cream.

⚜ PINEAPPLE SUNDAE

Put chopped pineapple marinated in Kirsch in the bottom of the coupe or glass. Add a scoop of pineapple ice or ice cream. Garnish with Chantilly Cream and top with a piece of glacéed pineapple.

⚜ VANDERBILT SUNDAE

Fill the coupe or glass half-full with Orange Ice. Cover with chopped fresh strawberries marinated in Grand Marnier. Just before serving pour in champagne. In France this is made with *fraises des bois* (wild strawberries).

Bombes

⚜ HOW TO MAKE A BOMBE

Use a round decorated mold or charlotte mold, preferably with a tight cover. Place the mold in a bowl of ice. Line the mold with any desired ice cream, coating the bottom thickly and spreading the ice cream evenly around the sides up to the edge, leaving a hollow space in the center for the filling. Fill with any desired Parfait, frozen mousse, or other filling and smooth off the top. Cover with waxed paper and then with the cover of the mold (or cover tightly with foil tied around the top) and put the bombe in the refrigerator. These operations must be performed as rapidly as possible to avoid melting. Freeze until firm. At least 1 hour before serving, take the mold out of the refrigerator, dip it quickly into hot water, dry, and unmold onto a round serving dish. Decorate as desired and return the bombe to the refrigerator until ready to serve. Cut into slices for serving. A 1½-quart mold makes 10 servings.

Bombes can be made with a wide variety of ice creams, fillings, and decorations, according to the taste and ingenuity of the maker.

⚜ BOMBE DIANE

1 quart vanilla ice cream
Mint Parfait
whipped cream
sugar
glacéed cherries
shaved unsweetened chocolate
deer-shape cookies

Line a chilled 1½-quart dome-shaped mold with vanilla ice cream. Fill the center with Mint Parfait (or parfait of other flavors). Spread vanilla ice cream over the top. Cover with the lid that fits the mold, or with foil tied around the top of the mold. Freeze until firm. At least 1 hour before serving unmold the Bombe onto a serving tray. Sweeten whipped cream to taste with sugar, put it in a decorator's tube fitted with a rosette nozzle, and decorate the Bombe with rosettes as desired. Return to the refrigerator until ready to serve; then garnish with shaved chocolate and thin cookies in the shape of deer. Makes 10 servings. (See illustration, page 910.)

⚜ BOMBE ESPERANZA

Marinate chopped glacéed fruit with Curaçao and mix with 1 pint Orange Ice. Line a mold as previously directed, using Pistachio Ice Cream. Fill the center with the fruit and ice mixture. Cover and refrigerate as previously directed.

⚜ BOMBE MARINETTE

Line a mold with Vanilla Ice Cream and fill the center with Strawberry Mousse, following the previous directions.

Special Ice-Cream Desserts

⚜ BAKED ALASKA (*Omelette Soufflée Norvégienne*)

- **1 9-inch Génoise layer, ¾ inch thick**
- **1 teaspoon salt**
- **5 large egg whites**
- **¼ teaspoon cream of tartar**
- **10 tablespoons sugar**
- **½ teaspoon vanilla extract**
- **1-quart brick ice cream**

Bake the Génoise in a square 9-inch pan (see recipe, page 965). Cool and place cake on a cutting board. Make it into an oval or oblong shape by cutting a strip 2 inches wide from each side and trimming the ends if desired. Set cake aside. Add the salt to the egg whites and beat them until they are foamy. Add the cream of tartar and beat until soft peaks form. Beat in the sugar, 1 tablespoon at a time. Continue beating until the egg whites stand in stiff peaks. Beat in the vanilla extract. Cut the brick of ice cream into slices 1 inch thick and arrange them over the cake. Trim the ice cream at the edges to conform with the shape of the cake. Cover completely with a thick layer of meringue. Put the leftover meringue in a pastry bag fitted with a star nozzle and pipe it over the top and sides in any pattern desired. Store the meringue-covered cake in the freezer until ready to serve it. Just before serving, place it in a preheated very hot oven (450° F.) 4 to 5 minutes, or until delicately browned. Serve at once. Makes 8 servings. (See illustration, page 900.)

Cherries Jubilee may be served with Baked Alaska.

⚜ NEAPOLITAN CASSATA

½ cup glacéed fruit
2 tablespoons rum
1 quart vanilla ice cream
1½ pints raspberry ice
1 pint coffee ice cream
1 cup heavy cream, whipped
citron
1 glacéed cherry

Soak glacéed fruit in rum while preparing the other ingredients. Line a 6-cup dome-shaped mold with a 1-inch layer of vanilla ice cream. (Return leftover vanilla ice cream to the freezer for use later.) Cover this with a 1-inch layer of raspberry ice. Cover the raspberry ice with a 1-inch layer of coffee ice cream, leaving a space in the center. Soften the reserved vanilla ice cream and fold into it the rum-soaked fruit and half the whipped cream. Spoon this mixture into the mold to finish filling it. Cover the mold with a lid or with foil and freeze until the ice cream is very firm. About an hour before serving, unmold onto a serving plate and frost with the remaining whipped cream. Return the mold to the freezer. When ready to serve, garnish mold with slices of citron and a glacéed cherry. Makes 10 servings. (See illustration, page 908.)

⚜ FROSTED LEMONS (*Citrons Givrés*)

6 large lemons
1 pint Lemon Ice
angelica

Wash the lemons and cut a lengthwise slice from the side of each. Remove the pulp and the juice and save them for other cooking purposes. (If you are making the Lemon Ice, part of the juice can be used in it.) Fill the lemon shells with Lemon Ice that is frozen very hard and replace the slices that were cut off the sides. Brush the outside of the lemon shells lightly with water. Store them in the freezer until ready to serve. Decorate with angelica. Makes 6 servings. (See illustration, page 909.)

Mandarin oranges or regular oranges may be prepared in the same way.

⚜ FROZEN TOURTE WITH ASSORTED FRUITS

1 thin round 9-inch Génoise layer
Sugar Syrup, flavored with Kirsch
1½ cups heavy cream
1 pint vanilla ice cream, softened
2 to 3 tablespoons Kirsch
½ cup diced fresh pineapple
¼ cup diced fresh strawberries
1 pint cherry ice cream, softened
1 pint chocolate ice cream, softened
Chantilly Cream
glacéed cherries

Place the Génoise layer in a round 9-inch spring-form pan. Sprinkle with the Kirsch-flavored Sugar Syrup. Whip ½ cup of the cream and fold it into the vanilla ice cream along with the Kirsch, pineapple, and strawberries. Spread over the cake layer. Freeze until firm. Whip another ½ cup of the cream and fold it into the softened cherry ice cream. Freeze until firm. Whip the remaining ½ cup cream and fold it into the softened chocolate ice cream. Spread over the cherry ice-cream layer. Freeze until firm. When ready to serve, transfer the tourte to a serving plate and garnish with rosettes of Chantilly Cream and glacéed cherries. Makes 12 to 16 servings. (See illustration, page 910.)

·21·
FRUIT DESSERTS

Fruit as a dessert may be served raw, poached or stewed in syrup, or as the chief component of more elaborate desserts.

Fresh ripe fruit in perfect condition has a triple appeal—to the eye, the nose, and the palate. It is one of the most popular everyday desserts in French homes, where a special fruit knife and fork are provided. For methods of peeling and serving oranges, see Culinary Techniques in Pictures. Cheese and wine frequently accompany fresh fruit (see Chapter 18).

Two or more fresh fruits cut up and flavored with a liqueur make a macédoine. Fruit cooked in sugar syrup is a compote. Other dessert dishes made with fresh fruit include pastries, fritters, puddings, and frozen desserts.

Additional recipes for desserts containing fruit appear in Chapters 20 and 22; fruit sauces are in Chapter 19.

⚜ HOW TO POACH OR STEW FRUITS

Fruit which is to be poached or stewed should not be overripe. The fruit may be left whole, halved, quartered, or sliced. It should be cooked in a fairly heavy sugar syrup, with a piece of vanilla bean cooked with the syrup or vanilla extract added after the fruit has finished cooking. Red or white wine is often used to replace all or part of the water. The fruit may be served in the syrup, or it may be transferred with a perforated spoon to a serving dish and the syrup reduced by one-fourth or one-half before it is poured over the fruit. Or the syrup may be thickened with a little cornstarch blended with water or wine, or by the addition of a little apricot jam or red-currant jelly. Cointreau, Crème de Menthe, Kirsch, or rum is often added to the syrup. Poached or stewed fruits are usually served cold.

⚜ BAKED APPLES (*Pommes Bonne Femme*)

6 tart baking apples
6 teaspoons butter
sugar
6 tablespoons dry white wine
2 tablespoons apricot jam

Wash and core apples, being careful not to break through the blossom end. Starting at the stem end, pare apples about ⅓ of the way down. Place them in a 10- by 7- by 2-inch baking pan, pared side up. Put a teaspoon of butter in the cavity of each apple and finish filling the cavity with sugar. Pour 1 tablespoon dry white wine over each. Pour hot water into the pan to a depth of ¼ inch. Cover pan with foil and bake in a preheated hot oven (400° F.) 25 minutes. Remove cover and baste with some of the liquid in the pan. Continue baking, uncovered, 15 to 20 minutes. Remove apples to individual serving dishes. Blend apricot jam with the liquid left in the pan. Heat and cook about 1 minute. Spoon over apples. Makes 6 servings.

⚜ APPLES BOURGEOISE

6 medium-sized tart apples
Vanilla Syrup
¾ cup mixed glacéed fruit
French Pastry Cream
toasted, slivered, blanched almonds, or Macaroon Crumbs
granulated sugar

Peel the apples, cut in half, and remove cores. Cook in Vanilla Syrup until apples are soft but still retain their shape. Cool them in the syrup. Transfer apples, cut side up, to a heatproof serving dish. Fill the apple cavities with mixed glacéed fruit and coat with French Pastry Cream. Sprinkle with toasted, slivered, blanched almonds, or with Macaroon Crumbs. Springle with sugar. Place in a preheated very hot oven (450° F.) 5 to 7 minutes, or until glazed. Makes 6 servings.

⚜ APPLES BRISSAC

6 medium-small apples
Vanilla Syrup
Grand Marnier
1 round Génoise layer
6-ounce glass currant jelly
1 tablespoon water
12 diamond-shaped pieces of angelica
Sabayon Sauce

Peel and core the apples and poach them in Vanilla Syrup until they are tender. Cool them in the syrup. Add Grand Marnier to taste to ¼ cup of the poaching syrup and sprinkle it over the Génoise layer. Place the cake on a serving plate. Melt the jelly with the water, brush it over the apples, and arrange them around the top of the cake. Decorate each apple with 2 diamond-shaped pieces of angelica. Serve with Sabayon Sauce flavored to taste with Grand Marnier. Makes 6 servings.

⚜ APPLES CHATEAUBRIAND

¾ cup sugar
2 cups water
2-inch vanilla bean
8 tart medium-sized apples
6 3-inch rounds of bread
butter
⅓ cup red-currant jelly

Combine the sugar, water, and vanilla bean in a 2-quart saucepan. Bring to boiling point and simmer 5 minutes. Peel and core apples and add 4 apples at a time to the hot syrup. Cook, uncovered, until apples are tender when pierced with a toothpick but still hold their shape. Cool them in the syrup. Fry the bread rounds in butter over moderate heat, turning to brown both sides. Put a round of bread in each of 8 serving dishes and place a well-drained apple on each round. Melt the jelly and spoon it over apples. Makes 8 servings.

⚜ APPLE COMPOTE

6 large apples
1 tablespoon lemon juice
½ cup water
¾ cup sugar
2 cups water
dash salt
2-inch piece vanilla bean, or 1 teaspoon vanilla extract

Peel apples, remove cores, and cut apples into quarters. Mix the lemon juice and the ½ cup water, and dip apples in this mixture to prevent discoloration.

Meanwhile, combine sugar, 2 cups water, salt and vanilla bean (if used) in a 2-quart saucepan and bring to boiling point. Reduce heat and boil slowly 5 minutes. Add apples, cover, and cook gently until they are tender but still hold their shape, basting occasionally or turning carefully. If the vanilla bean was not used, add the vanilla extract. Cool in the syrup. Serve as a meat accompaniment or as a dessert. Makes 6 servings.

SPICED APPLES

Prepare as in preceding recipe but add 2 sticks cinnamon, each 2 inches long, to the sugar and water and cook with the apples. Sprinkle each serving with a dash of nutmeg.

⚜ APPLE DUMPLINGS NORMANDE (*Douillons à la Normande*)

6 medium-large cooking apples (Rome Beauty, Jonathan, Northern Spy)
¾ cup sugar
¼ teaspoon salt
1¼ teaspoons ground cinnamon
Plain Pastry, using 3 cups flour
6 teaspoons butter
1 tablespoon milk
sugar
Chantilly Cream (optional)

Wash apples, peel, and core, being sure not to cut through the blossom end. Mix the next 3 ingredients and spoon 2 tablespoons into each of the apple cavities. Roll two-thirds of the pastry into a 15½-inch square, ⅛ inch thick. With a fluted pastry cutter, cut the pastry into 4 squares of equal size. Place an apple in the center of each and top with 1 teaspoon butter. Bring opposite corners of pastry together over the top, pressing the sides together firmly. Repeat with the remaining dough, cutting 2 squares and using the 2 remaining apples. With a fluted pastry cutter, cut 6 1-inch circles from the leftover dough and place one over the center top of each apple, pressing it down with the index finger. Brush the surface of each dumpling with milk and sprinkle lightly with sugar. Bake in a preheated hot oven (425° F.) 35 minutes, or until apples are tender and pastry is brown. Serve warm or cold, with Chantilly Cream if desired. Makes 6 servings.

⚜ APPLE FRITTERS (*Beignets aux Pommes*)

3 large firm tart apples
3 tablespoons sugar
½ teaspoon ground cinnamon
1 tablespoon rum or Kirsch
Fritter Batter

Peel and core apples, and cut into crosswise slices about ¼ inch thick. Combine the sugar and cinnamon and sprinkle 1 tablespoon over the apples. Sprinkle with rum or Kirsch and marinate 1 hour. Drain well, pouring the juice into the Fritter Batter. Dip a few apple slices at a time into the batter and fry in hot deep fat (375° F.) until they are golden brown. Drain fritters on paper towels and arrange them in a baking pan. Sprinkle them with the remaining sugar and cinnamon. Place in a preheated hot oven (450° F.) 5 minutes to glaze. Makes 6 to 8 servings. (See illustration, page 899.)

Vanilla Sugar may be used instead of the sugar and cinnamon.

⚜ APPLES MARIETTE

6 large whole poached apples
6 tablespoons Sweet Chestnut Purée
rum to taste
Apricot Jam Sauce
toasted, shredded, blanched almonds

Poach apples as directed in the recipe for Apples Chateaubriand. Flavor Sweet Chestnut Purée to taste with rum and spoon it into the cavities of the apples. Cover with Apricot Jam Sauce and sprinkle with almonds. Serve warm or cold. If desired, replace the Chestnut Purée with rum-flavored Nesselrode, which is available in most stores in the fancy food department. Makes 6 servings.

APRICOT JAM SAUCE

1 cup apricot jam
⅓ cup water
1½ tablespoons sugar
1½ tablespoons brandy, cognac, Kirsch, Maraschino, or rum

Combine apricot jam, water, and sugar in a small saucepan. Bring to boiling point. Stir and cook 4 to 5 minutes, or only until thickened. Rub through a sieve. Cool and add brandy, cognac, Kirsch, Maraschino, or rum. Makes approximately ¾ cup.

⚜ POACHED WHOLE APPLES

Small apples should be used for this recipe.

8 cooking apples, 2 inches in diameter
2 tablespoons lemon juice
½ cup cold water
1 cup sugar
⅛ teaspoon salt
2 cups water
2-inch piece of vanilla bean, or 1 teaspoon vanilla extract
2 teaspoons sugar (optional)
⅓ cup heavy cream (optional)

Peel the apples and remove cores, leaving the apples whole. Rinse apples in cold water. Combine 1 tablespoon of the lemon juice with the ½ cup cold water and dip the apples into this mixture to prevent them from discoloring. Meanwhile mix the remaining lemon juice, the sugar, salt, 2 cups water, and the vanilla bean (if used) in a saucepan, bring to boiling point, and add 2 or 3 apples at a time. Cover and simmer until apples are tender when pierced with a fork. Using a perforated spoon, transfer apples to a serving dish. Repeat until all apples are cooked. If vanilla bean was not used, add vanilla extract to the syrup. Serve the apples in individual dishes, 1 to a serving, with a little of the syrup poured over each. If desired, beat 2 teaspoons sugar with ⅓ cup of cream until the cream stands in soft peaks and serve on the apples. Makes 8 servings.

⚜ APPLE SNOW

2 cups unsweetened chilled applesauce
1½ teaspoon vanilla extract
1 tablespoon orange juice
dash of salt
3 egg whites, unbeaten
3 tablespoons sugar
ground nutmeg

Combine the first 3 ingredients and set aside. Add salt to egg whites and beat them until they stand in soft, stiff peaks. Gradually beat in sugar. Fold in the applesauce mixture. Pile into individual compotes and sprinkle each with nutmeg. Makes 6 servings.

⚜ APRICOTS BOURDALOUE

1 recipe Génoise
12 apricot halves poached in Vanilla Syrup
½ cup Apricot Sauce II
glacéed cherries
angelica
½ cup heavy cream, whipped
1 cup Frangipane Cream
2 tablespoons Macaroon Crumbs

Bake the Génoise in a 6-cup savarin mold (ring mold). Cool cake in the mold 10 minutes and turn it out onto cooling rack to finish cooling with the top side up. When it is cold, place it on a serving plate. Drain apricot halves well and arrange them around the top of the cake, having them slightly overlapping. Cover with Apricot Sauce II. Garnish with glacéed cherries and angelica. Fold the whipped cream into Frangipane Cream and fill the hole in the center of the cake. Sprinkle with Macaroon Crumbs. Makes 6 servings.

⚜ APRICOT COMPOTE

¾ cup sugar
2 cups water
1/16 teaspoon salt
1 tablespoon lemon juice
2-inch piece vanilla bean, or 1 teaspoon vanilla extract
12 fresh apricots

Combine the first 4 ingredients in a 1 ½-quart saucepan, with the vanilla bean (if used). Bring to boiling point and simmer 5 minutes. Peel apricots, remove seeds, and add apricots to the syrup. Cover and cook gently 5 minutes, or until apricots are tender. Add vanilla extract if vanilla bean was not used. Chill and serve in individual dishes. Makes 4 servings.

VARIATION

APRICOTS ANTOINETTE

Poach apricots as in Apricot Compote. For each serving, place 2 apricot halves in a serving dish and top them with a scoop of coffee or vanilla ice cream. Add 1 teaspoon Kirsch to 2 tablespoons of the syrup and pour it over the ice cream.

⚜ APRICOT NÉGUS

12 firm ripe apricots
Vanilla Syrup
chocolate ice cream
Apricot Sauce II
Chantilly Cream

Peel apricots, cut them into halves, and remove seeds. Place them in a saucepan with Vanilla Syrup and simmer until they are tender. Cool in the syrup. Line the bottoms of 6 individual serving dishes with chocolate ice cream and place 2 apricot halves in each. Cover with Apricot Sauce II. Put Chantilly Cream on top. Makes 6 servings.

⚜ APRICOTS SOBIESKI

6 large apricots
Vanilla Syrup
raspberry ice cream or ice
6-ounce glass currant jelly
Chantilly Cream
Anisette

Peel the apricots, cut them in half, remove the seeds, and poach the halves in Vanilla Syrup until tender. Drain. Put raspberry ice cream or ice in each of 6 individual serving dishes, filling them one-third full. Place 2 well-drained apricot halves in each dish. Force the jelly through a coarse sieve and spoon it over the apricots. Flavor Chantilly Cream with Anisette to taste, put it in a pastry bag, and pipe rosettes as desired over the jelly. Makes 6 servings.

⚜ BAKED BANANAS WITH ALMONDS

4 large bananas
1 tablespoon lemon juice
6 tablespoons butter
½ cup sliced blanched almonds
1 tablespoon rum or sherry
¼ cup light brown sugar

Peel the bananas and cut them into lengthwise halves. Place them in a shallow baking dish. Brush with the lemon juice. Melt the butter in a skillet. Add the almonds, stir, and cook until they have turned golden brown. Add rum or sherry and pour over bananas. Sprinkle with brown sugar. Bake in a preheated moderate oven (375° F.) 15 minutes. Serve as a dessert or a meat accompaniment. Makes 8 servings.

⚜ BANANAS BOURDALOUE

2 cups milk
2-inch piece vanilla bean, or 1½ teaspoons vanilla extract
4 tablespoons cornstarch
½ cup sugar
1/16 teaspoon salt
4 large egg yolks, beaten
9-inch baked Sweet Pastry tart (pie) shell
½ cup sugar
1 cup water
dash salt
1 teaspoon lemon juice
6 medium-sized bananas
½ cup Macaroon Crumbs
confectioners' sugar
2 tablespoons butter, melted
Apricot Sauce (optional)

Heat 1¾ cups of the milk, with the vanilla bean (if used), reserving the remaining ¼ cup of milk. Combine cornstarch, sugar, and salt in a saucepan, add the reserved ¼ cup of milk, and mix well. Gradually add the hot milk. Stir and cook until the mixture is very thick. Blend a little of the hot mixture with the beaten egg yolks and gradually stir them into remaining hot mixture. Stir and cook over low heat until mixture is about as thick as mayonnaise. Remove from heat and strain. If vanilla bean was not used, add vanilla extract now. Cool completely. Turn half of the pastry cream into the baked tart (pie) shell, reserving the remaining half to use later. Combine next 4 ingredients in a saucepan and bring to boiling point. Peel bananas, cut into crosswise halves, and then cut the halves in half lengthwise. Put half the bananas in the hot syrup and cook 2 to 3 minutes. Remove bananas from syrup, drain well, and set aside. Cook the remaining bananas. Place the drained bananas over the pie filling, covering the cream completely. Spread the remaining cream over the bananas, sprinkle with Macaroon Crumbs, and drizzle with melted butter. Place in preheated very hot oven (450° F.) 3 to 4 minutes to glaze. If desired, serve with Apricot Sauce. Makes 6 servings.

⚜ BANANAS COPACABANA

2 tablespoons rum
2½ cups Vanilla Syrup
3 bananas
vanilla ice cream
Chocolate Sauce
sliced toasted almonds

Place the rum and Vanilla Syrup in a 1-quart saucepan. Bring to boiling point. Peel the bananas, cut them into crosswise halves, and add them to the hot syrup. Cover and cook 2 to 3 minutes. Cool bananas in the syrup. Line the bottoms of 6 individual serving dishes with vanilla ice cream. Place a drained banana half in each. Cover with Chocolate Sauce. Sprinkle the tops with slivered toasted almonds. Makes 6 servings.

⚜ FLAMBÉED BANANAS MARTINIQUE

¼ cup (½ stick) butter
½ cup sugar
½ cup orange juice
1 tablespoon lemon juice
¼ cup apricot jam
6 large firm ripe bananas
¼ cup rum
toasted, slivered, blanched almonds

Melt the butter in a saucepan. Add the sugar and cook until the mixture begins to turn golden (caramelize), stirring constantly. Add the orange juice, lemon juice, and apricot jam. Stir and cook 1 to 2 minutes. Peel the bananas, cut them in half lengthwise, and place them in the sauce. Cook 3 to 4 minutes. Transfer bananas to a chafing dish or a serving dish. Heat the rum, ignite, and quickly pour it over the bananas. As soon as the flame is out, sprinkle with toasted, slivered, blanched almonds. Makes 6 servings.

⚜ BANANA FRITTERS

3 bananas
1 tablespoon sugar
1 tablespoon lemon juice
2 tablespoons rum or brandy
Sweet Fritter Batter
Lemon Sauce, Orange Sauce, or Rum Sauce

Peel the bananas and cut them into slices 1 inch thick. Add the next 3 ingredients and marinate 1 hour, turning occasionally. Drain the bananas well and dip the slices into Sweet Fritter Batter. Drop them, a few at a time, into deep fat preheated to (375° F.). Fry until golden brown. Drain on paper towels. Serve hot with Lemon Sauce, Orange Sauce, or Rum Sauce. Or, if desired, serve as an accompaniment to meats. Makes 6 to 8 servings.

⚜ BANANAS ORIENTAL STYLE

2 tablespoons lemon juice
1 slice of lemon
Vanilla Syrup
4 bananas
almond ice cream
Custard Sauce
rosewater (can be bought in drugstores)
slivered toasted almonds

Combine the first 3 ingredients in a 1½-quart saucepan and bring to boiling point. Peel the bananas and cut them into slices 1 inch thick. Add them to the syrup, cover, and cook 1 to 2 minutes. Cool in the syrup. Put almond ice cream in each of 6 individual serving dishes, filling them one-third full. Cover with well-drained bananas. Flavor Custard Sauce to taste with rosewater and spoon over the bananas. Sprinkle with slivered toasted almonds. Makes 6 servings.

⚜ CANTALOUPE BALLS AND STRAWBERRIES WITH KIRSCH

2 small cantaloupes
1½ cups sliced strawberries
3 tablespoons sugar
4 tablespoons Kirsch
fresh mint

Cut the cantaloupes in half. Remove the seeds and cut the flesh into balls with a French melon-ball cutter. Scoop out the meat that remains in the shells and save it to add to fruit cups and salads. Reserve the shells. Combine the cantaloupe balls, strawberries, sugar, and Kirsch and marinate 30 minutes. Notch the cantaloupe shells and fill them with the cantaloupe balls and strawberries. Garnish each with a sprig of mint. Makes 4 servings.

⚜ FLAMBÉED FRESH CHERRIES

1½ pounds fresh sweet cherries
¼ cup sugar
½ cup sweet red wine (not port)
¼ cup water
1 stick cinnamon
1 teaspoon cornstarch
1 tablespoon water or sweet red wine
2 tablespoons red-currant jelly
¼ cup Kirsch

Wash the cherries and remove stones. Combine the sugar, wine, water, and cinnamon in a saucepan. Bring to boiling point, reduce heat, and simmer 5 minutes. Add cherries and cook 5 minutes, or until cherries can be easily pierced with a toothpick. Transfer cherries to a large serving dish. Boil syrup gently 3 to 4 minutes. Blend the cornstarch with the 1 tablespoon water or wine, and add to the syrup. Bring to boiling point and cook about 1 minute. Stir in red-currant jelly and pour over cherries. Just before serving, heat the Kirsch, ignite, and quickly pour it over the cherries. Bring to the table flaming. The secret of success in making Flambéed Cherries is to have both the cherries and the Kirsch hot, and to ignite the Kirsch as it is being poured over the cherries. If this rule is followed, success should be achieved every time. Makes 6 servings.

⚜ CHERRIES JUBILEE

1 pint jar Bing cherries
1 teaspoon cornstarch
¼ cup Kirsch

Drain the juice from the cherries into a saucepan, or into the top pan of a chafing dish. Blend the cornstarch with 1 tablespoon of the juice and add to the rest of the juice. Stir and cook until juice has thickened slightly. Add cherries and cook until they are heated through. Heat the Kirsch, ignite, and quickly pour it over the cherries. Serve the flaming cherries and sauce over vanilla ice cream, or serve alone. Makes 4 servings.

⚜ CHERRIES IN KIRSCH

2½ pounds sweet cherries
½ cup sugar
¾ cup water
2 cups dry red wine
¼ cup Kirsch
vanilla ice cream (optional)

Wash and pit the cherries. Crack 18 of the pits and tie them up in a cheesecloth bag. Combine the next 3 ingredients, add the bag of pits, bring the mixture to boiling point, and cook 5 minutes. Add cherries, cover, and simmer 10 minutes. Using a perforated spoon, remove the cherries to a serving dish. Reduce the syrup to 1¾ cups and strain it through a fine sieve. Add the Kirsch to the syrup and pour over the cherries. Serve in individual dishes as a dessert. If desired, top with vanilla ice cream. Makes 10 servings.

⚜ CHERRIES VICTORIA

6 small round slices Brioche
¼ cup Kirsch
1½ pounds sweet cherries
¼ cup sugar
¼ cup water
½ cup sweet red wine (not port)
1½ cups fresh strawberries
sugar
dash of salt
¼ teaspoon vanilla extract
1 teaspoon lemon juice

Soak the Brioche slices in the Kirsch and place a slice in each of 6 custard cups. Pit the sweet cherries and cook them in the sugar, wine, and water, as in recipe for Flambéed Cherries. While hot, pour them over the Brioche slices. Wash and hull the strawberries, crush, and sweeten to taste with sugar. Add the salt, vanilla extract, and lemon juice. Pour over the cherries. Makes 6 servings.

⚜ FIG COMPOTE

1 quart ripe figs
¾ cup sugar
2 cups water
dash salt
1 tablespoon lemon juice
2-inch piece vanilla bean, or 1½ teaspoon vanilla extract
2 tablespoons Kirsch

Wash the figs, cut into lengthwise halves, and set aside. Combine the next 4 ingredients in a 2-quart saucepan, with the vanilla bean (if used). Mix well, bring to boiling point, and simmer, uncovered, 5 minutes. Add figs and cook 5 minutes. Add the Kirsch (and the vanilla extract if the vanilla bean was not used) and let the figs cool in the syrup. Serve as a dessert. Makes 8 servings.

⚜ GRAPEFRUIT IN STRAWBERRY SAUCE

3 large grapefruit
1½ cups strawberries
1 tablespoon orange juice
1 teaspoon lemon juice
3 tablespoons sugar
6 whole unhulled strawberries

Peel and section the grapefruit and arrange the sections in sherbet glasses. Wash the strawberries and remove hulls, then crush the strawberries and push them through a sieve. Add orange juice, lemon juice, and sugar. Mix well and spoon the purée over the grapefruit sections. Garnish each with a whole unhulled strawberry. Makes 6 servings.

⚜ NECTARINES BOURDALOUE

Use the recipe for Apricots Bourdaloue, replacing the apricots with nectarines. Makes 6 servings.

NECTARINES SOBIESKI

Use the recipe for Apricots Sobieski, replacing the apricots with nectarines.

⚜ ORANGE-COCONUT COMPOTE

6 medium-sized navel oranges
½ cup sugar
1 cup water
½ cup grated fresh coconut or flaked coconut

Peel and section the oranges. Set aside. Combine the sugar and water in a saucepan, bring to boiling point, and boil 1 minute. Add orange sections and simmer 1 minute. Cool. Chill in the syrup. Serve in tall sherbet glasses, each garnished with 1 tablespoon coconut. Makes 8 servings.

⚜ ORANGES RIVIERA

about ½ pound almond paste
green food coloring
12 medium-sized navel oranges
colored candy decorettes
3 pints orange ice cream, orange sherbet, or orange ice
assorted cookies or small cakes

Color the almond paste light green with green food coloring and shape it into 12 short stems and 12 small leaves to simulate orange stems and leaves. Set them aside. Wash and dry oranges and cut a slice from the top of each. Place an almond-paste stem and leaf in the center of each slice. Put the remaining almond paste in a pastry bag fitted with a fine nozzle and pipe small sprays on each slice. Decorate as desired with colored candy decorettes. Set the slices aside. Remove the pulp from the oranges with a sharp paring knife, leaving the shells intact. Chill the shells thoroughly. About one hour before serving, fill the shells with orange ice cream, orange sherbet, or orange ice. Cover the shells with the decorated orange slices and store them in the freezer until serving time. To serve, place the filled orange shells on laurel leaves or on candied sections of orange peel and arrange them on a round tray. Serve with cookies or small cakes. For a more fanciful presentation, fill a ceramic orange-shaped bowl with small cakes or cookies and place it in the center of the tray. If desired, put the same kind of almond-paste decoration on the ceramic cover as was put on the orange slices. Makes 12 servings. (See illustration, page 38.)

⚜ PEACHES BOURDALOUE

Use the recipe for Apricots Bourdaloue, replacing the apricots with peaches. Makes 6 servings.

⚜ PEACHES IN CHANTILLY CREAM

1 cup crushed fresh peaches
1 cup sifted confectioners' sugar
⅛ teaspoon salt
1⅓ cups heavy cream
1 teaspoon vanilla extract
1 tablespoon granulated sugar

Combine the peaches, ¼ cup of the confectioners' sugar, and the salt and set aside. Whip 1 cup of the cream until almost stiff and gradually beat in the remaining confectioners' sugar and the vanilla extract. Fold in the peaches. Turn the mixture into a serving bowl. Add the granulated sugar to the remaining ⅓ cup cream and beat until it stands in stiff peaks. Using a pastry bag, pipe whipped-cream rosettes over the top of the mixture. Makes 6 servings.

⚜ PEACH COMPOTE

In the recipe for Apricot Compote, replace the apricots with peaches. Makes 6 servings.

⚜ FLAMBÉED PEACHES I

6 large or 9 medium-sized peaches
¾ cup sugar
2 cups water
1 teaspoon lemon juice
dash of salt
1-inch piece of vanilla bean, or ½ teaspoon vanilla extract
¼ cup Kirsch

Dip the peaches in boiling water, then in cold water, and remove the skins. Cut peaches into halves and remove pits, reserving 4 of the pits. Place reserved peach pits, the next 4 ingredients and the vanilla bean (if used) in a 1½-quart saucepan, bring to boiling point and simmer 5 minutes. Add one-third of the peaches at a time and cook them until they are tender when pierced with a toothpick. As the peaches are cooked, transfer them to a serving dish. If vanilla extract is used instead of vanilla bean, add it to the syrup and pour syrup over the peaches. Heat the Kirsch, ignite, and pour over the peaches. Bring to the table flaming. Makes 6 servings.

⚜ FLAMBÉED PEACHES II

Poach 6 large or 9 medium-sized peaches as instructed for Flambéed Peaches I. Sweeten ½ cup crushed strawberries to taste with sugar, heat, put in a serving dish, and pour the hot poached peaches over the strawberries. Heat ¼ cup Kirsch, ignite, and pour over peaches and crushed strawberries. Bring to the table flaming. Makes 6 servings.

⚜ PEACHES MONTREAL

12 poached peach halves
12 almond macaroons
⅓ cup Benedictine
sugar
⅓ cup Kirsch

Drain the syrup from poached peaches and wipe them dry with paper towels. Soak the macaroons in Benedictine and sprinkle them with sugar. Arrange them in a serving dish large enough to accommodate the peaches, and place a poached peach half on each macaroon. Heat the Kirsch, ignite, and pour it over the peaches and macaroons. Bring to the table flaming. Makes 6 servings.

⚜ PRALINE PEACHES

12 poached peach halves
12 rounds Génoise, ½ inch thick and 3 inches in diameter
Praline Condé
sugar
2 tablespoons apricot jam

Poach the peach halves in syrup (see How to Poach Fruits), drain, and wipe dry with paper towels. Reserve the syrup. Place a peach half on each round of Génoise and spoon Praline Condé on top. Sprinkle with sugar. Place in a preheated hot oven (425° F.) 5 minutes, or until the surface has glazed. Arrange the peaches in a silver dish or an attractive china bowl. Simmer the poaching syrup 5 minutes, add apricot jam, and pour the mixture over the peaches. Makes 6 servings.

⚜ PEACHES SOBIESKI

Use the recipe for Apricots Sobieski, replacing the apricots with 6 medium-sized peaches.

⚜ PEACHES SURPRISE

6 stewed peach halves
vanilla ice cream
apricot jam
6 rounds of Génoise or Sponge Cake
Kirsch or Cointreau
sliced toasted almonds

Drain peaches and pat dry with paper towels. Fill cavity of each with a scoop of vanilla ice cream, rounding it high enough to make the peach look whole. Coat the ice cream and the sides of the peach with apricot jam. Sprinkle cake rounds with Kirsch or Cointreau and top each with an ice-cream-stuffed peach. Scatter slivered almonds over the top. Serve immediately. Makes 6 servings.

⚜ PEARS BOURDALOUE

1 cup milk
1 cup light cream
2-inch piece vanilla bean, or 1½ teaspoons vanilla extract
4 tablespoons cornstarch
½ cup sugar
1/16 teaspoon salt
4 large egg yolks, beaten
9-inch baked Plain Pastry tart (pie) shell
½ cup sugar
1 cup water
dash salt
1 teaspoon lemon juice
3 medium-sized firm ripe pears
½ cup Macaroon Crumbs
confectioners' sugar
2 tablespoons butter, melted
Apricot Sauce (optional)

Heat the milk and ¾ cup of the light cream, with vanilla bean (if used), reserving ¼ cup of the cream for later use. Combine cornstarch, sugar, and salt in a saucepan, add remaining ¼ cup of cream, and mix well. Gradually add the hot milk. Stir and cook until the mixture is very thick. Blend a little of the hot mixture with the beaten egg yolks and gradually stir them into the remaining hot mixture. Stir and cook over low heat until mixture is about as thick as mayonnaise. Remove from heat and strain. If vanilla bean was not used, add vanilla extract now. Cool completely. Turn half the pastry cream into the baked tart (pie) shell, reserving the remaining half to use later.

Combine the next 4 ingredients in a saucepan and bring to boiling point. Peel pears, cut them in lengthwise halves, and remove cores. Put half of the pears in the hot syrup, cover and cook 8 to 10 minutes, or until pears are tender when pierced with a toothpick. Remove pears from the syrup and set aside to drain. Repeat with the remaining pears. Place all the drained pears over the cream in the tart shell. Cover the pears with the remaining cream. Sprinkle with Macaroon Crumbs and drizzle with melted butter. Place in a preheated very hot oven (450° F.) 3 to 4 minutes to glaze. If desired, serve with Apricot Sauce. Makes 6 servings.

⚜ PEAR TARTLETS BOURDALOUE

Sweet Pastry
1 tablespoon cornstarch
⅓ cup flour
⅛ teaspoon salt
¾ cup sugar
5 egg yolks
1 cup milk
1 cup light cream
2-inch piece vanilla bean, or 1½ teaspoons vanilla extract
3 tablespoons butter
1 tablespoon cognac, Kirsch, or rum
8 poached pears
1 cup Macaroon Crumbs

Line 8 4-inch tart pans with Sweet Pastry rolled ⅛ inch thick. Bake in a preheated very hot oven (450° F.) for 5 minutes. Remove from the oven and set aside. Combine the next 4 ingredients in the top of a double boiler, or in a 1½-quart saucepan. Beat in the egg yolks and ¼ cup of the milk. Heat the remaining milk, the cream, and the vanilla bean (if used) together, and gradually beat into the sugar and egg mixture. Beat and cook over hot water (not boiling) or over very low heat until the cream is smooth and thickened. Strain into the top of a double boiler and place over hot water. If vanilla bean was not used, add vanilla extract now. Beat in butter and cognac, Kirsch or rum. Put 3 tablespoons of cream into each of the 8 semibaked tart shells and place a poached pear on top. Cover the pears with the remaining cream and sprinkle with Macaroon Crumbs. Return tarts to the very hot oven (450° F.) and bake 5 minutes. Chill and serve. Makes 8 servings.

⚜ PEAR COMPOTE

1¼ cups sugar
3 cups water
⅛ teaspoon salt
¼ cup lemon juice
2-inch piece vanilla bean, or 2 tablespoons vanilla extract
8 medium-sized pears
2 tablespoons cornstarch
2 tablespoons water
fresh mint

Combine the first 4 ingredients and the vanilla bean (if used) in a 1½-quart saucepan. Bring to boiling point and simmer, uncovered, 5 minutes. Peel, core, and quarter the pears. Add to the syrup, cover, and cook gently 20 to 25 minutes, or until pears are tender when pierced with a fork. If vanilla bean was not used, add vanilla extract. Cool and chill. Serve in compotes, garnished with fresh mint. Makes 6 servings.

⚜ FLAMBÉED PEARS

Follow directions for Flambéed Peaches I, replacing the peaches with 6 medium-large firm ripe pears. Makes 6 servings.

⚜ PEARS FLORETTA

¼ cup farina (semolina)
½ cup sugar
½ teaspoon salt
2 cups milk
2-inch piece vanilla bean, or 1½ teaspoon vanilla extract
1 envelope unflavored gelatin
¼ cup cold water
1 cup heavy cream, whipped
2½ pounds medium-small firm ripe pears
1 cup cold water
1 tablespoon lemon juice
½ cup sugar
2 cups red Bordeaux
1 stick cinnamon, 2 inches long
¼ cup red currant jelly
10 small circles candied orange peel
pistachio nuts

Combine the first 4 ingredients in a 1½-quart saucepan. Add vanilla bean (if used). Bring mixture to boiling point, reduce heat, and cook 5 to 10 minutes, or until the mixture thickens. Meanwhile, soften gelatin in cold water and blend with the hot cereal. If vanilla bean was used, remove it; if not, add vanilla extract now. Chill the mixture in a pan of ice water until it begins to set. Fold in whipped cream and turn the mixture into a lightly oiled 8-inch ring mold. Chill until firm.

Peel the pears, leaving them whole with stems attached. Combine the 1 cup of cold water and the lemon juice, and drop the pears into the mixture as they are peeled, to prevent discoloration. Combine the next 3 ingredients in a 1½-quart pan, mix well, and bring to boiling point. Add half the pears and simmer them 10 minutes, or until pears are tender (do not cook pears too much). Transfer pears to a bowl. Add remaining pears and cook them only until tender. Put pears in the bowl with the first lot. Return syrup to the heat and cook until it spins a short thread (230° F.). Add the jelly and mix well. Stir and cook slowly until the sauce coats a spoon. Unmold the farina onto a serving plate. Drain the pears. Dip 4 to 5 pears in the jelly glaze and place them in the center of the mold. Arrange the remaining pears around the outside of the mold. Garnish top of the mold with the circles of candied orange peel and with pistachio nuts. Makes 6 servings. (See illustration, page 905.)

⚜ PEARS SCHOUVALOFF

6 medium-small pears
½ cup sugar
2 cups water
1 teaspoon lemon juice
1/16 teaspoon salt
2-inch piece vanilla bean, or ½ teaspoon vanilla extract
8-inch round of Sponge Cake
⅓ cup apricot jam
Soft Meringue, made with 3 egg whites
red currant jelly
pistachio nuts
2 tablespoons Kirsch (optional)

Wash and peel the pears, cut them in halves crosswise, and remove the cores. Combine the sugar, water, lemon juice, salt, and vanilla bean (if used). Bring to the boiling point and simmer 5 minutes. Add half the pears. Cover and cook gently 8 to 10 minutes, or until pears are tender when tested with a toothpick. Transfer pears to a bowl. Add remaining pears to the syrup and cook gently until they are tender. Combine all the cooked pears in the syrup, add vanilla extract if vanilla bean was not used, and let pears cool. Place the Sponge Cake on a baking sheet. Spread it with apricot jam and arrange the pears on the jam, with stem ends pointing toward the center. Cover with two-thirds of the meringue and smooth it over the top. Put the remaining meringue in a pastry bag fitted with a star nozzle and pipe a lattice pattern over the top. Place in a preheated very slow oven (275° F.) 20 to 25 minutes, or until the meringue is dry and slightly colored. Cool. Place cake on a serving plate. Drop a bit of red currant jelly in each of the squares of the lattice pattern. Place a pistachio nut on each. If desired, mix Kirsch with the syrup in which the pears were poached and spoon over each serving. Makes 6 servings.

⚜ PEARS IN RED WINE

8 medium-sized firm ripe pears
½ cup water and 1 tablespoon lemon juice, mixed
¾ cup sugar
2 cups dry red wine
2 tablespoons Kirsch or Cointreau (optional)

Peel, quarter, and core pears and drop them into the water and lemon juice mixture to prevent discoloration. Combine sugar and wine and cook 5 minutes. Add pears, cover, and cook gently until they are tender when pierced with a fork. Transfer pears to a serving dish. Cook syrup until it has reduced to three-quarters the original amount. If desired, add Kirsch or Cointreau. Pour the syrup over the pears. Serve cold. Makes 8 to 10 servings.

⚜ FRESH PINEAPPLE COMPOTE

1 medium-sized fresh pineapple
¾ cup sugar
1½ cups water
1 tablespoon lemon juice
dash salt
2-inch piece vanilla bean, or 1½ teaspoons vanilla extract
2 tablespoons rum or Kirsch

Peel the pineapple, slice, cut into wedges, and remove core. Set aside. Combine the next 4 ingredients and the vanilla bean (if used) in a saucepan, bring to boiling point, and simmer 5 minutes. Add pineapple, cover, and cook 5 minutes, or until pineapple is tender. Using a perforated spoon, remove pineapple from syrup. Reduce syrup by one-fourth, add rum or Kirsch and vanilla extract if vanilla bean was not used, and pour over pineapple. Cool in the syrup. Serve as dessert or as a meat accompaniment. Makes 6 servings.

⚜ PINEAPPLE FRITTERS

1 medium-sized fresh pineapple
2 tablespoons sugar
2 tablespoons rum or cognac
Sweet Fritter Batter
Pineapple-Rum Sauce, or Lemon Sauce

Peel the pineapple and cut it into slices ¾ inch thick. Cut the slices into quarters and cut out and discard the cores. Sprinkle the pineapple with sugar and rum. Marinate 1 hour, turning occasionally. Drain pineapple well. Drop the pineapple quarters, a few at a time, into the Sweet Fritter Batter. Fry in deep fat preheated to 375° F. until golden brown. Drain on paper towels. Serve fritters with Pineapple-Rum Sauce or Lemon Sauce. Or, if desired, serve as an accompaniment to meats. Makes 6 to 8 servings.

⚜ PINEAPPLE AND STRAWBERRY CUP

¼ cup sugar
¾ cup water
1 teaspoon lemon juice
2-inch piece of vanilla bean, or 1 teaspoon vanilla extract
3 cups fresh pineapple wedges
1 cup sliced fresh strawberries
fresh mint

Combine the first 3 ingredients with the vanilla bean (if used) in a saucepan. Bring to boiling point and boil, uncovered, 2 minutes. Remove from heat and cool. Remove vanilla bean if used, or add vanilla extract now. Add fruit and chill. Serve in compotes, each garnished with a small sprig of mint. Makes 6 servings.

⚜ PLUM COMPOTE

In the recipe for Apricot Compote, replace the apricots with 2 pounds of plums. Makes 6 servings.

⚜ PRUNE COMPOTE

Cook prunes according to package directions, but replace water with dry red or white wine.

⚜ RASPBERRY COMPOTE

1 quart raspberries
¾ cup sugar
1 cup water
2 teaspoons cornstarch
2 tablespoons water

Wash raspberries and drain well. Set aside. Combine sugar and water in a 1-quart saucepan. Mix well and stir and cook to the soft-crack stage (290° F.). While syrup is still boiling, pour it over the raspberries. Cover and let stand until the raspberries have given up their juice. Using a perforated spoon, transfer raspberries to a serving dish. Blend the cornstarch with the 2 tablespoons water and add to the hot syrup. Bring to boiling point and cook until syrup has thickened slightly and is transparent. Pour over raspberries. Cool and chill. Makes 6 servings.

⚜ RHUBARB COMPOTE

2 pounds rhubarb
⅓ cup water
dash salt
1 cup sugar
2-inch piece vanilla bean, or 1½ teaspoons vanilla extract

Cut off the leaves and coarse big ends of the rhubarb stalks. Wash and peel the older stalks, but do not peel the young tender ones, since the peel turns pink when cooked. Cut stalks into 1-inch pieces. Add water, salt, sugar, and vanilla. Cover and cook over low surface heat 25 to 30 minutes. Or, if desired, omit water, mix salt with sugar and sprinkle over rhubarb, add vanilla, and bake in a covered casserole in a preheated moderate oven (375° F.) 45 to 50 minutes, or until rhubarb is tender. Do not stir. Serve as an accompaniment to meat or as a dessert. Makes 6 servings.

VARIATION

SPICED RHUBARB

Add 2 sticks cinnamon, each 2 inches long, and 4 whole cloves to rhubarb and cook in either of the ways described in recipe for Stewed Rhubarb.

⚜ STRAWBERRY COMPOTE

In the recipe for Raspberry Compote, replace raspberries with 1 quart of fresh strawberries. Add ¼ cup red currant jelly to the syrup before pouring over the drained strawberries. Makes 6 servings.

⚜ STRAWBERRY CREAM

1 quart strawberries
5 tablespoons granulated sugar
2 tablespoons Kirsch
1 cup heavy cream, whipped
2 tablespoons confectioners' sugar
½ teaspoon vanilla extract
6 whole unhulled strawberries

Wash, hull, and slice the 1 quart strawberries. Sprinkle with the granulated sugar and the Kirsch. Combine the whipped cream, confectioners' sugar, and vanilla extract. Fold in strawberries. Turn into a freezer tray and place in the freezer until very cold but not frozen. Remove and serve at once in tall sherbet glasses. Top each glass with a whole unhulled strawberry. Makes 6 servings.

⚜ STRAWBERRIES ROMANOFF

1 quart fresh strawberries
¼ cup orange juice
2 tablespoons Curaçao
1 pint vanilla ice cream
Chantilly Cream

Wash and hull the strawberries. Add the orange juice and Curaçao and marinate 1 hour in the refrigerator. Line serving dishes with vanilla ice cream and spoon the strawberries over it. Decorate with Chantilly Cream put through a pastry bag fitted with a fluted nozzle. Makes 6 servings.

⚜ COMPOTE OF MIXED FRUITS (*Macédoine*)

¾ cup sugar
2 cups water
dash salt
1 tablespoon lemon juice
2-inch piece vanilla bean, or 1½ teaspoons vanilla extract
2 peeled pears, quartered
2 peeled peaches, quartered
2 peeled nectarines or apricots, quartered
1 cup fresh pineapple wedges
sweet cherries (optional)

Combine the first 4 ingredients in a saucepan, with the vanilla bean (if used). Bring to boiling point and simmer, uncovered, 5 minutes. Add the pears, cover, and cook gently 10 minutes. Add the remaining fruit, cover, and cook 5 to 10 minutes, or until fruit is tender. If vanilla bean was not used, add vanilla extract. Cool in the syrup. If desired, add sweet cherries but cook them separately according to the recipe for Cherries in Kirsch, omitting the Kirsch. This method prevents the cherries from discoloring the other fruits. Makes 8 servings.

⚜ MIXED FRUITS IN CHAMPAGNE OR LIQUEUR (*Fruits Rafraîchis au Champagne ou à la Liqueur*)

Cook ½ cup sugar and 1½ cups water together for 5 minutes. Set aside to cool. Prepare a macédoine of fruit (orange sections, apple slices, pear slices, and banana slices) and place it in a large crystal bowl. Pour the cold syrup and 1 cup dry champagne or 1 cup of any desired liqueur over the fruit. Place the bowl in a pan of crushed ice and let it stand for 2 hours. Garnish the center with a Maraschino cherry or a whole unhulled strawberry. Allow ½ cup fruit for each serving. (See illustration, page 905.)

·22·

CAKES AND PASTRIES

In American cooking, the distinction between cake and pie is very definite, and the term pastry is usually applied to pie pastry, while a cake mixture is called a batter. In France, however, *gâteau*, which is translated as "cake," also covers concoctions made with puff pastry, chou pastry, and sweet pie pastry. The distinction in French culinary language is chiefly one of size, small cakes, cookies, tarts, etc., all being known as *petits gâteaux*. The American dessert pie is a *tarte* in France, the American tart a *tartelette*. Of the basic French pastry doughs, those for Génoise and sponge cake (*biscuit*) are given in this chapter; the others will be found in Chapter 3, under Doughs.

CAKES

⚜ GÉNOISE

Génoise is a very fine-textured French butter cake of which the only leavening agent is the air beaten into the eggs and the richness is due to having lukewarm melted butter folded into the batter near the end of the mixing period. It is light like a sponge cake but has a firmer and moister texture and cuts more easily. It is used as the basis of other fine French cakes, petits fours, and many French desserts for which a layer of cake firmer than sponge cake is required.

Génoise is more difficult to make than a regular sponge cake or a conventional butter cake; therefore it is important that all rules be followed carefully. The ingredients must be at room temperature. The eggs should be beaten with the sugar in a warm bowl until they have doubled in volume. If the beating is done by hand, the bowl should be placed over (not in) warm water. If an electric mixer is used (which shortens the beating time), both the bowl and the beater should be warm (not hot) before the ingredients are added. After the eggs have been beaten and the sugar added, the rest of the ingredients should be very carefully folded into the batter.

The amount made by this recipe may be baked in a 15½- by 10½- by 1-inch jelly-roll pan, in 2 round or square 9-inch layer-cake pans, or in 2 or 3 round or square 8-inch layer-cake pans, depending on the thickness of layer desired.

After the cake is baked, it must be removed from the pan immediately to prevent it from becoming damp and heavy.

6 large eggs
1 cup fine granulated sugar
1½ teaspoons vanilla extract
1 cup sifted cake flour
¼ cup (½ stick) butter, melted

Choose pans of the size desired, grease the bottoms lightly, line with waxed paper, and grease the paper lightly. Set aside.

Break eggs into the larger bowl of an electric mixer, having both bowl and beater warm (not hot). Or break eggs into a large warmed mixing bowl. If this cake is mixed by hand, place the bowl *over warm* water. (The water should not be hot and the bowl should not be placed down in the water.) Use a warm beater. Beat eggs until foamy. Gradually beat in sugar and beat at high speed on the electric mixer, or beat vigorously by hand until the volume of eggs and sugar has doubled. Scrape sides and bottom of the bowl frequently so that the sugar will be well blended with the eggs. The mixture should stand in stiff peaks when the beater is withdrawn. Beat in the vanilla extract. If the eggs were beaten by hand, remove the bowl from over the warm water. Sift the flour and carefully fold in 2 tablespoons at a time, using a rubber spatula. Cool the melted butter to lukewarm and fold in 1 teaspoon at a time, being careful not to include any of the residue that has settled to the bottom of the pan. Pour the batter into the prepared cake pans. Bake in a preheated moderate oven 35 to 40 minutes, or until a cake tester or toothpick inserted in the center of the cake comes out clean. Remove the cake from the pan immediately, strip off the paper from the bottom, and cool the cake on a cooling rack. Génoise may be frosted as desired and served as a dessert, or used in the preparation of other desserts, or for frosted Petits Fours. Makes one 15½- by 10½-inch layer, or two 9-inch layers, or two to three 8-inch layers, depending upon the thickness desired.

⚜ SPONGE CAKE

6 large eggs, separated
1¼ cups sugar
2 teaspoons grated lemon rind
1 tablespoon lemon juice
1 teaspoon vanilla extract
½ teaspoon salt
1½ cups sifted cake flour
confectioners' sugar (optional)

Beat the egg yolks over hot water (not in it), until they are very thick and lemon-colored. Gradually beat in the sugar and lemon rind, beating well after each addition. Beat in the lemon juice and vanilla extract. Add the salt to the egg whites and beat until they are stiff but not dry. Pile the whites on top of the egg-yolk mixture. Sift flour over the whites and carefully fold both into the egg-yolk mixture. Turn the batter into an ungreased 10- by 4-inch tube-cake pan that has been rinsed in cold water and well drained. Bake in a preheated slow oven (325° F.) 1 hour, or until the cake has browned and pulls away from the sides of the pan. Invert the cake on a cooling rack to cool. Loosen cake from the sides of the pan and tube with a spatula. Turn the cake top side up on the cooling rack and lift off the pan. If desired, dust the top with confectioners' sugar. Or if desired cut the cake into layers and put them together with apricot jam, currant jelly or any desired filling. Makes one 10-inch tube cake. (For Jelly-Roll Sponge Cake Layer, see page 886.)

⚜ ALMOND CAKE (*Gâteau Pithivers*)

Puff Pastry
½ cup almond paste
1 cup French Pastry Cream
1 egg
2 tablespoons milk
confectioners' sugar (optional)

Roll out Puff Pastry ¼ inch thick on a lightly floured board. Cut it into two 9-inch circles, using a 9-inch round layer-cake pan as a guide. Combine almond paste and French Pastry Cream and spread over one of the circles to within ½ inch of the edge of the pastry. Cover with the second circle of Puff Pastry. Moisten the edge of the pastry and seal it by pressing firmly all around with the thumb. Beat the egg and milk together and brush over the top of the pastry. With a sharp knife, make curving lines out from the center and cut a small hole in the center of the pastry. Place the cake on a greased baking sheet lined with heavy brown paper. Chill 30 to 40 minutes. Bake in a preheated very hot oven (450° F.) 10 minutes, or until pastry has puffed and has begun to brown. Reduce heat to 350° F. (moderate) and bake 25 minutes. Reduce temperature to 300° F. (slow) and bake 10 minutes, or until the cake is golden brown. Sprinkle with confectioners' sugar while hot, if desired. Makes one 9-inch cake. (See illustration, page 903.)

⚜ ALMOND RING (*Couronne aux Amandes*)

1 envelope active dry yeast
¼ cup lukewarm water
1 cup sugar
¾ cup shortening
1½ cups milk, scalded
3 egg yolks, beaten
1½ teaspoons salt
about 6 cups sifted all-purpose flour
¼ cup (½ stick) butter, melted
⅔ cup chopped blanched almonds
1 egg white
1 tablespoon water
⅓ cup slivered blanched almonds

Soften the yeast in the lukewarm water with 1 teaspoon of the sugar. Add the shortening to the milk, cool it to lukewarm, and add to the yeast along with the remaining sugar, the beaten egg yolks, the salt, and 2 cups of the flour. Beat the batter until it falls in sheets from a spoon. Gradually add the remaining flour, stirring and kneading until the dough can be handled. Knead a few seconds longer. Shape the dough into a ball and place it in a greased bowl. Grease the top of the dough. Cover and let rise in a warm place (80 to 85° F.) until it has doubled in bulk. Punch down dough, shape it into 2 balls, cover, and let it rest 10 minutes. Roll each ball of dough into a 16- by 8-inch rectangle ¼ inch thick. Brush each with melted butter and sprinkle each with half the chopped blanched almonds. Starting at the long side roll up each ball in jelly-roll fashion. Place them on a baking sheet and join the ends to form rings. With scissors cut 1½-inch slices on a slant almost through to the opposite side of the ring. Combine the egg white and 1 tablespoon water, beat until foamy, and brush over the tops of the rings. Sprinkle them with slivered blanched almonds. Cover the rings and let them rise in a warm place until they have doubled in size. Bake in a preheated moderate oven (375° F.) 25 to 30 minutes until browned. Makes 2 rings. (See illustration, page 975.)

⚜ CARAQUE CAKE

5½ squares (5½ ounces) semisweet chocolate
4 large eggs
½ cup sugar
⅔ cup sifted all-purpose flour
¼ cup strong black coffee
1 tablespoon Crème de Menthe
Fondant Cake Icing

Have all ingredients at room temperature. Butter a round 9-inch layer-cake pan, line it with waxed paper, and butter the paper. Set aside. Cut a circle of waxed paper 2 inches in diameter. Melt 1 square of the chocolate and spread it on the waxed-paper circle. Chill until cake is ready to be frosted.

Break the eggs in a mixing bowl and place it over (not in) a pan of hot water. Gradually beat in the sugar and continue beating until the eggs and sugar have doubled in volume and hold their shape when the beater is withdrawn. (If possible, use an electric beater since this requires much beating.) Sift the flour 4 times and carefully fold it into the eggs, using a rubber spatula. Melt 4 squares of the chocolate over hot water, cool about 2 minutes, and fold into the batter, along with the coffee. Pour the batter into the prepared cake pan. Bake in a preheated moderate oven (350° F.) 30 minutes or until a toothpick inserted in the center comes out clean. Cool the cake in the pan 10 minutes. Turn out onto a cooling rack to finish cooling. Transfer cake to a serving plate. Add the Crème de Menthe to semimelted Fondant (see recipe for Fondant Cake Icing). Pour the icing over the top of the cake, being careful not to let it run down the sides. Let the icing set. Melt the remaining ½ square of chocolate, mix with the remaining icing, and with a cake-decorating tube make a dainty design around the edge of the cake. Remove the chocolate circle from the waxed paper and place it in the center of the cake. Makes one round 9-inch cake. (See illustration, page 983.)

⚜ CARVELLE CAKE (*Swiss*)

2 round 9-inch Génoise layers
8 squares (½ pound) unsweetened chocolate
Butter Filling and Frosting
1 tablespoon butter
1 package chocolate decorettes

Have the cake layers completely cool. Add 1 square of the chocolate to the Butter Frosting mixture while it is still hot and stir until chocolate has melted and is well blended with the frosting. Beat 2 to 3 minutes. Chill and beat again 2 to 3 minutes. Spread frosting between the layers and over the top and sides of the cake. Melt the remaining chocolate with the butter in a small bowl over hot water (not boiling). Mix well. Cover the bottom of a round 9-inch layer-cake pan with waxed paper cut to fit. Pour the chocolate mixture into it. Cool 2 to 3 hours, or until chocolate has hardened. Remove chocolate from the pan and cut into wedges while still on the paper. Remove the wedges from the paper and arrange them over the frosting that is on the top layer, having them slightly overlapping. Sprinkle chocolate decorettes on the frosting around the sides. Makes one 2-layer 9-inch cake. (See illustration, page 980.)

⚜ CHOCOLATE CAKE (*Gâteau Chocolatine*)

3 round 8-inch Génoise layers
Chocolate Butter-Cream Filling and Frosting
toasted chopped blanched almonds

Have the layers completely cool. Spread Chocolate Butter-Cream Filling and Frosting between the layers and over the top and sides. Sprinkle the frosting on the sides of the cake with toasted chopped blanched almonds. Makes one 3-layer 8-inch cake.

⚜ CHRISTMAS LOG (*Bûche de Noël*)

3 large eggs
1 cup sugar
5 tablespoons water
1½ teaspoons vanilla extract
1 cup sifted cake flour
¼ teaspoon salt
1 teaspoon double-acting baking powder
Coffee Butter-Cream Filling and Frosting
3 tablespoons cocoa

Line a greased 15½- by 10½- by 1-inch jelly-roll pan with waxed paper and grease the paper lightly. Beat eggs until they are thick and lemon-colored. Gradually beat in sugar. Add the water and vanilla extract all at one time and beat. Sift together the next 3 ingredients and add to the beaten eggs all at one time. Beat mixture only until it is smooth. Pour the batter into the prepared jelly-roll pan. Bake cake in a preheated moderate oven (375° F.) 15 minutes. Turn out onto a towel sprinkled with confectioners' sugar. Trim crust from the edges. Roll up towel and cake together. Cool. Unroll cake and spread it with Coffee Butter-Cream Filling and Frosting. Roll up the cake jelly-roll fashion. Add the cocoa to the remaining frosting and spread over the outside of the roll. Run the tines of a fork down the length of the roll to simulate the bark on the log. Make knots on the log with frosting and run the tines of a fork over them. Place the roll on a serving tray and add Christmas decorations. Makes 10 servings. (See illustration, page 984.)

⚜ FRANKFURT CROWN (*German*)

½ cup (1 stick) softened butter
¾ cup sugar
1 teaspoon grated lemon rind
4 large eggs
¾ cup sifted all-purpose flour
½ cup sifted cornstarch
2 teaspoons double-acting baking powder
rum, Kirsch, or Grand Marnier
Butter-Cream Filling and Frosting
Praline Powder, glacéed cherries, and pistachio nuts

Have all ingredients at room temperature. Place the first 3 ingredients in a mixing bowl. Mix until fluffy and well blended. Beat in the eggs one at a time. Sift together flour, cornstarch, and baking powder and gradually add to the first mixture. Turn the batter into a well-greased lightly floured 8½-inch ring mold, or a 9-inch tube cake pan. Bake in a preheated slow oven (325° F.) 40 minutes or until a toothpick inserted in the center of the cake comes out clean. Cool the cake in the pan 10 minutes. Turn out of the pan onto a cooling rack. When cold, split the cake into 3 or 4 layers and sprinkle each with rum, Kirsch, or Grand Marnier. Put the layers together in layer-cake fashion with a Butter-Cream Filling and Frosting. Frost the top and sides of cake with the same frosting. Sprinkle with Praline Powder. Put remaining frosting into a pastry tube with a rosette nozzle and decorate the top of cake with rosettes. Garnish each with a glacéed cherry and 2 pistachio nuts. This cake is best eaten after it is 1 day old. Makes one 8½- or 9-inch cake. (See illustration, page 984.)

⚜ HUNGARIAN CAKE

9 egg whites
1½ cups sifted confectioners' sugar
½ cup fine cracker crumbs
8 squares (½ pound) unsweetened chocolate, grated
2 tablespoons flour
1 teaspoon double-acting baking powder
½ cup ground nuts (hazelnuts, almonds, walnuts, or pecans)
¼ cup sweet white or red wine
2 teaspoons vanilla extract
1 tablespoon lemon juice
Chocolate Butter-Cream Filling and Frosting
shaved chocolate
confectioners' sugar
glacéed cherries (optional)

Grease 2 round 9-inch layer-cake pans, or 3 round 8-inch layer-cake pans. Line them with waxed paper cut to fit the pans and grease the paper. Set aside.

Beat egg whites until they stand in soft stiff peaks and gradually fold in sugar. Combine the next 5 ingredients, mixing them well, and carefully fold them into the beaten egg whites. Fold in the wine, vanilla extract, and lemon juice. Turn the batter into the prepared cake pans. Bake in a preheated moderate oven (350° F.) 40 to 45 minutes, or until a cake tester inserted in the center comes out clean. Frost the layers with Chocolate Butter-Cream Filling and Frosting. Garnish each with shaved chocolate, sprinkle with confectioners' sugar, and if desired put a glacéed cherry in the center. This cake may also be stacked in conventional layer-cake fashion with the top decorated as described. Makes 2 9-inch layers or 3 8-inch layers. (See illustration, page 981.)

⚜ KUGELHOPF

1 envelope active dry yeast
¼ cup lukewarm water
½ cup sugar
1¼ cups milk, scalded
¾ cup (1½ sticks) butter
1 teaspoon salt
1½ teaspoons vanilla extract
2 teaspoons grated lemon rind
4 cups sifted all-purpose flour
2 large eggs
½ cup raisins
¼ cup chopped blanched almonds (optional)
about 3 dozen whole blanched almonds (optional)
confectioners' sugar (optional)

Soften the yeast in the lukewarm water with 1 teaspoon of the sugar. Combine the hot milk with the butter and cool to lukewarm. Add the remaining sugar, the salt, vanilla extract, lemon rind, and softened yeast. Stir in 2 cups of the flour and beat well. Beat in the eggs, one at a time. Continue beating 5 minutes. (The longer the batter is beaten, the better the cake.) Stir in the raisins and the chopped almonds, if used. (If the raisins are too dry, steam them in a sieve over boiling water for a few minutes.) Gradually add the remaining flour. Mix well. Cover the bowl and let the dough rise in a warm place (80° to 85° F.) until it has doubled in size, about 1½ hours.

Butter two 7-inch crown (Kugelhopf) pans generously. If desired, place a circle of whole blanched almonds in the bottom of each. Put half the dough in each pan. Cover and let dough rise in a warm place until it has doubled in bulk. (The dough should have risen enough to almost fill the pans.) Bake in a preheated moderate oven (350° F.) 40 to 45 minutes. Cool the cakes in the pans 5 minutes, then turn them out onto cooling racks, crown side up. Sprinkle generously with confectioners' sugar, if desired. Makes 2 7-inch cakes. (See illustration, page 975.)

VARIATION

CHOCOLATE KUGELHOPF

Make the Kugelhopf recipe, omitting the lemon rind, raisins, and almonds, and using 4¼ cups flour. Divide the dough in half. Melt 2 squares (2 ounces) of unsweetened chocolate with 3 tablespoons milk and 2 tablespoons sugar in a cup over hot water. Cool slightly and add to one part of the dough. Roll out each part of the dough ¼ inch thick on a lightly floured board, adding a little more flour if dough is too soft to roll. Place the chocolate dough over the white dough and roll it up jelly-roll fashion. Place the roll in a well-buttered 9-inch Kugelhopf or tube cake pan and allow it to rise in a warm place until double in bulk. Bake as directed in a preheated moderate oven (350° F.) 45 to 50 minutes. Cool and frost with Chocolate Glaze. Makes 1 9-inch cake.

⚜ LÉMANIA CAKE (*Swiss*)

½ cup (1 stick) softened butter
1 cup sifted fine granulated sugar
¾ teaspoon baking soda
¼ teaspoon salt
1 teaspoon grated lemon rind
3 large eggs, separated
1¾ cups sifted all-purpose flour
¼ cup sifted cornstarch
2½ tablespoons lemon juice
½ cup milk
Lemon Butter-Cream Filling and Frosting (optional)

Stir softened butter until it is fluffy and lemon-colored. Gradually blend in the sugar, soda, salt, and lemon rind. Beat until the mixture is smooth and creamy. Beat in the egg yolks, one at a time, beating vigorously after each addition. Sift the flour with the cornstarch. Combine the lemon juice and milk. Add the flour mixture to the butter and egg mixture alternately with the milk and lemon juice. Beat the egg whites until they stand in soft, stiff peaks, and carefully fold them into the batter. Pour into 2 well-buttered, lightly floured round 8-inch layer-cake pans. Bake in a preheated moderate oven (375° F.) 25 to 30 minutes, or until a toothpick inserted in the center comes out clean. Cool the cake in the pans 10 minutes. Turn out onto a cooling rack to finish cooling. If desired, put the layers together with Lemon Butter-Cream Filling and Frosting and decorate the top with alternating rows of sifted confectioners' sugar and glacéed cherries. Or omit the filling and treat each layer as a separate cake, decorating the tops with alternating rows of cherries and sugar. Makes 2 round 8-inch layers. (See illustration, page 976.)

⚜ LUTÉTIA CAKE

1 round 9-inch Génoise layer 2 inches thick
Walnut Butter Cream
Apricot Glaze
Chocolate Fondant Cake Icing
Sweet Chestnut Purée
½ cup confectioners' sugar
about 1½ teaspoons water
1 drop green food coloring
8 walnut halves
2 blanched almonds, chopped

When the Génoise is cold split it to make 3 layers of equal thickness. Spread Walnut Butter Cream between the layers. Spread a thin layer of Apricot

Glaze over the top and sides of the cake and frost with Chocolate Fondant Cake Icing. Put Sweet Chestnut Purée in a cake-decorating tube and pipe any design desired over the top. Combine the confectioners' sugar with enough water to make it of coating consistency. Add 3 to 4 walnut halves at a time to the mixture and mix until walnuts are well glazed. Transfer walnuts to waxed paper and let them set until they are dry. Decorate the walnuts with bits of chopped blanched almond and a little of the Chocolate Fondant and arrange them over the top of the cake. Makes one round 9-inch cake. (See illustration, page 982.)

⚜ MASCOTTE CAKE

8 large egg yolks
1 cup sifted confectioners' sugar
1 cup finely chopped blanched almonds
1 cup fine dry breadcrumbs
2 tablespoons rum
6 large egg whites
½ cup chopped toasted blanched almonds
2 cups Butter-Cream Filling and Frosting
toasted sliced blanched almonds
Praline Powder

Beat the egg yolks until fluffy. Gradually beat in the sugar and continue beating until the mixture is lemon-colored. Add the chopped blanched almonds and mix well. Gradually beat in the breadcrumbs and rum. Beat egg whites until they stand in soft stiff peaks and fold them into the mixture. Butter an 8-inch spring-form pan, dust it lightly with fine dry breadcrumbs, and pour in the batter. Bake in a preheated moderate oven (350° F.) 40 to 50 minutes, or until the cake springs back when pressed in the center with the index finger. Cool the cake in the pan. Remove it to a pastry board and split it into 3 layers of equal thickness. Stir the chopped toasted almonds into Butter-Cream Filling and Frosting. Spread it between the layers and over the top and sides. Sprinkle the frosting with toasted sliced blanched almonds. Sprinkle a circle of Praline Powder in the center of the cake. Makes one round 8-inch 3-layer cake. (See illustration, page 979.)

⚜ MOCHA CAKE

2 square 9-inch Génoise layers
Mocha Butter-Cream Filling and Frosting
toasted chopped blanched almonds

Have the cake layers completely cooled. Put them together with Mocha Butter-Cream Filling and Frosting in between and spread it over the top and sides. If desired, make an additional 1 cup of the frosting and using a cake-decorating tube with a rosette nozzle pipe rosettes over the top of the cake, covering it completely. Cover the sides of the cake with the chopped almonds. Makes one 2-layer 9-inch cake. (See illustration, page 978.)

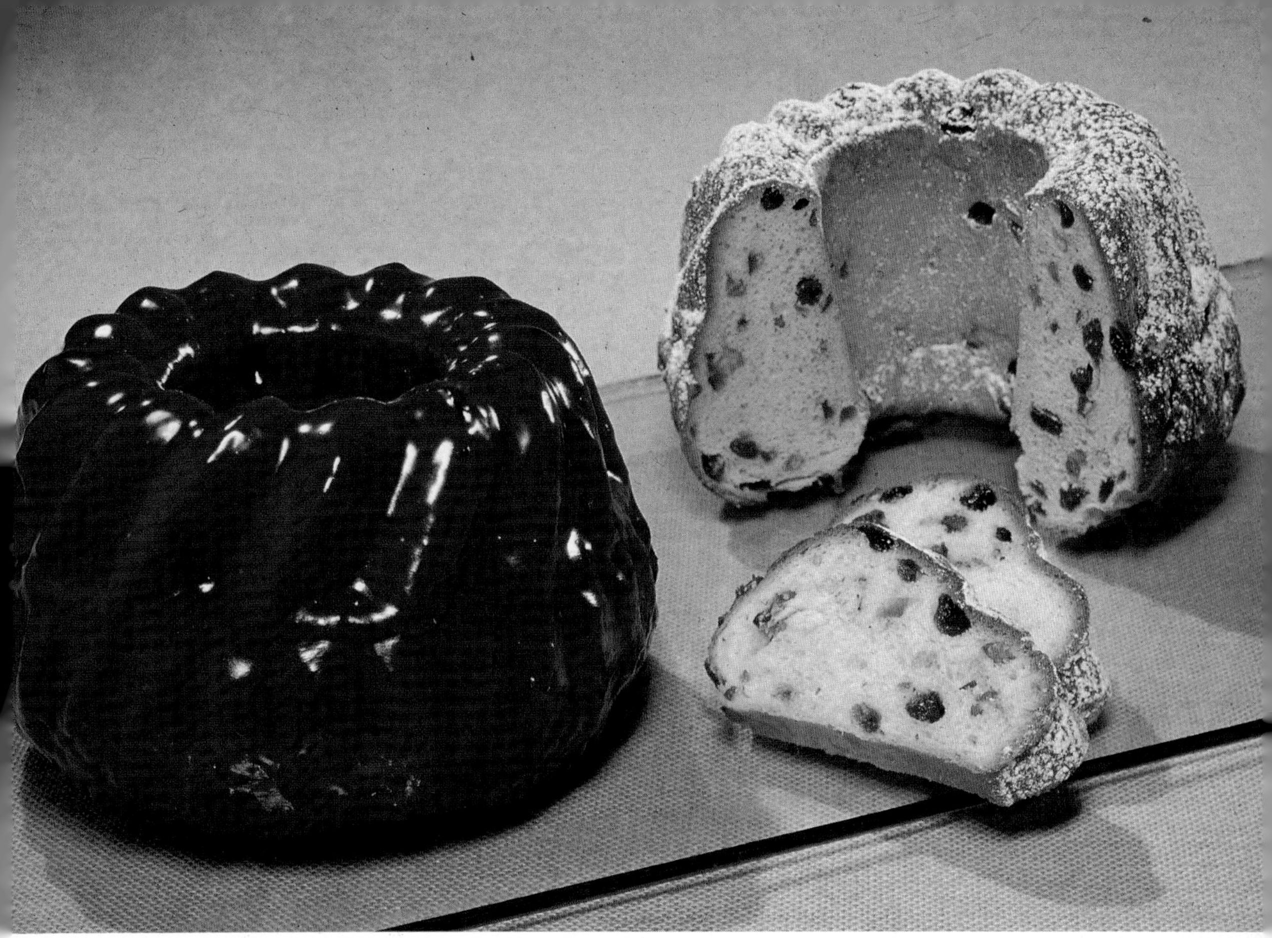

Kugelhopfs, page 972 ▲

▼ Almond Ring, page 968

▲ Lémania Cakes, page 973

Brioches, page 125 ▼

Small puff-paste pastries, pages 1019–22 ▲

▼ Niçoise Cakes, page 992

▲ Mocha Cake, page 974

Mexican Cake, page 991 ▼

Mascotte Cake, page 974 ▲

▼ Mocha Cake, Modern Style, page 991

▲ Kirsch Torte, page 995

Caravelle Cake, page 969 ▼

Hungarian Cake, page 971 ▲

▼ Black Forest Cherry Torte, page 994

▲ Zigomar Cake, page 993

Lutétia Cake, page 973 ▼

▼ Caraque Cake, page 968

Dobos Torta, page 995 ▲

984

▲ Christmas Log, page 970

Croquembouche, page 1018 ►

Frankfurt Crown, page 970 ▼

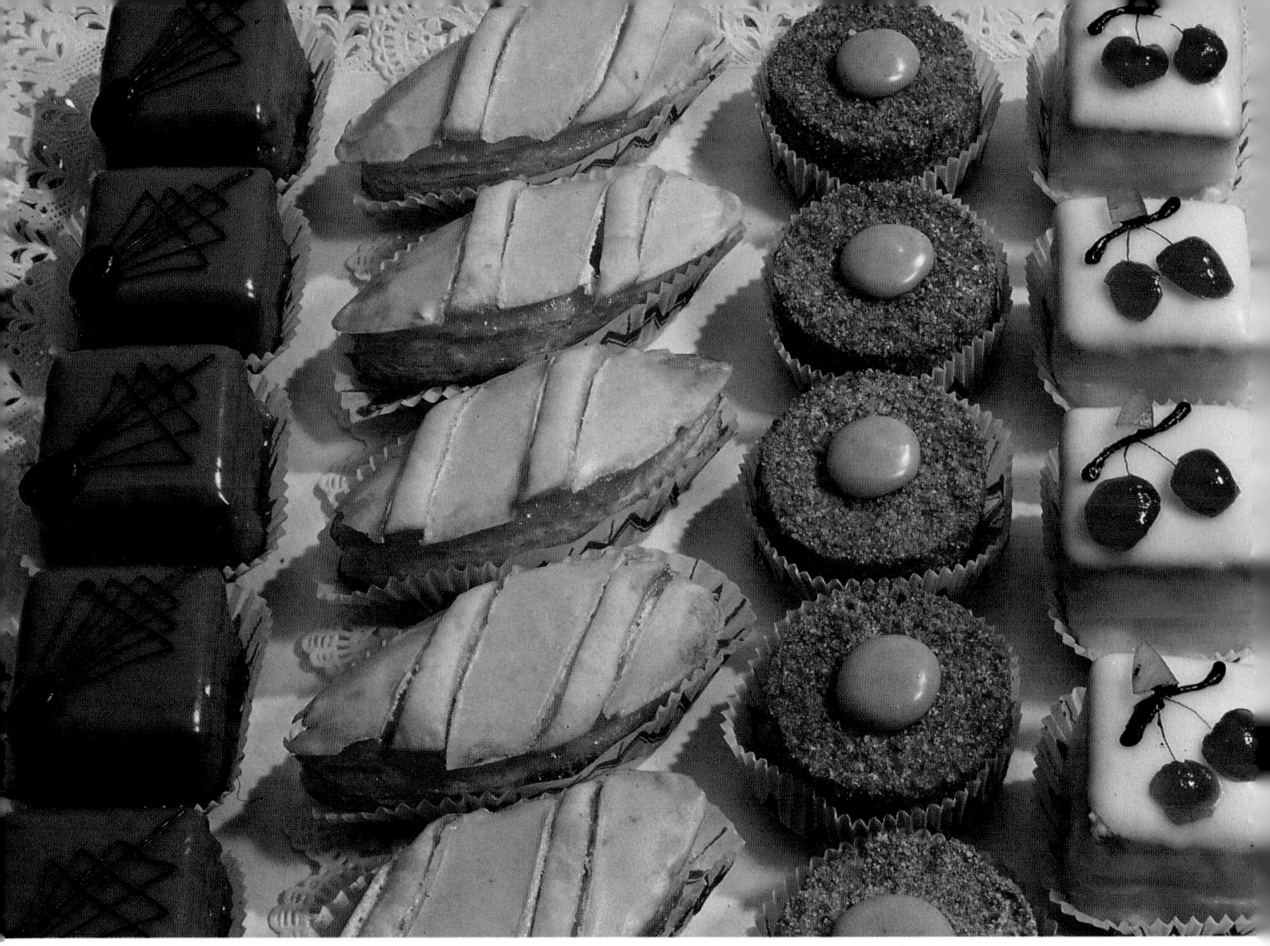

Assorted small cakes and tartlets, pages 1000–1005; 1033

Frosted Almond Pretzels, page 999 ▲

▼ Savarins and assorted pastries (see pages 998, 1017–18, 1033)

▲ Assortment of petits fours (see pages 1007–1009, 1041)

Frosted Petits Fours, pages 1012–15 ▼

Assortment of glacéed fruits, stuffed dates, pastries (see pages 1011, 1043–45) ▲

▼ Assortment of chocolate-covered candies (see pages 1039, 1043)

⚜ MOCHA CAKE, MODERN STYLE

Prepare 2 round 9-inch Génoise layers and allow them to cool completely. Frost with Coffee Fondant Cake Icing. Darken a little of the icing with a few drops of caramel or with one drop each red and yellow food coloring and use a decorator's tube to make any desired modern design on the cake. Decorate the center with citron, angelica, or other candied fruit cut in a modern design. Sprinkle toasted chopped blanched almonds around the sides. Makes one 2-layer 8-inch cake. (See illustration, page 979.)

⚜ MEXICAN CAKE

5 large egg yolks
⅔ cup sugar
¾ cup sifted all-purpose flour
3 tablespoons cocoa
¼ teaspoon salt
4 large egg whites
5 tablespoons butter, melted
1½ teaspoons vanilla extract
Chocolate Butter-Cream Filling and Frosting
Apricot Glaze
Chocolate Fondant Cake Icing
¾ cup Royal Icing

Beat egg yolks until they are light and lemon-colored. Gradually beat in sugar and continue beating until the mixture is thick and pale in color. Sift together the next 3 ingredients and gradually fold into the eggs and sugar. Beat egg whites until they stand in soft stiff peaks, and fold them into the mixture. Cool the melted butter and gently fold it and the vanilla extract into the batter. (Be careful not to include the sediment which collects in the bottom of the saucepan in which butter was melted.) Turn the batter into a buttered, lightly floured, round 8-inch cake pan. Bake in a preheated moderate oven (350° F.) 35 to 40 minutes, or until a toothpick inserted in the center comes out clean. Cool in pan 10 minutes. Remove cake from pan and cool on a wire rack. When the cake is cold, split into 2 or 3 layers as desired. Put the layers together with Chocolate Butter-Cream Filling and Frosting. Spread the top and sides of the cake with Apricot Glaze. Frost the cake with Chocolate Fondant Cake Icing. Before the fondant has set, put the Royal Icing into a pastry bag and pipe parallel lines across the top of the cake. Draw the point of a knife lightly across the lines at intervals to make an attractive decoration. Makes 8 servings. (See illustration, page 978; also Culinary Techniques in Pictures.)

◀ Confectioners' spun-sugar basket filled with Frosted Petits Fours

⚜ NIÇOISE CAKE

½ recipe Puff Pastry
¼ pound almonds, blanched
½ cup sugar
¼ cup finely chopped candied orange peel
1 teaspoon grated orange rind
1 large egg
Curaçao to taste
1 teaspoon milk
confectioners' sugar
shaved almonds
1 preserved orange slice
1 glacéed cherry

Roll half of the Puff Pastry ¼ inch thick and cut it into an 8-inch circle, using a round 8-inch cake pan as a guide. Place the circle on a cooky sheet that has been wet with water and well drained. Grind the blanched almonds fine, using the finest blade of the food chopper, or grind them fine in the electric blender, a few at a time. Add the next 4 ingredients and mix until smooth. Add Curaçao to taste. Spread the mixture over the pastry circle to within ½ inch of the edge. Brush the edge with water. Roll the remaining Puff Pastry a little less than ¼ inch thick and cut it into an 8-inch circle. Place it over the almond filling and press the edges together firmly. Chill. Brush the top with milk and sprinkle with confectioners' sugar and shaved almonds. Bake in a preheated moderate oven (350° F.) 1 hour, or until pastry is golden brown. Remove from the oven. Cool. Garnish center with the orange slice and the glacéed cherry. Makes 1 8-inch cake. (See illustration, page 977.)

⚜ SAINT-HONORÉ CAKE

Roll Plain Pastry, made with 2 cups flour, into a circle ¼ inch thick. Cut a 9-inch pastry circle, using a 9-inch cake pan as a guide. Transfer it to an ungreased cooky sheet. Fill a pastry bag with Chou Paste and pipe a rim of the paste 2 inches high around the pastry circle. Beat 1 egg yolk with 1 tablespoon milk and brush it over the pastry. Bake in a preheated hot oven (400° F.) 30 minutes, or until the bottom of the pastry is brown and the Chou Paste rim is well puffed.

Using the pastry bag, form Chou Paste into 17 small cream puffs on an ungreased baking sheet. Bake in a preheated hot oven (425° F.) 20 to 25 minutes. Turn off the oven heat. Prick puffs with a sharp knife to permit the escape of steam and leave them in the oven 15 minutes to dry out. Remove and let cool. Fill cold cream puffs with French Pastry Cream or with Chantilly Cream. Dip the top of each in Caramel Syrup and arrange them around the edge of the cake. Fill the center of cake with French Pastry Cream. Fill the spaces between the cream puffs with whipped cream or Chantilly Cream, piped through a pastry tube, and garnish with green and red glacéed cherries. Garnish the center with a preserved orange slice cut into quarters, with Chantilly Cream or whipped cream piped between the quarters and a small cream puff in the center. Makes 8 servings. (See illustration, page 902.)

⚜ ZIGOMAR CAKE (*Swiss*)

10 large eggs, separated
2 cups sugar
4½ squares (4½ ounces) unsweetened chocolate
3 teaspoons ground cinnamon
2 tablespoons lemon juice
1 teaspoon grated lemon rind
2 cups ground blanched almonds
½ cup apricot brandy or peach brandy
½ teaspoon salt
1 cup sifted fine cracker meal
2 cups Rum Butter-Cream Filling and Frosting
¼ cup chopped pistachio nuts
½ teaspoon instant coffee
Chocolate Fondant Cake Icing

Beat the egg yolks until they are well mixed. Gradually beat in the sugar. Continue beating until mixture is thick and lemon-colored. Grate 4 squares of the chocolate and add, with the next 5 ingredients. Mix well. Add the salt to the egg whites and beat them until they stand in soft stiff peaks. Fold them into the batter, alternating with the cracker meal. Turn the batter into a buttered 9-inch spring-form pan. Bake in a preheated moderate oven (350° F.) 50 to 60 minutes, or until a toothpick inserted in the center comes out clean. Cool the cake in the pan for 10 minutes, then remove it to a cooling rack. When the cake is cold split it into 3 layers. Reserve ⅔ cup of the Rum Butter-Cream Filling and Frosting. Melt the remaining ½ square of chocolate and add it to the rest of the frosting. Spread over the first layer of cake, reserving the remaining chocolate rum frosting. Cover with the second layer. Spread the reserved white rum frosting on the second layer and sprinkle it with chopped pistachio nuts. Cover with the remaining cake layer. Add the instant coffee to the reserved chocolate-rum frosting and spread it over the top and sides of the cake, reserving a small amount to use as decoration on top of the cake. Chill the cake 1 hour for frosting to set. Cover the top with Chocolate Fondant Cake Icing. Make a dainty design around the edge of cake with Chocolate Fondant Cake Icing put through a cake-decorating tube. Make a big "Z" in the center of the cake with the rest of the chocolate-rum frosting. Makes one 9-inch 3-layer cake. (See illustration, page 982.)

Tortes

⚜ BLACK FOREST CHERRY TORTE (*German*)

9 large eggs
1 tablespoon water
1 cup sugar
¾ cup fine dry breadcrumbs
½ cup ground blanched almonds
⅓ cup cocoa
½ cup sifted all-purpose flour
Cherry Filling
Chantilly Cream
unsweetened chocolate
red glacéed cherries

Separate 8 of the eggs and beat the yolks and the whole egg with the water. Gradually beat in the sugar. Add the breadcrumbs and almonds. Mix well. Sift the cocoa with the flour, add, and mix well. Beat the 8 egg whites until they stand in soft stiff peaks and fold them into the mixture. Turn into a greased and floured round 9-inch cake pan 2 inches deep. Bake in a preheated slow oven (350° F.) 30 minutes, or until a toothpick inserted in the center of the cake comes out clean. Cool the cake in the pan 5 minutes, then turn out onto a cooling rack to finish cooling. When cold, split the cake into 3 thin layers. Put layers together in layer-cake fashion, spreading the first layer with cold Cherry Filling and then with a layer of Chantilly Cream, and the second with Chantilly Cream. Spread Chantilly Cream over the top and sides of the cake. Make rosettes over the top with Chantilly Cream put through a cake-decorating tube fitted with a rosette nozzle. Garnish each rosette with a glacéed cherry. Decorate the center and around the edge with unsweetened Chocolate Curls. Sprinkle sides with shaved unsweetened chocolate. Makes one 9-inch 3-layer cake. (See illustration, page 981; also Culinary Techniques in Pictures.)

CHERRY FILLING

2 cups pitted fresh sweet red cherries
2 tablespoons water
¼ cup sugar
1 tablespoon cornstarch
dash salt
⅛ teaspoon almond extract

Put the cherries and the water in a heavy one-quart saucepan. Cover and cook over low heat 10 minutes, or until cherry juice has formed in the pan. Mix the sugar, cornstarch, and salt and add. Increase heat to moderate and stir and cook until the juice is clear and has thickened. Add the almond extract and cool. Use as filling for cake or spoon into baked small tart shells. Makes approximately 1 cup.

⚜ DOBOS TORTA (*Hungarian*)

This torte was created by a famous Hungarian pastry chef named Dobos. It consists of several thin layers of cake of sponge type spread with light chocolate butter-cream frosting and a layer of caramel glaze over the top.

5 large eggs, separated
½ cup sugar
1 tablespoon strained lemon juice
1 teaspoon vanilla extract
½ cup sifted cake flour
¼ teaspoon salt
Chocolate Butter-Cream Filling and Frosting
Caramel Glaze

Line 6 lightly greased round 8-inch layer cake pans with waxed paper and grease the paper. Set aside. With a wire whisk beat the egg yolks until they are fluffy. Gradually beat in the sugar. Beat in the lemon juice and vanilla extract and continue beating until the mixture is thick and lemon-colored. Sift the flour over the beaten egg yolks and fold it in very carefully. Add the salt to the egg whites and beat them until they stand in soft stiff peaks. With a rubber spatula carefully fold them into the cake mixture. Put an equal amount of the batter into each of the 6 prepared pans, spreading it over the bottoms to cover them uniformly. (If only 2 pans are available, bake 2 layers and repeat the operation until 6 layers have been baked.) Bake the cakes in a preheated moderate oven (350° F.) 5 to 8 minutes, or until the cake springs back when the center is pressed lightly with the index finger. Remove the cakes from the pans immediately and strip the paper off the bottoms. Cool on a cooling rack. When cakes are cold, spread 5 layers with Chocolate Butter-Cream Filling and Frosting and put them together with the sixth layer on top. Using a spatula, quickly spread the top with Caramel Glaze. When the glaze has hardened, heat a knife in hot water, wipe it dry, and make wedge-shaped incisions around the top, cutting through the glaze. Or glaze top layer before putting it on cake, cut it into wedges, and arrange them over top of cake between rows of frosting piped on with a cake-decorating tube, as illustrated on page 983. Makes one 6-layer 8-inch torte.

⚜ KIRSCH TORTE (*Swiss*)

1/16 teaspoon salt
5 large egg whites
½ teaspoon lemon juice
1 cup sugar
1½ teaspoons vanilla extract
¾ cup grated blanched almonds
1 round 8-inch Génoise layer
¼ cup heavy Sugar Syrup flavored with Kirsch
Kirsch Butter-Cream Filling and Frosting
confectioners' sugar
chopped blanched almonds
1 drop green food coloring

Add the salt to the egg whites and beat them until they stand in soft stiff peaks (not dry). Beat in the lemon juice. Beat in ¾ cup of the sugar, about 1 tablespoon at a time, and continue to beat until the meringue is thick and smooth. Fold in remaining ¼ cup of sugar, the vanilla extract, and the grated almonds. Cut a sheet of brown paper to fit a baking sheet. Trace two 8-inch circles, about 1 inch apart on the paper, using an 8-inch round layer-cake pan as a guide. Spread the circles with the meringue, to a thickness of about ⅜ inch. Bake in a preheated moderate oven (350° F.) 10 minutes. Remove from the oven and strip off brown paper. Cool meringues on racks until crisp. Meanwhile, place the Génoise layer on a cooking rack with a baking pan underneath it. Sprinkle the syrup over it, spooning any syrup that drips into the pan over the cake. Place 1 cold meringue circle on a serving plate and spread it with a layer of Kirsch Butter-Cream Filling and Frosting. Cover it with the Génoise layer, spread cake with the frosting, and place the remaining meringue circle on top. Frost the top and sides. Sprinkle the sides with toasted chopped blanched almonds. Sprinkle the top with a thick layer of sifted confectioners' sugar. Color about 2 teaspoons chopped blanched almonds with 1 drop of green food coloring and sprinkle them in the center of the cake. This cake should stand in a cool place for at least 6 hours, or overnight, before serving. Makes one 8-inch round cake. (See illustration, page 980.)

⚜ SACHER TORTE (*Austrian*)

¾ cup sugar
¾ cup (1½ sticks) softened butter
1½ teaspoons vanilla extract
6 eggs, separated
6 squares (6 ounces) semisweet chocolate
2 cups sifted cake flour
apricot jam
chocolate frosting (any kind)

Gradually blend the sugar with the softened butter and vanilla extract. Beat in the egg yolks, one at a time. Melt the chocolate over hot water and cool slightly. Beat the egg whites until they stand in soft peaks, then fold in the cooled melted chocolate and add. Fold in the cake flour. Turn the batter into 2 well-buttered, lightly floured, round 9-inch layer-cake pans. Bake in a preheated moderate oven (350° F.) 25 to 30 minutes. Remove the tortes from the pans and place them on a rack to cool. Spread apricot jam between the layers and over the top. Frost with any desired chocolate frosting. Makes one 9-inch 2-layer torte.

Babas and Savarins

⚜ BABA AU RHUM

1 envelope active dry yeast
¼ cup lukewarm water
1 tablespoon (3 teaspoons) sugar
¼ cup lukewarm milk
2 cups sifted all-purpose flour
½ teaspoon salt
⅔ cup butter, melted
2 tablespoons raisins
1 tablespoon currants
½ cup sugar
¾ cup water or apricot juice
1 teaspoon lemon juice
¼ cup rum
fruit, ice cream, or Chantilly Cream

Soften the yeast in the lukewarm water with 1 teaspoon of the sugar. Add the remaining 2 teaspoons sugar and the milk. Stir in the flour and the eggs and beat about 2 minutes. Cover the bowl and let the dough rise in a warm place (80° to 85° F.) until it has doubled in bulk. Punch down the dough, add the salt, butter, raisins, and currants, and work these ingredients into the dough. Put the dough into a well-buttered 8½-inch ring mold, filling it two-thirds full, or put it into 8 individual buttered ring molds or baking cups, filling each two-thirds full. Cover and let dough rise until it fills the mold or molds. Bake in a preheated hot oven (400° F.), the larger mold 25 to 30 minutes, the smaller molds or cups about 15 minutes, or until a toothpick inserted in the center comes out clean.

While the Baba is baking, mix the ½ cup sugar, ¾ cup water or apricot juice, and the lemon juice in a saucepan. Stir and cook until boiling point is reached. Continue cooking without stirring for 5 minutes. Remove from heat and add ¼ cup rum. Invert the hot Baba on a serving plate and pour the rum syrup over it. If desired, just before serving, heat 2 tablespoons rum, ignite, pour over the Baba, and bring it to the table flaming. The center may be filled with fruit, such as pitted black cherries, berries, sliced bananas, apricots or peaches, piled high, or with ice cream. The small Babas may be filled with fruit, ice cream, or Chantilly Cream. Or, if desired, sprinkle the top with chopped pistachio nuts and sprinkle chopped toasted blanched almonds around the sides at the bottom of the Baba. Makes one 8½-inch Baba, or 8 individual Babas. (See illustration, page 901; also Culinary Techniques in Pictures.)

⚜ SAVARIN

Make the dough for Baba au Rhum, omitting the raisins and currants. Bake. Unmold, puffed side up. Sprinkle with confectioners' sugar. If desired, fill the center of the mold with fruit marinated in brandy, Kirsch, or rum. Makes one 8½-inch Savarin, or 8 individual Savarins.

⚜ SAVARINS CHANTILLY

Bake Savarin dough in individual Savarin molds (small ring molds). Place the Savarins on a plate, puffed side up. Prick the tops with a fork and pour warm heavy Kirsch-flavored Sugar Syrup over them. Let stand 30 minutes. Coat with Apricot Glaze. Put Chantilly Cream in a pastry bag fitted with a star nozzle, and pipe it into the center of each Savarin, piling it high. If desired, soak half the Savarins in heavy Sugar Syrup flavored with dark rum to taste. Allow 1 Savarin per serving. (See illustrations, pages 901, 987.)

⚜ KIRSCH SAVARINS

Place a seedless muscatel raisin in the bottom of each greased, individual Savarin mold (small ring mold). Fill the molds with Savarin dough. Cover and let rise in a warm place (80 to 85° F.) until doubled in bulk. Bake in a preheated hot oven (400° F.) 15 minutes, or until a toothpick inserted in the center comes out clean. Unmold. Place the hot Savarins on a plate, puffed side up. Prick them with a fork and pour warm Kirsch-flavored Sugar Syrup over them. Let them stand 30 minutes. Frost half of the Savarins with white Fondant Icing and the remainder with pink Fondant Icing (made by adding 1 to 2 drops of red food coloring to white Fondant). Allow 1 Savarin for each serving.

⚜ PINEAPPLE CROÛTE

8 fresh pineapple rings or large canned pineapple rings
8 individual Savarins
French Pastry Cream
1 to 2 tablespoons rum
Apricot Sauce
8 glacéed cherries
Pineapple-Rum Sauce

If fresh pineapple is used, poach the whole rings as directed in the recipe for Fresh Pineapple Compote. Fill the centers of small Savarins with French Pastry Cream flavored with rum to taste. Cover each with a drained pineapple ring. Spread with Apricot Sauce. Put a glacéed cherry in the center of each pineapple ring. Serve with Pineapple-Rum Sauce. Makes 8 servings. (See illustration, page 904.)

COOKIES AND SMALL CAKES

⚜ ALMOND PRETZELS

1 cup (2 sticks) softened butter
1 cup sugar
1 teaspoon grated lemon rind
3 large egg yolks
1 cup ground unblanched almonds
¼ teaspoon almond extract
about 2½ cups sifted all-purpose flour
confectioners' sugar

Stir the butter until it is creamy. Gradually add the sugar and lemon rind, mixing well after each addition. Beat in the egg yolks, one at a time. Add the almonds and almond extract and mix well. Gradually stir in the flour, using only enough to make a soft stiff dough. Chill until dough can be handled, 2 to 3 hours. Shape the dough into long, thin rolls, the diameter of a pencil. Cut them into 3- to 4-inch lengths and shape them into pretzels or figure 8's. Place the pretzels on a greased baking sheet and bake in a preheated moderate oven (350° F.) about 8 minutes, or until lightly browned. Remove the pretzels from the baking sheet and while they are still warm roll them in sifted confectioners' sugar. Or, if desired, frost with Fondant Cake Icing, made with plain or Chocolate Fondant. Makes approximately 3 dozen. (See illustration, page 987.)

⚜ APRICOT DAINTIES (*Beignets d'Abricots*)

These dainty little cookies will keep for weeks if stored in a cool place in tightly covered containers.

¾ cup finely ground blanched almonds
½ cup sugar
¼ cup sifted all-purpose flour
3 egg whites
½ teaspoon vanilla extract
¼ teaspoon almond extract
confectioners' sugar
apricot jam

Combine the first 3 ingredients and set aside. Beat the egg whites until they stand in soft stiff peaks. Carefully fold in the almond-sugar mixture, along with the vanilla and almond extract. Using a teaspoon, or a pastry bag fitted with a ½-inch plain nozzle, drop small mounds of the mixture on a buttered and lightly floured baking sheet. Sprinkle confectioners' sugar over each, and bake in a preheated moderate oven (350° F.) 8 to 10 minutes. Cool on the baking sheet for about 1 minute, and transfer to a cooling rack. If the cookies cool before you can remove them from the baking sheet, return them to the oven for about ½ minute. Put cookies together in pairs with apricot jam spread between them. Makes approximately 2½ dozen.

⚜ CARAQUES

1¾ cups (3½ sticks) softened butter
¼ teaspoon salt
1½ teaspoons vanilla extract
¾ cup sugar
6 large egg yolks
3¾ cups sifted all-purpose flour
Ganache Cream
Pistachio Fondant

Mix the butter with the salt and vanilla and gradually blend in the sugar. Beat in the egg yolks 2 at a time. Gradually stir in the flour, mixing well after each addition. Shape the dough into a ball. Place on a pastry board, invert a bowl over the dough, and let rest for 1 hour. Divide the dough into 3 equal parts. Place 1 part at a time on a lightly floured board, keeping the remaining dough under the bowl. Roll each part ⅛ inch to ¼ inch thick Cut into round cookies with a 1½-inch cookie cutter. Place on a lightly buttered baking sheet and bake in a preheated moderate oven (350° F.) 10 to 15 minutes or until cookies are lightly browned. Transfer to a cooling rack. Repeat until all dough is used. After all the cookies have been baked and cooled, make them into sandwiches with Ganache Cream as the filling. Let stand until filling is set. Ice the tops with Pistachio Fondant and put a large dollop of Ganache Cream in the center of each. Allow frosting to set, then store in a tightly covered container in a cool place. Makes approximately 4 dozen. (See illustration, page 986.)

GANACHE CREAM

Melt 5 squares (5 ounces) unsweetened chocolate and 3 tablespoons butter in the top of a 1-quart double boiler. Gradually stir in ⅓ cup heavy cream. Cool. When cold, use as a filling for Caraques or Petits Fours.

PISTACHIO FONDANT

Heat 1 cup Fondant (see page 1036) over hot water until semimelted. Stir in ¼ cup finely ground pistachio nuts. Makes enough frosting for 4 dozen Caraques.

⚜ CHOCOLATE PARFAITS

Make and bake round cookies, using the recipe for Caraques. When the cookies are cooled, make them into sandwiches, using Chocolate Butter-Cream Filling and Frosting as the filling. Let stand until filling is set. Frost the tops with Chocolate Glaze and top each with half a peeled blanched almond or sprinkle with finely chopped pistachio nuts. Makes about 4 dozen. (See illustration, page 986.)

⚜ CHOCOLATE PECAN SQUARES *(American)*

1 square (1 ounce) unsweetened chocolate
¼ cup (½ stick) butter
2 large eggs
1 cup sugar
¼ teaspoon salt
1½ teaspoons vanilla extract
¼ cup milk
1 cup sifted cake flour
1 cup pecans, chopped fine

Melt the chocolate and butter together over hot water (not boiling). Mix well. Beat the eggs until light and lemon-colored, then gradually beat in the sugar. Stir in the salt, vanilla extract, and milk. Gradually add flour. Add melted chocolate and butter. Stir in pecans. Line a buttered 8- by 8- by 2-inch pan with waxed paper cut to fit and lightly buttered. Pour in the batter. Bake in a preheated moderate oven (350° F.) 30 minutes, or until a toothpick inserted in the center comes out clean. Cool in the pan. Cut the cake into 1½-inch squares before removing from the pan. Store in a tightly covered container. Makes 25 squares.

⚜ FRENCH REFRIGERATOR COOKIES *(Petits Gâteaux Taillés)*

1 cup sugar
¼ teaspoon salt
1½ teaspoons vanilla extract
½ teaspoon almond extract
1 cup softened butter
2½ cups sifted all-purpose flour
1 tablespoon water

Gradually add the sugar, salt, vanilla extract, and almond extract to the butter and mix until creamy and fluffy. Add 1½ cups of the flour and then add the water. Stir in the remaining flour and mix well. (This makes a very stiff dough, but do not add more water.) Shape the dough into two rolls 1½ inches in diameter and 10 inches long. Wrap in waxed paper and chill 3 to 4 hours or overnight. With a sharp knife cut the rolls into slices 1/16 to ⅛ inch thick. Place the slices on lightly buttered baking sheets. Bake in a preheated hot oven (400° F.) 4 to 5 minutes or until cookies begin to brown around the edges. Do not bake too brown. Cool and store in an airtight container. Makes 8 dozen cookies.

⚜ JAPANESE FANCIES (*Japonais*)

¼ teaspoon salt
5 large egg whites
½ teaspoon lemon juice
1 cup sugar
1½ teaspoons vanilla extract
¾ cup ground pistachio nuts
Praline Butter-Cream Filling and Frosting
Fondant (page 1036)
pink food coloring

Add the salt to the egg whites and beat until foamy. Add the lemon juice. With an electric beater, beat at high speed until the egg whites are stiff enough to hold their shape but not dry. At low speed beat in ¾ cup of the sugar, 2 tablespoons at a time. Add the vanilla extract and continue beating until the egg whites stand in stiff peaks and are shiny and moist. Combine the remaining ¼ cup sugar with the pistachio nuts and carefully fold into the egg whites. Mark 1¾-inch circles on brown paper, using a cooky cutter or glass as a guide. Butter the paper lightly and dust lightly with cornstarch. Spread on each circle a layer of meringue ¼ inch thick. Place the paper on baking sheets. Bake in a preheated very slow oven (250° F.) 50 to 60 minutes. Turn off heat and cool in the oven ½ hour. When cool, remove to a tray or pastry board. Crumble enough of the meringues to make 1 cup fine meringue crumbs. Set aside. Make sandwiches of the remaining meringues with Praline Butter-Cream Filling and Frosting as the filling, and use it to frost the tops and sides, spreading it thinly. Sprinkle the tops and sides with the reserved meringue crumbs. Decorate the tops with a dollop of Fondant, colored as desired with pink food coloring. Place each Fancy in a paper case. Store in a tightly covered container in a cool place. Makes approximately 3 dozen. (See illustration, page 986.)

⚜ LADYFINGERS (*Biscuits à la Cuiller*)

⅛ teaspoon salt
3 large eggs, separated
2 tablespoons granulated sugar
1 cup sifted confectioners' sugar
¾ teaspoon vanilla extract
¾ cup sifted all-purpose flour

Add the salt to the egg whites and beat them until soft peaks form. Beat in the granulated sugar and continue beating until the whites are stiff but not dry. Beat the egg yolks and then beat the confectioners' sugar and vanilla extract into the beaten yolks. Continue beating until eggs are thick and lemon-colored. Add the egg-yolk mixture to the egg-white mixture all at one time and carefully fold it in. Fold in the flour. Drop the batter by rounded teaspoonfuls into greased ladyfinger pans, or put batter in a pastry bag and pipe it into the ladyfinger pans. If ladyfinger pans are not available, shape rounded teaspoons of the batter into fingers about 2½ inches long and place them on greased cooky sheets. Bake them in a preheated moderate oven (350° F.) 12 to 15 minutes, or until ladyfingers are lightly browned. Remove from pans or cooky sheets and immediately sprinkle the bottom of each ladyfinger with confectioners' sugar. To keep ladyfingers moist, store a slice of bread in the storage container. Makes 2½ dozen. (See Culinary Techniques in Pictures.)

⚜ MADELEINES

1¼ cups sifted cake flour
½ teaspoon double-acting baking powder
¼ teaspoon salt
3 large eggs
1 teaspoon vanilla extract
⅔ cup sugar
2 teaspoons grated lemon rind
¾ cup (1½ sticks) butter, melted and cooled
sifted confectioners' sugar

Sift the first 3 ingredients together and set them aside. Beat the eggs in a 2-quart mixing bowl until light and lemon-colored. Add the vanilla extract. Gradually beat in the sugar. Continue beating until the volume has increased to four times the original volume. Gradually fold in the flour mixture and the lemon rind. Stir in the melted butter. Brush madeleine pans with additional melted butter. Spoon 1 tablespoon of batter into each shell, filling it two-thirds full. Bake in a preheated moderate oven (350° F.) 12 minutes, or until a toothpick inserted in the center comes out clean. Remove the cakes from the pans onto cooling racks. Dust the tops with sifted confectioners' sugar. Makes 3 dozen Madeleines.

⚜ MOCHA PAVÉS

1 Génoise layer 15½ by 10 inches and 1 inch thick
Coffee Butter-Cream Filling and Frosting
Mocha Fondant Cake Icing
2 squares (2 ounces) semisweet chocolate

Split the Génoise into 2 thin layers and put them together with Coffee Butter-Cream Filling and Frosting between. Let the cake stand in a cool place until the filling is firm, then cut it into 2-inch squares. Frost the tops and sides with Mocha Fondant Cake Icing. Melt the chocolate and using a cake-decorating tube with the smallest nozzle make designs as desired on the tops of the cake squares. Makes about 3 dozen individual cakes. (See illustration, page 986.)

⚜ NUT CREAM ROLLS

5 large eggs, separated
½ cup sugar
¼ cup softened butter
1 teaspoon grated lemon rind
¼ teaspoon salt
⅓ cup sifted cake flour
⅓ cup fine dry breadcrumbs
½ cup finely chopped nuts (almonds, hazelnuts, pecans, or walnuts)
French Pastry Cream
confectioners' sugar

Beat the egg yolks and ⅓ cup of the sugar together until mixture is thick and lemon-colored. Beat in the butter, lemon rind, and salt. Combine the flour, breadcrumbs, and nuts and stir into the egg mixture. Beat the egg whites until they stand in soft stiff peaks, then beat in the remaining sugar. Fold the whites into the batter. Spread the batter in a greased, waxed-paper-lined, 15½- by 10½- by 1-inch jelly-roll pan. Bake in a preheated moderate oven (350° F.) 18 minutes or until a toothpick inserted in the center comes out clean. Immediately turn the cake upside down on a towel that has been sprinkled lightly with confectioners' sugar and remove the waxed paper. Roll up the cake, jelly-roll fashion, in the towel, to prevent the cake from sticking together. When the cake is cold, unroll it on a piece of waxed paper. Remove the towel and cut the cake in half crosswise. Spread each half with French Pastry Cream, roll up each half separately, and wrap in waxed paper. Let the rolls stand in a cool place 1 to 2 hours before serving. To serve, cut each roll into 4 2½-inch lengths. Lay a 1-inch strip of paper across the center of each. Dust the cake on each side of the paper with sifted confectioners' sugar. Remove paper. Makes 8 servings. (See illustration, page 986.)

⚜ RIBBON COOKIES

2 cups sifted all-purpose flour
2 teaspoons double-acting baking powder
½ teaspoon salt
1 teaspoon ground mace
1 cup (2 sticks) butter
½ cup sugar
2 teaspoons vanilla extract
1 large egg
colored candy decorettes
sifted confectioners' sugar (optional)

Sift the first 4 ingredients together and set aside. Soften the butter and gradually work the sugar into it, mixing well after each addition. Beat in vanilla extract and egg. Stir in the flour mixture and mix well. Cover the bowl and let the dough stand 30 minutes. Place one-fourth of the dough at a time in a cooky press fitted with the wide flat, ridged plate. Force the dough through the plate onto ungreased cooky sheets, moving the press back and forth to make rippled ribbons of dough 2 inches long. Sprinkle the ribbons with candy decorettes. Bake in a preheated hot oven (400° F.) 8 to 10 minutes, or until the cookies are light brown around the edges. Transfer cookies to cooling racks to cool. Sprinkle with confectioners' sugar, if desired. Makes 5 dozen cookies.

⚜ SOUVAROFF

1¾ cups (3½ sticks) softened butter
2 teaspoons vanilla extract
¾ cup sugar
5 cups sifted all-purpose flour
about 3 to 4 tablespoons light cream
apricot jam or currant jelly

Mix the butter and vanilla extract. Blend in the sugar gradually. Stir in the flour ¼ at a time until all has been added. Add just enough cream to make a dough that can be easily rolled. Shape the dough into a ball, invert a bowl over it, and let rest for 1 hour. Divide the dough into 3 equal parts. Roll 1 part at a time, keeping the rest covered with the bowl. Roll dough about ⅛ inch thick. Cut in rounds or ovals with a pastry cutter. Place the pastries on a lightly buttered baking sheet and bake in a preheated hot oven (400° F.) 8 to 10 minutes or until lightly browned. Transfer the pastries to rack to cool. Repeat until all the dough is used. After all the pastries are baked and cooled, make sandwiches of them, using apricot jam or currant jelly as the filling. If desired, sprinkle the tops with confectioners' sugar, or spread lightly with Caramel Glaze. Makes 4 dozen to 5 dozen. (See illustration, page 986.)

⚜ SPRITZ

1 cup (2 sticks) softened butter
½ cup sugar
1 large egg
1½ teaspoons vanilla extract
about 2½ cups sifted all-purpose flour

Stir the butter until it is fluffy. Gradually blend in the sugar. Beat in the egg and the vanilla extract. Stir in enough flour to make a dough that may be forced through a pastry bag. Using nozzles of various shapes, pipe the dough onto unbuttered cooky sheets. Bake in a preheated moderate oven (375° F.) 7 to 10 minutes, or until cookies are lightly browned. Transfer to cooling racks. When cold decorate as desired with melted semisweet chocolate, frosting, glacéed fruit, or nuts. Makes about 7 dozen cookies.

⚜ VIENNESE ANISE DROPS

These delicious little cookies have a cakelike base with a crisp meringuelike top.

1½ cups sifted all-purpose flour
¼ teaspoon double-acting baking powder
⅛ teaspoon salt
¼ teaspoon anise seed
2 large eggs
1 cup sugar

Sift together the first 3 ingredients. Crush the anise seed fine, sift into the flour mixture, and mix well. Set aside. Break the eggs into a measuring cup and add enough cold water to make ½ cup of liquid. Turn into a mixing bowl, add the sugar, and beat until mixture is very thick. Fold in the flour mixture, sifting in one-fourth at a time. Drop the batter from a teaspoon onto greased cooky sheets, allowing 2 inches space between cookies for spreading. Leave the cookies, uncovered, in a cool place (not in the refrigerator) 8 to 10 hours or overnight to dry a little. Bake in a preheated moderate oven (350° F.) 5 to 6 minutes. Cool on cooling racks. Makes approximately 4 dozen cookies.

⚜ VIENNESE JELLY BARS

2¼ cups sifted all-purpose flour
⅔ cup sugar
½ teaspoon double-acting baking powder
¼ teaspoon salt
1 large egg
2 teaspoons vanilla extract
¾ cup (1½ sticks) softened butter
jelly or apricot jam

Sift together the first 4 ingredients. Add the egg, vanilla extract, and butter. Mix well to form a soft dough. Divide dough into 4 equal parts on a lightly floured board. Shape each part into a roll 12 inches long and 1 inch in diameter. Place 2 rolls on each of 2 ungreased cooky sheets 3 inches apart and 2 inches from the edges of the cooky sheet. With a knife handle make a depression ½ inch deep lengthwise down the center of each roll. Fill the depression with jelly or apricot jam. Bake in a preheated moderate oven (350° F.) 15 to 20 minutes, or until lightly browned around the edges. While strips are still warm, cut them into diagonal bars. Cool on cooling racks. Store in airtight containers. Makes 3½ dozen bars.

PETITS FOURS

The name *petit four* is given to a wide variety of small cakes, pastries, and cookies, including fancy cookies, macaroons, tuiles, wafers, glacéed fruits etc., as well as frosted petits fours, which are usually Génoise cut into tiny squares or fancy shapes and coated with a fondant frosting. (See illustrations, pages 988–89.)

⚜ ALMOND WAFERS

¼ teaspoon salt
5 large egg whites
¾ cup sifted confectioners' sugar
⅓ cup sifted all-purpose flour
6 tablespoons butter, melted
2 tablespoons milk
1 teaspoon vanilla extract
4 tablespoons almond paste
½ cup blanched slivered almonds

Combine the first 3 ingredients and beat until the mixture is very light. Stir in the flour, butter, and milk. Add the vanilla extract and almond paste and beat until batter is smooth. Stir in the almonds. Drop the batter from a teaspoon onto lightly buttered cooky sheets, allowing 2 inches space between wafers for spreading. Bake in a preheated very hot oven (450° F.) 5 minutes, watching closely to prevent burning. Remove from oven and allow wafers to stand on the cooky sheets about ½ minute, then remove to racks to finish cooling. Store in tightly closed jars or tin boxes. Makes approximately 2 dozen.

ALMOND WAFER CORNETS

Drop Almond Wafer batter from a tablespoon onto a lightly buttered cooky sheet. Bake in a 450° F. oven about 6 minutes. After removing the wafers from the cooky sheet, and while they are still warm, shape them into cones over the index finger. Cool and store. Makes 1 dozen.

⚜ BROWN-SUGAR NUGGETS

1 cup (2 sticks) softened butter
½ cup light brown sugar
¼ teaspoon salt
2 teaspoons vanilla extract
2¼ cups sifted all-purpose flour
½ cup finely chopped almonds, hazelnuts, or pecans
confectioners' sugar, granulated sugar, or semisweet chocolate

Stir the softened butter until it is fluffy, then blend in the brown sugar, salt, and vanilla extract. Gradually stir in the flour and nuts, mixing well after each addition. Chill the dough 2 hours, or until it is stiff enough to handle. Shape into balls, crescents, or 1-inch nuggets. Place on ungreased cooky sheets. Bake in a preheated moderate oven (350° F.) 12 to 15 minutes, or until very lightly browned. Cool on cooling racks. Roll in sifted confectioners' sugar or granulated sugar, or frost with melted semisweet chocolate. Makes approximately 5 dozen cookies. (See illustration, page 988.)

⚜ CHOCOLATE WAFERS (*Chocolatines*)

1½ cups sifted all-purpose flour
¾ cup cocoa
1¼ teaspoons double-acting baking powder
⅛ teaspoon salt
1¼ cups sugar
¾ cups (1½ sticks) soft butter
1 tablespoon rum
1 egg

Sift together the first 4 ingredients and set them aside. Gradually blend the sugar with the butter. Beat in the rum and the egg. Stir in the dry mixture and mix well. Chill the dough until it is stiff enough to handle. Roll dough to ⅛ inch thickness on a lightly floured board, and shape the cookies with a 2-inch cooky cutter dipped in flour. Place on ungreased cooky sheets. Or, if desired, shape the dough into ½ inch balls, place on ungreased cooky sheets, and flatten to ⅛ inch thickness with a glass covered with a damp cloth. Bake cookies in a preheated hot oven (400° F.) 8 minutes. Makes approximately 3 dozen cookies. (See illustration, page 988.)

⚜ CIGARETTES

This fragile French cooky, shaped like a cigarette, breaks easily. It is wise to bake a test cooky before dropping all the cooky batter. If the test cooky breaks when it is rolled, add a little more flour (1 to 2 tablespoons). If the cooky is thick and difficult to roll, add 1 to 2 teaspoons more melted and cooled butter.

2 large egg whites
dash salt
½ cup sugar
about ⅓ cup sifted all-purpose flour
about 3 tablespoons butter, melted and cooled
½ teaspoon vanilla extract
confectioners' sugar

Combine the egg whites and salt and beat until stiff. Beat in the sugar, 1 tablespoon at a time. Sift the flour over the egg whites and carefully fold it into them. Fold in the butter and vanilla extract. Drop the cooky batter by the tablespoonful onto a buttered and lightly floured baking sheet and spread as thin as possible with a spatula. Bake in a preheated very hot oven (450° F.) 2 to 3 minutes or until cookies are golden brown around the edges. Remove cookies from baking sheets and quickly roll them around a pencil to shape them like a cigarette. Serve plain sprinkled with confectioners' sugar or fill them with whipped cream or French Pastry Cream, if desired. Makes 2 dozen.

These cookies may also be given cone shapes by wrapping them around the index finger. The large ends may be dipped in melted semisweet chocolate, Chocolate Glaze, or Chocolate Fondant Cake Icing, if desired. (See illustration, page 988.)

⚜ DÉLICES WITH JELLY

¾ cup (1½ sticks) softened butter
¾ cup finely ground almonds or hazelnuts
½ cup sugar
1½ cups sifted all-purpose flour
jelly or apricot jam

Combine the butter and nuts. Gradually add the sugar and flour and mix the dough until it is smooth. Chill the dough, if necessary, until it can be rolled. Roll on a lightly floured board to ⅛ inch thickness. Cut into round cookies with a scalloped 1½-inch cooky cutter. Cut a ¾-inch hole in the center of half of the cookies. Save the centers, roll out again to ⅛ inch thickness, and cut out additional cookies, making holes in half of them, until all the dough has been used. Place the cookies on a lightly greased cooky sheet and bake in a preheated moderate oven (350° F.) 7 to 8 minutes, or until they are golden brown. Cool on cooling racks. Spread the solid cookies with jelly or apricot jam, and cover them with those that have holes in them. Makes approximately 2½ dozen cookies. (See illustration, page 988.)

⚜ CHOCOLATE DÉLICES

Make the recipe for Délices with Jelly. Melt 4 squares (4 ounces) semisweet chocolate over hot water (not boiling). Cool slightly and spread over the solid cookies, instead of jelly or jam. Cover with those that have the holes in them. Makes approximately 2½ dozen cookies.

⚜ LANGUES DE CHAT (*Cat's Tongues*)

¼ cup (1 stick) softened butter
¼ cup sugar
1 teaspoon vanilla extract
2 egg whites
¼ cup sifted all-purpose flour

Stir the butter until it is creamy, then gradually beat in the sugar and vanilla extract. Beat the mixture until it is light and fluffy. Beat in the egg whites, one at a time, beating well. Sift the flour over the mixture and carefully fold it in. Put the batter in a pastry bag fitted with a small plain round nozzle, and pipe it onto buttered lightly floured baking sheets in strips about 2 inches long and the diameter of a pencil. Bake in a preheated hot oven (450° F.) 4 to 5 minutes, or until the edges are golden brown. (Do not bake too brown.) Transfer the cookies to paper towels to cool. Makes approximately 2 dozen cookies.

⚜ MACAROON BUTTER-CREAM SANDWICHES

1½ cups peeled almonds
1½ cups fine granulated sugar
2 egg whites
Butter-Cream Filling and Frosting with any desired flavoring

Blanch the almonds and dry with paper towels. Put them through a food chopper twice, using the finest blade; add the sugar while grinding the almonds the second time. Add the egg whites and gradually work the mixture to a smooth paste. Drop from a teaspoon or force through a pastry bag fitted with a fluted nozzle onto brown paper, allowing 2 inches between macaroons. Bake in a preheated slow oven (325° F.) 30 minutes, or until they begin to turn golden. Remove from the paper and cool. Mix Butter Cream Filling and Frosting with any desired flavoring—vanilla, Kirsch, Cointreau, rum, chocolate, coffee, etc.—and spread it between two macaroons in sandwich fashion. Store in a cool place in a tightly covered container. Makes approximately 1½ dozen.

⚜ MILANESE COOKIES (*Italian*)

2½ cups sifted all-purpose flour
¾ cup sugar
¼ teaspoon salt
1½ cups (3 sticks) softened butter
3 teaspoons grated lemon rind
2 tablespoons cognac or rum
4 large egg yolks
semisweet chocolate, melted (optional)

Sift together into a mixing bowl the first 3 ingredients. Add the remaining ingredients and mix well. Chill the dough until it is stiff enough to handle. Shape the dough into 1-inch balls, and place them on greased cooky sheets. Flatten the balls to ¼ inch thickness with a glass covered with a damp cloth. Bake the cookies in a preheated hot oven (400° F.) 10 to 12 minutes, or until the tops are golden brown. Cool on cooling racks. If desired, frost the tops with melted semisweet chocolate. Makes approximately 4½ dozen cookies.

⚜ PALAIS DE DAME

¼ cup dried currants
1 tablespoon rum
¼ cup (½ stick) softened butter
¼ teaspoon salt
6 tablespoons sugar
1 large egg
¾ cup sifted all-purpose flour

Soak the currants in the rum 30 minutes. Stir the butter with the salt until it is creamy. Gradually blend in the sugar. Beat in the egg. Add the currants and rum and mix well. Gradually stir in the flour. Drop the batter from a teaspoon onto lightly buttered baking sheets, 2½ inches apart. Bake in a preheated moderate oven (350° F.) 8 to 10 minutes, or until cookies have browned lightly around the edges. Transfer the cookies to cooling racks and when cold store them in a tightly closed container. Makes 2 dozen cookies.

⚜ PINEAPPLE PASTRIES

Cut Puff Pastry into ovals 1½ inches long and 1 inch wide. Place them on ungreased baking sheets, prick them generously with a fork, and bake in a preheated hot oven (425° F.) 5 to 8 minutes, or until golden brown. Transfer the pastries to a cooling rack. When they are cold, marinate wedges of candied pineapple in Kirsch for about 30 minutes, drain, and place a wedge on each pastry oval. Ice with Kirsch-flavored Fondant Icing. Decorate, if desired, with glacéed cherries and pistachio nuts, or with a little Chocolate Fondant. The pastry ovals may be stored in tightly covered containers and decorated when needed. Allow 2 per serving. (See illustration, page 989.)

⚜ TUILES WITH ALMONDS

½ cup sugar
2 large egg whites
½ cup sifted all-purpose flour
½ teaspoon almond extract
½ teaspoon vanilla extract
½ cup blanched almonds, finely shredded
¼ cup (½ stick) butter
confectioners' sugar

Beat the sugar with the egg whites until the egg whites are frothy. Stir in the next 5 ingredients. Mix well. Drop the batter from a teaspoon in mounds the size of a quarter, onto lightly buttered baking sheets, or pipe through a pastry bag, onto lightly buttered baking sheets, leaving 2 inches between cookies to allow room for spreading. Sprinkle tops with confectioners' sugar. Bake the cookies in a preheated moderate oven (350° F.) 8 minutes, or until they have browned lightly around the edges. Cool ½ minute on the baking sheets, then remove, and while the cookies are still hot, bend them around a small rolling pin or small glass to give them the shape of a curved roofing tile (*tuile*). Store cookies in a tightly closed container. Makes about 2½ dozen.

Frosted Petits Fours

Petits fours that are to be frosted are usually made of Génoise cut with a sharp knife or cooky cutters into small squares, rectangles, diamonds, triangles, rounds, or hearts. The pieces are coated with Apricot Glaze and covered with Fondant Frosting. (See illustration, page 988.)

⚜ HOW TO FROST PETITS FOURS

With a sharp knife carefully trim all ragged edges from a Génoise layer. Using the knife or cooky cutters cut the cake into 1½-inch squares or small rectangles, triangles, diamonds, hearts, etc. Insert a fork into each piece and dip into Apricot Glaze, covering the top and sides. Place the pieces with the uncoated side down 1 inch apart on wire racks placed on cooky sheets. Let stand about 1 hour for the glaze to set. Using a large metal kitchen spoon, pour warm Fondant Frosting over 1 piece at a time, letting the frosting run over the top and cover the sides smoothly. (The cooky sheet underneath will catch the excess frosting, which should be scraped up, returned to the top of the double boiler, and reheated just until thin enough to pour.) Let the Petits Fours dry on the racks 1 hour or longer. If any are not sufficiently covered, frost again and let dry. Decorate the tops as desired with glacéed fruit or nuts, or with Confectioners' Sugar Flower and Leaf Frosting put through a cake-decorating tube.

APRICOT GLAZE

1 cup sugar
1 cup boiling water
¾ cup apricot jam

Combine the sugar and water in a saucepan. Stir and cook over medium heat until the sugar is dissolved. Bring to boiling point, uncovered, and boil 10 minutes. Heat the apricot jam in a saucepan until it bubbles around the edge of the pan. Remove from heat and push the jam through a sieve into the syrup. Mix well. Keep warm over hot water until ready to use, or reheat just before using to make the glaze thin enough to pour. Makes enough for 2½ dozen Petits Fours.

FONDANT FROSTING FOR PETITS FOURS

2¾ cups granulated sugar
¼ teaspoon cream of tartar
dash salt
1½ cups water
4 to 5 cups sifted confectioners' sugar
½ teaspoon almond extract

Combine the first 4 ingredients in the top of a double boiler. Mix well. Stir and cook over direct low heat until the sugar is dissolved. Increase the heat to moderate and cook, without stirring, to 226° F. on a candy thermometer. Cool to 110° F., or until the bottom of the pan can rest comfortably in the palm of the hand. With a wooden spoon, beat in confectioners' sugar, using only enough to make a frosting that is still thin enough to pour. Add the almond extract. Let the frosting stand over hot water to keep it at pouring consistency until it is to be used. If it thickens, add a few drops of hot water; if it is too thin, add a little more confectioners' sugar. If colored frosting is desired, add a few drops of red, yellow, green, or blue food coloring. Makes enough for 2½ dozen Petits Fours.

COFFEE FONDANT FROSTING

In the recipe for Fondant Frosting, replace the water with the same amount of strong coffee, and use 1 teaspoon vanilla extract instead of the almond extract.

KIRSCH FONDANT FROSTING

Add 1 tablespoon Kirsch, or Kirsch to taste, to Fondant Frosting.

CONFECTIONERS' SUGAR FLOWER AND LEAF FROSTING

1 large egg white
2 to 2½ cups sifted confectioners' sugar
food coloring

Place the egg white in the smaller bowl of an electric mixer. Gradually beat in 2 cups confectioners' sugar. If frosting is not stiff enough to stand in stiff peaks when the beater is slowly raised, beat in more confectioners' sugar, about 2 tablespoons at a time, until desired stiffness is reached. To color frosting, place 2 tablespoons frosting in each of 4 custard cups and keep covered with a damp cloth to prevent drying. Color one portion green by adding 5 to 6 drops green food coloring; one yellow with 10 drops yellow food coloring; one pink with 4 drops red food coloring; one lavender with 2 drops blue food coloring and 4 drops red. Put a little frosting on the four corners of a piece of waxed paper and place it frosting side down on a cooky sheet. Put green frosting in a cake-decorating tube fitted with a leaf nozzle (No. 65) and pipe leaves onto the paper. Make flowers in the same manner, using a flower nozzle (No. 15) with yellow, pink, or lavender frosting. Let the leaves and flowers dry on the waxed paper, then remove them and arrange them on Petits Fours. If desired, freeze the leaves and flowers on a tray, wrap the tray for the freezer, and store in freezer until needed. Makes 2½ dozen flowers and leaves.

⚜ CHOCOLATE PETITS FOURS

Génoise
Chocolate Butter-Cream Filling and Frosting
finely chopped toasted blanched almonds
melted semisweet chocolate

Split the Génoise into 2 layers, and sandwich the layers together with a thick layer of Chocolate Butter-Cream Filling and Frosting. Chill until filling is firm. Cut into 1½-inch squares and glaze as previously directed. Frost with a thin layer of Chocolate Butter-Cream Filling and Frosting. Sprinkle the edges with finely chopped almonds. Decorate the top of each piece with a large drop of melted semisweet chocolate. Store, tightly covered, in a cool place.

⚜ COFFEE BUTTER-CREAM PETITS FOURS

Génoise
Coffee Butter-Cream Filling and Frosting
Coffee Fondant Frosting for Petits Fours
candy coffee beans

Split the Génoise into 2 layers and sandwich the layers together with Coffee Butter-Cream Filling and Frosting. Chill until filling is firm. Cut cake into 1½-inch squares, triangles, or rectangles. Glaze and frost as previously directed, using Coffee Fondant Frosting. Decorate the top of each piece with a candy coffee bean. Store, tightly closed, in a cool place.

VARIATION

KIRSCH BUTTER-CREAM PETITS FOURS

In the recipe for Coffee Butter-Cream Petits Fours, replace the Coffee Butter-Cream Filling and Frosting with Kirsch Butter-Cream Filling and Frosting, and Coffee Fondant Frosting with Kirsch Fondant Frosting. Decorate with bits of glacéed cherries.

⚜ PISTACHIO NUT PETITS FOURS

Add ¼ cup finely chopped pistachio nuts to Butter-Cream Filling and Frosting. Spread between 2 thin Génoise layers and over the top. Chill until the frosting is firm. Cut into squares or other shapes. Glaze and frost as previously directed, using Fondant Frosting to which 2 to 3 drops of light green food coloring have been added.

⚜ RUM PETITS FOURS

Spread Rum Butter-Cream Filling and Frosting between 2 thin Génoise layers and over the top. Chill until the frosting is firm. Cut into desired shapes. Glaze and frost as previously directed, using Coffee Fondant Frosting or Chocolate Glaze. Decorate each with a candy coffee bean.

⚜ MOCHATINE PETITS FOURS

Génoise
Coffee Butter-Cream Filling and Frosting
coarse granulated sugar, or chopped toasted blanched almonds

Split the Génoise into 2 layers, and sandwich the layers together with Coffee Butter-Cream Filling and Frosting. Chill until filling is firm. Cut into squares, triangles, or rectangles. Glaze and frost as previously directed, using Coffee Butter-Cream Filling and Frosting. Sprinkle the edges with coarse granulated sugar or chopped almonds. Decorate the top of each piece with a rosette of the frosting. Store, tightly covered, in a cool place.

⚜ ORANGE PETITS FOURS

Génoise
orange marmalade
Orange Butter-Cream Filling and Frosting
Chocolate Fondant Frosting
candied orange rind

Split the Génoise into 2 layers and sandwich the layers together with thick orange marmalade. Spread the top with Orange Butter-Cream Filling and Frosting. Chill until frosting is firm. Using cooky cutters or a sharp knife, cut into assorted shapes (round, crescent, square, rectangular, etc.). Glaze and frost as previously directed, using Chocolate Glaze for the frosting. Decorate each with a small piece of candied orange rind.

PASTRIES MADE OF CHOU PASTE

⚜ SMALL CREAM PUFFS

Make small cream puffs from Chou Paste (see page 126). Bake and cool. When cold, fill them with any of the following:

1. French Pastry Cream mixed with finely chopped candied fruit marinated in rum, Kirsch, or other liqueur. Ice with Fondant Cake Icing flavored the same as the filling. Decorate with glacéed cherries or other candied fruit.
2. Almond Pastry Cream flavored with rum. Sprinkle with sifted confectioners' sugar.
3. Butter-Cream Filling and Frosting flavored with rum, Kirsch, or other liqueur. If desired, add finely chopped candied fruit marinated in the same liqueur as used to flavor the filling. Ice with Fondant Cake Icing. Decorate each with a bit of angelica.
4. Chantilly Cream flavored with vanilla extract, rum, Kirsch, or other liqueur. Ice with chocolate-, mocha-, coffee-, or vanilla-flavored Fondant Cake Icing.

Allow 2 cream puffs per serving.

⚜ CHOCOLATE ÉCLAIRS

Chou Paste (page 126)
French Pastry Cream
Chocolate Fondant Cake Icing

Pastries Made of Chou Paste

Pipe Chou Paste through a pastry bag fitted with a ½-inch nozzle in 1- by 4-inch strips, 2 inches apart, on a greased baking sheet. Bake in a preheated hot oven (425° F.) 30 to 35 minutes, or until golden brown. Do not underbake. Turn off oven heat. Pierce the éclairs with a knife near the bottom to allow steam to escape. Leave them in the oven 20 minutes to dry out the centers. Cool, split, and fill with French Pastry Cream. Frost with Chocolate Fondant. Makes 2 dozen éclairs.

⚜ COFFEE ÉCLAIRS

Make the éclairs as directed in the recipe for Chocolate Éclairs. Fill with Mocha Pastry Cream. Frost with Coffee Fondant Cake Icing. Garnish each with a candy coffee bean. Makes 24 éclairs. (See illustration, page 987.)

⚜ FROSTED SMALL ÉCLAIRS

Make small éclairs, about 1½ inches long. Bake and cool. Fill them with Chantilly Cream or French Pastry Cream flavored with vanilla, rum, Kirsch, coffee, chocolate, or other desired flavoring. Frost with Fondant Cake Icing. Allow 1 to 2 per serving.

⚜ PROFITEROLES WITH CHOCOLATE SAUCE

Chou Paste (page 126)
1 egg, beaten with 1 tablespoon water
Chantilly Cream
Thick Chocolate Sauce

Make half the recipe for Chou Paste. Put it in a pastry bag fitted with a ¾-inch nozzle, and pipe small balls about the size of walnuts onto greased cooky sheets. Or drop the paste from a teaspoon. Brush beaten egg over the tops of the balls. Bake in a preheated hot oven (425° F.) 20 to 25 minutes. Turn off oven heat. Prick puffs with a knife to allow steam to escape and leave them in the oven 15 minutes to allow centers to dry out. Cool. Fill from underneath with Chantilly Cream. Arrange the little cream puffs in champagne glasses, 3 for each serving, and cover them with chilled Thick Chocolate Sauce. Makes 6 to 8 servings.

Profiteroles may also be filled with vanilla ice cream.

THICK CHOCOLATE SAUCE

1 cup milk
1 cup light cream
3-inch piece vanilla bean, or 2 teaspoons vanilla extract
⅔ cup sugar
½ teaspoon cornstarch
⅛ teaspoon salt
4 large egg yolks
2 squares (2 ounces) unsweetened chocolate

Heat milk and ¾ cup of the cream, with the vanilla bean (if used). Combine the next 3 ingredients in the top of a double boiler, or in a saucepan. Add the egg yolks and mix well. Stir in the remaining ¼ cup of cream. Then add the hot milk and cream. Stir and cook over hot water or very low heat until the custard coats a metal spoon. Add the chocolate and stir until it is melted. Cool. Strain. If vanilla bean was not used, stir in the vanilla extract. Makes approximately 2 ¼ cups.

⚜ RÉLIGIEUSES

6 baked Plain Pastry (Pâte Brisée) tartlets, 3 inches in diameter
18 small Éclairs, 3 inches long
6 Small Cream Puffs
French Pastry Cream
whipped cream, sweetened to taste
Caramel Syrup
Mocha Butter-Cream Filling and Frosting

For each serving you will need 1 baked pastry tartlet, 3 éclairs, and 1 cream puff. Fill the tartlets and éclairs with French Pastry Cream and the cream puff with whipped cream. Fit the ends of 3 filled éclairs into the filled tartlet shell, pushing them into the cream and bringing the tops together to form a pyramid. Dip the bottom of each cream puff in Caramel Syrup and place one on top of each pyramid. Put whipped cream in a cake-decorating tube and pipe it around the éclairs. Frost the top of the pyramid with Mocha Butter Cream Filling. Makes 6 servings. (See illustration, page 987.)

⚜ CROQUEMBOUCHE

Roll Puff Pastry in a circle ¼ inch thick on a lightly buttered baking sheet. Cut it into an 8-inch circle using a round 8-inch layer-cake pan as a guide. Remove the pastry trimmings. Prick the pastry over the top with a fork. Bake in a preheated hot oven (425° F.) 12 to 15 minutes, or until browned. Make 100 Small Cream Puffs (the size of walnuts) from Chou Paste, bake, and cool. Fill with French Pastry Cream. Mix 2 cups sugar, ⅔ cup water, and ½ teaspoon cream of tartar in a heavy 1½-quart saucepan. Stir and cook until boiling point is reached. Continue cooking, without stirring, until the syrup has thickened and turned amber color. Place the pastry base on a large serving plate. Invert a charlotte mold or other suitably shaped dish on the pastry base to serve as a foundation. Dip the bottoms of the cream puffs, one at a time, in the syrup and place them around the edge of the base, touching one another. Make a second row on top of the first, placing the cream puffs between those on the bottom. Continue in this manner, building a pyramid of the cream puffs. Top it with one cream puff. Or, if you are an artist with spun sugar, make a top as illustrated on page 985.

SMALL PUFF-PASTE PASTRIES

⚜ FROSTED BÂTONS

Roll Puff Pastry ¼ inch thick in an 8- by 12-inch rectangle. Prick the pastry all over with a fork. Spread thinly with Royal Icing. Using a sharp knife, dipped in water frequently to prevent the icing from sticking, cut the rectangle into 3- by 1-inch strips. Place the strips on a slightly moistened baking sheet and set aside for the icing to dry. Chill thoroughly. Bake in a preheated hot oven (400° F.) 10 to 12 minutes. Allow 2 per serving. (See Culinary Techniques in Pictures.)

⚜ CONDÉ

Roll Puff Pastry ¼ inch thick in an 8- by 12-inch rectangle. Place the pastry on a slightly moistened baking sheet. Prick it all over with a fork. Spread the top with Royal Icing. Sprinkle with chopped blanched almonds. Chill thoroughly. Bake in a preheated hot oven (400° F.) 10 to 12 minutes. Transfer the pastry to a pastry board. Using a very sharp knife, cut it into 4 strips 3 inches wide, then cut the strips crosswise into pieces 1 inch wide. Allow 2 to 3 pieces per serving.

⚜ COUQUES

Roll Puff Pastry ¼ inch thick. Using a 2-inch biscuit cutter with a scalloped edge, cut the pastry into biscuits. Shape them into ovals by rolling them over once on a pastry board sprinkled with granulated sugar. Place them on buttered baking sheets, sugared side up, and bake in a preheated very hot oven (450° F.) 8 to 10 minutes, or until the ovals are puffed and browned. Allow 2 to 3 per serving. (See illustration, page 977.)

⚜ PUFF-PASTRY CROISSANTS

Roll Puff Pastry 1/4 inch thick into 9-inch circles, using a round 9-inch cake pan as a guide. Cut each circle into 12 wedges. Starting at the widest end of the wedge, roll each loosely to form a cylinder thicker in the center than at the ends. Shape the rolls into crescents, sprinkle them lightly with confectioners' sugar, and place them on an ungreased baking sheet. Chill thoroughly. Bake in a preheated hot oven (400° F.) 5 minutes. Reduce heat to 350° F. and bake 10 to 15 minutes, or until the crescents have browned. Allow 2 to 3 per serving. (See illustration, page 977.)

⚜ PUFF-PASTE FANCIES

Roll Puff Pastry 1/8 inch thick in sheets 14 by 12 inches. Place on baking sheets lined with 3 to 4 layers of brown paper. Prick all over with a fork. Chill thoroughly. Bake the same as for Napoleons. The pastry should be light but not puffy. Put 2 or 3 layers together with French Pastry Cream or Almond Pastry Cream. Spread the top with Royal Icing, or sprinkle with confectioners' sugar. With a sharp knife dipped in boiling water, cut into oval-shaped pieces 1 1/2 inches wide. Allow 1 per serving.

⚜ HORSESHOES (*Fers à Cheval*)

Puff Pastry
apricot jam
1 egg
1 tablespoon milk
granulated sugar

Roll Puff Pastry 1/4 inch thick on a lightly floured board in 12- by 6-inch strips. Cut the dough into 3 lengthwise strips 2 inches wide. Pipe or spread a little apricot jam down the center of each strip. Fold the dough over and press the edges together. Cut each strip in half. Press the ends of the dough together to prevent the jam from seeping out while baking. Form the strips into horseshoe shape, and place them on a cooky sheet lined with 3 thicknesses of brown paper. Chill 2 hours. Brush with the egg beaten with the milk and sprinkle with granulated sugar. Bake in a preheated very hot oven (450° F.) 8 minutes. Reduce heat to 350° F. (moderate) and bake 5 minutes more.

Place a cold cooky sheet under the one on which the Horseshoes are baking, reduce heat to 300° F. (slow) and bake another 5 minutes, or until browned. Allow 2 horseshoes per serving. (See illustration, page 977.)

⚜ PUFFED JAM TURNOVERS

Roll Puff Pastry ¼ inch thick and cut into 3-inch rounds with a scalloped round cooky cutter. Place 1 rounded teaspoon of jam (any kind) in the center of each round. Dampen the edges of the rounds with water and fold the dough over to make them into half-moon shapes. Press the edges together. Place the turnovers on a lightly moistened baking sheet. Beat 1 egg with 1 tablespoon of milk and brush the tops. Chill thoroughly. Prick the top of each in one or two places with a fork. Bake in a preheated hot oven (425° F.) 5 minutes. Reduce heat to moderate (350° F.) and bake 12 to 15 minutes, or until turnovers have browned. Allow 2 turnovers per serving. (See illustration, page 977.)

⚜ NAPOLEONS

Roll Puff Pastry into a rectangle ¼ inch thick and cut it into strips 1½ inches wide and the length of the baking sheet. Place them on baking sheets lined with 3 to 4 layers of brown paper. Prick pastry all over with a fork and chill 1 to 2 hours. Bake in a preheated very hot oven (450° F.) 8 minutes. Reduce heat to 350° F. (moderate) and bake 8 to 10 minutes. Place cold baking sheets under the hot ones in the oven to prevent the bottoms of the Napoleons from becoming too brown and bake 8 to 10 more minutes. Transfer the strips to cooling racks. When they are cold, cut them into 3-inch pieces with a very sharp knife or a serrated knife. Make the small strips into sandwiches with French Pastry Cream as the filling. Spread the tops with Royal Icing or dust them with sifted confectioners' sugar. Allow 1 Napoleon per serving. (See illustration, page 977.)

⚜ PALMIERS

Roll Puff Pastry ¼ inch thick into an 8- by 15-inch rectangle. Sprinkle with granulated sugar. Fold each end of the dough to the center of the rectangle. Sprinkle with granulated sugar. Fold each end of the folded dough to center of the rectangle, making 4 layers of dough on each side of the center. Then fold the two sides of the dough together as in closing a book. Roll the rolling pin down the dough lightly once. With a sharp knife cut the dough into crosswise slices ½ inch thick. Place the slices about 1 inch apart on a baking sheet. Bake in a preheated hot oven (425° F.) 10 to 12 minutes, or until golden brown. Allow 2 Palmiers per serving. (See illustration, page 977; see also Culinary Techniques in Pictures.)

⚜ SACRISTAINS

Roll Puff Pastry ¼ inch thick into a rectangle 12 by 8 inches. Beat 1 egg with 1 tablespoon milk and brush the surface. Sprinkle with finely chopped almonds and dust with confectioners' sugar. Cut the pastry into crosswise strips ½ inch to ¾ inch wide. Shape them like corkscrews by taking one end of the strip in each hand and giving it a twist. Place them on baking sheets and bake in a preheated hot oven (400° F.) 10 to 12 minutes, or until they are golden brown. Allow 3 per serving. (See Culinary Techniques in Pictures.)

⚜ VIENNESE PASTRIES

Roll Puff Pastry ⅛ inch thick and cut it into 3- by 3-inch squares. Place 1 teaspoon of Almond Pastry Cream, French Pastry Cream, or jam in the center of each square. Bring the four corners of the square to the center, having them cover the filling. Beat 1 egg with 1 tablespoon water and brush the pastries. Sprinkle with chopped almonds and confectioners' sugar. Bake in a preheated hot oven (400° F.) 10 to 12 minutes, or until browned. Allow 2 pastries per serving.

CRÊPES AND WAFFLES

⚜ DESSERT CRÊPES

1 cup sifted all-purpose flour
½ teaspoon salt
1 tablespoon sugar
3 large eggs
2 cups milk
1 tablespoon rum or cognac
2 tablespoons butter, melted

Sift together the first 3 ingredients into a mixing bowl. Beat the eggs, add the milk and rum or cognac, and stir into the flour mixture. Blend in the melted butter. Let the batter stand 2 hours to improve the flavor and texture. Heat a 6-inch skillet or a French crêpe pan and brush the bottom lightly with melted butter. For each crêpe pour in 2 tablespoons of the batter. Quickly rotate the pan to spread the batter uniformly over the bottom. Cook over direct moderate heat 1 to 2 minutes or until the underside is brown and bubbles have formed over the top. Turn and cook ½ to 1 minute or until the other side has browned. When each crêpe is cooked, sprinkle confectioners' sugar on it. Stack the crêpes in pancake fashion in a pan lined with a clean towel and when all are cooked fold the ends of the towel over them. Just before serving, heat the crêpes, without unwrapping, in a preheated moderate oven (350° F.) only until they are hot (10 minutes). Serve sprinkled with confectioners' sugar or with syrup or honey. Or spread them with jelly or marmalade and roll them up, or serve them as Crêpes Suzette. Makes 18 crêpes or 6 servings.

⚜ CRÊPES SUZETTE (*Classic Method*)

Dessert Crêpes
Crêpes Suzette Sauce
brandy or Grand Marnier

Have the sauce hot and place the crêpes in it, spooning it over them until they are well covered. Fold them into quarters. Heat the brandy or Grand Marnier in a small saucepan, and ignite it, and quickly pour it over the crêpes. Bring the dish to the table flaming. Serve the crêpes with some of the sauce poured over them. The crêpes may be made ahead of time, but the sauce should be made just before it is used. Allow 3 crêpes to a serving. (See Culinary Techniques in Pictures.)

CRÊPES SUZETTE SAUCE

1 medium-sized navel orange
4 large-sized lumps sugar
4 tablespoons sweet butter
1 teaspoon lemon juice
¼ cup Cointreau or Curaçao
¼ cup Benedictine or Grand Marnier

Wash the orange well and dry it thoroughly. Rub the lumps of sugar over the skin, then place them on a board and crush them. Transfer the crushed sugar to a heatproof dish or to the inset pan of a chafing dish. Squeeze out the juice from the orange and discard the rind. (The rind is not used because the sugar has absorbed enough flavor.) Add the butter, orange juice, and lemon juice to the sugar and mix well. Cook until the sugar and butter have melted, then add the liqueurs and heat to boiling point. Makes enough sauce for 6 servings.

⚜ CRÊPES SUZETTE (*Quick Method*)

18 Dessert Crêpes
Quick Crêpes Suzette Sauce
brandy

Make the crêpes ahead of time. Immediately before ready to serve, wrap crêpes in a towel, place in a baking pan, and heat in a preheated moderate oven (350° F.). Remove the crêpes from the oven, spread them with the sauce, fold or roll them, and place them in a heatproof dish. Heat the brandy in a small saucepan, ignite it, and quickly pour it over the crêpes. Bring to the table flaming. Makes 6 servings.

QUICK CRÊPES SUZETTE SAUCE

½ cup (1 stick) softened sweet butter
½ cup sugar
1 tablespoon grated orange rind
⅓ cup orange juice
1 teaspoon lemon juice
¼ cup Cointreau, Curaçao, or Grand Marnier
¼ cup apricot brandy or peach brandy

Stir and beat the butter until it is creamy. Gradually blend in the sugar and orange rind. Add the orange juice, lemon juice, and liqueurs. Makes 6 servings.

⚜ PARISIAN WAFFLES (*Gaufres Parisienne*)

1 cup sugar
1 teaspoon vanilla extract
½ cup (1 stick) softened butter
4 large eggs, separated
1½ cups sifted all-purpose flour
⅓ cup milk

Gradually blend the sugar and vanilla extract with the butter. Stir and beat the mixture until it is creamy and lemon-colored. Beat in the egg yolks, one at a time. Add the flour and milk alternately to the mixture. Beat the egg whites until they stand in soft stiff peaks and carefully fold them into the batter. Set the heat control of the waffle iron to low and preheat it 5 minutes, or only until it is hot. Brush the iron lightly with melted butter. Spoon the batter into the hot waffle iron (the amount depends upon the size of the waffle iron). Bake 2 to 3 minutes or until waffles are brown. Cut each waffle into 4 sections. Serve hot or cold with ice cream. Or, if desired, put 2 sections together in shortcake fashion, with sliced ripe peaches, raspberries, or strawberries, sweetened to taste, and whipped cream. Makes 4 to 5 waffles.

VARIATION

FILLED WAFFLES

Make Parisian Waffles. While they are hot, cut each into 4 sections and cool them under a weight so that they will retain their shape. When they are cold, put each 2 sections together with Praline Butter-Cream Filling and Frosting between.

⚜ SPONGE-CAKE WAFFLES

4 large eggs, separated
1 cup sugar
¼ cup cold water
1 teaspoon vanilla extract
2 teaspoons grated orange rind
½ teaspoon grated lemon rind
¼ teaspoon salt
1 cup sifted cake flour

Beat the egg yolks until they are light and lemon-colored. Gradually beat in the sugar. Continue beating until the mixture is thick. Add the next 4 ingredients, and beat well. Add the salt to the egg whites and beat them until they stand in soft stiff peaks. Pile them on the beaten egg-yolk mixture, sift the flour over them, and carefully fold them into the mixture. Set the heat control on the waffle iron to low and preheat it 5 minutes, or until the iron is hot. Brush the iron lightly with melted butter. Spoon the batter into the iron (the amount depends upon the size of the waffle iron) and bake 2 to 3 minutes or until the steam subsides. Serve hot or cold with ice cream, or Chantilly Cream, or with sweetened berries, sliced apricots, nectarines, or peaches and Chantilly Cream. Makes 3 to 4 waffles.

⚜ RICH DESSERT WAFFLES

1 cup sifted cake flour
1 tablespoon sugar
1 teaspoon double-acting baking powder
1 teaspoon salt
2 large eggs, beaten
1 cup heavy cream

Sift the first four ingredients together into a mixing bowl. Beat the egg yolks with the cream and add to the dry ingredients. Mix the batter until it is smooth. Beat the egg whites until they stand in soft stiff peaks and carefully fold them into the batter. Spoon the batter into a preheated waffle iron and bake 3 to 4 minutes or until the steam subsides. Serve with Lemon Sauce, Orange Sauce, Chocolate Sauce, or any other desired dessert sauce. Makes 3 to 4 waffles.

TARTS AND TARTLETS

What Americans call a pie is a *tarte* in France and a tart in England. American tarts are small individual pies, which in France are *tartelettes*. Since the recipes here are French, the term tart has been used for the larger size and tartlet for the smaller. Oval or boat-shaped tartlets are called barquettes.

⚜ APPLE MERINGUE TART

1 9-inch baked Plain Pastry tart (pie) shell
cooked dried apricots, or apricot jam
4 cups thick sweetened applesauce
⅓ cup toasted blanched shredded almonds
1½ tablespoons each finely chopped candied pineapple, citron, and orange peel (optional)
⅛ teaspoon salt
2 large egg whites
5 tablespoons sugar

Spread the bottom of a baked 9-inch tart shell with dried apricots cooked and cooled according to package directions, or with apricot jam. Combine the applesauce, almonds, candied fruit (if used), and salt. Turn into the tart shell. Beat the egg whites until they stand in soft stiff peaks, then gradually beat in the sugar, beating well after each addition. Put the meringue in a pastry bag fitted with a star nozzle and pipe the meringue over the top in lattice fashion. Drop about ¼ teaspoon of apricot jam into each space left by the lattice. Bake in a preheated slow oven (325° F.) 15 minutes. Cool before serving. Makes one 9-inch tart. (See illustration, page 907.)

⚜ LATTICE-TOP APPLE TART

Plain Pastry for 2-crust 9-inch pie
3 cups thick unsweetened applesauce
1 teaspoon grated lemon rind
½ teaspoon ground cinnamon
¼ teaspoon ground mace
¼ teaspoon salt
1 cup sugar
3 large egg yolks
½ cup (1 stick) butter, melted
1 egg white, beaten with 1 tablespoon milk

Line a 9-inch pie plate or round 9-inch cake pan with one-half of the pastry. Combine the next 5 ingredients. Mix the sugar, egg yolks, and cooled melted butter, and blend with the applesauce. Turn the mixture into the pastry shell. Roll out the remaining pastry ⅛ inch thick, cut it into strips ½ inch wide, and arrange the strips over the top of the pie in lattice fashion. With the thumb press the ends of the lattice pastry against the pastry for the under crust, sealing it well. Turn up the edge and flute it with the thumb and index finger, or crimp it with a fork. Brush pastry with egg white beaten with the milk. Bake in a preheated hot oven (425° F.) for 15 minutes. Reduce heat to

350° F. (moderate) and bake 25 to 30 minutes, or until the crust has browned. Makes one 9-inch tart. (See illustration, page 906.)

⚜ APRICOT TART

1 9-inch Plain Pastry tart (pie) shell
½ cup apricot jam
French Pastry Cream
poached apricot halves, or canned apricots
2 tablespoons apple jelly
2 tablespoons water
confectioners' sugar (optional)
pistachio nuts (optional)
whipped cream (optional)

Bake the pastry shell and set it aside to cool. Spread the apricot jam over the pastry. Cover the jam with French Pastry Cream, filling the shell half full. Drain the apricot halves and arrange them decoratively over the filling. Combine the jelly and water and heat until jelly is melted. Let the jelly stand a few minutes to thicken slightly. Brush it over apricots. If desired, sift confectioners' sugar over the top and sprinkle with pistachio nuts, or decorate around the edges with whipped cream. Makes one 9-inch pie (tart).

⚜ CHEESE TART WITH ALMOND CRUST

¾ package zwieback
½ cup toasted blanched almonds
¼ cup (½ stick) butter (softened)
11 ounces cream cheese (one 8-ounce package and one 3-ounce package)
2 large eggs
1 teaspoon vanilla extract
1 cup sugar
1 cup sour cream

Put the zwieback and the almonds through a food chopper, using the finest blade, or grind a little at a time in an electric blender. Add the butter and mix well. Turn the mixture into a 9-inch pie plate and press it over the bottom and sides, making it of uniform thickness. Have the cheese at room temperature and place it in a mixing bowl. Beat in the eggs, one at a time, with an electric beater. Add the vanilla extract and ½ cup of the sugar. Beat until mixture is well blended. Spoon into the prepared pie crust. Bake in a preheated moderate oven (350° F.) 25 minutes. Reduce heat to 275° F. (very slow) and bake 5 minutes longer. Cool if desired. Blend the remaining ½ cup sugar with the sour cream and spread it over the hot or cold pie. Serve warm or chilled. Makes one 9-inch tart.

⚜ ORANGE TART

1 9-inch Sweet Pie Pastry tart shell
3 cups fresh orange segments
⅔ cup sugar
water, if needed
2 tablespoons cornstarch
1/16 teaspoon salt
½ teaspoon vanilla extract
apricot jam
preserved orange slices
glacéed cherries

Bake the tart shell and set it aside to cool. Combine the orange segments and sugar and let stand 30 minutes for juice to form, then turn them into a sieve and place it over a bowl for about 15 minutes to drain the juice. Measure the juice and add water, if necessary, to make 1 cup. Blend with the cornstarch and salt until mixture is smooth. Stir and cook in a small saucepan 3 to 4 minutes, or until thickened. Add the vanilla extract. Cool. Spread a layer of apricot jam over the tart shell. Add the orange segments and pour the thickened juice over the top. Chill for two hours. Garnish as desired with preserved orange slices and glacéed cherries. Serve cold. Makes one 9-inch tart. (See illustration, page 906.)

⚜ STRAWBERRY TART

1 9-inch tart shell made from Plain Pastry or Puff Pastry
3 pints fresh strawberries
1 cup sugar
water, if needed
1½ tablespoons cornstarch
1/16 teaspoon salt
½ cup heavy cream (optional)
1 tablespoon sugar (optional)
Kirsch to taste (optional)
confectioners' sugar, sifted

Bake the tart shell and set it aside to cool. Wash, hull, and slice enough strawberries to make 2 cups. Combine with ⅔ cup of sugar. Cut the remaining strawberries in half, combine with the remaining ⅓ cup sugar, and let strawberries stand about 30 minutes for juice to form. Put the sliced strawberries in a strainer over a bowl, for about 15 minutes, to drain the juice from them. Do the same with the halved strawberries in a separate strainer. Measure the juice and add water, if necessary, to make 1 cup. Blend the juice with the cornstarch until mixture is smooth. Stir and cook in a small saucepan 3 to 4 minutes, or until thickened. Cool. Place the sliced strawberries on the pastry shell and cover them with the strawberry halves, red rounded side up. Pour the thickened juice over the top. Chill two hours. Sprinkle the edge of the crust with sifted confectioners' sugar. If desired, combine cream and sugar and whip until it stands in soft stiff peaks, flavor to taste with Kirsch, and serve over the tart. Makes one 9-inch tart. (See illustration, page 907.)

VARIATION

STRAWBERRY TARTLETS

Bake 6 3-inch Plain Pastry tartlet shells. Prepare the strawberries as directed in the recipe for Strawberry Tart and divide them equally among the 6 tartlet shells. Proceed as directed in the recipe. Garnish with Kirsch-flavored whipped cream. Makes 6 tarts.

⚜ MILANESE PASTRY TART SHELLS

1½ cups sifted all-purpose flour
⅛ teaspoon salt
¼ cup sifted confectioners' sugar
½ teaspoon grated lemon rind
1 teaspoon grated orange rind
½ cup ground nuts (walnuts, pecans, almonds, or hazelnuts)
½ cup butter
about 3 tablespoons water

Sift together the first 3 ingredients. Add the lemon rind, orange rind, and nuts, and mix until well blended. Add the butter and cut it in with a pastry blender or with 2 knives. Gradually add enough water to hold the pastry together. Chill the dough 1 to 2 hours. Divide dough into 8 equal parts. Roll each part in a circle 1/16 inch thick. Fit the rounds into 8 tart pans 2 inches across the bottom and 3½ inches across the top. Turn the edges of the pastry rounds under and crimp them with the tines of a fork. Prick each with a fork in several places to prevent blistering. Bake in a preheated moderate oven (350° F.) 15 to 20 minutes. Store in the tart pans until ready to use. This pastry may also be baked in 12 very small tart pans. Makes 8 tart shells.

MILANESE PASTRY FLAN RINGS

Divide Milanese Pastry for tart shells into 2 equal parts. Roll each ⅛ inch thick in a circle large enough to fit a 9-inch flan ring and fit it in the flan ring. Prick the pastry in several places with a fork. Bake in a preheated moderate oven (325° F.) 15 to 20 minutes. Makes two 9-inch flan rings.

APPLE TARTLETS BULGARIAN STYLE

8 tart medium-sized apples
1 tablespoon lemon juice
½ cup cold water
⅔ cup sugar
1¼ cups water
⅔ cup dry red wine
¾ cup French Pastry Cream
¼ cup chopped muscat raisins
2 tablespoons chopped blanched toasted almonds
8 baked Milanese Pastry Tart Shells
¼ cup red currant jelly
1 teaspoon cornstarch

Peel and core the apples and immerse them in the lemon juice mixed with ½ cup of water, to prevent discoloration. Combine the sugar, the 1¼ cups of water, and ⅓ cup of the wine. Bring to boiling point. Add 4 apples at a time to the syrup and cook slowly about 10 minutes, or until apples are tender when pierced with a toothpick. Turn them in the syrup to cook them uniformly. Repeat with the remaining apples. Remove from heat and add the remaining wine. Cool the apples in the syrup and chill. Drain the apples, reserving the syrup. Combine the next 3 ingredients and spoon the mixture into the cavities of the apples, mounding it over the tops. Place an apple in each tart shell. Cook the syrup until it has reduced by one-fourth. Mix the red currant jelly with the cornstarch and add to the syrup. Bring to boiling point and spoon over the apples. Makes 8 servings.

APRICOT TARTLETS

Bake small square tartlet shells of Sweet Pie Pastry. Marinate candied apricots in Cointreau 30 minutes, drain well, and place one in each tartlet. Frost with Cointreau-flavored Fondant Cake Icing. Decorate each with a small piece of candied apricot and a pistachio nut in each corner. The icing may be omitted and each tart decorated with a glacéed cherry which has been marinated in Cointreau for 30 minutes. Allow 1 tartlet per serving. (See illustration, page 989.)

BANANA TARTLETS

3 tablespoons cornstarch
⅔ cup sugar
¼ teaspoon salt
2 cups milk
3 large eggs, lightly beaten
1 teaspoon vanilla extract

4 bananas
1 teaspoon lemon juice
6 4-inch baked tartlet shells
3 tablespoons currant jelly
⅓ cup heavy cream
1 tablespoon confectioners' sugar

Combine the first 3 ingredients in a saucepan. Add 1¾ cups of the milk and stir and cook over moderately low heat until the mixture has thickened. Mix the remaining ¼ cup milk with the beaten eggs and blend with the first mixture. Stir and cook over low heat until the mixture has the consistency of mayonnaise. Remove the saucepan from the heat and set it in a pan of ice water to chill the mixture. Mash 1 banana with lemon juice, add it to the chilled custard, and spoon the custard into the tartlet shells. Slice the remaining bananas ⅛ inch thick and place them over the filling. Melt the jelly over hot water and spread a thin layer over the bananas. Chill. Combine the cream and confectioners' sugar, beat until the cream stands in soft stiff peaks, put it into a pastry bag, and pipe a rosette over each tartlet. Makes 6 tartlets.

⚜ CHERRY PASTRIES

Fill cold baked 1½-inch tartlet shells with Kirsch Butter-Cream Filling and Frosting. Place half a glacéed cherry that has been marinated in Kirsch for 30 minutes in the center of each. Frost with Fondant Cake Icing flavored with Kirsch. Decorate with two lines of Chocolate Fondant. Allow 2 pastries for each serving.

⚜ CHERRY TARTLETS

8 baked tartlet or barquette shells
1 cup sugar
3 tablespoons cornstarch
⅛ teaspoon salt
1 cup pitted crushed fresh cherries
¼ cup water
3 cups pitted whole fresh cherries
¼ teaspoon almond extract
almonds or pistachio nuts (optional)
whipped cream (optional)

Combine the sugar, cornstarch, and salt in a saucepan. Add the crushed cherries and the water. Mix well. Stir and cook over moderate heat until the juice is clear and thick. Remove from heat, cover, and cool to lukewarm. Add the whole cherries and the almond extract. Mix well. Spoon the mixture into the baked tartlet or barquette shells. If desired, chop almonds or pistachio nuts and sprinkle around the edges, or serve topped with whipped cream. Makes 8 tartlets. (See illustration, page 908.)

⚜ FRUIT CREAM TARTLETS

Sweet Pie Pastry
¼ cup cornstarch
½ cup sugar
1⁄16 teaspoon salt
2 cups milk
4 large egg yolks
1 tablespoon Curaçao, or enough to taste, or 1½ teaspoons vanilla extract
about 1 cup green seedless grapes, strawberries, raspberries, orange sections, canned pineapple wedges, or sliced canned pears
1 tablespoon cornstarch
2 tablespoons sugar
¾ cup fruit juice
whipped cream

Make Sweet Pie Pastry. Divide the dough into 8 equal parts. Roll each 1⁄16 inch thick in a circle or an oval. Fit them into 8 tartlet pans measuring about 3 inches across the top, or into small barquette pans. Prick the pastry with a fork in several places, to prevent blistering. Bake in a preheated moderate oven (350° F.) 15 minutes or until browned. Remove from oven and cool thoroughly. Combine the cornstarch, sugar, and salt in the top of a double boiler or in a saucepan. Heat 1¾ cups of the milk and gradually add it to the sugar mixture. Stir and cook over low heat until mixture is very thick. Blend the remaining ¼ cup of milk with the egg yolks, gradually add to the hot mixture, and stir and cook until the mixture is about the consistency of thick mayonnaise. Add the Curaçao or vanilla extract. Cool completely. Spoon the mixture into the cold baked tart shells. Chill 3 to 4 hours. Before serving, arrange the desired fruit over the tops. Combine the 1 tablespoon cornstarch and the 2 tablespoons sugar in a small saucepan, add the fruit juice, and cook until the liquid is thick and clear. Cool slightly and spoon over the fruit tarts. Garnish with whipped cream, if desired. Makes 8 tarts. (See illustration, page 908.)

⚜ HAZELNUT BARQUETTES

Bake small boat-shaped Sweet Pastry tartlet shells and set aside to cool. Fill with Hazelnut Butter-Cream Filling and Frosting. Ice with Fondant Cake Icing. Sprinkle cocoa in a line down the center and garnish with half a hazelnut in each corner. Allow 1 barquette per serving.

⚜ LEMON TARTLETS

8 baked Sweet Pastry tartlet shells, 2 inches in diameter
5 large eggs, beaten
1½ cups sugar
¾ teaspoon ground mace
1½ tablespoons grated lemon rind
2 tablespoons butter
⅓ cup heavy cream, whipped
Chocolate Sauce

Bake the tartlet shells and set them aside to cool. Place the eggs and sugar in the top of a double boiler. Stir and cook over hot water (not boiling) 15 to 20 minutes, or until thickened. Add the next 3 ingredients, mix well, and cool. Spoon into the baked tart shells. Garnish with whipped cream and a little Chocolate Sauce. Makes 8 tartlets. (See illustration, page 987.)

⚜ LINZER TARTLETS (OR LINZER TORTE)

1½ cups unpeeled almonds, grated
1 cup sifted all-purpose flour
⅛ teaspoon salt
¼ teaspoon ground cinnamon
⅛ teaspoon ground cloves
1 cup (2 sticks) butter
½ cup granulated sugar
2 large egg yolks
raspberry or currant jam
1 egg white
confectioners' sugar (optional)

Prepare the almonds and set them aside. Sift together the next 4 ingredients. Add the butter and cut it into the flour with a pastry blender or 2 knives. Add the grated almonds and mix well. Blend the sugar with the egg yolks and stir into the flour mixture. Knead the dough until all the ingredients are well blended and the dough is smooth. Press two-thirds of the dough in 8 ungreased tartlet pans, about 2 inches in diameter, covering the bottom and sides well. Chill the remaining one-third of the dough. Spread raspberry or currant jam in the tart shells. Roll the chilled dough ⅛ inch thick and cut strips ⅜ inch wide and make a cross with 2 strips on the top of each tart. Crimp the edges with a fork or with a pastry cutter. Beat the egg white until foamy and brush it over the tops. Bake in a preheated slow oven (325° F.) 40 minutes or until pastry has browned. Cool. Before serving, sprinkle with confectioners' sugar, if desired. Makes 8 tartlets. (See illustration, page 986.)

This can also be baked in 8-inch pie plate to make a Linzer Torte.

⚜ NUT TARTLETS

Bake small Sweet Pastry tartlet shells. Cool. Add chopped nuts (almonds, hazelnuts, pecans, or pistachios) to Butter-Cream Filling and Frosting, and fill the tartlet shells. Frost with Fondant Cake Icing. Dip nut halves in caramel and place one on top of each tart. Allow 1 tartlet per serving.

⚜ PEACH TARTLETS

8 baked tartlet shells
1 cup sugar
3 tablespoons cornstarch
⅛ teaspoon salt
1 cup crushed fresh peaches
¼ cup water
3 cups sliced fresh peaches
whipped cream (optional)

Combine the sugar, cornstarch, and salt in a saucepan. Add the crushed peaches and the water and mix well. Stir and cook over moderate heat until the juice is clear and thick. Remove from heat, cover, and cool to lukewarm. Add the sliced peaches and mix well. Spoon into the baked tartlet shells. Serve topped with whipped cream, if desired. Makes 8 tartlets. (See illustration, page 908.)

⚜ NEAPOLITAN PEACH TARTLETS

6 Plain Pastry tartlet shells, 3 inches in diameter
6 large peach halves, poached, or 6 canned peach halves
Apricot Jam Sauce
6 almond halves

Bake the tartlet shells and set them aside to cool. Drain the peach halves well and place one in each tart shell, rounded side up. Coat with Apricot Jam Sauce. Garnish each with half an almond. Makes 6 servings.

TO POACH PEACHES

Combine ¾ cup sugar, 2 cups water, and a 2-inch piece of vanilla bean in a saucepan. Bring to boiling point and boil 5 minutes. Add 6 large raw peach halves and cook 5 to 8 minutes, or until tender when tested with a toothpick. Cool in the syrup.

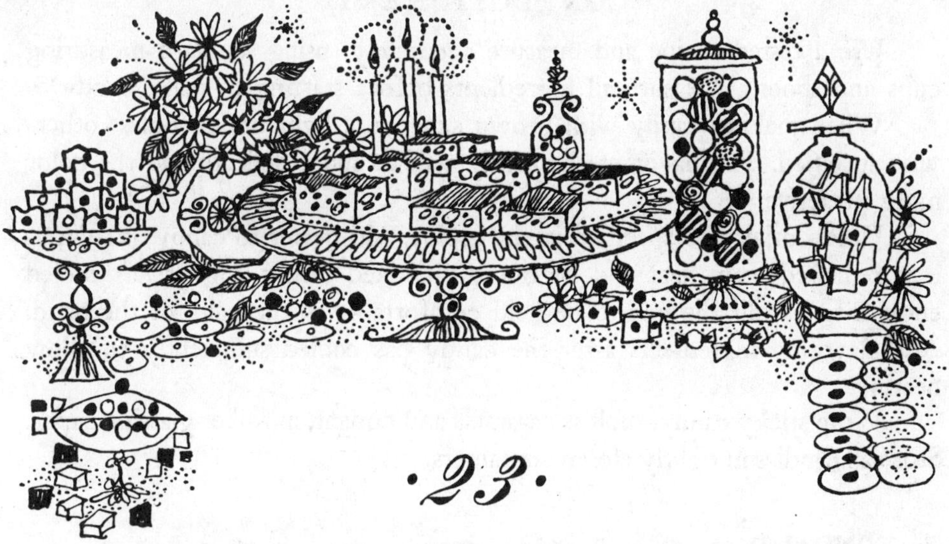

·23·

CONFECTIONERY

Excellent candies and other confectionery can be made at home if a few simple rules are followed.

Choose a clear, dry day, since candy picks up moisture from the air and becomes sticky. If you must make candy on a rainy day, cook it at a temperature about 2 degrees higher than is specified in the recipe.

Use a smooth-surfaced saucepan of the specified size and one heavy enough to prevent scorching.

A wooden spoon is best for stirring, since it can be handled comfortably in hot candy and does not scratch the pan. Use a strong spoon for beating a stiff cooled syrup mixture.

A candy thermometer gives the most accurate temperature check on boiling the syrup. However, a simple cold-water test may be used if a thermometer is not available. The directions for making the tests are given in each recipe. If a thermometer is used, be sure that the bulb is immersed in the syrup and does not touch the bottom of the pan. Read it at eye level.

A spatula with a flexible blade is best for taking candy from pans and platters and for beating fondant.

For working candy, use a smooth surface, such as a marble slab, a large platter, or a baking sheet.

Use a tested recipe and measure accurately, using standard measuring cups and spoons. Measure all ingredients before starting to make candy.

When making candy with brown sugar, use light brown unless otherwise specified. The flavor of the candy will be more delicate and the color more attractive.

Unless otherwise specified in the recipe, add butter to candy as soon as it is removed from heat and do not stir cooked candy until it has cooled enough to permit the pan to be held comfortably in the palm of the hand. Add flavoring ingredients after the candy has cooled sufficiently to allow beating.

Wrap sticky candy, such as caramels and nougat, in foil or glassine paper. Store all candies in tightly closed containers.

⚜ FONDANT

2 cups sugar
2 tablespoons light corn syrup
1¼ cups water
1 teaspoon vanilla extract

Place all ingredients in a heavy-bottomed 1½-quart saucepan. Mix well. Stir and cook until sugar has dissolved. Remove the spoon when boiling point is reached. Cover and cook 3 minutes. Steam condensing on the sides of the pan will wash down any sugar crystals that may have formed there. Place candy thermometer in the syrup, being sure that the bulb does not touch the bottom or sides of the pan. Cook uncovered, without stirring, until the thermometer registers 238° F., or until a soft ball forms when a little of the syrup is dropped in cold water. Wash away any sugar crystals from the sides of the pan with a swab or a pastry brush dipped in cold water. Pour the mixture into a large platter that has been rinsed in cold water, but not dried. Place platter on a wire rack to cool to 110° F., or until platter can be held in the palm of the hand without discomfort. (Do not stir or agitate fondant during the cooling period.) With a spatula or paddle, work the fondant back and forth until it is white and creamy. Spoon into a tightly covered jar and store in the refrigerator 24 hours or more to ripen. Fondant will keep several weeks if it is refrigerated. Use for stuffing dates, figs, for making mint patties, nut bars, and chocolate-dipped bonbons.

⚜ CHOCOLATE FONDANT

To the Fondant recipe add 1½ squares (1½ ounces) unsweetened chocolate along with the sugar and water. Cook as directed in the recipe. Sprinkle 1 teaspoon vanilla extract over the top of the Fondant before starting to beat or work it.

FONDANT MINT PATTIES

Melt 1 cup Fondant slowly over hot water. Add red, green, or yellow food coloring as desired, and peppermint or wintergreen flavoring to taste. Drop Fondant on waxed paper from the tip of a teaspoon, in patties the size of quarters. As soon as the patties are firm, loosen them with a spatula, since they may break if allowed to stand too long.

BROWN-SUGAR FONDANT

1 cup granulated white sugar
1 cup light brown sugar
1¼ cups water
1 teaspoon vanilla extract

Combine the first 3 ingredients in a heavy-bottomed 1½-quart saucepan. Mix well. Stir and cook over moderate heat until sugar is dissolved. Remove the spoon when boiling point is reached. Cover and cook 3 minutes. Steam condensing on the sides of the pan will wash down any sugar crystals that have formed there. Place a thermometer in the syrup, being sure that the bulb does not touch the bottom or sides of the pan. Cook without stirring until the thermometer reaches 238° to 240° F., or until the syrup forms a soft ball when half a teaspoonful of the syrup is dropped in cold water. The lower temperature produces a soft fondant while the higher temperature produces a firm one. With a swab or a pastry brush dipped in cold water, wash away any sugar crystals that form on the sides of the pan. Pour the mixture onto a large platter that has been rinsed in cold water but not dried. Place platter on a wire rack to cool to 110° F., or until platter can be held in the palm of the hand without discomfort. Work the fondant back and forth with a spatula or paddle until the fondant is light and creamy. Put fondant in a jar or bowl and cover tightly. Refrigerate 24 hours or more to ripen. Makes about 1 pound.

BROWN-SUGAR FONDANT PATTIES

Melt 1 cup Brown-Sugar Fondant at a time over hot water (just below boiling point). If the fondant does not hold its shape, let it stand 10 minutes over hot (not boiling) water. Drop mixture on waxed paper, from the tip of a teaspoon, in patties the size of a quarter. As soon as the patties are firm, loosen them with a spatula.

⚜ DATES STUFFED WITH BROWN-SUGAR FONDANT

Slit dates lengthwise and remove pits. Fill the cavity with fondant. Press dates into shape. Roll in coarse granulated sugar. If desired, knead chopped nuts or glacéed fruit into fondant and use for stuffing dates.

⚜ BROWN-SUGAR FONDANT NUT BARS

Knead ¾ cup chopped nuts (almonds, hazelnuts, pecans, pistachios, or walnuts) into 2 cups Brown-Sugar Fondant. Shape into a 6-inch square. Cut into ¾-inch squares.

⚜ HOW TO DIP CANDIES IN CHOCOLATE

To make home-dipped chocolates with a professional look, a special coating-chocolate used by candy manufacturers is required. It leaves the finished candy with a sheen that is impossible to obtain with the chocolate available in American supermarkets. This chocolate may be purchased from dealers specializing in candy-makers' supplies. However, if the professional appearance of the candy is not important, unsweetened or semisweet chocolate may be used. The chocolates will have a dull finish and will not look quite as attractive, but they will taste good.

Melting the chocolate. The following directions for melting chocolate must be carefully observed. Cut chocolate (not less than 1 pound) into fine pieces and put in the top of a small deep double boiler (about 1-quart capacity for 1 pound of chocolate). It is important that the pieces of chocolate be fine since less heat is required to melt them. Pour water into the bottom of the double boiler, filling it one-third full. Heat the water to 130° F. Add a little cold water if the temperature goes higher. Place the upper part of the double boiler, which contains the chocolate, over the warm water. Stir frequently so that the chocolate at the bottom will not be overheated. Use a candy thermometer and make sure that the temperature of the chocolate never exceeds 110° F. Test the water in the bottom part of the boiler occasionally. If it goes below 130° F., pour out some of the water and replace it with 130° F. water from another vessel. Stir and heat chocolate until it is melted and smooth. (Do not at any time add water to the chocolate.) Place melted chocolate over 85° F. water.

Dipping. Place the prepared centers (fondant, nut, or fruit) on a fork one at a time and dip into the melted chocolate. Lift out, scraping the bottom of the fork across the side of the boiler to remove excess chocolate. Place the dipped pieces on a tray covered with waxed paper. When the tray is filled, cool quickly in the refrigerator to prevent spots from forming on the chocolate. After it is chilled the candy may be stored in a tightly closed container in a cool place. Leftover chocolate may be remelted and used again. One pound of chocolate will cover 70 to 80 centers with one coat.

Centers for dipping in chocolate may be Fondant, Caramels, Nougat, nuts, raisins, and glacéed or preserved fruits. Some suggestions for Fondant centers follow; plain Fondant, Chocolate Fondant, or Brown-Sugar Fondant may be used for any of these. Examples of chocolate-covered candies in various shapes are shown in the illustration on page 989.

ALMOND FONDANT CHOCOLATES

To each cup of Fondant, add ¼ cup chopped almonds and 8 drops almond extract. Mix well.

FRUIT FONDANT CHOCOLATES

To each cup of Fondant, add ¼ cup finely chopped glacéed fruit. Mix well.

NUT FONDANT CHOCOLATES

To each cup of Fondant, add ¼ cup chopped pecans, hazelnuts, or walnuts. Mix well.

PEPPERMINT FONDANT CHOCOLATES

Flavor fondant with peppermint extract or oil of peppermint to taste. Mix well.

⚜ BRÉSILIENNES

1 cup finely ground blanched almonds
rum
2 teaspoons instant coffee, or instant coffee to taste
about 2 cups sifted confectioners' sugar
4 squares (4 ounces) unsweetened or semisweet chocolate, grated

Combine almonds, 1 tablespoon rum, and the coffee. Stir and mix well. Add the confectioners' sugar, a little at a time, and additional rum and coffee to taste. Shape the mixture into balls, adding more sugar if it is needed to make the balls hold their shape. Roll the balls in grated chocolate. Store in a cool place. Makes approximately 1 pound.

⚜ CARAMELS

2 cups sugar
¾ cup light corn syrup
¼ cup (½ stick) butter
2 cups heavy cream
2 teaspoons vanilla extract
⅔ cup chopped almonds, pecans, walnuts, or hazelnuts (optional)

Combine the first 3 ingredients and 1 cup of the cream in a heavy-bottomed 2-quart saucepan. Mix well. Stir and cook until mixture comes to a full rolling boil. Pour in the remaining cream so slowly that the boiling does not stop. Stir and cook to 250° F. on the candy thermometer, or until a hard ball forms when a little of the syrup is dropped in cold water. Remove from heat. Stir in vanilla extract and nuts (if used). Pour into a buttered 8-inch square pan. When the candy is cold, turn it out onto a slab and cut it into ¾-inch squares. Makes 2 pounds.

⚜ CHOCOLATE CARAMELS

2 cups sugar
¾ cup light corn syrup
¼ cup (½ stick) butter
3 squares (3 ounces) unsweetened chocolate
2 cups light cream
2 teaspoons vanilla extract
⅔ cup chopped nuts (optional)

Combine the first 4 ingredients and 1 cup of the cream in a heavy-bottomed 2-quart saucepan. Stir and cook until mixture has come to a rolling boil. Pour in remaining 1 cup of cream so slowly that the boiling does not stop. Stir and cook to 248° F. on the candy thermometer, or until a firm ball forms when a little of the mixture is dropped in cold water. Remove from heat. Stir in vanilla extract and nuts (if used). Pour into a buttered 8-inch square pan. When candy is cold, turn it out onto a slab and cut it into ¾-inch squares. Makes 2 pounds.

⚜ CARAMEL KISSES

1½ cups sugar
¼ cup honey
⅛ teaspoon salt
⅓ cup butter
½ cup light cream
¼ pound blanched, toasted, salted almonds

Combine the first 5 ingredients in a heavy-bottomed 2-quart saucepan. Mix well. Stir and cook until boiling point is reached. Cook, without stirring, over medium heat, to 255° F. on the candy thermometer, or until ½ teaspoon of the syrup forms a firm ball when dropped in cold water. Remove syrup from heat and pour at once into a buttered 15- by 12- by 1-inch pan. Cool until candy can be handled. Cut into 1-inch squares. Place a whole almond in the center of each square. Roll the candy around the almond (using the palms of both hands), keeping almond completely covered with the caramel. Wrap each piece in foil or glassine paper. Store in a tightly covered container. Makes 1¼ pounds.

⚜ CHOCOLATE NUT TRUFFLES

1 cup grated or very finely chopped nuts (almonds, hazelnuts, or pecans)
½ cup sugar
2 squares (2 ounces) semisweet chocolate
½ cup water
1½ teaspoons vanilla extract
cocoa
granulated sugar (optional)

Place the first 3 ingredients in a saucepan. Gradually add water, mixing well after each addition. Stir and cook over very low heat until the sugar dissolves and the chocolate melts, then add the vanilla extract. Cool. Shape the mixture into 1-inch balls and roll them in cocoa. If desired, roll them in granulated sugar. Makes 1½ dozen balls. (See illustration, page 988.)

⚜ MARZIPAN (*Massepain*)

This is an easy method of making marzipan. Almond paste may be purchased at bakeries or specialty food shops.

1 can almond paste (not filling)
1 large egg white
confectioners' sugar

Crumble the almond paste. Add egg white and mix well. Beat in enough confectioners' sugar to make a mixture that is too stiff to beat. Then knead in ½ cup sifted confectioners' sugar. Store the mixture in a tightly covered container in the refrigerator 5 to 6 hours to ripen. Form the paste into desired shapes. If desired, tint paste with food coloring diluted with a few drops of water, or paint with food coloring after shaping. Roll the pieces in colored granulated sugar. Makes approximately 1 pound.

⚜ NOUGAT (*Nougat de Montélimar*)

2 cups sugar
1 cup water
4 tablespoons light corn syrup
4 egg whites, beaten
1 cup honey
½ cup chopped blanched pistachio nuts
1 cup chopped toasted blanched almonds
1½ teaspoons vanilla extract

Place the sugar, water, and 2 tablespoons of the corn syrup in a 1½-quart saucepan. Mix well. Stir and cook until boiling point is reached. Cover and cook 3 minutes to dissolve any sugar crystals which form on the sides of the pan. Remove cover and place a candy thermometer in the syrup. Cook without stirring to 290° F., keeping the sugar crystals on the sides of the pan washed down with a swab or a pastry brush dipped in cold water. Beat the egg whites until they stand in soft stiff peaks. Pour the syrup in a fine stream into the beaten egg whites. Using an electric mixer, continue beating until the mixture is thick and the bowl is cool enough to be held in the palm of the hand without discomfort.

Put the honey and the 2 remaining tablespoons of corn syrup in a 1-quart saucepan. Cook to 270° F. on the candy thermometer (soft-crack stage). Pour in a fine stream into the egg-white mixture, beating constantly at medium speed, until the mixture has lost some of its gloss. Transfer it to the top of a large double boiler and place it over boiling water. Stir and cook 25 minutes or until mixture is no longer sticky when a small amount is cooled on a spoon. Gradually stir in nuts and vanilla extract. Turn mixture into a well-buttered 8-inch square pan. Cool 10 minutes. Press the nougat down firmly with the hands. Cool completely. Cover pan tightly and set it aside 24 hours for nougat to ripen. Turn candy onto a cutting board and cut into 1½- by 1-inch pieces. Wrap pieces in foil or glassine paper and store in a tightly covered container. Makes approximately 3½ dozen pieces.

VARIATION

⚜ CHOCOLATE-COATED NOUGAT

Cut nougat into ¾-inch squares and dip in melted unsweetened chocolate, as directed in How to Dip Candies in Chocolate, page 1038.

⚜ PRALINES

2 cups sugar	**¼ cup light cream**
½ cup boiling water	**2 tablespoons butter**
⅛ teaspoon baking soda	**1½ teaspoons vanilla extract**
1/16 teaspoon salt	**⅔ cup pecan halves**

Place ¼ cup of the sugar in a small heavy-bottomed saucepan. Stir and cook over moderate heat until sugar has melted. Stir in boiling water. Stir and cook 1 to 2 minutes or until lumps are dissolved. Pour syrup into a 1½-quart saucepan. Add the remaining sugar, soda, salt, and cream. Stir until well mixed. Bring mixture to boiling point over moderate heat, stirring constantly. Continue cooking, without stirring, to 242° F. on the candy thermometer, or until a firm ball forms when a half teaspoon of the syrup is dropped in cold water. Remove the candy from the heat and cool to 140° F.–about 15 minutes. Add butter, vanilla extract, and pecans. Stir until well mixed. Drop from a teaspoon onto waxed paper to form thin wafers 1½ to 2 inches in diameter. These harden quickly; therefore it is necessary to work fast when dropping them. Store in an airtight container. Makes 3 dozen pralines.

⚜ MARQUISE CHERRIES

Soak glacéed cherries in brandy at least 1 hour. Drain well and coat with Kirsch-flavored Fondant Cake Icing. Cool on a marble slab or waxed paper that has been dusted with confectioners' sugar.

⚜ CHOCOLATE-COATED MARQUISE CHERRIES

Make Marquise Cherries as directed. When they have dried, dip them in melted unsweetened chocolate. Place them on waxed paper. Chill quickly to prevent spotting. If the chocolate coating is not heavy enough, dip into melted chocolate again. Chill and dry as directed in How to Dip Candies in Chocolate. (See illustration, page 989.)

⚜ STUFFED DATES. (*Dattes farcies*)

Slit dates down one side and remove the pits. Insert into the cavities a roll of almond paste a little larger than the pit. Sprinkle with coarse granulated sugar, if desired. (See illustration, page 989.)

⚜ WALNUT-STUFFED DATES

Slit large dates down one side and remove the pits. Insert a small piece of Fondant into the cavity of each and place a walnut half over each. Roll in granulated sugar, if desired. (See illustration, page 989.)

⚜ CANDIED ORANGE PEEL

peel from 4 medium-sized navel oranges	**2⅔ cups sugar**
	⅛ teaspoon salt

Wash oranges and cut through the peel of the orange with a knife so that it can be removed in quarters. Place it in a 2-quart saucepan with enough cold water to cover. Bring water to boiling point and cook slowly 10 to 15 minutes, or until peel is tender. Drain, reserving the water.

Using a teaspoon, scrape out the white inner portion of the orange peel. With scissors, cut the peel into narrow strips. Pour the water in which the orange peel was cooked into a measuring cup and add water if necessary to make 1 cup. Pour it into a 2-quart saucepan. Add 2 cups of the sugar and the salt. Mix well. Stir and cook until the candy thermometer registers 238° F. (soft-ball stage). Add orange peel and cook slowly 20 to 30 minutes, or until peel has absorbed most of the syrup. Turn the peel into a coarse sieve to drain well. Put remaining ⅔ cup of sugar in a bowl, add a few pieces of orange peel at a time and mix until each piece is completely covered with sugar. Shake off excess sugar. Arrange in a single layer on waxed paper to dry. Store in a tightly covered container. Makes ½ pound.

⚜ GLACÉED CHERRIES

Wash and dry the cherries, leaving the stems attached. Chill. Make Glazing Syrup (see page 862) and place the saucepan over hot water. Hold each cherry by its stem and dip in the hot syrup. Drain well and put the cherries on an oiled platter or on waxed paper to dry, spacing them so that they do not touch. (See illustration, page 989.)

GLACÉED GRAPES

Cut the grapes from the bunch, leaving ½ inch of stem on each. Proceed as with Glacéed Cherries.

GLACÉED STRAWBERRIES

Use firm ripe strawberries, leaving the green hulls attached. Wash and dry the strawberries and chill them. Dip each up to the hull in hot Glazing Syrup. Proceed as with Glacéed Cherries.

GLACÉED TANGERINES OR TEMPLE ORANGES

Peel the fruit and separate the sections. Chill. Place each section on the tines of a fork and dip into the hot Glazing Syrup. Proceed as with Glacéed Cherries.

⚜ GLACÉED CHESTNUTS (*Marrons Glacés*)

Peel 1 pound chestnuts (see instructions on pages 777–78). Put chestnuts in a saucepan with ½ teaspoon salt and enough boiling water to cover them. Cover and simmer 8 to 20 minutes, or until they are tender when pierced with a fork. Drain well. Make Glazing Syrup and set it over hot water. Place chestnuts on a fork and dip them one at a time into the syrup. When chestnuts appear clear, lift them out, scraping the bottom of the fork across the side of the pan to remove excess syrup. Place chestnuts on a buttered baking sheet to dry. Makes about 1 pound Glazed Chestnuts.

MASKED NUTS

Roast shelled perfect halves of pecans and walnuts and whole shelled blanched almonds in a preheated moderate oven (325° F.) 30 minutes, or until the nuts are toasted. Dip them in melted semisweet chocolate as directed in How to Dip Candies in Chocolate, page 1038.

⚜ STUFFED NUTS

Put 2 walnut, pecan, or almond halves together with white or tinted almond paste or fondant. Roll in coarse granulated sugar, if desired. (See illustration, page 989.)

CULINARY TECHNIQUES IN PICTURES

Preparing turbot

Preparing fillets of sole

Sole Colbert

Preparing a large fish

Cold boiled rock lobster

Quenelles

Ravioli

Poached eggs

Puff Pastry

Puff-Pastry Bâtons and Sacristains

Classic Vol-au-Vent

Modern Vol-au-Vent

Larding

Paupiettes of Veal

Carving a saddle of lamb or mutton

Preparing a chicken for grilling

Disjointed raw chicken, French style

Chicken breasts (suprêmes)

Cold stuffed chicken or pheasant

Pâté en Croûte

Fluted mushrooms

Asparagus

Potato Fritters

Stuffed Peppers

Palmiers

Black Forest Cherry Torte

Babas

Ladyfingers

Mexican Cake

Serving Sole Meunière

Slicing a Chateaubriand

Carving a saddle of hare

Carving a roast chicken

Peeling and slicing an orange—two methods

Crêpes Suzette

PREPARING TURBOT

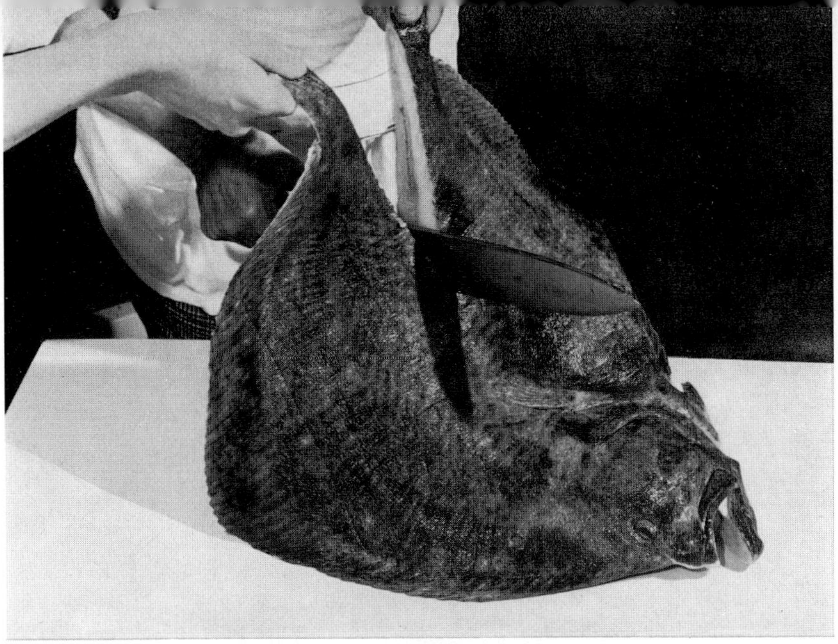

Slit the turbot through lengthwise, using a large sharp knife.

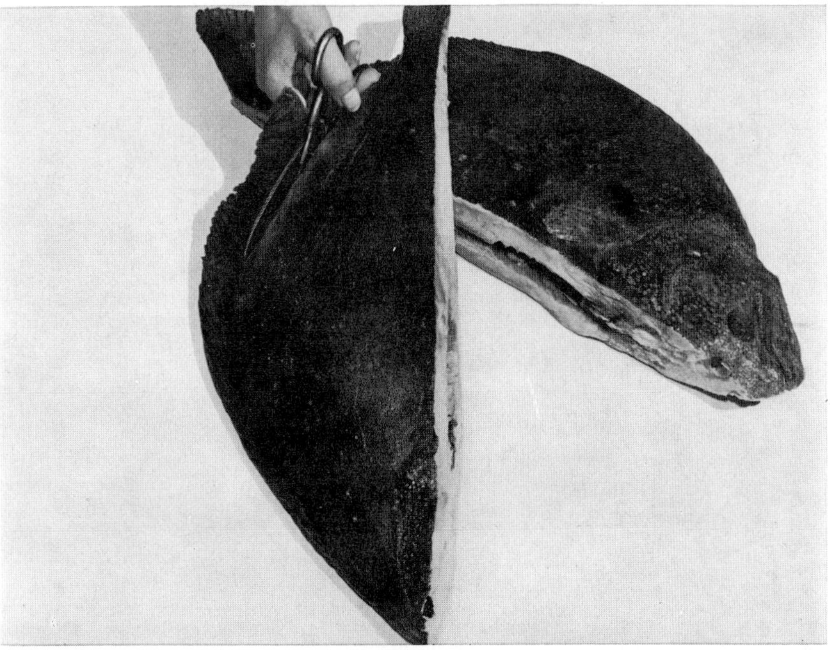

Cut off the fins with scissors.

Cut each half into thick steaks.

PREPARING FILLETS OF SOLE

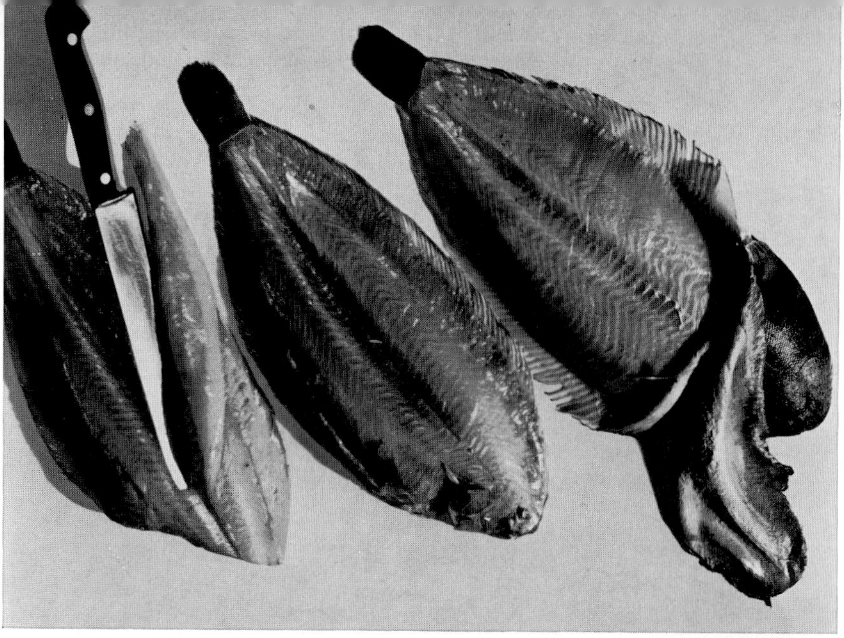

Remove the skin from both sides of the fish, pulling it off with a sharp jerk from the tail toward the head.

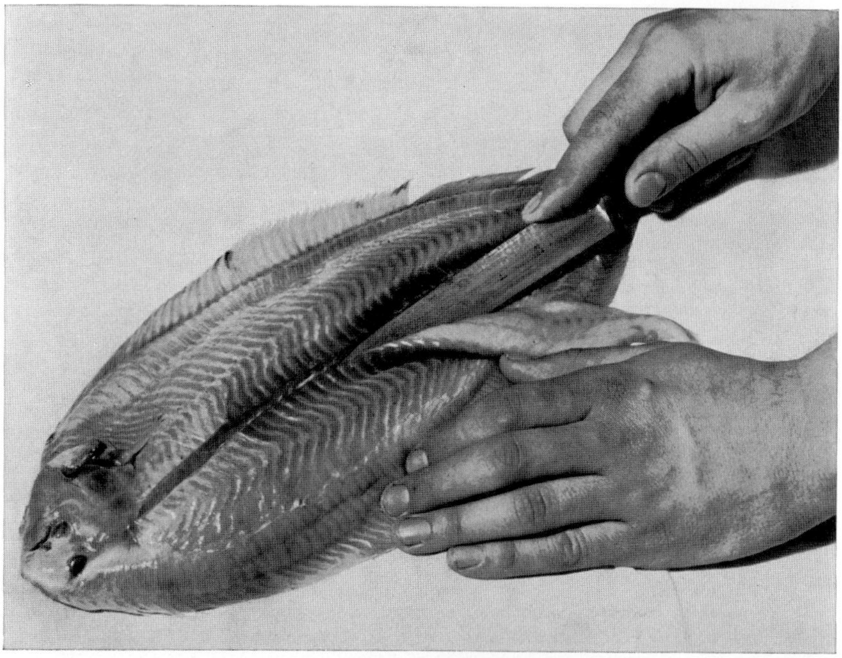

To fillet the fish, run a flexible knife under the flesh along the bone from the center outward.

Fold the fillets over, trim them, arrange them in a shallow buttered saucepan sprinkled with chopped shallots, and place a fluted mushroom cap on each. They are now ready for poaching.

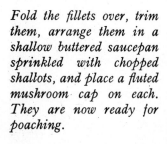

SOLE COLBERT

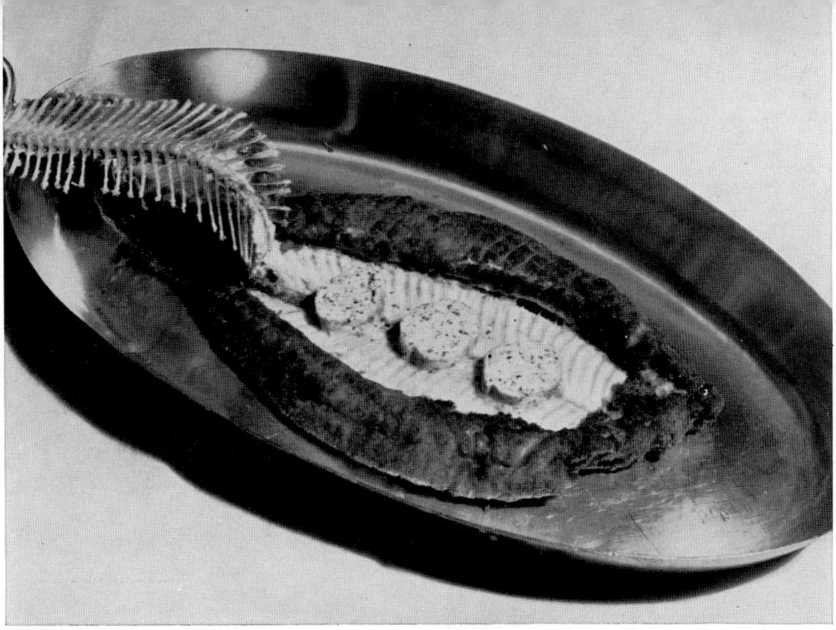

After frying the sole, carefully remove the bones and fill the center with Maître d'Hôtel Butter.

PREPARING A LARGE FISH

Cut off the fins with scissors.

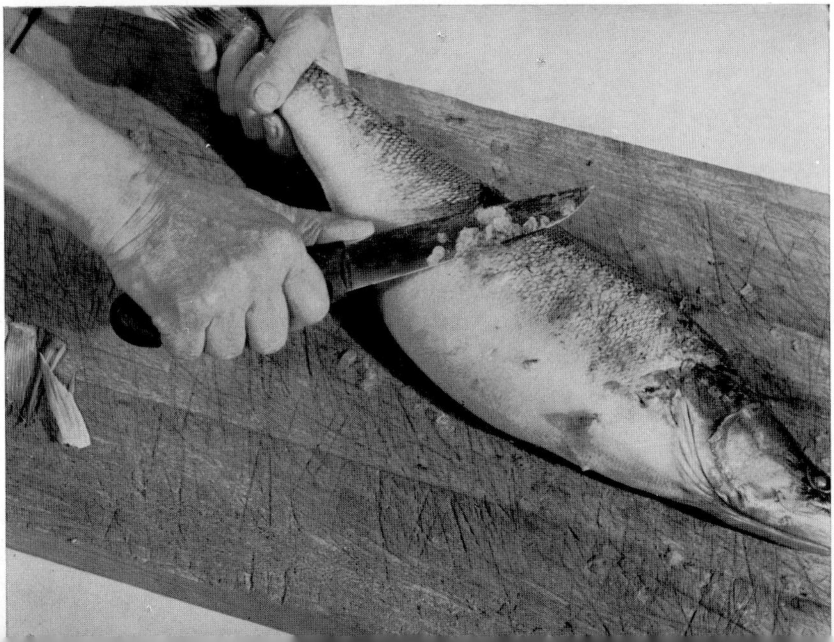

Use a firm knife or a fish scraper to remove the scales, holding the fish tightly to avoid damaging the flesh.

PREPARING A LARGE FISH
(concluded)

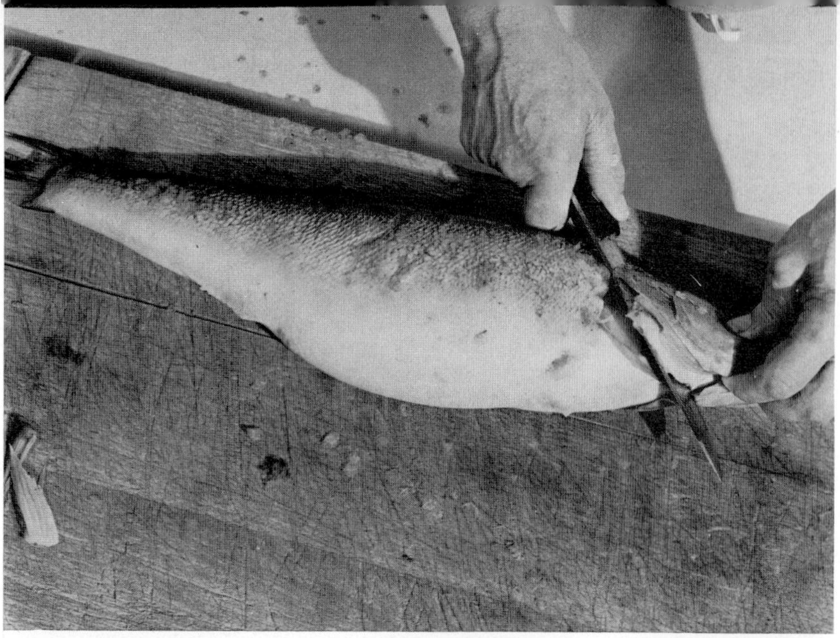

Cut off the head, running the knife along directly behind the gills.

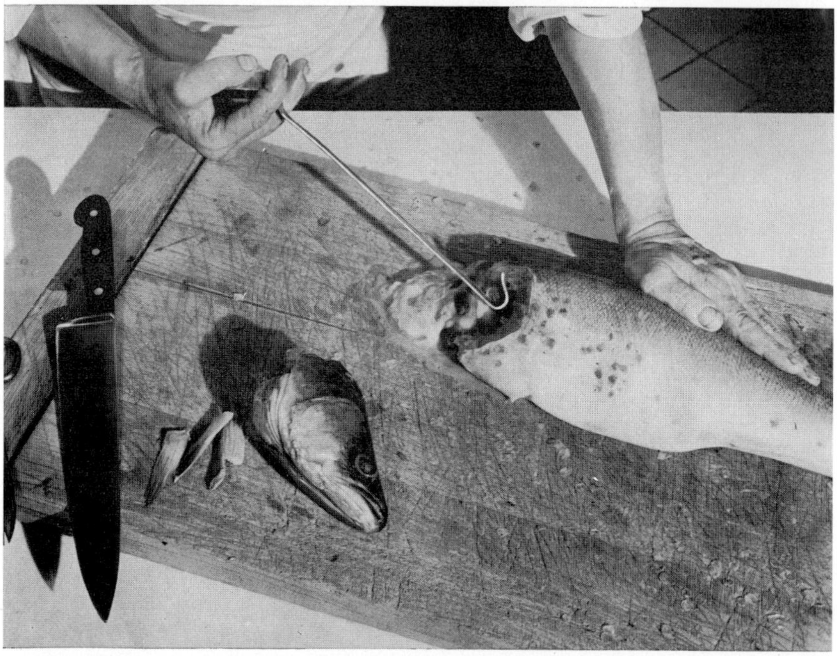

To gut the fish without slitting the abdomen, insert the hooked end of a skimming ladle and draw out the entrails.

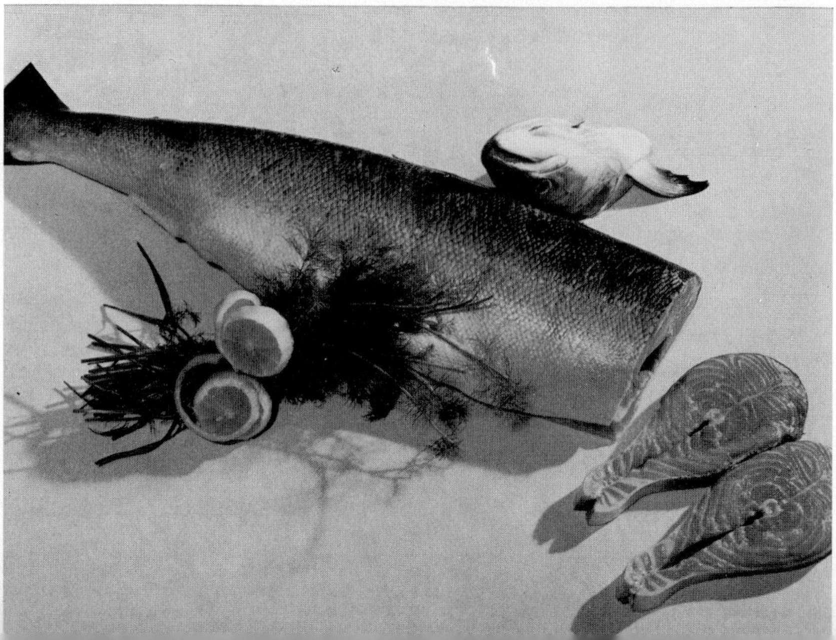

Wash the fish. Leave whole or cut into individual steaks.

COLD BOILED ROCK LOBSTER

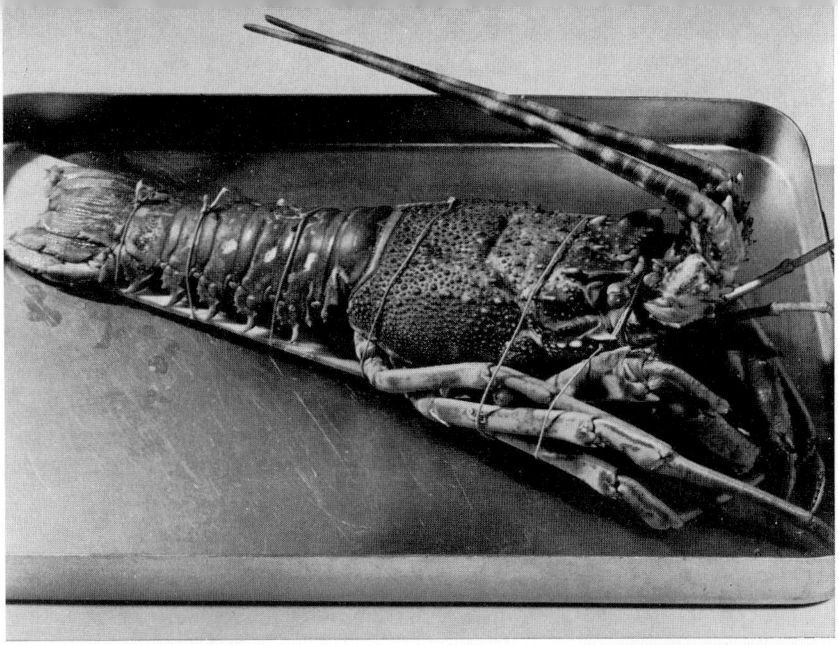

Tie the live rock lobster down on a small board with its tail extended to keep it straight while it is boiled.

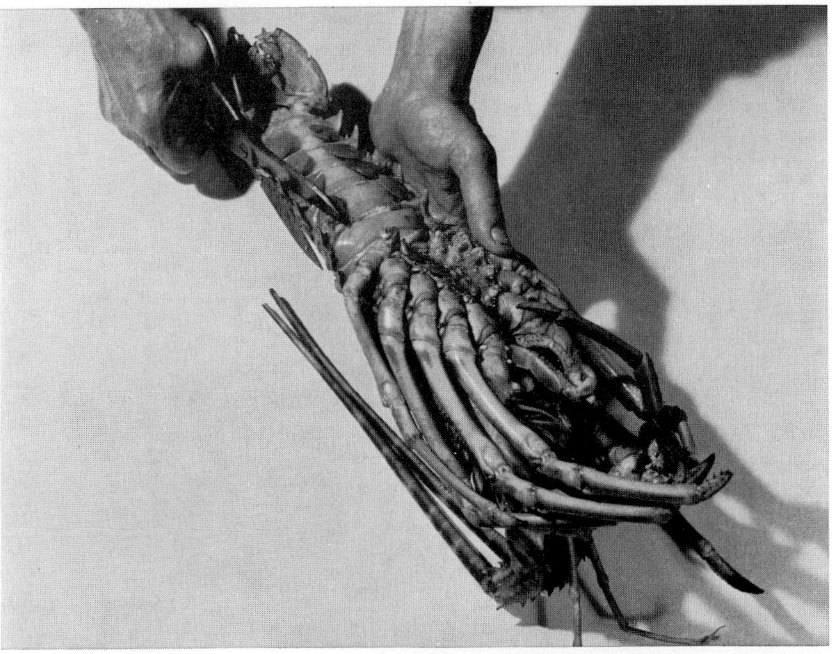

After boiling the rock lobster and letting it cool, make two incisions in the underside with scissors.

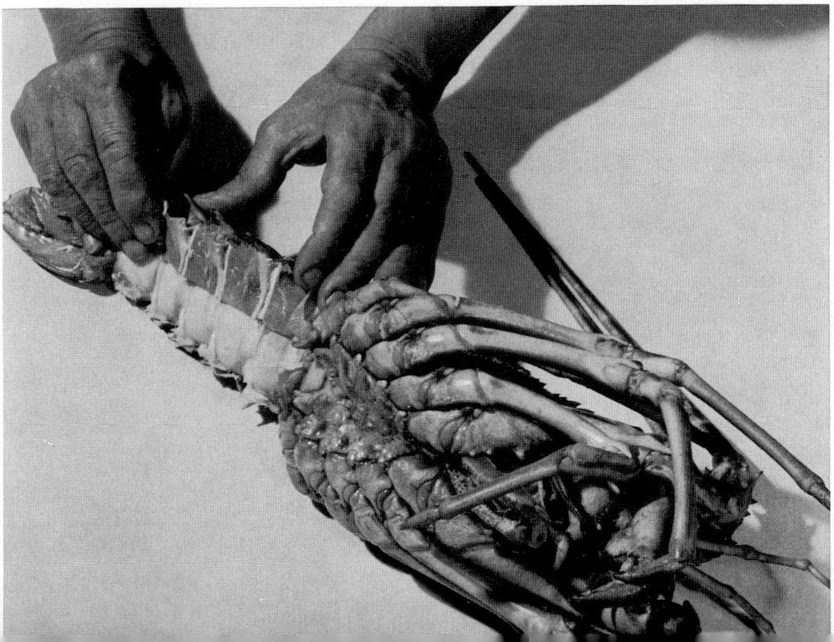

Carefully detach the shell.

COLD BOILED ROCK LOBSTER

(concluded)

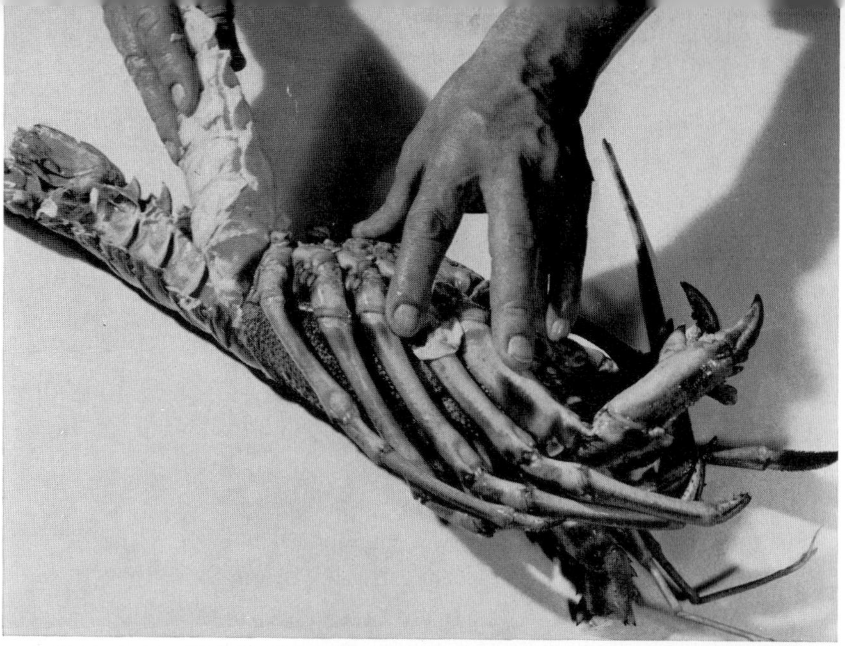

Gently remove the meat from the shell in one piece.

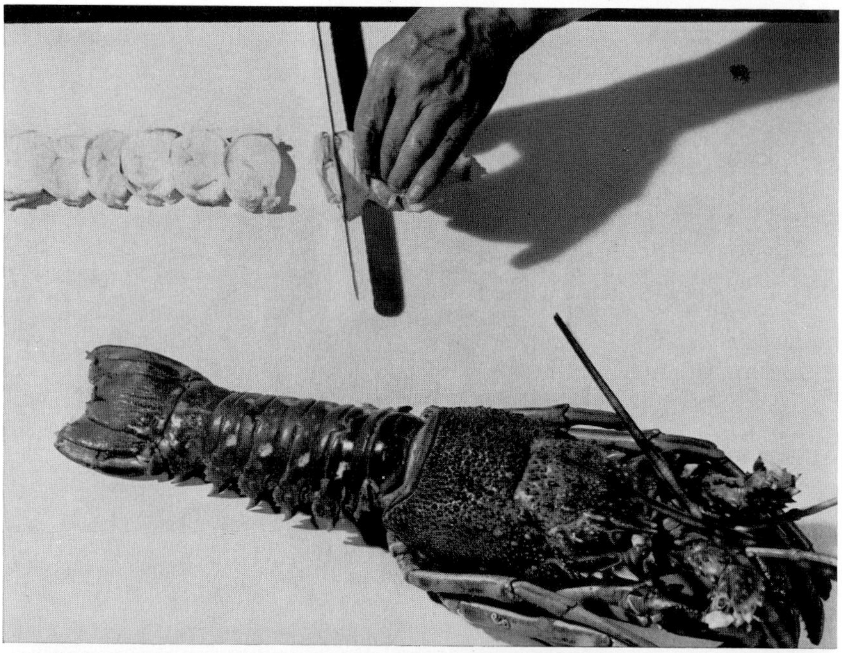

The meat may now be cut into round slices. The shell, which is kept intact, may be used to support an arrangement of the slices of meat or placed on the serving dish as a decoration.

QUENELLES

Quenelles are made in various sizes. They may be shaped by hand, with spoons or molds, or by forcing the mixture through a pastry bag, and may either be dropped straight into simmering liquid or piped onto a buttered saucepan and the simmering liquid poured over them.

RAVIOLI

Roll out noodle dough in a rectangle 1/8 inch thick. Mark one-half out into squares and pipe a little forcemeat onto each, using a pastry bag with a plain tube. Or drop the filling from a spoon. Lightly moisten the dough all round the filling.

Fold the remaining half of the dough over the half with the filling and press down, first with the hand and then with the back of a round cutter. Cut the squares apart with a pastry wheel.

POACHED EGGS

Break one egg at a time into a small bowl.

POACHED EGGS
(continued)

Slide the egg into simmering water to which a little vinegar may be added. Let the water come to a simmer again, then remove the pan from the heat.

Carefully remove the egg from the water with a perforated ladle or spoon.

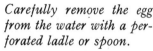

Dip the egg in cold water at once.

POACHED EGGS
(concluded)

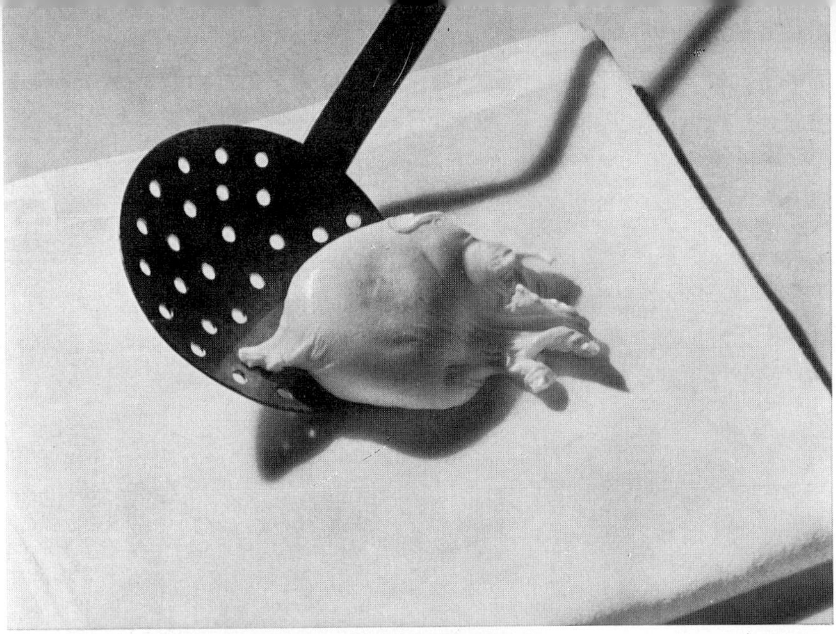

The egg should be trimmed before it is served.

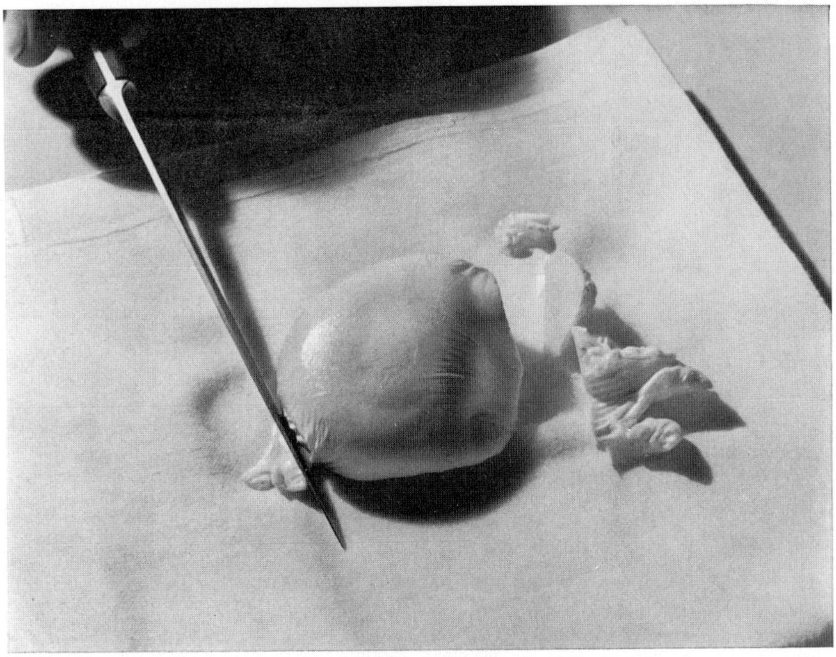

Use a knife or scissors to trim off the uneven edges.

Place the egg on a triangle or square of buttered toast or on a crouton. It may also be coated with sauce or served in various other ways.

PUFF PASTRY

Sift the flour onto a marble slab and make a well in the center.

Starting with the fingertips, mix the flour with a pinch of salt and some water to make a medium-firm dough.

Shape the dough into a ball and let it rest for 15 minutes. Then make two incisions with a knife.

PUFF PASTRY
(continued)

Have the butter the same temperature as the dough.

After rolling out the dough, fold it over to encase the butter.

Roll out the dough into a rectangular shape and fold the ends over to meet in the center.

PUFF PASTRY
(concluded)

Fold the two sides of the dough together at the center. Chill. Roll out, fold, and chill three more times, or as specified in the recipe.

PUFF PASTRY BÂTONS AND SACRISTAINS

Roll Puff Pastry 1/8 to 1/4 inch thick, brush with beaten egg, and sprinkle with chopped almonds or cheese. Cut into strips 1/2 to 3/4 inch wide.

To make Sacristains, hold each unbaked strip by the ends and twist into the shape of a corkscrew.

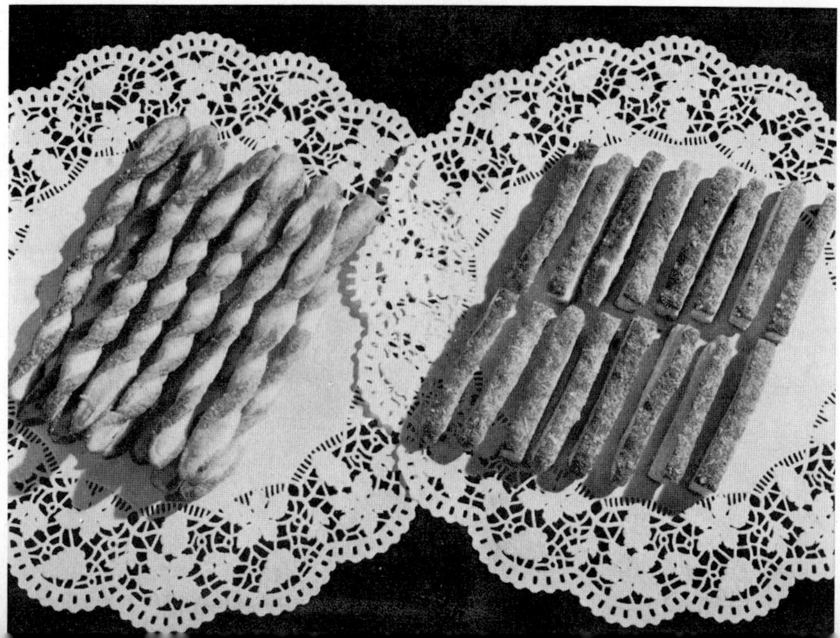

CLASSIC VOL-AU-VENT

Roll Puff Pastry 1/8 inch thick. Cut out a round base of desired size. Prick it all over with a fork and lightly moisten the edge.

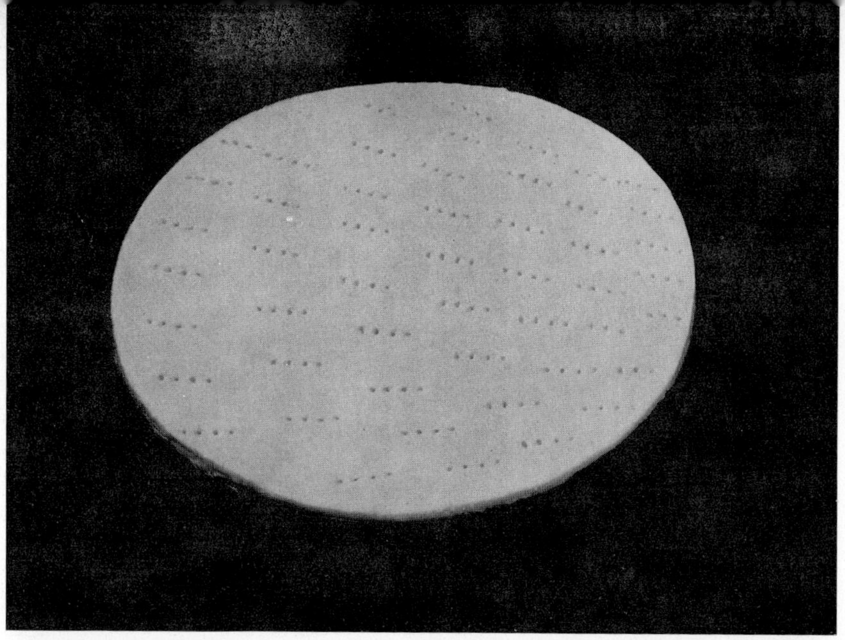

Place a ring of Puff Pastry 3/4 inch thick on the base, score lightly with a knife, and brush with beaten egg. The center of the ring can serve as the lid. Lightly score it across, notch the edges all around, brush with beaten egg, and put it on top of the ring.

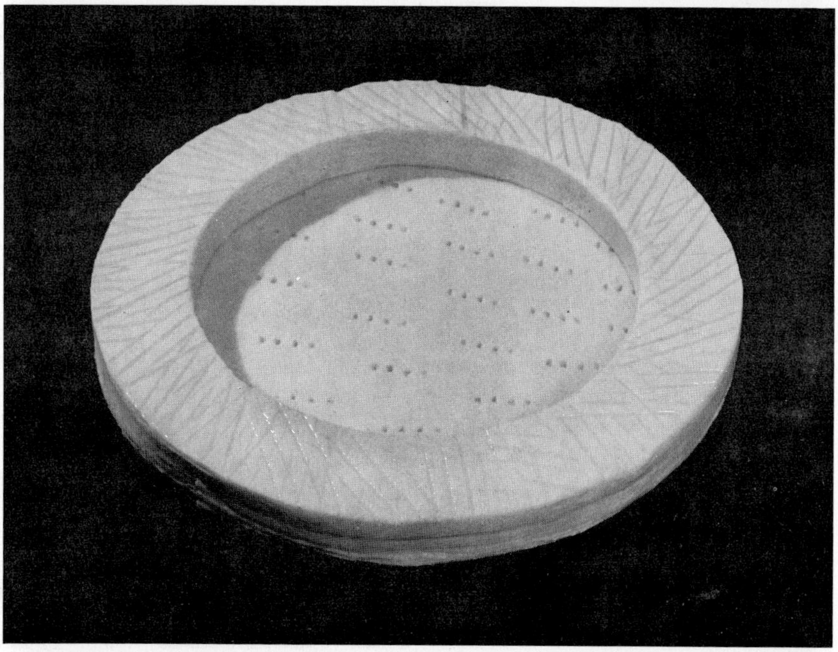

After baking, remove the lid carefully with the point of a knife. Fill the vol-au-vent with any desired mixture.

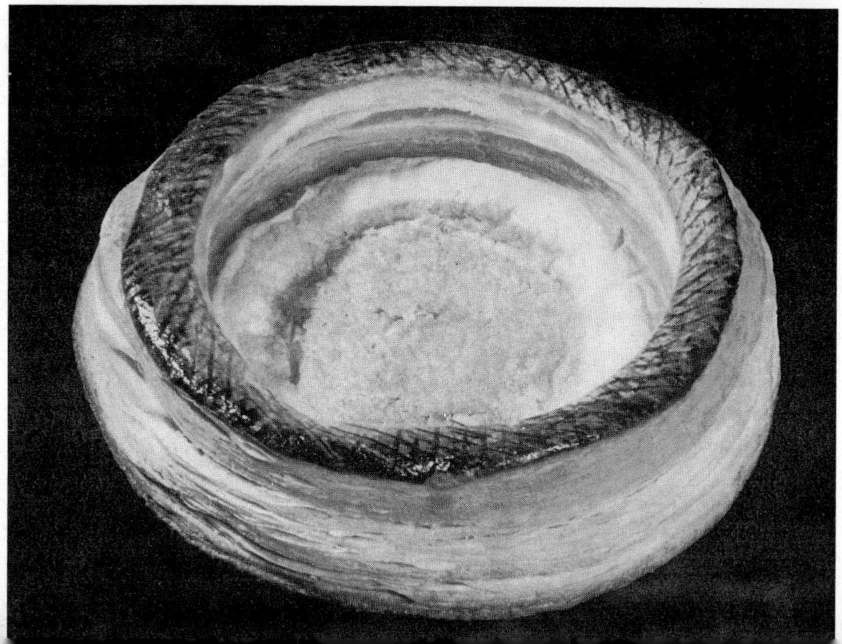

MODERN VOL-AU-VENT

Roll out Puff Pastry 1/8 inch thick and cut out a round base. Prick it all over with a fork. Make a ball of scraps of paper, wrap it in tissue paper, tie it with thin twine, and place it in the center of the circle of pastry. Brush the edge with water.

Cover the ball with a somewhat larger round of Puff Pastry and press down well all round.

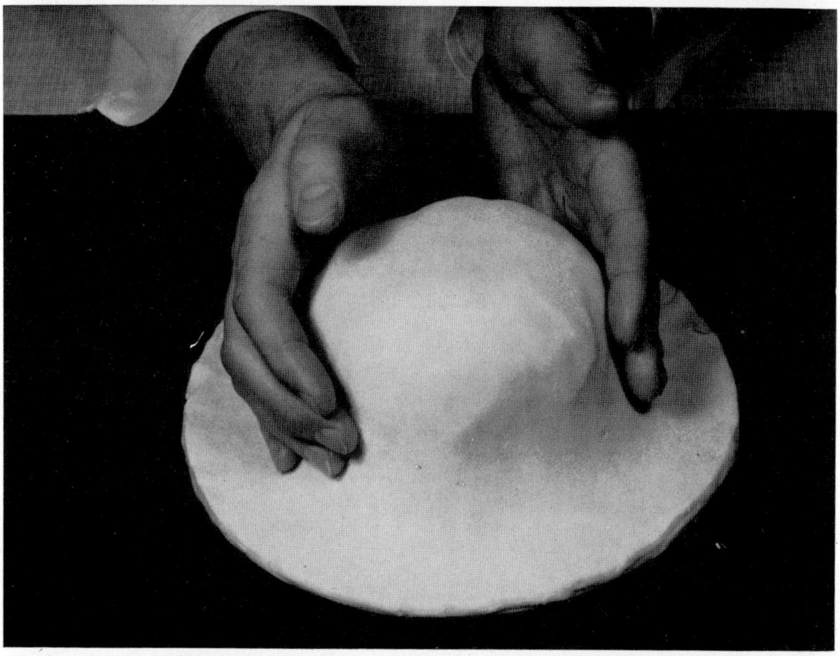

Brush with beaten egg and decorate with strips of Puff Pastry the width of the little finger.

MODERN VOL-AU-VENT
(concluded)

Cover the edge with a somewhat thicker ring of Puff Pastry and brush with beaten egg.

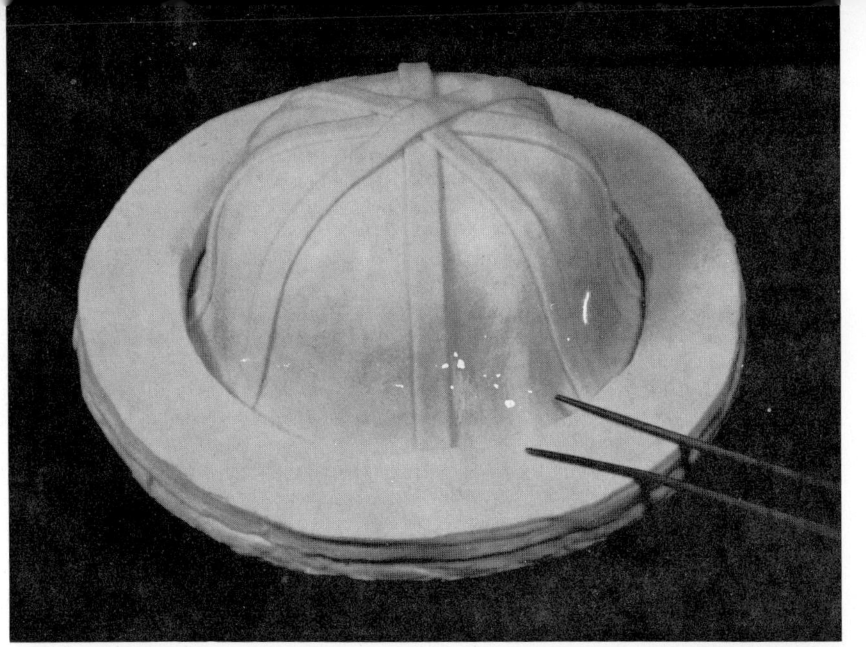

Place two thin cut-out rings of Puff Pastry on top around the center and decorate the lower edge and the sides with Puff Pastry cut-outs as desired. Prick the pastry with a fine needle in several places to prevent its splitting open while baking. Brush it all over with beaten egg and bake.

After baking, remove the lid with a sharp, pointed knife. Carefully remove the ball of paper and fill the case as desired.

LARDING

Top: *Draw long, thick strips of fat bacon through the meat.*

Center: *Venison—lard the saddle across the grain of the meat with thin strips of fat bacon.*

Bottom: *Fillet of beef or veal—lard lengthwise with thin strips of bacon.*

PAUPIETTES OF VEAL

Cut the veal into slices about 4 inches by 2 inches. Flatten slightly and spread with forcemeat.

Roll up the slices of veal and tie with twine.

CARVING A SADDLE OF LAMB OR MUTTON

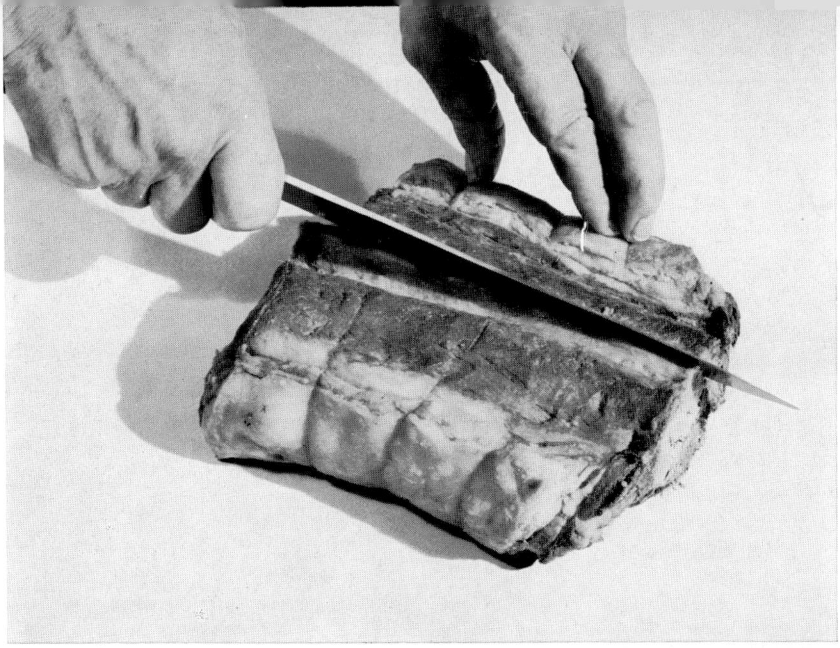

Using a long, slightly flexible knife, cut down into the two saddle fillets along the bone.

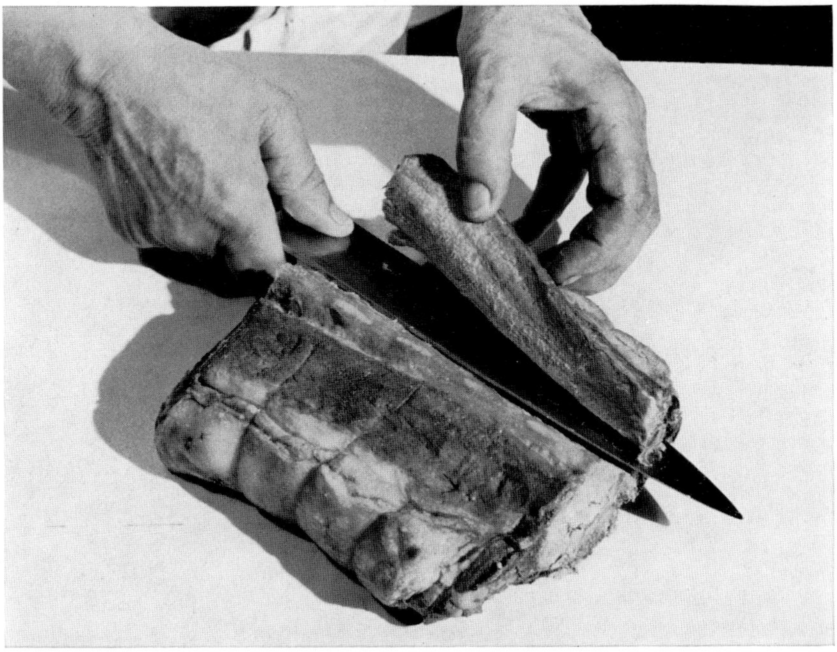

Carefully run the knife down the bone to remove the fillets.

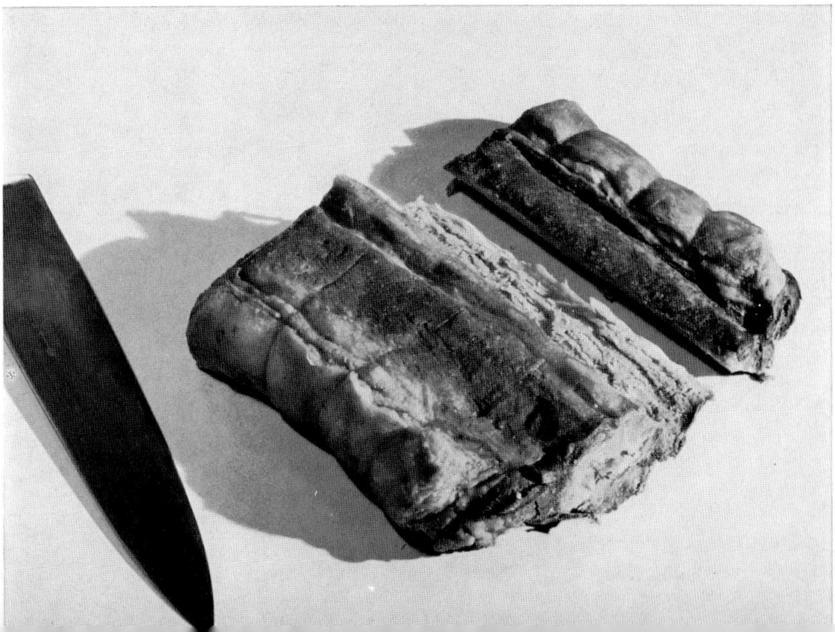

Now cut the fillets into thin slices lengthwise or into somewhat thicker slices diagonally.

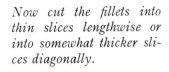

PREPARING A CHICKEN FOR GRILLING

After washing the cleaned bird, split it down the back with a sharp knife and cut off the backbone.

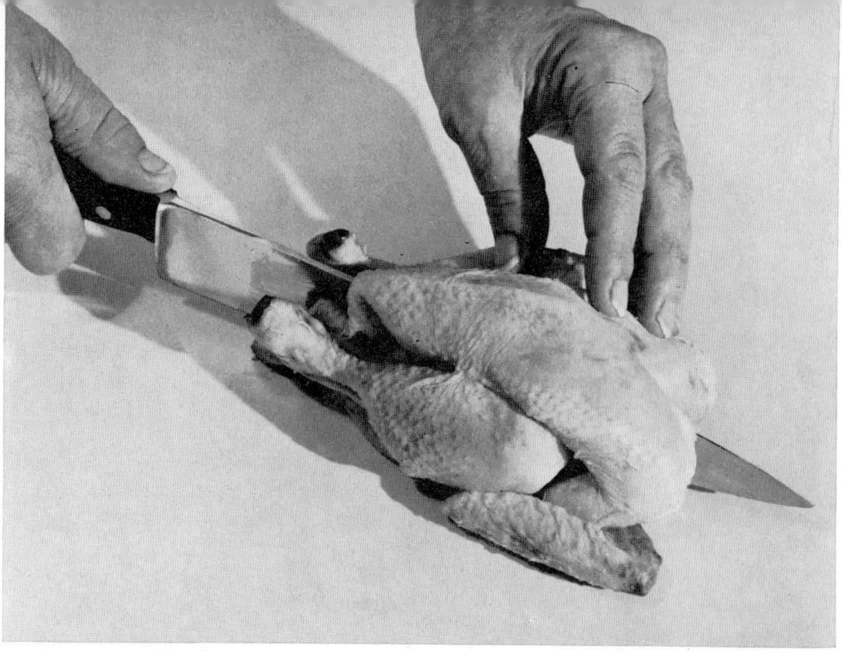

Lightly flatten the bird to make a level surface.

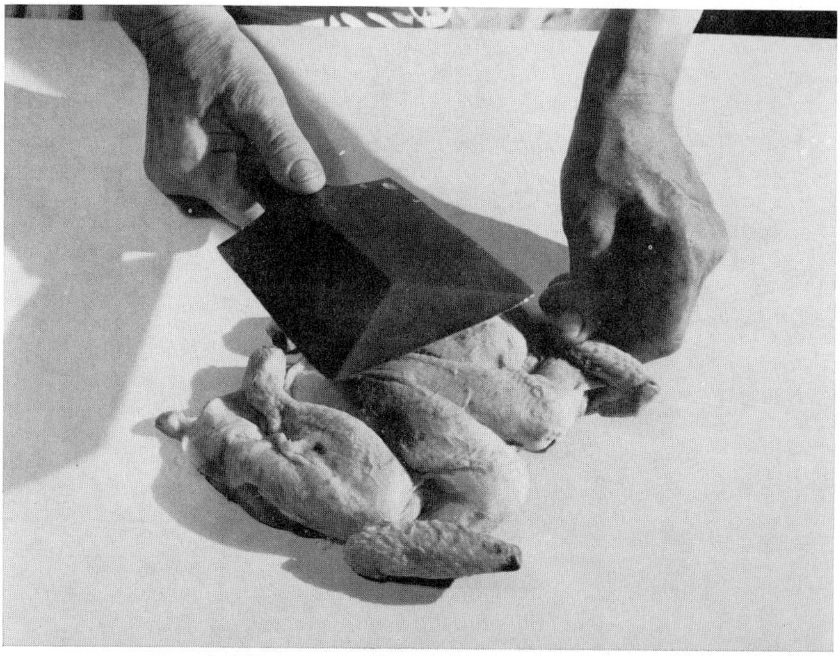

Hold the drumsticks down by passing them through an incision at the end of the skin covering the breast. The chicken must keep its shape while grilling.

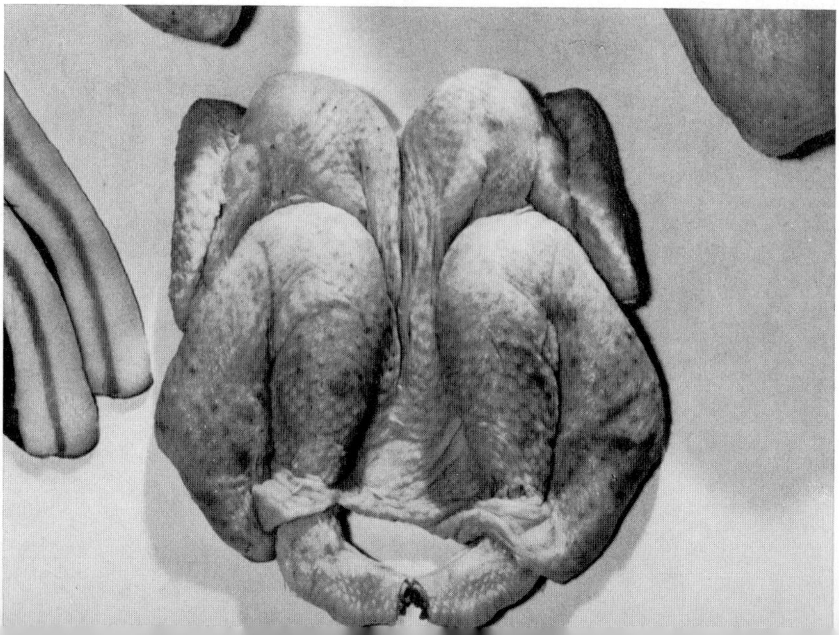

DISJOINTED RAW CHICKEN, FRENCH STYLE

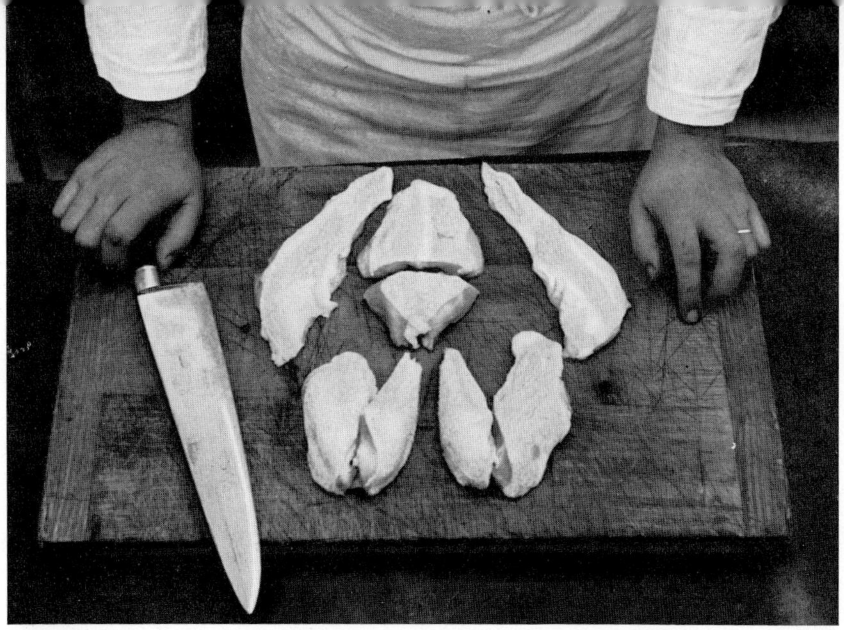

Serving pieces: drumsticks, thighs, half-breasts (suprêmes), breast with breastbone, cut in two crosswise. (The breast may be divided in either of these ways. The top parts of the wings, with strips of breast attached, may also be included with the serving pieces.)

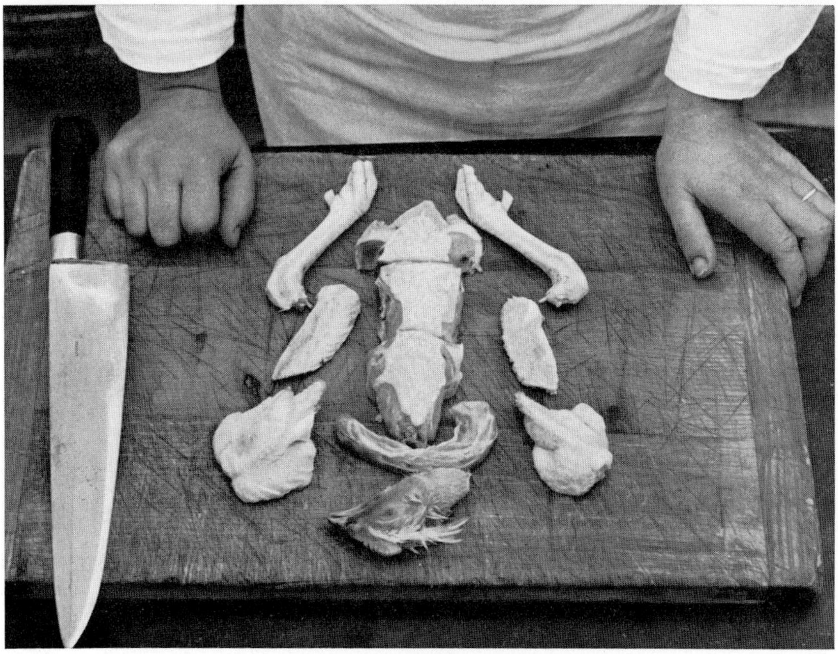

Offcuts (used for stock, soup, forcemeat, etc.): head, neck, wings (sometimes used as serving pieces), wingtips, back (cut in three pieces), feet.

CHICKEN BREASTS (Suprêmes)

The breasts with the top parts of the wings attached are placed, ready for cooking, in a frying pan with butter.

COLD STUFFED CHICKEN OR PHEASANT

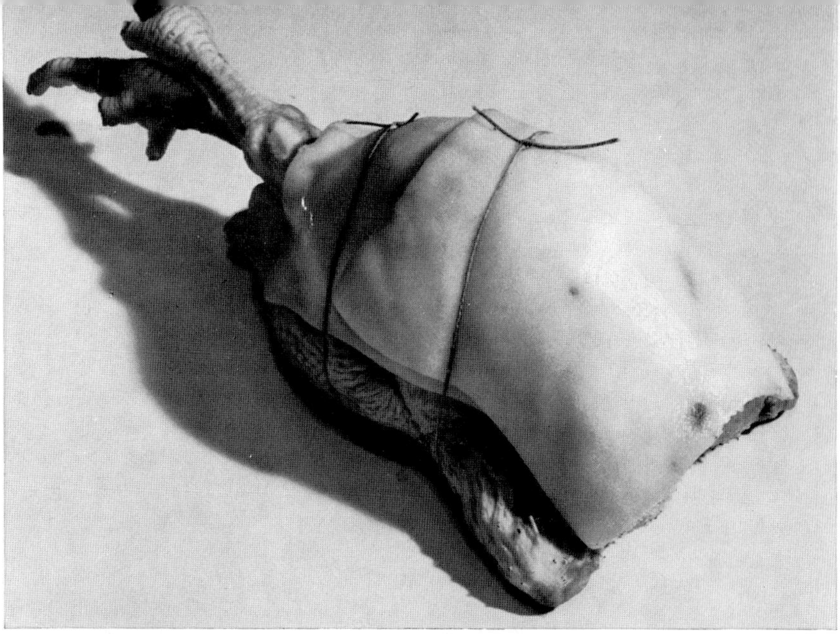

The bird ready for roasting, after trussing and larding.

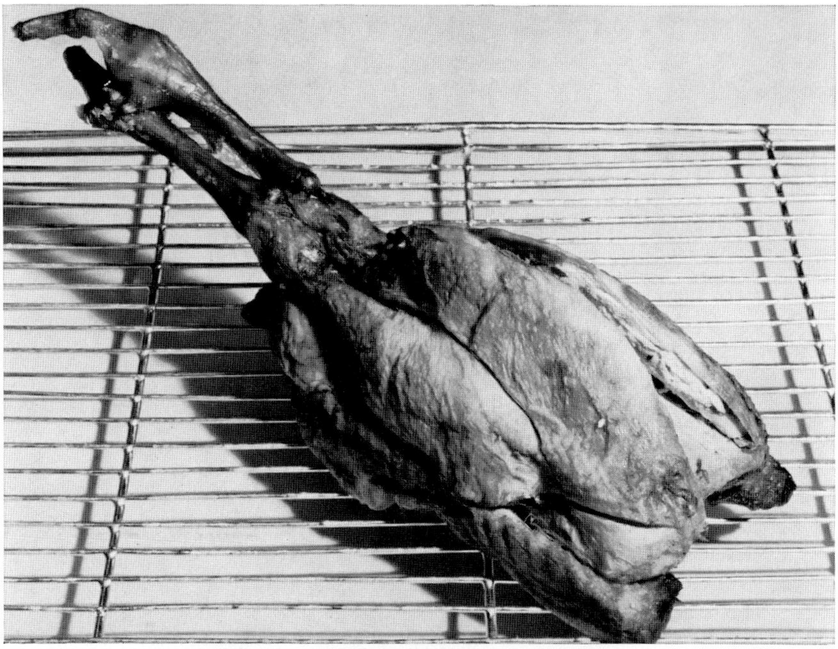

After roasting, let the bird cool, then remove the breast in one piece and cut out the breastbone with scissors.

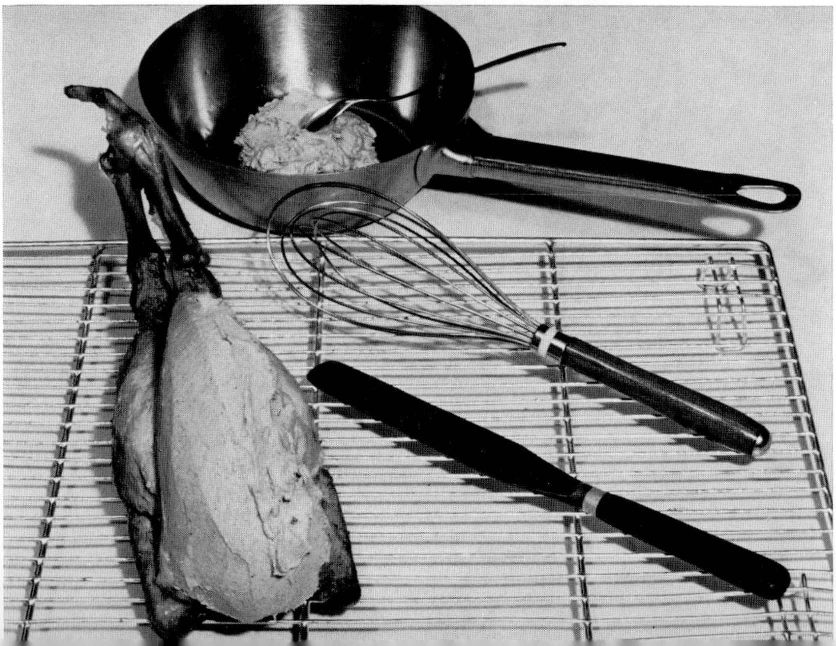

Fill the cavity with mousse or forcemeat, mold to the original shape of the breast, and chill in the refrigerator until firm.

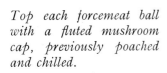

COLD STUFFED CHICKEN OR PHEASANT
(continued)

Cut the half-breasts (suprêmes) *diagonally into even slices and arrange the slices on the forcemeat.*

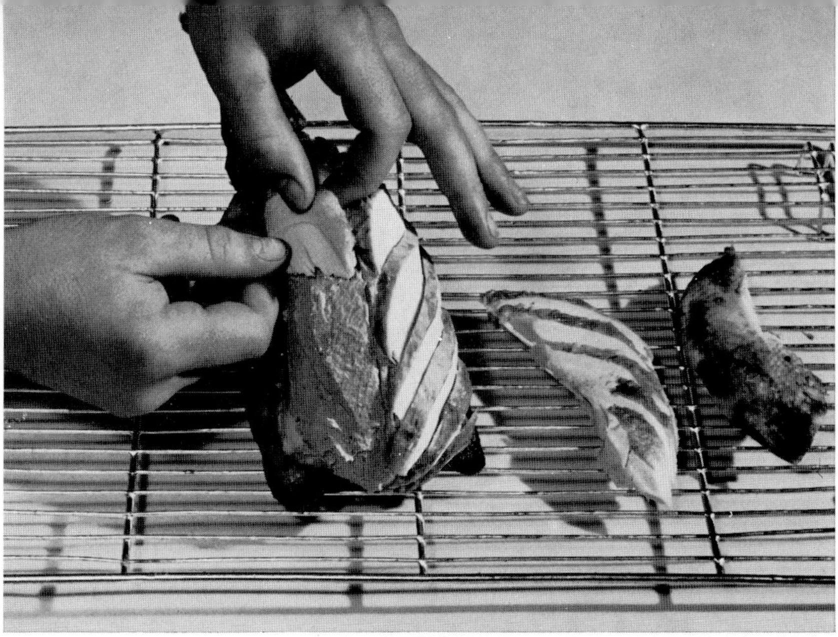

Using a pastry bag with a plain tube, pipe a line of forcemeat balls between the slices.

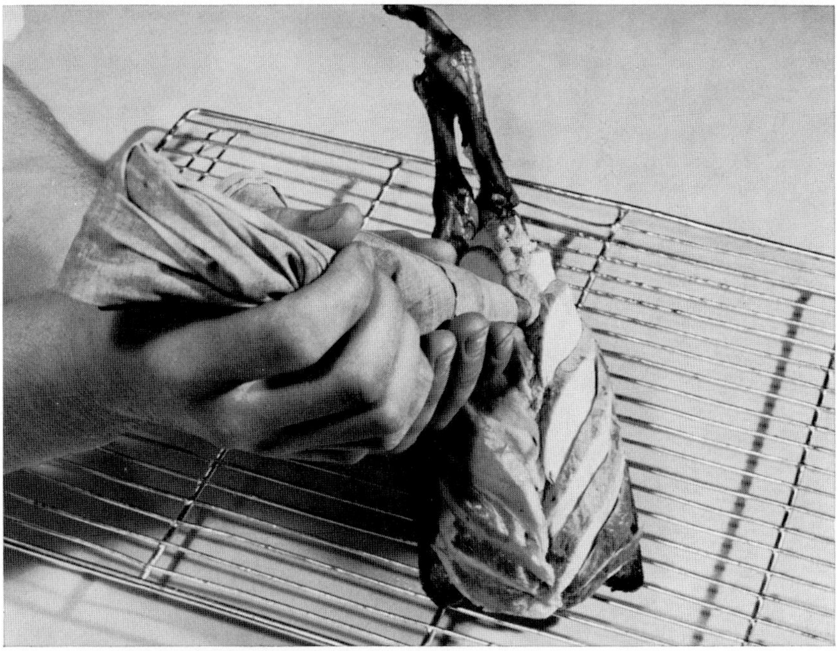

Top each forcemeat ball with a fluted mushroom cap, previously poached and chilled.

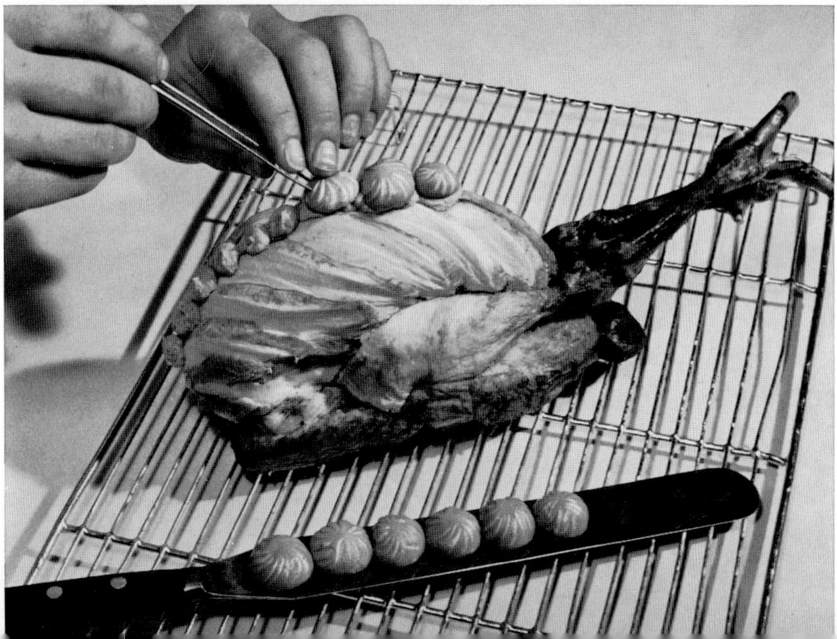

COLD STUFFED CHICKEN OR PHEASANT
(concluded)

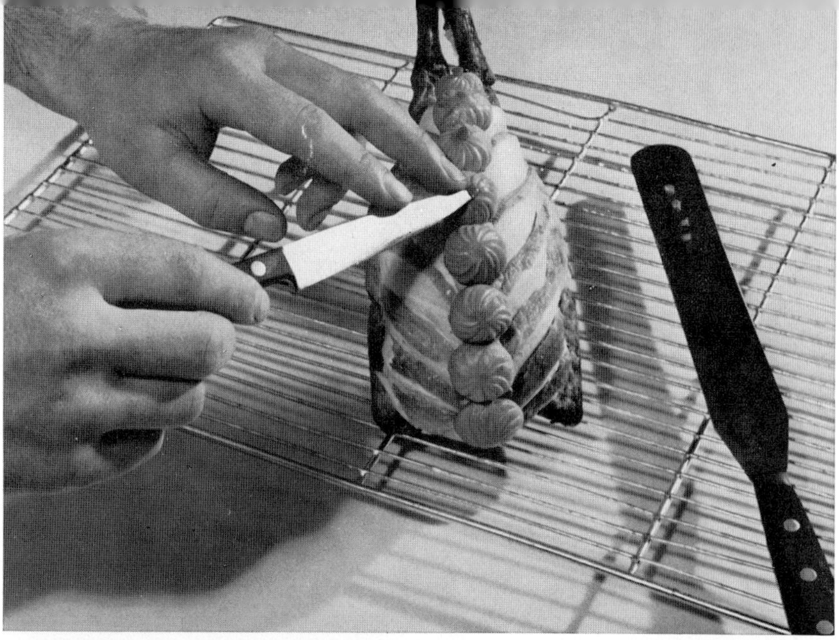

Place a tiny round of red pepper or tomato in the center of each mushroom cap.

Carefully glaze all over with aspic.

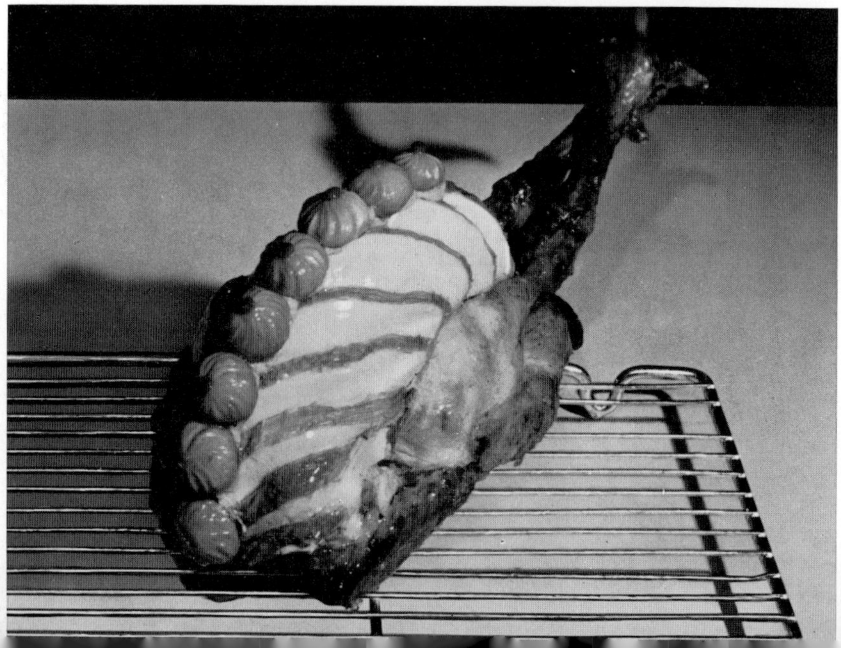

The bird is now ready to be placed on a serving dish.

PATÉ EN CROÛTE

Roll out the pastry to a thickness of 3/8 inch, flour lightly, and mark out the shape of the bottom of the loaf pan or mold on it four times.

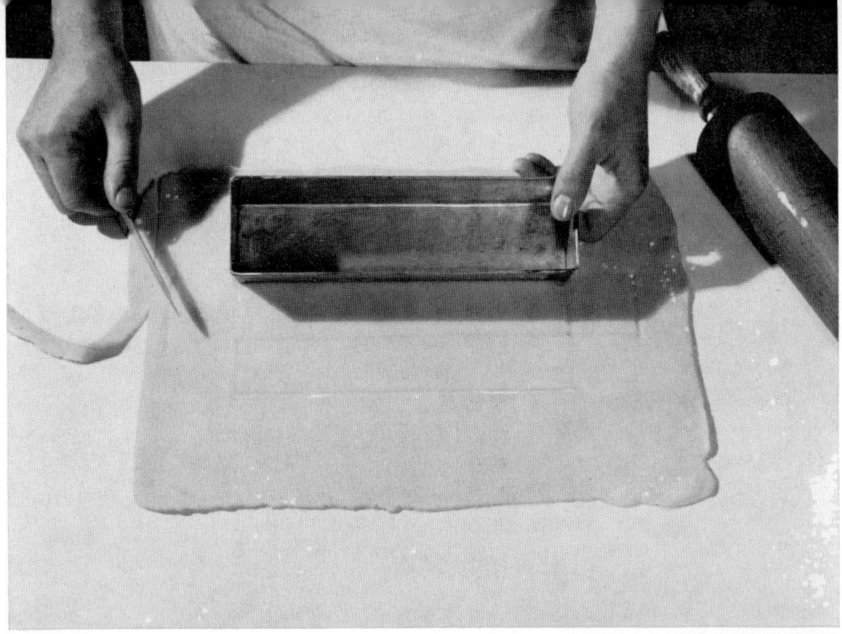

Cut off one of the four portions and set it aside to make the lid.

Line the greased, floured pan or mold with the remaining pastry.

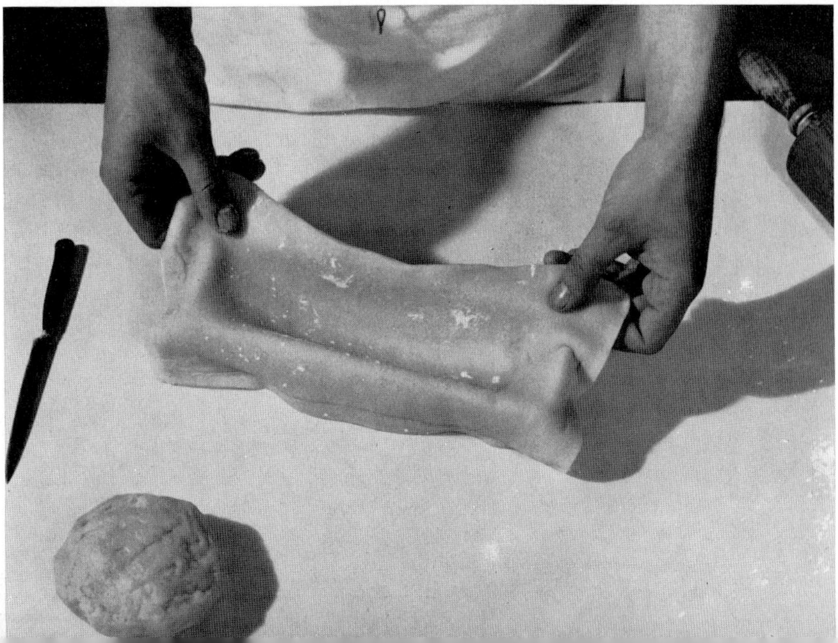

PATÉ EN CROÛTE
(continued)

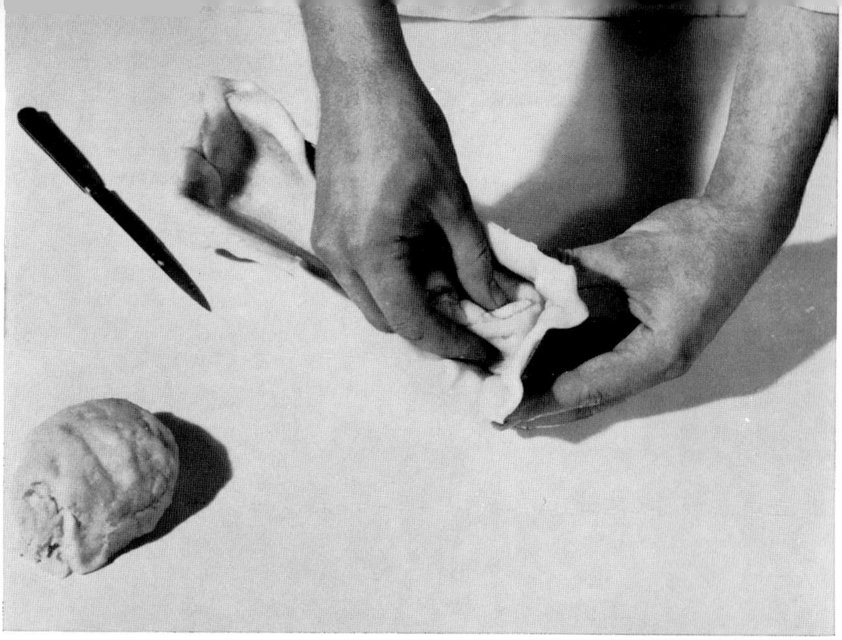

Use a ball of pastry to press the pastry lining firmly into the sides and bottom of the mold; the pastry must overlap the edges.

Cover the bottom and sides of the mold with thin slices of salt pork and half fill the mold with forcemeat.

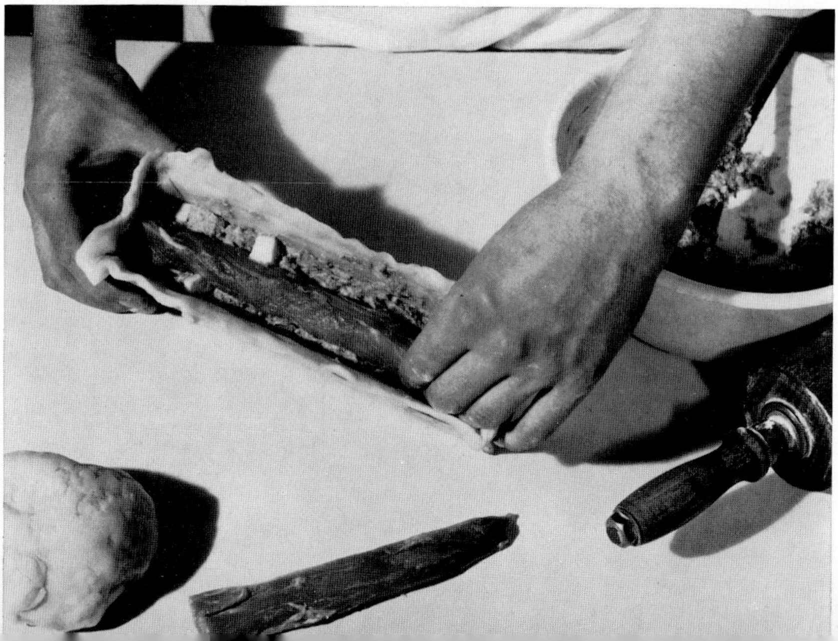

Garnish the center of the forcemeat with strips of venison, veal, chicken breast, etc., previously marinated in brandy and spices.

PATÉ EN CROÛTE
(continued)

Fill the mold with the remaining forcemeat, cover with thin slices of salt pork and fold the overlapping edges of paste toward the center.

Lightly moisten the edges of the pastry, cover the filling with the reserved piece of pastry, and press down well.

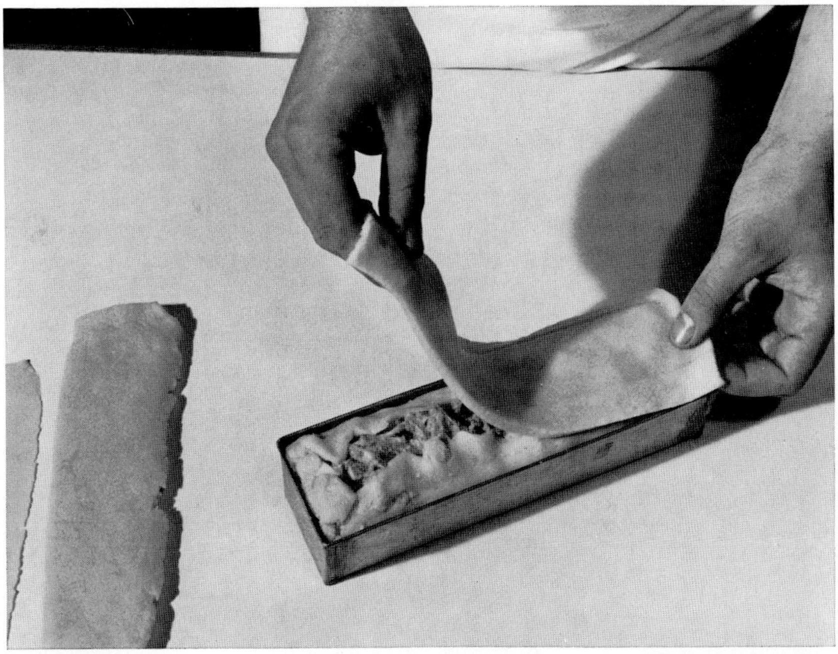

Pinch the edges together to fix the lid firmly in position and give a decorative finish to the edges.

PATÉ EN CROÛTE
(concluded)

Decorate with pastry cut-outs as desired, make a hole in the center to allow the steam to escape, and brush with beaten egg.

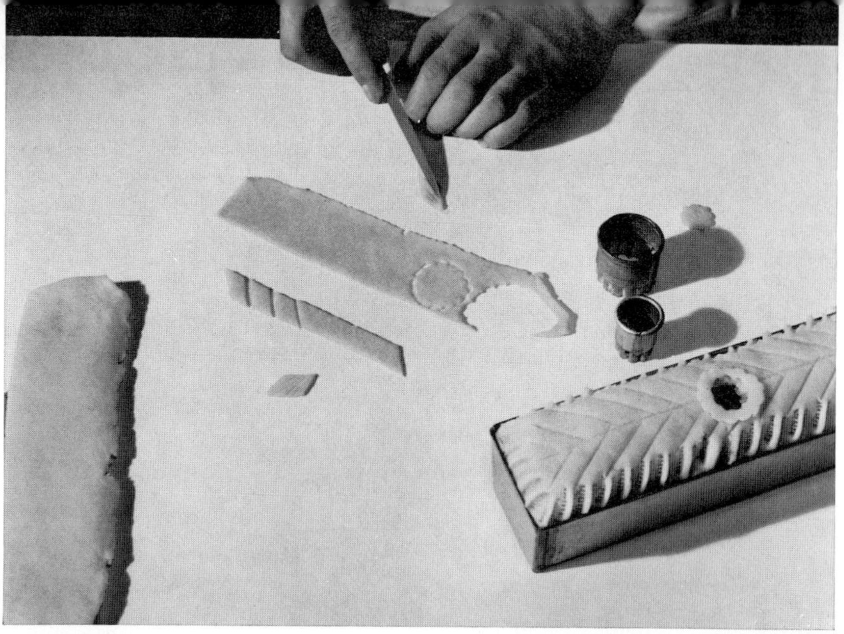

FLUTED MUSHROOMS

Peel the mushroom caps. Using a small knife held at an angle, score out semicircular ridges all around the caps.

ASPARAGUS

Scrap asparagus stalks from the top downward with a sharp paring knife. Tie the stalks in bunches for serving and cut off the ends evenly.

POTATO FRITTERS

Using a pastry bag with a star tube, pipe out the potato mixture in rings onto greased paper.

Slide the paper into hot deep fat. The potato rings will detach themselves and the paper can be pulled out by one corner. Fry the rings until they are golden brown on the bottom.

Turn the rings to brown the other side.

STUFFED PEPPERS

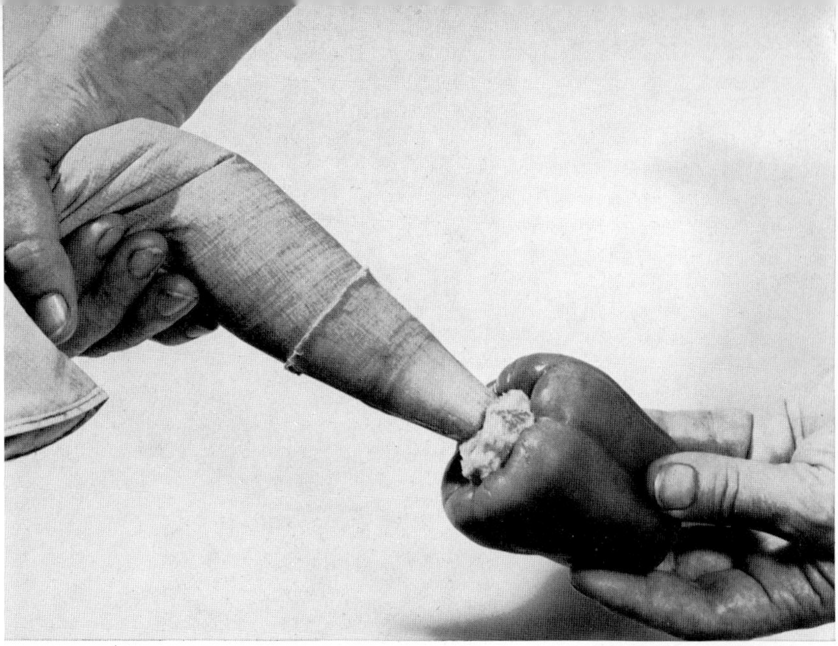

Using a pastry bag with a coarse plain tube, fill the peppers with rice stuffing.

The cooked stuffed peppers may be cut into thick slices and used as a garnish.

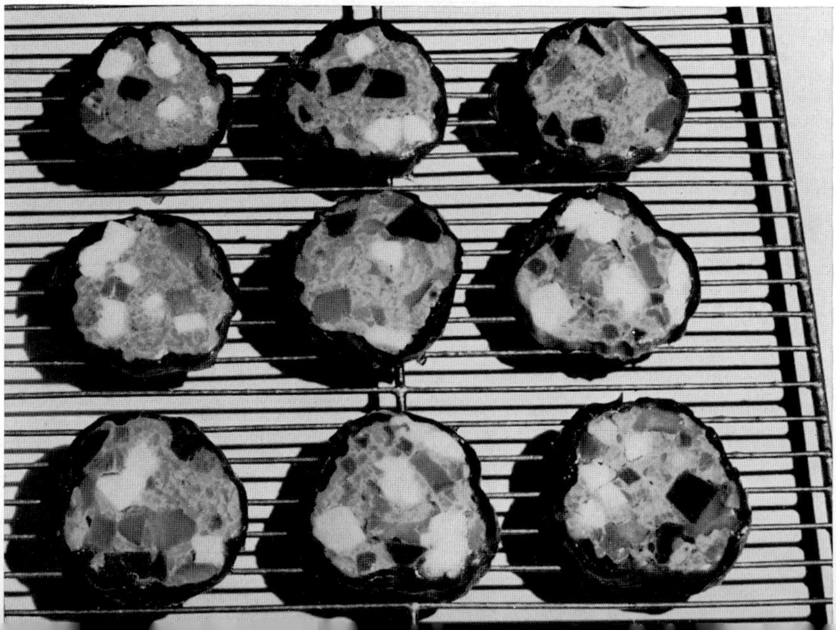

Halves of peppers may be stuffed with a pâté forcemeat and served as a cold hors d'œuvre or used to garnish cold dishes.

PALMIERS

Roll out and fold Puff Pastry only twice. Fold each end in two thicknesses (or in four thicknesses), sprinkling sugar generously between the folds, and fold the ends together. Chill in the refrigerator until firm. Slice, place on a lightly moistened baking sheet, and bake.

BLACK FOREST CHERRY TORTE

Cut the torte base into three layers of equal thickness. Cover the first layer with thickened stewed cherries (Cherry Filling) and spread Kirsch-flavored whipped cream or Chantilly Cream over them. Place the second layer on top and coat with the cream. Top with the third layer.

Coat the top and sides with the cream and sprinkle the sides with shaved chocolate. Using a pastry bag with a star tube, make rosettes of the cream around the edge of the top. Top each rosette with a glacéed cherry. Fill the center of the top with shaved chocolate and dust lightly with confectioners' sugar.

BABAS

Remove the babas from the molds, place them on a baking sheet with upturned sides, and pour sugar syrup over them.

Turn, place on a wire rack, sprinkle with spirits if desired, and spoon Apricot Glaze over them.

LADY FINGERS

Using a pastry bag with a coarse plain tube, pipe out the lady fingers on broad strips of greaseproof paper.

LADY FINGERS
(concluded)

Pick up each strip of paper carefully by the ends, turn over, and gently place in confectioners' sugar.

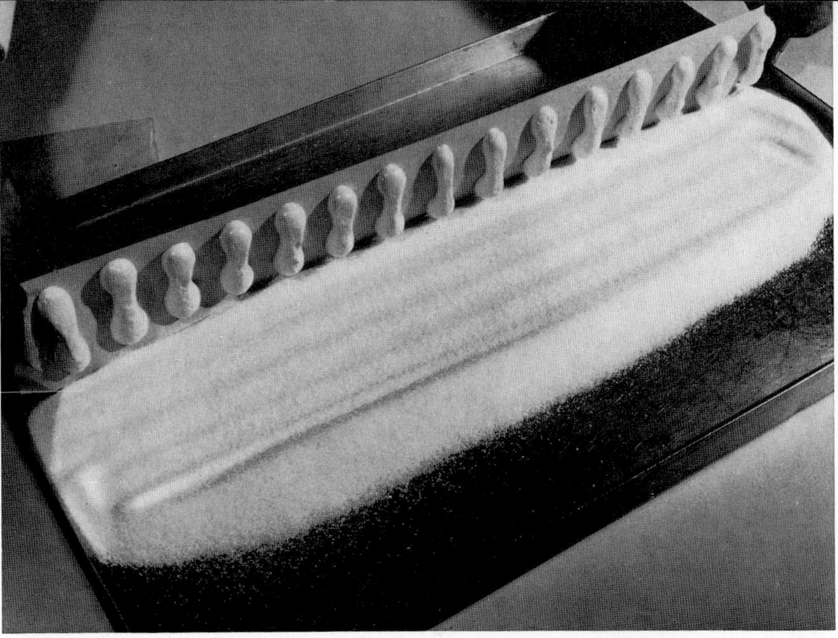

Leave the lady fingers in the sugar for a moment, then gently turn the paper back, and lay it on a baking sheet.

After baking, allow to cool, then remove the lady fingers from the paper by lightly pressing the latter over the edge of the baking sheet.

MEXICAN CAKE

Split the cake into two layers and sandwich them together with Butter-Cream Filling and Frosting. Then brush the top and sides with Apricot Glaze.

Spread Chocolate Fondant Cake Icing evenly all over with a spatula.

While the icing is still soft, pipe Royal Icing from a pastry bag onto it in parallel lines.

MEXICAN CAKE
(concluded)

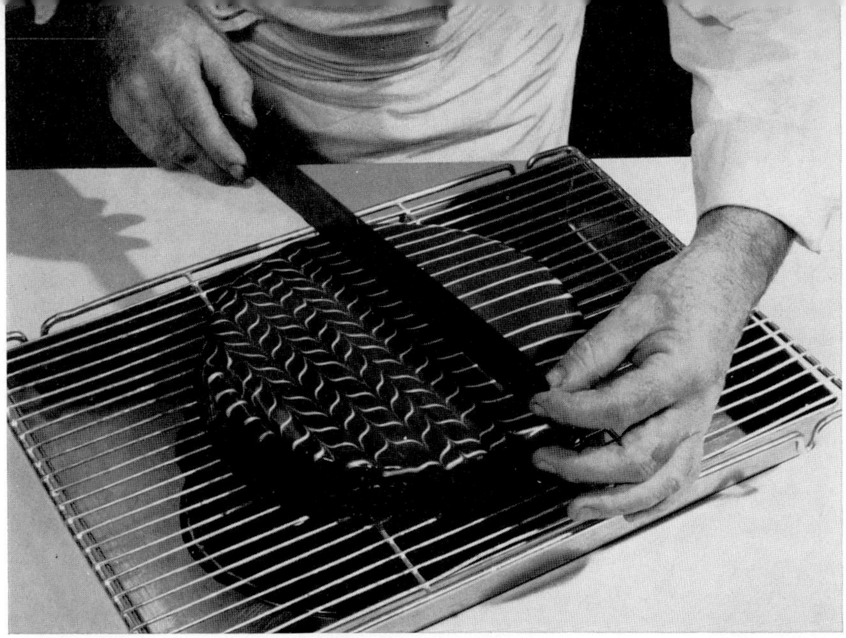

Make even breaks in the lines, working first upward and then downward with a palette knife or the point of a knife.

Alternative decoration: First pipe onto the Chocolate Fondant Cake Icing a spiral in Royal Icing.

Then make breaks in the spiral by drawing a knife in straight lines alternately from the center outward and vice versa.

SERVING SOLE MEUNIÈRE

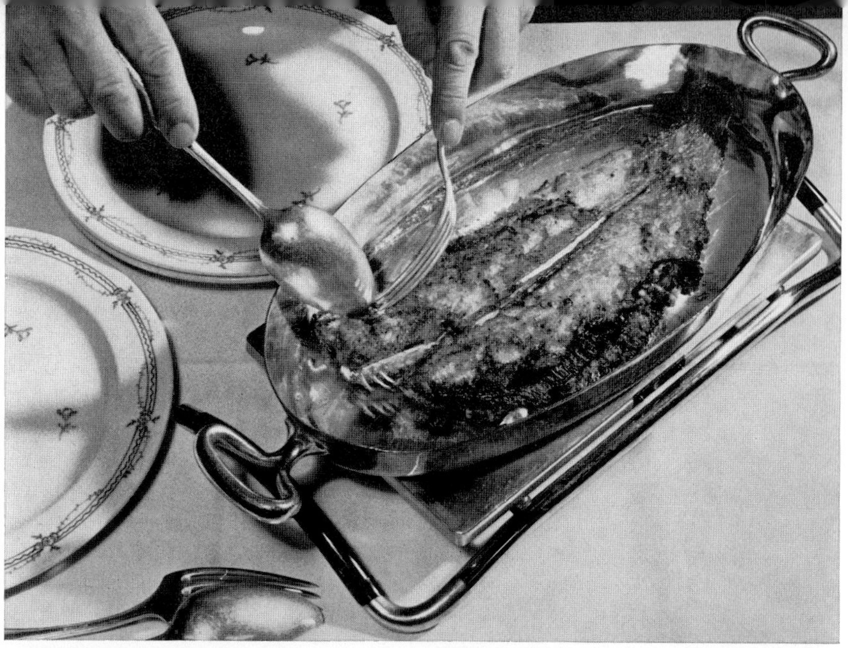

Hold the sole with a fork and remove the outside bones with a spoon.

Remove the outside bones from the dish.

Insert the fork into the middle of the center bone and use the spoon to slide the two fillets outward off the bone. After the upper fillets have been removed, slide those on the underside clear of the backbone.

SERVING SOLE MEUNIÈRE
(concluded)

Place the fillets on a warmed plate.

SLICING A CHATEAUBRIAND

Slide the carving knife under the meat, hold it steady with the back of a fork, and place it on the carving board.

Holding the meat with the back of the fork, slice it diagonally, letting the knife slide down without exerting any pressure so that the juices do not run out of the meat.

SLICING A CHATEAUBRIAND
(concluded)

To replace the meat on the serving dish, slip the knife under it again and steady the end slice with the back of the fork.

Serve two slices per person on warmed plates, leaving the third slice for a second helping.

CARVING A SADDLE OF HARE

Insert a fork in the backbone, lift the saddle with the aid of a spoon, drain, and place on the carving board.

CARVING A SADDLE OF HARE
(continued)

Holding the saddle in the center with a fork, detach the fillets with a spoon.

The fillet is easily removed with the spoon.

After removing the first fillet, detach and remove the second one.

CARVING A SADDLE OF HARE
(concluded)

Cut each fillet diagonally into four even slices, letting the knife slide along the meat without exerting any pressure.

CARVING A ROAST CHICKEN

Pick up the chicken on the point of a knife, hold it steady with a fork, drain, and transfer to the carving board.

Holding the wings with the fork, sever them at the joint with the knife.

CARVING A ROAST CHICKEN
(continued)

Turn the chicken on its side, insert the fork between the thigh and the drumstick and make an incision with the knife between the leg and the breast.

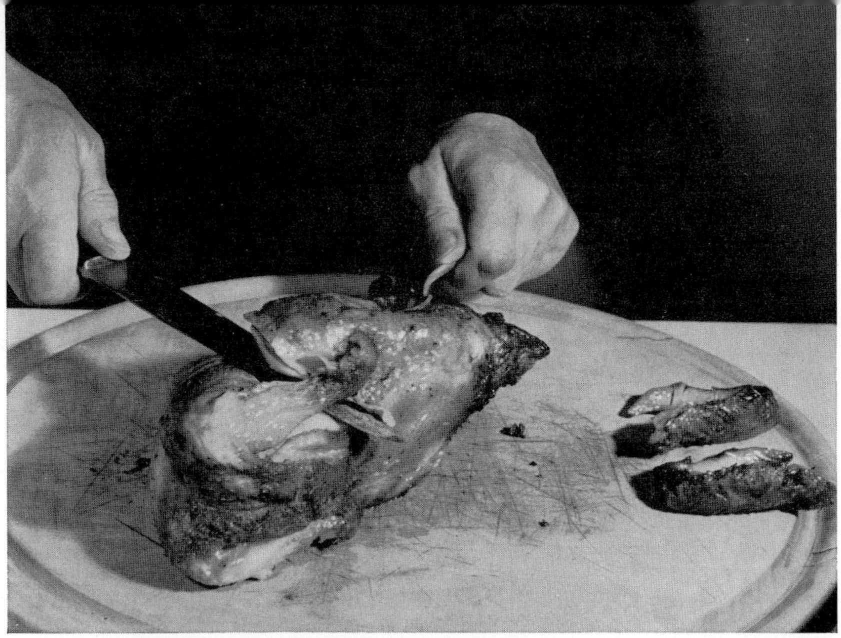

Remove the leg by prising it outward with the fork while holding the chicken with the side of the knife.

Repeat the procedure to remove the other leg.

CARVING A ROAST CHICKEN
(continued)

Turn the chicken on its back. Insert the fork at the place where one of the legs was removed and cut off the wing on the other side at the joint, together with a small piece of breast.

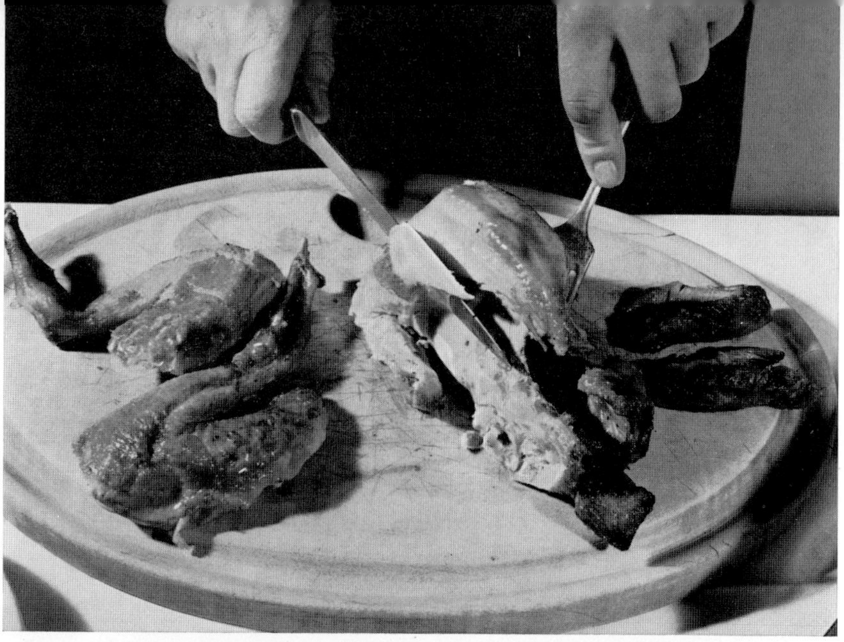

Cut off the tail where it joins on to the breast.

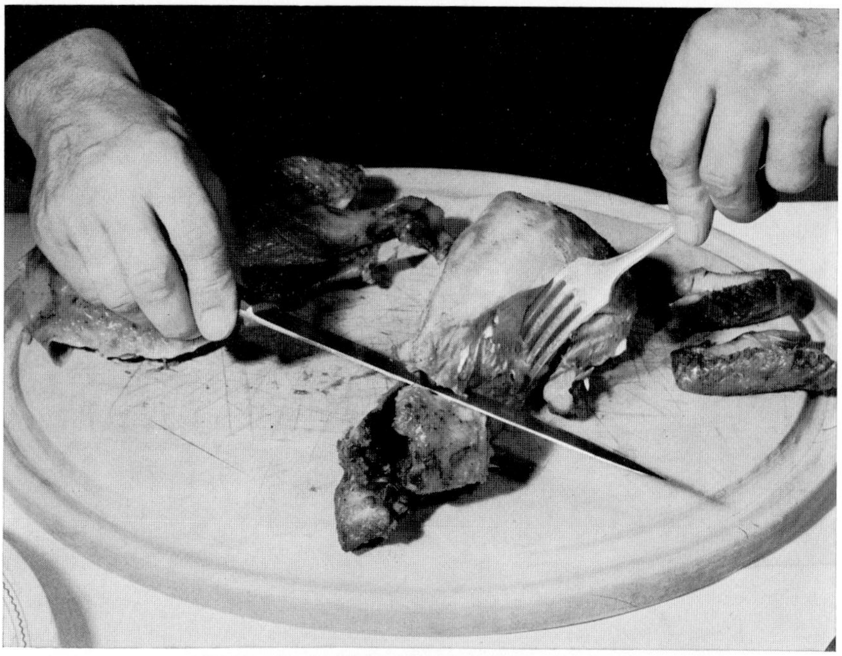

Cut off the second wing portion in the same way as the first.

CARVING A ROAST CHICKEN
(concluded)

Turn the chicken on its side again and cut through the crest of the breastbone with a sharp movement.

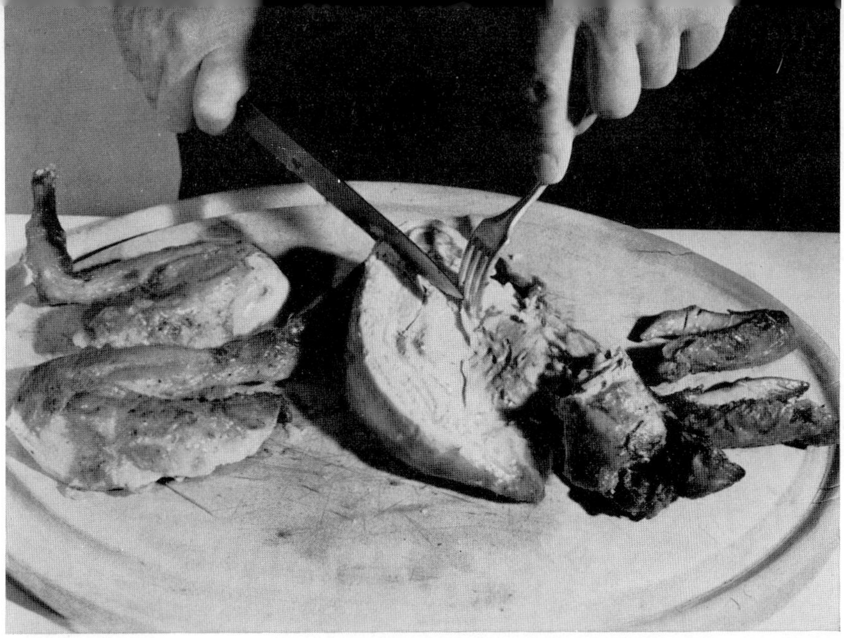

With the aid of the knife, the breast may now easily be removed from the carcass. If it is large, cut it in two.

Divide the drumsticks from the thigh by a clean cut through the joint.

PEELING AND SLICING AN ORANGE

First method

Mark out a cap shape at the top and bottom of the orange. Cut one of the caps off, invert it, impale it on a fork, and insert the fork through the cap into the other end of the orange.

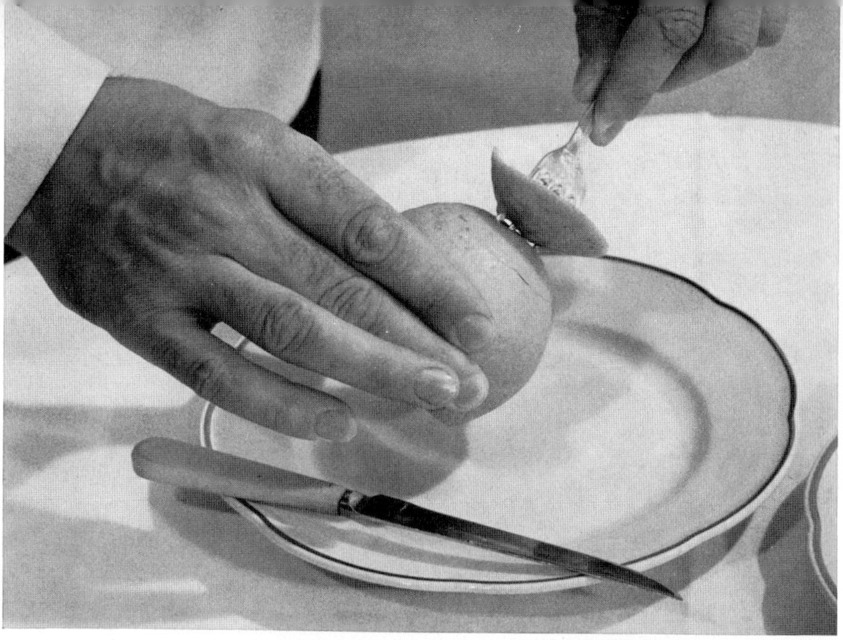

Using a sharp knife, peel the orange up to the level of the cap mark.

Slice the pulp of the orange thinly and sprinkle with the juice from the two caps.

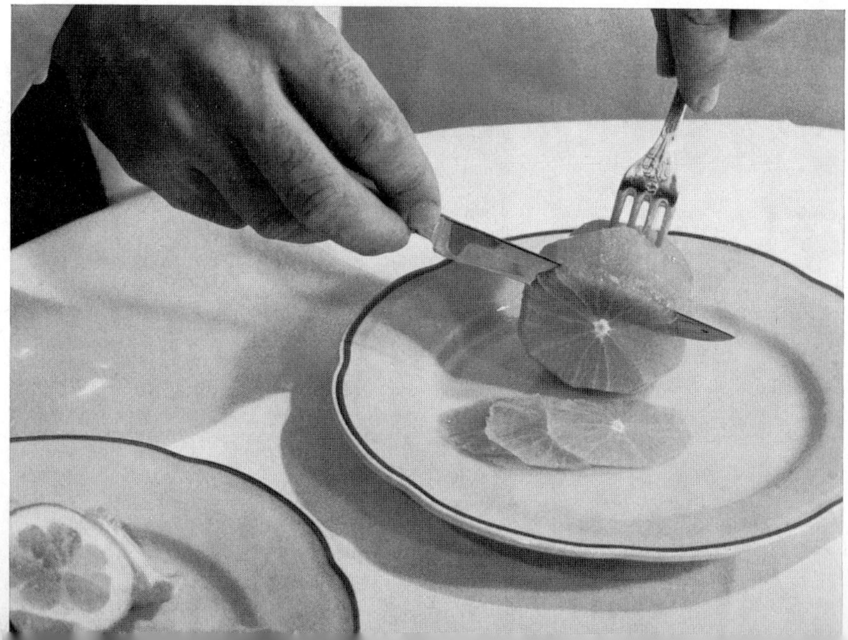

PEELING AND SLICING AN ORANGE

Second method

Cut the top off the orange. Insert a fork into the other end and peel the orange with a sharp knife, turning it with the fork and cutting the rind off the pulp in a spiral.

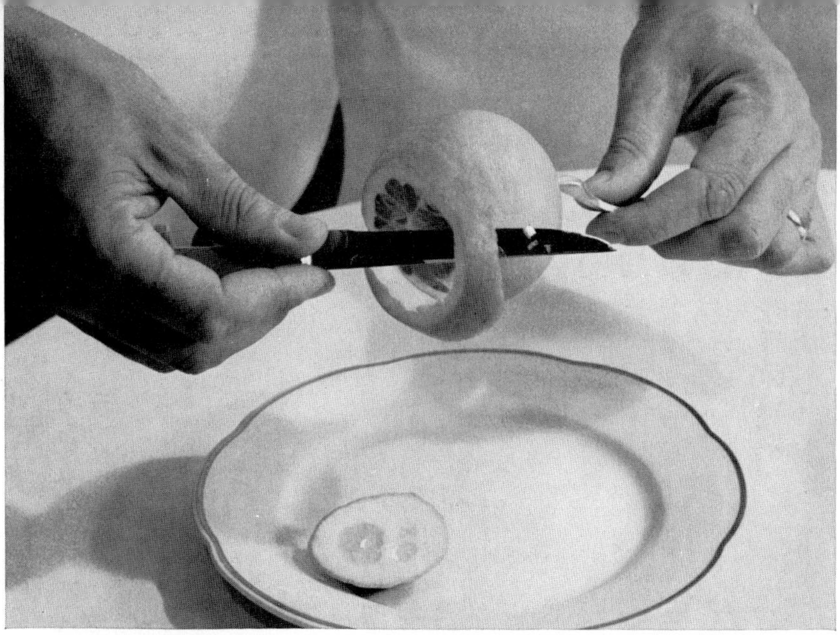

Remove the membrane from the segments and place the skinned segments on a plate.

Arrange the segments in a pattern, extract the juice from the top, and sprinkle it over them.

CRÊPES SUZETTE

For 4 portions, take 2 oranges, 1 lemon, and 24 lumps of sugar. Rub the orange and lemon zest off on to the lumps of sugar, using a napkin to avoid touching them with the hands.

Melt some butter in a shallow frying pan, add the sugar, and crush it.

Stir continuously until the sugar has caramelized slightly in the butter.

CRÊPES SUZETTE
(continued)

Add the juice of the lemon and oranges and cook briskly. The sauce should thicken a little.

Put the crêpes into the sauce one after another, folding them into quarters.

Turn them several times to steep them well in the sauce.

CRÊPES SUZETTE
(concluded)

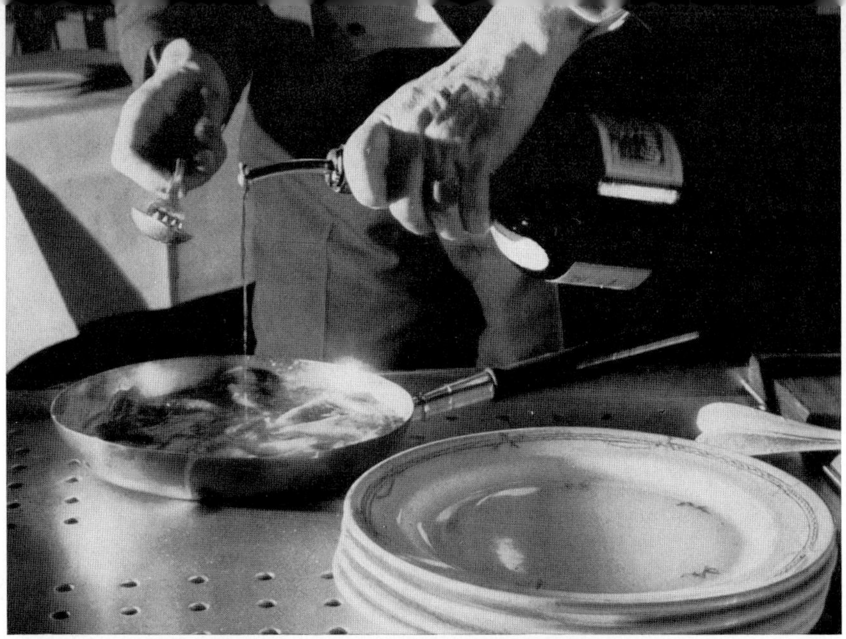

To "flame" the crêpes, pour Grand Marnier into the pan and set fire to it.

Remove the crêpes from the pan, open them out, and place them on warmed plates.

Coat each crêpe with a spoonful of the sauce.

Note: *Crêpes Suzette may be made in various ways, but the principle remains the same.*

GLOSSARY OF CULINARY TERMS

à la in the style of.

apéritif short alcoholic drink taken before a meal; appetizer or hors d'oeuvre.

appareil French term for a mixture used in the making of a dish. Such mixtures are of various kinds (see pages 147–50).

apricot glaze reduced, strained apricot jam used to coat cakes, petits fours, pastries, etc. The French term *abricoter* means to apply such a glaze.

aspic clear, brilliant jelly made from stock and used for glazing or dressing cold dishes. In French usage *aspic* applies to cold dishes molded with jelly; the term for jelly is *gelée*.

assaionnement salad dressing.

au, aux with, or cooked with.

au jus served with the natural juices (meat).

bain-marie vessel containing warm or hot water into which another utensil containing food is set while food is cooking.

ballottine piece of meat, poultry, etc., boned, stuffed, and rolled up—usually served hot. See also *galantine*.

Bar-le-Duc currant jam named for the town of Bar-le-Duc in Lorraine.

barquette small oval or boat-shaped pastry shell. Barquettes may be filled with various mixtures for hot or cold hors d'oeuvre or small entrées, or with fruit, custard, etc., for dessert. See Index for recipes.

baste (*arroser*) to moisten with pan drippings, fat, or liquid while cooking.

beard, debeard (*ébarber*) to remove the "beard" from oysters or mussels: to remove fins and small fin bones from fish.

beat (***fouetter***) to mix by long and vigorous stirring with a spoon, fork, whip, or electric beater or mixer.

beurre butter; see Butters and Butter Sauces, pages 197–200.

beurre manié butter thickened with flour, used for sauces.

beurre noir butter cooked to a very dark brown and mixed with chopped herbs and vinegar; served as a sauce.

bind (***lier***) thicken with flour, starch, eggs, cream, etc.; mix chopped meat, vegetables, etc., with a sauce.

biscuit American usage, a raised bread baked in small, round shapes; English usage, a cracker or a sweet wafer or cooky; French usage, sponge cake.

biscuit glacée ice cream shaped in molds.

blanch (***blanchir***) to scald or bleach by putting into boiling water.

blanquette white ragout or stew made with lamb, veal, or poultry.

blend (***melanger***) to mix gently.

boil (***bouillir***) to cook in boiling water.

bombe (***bombe glacée***) combination of ice creams or ices, fruits, creams, etc., made in a mold.

bone (***deosser***) to remove the bones from meat, poultry, or fish.

bouchées small puff-pastry patty shells.

bouillon strong, clear stock or broth.

bouquet garni herbs—usually parsley, thyme, and bay leaf—tied in a bunch and used for flavoring stews and sauces; the bouquet is removed before the dish is served.

braise (***braiser***) to brown meat or poultry in a little fat, then add a little water or other liquid and finish cooking with low heat.

brochette small spit or skewer used for broiling cubes of meat, shellfish, or vegetables. Food so cooked may be called *brochettes* or *en brochette*.

brunoise a mixture of vegetables, chopped or finely shredded and cooked in butter or other fats, used in forcemeats, sauces, etc.

canapé bread cut in fancy shapes, fried in butter or toasted and spread with a savory topping; served as an hors d'oeuvre.

caramel browned sugar.

cassolette individual heatproof dish; food cooked and served in such a dish.

chaud-froid literally "hot-cold"; a gelatin sauce used to coat cold cooked meat, poultry, or fish (see Index).

chiffonade leafy salad vegetables (especially lettuce and sorrel) cut into fine strips or shredded and simmered in butter.

chop coarsely (***concasser***) cut or break up a food into large pieces.

coat a spoon (***napper la cuillère***) method of determining the thickness of sauces, etc., by dipping a spoon into the liquid; the thickness can be judged by the amount that adheres to the spoon.

cocotte small individual heatproof dish in which food is cooked and served; food so presented is called *en cocotte*.

compote fresh or dried fruits cooked in syrup (see Index).

coquille scallop shell; by extension a dish so shaped, or food cooked or served in a natural scallop shell or a shell-shaped container.

cream (***crème***) butter cream or custard cream used for frosting and for filling cakes and pastries; custard cream sauce. The French term for the cream that rises from milk is *crème du lait*.

crêpe thin French pancake. Crêpes may be filled, rolled, and baked for an entrée; sweet crêpes are served as a dessert with confectioners' sugar or a sauce.

croissant crescent-shaped roll made of puff pastry or yeast pastry.

cromesqui mixture dipped in batter and fried in deep fat; similar to a croquette.

croustade small or large case made of rich pastry or puff pastry, or a hollowed-out toast case, used for serving various creamed mixtures.

croûte bread crust, pie crust, or crust formed on anything. Meat, *pâtés*, etc., baked in a crust are called *en croûte*.

crouton small cubes or other shapes of bread fried in butter or toasted and served in soups or as a garnish.

daube stew cooked in a hermetically sealed casserole to preserve the flavor.

decant (wine) to pour gently into another bottle to get rid of the sediment (see page 57).

degrease (*dégraisser*) to skim off excess fat from the surface of a liquid.

diable, à la deviled; method of preparing food. Sauce Diable (see Index).

émincer to cut meat or vegetables into very fine slices (*not* to mince).

émincé dish made with thinly sliced leftover cooked meat.

dice (*couper en dés*) to cut into small cubes.

fillet (*filet*) strip of meat or fish without bone.

fillet of beef tenderloin.

fines herbes finely chopped parsley and/or other herbs, used as a garnish.

flambéed (*flambé*) served with brandy or a liqueur poured on and set alight.

fleurons decorations made of puff pastry in fancy shapes, used as a garnish and to ornament *pâté en croûte* and dessert pastries.

Florentine cooked or served with spinach.

foie gras livers of duck or geese fattened in a special way (see page 745).

fold (*incorporer*) to blend a light mixture gently into a heavier mixture; most often used of beaten egg whites.

fondu melted.

fondue name given to various dishes in which the main ingredient is melted or (for vegetables) cooked to a pulp.

forcemeat (*farce*) meat or fish chopped fine and seasoned, used as a stuffing or garnish or in the making of other dishes.

four oven.

fruits de mer seafood.

galantine boned poultry or meat, stuffed, rolled, and cooked in a gelatinous stock (see Index).

garnish (*garniture*) various items of food used to decorate and to enhance the flavor of a dish (see pages 150–58).

gelée (adj.) frozen; (n.) jelly.

glacé frozen; iced; glazed; candied.

glacéed (*glacé*) glazed; candied.

gourmandises rich dainty tidbits, used of pastries and hors d'oeuvres.

gratin, au sprinkled with breadcrumbs and melted butter and browned. Cheese may or may not be added.

grill (*griller*) to broil.

hacher to chop or mince.

herbs aromatic plants used in cooking, salads, etc. (see pages 102–3).

jelly (*gelée*) aspic; preserve made of fruit juice and sugar.

julienne (food) cut in fine, short strips.

jus lié thickened meat juice; gravy.

lard (*larder*) to thread strips of pork fat into large pieces of meat with a larding needle (see Culinary Techniques in Pictures).

lardon strip of pork or bacon used for larding.

macédoine mixture of small or cut-up fruits or vegetables.

Madère, au with Madeira wine.

maigre meatless; term used for dishes that can be served in Lent and on fast days.

maître d'hôtel butter or **sauce** butter sauce with parsley and lemon juice.

marinade a seasoned liquid, cooked or uncooked, in which food is steeped for varying lengths of time.

marinate (*mariner, macérer*) to steep in a marinade.

marmite cooking pot of metal or earthenware, with a lid. This utensil has given its name to certain soups; see Grande Marmite, Petite Marmite.

mask (*masquer*) to cover or mask with a sauce.

medallion (*médaillon*) round slice.

meunière, à la way of preparing fish, in which the fish is rolled in flour, fried in butter, and garnished with lemon juice and chopped parsley.

mince (*hacher*) to cut into small pieces.

mode, à la in the style of, as Tripe à la Mode de Caen.

noisette hazelnut; small round slice cut from the fillet, rib, or leg of lamb, mutton, or veal.

papillote paper frill put on bones of cutlets, *suprêmes* of chicken, or croquettes in cutlet form; *en papillote*, baked in oiled or buttered paper, or, in America, in foil; method used for small cuts of meat or for fish.

Parmentier name applied to dishes that include potatoes, after Antoine-Auguste Parmentier (1737–1817), who popularized potatoes in France.

pastry base (*abaisse*) sweet pastry rolled to any desired thickness and used as a base for a dessert preparation. The French term is also applied to a layer of sponge cake similarly used.

pâte pastry, dough.

pâté originally a meat or fish dish enclosed in pastry, served hot or cold; now extended to meat or fish mixtures baked in a mold or loaf pan (see *terrine*) lined with strips of bacon and served cold (see pages 733–41).

pâtisserie pastries; the art of the pastry cook; pastry shop.

paupiette slice of meat spread with a filling, rolled, and braised.

petits pots de crème rich custards baked in individual custard cups (see pages 881–82).

petits fours small cookies, iced cakes, pastries, glacéed fruits, etc. (see pages 1007–1016). The name is said to have originated from the fact that the small cakes were baked in an oven that had been allowed to cool after large cakes had been baked.

pilaf rice cooked in stock with various seasonings; also spelled pilaff, pilau.

poach (*pocher*) to cook in liquid that has barely been brought to a simmer.

poivre pepper; *au poivre*, cooked or heavily seasoned with pepper.

pot-au-feu classic French soup, made with meat, poultry, and vegetables. The broth is served separately from the meat and vegetables, making two dishes in one (see Index).

profiteroles small balls of chou paste, baked, and filled either with cheese, puréed meat, and other savory mixtures for hors d'oeuvres or garnish, or with creams or ice cream as a dessert. For dessert, *profiteroles* may be frosted or served with a caramel or chocolate sauce.

puff pastry, puff paste (*pâte feuillitée*) delicate, rich pastry made with flour, water, and butter, rolled, folded, and chilled several times (see page 127 and Culinary Techniques in Pictures).

purée (*reduire en purée*) to mash solid foods by putting through a sieve, pounding in a mortar, or putting through an electric blender. A purée of anything is food that has been so treated.

quenelles dumplings made with various kinds of forcemeat bound with a panada or with eggs, used as a garnish or in soups (see pages 146–47).

quiche savory custard tart, originating in Lorraine.

ragout stew.

reduce (*réduire*) boil down to a sauce or other liquid in order to increase flavor and thicken the consistency.

rissole pastry filled with forcemeat and fried in deep fat.

roux cooked mixture of butter and flour used for thickening sauces (see pages 138–39).

Royale molded custard cut into various shapes and used to garnish soups (see Index); also a term applied to various main dishes and desserts.

sabayon see *zabaglione*.

salpicon preparation of diced foods bound with a sauce and used to fill pastry cases or made into croquettes, etc.

sauté (*sauter*) to brown or cook in a small amount of very hot fat.

scallop (*escalope, scaloppine*) thin slice of meat or fish cut slantwise; the method is most often used with veal.

scallop (*pétoncle*) bivalve mussel with ribbed, rounded shell (see *coquille*).

simmer (*mijoter*) to cook at a very slow boil.

spices seeds or other parts of aromatic plants used to season food (see pages 104–106).

subrics croquette-type mixtures that are not dipped in egg and breadcrumbs but fried in butter in a shallow frying pan; served as hors d'oeuvre or small entrées.

tart (*tarte*), tartlet (*tartelette*) pastry crust with fruit, custard, or other filling. In American usage the large version is called a pie, the small individual version a tart, but in French and English usage the large size is a *tarte* (tart) and the small a *tartelette* (tartlet). The terms "tart" and "tartlet" are used in this book.

Tartare, à la way of serving chopped raw beef, seasoned with salt and pepper and with a raw egg yolk on top.

Tartare Sauce mayonnaise-type sauce made with oil, finely chopped hard-cooked eggs, and chopped chives.

tartine slice of bread spread with butter, jam, or other spread.

terrine earthenware dish or mold in which pâté mixtures are cooked; the food cooked in such a dish (see pages 739–41).

torte, tourte tart, pie.

toss (*faire sauter*) to flip food over by tossing the pan.

tournedos (s. and pl.) small round steak cut from the tenderloin of beef.

truss (*brider*) to tie up or skewer a fowl for cooking (see page 644).

vacherin dessert made with rings ("crowns") of meringues or almond paste mounted one above the other on a sweet pastry base. The center is filled with pastry cream or ice cream.

vol-au-vent elaborate large or small puff-pastry shell filled with various creamed mixtures (see Index and Culinary Techniques in Pictures).

zabaglione (Italian; French *sabayon*) rich wine custard served hot in cups or as a sauce (see Index).

zest (*zeste*) peel of citrus fruit.

INDEX

[Page numbers in italic type indicate illustrations.]

A

B

C

D

E

F

G

H

I

J

K

L

M

N

O

P

Q

R

S

T

U

V

W

X

Y

Z